Philosophy of
Religion

Philosophy of Religion

SELECTED READINGS

FOURTH EDITION

Edited by

Michael Peterson
Asbury University

William Hasker
Huntington University

Bruce Reichenbach
Augsburg College

David Basinger
Roberts Wesleyan College

New York   Oxford
OXFORD UNIVERSITY PRESS
2010

Oxford University Press, Inc., publishes works that further Oxford University's
objective of excellence in research, scholarship, and education.

Oxford   New York
Auckland   Cape Town   Dar es Salaam   Hong Kong   Karachi
Kuala Lumpur   Madrid   Melbourne   Mexico City   Mumbai   Nairobi
New Delhi   Shanghai   Taipei   Toronto

With offices in
Argentina   Austria   Brazil   Chile   Czech Republic   France   Greece
Guatemala   Hungary   Italy   Japan   Poland   Portugal   Singapore
South Korea   Switzerland   Thailand   Turkey   Ukraine   Vietnam

Published by Oxford University Press, Inc.
198 Madison Avenue, New York, New York, 10016
http://www.oup.com

Oxford is a registered trademark of Oxford University Press

ISBN: 978-0-19-539359-0

Printing number: 9 8 7 6 5 4 3 2
Printed in the United States of America
on acid-free paper

CONTENTS

v

PREFACE TO THE FOURTH EDITION

We reflect with great satisfaction on the growth of philosophy of religion since the first edition of this book in 1996. That first Table of Contents reflected all standard issues as well as many new issues important at that time, thereby redefining what an anthology in this field could be. Interest in the field remains high and activity robust, making it imperative to keep this text of classical and contemporary readings at the forefront. With well over a century of teaching experience among the co-editors, and many years of getting both student and instructor feedback on this book, the new edition is designed as a complete introduction to the field. Insightful suggestions from reviewers and users of the book have also helped improve its pedagogical value. We would like to thank Simon Evnine at University of Miami, Thomas J. Fryc at Utica College, Matt Lawrence at Long Beach City College, and David McNaughton at Florida State University for their thoughtful comments in preparation for the fourth edition. We would also like to thank those who reviewed the second edition in preparation for the third: Philip Blosser at Lenoir-Rhyne College, Harry Gensler at John Carroll University, Kenneth Himma at Seattle Pacific University, the late Joseph Lynch at California Polytechnic State University, Ian Markham at the Hartford Seminary, and Gordon Pettit at Western Illinois University. We also deeply appreciate the work and encouragement of our editor, Robert Miller, who, as always, provided excellent advice. Kudos also to Christina Mancuso, our editorial assistant, who worked conscientiously on all the details of this large project.

We have continued popular hallmarks from previous editions, such as our fourteen thematic sections (more than other anthologies) that can be used in any order, according to instructor preference. This new edition also features seventy-eight readings (up from seventy-three) for depth and breadth of coverage; suggested reading after each section; study questions after each reading; and a glossary at the end of the book. For this edition, the consensus among reviewer recommendations was that student understanding would be greatly enhanced by including significantly more introductory material to each general topic to explain more fully how each reading relates to the issue at hand. In response to this, we have enlarged the section introductions to four times their previous size, thereby providing unparalleled pedagogical assistance. In addition, introductions to individual readings have been modestly enhanced, and the study questions, suggested reading lists, and glossary have been revised and updated.

Ten selections are new to the fourth edition: Daniel Dennett on religion as a delusion, Gottfried Leibniz on the best of all possible worlds, William Dembski and Philip Kitcher on the intelligent design debate, John Polkinghorne and John Lennox on arguments about intelligent design, the Buddha on the nature of religion, David Hume on the critique of the analogical teleological argument, an anonymous Buddhist piece on rebirth, and Stephen T. Davis on the claim for the resurrection of Jesus. This anthology covers all of the standard subjects—religious experience, theistic arguments, the problem of evil, miracles—as well as topics of more recent interest, such as the ontological status of religion, reformed epistemology, open theism, the kalam cosmological argument, divine action in the world, open theism, the science versus religion controversy, and religious diversity. Like previous editions, this fourth edition primarily contains readings from the Western tradition, many of which take an analytic approach, as the renaissance in philosophy of religion in our time has sprung largely from this particular practice. Yet it is often helpful to be able to compare and contrast Western ideas and interests with those of other traditions. For this reason, we include several continental, feminist, and Asian readings for diverse perspective and flavor.

We trust that instructors will find the organization, scope, depth, balance, and flexibility of *Philosophy of Religion: Selected Readings*, Fourth Edition, helpful in the way they teach their introductory courses. The book is designed to connect with students—to show them why each issue or topic is important and to provide them the opportunity to form their own opinions about key issues. *Philosophy of Religion*, Fourth Edition, is an excellent stand-alone primary source but is also compatible with the editors' textbook, *Reason and Religious Belief*, Fourth Edition (Oxford University Press, 2006). These two books share the same topical organization and make cross-referencing possible. Some instructors also use *Reason and Religious Belief* for their own background preparation.

May 2009

MP
Asbury University

WH
Huntington University

BR
Augsburg College

DB
Roberts Wesleyan College

Philosophy of
Religion

Exploring the Philosophy of Religion

PHILOSOPHY ENGAGES RELIGION

Is there a God? How would we know if there were? Do miracles occur? Has science discredited faith? If a loving God exists, why is there so much suffering? Thoughtful people ponder such big questions. The fundamental human drive to understand finds sophisticated expression in the discipline of philosophy, which aids the quest by transmitting the reflections of great thinkers and providing methods for clear, logical analysis. Academic philosophy can be divided into a number of subdisciplines according to the main subject matter: philosophy of science, philosophy of history, philosophy of art, and so forth. Our focus is philosophy of religion—the critical examination of religious concepts and beliefs.

The philosophy of religion is clearly a branch of philosophy and should not be confused with religion itself or even with theology. Although "religion" is notoriously difficult to define, it is, at the very least, a set of beliefs, actions, and experiences, both individual and collective, organized around some idea of Ultimate Reality that is recognized as sacred and in relation to which persons enter into a transformative process. Ultimate Reality may be understood as a unity or a plurality, as personal or nonpersonal, as divine or not, differing from religion to religion. But virtually every cultural phenomenon we call a religion contains these important elements.

Theology is a discipline that occurs largely within a given religious tradition. It is concerned with the conceptual development and systematization of the key beliefs and doctrines of that faith orientation. As justification for its claims, theology typically appeals to such sources as holy writings and accredited teachings. We might call this "sacred theology" since it is rooted in authoritative sources that contain sacred truths. Sometimes there is also appeal to what all persons can know through observing the world and employing human reason in order to arrive at some truths of religion—a project often labeled "natural theology."

Philosophy of religion, however, does not have to be viewed as having its exclusive home within some specific religious tradition. Certain religious traditions obviously nurture and support the life of the mind in general and the philosophical investigation of their teachings in

1

particular, while a few religious traditions discourage or disparage rational probing. Nevertheless, philosophy of religion is a bona fide academic field that is as objective, rigorous, and systematic as possible. As such, it is not a dogmatic or parochial enterprise but rather seeks to follow the best approaches to study and dialogue about religious beliefs. In this way, philosophy of religion takes its legitimate place seeking intellectual engagement with religion in the broad arena of ideas.

Robust intellectual examination of religion involves a rich variety of philosophical activities: assessing reasons that have been offered for and against religious belief; investigating the logic of such concepts as God and faith; exploring the meaning of theological terms such as "salvation" and "miracle"; and even comparing elements across religious traditions for additional perspective. Whether one is a religious believer or not, we are all invited to meet, discuss, and debate in the wide-open space of philosophy of religion.

The Resurgence of the Philosophy of Religion

For much of the twentieth century, the dominant approach to philosophy in the English-speaking world has been what we may call *analysis*. The analytic approach, broadly conceived, is concerned with the meaning, consistency, coherence, reasonableness, justification, and truth of our beliefs. Emphasis throughout is on the content of crucial concepts as well as on the structure and soundness of arguments. Yet analytic philosophy passed through various evolutionary phases during the twentieth century. Early analytic philosophers committed to positivism were determined to shape the field of philosophy according to the intellectual methods of modern science. Positivism embraced a very strict form of empiricism, an epistemological position that bases knowledge on sensory experience or what can be inferred from experience. This meant that the many nonempirical claims of religion could make no pretense to being knowledge. In its heyday, the influential positivist movement made it difficult and even embarrassing for any self-respecting intellectual to take religious claims seriously.

In the second half of the twentieth century, however, things began to change. In the 1960s and 1970s, many philosophers became interested in the work of the later Wittgenstein. They widely believed that sophisticated Wittgensteinian insights into the meaning and function of language in ordinary contexts provided a way to break from positivism's intellectual imperialism. Some philosophers who were interested in religion were able to apply these new insights to religious language and rehabilitate the respectability of discussing religion. About the only exceptions to these changing trends in the larger analytic movement were Catholic philosophers, who themselves had roots in more ancient ideas. Their more classical ideas—stemming from such thinkers as Aristotle, Augustine, and Aquinas—made them less susceptible to the impact of positivism, on the one hand, and less in need of the new Wittgensteinian ideas, on the other.

During the last several decades, the status of philosophy of religion drastically changed. For one thing, philosophers now know very well that the positivistic principle of verifiability was inadequate even for science, let alone religion. For another thing, freedom from positivism paved the way for a lot of new, quality work in other areas of philosophy, such as logic, epistemology, and metaphysics—work that has contributed to fresh investigations into religion that go far beyond the old questions of whether religious language has meaning. The situation has also changed because of the notable increase in the number of practicing philosophers who not only espouse some form of personal religious faith but also address issues of faith from within the discipline of philosophy. Moreover, many nonbelievers and outright opponents of religious faith have come to respect its rational integrity and are joining in vigorous discussion and debate. All of this brings an atmosphere of energy and vibrancy to philosophy of religion that is palpable. Not surprisingly, student interest in academic philosophy of religion, at both undergraduate and graduate levels, is at a measurable high.

These are exciting days in philosophy of religion. Academic publishing in the area has exploded. Over the past several decades, studies of eminent medieval philosophers (e.g., Augustine, Anselm, Boethius, Aquinas, Ockham) have blossomed. Many excellent treatments have appeared on how ideas of modern thinkers (e.g., Leibniz, Hume, and Reid) bear upon religious topics. And debates abound over the new and creative proposals that have been advanced by contemporary figures in philosophy (e.g., Hick, Plantinga, Swinburne, Mackie).

THE FOCUS OF PHILOSOPHY OF RELIGION AND THE PROJECT OF THIS BOOK

Philosophy of religion has gone from being a virtual outcast in analytic philosophy to being one of the most active areas in scholarship today. This change has mirrored a shift in the focus of research in the broader field. Instead of being driven by inordinate concern with whether nonempirical concepts can have meaning according to a very narrow standard, philosophy in general—and the philosophy of religion in particular—now pursues a more straightforward and more traditional interest in concerns about truth, knowledge, reality, and values. We might say that second-order obsessions have once again given way to first-order questions—and that this is all to the good.

In this context, the renewed philosophical interest in religion has largely focused on classical theism. *Classical theism* is the belief that a transcendent spiritual being exists who is omnipotent, omniscient, and perfectly good and who is the personal creator and sustainer of the world. Although theism itself is not a living religion, it is part of the essential belief-framework of three major religions: Judaism, Christianity, and Islam. The discussion of classical theism leads naturally in a number of important directions—to efforts that unfold and defend a theistic perspective as well as efforts to critique and refute it, to studies of how it is embedded within the larger ambit of full-blooded religious life, to proposals of modified versions of theism, and even to inquiries into nontheistic religious perspectives.

This book of readings is situated within the analytic tradition in the philosophy of religion and its strong interest in the beliefs, activities, and experiences that are tied to theistic religions. Many of the selections here also reflect the fact that the bulk of philosophical work in contemporary analytic philosophy of religion deals with specifically *Christian* theism. Since the nature of analytic philosophy is to be interested in all relevant concepts and arguments, the scope of this book seeks to include some works from other philosophical and religious traditions. Certainly, life today faces us with a wide diversity of people, cultures, and perspectives that provide important and stimulating material for philosophical analysis and reflection. New ideas, different methodologies, divergent world views, and challenging arguments must be taken into account. So, while remaining analytic in approach and theistic in central focus, the present anthology includes readings representing continental, feminist, and Asian contributions.

The best primary works on the important themes in the philosophy of religion today are included here. The comprehensive scheme of organization makes this anthology excellent as the sole text in a course or in conjunction with a secondary text. Naturally, there is a close fit between this book of primary source readings and our own secondary text, *Reason and Religious Belief* (OUP, 2006). Many courses use the two books together.

The structure of this anthology is straightforward. It consists of seventy-eight selections arranged into fourteen thematic parts: the nature of religion; religious experience; faith and reason; the divine attributes; arguments about God's existence; knowing God without arguments; the problem of evil; divine action; religious language; miracles; life after death; religion and science; religious diversity; and religion and morality. To maximize its pedagogical value, this new edition includes greatly expanded introductions to each of the fourteen major parts as well as an expanded synopsis of each individual selection. Study questions follow each selection; suggested readings are included at the end of each major part; and a glossary is provided at the end of the book.

Whether or not one has a religious point of view, the relevance of religion to human life is undeniable. To work through this anthology is to take a refreshing and worthwhile journey, a journey of the human intellect seeking philosophical understanding in religion. Thoughtful persons who explore the issues presented here will be rewarded with deeper insight into an important dimension of human existence.

PART ONE

The Nature of Religion

The philosophy of religion takes religious concepts and beliefs as the primary material for study. Although often unrecognized, behind the discussions and debates that normally occupy the philosophy of religion lurks a prior and important question: what is religion? For example, the philosophical analysis of such concepts as life after death and God, or the rigorous scrutiny of arguments for the existence of God or for possibility of miracles, assume some conception of the nature of religion. Indeed, even the acceptance or rejection of religious faith must be interpreted, even implicitly, in terms of some idea about what religion is. At the same time, the lack of consensus about the nature of religion further complicates the discussion of virtually all philosophical issues touching on religion.

One might broadly delineate two opposing positions, realism and nonrealism. *Realism*, whether in science or religion, affirms that our beliefs, theories, doctrines, and statements about unobservable things can be true or false and are made true or false by that to which they refer. This applies to beliefs and statements about electrons or about God. *Nonrealism*, in science or religion, holds that our theories, doctrines, and beliefs about unobservable things are nonreferential. Rather, they are human constructions that help us to understand and interpret our experience. They are tools for solving problems, whether scientific or about life, and hence can be assessed in terms of whether they are pragmatically useful in enabling us to better cope with our world. There are many versions of realism and nonrealism; our treatment will focus on the central core ideas of religious realism and nonrealism.

Religious Nonrealism

Religious nonrealists deny that religious beliefs and statements are about real unobservable entities, properties, or events. Religion is solely a human creation; people have constructed religious language and sets of beliefs that enable them to function effectively in their environment, but religious assertions do not make true or false claims about real spiritual beings, their properties, or unobservable events that include them or their activities.

The history of religion contains many nonrealist theories. Friedrich Nietzsche stated that religion was developed as a kind of fiction to support morality, which in turn aims at suppressing a desire for power in strong, creative persons. Sigmund Freud postulated that religion developed in response to neurotic feelings of helplessness in the face of a world that humans could not control; to think that religion is about the supernatural is to embrace an illusion. William James said that religious beliefs are evaluated pragmatically by the psychological health or ill health that they bring and are not to be gauged by correspondence to some transcendent reality.

Nonrealists frequently ground religion either in subjective psychological experiences (as with Freud) or in the structure and demands of society. The sociologist Émile Durkheim emphasized religion's sociological origin, holding that religious ideas result from personal interpretations of social feelings or sentiments that in turn connect us to other social phenomena. For Durkheim, interpretations of religious feelings link us to social entities that provide the basis of moral obligations. The group dictates to the individual the beliefs to be embraced, the rules to be followed, and the rites to be observed. Consequently, religion is not really about cosmic forces or metaphysical realities but arises out of society's need for individuals to comply with rules. Although religion engages in metaphysical speculation, the usefulness of religion does not depend on any given metaphysical structure; this metaphysical structure will eventually be abandoned. Religion is a natural, not supernatural, phenomenon, created by and for humans, and properly must be studied as a social discipline.

Although these examples seem dated, they are not; the nonrealist theme is repeated by contemporary authors and updated using contemporary models and language invoking market economics, philosophical notions of intentionality, Darwinian evolution, and sociological memes (units of cultural inheritance). The philosopher Daniel Dennett, in our first selection, suggests that for some people religion provides a benefit by helping them achieve a higher level of citizenship and morality; at the same time, nonreligious ideas can likewise benefit us, and religious ideas can be nonbeneficial by encouraging bigotry, oppressive behavior, and war. But since religion has survived by being beneficial, someone must have been benefited. Dennett suggests a number of possible survival/benefit theories: religion satisfies a genetically transmitted craving; sexual selection occurred when women preferred males who showed sensitivity to music and ceremony; religion was fostered by elites who benefited from controlling the ignorant and ill informed. Whatever the explanation, organized religion is rooted in and evolves out of folk religion, which itself has diverse roots. Humans tend to adopt what Dennett calls an "intentional stance" toward things: we view things, whether computers or animals, as agents with beliefs, acting intentionally or purposively out of their desires. With respect to religion, we view nature as populated with agents who have all the strategic information that we humans need to survive. Not only do we try to influence these agents, but special persons such as shamans use alleged communication from these agents to control others. Humans also construct stories about these causally empowered agents, which are then codified and passed on to subsequent generations because humans have a genetic interest in informing their young. Since generally it is selectively advantageous for the young to trust their parents, natural selection has built children's brains with a tendency to believe parents, and religious leaders thus get extra authority by taking on the title of "parent" (and especially "Father"). Religion becomes institutionalized when these competing culturally transmitted units (memes) are domesticated and obtain stewards who propagate them. Thus, the development of organized religion occurs both unconsciously by natural selection (memes that unite groups tend to survive) and by rational choice (stewards see a benefit to themselves and to the group from preserving these beliefs and practices).

The impact of the nonrealist interpretation is that religious beliefs and issues often transmute into something other than what religious believers originally thought them to be. Questions about the rationality of religious belief and life, for example, are no longer questions about whether there really are divine beings. Rather, issues of rationality are about whether certain beliefs and behaviors make sense of experience or serve a useful social function. Similarly, debates over theological beliefs may still be waged, but such debates have nothing to do with the existence of higher powers. Both believers and nonbelievers may marshal arguments to show that God does or does not exist. But the nonrealist holds that both sides of the dispute can be shown to be really talking only about human experience by shifting to a sociological or psychological perspective according to which the issues are not genuinely about an unobservable reality.

BUDDHIST NONREALISM

Nonrealism is especially manifest in Buddhism. This is nowhere more obvious than in its doctrine of no-self. In the famous passage from the *Milindapañha* (part of which makes up the fifth selection in Part Eleven of this anthology), King Milinda engages in a conversation with the venerable Nāgasena on the question of whether Nāgasena has a self. Nāgasena affirms that he has a name, but the name could have been any name; names are a "way of counting, a term, an appellation, a convenient designation, a mere name, . . . for there is no [Self] here to be found." Buddhist epistemic nonrealism extends to ordinary objects or things as well. The word "chariot" neither names nor refers to a persisting object or to a composite of its parts.

Buddhists hold that we construct our world out of our subjective factors, that is, our desires, hatred, and ignorance, using our experiences of groups of events (called attachment groups). We project selves and persistent objects because we are ignorant that all events are in constant flux and because we desire permanence and stability. Thus, liberation will be achieved not through changing the world but through changing ourselves, in particular, our outlook or perspective on things. The change comes when we realize that whatever exists is mutually conditioned and is what it is because of our conscious activity.

Buddhist nonrealism can be traced back to the Buddha's refusal to engage in metaphysical discussion, as shown in our second selection. The Buddha sought to use language without making ontological and theoretical commitments. Discourse about metaphysical issues—the nature of the Self, the eternality of the world, life after death—are not conducive to what really matters, namely, leading the religious life. Religious thought is directed toward the experiences of suffering and ending it, not toward the construction of true explanatory theories.

RELIGIOUS REALISM

In contrast to nonrealists, religious realists affirm a view that is consistent with the way that most Western religions or religious believers intend or interpret their beliefs. Religious realists agree with nonrealists that religions are psychological and sociological phenomena and are properly studied as such. They likewise agree with nonrealists that most aspects of religion are human creations. Rituals, symbols, traditions, practices, even beliefs are originated by human beings. They construct moral codes about actions that are permitted, forbidden, or obligatory. They write theologies or treatises that describe the human predicament and how it might be addressed. As such, there is little doubt that most of what we take to be religion in structure and function, concept and system is of human origin. However, for realists the critical question of the nature of religious beliefs, theories, or doctrines is not merely about the origin of religious beliefs and practices; it concerns the content, meaning, and referent of those beliefs and doctrines, about what really exists independent of us and makes those beliefs true or false. In this respect, religious realism parallels scientific realism: although science and religion arise from and are conditioned by human experience, they are descriptively informative about the world, both seen and unseen, and their theories or doctrines are truth determinable.

Although religious beliefs address human personal and social experience, they also speak about the transempirical, in particular, about God, about experiences of encounters with God, and about events that involve God's actions in the world. These beliefs are conveyed in language that contains assertions that are taken as making truth claims, and they are defended by arguments meant to show that there is good reason to think that these beliefs are true. The assertions are true if there actually are referents with the properties indicated by these assertions; false, if not. Statements about the existence and nature of God are true if and only if there is a divine being with such properties. Statements about actually experiencing the Transcendent are true if and only if there is a Transcendent to be experienced. The claim that God answers prayer is true if and only if there is a God who answers prayer. The claim that humans exist after death is true if and only if humans do in fact live subsequent to their death. In short, religious realists hold that the concepts, beliefs, assertions, doctrines, and worldviews of a religion refer to an actually existing transcendent God, God's properties, and God's actions that cause phenomenal states.

Realists, like Roger Trigg in the third selection, argue that religious nonrealists confuse the origin or function of religious claims with the content of these claims. Although it may be true that religion promotes social solidarity and contributes to social stability, religious claims are not about these functions or effects. One can see this by the fact that what would justify the truth of a religious claim would differ significantly from what would justify the claim that religions are psychologically and socially propitious. For example, arguments to show that God exists are completely different from and irrelevant to arguments showing that belief in God is functionally beneficial.

The move from content to function of beliefs has the further consequence of negating the significance of the differences in the content of religious beliefs. The reduction of content to function means that differences in content are real differences only if they make a difference in practice, in how those beliefs function is society. But different religions propose diverse accounts of the human predicament and how to address it. These accounts differ widely on the nature of the perceptual unobservables involved and how they function. For some, there is a God; for others, not. For some, God enters in an incarnate fashion into history; for others not. So in terms of explanatory power, propositional content, not mere function, matters. On the realist view, then, religious doctrines or theories refer to transcendent (as well as empirical) realities and thus deserve close and careful analysis and defense or critique of their truth.

WITTGENSTEIN'S NONREALISM

Any philosophical discussion of how to understand the nature of religion would be incomplete without introducing the thinking of the later Wittgenstein and his intellectual followers. Wittgenstein's approach, discussed by D. Z. Phillips in our fourth selection, is often characterized as nonrealism because it so thoroughly criticizes what it takes to be the confusions of realism, although Wittgensteinians themselves deny that they are either realist or nonrealist. The general confusion of realism is that it takes belief to be private mental states whose meaning lies in correspondence to an object. This would apply equally to beliefs about mathematical theorems and beliefs about material things in the local environment and beliefs about the identity of some person. Norman Malcolm, John Searle, D. Z. Phillips, and other followers urge us to look at the "grammar" of belief, which involves studying the dynamic, living context of its application. This includes all beliefs, not just religious beliefs. On their view, the meaning of religious belief is found in its use, rather than in relation to an external object. The primary concern is with how a person who has a particular belief lives—that is, what difference this belief makes in his or her life, not what reality the belief corresponds to.

As we begin our study of important issues in the philosophy of religion, it is fitting that we begin by considering this pressing prior question: what is the nature of religion? For how we think about this question will affect how we understand the role and significance of the issues that are addressed throughout this anthology. In particular, it affects whether we see religion as making truth claims about some transcendent reality and whether these claims can be justified. And it affects how we assess religions. Do we only attend to whether religions are practically useful in enabling us to cope with existence, or do we assess religions in terms of consistent truth claims about that which transcends human experience?

Daniel C. Dennett

An Evolutionary Account of Religion

Daniel Dennett (b. 1942) pushes his readers to investigate their religion in the same way they would investigate anything else. For him, the best way to investigate it is by invoking an evolutionary explanation in terms of memes, cultural units that are replicated and transmitted often unconsciously. He wonders why religion, since it is so costly, has survived. Religion probably arose when people developed the hyperactive intentional stance, enhanced by language, which attributes agency to a wide variety of things, animate or inanimate, that are puzzling or frightening to us. The rituals and beliefs, as memes, were passed on from parents to children in ways that protected even the weakest memes (those that did not work). As folk religion transmuted into organized religion, religious authorities, with self-interest playing a role, became stewards of the memes and protected them. In the end, Dennett returns to his concern that if religion has survived, it must be beneficial in some way. He thinks that religion might be good for one's health and morale, although not necessarily better than disbelief. But he is skeptical of the claim that religion makes one morally better. Throughout, Dennett is not concerned with the truth of religious beliefs but rather with their function in culture.

WHY GOOD THINGS HAPPEN

Religion can certainly bring out the best in a person, but it is not the only phenomenon with that property. Having a child often has a wonderfully maturing effect on a person,... but for day-in, day-out lifelong bracing, there is probably nothing so effective as religion: it makes powerful and talented people more humble and patient, it makes average people rise above themselves, it provides a sturdy support for many people who desperately need help staying away from drink or drugs or crime. People who would otherwise be self-absorbed or shallow or crude or simply quitters are often ennobled by their religion, given a perspective on life that helps them make the hard decisions that we all would be proud to make.

No all-in value judgment can be based on such a limited and informal survey, of course. Religion does all this good and more, no doubt, but something else we could devise might do it as well or better. There are many wise, engaged, morally committed atheists and agnostics, after all. Perhaps a survey would show that

From Daniel C. Dennett, *Breaking the Spell: Religion as a Natural Phenomenon* (New York: Viking, 2006).

as a group, atheists and agnostics are more respectful of the law, more sensitive to the needs of others, or more ethical than religious people. Certainly no reliable survey has yet been done that shows otherwise.

Among the questions that we need to consider, objectively, are whether Islam is more or less effective than Christianity at keeping people off drugs and alcohol (and whether the side effects in either case are worse than the benefits), whether sexual abuse is more or less of a problem among Sikhs than among Mormons, and so forth. You don't get to advertise all the good your religion does without first scrupulously subtracting all the harm it does and considering seriously the question of whether some other religion, or no religion at all, does better. World War II certainly brought out the best in many people, and those who lived through it often say that it was the most important thing in their lives, without which their lives would have no meaning; but it certainly doesn't follow from this that we should try to have another world war. The price you must pay for *any* claim about the virtue of your religion or any other religion is the willingness to see your claim put squarely to the test. My point here at the outset is just to acknowledge that we already know enough about religion to know that, however terrible its negative effects are—bigotry, murderous fanaticism, oppression, cruelty, and enforced ignorance, to cite the obvious—the people who view religion as the most important thing in life have many good reasons for thinking so....

Lawyers have a stock Latin phrase, *Cui bono?* which means "Who benefits from this?" a question that is even more central in evolutionary biology than in the law. Any phenomenon in the living world that *apparently* exceeds the functional cries out for explanation. The suspicion is always that we must be missing something, since a gratuitous outlay is, in a word, uneconomical, and as economists are forever reminding us, there is no such thing as a free lunch.... Evolution is remarkably efficient at sweeping pointless accidents off the scene, so if we find a *persistent pattern* of expensive equipment or activity, we can be quite sure that something benefits from it in the only stocktaking that evolution honors: differential reproduction. We should cast our nets widely when hunting for the beneficiaries, since they are often elusive....

Whatever else religion is as a human phenomenon, it is a hugely costly endeavor, and evolutionary biology shows that nothing so costly just happens. Any such regular expenditure of time and energy has to be balanced by something of "value" obtained, and the ultimate measure of evolutionary "value" is fitness: the capacity to replicate more successfully than the competition does. (This does not mean that we ought to value replication above all! It means only that nothing can evolve and persist for long in this demanding world unless it somehow provokes its own replication better than the replication of its rivals.) Since money is such a recent innovation from the perspective of evolutionary history, it is weirdly anachronistic to ask *what pays for* one evolved biological feature or another, as if there were actual transactions and ledgers in Darwin's countinghouse. But this metaphor nevertheless nicely captures the underlying balance of forces observed everywhere in nature, and *we know of no exceptions to the rule*. So, ... I ask, what pays for religion? Abhor the language if you must, but that gives you no good reason to ignore the question. Any claim to the effect that religion—your religion or all religion—stands above the biosphere and does not have to answer to this demand is simply bluster. It might be that God implants each human being with an immortal soul that thirsts for opportunities to worship God. That would indeed explain the bargain struck, the exchange of human time and energy for religion. The only honest way to defend that proposition, or anything like it, is to give fair consideration to alternative theories of the persistence and popularity of religion and rule them out by showing that they are unable to account for the phenomena observed. Besides, you might want to defend the hypothesis that God set up the universe so that we would evolve to have a love of God. If so, we would want to understand how that evolution occurred....

Can't we just accept the obvious fact that religion is a human phenomenon and that humans are mammals, and hence products of evolution, and then leave the biological underpinnings of religion at that? People make religions, but they also make automobiles and literature and sports, and surely we don't need to look deep into biological prehistory to understand the differences between a sedan, a poem, and a tennis tournament. Aren't most of the religious phenomena that need investigation *cultural* and *social*—hence somehow "above" the biological level?

This is a familiar presumption among researchers in the social sciences and humanities, who often deem it "reductionistic" (and very bad form) even to *pose* questions about the biological bases of these delightful and important phenomena....But the disciplinary isolation it motivates has become a major obstacle to good scientific practice, a poor excuse for ignorance, an ideological crutch that should be thrown away.

We have particularly compelling reasons for investigating the biological bases of religion *now*. Sometimes—rarely—religions go bad, veering into something like group insanity or hysteria, and causing great harm. Now that we have created the technologies to cause global catastrophe, our jeopardy is multiplied to the maximum: a toxic religious mania could end human civilization overnight. We need to understand what makes religions work, so we can protect ourselves in an informed manner from the circumstances in which religions go haywire. What is religion composed of? How do the parts fit together? How do they mesh? Which effects depend on which causes? Which features, if any, invariably occur together? Which exclude each other? What constitutes the health and pathology of religious phenomena? These questions can be addressed by anthropology, sociology, psychology, history, and any other variety of cultural studies that you like, but it is simply inexcusable for researchers in these fields to let disciplinary jealousy and fear of "scientific imperialism" create an ideological iron curtain that could conceal important underlying constraints and opportunities from them....

A culturally transmitted design can...have a free-floating rationale in exactly the same way a genetically transmitted design does....And the reason the process can work is exactly the same in human culture as it is in genetics: *differential replication*. When copies are made with variation, and some variations are in some tiny way "better" (just better enough so that more copies of *them* get made in the next batch), this will lead inexorably to the ratcheting process of design improvement Darwin called evolution by

natural selection. What gets copied doesn't have to be genes. It can be anything at all that meets the basic requirements of the Darwinian algorithm.

This concept of cultural replicators—items that are copied over and over—has been given a name by Richard Dawkins, who proposed to call them *memes*.... Cultural transmission can *sometimes* mimic genetic transmission, permitting competing variants to be copied at different rates, resulting in gradual revisions in features of those cultural items, and *these revisions have no deliberate, foresighted authors*. The most obvious and well-researched examples are natural languages. The Romance languages—French, Italian, Spanish, Portuguese, and a few other variants—all descend from Latin, preserving many of the basic features while revising others.

THE ROOTS OF RELIGION

Your religion, you may believe, came into existence when its fundamental truth was revealed by God to somebody, who then passed it along to others. It flourishes today because you and others of your faith know that it is the truth, and God has blessed you and encouraged you to keep the faith. For you, it is as simple as that. And why do all the other religions exist? If those people are just wrong, why don't their creeds crumble as readily as false ideas about farming or obsolete building practices? They will crumble in due course, you may think, leaving only the true religion, your religion, standing. Certainly there is some reason to believe this. In addition to the few dozen major religions in the world today—those whose adherents number in the hundreds of thousands or millions—there are thousands of less populous religions recognized. Two or three religions come into existence every day, and their typical life span is less than a decade. There is no way of knowing how many distinct religions have flourished for a while during the last ten or fifty or a hundred thousand years, but it might even be millions, of which all traces are now lost forever.

Some religions have confirmed histories dating back for several millennia—but only if we are generous with our boundaries....These are short periods of time, biologically speaking. They are not even long compared with the ages of other features of human culture. Writing is more than five thousand years old, agriculture is more than ten thousand years old, and language is—who knows?—maybe "only" forty thousand years old and maybe ten or twenty times older than that.... Is language older than religion? However we date its beginnings, language is much, much older than any existing religion, or even any religion of which we have any historical or archeological knowledge....

What, then, could explain both the diversity and the similarities in the religious ideas we observe around the world? Are the similarities due to the fact that all religious ideas spring from a common ancestor idea, passed on over the generations as people spread around the globe, or are such ideas independently rediscovered by just about every culture because they are simply the truth and obvious enough to occur to people in due course? These are obviously naïve oversimplifications, but at least they are attempts to ask and answer explicit questions often left unexamined....

The first thing we have to understand about human minds as suitable homes for religion is how our minds understand *other* minds! Everything that moves needs something like a mind to keep it out of harm's way and help it find the good things; even a lowly clam, which tends to stay in one place, has one of the key features of a mind—a harm-avoiding retreat of its feeding "foot" into its shell when something alarming is detected. Any vibration or bump is apt to set it off, and probably most of these are harmless, but *better safe than sorry* is the clam's motto (the free-floating rationale of the clam's alarm system). More mobile animals have evolved more discriminating methods; in particular, they tend to have the ability to divide detected motion into the banal (the rustling of the leaves, the swaying of the seaweed) and the potentially vital: the "*animate* motion" (or "biological motion") of another *agent*, another animal, with a mind, who might be a predator, or a prey, or a mate, or a rival conspecific. This makes economic sense, of course. If you startle at every motion you detect, you'll never find supper, and if you don't startle at the dangerous motions, you'll soon be somebody else's supper. This is another Good Trick, an evolutionary innovation—like eyesight itself, or flight—that is so useful to so many different ways of life that it evolves over and over again in many different

species. Sometimes this Good Trick can be too much of a good thing; then we have what Justin Barrett calls a *hyperactive agent detection device*, or HADD. This overshooting is not restricted to human beings. When your dog leaps up and growls when some snow falls off the eaves with a thud that rouses him from his nap, he is manifesting a "false positive" orienting response triggered by his HADD.

Recent research on animal intelligence has shown that some mammals and birds, and perhaps some other creatures as well, carry these agent-discriminations into more sophisticated territory. Evidence shows that they not only distinguish the animate movers from the rest but draw distinctions between the likely *sorts* of motions to anticipate from the animate ones; will it attack me or flee, will it move left or right, will it back down if I threaten, does it see me yet, does it want to eat me or would it prefer to go after my neighbor. These cleverer animal minds have discovered the further Good Trick of *adopting the intentional stance*: they treat some other things in the world as agents....

Whenever an animal treats something as an *agent*, with beliefs and desires (with knowledge and goals), I say that it is *adopting the intentional stance* or treating that thing as an *intentional system*. The intentional stance is a useful perspective for an animal to take in a hostile world, since there are things out there that may *want* it and may have *beliefs* about where it is heading....

There is no doubt at all that normal human beings do not have to be *taught* how to conceive of the world as containing lots of agents who, like themselves, have beliefs and desires, as well as beliefs and desires about the beliefs and desires of others.... This virtuoso use of the intentional stance comes naturally, and it has the effect of saturating the human environment with *folk psychology*.... So powerful is our innate urge to adopt the intentional stance that we have real difficulty turning it off when it is no longer appropriate....

Extrapolating back to human prehistory with the aid of biological thinking, we can surmise how folk religions emerged without conscious and deliberate design, just as languages emerged, by interdependent processes of biological and cultural evolution. At the root of human belief in gods lies an instinct on a hair trigger: the disposition to attribute *agency*—beliefs and desires and other mental states—to anything complicated that moves....

Religion, the Early Days

Simple forms of what we might call *practical animism* are arguably not mistakes at all, but extremely useful ways of keeping track of the tendencies of designed things, living or artifactual....But sometimes the tactic of seeking an intentional-stance perspective comes up dry. Much as our ancestors would have loved to predict the weather by figuring out what it *wanted* and what *beliefs* it harbored about them, it simply didn't work. It no doubt *seemed* to work, however. Every now and then the rain dances were rewarded by rain....

Put these two ideas together—a hyperactive agent-seeking bias and a weakness for certain sorts of memorable combos—and you get a kind of fiction-generating contraption. Every time something puzzling happens, it triggers a sort of curiosity startle, a "Who's there?" response that starts churning out "hypotheses" of sorts: "Maybe its Sam, maybe it's a wolf, maybe its...a tree that can walk—*hey, maybe it's a tree that can walk!*" We can suppose that this process *almost never* generates anything with any staying power—millions or billions of little stretches of fantasy that almost instantly evaporate beyond recall until, one day, one happens to occur at just the right moment, with just the right sort of zing, to get rehearsed not just once and not just twice, but many times. A line of ideas—the walking-tree lineage—is born. Every time the initiator's mind is led to review the curious idea, not deliberately but just idly, the idea gets a little stronger—in the sense of a little more likely to occur in the initiator's mind again. And again. It has a little self-replicative power, a little *more* self-replicative power than the other fantasies it competes with for time in the brain. It is not yet a meme, an item that escapes an individual mind and spreads through human culture, but it is a good proto-meme....

To sum up the story so far: The memorable nymphs and fairies and goblins and demons that crowed the mythologies of every people are the imaginative offspring of a hyperactive habit of finding agency wherever anything puzzles or frightens us. This mindlessly generates a vast overpopulation of agent-ideas, most of which are too stupid to hold our attention for an instant....

It is in the genetic interests of parents...to inform—not misinform—their young, so it is efficient (and relatively safe) to *trust* one's parents....Once the information superhighway between parent and child is established by genetic evolution, it is ready to be used—or abused—by any agents with agendas of their own, *or by any memes that happen to have features that benefit from the biases built into the highway.*

"Natural selection builds child brains with a tendency to believe whatever their parents and tribal elders tell them" (Dawkins). It is not surprising, then, to find religious leaders in every part of the world hitting upon the extra authority provided them by their taking on the title "Father."...

People have been taught since childhood, and hence will avow, that God knows *everything*....But what good to us is the gods' knowledge if we can't get it from them? How could one communicate with the gods? Our...ancestors stumbled on an extremely ingenious solution: *divination*. We all know how hard it is to make the major decisions of life: Should I hang tough or admit my transgression? Should I move or stay in my present position? . . . We still haven't figured out any satisfactory systematic way of deciding these things. Anything that can relieve the burden of figuring out how to make these hard calls is bound to be an attractive idea. Consider flipping a coin, for instance. Why do we do it? To take away the burden of having to *find a reason* for choosing A or B. We like to have reasons for what we do, but sometimes nothing sufficiently persuasive comes to mind, and we recognize that we have to decide soon, so we concoct a little gadget, an external thing that will make the decision for us. But if the decision is about something momentous, like whether to go to war, or marry, or confess, anything like flipping a coin would just be too, well, flippant. In such a case, choosing for *no good reason* would be too obviously a sign of incompetence....Something more ceremonial, more impressive is needed, like divination, which not only tells you what to do, but gives you a reason (if you squint just right and use your imagination)....

Even if people are not, in general, capable of making good decisions on the information they have, it may *seem to them* that divination helps them think about their strategic predicaments, and this may provide the motivation to cling to the practice. For reasons they cannot fathom, divination provides relief and makes them feel good—rather like tobacco. And note that none of this is genetic transmission. We're talking about a culturally transmitted practice of divination, not an instinct. We don't have to settle the empirical question now of whether divination memes are mutualist memes that actually enhance the fitness of their hosts or parasite memes that they'd be better off without. Eventually it would be good to get an evidence-based answer to this question, but for the time being it is the question I am interested in. Notice, too, that this leaves wide open the possibility that divination (under specific circumstances, to be discovered and confirmed) is a mutualist meme because it's *true*—because there *is* a God who knows what is in everyone's heart and on special occasions tells people what to do. After all, the reason why water is deemed essential to life in every human culture is that it *is* essential to life. For the moment, my point is just that divination, which appears just about everywhere in human culture, could be understood as a natural phenomenon paying for itself in the biological coin of replication, whether or not it is actually a source of reliable information, strategic or otherwise....

Every folk religion has rituals. To an evolutionist, rituals stand out like peacocks in a sunlit glade. They are usually stunningly expensive: they often involve the deliberate destruction of valuable food and other property—to say nothing of human sacrifices—are often physically taxing or even injurious to the participants, and typically require impressive preparation time and effort. Who or what is the beneficiary of all this extravagant outlay? We have already seen two ways rituals might pay for themselves, as psychologically necessary features of divination techniques, or hypnotic induction procedures in shamanic healing. Once they were established on the scene for these purposes, they would be available to be adapted for other uses.... But there are other possibilities to explore....

People run and jump and throw stones pretty much the same way everywhere, and this regularity is explained by the physical properties of human limbs and musculature and the uniformity of wind resistance around the globe, not a tradition somehow passed down from generation to generation. On the other hand, where no constraints ensure reinvention, items of culture will be able to wander swiftly, widely, and unrecognizably in the absence of mechanisms of copying fidelity. And wherever this wandering transmission occurs, there will automatically be selection for mechanisms that enhance copying fidelity whenever they arise, *whether or not people care*, since any such mechanisms will tend to persist longer in the cultural medium than alternative (and no less costly) mechanisms that get themselves copied indifferently.

One of the best ways of ensuring copying fidelity over many replications is the "majority rule" strategy that is the basis for the uncannily reliable behavior of computers. It was the great mathematician John von Neumann who saw a way of applying this trick in the real world of engineering so that Alan Turing's imaginary computing machine could become a reality, permitting us to manufacture highly reliable computers out of unavoidably unreliable parts. Practically perfect transmission of trillions of bits is routinely executed by even the cheapest computers these days,... but this trick has been invented and reinvented over the centuries in many variations....

Long before it was consciously invented or discovered, this Good Trick (a move in design space that will be "discovered" again and again by blind evolutionary processes simply because so many different adaptive paths lead to it and thereby endorse it) was already embodied as an adaptation of memes. It can be seen at work in any oral tradition, religious or secular, in which people act in unison—praying or singing or dancing, for instance. Not everybody will remember the words or the melody or the next step, but most will, and those who are out of step will quickly correct themselves to join the throng, preserving the traditions much more reliably than any of them could do on their own. It doesn't depend on virtuoso memorizers scattered among them; nobody needs to be better than average. It is mathematically provable that such "multiplexing" schemes can overcome the "weakest link" phenomenon, and make a mesh that is much *stronger* than its weakest links. It is no accident that religions all have occasions on which the adherents come together to act in public unison in rituals. Any religion without such occasions would already be extinct.

A public ritual is a great way of preserving content with high fidelity, but why are people so eager to participate in rituals in the first place? Since we are presuming that they are *not* intent on preserving the fidelity of their meme-copying by constituting a sort of social computer-memory, what motivates them to join in? Here, there are currently a welter of conflicting hypotheses that will take some time and research to resolve, an embarrassment of riches in need of culling. Consider what we can call the shamanic-advertising hypothesis. Shamans the world over conduct much of their medicine in public ceremonies, and they are adept at getting the local people not just to watch while they induce a trance in themselves or their clients but to participate, with drumming, singing, chanting, and dancing....Innate curiosity, stimulated by music and rhythmic dancing and other forms of "sensory pageantry," could probably account for the initial motivation to join the chorus....

Doesn't there have to be some*one* to prime the pump? How would this initially get started unless there were some people, some agents, who *wanted* to start a ritual tradition As usual, this hunch betrays a failure of evolutionary imagination. It is of course possible—and in some instances surely *likely* or even *proven*—that some community leader or other agent set out to design a ritual to serve a particular purpose, but we have seen that such an author is not strictly necessary. Even elaborate and expensive rituals of public rehearsal could *emerge* out of earlier practices and habits without conscious design....

Note that, so far, the adaptations that we have uncovered as likely contributors to the survival of religions have been neutral on the subject of whether or not *we* are beneficiaries. They are features of the medium, not the message, designed to ensure the transmission fidelity—a requirement of evolution—while almost entirely neutral with regard to whether what is transmitted is good (a mutualist), bad (a parasite), or neutral (a commensal)....

THE EVOLUTION OF STEWARDSHIP

How long could folk religion be carried along by our ancestors before reflection began to transform it? We may get some perspective on this by looking at other species. It is obvious that birds don't need

to understand the principles of aerodynamics that dictate the shapes of their wings. It is less obvious—but still true—that birds can be uncomprehending participants in such elaborate rituals as *leks*—the mating meeting places sometimes called "nature's nightclubs"—where females of a local population of a species gather to observe the competitive performances by the males, who strut their stuff. The rationale for leks, which are also found in some mammals, fish, and even insects, is clear: leks *pay for themselves* as efficient methods of male selection under specifiable conditions. But the animals that participate in leks don't need to have any understanding of why they do what they do. The males show up and show off, and the females pay attention and let their choices be guided by the "dictates of their heats," which, unbeknownst to them, have been shaped by natural selection over many generations.

Could our proclivity for participating in religious rituals have a similar explanation? The fact that our rituals are passed on through culture, not genes, doesn't rule out this prospect at all. We know that specific languages are passed on through culture, not genes, but there has also been genetic evolution that has tuned our brains for ever more adept acquisition and use of language. Our brains have evolved to become more effective word processors, and they may also have evolved to become more effective implementers of the culturally transmitted habits of folk religions....Sensitivity to ritual...could be part of that package....

Folk religions emerge out of the daily lives of people living in small groups, and they share common features the world over. How and when did these metamorphose into organized religions? There is a general consensus among researchers that the big shift responsible was the emergence of agriculture and the larger settlements that this made both possible and necessary....

What I now want to suggest is that, alongside the domestication of animals and plants, there was a gradual process in which the wild (self-sustaining) memes of folk religion became thoroughly domesticated. They acquired stewards. Memes that are fortunate enough to have stewards, people who will work hard and use their intelligence to foster their propagation and protect them from their enemies, are relieved of much of the burden of keeping their own lineages going.... The wild memes of language and folk religion, in other words, are like rats and squirrels, pigeons and cold viruses—magnificently adapted to living with us and exploiting us, whether we like them or not. The domesticated memes, in contrast, depend on help from human guardians to keep going....

So we find the same devices invented over and over again, in just about every religion, and many nonreligious organizations as well.... For instance, *accepting inferior status to an invisible god* is a cunning stratagem, whether or not its cunning is consciously recognized by those who stumble upon it. Those who rely on it will thrive, wittingly or otherwise. As every subordinate knows, one's commands are more effective than they might otherwise be if one can accompany them with a threat to tell the bigger boss if disobedience ensues. (Variations on this stratagem are well known to Mafia underlings and used-car salesmen, among others—"I myself am not authorized to make such an offer, so I'll have to check with my boss. Excuse me for a minute.")....

The gods will get you if you try to cross either one of us. We have already noted the role of rituals, both individual rehearsals and unison error-absorption sessions, in enhancing the fidelity of memetic transmission, and noted that these are enforced by making nonparticipation costly in one way or another....

The transmission of religion has been attended by voluminous revision, often deliberate and foresighted, as people became stewards of the ideas that had entered them, domesticating them. Secrecy, deception, and systematic invulnerability to disconfirmation are some of the features that have emerged, and these have been designed by processes that were sensitive to new answers to the "who benefits" question, as the stewards' motives entered the process....

Belief in Belief

It has been noted by many commentators that typical, canonical religious beliefs cannot be tested for truth. As I suggested earlier, this is as good as a defining characteristic of religious creeds. They have to be "taken on faith" and are not subject to (scientific, historical) confirmation. But, more than that, for this reason and others, religious-belief *expressions* cannot really be taken at face value. The anthropologists Craig Palmer and Lyle Steadman [argue for] the need to recast anthropological theories as accounts of religious behavior, not religious belief: "While religious beliefs are not identifiable, religious behavior is, and this aspect of human experience can be comprehended. What is needed is an explanation of this observable religious behavior that is restricted to what can be observed."...

[It is not just anthropologists who are outsiders.] When it comes to interpreting religious avowals of others, *everyone is an outsider*. Why? Because religious avowals concern matters that are beyond observation, beyond meaningful test, so the only thing *anybody* can go on is religious behavior, and, more specifically, the behavior of *professing*. A child growing up in a culture is like an anthropologist, after all, surrounded by informants whose professings stand in need of interpretation. The fact that your informants are your father and mother, and speak in your mother tongue, does not give you anything more than a slight circumstantial advantage over the adult anthropologist who has to rely on a string of bilingual interpreters to query the informants. (And think about your own case: weren't you ever baffled or confused about just what you were supposed to believe? You know perfectly well that *you* don't have privileged access to the tenets of the faith you were raised in. I am just asking you to generalize the point, to recognize that others are in no better position.)....

Toward a Buyer's Guide to Religion

Does religion *make us better*? William James distinguished two main ways in which this might be true. It might make people *more effective* in their daily lives, healthier, both physically and mentally, more steadfast and composed, more strong-willed against temptation, less tormented by despair, better able to bear their misfortunes without giving up. He calls this the "mind-cure movement." Or it might make people *morally* better. The ways in which religion purports to accomplish this he calls "saintliness." Or it could accomplish both ends, in varying degrees under different circumstances....

So is religion good for your health? There is growing evidence that many religions have succeeded remarkably well on this score, improving both the health and morale of their members, quite independently of the good works they may have accomplished to benefit others. For instance, eating disorders such as anorexia nervosa and bulimia are much less common among women in Muslim countries, in which the physical attractiveness of women plays a muted role relative to that in Westernized countries.... [These] questions are [independent] from whether or not any religious beliefs are *true*.... The results so far are strong but in need of further investigation....

MORALITY AND RELIGION

Religion plays its most important role in supporting morality, many think, by giving people an unbeatable reason to do good: the promise of an infinite reward in heaven, and (depending on tastes) the threat of an infinite punishment in hell if they don't. Without the divine carrot and stick, goes this reasoning, people would loll about aimlessly or indulge their basest desires, break their promises, cheat on their spouses, neglect their duties, and so on. There are two well-known problems with this reasoning: (1) it doesn't seem to be true, which is good news, since (2) it is such a demeaning view of human nature.

I have uncovered no evidence to support the claim that people, religious or not, who *don't* believe in reward in heaven and/or punishment in hell are more likely to kill, rape, rob, or break their promises than people who do. The prison population in the United States shows Catholics, Protestants, Jews, Muslims, and others—including those with no religious affiliation—represented about as they are in the general population. Brights (nonbelievers) and others with no religious affiliation exhibit the same range of moral excellence and turpitude as born-again Christians, but, more to the point, so do members of religions that deemphasize or actively deny any relationship between moral behavior "on earth" and eventual postmortem reward and punishment. And when it comes to "family values," the available evidence to date supports the hypothesis that brights (nonbelievers) have the lowest divorce rate in the United States, and born-again Christians, the highest....

But what about that hunger for spirituality that so many of my informants think is the mainspring of religious allegiance? The good news is that people really do want to be good. Believers and brights alike deplore the crass materialism of popular culture and yearn not just to enjoy the beauty of genuine love but to bring that joy to others. It may often have been true in the past that for most people the only available road to that fulfillment involved a commitment to the supernatural, and more particularly to a specific institutional version of the supernatural, but today we can see that there is a bounty of alternative highways and footpaths to consider.

The widely prevailing opinion that religion is the bulwark of morality is problematic at best. The idea that heavenly reward is what motivates good people is demeaning and unnecessary; the idea that religion at its best gives meaning to a life is jeopardized by the hypocrisy trap into which we have fallen; the idea that religious authority grounds our moral judgments is useless in genuine ecumenical exploration; and the presumed relation between spirituality and moral goodness is an illusion.

STUDY QUESTIONS

1. How does Dennett connect evolution with religion?
2. How does Dennett see folk religion developing, and how does he assess its success?
3. How does Dennett assess the benefit of religion, and what might be his prognostication for its survival?
4. What in Dennett's presentation makes him a nonrealist on religion?

The Buddha

BUDDHIST NONREALISM

A meditator and an ascetic express dissatisfaction with the Buddha's failure to provide them with answers to metaphysical questions about the nature of the world, the soul and the body, and life after death. The Buddha replies that he does not propose theories, in particular about the unobservable. What he knows and speaks about is the unsatisfactoriness of life and how to resolve it by controlling the events (attachment groups) that govern our lives. The religious life thus is directed toward the removal of pain and suffering caused by ignorance, cravings, and hatred. Its language is not meant to be metaphysical, discussing whether theories are true or false, but rather tries to address human experience. It succeeds insofar as it resolves the difficulties we face in our painful experience and ultimately leads to the cessation of passion, to wisdom, and to Nirvana.

QUESTIONS THAT DON'T TEND TO EDIFICATION

Sermon 1

On a certain occasion the Blessed One was dwelling at Sāvatthi in Jetavana monastery.... Now it happened to the venerable Māluñkyāputta, being in seclusion and plunged in meditation, that a consideration presented itself to his mind, as follows:

"These theories which the Blessed One has left unelucidated, has set aside and rejected—that the world is eternal, the world is not eternal, that the world is finite, that the world is infinite, that the soul and the body are identical, that the soul is one thing and the body another, that the saint exists after death, that the saint does not exist after death, that the saint both exists and does not exist after death, that the saint neither exists nor does not exist after death—these the Blessed One does not elucidate to me...."

"Pray, Māluñkyāputta, did I ever say to you, 'Come, Māluñkyāputta, lead the religious life under me, and I will elucidate to you either that the world is eternal, or that the world is not eternal,... or that the saint neither exists nor does not exist after death'?"

"No, truly, Reverend Sir."

"Or did you ever say to me, 'Reverend Sir, I will lead the religious life under the Blessed One, on condition that the Blessed One elucidate to me either that the world is eternal, or that the world is not eternal,... or

Majjima-Nikaya, Suttas 63 and 72. In *Buddhism in Translations*, ed. and trans. by Henry Clarke Warren (New York: Atheneum), 1973.

that the saint neither exists nor does not exist after death'?"

"No, truly, Reverend Sir."...

"It is as if, Māluñkyāputta, a man had been wounded by an arrow thickly smeared with poison, and his friends and companions, his relatives and kinsfolk, were to procure for him a physician or surgeon; and the sick man were to say, 'I will not have this arrow taken out until I have learned whether this man who wounded me belonged to the warrior caste, or to the Brahman caste, or to the agricultural caste, or to the menial cast.'

"Or again he were to say, 'I will not have this arrow taken out until I have learned whether the man who wounded me was tall, or short, or of the middle height.'...

"The religious life does not depend on the dogma that the world is eternal; nor does the religious life depend on the dogma that the world is not eternal. Whether the dogma obtain, Māluñkyāputta, there still remain birth, old age, death, sorrow, lamentation, misery, grief, and despair, for the extinction of which in the present life I am prescribing.

"The religious life does not depend on the dogma that the world is finite,...or that the soul and body are identical,...or that the saint exists after death....

"Accordingly, Māluñkyāputta, bear always in mind what it is that I have not elucidated, and what it is that I have elucidated. And what have I not elucidated? I have not elucidated that the world is eternal; I have not elucidated that the world is not eternal; I have not elucidated that the world is finite; I have not elucidated that the world is infinite; I have not elucidated that the soul and body are identical; I have not elucidated that the soul is one thing and the body another; I have not elucidated that the saint exists after death; I have not elucidated that the saint does not exist after death; I have not elucidated that the saint neither exists nor does not exist after death. And why, Māluñkyāputta, have I not elucidated this? Because this profits not, nor has to do with the fundamentals of religion, nor tends to aversion, absence of passion, cessation, quiescence, the supernatural faculties, supreme wisdom, and Nirvana; therefore have I not elucidated it.

"And what have I elucidated? Misery have I elucidated; the origin of misery have I elucidated; the cessation of misery have I elucidated; and the path leading to the cessation of misery have I elucidated. And why have I elucidated this? Because this does profit, has to do with the fundamentals of religion, and tends to aversion, absence of passion, cessation, quiescence, knowledge, supreme wisdom, and Nirvana; therefore have I elucidated it. Accordingly, Māluñkyāputta, bear always in mind what it is that I have not elucidated, and what it is that I have elucidated."

Sermon 2

Vaccha, the wandering ascetic, spoke to the Blessed One as follows:

"How is it, Gotama? Does Gotama hold that the world is eternal, and that this view alone is true, and every other false?"

"Nay, Vaccha. I do not hold that the world is eternal and that this view alone is true, and every other false."

"But how is it, Gotama? Does Gotama hold that the world is not eternal, and that this view alone is true, and every other false?"

"Nay, Vaccha. I do not hold that the world is not eternal and that this view alone is true, and every other false."

"How is it, Gotama? Does Gotama hold that the world is finite,...that the soul and the body are identical,...the saint exists after death,...that the saint both exists and does not exist after death, and that this view alone is true, and every other false?"

"Nay Vaccha. I do not hold that the saint both exists and does not exist after death, and that this view alone is true, and every other false....

"Vaccha, the theory that the world is eternal, (that the world is finite, that the soul and body are identical, that the saint exists after death) is a jungle, a wilderness, a puppet show, a writhing, and a fetter, and is coupled with misery, ruin, despair, and agony, and does not tend to aversion, absence of passion, cessation, quiescence, knowledge, supreme wisdom, and Nirvana....

"The Tathāgata (one who has passed over), O Vaccha, is free from theories; but this does the Tathāgata know,—the nature of form, and how form arises, and how form perishes; the nature of sensation, and how sensation arises, and how sensation perishes; the nature of perception (predispositions, consciousness), and how perception (predispositions, consciousness) arises, and how perception (predispositions, consciousness) perishes. Therefore say I that the Tathāgata has attained deliverance and is free from attachment, inasmuch as all imaginings, or agitations, or proud thoughts concerning an ego or anything pertaining to an ego, have perished, have faded away, have ceased, have been given up and relinquished."

STUDY QUESTIONS

1. What are the worries of the two questioners of the Buddha?
2. How does the Buddha respond to these worries?
3. What does this discourse tell us about the way the Buddha was concerned with metaphysical or religious theories and language?

Roger Trigg

A Defense of Religious Realism

Roger Trigg (b. 1941) argues that not only can we study religion as a social phenomenon, we can rightly raise questions about whether it is rational to hold religious beliefs and whether those beliefs are true. The social science approach to religion ignores the content of the beliefs but treats the beliefs and institutions of religion as another social fact that arises for social reasons. Trigg points out the paradox that those who try to explain religion *merely* as a social fact and reject its claims about truth are subject to the same account of their work—namely, that their view of religion has nothing to do with claims to truth or rationality and everything to do with being the product of social forces. Rather, he wants to maintain both that religion has a social function and that questions about the truth and rationality of religious beliefs can be raised. Thus, religious beliefs might be held not only because they are useful, but because they are true.

1. Reasoning About Religion

The issue of what kind of truth a religion can lay claim to is hotly contested. There is, however, a prevalent temptation to avoid the question by changing the subject. This becomes particularly apparent when different religions are studied and compared. Religion, whatever else it may be, clearly embodies social practices and bodies of belief expressed in particular ways of life. Social scientists and those studying different religions are therefore going to be drawn into concentrating on these unquestioned social effects. They will quite rightly feel that consideration of religious claims to truth will involve them in matters that are more properly the preserve of philosophy or

even theology. The fear of some hidden "theological agenda" makes them very jealous of their status as independent scholars and "scientists." What people believe and the reasons they give for so doing will tend to be ignored. The mere fact that they have those beliefs and that they are encapsulated in public, social practices will be enough. Yet the problem that must be confronted is whether such an approach does violence to important features of religion. For one thing, it appears to ignore the claim that religious beliefs can themselves be held on rational grounds and hence have a right to claim truth.

The claim that it is rational to hold a religious belief must be sharply distinguished from a parallel argument. Can we study the nature of religion in a

Roger Trigg, *Rationality and Religion* (Oxford: Blackwell, 1998), pp. 29–36, 39–41.

rational way? How far can we capture its nature if we view it simply as one among many kinds of social phenomena? Is it possible to talk of the scientific study of religion, and accept the possibility of a rational examination of religion in a dispassionate and objective manner? For those who doubt whether social science should be modelled on a science like chemistry, this will be one more example of a more general problem. There is a perpetual tug between those who wish to understand human behaviour and those who want to explain it. Some have the goal of interpretative understanding, stemming from a hermeneutical approach. Others wish to provide a causal explanation, integrating human social activity firmly in the natural world. Whatever difficulties arise from the standpoint of social science, religion brings additional complications. A social scientific approach to religion must treat religious beliefs and institutions as social facts. In other words, it is not dealing with the content of such belief, but its context. Religion, it may be held, promotes social solidarity and contributes to the stability of a society. Whether true or not, this is a thesis about the effects of religious belief and the function religion plays in a society. It has such effects and functions whether it is true or false. Social science has no need to assess the rationality of a belief to see the role it plays in society.

The sociology of religion becomes a species of the sociology of knowledge, so long as the latter is understood in a benign way. One classic statement of the phenomenological brand of the sociology of knowledge is that given by Berger and Luckmann. They say: "It is our contention that the sociology of knowledge must concern itself with whatever passes for 'knowledge' in a society, regardless of the ultimate validity or invalidity (by whatever criterion) of such 'knowledge.'"[1] This brand of the sociology of knowledge looks at how reality is constructed in a given society. Its role will, given its "bracketing off" of questions of truth and falsity, be ultimately descriptive. It will show how systems of belief are held and unfold their nature. Such phenomenological analysis, according to Berger and Luckmann, "refrains from any causal or genetic hypotheses, as well as from assertions about the ontological status of the phenomenon analysed." Clearly if this method

is applied to the study of religion, it can be both liberating and restricting. It enables students of religion to look at what religious belief means to the participants of a particular religious way of life, without getting involved in theological judgements about what is true. At the same time, however, many would find such an analysis too bland, since it aims at nothing deeper than description. It is certainly empirical in that "fieldwork" of various kinds would be essential to find out how beliefs and purported knowledge appear to those who hold them. Yet if science aims to do more than show what happens, and if it aims at some deeper form of understanding and explanation, this kind of survey of religions may not seem to get very far. As one writer says: "To restrict the study of religion to pure description precludes what seems to be of the essence of science, namely explanation and theory."[2] This argument about the proper way to approach religion is, of course, one instance of a general dispute about the role of social science.

Endemic in such disputes is the question of the "insider" and the "outsider." Accounts of social science derived from the views of the later Wittgenstein on meaning stress the fact that the only way to understand a concept is to learn how to use it. At first sight, this merely shows the importance of fieldwork in placing concepts in their proper contexts. Yet what is really at issue is whether someone coming to a society, whether that of a remote tribe, or merely a particular religious institution, can be in a better position to know what is going on than a participant. Again the problem of whether social science is more than elucidation and description arises. This is particularly important in the case of religion, since the issue of whether anyone else can explain religion in terms that would be rejected by the participants is a crucial one. Phenomenological analysis will, by its very nature, be in no danger of challenging the beliefs of the people it is investigating. By its procedure of "bracketing off" questions of truth, it practises a methodological agnosticism about the substantive issues. Yet the question must remain how much it can achieve. It would certainly seem difficult for it to add anything to an understanding of religion which was not already implicit in the believer's own perspective.

For anyone schooled in the idea that we should be able to reason about anything, it may seem odd if religious beliefs, together with the other elements of human culture, cannot themselves be an object of our reasoning. Why, it may be asked, should there not be a clear demarcation between being religious and studying religion? This becomes impossible, if religion can only be understood from the inside. One either understands and believes, or one fails to understand. In that case, atheism would be impossible, since no one could understand enough to deny the truth of what is understood. The assumption, however, in the case of those who would study religion is not that they are confronting internal questions of truth and falsity. Instead they wish to take up an external position and look at religion and its role purely as a cultural construction. The whole point of this approach is that the observer takes up a different stance from that of the participant. A certain distance is needed to look at the religion and its effects. The question, however, must be whether this distancing can allow us to do justice to the object of our study. Since the fact of belief becomes more important than what is believed, the inevitable tendency will be to look for explanations of the belief elsewhere in society and in the human mind. The very fact that we stand back from the beliefs, and refuse to examine their truth, will have the result that scientific explanations of such belief will have to dismiss any idea that a belief is held because it is true....

2. EXPLAINING RELIGION

The sociology of science has often taken a strong explanatory line instead of a neutral descriptive one in its approach to the physical sciences. Yet it seems set on a self-defeating course if it holds that no scientist can ever hold a belief simply because it is true. There will always be some other explanation why it is thought true. The same mode of argument will then be used about the sociologist who has been conditioned to see things in one way rather than another. Does the study of religion fall into the same trap, holding that a religious person is somehow the product of social forces when the student of religion is miraculously not? The more this question is pursued, the clearer it becomes that an invocation of

science is in fact promoting it above religion. What is being proclaimed is a scientistic attitude according to which knowledge is restricted to what can be produced by human scientific method. There is an echo here of the old positivist insistence on science being restricted to empirical data, which were public and could be shared, to experiments that could be repeated, and to observations which were accessible to all. Positivism lives on in a naturalism that refuses to countenance specifically religious claims to truth, but restricts itself to what is within the province of science. "Naturalists" of this kind will inevitably want explanations as to why anyone should have peculiar beliefs of the kind afforded by religion. For many such thinkers rationality demands evidence, but the evidence produced in favour of religious faith would be regarded as inadmissible. Appeals to revelation would be seen as private, idiosyncratic beliefs which cannot be validated in a manner which enables them to be shared with others. Even when such beliefs are held by a community, there still remains the question how they can be discussed with those outside the community. At the root of such an attitude is a view of reason which stems from the Enlightenment, with its opposition of reason to revelation and of the natural to the supernatural. The consequence is to assume that religions are cultural constructions. All that can be known about a religion will, it is said, be known scientifically. Science can have no access to whatever transcendent reality is proclaimed by religion, and there will be no difference to the scholar whether it exists or not. It can only be understood within the ideological context of the religious life.

The problem is that it is always easier to accept such an approach to a religion that appears primitive and superstitious than to the "higher" religions. Even a Christian theologian might be willing to accept a naturalistic explanation (in terms, say, of social function) for an African tribal religion, while indignantly refusing to accept that similar explanations can exhaust what can be said about Christianity. The field of comparative religion has produced those who want to give a naturalistic account of all religion. Anyone wanting a scientific theory of religion would want a general account which could be genuinely transcultural. Accounts on the other hand which insist on appealing to the conceptual scheme of the participants could never get beyond the bounds of the culture they were investigating. Yet once the student occupies a vantage point beyond religion, the pressure will undoubtedly exist to give reductionist theories of religion which deliberately ignore the particular claims of particular religions. Social scientists have often been drawn to functionalist accounts which focus on the functions a religion may serve in society. They stress its role in promoting social solidarity, although it is also rather obviously a source of division and dispute in many societies. They also stress its contribution to the maintenance of social order. The point of such explanations is that they can be applied to any religion regardless of the content of its beliefs. Sacrificing to the Roman emperor could serve the same function as a great state occasion organized by the Church of England. Both serve to uphold the established order, and yet may be motivated by different beliefs. Some participants may be taking part in a ritual for its own sake, but in the latter case a belief in the truth of Christian doctrine would surely be motivating some of the participants. The function may not be the purpose, and even unacknowledged or latent functions may not provide a full explanation of what is occurring. Applause at a central meeting of the old Soviet Communist Party may have fulfilled a similar function to the singing of the Gloria in church. Yet the systems of belief being upheld are markedly different. Even if the fulfilment of function might serve to perpetuate the holding of the belief, it fails to explain its origins. Why should people hold one set of beliefs rather than another? The danger of accounts given by social scientists (and scientists of other kinds) is that they tend to flatten out differences in belief as being of little account. Since what matters to them are the social effects of religion what is believed is subordinated to the fact of belief.

A naturalistic approach certainly encourages this process. Religion has to be explained in ways that take no account of the object of belief, if it is assumed that there is no such thing as the supernatural (however defined), or that if there is such a thing, it cannot be in contact with us. This approach is summed up by Drees when he says: "I do not see religiously relevant gaps in the natural and human world, where the divine could somehow interfere with natural reality."[3] He concludes that as a result of this "the origins and functions of religions may be intelligible." Without the possibility of divine intervention, the origins of religious belief clearly lie wholly in this world. On the other hand, if there is a God who is revealed to some in a special way, we may feel that we need look no further for an explanation for the sparking of religious faith. In other words, it may seem as if the question of the scope of the scientific explanation for religion comes down to whether religious claims are true or not. If they are, that is their justification. If not, we then need some further reason as to why people should produce and hold to such beliefs. A similar pattern of reasoning has marked the development of the sociology of science. It was tacitly assumed at first that truth was its own explanation while the occurrence of scientific error seemed to demand a special explanation. The so-called "strong programme" in the sociology of knowledge[4] undertook to provide a causal account of all scientific beliefs. The weight of explanation was moved from truth to what is considered true, and that was thought to be wholly within the scope of sociological investigation. Truth, it was thought, could not be abstracted from what is held true. All emphasis was put on the social environment and the agreements negotiated, not on the internal character of the beliefs themselves.

This way of looking at things must become profoundly anti-realist in that no distinction is drawn between what is the case and what is believed to be the case. Reality drops out in favour of understandings of reality. The latter seem to be firmly within the province of the social scientists. Yet in the end it has to be realized that a distinction has to be drawn between the object, of whatever kind, under study and the beliefs of the sociologist or anthropologist conducting the study. At that point, the very same distinction between the subject and the object of belief is bound to re-emerge. Social scientists cannot claim validity for their discipline without allowing that it is motivated by the very same search for truth that they wish to suggest in others is merely the expression of social or psychological conditions.

Dangers of self-reference arise when truth is reduced to issues about the causes of belief. There is a further difficulty which arises when a stark contrast is made between the insider and the outsider. It can look as if a choice is being forced between service of the interests of an ideology or a critical stance. We must either be prepared to accept without question the claims of a religion or stand outside and unmask it as a rationalization of deeper social pressures. It is either absolute knowledge of the divine or a sham. Yet, it will be pointed out, a subservient commitment to an authoritarian structure or received dogma is the antithesis of the questioning of the scientific spirit. We are brought back once again to the values of the Enlightenment. A sleight of hand has made reason the enemy of religion. Even though criticisms of religion are being made in the name of rationality, little credence in all this is in fact being given to the powers of human rationality.

Much of the motivation for the sociology of science and for the study of religion comes from the assumption that most scientific and religious belief has proved to be mistaken. Such a conclusion would seem inevitable given the plurality of such belief. If the earth is round, those who believed it flat were in error. If there is one God, polytheists have always been wrong. If there is no God at all, most of humanity has been mistaken. Error is widespread. Once it appears to be wrong to talk of simple error in such contexts, that position can easily degenerate into relativism. The study of religion, however, has undoubtedly gained impetus from the fact of the multiplicity of religions and the ensuing conclusion that they are all held on grounds far removed from issues concerning truth. Yet it is unwise to assume that the possession of rationality can be identified with the acquisition of truth. People can stumble on the truth by accident, and it is also possible that they can be perfectly rational but be constrained by the imperfect information available to them. Given what they do know, their beliefs may be not only intelligible, but even rational. This ground alone should make us hesitate in assuming that all religious beliefs must lie beyond the bounds of rationality.

3. THE AUTONOMY OF RELIGION

Many students of religion find it convenient not so much to hold that every religion is fundamentally in error, but to conclude that in fact a religious attitude to the world can have no cognitive basis. . . . Religious belief is not to be understood as a reflection of some transcendent reality but a projection of human needs and aspirations. It might, for instance, reflect human feelings of vulnerability and dependence in the face of a natural world that can be capricious in its effects. One anthropologist is quite explicit about this. He says: "Few anthropologists appear to subscribe to the theory that humanity has religion because it was originally given or established by God. Rather, most account religion to be a variable cultural creation."[5] What is claimed within a religion is only relevant in so far as a theory can be produced as to why such things are ever claimed. The content becomes the mere projection of some feature of the human condition. . . .

This view brings us back to the issue of realism which must reoccur at every level of study. How far does what we are investigating exist in its own right or merely as a construction out of our own presuppositions? The temptation for any investigator is to treat the object of study as a product of construction, while assuming that the investigation itself is in the business of discovery. The question of levels is important. If I am investigating an independent reality, namely the beliefs and practices of a people, why should I be reluctant to accept that their beliefs in turn at least purport to be about an independent reality? Conversely, if I am convinced that the content of their beliefs is the projection of a conceptual scheme, how confident ought I to be that my own anthropological or other theories are not similarly involved in projection? It is received wisdom nowadays that all categories are rooted in some conceptual scheme, and are never just read off the world. Theory imbues them at every level. Religion will itself, it will be said, be an example of this. Yet if such a view is pushed too far, we can never discover anything, but in every context merely inhabit a world of our own construction.

Anthropology reduces content to context whereas if truth is ever to be an issue, what is asserted at any level must be detachable from the circumstances in which it is asserted. This is as important for the history of science as the study of religion. Unless the same content can be passed on through different generations and in different contexts, one cannot refer to the development of a particular scientific theory rather than a succession of different ones. In the same way, one would be unable to distinguish between differing forms of the same religion rather than a succession of different religions. The very notion of Christianity, for example, would become problematic, as would the idea of religion itself. The concept of a social fact existing independently of the investigator, and perhaps detachable from its surroundings, would be dissolved....

We can distance ourselves from all religion and reason about it. The assumption, however, that anthropological and other explanations will not only be forthcoming but will be wholly adequate to explain the origins and persistence of religion not only assumes the falsity of religious claims but also relies on the truth of anthropological ones. Yet why is religion untrustworthy and social science trustworthy? Allegations of a "theological agenda" made against those who are not willing to assume the falsity of religious claims from the outset rather invite the rejoinder that there seems to be an anti-theological agenda in place. Why should it be taken for granted that claims to truth can be rejected at one level and yet be accepted at the next? When postmodernists query anyone's right to occupy a "God's eye view" and enunciate the truth, this is not an idle debating point.

The very distinction between levels of belief, between religious belief and the study of it, indicates that truth cannot be arbitrarily claimed for one level and denied at the other. Once truth is denied at one level, the same form of argumentation may be repeated at the next.

If we acknowledge that humans are capable of reasoning about what is true, one explanation for a belief may be that it is held because it is true. The blanket assumption that all religious beliefs are mistaken and stand in further need of explanation itself stands in need of further justification. It does not follow from the mere fact of human rationality that there is no transcendent reality of the kind sought after in the religions of the world. That assumption was the product of the Enlightenment. However that may be, we can still reason about religious beliefs in a critical way. Such reasoning does not, however, have to conclude that their content is irrelevant to the fact of their being held. Social scientists may not like that, because it may put limits on the scope of their investigations. They may not be able to explain everything about religion. Yet even if a particular religious belief were true, there would still be matters that social science could tell us about. True or not, the belief would still have a function in society.

NOTES

1. Peter L. Berger and Thomas Luckmann, *The Social Construction of Reality* (New York: Anchor Books, 1966), p.15.
2. Donald Wiebe, *Beyond Legitimation* (London: Macmillan, 1994), p.121.
3. Willem B. Drees, *Religion, Science, and Naturalism* (Cambridge, England: Cambridge University Press), p.xi.
4. See D. Bloor, *Knowledge and Social Imagery* (Chicago: University of Chicago Press, 1991), and my *Understanding Social Science* (Oxford, England: Blackwell, 2001), pp.27ff.
5. Benson Saler, *Conceptualising Religion* (Leiden, the Netherlands: Brill, 1995), p.5.

STUDY QUESTIONS

1. How does Trigg view the difference between the fact *that* someone believes and *what* someone believes? How does the question of truth differ in the two cases?
2. How does Trigg turn the social scientist's reductivist view of religion (religion is to be explained by its social function in society) back on the explanatory program of the social scientists (what he refers to as the problem of self-reference)?
3. What reply does Trigg give to the argument that if religion arose from concerns for truth, there would not be such a diversity of religions and religious beliefs?

D. Z. Phillips

The Meaning of Religious Beliefs
Is Their Use

According to D. Z. Phillips (1934–2006), realists require that facts or objects actually exist for beliefs to be truth. In holding this view, Phillips claims, realists make an illicit distinction between the belief that is held (a mental state) and the actions that follow from it. To the contrary, a belief is not a report of a mental state, but is, in fact, an action, e.g., the making of an assertion. There are not, as realists hold, two things involved, an internal acceptance and a religious response, but a response in terms of actions and practices in a particular context. So, what believing manifests itself as varies according to the context that calls for action. Thus, different kinds of beliefs are shown by different kinds of practices in which we engage. With respect to belief in God, if such a belief involved picturing or referring, we could have no beliefs about God, for God is not a picturable being. In short, religious beliefs have their meaning in practices and actions, not in referring to or picturing particular objects.

It is widely assumed in contemporary philosophy of religion that if a philosopher wishes to give an analytic account of religious belief, one which seeks to clarify the grammar of that belief, he must choose between realism and nonrealism. These, it is thought, are the only philosophical alternatives open to him.... According to realists, the non-realist analyses fail to capture the essence of belief and atheism.

What is the theological realist's account of believing in God? According to Penelhum, anyone committed to realism

> would hold that the supernatural facts which he thinks faith requires must indeed *be* facts for faith to be true, so that if they are not facts, but fantasies (or, even worse, not coherently expressible), then faith is unjustified.[1]

The realist admits that faith, believing, has consequences which constitute the commitments which make up living religiously, but he insists...that "the belief is distinct from the commitment which may follow it, and is the justification for it."[2] The nonrealist's sin, it is said, is to conflate believing with the consequences of believing, so making the realist's conception of belief redundant.

For the realist, the non-realist analyses of religious belief are reductionist in character. These analyses have been arrived at as a result of the alleged difficulties created for a belief in the existence of God by the demands of verificationism. Many non-realists concur with this view. They are prepared to admit that realism portrays what faith once meant for

D. Z. Phillips, *Wittgenstein and Religion* (New York: St. Martin's Press, 1993), pp. 33–38, 40–45, 55 (edited).

people, but argue that this conception of faith cannot be sustained today. In this respect, non-realists are revisionists.... They all dispense with something, which they admit was once integral to faith, "in the interest of preserving and revitalizing the rest of it" (Penelhum, p. 163). The realist claims that what the non-realist dispenses with is logically indispensable for any notion of belief.

In contemporary philosophy of religion there has been a Wittgensteinian critique of realism. Given the assumption that philosophers have to choose between realism and non-realism, it is not surprising to find this critique discussed in these terms. The criticisms...are firmly in the non-realist camp....

What I shall show in this essay is that Wittgenstein's critique of realism is far more radical than Penelhum and Trigg suspect.... They do not realize that, for Wittgenstein, realism and non-realism are equally confused. Further, what Wittgenstein is saying is not that realism is a correct analysis of ordinary beliefs but not of religious beliefs. His view is that realism is a confused account of *any* kind of belief: believing that my brother is in America, that a theorem is valid, that fire will burn me. In short, realism is not coherently expressible.

I

Consider the following remarks by Wittgenstein:

> One man is a convinced realist, another a convinced idealist and teaches his children accordingly. In such an important matter as the existence or nonexistence of the external world they don't want to teach their children anything wrong....
>
> But the idealist will teach his children the word "chair" after all, for of course he wants to teach them to do this and that, e.g. to fetch the chair. Then there will be the difference between what the idealist-educated children say and the realist ones. Won't the difference only be one of battle cry? (*Zettel*, 413–14)

Rightly or wrongly, Wittgenstein is accusing realism and non-realism of being idle talk; talk which takes us away from the directions in which we should be looking if we want to clarify the grammar of our beliefs concerning chairs. Similarly, the accusation

against theological realism is that it is idle talk. If this accusation is a just one, realism has never been integral to faith. This does not mean that we must embrace non-realism....

Why have [realists] failed to appreciate the radical character of Wittgenstein's critique? A large part of the answer lies in their neglect of the grammatical issues involved in "believing." They take themselves to be reflecting, philosophically, a straightforward relation between belief and its object. Similarly, theological realism takes itself to be the expression of a truism: we cannot believe in God unless we believe there is a God to believe in. If that were denied, it seems belief would be robbed of its object. Aren't we all realists? What we need to realize is that, as yet *no* grammatical work has been done to elucidate the relations between belief and its object....

Realists speak of the relation between belief and its object as though the character of that relation can be taken for granted. But is the relation between belief and its object the same no matter what the character of what is believed? Realism prevents us from answering this question by ignoring the very circumstances which would enable us to answer it; the circumstances in which "really believing" has its sense....

If I say, "I believe it will rain," I am not referring to my state of mind. "I believe it will rain" can be replaced by "It'll rain." Wittgenstein writes:

> What does it mean to say that "I believe p" says roughly the same as "p"? We react in roughly the same way when anyone says the first and when he says the second: if I said the first, and someone didn't understand the words "I believe," I should repeat the sentence in the second form and so on. As I'd also explain the words "I wish you'd go away" by means of the words "Go away." (*Remarks on the Philosophy of Psychology*, vol. I, para. 477)

"I believe" is not a report or description of a mental state. It is doing something, making an assertion. But, according to [the realists], the essence of "believing" cannot be found in action, in doing anything, since, according to them, action is itself based on something called "belief." But, once again, what does this conception of belief amount to? Is it not entirely vacuous? Wittgenstein imagines someone saying, "'If I look outside, I see that it's raining; if I look within myself, I see that I believe it.' And what is one supposed to do with this information?" (*R.P.P.*, vol. I, para. 823). Wittgenstein is challenging this whole way of thinking....

But the realist divorces "believing" from the situations in human life in which [it has its] sense. On the realist's view, our actions are based on the trustworthiness of our beliefs. This means, as Wittgenstein says:

> I should have to be able to say: "I believe that it's raining, and my belief is trustworthy, so I trust it." As if my belief were some kind of sense-impression. Do you say, e.g., "I believe it, and as I am reliable, it will presumably be so"? That would be like saying: "I believe it—therefore I believe it." (*R.P.P.*, vol. I, paras. 482–83)

One way of referring to the criticisms Wittgenstein makes of realism is to say that the realist wishes to speak of the relation of belief to its object, without specifying the context of application which specifies what the relation comes to. As a result, what [the realists] mean by the relation of belief to its object remains completely obscure. Wittgenstein asks,

> How do you know that you believe that your brother is in America?... Suppose we say that the thought is some sort of process in his mind, or his saying something, etc.—then I could say: "All right, you call this a thought of your brother in America, well, what is the connection between this and your brother in America?" (*Lectures on Religious Belief*, p. 66)

If we simply say that the thought pictures the fact, this obscures the fact that it is only within a context of application that the distinction between successful and unsuccessful picturing has any application.... Wittgenstein describes the realist's dilemma as follows:

> The first idea [you have] is that you are looking at your own thought, and are absolutely sure that it is a thought that so and so. You are looking at some mental phenomenon, and you say to yourself "obviously this is a thought of my brother being in America." It seems to be a super-picture. It seems, with thought, there is no doubt whatever. With a picture, it still depends on the method of projection, whereas here it seems you get rid of the

projecting relation, and are absolutely certain that this is a thought of that.... (*L.R.B.*, p. 66)

The theological realist argues, as Trigg does: "It must be recognised that there are two distinct parts in religious commitment, the acceptance of certain propositions as true, and, as a result, a religious response, expressed in both worship and action" (p. 42). The realist argues that the same distinction can be made with respect to all our beliefs. On the one hand we believe certain things are true, and on the other hand we commit ourselves and act accordingly. But what is involved in believing something to be true? The realist can give no intelligible answer to this question. His failure is due to his exclusion of the mode of projection within which the relation of belief to its object has its sense. So when the theological realist seeks to divorce the meaning of believing from our actions and practices, he effects a divorce between belief and practice which would render *any* kind of believing unintelligible.

We cannot, as the realist supposes, give the same kind of account of belief in every context. To say that the relation between belief and its object varies is to say that contexts of application vary. Wittgenstein gives us numerous examples to illustrate this....

> Ask yourself: What does it mean to *believe* Goldbach's theorem? What does this *belief* consist in? In a feeling of certainty as we state, hear, or think of the theorem? (That would not interest us.) And what are the characteristics of this feeling? Why I don't even know how far the feeling may be caused by the proposition itself.
>
> Am I to say that belief is a particular colouring of our thoughts? Where does this idea come from? Well, there is a tone of belief, as of doubt.
>
> I should like to ask: how does the belief connect with this proposition? Let us look and see what are the consequences of this belief, where it takes us. "It makes me search for a proof of the proposition."—Very well: and now let us look and see what your searching really consists in. Then we shall know what belief in the proposition amounts to. (*Philosophical Investigations*, I, para. 578)

But now, contrast these examples with the following:

> A man would fight for his life not to be dragged into the fire. No induction. Terror. That is, as it were, part of the substance of the belief. (*L.R.B.*, p. 56)

The differences in the character of these beliefs is shown by the practices of which they are a part. The practices cannot be cut off from the beliefs in the way suggested by the realist's account of "believing." What would "believing" be after such a divorce?...

But it is to practice, what a man does, that one would look to determine whether he believes something or not. What kind of example would one have to think of to imagine a severe dislocation between a man's words and his beliefs? Consider the following:

> Imagine an observer who, as it were automatically, says what he is observing. Of course he hears himself talk, but, so to speak, he takes no notice of that. He sees that the enemy is approaching and reports it, describes it, but like a machine. What would that be like? Well, he does not act according to his observation. Of him, one might say that he speaks what he sees, but that he does not *believe* it. It does not, so to speak, get inside him. (*R.P.P.*, vol. I, para. 813)

Notice that Wittgenstein does not object to saying that the belief does not get inside this man. He might also have said that the man had not made the words he spoke his own. But it is what surrounds the words, or rather, in this case, the absence of expected surroundings, which leads to his characterisation of the words....

In all these examples, it can be seen that what the relation between belief and its object amounts to can only be seen within the context of application within which the belief has its sense. The reason why I have dwelt on so many non-religious examples is that the theological realist speaks as though, in relation to religion, philosophers of religion, influenced by Wittgenstein, have introduced a way of discussing what believing amounts to which departs from the ordinary meanings of believing. It has been said that Wittgensteinian philosophers had a motive for doing this, namely, their desire to protect religious beliefs from the stringent tests to which beliefs are subject in other spheres. As we have seen, these tests vary. To see what our beliefs come to, we must turn to the very contexts which the realists want to rule out of consideration, namely, the actions and practices we engage in. We cannot appreciate the relation between belief and its object while ignoring the appropriate context of application. These contexts vary. In bringing out differences between them, we can also bring out the grammatical differences between various beliefs. This is the philosopher's task where religious belief is concerned, not because it is a distinctive kind of belief, true though that is, but because this is the philosopher's task in endeavouring to understand what is involved in *any* kind of believing.

II

Let us suppose that someone who says that "I believe in God" pictures the object of belief, or refers to it. How is the "picturing" or "referring" to be understood? As we have seen, this involves exploring the context of application involved. This context cannot be taken for granted. We have yet to explore the relation between "I believe in God" and the object of the belief. The relation can be explored by asking how we would set about deciding whether two people believe in the same God. Rush Rhees has shown how *not* to answer this question:

> If one lays emphasis...on the fact that "god" is a substantive, and especially if one goes on...to say that it is a proper name, then the natural thing will be to assume that meaning the same by "God" is something like meaning the same by "the sun" or meaning the same by "Churchill." You might even want to use some such phrase as "stands for" the same. But nothing of that sort will do here. Questions about "meaning the same" in connexion with the names of physical objects are connected with the kind of criteria to which we may appeal in saying that this is the same object—"that is the same planet as I saw in the south west last night," "that is the same car that was standing here this morning." Supposing someone said "the word 'God' stands for a different object now." What could that mean? I know what it means to say that "the Queen" stands for a different person now, and I know what it means to say that St. Mary's Church is not the St. Mary's Church that was here in So-and-So's day. I know the sort of thing that might be said if I were to question either of these statements. But *nothing* of that sort could be said in connexion with any question about the meaning of "God." It is not by having someone point and say "That's God." Now this is not a trivial or inessential matter. It hangs together in very important ways with what I call the grammar of the

word "God." And it is one reason why I do not think it is helpful just to say that the word is a substantive.[3]

Another way of making the same point is to say that "I believe in God" does not picture its object as a photograph does. In the latter relation, the criterion of likeness is central. For example, Wittgenstein says, "I could show Moore the picture of a tropical plant. There is a technique of comparison between picture and plant" (*L.R.B.*, p. 63). Believing that a particular picture is in fact a picture of the plant has its sense from the technique in which likenesses and comparisons play a central role. But such techniques have nothing to do with belief in God even when religious pictures are involved. Wittgenstein gives the following example:

> Take "God created man." Pictures of Michelangelo showing the creation of the world. In general, there is nothing which explains the meanings of words as well as a picture, and I take it that Michelangelo was as good as anyone can be and did his best, and here is the picture of the Deity creating Adam. (*L.R.B.*, p. 63)

Wittgenstein is saying, ironically, that if we did think this was a photograph or the representation of a likeness, we could trust Michelangelo to have made a good job of it! But, of course, we do not treat it in this way. "If we ever saw this, we certainly wouldn't think this the Deity. The picture has to be used in an entirely different way if we are to call the man in that queer blanket 'God,' and so on. You could imagine that religion was taught by means of these pictures" (*L.R.B.*, p. 63). To say that God is in the picture, is not to say that it is a picture of God. To believe in the truth of such a picture is to adopt what it says as one's norm of truth. To say God is in the picture is a confession of faith.

The realist will not wait on the language of religion. Even when some of its central features are pointed out to him, he draws the wrong conclusions from them. Wittgenstein provides the reminder: "The word 'God' is amongst the earliest learnt—pictures and catechisms, etc. But not the same consequences as with pictures of aunts. I wasn't shown [that which the picture pictured]" (*L.R.B.*, p. 59). The realist takes this to mean that we *could* have been shown that which the picture pictures, but, as it happens, we were not. It is as if one said, "We *could* have had a picture of God creating Adam (after all, it must have looked like something) but Michelangelo's picture does not represent it." Perhaps the realist will say that because God is transcendent, it is hardly surprising that this should be so. Wittgenstein imagines someone saying: "Of course, we can only express ourselves by means of these pictures....I can't show you the real thing, only the picture," and he responds, "The absurdity is, I've never taught him the technique of using this picture" (*L.R.B.*, p. 63).

The realist does not appreciate that when Wittgenstein says we were not shown that which the picture pictured, he is not referring to an omission which ought to be rectified. He is not referring to an omission at all. Rather, he is remarking on the *kind* of picture he is talking about, namely, one which does not have its sense in a context of application in which the important criterion is the likeness of the picture to what it pictures. If the latter relation is what we are looking for, Wittgenstein's point is that there is nothing for the picture to be compared or likened to— that is part of the grammar of the picture.

What, then, is involved in believing the picture? Wittgenstein replies:

> Here believing obviously plays much more this role: suppose we said that a certain picture might play the role of constantly admonishing me, or I always think of it. Here, an enormous difference would be between those people for whom the picture is constantly in the foreground, and the others who just didn't use it at all. (*L.R.B.*, p. 56)

But this is precisely what Trigg denies. He argues: "The important thing about talk of God is that it is about God. The place it holds in the life of an individual must be a secondary consideration" (pp. 74–75). But, as we have seen, on this view we are unable to give a coherent account of what believing in God amounts to. Further, no way could be found of determining whether two people are worshipping the same God, since, here, too, what we would refer to is what belief comes to in the believer's life, to what spiritual matters amount to for him.

Why are realists so reluctant to embrace these conclusions? They fear that the fruits of belief are emphasised in such a way as to neglect, or even ignore, the object of the belief, namely, God. Some nonrealist accounts of religious belief have fuelled these fears. The most well-known of these is R. B. Braithwaite's notorious suggestion that it is unnecessary for believers to assent to the truth of religious beliefs. Braithwaite characterises these religious beliefs as stories, the essential function of which is to give psychological aid to moral endeavour. It is conceivable that this endeavour should be aided by stories and beliefs other than religious ones. Little wonder, then, that this leads the realist to conclude that, on this view, religious belief could be dispensed with altogether. What is essential is the efficacy of moral endeavour. The nonrealist gives a reductionist account of religious belief. Religious concepts are explained away in non-religious terms. This is the root of the realist's fears....

Wittgenstein is insisting on the irreducibility of religious pictures. He is not giving a reductionist account of them. In [some] cases, religious cases included, he says, "The whole *weight* may be in the picture...." (*L.R.B.*, pp. 71–72)

Wittgenstein's remarks show how different he is from those nonrealists...who argue that religious beliefs are simply the outward forms of attitudes which can survive their demise....Wittgenstein, on the other hand, is insisting that the whole weight may be in the picture. In that case, the loss of the picture may constitute the loss of what is essential in a belief. When a picture is lost, a truth may be lost which cannot be replaced. This is a far cry from the view of Wittgenstein as a nonrealist who sees religious beliefs as expressive attitudes that have no necessary relation to the object of the belief. It is in the use of the picture that the relation of belief to its object is to be understood. It is this use, this context of application, which the realist ignores. Wittgenstein is not trying to get the realist to embrace nonrealism. Rather, he is trying to get him or her to look in a certain direction, to our actions and practices, where religious belief has its sense.

Notes

1. Terence Penelhum, *God and Skepticism* (Dordrecht, the Netherlands: Reidel, 1983), p. 151.
2. Roger Trigg, *Reason and Commitment* (Cambridge, England: Cambridge University Press, 1973), p. 75. All quotations from Penelhum and Trigg are from the two works cited.
3. Rush Rhees, "Religion and Language, in *Without Answers* (New York: Routledge, 1969), pp. 127–28.

Study Questions

1. What is the realist view of beliefs that Phillips critiques?
2. What objection does Phillips raise against the realist view?
3. How would Wittgenstein's view of beliefs provide meaning for religious beliefs such as "God exists" or "God loves me"?

Suggested Reading

Adler, Mortimer. *Truth in Religion: The Diversity of Religions and the Unity of Truth.* New York: Macmillan, 1990.
Byrne, Peter. *God and Realism.* Burlington, Vt.: Ashgate, 2003.
Dennett, Daniel. *Breaking the Spell: Religion as a Natural Phenomenon.* London: Viking Press, 2006.
Trigg, Roger. *Rationality and Religion.* Oxford, England: Blackwell, 1998.
Zuckerman, Phil. *Invitation to the Sociology of Religion.* New York: Routledge, 2003.

PART TWO

Religious Experience

According to William James, religious experiences are significant because they form the root of religion. In many religions, believers claim that special kinds of experiences provide meaning and direction to their lives or insight into reality. These kinds of experiences are variously (but not synonymously) termed religious, mystical, numinous, or meditative experiences.

DIVERSE TYPES OF RELIGIOUS METHODS AND EXPERIENCES

Some religions cultivate particular techniques to facilitate having religiously important experiences. For example, the Hindu school of yoga divides the techniques for achieving release from bondage into eight groups. The first five (sometimes referred to as external aids)—moral restraints, spiritual observances, postures, disciplined breathing, and withdrawal of the senses—are preliminary to the more specifically meditative techniques of concentration, meditation, and contemplation (*samādhi*), which lead to the ultimate achievement of pure consciousness. In Buddhism, the Eightfold Path culminates in right mindfulness and right concentration. In right mindfulness, one focuses one's undivided attention on all affairs in life to achieve equanimity. In right concentration, one focuses on particular objects until one achieves a complete end of seeing and of self.

Accounts of religious experiences in the Western theistic traditions vary widely. Some people speak about experiencing God through public, common things like icons or sunsets; others maintain that they experience God through unusual objects like weeping statues or faces in clouds. Some people report instances when the divine is mediated through private, inner experiences, while others experience God or Ultimate Reality in ways unmediated by anything describable in sensory language. An example of the latter types of religious experience can be found in St. Teresa of Avila, in our first selection. Teresa described two religious experiences, one in which she had an awareness that Christ was beside her even though she had no visual sensation of him. In the other vision, Christ revealed himself to her in his humanity. In this case she saw Christ not with her physical eyes, but with the eyes of her soul. When pressed regarding the authenticity of the vision, Teresa appealed to the significant changes for the better in her life that attested to its authenticity. That is, Teresa presented a pragmatic test for the truth of her claims to have seen Christ with the eyes of her soul.

Religious Experience as a Complex of Feelings

Philosophers of religion have several concerns about religious experiences. First, what kind of event is a religious experience? Theologians such as Friedrich Schleiermacher believed that religious experience is not a cognitive experience but "a feeling of absolute or total dependence upon a source or power that is distinct from the world." In his classic work, *The Idea of the Holy*, Rudolph Otto speaks about three types of feelings: the feeling of dependence [that we are mere creatures "submerged and overwhelmed by (our) own nothingness"], the feeling of religious dread or awe, and the feeling of longing for the transcendent being that fascinates us.

William James develops this idea of religious as feeling in our second selection. For him, "feeling is the deeper source of religion," so that cognitive formulations of religion are secondary by-products of the feelings. As such, it is inappropriate to attempt to find a rational justification of these experiences. They are authoritative for the individual who has mystical experiences, even though they may not be authoritative for anyone else.

But if religious experiences are mere feelings, from where does the cognitive content arise that provides the stuff of theology and religion? It is difficult to see how one can generate the cognitive religious truth-claims found in theology and religious philosophy out of noncognitive feelings.

Religious Experience as a Type of Perception

Other philosophers, like William Alston in our third selection, understand some religious experiences as a type of perception, for many experiences of God have a structure similar to sense experience (perceiver, object perceived, and appearance). Alston argues that the fact that the experience of God may be an uncommon experience should not count against understanding it as a type of perception. The fact that blind and deaf people have limited sensory capabilities does not affect the claim that seeing and hearing are forms of perception.

But since God is not a sensory object, how can we perceive God? It would seem that not being a sensory experience would count against its being a perceptual experience, for what is perceived would be very different from that available in ordinary experience. Alston agrees that the perceived qualities of God, such as power, goodness, and love, are not sensory. However, if we use comparative concepts to report our experiences of God, rather than phenomenal (what something looks like) concepts, we can describe experiencing God in nonsensory fashion. The report concerns how one would experience God under normal experiences. But what would these normal experiences be like? Alston suggests that although it is hard to know ahead of time, our experience of other humans provides a clue about what we would experience when encountering God. Knowing how good people act gives us some idea (a comparison) of what experiencing a good God would be like. We move comparatively from sensory experience of how good people act to the nonsensory experience of God's action in order to anticipate how God would manifest his goodness under normal circumstances.

However, describing the experience as a type of perception does not entail that religious experiences are genuine, that is, that there really is a God who is experienced. All Alston wants to show is that if God exists, religious experiences are "the right sort of experience to constitute a genuine perception of God."

RELIGIOUS EXPERIENCE AS AN INTERPRETIVE ACCOUNT

Wayne Proudfoot contends that treating religious experiences as perceptual experiences begs the question of their genuineness, for in doing so we could not grant that people have religious experiences without granting that they really encountered God. Rather, Proudfoot argues in our fourth selection, we should view religious experiences as interpretative accounts of our experience. It is true that in order for an experience to be religious, persons must understand or describe the experience as being of something transcendent. Purely naturalistic accounts are inadequate. However, it is important to distinguish the *description* of the experience from its *explanation*. The fact that the believer describes the experience as being of the transcendent tells us nothing about whether it is so. We need to ask why the person uses a particular set of concepts and beliefs to describe the experience. The explanation for the interpretation can be understood best in terms of the history of the individuals who give the description: their biography, culture, context, religious practices (e.g., study under a guru), psychology, and the concepts available to them. Once these are understood, we can then understand why these people interpreted the experience as they did.

Proudfoot's analysis leaves us with the question of whether we can really experience God. On his view there is no way of knowing, for each person's concepts and beliefs shape each person's religious experience. But then there is no reason to assume that a historical or cultural explanation of the experience is more relevant than a supernatural explanation. We thus have returned to a nonrealist view of religion, in that we invoke language about the transcendent but that language lacks referential meaning.

CAN RELIGIOUS EXPERIENCE JUSTIFY RELIGIOUS BELIEFS?

This brings us to a second concern, namely, can religious experience be used to justify religious beliefs, such as the belief that God exists? On the one hand, if the experience is merely an ineffable feeling, little that is cognitive follows from it. It could not function as the basis for religious truths. This accords with what we noted in Part One, namely, that nonrealists are not interested in the truth of religious claims, but in religion's pragmatic function in helping us to better adapt to our situation. On the other hand, those who understand religious experiences as a type of perceptual experience might use such experiences to argue for God's existence, much as one would use the visual experience of a cat sitting on a porch chair as evidence for the existence of a cat on the porch.

This latter view faces the challenge of philosophers, like Michael Martin in our fifth selection, who think it is more likely that those who have religious experiences are mistaken than that they have an authentic experience of God. Martin agrees with Proudfoot that religious experience must be described in terms of encountering something supernatural, but that such a description should not commit us to the view that we actually experience the supernatural or that the supernatural exists. Religious experiences are best explained in terms of a psychological or natural phenomenon rather than an encounter with the divine, for there is no consistency among the diverse experiences, something one would expect if they reported genuine encounters. Indeed, even St. Teresa's appeal to moral improvement does not establish that her experiences were genuine, for there is no necessary connection between moral improvement and the genuineness of her experience.

Richard Swinburne acknowledges that although we could be mistaken about what we experience, there is reason to suppose that when it seems to persons that they experience something, unless special considerations mitigate the claim, it is probably the case that they do experience it. He terms this the *Principle of Credulity* and applies it to religious as well as to ordinary experience. Of course, there are limits to the principle. If one can show that the context of the experience has made such experiences unreliable in the past, or if one has independent evidence to show that what is allegedly perceived does not exist, these factors would override the Principle. However, these limits do not function to generally exclude religious experiences of God as authenticating that which is experienced.

Martin counters by proposing a Negative Principle of Credulity, such that when it seems to someone that something is not the case, it is likely not the case. For those who have had no religious experience of a god, it is likely that there is no god to be experienced. Whether the Negative Principle of Credulity is really a complement to the Principle of Credulity or a separate principle is a subject of legitimate debate. Would one really know what to expect (and not find) if God did exist?

RELIGIOUS DIVERSITY AND RELIGIOUS EXPERIENCES

What bothers many philosophers is the diversity of religious experiences. As we noted above, religious experiences of diverse types can be found in monotheistic, polytheistic, monistic, and nontheistic religions alike. If experiences are prima facie reliable, how can one account for the diversity of truth claims that arise from such experiences? It is not the mere diversity, however, that is problematic, but the apparent incompatibility of the religious claims based on these experiences. What beliefs could religious experiences establish if the religious claims they apparently support not only radically differ but contradict each other? Of course, merely noting that religious experiences involve interpretation will not allow us to dispose of religious experiences. Although all experiences involve interpretation, we still are willing to affirm that experiences can provide authentic information about reality.

IS THERE A COMMON CORE TO RELIGIOUS EXPERIENCE?

This raises a final question, namely, is there a common core to religious experience? Some argue that once we get behind the diverse languages, concepts, and metaphors employed by people from their respective religious traditions, the experiences themselves do not differ. Walter T. Stace, for example, distinguishes between the interpretation of the (mystical) experience and the (mystical) experience itself. The interpretation is provided to enable the person who had the experience to communicate it. But the core (mystical) experiences cross religious and conceptual boundaries. At the core of mystical experiences, he finds a Unitary Consciousness (the One) that is nonspatial and nontemporal, a sense of objectivity and blessedness, a feeling of the holy or divine, paradox, and an inability to conceptually communicate what is experienced.

Others, such as Steven Katz and Proudfoot, contend that concepts and beliefs mediate all experiences. Our prior beliefs are formed by our interaction with our religious traditions and are shaped by them. Indeed, they would argue, Stace's analysis of mystical experiences is itself an interpretation. Accordingly, one cannot separate the experience from the interpretative (or explanatory) element. In fact, the similarities Stace identifies are more apparent than real, hidden by use of the same words but with possibly very different meanings in the different traditions. Thus, people in different traditions experience things differently, such that one cannot use religious experience to justify religious beliefs.

Mystics themselves contend that their experiences are transconceptual, which is why they cannot discourse about them. As such, they contend, these experiences are not conditioned by subjective conditions but only by what is experienced. Even if this is not so, one might suggest that the dichotomy of complete objectivity/complete subjectivity must be mediated. That there is a subjective component in our experience does not mean that the experience cannot be used to justify our beliefs. That I have learned to categorize lions as carnivorous and have theories about what animals do with pointed teeth does not mean that I am not justified in taking precautions when walking on a safari in Kenya.

THE PHENOMENOLOGY OF RELIGIOUS EXPERIENCE

Instead of asking what religious experience justifies, phenomenologists like Merold Westphal in our sixth selection argue that the most fruitful approach is to provide a phenomenological description of the experiences. Religious experiences are best understood as the opening of oneself to the transcendent Other. Whether this self-transcendence is an authentic experience of God is not easily decidable, for self-deception is always possible. Rather, what is important is restoring subjectivity to religious experience, which reveals religious experiences in all traditions as acts of genuine self-transcendence.

Because many points—the nature of religious experience, the role of interpretation in experience, whether a common core underlies all religious experience, and whether we should invoke a Principle of Credulity that presupposes a prima facie trust in experiential reports—need clarification and defense, significant opportunity remains for philosophical reflection on the topic of religious experience.

Saint Teresa of Jesus

Religious Experiences

St. Teresa (1515–1582) describes two different types of religious experience. In reporting her experience of the first type, she claims to have been conscious of Jesus Christ's appearing and speaking to her. Although she did not see him with either her physical eyes or the eyes of her soul, she felt an internal illumination and a change in her prayers that convinced her that he was beside her. Teresa goes on to describe an experience of the second type in which she gradually came to see the resurrected Jesus and his glory and majesty with the eyes of her soul. Although this vision was "imaginary" (i.e., accompanied by images) and hence subject to description, she was sure that it came from God and not the devil because what she saw transcended anything that she could have imagined and because it made significant changes for the better in her life.

XXVII

At the end of two years, during the whole of which time both other people and myself were continually praying for what I have described—that the Lord would either lead me by another way or make plain the truth: and these locutions which, as I have said, the Lord was giving me were very frequent—I had the following experience. I was at prayer on a festival of the glorious Saint Peter when I saw Christ at my side—or, to put it better, I was conscious of Him, for neither with the eyes of the body nor with those of the soul did I see anything. I thought He was quite close to me and I saw that it was He Who, as I thought, was speaking to me. Being completely ignorant that visions of this kind could occur, I was at first very much afraid, and did nothing but weep, though, as soon as He addressed a single word to me to reassure me, I became quiet again, as I had been before, and was quite happy and free from fear. All the time Jesus Christ seemed to be beside me, but, as this was not an imaginary vision, I could not discern in what form: what I felt very clearly was that all the time He was at my right hand, and a witness of everything that I was

From *The Life of Teresa of Jesus*, trans. and ed. E. Allison Peers. Copyright © 1960 by Sheed & Ward. Reprinted by permission of Sheed & Ward.

doing, and that, when ever I became slightly recollected or was not greatly distracted, I could not but be aware of His nearness to me.

Sorely troubled, I went at once to my confessor, to tell him about it. He asked me in what form I had seen Him. I told him that I had not seen Him at all. Then he asked me how I knew it was Christ. I told him that I did not know how, but that I could not help realizing that He was beside me, and that I saw and felt this clearly; that when in the Prayer of Quiet my soul was now much more deeply and continuously recollected; that the effects of my prayer were very different from those which I had previously been accustomed to experience; and that the thing was quite clear to me. I did nothing, in my efforts to make myself understood, but draw comparisons—though really, for describing this kind of vision, there is no comparison which is very much to the point, for it is one of the highest kinds of vision possible....

XXVIII

One day, when I was at prayer, the Lord was pleased to reveal to me nothing but His hands, the beauty of which was so great as to be indescribable. This made me very fearful, as does every new experience that I have when the Lord is beginning to grant me some supernatural favour. A few days later I also saw that Divine face, which seemed to leave me completely absorbed. I could not understand why the Lord revealed Himself gradually like this since He was later to grant me the favour of seeing Him wholly, until at length I realized that His Majesty was leading me according to my natural weakness. May He be blessed for ever, for so much glory all at once would have been more than so base and wicked a person could bear: knowing this, the compassionate Lord prepared me for it by degrees.

Your Reverence may suppose that it would have needed no great effort to behold those hands and that beauteous face. But there is such beauty about glorified bodies that the glory which illumines them throws all who look upon such supernatural loveliness into confusion. I was so much afraid, then, that I was plunged into turmoil and confusion, though

later I began to feel such certainty and security that my fear was soon lost.

One year, on Saint Paul's Day, when I was at Mass, I saw a complete representation of this most sacred Humanity, just as in a picture of His resurrection body, in very great beauty and majesty; this I described in detail to Your Reverence in writing, at your very insistent request. It distressed me terribly to have to do so, for it is impossible to write such a description without a disruption of one's very being, but I did the best I could and so there is no reason for me to repeat the attempt here. I will only say that, if there were nothing else in Heaven to delight the eyes but the extreme beauty of the glorified bodies there, that alone would be the greatest bliss. A most especial bliss, then, will it be to us when we see the Humanity of Jesus Christ; for, if it is so even on earth, where His Majesty reveals Himself according to what our wretchedness can bear, what will it be where the fruition of that joy is complete? Although this vision is imaginary, I never saw it, or any other vision, with the eyes of the body, but only with the eyes of the soul.

Those who know better than I say that the type of vision already described [in part XXVII] is nearer perfection than this, while this in its turn is much more so than those which are seen with the eyes of the body....

I will describe, then, what I have discovered by experience. How the Lord effects it, Your Reverence will explain better than I and will expound everything obscure of which I do not know the explanation. At certain times it really seemed to me that it was an image I was seeing; but on many other occasions I thought it was no image, but Christ Himself, such was the brightness with which He was pleased to reveal Himself to me. Sometimes, because of its indistinctness, I would think the vision was an image, though it was like no earthly painting, however perfect, and I have seen a great many good ones. It is ridiculous to think that the one thing is any more like the other than a living person is like his portrait: however well the portrait is done, it can never look completely natural: one sees, in fact, that it is a dead thing. But let us pass over that, apposite and literally true though it is.

I am not saying this as a comparison, for comparisons are never quite satisfactory: it is the actual truth.

The difference is similar to that between something living and something painted, neither more so nor less. For if what I see is an image it is a living image—not a dead man but the living Christ. And He shows me that He is both Man and God—not as He was in the sepulchre, but as He was when He left it after rising from the dead. Sometimes He comes with such majesty that no one can doubt it is the Lord Himself; this is especially so after Communion, for we know that He is there, since the Faith tells us so. He reveals Himself so completely as the Lord of that inn, the soul, that it feels as though it were wholly dissolved and consumed in Christ. O my Jesus, if one could but describe the majesty with which Thou dost reveal Thyself! ...

The soul is now a new creature: it is continuously absorbed in God; it seems to me that a new and living love of God is beginning to work within it to a very high degree; for, though the former type of vision which, as I said, reveals God without presenting any image of Him, is of a higher kind, yet, if the memory of it is to last, despite our weakness, and if the thoughts are to be well occupied, it is a great thing that so Divine a Presence should be presented to the imagination and should remain within it. These two kinds of vision almost invariably occur simultaneously, and, as they come in this way, the eyes of the soul see the excellence and the beauty and the glory of the most holy Humanity. And in the other way which has been described it is revealed to us how He is God, and that He is powerful, and can do all things, and commands all things, and rules all things, and fills all things with His love.

This vision is to be very highly esteemed, and, in my view, there is no peril in it, as its effects show that the devil has no power over it....

Of all impossibilities, the most impossible is that these true visions should be the work of the imagination. There is no way in which this could be so: by the mere beauty and whiteness of a single one of the hands which we are shown the imagination is completely transcended. In any case, there is no other way in which it would be possible for us to see in a moment things of which we have no recollection, which we have never thought of, and which, even in a long period of time, we could not invent with our imagination, because, as I have already said, they far transcend what we can comprehend on earth....

I used to put forward this argument together with others, when they told me, as they often did, that I was being deceived by the devil and that it was all the work of my imagination. I also drew such comparisons as I could and as the Lord revealed to my understanding....

I once said to the people who were talking to me in this way that if they were to tell me that a person whom I knew well and had just been speaking to was not herself at all, but that I was imagining her to be so, and that they knew this was the case, I should certainly believe them rather than my own eyes. But, I added, if that person left some jewels with me, which I was actually holding in my hands as pledges of her great love, and if, never having had any before, I were thus to find myself rich instead of poor, I could not possibly believe that this was delusion, even if I wanted to. And, I said, I could show them these jewels—for all who knew me were well aware how my soul had changed: my confessor himself testified to this, for the difference was very great in every respect, and no fancy, but such as all could clearly see. As I had previously been so wicked, I concluded, I could not believe that, if the devil were doing this to delude me and drag me down to hell, he would make use of means which so completely defeated their own ends by taking away my vices and making me virtuous and strong; for it was quite clear to me that these experiences had immediately made me a different person.

Study Questions

1. How do the two types of mystical experience St. Teresa reports differ?
2. When she is questioned, how does St. Teresa defend these religious experiences as authentic experiences of Christ?

William James

Religious Experiences as Feelings Forming the Root of Religion

William James (1842–1910) notes four characteristics of mystical experiences: they are inexpressible in words, yield knowledge, are of short duration, and happen to us independent of our wills. He illustrates these characteristics by examples drawn from mystical experiences from diverse traditions. He concludes that although a mystical experience is authoritative for those who experience it, it need not be authoritative for others. He also argues that rationally cognitive states are not the sole mediators of reality. This is particularly true for religion, whose deeper source is feeling. Philosophical and theological formulations are secondary to and derived from religious feelings, but because they are rational, they are subject to analysis and criticism.

One may say truly, I think, that personal religious experience has its root and centre in mystical states of consciousness; so for us, who in these lectures are treating personal experience as the exclusive subject of our study, such states of consciousness ought to form the vital chapter from which the other chapters get their light....

First of all, then, I ask, What does the expression "mystical states of consciousness" mean? How do we part off mystical states from other states?...I propose to you four marks which, when an experience has them, may justify us in calling it mystical for the purpose of the present lectures.

1. *Ineffability*. The handiest of the marks by which I classify a state of mind as mystical is negative. The subject of it immediately says that it defies expression, that no adequate report of its contents can be given in words. It follows from this that its quality must be directly experienced; it cannot be imparted or transferred to others. In this peculiarity mystical states are more like states of feeling than like states of intellect. No one can make clear to another who has never had a certain feeling, in what the quality or worth of it consists....

2. *Noetic quality*. Although so similar to states of feeling, mystical states seem to those who experience them to be also states of knowledge. They are states of insight into depths of truth unplumbed by the discursive intellect. They are illuminations, revelations, full of significance and importance, all inarticulate

From *The Varieties of Religious Experience*, copyright © 1923. New York: Longmans, Green, and Co.

though they remain; and as a rule they carry with them a curious sense of authority for after-time.

These two characters will entitle any state to be called mystical, in the sense in which I use the word. Two other qualities are less sharply marked, but are usually found. These are:

3. *Transiency*. Mystical states cannot be sustained for long. Except in rare instances, half an hour, or at most an hour or two, seems to be the limit beyond which they fade into the light of common day. Often, when faded, their quality can but imperfectly be reproduced in memory; but when they recur it is recognized; and from one recurrence to another it is susceptible of continuous development in what is felt as inner richness and importance.

4. *Passivity*. Although the oncoming of mystical states may be facilitated by preliminary voluntary operations, as by fixing the attention, or going through certain bodily performances, or in other ways which manuals of mysticism prescribe; yet when the characteristic sort of consciousness once has set in, the mystic feels as if his own will were in abeyance, and indeed sometimes as if he were grasped and held by a superior power. This latter peculiarity connects mystical states with certain definite phenomena of secondary or alternative personality, such as prophetic speech, automatic writing, or the mediumistic trance. When these latter conditions are well pronounced, however, there may be no recollection whatever of the phenomenon, and it may have no significance for the subject's usual inner life, to which, as it were, it makes a mere interruption. Mystical states, strictly so called, are never merely interruptive. Some memory of their content always remains, and a profound sense of their importance. They modify the inner life of the subject between the times of their recurrence. Sharp divisions in this region are, however, difficult to make, and we find all sorts of gradations and mixtures.

These four characteristics are sufficient to mark out a group of states of consciousness peculiar enough to deserve a special name and to call for careful study. Let it then be called the mystical group.

Our next step should be to gain acceptance with some typical examples. Professional mystics at the height of their development have often elaborately organized experiences and a philosophy based thereupon....

The simplest rudiment of mystical experience would seem to be that deepened sense of the significance of a maxim or formula which occasionally sweeps over one. "I've heard that said all my life," we exclaim, "but I never realized its full meaning until now." "When a fellow-monk," said Luther, "one day repeated the words of the Creed: 'I believe in the forgiveness of sins,' I saw the Scripture in an entirely new light; and straightway I felt as if I were born anew. It was as if I had found the door of paradise thrown wide open." This sense of deeper significance is not confined to rational propositions. Single words, and conjunctions of words, effects of light on land and sea, odors and musical sounds, all bring it when the mind is tuned aright. Most of us can remember the strangely moving power of passages in certain poems read when we were young, irrational doorways as they were through which the mystery of fact, the wildness and the pang of life, stole into our hearts and thrilled them. The words have now perhaps become mere polished surfaces for us; but lyric poetry and music are alive and significant only in proportion as they fetch these vague vistas of a life continuous with our own, beckoning and inviting, yet ever eluding our pursuit. We are alive or dead to the eternal inner message of the arts according as we have kept or lost this mystical susceptibility.

A more pronounced step forward on the mystical ladder is found in an extremely frequent phenomenon, that sudden feeling, namely, which sometimes sweeps over us, of having "been here before," as if at some indefinite past time, in just this place, with just these people, we were already saying just these things....

Somewhat deeper plunges into mystical consciousness are met with in yet other dreamy states. Such feelings as these which Charles Kingsley describes are surely far from being uncommon, especially in youth:

> When I walk the fields, I am oppressed now and then with an innate feeling that everything I see has a meaning, if I could but understand it. And this feeling of being surrounded with truths which I cannot grasp amounts to indescribable awe sometimes....Have you not felt that your real soul was imperceptible to your mental vision, except in a few hallowed moments?...

Certain aspects of nature seem to have a peculiar power of awakening such mystical moods. Most of the striking cases which I have collected have occurred out of doors....

Here is a...record from the memoirs of that interesting German idealist, Malwida von Meysenbug:

> I was alone upon the seashore as all these thoughts flowed over me, liberating and reconciling; and now again, as once before in distant days in the Alps of Dauphiné, I was impelled to kneel down, this time before the illimitable ocean, symbol of the Infinite. I felt that I prayed as I had never prayed before, and knew now what prayer really is: to return from the solitude of individuation into the consciousness of unity with all that is, to kneel down as one that passes away, and to rise up as one imperishable. Earth, heaven, and sea resounded as in one vast world-encircling harmony. It was as if the chorus of all the great who had ever lived were about me. I felt myself one with them, and it appeared as if I heard their greeting: "Thou too belongest to the company of those who overcome."...

We have now seen enough of this cosmic or mystic consciousness, as it comes sporadically. We must next pass to its methodical cultivation as an element of the religious life. Hindus, Buddhists, Mohammedans, and Christians all have cultivated it methodically.

In India, training in mystical insight has been known from time immemorial under the name of yoga. Yoga means the experimental union of the individual with the divine. It is based on persevering exercise; and the diet, posture, breathing, intellectual concentration, and moral discipline vary slightly in the different systems which teach it. The yogi, or disciple, who has by these means overcome the obscurations of his lower nature sufficiently, enters into the condition termed *samâdhi*, "and comes face to face with facts which no instinct or reason can ever know." He learns

> that the mind itself has a higher state of existence, beyond reason, a superconscious state, and that when the mind gets to that higher state, then this knowledge beyond reasoning comes....All the different steps in yoga are intended to bring us scientifically to the superconscious state or samâdhi....Just as unconscious work is beneath consciousness, so there is another work which is above consciousness, and which, also, is not

accompanied with the feeling of egoism....There is no feeling of I, and yet the mind works, desireless, free from restlessness, objectless, bodiless. Then the Truth shines in its full effulgence, and we know ourselves—for Samâdhi lies potential in us all—for what we truly are, free, immortal, omnipotent, loosed from the finite, and its contrasts of good and evil altogether, and identical with the Atman or Universal Soul.

The Vedantists say that one may stumble into superconsciousness sporadically, without the previous discipline, but it is then impure. Their test of its purity, like our test of religion's value, is empirical: its fruits must be good for life. When a man comes out of samâdhi, they assure us that he remains "enlightened, a sage, a prophet, a saint, his whole character changed, his life changed, illumined."

The Buddhists use the word "samâdhi" as well as the Hindus; but "dhyâna" is their special word for higher states of contemplation. There seem to be four stages recognized in dhyâna. The first stage comes through concentration of the mind upon one point. It excludes desire, but not discernment or judgment: it is still intellectual. In the second state the intellectual functions drop off, and the satisfied sense of unity remains. In the third stage the satisfaction departs, and indifference begins, along with memory and self-consciousness. In the fourth stage the indifference, memory, and self-consciousness are perfected. [Just what "memory" and "self-consciousness" mean in this connection is doubtful. They cannot be the faculties familiar to us in the lower life.] Higher stages still of contemplation are mentioned—a region where there exists nothing, and where the meditator says: "There exists absolutely nothing," and stops. Then he reaches another region where he says: "There are neither ideas nor absence of ideas," and stops again. Then another region where, "having reached the end of both idea and perception, he stops finally." This would seem to be, not yet Nirvâna, but as close an approach to it as this life affords.

In the Mohammedan world the Sufi sect and various dervish bodies are the possessors of the mystical tradition. The Sufis have existed in Persia from the earliest times, and as their pantheism is so at variance with the hot and rigid monotheism of the Arab mind, it has been suggested that Sufism must have been inoculated into Islam by Hindu influences. We Christians know little of Sufism, for its secrets are disclosed only to those initiated. To give its existence a certain liveliness in your minds, I will quote a Moslem document, and pass away from the subject.

Al-Ghazzali, a Persian philosopher and theologian, who flourished in the eleventh century, and ranks as one of the greatest doctors of the Moslem church, has left us one of the few autobiographies to be found outside of Christian literature.

"The Science of the Sufis," says the Moslem author, "aims at detaching the heart from all that is not God, and at giving to it for sole occupation the meditation of the divine being....What pertains most exclusively to their method is just what no study can grasp, but only transport, ecstasy, and the transformation of the soul.

"The first condition for a Sufi is to purge his heart entirely of all that is not God. The next key of the contemplative life consists in the humble prayers which escape from the fervent soul, and in the meditations on God in which the heart is swallowed up entirely. But in reality this is only the beginning of the Sufi life, the end of Sufism being total absorption in God. The intuitions and all that precede are, so to speak, only the threshold for those who enter. From the beginning, revelations take place in so flagrant a shape that the Sufis see before them, whilst wide awake, the angels and the souls of the prophets. They hear their voices and obtain their favors. Then the transport rises from the perception of forms and figures to a degree which escapes all expression, and which no man may seek to give an account of without his words involving sin.

"The chief properties of prophetism are perceptible only during the transport, by those who embrace the Sufi life. The prophet is endowed with qualities to which you possess nothing analogous, and which consequently you cannot possibly understand. How should you know their true nature, since one knows only what one can comprehend? But the transport which one attains by the method of the Sufis is like an immediate perception, as if one touched the objects with one's hand."

This incommunicableness of the transport is the keynote of all mysticism. Mystical truth exists for the individual who has the transport, but for no one else. In this, as I have said, it resembles the knowledge given to us in sensations more than that given by conceptual thought. Thought, with its remoteness and abstractness, has often enough in the history of philosophy been contrasted unfavorably with sensation. It is a commonplace of metaphysics that God's knowledge cannot be discursive but must be intuitive, that is, must be constructed more after the pattern of what in ourselves is called immediate feeling, than after that of proposition and judgment. But our immediate feelings have no content but what the five senses supply; and we have seen and shall see again that mystics may emphatically deny that the senses play any part in the very highest type of knowledge which their transports yield.

In the Christian church there have always been mystics. Although many of them have been viewed with suspicion, some have gained favor in the eyes of the authorities. The experiences of these have been treated as precedents, and a codified system of mystical theology has been based upon them, in which everything legitimate finds its place. The basis of the system is "orison" or meditation, the methodical elevation of the soul towards God. Through the practice of orison the higher levels of mystical experience may be attained.

The first thing to be aimed at in orison is the mind's detachment from outer sensations, for these interfere with its concentration upon ideal things. Such manuals as Saint Ignatius's Spiritual Exercises recommend the disciple to expel sensation by a graduated series of efforts to imagine holy scenes. The acme of this kind of discipline would be a semi-hallucinatory mono-ideism—an imaginary figure of Christ, for example, coming fully to occupy the mind. Sensorial images of this sort, whether literal or symbolic, play an enormous part in mysticism. But in certain cases imagery may fall away entirely, and in the very highest raptures it tends to do so. The state of consciousness becomes then insusceptible of any verbal description. Mystical teachers are unanimous as to this. Saint John of the Cross, for instance, one of the best of them, thus describes the condition called the "union of love," which, he says, is reached by "dark contemplation."...

I have now sketched with extreme brevity and insufficiency, but as fairly as I am able in the time allowed, the general traits of the mystic range of consciousness. *It is on the whole pantheistic and optimistic, or at least the opposite of pessimistic. It is anti-naturalistic, and harmonizes best with twice-bornness and so-called otherworldly states of mind.*

My next task is to inquire whether we can invoke it as authoritative. Does it furnish any *warrant for the truth* of the twice-bornness and supernaturality and pantheism which it favors? I must give my answer to this question as concisely as I can.

In brief my answer is this, and I will divide it into three parts:

1. Mystical states, when well developed, usually are, and have the right to be, absolutely authoritative over the individuals to whom they come.
2. No authority emanates from them which should make it a duty for those who stand outside of them to accept their revelations uncritically.
3. They break down the authority of the non-mystical or rationalistic consciousness, based upon the understanding and the senses alone. They show it to be only one kind of consciousness. They open out the possibility of other orders of truth, in which, so far as anything in us vitally responds to them, we may freely continue to have faith.

I will take up these points one by one.

1

As a matter of psychological fact, mystical states of a well-pronounced and emphatic sort *are* usually authoritative over those who have them. They have been "there," and know. It is vain for rationalism to grumble about this. If the mystical truth that comes to a man proves to be a force that he can live by, what mandate have we of the majority to order him to live in another way? We can throw him into a prison or a madhouse, but we cannot change his mind—we commonly attach it only the more stubbornly to its beliefs. It mocks our utmost efforts, as a matter of fact, and in point of logic it absolutely escapes our jurisdiction. Our own more "rational" beliefs are based on evidence exactly similar in nature to that which mystics quote for theirs. Our senses, namely, have assured us of certain states of fact; but mystical experiences are as direct perceptions of fact for those who have them as any sensations ever were for us. The records show that even though the five senses be in abeyance in them, they are absolutely sensational in their epistemological quality, if I may be pardoned the barbarous expression—that is, they are face to face presentations of what seems immediately to exist.

The mystic is, in short, *invulnerable*, and must be left, whether we relish it or not, in undisturbed enjoyment of his creed. Faith, says Tolstoy, is that by which men live. And faith state and mystic state are practically convertible terms.

2

But I now proceed to add that mystics have no right to claim that we ought to accept the deliverance of their peculiar experiences, if we are ourselves outsiders and feel no private call thereto. The utmost they can ever ask of us in this life is to admit that they establish a presumption. They form a consensus and have an unequivocal outcome; and it would be odd, mystics might say, if such a unanimous type of experience should prove to be altogether wrong. At bottom, however, this would only be an appeal to numbers, like the appeal of rationalism the other way; and the appeal to numbers has no logical force. If we acknowledge it, it is for "suggestive," not for logical reasons: we follow the majority because to do so suits our life.

But even this presumption from the unanimity of mystics is far from being strong. In characterizing mystic states as pantheistic, optimistic, etc., I am afraid I over-simplified the truth. I did so for expository reasons, and to keep the closer to the classic mystical tradition. The classic religious mysticism, it now must be confessed, is only a "privileged case." It is an *extract*, kept true to type by the selection of the fittest specimens and their preservation in "schools." It is carved out from a much larger mass; and if we take the larger mass as seriously as religious mysticism has historically taken itself, we find that the supposed unanimity largely disappears. To begin with, even religious mysticism itself, the kind that accumulates traditions and makes schools, is much less unanimous than I have allowed. It has been both ascetic and anti-nomianly self-indulgent within the Christian church. It is dualistic in Sankhya, and monistic in Vedanta philosophy. I called it pantheistic; but the great Spanish mystics are anything but pantheists. They are with few exceptions nonmetaphysical minds, for whom "the category of personality" is absolute. The "union" of man with God is for them much more like an occasional miracle than like an original identity.... The fact is that the mystical feeling of enlargement, union, and emancipation has no specific intellectual content whatever of its own. It is capable of forming matrimonial alliances with material furnished by the most diverse philosophies and theologies, provided only they can find a place in their framework for its peculiar emotional mood. We have no right, therefore, to invoke its prestige as distinctively in favor of any special belief, such as that in absolute idealism, or in the absolute monistic identity, or in the absolute goodness, of the world. It is only relatively in favor of all these things—it passes out of common human consciousness in the direction in which they lie.

So much for religious mysticism proper. But more remains to be told, for religious mysticism is only one half of mysticism. The other half has no accumulated traditions except those which the textbooks on insanity supply. Open any one of these, and you will find abundant cases in which "mystical ideas" are cited as characteristic symptoms of enfeebled or deluded states of mind. In delusional insanity, as they sometimes call it, we may have a *diabolical* mysticism, a sort of religious mysticism turned upside down. The same sense of ineffable importance in the smallest events, the same texts and words coming with new meanings, the same voices and visions and leadings and missions, the same controlling by extraneous powers; only this time the emotion is pessimistic: instead of consolations we have desolations; the meanings are dreadful; and the powers are enemies to life. It is evident that from the point of view of their psychological mechanism, the classic

mysticism and these lower mysticisms spring from the same mental level, from that great subliminal or transmarginal region of which science is beginning to admit the existence, but of which so little is really known. That region contains every kind of matter: "seraph and snake" abide there side by side. To come from thence is no infallible credential. What comes must be sifted and tested, and run the gauntlet of confrontation with the total context of experience, just like what comes from the outer world of sense. Its value must be ascertained by empirical methods, so long as we are not mystics ourselves.

3

Yet, I repeat once more, the existence of mystical states absolutely overthrows the pretension of non-mystical states to be the sole and ultimate dictators of what we may believe. As a rule, mystical states merely add a supersensuous meaning to the ordinary outward data of consciousness. They are excitements like the emotions of love or ambition, gifts to our spirit by means of which facts already objectively before us fall into a new expressiveness and make a new connection with our active life. They do not contradict these facts as such, or deny anything that our senses have immediately seized. It is the rationalistic critic rather who plays the part of denier in the controversy, and his denials have no strength, for there never can be a state of facts to which new meaning may not truthfully be added, provided the mind ascend to a more enveloping point of view. It must always remain an open question whether mystical states may not possibly be such superior points of view, windows through which the mind looks out upon a more extensive and inclusive world. The difference of the views seen from the different mystical windows need not prevent us from entertaining this supposition. The wider world would in that case prove to have a mixed constitution like that of this world, that is all.... The counting in of that wider world of meanings, and the serious dealing with it, might, in spite of all the perplexity, be indispensable stages in our approach to the final fullness of the truth.

In this shape, I think, we have to leave the subject. Mystical states indeed wield no authority due simply to their being mystical states. But the higher ones among them point in directions to which the religious sentiments even of nonmystical men incline. They tell of the supremacy of the ideal, of vastness, of union, of safety, and of rest. They offer us *hypotheses*, hypotheses which we may voluntarily ignore, but which as thinkers we cannot possibly upset. The super-naturalism and optimism to which they would persuade us may, interpreted in one way or another, be after all the truest of insights into the meaning of this life....

The subject of Saintliness left us face to face with the question, Is the sense of divine presence a sense of anything objectively true? We turned first to mysticism for an answer, and found that although mysticism is entirely willing to corroborate religion, it is too private (and also too various) in its utterances to be able to claim a universal authority. But philosophy publishes results which claim to be universally valid if they are valid at all, so we now turn with our question to philosophy. Can philosophy stamp a warrant of veracity upon the religious man's sense of the divine?...

I do believe that feeling is the deeper source of religion, and that philosophic and theological formulas are secondary products, like translations of a text into another tongue. But all such statements are misleading from their brevity, and it will take the whole hour for me to explain to you exactly what I mean.

When I call theological formulas secondary products, I mean that in a world in which no religious feeling had ever existed, I doubt whether any philosophic theology could ever have been framed. I doubt if dispassionate intellectual contemplation of the universe, apart from inner unhappiness and need of deliverance on the one hand and mystical emotion on the other, would ever have resulted in religious philosophies such as we now possess. Men would have begun with animistic explanations of natural fact, and criticised these away into scientific ones, as they actually have done. In the science they would have left a certain amount of "psychical research," even as they now will probably have to re-admit a certain amount. But high-flying speculations like those of either dogmatic or idealistic theology, these they would have had no motive to venture on, feeling no need of commerce with such deities. These speculations must, it seems to me, be classed as over beliefs,

buildings—outperformed by the intellect into directions of which feeling originally supplied the hint.

But even if religious philosophy had to have its first hint supplied by feeling, may it not have dealt in a superior way with the matter which feeling suggested? Feeling is private and dumb, and unable to give an account of itself. It allows that its results are mysteries and enigmas, declines to justify them rationally, and on occasion is willing that they should even pass for paradoxical and absurd. Philosophy takes just the opposite attitude. Her aspiration is to reclaim from mystery and paradox whatever territory she touches. To find an escape from obscure and wayward personal persuasion to truth objectively valid for all thinking men has ever been the intellect's most cherished ideal. To redeem religion from unwholesome privacy, and to give public status and universal right of way to its deliverances, has been reason's task.

I believe that philosophy will always have opportunity to labor at this task. We are thinking beings, and we cannot exclude the intellect from participating in any of our functions. Even in soliloquizing with ourselves, we construe our feelings intellectually. Both our personal ideals and our religious and mystical experiences must be interpreted congruously with the kind of scenery which our thinking mind inhabits. The philosophic climate of our time inevitably forces its own clothing on us. Moreover, we must exchange our feelings with one another, and in doing so we have to speak, and to use general and abstract verbal formulas. Conceptions and constructions are thus a necessary part of our religion; and as moderator amid the clash of hypotheses, and mediator among the criticisms of one man's constructions by another, philosophy will always have much to do. It would be strange if I disputed this, when these very lectures which I am giving are (as you will see more clearly from now onwards) a laborious attempt to extract from the privacies of religious experience some general facts which can be defined in formulas upon which everybody may agree.

Religious experience, in other words, spontaneously and inevitably engenders myths, superstitions, dogmas, creeds, and metaphysical theologies, and criticisms of one set of these by the adherents of another.

Study Questions

1. To what four marks does James appeal to identify mystical experiences? In what ways do the religious experiences of St. Teresa in the previous reading satisfy these four marks?

2. James's descriptions of religious experience cover a broad spectrum of experiences from mystical insights to deep religious practices. What features, if any, of mystical experience can you identify within these diverse examples?

3. What justified claims does James think persons who have a religious experience can make about their experience? What limits on these claims does James propose?

4. With respect to religion, what roles does James see for religious experience and philosophy?

William P. Alston

Religious Experience as Perception of God

After noting that he wants to consider direct rather than indirect awareness of God, William Alston (1921–2009) briefly sketches his "Theory of Appearing" model of perception, according to which perception consists of something presenting itself to me in a certain way, apart from my conceptualizing it or making judgments about it. Alston then applies this model to direct religious experience, showing that many who have religious experiences understand their experiences along similar lines, saying that it is possible to have a direct, genuine perception of God. To the objection that the properties by which God presents himself to us are very different from those presented by sensory objects, Alston replies that we often report appearances by using comparative concepts rather than phenomenal (appearance) concepts. In religious experience, people use comparative concepts to report how God presents himself to our experience, i.e., as good, powerful, and loving in ways that one would expect good, powerful, and loving beings to appear. Finally, religious experience provides personal communication between God and us; whether such experience is genuine depends on whether what is experienced is what the subject takes it to be. The problems that arise when one attempts to establish the veridicality of religious experience are in principle no different from those that arise from ordinary perceptual experience.

I

I pick out what I am calling "experience of God" by the fact that the subject takes the experience (or would take it if the question arose) to be a direct awareness of God. Here is a clear example cited in William James's *The Varieties of Religious Experience.*

(1)…all at once I…felt the presence of God—I tell of the thing just as I was conscious of it—as if his goodness and his power were penetrating me altogether.

Then, slowly, the ecstasy left my heart; that is, I felt that God had withdrawn the communion which he had granted.…I asked myself if it were possible that Moses on Sinai could have had a more intimate communication with God. I think it well to add that in this ecstasy of mine God had neither form, color, odor, nor taste; moreover, that the feeling of his presence was accompanied by no determinate localization.… But the more I seek words to express this intimate intercourse, the more I feel the impossibility of describing the thing by any of our usual images.

Reprinted by permission of William P. Alston.

At bottom the expression most apt to render what I felt is this: God was present, though invisible; he fell under no one of my senses, yet my consciousness perceived him.

Note that I do not restrict "experience of God" to cases in which it is really God of whom the subject is aware. The term, as I use it, ranges over all experiences that the subject *takes* to have this status. Thus the general category would be more exactly termed "*supposed* experience of God," where calling it "*supposed*" does not prejudice the question of whether it is genuine or not. However, I will generally omit this qualification. Note too that my category of "experience of God" is much narrower than "religious experience," which covers a diverse and ill-defined multitude of experiences.

In restricting myself to *direct* awareness of God I exclude cases in which one takes oneself to be aware of God through the beauties of nature, the words of the Bible or of a sermon, or other natural phenomena. For example:

> (2) I feel him [God] in the sunshine or rain; and awe mingled with a delicious restfulness most nearly describes my feelings.

My reason for concentrating on direct experience of God, where there is no other object of experience in or through which God is experienced, is that these experiences are the ones that are most plausibly regarded as *presentations* of God to the individual, in somewhat the way in which physical objects are presented to sense perception, as I will shortly make explicit.

Within this territory I will range over both lay and professional examples, both ordinary people living in the world and monastics who more or less devote their lives to attaining union with God. The category also embraces both focal and background experiences; though in order to discern the structure of the phenomenon we are well advised to concentrate on its more intense forms.

There is also the distinction between experiences with and without sensory content. In (1) the subject explicitly denies that the experience was sensory in character. Here is an example that does involve sensory content.

> (3) During the night…I awoke and looking out of my window saw what I took to be a luminous star which gradually came nearer, and appeared as a soft slightly blurred white light. I was seized with violent trembling, but had no fear. I knew that what I felt was great awe. This was followed by a sense of overwhelming love coming to me, and going out from me, then of great compassion from this Outer Presence. (Cited in T. Beardsworth, *A Sense of Presence.*)

In this discussion I will concentrate on nonsensory experiences. The main reason for this choice is that since God is purely spiritual, a nonsensory experience has a greater chance of presenting Him as He is than any sensory experience. If God appears to us as bearing a certain shape or as speaking in a certain tone of voice, that is a long way from representing Him as He is in Himself. I shall refer to nonsensory experience of God as "mystical experience," and the form of perception of God that involves that experience as "mystical perception." I use these terms with trepidation, for I do not want them to carry connotations of the merging of the individual subject into the One, or any of the other salient features of what we may term "classical mystical experience." (See William James.) They are to be understood simply as shorthand for "supposed nonsensory experience (perception) of God."

Many people find it incredible, unintelligible, or incoherent to suppose that there could be something that counts as *presentation*, that contrasts with abstract thought in the way sense perception does, but is devoid of sensory content. However, so far as I see, this simply evinces lack of speculative imagination or perhaps a mindless parochialism. Why should we suppose that the possibilities of experiential givenness, for human beings or otherwise, are exhausted by the powers of *our* five senses. Surely it is possible, to start with the most obvious point, that other creatures should possess a sensitivity to other physical stimuli that play a role in their functioning analogous to that played by our five senses in our lives. And, to push the matter a bit further, why can't we also envisage presentations that do not stem from the activity of any physical sense organs, as is apparently the case with mystical perception?

II

As the title indicates, I will be advocating a "perceptual model" of mystical experience. To explain what I mean by that, I must first say something about sense perception, since even if we suppose, as I do, that perception is not restricted to its sensory form, still that is the form with which we are far and away most familiar, and it is by generalizing from sense perception that we acquire a wider concept of perception.

As I see the matter, at the heart of perception (sensory or otherwise) is a phenomenon variously termed *presentation, appearance,* or *givenness.* Something is presented to one's experience (awareness) *as* so-and-so, as blue, as acrid, as a house, as Susie's house, or whatever. I take this phenomenon of *presentation* to be essentially independent of conceptualization, belief, or judgment. It is possible, in principle, for this book to visually present itself to me as blue even if I do not *take* it to be blue, *think* of it as blue, *conceptualize* it as blue, *judge* it to be blue, or anything else of the sort. No doubt, in mature human perception presentation is intimately intertwined with conceptualization and belief, but presentation does not consist in anything like that. The best way to see this is to contrast actually seeing the book with thinking about the book, or making judgments about it, in its absence. What is involved in the former case but not in the latter that makes the difference? It can't be anything of a conceptual or judgmental order, for anything of that sort can be present in the latter case when the book is not seen. Reflection on this question leads me to conclude that what makes the difference is that when I see the book it is *presented* to my awareness; it occupies a place in my visual field. This crucial notion of presentation cannot be analyzed; it can be conveyed only by helping another to identify instances of it in experience, as I have just done.

On the view of perception I favor, the "Theory of Appearing," perceiving X simply consists in X's appearing to one a subject S, for example, or being presented to one, as so-and-so. That's all there is to it, as far as what perception is, in contrast to its causes and effects. Where X is an external physical object like a book, to perceive the book is just for the book to appear to one in a certain way.

In saying that a direct awareness that does not essentially involve conceptualization and judgment is at the heart of perception, I am *not* denying that a person's conceptual scheme, beliefs, cognitive readinesses, and so on, can affect the *way* an object presents itself to the subject, what it presents itself *as.* Things do look and sound differently to us after we are familiar with them, have the details sorted out, can smoothly put everything in its place without effort. My house presents a different appearance to me now after long habituation than it did the first time I walked in. Whereas Stravinski's *The Rite of Spring* sounded like a formless cacophony the first time I heard it, it now presents itself to me as a complex interweaving of themes. In saying this I am not going back on my assertion that X's presenting itself to one's awareness as P is not the same as S's *taking* X to be P. The latter involves the application of the concept of P to X, but the former does not, even though the character of the presentation can be influenced by one's conceptual repertoire and one's beliefs. But though my conceptual capacities and tendencies can affect the *way* objects appear to me, they have no power over *what object it is* that looks (sounds…) that way. When I look at my living room, the same objects present themselves to my visual awareness as when I first saw it. It is essential not to confuse *what* appears with what it appears *as.*

Even if to perceive X is simply for X to appear to one in a certain way, there can be further necessary conditions for someone to perceive X, for there can be further conditions for X's appearing to one. First, and this is just spelling out one thing that is involved in X's appearing to one, X must exist. I can't (really) perceive a tree unless the tree is there to be perceived. Second, it seems to be necessary for X's appearing to me (for my perceiving X) that X make an important *causal* contribution to my current experience. If there is a thick concrete wall between me and a certain house, thereby preventing light reflected from the house from striking my retina, then it couldn't be that that house is visually presented to me. I will assume such a causal condition in this discussion. Third, I will also assume a doxastic condition, that perceiving X at least tends to give rise to beliefs about X. This is much more questionable than the causal condition, but in any event we are concerned here with cases in which perception does give rise to beliefs about what is perceived.

III

Now we are ready to turn to the application of the perceptual model to mystical experience. In this essay I will not try to show that mystical experience (even sometimes) constitutes (genuine) perception of God. Remembering the necessary conditions of perception just mentioned, this would involve showing that God exists and that He makes the right kind of causal contribution to the experiences in question. What I will undertake here is the following. (1) I will argue that mystical experience is the right sort of experience to constitute a genuine perception of God if the other requirements are met. (2) I will argue that there is no bar in principle to these other requirements' being satisfied if God does exist. This adds up to a defence of the thesis that it is quite possible that human beings do sometimes perceive God if God is "there" to be perceived. In other words, the thesis defended is that if God exists, then mystical experience is quite properly thought of as mystical perception.

If mystical experience is not construed perceptually, how can it be understood? The most common alternative is to think of it as made up of purely subjective feelings and sensations, to which is added an *explanation* according to which the experience is due to God. A recent example of this approach is the important book, *Religious Experience*, by Wayne Proudfoot. Proudfoot goes so far as to identify the "noetic" quality that James and many others have noted in mystical experience with the supposition by the subject that the experience must be given a theological rather than a naturalistic explanation.

It is not difficult to show that the people I have quoted and countless others take their mystical experiences to be perceptual, to involve what I have been calling a direct presentation of God to their awareness, though they do not typically use this terminology. They take their experience to contrast with thinking about God, calling up mental images, entertaining propositions, reasoning, or remembering something

about God, just as seeing a tree contrasts with these other cognitive relations to it. They take it that God has been *presented* or *given* to their consciousness in generically the same way as that in which objects in the environment are *presented* to one's consciousness in sense perception. They emphasize the difference between presence to consciousness and absence. Saint Teresa says that God "presents Himself to the soul by a knowledge brighter than the sun." Again she contrasts a "consciousness of the presence of God" with "spiritual feelings and effects of great love and faith of which we become conscious," and with "the fresh resolutions which we make with such deep emotion." Although she takes it that the latter is a "great favour" that "comes from God," still it does not amount to God's actually being present. Another writer who clearly makes this distinction is Angela of Foligno.

> (4) At times God comes into the soul without being called; and He instills into her fire, love, and sometimes sweetness; and the soul believes this comes from God, and delights therein. But she does not yet know, or see, that He dwells in her; she perceives His grace, in which she delights....And beyond this the soul receives the gift of seeing God. God says to her "Behold Me!" and the soul sees Him dwelling within her. She sees Him more clearly than one man sees another. For the eyes of the soul behold a plenitude of which I cannot speak: a plenitude which is not bodily but spiritual, of which I can say nothing. And the soul rejoices in that sight with an ineffable joy; and this is the manifest and certain sign that God indeed dwells in her.

Thus it is quite clear that the people cited, who are representative of a vast throng, take their experiences to be structured the way, on my view, perception generally is structured. In fact, it may be thought that it is too easy to show this, too much like shooting fish in a barrel. For haven't I chosen my cases on the basis of the subjects' taking themselves to be directly aware of God? They are tailor-made for my purpose. I must plead guilty to picking cases that conform to my construal. But the significant point is that it is so easy to find such cases and that they are so numerous, given the fact that most mystical experiences are not reported at all. As pointed out earlier, I do not wish to deny that there are other forms of "religious experience" and even other forms of experience of God, such as the indirect experiences of God mentioned earlier. My contention is that there is a large body of experiences of God that are perceptual in character, and that they have played a prominent role in Christianity and other religions.

I don't know what could be said against this position except to claim that people who report such experiences are all confused about the character of their experience. Let's consider the following charge.

These people were all having strongly affective experiences that, because of their theological assumptions and preoccupations, they confused with a direct experience of God. Thus (1) was in an unusual state of exaltation that he interpreted as the power and goodness of God penetrating him. In (4) the "ineffable joy" that Angela says to be "the manifest and certain sign that God indeed dwells in her" is simply a state of feeling that her theological convictions lead her to *interpret* as an awareness of the presence of God. Another possibility is that the person is suddenly seized with an extremely strong conviction of the presence of God, together with sensations and feelings that seem to confirm it. Thus Teresa says that she "had a most distinct feeling that He was always on my right hand, a witness of all I did."

It is conceivable that one should suppose that a purely affective experience or a strongly held conviction should involve the experiential presentation of God when it doesn't, especially if there is a strong need or longing for the latter. But, even if an individual's account of the character of his/her own experience is not infallible, it must certainly be taken seriously. Who is in a better position to determine whether S is having an experience as of something's presenting itself to S as divine than S? We would need strong reasons to override the subject's confident report of the character of her experience. And where could we find such reasons? I suspect that most people who put forward these alternative diagnoses do so because they have general philosophical reasons for supposing either that God does not exist or that no human being could perceive Him, and they fail to recognize the difference between a *phenomenological* account of object presentation, and the occurrence of veridical perception. In any event, once we get straight about all this, I cannot see any reason for doubting the subjects' account of the character of their experience,

whatever reasons there may be for doubting that God Himself does in fact appear to them.

If these cases are to conform to our account of perceptual consciousness, they must seem to involve God's appearing to the person as being and/or doing so-and-so. And our subjects do tell us this. God is experienced as good, powerful, loving, compassionate, and as exhibiting "plenitude." He is experienced as speaking, forgiving, comforting, and strengthening. And yet how can these be ways in which God presents Himself to experience? Power and goodness are complex dispositional properties or bases thereof, dispositions to act in various ways in various situations. And to forgive or to strengthen someone is to carry out a certain intention. None of this can be read off the phenomenal surface of experience. This is quite different from something's presenting itself to one's sensory consciousness as red, round, sweet, loud, or pungent. Isn't it rather that the subject is *interpreting*, or *taking*, what she is aware of as being good or powerful, as forgiving or strengthening? But then what is God *experienced* as being or doing? We seem to still lack an answer.

But that charge misconstrues the situation. The basic point is that we have different sorts of concepts for specifying how something looks, sounds, tastes, or otherwise perceptually appears. There are *phenomenal* concepts that specify the felt qualities that objects present themselves as bearing—round, red, acrid, etc. But there are also *comparative* concepts that specify a mode of appearance in terms of the sort of objective thing that typically appears in that way. In reporting sensory appearances we typically use comparative concepts whenever the appearances involve something more complex than one or two basic sensory qualities. Thus we say, "She looks like Susie," "It tastes like a pineapple," "It sounds like Bach." In these cases there undoubtedly is some complex pattern of simple sensory qualities, but it is beyond our powers to analyze the appearance into its simple components. We are thrown back on the use of comparative concepts to report how something looks, sounds, or tastes. And so it is in our religious cases. Our subjects tell us that God presented Himself to their experience as a good, powerful, compassionate, forgiving being could be expected to appear. In reporting modes of divine appearance in this way, they are proceeding just as we typically do in reporting modes of sensory appearance.

IV

Now for the task of showing that if God exists there is no bar to the (not infrequent) satisfaction of the causal and doxastic conditions by the subject of mystical experience. First consider the doxastic condition. It is clear that mystical experience typically gives rise to beliefs about God. To be sure, those who perceive God as loving, powerful, and so on, usually believed that God is that way long before they had that experience. But the same is true of sense perception. My 50,000th look at my house doesn't generate any important new beliefs. I knew just what my house looks like long before that 50,000th look. That is why I put the doxastic condition in terms of a "tendency" to engender beliefs about what is perceived. However, in both sensory and mystical cases some kinds of new beliefs will almost always be produced. Even if I don't see anything new about my house on that umpteenth look, I at least learn that it is blue and tall *today*. When what we perceive is a person the new beliefs will be more interesting. On my 50,000th look at my wife I not only learn that she is still beautiful today, but I learn what she is doing right now. And similarly with God. One who perceives God will thereby come to learn that God is strengthening her or comforting her *then*, or telling her so-and-so *then*. There is, if anything, even less of a problem with the doxastic condition here.

The causal condition calls for a bit more discussion. First, there is no reason to think it impossible that God, if He exists, does causally contribute to the occurrence of mystical experiences. Quite the contrary. If God exists and things are as supposed by classical theism, God causally contributes to everything that occurs. That follows just from the fact that nothing would exist without the creative and sustaining activity of God. And with respect to many things, including mystical experiences, God's causality presumably extends farther than that, though the precise story will vary from one theology to another. To fix our thoughts let us say that it is possible (and remember that we are concerned here only with whether this causal condition *can* be satisfied) that at least some of these experiences occur only because God intentionally presents Himself to the subject's awareness as so-and-so.

It may well be pointed out that not every causal contributor to an experience is perceived via that experience. When I see a house, light waves and goings on in my nervous system form parts of the causal chain leading to the visual experience, but I don't see them. Thus it is not enough that God figures somehow or other in the causes of the experience; He would have to make the right kind of causal contribution. But what is the right kind? There is no one answer to this question for all perceptual modalities. The causal contribution a seen object makes to the production of visual experience (transmitting light to the retina) is different from the causal contribution a felt object makes to tactile experience, and different from the causal contribution a heard object makes to aural experience. And how do we tell, for each modality, what the crucial causal contribution is? We have no a priori insight into this. We cannot abstract from everything we have learned from perception and still ascertain how an object must be causally related to a visual experience in order to be what is seen in that experience. Quite the contrary. We learn this by first determining in many cases what is *seen*, felt, or heard in those cases, and then looking for some causal contribution that is distinctive of the object perceived. That is, we have first to be able to determine *what is seen*; then on the basis of that we determine how an entity has to be causally related to the visual experience to be seen therein. We have no resources for doing it the other way around, first determining the specific causal requirement and then picking out objects seen on the basis of what satisfies that requirement.

The application of this to divine perception is as follows. We will have a chance of determining how God has to be causally related to an experience in order to be perceived only if we can first determine in a number of cases that it is God who is being perceived. And since that is so, we can't rule out the possibility of perceiving God on the grounds that God can't be related to the relevant experience in the right way. For unless we do sometimes perceive God we are unable to determine what the right way is. Hence, so long as God does make some causal contribution to the relevant experiences, we can't rule out God's being perceived in those experiences on the grounds that He isn't causally related to them in the right way. To be sure, by the same token we cannot show that we do perceive God by showing that God is causally related to the experiences in the right way. But showing that is no part of our purpose here. It will be sufficient to show that, so far as we can see, there is no reason to doubt that it is possible that God should satisfy an appropriate causal requirement for being perceived in at least some of the cases in which people take themselves to be directly aware of Him.

V

If my arguments have been sound, we are justified in thinking of the experience of God as a mode of perception in the same generic sense of the term as sense perception. And if God exists, there is no reason to suppose that this perception is not sometimes veridical rather than delusory. I will conclude by mentioning a couple of respects in which this conclusion is of importance.

First, the main function of the experience of God in theistic religion is that it constitutes a mode, an avenue of communion between God and us. It makes it possible for us to enter into personal interaction with God. And if it involves our directly perceiving God in a sense generically the same as that in which we

perceive each other, this can be personal intercourse in a literal sense, rather than some stripped down, analogical or symbolic reconception thereof. We can have the real thing, not a metaphorical substitute.

Second, there are bearings on the cognitive significance of this mode of experience. If it is perceptual in character, and if it is possible that the other requirements should be satisfied for it to be a genuine perception of God, then the question of whether it is genuine is just a question of whether it is what it seems to its subject to be. Thus the question of genuineness arises here in just the same way as for sense perception, making possible a uniform treatment of the epistemology of the two modes of experience. This is not to beg the question of the genuineness of mystical perception. It could still be true that sense perception is the real thing, whereas mystical perception is not. And it could still be true that sense perception provides knowledge about its objects, whereas mystical perception yields no such results. The point is only that the *problems*, both as to the status of the perception and as to the epistemic status of perceptual beliefs, arise in the same form for both. This contrasts with the situation on the widespread view that "experience of God" is to be construed as purely subjective feelings and sensations to which supernaturalistic causal hypotheses are added. On that view the issues concerning the two modes of experience will look very different, unless one is misguided enough to treat sense perception in the same fashion. For on this subjectivist construal the subject is faced with the task of justifying a causal hypothesis before he can warrantedly claim to be perceiving God. Whereas if the experience is given a perceptual construal from the start, we will at least have to take seriously the view that a claim to be perceiving God is prima facie acceptable on its own merits, pending any sufficient reasons to the contrary.[1]

Note

1. See my *Perceiving God* (Ithaca, N.Y.: Cornell University Press, 1991) for a development of this last idea.

STUDY QUESTIONS

1. What are the features of the "Theory of Appearing" perceptual model used by Alston to understand our sensory experience?
2. How does Alston see accounts of the direct perception of God fitting into this "Theory of Appearing" model of perception?
3. How does Alston respond to the charge that in our experience of God we are merely providing a subjective interpretation of our experience?
4. How would you summarize Alston's overall thesis regarding religious experience?

Wayne Proudfoot

Religious Experiences as Interpretative Accounts

Wayne Proudfoot (b. 1939) holds that a description of religious experience must include reference to the experiencer's belief system, which is not neutral. Since religious experience has this connection with beliefs, it is similar to perceptual experience in that it includes reference to the cause or origin of the experience. It differs from perception, however, in that perceiving a tree, for example, requires that a tree be present and that it be noticed by the person. To place this same requirement on religious experience would be to impose too narrow a restriction, for to admit that others had a religious experience would be to grant that the object of their experience (e.g., Jesus, Krishna) existed. Rather, a religious experience is an experience that the subject *takes as* religious, as being incapable of being accounted for or explained in natural terms, without reference to religious beliefs. The concepts and beliefs constitute the experience and hence give rise to different experiences. According to Proudfoot, the remaining task is that of understanding why persons explain their experience in terms of the particular beliefs and concepts that they use. Here an appeal to historical, psychological, and social factors may be helpful.

We have seen that James describes the common core of religious experience as a sense or consciousness of the presence of a reality of power that transcends the self and its ordinary world. This sense or consciousness is said to be more like a sensation than like an intellectual operation. It is formative of, rather than consequent upon, religious belief. But the examples James gives of a sense of reality or consciousness of a presence suggest that intellectual operations are involved, and that what he has called a sense is really a thought or belief. He proposes that questions of origin and questions of evaluation be radically separated in the study of religious experience. But his observation that that experience is characterized by a noetic quality similar to that of sense perception suggests that matters of assessment and explanation cannot be kept as clearly distinct as he would like. To that question we now turn.

SENSIBLE AUTHORITY

The analogy James draws between mystical experience and sense perception is weakened by his assumption that perceptual experience is unmediated by concepts and beliefs, but his observation is accurate. The contrast he makes between the authority of the experience for the subject and its authority for an observer is important, and it does parallel the case of ordinary perception. There is a noetic quality to the experience, a sense of authority that distinguishes the attitude of the subject of the experience from that of an observer. An analysis of this characteristic of the experience will demonstrate the impossibility of following James in his proposal to exclude questions about the cause or origin of the experience.

An important distinction that will help to capture the noetic quality or the authority of perceptual experience is that drawn by Chisholm...between the *epistemic* and comparative uses of what he calls "appear words."[1] When I say that the table across the room appears to be round, I am using *appears* to report what I am inclined to believe on the basis of my present sensory experience. I believe that the table is round even though its image on my retina is elliptical. When I say that the tree in the distance appears to be as tall as the one under which I am standing, I am reporting my belief about the actual size of the tree. In both cases I have already made corrections for parallax and distance, and I am stating what appears to me to be the case. Such adjustments have become habitual in my learning to use the relevant words and to report what I see. Now I am making a judgment and a claim. When, however, I report that the table appears elliptical even though I believe it really to be round, or that the stick I have just dropped into the water appears to be bent, I am employing what Chisholm calls the comparative use of *appears*. I am stating that the table looks to me as it would look if it were an ellipse and were viewed under standard conditions, or the stick appears as it would if it were out of the water and bent. I am not making a judgment about the actual characteristics of the table or the stick; I am reporting an image by comparing it with other known images. The epistemic use is a report of what the subject is inclined to believe on the basis of the present experience, and

thus it assumes habits of inference and of explanation which are relevant for arriving at beliefs on the basis of this data. The comparative use is a report of how the image appears to the subject, despite what he may believe about the actual state of affairs. The epistemic use assumes a theoretical interest and an inference to the best explanation, whereas the comparative use does not. Ordinary perceptual judgments include an epistemic component. This is what James refers to as the noetic quality of religious experience....

James understands that the religious consciousness is more than a way of seeing, that it includes a claim about the nature of things....Religious experience includes a judgment about how things actually are. Stephen Bradley's accelerated heart rate appeared to him to be the result of the operation of the Holy Spirit. His belief that it was to be explained that way was a constitutive part of his experience. Schleiermacher's pious theist experiences every event in the light of the sense of absolute dependence. For him, every event is a miracle. It is to be ascribed to a power on which the entire nexus of natural causes is dependent....

A noetic quality is an essential part of the experience. Once we recognize this noetic or epistemic quality in the religious experience, it is not possible to maintain the sharp separation James proposes between inquiry into its significance or value. When he introduces this distinction, James says that it is drawn in recent books on logic. His reference here is probably to Peirce....Peirce argues that the origin of a hypothesis is altogether irrelevant to the issue of its truth or falsity. A physicist might arrive at a novel hypothesis in a dream, by painstaking calculation, or he might derive it from some mystical interpretation of ancient texts. But the hypothesis must be assessed only according to the results of an experiment designed to test it, without regard for its origin. The justification of a belief and the explanation of how one came to hold it must be kept distinct. The criteria for empirical inquiry are orthogonal to the criteria appropriate for the causal explanation of a belief. The scientist is and should be indifferent to the origin of his hypotheses....

Granted Peirce's point that the evaluation of a belief should be independent of its origin, does this apply to religious experience as well? Were religious experience a matter of a simple feeling more akin to a physiological sensation than to an intellectual process, it is possible that it could be evaluated without reference to its origin. A particular shade of blue, the taste of honey, the scent of eucalyptus, or a lowered body temperature or accelerated heart rate can each be described and, for some purposes, assessed without attention to their causes. A high body temperature may be desirable in order to combat a particular virus, and that judgment can be made independently of the means used to achieve that end. A certain shade of blue might be preferred to another....

If we consider, not a particular shade of blue or a taste of honey, but the perceptual judgment that this sample is blue and this liquid contains honey, then the situation is different. Beliefs can ordinarily be assessed without regard to the origin or cause of the experience that gave rise to those beliefs. But an exception must be made in the case of beliefs that include claims about the cause of an experience. Perceptual beliefs and judgments are of this kind. A perceptual judgment includes an embedded claim about the cause or origin of the perceptual experience. What are the conditions under which we identify an experience as a perception? My having a visual image of a tree, believing that I see a tree, and possessing evidence to justify my belief are not jointly sufficient to constitute a perception of the tree. My belief may be mistaken; perhaps there is no tree there at all. More surprisingly, my having a visual image of a tree, believing that I see that tree, having evidence to justify my belief, and the actual existence of a tree at the point at which I think I see one are not sufficient for the conclusion that I am seeing the tree. Each of these conditions could be fulfilled and yet the circumstances be such that we would not call it a perception.

Consider the following example: I have a visual image of a tree, and on the basis of that image, my beliefs about my visual capacities, my waking state, and other background assumptions, I believe I see a tree thirty yards ahead. It is possible that a tree exactly matching the description of the tree I think I see does stand at that point thirty yards away, thus that my belief is both justified and true, and yet that I have not perceived the tree. Suppose that, unknown to me, halfway between where I stand and the tree is a large mirror. This mirror blocks my vision of the tree but reflects a tree of exactly the same description placed off to the side at such a distance that the reflected image exactly simulates the image I would have received had the mirror not been interposed. I have not actually perceived the tree because the relevant causal conditions have not been fulfilled. The tree has not entered in the requisite way into my coming to believe there is a tree at that spot. Most important, were the tree that I think I perceive not there, I would have the same experience I now have. Should I come to know the actual conditions that have produced my visual image of the tree and my belief, I would conclude that I had not perceived the tree that I had supposed, but that I did perceive another tree. Reflection on such examples has led to the recent revival of the causal theory of perception.

The authority of the perceptual judgment is dependent on an assumed causal relation. It is the assumption of such a relation which gives the perceptual experience its noetic quality. If James is correct in saying that the noetic quality and the authority of religious experience are analogous to that of sense perception, then a similar assumption about the cause of the experience may be embedded in reports of religious experience. Consider religious conversion....

For the subject, the identification of an experience as religious assumes an embedded causal claim; consequently the experience has an epistemic quality, as in the case of sense perception. But what are the conditions under which an observer would identify an experience as religious? Here the cases of sense perception and religious experience diverge in an important way. *To perceive* is what Ryle[2] calls an achievement verb. The criteria for saying that someone has perceived an object include the assumption that the object is really there to be perceived and that he has perceived it. If you claim you see a table, and I think there is no table there to be seen and you are hallucinating, I will not identify your experience as a perception of the table. I will say that you think (wrongly) that you see the table. The identification by an observer of a subject's experience as a perception includes an endorsement by the observer of the subject's perpetual claims. The subject believes the tree or table is there and he has seen it, and the observer identifies the experience as a perception only if he endorses that belief. If a person erroneously believes he has seen a table, or if he has been to Rouen and is confusing that town with Chartres, we would not claim he has seen the table or the cathedral at Chartres.

One could follow a similar policy with respect to the identification of a religious experience, but the result would be too restrictive. Were we to require the existence of the object or the accuracy of the subject's embedded claim as a criterion for the identification of an experience as religious, then the very existence of religious experiences would depend on the existence of God, Krishna, or other objects people have claimed to experience. Edwards did require that an affection be caused by the operation of the Holy Spirit for it to be identified as a religious affection. By that criterion, the identification of an experience as religious presupposes belief in God and his Spirit. We want to admit, however, that there are religious experiences. Reports of them abound in religious literature. People identify their experiences as religious, though, as we shall see, not often in those terms. But we want to identify certain experiences as religious without committing ourselves to endorsing the claims that are constitutive of those experiences. Perceptual experience and religious experience are similar in that the experience is constituted by certain embedded claims. The subject assumes certain beliefs in identifying his experience as perceptual or religious. But they differ in that the observer's identification of a perceptual experience does, and his identification of a religious experience does not, imply an endorsement of the claims assumed by the subject which constitute the experience.

RELIGIOUS EXPERIENCE

We can now return to the question with which we began this chapter: What are the distinguishing marks of a religious experience? The aim of the question is not to arrive at a definition that will capture the real essence of religious experience. There is no

such essence to capture. Our aim is rather to explicate the concept....

The concept of religious experience is a difficult one to make precise, as much because of the term experience as because of anything to do with religion. *Experience* covers a wide variety of phenomena, from ordinary sense experience to dreams, fantasies, and extraordinary states that may be either spontaneously induced or highly contrived. This is not the place to enter into an elaborate analysis of the term. We might agree, however, that anything that is described as an experience must be specified under a description that is given from the subject's point of view....

Religious experience must be characterized from the perspective of the one who has that experience. It is an experience that the subject apprehends as religious....

Even from the subject's perspective, religious content is not enough to identify an experience as religious. The intellectual or imagistic content of an experience does not suffice to identify it as religious....One would not want to characterize religious experience in this way. Were we to do so, visiting Borobodur, listening to Bach, admiring a painting by Piero della Francesca, wishing there were a God, and tracing the history of the concept of nirvana would all be religious experiences. Any of these might be a religious experience, but it is not made such by the fact that the person attends to concepts or images that derive from a religious tradition. The experience must be one that the subject takes to have religious significance or import.

What does it mean to say that an experience has religious import, if this is to be identified with the subject matter of the experience? This is the noetic quality or authority described above, the basis for the analogy with perception....Religion refers to the feelings, acts, and experiences of persons "so far as they apprehend themselves to stand in relation to whatever they may consider the divine." "Apprehend" includes a judgment about what is real and its relation to the subject. In order to do justice to the authority of the experience, the subject must be convinced that the experience could not be accounted for without reference to religious beliefs. This does not mean only that it could not be described without reference to religious concepts or beliefs. That would be true of Borobodur, of a performance of the Bach B-minor Mass, or of an exhibition of Islamic calligraphy. It must also be the case that the experience cannot be explained without such a reference. We saw that the noetic quality of sense perception and of mystical experience assumes a judgment about the proper explanation of that experience. The subject matter on which attention is focused might not be distinctively religious at all,…but the one who has the experience must be convinced that it cannot be exhaustively accounted for without reference to religious beliefs.…

A religious experience is an experience that is identified by its subject as religious, and this identification must be based not on the subject matter or content of the experience, but on its noetic quality or its significance for the truth of religious beliefs.…

We have discovered that our concept of religious experience includes a noetic quality or epistemic element, and that that component is best analyzed as an assumed claim about the proper explanation of the experience. We have found this in various guises in Schleiermacher, Otto, and James, and in accounts of mystical experiences. More specifically, we have seen that Otto includes among the criteria for the identification of the religious moment the condition that it cannot be explained exhaustively in natural terms. Schleiermacher describes the experience as one of the utter dependence of oneself and the nexus of natural causes on some other power. James includes in his description of the common element in all religious experience a consciousness of a "More" that is operative in the universe beyond the self and its ordinary world. He thinks it is best understood as a straightforward supernaturalism, though he says this is an Overbelief that goes beyond the data. In the discussion of mystical experience, we saw that the noetic quality of the experience seems to derive from an assumption that naturalistic explanations are insufficient. This assumption accords with the way in which the concept of religious experience is ordinarily used. We would think it odd if someone claimed to have had a religious experience and then argued that the experience could be exhaustively explained as the effect of a pill he had ingested. It would be strange for someone

to report a religious experience and to subscribe to a psychoanalytic or sociological explanation as providing a complete account of that experience. The words *exhaustive* and *complete* are important here. Mystical regimens and other disciplines for prayer and meditation do prescribe exercises and conditioning that powerfully affect both mind and body, and the meditator is normally aware of such effects. But in the doctrine that governs those practices, and in the beliefs of the adept, those manipulations are viewed as catalysts. They are required for the experience, but they don't constitute a sufficient explanation. If it was thought that an experience could be exhaustively explained by these manipulations, then it could not be apprehended by the subject as religious.

EXPLAINING RELIGIOUS EXPERIENCE

The term *experience* is ambiguous. When I inquire about what a person has experienced at a certain moment, my question is ambiguous between two meanings: (1) how it seemed to that person at that time; and (2) the best explanation that can be given of the experience. This ambiguity is present in our ordinary talk about perception. I may have been frightened by the bear that I saw up ahead on the trail. My friend points out to me that it is not a bear but a log, and my fear subsides. What did I really see up ahead? By one interpretation of the word *see*, I saw a bear. That is the way I apprehended it, and that apprehension accounts for my fear and behavioral response. By another interpretation, what I really saw was a log, and I took it for a bear. I was wrong about what I experienced, and now that I can explain what happened I can correct my mistake.

This distinction is similar to, but differs from, Chisholm's distinction between the comparative and epistemic uses of "appear" words. It differs because Chisholm suggests that the comparative use, the description of how it appears to the subject, is a report of an immediate experience that is independent of interpretation or other beliefs. No such unmediated experience is possible. The distinction drawn here is between one interpretation, which presupposes a particular explanation of the experience, and another interpretation, also assuming an explanation, which is adopted by another person or by the same person at a later time. The perception of the object ahead as a bear was one explanation, and that was replaced by a better explanation when more information became available. That better explanation led to a reinterpretation of the experience.

It is important to note that both senses of *experience* assume explanations. It is not the case that explanation enters only into the second sense. The first, the description of his or her experience as assumed by the subject at the time of the experience, presupposes an explanation. If the distinguishing mark of the religious is that it is assumed to elude natural explanation, then the labeling of the experience as religious by the subject includes the belief that it cannot be exhaustively explained in naturalistic terms....

The distinction we have drawn between descriptive and explanatory reduction is tailored to meet this ambiguity. Descriptive reduction is inappropriate because the experience must be identified under a description that can be ascribed to the subject at the time of the experience. The experience must be described with reference to its intentional object. In the example given above, my fright was the result of noticing a bear ahead of me. The fact that the analyst must attempt to formulate a description of the experience which captures the way it was apprehended by the subject does not mean that no explanation is incorporated into the subject's description, nor does it mean that the analyst is not engaged in an inference toward the best explanation in his attempt to arrive at that formulation.

The identification of an experience under a description that can be ascribed to the subject is required before any explanation of the experience can be proposed. Every explanation assumes a description of that which is to be explained. One cannot explain phenomena as such but only phenomena under a description.... An event, action, emotion, or experience can be identified only under a certain description, and reference must be made to that description in any explanation that is offered. If the relevant description is not acknowledged, it will be tacitly assumed. The analyst's choice of the appropriate description of an experience or action is not

entirely independent of the explanation he goes on to offer. If a practice is completely baffling to me under a certain description, and would be recognizable as a practice common to the culture in which it is ensconced if the description were altered slightly, then I will be tempted to alter it and to ascribe the discrepancy to defects in my observation or in the reports from which I am working. If the evidence for the original description is compelling, I must accept the anomaly and search further for an explanation; if it is weak, I may adjust the description in the interest of overall plausibility. This is the proper point at which to invoke Quine's Principle of Charity. I want my total account, with its descriptive and explanatory components, to be the most plausible of the available alternatives. I adjust each until I reach a reflective equilibrium.

The recognition that religious experience is constituted by concepts and beliefs permits an optimism with respect to the descriptive task which would not otherwise be possible. There is no reason, in principle, to despair about the possibility of understanding the experience of persons and communities that are historically and culturally remote from the interpreter. The difficulty is not posed by an unbridgeable gap between an experience that can only be known by acquaintance and the concepts in which that experience is expressed. Because the concepts and beliefs are constitutive of the experience, careful study of the concepts available in a particular culture, the rules that govern them, and the practices that are informed by them will provide access to the variety of experiences available to persons in that culture. Though it may be difficult to reconstruct, the evidence required for understanding the experience is public evidence about linguistic forms and practices. We attempt to formulate a description of the experience from the perspective of the subject, but the evidence is, in principle, accessible to us.

This conception of religious experience also shows that the variety of that experience is much greater and richer than has been suggested by those who claim that a single experience of the numinous or sacred, or a few such types, underlie all the diverse reports in different traditions. Just as the experiences of nirvana and devekuth differ because they are informed by different concepts and beliefs, so the often rather subtle doctrinal differences between religious communities, or subgroups of the same community, will give rise to different experiences.... The catalogue of varieties can never be completed.

If explanation is as central to the study of religious experience as this account suggests, then why has it not been recognized as such? Why is the explanatory component so often disguised or ignored in favor of appeals to a sense or a consciousness that is contrasted with belief? There are two motivations for this procedure: phenomenological accuracy and a protective strategy adopted for apologetic purposes. The first arises from the fact that those who report religious experiences typically take them to be independent of and more fundamental than beliefs or theories. The sense of the infinite or the consciousness of finitude is not apprehended as a theoretical commitment but as an inchoate sense that provides a practical orientation. It seems to the subject to be inaccurate to classify it with inference, inquiry, and hypothesis. Since an understanding of the experience requires that it be identified under a description that accords with that of the subject, it is tempting to assimilate it to the case of sensations, and to assume that sensations are independent of practices and beliefs. For these reasons, phenomenological accuracy appears to some to require that the experience be described so as to make it independent of beliefs.

The appeal to a sense of consciousness that is allegedly innocent of explanatory commitments has an apologetic advantage. If such an appeal could be made, it would be unaffected by any developments in science or other kinds of inquiry. It would, as Schleiermacher said, leave one's physics and psychology unaffected. Religious belief and practice could be seen as derived from this independent experience, and the difficult questions that have been raised for religion by changes in our other beliefs could be circumvented. Rather than seeing the experience as constituted by the beliefs, one could view the beliefs as expressive of the experience. The direction of derivation would be reversed, and that would serve the task of apologetics. If it did not provide a way of justifying religious beliefs and practices, it would at least

protect them from the criticism that they conflict with ordinary and scientific beliefs....

A consequence of such strategies is that language that appears to be descriptive may be intended to evoke or reproduce the experience that is purportedly described.

Such terms as *numinous, holy*, and *sacred* are presented as descriptive or analytical tools, but in conjunction with warnings against reductionism they function to preclude explanation and evoke a sense of mystery or awe. They are used to persuade the reader that the distinguishing mark of the religious is some quality that eludes description and analysis in nonreligious terms. Otto's use of *numinous* is an example of how one can employ the term to create a sense of mystery and present it as analysis. Such approaches to the study of religion are offered as neutral descriptions, but they assume not only a theory of religion but also religious theory.

We have distinguished the tasks of description and explanation and have argued that explanation is central both to religious experience and to its study. What kind of explanation, then, might we expect to construct for religious experience? An experience or an event can be explained only when it is identified under a description. And we have concluded that the distinguishing mark of religious experience is the subject's belief that the experience can only be accounted for in religious terms. It is this belief, and the subject's identification of his or her experience under a particular description, which makes it religious. If the concepts and beliefs under which the subject identifies his or her experience determine whether or not it is a religious experience, then we need to explain why the subject employs those particular concepts and beliefs. We must explain why the subject was confronted with this particular set of alternative ways of understanding his experience and why he employed the one he did. In general, what we want is a historical or cultural explanation.

This holds both for discrete, datable religious experiences, of the sort on which James concentrates, and for the identification of an underlying and pervasive religious moment in experience. Why did Stephen Bradley identify his accelerated heart rate as the work of the Holy Spirit? What caused Astor to regard what he saw as a miracle whereas Bingham remained skeptical? Why did Schleiermacher apprehend the moment that precedes thought as a sense of the infinite and discern a feeling of absolute dependence which accompanies all consciousness of the polarity of self and world? For Bradley, we would need to know something about Methodist revivalism in early nineteenth-century New England, about the particular meeting he attended earlier in the evening, and about the events in his life up to that moment. To explain Astor's beliefs about what he saw it would be necessary to acquaint oneself with Roman Catholic teachings on miracles, the significance of the shrine at Lourdes, and the details of Astor's background. To explain Schleiermacher's sense of the infinite, his feeling of absolute dependence, and his apprehension of all events as miracles one would need to know more about his early years among the Moravians, his study of Spinoza, and the circle of friends in Berlin for whom he wrote *On Religion*. Each of these instances requires acquaintance with the Christian tradition and with the particular forms of that tradition which shaped the person and his experience.

For experiences sought in highly manipulative settings, as in meditative traditions where the training is carefully prescribed and a person is guided by a spiritual director in the interpretation of the states of mind and body achieved by the regimen, explanations of the sort suggested by Schachter's experiment seem clearly relevant. The novice learns to make attributions that accord with the tradition, and he engages self-consciously in manipulations to attain states that confirm those attributions. For seemingly more spontaneous but still relatively discrete and datable experiences in less contrived settings, one would still look to explain the experience by accounting for why the subject makes these particular attributions. Just as Schachter's experiment sheds light on the experience of emotions in natural settings, attention to the meditative traditions may provide insight into the allegedly natural, spontaneous examples of religious experience. The phenomenologist of religion has often claimed that elaborately contrived ritualistic settings are expressions of the pervasive sense of the sacred or the infinite in human experience, but it seems more likely that the supposedly natural and spontaneous experiences are derived from beliefs and practices in much the same way that an experience is produced in the more disciplined traditions of meditative practice. How did Schleiermacher and others come to think that the sense of the infinite or the sense of finitude was independent of and prior to the beliefs and practices of a culture shaped by theism? His identification of what he takes to be a universal moment in human experience seems clearly to reflect the concept of God as Creator and Governor derived from the Hebrew Bible and the traditions it formed. The consciousness Schleiermacher accurately describes may, upon investigation, turn out to be the product of prior religious beliefs and practices....

It seems quite likely that the feeling of absolute dependence and Otto's sense of the numinous are legacies of belief in the God of the Hebrew Bible and Christian tradition and of the practices informed by that belief. These experiences now appear to be autonomous and independent of that belief and that tradition. At a time in which belief in a transcendent Creator and associated metaphysical doctrines have been rejected by many, the habits of interpretation informed by those beliefs remain firmly entrenched in cultural patterns of thought, action, and feeling. Belief in God as Creator once provided the justifying context for these affections and practices. Now the direction of justification is reversed, and attempts are made to defend the beliefs by appeal to the affective experiences and practices. The sense of finitude, the feeling of absolute dependence, the practice of worship, and the grammar that governs the use of the word *God* are appealed to in order to justify the traditional religious statements without which this sense, feeling, practice, and grammar would not be intelligible.

These are only some suggestions of the kind of explanation that might be offered of religious experience. While one might venture a hypothesis to account for Bradley's accelerated heart rate or the recovery that Astor witnessed, that approach will not yield an explanation of their experiences. What must be explained is why they understood what happened to them or what they witnessed in religious terms. This requires a mapping of the concepts and beliefs that were available to them, the commitments they brought to the experience, and the contextual conditions that might have supported their identification of their experiences in religious terms. Interest in explanations is not an alien element that is illegitimately introduced into the study of religious experience. Those who identify their experiences in religious terms are seeking the best explanations for what is happening to them. The analyst should work to understand those explanations and discover why they are adopted.

NOTES

1. Roderick Chisholm, *Perceiving: A Philosophical Study* (Ithaca, N.Y.: Cornell University Press, 1957), pp. 43–55.
2. Gilbert Ryle, *The Concept of God* (London: Hutchinson & Co., Ltd., 1949), pp. 130–154.

STUDY QUESTIONS

1. What is the causal theory of perception developed by Proudfoot? In what ways is the causal theory similar to or different from the Theory of Appearing developed by Alston in the previous reading?
2. Given the causal theory of perception, what differences does Proudfoot see between ordinary perceptual experience and religious experience?
3. How does Proudfoot differentiate between the descriptive and the explanatory accounts of an experience? What role does this distinction play in Proudfoot's account of religious experience?
4. What objection does Alston (in the previous reading) raise against Proudfoot's analysis of religious experience?

Michael Martin

Critique of Religious Experience

After briefly describing the argument for God's existence from religious experience, Michael Martin (b. 1932) proceeds to criticize its first premise. Under certain conditions, religious beliefs generated by religious experience are likely to be true. For Martin, it is just as likely that religious experience is have a psychological explanation as that they have an external cause, for they are unreasonably inconsistent with each other. Even personal moral improvement does not prove that a religious experience is genuine, for the two might only be correlatively connected. He notes that even the experience of a public physical object is open to different interpretations and maintains that mystical experiences fare no better. Considering Swinburne's Principle of Credulity—when something seems to someone to be present, it probably is present, Martin suggests a parallel Negative Principle of Credulity such that the absence of any experience of God would count strongly against there being a God. He also points out that applying an unqualified Principle of Credulity to diverse and incompatible religious experiences actually proves too much, for it would legitimate incompatible claims about the nature of what is real (a monotheistic God, Brahma, etc.).

I. Religious Experience Defined

Down through the ages religious believers have had a variety of religious experiences and have used these to justify their belief in God. What is the religious experience? Although the notion is difficult to define, for my purpose here a religious experience is understood as an experience in which one senses the immediate presence of some supernatural entity.[1] But what does this involve?

As I am using the term "sense," if someone senses the immediate presence of some entity, this does *not* entail that it exists. It does entail that the person either believes or is inclined to believe that the entity exists, at least partly on the basis of the person's experience.[2] For example, if Jones senses the immediate presence of the angel Gabriel, this does not entail that the angel Gabriel exists, but it does entail that Jones believes or is inclined to believe that the angel Gabriel exists, at least in part on the basis of his experience. However, the entailment can not be reversed. One may believe that an entity is present or be inclined to believe that it is present and yet not do so on the basis of one's religious experience if, for example, one's belief is based entirely on faith or indirect evidence. Furthermore, by "some supernatural entity" I mean to include more than God, in the sense of an all-good, all-knowing, all-powerful being. For example, one could sense the immediate presence of an angel or a finite god. In addition, by sensing the immediate presence of some supernatural being I do not mean to imply that the being whose immediate presence is sensed is experienced as distinct or separate from the person who is having the experience. I mean rather to include phenomena in which the person experiences a union or a merging with the divine.

II. Types of Religious Experience

There are several types of religious experience in the sense defined above. It is useful to consider Swinburne's classification of religious experience, which is one of the most extensive and illuminating schemes to appear in recent literature.[3]

Type 1. One can experience an ordinary nonreligious object *as* a supernatural being—for example, a dove as an angel. The experience is of a public object, an object that ordinary observers would experience under normal conditions. For example, ordinary observers under normal conditions would experience the dove, although they would not experience it as an angel.

Type 2. One can experience some supernatural being that is a public object and use ordinary vocabulary to describe the experience. This experience would not be of some ordinary object *as* a supernatural being but of a supernatural being in its normal guise. Thus a person P can experience an angel in its normal guise as a beautiful being with wings, and the object of P's experience can be such that any ordinary

observer would experience what P would experience under ordinary circumstances. For example, Joseph Smith, the founder of the Mormon Church, had an experience of the angel Moroni "standing in the air" by his beside on September 21, 1823.[4] If we assume that any normal observer who had been in Joseph Smith's bedroom on the night of September 21, 1823, would have experienced the angel Moroni standing in the air near Smith's bed, then Smith's experience would be of type 2.

Type 3. This is like type 2 experiences except that the experience is not of a public object. One can experience some supernatural being in its standard guise, not some ordinary object as a supernatural being, and use ordinary vocabulary to describe the experience, although this being could not be experienced by ordinary observers under normal conditions....

Type 4. Another kind of experience entails sensations that are not describable by the normal vocabulary. Mystical experiences, for example, are sometimes so difficult to describe that the mystic is forced to use paradoxical and negative terms....

Type 5. The experience of a supernatural being can involve no sensations at all. A person may experience God and not claim to have had any particular sensations either of the typical sort or of some sort that is difficult to describe.[5] For example, it is likely that one of the experiences of St. Teresa of Avila, a Spanish nun of the sixteenth century, was of this kind, for she described it in this way:

> I was at prayer on a festival of the glorious Saint Peter when I saw Christ at my side—or, to put it better, I was conscious of Him, for neither with the eyes of the body nor with those of the soul did I see anything. I thought He was quite close to me and I saw that it was He Who, as I thought, was speaking to me.[6]

This last type of experience is also of a nonpublic object. Her nonsensory experience of Christ is not something that ordinary people could have had.

The Argument in Brief

Although religious experiences have been used to justify religious belief, such as belief in the existence of God, it is sometimes maintained that this use does not constitute an *argument* for the existence of God because when one senses the presence of God, no inference is involved. Religious belief based on religious experience, it is said, is like a perceptual belief of tables and chairs; because it is immediate and non-inferential, it cannot be construed as being based on an argument. Consequently, there is no argument from religious experience.

However, the thesis that appeals to religious experience to justify religious belief does not constitute an argument is much less compelling than it may seem. Its apparent plausibility rests on a confusion between how a belief is arrived at—that is, the genesis of the belief—and how it is justified. For it may well be true that a person who arrives at his or her beliefs by means of religious experience or ordinary perceptual experience does so without using inferences or arguments, but it is not obviously true that this person could justify those beliefs without using inferences or arguments.[7] For example, in order to be able to justify my spontaneous perceptual belief that there is a brown table in front of me, it would seem to be necessary in principle to be able to argue thus: Spontaneous beliefs of a certain sort occurring under certain conditions are usually true, and my belief that there is a brown table in front of me is of this sort and occurs under these conditions. Consequently, my belief is probably true....

Given that religious beliefs based on religious experiences need to be justified by an argument, what kind would be appropriate? I suggest that the following sort is basic to justifying belief in God on the basis of religious experience:

(1′) Under certain conditions C_1, religious beliefs of type K_1—that is, beliefs generated by religious experience—are likely to be true.

(2′) Condition C_1 obtains.

(3′) My religious belief that God exists is of type K_1.

(4′) Hence my religious belief that God exists is likely to be true.

Evaluation of the Argument

Clearly the crucial premise of the argument is premise (1′). What reason can we have for supposing the religious beliefs generated by certain types of religious experiences under certain conditions are likely to be true? One general problem with the several types of experience considered above is that they are concerned with nonpublic objects. In order for us to suppose that beliefs generated by these experiences are likely to be true, we must assume that each experience is caused by a reality external to the person who is having it, a reality that does not cause ordinary persons to experience something similar. Let us call this supposition the external cause hypothesis (H_1).

The problem arising in relation to premise (1′) is that there is a rival hypothesis. One might suppose that a person's religious experience is caused not by some external reality but by the workings of the person's own mind. On this theory, a religious experience would have an origin similar to that of delusion and delirium. But then religious experience would have no objective import and would not be trustworthy at all. Let us call this the psychological hypothesis (H_2).

Which hypothesis should be accepted? Consider first the reasons why we do not use the external cause hypothesis (H_1) to explain the experiences that result from the use of certain drugs, from mental illness, and from going without sleep for long periods of time. Why could not one argue that these experiences are caused by some external reality and that they provide evidence of the nature of such a reality? It may be suggested that when one takes certain drugs, has a mental illness, or goes without sleep the mind is opened to this reality and ordinary perception is unable to make contact with it. Certainly, people who have such experiences often interpret them as experiences of objects external to their minds. We have good reasons to suppose, however, that such an interpretation is mistaken and thus good reason not to use (H_1) to explain these experiences. Why? The primary reason is that experiences induced by drugs, alcohol, sleep deprivation, and mental illness tell no uniform or coherent story of a supposed external reality that one can experience only in these extraordinary ways....

Religious experiences are like those induced by drugs, alcohol, mental illness, and sleep deprivation: They tell no uniform or coherent story, and there is no plausible theory to account for discrepancies among them. Again the situation could be different. Imagine a possible world where part of reality can only be known through religious experiences. There religious experiences would tend to tell a coherent story. Not only would the descriptions of each religious experience be coherent, but the descriptions of the experiences of different people would tend to be consistent with one another. Indeed, a religious experience in one culture would generally corroborate a religious experience in another culture. When there was a lack of corroboration, there would be a plausible explanation for the discrepancy. For example, it might be known that the experiences of a person who had not performed certain spiritual exercises for at least three months would be untrustworthy. Moreover, if first-hand descriptions of religious experience made no sense, there would be a ready explanation. For instance, the person might not be properly trained to describe such experiences but, once trained, would be able to provide coherent descriptions. Indeed, there might be independent reason to suppose that the incoherent descriptions could be translated into coherent terms. In this possible world the external cause hypothesis might well be the best explanation of religious experiences.

Once again, this possible world is not ours. In our world, descriptions of religious experience sometimes make no sense, yet we have no ready explanation of this incoherence and no reason to suppose that some suggested coherent translation captures the meaning of the description. Furthermore, religious experiences in one culture often conflict with those in another. One cannot accept all of them as veridical, yet there does not seem to be any way to separate the veridical experiences from the rest. With the possible exception of mystical experiences in our world, the psychological hypothesis is therefore the best explanation of these experiences. In a moment I will take up the claim made by some scholars that mystical experience is uniform over cultures and time. Even if it is correct, other types of religious experience of nonpublic objects tell no uniform or coherent story.

But is there really no way to determine which religious experiences should be considered trustworthy and which should be rejected? St. Teresa suggested several ways of ruling out deceptive religious experiences. These techniques have been adopted by other religious believers,[8] and two of them are especially important. If the content of a religious experience is incompatible with Scripture, she says, it should be considered nonveridical. She also maintained that if a religious experience has a bad effect on one—for example, if a person becomes less humble or loving or fervent in faith after the experience—then the experience is deceptive.

Unfortunately, these tests for separating deceptive from trustworthy religious experiences will not do. Since the test of scriptural compatibility already presumes that the Bible is the revealed word of God and therefore that the Christian God exists, it cannot be used to support an argument from religious experience for the existence of God. Further, it would hardly be surprising on the psychological hypothesis (H_2) that people raised in the Christian tradition should tend to have religious experiences that are compatible with Christian Scripture. This hypothesis, combined with plausible auxiliary hypotheses such as that people's delusions tend to be strongly influenced by their training and culture, predicts that in general people raised in a certain religious tradition tend to have religious experiences compatible with the religious literature of this tradition. This is exactly what one finds. Divergences from this prediction are rare and in any case can be accounted for in terms of individual psychological factors and the influence of other traditions.

Unless we grant large and dubious assumptions about the relations between religious experience and conduct, St. Teresa's test of conduct will not work either. Why should one assume that a vision of ultimate reality will always or even usually make a person better? One could have a vision of God and yet, on account of weakness of will or the overpowering and dreadful nature of the vision, degenerate morally. Furthermore, there is no a priori reason why a person might not show moral improvement after an illusory religious experience. It might just be the catalyst needed to change the person's life. St. Teresa wrongly seemed to think that the only deception possible in a religious experience is brought about by the devil. But the deceptive nature of such experience could have purely psychological causes, and the moral improvement that results could have such causes as well. In addition to these problems, the test of conduct surely proves too much. Since religious experiences occur in the context of different religious, it would not be surprising to discover that, for example, Christian, Islamic, and Hindu religious experiences have all resulted in improved conduct. However, since they seem to be incompatible, it can hardly be claimed that all these experiences are trustworthy. I must conclude, therefore, that St. Teresa's tests of veridical religious experience are unsatisfactory.

As we have seen, two kinds of religious experience, type 1 and type 2, are of public objects. Could these provide the corroboration needed to claim that some religious experience is trustworthy? Although this is possible in principle, as a matter of fact the ingredients necessary for the experience of a public object are missing. Consider, for example, a type 1 experience of a black cat as the devil. We have here the same problem as in the case of nonpublic objects. There is no agreement among observers and no plausible theory to explain disagreement. To be sure, there is agreement among observers that a black cat is seen. However, there is no agreement that the devil is seen and no plausible theory to account for discrepancies. Because of this, the experience of seeing the black cat as the devil is better explained by the psychological hypothesis (H_2) than by the external cause hypothesis (H_1)....

Turning now to experiences of type 2, we must distinguish two different cases. In the first, several people experience some supernatural being at the same time. In the second, some lone individual P experiences a supernatural being, but it is claimed that if other normal people had been with P, they would have experienced what P did. Since the second case can for all practical purposes be treated as a type 3 experience, it can be ignored here.

The first kind of type 2 experience seems important, however. For it may be maintained that if there were clear and uncontroversial cases of type 2 religious experiences, there would be strong evidence for the existence of God. Furthermore, it might be claimed by religious believers that there have been such cases. One example that could be cited is the appearance of Jesus to several of his disciples after his resurrection. It could be maintained that Jesus was a public object capable of being observed by all normal observers. Furthermore, he was surely a supernatural being, since he arose from the dead. Moreover, religious believers could claim that this case provides evidence for the existence of God, since Jesus' appearance after his resurrection is best explained by the hypothesis that he was God incarnate.

But have there been clear and uncontroversial cases of type 2 religious experience? Certainly the case of Jesus' alleged resurrection is not one of them. Indeed, there is little reason to accept this story as true. The accounts of Jesus' resurrection in different gospels contradict each other;[9] the story is not supported by Paul's letters, which many scholars believe were written earlier;[10] and the story is not supported by Jewish and Roman sources.[11] Furthermore, I know of no clear and uncontroversial cases of type 2 religious experiences.

However, suppose that there were good grounds to suppose that Jesus appeared to several of his disciples after his death on the cross. Would this be strong evidence that God, an all-powerful, all-knowing, all-good being, exists? This would, indeed, be strong evidence that Jesus was a supernatural being, but it would not be strong evidence for the existence of an all-good, all-powerful, all-knowing being. This is because Jesus' appearance is compatible with many different supernatural explanations. For example, Jesus may have been the incarnation of a finite god or one of many gods or even of the devil. This is a basic problem in appealing to any religious experience—even type 2 religious experiences—as evidence for the existence of God. Even if one has good grounds for supposing a religious experience cannot be explained by (H_2) and must be explained by (H_1), this is compatible with various alternative supernatural explanations.

So although type 2 religious experiences could in principle provide support for belief in *some* supernatural being, in fact it remains to be shown that they do. And in any case it remains dubious that, even if such experience supported the belief that some supernatural being exists, it could provide more support for the existence of an all-good, all-powerful, all-knowing God than for the existence of some other supernatural being.

III. Mystical Experience

Mystical experiences are typically type 4 religious experiences in which a person has sensations that are not describable by our normal vocabulary. Some scholars of mysticism maintain that there is a common core of mysticism. They maintain that, although there are cultural differences among mystics, mystical experiences in different times and in different religions have important and fundamental similarities. If these scholars are correct, then perhaps these similarities provide the basis for a sound argument from mystical experiences to the existence of God.

Consider the following argument:

(1) All mystical experiences are basically the same.
(2) This similarity is better explained in terms of the external cause hypothesis (H_1) than of the psychological hypothesis (H_2).
(3) The most adequate version of (H_1) is that God causes the mystical experience (H_1').
(4) Therefore, mystical experiences provide inductive support for (H_1').

Walter Stace has argued for premise (1). According to Stace, all mystical experiences "involve the apprehension of *an ultimate nonsensuous unity of all things,* a oneness or a One to which neither the senses or the reason can penetrate."[12] He distinguishes two kinds of mysticism: extrovertive and introvertive. In extrovertive mysticism the mystic "looks outward and through the physical sense into the external world and finds the One there. The introvertive way turns inward, introspectively, and finds the One at the bottom of the self, at the bottom of the human personality."...

Stace's view is not shared by all scholars of mysticism. For example, Steven Katz maintains that there is no clear way of distinguishing the mystical experience itself from the interpretation of it.[13] Consequently, the meaning of the experience and even the meaning of the language used to describe the experience vary from context to context. For example, Katz argues that although all mystics claim that they experience a sense of objective reality (characteristic 3), what they mean differs radically from context to context and, indeed,

their interpretations are often mutually incompatible.... Fortunately, we do not have to settle the debate between Stace and his defenders on the one hand[14] and his critics on the other, for whether the critics are correct or not, the argument fails. Suppose that critics such as Steven Katz are correct that mystics in different religious traditions experience different realities. Then the first premise of the above argument fails, and in order to argue from mystical experiences to the existence of God, a new one would have to be constructed. Suppose now that Stace's critics are mistaken and that mystical experiences in different religious traditions show significant similarities. Then premise (1) would be true. What about premise (2)? It is possible that the similarity of mystical experience in different religious traditions can be explained in terms of the psychological hypothesis. There have been attempts, for example, to explain mystical experiences in terms of sexual repression and to show that mystical experiences are similar to ones that are caused by psychedelic drugs.[15] But even if these explanations are valid, given the alleged striking similarity of all mystical experiences, the external cause hypothesis is not ruled out. Sexual repression may be necessary if certain individuals are to have access to ultimate reality; and psychedelic drugs, as we have already argued, may provide this access.

The problem with the external cause hypothesis in the case of mystical experiences, and the reason for preferring the psychological hypothesis over the external cause hypothesis, is the difficulty of making sense of these experiences. As we have seen, for the external cause hypothesis to apply, not only must the experiences of different people usually cohere with one another, and not only must there be a plausible theory to explain cases where there are discrepancies, but the individual experiences themselves must be coherent or else there must be some plausible way to account for the incoherence. According to Stace, mystics claim that their experience is ineffable and yet describe it....So his characteristics of mystical experience seem prima facie contradictory. Further, according to Stace, the mystical experience itself has paradoxicality. By this he means that many mystics describe their experience in seemingly paradoxical language. For example, Dionysius the Aeropagite described his experience of God as "the dazzling obscurity of the

Secret Silence, outshining all brilliance with the intensity of their darkness."[16] Taken literally, descriptions of this sort are nonsense. The mystic who gives them cannot be interpreted as making any factual claims.[17] Further, there is no widely accepted theory to account for the incoherences[18] and no objective way of translating such nonsensical statements into statements that are not. Without such a theory and method of translation, the external cause hypothesis is not to be preferred to the psychological hypothesis.

However, let us suppose that there is some good reason to prefer the external cause hypothesis to the psychological hypothesis. This would establish premise (2) in the above argument but not premise (3) (the most adequate version of (H_1) is that God causes the mystical experience (H_1')). However, it is difficult to see why God should be postulated as the external cause rather than the Tao, nirvana, or nature.[19] Indeed, if the paradoxical language of mystical experience points beyond itself to some external cause, this external cause would have to be very obscure and difficult to understand. To suppose that this external cause is God, an all-good, all-powerful, all-knowing being, is surely unwarranted. Thus there seems to be no good reason to suppose that (H_1') is the most plausible version of (H_1). Consequently, even if the argument is successful in providing evidence for an external cause of mystical experience, it fails as an argument for God.

IV. Swinburne's Principle of Credulity and Religious Experience

...In his argument from religious experience Swinburne makes use of what he calls the principle of credulity, which allows one to infer from the fact that it seems to a person that something is present to the probability that it is present. Let us evaluate this principle and the use Swinburne makes of it.

The Principle of Credulity and Its Limitations

Traditionally, critics of the argument from religious experience have maintained that it is a fallacy to argue from a psychological experience of x to x—for example, from the fact that it appears to you that God is present to the probability that God is present.[20] Maintaining, however, that the way things seem is indeed good grounds for belief about the way things are, Swinburne calls the general principle that guides our inferences the Principle of Credulity. It can be formulated as follows:

> (PC) If it seems (epistemically) to a subject S that x is present, then probably x is present.

By the expression "seems (epistemically)" Swinburne means that the subject S is inclined to believe what appears to S on the basis of his or her present sensory experience. Swinburne contrasts this sense of "seems" with the comparative sense in which one compares the way an object looks with the way other objects normally look. Thus when S says, "It seemed that the Virgin Mary was talking to me," S is using "seemed" epistemically. But if S says, "The figure seemed like a beautiful lady bathed in a white light," S is using "seemed" comparatively.

Swinburne gives two basic reasons for advocating (PC). The first one is that without such a means of arguing, we would land in a "skeptical bog."[21] Unfortunately, he does not expand on this reason, but one can assume he means something like this: Without (PC) we would be unable ever to get outside our own experiences and make justified judgments about how things really are; we would be restricted to how things appear to us. However, if we are restricted to how things appear to us, skepticism about the world is the only justified position to take. But with (PC) we can say how things really are and avoid skepticism.

The second reason Swinburne gives for advocating (PC) is that the attempt to restrict it so that it does not apply to religious experience is arbitrary. He considers only two attempts to restrict the range of application. First one might argue that (PC) is not an ultimate principle of rationality but must itself be justified on inductive grounds; in other words, by showing that appearances have in general proved reliable in the past. But, the argument continues, although this reliability has been demonstrated in the case of the appearance of ordinary things, it has not been in the case of religious experience. So (PC) should be restricted to ordinary appearances. Swinburne rejects this restriction on two grounds. He maintains that people are justified in taking what looks like a table to be a table "even if they do not recall their past experience with tables,"[22] and in any case this attempt to restrict the range of application would not allow us to deal with cases where the subject has no experience of x's but does have experiences of the properties in terms of which x is defined.

Another objection to the use of (PC) with respect to religious experiences that Swinburne discusses is based on the distinction between experience and the interpretation of experience. One might argue, he says, that (PC) should be used only when one is experiencing certain properties—for example, the so-called sensible properties of red, brown, soft, hard, left, right—but that it should not be used when one makes interpretations. Thus if it seems that x is red, one can infer that probably it is red since the inference entails no interpretation. But if it seems x is a Russian ship, then one cannot infer that it probably is since one is interpreting. Using this argument one could argue that (PC) cannot be used to infer from the appearance of God that probably God exists, since interpretation is involved. Swinburne rejects this line of argument, maintaining that it rests on the dubious distinction between experience and interpretation. There is no way, he claims, of making this distinction without being arbitrary.

Swinburne of course believes that (PC) is limited in its application by some special considerations. On his view there are in fact four special considerations that limit (PC). First, one can show that the subject S was unreliable or that the experience occurred under conditions that in the past have been unreliable. For example, if S was subject to hallucinations or delusions or was under the influence of a drug such as LSD, this would limit the application of (PC). Second, one can show that the perceptual claim was to have perceived an object of a certain kind in circumstances where similar perceptual claims have proved false. For example, one might show that the perceiver did not have the experience necessary to make reliable perceptual claims in these circumstances. Swinburne argues, however, that what experiences are necessary in order to recognize something is often unclear, and

in any case the ability to recognize something, given certain experiences, varies widely from person to person....

A third circumstance in which (PC) would be limited is one in which there was strong evidence that x did not exist. Because he believes that S's experience has a very strong evidential force, Swinburne emphasizes that this evidence would have to be very, very strong. Finally, a fourth way to limit (PC) would be to show that although x is present, the appearance of x can be accounted for in other ways.

Swinburne believes that these four special considerations do not apply to religious experiences. Although the first special consideration may rule out some religious experience, most religious experiences are not affected, he says. Thus most people who claim that they have had a religious experience are not subject to hallucinations or delusions and are not on drugs such as LSD. Swinburne also argues that the second special consideration does not apply. He maintains that one cannot argue that someone who claims to experience God could not recognize God; nor can one argue that many religious experiences are incompatible. For example, it may be argued that in order to recognize God one would have to have previously perceived God or been given a detailed description of Him. But since people have not previously experienced God and do not have a detailed description of Him, they could not recognize Him. Swinburne rejects this contention and argues that the description of God as an omnipotent, omniscient, and perfectly free person may be sufficient for S to recognize God "by hearing his voice, or feeling his presence, or seeing his handiwork or by some sixth sense."...[23]

The Negative Principle of Credulity

One obvious critical question that can be raised about Swinburne's argument is this: Since experiences of God are good grounds for the existence of God, are not experiences of the absence of God good grounds for the nonexistence of God? After all, many people have tried to experience God and have failed. Cannot these experiences of the absence of God be used by atheists to counter the theistic argument based on experience of the presence of God? Swinburne thinks they cannot be so used.

In ordinary life we suppose that the experience of a chair is a good ground for believing that the chair is present. But we also believe that the experience of the absence of a chair is a good ground for supposing that a chair is absent. If Swinburne is correct that the way things appear is good ground for the way they are, then surely the way things do not seem is good ground for the way they are not. Indeed, if (PC) is a legitimate principle of inference, then one would suppose that there is a Negative Principle of Credulity that can be formulated as follows:

> (NPC)   If it seems (epistemically) to a subject S that x is absent, then probably x is absent....

Swinburne does not explicitly formulate a negative credulity principle. Whether he would be opposed to one as such or merely to the applications I have made of it is unclear. But let us try to understand his objection to the use of (NPC) to argue that probably God does not exist.

His objection to the use of (NPC) in showing the nonexistence of God based on the experience of God's absence turns on the alleged disanalogy between ordinary perceptual claims that can legitimately be made about the absence of something, such as the absence of a chair, and a perceptual claim in the context of religion that cannot be made, such as the absence of God. Swinburne sees the difference in this way: In the case of a chair one can know under what conditions one would see a chair if a chair was there. But in the case of God one cannot know under what conditions one would see God if God existed. Swinburne seems to believe that since we do not know under what conditions God would appear if He existed, experience of the absence of God cannot be used as evidence that God does not exist. But he maintains that this lack of knowledge only "*somewhat* lessens" the evidential value of perceptual claims of God's presence.[24]

It is difficult to understand why, if there were this difference, it would affect the evidential value of perceptual claims in religious contexts in the way Swinburne says. One would suppose that if one did not know under what conditions a subject could expect to see x if x existed, this would affect both the evidential value of S's claim that it seemed that x is present and S's claim that it seemed that x is not present, and to the same extent. Yet Swinburne maintains that since we do not know under what conditions someone would see God if God existed, this only somewhat lessens the evidential value of a perceptual claim that it seems to S that God is present, but it completely negates the evidential value of the perceptual claim that it seems to S that God is not present. Perceptual judgments of both the absence and the presence of God seem equally suspect, yet Swinburne finds a great disanalogy....

The Reliability of Religious Experiences

As I have indicated, Swinburne does not believe it possible to show that religious experience is unreliable by arguing that different religious experiences are incompatible. He maintains that religious experiences stemming from non-Christian traditions are of a being who is supposed to have "similar properties to those of God" or "experiences of apparently lesser beings."[25] Swinburne admits that if there were religious experiences of an all-powerful devil, they would conflict with religious experiences of God. But he argues that no such experiences exist.

However, it is not necessary to have experiences of an all-powerful devil to claim that religious experiences are systematically incompatible. Swinburne must do more than argue that the beings described in the religious experience of non-Western cultures have properties similar to those of God in the Western tradition in order to show no incompatibility. He must show that these beings do not have *any* properties that are incompatible with properties of God.

Prima facie there does seem to be a remarkable incompatibility between the concept of God in the Western tradition and the concept of Brahma, the absolute, and so on in Eastern thought. In the Western tradition, God is a person distinct from the world and from His creatures. Not surprisingly, many religious experiences within the Western tradition, especially nonmystical ones such as the experience of God speaking to someone and giving advice and counsel, convey this idea of God. On the other hand, mystical religious experience within the Eastern tradition tends to convey a pantheistic and impersonal God. The experience of God in this tradition typically is not that of a caring, loving person but of an impersonal absolute and ultimate reality. To be sure, this difference is not uniform: There are theistic trends in Hinduism and pantheistic trends in Christianity. But the differences between East and West are sufficiently widespread to be noted by scholars, and they certainly seem incompatible. A God that transcends the world seemingly cannot be identical with the world; a God that is a person can apparently not be impersonal. Indeed, Christians who have held pantheistic and impersonal views about God have typically been thought to be heretics by Christian orthodoxy. So there do seem to be incompatible differences in the religious experiences of different cultures....

V. Conclusion

I do not wish to deny that (PC) operates in ordinary life and science. But there are more limitations on its use than Swinburne imagines, and they need to be more tightly drawn. If without PC we might land in a skeptical bog, without tighter restrictions on (PC) we would find ourselves in a cluttered ontological landscape. Given Swinburne's version of (PC), there would indeed be more things in heaven and earth than are dreamt of in anyone's philosophy.

Notes

1. I am indebted here to William Rowe's illuminating discussion of the meaning of religious experience. See William L. Rowe, *Philosophy of Religion: An Introduction* (Belmont, Calif.: Wadsworth, 1978), pp. 63–64.
2. Cf. R. M. Chisholm, *Perception* (Ithaca, N.Y.: Cornell University Press, 1957), chap. 4.
3. See Richard Swinburne, *The Existence of God* (Oxford, England: Clarendon Press, 1979), pp. 249–253.
4. Quoted in Paul Kurtz, *The Transcendental Temptation* (Buffalo, N.Y.: Prometheus Books, 1986), p. 237.
5. See also Gary Gutting, *Religious Belief and Religious Skepticism* (Notre Dame, Ind.: University of Notre Dame Press, 1982), chap. 5, for further discussion of this type of experience.
6. St. Teresa, *The Life of Teresa of Jesus*, trans. and ed. by E. Allison Peers (Garden City, N.Y.: Image Books, 1960), p. 249. Quoted by George Mavrodes in "Real v. Deceptive Mystical Experiences," *Mysticism and Philosophical Analysis* (New York: Oxford University Press, 1978), p. 238.
7. See Laurence BonJour, *The Structure of Empirical Knowledge* (Cambridge, Mass.: Harvard University Press, 1985), p. 112.
8. Cf. Mavrodes, "Real v. Deceptive Mystical Experiences."
9. Kurtz, *Transcendental Temptation*, pp. 153–159.
10. G. A. Wells, *The Historical Evidence for Jesus* (Buffalo, N.Y.: Prometheus Books, 1982), pp. 22–25.
11. R. Joseph Hoffman, *Jesus Outside the Gospels* (Buffalo, N.Y.: Prometheus Books, 1984).
12. W. T. Stace, *The Teachings of the Mystics* (New York: New American Library, 1960), p. 14.
13. Steven Katz, "Language, Epistemology and Mysticism," *Mysticism and Philosophical Analysis*, pp. 22–74.
14. See, for example, Gary E. Kessler and Normal Prigge, "Is Mystical Experience Everywhere the Same?" *Sophia*, 21, 1982, pp. 39–55. They argue against Katz, maintaining that mystical experience is contentless consciousness, and such experience is found in all cases of introvertive mysticism. See also Agehananda Bharati, *The Light at the Center* (Santa Barbara, Calif.: Ross-Erikson, 1976), chap. 2. Bharati maintains that his mystical experience and that of others are a "zero experience," by which he means an experience that has zero cognitive content.
15. See, for example, Kurtz, *Transcendental Temptation*, pp. 97–102.
16. Stace, *Teachings of the Mystics*, p. 135. Whether this means that the experience seems to the mystic to have contradictory features or whether, as Katz has suggested, the paradoxical language cloaks the content, we need not decide here. We are assuming for the sake of argument that the experience seems contradictory. See also Katz, "Language, Epistemology and Mysticism," *Mysticism and Philosophical Analysis*, p. 54.
17. Robert Hoffman, "Logic, Meaning and Mystical Intuition," *Philosophical Studies*, 5, 1960, pp. 65–70.

18. For one interesting attempt to account for the incoherence of the descriptions of mystical experiences, see Paul Henle, "Mysticism and Semantics," *Philosophy and Phenomenological Research*, 9, 1948–1949, pp. 416–422.
19. In *Teachings of the Mystics*, p. 27, Stace admits that mystical experiences can be interpreted in terms of many religious traditions.
20. Indeed, I have argued something similar above: In order to justify my spontaneous perceptual belief, for example, that there is a brown table in front of me, it is necessary to give some sort of argument. Moreover, as my criticism of Swinburne's argument makes clear, I do not believe that the way things appear is *by itself* good grounds for believing how they are. A sound argument is needed that enables one to infer from the appearance of x to x.
21. Swinburne, *Existence of God*, p. 254, n. 1.
22. Ibid., p. 255.
23. Ibid., p. 268.
24. Ibid., p. 263.
25. Ibid., p. 267.

STUDY QUESTIONS

1. In your own words, explain Martin's reasoning that we need an argument to justify our belief that we are experiencing God when we claim to have a religious experience.
2. What argument does Martin give against the thesis that an external cause is the best hypothesis to explain religious experiences of his types 1 and 2?
3. What argument does Martin give against the thesis that an external cause is the best hypothesis to explain religious experiences of his types 4 and 5?
4. What is the Principle of Credulity? What objection does Martin raise against applying the Principle of Credulity to religious experience? If Swinburne had a voice in this book, what response might he make to Martin's Negative Principle of Credulity?

Merold Westphal

A Phenomenological Account of Religious Experience

Merold Westphal (b. 1940) characterizes religious experience as self-transcendence, moving from self-preoccupation to opening oneself to the Other who transcends the self. He believes that understanding religious experience as self-transcendence has three advantages: it shows that religious experiences are mediated by our concepts and feelings, it allows one to understand religious experiences from a diversity of religious perspectives, and it gives a criterion for distinguishing genuine religious experiences from imitations. Westphal goes on to describe the immediacy and givenness of the encounter with the Other in analogy with our experience with other persons. He concludes with the observation that since the experience of self-transcendence cannot be guaranteed against self-deception, the task of attaining authentic self-transcendence is lifelong. Hence, before we can consider how to use religious experience to justify religious beliefs, we have to attend to our own subjectivity.

The concluding line, taken from one of Pasternak's poems, was utterly shattering and unforgettable. "To live life to the end is no childish task."

Kierkegaard expresses this same conviction that life is the task of a lifetime by satirizing those for whom most of life is supposed to consist in living happily ever after. For such,

> when they have arrived at a certain point in their search for truth, life takes on a change. They marry, and they acquire a certain position, in consequence of which they feel that they must in all honor have something finished, that they must have result....And so they come to think of themselves as really finished....Living in this manner, one is relieved of the necessity of becoming executively aware of the strenuous difficulties which the simplest of propositions about existing qua human-being involves.[1]

By arguing that such persons are strangers to religion, no matter how orthodox or pious, Kierkegaard suggests that this enduring adult task has religious import. But what is this task, which is the sine qua non of religion, and from which, apparently, only death can release us? The Augustinian tradition, to which Kierkegaard belongs, is united in its answer:

Merold Westphal, "Religious Experience as Self-Transcendence and Self-Deception," *Faith and Philosophy* 9, no. 2 (April 1992). Edited, with author's additions.

self-transcendence. This is why Augustine speaks of the incarnation as the means by which Jesus "might detach from themselves those who were to be subdued and bring them over to Himself, healing the swelling of their pride and fostering their love so that instead of going further in their own self-confidence, they should put on weakness…should cast themselves down upon that divinity which, rising would bear them up aloft."[2] From this perspective follows the Augustinian beatitude: "Blessed is the man who loves you, who loves his friend in you, and his enemy because of you."

Thomas Merton gives the same answer when he writes, "We do not detach ourselves from things in order to attach ourselves to God, but rather we become detached *from ourselves* in order to see and use all things in and for God."[3]

[Kierkegaard's] definitions of the self and of faith spell out his understanding of self-transcendence as the lifelong task of life. The self is "a relation that relates itself to itself and in relating itself to itself relates itself to another."[4] This latter relation is faith when "in relating itself to itself and in willing to be itself, the self rests transparently in the power that established it."[5]

Augustine and Merton introduce the basic notion of becoming detached from ourselves. [Gabriel] Marcel makes it clear that this involves the transition from a self preoccupied with itself and its position as the center to a self capable of giving itself in admiration and creative fidelity to another. From the point of view of the point of departure, this is a humiliating tearing away from that to which I cling with all my might. From the point of view of the destination, this is a liberating elevation above the narrow horizons defined by the question, "But what about me?" In short, self-transcendence is the journey from the false self to the true self, with all of its agony and its ecstasy.

In spite of its austere form, Kierkegaard's formula for faith recapitulates these themes and introduces another. First, with Augustine and Merton he is explicit that we are to be detached from ourselves in order to be attached to God. "Freedom from" is in the service of "freedom for." Here we encounter the wonderful ambiguity of the term "transcendence."

It can mean that which is beyond, the transcendent. Or it can mean going beyond, transcending. For the Augustinian tradition the two are united, and transcending is toward the transcendent. What is beyond my false self is not simply my true self, but the not-myself in proper relation to which it first becomes possible for me to be my true self. Only by losing myself, in the sense of going beyond myself, do I ever truly find myself.

Second, with Marcel, Kierkegaard is explicit that the relation to the other is a humble, decentering relation. (This is why it is experienced by pride as humiliation.) Self-transcendence means willing to be myself while at the same time willing to let God be God, that is, willing to be myself without insisting on being God. It is the exact opposite of Nietzsche's Zarathustra, who says, "*if* there were gods, how could I endure not to be a god! *Hence* there are no gods."[6] It means learning to pray, "Hallowed be Thy name; *Thy* kingdom come; *Thy* will be done" without surreptitiously co-opting the name and the kingdom so that *my* will may be done on earth and in heaven.

Finally, for all of its emphasis on the role of the transcendent in self-transcendence, Kierkegaard's account explicitly links relation-to-an-other to self-relation. Only as self-relating selfhood does the self transcend itself toward its true self in relation to the transcendent.…

On the other hand, by making self-presence itself a task rather than an achievement, Kierkegaard excludes that total self-presence by virtue of which the self could claim to be the center. This expresses the great gulf fixed between his Augustinianism and its modern, secular counterpart, the Cartesian Humean (Husserlian-positivist) tradition. In its self-relation, the self is not posited as the ground of certainty, the criterion of truth, the self-sufficient and absolute mode of being, in short, the center.…To express the point oxymoronically,…Kierkegaard develops the inwardness of a decentered Cartesianism. The I of the Augustinian "I think" is always a problem, never a possession nor an Archimedean *pou sto* (Grk., standing place).

Having given this somewhat extended Augustinian definition of self-transcendence, I now want to suggest that we use it as at least a working definition of what we mean by religious experience. Religious experience is by definition self-transcendence, the self-aware, self-involving, self-transforming relation to the ultimately transcendent. I also want to suggest, in order of increasing importance, three advantages of this conceptual strategy. The first two operate at the descriptive level; the third arises from recognizing that this account of religious experience is essentially prescriptive.

The first advantage of construing religious experience as self-transcendence is that it permits us, even requires us, to recognize the thoroughly mediated character of religious experience. The conceptual strategy I am recommending is the wholehearted abandonment of all attempts to import the "myth of the given," in either its empiricist (Sellars) or its phenomenological (Derrida) form, into the interpretation of religion.

Since at least the time of Schleiermacher there have been two ways of doing this, not always clearly separated. One is the attempt to isolate the affective moment of the religious life from the cognitive and volitional and to identify religious experience with the former. The other is the attempt to identify religious experience with mystical experience. In either case the attempt is to identify some region of feeling or intuition which is immediate in the Hegelian sense of the term, namely the originality and self-sufficiency of that for which "there is yet no other."[7] The primary other that is excluded here is language, and the designation of feeling or intuition as immediate postulates a pre-predicative, pre-linguistic domain in which experience is fully prior to judgment. The other that is excluded by the claim to immediacy is volition, whether in the form of inner decision or of outward behavior. By virtue of their alleged immediacy the affections or intuition that constitute religious experience can give rise to linguistic and volitional expression, but they are not in any way shaped or constituted by language or will. The relation is strictly asymmetrical....

While the identification of religious experience with self-transcendence has the advantage of not getting entangled in untenable appeals to immediacy of one sort or another, it does not fall back into that from which Schleiermacher originally wanted to

escape, the identification of religion with doctrinal assent or moral behavior. In the first place, the philosophical repudiation of immediacy for the affective moment equally entails that neither the cognitive nor the volitional enjoy an immediacy that isolates them either from each other or from the affective. Moreover, the concept of self-transcendence as given in the brief, basic account above readily welcomes the more general notion of the thoroughly mediated character of human experience in which there are no one-way streets. No account of becoming detached from myself as center that does not include cognitive, volitional, and affective aspects is likely to be very persuasive....

The second advantage of defining religious experience in terms of self-transcendence is that this notion, in spite of our derivation of it from Augustinian Christianity, has the kind of scope required of the very generic and ecumenical concept of religious experience....

Self-transcendence works equally well for each of the three basic types of religious experience I sought to distinguish [elsewhere].[8] Exilic religion is antiworldly religion; it views the world as a place of exile. The false self is the worldly self, while the true self is not the otherworld self but the worldless self. The purest forms of exilic religion are found in the Hindu aspiration for absorption into Brahman and the Buddhist pursuit of Nirvana. In each case the transcendent toward which the self transcends is so radically beyond name and form as to be the transcendental condition for the impossibility of being in the world....

While the ultimately transcendent for these traditions differs dramatically from that of our Augustinian point of departure, religious experience is self-transcendence, going beyond my immediate false self toward my true "self," which can only be designated with reference to what is ultimately transcendent and quite definitely other to my original self. This is why the journey is so difficult and requires such discipline. The pseudo-self, which the Buddhists designate as the five modes or systems of grasping, must be completely dismantled.

Mimetic religion is the civil religion of law and order. It dissolves the self into the sacred in a very different way. The ultimately transcendent is a cosmic order whose eternal perfection is portrayed in myth. The penultimately transcendent is the social order that *participates* in eternal perfection by means of ritual *imitation* and observance of the taboos associated therewith....The social order (tribe, state, church) is the mediator between the human and the divine. Whether my integration into the social order has a punctiliar character, as in initiation rites or conversion experiences, or a process character, as in moral and spiritual formation, socialization is the path to salvation.

Here the false self is not the worldly self,...but rather the autonomous self and the true self is the self that finds its law outside of itself, first in the social order, but ultimately in the cosmic order it purports to embody. By participating in society's imitation of this cosmic order, the self transcends itself toward that which is ultimately transcendent....

I have given the name covenantal religion to the dominant spirituality of biblical faith. Since the Augustinian tradition from which we began is itself an expression of covenantal religion, it hardly needs to be argued that the concept of self-transcendence derived from the former applies to the latter....Like mimetic religion, covenantal religion does not share the exilic goal of dismantling the self as such in order to become worldless "experience"; it only requires the demise of the autonomous self....

As the third advantage that accrues to its employment,...it tells us what religious experience intends and purports to be, thereby giving us a criterion for distinguishing between the genuine article and various imitations. Not all the beliefs, practices, and feelings that are easily recognized as religious are acts of self-transcendence. Prayer, for example, can easily be "a burning preoccupation with self," a solemn repetition of the question, "But what about me, what becomes of me in that case?"...

Reflection on specifically religious experience can make an important contribution to the wider discussion of otherness in general. For in the first place, the holy, the ultimately transcendent, has appropriately been designated, not merely as other but as "wholly other." It is quintessentially transcendent. Secondly, self-transcendence may be more than casually linked to the transcendent; it may well be the condition and

measure of the transcendent. This would mean...that we experience the transcendent as such, as truly other, only to the degree that we are able to transcend ourselves. Conversely, to the degree that self-transcendence fails, transcendence is only apparent....

[To help understand] the idea that it is in the form of a claim upon us that we encounter the otherness of the other, we can turn to Levinas's account of metaphysical desire as directed toward "*something else entirely*, toward the *absolutely other*."[9] His analysis of enjoyment as involving self-centering rather than self-transcendence is one of several foils against which he develops the thesis that "the absolutely other is the Other" (Levinas, 39).

Who is this Other? In the first instance it is the one whom I encounter face to face in conversation.[10] In other words, the Other is another human being. Because our encounter takes place in language, it can be no animal other, and because it takes place face to face it can be no divine other. Rather, "it is only man who could be absolutely foreign to me."[11]

Secondly, the Other is the one whose face and speech I first encounter, beyond all knowing, all using, and all enjoying,[12] as a claim, the unconditional constraint upon my freedom that leaves me fully free to accept or reject it and that is expressed in the word, "You shall not commit murder."[13] Only in the realm of ethics, only in "the ethical impossibility of killing [the Other],"[14] do I encounter otherness as truly other.

This claim has a radically decentering intent. "To welcome the Other is to put in question my freedom."[15] It is reminds me that I am not the center to which all else is peripheral, the end to which all else is the means. In the claims of the other I am suddenly beyond all objects to be known, all tools to be used, and all elements on which to feed either body or soul.

What is worse, from the perspective of the "dear self," the relation is asymmetrical. It is not a prudent, contractual arrangement among equals in which I offer to spare your life (and liberty) if you agree to spare mine. The unconditional character of the Other's claim can only be expressed in images of height and authority. For this reason, although the Other is human and not divine, Levinas speaks of the Other as "Most-High" (34) and "Master."[16] On the other hand, there is the asymmetry of indigence. This is why

Levinas also refers to the Other first as the stranger, the widow, the orphan, and the poor.[17] The other has nothing to offer in exchange for my welcoming, least of all a bribe....

Finally, the face of the Other "*expresses itself*," manifests itself,...through itself and not through another....Its manifestation per se consists in a being telling itself to us independently of every position we would have taken in its regard, "*expressing itself*."[18] ...

Levinas knows exactly what he is doing here. He is claiming immediacy for the Other's self-expression. "The immediate is the face to face."[19] In spite of all attacks on the "myth of the given," he is claiming that the face is a theory-free datum. In willful disregard for the alleged inescapability of the hermeneutical circle, he finds us pointed toward "the possibility of *signification without a context*."[20] And in spite of all attacks on the metaphysics of presence and the transcendental signifier, he insists that "the signification of the face is due to an essential coinciding of the existent and the signifier. Signification is not added to the existent. To signify is not equivalent to presenting oneself as a sign, but to expressing oneself, that is presenting oneself in person."...[21]

Without self-expression per se, I could not welcome the Other *as such*....

Here we have the model we have been seeking to help us clarify the Augustinian notion of self-transcendence. This is an Other whose transcendence consists in an unconditional claim that removes me from the center of the universe both ethically by constraining my will and epistemologically by refusing to be constrained by the cultural codes of the world in which I recognize myself....

The Other whose transcendence Levinas has helped us to specify provides us with the opportunity for a unique self-transcendence. To welcome an Other so unwelcome to the pride that the Augustinian tradition finds to be the heart of our darkness and the darkness of our heart is to become a new person indeed. We are, of course, still in the realm of ethics and not yet talking about religious experience. For this Other is human and not divine. But all we have to do is replace the human with the divine Other to have the normative concept of religious experience we are looking for. Genuine religious experience is the self-transcendence in relation to a divine transcendence that radically decenters us as will, and, correspondingly, as belief and affection....

Let us suppose, then, that at least such religions as Buddhism and Christianity...define themselves in terms of the transcendence that evokes decentering self-transcendence. Will religious experience within the conceptual and communal framework of such religions be immune to self-deception? Will it no longer be necessary to ask Nietzsche's question, "What did I really experience?"...

Suppose that I am Thomas à Kempis, and that I offer the following prayer in all sincerity. "O Lord, Thou knowest what is the better way, let this or that be done, as Thou shalt please. Give what Thou wilt, and how much Thou wilt, and when Thou wilt. Deal with me as Thou knowest, and as best pleaseth Thee, and is most for Thy honour. Set me where Thou wilt, and deal with me in all things just as Thou wilt. I am in Thy hand: turn me round, and turn me back again, even as a wheel. Behold, I am Thy servant, prepared for all things; for I desire not to live unto myself, but unto Thee; and O that I could do it worthily and perfectly."[22] Can we be confident that this prayer is offered to a truly transcendent God, rather than an idol, and that the prayer belongs to an experience of genuine self-transcendence?

Unfortunately not. To the objection that these are but words, which might be deceitful, it can be replied that we have already stipulated that they are sincere. We can further stipulate that their sincerity is attested by the appropriate deeds. Our Thomas lives, let us say, an exemplary life of poverty, chastity, and obedience....How could such words and deeds fail to express a decentering surrender of oneself to God?

The answer is simple. Sincerity is no guarantee against deception....This piety...[might have] the form [of true godliness, decentering self-transcendence] so conspicuously that it could be used as its paradigm. But that form may still be but appearance not supported by the reality it professes. Our Thomas may unconsciously be a hypocrite....

The form of his piety might be that of a decentering self-transcendence. Its inner content may or may not correspond. The form is visible, to others and to him. The content may be hidden from both. If it does not correspond and if he has managed not to notice this, he is self-deceived and the god he serves, so far from being genuinely transcendent, is not only constituted by his intentionality but also constructed by his (hidden) intentions....

Perhaps we can see now why self-transcendence is the task of a lifetime. It is because genuine transcendence is so elusive....

I want to suggest two conclusions for the philosophy of religion that seem to me to follow from these reflections....It may seem as if our phenomenological reflections have ignored one of the most intensely debated philosophical questions relating to religious experience, namely, whether it can provide good reasons to support religious beliefs. But this is not so. Instead, the account of religious experience we have developed together would seem to place a major obstacle in the way of any positive answer to this question we might seek to develop. Our normative concept suggests that the intentional object of religious experience that lacks either the form or the substance of true godliness will be an idol of one sort or another. Such experience can hardly provide rational support for beliefs that purport to express the genuine transcendence of the truly divine. For religious experience to have any evidential value, it will first have to be shown to be authentic.

There are perhaps two reasons why this task has been conspicuously absent from most discussions.

One is its obvious difficulty. The other is the Principle of Charity, the tendency to consider religious experience innocent until proven guilty. But neither of these is a good reason. An essential task becomes less essential because of its difficulty only in the presence of self-deceptive laziness....The innocent-until-proven-guilty principle simply ignores (1) the biblical claim that "the heart is deceitful above all things, and desperately corrupt" (Jer. 17:9), (2) the powerful theoretical analyses...of self-deception whenever self-transcendence is at tissue, and (3) our own "thou art the man" experience in the presence of such analyses.

One way to put this point would be to say that religious experience cannot provide any evidence for truth as objectivity until it has passed the test of truth as subjectivity. This link between the hermeneutics of suspicion and questions of inwardness and authenticity leads to a second conclusion. It puts in question the wisdom of doing business as usual within the religious epistemology industry. No doubt reflection is and ought to be *ancilla vitae* (Latin, aid to life). But when the philosophy of religion...so focuses on objectivity as to let issues of subjectivity get forgotten or rendered peripheral, it shows itself to be ancillary to the life of some objectivist culture...that is systematically prejudiced against religious experience in general and the life of Christian faith in particular. This fact, if it is indeed a fact, is deserving of more attention than it usually gets among Christians in philosophy.

Notes

1. Søren Kierkegaard, *Concluding Unscientific Postscript,* trans. David Swenson and Walter Lowrie (Princeton, N.J.: Princeton University Press, 1941), pp. 18–19. See Søren Kierkegaard, *The Sickness Unto Death*, trans. Howard V. Hong and Edna H. Hong (Princeton, N.J.: Princeton University Press, 1980), pp. 55–56.
2. Augustine, *The Confessions of St. Augustine*, trans. Rex Warner (New York: New American Library, 1960), p. 155.
3. Thomas Merton, *New Seeds of Contemplation* (New York: New Directions Books, 1972), p. 21.
4. Kierkegaard, *Sickness*, pp. 13–14.
5. Kierkegaard, *Sickness*, p. 49.
6. Friedrich Nietzsche, *Thus Spake Zarathustra,* trans. Walter Kaufmann (New York: Viking Press, 1966), p. 86, "Upon the Blessed Isles."
7. W.F. Hegel, *The Logic of Hegel*, trans. William Wallace (Oxford, England: Oxford University Press, 1959), par. 86, Zusatz 1.
8. Merold Westphal, *God, Guilt and Death* (Bloomington, Ind.: Indiana University Press, 1984), ch. 9–11.
9. Emmanuel Levinas, *Totality and Infinity,* trans. Alfonso Lingis (Pittsburgh, Pa.: Duquesne University Press, 1969), p. 33.
10. Levinas, pp. 39, 71.
11. Levinas, p. 73.

12. Levinas, p. 38.
13. Levinas, pp. 199, 216, 262, 303.
14. Levinas, p. 87.
15. Levinas, p. 85.
16. Levinas, pp. 72, 75, 80.
17. Levinas, pp. 77–78.
18. Levinas, p. 65.
19. Levinas, p. 52.
20. Levinas, p. 23.
21. Levinas, p. 262.
22. Thomas à Kempis, *The Imitation of Christ* (London: Oxford University Press, 1900), p. 127.

STUDY QUESTIONS

1. What task does Westphal assign to all individuals, and what are the three features of that task?
2. How does Levinas's concept of the Other help us to understand religious experience as self-transcendence?
3. What two things does Westphal conclude from the fact that we cannot guarantee against self-deception in religious experience?
4. What is Westphal's view of Swinburne's Principle of Credulity (as discussed in the previous reading)? With which writer do you side, and why?

SUGGESTED READING

Alston, William. *Perceiving God*. Ithaca, N.Y.: Cornell University Press, 1991.

Bloechl, Jeffrey, ed. *Religious Experience and the End of Metaphysics*. Bloomington: Indiana University Press, 2003.

Brakenhielm, Carl. *Problems of Religious Experience*. Uppsala, Sweden: University of Uppsala, 1985.

Davis, Caroline Franks. *The Evidential Force of Religious Experience*. Oxford, England: Clarendon Press, 1989.

Dupré, Wilhelm. *Experience and Religion: Configurations and Perspectives*. New York: Peter Lang, 2005.

Ingram, Paul. *Wrestling with the Ox: A Theology of Religious Experience*. New York: Continuum, 1997.

James, William. *The Varieties of Religious Experience*. New York: New American Library, 1958.

Katz, Steven T., ed. *Mysticism and Philosophical Analysis*. Oxford, England: Oxford University Press, 1978.

Lewis, H. D. *Our Experience of God*. London: Allen and Unwin, 1959.

Otto, Rudolf. *The Idea of the Holy*. London: Oxford University Press, 1958.

Proudfoot, Wayne. *Religious Experience*. Berkeley: University of California Press, 1985.

Smart, Ninian. *The Religious Experience*. London: Macmillan, 1991.

Stace, W. T. *Mysticism and Philosophy*. New York: Macmillan, 1960.

Steinbock, Anthony J. *Phenomenology and Mysticism: The Verticality of Religious Experience*. Bloomington: Indiana University Press, 2007.

Swinburne, Richard. *The Existence of God*, ch. 13, London: Oxford University Press, 1979.

Wainwright, William. *Mysticism: A Study of Its Nature, Cognitive Value, and Moral Implications*. Madison: University of Wisconsin Press, 1981.

Yandell, Keith. *The Epistemology of Religious Experience*. Cambridge, England: Cambridge University Press 1993.

PART THREE

Faith and Reason

For a great many religious people, religion is fundamentally a matter of *faith*—of belief and trust in God, in the teachings of one's religion, and in the institutions and practices the religion holds to be important. For some of these people, "faith is enough," and they may feel little need to engage their reasoning capacity in dealing with their religious faith. But there are compelling reasons why religion and reason can't easily be kept apart. Some religious teachings can be quite difficult to understand, and the injunction, "Don't worry about it, just accept it," can be decidedly frustrating. Yet if you are not content to "just accept it," reasoning is about the only remaining option; it takes serious thinking, in many instances, to understand just what the religious teaching is saying. Sometimes, on the other hand, it seems that what the religious teaching is telling us comes into conflict with what we have come to believe in other ways. This is known as *cognitive dissonance*, and only thinking about the issue—sometimes, difficult and demanding thinking—offers hope for a resolution. Then there is the whole question of *evidence* for one's religious beliefs. Often it seems that the appeal to "faith" is meant to forestall the demand for evidence—what you "have faith in" is precisely what you don't *need* evidence for. But once we have become accustomed to the role of evidence in other areas—science and history, for example—the question of the evidence, or lack of evidence, for one's religious faith is not easily silenced. For all these reasons, faith and reason are not easy to keep separate from each other.

But the fact that faith and reason can't be kept separate does not mean that they always get along well together. (In the same way, members of a family can't easily avoid each other, but that does not automatically mean that they get along well with one another!) In fact, the relationship between faith and reason has often been a rather stormy one. And the way we view this relationship is obviously crucial for a subject such as the philosophy of religion—thus, the present section.

As already indicated, one of the most crucial questions concerns the role of, and the need for, *evidence* in religious matters. Just what is required of a person, if she is going to be responsible in the religious beliefs that she holds? We can all see that certain sorts of belief are irresponsible. That would be a fair description, for example, of someone who hears a fiery sermon by a TV preacher and, without any further thought or inquiry, immediately decides to completely change his lifestyle and his goals in life. Even if the change seems on the whole beneficial, we are likely to think he should have looked more closely before making such a radical decision. But what does the other end of the scale look like? What really is required of a person who wants to be responsible in what she believes? There have been a great many answers to this question, but the main options can be sorted into a few general types, and it is these types that will occupy us in this section.

Strong Rationalism

One type of answer to our question can be labeled as *strong rationalism*. The answer of strong rationalism to the question about evidence is straightforward: in order for someone to be rational and responsible in holding a religious belief, the belief must be able to be proved true. There are different explanations of just what the proof must consist of, but a couple of things are reasonably clear. First of all, the evidence, whatever it is, must be *available to all rational people*. That does not mean that everyone must actually possess the evidence. For example, the evidence might be historical in nature, and thus would be known only to those who had familiarized themselves with the relevant segment of history. But it is *available* to all; anyone who chooses to find out about it has the opportunity to do so. In contrast to this, an alleged divine revelation, given to a single person or to a small group, would *not* count as evidence. Rather, such a revelation would itself need to be attested by generally available evidence—here miracles have often been appealed to—in order to be accepted as revealed by God. Furthermore, the evidence must at least *strongly indicate* the truth of the religious doctrine in question; we might say that the evidence must establish the doctrine as highly probable.

Some exponents of strong rationalism have been devout religious believers, ready and eager to offer on behalf of their own beliefs the proof that is called for. At least as often, however, strong rationalists have been religious skeptics, and have argued that no religious belief meets the requirements and therefore no religious belief can be reasonably and responsibly accepted. It is fair to say that today, in the twenty-first century, most strong rationalists fall into the latter camp. The "proofs" given for religious beliefs always seem to be open to challenge in one way or another, so the quest for such proof tends to be frustrating.

There is, however, an important problem that needs to be faced by strong rationalists, whether they are believers or religious skeptics. One of the things the history of philosophy seems to have shown us is that it is extremely difficult—and may well be impossible—to "prove" *any* wide-ranging philosophical or religious view of the world in the way required by strong rationalism. To be sure, philosophers have often enough thought the opposite; many philosophers have presented what seemed to them compelling, completely convincing arguments for why their view of things, and theirs only, should be rationally accepted. Over time, however, these attempts have not fared very well. Later philosophers, even when they largely agree with the view in question, are forced to admit that there is room for someone to reasonably disagree with the view; the more closely we look, the more elusive the goal of "proof" seems to become. That does not mean that there are no good reasons for holding a particular belief, much less that no belief is better or worse than any other. But the requirements set by strong rationalism may be too demanding to be met by human beings—and this holds true quite generally, not just for religious beliefs. If this is so, then we must look elsewhere for an answer to our question about evidence.

FIDEISM

At the opposite end of the scale from strong rationalism, there is *fideism* ("fee-day-ism," from the Latin *fides*, meaning "faith"). The basic idea of fideism is simple: whenever faith and reason clash, we must follow faith rather than reason. Faith, after all, is concerned with God, God's word, and God's revelation, and what God tells us is certainly true, whereas human reason can often be mistaken. (If a philosopher disagrees with God, the philosopher is not going to win the argument!) And the idea that God's word needs proof by human beings in order to validate it is absurd—or more likely, it is idolatrous; it means that our faith is really in human reason rather than in God.

Fideism, to be sure, comes in more than one variety. What may be termed "simple fideism" is most common among people who have not devoted a lot of study to matters of religion and philosophy; for them, "faith is enough," and they simply don't care to engage the sorts of problems philosophers of religion spend their time on. But there are also sophisticated fideists, who do make a serious effort to engage other philosophers and theologians. They will give a careful account of their understanding of faith, and of why faith should take precedence over reason and philosophy. And they often engage in extensive critiques of other, more rationalistic, versions of philosophy and theology. (It may sound strange to use one's reason to defend the idea that reason should give way to something else, but in fact this is a perfectly possible thing to do.)

Fideism's answer to the question of evidence is straightforward: Faith has no need to be justified by reason or rational arguments. The right way to proceed in religious matters is simply to believe what God has told us and go on from there; trying to "prove" God's word by rational arguments is unnecessary, futile, and even dangerous, since doing this tempts us to put our own reasoning in the highest place that should be reserved for God. To be sure, we can and must use our intelligence to understand a religious teaching and to draw out its implications for our lives. But the foundation is laid by faith, and faith alone.

Fideism, however, encounters some serious problems. Sometimes the secular belief systems that come into conflict with religious beliefs can be pretty compelling, and hard to simply dismiss. Fundamentalists who believe that the earth is only a few thousand years old don't usually just say, "So much the worse for science!" Instead, they devise a "scientific creationism," which allows them to argue that "real science" supports their view rather than that held by the mainstream scientific community. (See Part Twelve of this anthology for more on religion–science issues.) Another problem is, *which* faith should be held supreme? If someone is seriously considering which faith to embrace among a number of contenders, it seems that the only sensible approach is to compare them to see which seems most likely to be true. But to do this is to engage in the rational evaluation of belief systems, which is just what the fideist refuses to do.

CRITICAL RATIONALISM

If neither strong rationalism nor fideism seems to be a workable approach, there is a middle ground between them that may offer more promise. This middle ground has been labeled in various ways; it may be termed *critical rationalism, soft rationalism,* or *critical dialog.* This view agrees with strong rationalism against fideism in holding that it is reasonable, appropriate, and necessary to subject religious beliefs to rational assessment. But it recognizes that when there is disagreement on matters of fundamental importance, issues are not likely to be settled by conclusive arguments that convince all persons regardless of their previous state of belief or disbelief. "Critical rationalism," as we shall term it, is critical in two different ways. It assumes a responsibility to criticize, that is to critically evaluate, the fundamental assumptions of religious belief systems, as well as of secular systems that may conflict with them. But it is also critical of reason itself; it takes a more modest view of reason's capabilities, in contrast to the excessive confidence in reason that is characteristic of strong rationalism. Because no single argument or piece of evidence is able to bear the full weight of either supporting or refuting belief, some critical rationalists seek to develop a "cumulative case" to show that their belief system does a better job than its rivals of explaining the "total evidence" provided by life in all its complexity. When there is conflict between religious belief and beliefs derived from other sources, critical rationalists have several options. They may try to show that the secular belief in question is not well supported, or they may argue that the religious belief has been misinterpreted, or that the belief can be modified without serious damage to the religious belief system. The goal is to show due respect both to the religious belief, which has been thought to be supported by divine revelation, and to secular sources of knowledge that have a proven record of success and are worthy of our trust. Obviously, these general statements don't solve the problems; they leave the hard work to be done in the discussion of particular issues. But critical rationalism has the advantage that it promotes an open dialogue between different belief systems, in contrast with the "my way or the highway" approaches that characterize, in their different ways, both strong rationalism and fideism.

Our first selection is from the great medieval Christian thinker Thomas Aquinas, who develops what has become a traditional view of the relationship of reason and revelation. There are some truths about God that can be learned through human reason, and others that are known only through divine revelation. However, there are compelling arguments showing that the revelation really does come from God, so there is no offense to reason from accepting the truths of revelation as such. Thomas, then, is a strong rationalist in terms of our classification, but he insists that it is not necessary that each and every person should grasp the proofs for himself or herself. Even the truths that are knowable through reason may properly be accepted by faith, on the authority of the church, by those who are unable or have not yet had the opportunity to work through the proofs for themselves.

In the next selection, the seventeenth-century French thinker Blaise Pascal makes a radical thought experiment: suppose we have no evidence whatsoever concerning the existence or nonexistence of God. Under these conditions, which belief should we accept? Pascal argues that one who believes in God stands to gain an enormous benefit, namely, a happy eternal life, if she is right, whereas she will lose at most a little (mainly some worldly pleasures) if she is mistaken. On the other hand, one who rejects belief in God gains very little if he is right (again, mainly some pleasures that he might have to give up as a Christian), whereas he stands to lose a tremendous good if he is wrong. Thus, good sense and reason require that we should believe in God (or should endeavor to get ourselves to believe in God), even in the total absence of evidence either for or against this belief.

The English mathematician William Clifford presents one of the clearest and most forceful arguments for strong rationalism: it is simply wrong for anyone to believe anything without sufficient evidence. He gives examples of persons who do so believe and as a result take actions that prove harmful to many other people. Clifford's main attack is directed against religious belief, which he thinks is never based on adequate evidence and is therefore always morally wrong. Unlike Thomas Aquinas, Clifford requires that each and every person who accepts a belief should do so on the basis of reason and evidence—a stringent requirement that would mean, at best, that religion could only be taught to a small number of people, namely, those who are sufficiently intelligent and educated to evaluate the arguments in its favor.

In our fourth selection, the American philosopher William James argues against Clifford on behalf of our "right to believe" in some instances where Clifford's demand for convincing evidence cannot be met. Under certain circumstances, according to James, it is perfectly proper to make decisions about belief and unbelief based on our "passional nature." James, however, is not a fideist; he insists that where adequate evidence is available, we must follow it. But his argument provides a potent challenge to the strong rationalism of Clifford.

In the fifth selection, the nineteenth-century Danish thinker Søren Kierkegaard writes under the pseudonym Johannes Climacus. "Climacus" insists that where religious truth is concerned, what matters more than the actual content of the belief is *the way in which the inquirer is related to the truth that he believes.* Passionate commitment is the key to "truth" in religion; if one were actually able to prove the truth of one's belief, this would be the death of faith. It should be noted that Kierkegaard's overall position is quite complex and may not be fully represented by this selection from "Climacus." That said, the statement remains a powerful assertion of the inner logic of one kind of fideism.

The final selection in this section, by C. Stephen Evans, is an effective presentation of the approach of critical rationalism or, as he terms it, *critical dialog.* Evans begins by criticizing both fideism and what he terms *neutralism,* which is closely related to strong rationalism. He then elaborates the process of critical dialog, in which we rationally test our religious beliefs even though we recognize our inability to conclusively prove them. He admits that critical dialog can be risky but claims that "a genuine and robust faith will not shrink from the process of testing."

Thomas Aquinas

The Harmony of Reason and Revelation

In this selection, Thomas Aquinas (1224–1274) articulates a classical position concerning the relationship between reason and revelation. He says that there are some truths about God that can be learned through human reasoning, and other truths that can be known only because God has disclosed them through revelation. Both kinds are worthy of our belief, and even the truths that are knowable by reason may and should be accepted on faith by those who lack the time, opportunity, or ability to verify them for themselves. Although the sources of the two kinds of truth are different, they are not and cannot be in disagreement with each other, since "only the false is opposed to the true."

There is a twofold mode of truth in what we profess about God. Some truths about God exceed all the ability of the human reason. Such is the truth that God is triune. But there are some truths which the natural reason also is able to reach. Such are that God exists, that He is one, and the like. In fact, such truths about God have been proved demonstratively by philosophers, guided by the light of natural reason.

That there are certain truths about God that totally surpass man's ability appears with the greatest evidence.... For the human intellect is not able to reach a comprehension of the divine substance through its natural power. For, according to its manner of knowing in the present life, the intellect depends on the sense for the origin of knowledge; and so those things that do not fall under the senses cannot be grasped by the human intellect except in so far as the knowledge of them is gathered from sensible things. Now, sensible things cannot lead the human intellect to the point of seeing in them the nature of the divine substance; for sensible things are effects that fall short of the power of their cause. Yet, beginning with sensible things, our intellect is led to the point of knowing about God that He exists, and other such characteristics that must be attributed to the First Principle. There are, consequently, some intelligible truths about God that are open to the human reason; but there are others that absolutely surpass its power....

Sacred Scripture also gives testimony to this truth. We read in Job: "Peradventure thou wilt comprehend

From *Summa Contra Gentiles* by Thomas Aquinas, trans. A. C. Pegis (Notre Dame, Ind.: University of Notre Dame Press), 1975.

the steps of God, and wilt find out the Almighty perfectly?" (11:7). And again: "Behold, God is great, exceeding our knowledge" (Job 36:26). And St. Paul: "We know in part" (I Cor. 13:9). We should not, therefore, immediately reject as false, following the opinion of the Manicheans and many unbelievers, everything that is said about God even though it cannot be investigated by reason.

Since, therefore, there exists a twofold truth concerning the divine being, one to which the inquiry of the reason can reach, the other which surpasses the whole ability of the human reason, it is fitting that both of these truths be proposed to man divinely for belief. This point must first be shown concerning the truth that is open to the inquiry of the reason; otherwise, it might perhaps seem to someone that, since such a truth can be known by the reason, it was uselessly given to men through a supernatural inspiration as an object of belief.

Yet, if this truth were left solely as a matter of inquiry for the human reason, three awkward consequences would follow. The first is that few men would possess the knowledge of God. For there are three reasons why most men are cut off from the fruit of diligent inquiry which is the discovery of truth. Some do not have the physical disposition for such work. As a result, there are many who are naturally not fitted to pursue knowledge; and so, however much they tried, they would be unable to reach the highest level of human knowledge which consists in knowing God. Others are cut off from pursuing this truth by the necessities imposed upon them by their daily lives. For some men must devote themselves to taking care of temporal matters. Such men would not be able to give so much time to the leisure of contemplative inquiry as to reach the highest peak at which human investigation can arrive, namely, the knowledge of God. Finally, there are some who are cut off by indolence. In order to know the things that the reason can investigate concerning God, a knowledge of many things must already be possessed. For almost all of philosophy is directed towards the knowledge of God, and that is why metaphysics, which deals with divine things, is the last part of philosophy to be learned. This means that we are able to arrive at the inquiry concerning the aforementioned truth only on the basis of a great deal of labor spent in study. Now, those who wish to undergo such a labor for the mere love of knowledge are few, even though God has inserted into the minds of men a natural appetite for knowledge.

The second awkward effect is that those who would come to discover the abovementioned truth would barely reach it after a great deal of time.... If the only way open to us for the knowledge of God were solely that of the reason, the human race would remain in the blackest shadows of ignorance. For then the knowledge of God, which especially renders men perfect and good, would come to be possessed only by a few, and these few would require a great deal of time in order to reach it.

The third awkward effect is this. The investigation of the human reason for the most part has falsity present within it, and this is due partly to the weakness of our intellect in judgment, and partly to the admixture of images. The result is that many, remaining ignorant of the power of demonstration, would hold in doubt those things that have been most truly demonstrated. This would be particularly the case since they see that, among those who are reputed to be wise men, each one teaches his own brand of doctrine. Furthermore, with the many truths that are demonstrated, there sometimes is mingled something that is false, which is not demonstrated but rather asserted on the basis of some probable or sophistical argument, which yet has the credit of being a demonstration. That is why it was necessary that the unshakeable certitude and pure truth concerning divine things should be presented to men by way of faith.

Beneficially, therefore, did the divine Mercy provide that it should instruct us to hold by faith even those truths that the human reason is able to investigate. In this way, all men would easily be able to have a share in the knowledge of God, and this without uncertainty and error....

Now, perhaps some will think that men should not be asked to believe what the reason is not adequate to investigate, since the divine Wisdom provides in the case of each thing according to the mode of its nature. We must therefore prove that it is necessary for man to receive from God as objects of belief even those truths that are above the human reason.

No one tends with desire and zeal towards something that is not already known to him. But, as we shall examine later on in this work, men are ordained by the divine Providence towards a higher good than human fragility can experience in the present life. That is why it was necessary for the human mind to be called to something higher than the human reason here and now can reach, so that it would thus learn to desire something and with zeal tend towards something that surpasses the whole state of the present life. This belongs especially to the Christian religion, which in a unique way promises spiritual and eternal goods. And so there are many things proposed to men in it that transcend human sense. The Old Law, on the other hand, whose promises were of a temporal character, contained very few proposals that transcended the inquiry of the human reason. Following this same direction, the philosophers themselves, in order that they might lead men from the pleasure of sensible things to virtue, were concerned to show that there were in existence other goods of a higher nature than these things of sense, and that those who gave themselves to the active or contemplative virtues would find much sweeter enjoyment in the taste of these higher goods.

It is also necessary that such truth be proposed to men for belief so that they may have a truer knowledge of God. For then only do we know God truly when we believe Him to be above everything that it is possible for man to think about Him; for, as we have shown, the divine substance surpasses the natural knowledge of which man is capable. Hence, by the fact that some things about God are proposed to man that surpass his reason, there is strengthened in man the view that God is something above what he can think.

Another benefit that comes from the revelation to men of truths that exceed the reason is the curbing of presumption, which is the mother of error. For there are some who have such a presumptuous opinion of their own ability that they deem themselves able to measure the nature of everything; I mean to say that, in their estimation, everything is true that seems to them so, and everything is false that does not. So that the human mind, therefore, might be freed from this presumption and come to a humble inquiry after

truth, it was necessary that some things should be proposed to man by God that would completely surpass his intellect.... From all these considerations it is clear that even the most imperfect knowledge about the most noble realities brings the greatest perfection to the soul. Therefore, although the human reason cannot grasp fully the truths that are above it, yet, if it somehow holds these truths at least by faith, it acquires great perfection for itself....

Those who place their faith in this truth, however, "for which the human reason offers no experimental evidence," do not believe foolishly, as though "following artificial fables" (II Peter 1:16). For these "secrets of divine Wisdom" (Job 11:6) the divine Wisdom itself, which knows all things to the full, has deigned to reveal to men. It reveals its own presence, as well as the truth of its teaching and inspiration, by fitting arguments; and in order to confirm those truths that exceed natural knowledge, it gives visible manifestation to works that surpass the ability of all nature. Thus, there are the wonderful cures of illnesses, there is the raising of the dead, and the wonderful immutation in the heavenly bodies; and what is more wonderful, there is the inspiration given to human minds, so that simple and untutored persons, filled with the gift of the Holy Spirit, come to possess instantaneously the highest wisdom and the readiest eloquence. When these arguments were examined, through the efficacy of the abovementioned proof, and not the violent assault of arms or the promise of pleasures, and (what is most wonderful of all) in the midst of the tyranny of the persecutors, an innumerable throng of people, both simple and most learned, flocked to the Christian faith. In this faith there are truths preached that surpass every human intellect; the pleasures of the flesh are curbed; it is taught that the things of the world should be spurned. Now, for the minds of mortal men to assent to these things is the greatest of miracles, just as it is a manifest work of divine inspiration that, spurning visible things, men should seek only what is invisible. Now, that this has happened neither without preparation nor by chance, but as a result of the disposition of God, is clear from the fact that through many pronouncements of the ancient prophets God had foretold that He would do this. The books of these prophets are held in veneration among us Christians, since they give witness to our faith. . . .

This wonderful conversion of the world to the Christian faith is the clearest witness of the signs given in the past; so that it is not necessary that they should be further repeated, since they appear most clearly in their effect. For it would be truly more wonderful than all signs if the world had been led by simple and humble men to believe such lofty truths, to accomplish such difficult actions, and to have such high hopes. Yet it is also a fact that, even in our own time, God does not cease to work miracles through His saints for the confirmation of the faith. . . .

Now, although the truth of the Christian faith which we have discussed surpasses the capacity of the reason, nevertheless that truth that the human reason is naturally endowed to know cannot be opposed to the truth of the Christian faith. For that with which the human reason is naturally endowed is clearly most true; so much so, that it is impossible for us to think of such truths as false. Nor is it permissible to believe as false that which we hold by faith, since this is confirmed in a way that is so clearly divine. Since, therefore, only the false is opposed to the true, as is clearly evident from an examination of their definitions, it is impossible that the truth of faith should be opposed to those principles that the human reason knows naturally.

Study Questions

1. Aquinas, unlike Clifford, does not require that each individual person have good reasons for what he or she believes. What is Aquinas's reason for this view? Does the reason strike you as a good one? Why, or why not?
2. According to Aquinas, there are certain "truths of faith" that we should accept even though we are unable, by human reason, to see that they are true. What are his reasons for this view?

Blaise Pascal

The Wager

In his famous "Wager," Blaise Pascal (1623–1662) poses the question: if you had to decide for or against belief in the Christian God with no evidence whatsoever—no reason either to believe that God exists or to believe that he does not—which should you choose? Basing his case on probability theory, Pascal argues that the only rational choice under such circumstances is to believe. Note, however, that Pascal does not think that it really is in our power simply to "decide to believe." On the contrary, he thinks that our desires may keep us from believing even when we can clearly see that this is the rational choice; thus, we must purify our hearts so as to be able to believe. Nor does he really think that the believer has no good reasons in support of his or her faith; Pascal's *Pensées* as a whole constitutes a forceful defense of the truth of Christianity.

If there is a God, He is infinitely incomprehensible, since, having neither parts nor limits, He has no affinity to us. We are then incapable of knowing either what He is or if He is. This being so, who will dare to undertake the decision of the question? Not we, who have no affinity to Him.

Who then will blame Christians for not being able to give a reason for their belief, since they profess a religion for which they cannot give a reason? They declare, in expounding it to the world, that it is a foolishness, *stultitiam;* and then you complain that they do not prove it! If they proved it, they would not keep their word; it is in lacking proofs that they are not lacking in sense. "Yes, but although this excuses those who offer it as such, and takes away from them the blame of putting it forward without reason, it does not excuse those who receive it." Let us then examine this point, and say, "God is, or He is not." But to which side shall we incline? Reason can decide nothing here. There is an infinite chaos which separated us. A game is being played at the extremity of this infinite distance where heads or tails will turn up. What will you wager? According to reason, you can do neither the one thing nor the other; according to reason, you can defend neither of the propositions.

Do not then reprove for error those who have made a choice; for you know nothing about it. "No, but I blame them for having made, not this choice, but a choice; for again both he who chooses heads and he who chooses tails are equally at fault, they are both in the wrong. The true course is not to wager at all."

From Pensées in *Pensées and the Provincial Letters* by Blaise Pascal, trans. W. F. Trotter (New York: Modern Library), 1941.

Yes; but you must wager. It is not optional. You are embarked. Which will you choose then? Let us see. Since you must choose, let us see which interests you least. You have two things to lose, the true and the good; and two things to stake, your reason and your will, your knowledge and your happiness; and your nature has two things to shun, error and misery. Your reason is no more shocked in choosing one rather than the other, since you must of necessity choose. This is one point settled. But your happiness? Let us weigh the gain and the loss in wagering that God is. Let us estimate these two chances. If you gain, you gain all; if you lose, you lose nothing. Wager, then, without hesitation that He is.—"That is very fine. Yes, I must wager; but I may perhaps wager too much."—Let us see. Since there is an equal risk of gain and of loss, if you had only to gain two lives, instead of one, you might still wager. But if there were three lives to gain, you would have to play (since you are under the necessity of playing), and you would be imprudent, when you are forced to play, not to chance your life to gain three at a game where there is an equal risk of loss and gain. But there is an eternity of life and happiness. And this being so, if there were an infinity of chances, of which one only would be for you, you would still be right in wagering one to win two, and you would act stupidly, being obliged to play, by refusing to stake one life against three at a game in which out of an infinity of chances there is one for you, if there were an infinity of an infinitely happy life to gain. But there is here an infinity of an infinitely happy life to gain, a chance of gain against a finite number of chances of loss, and what you stake is finite. It is all divided; wherever the infinite is and there is not an infinity of chances of loss against that of gain, there is no time to hesitate, you must give all. And thus, when one is forced to play, he must renounce reason to preserve his life, rather than risk it for infinite gain, as likely to happen as the loss of nothingness.

For it is no use to say it is uncertain if we will gain, and it is certain that we risk, and that the infinite distance between the *certainty* of what is staked and the *uncertainty* of what will be gained, equals the finite good which is certainly staked against the uncertain infinite. It is not so, as every player stakes a certainty to gain an uncertainty, and yet he stakes a finite certainty to gain a finite uncertainty, without transgressing against reason. There is not an infinite distance between the certainty staked and the uncertainty of the gain; that is untrue. In truth, there is an infinity between the certainty of gain and the certainty of loss. But the uncertainty of the gain is proportioned to the certainty of the stake according to the proportion of the chances of gain and loss. Hence it comes that, if there are as many risks on one side as on the other, the course is to play even; and then the certainty of the stake is equal to the uncertainty of the gain, so far is it from fact that there is an infinite distance between them. And so our proposition is of infinite force, when there is the finite to stake in a game where there are equal risks of gain and of loss, and the infinite to gain. This is demonstrable: and if men are capable of any truths, this is one.

"I confess it, I admit it. But, still, is there no means of seeing the faces of the cards?"—Yes, Scripture and the rest, etc. "Yes, but I have my hands tied and my mouth closed; I am forced to wager, and am not free. I am not released, and am so made that I cannot believe. What, then, would you have me do?"

True. But at least learn your inability to believe, since reason brings you to this, and yet you cannot believe. Endeavour then to convince yourself, not by increase of proofs of God, but by the abatement of your passions. You would like to attain faith, and do not know the way; you would like to cure yourself of unbelief, and ask the remedy for it. Learn of those who have been bound like you, and who now stake all their possessions. These are people who know the way which you would follow, and who are cured of an ill of which you would be cured. Follow the way by which they began; by acting as if they believed, taking the holy water, having masses said, etc. Even this will naturally make you believe, and deaden your acuteness.—"But this is what I am afraid of."—And why? What have you to lose?

But to show you that this leads you there, it is this which will lessen the passions, which are your stumbling-blocks.

Study Questions

1. Pascal argues that if one has no good reasons either for or against the existence of the Christian God, it is more reasonable to believe than to disbelieve. Why does he think this? Do you find the argument convincing? Why, or why not?

2. What is Pascal's explanation for the fact that some persons find themselves unable to believe, even when they can see that it would be advantageous for them to do so?

William Clifford

The Ethics of Belief

What moral obligations pertain to our decisions about what to believe and what not to believe? Although many people think that moral obligations are irrelevant to belief, William Clifford (1845–1879) argues that "it is wrong always, everywhere, and for anyone, to believe anything upon insufficient evidence." This is true, first of all, because if we act on poorly supported beliefs, we are very likely to harm others as well as ourselves. But also, and more fundamentally, by habitually accepting beliefs that are not supported by evidence, we make ourselves and other people credulous, so that we and they will more easily be seduced by falsehood in the future. But what if a person has no time for the extensive study required to judge concerning certain complicated matters? (Clifford clearly has religious beliefs in mind, though perhaps not only those.) Clifford answers curtly, "Then he should have no time to believe."

THERE IS A MORAL DUTY TO BELIEVE ACCORDING TO THE EVIDENCE

A shipowner was about to send to sea an emigrant ship. He knew that she was old, and not over-well built at the first; that she had seen many seas and climes, and often had needed repairs. Doubts had been suggested to him that possibly she was not seaworthy. These doubts preyed upon his mind, and made him unhappy; he thought that perhaps he ought to have her thoroughly overhauled and refitted, even though this should put him to great expense. Before the ship sailed, however, he succeeded in overcoming these melancholy reflections. He said to himself that she had gone safely through so many voyages and weathered so many storms that it was idle to suppose she would not come safely home from this trip also. He would put his trust in Providence, which could hardly fail to protect all these unhappy families that were leaving their fatherland to seek for better times elsewhere. He would dismiss from his mind all ungenerous suspicions about the honesty of builders and contractors. In such ways he acquired a sincere and comfortable conviction that his vessel was thoroughly safe and seaworthy; he watched her departure with a light heart, and benevolent wishes for the success of the exiles in their strange new home that was to be; and he got his insurance money when she went down in mid-ocean and told no tales.

From *Lectures and Essays* (New York: Macmillan), 1974.

What shall we say of him? Surely this, that he was verily guilty of the death of those men. It is admitted that he did sincerely believe in the soundness of his ship; but the sincerity of his conviction can in no wise help him, because *he had no right to believe on such evidence as was before him.* He had acquired his belief not by honestly earning it in patient investigation, but by stifling his doubts. And although in the end he may have felt so sure about it that he could not think otherwise, yet inasmuch as he had knowingly and willingly worked himself into that frame of mind, he must be held responsible for it.

Let us alter the case a little, and suppose that the ship was not unsound after all; that she made her voyage safely, and many others after it. Will that diminish the guilt of her owner? Not one jot. When an action is once done, it is right or wrong for ever; no accidental failure of its good or evil fruits can possibly alter that. The man would not have been innocent, he would only have been not found out. The question of right or wrong has to do with the origin of his belief, not the matter of it; not what it was, but how he got it; not whether it turned out to be true or false, but whether he had a right to believe on such evidence as was before him.

There was once an island in which some of the inhabitants professed a religion teaching neither the doctrine of original sin nor that of eternal punishment. A suspicion got abroad that the professors of this religion had made use of unfair means to get their doctrines taught to children. They were accused of wresting the laws of their country in such a way as to remove children from the care of their natural and legal guardians; and even of stealing them away and keeping them concealed from their friends and relations. A certain number of men formed themselves into a society for the purpose of agitating the public about this matter. They published grave accusations against individual citizens of the highest position and character, and did all in their power to injure these citizens in the exercise of their professions. So great was the noise they made, that a Commission was appointed to investigate the facts; but after the Commission had carefully inquired into all the evidence that could be got, it appeared that the accused were innocent. Not only had they been accused on insufficient evidence, but the evidence of their innocence was such as the agitators

might easily have obtained, if they had attempted a fair inquiry. After these disclosures the inhabitants of that country looked upon the members of the agitating society, not only as persons whose judgment was to be distrusted, but also as no longer to be counted honourable men. For although they had sincerely and conscientiously believed in the charges they had made, yet *they had no right to believe on such evidence as was before them.* Their sincere convictions, instead of being honestly earned by patient inquiring, were stolen by listening to the voice of prejudice and passion.

Let us vary this case also, and suppose, other things remaining as before, that a still more accurate investigation proved the accused to have been really guilty. Would this make any difference in the guilt of the accusers? Clearly not; the question is not whether their belief was true or false, but whether they entertained it on wrong grounds. They would no doubt say, "Now you see that we were right after all; next time perhaps you will believe us." And they might be believed, but they would not thereby become honourable men. They would not be innocent, they would only be not found out. Every one of them, if he chose to examine himself *in foro conscientiæ*, would know that he had acquired and nourished a belief, when he had no right to believe on such evidence as was before him; and therein he would know that he had done a wrong thing.

The Duty Applies to Belief Itself, Not Only to Action

It may be said, however, that in both of these supposed cases it is not the belief which is judged to be wrong, but the action following upon it. The shipowner might say, "I am perfectly certain that my ship is sound, but still I feel it my duty to have her examined, before trusting the lives of so many people to her." And it might be said to the agitator, "However convinced you were of the justice of your cause and the truth of your convictions, you ought not to have made a public attack upon any man's character until you had examined the evidence on both sides with the utmost patience and care."

In the first place, let us admit that, so far as it goes, this view of the case is right and necessary; right, because even when a man's belief is so fixed that he cannot think otherwise, he still has a choice in regard to the action suggested by it, and so cannot escape the duty of investigating on the ground of the strength of his convictions; and necessary, because those who are not yet capable of controlling their feelings and thoughts must have a plain rule dealing with overt acts.

But this being premised as necessary, it becomes clear that it is not sufficient, and that our previous judgment is required to supplement it. For it is not possible so to sever the belief from the action it suggests as to condemn the one without condemning the other. No man holding a strong belief on one side of a question, or even wishing to hold a belief on one side, can investigate it with such fairness and completeness as if he were really in doubt and unbiassed; so that the existence of a belief not founded on fair inquiry unfits a man for the performance of this necessary duty.

Nor is that truly a belief at all which has not some influence upon the actions of him who holds it. He who truly believes that which prompts him to an action has looked upon the action to lust after it, he has committed it already in his heart. If a belief is not realized immediately in open deeds, it is stored up for the guidance of the future. It goes to make a part of that aggregate of beliefs which is the link between sensation and action at every moment of all our lives, and which is so organized and compacted together that no part of it can be isolated from the rest, but every new addition modifies the structure of the whole. No real belief, however trifling and fragmentary it may seem, is ever truly insignificant; it prepares us to receive more of its like, confirms those which resembled it before, and weakens others; and so gradually it lays a stealthy train in our inmost thoughts, which may some day explode into overt action, and leave its stamp upon our character for ever.

And no one man's belief is in any case a private matter which concerns himself alone. Our lives are guided by that general conception of the course of things which has been created by society for social purposes. Our words, our phrases, our forms and processes and modes of thought, are common property, fashioned and perfected from age to age; an heirloom which every succeeding generation inherits as a precious deposit and a sacred trust to be handed on to the next one, not unchanged but enlarged and purified, with some clear marks of its proper handiwork. Into this, for good or ill, is woven every belief of every man who has speech of his fellows. An awful privilege, and an awful responsibility, that we should help to create the world in which posterity will live.

In the two supposed cases which have been considered, it has been judged wrong to believe on insufficient evidence, or to nourish belief by suppressing doubts and avoiding investigation. The reason of this judgment is not far to seek: it is that in both these cases the belief held by one man was of great importance to other men. But forasmuch as no belief held by one man, however seemingly trivial the belief, and however obscure the believer, is ever actually insignificant or without its effect on the fate of mankind, we have no choice but to extend our judgment to all cases of belief whatever. Belief, that sacred faculty which prompts the decisions of our will, and knits into harmonious working all the compacted energies of our being, is ours not for ourselves, but for humanity. It is rightly used on truths which have been established by long experience and waiting toil, and which have stood in the fierce light of free and fearless questioning. Then it helps to bind men together, and to strengthen and direct their common action. It is desecrated when given to unproved and unquestioned statements, for the solace and private pleasure of the believer; to add a tinsel splendour to the plain straight road of our life and display a bright mirage beyond it; or even to drown the common sorrows of our kind by a self-deception which allows them not only to cast down, but also to degrade us. Whoso would deserve well of his fellows in this matter will guard the purity of his belief with a very fanaticism of jealous care, lest at any time it should rest on an unworthy object, and catch a stain which can never be wiped away.

THE DUTY APPLIES TO EVERYONE, NOT ONLY TO THE EDUCATED

It is not only the leader of men, statesman, philosopher, or poet, that owes this bounden duty to mankind.

Every rustic who delivers in the village alehouse his slow, infrequent sentences, may help to kill or keep alive the fatal superstitions which clog his race. Every hard-worked wife of an artisan may transmit to her children beliefs which shall knit society together, or rend it in pieces. No simplicity of mind, no obscurity of station, can escape the universal duty of questioning all that we believe.

It is true that this duty is a hard one, and the doubt which comes out of it is often a very bitter thing. It leaves us bare and powerless where we thought that we were safe and strong. To know all about anything is to know how to deal with it under all circumstances. We feel much happier and more secure when we think we know precisely what to do, no matter what happens, than when we have lost our way and do not know where to turn. And if we have supposed ourselves to know all about anything, and to be capable of doing what is fit in regard to it, we naturally do not like to find that we are really ignorant and powerless, that we have to begin again at the beginning, and try to learn what the thing is and how it is to be dealt with—if indeed anything can be learnt about it. It is the sense of power attached to a sense of knowledge that makes men desirous of believing, and afraid of doubting.

The sense of power is the highest and best of pleasures when the belief on which it is founded is a true belief, and has been fairly earned by investigation. For then we may justly feel that it is common property, and holds good for others as well as for ourselves. Then we may be glad, not that I have learned secrets by which I am safer and stronger, but that *we men* have got mastery over more of the world; and we shall be strong, not for ourselves, but in the name of Man and in his strength. But if the belief has been accepted on insufficient evidence, the pleasure is a stolen one. Not only does it deceive ourselves by giving us a sense of power which we do not really possess, but it is sinful, because it is stolen in defiance of our duty to mankind. That duty is to guard ourselves from such beliefs as from a pestilence, which may shortly master our own body and then spread to the rest of the town. What would be thought of one who, for the sake of a sweet fruit, should deliberately run the risk of bringing a plague upon his family and his neighbours?

It Is Wrong to Believe Without Good Evidence Even If Our Belief Turns Out to Be True After All

And, as in other such cases, it is not the risk only which has to be considered; for a bad action is always bad at the time when it is done, no matter what happens afterwards. Every time we let ourselves believe for unworthy reasons, we weaken our powers of self-control, of doubting, of judicially and fairly weighing evidence. We all suffer severely enough from the maintenance and support of false beliefs and the fatally wrong actions which they lead to, and the evil born when one such belief is entertained is great and wide. But a greater and wider evil arises when the credulous character is maintained and supported, when a habit of believing for unworthy reasons is fostered and made permanent. If I steal money from any person, there may be no harm done by the mere transfer of possession; he may not feel the loss, or it may prevent him from using the money badly. But I cannot help doing this great wrong towards Man, that I make myself dishonest. What hurts society is not that it should lose its property, but that it should become a den of thieves; for then it must cease to be society. This is why we ought not to do evil that good may come; for at any rate this great evil has come, that we have done evil and are made wicked thereby. In like manner, if I let myself believe anything on insufficient evidence, there may be no great harm done by the mere belief; it may be true after all, or I may never have occasion to exhibit it in outward acts. But I cannot help doing this great wrong towards Man, that I make myself credulous. The danger to society is not merely that it should believe wrong things, though that is great enough; but that it should become credulous, and lose the habit of testing things and inquiring into them; for then it must sink back into savagery.

The harm which is done by credulity in a man is not confined to the fostering of a credulous character in others, and consequent support of false beliefs. Habitual want of care about what I believe leads to habitual want of care in others about the truth of what is told to me. Men speak the truth to one another when each reveres the truth in his own mind and in the other's mind; but how shall my friend revere the truth in my mind when I myself am careless about it, when I believe things because I want to believe them, and because they are comforting and pleasant? Will he not learn to cry, "Peace," to me, when there is no peace? By such a course I shall surround myself with a thick atmosphere of falsehood and fraud, and in that I must live. It may matter little to me, in my cloud-castle of sweet illusions and darling lies; but it matters much to Man that I have made my neighbours ready to deceive. The credulous man is father to the liar and the cheat; he lives in the bosom of this his family, and it is no marvel if he should become even as they are. So closely are our duties knit together, that whoso shall keep the whole law, and yet offend in one point, he is guilty of all.

To sum up: it is wrong always, everywhere, and for anyone, to believe anything upon insufficient evidence.

If a man, holding a belief which he was taught in childhood or persuaded of afterwards, keeps down and pushes away any doubts which arise about it in his mind, purposely avoids the reading of books and the company of men that call in question or discuss it, and regards as impious those questions which cannot easily be asked without disturbing it—the life of that man is one long sin against mankind.

If this judgment seems harsh when applied to those simple souls who have never known better, who have been brought up from the cradle with a horror of doubt, and taught that their eternal welfare depends on *what* they believe, then it leads to the very serious question, *Who hath made Israel to sin?*

It may be permitted me to fortify this judgment with the sentence of Milton.[1]

> A man may be a heretic in the truth; and if he believe things only because his pastor says so, or the assembly so determine, without knowing other reason, though his belief be true, yet the very truth he holds becomes his heresy.

And with this famous aphorism of Coleridge.[2]

> He who begins by loving Christianity better than Truth, will proceed by loving his own sect or Church better than Christianity, and end in loving himself better than all.

Inquiry into the evidence of a doctrine is not to be made once for all, and then taken as finally settled. It is never lawful to stifle a doubt; for either it can be honestly answered by means of the inquiry already made, or else it proves that the inquiry was not complete.

"But," says one, "I am a busy man; I have no time for the long course of study which would be necessary to make me in any degree a competent judge of certain questions, or even able to understand the nature of the arguments." Then he should have no time to believe.

Notes

1. *Areopagitica.*
2. *Aids to Reflection.*

Study Questions

1. In sharp contrast to both Pascal and Aquinas, Clifford holds that it is morally wrong to accept any belief for which one does not have convincing rational evidence. What is his reason for this view? Explain why you do or do not find this reason persuasive.
2. Many people would agree with Clifford that it is wrong to take some action that may harm or endanger others, on the basis of a belief that lacks rational support. Clifford, however, goes further and insists that the moral wrong attaches to the mere holding of the belief, not only to actions that are based on it. Explain his reasons for this argument.
3. Does Clifford seem to have a particular kind of evidence for beliefs in mind—and, if so, what kind? Also, evaluate Clifford's understanding of sufficient evidence.

William James

The Will to Believe

In this essay, William James (1842–1910) is responding to William Clifford, who had argued that "it is wrong always, everywhere, and for anyone, to believe anything on insufficient evidence." (Clifford strongly suggests that religious beliefs will fail to meet this test.) In reply, James argues for the "will to believe"—or, more accurately, the *right* to believe—in some cases in which we lack the strong supporting evidence Clifford considers essential. In the case of "genuine options"—choices that are "living, forced, and momentous"—we may and indeed must make our decisions to believe or disbelieve with our "passional nature." It should be noted, however, that James endorses this conclusion only when clear-cut, objective evidence is unavailable; he does not advocate ignoring or denying the evidence.

Let us give the name of *hypothesis* to anything that may be proposed to our belief; and just as the electricians speak of live and dead wires, let us speak of any hypothesis as either *live* or *dead*. A live hypothesis is one which appeals as a real possibility to him to whom it is proposed. If I ask you to believe in the Mahdi, the notion makes no electric connection with your nature—it refuses to scintillate with any credibility at all. As an hypothesis it is completely dead. To an Arab, however (even if he be not one of the Mahdi's followers), the hypothesis is among the mind's possibilities: it is alive. This shows that deadness and liveness in an hypothesis are not intrinsic properties, but relations to the individual thinker. They are measured by his willingness to act. The maximum of liveness in an hypothesis means willingness to act irrevocably. Practically, that means belief; but there is some believing tendency wherever there is willingness to act at all.

Next, let us call the decision between two hypotheses an *option*. Options may be of several kinds. They may be—first, *living* or *dead*; secondly, *forced* or *avoidable*; thirdly, *momentous* or *trivial*; and for our purposes we may call an option a *genuine* option when it is of the forced, living, and momentous kind.

1. A living option is one in which both hypotheses are live ones. If I say to you: "Be a theosophist or be a Mohammedan," it is probably a dead option, because for you neither hypothesis is likely to be alive. But if I say: "Be an agnostic or be a Christian," it is

From *Essays in Pragmatism* (New York: Hafner), 1969.

otherwise: trained as you are, each hypothesis makes some appeal, however small, to your belief.

2. Next, if I say to you: "Choose between going out with your umbrella or without it," I do not offer you a genuine option, for it is not forced. You can easily avoid it by not going out at all. Similarly, if I say, "Either love me or hate me," "Either call my theory true or call it false," your option is avoidable. You may remain indifferent to me, neither loving nor hating, and you may decline to offer any judgment as to my theory. But if I say, "Either accept this truth or go without it," I put on you a forced option, for there is no standing place outside of the alternative. Every dilemma based on a complete logical disjunction, with no possibility of not choosing, is an option of this forced kind.

3. Finally, if I were Dr. Nansen and proposed to you to join my North Pole expedition, your option would be momentous; for this would probably be your only similar opportunity, and your choice now would either exclude you from the North Pole sort of immortality altogether or put at least the chance of it into your hands. He who refuses to embrace a unique opportunity loses the prize as surely as if he tried and failed. *Per contra*, the option is trivial when the opportunity is not unique, when the stake is insignificant, or when the decision is reversible if it later proves unwise. Such trivial options abound in the scientific life. A chemist finds an hypothesis live enough to spend a year in its verification: he believes in it to that extent. But if his experiments prove inconclusive either way, he is quit for his loss of time, no vital harm being done.

It will facilitate our discussion if we keep all these distinctions well in mind.

The next matter to consider is the actual psychology of human opinion....Evidently...our non-intellectual nature does influence our convictions. There are passional tendencies and volitions which run before and others which come after belief, and it is only the latter that are too late for the fair; and they are not too late when the previous passional work has been already in their own direction....The state of things is evidently far from simple; and pure insight and logic, whatever they might do ideally, are not the only things that really do produce our creeds.

Our next duty, having recognized this mixed-up state of affairs, is to ask whether it be simply reprehensible and pathological, or whether, on the contrary, we must treat it as a normal element in making up our minds. The thesis I defend is, briefly stated, this: *Our passional nature not only lawfully may, but must, decide an option between propositions, whenever it is a genuine option that cannot by its nature be decided on intellectual grounds; for to say, under such circumstances, "Do not decide but leave the question open, is itself a passional decision—just like deciding yes or no—and attended with the same risk of losing the truth.* The thesis thus abstractly expressed will, I trust, soon become become quite clear....

There are two ways of looking at our duty in the matter of opinion—ways entirely different, and yet ways about whose difference the theory of knowledge seems hitherto to have shown very little concern. *We must know the truth*; and *we must avoid error*—these are our first and great commandments as would-be knowers; but they are not two ways of stating an identical commandment, they are two separable laws. Although it may indeed happen that when we believe the truth *A*, we escape as an incidental consequence from believing the falsehood *B*, it hardly ever happens that by merely disbelieving *B* we necessarily believe *A*. We may in escaping *B* fall into believing other falsehoods, *C* or *D*, just as bad as *B*; or we may escape *B* by not believing anything at all, not even *A*.

Believe truth! Shun error!—these, we see, are two materially different laws; and by choosing between them we may end by coloring differently our whole intellectual life. We may regard the chase for truth as paramount, and the avoidance of error as secondary; or we may, on the other hand, treat the avoidance of error as more imperative, and let truth take its chance. Clifford...exhorts us to the latter course. Believe nothing, he tells us, keep your mind in suspense forever, rather than by closing it on insufficient evidence incur the awful risk of believing lies. You, on the other hand, may think that the risk of being in error is a very small matter when compared with the blessings of real knowledge, and be ready to be duped many times in your investigation rather than postpone indefinitely the chance of guessing true. I myself find it impossible to go with Clifford. We must remember that these feelings of our duty about either truth or error are in any case only expressions of our passional life. Biologically considered, our minds are as ready to grind out falsehood as veracity, and he who says, "Better go without belief forever than believe a lie!" merely shows his own preponderant private horror of becoming a dupe. He may be critical of many of his desires and fears, but this fear he slavishly obeys. He cannot imagine any one questioning its binding force. For my own part, I have also a horror of being duped; but I can believe that worse things than being duped may happen to a man in this world: so Clifford's exhortation has to my ears a thoroughly fantastic sound. It is like a general informing his soldiers that it is better to keep out of battle forever than to risk a single wound. Not so are victories either over enemies or over nature gained. Our errors are surely not such awfully solemn things. In a world where we are so certain to incur them in spite of all our caution, a certain lightness of heart seems healthier than this excessive nervousness on their behalf. At any rate, it seems the fittest thing for the empiricist philosopher.

And now, after all this introduction, let us go straight at our question. I have said, and now repeat it, that not only as a matter of fact do we find our passional nature influencing us in our opinions, but that there are some options between opinions in which this influence must be regarded both as an inevitable and as a lawful determinant of our choice.

I fear here that some of you my hearers will begin to scent danger, and lend an inhospitable ear. Two first steps of passion you have indeed had to admit as necessary—we must think so as to avoid dupery, and we must think so as to gain truth; but the surest path to those ideal consummations, you will probably consider, is from now onwards to take no further passional step.

Well, of course, I agree as far as the facts will allow. Wherever the option between losing truth and gaining it is not momentous, we can throw the chance of *gaining truth* away, and at any rate save ourselves from any chance of *believing falsehood*, by not making up our minds at all till objective evidence has come. In scientific questions, this is almost always the case; and even in human affairs in general, the need of acting is seldom so urgent that a false belief to act on is better than no belief at all. Law courts, indeed, have to decide on the best evidence attainable for the moment, because a judge's duty is to make law as well as to ascertain it, and (as a learned judge once said to me) few cases are worth spending much time over: the great thing is to have them decided on any acceptable principle, and got out of the way. But in our dealings with objective nature we obviously are recorders, not makers, of the truth; and decisions for the mere sake of deciding promptly and getting on to the next business would be wholly out of place. Throughout the breadth of physical nature facts are what they are quite independently of us, and seldom is there any such hurry about them that the risks of being duped by believing a premature theory need be faced. The questions here are always trivial options, the hypotheses are hardly living (at any rate not living for us spectators), the choice between believing truth or falsehood is seldom forced. The attitude of sceptical balance is therefore the absolutely wise one if we would escape mistakes. What difference, indeed, does it make to most of us whether we have or have not a theory of the Röntgen rays, whether we believe or not in mind-stuff, or have a conviction about the causality of conscious states? It makes no difference. Such options are not forced on us. On every account it is better not to make them, but still keep weighing reasons *pro et contra* with an indifferent hand.

I speak, of course, here of the purely judging mind. For purposes of discovery such indifference is to be less highly recommended, and science would be far less advanced than she is if the passionate desires of individuals to get their own faiths confirmed had been kept out of the game. See for example the sagacity which Spencer and Weismann now display. On the other hand, if you want an absolute duffer in an investigation, you must, after all, take the man who has no interest whatever in its results: he is the warranted incapable, the positive fool. The most useful investigator, because the most sensitive observer, is always he whose eager interest in one side of the question is balanced by an equally keen nervousness lest he become deceived. Science has organized this nervousness into a regular *technique*, her so-called method of verification; and she has fallen so deeply in love with the method that one may even say she has ceased to care for truth by itself at all. It is only truth as technically verified that interests her. The truth of truths might come in merely affirmative form, and she would decline to touch it. Such truth as that, she might repeat with Clifford, would be stolen in defiance of her duty to mankind. Human passions, however, are stronger than technical rules. "*Le cœur a ses raisons,*" as Pascal says, "*que la raison ne connaît pas*"; and however indifferent to all but the bare rules of the game the umpire, the abstract intellect, may be, the concrete players who furnish him the materials to judge of are usually, each one of them, in love with some pet "live hypothesis" of his own. Let us agree, however, that wherever there is no forced option, the dispassionately judicial intellect with no pet hypothesis, saving us, as it does, from dupery at any rate, ought to be our ideal.

The question next arises: Are there not somewhere forced options in our speculative questions, and can we (as men who may be interested at least as much in positively gaining truth as in merely escaping dupery) always wait with impunity till the coercive evidence shall have arrived? It seems a priori improbable that the truth should be so nicely adjusted to our needs and powers as that. In the great boarding-house of nature, the cakes and the butter and the syrup seldom come out so even and leave the plates so clean. Indeed, we should view them with scientific suspicion if they did.

Moral questions immediately present themselves as questions whose solution cannot wait for sensible proof. A moral question is a question not of what sensibly exists, but of what is good, or would be good if it did exist. Science can tell us what exists; but to compare the *worths*, both of what exists and of what does not exist, we must consult not science, but what Pascal calls our heart. Science herself consults her heart when she lays it down that the infinite ascertainment of fact and correction of false belief are the supreme goods for man. Challenge the statement, and science can only repeat it oracularly, or else prove it by showing that such ascertainment and correction bring man all sorts of other goods which man's heart in turn declares. The question of having moral beliefs at all or not having them is decided by our will. Are our moral preferences true or false, or are they only odd biological phenomena, making things good or bad for *us*, but in themselves indifferent? How can your pure intellect decide? If your heart does not *want* a world of moral reality, your head will assuredly never make you believe in one. Mephistophelian scepticism, indeed, will satisfy the head's play-instincts much better than any rigorous idealism can. Some men (even at the student age) are so naturally cool-hearted that the moralistic hypothesis never has for them any pungent life, and in their supercilious presence the hot young moralist always feels strangely ill at ease. The appearance of knowingness is on their side, of naïveté and gullibility on his. Yet, in the inarticulate heart of him, he clings to it that he is not a dupe, and that there is a realm in which (as Emerson says) all their wit and intellectual superiority is no better than the cunning of a fox. Moral scepticism can no more be refuted or proved by logic than intellectual scepticism can. When we stick to it that there is truth (be it of either kind), we do so with our whole nature, and resolve to stand or fall by the results. The sceptic with his whole nature adopts the doubting attitude; but which of us is the wiser, Omniscience only knows.

Turn now from these wide questions of good to a certain class of questions of fact, questions concerning personal relations, states of mind between one man and another. *Do you like me or not?*—for example. Whether you do or not depends, in countless instances, on whether I meet you half-way, am willing to assume that you must like me, and show you trust and expectation. The previous faith on my part in your liking's existence is in such cases what makes your liking come. But if I stand aloof, and refuse to budge an inch until I have objective evidence, until you shall have done something apt, as the absolutists say, *ad extorquendum assensum meum,* ten to one your liking never comes. How many women's hearts are vanquished by the mere sanguine insistence of some man that they *must* love him! He will not consent to the hypothesis that they cannot. The desire for a certain kind of truth here brings about that special truth's existence; and so it is in innumerable cases of other sorts. Who gains promotions, boons, appointments, but the man in whose life they are seen to play the part of live hypotheses, who discounts them, sacrifices other things for their sake before they have come, and takes risks for them in advance? His faith acts on the powers above him as a claim, and creates its own verification.

A social organism of any sort whatever, large or small, is what it is because each member proceeds to his own duty with a trust that the other members will simultaneously do theirs. Wherever a desired result is achieved by the cooperation of many independent persons, its existence as a fact is a pure consequence of the precursive faith in one another of those immediately concerned. A government, an army, a commercial system, a ship, a college, an athletic team, all exist on this condition, without which not only is nothing achieved, but nothing is even attempted. A whole train of passengers (individually brave enough) will be looted by a few highwaymen, simply because the latter can count on one another, while each passenger fears that if he makes a movement of resistance, he will be shot before any one else backs him up. If we believed that the whole car-full would rise at once with us, we should each severally rise, and train-robbing would never even be attempted. There are, then, cases where a fact cannot come at all unless a preliminary faith exists in its coming. *And where faith in a fact can help create the fact,* that would be an insane logic which should say that faith running ahead of scientific evidence is the "lowest kind of immorality" into which a thinking being can fall. Yet such is the logic by which our scientific absolutists pretend to regulate our lives!

In truths dependent on our personal action, then, faith based on desire is certainly a lawful and possibly an indispensable thing.

But now, it will be said, these are all childish human cases, and have nothing to do with great cosmical matters, like the question of religious faith. Let us then pass on to that. Religions differ so much in their accidents that in discussing the religious question we must make it very generic and broad. What then do we now mean by the religious hypothesis? Science says things are; morality says some things are better than other things; and religion says essentially two things.

First, she says that the best things are the more eternal things, the overlapping things, the things in the universe that throw the last stone, so to speak, and say the final word. "Perfection is eternal"—this phrase of Charles Secrétan seems a good way of putting this first affirmation of religion, an affirmation which obviously cannot yet be verified scientifically at all.

The second affirmation of religion is that we are better off even now if we believe her first affirmation to be true.

Now, let us consider what the logical elements of this situation are *in case the religious hypothesis in both its branches be really true.* (Of course, we must admit that possibility at the outset. If we are to discuss the question at all, it must involve a living option. If for any of you religion be a hypothesis that cannot, by any living possibility, be true, then you need go no farther. I speak to the "saving remnant" alone.) So proceeding, we see, first, that religion offers itself as a *momentous* option. We are supposed to gain, even now, by our belief, and to lose by our non-belief, a certain vital good. Secondly, religion is a *forced* option, so far as that good goes. We cannot escape the issue by remaining sceptical and waiting for more light, because, although we do avoid error in that way *if religion be untrue,* we lose the good, *if it be true,* just as certainly as if we positively chose to disbelieve. It is as if a man should hesitate indefinitely to ask a certain woman to marry him because he was not perfectly sure that she would prove an angel after he brought her home. Would he not cut himself off from that particular angel-possibility as decisively as if he went and married some one else? Scepticism, then, is not avoidance of option; it is option of a certain particular kind of risk. *Better risk less of truth than chance of error*—that is your faith-vetoer's exact position. He is actively playing his stake as much as the believer is; he is backing the field against the religious hypothesis, just as the believer is backing the religious hypothesis against the field. To preach scepticism to us as a duty until "sufficient evidence" for religion be found, is tantamount therefore to telling us, when in presence of the religious hypothesis, that to yield to our fear of its being error is wiser and better than to yield to our hope that it may be true. It is not intellect against all passions, then; it is only intellect with one passion laying down its law. And by what, forsooth, is the supreme wisdom of this passion warranted?

Dupery for dupery, what proof is there that dupery through hope is so much worse than dupery through fear? I, for one, can see no proof; and I simply refuse obedience to the scientist's command to imitate his kind of option, in a case where my own stake is important enough to give me the right to choose my own form of risk. If religion be true and the evidence for it be still insufficient, I do not wish, by putting your extinguisher upon my nature (which feels to me as if it had after all some business in this matter), to forfeit my sole chance in life of getting upon the winning side—that chance depending, of course, on my willingness to run the risk of acting as if my passional need of taking the world religiously might be prophetic and right.

All this is on the supposition that it really may be prophetic and right, and that, even to us who are discussing the matter, religion is a live hypothesis which may be true. Now, to most of us religion comes in a still further way that makes a veto on our active faith even more illogical. The more perfect and more eternal aspect of the universe is represented in our religions as having personal form. The universe is no longer a mere *It* to us, but a *Thou*, if we are religious; and any relation that may be possible from person to person might be possible here. For instance, although in one sense we are passive portions of the universe, in another we show a curious autonomy, as if we were small active centres on our own account. We feel, too, as if the appeal of religion to us were made to our own active goodwill, as if evidence might be forever withheld from us unless we met the hypothesis halfway. To take a trivial illustration: just as a man who in a company of gentlemen made no advances, asked a warrant for every concession, and believed no one's word without proof, would cut himself off by such churlishness from all the social rewards that a more trusting spirit would earn—so here, one who should shut himself up in snarling logicality and try to make the gods extort his recognition willy-nilly, or not get it at all, might cut himself off forever from his only opportunity of making the gods' acquaintance. This feeling, forced on us we know not whence, that by obstinately believing that there are gods (although not to do so would be so easy both for our logic and our life) we are doing the universe the deepest service we can, seems part of the living essence of the religious hypothesis. If the hypothesis *were* true in all its parts, including this one, then pure intellectualism, with its veto on our making willing advances, would be an absurdity; and some participation of our sympathetic nature would be logically required. I, therefore, for one, cannot see my way to accepting the agnostic rules for truth seeking, or wilfully agree to keep my willing nature out of the game. I cannot do so for this plain reason, that *a rule of thinking which would absolutely prevent me from acknowledging certain kinds of truth if these kinds of truth were really there, would be an irrational rule.* That for me is the long and short of the formal logic of the situation, no matter what the kinds of truth might materially be.

I confess I do not see how this logic can be escaped. But sad experience makes me fear that some of you may still shrink from radically saying with me, *in abstracto*, that we have the right to believe at our own risk any hypothesis that is live enough to tempt our will. I suspect, however, that if this is so, it is because you have got away from the abstract logical point of view altogether, and are thinking (perhaps without realizing it) of some particular religious hypothesis which for you is dead. The freedom to "believe what we will" you apply to the case of some patent superstition; and the faith you think of is the faith defined by the schoolboy when he said, "Faith is when you believe something that you know ain't true." I can only repeat that this is misapprehension. *In concreto*, the freedom to believe can only cover living options which the intellect of the individual cannot by itself resolve; and living options never seem absurdities to him who has them to consider. When I look at the religious question as it really puts itself to concrete men, and when I think of all the possibilities which both practically and theoretically it involves, then this command that we shall put a stopper on our hearts, instincts, and courage, and *wait*—acting of course meanwhile more or less as if religion were *not* true[1]—till doomsday, or till such time as our intellect and senses working together may have raked in evidence enough—this command, I say, seems to me the queerest idol ever manufactured in the philosophic cave. Were we scholastic absolutists, there might be more excuse. If we had an infallible intellect with its objective certitudes, we might feel ourselves disloyal to such a perfect organ of knowledge in not trusting to it exclusively, in not waiting for its releasing word. But if we are empiricists, if we believe that no bell in us tolls to let us know for certain when truth is in our grasp, then it seems a piece of idle fantasticality to preach so solemnly our duty of waiting for the bell. Indeed we *may* wait if we will—I hope you do not think that I am denying that—but if we do so, we do so at our peril as much as if we believed. In either case we *act*, taking our life in our hands. No one of us ought to issue vetoes to the other, nor should we bandy words of abuse. We ought, on the contrary, delicately and profoundly to respect one another's mental freedom: then only shall we bring about the intellectual republic; then only shall we have that spirit of inner tolerance without which all our outer tolerance is soulless, and which is empiricism's glory; then only shall we live and let live, in speculative as well as in practical things.

Note

1. Since belief is measured by action, he who forbids us to believe religion to be true, necessarily also forbids us to act as we should if we did believe it to be true. The whole defence of religious faith hinges upon action. If the action required or inspired by the religious hypothesis is in no way different from that dictated by the naturalistic hypothesis, then religious faith is a pure superfluity, better pruned away, and controversy about its legitimacy is a piece of idle trifling, unworthy of serious minds. I myself believe, of course, that the religious hypothesis gives to the world an expression which specifically determines our reactions, and makes them in a large part unlike what they might be on a purely naturalistic scheme of belief.

Study Questions

1. Explain what James means by a "genuine option." Why is it especially in cases involving such an option that one may be rational in accepting a belief that goes beyond the evidence one has?
2. James points out that sometimes "faith in a fact can help to create the fact" and uses this view to justify faith that goes beyond one's present evidence. Is James correct to extend this reasoning to the case of religious belief?
3. James argues that our interests and desires—our "passional nature"—do, in fact, have a considerable influence on what we believe and disbelieve. Is James right about this? If he is, do you also agree with him that this influence is legitimate?
4. Explain what James calls the different values in the search for truth and how giving on one value priority over the other may lead to different beliefs.

Søren Kierkegaard

Truth Is Subjectivity

In this selection, Søren Kierkegaard (1813–1855), writing under the pseudonym Johannes Climacus, strongly emphasizes the deeply subjective and personal nature of religious truth. While he does not deny that there is a difference between truth and falsehood, he insists that an attitude of detached, objective inquiry is totally inappropriate in religious matters. In religion, he maintains, what is crucial is the *way in which one is related* to the truth that one believes. Interestingly, "Climacus" stresses that in order to have a vital *faith*, it is essential that one should *not* be able to prove that one's belief is true. A point that should be kept in mind is that views expressed under a pseudonym (such as Johannes Climacus) are not necessarily those of Kierkegaard himself, and recent scholarship suggests that Kierkegaard's overall attitude toward reason is less negative than the view "Climacus" expresses here. Nevertheless, this selection remains a powerful statement of the attitude towards faith and reason known as *fideism*—"faithism."

In an attempt to make clear the difference of way that exists between an objective and a subjective reflection, I shall now proceed to show how a subjective reflection makes its way inwardly in inwardness. Inwardness in an existing subject culminates in passion; corresponding to passion in the subject the truth becomes a paradox; and the fact that the truth becomes a paradox is rooted precisely in its having a relationship to an existing subject. Thus the one corresponds to the other. By forgetting that one is an existing subject, passion goes by the board and the truth is no longer a paradox; the knowing subject becomes a fantastic entity rather than a human being, and the truth becomes a fantastic object for the knowledge of this fantastic entity.

When the question of truth is raised in an objective manner, reflection is directed objectively to the truth, as an object to which the knower is related. Reflection is not focussed upon the relationship, however, but upon the question of whether it is the truth to which the knower is related. If only the object to which he is related is the truth, the subject is accounted to be in the truth. When the question of the truth is raised subjectively, reflection is directed subjectively to the nature of the individual's relationship; if only the mode of this relationship is in the truth, the individual is in the truth

Swenson, David; *Concluding Unscientific Postscript* by Soren Kierkegaard. © 1941 Princeton University Press, 1969 renewed. Reprinted by permission of Princeton University Press.

even if he should happen to be thus related to what is not true. Let us take as an example the knowledge of God. Objectively, reflection is directed to the problem of whether this object is the true God; subjectively, reflection is directed to the question whether the individual is related to a something *in such a manner* that his relationship is in truth a God-relationship. On which side is the truth now to be found? Ah, may we not here resort to a mediation, and say: It is on neither side, but in the mediation of both? Excellently well said, provided we might have it explained how an existing individual manages to be in a state of mediation. For to be in a state of mediation is to be finished, while to exist is to become. Nor can an existing individual be in two places at the same time—he cannot be an identity of subject and object. When he is nearest to being in two places at the same time he is in passion; but passion is momentary, and passion is also the highest expression of subjectivity.

The existing individual who chooses to pursue the objective way enters upon the entire approximation process by which it is proposed to bring God to light objectively. But this is in all eternity impossible, because God is a subject, and therefore exists only for subjectivity in inwardness. The existing individual who chooses the subjective way apprehends instantly the entire dialectical difficulty involved in having to use some time, perhaps a long time, in finding God objectively; and he feels this dialectical difficulty in all its painfulness, because every moment is wasted in which he does not have God. That very instant he has God, not by virtue of any objective deliberation, but by virtue of the infinite passion of inwardness. The objective inquirer, on the other hand, is not embarrassed by such dialectical difficulties as are involved in devoting an entire period of investigation to finding God—since it is possible that the inquirer may die tomorrow; and if he lives he can scarcely regard God as something to be taken along if convenient, since God is precisely that which one takes *à tout prix*, which in the understanding of passion constitutes the true inward relationship to God.

It is at this point, so difficult dialectically, that the way swings off for everyone who knows what it means to think, and to think existentially; which is something very different from sitting at a desk and writing about what one has never done, something very different from writing *de omnibus dubitandum* and at the same time being as credulous existentially as the most sensuous of men. Here is where the way swings off, and the change is marked by the fact that while objective knowledge rambles comfortably on by way of the long road of approximation without being impelled by the urge of passion, subjective knowledge counts every delay a deadly peril, and the decision so infinitely important and so instantly pressing that it is as if the opportunity had already passed.

Now when the problem is to reckon up on which side there is most truth, whether on the side of one who seeks the true God objectively, and pursues the approximate truth of the God-idea; or on the side of one who, driven by the infinite passion of his need of God, feels an infinite concern for his own relationship to God in truth (and to be at one and the same time on both sides equally, is as we have noted not possible for an existing individual, but is merely the happy delusion of an imaginary I-am-I): the answer cannot be in doubt for anyone who has not been demoralized with the aid of science. If one who lives in the midst of Christendom goes up to the house of God, the house of the true God, with the true conception of God in his knowledge, and prays, but prays in a false spirit; and one who lives in an idolatrous community prays with the entire passion of the infinite, although his eyes rest upon the image of an idol: where is there most truth? The one prays in truth to God though he worships an idol; the other prays falsely to the true God, and hence worships in fact an idol.

When one man investigates objectively the problem of immortality, and another embraces an uncertainty with the passion of the infinite: where is there most truth, and who has the greater certainty? The one has entered upon a never-ending approximation, for the certainty of immortality lies precisely in the subjectivity of the individual; the other is immortal, and fights for his immortality by struggling with the uncertainty. Let us consider Socrates. Nowadays everyone dabbles in a few proofs; some have several such proofs, other fewer. But Socrates! He puts the question objectively in a problematic manner: *if* there is an immortality. He must therefore be accounted a doubter in comparison with one of our modern thinkers with the three proofs? By no means. On this "if" he risks his entire life, he has the courage to meet death, and he has with the passion of the infinite so determined the pattern of his life that it must be found acceptable—*if* there is an immortality. Is any better proof capable of being given for the immortality of the soul? But those who have the three proofs do not at all determine their lives in conformity therewith; if there is an immortality it must feel disgust over their manner of life: can any better refutation be given of the three proofs? The bit of uncertainty that Socrates had, helped him because he himself contributed the passion of the infinite; the three proofs that the others have do not profit them at all, because they are dead to spirit and enthusiasm, and their three proofs, in lieu of proving anything else, prove just this. A young girl may enjoy all the sweetness of love on the basis of what is merely a weak hope that she is beloved, because she rests everything on this weak hope; but many a wedded matron more than once subjected to the strongest expressions of love, has in so far indeed had proofs, but strangely enough has not enjoyed *quod erat demonstrandum*. The Socratic ignorance, which Socrates held fast with the entire passion of his inwardness, was thus an expression for the principle that the eternal truth is related to an existing individual, and that this truth must therefore be a paradox for him as long as he exists; and yet it is possible that there was more truth in the Socratic ignorance as it was in him, than in the entire objective truth of the System, which flirts with what the times demand and accommodates itself to *Privatdocents*.

The objective accent falls on WHAT is said, the subjective accent on HOW it is said. This distinction holds even in the aesthetic realm, and receives definite expression in the principle that what is in itself true may in the mouth of such and such a person become untrue. In these times this distinction is particularly worthy of notice, for if we wish to express in a single sentence the difference between ancient times and our own, we should doubtless have to say: "In ancient times only an individual here and there knew the truth; now all know it, except that the inwardness of its appropriation stands in an inverse relationship to the extent of its dissemination." Aesthetically the contradiction that truth becomes untruth in this or that person's mouth, is best construed comically: In the ethico-religious sphere, accent is again on the "how." But this is not to be understood as referring to demeanor, expression, or the like; rather it refers to the relationship sustained by the existing individual, in his own existence, to the content of his utterance. Objectively the interest focussed merely on the thought-content, subjectively on the inwardness. At its maximum this inward "how" is the passion of the infinite, and the passion of the infinite is the truth. But the passion of the infinite is precisely subjectivity, and thus subjectivity becomes the truth. Objectively there is no infinite decisiveness, and hence it is objectively in order to annul the difference between good and evil, together with the principle of contradiction, and therewith also the infinite difference between the true and the false. Only in subjectivity is there decisiveness, to seek objectivity is to be in error. It is the passion of the infinite that is the decisive factor and not its content, for its content is precisely itself. In this manner subjectivity and the subjective "how" constitute the truth.

But the "how" which is thus subjectivity accentuated precisely because the subject is an existing individual, is also subject to a dialectic with respect to time. In the passionate moment of decision, where the road swings away from objective knowledge, it seems as if the infinite decision were thereby realized. But in the same moment the existing individual finds himself in the temporal order, and the subjective "how" is transformed into a striving, a striving which receives indeed its impulse and a repeated renewal from the decisive passion of the infinite, but is nevertheless a striving.

When subjectivity is the truth, the conceptual determination of the truth must include an expression for the antithesis to objectivity, a memento of the fork in the road where the way swings off; this expression will at the same time serve as an indication of the tension of the subjective inwardness. Here is such a definition of truth: *An objective uncertainty held fast in an appropriation-process of the most passionate inwardness is the truth*, the highest truth attainable for an *existing* individual. At the point where the way swings off (and where this is cannot be specified objectively, since it is a matter of subjectivity), there objective knowledge is placed in abeyance. Thus the subject merely has, objectively, the uncertainty; but it is this which precisely increases the tension of that infinite passion which constitutes his inwardness. The truth is precisely the venture which chooses an objective uncertainty with the passion of the infinite. I contemplate the order of nature in the hope of finding God, and I see omnipotence and wisdom; but I also see much else that disturbs my mind and excites anxiety. The sum of all this is an objective uncertainty. But it is for this very reason that the inwardness becomes as intense as it is, for it embraces this objective uncertainty with the entire passion of the infinite. In the case of a mathematical proposition the objectivity is given, but for this reason the truth of such a proposition is also an indifferent truth.

But the above definition of truth is an equivalent expression for faith. Without risk there is no faith. Faith is precisely the contradiction between the infinite passion of the individual's inwardness and the objective uncertainty. If I am capable of grasping God objectively, I do not believe, but precisely because I cannot do this I must believe. If I wish to preserve myself in faith I must constantly be intent upon holding fast the objective uncertainty, so as to remain out upon the deep, over seventy thousand fathoms of water, still preserving my faith.

Study Questions

1. Does Kierkegaard's description of religious faith seem to be true to faith as you have observed it in religious persons you have known? Why, or why not?
2. Explain Kierkegaard's reasons against the view that religious beliefs ought to be arrived at through an "objective" process of reflection on the available evidence.
3. What does Kierkegaard mean by saying that someone who is worshiping an idol may all the same "pray in truth to God"?

C. Stephen Evans

Critical Dialog in Philosophy of Religion

What should our attitude be as we attempt to philosophize about religious matters? In this selection C. Stephen Evans (b. 1948) rejects fideism (seen here in Kierkegaard-writing-as-Climacus), and also neutralism (as advocated by Clifford), which would demand that we begin our thinking by setting aside all previous commitments and adopting a completely neutral, impartial standpoint. Instead, he recommends an approach he terms "*critical dialog*," in which we begin by accepting and acknowledging our own commitments and convictions but are ready and willing to test them by critical reflection and by engaging in vigorous dialog with those whose commitments are different than our own.

In comparison with theology...the philosophy of religion appears to aim for a neutral stance. But is such neutrality with respect to religious matters really possible? Some religious thinkers have denied that it is, claiming, for example, that a human being cannot be neutral with respect to God. The person who is not properly submissive to God is, they claim, a rebel. "He who is not for us is against us."

Even more radically, one might ask whether such neutrality is desirable. Is it not possible that those who attempt to adopt a neutral, disinterested posture cut themselves off from the possibility of even understanding what religion is all about?...

...Some religious believers hold a view of faith and reason which claims that rational reflection on religion is impossible, useless, or even harmful. In effect, they call into question the very legitimacy of philosophy of religion. Hence some consideration of their view is in order if we are to be truly reflective and critical....I shall approach this issue by sketching two opposing viewpoints, *fideism* and *neutralism*. These I will criticize and reject. I will then propose an alternative which will, I hope, preserve the strengths and eliminate the weaknesses of the initial theories. This constructive proposal will be termed *critical dialog*.

FIDEISM

Many theologians have claimed that human beings are inherently religious. If they do not worship the true God, then they worship false gods—themselves,

C. Stephen Evans, *Philosophy of Religion: Thinking about Faith* (Downers Grove, Ill.: InterVarsity Press, 1985), pp. 17–29.

or things of their own making. On this view a human being is never religiously neutral; he is always either a faithful servant or a rebel against the Creator. The faithful servant functions as he was meant to function and fulfills his created destiny. The rebel, however, is always "kicking against the pricks." All her activities reflect the distorted and twisted character she has given to life.

Some have concluded from this that the thinking of the unbeliever is also twisted and distorted, either in all areas or at least with respect to essential moral and religious truth. Although the reasoning of rebellious humans makes a pretense of neutrality, this neutrality is in fact an illusion. Indeed, the very attempt of humans to think about God "for themselves," independently and autonomously, is proof of their rebelliousness. It represents an attempt on the part of man to put his own thought and reason above God.

This view implies that human attempts to reflect on the truth of religious beliefs are disastrous. It is impossible for the unbeliever as an unbeliever to reflect on the reasonableness of religious belief and thereby become a believer. Rather, the unbeliever's only hope is first to *believe* and then perhaps come to see the reasonableness of the belief. If God in his mercy reveals to the unbeliever the truth about himself and the unbeliever, the unbeliever must humbly accept this truth. God must "force an entry." The unbeliever's twisted thinking can only be straightened out as his status and life change from that of rebel to servant. Only the regenerate mind can see the truth.

This view implies that one cannot arrive at true religious beliefs as a result of rational reflection. The starting place for any correct thinking about religion is rather a genuine faith, a personal commitment. Fideism claims that faith is the precondition for any correct thinking about religion.

Fideism puts its critics in an awkward spot, for all criticism of the view can easily be written off as the product of unbelief. It thus gains an invulnerable status against all attacks. But it gains this status at a rather high cost; the fideist cannot attempt to win over his critics by rational argument or even attempt to engage in rational dialog with those who disagree. The presupposition of such dialog and argument is

the possibility of common ground, some point of agreement which can be reflected on or appealed to. But it is just this kind of common ground which the fideist denies...

In effect, the fideist says, "Commit yourself and you will see that what I say is true." The problem is that *many* people say that, asking for commitment to many different things. One can demand commitment to creeds, books, churches or popes. Religious sects, political ideologies (like Marxism), psychological cults and non-Christian religions all make their appeals.

The Christian fideist may, of course, respond that there is an important difference between his commitments and those of all other faiths. He holds to the *true* set of beliefs, the *right* presuppositions. He can see the truth because he has been regenerated; he has the witness of the Spirit. Of course, these claims may be correct, but how does one know them to be correct? Adherents of other religions can easily make similar claims.

It seems to me that in a pluralistic culture it is almost impossible *not* to reflect critically on where one should place one's trust. And even if it is possible to make a commitment apart from critical reflection, the existence of even one Jonestown horror would make it clear that it is irresponsible not to exercise critical judgment when asked for commitment. To the sincere individual who really wants truth, the fideist offers no help; he offers only another voice crying out in the middle of the modern religious babel.

Perhaps the mistake of the fideist is to overestimate dogmatically the impact of unbelief. For the moment let us concede that most (or all) human beings are rebels against God. Let us further concede that this status impairs their personality in all its functions, including their reasoning. From this it follows only that it may be difficult for human beings in this condition to think rightly about God. Their thinking may be harmed and limited in all kinds of ways, but it does not necessarily follow that such thinking is useless. After all, God remains God, the Creator, and he may well establish limits to the ways in which even a rebellious creature may run amuck in his thinking.

At the very least it seems wrong-headed to conclude at the outset that human thinking about God is worthless. Perhaps this is a conclusion one might be wearily driven to accept, after many efforts, but even then it would appear that human thinking would have to have a certain competence *even to recognize its incompetence*. Such a negative result might, in fact, be a valuable conclusion, analogous to the wisdom of Socrates, who surpassed his contemporaries by recognizing what he did not know.

But what about the charge of the fideist that critical thinking about religious belief is impious or presumptuous, an arrogant placing of human reason above God? It would seem that whether critical reflection about religious questions is presumptuous depends chiefly on two factors. The first is whether God, if real, wants humans to reflect about religious truth. If God had forbidden humans to think critically about religious questions, then perhaps it would be impious to do so, provided one had some way of knowing about the prohibition. But I see absolutely no reason to think that God wishes human beings to suppress their critical faculties. After all, our ability to think is a gift from God, and it seems proper to assume that this gift, like others God has bestowed, is intended to be used if used properly. And it would certainly appear to be a proper use of reason, when confronted by a plurality of competing truth-claims, to reflect on matters as important as religious belief.

The second factor which would affect whether critical thinking about religion is legitimate is the manner in which the thinking is carried on. Clearly it is possible to think about God (or anything else) in an arrogant or presumptuous manner. No doubt much actual human thinking about God is of this character. But this is surely a temptation to combat, not a necessary feature of critical thought about religion. A person who sincerely wants to know whether God is real, who is willing to recognize his own inferior status in relation to God, who recognizes the fallibility and possible bias of his own thinking, who understands that it is unlikely that he will be able to gain a fully adequate understanding of God, who is open to the possibility that his thinking may have to be aided by God to be successful, and who thereby

does not rule out the possibility of a revelation—such a person's thinking about God would hardly appear to be impious or presumptuous.

NEUTRALISM

The opposite pole from the fideist is the philosopher who insists that our thinking about religious matters must be presuppositionless. The neutralist believes that our critical thinking will only be likely to help us toward the truth if it is completely impartial and unbiased. Thus to think rightly about religious matters we must put aside all our commitments, or at least those commitments which are religiously "loaded," and adopt a completely neutral stance.

The neutralist in effect claims that to be reasonable is to think without making any "risky" assumptions. Two sorts of questions must be asked about this. First, if the neutralist is right, is it possible to think reasonably? *Can* human beings think in a purely neutral, disinterested manner? Second, is the neutralist right? Does reason require that one jettison all prior commitments and assumptions?

With regard to the first type of question, it is painfully obvious that human thinking is very much affected by all sorts of nonrational factors. Our thought is colored not only by our prior experiences but by our emotions, our upbringing and education, the ideas and attitudes of our friends, our historical situation, and a host of other factors. It is true that by reflection we can become conscious of some of these factors and negate or reduce their influence. But it seems unlikely that a person could ever do this completely. Indeed, it would seem foolish and unreasonable for a person to believe she has done this, for such a self-satisfied attitude would harm her chances of uncovering other nonrational influences. I conclude that the proposal of the neutralist cannot be accepted as a condition or requirement of rational thought. It can be at most an ideal which one should strive to approximate.

But, second, is neutralism even valid as an ideal? Is the neutralist right to insist that rational thought be presuppositionless? A full treatment of this question would require a detailed discussion of the central issues in the theory of knowledge. Such an excursion into epistemology is hardly possible here, but it is necessary to say something about these questions, even if what is said is very sketchy.

A long and venerable philosophical tradition holds that genuine knowledge must consist of truths which are known with absolute certainty. We shall term this view *foundationalism,* using the term in a "strong" sense. To know something, one must have a conclusive reason to think it is true. But of course one must also know that the reason is a good one, and therefore one must know it to be true, which may require a reason for one's reason. This threatens to become an infinite regress unless one knows some things directly or immediately, things which therefore can be said to be basic or foundational to knowledge. If this foundational knowledge is not really known but is merely believed or assumed, then the whole structure of knowledge becomes insecure. For this reason, the foundationalist insists that this basic knowledge must be certain. Any proposal to begin with unjustified or unproven assumptions, as the fideist recommends, is disastrous. Only what can be recognized to be true with certainty by a purely objective thinker will do.

We have already discussed whether such thinking is really possible. We are now asking whether it is desirable. Perhaps one way of getting a handle on this question is to see how well the foundationalist ideal accurately describes the work of natural scientists. Most people would agree that in the natural sciences people are working toward knowledge in a rational manner. However, many philosophers of science would today question whether scientists follow the foundationalist ideal.

It has always been evident that scientists make some assumptions which do not seem unquestionable and which cannot really be proven to be true. They assume that nature is basically intelligible and orderly. A uniformity of natural processes and of experience is also assumed as a basis for making generalizations. However, in addition to these very general assumptions, it seems quite plausible to claim that science only progresses if more specific kinds of commitments are made. T. S. Kuhn, in his book *The Structure of Scientific Revolutions*, has called attention

to the way "normal science" depends on what he terms a *paradigm*, a basic set of assumptions which is embodied in the practices of a scientific community. Kuhn argues convincingly that the acceptance of such a paradigm is not simply a matter of "checking it by the facts," as the foundationalist might wish to claim, since the basic paradigm beliefs have at least some bearing on what is to count as a fact and how the facts are to be described. As some interpret him, Kuhn goes on to make the extreme and questionable claim that the adoption of a paradigm is a nonrational matter governed by sociological factors. Even if one does not accept this extreme claim, Kuhn's work still implies that science, far from precluding less-than-certain commitments, actually depends on such commitments.

The history of philosophy also provides an interesting way of testing the claims of the foundationalist. Perhaps the philosopher who most rigorously attempted to follow the foundationalist program was René Descartes (1596–1650). Descartes attempted to realize the ideal of pure objectivity by methodically subjecting all his beliefs to doubt. By supposing that all his experiences might be dream experiences and that it was possible that he was constantly being deceived by an evil being of great power, Descartes rejected almost all his previous beliefs as uncertain. All that remained was the certain truth of his own existence, which he affirmed to be undoubtable as long as he was conscious.

With this slender foundation of "I think, therefore I am," Descartes attempted to prove the existence of God, the external world, and his own immaterial soul. However, almost no one today finds Descartes' arguments convincing. It seems evident, rather, that David Hume was correct in asserting that Cartesian doubt would be incurable if attainable. Rather than laying a foundation for knowledge, Descartes' doubt seems a sure road to total skepticism.

CRITICAL DIALOG

What option remains? We have rejected both fideism and neutralism, the former because it precludes rational reflection, the latter because it places impossible demands on rational reflection. But there is something correct about both these viewpoints. It can be seen from our criticism of neutralism that the fideist has a valid point when he stresses the way our thought is conditioned by basic assumptions and attitudes. And surely the neutralist has a point against the fideist in stressing the value of honest, no-holds-barred, critical reflection on our commitments. How then can reason and commitment be combined?

Perhaps the two can be brought into a happy if sometimes tension-filled alliance by rethinking what it means to be reasonable. Instead of seeing reason as presuppositionless thinking, suppose we view reason as *a willingness to test one's commitments*. Perhaps the fideist is right in claiming that it is impossible to begin without commitments; perhaps it is not even desirable. But it is a mistake to claim that commitments, even fundamental ones, are impervious to criticism and modification. Perhaps the neutralist is right in urging us to strive to rationally evaluate our commitments, to reflect on them critically and honestly in the light of evidence and argument. But it is a mistake to think that this process of testing can or should proceed from a totally neutral standpoint, the standpoint of a person without any convictions. Although any belief can in principle be doubted, we cannot doubt all our beliefs at once without undermining the possibility of overcoming the doubt.

How does one go about testing one's beliefs? Simple beliefs about particular matters of fact are subject to fairly direct experiential tests. More general and comprehensive scientific theories can only be tested indirectly. One looks for theoretical coherence, predictive power, the ability to illuminate what was previously unintelligible. Usually a theory must be tested relative to its rivals. A scientific theory which explains a great deal will be accepted even if it faces serious objections as long as there is no viable alternative. Sometimes the decision to continue to accept a theory requires one to discount or reinterpret what purport to be facts; at other times it seems more reasonable to accept the fact and reject or modify the theory. In short, the testing of theories is a complicated affair, requiring an element of good judgment as well as honesty and concern for truth. One assumes that experience is not infinitely plastic; some theories

fit the facts better than others. But the process of testing is not one for which formal rules can be given.

The testing of basic religious beliefs seems to me to be basically a similar matter, although the kinds of experiences which are relevant as evidence is far broader. The testing of religious beliefs is, of course, likely to be even more difficult than the testing of scientific theories. The reasons for this are many, but they include the point with which the fideist begins. Few if any people are indifferent to religious matters. Since religion bears on a person's life in a far more direct and personal way than science, one can expect it to be correspondingly more difficult to reach agreement on religious matters. Common ground may be hard to find, and rational discussion may sooner or later reach an impasse where both sides say, "This is how it appears to me."

But though common ground may be difficult to find (or even impossible, as the fideist claims), that is no reason not to *look*. Each person is an individual and no doubt must make a final judgment about "the way things appear to him." But to the extent that one individual has made an effort to engage others in critical dialog, he is entitled to regard his commitments as no longer mere prejudices but as convictions which have withstood a process of critical testing and are so far reasonable. In the process of critical dialog the individual attempts to think through the alternatives and the objections to his own view which those alternatives put forward. In the course of such a process a person's views may be modified or abandoned. What survives is not merely prejudice or bias but, subject to a continued willingness to test what appears doubtful, reasoned conviction.

Such a process cannot be guaranteed to work successfully, of course. Finite, fallible human beings cannot survey all the alternatives or assess those they do examine with total accuracy. And the process of reflection cannot be extended indefinitely. The purpose of our religious beliefs is ultimately to guide our lives; if a person spent all his time critically reflecting on his beliefs, there would be no point in having any in the first place.

Philosophy of religion, I believe, is best viewed as a process of critical dialog. Obviously each participant in the dialog approaches it from her own unique perspective. This means that even her critical reflections about her faith are shaped somewhat by her attitudes, basic convictions, and previous experiences. In short, people participate as whole persons, not calculating machines. But the honest participant does not shrink from self-consciously examining any part of what he brings to the encounter. No commitments can be taken off the table as not subject to discussion. And although it may not be possible to be neutral, it is possible for the participants in the dialog to be honest with themselves and others. This honesty requires a willingness to see if the evidence really is best interpreted and explained according to one's own theory.

Such a critical dialog is risky. Probably everyone has heard a story of a student in a strict religious environment who loses his faith as a result of the critical challenges hurled at him at a university. But there is something unhealthy and even dishonest about a faith which hides from such a challenge. Can one really believe in God wholeheartedly and at the same time assert that one can only continue to believe by refusing to consider the evidence against one's belief? Such a "belief" seems perilously close to a half-conscious conviction that in fact God may not be real, combined with a wish to hide this truth from oneself. (Although a decision to ignore evidence must not be confused with an honest recognition of one's inability to properly evaluate evidence, it might be entirely proper for an uneducated person to refuse to consider complicated, abstract arguments which would only confuse and bewilder him.)

A genuine and robust faith will not shrink from the process of testing, for it is confident that it will indeed pass the test. If I genuinely believe that God is real (or that he is an illusion), I will not be afraid to examine alternative views and listen to problems and objections raised by others. Through this process I am confident that my faith will be deepened and strengthened. Furthermore, by listening to my opponent and by looking for common ground on which to show her the superiority of my belief, I gain the possibility of making my opponent into a friend and ally. Instead of churlishly telling those who have other views that they must begin by accepting my presuppositions—an action which is probably not possible even if it were desirable, since belief is not usually under voluntary control—I attempt to find ground on which we both are comfortable. The process may be difficult, and with some it is doubtless impossible. I must not allow my opponent to lure me over the cliff into the thin air of neutralism, where no living human being can stand. But the search for common ground is worth making.

Study Questions

1. What are Evans's objections to fideism, represented here by Kierkegaard/Climacus?
2. What are Evans's objections to neutralism, as represented by Clifford?
3. Explain what Evans means by "critical dialog" as an approach to reasoning about religious matters. Discuss the advantages and disadvantages of this approach.

Suggested Reading

Abraham, William. *An Introduction to the Philosophy of Religion.* Englewood Cliffs, N.J.: Prentice-Hall, 1985.

Allen, Diogenes. *Christian Belief in a Postmodern World: The Full Wealth of Conviction.* Louisville, Ky.: Westminster/John Knox Press, 1989.

Evans, C. Stephen. *Kierkegaard's "Fragments" and "Postscript: The Religious Philosophy of Johannes Climacus.* Atlantic Highlands, N.J.: Humanities Press, 1983.

———. *Philosophy of Religion: Thinking About Faith.* Downers Grove, Ill.: InterVarsity Press, 1985.

Helm, Paul, ed. *Faith and Reason.* Oxford, England: Oxford University Press, 1999.

———. *Faith and Understanding.* Grand Rapids, Mich.: William B. Eerdmans, 1997.

Hick, John. *Faith and Knowledge.* 2nd ed. London: Macmillan, 1966.

Kierkegaard, Søren. *Concluding Unscientific Postscript,* trans. David P. Swenson and Walter Lowrie. Princeton, N.J.: Princeton University Press, 1941.

Mavrodes, George I. *Belief in God.* New York: Random House, 1970.

Mitchell, Basil. *The Justification of Religious Belief.* Oxford, England: Oxford University Press, 1981.

Pascal, Blaise. *Penseés,* trans. W. F. Trotter. New York: Random House, 1941.

Penelhum, Terence. *God and Skepticism.* Dordrecht, the Netherlands: Riedel, 1983.

———. *Reason and Religious Faith.* Boulder, Colo.: Westview, 1995.

Phillips, D. Z. *Religion Without Explanation.* Oxford, England: Blackwell, 1976.

Placher, William C. *Unapologetic Theology: A Christian Voice in a Pluralistic Conversation.* Louisville, Ky.: Westminster/John Knox Press, 1989.

Pojman, Louis P. *Religious Belief and the Will.* New York: Routledge and Kegan Paul, 1986.

Swinburne, Richard. *The Existence of God.* Oxford, England: Oxford University Press, 1979.

———. *Faith and Reason.* Oxford, England: Oxford University Press, 1981.

Wainwright, William. *Reason and the Heart: A Prolegomenon to a Critique of Passional Reason.* Ithaca, N.Y.: Cornell University Press, 1995.

PART FOUR

The Divine Attributes

The most central idea in all of philosophy of religion is the concept of God. We need to be clear about what we mean by "God" before we even raise the question of whether God exists or not; otherwise, we don't really know what question we are asking. (Even an atheist needs to be clear about what sort of god it is in which she doesn't believe!) So we have to ask, what are the "attributes" of God—the characteristics that, so to speak, qualify God as really being God?

In a sense, of course, there is no one answer to this question. There are a number of different conceptions of God on offer, and because of this there are different, competing lists of divine attributes. However, there is a sort of generic concept of God that, with some variations, is common to the monotheistic religions of Christianity, Judaism, and Islam. This generic conception is known as *theism,* and while religious believers typically believe *more* about God than is contained in this concept, it does serve to spell out the essential core of what many religious people have in mind when they speak of God. It is this common core, together with some variations and deviations from it, that is the subject of the selections in this section.

GOD AS PERSONAL CREATOR

An initial component in this theistic conception of God is that God is a *personal* being, one who is capable of knowing, experiencing, making decisions, and performing actions, as well as relating personally to human beings: God loves us, cares for us, and holds us responsible if we act wrongly and harmfully. As a personal being, God is referred to using personal pronouns, and the traditional way of doing this is by speaking of God as "he," even though God, by common consent, is not a sexual being. This practice has been criticized by feminists, who suggest that God might equally well be called "she"; some have also tried to invent new, gender-free pronouns for use in referring to God. In this text, we have followed the traditional practice for the sake of simplcity, but we do not mean to imply that we are endorsing a view that God is male.

Another important attribute is that God is the *creator* of everything that exists other than God. This means that the most fundamental division in all of reality is between God, the uncreated Creator, and everything else—that is, everything God has created. God's creating, however, is not like our own making of things from already-existing materials. Rather, God is said to create "out of nothing" (*ex nihilo* is the Latin phrase); God simply wills that things come into being, and it happens as he wills. (In the Bible, God *speaks*: God said, "Let there be light," and there was light.) Furthermore, God's creating is not something he does once for all and then the things created go ahead "on their own steam," so to speak. Rather, God *sustains* the created world in existence from moment to moment; were God not to do this, the world would cease to exist. It is clear, then, that when we speak of God's "creating," we have in mind something rather different than when we talk about human beings' creating. We have here an example of the way in which many of the terms we use to describe the uncreated God have to be understood somewhat differently than they are when applied to human persons and other created beings. (For another example, God's "power" is not exercised by using his muscles to move things about, as ours usually is.) This brings up the important topic of religious language, the special ways in which language has to be used in speaking about God, which is the subject of Part Nine of this book.

GOD AS ALL POWERFUL, ALL KNOWING, AND MORALLY PERFECT

God, then, is the personal Creator of everything that is not God; furthermore, God is said to be perfect in power, knowledge or wisdom, and goodness. More precisely, God is said to be *omnipotent*, or all-powerful, *omniscient*, or all-knowing, and *perfectly morally good*. But questions arise concerning the right way to understand these attributes. If God can "do anything," does this include making a square circle, or making two plus two equal to seventeen? Most philosophers have thought that this sort of "power" is *not* included in omnipotence. A square circle is not a possible thing to exist or to be made, so God's not being able to make one is not in any real sense a limitation on God's power. Since the time of Thomas Aquinas, it has been customary to say that God can bring about any state of affairs that is logically possible—that does not involve a contradiction. Still, puzzles can arise that challenge this definition, as we will see in some of the selections below.

Somewhat similar questions come up concerning God's *omniscience*. If God "knows everything," just what is included in "everything"? If we accept that there are things God cannot do (such as making a square circle), because doing them is logically impossible, are there also truths God cannot know, because knowing them is logically impossible? Several suggestions have been made along this line, but the one that has drawn the greatest attention concerns the future free actions of human beings (and other free creatures, if there are any). According to a widely accepted view of free will, when a person makes a free choice, it is entirely possible, and fully within the person's power, to choose in any of two or more different ways, *given the exact situation in which the person makes her choice*. (This is called a *libertarian* view of free will.) But if this is so, then it seems that, until the person has made her choice, there is *no correct answer* to the question of what she will choose. Some philosophers, accordingly, have said that until the choice is made, *there is no truth for God to know* concerning that choice. God knows "everything"—that is, he knows all the truths there are to know—but there just *is no truth* concerning the decision in question. But this means that, with respect to the future of our world, there will be large stretches that, in God's view of them, are blank or at least very indistinct, because what will go on then depends, to a very considerable extent, on these free choices about which there is at present no truth to be known. Many philosophers and theologians, however, reject this conclusion. Some of them reject the whole idea of libertarian free will and insist that everything that happens is the result of God's infallible decrees. (And in that case, there is no question about how God knows what will happen: he knows, because he has predetermined how things will turn out.) Others have claimed that it is entirely possible for it to be true both that (a) it is often entirely possible for a person to choose in any of two or more different ways *and* that (b) God nevertheless knows with certainty in which of those ways the person will in fact choose. This question has given rise to an intense controversy that can only be sampled in a comprehensive text such as this one.

God, it is agreed, is perfectly morally good. But what that implies in more concrete terms is seen differently according to different theologies. Is justice more important as an attribute of God than mercy, or vice versa, or are they both equally important? And what is the relationship between God and morality as we know it in everyday life? Some matters related to this topic are discussed in Part Fourteen of this book.

God as Necessary

One of the more difficult attributes of God to understand is God's *necessity*, or *necessary existence*. This can be approached by contrasting God's existence with that of ourselves and all other created things. We human beings, along with other animals, trees, rocks, mountains, and so on, all depend on other things in order to exist. We need food, shelter, and protection, and we would not exist at all without the parents that brought us into this world, and their parents before them. The same is true of other animals; plants come from seeds that come from other plants, and so on. Even mountains are dependent on the geological processes that brought them into being, and they will eventually be worn down by processes of erosion. That is to say, all these beings are *contingent*–they *might or might not exist*, and their existence is dependent on all manner of other things. And of course, if theism is true, then all of this depends upon God, who has created it and sustains it in existence from moment to moment. But nothing like this is true of God. God did not come into existence, he needs nothing outside of himself in order to exist, and nothing whatever can threaten or endanger his existence. God, we may say, is a *necessary being*; it is impossible that God should not exist. But how are we to understand this "necessity"? It's not as though something forces God to exist; quite the contrary. Many have compared it to logical or mathematical necessity, like the necessity that two plus two equals four, but others have considered this comparison inappropriate. The topic continues to be discussed, and it is sampled briefly in this section.

God as Eternal

Everyone says that God is eternal, but two very different conceptions of eternity are in play. Probably the majority view in the history of theology is that God is eternal in the sense of being *timeless*; for God, there is no "before" and "after," but all things and events are experienced by God as if in a single "present moment." This is a difficult idea to grasp; it means that all of the actions and events that, as of now, lie in your future, are nevertheless timelessly "present" to God in God's eternity. In recent times, however, support has been growing for the view that God is *everlasting*: God always has existed and always will exist, but God experiences the events of time one after another, just as we do. A number of thinkers have alleged that if we fail to see God as living and acting in time, we undermine the biblical message of God's working in history on behalf of human beings.

ALTERNATIVES TO THE THEISTIC GOD

All of these questions pertain to the traditional, theistic conception of God. But there are also alternative conceptions that are important for us to understand. A view that has become somewhat popular in both Christian and Jewish circles is entitled *process theism*. This view, which is heavily dependent on the philosophy of Alfred North Whitehead, is similar to traditional theism in many ways, but its conception of God's relationship to the world is strikingly different. God does not, on this view, create the world out of nothing; rather he *guides the development* of a reality distinct from God, a reality that is eternally in being. According to *process theism*, God is not omnipotent in the traditional sense. God does not unilaterally control anything that happens in the world; however, God can influence the world and "lure" it to develop in the direction he desires it to go. This view brings with it some advantages; for instance, if God has less control than has often been thought, God is less responsible for the evil that takes place in the world. But it also means that God is less able to act on behalf of human beings and others than he has generally been thought to be. Process theism is represented in this text by the selection from Cobb and Griffin in Part Eight, on divine action.

Still more distant from the traditional theistic conception is the *monistic* or *pantheistic* view that is characteristic of some varieties (but not all) of Hinduism. One version of this view holds that Brahman, the sole ultimate reality, is an impersonal unity that underlies the entire universe with all its multiplicity and variety—a multiplicity and variety that are understood by the enlightened to be ultimately illusory.

The first selection is by John Hick, and concerns God's necessary existence. Hick reviews the conception of God's existence as logically necessary, as discussed by J. N. Findlay. Hick agrees with Findlay that this conception is logically incoherent. (The reader should be aware, however, that this conclusion is controversial. A good many philosophers affirm and defend a conception very like the one that Hick and Findlay are rejecting.) Instead, Hick proposes the idea of "ontological or factual necessity" as better capturing the concept of God held by the writers of the Bible.

Next in order is a selection from Moses Maimonides, probably the greatest Jewish scholar and theologian of the Middle Ages. (There is a Jewish saying, "From Moses to Moses, there is no one like Moses.") In it Maimonides develops a rather extreme version of *negative theology*. Negative theology expresses the idea that, because God is so radically different from human beings and from all created things, any statement we make about God in human language is misleading and contains more falsehood than truth. So the path of spiritual wisdom is best followed by the person who comes to realize this and who knows that the attributes we ascribe to God are not actually true of him; the truest way to speak of God is to say what God is *not*. It should be noted, however, that Maimonides continued to make use of the Jewish Bible, which does speak freely about God in terms of human language!

From the greatest medieval Jewish theologian, we move on to the greatest medieval Christian thinker, Thomas Aquinas. In this selection, Thomas confronts the difficulties involved in explaining God's omnipotence. God cannot, according to Thomas, do things that involve a contradiction; such actions are "absolutely impossible," and it would not make sense to ascribe them to God. Nor can God sin, for sin falls short of a perfect action, and to be able to sin is to be able to fall short of perfection—and for God, the perfect being, this is impossible.

Continuing on the subject of omnipotence, George Mavrodes confronts one of the many puzzles philosophers have contrived in order to test the definition of that attribute. Can God create a stone that God cannot lift? Making something one cannot lift certainly seems to be a possible action; home builders, for instance, do this on a regular basis. So if God cannot create such a stone, there is something God cannot do. But if God were able to make such a stone, God would be unable to lift it, and still there would be something God cannot do. Mavrodes argues, however, that this dilemma can be resolved and that Aquinas's definition of omnipotence stands the test of the example.

The next article, by Nelson Pike, touched off a revival of interest in an old argument to the effect that if God exists and is omniscient, then no human action is free or voluntary. Pike seems to have shown that if certain additional assumptions are made, the argument is successful. Pike, however, does not himself endorse the conclusion of the argument; he suggests that the conclusion can be avoided by rejecting some of the additional assumptions made in the argument. But all of those assumptions seem fairly plausible, so the argument presents a formidable challenge to anyone who would reject its conclusion.

The selection from Boethius, one of the important Christian thinkers of the early Middle Ages, is a classic presentation of the notion of divine eternity as *timelessness*. According to his often-quoted definition, "eternity is the complete possession of an endless life enjoyed as one simultaneous whole." For God, then, nothing is past and nothing is future; all objects and events are present *now*—in the "now" of God's eternity. Furthermore, God's knowledge "views with its own simple comprehension all things as if they were taking place in the present." And this, according to Boethius and many others, resolves the difficult problem of combining free will with divine knowledge of the future posed by Pike in the preceding article. Just as you or I, by seeing that another person is sitting down, do not force that person to be sitting rather than standing, in the same way, God, by seeing in eternity what we are doing, does not force us to act as we do.

The following selection, by the contemporary Christian philosopher Nicholas Wolterstorff, argues that the view of God as timeless is inadequate and should be rejected. His primary reason for this is the biblical accounts in which God acts and responds to human actions. According to Wolterstorff, the view of God as timeless cannot in the end make sense of these accounts. God, then, must be seen as temporal rather than timeless; but God is the Lord of time, and the whole array of temporal events lie within his power.

The final selection comes from a Hindu sacred text, the *Chandoya Upanishad*, and presents the view that the sole ultimate reality is the impersonal underlying unity, Brahman. This view is presented in the form of a conversation between a young student and his father and teacher, who seeks to awaken in him the realization that in his deepest self, the student's soul (*Atman*) is identical with the world-all or *Brahman*.

John Hick

God's Necessary Existence

Theists commonly hold that God is a *necessary being*, one that could not possibly fail to exist. But in what sense is God's existence necessary? John Hick (b. 1922) is one of the best-known philosophers of religion in the past half century. In this essay, he agrees with J. N. Findlay that it does not make sense to say that God's existence is logically necessary. However, Hick distinguishes *logical necessity* from *ontological* or *factual necessity* and holds that the latter is correctly attributed to God.

I

The two concepts of "necessary being" or "necessary existence" employ the quite distinct notions of logical necessity and ontological or factual necessity.

Consider first the notion of logical necessity, and its much discussed application by J. N. Findlay to the question of divine existence. In contemporary philosophical literature to say that a given proposition is logically true, or logically necessary, or analytic, is generally intended to signify that it is true by virtue of the meanings of the terms which compose it. Applying this usage in theology, to say that God has (logically) necessary being, or that his existence is (logically) necessary, would be to say that the meaning of "God" is such that the proposition "God

exists" is a logical, analytic, or a priori truth; or again that the proposition "God does not exist" is a self-contradiction, a statement of such a kind that it is logically impossible for it to be true. It is an implication of this contemporary empiricist view of logical necessity as analytic that an existential proposition (i.e., a value of the propositional function "x exists") cannot be logically necessary. On this view, the correct analysis of "a exists" is that the concept of a is instantiated; and the role of the word "exists" is to register this assertion. Such an analysis implies that existence cannot properly be included among the defining properties of a—except of course in the trivial sense that only existing entities can be instances of anything. Thus within the thought-world of modern empiricism the notion of logically necessary existence is not admissible, and cannot be employed as the foundation of a valid theistic argument.

This fact is used by J. N. Findlay in his much discussed article, "Can God's Existence Be Disproved?" (and often reprinted), as the foundation of a strict disproof of divine existence. Findlay puts the ontological argument into reverse by contending that the concept of a deity whose existence is logically necessary, so far from guaranteeing the existence of an entity corresponding to it, is such as to guarantee that nothing corresponds to it.

Findlay defines the concept of God as that of the adequate object of religious attitudes, a religious attitude being described as one in which we tend "to abase ourselves before some object, to defer to it wholly, to devote ourselves to it with unquestioning enthusiasm, to bend the knee before it, whether literally or metaphorically."[1] Such an attitude is rationally adopted only by one who believes that the object to which he thus relates himself as a worshiper has certain very remarkable characteristics. Findlay lists the most important of these characteristics. First, an adequate object of religious attitudes must be conceived as being infinitely superior to ourselves in value or worth. (Accordingly, Findlay refers to this object as "he" rather than as "it.") Second, he must be conceived as being unique: God must not merely be one of a class of beings of the same kind, but must stand in an asymmetrical relationship to all other objects as the source of whatever value they may have. Third, says Findlay, the adequate object of religious attitudes must be conceived as not merely happening to exist, but as existing necessarily; if he merely happened to exist, he would not be worthy of the full and unqualified attitude of worship. And fourth, this being must be conceived as not merely happening to possess his various characteristics, but as possessing them in some necessary manner. For our present purpose we may conflate these two necessities, necessary existence and the necessary possession of properties, and treat them as one. It should be borne in mind throughout that in Findlay's argument "necessary" means "logically necessary."

It is the last two in his list of requirements that provide the ground for Findlay's ontological disproof of theism. "For if God is to satisfy religious claims and needs, he must be a being in every way inescapable, one whose existence and whose possession of certain excellencies we cannot possibly conceive away. And modern views make it self-evidently absurd (if they don't make it ungrammatical) to speak of such a Being and attribute existence to him."[2] For no propositions of the form "x exists" can be analytically true. Hence, Findlay argues, the concept of an adequate object of religious attitudes, involving as it does the notion of a necessarily existent being who possesses his characteristic in some necessary manner, is a self-contradictory concept. We can know a priori, from inspection of the idea itself, that there is and can be no such being.

We may distinguish in Findlay's argument a philosophical premise to the effect that no existential proposition can be an analytic truth, and a theological premise to the effect that an adequate object of religious worship must be such that it is logically necessary that he exists. Of these two premises, I suggest that the former should be accepted but the latter rejected. We must deny, that is to say, the theological doctrine that God must be conceived, if at all, in such a way that "God exists" is a logically necessary truth. We must deny this for precisely the same reason as Findlay, namely, that the demand that "God exists" should be a necessary truth is like the demand that a circle should be square, not a proper demand at all but a misuse of language. Only, whereas Findlay concludes that the notion of an adequate object of religious attitudes is an absurdity, we should conclude that that of which the idea is an absurdity cannot be an adequate object of religious attitudes; it would on the contrary be an unqualifiedly inadequate object of worship.

Let us then ask the question, which seems highly appropriate at this point, as to how religious persons actually think of the Being whom they regard as the adequate object of their worship. What aspect of the Judeo-Christian experience of God lies behind the idea of necessary being?

The concept of God held by the biblical writers was based upon their experience of God as awesome power and holy will confronting them and drawing them into the sphere of his ongoing purpose. God was known as a dynamic will interacting with their own wills; a sheer given reality, as inescapably to be reckoned with as destructive storm and life-giving sunshine, the fixed contours of the land, or the hatred of their enemies and the friendship of their neighbors. God was not for them an inferred entity; he was an experienced reality. The biblical writers were (sometimes, although doubtless not at all times) as vividly conscious of being in God's presence as they were of living in a material environment. Their pages resound and vibrate with the sense of God's presence, as a building might resound and vibrate from the tread of some great being walking through it. They thought of this holy Presence as unique—as the maker and ruler of the universe, the sole rightful sovereign of men and angels, eternal and infinite, and as the ultimate reality and determining power, in relation to whom his creatures have no standing except as the objects of his grace. But nowhere in the biblical thought about God is use made of the idea of logical necessity. The notion is quite foreign to the characteristically Hebraic and concrete utterances found in the Bible, and forms no part of the biblical concept or concepts of God.

But, it might be said, was it not to the biblical writers inconceivable that God should not exist, or that he should cease to exist, or should lose his divine powers and attributes? Would it not be inconceivable to them that God might one day go out of existence, or cease to be good and become evil? And does not this attitude involve an implicit belief that God exists necessarily and possesses his divine characteristics in some necessary manner? The answer, I think, is that it was to the biblical writers psychologically inconceivable—as we say colloquially, unthinkable—that God might not exist, or that his nature might undergo change. They were so vividly conscious of God that they were unable to doubt his reality, and they relied so firmly upon his integrity and faithfulness that they could not contemplate his becoming other than they knew him to be. They would have allowed as a verbal concession only that there might possibly be no God; for they were convinced that they were at many times directly aware of his presence and of his dealings with them. But the question whether the nonexistence of God is

logically inconceivable, or logically impossible, is a philosophical puzzle which could not be answered by the prophets and apostles out of their own first-hand religious experience. This does not of course represent any special limitation of the biblical figures. The logical concept of necessary being cannot be given in religious experience. It is a product—as Findlay argues, a malformed product—of reflection. A religious person's reply to the question, Is God's existence logically necessary? will be determined by his view of the nature of logical necessity; and this is not part of his religion but of his system of logic. The biblical writers do not display any view of the nature of logical necessity, and would doubtless have regarded the topic as of no religious significance. It cannot reasonably be claimed, then, that logically necessary existence was part of their conception of the adequate object of human worship.

Nevertheless, the biblical tradition, in its subsequent theological development, does contain an increasingly explicit "understanding of" God as necessary being. In this concept it is not logical but ontological or factual necessity that is attributed to the object of man's worship. More than one type of nonlogical necessity have been distinguished in philosophical literature. Kant, for example, speaks in the *Critique of Pure Reason* of "material necessity in existence (*die materiale Notwendigkeit im Dasein*) and not merely formal and logical necessity in the connection of concepts" (2d ed., p. 279), this material necessity being equivalent to what is sometimes termed causal necessity, i.e., participation in the universal causal system of nature. Kant also speaks in the same work of another kind of factual necessity when he treats of the three modal categories of possibility, existence, and necessity. He derives the latter from the necessary or analytic proposition in formal logic; but its schema in time is the existence of an object throughout all time (2d ed., p. 184). This notion of necessary existence as existence throughout all time suggests the idea of a temporally unlimited Being, and this is an important part, although, not the whole, of the concept of divine existence as ontologically necessary. The concept first appears in Anselm, in *Proslogion* III and especially in his *Reply* to Gaunilo. In

Proslogion III, we read that "it is possible to conceive of a being which cannot be conceived not to exist." As most naturally understood by a twentieth-century philosopher, "a being which cannot be conceived not to exist" would be presumed to mean "a being whose nonexistence is logically inconceivable, i.e., logically impossible, or self-contradictory." However, when we turn to Anselm's *Reply* to Gaunilo, we find that he states explicitly what he means by the notion of beings which can and which cannot be conceived not to exist. "All those objects, and those alone," he says, "can be conceived not to exist, which have a beginning or end or composition of parts: also ... whatever at any place or at any time does not exist as a whole. That being alone, on the other hand, cannot be conceived not to exist, in which any conception discovers neither beginning nor end nor composition of parts (*nec initium nec finem nec partium conjunctionem*), and which any conception finds always and everywhere as a whole."[3]

Here we have something quite different from the distinctively modern thought of "God exists" as a logically necessary truth. We have instead the essence of the contrasting notion of God as sheer, ultimate, unconditioned reality, without origin or end.

Thomas Aquinas also uses the term "necessary being" and uses it, I believe, in the sense of ontological or factual necessity. The conclusion of the Third Way is that "there must exist something the existence of which is necessary (*oportet aliquid esse necessarium in rebus*)."[4] In the preceding argument the mark of contingency is transiency or temporal finitude; and, by contrast, the mark of noncontingency, or of the necessary being of God, is existence without beginning or end—in other words, eternal being.

Another, and indeed more fundamental, aspect of the distinctively theological form of ontological or factual necessity is contributed by Anselm in the *Monologion*, where he draws the distinction between existence *a se* and existence *ab alio*. He says of God, "The supreme Substance, then, does not exist through any efficient agent, and does not derive existence from any matter, and was not aided in being brought into existence by any external causes. Nevertheless, it by no means exists through

nothing, or derives existence from nothing; since, through itself and from itself, it is whatever it is" (*per seipsam et ex seipsa est quidquid est*). Thus, aseity (*a se esse*) is central to the notion of the necessary being of God.

From God's aseity, or ontic independence, his eternity, indestructibility, and incorruptibility can be seen to follow. A self-existent being must be eternal, i.e., without temporal limitation. For if he had begun to exist, or should cease to exist, he must have been caused to exist, or to cease to exist, by some power other than himself; and this would be inconsistent with his aseity. By the same token, he must be indestructible, for to say that he exists in total ontic independence is to say that there is and could be no reality able to constitute or to destroy him; and likewise he must be incorruptible, for otherwise his aseity would be qualified as regards its duration.

Again, to refer back to Findlay's discussion, it is meaningless to say of the self-existent being that he might not have existed or that he merely happens to exist. For what could it mean to say of the eternal, uncreated Creator of everything other than himself that he "merely happens to exist"? When we assert of a dependent and temporarily finite being, such as myself, that I only happen to exist, we mean that if such-and-such an event had occurred in the past, or if such-and-such another event had failed to occur, I should not now exist. But no such meaning can be given to the statement, "A self-existent being only happens to exist," or "might not have existed." There is no conceivable event such that if it had occurred, or failed to occur, a self-existent being would not have existed; for the concept of aseity is precisely the exclusion of such dependence. There is and could be nothing that would have prevented a self-existent being from coming to exist, for it is meaningless even to speak of a self-existent being as *coming* to exist.

What may properly be meant, then, by the statement that God is, or has, necessary rather than contingent being is that God *is*, without beginning or end, and without origin, cause, or ground of any kind whatsoever. He *is*, as the ultimate, unconditioned, absolute, unlimited reality.

NOTES

1. *Mind*, vol. 57, no. 226 (April 1948), p. 177. Reprinted in Antony Flew and Alasdair MacIntyre, eds., *New Essays in Philosophical Theology* (London: SCM, 1955), p. 49.
2. Ibid., p. 55.
3. Ch. IV. Cf. Ch. I.
4. *Summa theologica*, Pt. I. Q. 2, Arg. 3. For support for the nonlogical interpretation of *necessarium* here see Peter Geach in *Three Philosophers*, by Anscombe and Geach (Oxford, England: Blackwell, 1961), pp. 114–115.

STUDY QUESTIONS

1. According to Hick, the Bible supports the idea of God as a "necessary Being." What is it that the Bible says that provides a basis for this conclusion?
2. What does it mean to say that a being's existence is logically necessary? Why does Hick (in agreement with Findlay) hold that God's existence is not logically necessary?
3. What is meant by saying that God's existence is "ontologically or factually necessary"? Why does Hick think that this is the right way to understand God's "necessary existence"?

Moses Maimonides

Negative Theology

Moses Maimonides (1135–1204) develops an approach to the nature of God known as the *via negativa*—the "way of negation." On this view, the correct way of characterizing God is by means of negations: we can say what God *is* only by saying what God is *not*. According to Maimonides, those who think God can be described through positive attributes have been misled by the "external sense" of biblical texts. But "the Torah speaketh in the language of the sons of man," and a correct understanding will recognize that the positive attributes ascribed to God in Scripture are not truly descriptive of God himself. Since the only correct description of God is by means of negations, an interesting result follows for the growth of religious knowledge: to grow in the knowledge of God is precisely to increase in the number of attributes one realizes *cannot* be ascribed to God.

The reasons that led those who believe in the existence of attributes belonging to the Creator to this belief are akin to those that led those who believe in the doctrine of His corporeality to that belief. For he who believes in this doctrine was not led to it by intellectual speculation; he merely followed the external sense of the texts of the Scriptures. This is also the case with regard to the attributes. For inasmuch as the books of the prophets and the revealed books existed, which predicated attributive qualifications of Him, may He be exalted, these were taken in their literal sense; and He was believed to possess attributes. The people in question have, as it were, divested God of corporeality but not of the modes of corporeality, namely, the accidents—I mean the aptitudes of the soul, all of which are qualities. For with regard to every attribute that the believer in attributes considers to be essential in respect to God, may He be exalted, you will find that the notion of it is that of a quality, even if these people do not state it clearly; for they in fact liken the attribute in question to what they meet with in the various states of all bodies endowed with an animal soul. Of all this it is said: *The Torah speaketh in the language of the sons of man.* The purpose for which all these attributes are used is to predicate perfection of Him, but not the particular

From *Guide of the Perplexed*, trans. S. Pines (Chicago; University of Chicago Press, 1963), Chapters 53, 58, 59. Reprinted by permission.

notion that is a perfection with respect to creatures possessing a soul. Most of these attributes are attributes pertaining to His diverse actions. Now there need not be a diversity in the notions subsisting in an agent because of the diversity of his various actions. Of this I shall give you an instance taken from things that are to be found with us—I mean an example of the fact that though an agent is one, diverse actions may proceed from him, even if he does not possess will and all the more if he acts through will. An instance of this is fire: it melts some things, makes others hard, cooks and burns, bleaches and blackens. Thus if some man would predicate of fire that it is that which bleaches and blackens, which burns and cooks, which makes hard and which melts, he would say the truth. Accordingly he who does not know the nature of fire thinks that there subsist in it six diverse notions, by means of one of which it blackens, whereas it bleaches by means of another, cooks by means of a third, burns by means of a fourth, melts by means of a fifth, and makes hard by means of a sixth—all these actions being opposed to one another, for the meaning of any one of them is different from that of any other. However, he who knows the nature of fire, knows that it performs all these actions by virtue of one active quality, namely, heat. If, however, such a state of affairs exists with respect to a thing acting by virtue of its nature, it exists all the more with respect to one who acts through will, and again all the more with respect to Him, may He be exalted, who is above every attributive qualification. We have grasped with regard to Him relations having corresponding diverse notions—for the notion of knowledge is in us other than the notion of power, and the latter other than the notion of will. Yet how can we regard as a necessary consequence of this the subsistence in Him of diverse notions that are essential to Him, so that there would subsist in Him something by virtue of which He knows as well as something by virtue of which He wills and something by virtue of which He has power, for this is the meaning of the attributes whose existence is asserted by the people in question? Some of them state this clearly, enumerating the notions that are superadded to the essence. Others belonging to them do not state this clearly; however it is quite clear in their belief, even if it is not expressed

in comprehensible language. This is the case when some of them assert that He possesses power because of His essence, possesses knowledge because of His essence, is living because of His essence, possesses will because of His essence.

I shall illustrate this by the example of the rational faculty subsisting in man. It is one faculty with regard to which no multiplicity is posited. Through it he acquires the sciences and the arts; through the same faculty he sews, carpenters, weaves, builds, has a knowledge of geometry, and governs the city. Those very different actions, however, proceed from one, simple faculty in which no multiplicity is posited. Now these actions are very different, and their number is almost infinite—I mean the number of the arts brought forth by the rational faculty. It accordingly should not be regarded as inadmissible in reference to God, may He be magnified and honored, that the diverse actions proceed from one simple essence in which no multiplicity is posited and to which no notion is superadded. Every attribute that is found in the books of the deity, may He be exalted, is therefore an attribute of His action and not an attribute of His essence, or it is indicative of absolute perfection....

Know that the description of God, may He be cherished and exalted, by means of negations is the correct description—a description that is not affected by an indulgence in facile language and does not imply any deficiency with respect to God in general or in any particular mode. On the other hand, if one describes Him by means of affirmations, one implies, as we have made clear, that He is associated with that which is not He and implies a deficency in Him. I must make it clear to you in the first place how negations are in a certain respect attributes and how they differ from the affirmative attributes. After that I shall make it clear to you that we have no way of describing Him unless it be through negations and not otherwise.

I shall say accordingly that an attribute does not particularize any object of which it is predicated in such a way that it is not associated by virtue of that particular attribute with other things. On the contrary, the attribute is sometimes attributed to the object of which it is predicated in spite of the fact that the latter has it in common with other things and is not particularized through it. For instance, if you would see a man at some distance and if you would ask: What is this thing that is seen? and were told: This is a living being—this affirmation would indubitably be an attribute predicated of the thing seen though it does not particularize the latter, distinguishing it from everything else. However, a certain particularization is achieved through it; namely, it may be learnt from it that the thing seen is not a body belonging to the species of plants or to that of the minerals. Similarly if there were a man in this house and you knew that some body is in it without knowing what it is and would ask, saying: What is in this house? and the one who answered you would say: There is no mineral in it and no body of a plant—a certain particularization would be achieved and you would know that a living being is in the house though you would not know which animal. Thus the attributes of negation have in this respect something in common with the attributes of affirmation, for the former undoubtedly bring about some particularization even if the particularization due to them only exists in the exclusion of what has been negated from the sum total of things that we had thought of as not being negated. Now as to the respect in which the attributes of negation differ from the attributes of affirmation: The attributes of affirmation, even if they do not particularize, indicate a part of the thing the knowledge of which is sought, that part being either a part of its substance or one of its accidents; whereas the attributes of negation do not give us knowledge in any respect whatever of the essence the knowledge of which is sought, unless this happens by accident as in the example we have given.

After this preface, I shall say that it has already been demonstrated that God, may He be honored and magnified, is existent of necessity and that there is no composition in Him, as we shall demonstrate, and that we are only able to apprehend the fact that He is and cannot apprehend His quiddity. It is consequently impossible that He should have affirmative attributes. For he has no "That" outside of His "What," and hence an attribute cannot be indicative of one of the two; all the more His "What" is not compound so that an attribute cannot be indicative of its two parts; and all the more, He cannot have accidents so that an attribute cannot be indicative of them.

Accordingly He cannot have an affirmative attribute in any respect.

As for the negative attributes, they are those that must be used in order to conduct the mind toward that which must be believed with regard to Him, may He be exalted, for no notion of multiplicity can attach to Him in any respect on account of them; and, moreover, they conduct the mind toward the utmost reach that man may attain in the apprehension of Him, may He be exalted. For instance, it has been demonstrated to us that it is necessary that something exists other than those essences apprehended by means of the senses and whose knowledge is encompassed by means of the intellect. Of this thing we say that it exists, the meaning being that its nonexistence is impossible. We apprehend further that this being is not like the being of the elements, for example, which are dead bodies. We say accordingly that this being is living, the meaning being that He, may He be exalted, is not dead. We apprehend further that this being is not like the being of the heaven, which is a living body. We say accordingly that He is not a body. We apprehend further that this being is not like the being of the intellect which is neither a body nor dead, but is caused. We say accordingly that He, may He be exalted, is eternal, the meaning being that He has no cause that has brought Him into existence. We apprehend further that the existence of this being, which is its essence, suffices not only for His being existent, but also for many other existents flowing from it, and that this overflow—unlike that of heat from fire and unlike the proceeding of light from the sun—is an overflow that, as we shall make clear, constantly procures for those existents duration and order by means of wisely contrived governance. Accordingly we say of Him, because of these notions, that He is powerful and knowing and willing. The intention in ascribing these attributes to Him is to signify that He is neither powerless nor ignorant nor inattentive nor negligent. Now the meaning of our saying that He is not powerless is to signify that His existence suffices for the bringing into existence of things other than He. The meaning of our saying that He is not ignorant is to signify that He apprehends—that is, is living, for every apprehending thing is living. And the meaning of our saying that He is not inattentive or negligent is to signify that all the existent things in question proceed from their cause according to a certain order and governance—not in a neglected way so as to be generated as chance would have it, but rather as all the things are generated that a willing being governs by means of purpose and will. We apprehend further that no other thing is like that being. Accordingly our saying that He is one signifies the denial of multiplicity.

It has thus become clear to you that every attribute that we predicate of Him is an attribute of action or, if the attribute is intended for the apprehension of His essence and not of His action, it signifies the negation of the privation of the attribute in question. Moreover, even those negations are not used with reference to or applied to Him, may He be exalted, except from the following point of view, which you know: one sometimes denies with reference to a thing something that cannot fittingly exist in it. Thus we say of a wall that it is not endowed with sight. Now you who read this Treatise with speculative intent know that whereas this heaven is a moving body of which we have measured the cubits and inches and in regard to which we have moreover achieved knowledge of the dimension of certain of its parts and of most of its movements, our intellects are quite incapable of apprehending its quiddity. And this, in spite of our knowing that it has of necessity matter and form, for its matter is not like that which is in us. For this reason we are unable to predicate of it any attributes except in terms whose meaning is not completely understood, but not by means of affirmations that are completely understood. Accordingly we say that the heavens are neither light nor heavy nor acted upon and consequently not receptive to external impressions, that they have no taste and no smell; and we make other negations of this kind. All this is due to our ignorance with regard to that matter.

What then should be the state of our intellects when they aspire to apprehend Him who is without matter and is simple to the utmost degree of simplicity, Him whose existence is necessary, Him who has no cause and to whom no notion attaches that is superadded to His essence, which is perfect—the meaning of its perfection being, as we have made clear, that all deficiences are negated with respect to

it—we who only apprehend the fact that He is? There is accordingly an existent whom none of the existent things that He has brought into existence resembles, and who has nothing in common with them in any respect; in reference to whom there is no multiplicity or incapacity to bring into existence things other than He; whose relation to the world is that of a captain to his ship. Even this is not the true relation and a correct likeness, for this likeness has been used in order to lead the mind toward the view that He, may He be exalted, governs the existent things, the meaning of this being that He procures their existence and watches over their order as it ought to be watched over. This notion will be made clear more completely than it is here.

Glory then to Him who is such that when the intellects contemplate His essence, their apprehension turns into incapacity; and when they contemplate the proceeding of His actions from His will, their knowledge turns into ignorance; and when the tongues aspire to magnify Him by means of attributive qualifications, all eloquence turns into weariness and incapacity!

Someone may ask and say: If there is no device leading to the apprehension of the true reality of His essence and if demonstration proves that it can only be apprehended that He exists and that it is impossible, as has been demonstrated, to ascribe to Him affirmative attributes, in what respect can there be superiority or inferiority between those who apprehend Him? If, however, there is none, *Moses our Master* and *Solomon* did not apprehend anything different from what a single individual among the pupils apprehends, and there can be no increase in this knowledge.

Now it is generally accepted by the men of the Law, nay even by the philosophers, that there exist numerous differences of degree in this respect. Know, therefore, that this is indeed so and that the differences of degree between those who apprehend are very great indeed. For the thing of which attributes are predicated becomes more particularized with every increase in attributes that are predicated of it, and he who predicates these attributes accordingly comes nearer to the apprehension of the true reality of the thing in question. In a similar way, you come nearer to the apprehension of Him, may He be exalted, with every increase in the negations regarding Him; and you come nearer to that apprehension than he who does not negate with regard to Him that which, according to what has been demonstrated to you, must be negated. For this reason a man sometimes labors for many years in order to understand some science and to gain true knowledge of its premises so that he should have certainty with regard to this science, whereas the only conclusion from this science in its entirety consists in our negating with reference to God some notion of which it has been learnt by means of a demonstration that it cannot possibly be ascribed to God. To someone else who falls short in his knowledge of speculation, this demonstration will not be clear; and he will consider it doubtful whether or not this notion exists with reference to God. Again another one belonging to those who are struck with intellectual blindness ascribes to Him that notion which has been demonstrated should rather be negated with reference to Him. For instance, I shall demonstrate that He is not a body, whereas another

man will doubt and not know whether or not He is a body, and a third one will categorically decide that He is a body and will seek to approach God by means of this belief. How great is the difference between the three individuals! The first is undoubtedly nearer to God, while the second is far away from Him, and the third still farther away. Similarly if we may suppose a fourth one to whom the impossibility of affections in Him, may He be exalted, has become clear by demonstration—whereas this was not the case with regard to the first one who denied His corporeality—this fourth individual would undoubtedly be nearer to God than the first. And so on always; so that if an individual exists to whom it has been made clear by demonstration that many things, whose existence with reference to Him or whose proceeding from Him we hold possible, are, on the contrary, impossible with reference to Him, may He be exalted—and this applies of course all the more if we believe that these things are necessarily attached to Him—that individual will undoubtedly be more perfect than we....

STUDY QUESTIONS

1. Why does Maimonides insist that a correct description of God must be in terms of negative statements (negations), rather than in terms of affirmations?
2. Maimonides and other Jewish thinkers do say of God that God is "powerful and knowing and willing." Yet these are positive statements and so (according to him) do not properly apply to God. What is it, then, that is being said about God when these statements are made?

Thomas Aquinas

God Is Omnipotent

Thomas Aquinas (1224–1274), the greatest Christian philosopher-theologian of the Middle Ages, addresses here the question of what it means to say that God is omnipotent. He argues that omnipotence does not imply that God can do what is "impossible absolutely" (such as creating a square circle), because that is to do something contradictory. Nor does omnipotence imply that God can do evil, for to do evil would imply imperfection in God, which contradicts God's perfect nature.

We proceed thus to the Third Article:

Objection 1. It seems that God is not omnipotent. For movement and passiveness belong to everything. But this is impossible for God, since He is immovable, as was said above. Therefore He is not omnipotent.

Obj. 2. Further, sin is an act of some kind. But God cannot sin, nor *deny Himself,* as it is said 2 *Tim.* ii. 13. Therefore He is not omnipotent.

Obj. 3. Further, it is said of God that He manifests His omnipotence *especially by sparing and having mercy*. Therefore the greatest act possible to the divine power is to spare and have mercy. There are things much greater, however, than sparing and having mercy; for example, to create another world, and the like. Therefore God is not omnipotent.

Obj. 4. Further, upon the text, *God hath made foolish the wisdom of this world* (I *Cor.* i. 20), the *Gloss* says: *God hath made the wisdom of this world foolish* by showing those things to be possible which it judges to be impossible. Whence it seems that nothing is to be judged possible or impossible in reference to inferior causes, as the wisdom of this world judges them; but in reference to the divine power. If God, then were omnipotent, all things would be possible; nothing, therefore, impossible. But if we take away the impossible, then we destroy also the necessary; for what necessarily exists cannot possibly not exist. Therefore, there would be nothing at all that is necessary in things if God were omnipotent. But this is an impossibility. Therefore God is not omnipotent.

On the contrary, It is said: *No word shall be impossible with God* (Luke i. 37).

I answer that, All confess that God is omnipotent; but it seems difficult to explain in what His

From *Summa Theologica* by Thomas Aquinas, trans. Fathers of the English Dominican Province (London: R. and T. Washbourne), 1911.

omnipotence precisely consists. For there may be a doubt as to the precise meaning of the word "all" when we say that God can do all things. If, however, we consider the matter aright, since power is said in reference to possible things, this phrase, *God can do all things*, is rightly understood to mean that God can do all things that are possible; and for this reason He is said to be omnipotent. Now according to the Philosopher a thing is said to be possible in two ways. First, in relation to some power; thus whatever is subject to human power is said to be possible to man. Now God cannot be said to be omnipotent through being able to do all things that are possible to created nature; for the divine power extends farther than that. If, however, we were to say that God is omnipotent because He can do all things that are possible to His power, there would be a vicious circle in explaining the nature of His power. For this would be saying nothing else but that God is omnipotent because He can do all that He is able to do.

It remains, therefore, that God is called omnipotent because He can do all things that are possible absolutely; which is the second way of saying a thing is possible. For a thing is said to be possible or impossible absolutely, according to the relation in which the very terms stand to one another: possible, if the predicate is not incompatible with the subject, as that Socrates sits; and absolutely impossible when the predicate is altogether incompatible with the subject, as, for instance, that a man is an ass.

It must, however, be remembered that since every agent produces an effect like itself, to each active power there corresponds a thing possible as its proper object according to the nature of that act on which its active power is founded; for instance, the power of giving warmth is related, as to its proper object, to the being capable of being warmed. The divine being, however, upon which the nature of power in God is founded, is infinite; it is not limited to any class of being, but possesses within itself the perfection of all being. Whence, whatsoever has or can have the nature of being is numbered among the absolute possible, in respect of which God is called omnipotent.

Now nothing is opposed to the notion of being except non-being. Therefore, that which at the same time implies being and non-being is repugnant to the notion of an absolute possible, which is subject to the divine omnipotence. For such cannot come under the divine omnipotence; not indeed because of any defect in the power of God, but because it has not the nature of a feasible or possible thing. Therefore, everything that does not imply a contradiction in terms is numbered among those possibles in respect of which God is called omnipotent; whereas whatever implies contradiction does not come within the scope of divine omnipotence, because it cannot have the aspect of possibility. Hence it is more appropriate to say that such things cannot be done, than that God cannot do them. Nor is this contrary to the word of the angel, saying: *No word shall be impossible with God* (*Luke* i. 37). For whatever implies a contradiction cannot be a word, because no intellect can possibly conceive such a thing.

Reply Obj. 1. God is said to be omnipotent in respect to active power, not to passive power, as was shown above. Whence the fact that He is immovable or impassible is not repugnant to His omnipotence.

Reply Obj. 2. To sin is to fall short of a perfect action; hence to be able to sin is to be able to fall short in action, which is repugnant to omnipotence. Therefore it is that God cannot sin, because of His omnipotence. Now it is true that the Philosopher says that *God can deliberately do what is evil*. But this must be understood either on a condition, the antecedent of which is impossible—as, for instance, if we were to say that God can do evil things if He will. For there is no reason why a conditional proposition should not be true, though both the antecedent and consequent are impossible: as if one were to say: *If man is an ass, he has four feet*. Or he may be understood to mean that God can do some things which now seem to be evil: which, however, if He did them, would then be good. Or he is, perhaps, speaking after the common manner of the pagans, who thought that men became gods, like Jupiter or Mercury.

Reply Obj. 3. God's omnipotence is particularly shown in sharing and having mercy, because in this it is made manifest that God has supreme power, namely, that He freely forgives sins. For it is not for one who is bound by laws of a superior to forgive sins of his own free choice. Or, it is thus shown because by sparing and having mercy upon men, He leads them to the participation of an infinite good; which is the ultimate effect of the divine power. Or it is thus shown because, as was said above, the effect of the divine mercy is the foundation of all the divine works. For nothing is due anyone, except because of something already given him gratuitously by God. In this way the divine omnipotence is particularly made manifest, because to it pertains the first foundation of all good things.

Reply Obj. 4. The absolute possible is not so called in reference either to higher causes, or to inferior causes, but in reference to itself. But that which is called possible in reference to some power is named possible in reference to its proximate cause. Hence those things which it belongs to God alone to do immediately—as, for example, to create, to justify, and the like—are said to be possible in reference to a higher cause. Those things, however, which are such as to be done by inferior causes, are said to be possible in reference to those inferior causes. For it is according to the condition of the proximate cause that the effect has contingency or necessity, as was shown above. Thus it is that the wisdom of the world is deemed foolish, because what is impossible to nature it judges to be impossible to God. So it is clear that the omnipotence of God does not take away from things their impossibility and necessity.

Study Questions

1. When we say that God is omnipotent and can do "all things," why is it necessary to state clearly what is included under the word "all"?
2. Explain as clearly as you can what is meant, according to Aquinas, by saying that God can do everything.
3. One thing that human beings can do is commit sins, and Aquinas (like most other theists) holds that God cannot sin. How does Aquinas reconcile this fact with his claim that God is omnipotent?

George I. Mavrodes

Some Puzzles Concerning Omnipotence

In this article, George Mavrodes (b. 1926) explores the "paradox of the stone," one of a number of puzzles that have been devised by philosophers attempting to clarify the concept of omnipotence. Can God make a stone that he is unable to lift? If he cannot, then there is something he is unable to do. On the other hand, if God can make such a stone, then there is still something he cannot do, namely, lift the stone after he has made it. Mavrodes argues that if God is omnipotent, then the idea of "a stone God cannot lift" is self-contradictory. And as Aquinas has said, omnipotence does not mean that God can do what is self-contradictory.

The doctrine of God's omnipotence appears to claim that God can do anything. Consequently, there have been attempts to refute the doctrine by giving examples of things which God cannot do; for example, He cannot draw a square circle.

Responding to objections of this type, St. Thomas pointed out that "anything" should be here construed to refer only to objects, actions, or states of affairs whose descriptions are not self-contradictory.[1] For it is only such things whose nonexistence might plausibly be attributed to a lack of power in some agent. My failure to draw a circle on the exam may indicate my lack of geometrical skill, but my failure to draw a square circle does not indicate any such lack. Therefore, the fact that it is false (or perhaps meaningless) to say that God could draw one does no damage to the doctrine of His omnipotence.

A more involved problem, however, is posed by this type of question: can God create a stone too heavy for Him to lift? This appears to be stronger than the first problem, for it poses a dilemma. If we say that God can create a stone, then it seems that there might be such a stone. And if there might be a stone too heavy for Him to lift, then He is evidently not omnipotent. But if we deny that God can create such a stone, we seem to have given up His omnipotence already. Both answers lead us to the same conclusion.

Further, this problem does not seem obviously open to St. Thomas' solution. The form "*x* is able to draw a square circle" seems plainly to involve a contradiction, while "*x* is able to make a thing too heavy

Originally published in *Philosophical Review* 72 (1963).

for *x* to lift" does not. For it may easily be true that I am able to make a boat too heavy for me to lift. So why should it not be possible for God to make a stone too heavy for Him to lift?

Despite this apparent difference, this second puzzle *is* open to essentially the same answer as the first. The dilemma fails because it consists of asking whether God can do a self-contradictory thing. And the reply that He cannot does no damage to the doctrine of omnipotence.

The specious nature of the problem may be seen in this way. God is either omnipotent or not.[2] Let us assume first that He is not. In that case the phrase "a stone too heavy for God to lift" may not be self-contradictory. And then, of course, if we assert either that God is able or that He is not able to create such a stone, we may conclude that He is not omnipotent. But this is no more than the assumption with which we began, meeting us again after our roundabout journey. If this were all that the dilemma could establish it would be trivial. To be significant it must derive this same conclusion *from the assumption that God is omnipotent*; that is, it must show that the assumption of the omnipotence of God leads to a *reductio*. But does it?

On the assumption that God is omnipotent, the phrase "a stone too heavy for God to lift" becomes self-contradictory. For it becomes "a stone which cannot be lifted by Him whose power is sufficient for lifting anything." But the "thing" described by a self-contradictory phrase is absolutely impossible and hence has nothing to do with the doctrine of omnipotence. Not being an object of power at all, its failure to exist cannot be the result of some lack in the power of God. And, interestingly, it is the very omnipotence of God which makes the existence of such a stone absolutely impossible, while it is the fact that I am finite in power which makes it possible for me to make a boat too heavy for me to lift.

But suppose that some die-hard objector takes the bit in his teeth and denies that the phrase "a stone too heavy for God to lift" is self-contradictory, even on the assumption that God is omnipotent. In other words, he contends that the description "a stone too heavy for an omnipotent God to lift" is self-coherent and therefore describes an absolutely possible object.

Must I then attempt to prove the contradiction which I assume above as intuitively obvious? Not necessarily. Let me reply simply that if the objector is right in this contention, then the answer to the original question is "Yes, God can create such a stone." It may seem that this reply will force us into the original dilemma. But it does not. For now the objector can draw no damaging conclusion from this answer. And the reason is that he has just now contended that such a stone is compatible with the omnipotence of God. Therefore, from the possibility of God's creating such a stone it cannot be concluded that God is not omnipotent. The objector cannot have it both ways. The conclusion which he himself wishes to draw from an affirmative answer to the original question is itself the required proof that the descriptive phrase which appears there is self-contradictory. And "it is more appropriate to say that such things cannot be done, than that God cannot do them."[3]

The specious nature of this problem may also be seen in a somewhat different way.[4] Suppose that some theologian is convinced by this dilemma that he must give up the doctrine of omnipotence. But he resolves to give up as little as possible, just enough to meet the argument. One way he can do so is by retaining the infinite power of God with regard to lifting, while placing a restriction on the sort of stone He is able to create. The only restriction required here, however, is that God must not be able to create a stone too heavy for Him to lift. Beyond that the dilemma has not even suggested any necessary restriction. Our theologian has, in effect, answered the original question in the negative, and he now regretfully supposes that this has required him to give up the full doctrine of omnipotence. He is now retaining what he supposes to be the more modest remnants which he has salvaged from that doctrine.

We must ask, however, what it is which he has in fact given up. Is it the unlimited power of God to create stones? No doubt. But what stone is it which God is now precluded from creating? The stone too heavy for Him to lift, of course. But we must remember that nothing in the argument required the theologian to admit any limit on God's power with regard to the lifting of stones. He still holds that to be unlimited. And if God's power to lift is infinite, then His power to create may run to infinity also without outstripping that first power. The supposed limitation turns out to be no limitation at all, since it is specified only by reference to another power which is itself infinite. Our theologian need have no regrets, for he has given up nothing. The doctrine of the power of God remains just what it was before.

Nothing I have said above, of course, goes to prove that God is, in fact, omnipotent. All I have intended to show is that certain arguments intended to prove that He is not omnipotent fail. They fail because they propose, as tests of God's power, putative tasks whose descriptions are self-contradictory. Such pseudo-tasks, not falling within the realm of possibility are not objects of power at all. Hence the fact that they cannot be performed implies no limit on the power of God, and hence no defect in the doctrine of omnipotence.

NOTES

1. St. Thomas Aquinas, *Summa Theologiae*, Ia, q. 25, a. 3.
2. I assume, of course, the existence of God, since that is not being brought in question here.
3. St. Thomas Aquinas, *Summa Theologiae*.
4. But this method rests finally on the same logical relations as the preceding one.

STUDY QUESTIONS

1. Mavrodes considers the question, "Can God make a stone he cannot lift?" Explain why this question poses a problem for the doctrine of God's omnipotence.
2. Give a brief but clear explanation of Mavrodes' answer to the question, and explain why (according to him) this puzzle does not undermine the claim that God is omnipotent.

Nelson Pike

Divine Omniscience and Voluntary Action

If God knows the future completely, can human beings be completely free in deciding what to do? In a widely discussed article, Nelson Pike (b. 1930) argues that if God is omniscient, free choice is impossible. Suppose you are making a decision about what flavor of ice cream to have for dessert, and God knew eighty years ago that you would choose strawberry. Is it nevertheless in your power to choose vanilla instead? According to Pike, if it is in your power to choose vanilla, then you also have the power to do one of three additional things, You may have the power to bring about that a belief held by God in the past was false. Or, you may have the power to bring about, retroactively as it were, that God did not in fact have the belief in the past that he actually had. Or perhaps you have the power to bring about, again retroactively, that eighty years ago God did not exist. But none of these seem at all plausible as something that would be in your power as you decide about the ice cream. Pike left this argument as a problem to be worked out by other philosophers and theologians.

In Book V, sec. 3, of his *Consolatio Philosophiae,* Boethius entertained (though he later rejected) the claim that if God is omniscient, no human action is voluntary. This claim seems intuitively false. Surely, given only a doctrine describing God's *knowledge,* nothing about the voluntary status of human actions will follow. Perhaps such a conclusion would follow from a doctrine of divine omnipotence or divine providence, but what connection could there be between the claim that God is *omniscient* and the claim that human actions are determined? Yet Boethius thought he saw a problem here. He thought that if one collected together just the right assumptions and principles regarding God's knowledge, one could derive the conclusion that if God exists, no human action is voluntary. Of course, Boethius did not think that all the assumptions and principles required to reach this conclusion are true (quite the contrary), but he thought it important to draw attention to them nonetheless. If a theologian is to construct a doctrine of God's knowledge which does not commit him to determinism, he must first understand that there is a way of thinking about God's knowledge which would so commit him.

Originally published in *Philosophical Review* 74 (1965).

In this paper, I shall argue that although his claim has a sharp counterintuitive ring, Boethius was right in thinking that there is a selection from among the various doctrines and principles clustering about the notions of knowledge, omniscience, and God which, when brought together, demand the conclusion that if God exists, no human action is voluntary. Boethius, I think, did not succeed in making explicit all of the ingredients in the problem. His suspicions were sound, but his discussion was incomplete. His argument needs to be developed. This is the task I shall undertake in the pages to follow. I should like to make clear at the outset that my purpose in rearguing this thesis is not to show that determinism is true, nor to show that God does not exist, nor to show that either determinism is true or God does not exist. Following Boethius, I shall not claim that the items needed to generate the problem are either philosophically or theologically adequate. I want to concentrate attention on the implications of a certain set of assumptions. Whether the assumptions are themselves acceptable is a question I shall not consider....

Last Saturday afternoon, Jones mowed his lawn. Assuming that God exists and is (essentially) omniscient in the sense outlined above, it follows that (let us say) eighty years prior to last Saturday afternoon, God knew (and thus believed) that Jones would mow his lawn at that time. But from this it follows, I think, that at the time of action (last Saturday afternoon) Jones was not *able*—that is, it was not *within Jones's power*—to refrain from mowing his lawn.[1] If at the time of action, Jones had been able to refrain from mowing his lawn, then (the most obvious conclusion would seem to be) at the time of action, Jones was able to do something which would have brought it about that God held a false belief eighty years earlier. But God cannot in anything be mistaken. It is not possible that some belief of His was false. Thus, last Saturday afternoon, Jones was not able to do something which would have brought it about that God held a false belief eighty years ago. To suppose that it was would be to suppose that, at the time of the action, Jones was able to do something that would have brought it about that one of God's beliefs was false. Hence, given that God believed eighty years ago that Jones would mow his lawn on Saturday, if we are to assign

Jones the power on Saturday to refrain from mowing his lawn, this power must not be described as the power to do something that would have rendered one of God's beliefs false. How then should we describe it vis-a-vis God and His belief? So far as I can see, there are only two other alternatives. First, we might try describing it as the power to do something that would have brought it about that God believed otherwise than He did eighty years ago; or, secondly, we might try describing it as the power to do something that would have brought it about that God (Who, by hypothesis, existed eighty years earlier) did not exist eighty years earlier—that is, as the power to do something that would have brought it about that any person who believed eighty years ago that Jones would mow his lawn on Saturday (one of whom was, by hypothesis, God) held a false belief, and thus was not God. But again, neither of these latter can be accepted. Last Saturday afternoon, Jones was not able to do something that would have brought it about that God believed otherwise than He did eighty years ago. Even if we suppose (as was suggested by Calvin) that eighty years ago God knew Jones would mow his lawn on Saturday in the sense that He "saw" Jones mowing his lawn as if this action were occurring before Him, the fact remains that God knew (and thus believed) eighty years prior to Saturday that Jones would mow his lawn. And if God held such a belief eighty years prior to Saturday, Jones did not have the power on Saturday to do something that would have made it the case that God did not hold this belief eighty years earlier. No action performed at a given time can alter the fact that a given person held a certain belief at a time prior to the time in question. This last seems to be an a priori truth. For similar reasons, the last of the above alternatives must also be rejected. On the assumption that God existed eighty years prior to Saturday, Jones on Saturday was not able to do something that would have brought it about that God did not exist eighty years prior to that time. No action performed at a given time can alter the fact that a certain person existed at a time prior to the time in question. This, too, seems to me to be an a priori truth. But if these observations are correct, then, given that Jones mowed his lawn on Saturday, and given that God exists and is (essentially) omniscient, it seems to follow that at the time of action, Jones did not have the power to refrain from mowing his lawn. The upshot of these reflections would appear to be that Jones's mowing his lawn last Saturday cannot be counted as a voluntary action. Although I do not have an analysis of what it is for an action to be *voluntary*, it seems to me that a situation in which it would be wrong to assign Jones the *ability* or *power* to do *other* than he did would be a situation in which it would also be wrong to speak of his action as voluntary. As a general remark, if God exists and is (essentially) omniscient in the sense specified above, no human action is voluntary.[2]

As the argument just presented is somewhat complex, perhaps the following schematic representation of it will be of some use.

1. "God existed at t_1" entails "If Jones did X at t_2, God believed at t_1 that Jones would do X at t_2."
2. "God believes X" entails "X is true."
3. It is not within one's power at a given time to do something having a description that is logically contradictory.
4. It is not within one's power at a given time to do something that would bring it about that someone who held a certain belief at the time prior to the time in question did not hold that belief at the time prior to the time in question.
5. It is not within one's power at a given time to do something that would bring it about that a person who existed at an earlier time did not exist at that earlier time.
6. If God existed at t_1 and if God believed at t_1 that Jones would do X at t_2 then if it was within Jones's power at t_2 to refrain from doing X, then (1) it was within Jones's power at t_2 to do something that would have brought it about that God held a false belief at t_1 or (2) it was within Jones's power at t_2 to do something which would have brought it about that God did not hold the belief He held at t_1, or (3) it was within Jones's power at t_2 to do something that would have brought it about that any person who believed at t_1 that Jones would do X at t_2 (one of whom was, by hypothesis, God) held a false belief and thus was not God—that is, that God (who by hypothesis existed at t_1) did not exist at t_1.

7. Alternative 1 in the consequent of item 6 is false. (from 2 and 3)
8. Alternative 2 in the consequent of item 6 is false. (from 4)
9. Alternative 3 in the consequent of item 6 is false. (from 5)
10. Therefore, if God existed at t_1 and if God believed at t_1 that Jones would do X at t_2, then it was not within Jones's power at t_2 to refrain from doing X. (from 6 through 9)
11. Therefore, if God existed at t_1, and if Jones did X at t_2, it was not within Jones's power at t_2 to refrain from doing X. (from 1 and 10)

In this argument, items 1 and 2 make explicit the doctrine of God's (essential) omniscience with which I am working. Items 3, 4, and 5 express what I take to be part of the logic of the concept of ability or power as it applies to human beings. Item 6 is offered as an analytic truth. If one assigns Jones the power to refrain from doing X at t_2 (given that God believed at t_1 that he would do X at t_2), so far as I can see, one would have to describe this power in one of the three ways listed in the consequent of item 6. I do not know how to argue that these are the only alternatives, but I have been unable to find another. Item 11, when generalized for all agents and actions, and when taken together with what seems to me to be a minimal condition for the application of "voluntary action," yields the conclusion that if God exists (and is essentially omniscient in the way I have described) no human action is voluntary.

It is important to notice that the argument given in the preceding paragraphs avoids use of two concepts that are often prominent in discussions of determinism.

In the first place, the argument makes no mention of the causes of Jones's action. Say (for example, with St. Thomas)[3] that God's foreknowledge of Jones's action was, itself, the cause of the action (though I am really not sure what this means). Say, instead, that natural events or circumstances caused Jones to act. Even say that Jones's action had no cause at all. The argument outlined above remains unaffected. If eighty years prior to Saturday, God believed that Jones would mow his lawn at that time, it was not within Jones's power at the time of action to refrain from mowing his lawn. The reasoning that justifies this assertion makes no mention of a causal series preceding Jones's action.

Secondly, consider the following line of thinking. Suppose Jones mowed his lawn last Saturday. It was then *true* eighty years ago that Jones would mow his lawn at that time. Hence, on Saturday, Jones was not able to refrain from mowing his lawn. To suppose that he was would be to suppose that he was able on Saturday to do something that would have made false a proposition that was *already true* eighty years earlier. This general kind of argument for determinism is usually associated with Leibniz, although it was anticipated in chapter ix of Aristotle's *De Interpretatione*. It has been used since, with some modification, in Richard Taylor's article, "Fatalism."[4] This argument, like the one I have offered above, makes no use of the notion of causation. It turns, instead, on the notion of its being *true eighty years ago* that Jones would mow his lawn on Saturday.

I must confess that I share the misgivings of those contemporary philosophers who have wondered what (if any) sense can be attached to a statement of the form "It was true at t_1 that E would occur at t_2."[5] Does this statement mean that had someone believed, guessed, or asserted at t_2 that E would occur at t_2, he would have been right?[6] (I shall have something to say about this form of determinism later in this paper.) Perhaps it means that at t_1 there was sufficient evidence upon which to predict that E would occur at t_2.[7] Maybe it means neither of these. Maybe it means nothing at all.[8] The argument presented above presupposes that it makes a straightforward sense to suppose that God (or just anyone) held a true belief eighty years prior to Saturday. But this is not to suppose that *what* God believed *was true eighty years prior to Saturday*. Whether (or in what sense) it was true eighty years ago that Jones would mow his lawn on Saturday is a question I shall not discuss. As far as I can see, the argument in which I am interested requires nothing in the way of a decision on this issue....

To conclude: I have assumed that any statement of the form "A knows X" entails a statement of the form "A believes X" as well as a statement of the form "'X' is true." I have then supposed (as

an analytic truth) that if a given person is omniscient, that person (1) holds no false beliefs, and (2) holds beliefs about the outcome of human actions in advance of their performance. In addition, I have assumed that the statement "If a given person is God that person is omniscient" is an a priori statement. (This last I have labeled the doctrine of God's essential omniscience.) Given these items (plus some premises concerning what is and what is not within one's power), I have argued that if God exists it is not within one's power to do other than [He] does. I have inferred from this that if God exists, no human action is voluntary.

As emphasized earlier, I do not want to claim that the assumptions underpinning the argument are acceptable. In fact, it seems to me that a theologian interested in claiming both that God is omniscient and that men have free will could deny any one (or more) of them. For example, a theologian might deny that a statement of the form "A knows X" entails a statement of the form "A believes X" (some contemporary philosophers have denied this) or, alternatively, he might claim that this entailment holds in the case of human knowledge but fails in the case of God's knowledge. This latter would be to claim that when knowledge is attributed to God, the term "knowledge" bears a sense other than the one it has when knowledge is attributed to human beings. Then again, a theologian might object to the analysis of "omniscience" with which I have been working. Although I doubt if any Christian theologian would allow that an omniscient being could believe something false, he might claim that a given person could be omniscient although he did not hold beliefs about the outcome of human actions *in advance* of their performance. (This latter is the way Boethius escaped the problem.) Still again, a theologian might deny the doctrine of God's essential omniscience. He might admit that if a given person is God that person is omniscient, but he might deny that this statement formulates an a priori truth. This would be to say that although God is omniscient, He is not *essentially* omniscient. So far as I can see, within the conceptual framework of theology employing any one of these adjustments, the problem of divine foreknowledge outlined in this paper could not be formulated. There thus appears to be a rather wide range of alternatives open to the theologian at this point. It would be a mistake to think that commitment to determinism is an unavoidable implication of the Christian concept of divine omniscience.

But having arrived at this understanding, the importance of the preceding deliberations ought not to be overlooked. There is a pitfall in the doctrine of divine omniscience. That knowing involves believing (truly) is surely a tempting philosophical view (witness the many contemporary philosophers who have affirmed it). And the idea that God's attributes (including omniscience) are essentially connected to His nature, together with the idea that an omniscient being would hold no false beliefs and would hold beliefs about the outcome of human actions in advance of their performance, might be taken by some theologians as obvious candidates for inclusion in a finished Christian theology. Yet the theologian must approach these items critically. If they are embraced together, then if one affirms the existence of God, one is committed to the view that no human action is voluntary.

Notes

1. The notion of someone being *able* to do something and the notion of something being *within one's power* are essentially the same. Traditional formulations of the problem of divine foreknowledge (e.g., those of Boethius and Augustine) made use of the notion of what is (and what is not) *within one's power*. But the problem is the same when framed in terms of what one is (and one is not) able to do. Thus, I shall treat the statements "Jones was able to do *X*," "Jones had the ability to do *X*," and "It was within Jones's power to do *X*" as equivalent. Richard Taylor, in "I Can," *Philosophical Review*, 69 (1960): 78–89, has argued that the notion of ability or power involved in these last three statements is incapable of philosophical analysis. Be this as it may, I shall not here attempt such an analysis. In what follows I shall, however, be careful to affirm only those statements about what is (or is not) within one's power that would have to be preserved on any analysis of this notion having even the most distant claim to adequacy.

2. In Bk. II, ch. xxi, secs. 8–11 of *An Essay*, Locke says that an agent is not free with respect to a given action (e.g., that an action is done "under necessity") when it is not within the agent's power to do otherwise. Locke allows a special kind of case, however, in which an action may be *voluntary* though done under necessity. If a man chooses to do something without knowing that it is not within his power to do otherwise (e.g., if a man chooses to stay in a room without knowing that the room is locked), his action may be voluntary though he is not free to forbear it. If Locke is right in this (and I shall not argue the point one way or the other), replace "voluntary" with (let us say) "free" in the above paragraph and throughout the remainder of this paper.

3. Aquinas, *Summa Theologicae*, Pt. I, q. 14, a. 8.

4. Richard Taylor, "Fatalism," *Philosophical Review*, 71 (1962): 56–66. Taylor argues that if an event *E* fails to occur at *t*, then at *t*, it was true *E* would fail to occur at *t*. Thus, at *t*, no one could have the power to perform an action that would be sufficient for the occurrence of *E* at *t*. Hence, no one has the power at *t* to do something sufficient for an event that is not going to happen. The parallel between this argument and the one recited above can be seen very clearly if one reformulates Taylor's argument, pushing back the time at which it was true that *E* would not occur at *t*.

5. For a helpful discussion of difficulties involved here, see Rogers Albritton's "Present Truth and Future Contingency," a reply to Richard Taylor's "The Problem of Future Contingency," both in *Philosophical Review*, 66 (1957): 1–28.

6. Gilbert Ryle interprets it this way. See "It Was to Be," in *Dilemmas* (Cambridge, England, 1954).

7. Richard Gale suggests this interpretation in "Endorsing Predictions," *Philosophical Review*, 70 (1961): 376–85.

8. This view is held by John Turk Saunders in "Sea Fight Tomorrow?" *Philosophical Review*, 67 (1958): 367–78.

Study Questions

1. The subject of Pike's article is the idea that "if God is omniscient [all-knowing], no human action is voluntary." Explain briefly why this claim has seemed plausible to many thinkers of the past and present.

2. Suppose Pike's argument is correct, and it cannot be true both that God knows everything that will happen in the future and that human beings have free will. Which of the following three options would be best for theists to accept? (Give reasons for your answer.)

    A. God's knowledge of the future is limited, not complete.
    B. Humans do not really have free will; everything we do is predestined.
    C. Since we are talking about God and his nature, logical arguments do not apply; we simply do not have to pay attention to the argument given by Pike.

Boethius

God Is Timeless

In this selection, Boethius (c. 480–c. 524) presents the view of God's eternity that has been most widely accepted in Christian theology. According to this view, God lives completely outside of time, in a changeless "eternal now" that contains all of time within itself. Boethius argues that this view of divine timelessness affords an answer to the dilemma of foreknowledge and free will discussed in the previous selection. God, according to this view, does not know *beforehand* what humans will do, for this would place God in the time sequence, and God is not in time. Rather, God know what humans do *eternally*, in his "eternal now," which is simultaneous with every moment of time at which they act. And just as our freedom is not taken away if others know what we do when we do it, neither is it taken away by God's knowing all our actions in his "eternal present."

"Since...everything that is known is apprehended not according to its own nature but according to that of the knower, let us examine now, so far as we lawfully may, what is the state of the divine substance, so that we may be able to learn also what its knowledge is. The common opinion, according to all men living, is that God is eternal. Let us therefore consider what eternity is, for this will make clear to us at the same time the divine nature and the divine knowledge. Now, eternity is the complete possession of an endless life enjoyed as one simultaneous whole; this will appear clearer from a comparison with temporal things. For whatever is living in time proceeds in the present from times past to times future; and nothing existing in time is so constituted as to embrace the whole span of its life at once, but it has not yet grasped tomorrow, while it has already lost yesterday. In this life of today you are living in no more than a fleeting, transitory moment. And so it is with everything that is subject to the condition of time: even if it should never have begun and would never cease to be—which Aristotle believed of the universe—even if its life were to be co-extensive with the infinity of time, yet it could not rightly be held to be eternal. For, even granted that it has an infinite lifetime, it does not embrace this life as a simultaneous

From *The Consolation of Philosophy*, ed. James T. Buchanan (New York: Frederick Ungar, 1957).

whole; it does not now have a grasp of the future, which is yet to be lived through. What is rightly called eternal is that which grasps and possesses simultaneously the entire fullness of an unending life, a life which lacks nothing of the future and has lost nothing of the fleeting past. Such a being must necessarily always be its whole self, unchangingly present to itself, and the infinity of changing time must be as one present before him. Wherefore they are mistaken who, hearing that Plato thought this world had no beginning in time and would have no end, think that in this way the created universe is co-eternal with the Creator. For to pass step by step through an unending life, a process ascribed by Plato to the universe, is one thing; to embrace simultaneously the whole of an unending life in one present, an act manifestly peculiar to the divine mind, is quite another thing. And, further, God should not be regarded as older than His creations by any quantity of time but rather by the peculiar quality of simplicity in His nature. For the infinite motion of temporal things tries to imitate the ever present immobility of His life, does not succeed in copying or equalling it, sinks from immobility into motion, and falls from the simplicity of the present to the infinite stretch of future and past; and since it cannot possess its life completely and simultaneously it seems to emulate, by the very fact that it somehow exists forever without ceasing, what it cannot fully attain and express, clinging as it does to the so-called present of this short and fleeting moment, which, inasmuch as it bears a certain resemblance to that abiding present, makes those to whom it comes appear to exist. But, since this present could not be abiding, it took to the infinite journey through time, and so it has come to pass that, by journeying on, it continues that life the fullness of which it could not grasp by staying. Thus if we would apply proper epithets to these subjects we would say, following Plato, that God is eternal, while the universe is perpetual.

"Since, then, every judgment comprehends the objects of its thought according to its own nature, and since God has an ever present and eternal state, His knowledge also, surpassing every temporal movement, remains in the simplicity of its own present and, embracing infinite lengths of past and future, views with its own simple comprehension all things as if they were taking place in the present. If you will weigh the foresight with which God discerns all things, you will rightly esteem it to be the knowledge of a never fading instant rather than a foreknowledge of the 'future.' It should therefore rather be called *provision* than *prevision* because, placed high above lowly things, it looks out over all as from the loftiest mountain top. Why then do you demand that those things which are translucent to the divine mind's light be necessary if not even men make necessary the things they see? Because you can see present things, does your sight impose upon them any necessity?"

"Surely not."

"Yet, if one may not unworthily compare the human present with the divine, just as you see certain things in this, your temporal present, so God sees all things in His eternal present. Wherefore this divine foreknowledge does not change the nature or properties of things: it sees things present to its contemplation just as they will turn out some time in the future. Neither is there any confusion in its judgment of things: with one glimpse of the mind it distinguishes what will happen necessarily and what will happen non-necessarily. For example, when you observe at the same time a man walking on the earth and the sun rising in the sky, although you see both sights simultaneously, nevertheless you distinguish between them and judge that the one is moving voluntarily, the other necessarily; in like manner the intuition of God looks down upon all things without at all disturbing their nature, yet they are present to Him and future in relation to time. Wherefore it is not opinion but knowledge grounded in truth when He knows that something will occur in the future and knows as well that it will not occur of necessity. If you say at this point that what God sees as about to happen cannot but happen and that what cannot but happen happens, and you pin me down to this definition of necessity, I will confess a matter of the firmest truth but one which scarcely any one save a contemplator of the divine can reach: i.e., I shall answer that one and the same future event is necessary with respect to God's knowledge of it but absolutely free and unrestrained when it is examined in its own nature.

"For there are two kinds of necessity. One is simple: for instance, it is necessary that all men are mortal. The other is conditional: for instance, if you really know that a man is walking, he must be walking. For what a man really knows cannot be otherwise than it is known to be. But the conditional kind of necessity by no means implies the simple kind, for the former is not based on the very nature of the thing called necessary but on the addition of an 'if.' For example, no necessity compels a man who is walking of his own accord to proceed, though it is necessary that, *if* he is walking, he should be proceeding. In the same way, if Providence sees any thing as present, that thing must be, though it has no necessity of its own nature; and, of course, God sees as present those future things which come to pass through free will. Therefore free acts, when referred to the divine intuition, become necessary in the conditional sense because God's knowledge provides that condition; on the other hand, viewed by themselves, they do not lose the perfect freedom of their nature. Without doubt, then, all things which God foreknows do come to pass, but certain of them proceed from free will. And these free acts, though they come to pass, do not by actually occurring lose their proper nature, because of which, before they come to pass, they could also not have come to pass....

"'But,' you will say, 'if it is within my power to change my mind I can make Providence void, for I may change what she foreknows.' To this I will answer that you can indeed change your mind but, since Providence truly sees in her present that you can change it, whether you will change it, and whither you may change it, you cannot avoid the divine foreknowledge any more than you can avoid the glance of an eye which is present, though you may by your free will turn yourself to various different actions. You will then say, 'Will the divine foreknowledge be altered by my own disposition, so that when I choose now one thing, now another, it too will seem to undergo alternations in its own cognition?' By no means; for the divine insight precedes the future and recalls it to the one present of its own proper cognition. It does not alternate, as you suppose, between this and that in its foreknowledge, but it is constantly preceding and grasping with one glance all mutations. This presence of comprehending and witnessing all things is not based on the actual occurrence of future events but on God's own peculiar simplicity—which fact also resolves that problem which you posed a little while ago when you said that it is shameful to maintain that our future acts are the cause of God's knowledge. For this power of knowledge to take cognizance, with one ever present glance, of all things has itself determined for each thing its mode of existence and owes nothing more to future things. Since this is so, mortal man's freedom of judgment remains inviolate and, because his will is free from any necessity, the laws which propose rewards and punishments are not unjust. God is the ever prescient spectator of all things, and the eternity of His vision, which is ever present, runs in unison with the future nature of our acts, dispensing rewards to the good, punishments to the evil. Hopes are not vainly put in God nor prayers vainly offered which, if they be right, cannot be ineffective. Therefore turn from vice, cultivate virtue, raise your heart to legitimate hope, direct humble prayers to the heavens. If you will only take notice and not dissemble, a great necessity for righteousness is laid upon you, since you live under the eyes of a Judge who discerns all."

STUDY QUESTIONS

1. Boethius long ago considered the problem posed by Pike in the previous selection, and he agreed that *if* God knows beforehand everything we will do, our actions cannot be free. His solution is that God is timeless, "outside of time." Explain what this means.
2. Explain why Boethius thinks that if God *timelessly* knows all human actions (past, present, and future), human free will is not threatened.

Nicholas Wolterstorff

God Is Everlasting

In this essay, Nicholas Wolterstorff (b. 1932) argues that rather than existing timelessly, as Boethius, Augustine, and many others have asserted, God is everlasting. That is to say, God exists *in time* without beginning or end. The belief in timeless divine eternity, he argues, is the result of excessive reliance by the early church fathers on ancient Greek philosophy. Presenting various facets of the picture of God's nature and actions found in the Bible, Wolterstorff maintains that these aspects of biblical teaching cannot be explained adequately on the assumption that God is timeless. For example, the God portrayed as a redeemer by classical theology is a God who *changes* and therefore cannot be timelessly eternal.

All Christian theologians agree that God is without beginning and without end. The vast majority have held, in addition, that God is *eternal*, existing outside of time. Only a small minority have contended that God is *everlasting*, existing within time.[1] In what follows I shall take up the cudgels for that minority, arguing that God as conceived and presented by the biblical writers is a being whose own life and existence is temporal.

The biblical writers do not present God as some passive factor within reality but as an agent in it. Further, they present him as acting within *human* history. The god they present is neither the impassive god of the Oriental nor the nonhistorical god of the Deist. Indeed, so basic to the biblical writings is their speaking of God as agent within history that if one viewed God as only an impassive factor in reality, or as one whose agency does not occur within human history, one would have to regard the biblical speech about God as at best one long sequence of metaphors pointing to a reality for which they are singularly inept, and as at worst one long sequence of falsehoods.

More specifically, the biblical writers present God as a redeeming God. From times most ancient, man has departed from the pattern of responsibilities awarded him at his creation by God. A multitude of evils has followed. But God was not content to leave man in the mire of his misery. Aware of what is going on, he has resolved, in response to man's sin and its resultant evils, to bring about renewal. He has, indeed, already been acting in accord with that resolve, centrally and decisively in the life, death, and resurrection of Jesus Christ.

What I shall argue is that if we are to accept this picture of God as acting for the renewal of human life, we must conceive of him as everlasting rather than eternal. God the Redeemer cannot be a God eternal. This is so because God the Redeemer is a God who *changes*. And any being which changes is a being among whose states there is temporal succession. Of course, there is an important sense in which God as presented in the Scriptures is changeless: he is steadfast in his redeeming intent and ever faithful to his children. Yet, *ontologically*, God cannot be a redeeming God without there being changeful variation among his states.

If this argument proves correct the importance of the issue here confronting us for Christian theology can scarcely be exaggerated. A theology which opts for God as eternal cannot avoid being in conflict with the confession of God as redeemer. And given the obvious fact that God is presented in the Bible as a God who redeems, a theology which opts for God as eternal cannot be a theology faithful to the biblical witness.

Our line of argument will prove to be neither subtle nor complicated. So the question will insistently arise, why have Christian theologians so massively contended that God is eternal? Why has not the dominant tradition of Christian theology been that of God everlasting?

Our argument will depend heavily on taking with seriousness a certain feature of temporality which has been neglected in Western philosophy. But the massiveness of the God eternal tradition cannot, I am persuaded, be attributed merely to philosophical oversight. There are, I think, two factors more fundamental. One is the feeling, deep-seated in much of human culture, that the flowing of events into an irrecoverable and unchangeable past is a matter for deep regret. Our bright actions and shining moments do not long endure. The gnawing tooth of time bites all. And our evil deeds can never be undone. They are forever to be regretted. Of course, the philosopher is inclined to distinguish the mere fact of temporality from the actual pattern of the events in history and to argue that regrets about the latter should not slosh over into regrets about the former. The philosopher is right. The regrettableness of what transpires in time is not good ground for regretting that there is time. Yet where the philosopher sees the possibility and the need for a distinction, most people have seen none. Regrets over the pervasive pattern of what transpires within time have led whole societies to place the divine outside of time—freed from the "bondage" of temporality.

But I am persuaded that William Kneale is correct when he contends that the most important factor accounting for the tradition of God eternal within Christian theology was the influence of the classical Greek philosophers on the early theologians.[2] The distinction between eternal being and everlasting being was drawn for the first time in history of thought by Plato (*Timaeus* 37–38), though the language he uses is reminiscent of words used still earlier by Parmenides. Plato does not connect eternity and divinity, but he does make clear his conviction that eternal being is the highest form of reality. This was enough to influence the early Christian theologians, who did their thinking within the milieu of Hellenic and Hellenistic thought, to assign eternity to God. Thus was the fateful choice made.

A good many twentieth-century theologians have been engaged in what one might call the dehellenization of Christian theology. If Kneale's contention is correct, then in this essay I am participating in that activity. Of course, not every bit of dehellenization is laudatory from the Christian standpoint, for not everything that the Greeks said is false. What is the case, though, is that the patterns of classical Greek thought are incompatible with the pattern of biblical thought. And in facing the issue of God everlasting versus God eternal we are dealing with the fundamental pattern of biblical thought. Indeed, I am persuaded that unless the tradition of God eternal is renounced, fundamental dehellenizing will perpetually occupy itself in the suburbs, never advancing to the city center. Every attempt to purge Christian theology of the traces of incompatible Hellenic patterns of thought must fail unless it removes the roadblock of the God eternal tradition. Around this barricade there are no detours....

It might seem obvious that God, as described by the biblical writers, is a being who changes, and who accordingly is fundamentally noneternal. For God is described as a being who *acts*—in creation, in providence, and for the renewal of mankind. He is an agent, not an impassive factor in reality. And from the manner in which his acts are described, it seems obvious that many of them have beginnings and endings, that accordingly they stand in succession relations to each other, and that these successive acts are of such a sort that their presence and absence on God's time-strand constitutes changes thereon. Thus it seems obvious that God is fundamentally noneternal.

God is spoken of as calling Abraham to leave Chaldea and later instructing Moses to return to Egypt. So does not the event of *God's instructing Moses* succeed that of *God's calling Abraham*? And does not this sort of succession constitute a change on God's time-strand—not a change in his "essence," but nonetheless a change on his time-strand? Again, God is spoken of as leading Israel through the Red Sea and later sending his Son into the world. So does not his doing the latter succeed his doing the former? And does not the fact of this sort of succession constitute a change along God's time-strand?

In short, it seems evident that the biblical writers regard God as having a time-strand of his own on which actions on his part are to be found, and that some at least of these actions vary in such a way that there are changes along the strand. It seems evident that they do not regard changes on time-strands as confined to entities in God's creation. The God who acts, in the way in which the biblical writers speak of God as acting, seems clearly to change.

Furthermore, is it not clear from how they speak that the biblical writers regarded many of God's acts as bearing temporal order-relations to events which are not aspects of him but rather aspects of the earth, of ancient human beings, and so forth? The four cited above, for example, seem all to be described thus. It seems obvious that God's actions as described by the biblical writers stand in temporal order-relations to all the other events in our own time-array.

However, I think it is not at all so obvious as on first glance it might appear that the biblical writers do in fact describe God as changing. Granted that the language they use suggests this. It is not at once clear that this is what they wished to say with this language. It is not clear that this is how they were describing God. Let us begin to see why this is so by reflecting on the following passage from St. Thomas Aquinas:

> Nor, if the action of the first agent is eternal, does it follow that His effect is eternal,... God acts voluntarily in the production of things,... God's act of understanding and willing is, necessarily, His act of making. Now, an effect follows from the intellect and the will according to the determination of the intellect and the command of the will. Moreover, just as the intellect determines every other condition of the thing made, so does it prescribe the time of its making; for art determines not only that this thing is to be such and such, but that it is to be at this particular time, even as a physician determines that a dose of medicine is to be drunk at such and such a particular time, so that, if his act of will were of itself sufficient to produce the effect, the effect would follow anew from his previous decision, without any new action on his part. Nothing, therefore, prevents our saying that God's action existed from all eternity, whereas its effect was not present from eternity, but existed at that time when, from all eternity, He ordained it (SCG II.35; cf. II.36, 4).

Let us henceforth call an event which neither begins nor ends an *everlasting* event. And let us call an event which either begins or ends, a *temporal* event. In the passage above, St. Thomas is considering God's acts of bringing about temporal events. So consider some such act; say, that of God's bringing about Israel's deliverance from Egypt. The temporal event in question, Israel's deliverance from Egypt, occurred (let us say) in 1225 B.C. But from the fact that what God brought about occurred in 1225 it does not follow, says Aquinas, that God's act of bringing it about occurred in 1225. In fact, it does not follow that this act had any beginning or ending whatsoever. And in general, suppose that God brings about some temporal event *e*. From the fact that *e* is temporal it does not follow, says Aquinas, that God's act of bringing about *e*'s occurrence is temporal. The temporality of the event which God brings about does not infect God's act of bringing it about. God's act of bringing it about may well be everlasting. This can perhaps more easily be seen, he says, if we remember that God, unlike us, does not have to "take steps" so as to bring about the occurrence of some event. He need only will that it occur. If God just wants it to be the case that e occur at t, e occurs at t.

Thus God can bring about changes in our history without himself changing. The occurrence of the event of Israel's deliverance from Egypt constitutes a change in our history. But there is no counterpart change among God's aspects by virtue of his bringing this event about.

Now let us suppose that the four acts of God cited above—instructing Moses, calling Abraham, leading Israel through the Red Sea, and sending his Son into the world—regardless of the impression we might gain from the biblical language used to describe them, also have the structure of God's bringing about the occurrence of some temporal event. Suppose, for example, that God's leading Israel through the Red Sea has the structure of God's bringing it about that Israel's passage through the Red Sea occurs. And suppose Aquinas is right that the temporality of Israel's passage does not infect with temporality God's act of bringing about this passage. Then what is strictly speaking the case is not that God's leading Israel through the Red Sea occurs during 1225. What is rather the case is that Israel's passage through the Red Sea occurs during 1225, and that God brings this passage about. And the temporality of the passage does not entail the temporality of God's bringing it about. This latter may be everlasting. So, likewise, the fact that the occurrence of this passage marks a change in our history does not entail that God's bringing it about marks a change among God's aspects. God may unchangingly bring about historical changes.

It is natural, at this point, to wonder whether we do not have in hand here a general strategy for interpreting the biblical language about God acting. Is it not perhaps the case that all those acts of God which the biblical writers speak of as beginning or as ending really consist in God performing the everlasting event of bringing about the occurrence of some temporal event?

Well, God does other things with respect to temporal events than bringing about their occurrence. For example, he also *knows* them. Why then should it be thought that the best way to interpret all the temporal-event language used to describe God's actions is by reference to God's action of bringing about the occurrence of some event? May it not be that the best way to interpret what is said with some of such language is by reference to one of those other acts which God performs with respect to temporal events? But then if God is not to change, it is not only necessary that the temporality of e not infect God's act of *bringing about* the occurrence of e, but also that *every* act of God such that he performs it with respect to e not be infected by the temporality of e. For example, if God *knows* some temporal event e, his knowledge of e must not be infected by the temporality of e.

So the best way of extrapolating from Aquinas's hint would probably be along the lines of the following theory concerning God's actions and the biblical speech about them. All God's actions are everlasting. None has either beginning or ending. Of these everlasting acts, the structure of some consists in God's performing some action with respect to some event. And at least some of the events that God acts with respect to are temporal events. However, in no case does the temporality of the event that God acts with respect to infect the event of his acting. On the contrary, his acting with respect to some temporal event is itself invariably an everlasting event. So whenever the biblical writers use temporal-event language to describe God's actions, they are to be interpreted as thereby claiming that God acts with respect to some temporal event. They are not to be interpreted as claiming that God's acting is itself a temporal event. God as described by the biblical writers is to be interpreted as acting, and as acting with respect to temporal events. But he is not to be interpreted as changing. All his acts are everlasting.

This, I think is a fascinating theory. If true, it provides a way of harmonizing the fundamental biblical teaching that God is a being who acts in our history, with the conviction that God does not change. How far the proposed line of biblical interpretation can be carried out, I do not know. I am not aware of any theologian who has ever tried to carry it out, though there are a great many theologians who might have relieved the tension in their thought by developing and espousing it. But what concerns us here is not so much what the theory can adequately deal with as what it cannot adequately deal with. Does the theory in fact provide us with a wholly satisfactory way of harmonizing the biblical presentation of God as acting in history with the conviction that God is fundamentally eternal?...

To refute the...Thomistic theory we would have to do one or the other of two things. We would have to show that some of the temporal-event language the biblical writers use in speaking of God's actions cannot properly be construed in the suggested way—that is, cannot be construed as used to put forth the claim that God acts in some way with respect to some temporal events. Or, alternatively, we would have to show that some of the actions that God performs with respect to temporal events are themselves temporal, either because they are infected by the temporality of the events or for some other reason.

One way of developing this latter alternative would be to show that some of God's actions must be understood as a response to the free actions of human beings—that what God does he sometimes does in response to what some human being does. I think this is in fact the case. And I think it follows, given that all human actions are temporal, that those actions of God which are "response" actions are temporal as well. But to develop this line of thought would be to plunge us deep into questions of divine omniscience and human freedom. So I shall make a simpler, though I think equally effective objection to the theory, arguing that in the case of certain of God's actions the temporality of the event that God acts on infects his own action with temporality.

Three such acts are the diverse though similar acts of knowing about some temporal event that it is occurring (that it is *present*), of knowing about some temporal event that it was occurring (that it is *past*), and of knowing about some temporal event that it will be occurring (that it is *future*). Consider the first of these. No one can know about some temporal event *e* that it is occurring except when it is occurring. Before *e* has begun to occur one cannot know that it is occurring, for it is not. Not after *e* has ceased to occur can one know that it is occurring, for it is not. So suppose that *e* has a beginning. Then P's knowing about *e* that it is occurring cannot occur until *e* begins. And suppose that *e* has an ending. Then P's knowing about *e* that it is occurring cannot

occur beyond *e*'s cessation. But every temporal event has (by definition) either a beginning or an ending. So every case of knowing about some temporal event that it is occurring itself either begins or ends (or both). Hence the act of knowing about *e* that it is occurring is infected by the temporality of *e*. So also, the act of knowing about *e* that it was occurring, and the act of knowing about *e* that it *will be* occurring, are infected by the temporality of *e*.

But, God, as the biblical writers describe him, performs all three of these acts, and performs them on temporal events. He knows what is happening in our history, what has happened, and what will happen. Hence, some of God's actions are themselves temporal events. But surely the nonoccurrence followed by the occurrence followed by the nonoccurrence of such knowings constitutes a change on God's time-strand. Accordingly, God is fundamentally noneternal....

God is also described by the biblical writers as planning that he would bring about certain events which he does. This, too, is impossible if God does not change. For consider some event which someone brings about, and suppose that he planned to bring it about. His planning to bring it about must occur before the planned event occurs. For otherwise it is not a case of planning.

So in conclusion, if God were eternal he could not be aware, concerning any temporal event, that it is occurring nor aware that it was occurring nor aware that it will be occurring; nor could he remember that it has occurred; nor could he plan to bring it about and do so. But all of such actions are presupposed by, and essential to, the biblical presentation of God as a redeeming God. Hence God as presented by the biblical writers is fundamentally noneternal. He is fundamentally in time.

As with any argument, one can here choose to deny the premises rather than to accept the conclusion. Instead of agreeing that God is fundamentally noneternal because he changes with respect to his knowledge, his memory, and his planning, one could try to save one's conviction that God is eternal by denying that he knows what is or was or will be occurring, that he remembers what has occurred, and that he brings about what he has planned. It seems to me, however, that this is clearly to give up the notion of God as a redeeming God; and in turn it seems to me that to give this up is to give up what is central to the biblical vision of God....

I have been arguing that God as described by the biblical writers is a being who changes. That, we have seen, is not self-evidently and obviously so, though the mode of expression of the biblical writers might lead one to think it was. Yet it is so nonetheless.

But are there not explicit statements in the Bible to the effect that God does not change? If we are honest to the evidence, must we not acknowledge that on this matter the biblical writers contradict each other? Let us see.

Surprisingly, given the massive Christian theological tradition in favor of God's ontological immutability, there are only two passages (to the best of my knowledge) in which it is directly said of God that he does not change. One of these is Malachi 3:6. The prophet has just been saying to the people that God is wearied by their hypocrisy; however (he goes on), God will send his messenger to clear a path before him; and "he will take his seat, refining and purifying." As a result of this cleansing, the "offerings of Judah and Jerusalem shall be pleasing to the Lord as they were in days of old." And then comes this assurance: "I am the Lord, unchanging; and you, too, have not ceased to be sons of Jacob. From the days of your forefathers you have been wayward and have not kept my laws. If you will return to me, I will return to you, says the Lord of Hosts" (NEB).

Surely it would be a gross misinterpretation to treat the prophet here as claiming that God is ontologically immutable. What he says, on the contrary, is that God is faithful to his people Israel—that he is unchanging in his fidelity to the covenant he has made with them. All too often theologians have ontologized the biblical message. Malachi 3:6 is a classic example of a passage which, cited out of context, would seem to support the doctrine of God's ontological immutability. Read in context, however, it supports not that but rather the doctrine of God's unswerving fidelity. No ontological claim whatever is made.

The other passage in which it is said of God that he is unchanging is to be found in Psalm 102:27. Again we must set the passage in its context:

My strength is broken in mid course;
the time allotted me is short.
   Snatch me not away before half my days are done,
   for thy years last through all generations.
   Long ago thou didst lay the foundations of the
      earth,
   and the heavens were thy handiwork.
They shall pass away, but thou endurest;
   like clothes they shall all grow old;
   thou shalt cast them off like a cloak,
   and they shall vanish;
but thou art the same and thy years shall have no end;
   thy servants' children shall continue,
and their posterity shall be established in thy
presence. (NEB)

Here, too, it would be a gross misinterpretation to regard the writer as teaching that God is ontologically immutable. The Psalmist is making an ontological point of sorts, though even so the ontological point is set within a larger context of religious reflection. He is drawing a contrast between God on the one hand and his transitory creation on the other. And what he says about God is clearly that God is without end— "Thy years shall have no end." He does not say that God is ontologically immutable.

In short, God's ontological immutability is not a part of the explicit teaching of the biblical writers. What the biblical writers teach is that God is faithful and without beginning or end, not that none of his aspects is temporal. The theological tradition of God's ontological immutability has no explicit biblical foundation.[3]

The upshot of our discussion is this: the biblical presentation of God presupposes that God is everlasting rather than eternal. God is indeed without beginning and without end. But at least some of his aspects stand in temporal order-relations to each other. Thus God, too, has a time-strand. His life and existence is itself temporal. (Whether his life and existence always was and always will be temporal, or whether he has taken on temporality, is a question we have not had time to consider.) Further, the events to be found on God's time-strand belong within the same temporal array as that which contains our time-strands. God's aspects do not only bear temporal order-relations to each other but to the aspects of created entities as well. And the aspects and succession of aspects to be found on God's time-strand are such that they constitute *changes* thereon. God's life and existence incorporates changeful succession.

Haunting Christian theology and Western philosophy throughout the centuries has been the picture of time as bounded, with the created order on this side of the boundary and God on the other. Or sometimes the metaphor has been that of time as extending up to a horizon, with all creaturely reality on this side of the horizon and God on the other. All such metaphors, and the ways of thinking that they represent, must be discarded. Temporality embraces us along with God.

This conclusion from our discussion turns out to be wholly in accord with that to be found in Oscar Cullmann's *Christ and Time*. From his study of the biblical words for time Cullmann concluded that, in the biblical picture, God's "eternity" is not qualitatively different from our temporality. Cullmann's line of argument (though not his conclusion) has been vigorously attacked by James Barr on the ground that from the lexicographical patterns of biblical language

we cannot legitimately make inferences as to what was being said by way of that language.[4] Verbal similarities may conceal differences in thought, and similarities in thought may be clothed with verbal differences. Barr's objection is *apropos*. But though we have traveled a very different route from Cullmann's we have come out at the same place. We have not engaged in any word studies. Yet, by seeing that God's temporality is presupposed by the biblical presentation of God as redeemer, we too have reached the conclusion that we share time with God. The lexicographical and philosophical cases coincide in their results.

Though God is within time, yet he is Lord of time. The whole array of contingent temporal events is within his power. He is Lord of what occurs. And that, along with the specific pattern of what he does, grounds all authentically biblical worship of, and obedience to, God. It is not because he is outside of time—eternal, immutable, impassive—that we are to worship and obey God. It is because of what he can and does bring about within time that we mortals are to render him praise and obedience.

Notes

1. The most noteworthy contemporary example is Oscar Cullmann, *Christ and Time* (Philadelphia: Westminster Press, 1950).
2. William Kneale, "Time and Eternity in Theology," *Proceedings of the Aristotelian Society* (1961).
3. "I am that I am" (Exod. 3:13) has also sometimes been used to support the doctrine of God's immutability. However, this is one of the most cryptic passages in all of Scripture; and—to understate the point—it is not in the least clear that what is being proclaimed is God's ontological immutability. There is a wealth of exegetical material on the passage, but see especially the comments by J. D. Murray, *The Problem of God* (New Haven, Conn.: Yale University Press, 1967), ch. 1.
4. *Biblical Words for Time* (London: SCM, 1962).

Study Questions

1. Wolterstorff argues that God must be thought of as "everlasting," rather than "eternal." Explain what is meant by these two contrasting terms.
2. Wolterstorff lays great emphasis on the Bible's depiction of God as acting within human life and history. Why does this depiction lead him to say that God must be understood as temporal (everlasting), rather than eternal (timeless)?
3. Given the contrast between God as temporal, living and acting in time, and God as eternal and outside time, which view do you think is better for a religious believer to take? Provide good reasons for your answer.
4. Explore the basis in classical thought—down through Plato and Boethius and others—for why a majority of Christian theologians down through the centuries have asserted God's timelessness.

The Upanishads

Atman Is Brahman

This text from the *Chandoya Upanishad* (written about 500 B.C.) expresses what became a fundamental teaching of the "advaita" school of Hinduism: Atman, the true inner self of each person, is identical with Brahman, the infinite divine reality behind all existence. The reader will note that this selection does not match the logical, analytical style of many others in this collection. Instead, it is a presentation adapted for practical religious teaching. It conveys the core doctrine forcefully and effectively, but much more would need to be said for an adequate analysis of this very difficult doctrine. It is the narrative of a young boy, Svetaketu, whose father impresses the truth upon him by a series of metaphorical examples, concluding each with the admonition, "*You are that*, Svetaketu."

"Just as the bees prepare honey by collecting the juices of all manner of trees and bring the juice to one unity, and just as the juices no longer distinctly know that the one hails from this tree, the other from that one, likewise, my son, when all these creatures have merged with the Existent they do not know, realizing only that they have merged with the Existent.

"Whatever they are here on earth, tiger, lion, wolf, boar, worm, fly, gnat, or mosquito, they become that.

"It is this very fineness which ensouls all this world, it is the true one, it is the soul. *You are that*, Svetaketu."

"Instruct me further, sir."

"So I will, my son," he said.

"The rivers of the east, my son, flow eastward, the rivers of the west flow westward. From ocean they merge into ocean, it becomes the same ocean. Just as they then no longer know that they are this river or that one, just so all these creatures, my son, know no more, realizing only when having come to the Existent that they have come to the Existent. Whatever they are here on earth, tiger, lion, wolf, boar, worm, fly, gnat or mosquito, they become that.

"It is this very fineness which ensouls all this world, it is the true one, it is the soul. *You are that*, Svetaketu."

"Instruct me further, sir."

"So I will, my son," he said.

Reprinted from Eliot Deutsch and J. A. B. van Buitenen, *A Source Book of Advaita Vedanta* (Honolulu: The University Press of Hawaii, 1971), pp. 14–16.

"If a man would strike this big tree at the root, my son, it would bleed but stay alive. If he struck it at the middle, it would bleed but stay alive. If he struck it at the top, it would bleed but stay alive. Being entirely permeated by the living soul, it stands there happily drinking its food.

"If this life leaves one branch, it withers. If it leaves another branch, it withers. If it leaves a third branch, it withers. If it leaves the whole tree, the whole tree withers. Know that it is in this same way, my son," he said, "that this very body dies when deserted by this life, but this life itself does not die.

"This is the very fineness which ensouls all this world, it is the true one, it is the soul. *You are that*, Svetaketu."

"Instruct me further, sir."

"So I will, my son," he said.

"Bring me a banyan fruit."

"Here it is, sir."

"Split it."

"It is split, sir."

"What do you see inside it?"

"A number of rather fine seeds, sir."

"Well, split one of them."

"It is split, sir."

"What do you see inside it?"

"Nothing, sir."

He said to him, "This very fineness that you no longer can make out, it is by virtue of this fineness that this banyan tree stands so big.

"Believe me, my son. It is this very fineness which ensouls all this world, it is the true one, it is the soul. *You are that*, Svetaketu."

"Instruct me further, sir."

"So I will, my son," he said.

"Throw this salt in the water, and sit with me on the morrow." So he did. He said to him, "Well, bring me the salt that you threw in the water last night." He looked for it, but could not find it as it was dissolved.

"Well, taste the water on this side.—How does it taste?"

"Salty."

"Taste it in the middle.—How does it taste?"

"Salty."

"Taste it at the other end.—How does it taste?"

"Salty."

"Take a mouthful and sit with me." So he did.

"It is always the same."

He said to him, "You cannot make out what exists in it, yet it is there.

"It is this very fineness which ensouls all this world, it is the true one, it is the soul. *You are that*, Svetaketu."

"Instruct me further, sir."

"So I will, my son," he said.

"Suppose they brought a man from the Gandhāra country, blindfolded, and let him loose in an uninhabited place beyond. The man, brought out and let loose with his blindfold on, would be turned around, to the east, north, west, and south.

"Then someone would take off his blindfold and tell him, 'Gandhāra is that way, go that way.' Being a wise man and clever, he would ask his way from village to village and thus reach Gandhāra. Thus in this world a man who has a teacher knows from him, 'So long will it take until I am free, then I shall reach it.'

"It is this very fineness which ensouls all this world, it is the true one, it is the soul. *You are that*, Svetaketu."

"Instruct me further, sir."

"So I will, my son," he said.

"When a man is dying, his relatives crowd around him: 'Do you recognize me? Do you recognize me?' As long as his speech has not merged in his mind, his mind in his breath, his breath in Fire, and Fire in the supreme deity, he does recognize.

"But when his speech has merged in the mind, the mind in the breath, the breath in Fire, and Fire in the supreme deity, he no longer recognizes.

"It is this very fineness which ensouls all this world, it is the true one, it is the soul. *You are that*, Svetaketu."

"Instruct me further, sir."

"So I will, my son," he said.

"They bring in a man with his hands tied, my son: 'He has stolen, he has committed a robbery. Heat the ax for him!' If he is the criminal, he will make himself untrue. His protests being untrue, and covering himself with untruth, he seizes the heated ax. He is burnt, and then killed.

"If he is not the criminal, he makes himself true by this very fact. His protests being true, and covering himself with truth, he seizes the heated ax. He is not burnt, and then set free.

"Just as he is not burnt—that ensouls all this world, it is the true one, it is the soul. *You are that*, Svetaketu."

This he knew from him, from him.

STUDY QUESTIONS

1. In your own words, what is the message that Svetaketu's father is trying to get across to him? Why does his father need to repeat the message a number of times in different ways?
2. What is the main difference between the Hindu concept of Brahman, as seen in this selection, and the conception of God in Western religions, such as Judaism and Christianity?

SUGGESTED READING

Basinger, David. *Divine Power in Process Theism: A Philosophical Critique.* Albany, N.Y.: State University of New York Press, 1988.

Beilby, James K., and Paul Rhodes Eddy, eds. *Divine Foreknowledge: Four Views.* Downers Grove, Ill.: InterVarsity Press, 2001.

Billington, Ray. *Understanding Eastern Philosophy.* London: Routledge, 1997.

Cobb, John B., and David Ray Griffin. *Process Theology: An Introductory Exposition.* Philadelphia: Westminster Press, 1976.

Creel, Richard. *Divine Impassibility.* Cambridge, England: Cambridge University Press, 1986.

Davis, Stephen T. *Logic and the Nature of God.* Grand Rapids, Mich.: Eerdmans, 1983.

Gale, Richard M. *On the Nature and Existence of God.* New York: Cambridge University Press, 1991.

Ganssle, Gregory E., ed. *God and Time: Four Views.* Downers Grove, Ill.: InterVarsity Press, 2001.

Hartshorne, Charles. *Omnipotence and Other Theological Mistakes.* Albany, N.Y.: State University of New York Press, 1984.

Hasker, William. *God, Time, and Knowledge.* Ithaca, N.Y.: Cornell University Press, 1989.

Kenny, Anthony. *The God of the Philosophers.* Oxford, England: Oxford University Press, 1979.

Koller, John M. *Oriental Philosophies.* 2nd ed. New York: Scribners, 1985.

Leftow, Brian. *Time and Eternity.* Ithaca, N.Y.: Cornell University Press, 1991.

MacDonald, Scott, ed. *Being and Goodness.* Ithaca, N.Y.: Cornell University Press, 1991.

Morris, Thomas. *Our Idea of God: An Introduction to Philosophical Theology.* Downers Grove, Ill.: InterVarsity Press, 1994.

Pinnock, Clark. *Most Moved Mover: A Theology of God's Openness.* Grand Rapids, Mich.: Baker Books, 2001.

Rogers, Katherin A. *Anselm on Freedom.* Oxford, England: Oxford University Press, 2008.

Rowe, William. *Can God Be Free?* Oxford, England: Clarendon Press, 2004.

Stump, Eleonore, and Norman Kretzmann. "Eternity." *Journal of Philosophy* 79 (1981): 429–58.

Swinburne, Richard. *The Coherence of Theism.* Oxford, England: Oxford University Press, 1979.

———. *The Christian God.* Oxford, England: Oxford University Press, 1994.

Urban, Linwood, and Douglas Walton., eds. *The Power of God.* New York: Oxford University Press, 1978.

Wierenga, Edward R. *The Nature of God: An Inquiry into Divine Attributes.* Ithaca, N.Y.: Cornell University Press, 1989.

Zagzebski, Linda. *The Dilemma of Freedom and Foreknowledge.* New York: Oxford University Press, 1991.

PART FIVE

Arguments About God's Existence

The question of whether we can have any reason to believe that God or some Ultimate Reality exists is central to the philosophy of religion. Over the centuries, philosophers and theologians have advanced numerous arguments for God's existence. A few contemporary philosophers of religion believe that the evidence provided by particular arguments is persuasive enough; others are interested in seeing whether a cumulative case, like that given in support of theories in science or history, can be constructed for God's existence, since the evidence from any one argument is not definitive. On the other hand, nontheists as well as many theists view the evidence presented by the arguments, individually or collectively, as quite weak. As Antony Flew once suggested, ten leaky buckets, even stacked together, ultimately cannot hold water (although more recently even he has changed his view about the evidence for God's existence).

Traditionally, theists have proposed two broad types of arguments for God's existence: *a priori* arguments and *a posteriori* arguments. *Ontological* and *moral* arguments are a priori arguments because they move from premises about concepts—for example, from an idea of God's nature or perfections—to a claim that something (a god) really exists. *Cosmological* and *teleological* arguments are a posteriori arguments that begin with premises about what exists—for example, affirming that the universe exists or has order. Each of these argument types comes in many versions, only a few of which can be presented in our anthology.

ONTOLOGICAL ARGUMENTS

The eleventh-century theologian Anselm formulated the intriguing ontological argument given in our first selection. Its basic idea is that from an understanding of God's nature, for example, that God is a being than which one cannot conceive a greater being, one can show that God exists. Since real existence is greater than mere existence in the mind, if God only existed as a concept, one could conceive of a being greater than God, one that also really existed. But this is contradictory: by definition, God is that than which one cannot conceive a greater. Hence, God must exist in reality as well as in concept. We might put the argument this way.

1. Persons have the idea of a being than which one cannot conceive a greater.
2. Suppose this being exists only as an idea in the mind.
3. Real existence is greater than mere mental existence.
4. Therefore, we can conceive of a being greater than the being of which we cannot conceive a greater, that is, a being that also exists in reality.
5. But there can be no being greater than the being of which we cannot conceive a greater.
6. Therefore, the being of which we cannot conceive a greater exists in reality.

Critics have raised numerous objections to the ontological argument. Many have maintained that any move from pure concepts to a claim about reality is suspect; were we able to do this, as Gaunilo suggests in our second selection, we could prove the existence of all sorts of unreal things, such as the greatest possible island, merely by conceiving them. Alvin Plantinga, in our third selection, responds that this objection is irrelevant since Anselm's move only applies in cases where the properties in question have an intrinsic maximum, which is not the case with the properties one ascribes to islands.

Others have argued that the ontological argument trades on a misunderstanding of the word "exist." Generally, properties of things can be treated as predicates: goodness is a property and hence can be predicated of people—Jake is good. In the ontological argument, existence is treated as a property and hence as a predicate of things. René Descartes argued that God as infinite has all perfections, and since to exist is better for something than not to exist, existence is a perfection. Hence, it follows from the concept of God that God exists. But as Kant argued long ago, existence does not add to the concept of anything: to say that $100 exists does not add anything to the concept of $100; the same amount of money is involved. Similarly, to say that existence is a perfection that God possesses does not add anything to the concept of God in the way that to say God has the perfection of goodness does add to the concept of God. Some have replied that this objection, though powerful, only shows that *existence* functions as a strange predicate, not that it is not a proper predicate.

The twentieth century saw the revitalization of the ontological argument. Charles Hartshorne suggested that while existence might not be a proper predicate, necessary existence or maximal greatness is, so that the ontological argument can be reconstructed using the concept of maximal greatness. On this view, as Plantinga argues, a being is maximally great only if it has maximal excellence in every possible world. Hence, if it is possible that God exists and has maximal greatness in every possible world, it follows that God necessarily exists. But like most others, Plantinga remains hesitant about the ontological argument, since not everyone would accept the claim that being maximally great is possible.

COSMOLOGICAL ARGUMENTS

The cosmological argument likewise appears in many forms. It concerns explanations, either of the universe or of particular contingent phenomena within it. The central thesis of the argument is that contingent beings alone cannot explain the existence of other contingent beings; what best explains their existence must include a necessary being. This necessary being does not need a cause, since the Principle of Causation—that every contingent thing needs a cause of its existence or continuing to exist—applies only to contingent beings. Hence, the question of what caused the necessary being is meaningless.

Thomas Aquinas, in our fourth selection, presents a deductive version of the cosmological argument that asks for the cause of something in motion. That when something is moved it is moved by another is shown by the fact that something cannot contain within itself the principle of its own motion. Further, since a timeless infinite series of contingent causal conditions cannot account for any effect, Aquinas concludes that a first cause or self-existent necessary being must exist now to explain why the effect is produced now. Thomas's argument is not for a first cause in time but for a sustaining cause of whatever is moved. It is like this: if a lamp is hung from a hook, and the hook from the ceiling, and the ceiling from a beam, and the beam from the house frame, one cannot keep going; there must be something that itself is not hung on something else to explain why the lamp remains hung.

Contemporary versions update Thomas's cosmological argument by using a conceptual schema that avoids Aristotelian thought forms. The argument commences from the contention that contingent phenomena require a cause or sufficient reason to be what they are. This explanation cannot come from themselves or from other contingent beings but must include a necessary being. An outline of this argument can be found in the fifth selection, by Bruce Reichenbach. Philosophers like Richard Swinburne distinguish between two kinds of explanation, scientific or natural explanation and personal explanation. The kind of explanation provided by God is not a natural or scientific explanation but a personal one that properly invokes intentions.

Numerous objections have been raised against the cosmological argument. For one, as John Mackie argues in our seventh selection, why should we think that everything must have a cause or sufficient reason? Couldn't things just simply exist? And even if we require a cause or sufficient reason, can we not hold that an individual's existence is explained by the presence of other contingent beings? An explanation in terms of an infinite regress of causal conditions suffices to account for it. If the contingent being is the universe, then its existence is explained by the presence of all the parts.

Defenders of the cosmological argument reject both of Mackie's options, the former on the grounds that contingent things, even if infinite, cannot explain anything; the latter on the grounds that although the parts explain why the collection is what it is, the parts do not explain why the whole exists in the first place. Appeal must be made to something other than the collected parts.

A different form of the cosmological argument (the kalam argument, developed by William Craig in the sixth selection) contends that whatever begins to exist must have a cause of its beginning. Since the universe began to exist, the universe must have an initial cause of its coming to be. The universe could not have existed infinitely in the past for several reasons. One argument is that whereas a potential infinite is possible, an actual infinite—which would be what an infinitely enduring universe would be—is impossible in reality because the concept of an actual infinite generates a contradiction. In particular, it leads to the absurdity that the whole is not greater than any of its infinite parts, so that removing an infinite number of its parts (as one might do in having an infinite number of guests leave a hotel that has an infinite number of rooms) would not diminish the whole (the hotel would still have the same number of guests). Other arguments in defense of the thesis that the universe began invoke the Big Bang theory of cosmology, which points to a beginning. Further, if the universe existed from infinity, according to the second law of thermodynamics the universe would by now have reached a state of thermodynamic equilibrium, which fortunately it has not. (An outline of this argument can be found in the sixth selection.)

Critics of the kalam cosmological argument express numerous worries. For one thing, they suggest that the principle of causation is either not necessarily true or inapplicable to the universe as a whole, for we have no experience of universes coming into existence from which to draw a conclusion about the Principle of Causation. Some also suggest that since time began with the universe, it makes little sense to ask what brought the universe into existence, since nothing can be before the universe. The universe just is and is all there is. Still others hold that the universe simply came to be out of nothing, understood perhaps as a vacuum with virtual energy. Parmenides' principle that out of nothing nothing comes does not hold for this initial, singular event.

TELEOLOGICAL ARGUMENTS

The teleological argument likewise comes in various forms. Thomas Aquinas developed a deductive version in the thirteenth century. All things have a final cause; they act for an end. But since things in nature lack knowledge, they must be directed by some intelligent being toward their end. Hence, an intelligent being, called God, exists. By the seventeenth century, the Aristotelian concept of final causes fell out of favor and was replaced by a more mechanical view of nature and the world.

In the early nineteenth century, William Paley (author of our eighth selection) constructed a widely read analogical version that likened natural organs and organisms to machine-like things (e.g., a watch or a telescope) with means–end ordering. Since a complex system like a watch cannot come into being by chance but must have an intelligent cause, nature and its impressively ordered contents must also have an intelligent cause. Means–ends ordering requires a designer.

A quarter century before Paley wrote, David Hume anticipated this argument, which had already been popularized by Isaac Newton and the Dutch theologian Bernard Nieuwentyt. In our ninth selection, Hume argues that the analogy between the universe and human artifacts, at the heart of the argument, is woefully deficient. For one thing, there are too many differences between the analogues: the universe is just not like houses, watches, and ships. For another, the generalization from the analogue to its properties is suspect. Just because humans use reason to create artifacts does not mean that this is the primary principle to be found in all of nature. Nature invokes many principles, including vegetation, generation, and magnetism, to create order. Indeed, it is possible that matter can organize itself; we have not achieved any advance in explanation when we explain natural order by appealing to mind, which itself requires an ordering principle. It is just that Hume did not know how this natural ordering could come about. In the nineteenth century, Charles Darwin attributed biological order to a process of "natural selection": biological order is present in the universe because the environment selects out those organisms that are best fitted to survive. But natural selection is a random adaptive process in response to environmental changes, not requiring an intelligent designer. One need not have a God to have an orderly, means–ends structured universe.

Contemporary versions of the teleological argument take into account Darwin's thesis that nature can organize itself. They argue that although Darwin is generally correct in regard to particular biological phenomena, chance fails to provide the best explanation for certain features, such as the origin of RNA in nonliving things, the ordering principles of nature, or the narrow window of physical constants such as the mass and charge of the proton, the gravitational constant, and the strengths of the weak and strong forces that are necessary for humans to witness the universe. According to this anthropic teleological argument, which is developed in the tenth selection by Betty and Cordell, the extreme unlikelihood of these events—the odds of their occurring together are astronomical—means that the existence of an intelligent orderer provides the best explanation for them.

On the other hand, nontheists, such as Stephen Jay Gould, argue that the fact that we as conscious beings witness the universe is not very remarkable. Something, no matter how improbable, had to happen. The point simply is that the universe has evolved to its present state, but this point fails to establish anything about why the present state rather than another resulted. Theists reply that although something had to happen, the combination of factors that together are necessary for conscious life are truly remarkable and therefore beg for a explanation that appeals to intelligence.

A version of the teleological argument is also found in defenders of intelligent design, whose contention that although a Darwinian evolutionary account can be given for microevolutionary changes, it cannot account for the development of complex adaptive systems. No satisfactory explanation can be found for how, for example, life (RNA) arose out of inert chemicals; neither can gradual development preserve the features necessary for the complex system to function, for in the earlier stages these features allegedly served no useful function. This approach and the questions raised are presented to some extent in Betty's article and considered more fully in Part Twelve, which deals with the relationship between religion and science.

Moral Arguments

The moral argument likewise comes in many forms, both deductive (Thomas Aquinas) and postulational (Immanuel Kant). According to Kant, since we are under the moral law, it is our duty to promote the highest good, which for him is virtue plus happiness. Since *ought* implies *can*, we must be able to be both virtuous and happy. But our happiness depends on our harmonious relations with nature. Unfortunately, nature is not in our control, which means that we cannot harmonize nature with our ends. Thus, we must postulate a cause of all nature, distinct from nature since it causes nature.

Several objections have been raised against this argument. For one, is it really the case that *ought* implies *can*? Furthermore, from within the Kantian framework, causation is a category of understanding properly applied to the phenomenal world, but causation of the world is not a phenomenal but a noumenal property. Hence, it is illegitimate for Kant to argue to a cause of the world.

Robert Adams, in our eleventh selection, presents several versions of the moral argument. He notes that the divine command theory of ethics is an adequate theory of morality, and since it entails the existence of God, it provides a reason for thinking that God exists. Further, to believe that there is no moral order—that as Sartre puts it, if God does not exist, all is possible—is demoralizing. Since this belief is undesirable, it provides a reason for thinking that God exists. At the same time, philosophers have challenged the key assumptions of both arguments, namely, the divine command theory of ethics and that there exists a moral law that is universal, objective, or not the product of human creation. Morality, like religion itself, is a conventional human creation that need not appeal to any external, normative law or ground.

THE ARGUMENTS AND THE GOD OF RELIGION

A final issue, not addressed in our readings, concerns whether the being to which the theistic arguments point—whether a necessary being, first cause, or mind that orders the universe and commands the moral law—is to be identified with the God of religion. To what extent can the detached, objective metaphysical description of the absolute being coincide with the involved religious believer's idea of a partially accessible, loving and caring God? Some sort of endeavor that correlates the properties of each must be invoked to assess any claims of identity.

That the debate over the soundness or cogency of these arguments continues shows that the central questions of philosophy of religion are alive and well. Although the theistic arguments are not convincing to everyone—and perhaps not even to most people—the lack of universal consent should not deter the serious questioner from investigating the claims. Whatever one concludes about the strength of the arguments, those who analyze them must pay close attention to the broader philosophical milieu in which the arguments are advanced and critiqued, as well as to the important philosophical questions they raise.

Saint Anselm

The Classical Ontological Argument

Anselm (1033–1109) argues that we understand God as a being than which we cannot conceive a greater. Yet, if we conceive of such a being as existing only in the understanding, a greater being could be conceived, namely, one that also exists in reality. But this would be contradictory. Hence, God as the being than which we cannot conceive a greater being must exist. Anselm's strategy, then, is to move from the admission that we have the concept of a being than which we cannot conceive a greater to the conclusion that God cannot be understood not to exist. For those who already believe that God exists, Anselm's argument provides a better understanding of God's existence.

For I do not seek to understand in order to believe; I believe in order to understand. For I also believe that "Unless I believe, I shall not understand."

CHAPTER 2. THAT GOD TRULY EXISTS

Therefore, Lord, you who grant understanding to faith, grant that, insofar as you know it is useful for me, I may understand that you exist as we believe you exist, and that you are what we believe you to be. Now we believe that you are something than which nothing greater can be thought. So can it be that no such nature exists, since "The fool has said in his heart,

'There is no God'" (Psalm 14:1; 53:1)? But when this same fool hears me say "something than which nothing greater can be thought," he surely understands what he hears; and what he understands exists in his understanding, even if he does not understand that it exists [in reality]. For it is one thing for an object to exist in the understanding and quite another to understand that the object exists [in reality]. When a painter, for example, thinks out in advance what he is going to paint, he has it in his understanding, but he does not yet understand that it exists, since he has not yet painted it. But once he has painted it, he both has it in his understanding and understands that it exists because he has painted it. So even the fool must admit that something than which nothing greater can be thought exists at least in his understanding, since he understands this when he hears it, and whatever is understood exists in the understanding. And surely that than which a greater cannot be thought cannot exist only in the understanding. For if it exists only in the understanding, it can be thought to exist in reality as well, which is greater. So if that than which a greater cannot be thought exists only in the understanding, then that than which a greater *cannot* be thought is that than which a greater *can* be thought. But that is clearly impossible. Therefore, there is no doubt that something than which a greater cannot be thought exists both in the understanding and in reality.

CHAPTER 3. THAT HE CANNOT BE THOUGHT NOT TO EXIST

This [being] exists so truly that it cannot be thought not to exist. For it is possible to think that something exists that cannot be thought not to exist, and such a being is greater than one that can be thought not to exist. Therefore, if that than which a greater cannot be thought can be thought not to exist, then that than which a greater cannot be thought is *not* that than which a greater cannot be thought; and this is a contradiction. So that than which a greater cannot be thought exists so truly that it cannot be thought not to exist.

And this is you, O Lord our God. You exist so truly, O Lord my God, that you cannot be thought not to exist. And rightly so, for if some mind could think something better than you, a creature would rise above the Creator and sit in judgment upon him, which is completely absurd. Indeed, everything that exists, except for you alone, can be thought not to exist. So you alone among all things have existence most truly, and therefore most greatly. Whatever else exists

has existence less truly, and therefore less greatly. So then why did "the fool say in his heart, 'There is no God,'" when it is so evident to the rational mind that you among all beings exist most greatly? Why indeed, except because he is stupid and a fool?

CHAPTER 4. HOW THE FOOL SAID IN HIS HEART WHAT CANNOT BE THOUGHT

But how has he said in his heart what he could not think? Or how could he not think what he said in his heart, since to say in one's heart is the same as to think? But if he really—or rather, *since* he really—thought this, because he said it in his heart, and did not say it in his heart, because he could not think it, there must be more than one way in which something is "said in one's heart" or "thought." In one sense of the word, to think a thing is to think the word that signifies that thing. But in another sense, it is to understand what exactly the thing is. God can be thought not to exist in the first sense, but not at all in the second sense. No one who understands what God is can think that God does not exist, although he may say these words in his heart with no signification at all, or with some peculiar signification. For God is that than which a greater cannot be thought. Whoever understands this properly, understands that his being exists in such a way that he cannot, even in thought, fail to exist. So whoever understands that God exists in this way cannot think that he does not exist.

Thanks be to you, my good Lord, thanks be to you. For what I once believed through your grace, I now understand through your illumination, so that even if I did not want to *believe* that you exist, I could not fail to *understand* that you exist.

STUDY QUESTIONS

1. In your own words, explain how Anselm argues for God's existence.
2. What does Anselm think allows the fool to persist in his claim that God does not exist?

Gaunilo

Critique of Anselm's Argument

The monk Gaunilo (eleventh century) raises a number of objections to Anselm's argument. First, Gaunilo charges that Anselm has confused having a concept of something with discovering whether that thing exists; they are two different things. Second, Guanilo claims that if Anselm is correct, we cannot deny that God exists, which would make his argument for God's existence useless. Third, he states that Anselm wrongly presupposes that we are able to conceive of or understand God himself. Finally, Gaunilo argues that we cannot reason from the existence of something in our understanding to the fact that it exists in extramental reality, for by such reasoning we could show that unreal objects like an island with unsurpassable attributes exists. One has to show that it exists in reality first.

The fool can perhaps reply, "The only reason this is said to exist in my understanding is that I understand what is said. But in the same way, could I not also be said to have in my understanding any number of false things that have no real existence at all in themselves, since if someone were to speak of them I would understand whatever he said? Unless perhaps it is established that this being is such that it cannot be had in thought in the same way that any false or doubtful things can, and so I am not said to think of what I have heard or to have it in my thought, but to understand it and have it in my understanding, since I cannot think of it in any other way except by understanding it, that is, by comprehending in genuine knowledge the fact that it actually exists.

"But first of all, if this were true, there would be no difference in this case between having the thing in the understanding at one time and then later understanding that the thing exists, as there is in the case of a painting, which exists first in the mind of the painter and then in the finished work.

"Furthermore, it is nearly impossible to believe that this being, once someone had heard it spoken of, cannot be thought not to exist, in just the same way that even God can be thought not to exist. For if that were so, why bother with all this argument against someone who denies or doubts that such a nature exists?

"Finally, it must be proved to me by some unassailable argument that this being merely needs to be thought in order for the understanding to perceive with complete certainty that it undoubtedly exists. It is not enough to tell me that it exists in my understanding, since I understand it when I hear about it. I still think I could likewise have any number of other doubtful or even false things in my understanding if I heard them spoken of by someone whose words I understand, and especially if I am so taken in by him that, as often happens, I believe him—as I still do not believe in that being....

"There is a further argument, which I mentioned earlier. When I hear someone speak of that which is greater than everything else that can be thought (which, it is alleged, can be nothing other than God himself), I can no more think of it or have it in my understanding in terms of anything whose genus or species I already know, than I can think of God himself—and indeed, for this very reason I can also think of God as not existing. For I do not know the thing itself, and I cannot form an idea of it on the basis of something like it, since you yourself claim that it is so great that nothing else could be like it. Now if I heard something said about a man I do not know at all, whose very existence is unknown to me, I could think of him in accordance with that very thing that a man is, on the basis of that knowledge of genus or species by which I know what a man is or what men are. Nonetheless, it could happen that the one who spoke of this man was lying, and so the man whom I thought of would not exist. But I would still be thinking of him on the basis of a real thing: not what that particular man would be, but what any given man is.

"But when I hear someone speak of 'God' or 'something greater than everything else,' I cannot have it in my thought or understanding in the same way as this false thing. I was able to think of the false thing on the basis of some real thing that I actually knew. But in the case of God, I can think of him only on the basis of the word. And one can seldom or never think of any truth solely on the basis of a word. For in thinking of something solely on the basis of a word, one does not think so much of the word itself (which is at least a real thing: the sound of letters or syllables) as of the meaning of the word that is heard. And in the present case, one does not do this as someone who

knows what is customarily meant by the word and thinks of it on the basis of a thing that is real at least in thought. Instead, one thinks of it as someone who does not know the meaning of the word, who thinks only of the impression made on his mind by hearing the word and tries to imagine its meaning. It would be surprising if one ever managed to reach the truth about something in this way. Therefore, when I hear and understand someone saying that there exists something greater than everything else that can be thought, it is in this way, and this way only, that it is present in my understanding....

"Then I am offered the further argument that this thing necessarily exists in reality, since if it did not, everything that exists in reality would be greater than it. And so this thing, which of course has been proved to exist in the understanding, would not be greater than everything else. To that argument I reply that if we are to say that something exists in the understanding that cannot even be thought on the basis of the true nature of anything whatever, then I shall not deny that even this thing exists in my understanding. But since there is no way to derive from this the conclusion that this thing also exists in reality, there is simply no reason for me to concede to him that this thing exists in reality until it is proved to me by some unassailable argument.

"And when he says that this thing exists because otherwise that which is greater than everything else would not be greater than everything else, he does not fully realize whom he is addressing. For I do not yet admit—indeed, I actually deny, or at least doubt—that this being is greater than any real thing. Nor do I concede that it exists at all, except in the sense that something exists (if you want to call it 'existence') when my mind tries to imagine some completely unknown thing solely on the basis of a word that it has heard. How, then, is the fact that this greater being has been proved to be greater than everything else supposed to show me that it exists in actual fact? For I continue to deny, or at least doubt, that this has been proved, so that I do not admit that this greater being exists in my understanding or thought even in the way that many doubtful and uncertain things exist there. First I must become certain that this greater being truly exists somewhere, and only then will the fact that it is greater than everything else show clearly that it also subsists in itself.

"For example, there are those who say that somewhere in the ocean is an island, which, because of the difficulty—or rather, impossibility—of finding what does not exist, some call 'the Lost Island.' This island (so the story goes) is more plentifully endowed than even the Isles of the Blessed with an indescribable abundance of all sorts of riches and delights. And because it has neither owner nor inhabitant, it is everywhere superior in its abundant riches to all the other lands that human beings inhabit.

"Suppose someone tells me all this. The story is easily told and involves no difficulty, and so I understand it. But if this person went on to draw a conclusion, and say, 'You cannot any longer doubt that this island, more excellent than all others on earth, truly exists somewhere in reality. For you do not doubt that this island exists in your understanding, and since it is more excellent to exist not merely in the understanding, but also in reality, this island must also exist in reality. For if it did not, any land that exists in reality would be greater than it. And so this more excellent thing that you have understood would not in fact be more excellent.'—If, I say, he should try to convince me by this argument that I should no longer doubt whether the island truly exists, either I would think he was joking, or I would not know whom I ought to think more foolish: myself, if I grant him his conclusion, or him, if he thinks he has established the existence of that island with any degree of certainty, without first showing that its excellence exists in my understanding as a thing that truly and undoubtedly exists and not in any way like something false or uncertain."

Study Questions

1. On what grounds does Gaunilo question whether he can have the understanding of God that Anselm thinks leads to showing that God exists, and what does Gaunilo think follows from this questioning?
2. How does Gaunilo think that his example of the most excellent island refutes Anselm's inference from the concept of a greatest possible being to this being's reality?

Alvin Plantinga

A Contemporary Modal Version
of the Ontological Argument

Alvin Plantinga (b. 1932) rejects Gaunilo's objections to Anselms's argument. As he sees it, Gaunilo's argument would work only with properties that have an intrinsic maximum, but the unsurpassable properties of Gaunilo's island have no intrinsic maximum: there could always be a greater. He proceeds to evaluate several versions of the ontological argument before developing his own version. According to Plantinga, it is possible that some being has maximal greatness. However, if a being has this property, then it has it in every possible world. So, reasons Plantinga, if it is possible that God exists with this property, it is necessary that God exists. However, in the end Plantinga remains skeptical of the ontological argument, for it requires that one accept the premise that a being with maximal greatness is possible.

I wish to discuss the famous "ontological argument" first formulated by Anselm of Canterbury in the eleventh century. This argument for the existence of God has fascinated philosophers ever since Anselm first stated it.... Although the argument certainly looks at first sight as if it ought to be unsound, it is profoundly difficult to say what, exactly, is wrong with it. Indeed, I do not believe that any philosopher has ever given a cogent and conclusive refutation of the ontological argument in its various forms....

How can we outline Anselm's argument? It is best construed, I think, as a *reductio ad absurdum* argument. In a *reductio* you prove a given proposition *p* by showing that its denial, *not-p*, leads to (or more strictly, entails) a contradiction or some other kind of absurdity. Anselm's argument can be seen as an attempt to deduce an absurdity from the proposition that there is no God. If we use the term "God" as an abbreviation for Anselm's phrase "the being than which nothing greater can be conceived," then the argument seems to go approximately as follows: Suppose

(1) God exists in the understanding but not in reality.
(2) Existence in reality is greater than existence in the understanding alone. (premise)
(3) God's existence in reality is conceivable. (premise)
(4) If God did exist in reality, then He would be greater than He is. [from (1) and (2)]

(5) It is conceivable that there is a being greater than God is. [(3) and (4)]

(6) It is conceivable that there be a being greater than the being than which nothing greater can be conceived. [(5) by the definition of "God"]

But surely (6) is absurd and self-contradictory; how could we conceive of a being greater than the being than which none greater can be conceived? So we may conclude that

(7) It is false that God exists in the understanding but not in reality.

It follows that if God exists in the understanding, He also exists in reality; but clearly enough He *does* exist in the understanding, as even the fool will testify; therefore, He exists in reality as well.

Now when Anselm says that a being *exists in the understanding*, we may take him, I think, as saying that someone has *thought of* or thought about that being. When he says that something *exists in reality*, on the other hand, he means to say simply that the thing in question really does exist. And when he says that a certain state of affairs is *conceivable*, he means to say, I believe, that this state of affairs is possible in our broadly logical sense; there is a possible world in which it obtains. This means that step (3) above may be put more perspicuously as

(3′) It is possible that God exists

and step (6) as

(6′) It is possible that there be a being greater than the being than which it is not possible that there be a greater.

An interesting feature of this argument is that all of its premises are *necessarily* true if true at all. (1) is the assumption from which Anselm means to deduce a contradiction. (2) is a premise, and presumably necessarily true in Anselm's view; and (3) is the only remaining premise (the other items are consequences of preceding steps); it says of some *other* proposition (*God exists*) that it is possible. Propositions which thus ascribe a modality—possibility, necessity, contingency—to another proposition are themselves either necessarily true or necessarily

false. So all the premises of the argument are, if true at all, necessarily true. And hence if the premises of this argument are true, then [provided that (6) is really inconsistent] a contradiction can be deduced from (1) together with necessary propositions; this means that (1) entails a contradiction and is, therefore, necessarily false.

GAUNILO'S OBJECTION

Gaunilo, a contemporary of Anselm's, wrote a reply which he entitled *On Behalf of the Fool*....

Gaunilo was the first of many to try to discredit the ontological argument by showing that one can find similar arguments to prove the existence of all sorts of absurd things—a greatest possible island, a highest possible mountain, a greatest possible middle linebacker, a meanest possible man, the like. But Anselm was not without a reply.

He points out, first, that Gaunilo misquotes him. What is under consideration is not a being that is *in fact* greater than any other, but one such that a greater *cannot be conceived*; a being than which it's *not possible* that there be a greater. Gaunilo seems to overlook this. And thus his famous lost island argument isn't strictly parallel to Anselm's argument; his conclusion should be only that there is an island such that no other island is greater than it—which, if there are any islands at all, is a fairly innocuous conclusion.

But obviously Gaunilo's argument can be revised. Instead of speaking, as he did, of an island that is more excellent than all others, let's speak instead of an island than which a greater or more excellent cannot be conceived—an island, that is, than which it's not possible that there be a greater. Couldn't we use an argument like Anselm's to "establish" the existence of such an island, and if we could, wouldn't that show that Anselm's argument is fallacious?

ANSELM'S REPLY

Not obviously. Anselm's proper reply, it seems to me, is that it's impossible that there be such an island.

The idea of an island than which it's not possible that there be a greater is like the idea of a natural number than which it's not possible that there be a greater, or the idea of a line than which none more crooked is possible. There neither is nor could be a greatest possible natural number; indeed, there isn't a greatest, *actual* number, let alone a greatest possible. And the same goes for islands. No matter how great an island is,…there could always be a greater.…The qualities that make for greatness in islands—number of palm trees, amount and quality of coconuts, for example—most, of these qualities have no *intrinsic maximum*. That is, there is no degree of productivity or number of palm trees (or of dancing girls) such that it is impossible that an island display more of that quality. So the idea of a greatest possible island is an inconsistent or incoherent idea; it's not possible that there be such a thing. And hence the analogue of step (3) of Anselm's argument (it is possible that God exists) is not true for the perfect island argument; so that argument fails.

But doesn't Anselm's argument itself founder upon the same rock? If the idea of a greatest possible island is inconsistent, won't the same hold for the idea of a greatest possible being? Perhaps not. For what are the properties in virtue of which one being is greater, just as a being, than another? Anselm clearly has in mind such properties as wisdom, knowledge, power, and moral excellence or moral perfection. And certainly knowledge, for example, does have an intrinsic maximum: if for every proposition p, a being B knows whether or not p is true, then B has a degree of knowledge that is utterly unsurpassable. So a greatest possible being would have to have this kind of knowledge: it would have to be *omniscient*. Similarly for *power*; omnipotence is a degree of power that can't possibly be excelled. Moral perfection or moral excellence is perhaps not quite so clear; still a being could perhaps always do what is morally right, so that it would not be possible for it to be exceeded along those lines.…

The usual criticisms of Anselm's argument, then, leave much to be desired. Of course, this doesn't mean that the argument is successful, but it does mean that we shall have to take an independent look at it. What about Anselm's argument? Is it a good one? The first thing to recognize is that the ontological argument comes in an enormous variety of versions, some of which may be much more promising than others. Instead of speaking of *the* ontological argument, we must recognize that what we have here is a whole family of related arguments. (Having said this I shall violate my own directive and continue to speak of *the* ontological argument.)

THE ARGUMENT RESTATED

Let's look once again at our initial schematization of the argument. I think perhaps it is step (2)

(2) Existence in reality is greater than existence in the understanding alone

that is most puzzling here. Earlier we spoke of the properties in virtue of which one being is greater, just as a being, than another. Suppose we call them *great-making properties*. Apparently Anselm means to suggest that *existence* is a great-making property. He seems to suggest that a nonexistent being would be greater than in fact it is, if it did exist. But how can we make sense of that? How could there be a nonexistent being anyway? Does that so much as make sense?

Perhaps we can put this perspicuously in terms of possible worlds. An object may exist in some possible worlds and not others. There are possible worlds in which you and I do not exist; these worlds are impoverished, no doubt, but are not on that account impossible. Furthermore, an object can have different properties in different worlds. In the actual world Paul J. Zwier is not a good tennis player; but surely there are worlds in which he wins the Wimbledon Open. Now if a person can have different properties in different worlds, then he can have different degrees of greatness in different worlds. In the actual world Raquel Welch has impressive assets; but there is a world RW_f in which she is fifty pounds overweight and mousy. Indeed, there are worlds in which she does not so much as exist. What Anselm means to be suggesting, I think, is that Raquel Welch enjoys very little greatness in those worlds in which she does not exist. But of course this condition is not restricted to Miss Welch. What Anselm means to say, more generally, is that for any being x and worlds W and W', if x exists in W but not in W', then x's greatness in W exceeds x's greatness in W'. Or, more modestly, perhaps he means to say that if a being x does not exist in a world W (and there is a world in which x does exist), *then there is at least one world* in which the greatness of x exceeds the greatness of x in W. Suppose Raquel Welch does not exist in some world W. Anselm means to say that there is at least one possible world in which she has a degree of greatness that exceeds the degree of greatness she has in that world W. (It is plausible, indeed, to go much further and hold that she has *no greatness at all* in worlds in which she does not exist.)

But now perhaps we can restate the whole argument in a way that gives us more insight into its real structure. Once more, use the term "God" to abbreviate the phrase "the being than which it is not possible that there be a greater." Now suppose

(13) God does not exist in the actual world.

Add the new version of premise (2):

(14) For any being x and world W, if x does not exist in W, then there is a world W' such that the greatness of x in W' exceeds the greatness of x in W.

Restate premise (3) in terms of possible worlds:

(15) There is a possible world in which God exists.

And continue on:

(16) If God does not exist in the actual world, then there is a world W' such that the greatness of God in W' exceeds the greatness of God in the actual world. [from (14)]

(17) So there is a world W' such that the greatness of God in W' exceeds the greatness of God in the actual world. [(13) and (16)]

(18) So there is a possible being x and a world W' such that the greatness of x in W' exceeds the greatness of God in actuality. [(17)]

(19) Hence it's possible that there be a being greater than God is. [(18)]

(20) So it's possible that there be a being greater than the being than which it's not possible

that there be a greater. [(19), replacing "God" by what it abbreviates]

But surely

(21) It's not possible that there be a being greater than the being than which it's not possible that there be a greater.

So (13) [with the help of premises (14) and (15)] appears to imply (20), which, according to (21), is necessarily false. Accordingly, (13) is false. So the actual world contains a being than which it's not possible that there be a greater—that is, God exists.

Now where, if anywhere, can we fault this argument? Step (13) is the hypothesis for *reductio*, the assumption to be reduced to absurdity, and is thus entirely above reproach. Steps (16) through (20) certainly look as if they follow from the items they are said to follow from. So that leaves only (14), (15), and (20). Step (14) says only that it is possible that God exists. Step (15) also certainly seems plausible: if a being doesn't even *exist* in a given world, it can't have much by way of greatness in that world. At the very least it can't have its *maximum* degree of greatness—a degree of greatness that it does not excel in any other world—in a world where it doesn't exist. And consider (20): surely it has the ring of truth. How could there be a being greater than the being than which it's not possible that there be a greater? Initially, the argument seems pretty formidable.

Its Fatal Flaw

But there is something puzzling about it. We can see this if we ask what sorts of things (14) is supposed to be about. It starts off boldly: "For any being x and world W...." So (14) is talking about worlds and beings. It says something about each world-being pair. And (16) follows from it, because (16) asserts of *God* and *the actual world* something that according to (14) holds of every being and world. But then if (16) follows from (14), God must be a *being*. That is, (16) follows from (14) only with the help of the additional premise that God is a being. And doesn't this statement—that God is a being—imply that *there is* or *exists* a being than which it's not possible that there be a greater? But if so, the argument flagrantly begs the question; for then we can accept the inference from (14) to (16) only if we already know that the conclusion is true.

We can approach this same matter by a slightly different route. I asked earlier what sorts of things (14) was *about*; the answer was: beings and worlds. We can ask the same or nearly the same question by asking about the *range* of the *quantifiers*—"for any being," "for any world"—in (14). What do these quantifiers range over? If we reply that they range over possible worlds and beings—*actually existing* beings—then the inference to (16) requires the additional premise that God is an actually existing being, that there *really* is a being than which it is not possible that there be a greater. Since this is supposed to be our conclusion, we can't very gracefully add it as a *premise*. So perhaps the quantifiers don't range just over actually existing beings. But what else is there? Step (18) speaks of a *possible being*—a thing that may not in fact exist, but *could* exist. Or we could put it like this. A possible being is a thing that exists in some possible world or other; a thing *x* for which there is a world *W*, such that if *W* had been actual, *x* would have existed. So (18) is really about worlds and *possible beings*. And what it says is this: take any possible being *x* and any possible world *W*. If *x* does not exist in *W*, then there is a possible world *W'* where *x* has a degree of greatness that surpasses the greatness that it has in *W*. And hence to make the argument complete perhaps we should add the affirmation that God is a *possible being*.

But *are* there any possible beings—that is, *merely* possible beings, beings that don't in fact exist? If so, what sorts of things are they? Do they have properties? How are we to think of them? What is their status? And what reasons are there for supposing that there are any such peculiar items at all?

These are knotty problems. Must we settle them in order even to consider this argument? No. For instead of speaking of *possible beings* and the worlds in which they do or don't exist, we can speak of *properties* and the worlds in which they do or don't *have instances*, are or are not *instantiated* or *exemplified*. Instead of speaking of a possible being named by the phrase, "the being than which it's not possible that

there be a greater," we may speak of the property *having an unsurpassable degree of greatness*—that is, *having a degree of greatness such that it's not possible that there exist a being having more*. And then we can ask whether this property is instantiated in this or other possible worlds. Later on I shall show how to restate the argument this way. For the moment please take my word for the fact that we can speak as freely as we wish about possible objects; for we can always translate ostensible talk about such things into talk about properties and the worlds in which they are or are not instantiated.

The argument speaks, therefore, of an unsurpassably great being—of a being whose greatness is not excelled by any being in any world. This being has a degree of greatness so impressive that no other being in any world has more. But here we hit the question crucial for this version of the argument. *Where* does this being have that degree of greatness? I said above that the same being may have different degrees of greatness in different worlds; in which world does the possible being in question have the degree of greatness in question? All we are really told, in being told that God is a possible being, is this: among the possible beings there is one that in some world or other has a degree of greatness that is nowhere excelled.

And this fact is fatal to this version of the argument. I said earlier that (21) has the ring of truth; a closer look (listen?) reveals that it's more of a dull thud. For it is ambiguous as between

(21′) It's not possible that there be a being whose greatness surpasses that enjoyed by the unsurpassably great being *in the worlds where its greatness is at a maximum*

and

(21″) It's not possible that there be a being whose greatness surpasses that enjoyed by the unsurpassably great being *in the actual world*.

There is an important difference between these two. The greatest possible being may have different degrees of greatness in different worlds. Step (21′) points to the worlds in which this being has its maximal greatness; and it says, quite properly, that the degree of greatness this being has in those worlds is nowhere excelled. Clearly this is so. The greatest possible being is a possible being who in some world or other has unsurpassable greatness. Unfortunately for the argument, however, (21′) does not contradict (20). Or to put it another way, what follows from (13) [together with (14) and (15)] is not the denial of (21′). If that *did* follow, then the *reductio* would be complete and the argument successful. But what (20) says is not that there is a possible being whose greatness exceeds that enjoyed by the greatest possible being *in a world where the latter's greatness is at a maximum*; it says only that there is a possible being whose greatness exceeds that enjoyed by the greatest possible being *in the actual world*—where, for all we know, its greatness is *not* at a maximum. So if we read (21) as (21′) the *reductio* argument falls apart.

Suppose instead we read it as (21″). Then what it says is that there couldn't be a being whose greatness surpasses that enjoyed by the greatest possible being in Kronos, the actual world. So read, (21) does contradict (20). Unfortunately, however, we have no reason, so far, for thinking that (21″) is true at all, let alone necessarily true. If, among the possible beings, there is one whose greatness *in some world or other* is absolutely maximal—such that no being in any world has a degree of greatness surpassing it—then indeed there couldn't be a being that was greater than *that*. But it doesn't follow that this being has that degree of greatness in the *actual* world. It has it *in some world or other* but not necessarily in Kronos, the actual world. And so the argument fails. If we take (21) as (21′) then it follows from the assertion that God is a possible being; but it is of no use to the argument. If we take it as (21″), on the other hand, then indeed it is useful in the argument, but we have no reason whatever to think it true. So this version of the argument fails.[1]

A MODAL VERSION
OF THE ARGUMENT

But of course there are many other versions; one of the argument's chief features is its many-sided diversity. The fact that *this* version is unsatisfactory does not show that *every* version is or must be. Professors Charles Hartshorne[2] and Normal Malcolm[3] claim to detect two quite different versions of the argument in Anselm's work. In the first of these versions *existence* is held to be a perfection or a great-making property; in the second it is *necessary existence*. But what could *that* amount to? Perhaps something like this. Consider a pair of beings A and B that both do in fact exist. And suppose that A exists in every other possible world as well—that is, if any other possible world has been actual, A would have existed. On the other hand, B exists in only some possible worlds; there are worlds W such that had any of *them* been actual, B would not have existed. Now according to the doctrine under consideration, A is so far greater than B. Of course, *on balance* it may be that A is not greater than B; I believe that the number seven, unlike Spiro Agnew, exists in every possible world; yet I should be hesitant to affirm on that account that the number seven is greater than Agnew. Necessary existence is just one of several great-making properties, and no doubt Agnew has more of some of these others than does the number seven. Still, all this is compatible with saying that necessary existence is a great-making property. And given this notion, we can restate the argument as follows:

(22) It is possible that there is a greatest possible being.

(23) Therefore, there is a possible being that in some world W' or other has a maximum degree of greatness—a degree of greatness that is no where exceeded.

(24) A being B has the maximum degree of greatness in a given possible world W only if B *exists in every possible world*.

(22) and (24) are the premises of this argument; and what follows is that if W' had been actual, B would have existed in every possible world. That is, if W' had been actual, B's nonexistence would have been impossible. But logical possibilities and impossibilities do not vary from world to world. That is to say, if a given proposition or state of affairs is impossible in at least one possible world, then it is impossible in every possible world. There are no propositions that in fact are possible but could have been impossible; there are none that are in fact impossible but could have been possible.[4] Accordingly, B's nonexistence is impossible

in every possible world; hence it is impossible in *this* world; hence *B* exists and exists necessarily.

A Flaw in the Ointment

This is an interesting argument, but it suffers from at least one annoying defect. What it shows is that if it is possible that there be a greatest possible being (if the idea of a greatest possible being is coherent) and if that idea includes necessary existence, then in fact there is a being that exists in every world and in *some* world has a degree of greatness that is nowhere excelled. Unfortunately it doesn't follow that the being in question has the degree of greatness in question in Kronos, the actual world. For all the argument shows, this being might *exist* in the actual world but be pretty insignificant here. In some world or other it has maximal greatness; how does this show that it has such greatness in Kronos? . . .

In determining the greatness of a being *B* in a world *W*, what counts is not merely the qualities and properties possessed by *B* in *W*; what *B* is like in *other* worlds is also relevant. Most of us who believe in God think of Him as a being than whom it's not possible that there be a greater. But we don't think of Him as a being who, had things been different, would have been powerless or uninformed or of dubious moral character. God doesn't *just happen* to be a greatest possible being; He couldn't have been otherwise.

Perhaps we should make a distinction here between *greatness* and *excellence*. A being's excellence in a given world *W*, let us say, depends only upon the properties it has in *W*; its *greatness* in *W* depends upon these properties but also upon what it is like in other worlds. Those who are fond of the calculus might put it by saying that there is a function assigning to each being in each world a degree of excellence; and a being's *greatness* is to be computed (by someone unusually well informed) by integrating its excellence over all possible worlds. Then it is plausible to suppose that the maximal degree of greatness entails *maximum excellence in every world*. A being, then, has the maximal degree of *greatness* in a given world *W* only if it has *maximal excellence in every possible world*. But *maximal excellence* entails *omniscience, omnipotence, and*

moral perfection. That is to say, a being *B* has maximal excellence in a world *W* only if *B* has omniscience, omnipotence, and moral perfection in *W*—only if *B* would have been omniscient, omnipotent, and morally perfect if *W* had been actual.

The Argument Restated

Given these ideas, we can restate the present version of the argument in the following more explicit way.

(25) It is possible that there be a being that has maximal greatness.

(26) So there is a possible being that in some world *W* has maximal greatness.

(27) A being has maximal greatness in a given world only if it has maximal excellence in every world.

(28) A being has maximal excellence in a given world only if it has omniscience, omnipotence, and moral perfection in that world.

And now we no longer need the supposition that necessary existence is a perfection; for obviously a being can't be omnipotent (or for that matter omniscient or morally perfect) in a given world unless it *exists* in that world. From (25), (27), and (28) it follows that there actually exists a being that is omnipotent, omniscient, and morally perfect; this being, furthermore, exists and has these qualities in every other world as well. For (26), which follows from (25), tells us that there is a possible world *W'*, let's say, in which there exists a being with maximal greatness. That is, had *W'* been actual, there would have been a being with maximal greatness. But then according to (27) this being has maximal excellence in every world. What this means, according to (28), is that in *W'* this being has omniscience, omnipotence, and moral perfection *in every world*. That is to say, if *W'* had been actual, there would have existed a being who was omniscient and omnipotent and morally perfect and who would have had these properties in every possible world. So if *W'* had been actual, it would have been *impossible* that there be no omnipotent, omniscient, and morally perfect being: But . . . while *contingent* truths vary from world to world, what is logically impossible does not. Therefore, in every possible world W it is impossible that there be no such being; each possible world W is such that if it had been actual, it would have been impossible that there be no such being. And hence it is impossible in the *actual* world (which is one of the possible worlds) that there be no omniscient, omnipotent, and morally perfect being. Hence there really does exist a being who is omniscient, omnipotent, and morally perfect and who exists and has these properties in every possible world. Accordingly these premises, (25), (27), and (28), entail that God, so thought of, exists. Indeed, if we regard (27) and (28) as consequences of a *definition*—a definition of maximal greatness—then the only premise of the argument is (25).

But now for a last objection suggested earlier. What about (25)? It says that there is a *possible being* having such and such characteristics. But what *are* possible beings? We know what *actual* beings are—the Taj Mahal, Socrates, you and I, the Grand Teton—these are among the more impressive examples of actually existing beings. But what is a *possible* being? Is there a possible mountain just like Mt. Rainier two miles directly south of the Grand Teton? If so, it is located at the same place as the Middle Teton. Does that matter? Is there another such possible mountain three miles east of the Grand Teton, where Jenny Lake is? Are there possible mountains like this all over the world? Are there also possible oceans at all the places where there are possible mountains? For any place you mention, of course, it is *possible* that there be a mountain there; does it follow that in fact *there is* a possible mountain there?

These are some questions that arise when we ask ourselves whether there are merely possible beings that don't in fact exist. And the version of the ontological argument we've been considering seems to make sense only on the assumption that there are such things. The earlier versions also depended on that assumption; consider for example, this step of the first version we considered:

(18) So there is a possible being x and a world W' such that the greatness of x in W' exceeds the greatness of God in actuality.

This possible being, you recall, was God Himself, supposed not to exist in the actual world. We can make

sense of (18), therefore, only if we are prepared to grant that there are possible beings who don't in fact exist. Such beings exist in other worlds, of course; had things been appropriately different, they would have existed. But in fact they don't exist, although nonetheless there *are* such things.

I am inclined to think the supposition that there are such things—things that are possible but don't in fact exist—is either unintelligible or necessarily false. But this doesn't mean that the present version of the ontological argument must be rejected. For we can restate the argument in a way that does not commit us to this questionable idea. Instead of speaking of *possible beings* that do or do not exist in various possible worlds, we may speak of *properties* and the worlds in which they are or are not *instantiated*. Instead of speaking of the possible fat man in the corner, noting that he doesn't exist, we may speak of the property *being a fat man in the corner*, noting that it isn't instantiated (although it could have been). Of course, the *property* in question, like the property *being a unicorn*, exists. It is a perfectly good property which exists with as much equanimity as the property of equininity, the property of being a horse. But it doesn't happen to apply to anything. That is, in *this* world it doesn't apply to anything; in other possible worlds it does.

THE ARGUMENT TRIUMPHANT

Using this idea we can restate this last version of the ontological argument in such a way that it no longer matters whether there are any merely possible beings that do not exist. Instead of speaking of the possible being that has, in some world or other, a maximal degree of greatness, we may speak of *the property of being maximally great* or *maximal greatness*. The premise corresponding to (25) then says simply that maximal greatness is possibly instantiated, i.e., that

(29) There is a possible world in which maximal greatness is instantiated.

And the analogues of (27) and (28) spell out what is involved in maximal greatness:

(30) Necessarily, a being is maximally great only if it has maximal excellence in every world

and

(31) Necessarily, a being has maximal excellence in every world only if it has omniscience, omnipotence, and moral perfection in every world.

Notice that (30) and (31) do not imply that there are possible but nonexistent beings—any more than does, for example,

(32) Necessarily, a thing is a unicorn only if it has one horn.

But if (29) is true, then there is a possible world W such that if it had been actual, then there would have existed a being that was omnipotent, omniscient, and morally perfect; this being, furthermore, would have had these qualities in every possible world. So it follows that if W had been actual, it would have been *impossible* that there be no such being. That is, if W had been actual,

(33) There is no omnipotent, omniscient, and morally perfect being

would have been an impossible proposition. But if a proposition is impossible in at least one possible world, then it is impossible in every possible world; what is impossible does not vary from world to world. Accordingly (33) is impossible in the *actual* world, i.e., impossible *simpliciter*. But if it is impossible that there be no such being, then there actually exists a being that is omnipotent, omniscient, and morally perfect; this being, furthermore, has these qualities essentially and exists in every possible world.

What shall we say of this argument? It is certainly valid; given its premise, the conclusion follows. The only question of interest, it seems to me, is whether its main premise—that maximal greatness is possibly instantiated—is *true*. It think it *is* true; hence I think this version of the ontological argument is sound.

But here we must be careful; we must ask whether this argument is a successful piece of natural theology, whether it *proves* the existence of God. And the answer must be, I think, that it does not. An argument for God's existence may be *sound*, after all, without in any useful sense proving God's existence.[5] Since I believe in God, I think the following argument is sound:

Either God exists or 7 + 5 = 14.
It is false that 7 + 5 = 14.
Therefore God exists.

But obviously this isn't a *proof*; no one who didn't already accept the conclusion, would accept the first premise. The ontological argument we've been examining isn't just like this one, of course, but it must be conceded that not everyone who understands and reflects on its central premise—that the existence of a maximally great being is *possible*—will accept it. Still, it is evident, I think, that there is nothing *contrary to reason* or *irrational* in accepting this premise.[6] What I claim for this argument, therefore, is that establishes, not the *truth* of theism, but its rational acceptability. And hence it accomplishes at least one of the aims of the tradition of natural theology.

Notes

1. This criticism of this version of the argument essentially follows David Lewis, "Anselm and Actuality," *Noûs* 4 (1970): 175–188. See also Alvin Plantinga, *The Nature of Necessity* (Oxford, England: Clarendon Press, 1974), pp. 202–205.
2. Charles Hartshorne, *Man's Vision of God* (New York: Harper and Row, 1941). Portions reprinted in Plantinga, ed., *The Ontological Argument* (Garden City, N.Y.: Doubleday, 1965), pp. 123–135.
3. Norman Malcolm, "Anselm's Ontological Arguments," *Philosophical Review* 69 (1960); reprinted in Plantinga, *The Ontological Argument,* pp. 136–139.
4. See Plantinga, "World and Essence," *Philosophical Review* 79 (October 1970): 475; and Plantinga, *The Nature of Necessity,* chap. 4, sec. 6.
5. See George Mavrodes, *Belief in God* (New York: Macmillan 1970), pp. 22ff.
6. For more on this see Plantinga, *The Nature of Necessity,* chap. 10, sec. 8.

Study Questions

1. How does Plantinga respond to Gaunilo's criticism of Anselm's ontological argument?
2. How does Plantinga reformulate the ontological argument in terms of possible worlds? Put his argument in your own words.
3. What is the confusion on which Plantinga thinks the traditional ontological argument rests?
4. How does Plantinga reformulate the ontological argument in terms of God's maximal greatness? What does Plantinga conclude about the success of his version of the ontological argument?

Thomas Aquinas

The Classical Cosmological Argument

In this selection, Thomas Aquinas (1224–1274) offers a deductive version of the cosmological argument. He states that we witness things in motion. For something to move, it must be moved by something else, a view for which Aquinas gives three arguments. That which moves things either is moved by another thing in motion or is itself unmoved (in which case an unmoved mover exists). The former option invokes an infinite regress of movers, which is impossible. For one thing, it would involve moving an infinite number of things in a finite time. For another, if one removes the cause one removes the effect. But an infinite series has no first cause, and thus can have no effect. Finally, if all the causes are instrumental causes, there is no first cause to bring about the effect. Hence, there must be an unmoved mover, which religious believers understand to be God.

ARGUMENTS IN PROOF OF THE EXISTENCE OF GOD

[1] We have now shown that the effort to demonstrate the existence of God is not a vain one. We shall therefore proceed to set forth the arguments by which both philosophers and Catholic teachers have proved that God exists....

[3] Of these ways the first is as follows.[1] Everything that is moved is moved by another. That some things are in motion—for example, the sun—is evident from sense. Therefore, it is moved by something else that moves it. This mover is itself either moved or not moved. If it is not, we have reached our conclusion—namely, that we must posit some unmoved mover. This we call God. If it is moved, it is moved by another mover. We must, consequently, either proceed to infinity, or we must arrive at some unmoved mover. Now, it is not possible to proceed to infinity. Hence, we must posit some prime unmoved mover.

[4] In this proof, there are two propositions that need to be proved, namely, that *everything that is moved is moved by another*, and that *in movers and things moved one cannot proceed to infinity*.

[5] The first of these propositions Aristotle proves in three ways. The *first* way is as follows. If something moves itself, it must have within itself the principle of its own motion; otherwise, it is clearly moved by another. Furthermore, it must be primarily moved.

From *Summa Contra Gentiles* I, chap. 13, by Thomas Aquinas, trans. A. C. Pegis (Notre Dame, Ind.: University of Notre Dame Press), 1975.

This means that it must be moved by reason of itself, and not by reason of a part of itself, as happens when an animal is moved by the motion of its foot. For, in this sense, a whole would not be moved by itself, but a part, and one part would be moved by another. It is also necessary that a self-moving being be divisible and have parts, since, as it is proved in the *Physics*,[2] whatever is moved is divisible.

[6] On the basis of these suppositions Aristotle argues as follows. That which is held to be moved by itself is primarily moved. For if, while one part was at rest, another part in it were moved, then the whole itself would not be primarily moved; it would be that part in it which is moved while another part is at rest. But nothing that is at rest because something else is at rest is moved by itself; for that being whose rest follows upon the rest of another must have its motion follow upon the motion of another. It is thus not moved by itself. Therefore, that which was posited as being moved by itself is not moved by itself. Consequently, everything that is moved must be moved by another....

[8] In the *second* way, Aristotle proves the proposition by induction.[3] Whatever is moved by accident is not moved by itself, since it is moved upon the motion of another. So, too, as is evident, what is moved by violence is not moved by itself. Nor are those beings moved by themselves that are moved by their nature as being moved from within; such is the case with animals, which evidently are moved by the soul. Nor, again, is this true of those beings, such as heavy and light bodies, which are moved through nature. For such beings are moved by the generating cause and the cause removing impediments. Now, whatever is moved is moved through itself or by accident. If it is moved through itself, then it is moved either violently or by nature; if by nature, then either through itself, as the animal, or not through itself, as heavy and light bodies. Therefore, everything that is moved is moved by another.

[9] In the *third* way, Aristotle proves the proposition as follows.[4] The same thing cannot be at once in act and in potency with respect to the same thing. But everything that is moved is, as such, in potency. For motion is *the act of something that is in potency inasmuch as it is in potency*.[5] That which moves, however, is as such in act, for nothing acts except according as it is in act. Therefore, with respect to the same motion, nothing is both mover and moved. Thus, nothing moves itself....

[11] The second proposition, namely, *that there is no procession to infinity among movers and things moved*, Aristotle proves in three ways.

[12] The *first* is as follows.[6] If among movers and things moved we proceed to infinity, all these infinite beings must be bodies. For whatever is moved is divisible and a body, as is proved in the *Physics*.[7] But every body that moves some thing moved is itself moved while moving it. Therefore, all these infinites are moved together while one of them is moved. But one of them, being finite, is moved in a finite time. Therefore, all those infinites are moved in a finite time. This, however, is impossible. It is, therefore, impossible that among movers and things moved one can proceed to infinity.

[13] Furthermore, that it is impossible for the above-mentioned infinites to be moved in a finite time Aristotle proves as follows. The mover and the thing moved must exist simultaneously. This Aristotle proves by induction in the various species of motion. But bodies cannot be simultaneous except through continuity or contiguity. Now, since, as has been proved, all the aforementioned movers and things moved are bodies, they must constitute by continuity or contiguity a sort of single mobile. In this way, one infinite is moved in a finite time. This is impossible, as is proved in the *Physics*.[8]

[14] The *second* argument proving the same conclusion is the following.[9] In an ordered series of movers and things moved (this is a series in which one is moved by another according to an order), it is necessarily the fact that, when the first mover is removed or ceases to move, no other mover will move or be moved. For the first mover is the cause of motion for all the others. But, if there are movers and things moved following an order to infinity, there will be no first mover, but all would be as intermediate movers. Therefore, none of the others will be able to be moved, and thus nothing in the world will be moved.

[15] The *third* proof comes to the same conclusion, except that, by beginning with the superior, it has a

reversed order. It is as follows. That which moves as an instrumental cause cannot move unless there be a principal moving cause. But, if we proceed to infinity among movers and things moved, all movers will be as instrumental causes, because they will be moved movers and there will be nothing as a principal mover. Therefore, nothing will be moved.

[16] Such, then, is the proof of both propositions assumed by Aristotle in the first demonstrative way by which he proved that a first unmoved mover exists.

NOTES

1. Aristotle, *Physics*, VII, 1 (241b 24).
2. Aristotle, *Physics*, VI, 4 (234b 10).
3. Aristotle, *Physics*, VIII, 4 (254b 8).
4. Aristotle, *Physics*, VIII, 5 (257a 39).
5. Aristotle, *Physics*, III, 1 (201a 10).
6. Aristotle, *Physics*, VII, 1 (241b 24).
7. Aristotle, *Physics*, VI, 4 (234b 10).
8. Aristotle, *Physics*, VII, 1 (241b 12); VI, 7 (237b 23ff.).
9. Aristotle, Physics, VIII, 5 (256a 12).

STUDY QUESTIONS

1. What is Aquinas's argument for the existence of God from motion?
2. Aquinas identifies two major presuppositions in the argument. In your own words, present one of his arguments in defense of each of these key presuppositions.

Bruce R. Reichenbach

The Cosmological Argument

Some theists claim that God's existence best explains the existence of our contingent universe. Bruce Reichenbach (b. 1943) explores the need for explanation, noting the defenses given for versions of the Principles of Sufficient Reason and Causation. The moderate version of the Principle of Sufficient Reason, according to which whatever is contingent or comes into being needs an explanation—is what the cosmological argument must invoke to succeed. After distinguishing scientific from personal explanation in terms of intention, he notes that theists have held that a variety of things, including individual contingent things and the universe, require an explanation. He then presents a version of the cosmological argument from contingency and defends it against three serious objections. The first is that the universe just is, the second is that one explains the whole by explaining the parts, and the third is that the conclusion of the argument is contradictory. In the end, Reichenbach suggests that a necessary being or God, to whom the Principle of Sufficient Reason is inapplicable, provides the best explanation in the cases he considers.

Theists are in good company when they look for explanations either of the universe or of particular phenomena within it. Historians search for explanations of why Hitler invaded Russia, economists for fluctuations in the GNP, psychologists for why some teens commit suicide, and natural scientists for why Eastern songbirds experience reduced breeding. Some invoke personal explanations, other natural or scientific explanations; yet all strive for the best explanation of what exists or happens or what they experience. In what follows I will say something about the nature of explanation, discuss what in the universe needs explanation that is best provided by the activity of God, and suggest why it is that God provides the best explanation of specific things or events.

1. The Need for Explanation

Explanatory reasoning that infers God's existence and activity has a long and distinguished career. Although Thomas Aquinas's thirteenth-century *Summae* contain the classical Western formulations, his arguments are firmly rooted in Aristotelian physics. Aristotle held

Chapter by Bruce Reichenbach in Michael Peterson and Raymond Vanarragon, eds. *Contemporary Debates in the Philosophy of Religion* (Oxford, England: Blackwell, 2003).

that to understand or explain why something exists as it does, one must appeal to the three principles (form, matter, privation) and the four causes. Aquinas uses this structure, especially efficient and final causes, to construct his arguments for God's existence. For Aquinas, the existence of things in motion, of effects, and of contingent beings requires the causal activity of other things, for something must already be actual to realize another's potency, and if what is actual is itself an effect, it too requires a causal explanation for its existence and causal efficacy (for example, as an intermediate mover). The process proceeds until we must invoke the existence of something that causes but is itself not an effect.

Subsequent Enlightenment versions of this argument gradually depart from Aristotelian physics and instead appeal to a more general principle called the Principle of Sufficient Reason, according to which "no fact can be real or existing and no statement true unless it has a sufficient reason why it should be thus and not otherwise."[1] The contingent has causes, which themselves stand in need of causal explanation. Since an explanation in terms of other things that need explanation cannot sufficiently account for the existent if the series of explanations proceeds to infinity, that which ultimately explains any contingent fact must stand outside this infinity of contingent causes; the ultimate cause must be a necessary being that "has the reason for its existence in itself."[2]

Contemporary philosophers have distinguished among versions of the Principle of Sufficient Reason. On the one hand, William Rowe questions the rational defense, intuitiveness, and necessary truth of Leibniz's strong version of the principle, according to which all existents must have a cause of their existence.[3] However, this version of the principle is stronger than the cosmological argument actually requires. On the other hand, the very weak version suggested by Richard Gale—namely, that it is *possible* that every fact has an explanation—is too weak to sustain the deductive cosmological argument, for since this weak version would not require an explanation for the contingent, it could at best lead to the conclusion that if the contingent has an explanation, the best explanation would be based on God's activity.[4] The cosmological argument requires a moderate version of the principle, which holds that

what is contingent or what comes into being requires a sufficient reason for why it exists or comes into being. The *contingent* needs an explanation because, although it exists, it could have not existed, and hence an explanation of why it exists rather than not is a reasonable demand. *What comes into existence* needs an explanation because, since things cannot bring themselves into existence or spring out of nothing, they must have a cause for their coming to be.

The moderate version of the Principle of Sufficient Reason is not derivable from more basic principles; an argument to derive it would ultimately invoke the principle itself, and hence beg the question. However, this is not to say that the principle is unjustified; its justification is located not only in the pragmatics of explanation[5] but also in the metaphysics of contingency. When so placed in metaphysics, it is perhaps better to speak about the Principle of Causation, according to which whatever exists contingently cannot have its existence from itself but is dependent upon something else for its existence, either at the moment of its conception or continuously. Since dependency is a causal notion, contingency itself requires that the cause be sufficient to bring about the effect.[6]

The classic argument against the necessity of the Principle of Causation is found in David Hume, who argues that "as all distinct ideas are separable from each other, and as the ideas of cause and effect are evidently distinct, 'twill be easy for us to conceive any object to be non-existent this moment, and existent the next, without conjoining to it the distinct idea of a cause or productive principle. The separation, therefore, of the idea of a cause from that of a beginning of existence, is plainly possible for the imagination; and consequently the actual separation of these objects is so far possible, that it implies no contradiction nor absurdity."[7] Hume's argument is that whatever items are distinguishable can be conceived to be separate from each other. Since cause and effect are distinguishable, they can be conceived to be separate. Since whatever is conceivable is possible in reality, cause and effect are separable, and the Principle of Causation is not necessarily true. For Hume, the criterion for deciding whether two things are distinguishable is whether we can entertain separate impressions of them. Distinguishability, therefore, is an epistemic category. Separability, however, is an ontological category, meaning that one thing can exist entirely independent of the other thing. But, so understood, Hume's critical premise that what is distinguishable is separable confuses epistemic with ontological conditions, and hence is not sound. The fact that we can have distinct impressions of things does not mean that those things are more than conceptually separable.[8]

In sum, there are two possible grounds for the Principle of Sufficient Reason: epistemic requirements for explanation and the ontology of contingency. Since reality need not meet subjective demands, an explanation grounded in ontological considerations leads to a stronger justification than that which places explanation merely within the subjective demand of rational endeavors. At the same time, an ontological grounding makes metaphysical commitments beyond those needed when grounding the principle in epistemic considerations.

2. Partial and Full Explanations

Theists construct both cosmological and teleological arguments around causal explanations for particular phenomena. Explanation contains two components: a description of what brought about the effect (the cause) and why the effect occurred. The causal factors are independent of the effect; otherwise there is no bringing about. A partial explanation appeals to some, often notable, causal condition that is partly responsible for the effect. That the boy played with matches partially but satisfactorily accounts for why the building burned, all things being equal (that the building was constructed of flammable material, oxygen was present, etc.). But a partial explanation, though often adequate from an epistemic or interest point of view, is inadequate when one wants to discover the ontology of the situation. Such requires a full explanation, which includes a *full* cause (the set of causal conditions that were individually necessary and jointly sufficient for the effect to occur) and "the reason why the cause, under the specified conditions, had the effect that it had."[9] The theistic arguments demand that whatever exists contingently or arises have a full explanation; otherwise there is no reason why something would exist or arise rather than not exist or arise.[10]

3. Scientific Explanation and Personal Explanation

Richard Swinburne distinguishes two types of explanation, the scientific and the personal. In a scientific explanation, the causes are natural features, events, processes, or conditions, and the "whys" are natural laws stating that events or things of a certain sort under specified conditions bring about effects of a certain sort. In a scientific explanation, given the causal conditions and the scientific laws operative at the time, the effect will—or perhaps better, given quantum and chaotic indeterminacy, probably will—occur.

A personal explanation, on the other hand, provides an "explanation in terms of the intentional action of a person."[11] It is appropriately invoked when scientific explanations do not suffice or when the personal explanation is simpler and no explanatory power is lost. Yet a personal explanation provides as legitimate an explanation as a scientific one.

Swinburne argues that personal explanations are not reducible to scientific explanations. That an action results from an agent having a specific intention is not equivalent to the action being brought about by a person's brain states, for a brain state could bring about an event without the person intending to bring it about. Intention does not belong to the "what" of the explanation but to why persons act as they do.[12] Yet, "the fact that personal explanation cannot be analyzed in terms of scientific explanation does not mean that its operation on a particular occasion cannot be given a scientific explanation."[13] In the case of certain phenomena, this inability to give a scientific explanation, or the unsatisfactoriness or incompleteness of such explanations, is crucial to inferring the existence and activity of God from a particular effect.

4. What Needs Theistic Explanation?

In the history of the cosmological and teleological arguments, theists have contended that a variety of things cannot satisfactorily receive their needed explanation from a fully naturalistic account. In general, theists have used two types of things in the initial premises of the cosmological argument. One is the *existence* of certain things—individual contingent beings, the universe, natural laws, or principles that govern events; the other, the *coming to be* of certain things, either the universe itself or its contents. This has led to two types of cosmological argument: arguments for a sustaining cause and arguments for an initiating cause.

With regard to the first type of argument, Thomas Aquinas held that among the things that need explanation for their existence are contingent beings, for such beings are dependent for their existence upon other beings. Richard Taylor and others argue that the universe (meaning everything that ever existed) as contingent needs explanation. William Rowe, arguing that the term "universe" refers to an abstract entity or set, rephrases the issue, "Why does that set (the universe) have the members that it does rather than some other members or none at all?"[14] That is, "Why is there something rather than nothing?"

With regard to the second type of argument, theists focus on the coming to be of the universe or of certain of its features. William Craig, for example, in his version of the Islamic Kalam argument, argues that since whatever begins to exist must have a cause, and since the universe began to exist, the universe had a cause.[15] ...

The danger in the versions of the theistic argument that commence from specific natural phenomena is that they smack of the appeal to a god of the gaps. The history of rational theology is fraught with examples where individuals invoke the activity of God to explain events for which scientific reasoning at the time could not account. As scientific knowledge progressed, however, explanations were forthcoming, and the invocation of God as an explanatory hypothesis was no longer necessary. If the above arguments are to avoid this troubled past, the events in question must be intrinsically, and not merely accidentally, completely inexplicable by scientific or naturalistic accounts. For example, Russell and Polkinghorne argue that it is not the case that we merely do not yet possess enough information to understand how particular effects arise from quantum causes; the indeterminacy resides in nature itself. Any quantum explanation has "intrinsic gaps."[16] Similarly, Craig argues that it is not simply our limited knowledge that prevents us from exploring the cause of the universe at the moment of its inception at the Big Bang. For the universe to develop out of infinite density is for it to develop out of nothing, and out of nothing, nothing comes.[17]

The point (and problem) here is to determine whether one has encountered an intrinsic gap in our ontology or whether the gap lies in our epistemic state. In this sense, Gale wisely warns the theist about developing arguments where the explanation in terms of God competes with that of science.[18] At the same time, it is not clear that explaining in terms of divine intention the origin of the Big Bang, the origin of life from nonliving physical/chemical elements, or why particular events arise out of quantum events competes with science, provided one can show ontological incongruity at these junctures....

5. Deductive and Inductive Inferences

The classical versions of the cosmological argument, which hold that the sufficient explanation for the existence or arising of contingencies necessitates the existence and activity of God, are deductive. The conclusion that God (or a necessary being) exists follows necessarily from either the existence or arising of contingent beings (whether individual contingent beings or the universe as a whole), the invocation of the Principle of Sufficient Reason in one of its forms (e.g., Aristotelian act/potency, the Leibnizian strong version, or the Principle of Causation), and the denial that an infinity of contingent beings or causal conditions can supply the requisite sufficient explanation.

Some contemporary versions of the cosmological argument are weaker. For one thing, the claim is not that the existence of God provides the *only* explanation, but rather that it provides the *best* explanation of the things or events in question. God's existence is simpler and has greater explanatory power.[19] For another, theists appeal not to one particular event requiring nonnatural explanation, but rather to a variety of phenomena for which the best explanation is a personal, intelligent supernatural being. From such a cumulative case that combines cosmological and teleological arguments with religious experience, they conclude that it is probable or more likely than not that God exists, given the total data. Should some of the data find their explanation elsewhere, the argument is not significantly affected, since sufficient other data point to the theistic conclusion as the best explanation.

In what follows we first consider the approach that the existence of a necessary being (what we will term God, though one need not use that term[20]) follows deductively from certain premises. The inductive approach, arguing that certain contingent phenomena find their best explanation in an appeal to the existence and activity of a supernatural being, we will not address.

6. THE DEDUCTIVE COSMOLOGICAL ARGUMENT FROM CONTINGENCY

Although the cosmological argument appears in various writers with different first premises, the fundamental structure and resulting issues are basically the same.

1. A contingent being (a being which, if it exists, can not-exist) exists.
2. This contingent being has a cause or explanation[21] of its existence.
3. The cause or explanation of its existence is something other than the contingent being itself.
4. What causes or explains the existence of this contingent being must either be solely other contingent beings or include a non-contingent (necessary) being.
5. Contingent beings alone cannot cause or explain the existence of a contingent being.
6. Therefore, what causes or explains the existence of this contingent being must include a non-contingent (necessary) being.
7. Therefore, a necessary being (a being which, if it exists, cannot not-exist) exists.

Premises 1 and 3 seem true, although objection has been raised to 3 on the grounds that certain complex things can be explained in terms of their components. We will look at this objection shortly. Premise 2 is seen by many to follow from the moderate version of the Principles of Sufficient Reason and Causation. If something is contingent, there must be a cause of its existence or a reason why it exists rather than not-exists. Premise 4 is true by virtue of the Principle of the Excluded Middle. Premises 6 and 7 follow validly from the respective premises.

For many critics, premise 5 is the key to the argument's success or failure. Whether it is true depends upon the requirements for an adequate explanation. We have already noted that, according to the Principle of Sufficient Reason, at a minimum what is required is a *full explanation*—that is, an explanation that includes a full cause and the reason why the cause had the effect it did. If the contingent being in premise 1 is the universe, then a full explanation would require something beyond the contingent factors that, as part of the universe, are what are to be explained. That there has always been a magnetic field around the earth does not explain why there is a magnetic field. Similarly, that contingent or dependent things (a universe) have always existed fails to provide a sufficient reason for why the universe exists rather than not. A full explanation of the universe, then, would require the existence of a non-contingent causal condition—namely, a necessary being.

Finally, it should be noted in 7 that if the contingent being identified in 1 is the universe, the necessary being cannot provide a natural explanation for it, for no natural, non-contingent causes and laws or principles exist from which the existence of the universe follows. What remains is a personal explanation in terms of the intentional acts of some supernatural being that is eternal and *a sei*, properties that follow necessarily from its being essentially non-contingent.

6.1 First Objection: The Universe Just Is

Of the many objections to the argument, we will consider three major ones. First, over the centuries philosophers have suggested various instantiations for the contingent being noted in premise 1. The Thomistic form of the argument focuses on providing a causal explanation for particular contingent beings: something in motion, something caused, and a contingent being. Others, such as Samuel Clarke, suppose that the contingent being referred to in premise 1 is the universe. Due to considerations of space, we will focus on the second of these options.[22]

Bertrand Russell denies that the universe needs an explanation; it just is. His argument takes two forms. In the first version, Russell contends that since we derive the concept of cause from our observation of particular things, we cannot ask about the cause of the universe, which we cannot experience. The universe is "just there, and that's all."[23] Those who reason that we can apply the causal principle (that every contingent being requires a cause of its existence) to the universe commit the Fallacy of Composition, which mistakenly concludes that since the parts have a certain property, the whole likewise has that property. Applied to the cosmological argument, Russell contends that the move from the contingency of the elements of the universe to that of the universe is likewise fallacious. Hence, whereas we can ask for the cause of particular things, there is no reason to think we can ask for the cause of the universe or the set of all contingent beings.

Russell correctly notes that arguments of the part–whole type can commit the Fallacy of Composition. For example, the argument that since all the bricks in the wall are small, the wall is small, is fallacious. Yet sometimes the totality has the same character as the parts on account of the parts—the wall is brick because we built it out of bricks. The universe's contingency, theists argue, resembles the second case. If all the contingent things in the universe, including matter and energy, ceased to exist simultaneously, the universe itself, as the totality of these things, would cease to exist. But if the universe can cease to exist, it is contingent and requires an explanation for its existence.[24]

Some reply that this argument for the contingency of the universe is still fallacious, for even if every contingent being fails to exist in some possible world, it may be the case that there is no possible world that lacks a contingent being. That is, though no being would exist in every possible world, every world would possess at least one contingent being. Rowe

gives the example of a horse race. "We know that although no horse in a given horse race necessarily will be the winner, it is, nevertheless, necessary that some horse in the race will be the winner."[25]

Rowe's example fails, however, for it is possible that all the horses break a leg and none finishes the race. That is, the necessity that some horse will win follows only if there is some reason to think that some horse must finish the race. Similarly, the objection to the universe's contingency will hold only if there is some reason to think that the existence of something is necessary. One reason given is that the existence of one contingent being may be necessary for the nonexistence of some other contingent being.[26]

But though the fact that something's existence is necessary for the existence of something else holds for certain properties (for example, the existence of siblings is necessary for someone not to be an only child), it is doubtful that something's existence is necessary for something else's nonexistence *per se*, which claim is needed to support the argument denying the contingency of the universe. Hence, with no good reason to the contrary, given the contingency of everything in the universe, it remains that there is a possible world without any contingent beings.[27]

Further, given contemporary accounts both of the origin of the universe and, in some quarters, its probable demise, it is reasonable to think that the universe is the sort of thing that is contingent (it could conceivably not be) and hence requires an explanation. The very meaningfulness of the discussion mutes the view that the universe is an abstraction, like the human race. Behind Russell's denial of causal predicates to the universe lies a positivism that presumes that the only meaningful causal accounts are those that invoke natural or scientific explanations. But such a presumption begs the question, especially if we admit personal explanations as genuine explanations. In short, contrary to Russell, the theist commits neither a fallacy nor a category mistake in asking for an explanation of the existence of the universe.

Russell's second version appeals to quantum physics.[28] He notes that physicists find indetermination on the subatomic level. For example, it appears that electrons can pass out of existence at one point and then come back into existence elsewhere. One cannot trace their intermediate existence or determine what causes them to come into existence at one point rather than another. Their location is only statistically probable.[29] Since the singular event of the Big Bang is a microscopic event on the level where quantum principles apply, the cosmological argument cannot defend premise 2, and hence the argument fails.

Given our present knowledge, it is difficult to know what to say about this argument from quantum physics. As some wag quipped, "one who claims to understand quantum physics does not understand quantum physics."[30] Some argue that the phenomenon of indeterminacy results from the limits of our investigative equipment. We simply are unable at this time to discern the intermediate states of the electron's existence. According to a second view, termed "the Copenhagen interpretation" of quantum physics, the very introduction of the observer into the arena so affects what is observed that it gives the appearance that effects exist without causes. But one cannot know what is happening without introducing observers and the changes they bring. A third view is that the indeterminacy is real, but that the evidence of particles or energy coming into existence out of vacuum fluctuation is not equivalent to showing that they are uncaused. "Virtual particles do not literally come into existence spontaneously out of nothing.... 'The quantum vacuum states... are defined simply as local, or global, energy minima.' The microstructure of the quantum vacuum is a sea of continually forming and dissolving particles which borrow energy from the vacuum for their brief existence.... Thus vacuum fluctuations do not constitute an exception to the principle that whatever begins to exist has a cause."[31] In each of these three explanations of quantum phenomena, premise 2 holds. A fourth view is that we have no idea what laws of physics applied in the very early stages of the universe, and hence no reason to deny that the Causal Principle applied at that stage.

At the same time, it should be recognized that showing that indeterminacy is a real feature of the world at the quantum level would have significant negative implications for the more general Causal Principle that underlies the deductive cosmological argument.[32] Quantum accounts allow for additional speculation regarding origins and structures of universes (for example, Hawking's theory that the finite universe has no space-time boundaries and hence, without an initial singularity, requires no cause[33]).

6.2 Second Objection: Explaining The Individual Constituents Is Sufficient

A second objection, originally raised by David Hume, is that the whole is explained when the parts are explained. "But the *whole*, you say, wants a cause. I answer that the uniting of these parts into a whole...is performed merely by an arbitrary act of the mind, and has no influence on the nature of things. Did I show you the particular causes of each individual in a collection of twenty particles of matter, I should think it very unreasonable should you afterwards ask me what was the cause of the whole twenty. This is sufficiently explained in explaining the parts."[34]

On the one hand, it is not always true that the whole is sufficiently explained in explaining its parts. An explanation of the parts may provide a partial but incomplete explanation; what remains unexplained is why these parts exist rather than others, why they exist rather than not, or why the parts are arranged as they are. With respect to the latter, Gale gives the example of a heap of rocks. While a prisoner swinging a sledgehammer may explain the existence of each individual rock in the pile, it does not explain the existence of the heap assembled by another prisoner.[35]

However, although this shows that Hume's principle that the whole is explained in explaining the parts is sometimes false, it does not show that it is false in the case under consideration: namely, that of the universe treated as a set rather than as an aggregate. But suppose one invokes the explanation of the parts to explain the whole. In terms of what are the parts themselves explained? Each is explained either in terms of itself or in terms of something else. The former would make them necessary beings, contrary to their contingency. If they are explained in terms of something else, the entire collection still remains unaccounted for. "When the existence of each member of a collection is explained by reference to some other member *of that very same collection* then it does not follow that the collection itself has an explanation. For it is one thing for there to be an explanation of the existence of each dependent being and quite another thing for there to be an explanation of why there are dependent beings at all."[36] Swinburne notes that an explanation is complete when "any attempt to go beyond the factors which we have would result in no gain of explanatory power or prior probability."[37] But explaining why something exists rather than nothing, and why it is as it is, gives additional explanatory power in explaining why a universe exists at all. Hence, to explain the parts of the universe and their particular concatenation, appeal must be made to something other than those parts.[38]

6.3 Third Objection: The Conclusion Is Contradictory

Some, like Immanuel Kant and, more recently, Richard Gale, object to the conclusion that a necessary being exists. They contend that when the cosmological argument concludes to the existence of a necessary being, it argues for the existence of a being whose nonexistence is absolutely inconceivable. But the only being that meets this condition is the most real or maximally excellent being, the concept that lies at the heart of the ontological argument. Accordingly, they claim, the cosmological argument presupposes the cogency of the ontological argument. But since the ontological argument is suspect, the cosmological argument that depends on it must likewise be suspect.[39] Indeed, Gale argues, since it is impossible for an unsurpassably great necessary being to exist, the conclusion of the argument is necessarily false, and the argument unsound.[40]

However, the contention that the cosmological argument depends on the ontological argument is based on a confusion. The term *necessary being* can be understood in different ways. Kant, like some modern defenders of the ontological argument, understands "necessary being" as having to do with logically necessary existence—that is, with existence that is logically undeniable. But this is not the sense in which "necessary being" is understood in the cosmological argument. Necessity is understood in the

sense of ontological or factual necessity. A necessary being is one that *if* it exists, it cannot not-exist; as self-sufficient and self-sustaining, its inability to not-exist flows from its nature. Since such a concept is not self-contradictory, the existence of a necessary being is not intrinsically impossible...

9 WHY GOD PROVIDES THE BEST EXPLANATION

But why does God provide the best or ultimate explanation in the cases we have considered? Part of the answer is that God, or the necessary being, is a being who is not only uncaused but to whom the Principle of Causation is inapplicable. On the one hand, there can be no scientific explanation of God's existence, for there are no antecedent beings or scientific principles from which God's existence follows. On the other hand, the Principle of Causation applies only to contingent, and not to necessary, beings. Explanation is required only of those things that are contingent—that is, those things that if they do exist, could possibly not have existed. It is not that God's existence is logically necessary, but that if God exists, he cannot not-exist. God is both eternal and does not depend on anything for his existence. These, however, are not reasons for his existence, but his properties.

Another part of the answer is that explanation can be reasonably thought to have achieved finality when a personal explanation has been provided that appeals to the intentions of a conscious agent. One may, of course, attempt to provide a scientific account of why someone has the intentions that he or she has, but there is no requirement that such an account be supplied, let alone even be possible. We may not achieve any more explanatory value by trying to explain physically why persons intended to act as they did. However, when we claim that something happened because persons intended it and acted on their intentions, we can achieve a complete explanation of why that thing happened.

Third, appeal to God as an intentional agent leads us to have certain expectations about the universe: that it manifests order, that it is comprehensible, that it favors the existence of beings that can comprehend it. The presence of these features helps to satisfy 11 above.

Swinburne and Haldane introduce a fourth feature: namely, the simplicity of God that, by its very nature, makes further explanation either impossible or makes theism the best explanation, thereby satisfying 12 above. But that leads to a whole other set of issues regarding God's properties and the nature of simplicity, a fit subject for another time and place.

Much more can be said. In particular, it remains to be shown that the necessary being is the God of religion. This is not the task of the cosmological argument, but requires employment of the method of correlation, whereby the properties of the necessary being are correlated with those of the God of religion. But enough has been presented to indicate that the deductive and inductive cosmological arguments provide part of a cumulative justification for theistic belief.

NOTES

1. Gottfried Leibniz, *Monadology,* trans. George Hendrix (Chicago: Open Court, 1992), p. 32.
2. Ibid., p. 45.
3. William Rowe, *The Cosmological Argument* (Princeton, N.J.: Princeton University Press, 1975), pp. 73–94.
4. Richard Gale, *On the Nature and Existence of God* (Cambridge, England: Cambridge University Press, 1991), pp. 279–80.
5. Richard Taylor, *Metaphysics,* 4th ed. (Englewood Cliffs, N.J.: Prentice-Hall, 1992), pp. 88–89.
6. Joseph Owens, "The Causal Proposition—Principle or Conclusion?" *Modern Schoolman,* 32 (1955): 159–71, 257–70, 323–39.
7. David Hume, *Treatise of Human Nature* (Oxford, England: Clarendon Press, 1888), p. 79.
8. Bruce R. Reichenbach, *The Cosmological Argument: A Reassessment* (Springfield, Ill.: Charles Thomas, 1972), pp. 56–60.
9. Richard Swinburne, *The Existence of God* (Oxford, England: Oxford University Press, 1979), p. 24.
10. The fact that often it is impossible to specify the full cause in any given case does not affect the ontological requirement that there be such a full cause in order to bring about the effect.
11. Swinburne, *Existence of God,* p. 22.
12. For a fuller defense of these theses, see ibid., pp. 36–42.
13. Ibid., p. 47.
14. Rowe, *Cosmological Argument,* p. 136.
15. William Craig, *The Kalam Cosmological Argument* (London: Macmillan, 1979), p. 63.
16. John Polkinghorne, "Theological Notions of Creation and Divine Causality," in Murray Rae, Hilary Regan, and John Stenhouse, eds., *Science and Theology* (Grand Rapids, Mich.: William B. Eerdmans, 1994), p. 237.
17. William Lane Craig and Quentin Smith, *Theism, Atheism, and Big Bang Cosmology* (New York: Oxford University Press, 1993), pp. 43–444.
18. Gale, *On the Nature and Existence of God,* pp. 240–411.
19. Swinburne, *Existence of God,* ch. 7.
20. One must carefully distinguish between the contention that x exists and what x is, although the second is related to the first in that certain properties of x are required to make the cosmological argument work. See Smart and Haldane, *Atheism and Theism,* pp. 140–48.
21. I include the disjunct "cause or explanation" because not all versions of the cosmological argument invoke the Principle of Sufficient Reason expressed in the Enlightenment sense. The Thomistic arguments emphasize a causal account. Since an explanation is usually (but not always) given in causal language, we will not exploit the difference.
22. For a more detailed consideration of the Thomistic version of the argument, see Michael Peterson et al., *Reason and Religious Belief* (New York: Oxford University Press, 1991), pp. 76–79; Reichenbach, *Cosmological Argument*; Swinburne, *Existence of God,* pp. 87–89; Anthony Kenny, *The Five Ways* (Boston: Schocken Books, 1969).

23. Bertrand Russell and Frederick Copleston, "A Debate on the Existence of God," in John Hick, ed., *The Existence of God* (New York: Macmillan, 1964), p. 175.
24. Reichenbach, *Cosmological Argument,* ch. 6.
25. Rowe, *Cosmological Argument,* p. 164.
26. This reason was suggested to me by James Sadowsky.
27. The theist need not establish that in fact this is the case, only that it is possible. William Rowe (*Cosmological Argument,* p. 166) develops a different argument to support the thesis that the universe must be contingent. He argues that it is necessary that if God exists, then it is possible that no dependent beings exist. Since it is possible that God exists, it is possible that no dependent beings exist, and hence the universe is contingent. Rowe takes the conditional as necessarily true in virtue of the concept of God. That is, given who God is, it is up to God whether dependent beings exist or not.
28. See also Paul Davies, *Superforce* (New York: Simon and Schuster, 1984), p. 200.
29. Craig and Smith, *Theism, Atheism, and Big Bang Cosmology,* pp. 182, 121–23.
30. "The greatest paradox about quantum theory is that after more than fifty years of successful exploitation of its techniques its interpretation still remains a matter of dispute" (John Polkinghorne, *One World* (London: SPCK, 1986), p. 47).
31. Craig and Smith, *Theism, Atheism, and Big Bang Cosmology,* pp. 143–44.
32. Mark William Worthing, *God, Creation, and Contemporary Physics* (Minneapolis: Fortress, 1996), p. 50.
33. Stephen Hawking, *A Brief History of Time* (New York: Bantam Books, 1988), p. 136.
34. David Hume, *Dialogues Concerning Natural Religion,* part IX.
35. Gale, *On the Nature and Existence of God,* pp. 253–54.
36. Rowe, *Cosmological Argument,* p. 264.
37. Swinburne, *Existence of God,* p. 86.
38. Gale, *On the Nature and Existence of God,* pp. 257–58.
39. Immanuel Kant, *Critique of Pure Reason,* tr. Norman Kemp Smith (New York: St. Martin's Press, 1929), p. A606.
40. Gale, *On the Nature and Existence of God,* pp. 282–84.

Study Questions

1. In your own words, what is the cosmological argument? How does it differ from the ontological argument?
2. What are the Principles of Sufficient Reason and Causation to which the theist appeals in constructing the cosmological argument? How does the theist propose to defend the truth of these principles?
3. Reconstruct Russell's and Hume's arguments against the cosmological argument. What reply might the theist make to these arguments? Which do you think is more sound?
4. Why does the theist hold that the appeal to God provides a better explanation for the contingent universe than the appeal to any other cause?

William Lane Craig

The Kalam Cosmological Argument

According to the kalam cosmological argument developed by medieval Arabic philosophers, the universe had a cause of its existence because it had a beginning, and whatever has a beginning must have a cause. William Lane Craig (b. 1949) presents four arguments, two from philosophy and two from physics, to support the claim that the universe had a beginning. One philosophical argument shows that an actual infinite cannot exist because it leads to the absurdity that the whole is not greater than its part. The other shows that if an actual infinite could exist, one could not traverse it, which would mean that one could not reach this particular point in time; in an infinite time one would have already reached it. The dual supporting arguments from physics appeal to the Big Bang model of the origin of the universe to confirm a beginning of the universe, and that according to the second law of thermodynamics, if the universe has existed infinitely, by now we should have already been gobbled up by black holes or suffered a "heat death." In the end, Craig concludes that since the universe had a beginning, it was caused, and that the cause had to be personal, not natural.

"The first question which should rightly be asked," wrote G. W. F. Leibniz, is "*Why is there something rather than nothing?*"[1] This question does seem to possess a profound existential force, which has been felt by some of mankind's greatest thinkers.... Now there is one form of the cosmological argument that aims precisely at the demonstration that the universe had a beginning in time.[2] Originating in the efforts of Christian theologians to refute the Greek doctrine of the eternity of matter, this argument was developed into sophisticated formulations by medieval Islamic and Jewish theologians, who in turn passed it back to the Latin West. The argument thus has a broad intersectarian appeal, having been defended by Muslims, Jews, and Christians, both Catholic and Protestant. This argument, which I have called the kalam cosmological argument, can be exhibited as follows:

(1.) Whatever begins to exist has a cause of its existence.
(2.) The universe began to exist.
  (2.1) Argument based on the impossibility of an actual infinite.
    (2.11) An actual infinite cannot exist.

From William Lane Craig, "The Existence of God and the Beginning of the Universe," *Truth: A Journal of Modern Thought* 3 (1991): 85–96 (posted on his website).

(2.12) An infinite temporal regress of events is an actual infinite.

(2.13) Therefore, an infinite temporal regress of events cannot exist.

(2.2) Argument based on the impossibility of the formation of an actual infinite by successive addition.

(2.21) A collection formed by successive addition cannot be actually infinite.

(2.22) The temporal series of past events is a collection formed by successive addition.

(2.23) Therefore, the temporal series of past events cannot be actually infinite.

(3.) Therefore, the universe has a cause of its existence.

Let us examine this argument more closely.

DEFENSE OF THE KALAM COSMOLOGICAL ARGUMENT

Second Premise

Clearly, the crucial premise in this argument is (2), and two independent arguments are offered in support of it. Let us therefore turn first to an examination of the supporting arguments.

First Supporting Argument

In order to understand (2.1), we need to understand the difference between a potential infinite and an actual infinite. Crudely put, a potential infinite is a collection which is increasing toward infinity as a limit but never gets there. Such a collection is really indefinite, not infinite.... An actual infinite is a collection in which the number of members really *is* infinite. The collection is not growing toward infinity; it is infinite, it is "complete."... Now (2.11) maintains not that a potentially infinite number of things cannot exist, but that an actually infinite number of things cannot exist. For if an actually infinite number of things could exist, this would spawn all sorts of absurdities.

Perhaps the best way to bring home the truth of (2.11) is by means of an illustration. Let me use one

of my favorites, Hilbert's Hotel, a product of the mind of the great German mathematician, David Hilbert. Let us imagine a hotel with a finite number of rooms. Suppose, furthermore, that *all the rooms are full.* When a new guest arrives asking for a room, the proprietor apologizes, "Sorry, all the rooms are full." But now let us imagine a hotel with an infinite number of rooms and suppose once more that all the rooms are full. There is not a single vacant room throughout the entire infinite hotel. Now suppose a new guest shows up, asking for a room. "But of course!" says the proprietor, and he immediately shifts the person in room #1 into room #2, the person in room #2 into room #3, the person in room #3 into room #4, and so on, out to infinity. As a result of these room changes, room #1 now becomes vacant and the new guest gratefully checks in. But remember, before he arrived, all the rooms were full! Equally curious, according to the mathematicians, there are now no more persons in the hotel than there were before: the number is just infinite. But how can this be? The proprietor just added the new guest's name to the register and gave him his keys—how can there not be one more person in the hotel than before? But the situation becomes even stranger. For suppose an infinity of new guests show up the desk, asking for a room. "Of course, of course!" says the proprietor, and he proceeds to shift the person in room #1 into room #2, the person in room #2 into room #4, the person in room #3 into room #6, and so on out to infinity, always putting each former occupant into the room number twice his own. As a result, all the odd numbered rooms become vacant, and the infinity of new guests is easily accommodated. And yet, before they came, all the rooms were full! And again, strangely enough, the number of guests in the hotel is the same after the infinity of new guests check in as before, even though there were as many new guests as old guests. In fact, the proprietor could repeat this process *infinitely many times*, and yet there would never be one single person more in the hotel than before.

But Hilbert's Hotel is even stranger than the German mathematician made it out to be. For suppose some of the guests start to check out. Suppose the guest in room #1 departs. Is there not now one less person in the hotel? Not according to the mathematicians—but just ask the woman who makes the beds! Suppose the guests in room numbers 1, 3, 5, etc., check out. In this case, an infinite number of people have left the hotel, but according to the mathematicians there are no less people in the hotel—but don't talk to that laundry woman! In fact, we could have every other guest check out of the hotel and repeat this process infinitely many times, and yet there would never be any less people in the hotel....Can anyone sincerely believe that such a hotel could exist in reality? These sorts of absurdities illustrate the impossibility of the existence of an actually infinite number of things.

That takes us to (2.12). The truth of this premise seems fairly obvious. If the universe never began to exist, then prior to the present event there have existed an actually infinite number of previous events. Hence, a beginningless series of events in time entails the existence of an actually infinite number of things, namely, past events.

Given the truth of (2.11) and (2.12), the conclusion (2.13) logically follows. The series of past events must be finite and have a beginning. But since the universe is not distinct from the series of events, it follows that the universe began to exist.

At this point, we might find it profitable to consider several objections that might be raised against the argument. First, let us consider objections to (2.11). Wallace Matson objects that the premise must mean that an actually infinite number of things is *logically* impossible; but it is easy to show that such a collection is logically possible. For example, the series of negative numbers $\{\ldots -3, -2, -1\}$ is an actually infinite collection with no first member.[3] Matson's error here lies in thinking that (2.11) means to assert the *logical* impossibility of an actually infinite number of things. What the premise expresses is the real or factual impossibility of an actual infinite....

The late J. L. Mackie also objected to (2.11), claiming that the absurdities are resolved by noting that for infinite groups the axiom "the whole is greater than its part" does not hold, as it does for finite groups.[4] Similarly, Quentin Smith comments that once we understand that an infinite set has a proper subset which has the same number of members as the set itself, the purportedly absurd situations become "perfectly believable."[5] But to my mind, it is precisely

this feature of infinite set theory which, when translated into the realm of the real, yields results which are perfectly incredible, for example, Hilbert's Hotel. Moreover, not all the absurdities stem from infinite set theory's denial of Euclid's axiom: the absurdities illustrated by guests checking out of the hotel stem from the self-contradictory results when the inverse operations of subtraction or division are performed using transfinite numbers. Here the case against an actually infinite collection of things becomes decisive....

With regard to (2.12), the most frequent objection is that the past ought to be regarded as a potential infinite only, not an actual infinite. This was Aquinas's position versus Bonaventure, and the contemporary philosopher Charles Hartshorne seems to side with Thomas on this issue.[6] Such a position is, however, untenable. The future is potentially infinite, since it does not exist; but the past is actual in a way the future is not, as evidenced by the fact that we have traces of the past in the present, but no traces of the future. Hence, if the series of past events never began to exist, there must have been an actually infinite number of past events.

The objections to either premise therefore seem to be less compelling than the premises themselves. Together they imply that the universe began to exist. Hence, I conclude that this argument furnishes good grounds for accepting the truth of premise (2) that the universe began to exist.

Second Supporting Argument

The second argument (2.2) for the beginning of the universe is based on the impossibility of forming an actual infinite by successive addition. This argument is distinct from the first in that it does not deny the possibility of the existence of an actual infinite, but the possibility of its being *formed* by successive addition.

Premise (2.21) is the crucial step in the argument. One cannot form an actually infinite collection of things by successively adding one member after another. Since one can always add one more before arriving at infinity, it is impossible to reach actual infinity. Sometimes this is called the impossibility of "counting to infinity" or "traversing the infinite." It is important to understand that this impossibility has nothing to do with the amount of time available: it belongs to the nature of infinity that it cannot be so formed.

Now someone might say that while an infinite collection cannot be formed by beginning at a point and adding members, nevertheless an infinite collection could be formed by never beginning but ending at a point, that is to say, ending at a point after having added one member after another from eternity. But this method seems even more unbelievable than the first method. If one cannot count to infinity, how can one count down from infinity? If one cannot traverse the infinite by moving in one direction, how can one traverse it by simply moving in the opposite direction?

Indeed, the idea of a beginningless series ending in the present seems to be absurd. To give just one illustration: suppose we meet a man who claims to have been counting from eternity and is now finishing: ..., −3, −2, −1, 0. We could ask, why did he not finish counting yesterday or the day before or the year before? By then, an infinite time had already elapsed, so that he should already have finished. Thus, at no point in the infinite past could we ever find the man finishing his countdown, for by that point he should already be done! In fact, no matter how far back into the past we go, we can never find the man counting at all, for at any point we reach, he will have already finished. But if at no point in the past do we find him counting, this contradicts the hypothesis that he has been counting from eternity. This illustrates the fact that the formation of an actual infinite by successive addition is equally impossible whether one proceeds to or from infinity. . . .

Given the truth of (2.21) and (2.22), the conclusion (2.23) logically follows. If the universe did not begin to exist a finite time ago, then the present moment could never arrive. But obviously, it has arrived. Therefore, we know that the universe is finite in the past and began to exist.

Again, it would be profitable to consider various objections that have been offered against this reasoning. Against (2.21), Mackie objects that the argument illicitly assumes an infinitely distant starting point in the past and then pronounces it impossible to travel from that point to today. But there would in an infinite past be no starting point, not even an infinitely distant one. Yet from any given point in the infinite past, there is only a finite distance to the present.[7] Now it seems to me that Mackie's allegation that the argument presupposes an infinitely distant starting point is entirely groundless. The beginningless character of the series only serves to accentuate the difficulty of its being formed by successive addition. The fact that there is *no beginning at all*, not even an infinitely distant one, makes the problem more, not less, nettlesome. And the point that from any moment in the infinite past there is only a finite temporal distance to the present may be dismissed as irrelevant. The question is not how any finite portion of the temporal series can be formed, but how the whole infinite series can be formed. If Mackie thinks that because every segment of the series can be formed by successive addition and therefore the whole series can be so formed, then he is simply committing the fallacy of composition. . . .

As for premise (2.22), many thinkers have objected that we need not regard the past as a beginningless infinite series with an end in the present. Popper, for example, admits that the *set* of all past events is actually infinite, but holds that the *series* of past events is potentially infinite. This may be seen by beginning in the present and numbering the events backwards, thus forming a potential infinite. Therefore, the problem of an actual infinite's being formed by successive addition does not arise. . . .[8] This objection, however, clearly confuses the *mental regress* of counting with the *real progress* of the temporal series of events itself. Numbering the series from the present backwards only shows that if there are an infinite number of past events, then we can denumerate an infinite number of past events. But the problem is, how can this infinite collection of events come to be *formed* by successive addition? How we mentally conceive the series does not in any way affect the ontological character of the series itself as a series with no beginning but an end, or in other words, as an actual infinite completed by successive addition.

Once again, then, the objections to (2.21) and (2.22) seem less plausible than the premises themselves. Together they imply (2.23), or that the universe began to exist.

First Scientific Confirmation

These purely philosophical arguments for the beginning of the universe have received remarkable confirmation from discoveries in astronomy and astrophysics during this century. These confirmations might be summarized under two heads: the confirmation from the expansion of the universe and the confirmation from thermodynamic properties of the universe.

With regard to the first, Hubble's discovery in 1929 of the red-shift in the light from distant galaxies began a revolution in astronomy perhaps as significant as the Copernican revolution. Prior to this time, the universe as a whole was conceived to be static; but the startling conclusion to which Hubble was led was that the red-shift is due to the fact that the universe is in fact *expanding*. The staggering implication of this fact is that as one traces the expansion back in time, the universe becomes denser and denser until one reaches a point of infinite density from which the universe began to expand. The upshot of Hubble's discovery is that at some point in the finite past— probably around 15 billion years ago—the entire known universe was contracted down to a single mathematical point which marked the origin of the universe. That initial explosion has come to be known as the "Big Bang." Four of the world's most prominent astronomers described that event:

> The universe began from a state of infinite density.... Space and time were created in that event and so was all the matter in the universe. It is not meaningful to ask what happened before the Big Bang; it is like asking what is north of the North Pole. Similarly, it is not sensible to ask where the Big Bang took place. The point-universe was not an object isolated in space; it was the entire universe, and so the answer can only be that the Big Bang happened everywhere.[9]

This event that marked the beginning of the universe becomes all the more amazing when one reflects on the fact that a state of "infinite density" is synonymous to "nothing." There can be no object that possesses infinite density, for if it had any size at all it could still be even more dense. Therefore, as the Cambridge astronomer Fred Hoyle points out, the Big Bang theory requires the creation of matter from nothing.

This is because as one goes back in time, one reaches a point at which, in Hoyle's words, the universe was "shrunk down to nothing at all."[10] Thus, what the Big Bang model of the universe seems to require is that the universe began to exist and was created out of nothing.

Some theorists have attempted to avoid the absolute beginning of the universe implied by the Big Bang theory by speculating that the universe may undergo an infinite series of expansions and contractions. There are, however, good grounds for doubting the adequacy of such an oscillating model of the universe: (i) The oscillating model appears to be physically impossible. For all the talk about such models, the fact seems to be that they are only theoretically, but not physically, possible. As the late Professor [Beatrice] Tinsley of Yale explains, in oscillating models, "even though the mathematics say that the universe oscillates, there is no known physics to reverse the collapse and bounce back to a new expansion. The physics seems to say that those models start from the Big Bang, expand, collapse, then end."[11] In order for the oscillating model to be correct, it would seem that the known laws of physics would have to be revised. (ii) The oscillating model seems to be observationally untenable. Two facts of observational astronomy appear to run contrary to the oscillating model. First, the observed homogeneity of matter distribution throughout the universe seems unaccountable on an oscillating model. During the contraction phase of such a model, black holes begin to gobble up surrounding matter, resulting in an inhomogeneous distribution of matter. But there is no known mechanism to "iron out" these inhomogeneities during the ensuing expansion phase. Thus, the homogeneity of matter observed throughout the universe would remain unexplained. Second, the density of the universe appears to be insufficient for the re-contraction of the universe. For the oscillating model to be even possible, it is necessary that the universe be sufficiently dense such that gravity can overcome the force of the expansion and pull the universe back together again. However, according to the best estimates, if one takes into account both luminous matter and nonluminous matter (found in galactic halos) as well as any possible contribution of neutrino particles to total mass, the universe is still only about one-half of that needed for re-contraction.[12] Moreover, recent work on calculating the speed and deceleration of the expansion confirms that the universe is expanding at, so to speak, "escape velocity" and will not therefore re-contract. According to Sandage and Tammann, "Hence, we are forced to decide that . . . it seems inevitable that the Universe will expand forever"; they conclude, therefore, that "the Universe has happened only once."[13]

Second Scientific Confirmation

As if this were not enough, there is a second scientific confirmation of the beginning of the universe, based on the thermodynamic properties of various cosmological models. According to the second law of thermodynamics, processes taking place in a closed system always tend toward a state of equilibrium. Now our interest is in what implications this has when the law is applied to the universe as a whole. For the universe is a gigantic closed system, since it is everything there is and no energy is being fed into it from without. The second law seems to imply that, given enough time, the universe will reach a state of thermodynamic equilibrium, known as the "heat death" of the universe. This death may be hot or cold, depending on whether the universe will expand forever or eventually re-contract. On the one hand, if the density of the universe is great enough to overcome the force of the expansion, then the universe will re-contract into a hot fireball. As the universe contracts, the stars burn more rapidly until they finally explode or evaporate. As the universe grows denser, the black holes begin to gobble up everything around them and begin themselves to coalesce, until all the black holes finally coalesce into one gigantic black hole which is coextensive with the universe, from which it will never reemerge. On the other hand, if the density of the universe is insufficient to halt the expansion, as seems more likely, then the galaxies will turn all their gas into stars and the stars will burn out. At 10^{30} years, the universe will consist of 90 percent dead stars, 9 percent supermassive black holes, and 1 percent atomic matter. Elementary particle physics suggests that thereafter protons will

decay into electrons and positrons, so that space will be filled with a rarefied gas so thin that the distance between an electron and a positron will be about the size of the present galaxy. At 10^{100} years some scientists believe that the black holes themselves will dissipate into radiation and elementary particles. Eventually, all the matter in the dark, cold, ever-expanding universe will be reduced to an ultrathin gas of elementary particles and radiation. Equilibrium will prevail throughout, and the entire universe will be in its final state, from which no change will occur.

Now the question which needs to be asked is this: if, given sufficient time, the universe will reach heat death, then why is it not now in a state of heat death if it has existed for infinite time? If the universe did not begin to exist, then it should now be in a state of equilibrium. Some theorists have suggested that the universe escapes final heat death by oscillating from eternity past to eternity future. But we have already seen that such a model seems to be physically and observationally untenable. But even if we waive those considerations and suppose that the universe does oscillate, the fact is that the thermodynamic properties of this model imply the very beginning of the universe which its proponents seek to avoid. For the thermodynamic properties of an oscillating model are such that the universe expands farther and farther with each successive cycle. Therefore, as one traces the expansions back in time, they grow smaller and smaller. As one scientific team explains, "The effect of entropy production will be to enlarge the cosmic scale, from cycle to cycle. . . . Thus, looking back in time, each cycle generated less entropy, had a smaller cycle time, and had a smaller cycle expansion factor than the cycle that followed it."[14] Novikov and Zeldovich of the Institute of Applied Mathematics of the Russian Academy of Sciences therefore conclude, "The multicycle model has an infinite future, but only a finite past."[15] As another writer points out, the oscillating model of the universe thus still requires an origin of the universe prior to the smallest cycle.[16]

So whatever scenario one selects for the future of the universe, thermodynamics implies that the universe began to exist. According to physicist P. C. W. Davies, the universe must have been created a finite time ago and is in the process of winding down. Prior to the creation, the universe simply did not exist. Therefore, Davies concludes, even though we may not like it, we must conclude that the universe's energy was somehow simply "put in" at the creation as an initial condition.[17]

We therefore have both a philosophical argument and scientific confirmation for the beginning of the universe. On this basis, I think that we are amply justified in concluding the truth of premise (2) that the universe began to exist.

First Premise

Premise (1) strikes me as relatively noncontroversial. It is based on the metaphysical intuition that something cannot come out of nothing. Hence, any argument for the principle is apt to be less obvious than the principle itself. Even the great skeptic David Hume admitted that he never asserted so absurd a proposition as that something might come into existence without a cause; he only denied that one could *prove* the obviously true causal principle.[18] With regard to the universe, if originally there were absolutely *nothing*—no God, no space, no time—then how could the universe possibly come to exist? The truth of the principle *ex nihilo, nihil fit* (out of nothing, nothing comes) is so obvious that I think we are justified in foregoing an elaborate defense of the argument's first premise.

Nevertheless, some thinkers, exercised to avoid the theism implicit in this premise within the present context, have felt driven to deny its truth. In order to avoid its theistic implications. Davies presents a scenario which, he confesses, "should not be taken too seriously," but which seems to have a powerful attraction for Davies.[19] He has reference to a quantum theory of gravity according to which space-time itself could spring uncaused into being out of absolutely nothing. While admitting that there is "still no satisfactory theory of quantum gravity," such a theory "would allow spacetime to be created and destroyed spontaneously and uncaused in the same way that particles are created and destroyed spontaneously and uncaused. The theory would entail a certain mathematically determined probability that,

for instance, a blob of space would appear where none existed before. Thus, spacetime could pop out of nothingness as the result of a causeless quantum transition."[20]

Now in fact particle pair production furnishes no analogy for this radical *ex nihilo* becoming, as Davies seems to imply. This quantum phenomenon, even if an exception to the principle that every event has a cause, provides no analogy to something's coming into being out of nothing. Although physicists speak of this as particle pair creation and annihilation, such terms are philosophically misleading, for all that actually occurs is conversion of energy into matter or vice versa. As Davies admits, "The processes described here do not represent the creation of matter out of nothing, but the conversion of pre-existing energy into material form."[21] Hence, Davies greatly misleads his reader when he claims that "particles...can appear out of nowhere without specific causation" and again, "yet the world of quantum physics routinely produces something for nothing."[22] On the contrary, the world of quantum physics *never* produces something for nothing....

Conclusion

Given the truth of premises (1) and (2), it logically follows that (3) the universe has a cause of its existence. In fact, I think that it can be plausibly argued that the cause of the universe must be a personal Creator. For how else could a temporal effect arise from an eternal cause? If the cause were simply a mechanically operating set of necessary and sufficient conditions existing from eternity, then why would not the effect also exist from eternity?...The only way to have an eternal cause but a temporal effect would seem to be if the cause is a personal agent who freely chooses to create an effect in time....Thus, we are brought not merely to the first cause of the universe, but to its personal Creator.

SUMMARY AND CONCLUSION

We have seen on the basis of both philosophical argument and scientific confirmation that it is plausible that the universe began to exist. Given the intuitively obvious principle that whatever begins to exist has a cause of its existence, we have been led to conclude that the universe has a cause of its existence. On the basis of our argument, this cause would have to be uncaused, eternal, changeless, timeless, and immaterial. Moreover, it would have to be a personal agent who freely elects to create an effect in time. Therefore, on the basis of the *kalam* cosmological argument, I conclude that it is rational to believe that God exists.

Notes

1. G. W. Leibniz, "The Principles of Nature and of Grace, Based on Reason," in *Leibniz Selections*, ed. Philip P. Wiener, *The Modern Student's Library* (New York: Scribners, 1951), p. 527.
2. See William Lane Craig, *The Cosmological Argument from Plato to Leibniz*, Library of Philosophy and Religion (London: Macmillan, 1980), pp. 48–58, 61–76, 98–104, 128–31.
3. Wallace Matson, *The Existence of God* (Ithaca, N.Y.: Cornell University Press, 1965), pp. 58–60.
4. J. L. Mackie, *The Miracle of Theism* (Oxford, England: Clarendon Press, 1982), p. 93.
5. Quentin Smith, "Infinity and the Past," *Philosophy of Science* 54 (1987): 69.
6. Charles Hartshorne, *Man's Vision of God and the Logic of Theism* (Chicago: Willett, Clark, & Co., 1941), p. 37.
7. Mackie, *Theism*, p. 93.
8. K. R. Popper, "On the Possibility of an Infinite Past: A Reply to Whitrow," *British Journal for the Philosophy of Science* 29 (1978): 47–48.
9. Richard J. Gott, et al., "Will the Universe Expand Forever?" *Scientific American* (March 1976), p. 65.
10. Fred Hoyle, *From Stonehenge to Modern Cosmology* (San Francisco, Calif: W. H. Freeman, 1972), p. 36.
11. Beatrice Tinsley, personal letter.
12. David N. Schramm and Gary Steigman, "Relic Neutrinos and the Density of the Universe," *Astrophysical Journal* 243 (1981): 1–7.
13. Alan Sandage and G. A. Tammann, "Steps toward the Hubble Constant: VII," *Astrophyscial Journal* 210 (1976): 23, 7; see also idem, "Steps toward the Hubble Constant: VIII," *Astrophysical Journal* 256 (1982): 339–45.
14. Duane Dicus, et al. "Effects of Proton Decay on the Cosmological Future." *Astrophysical Journal* 252 (1982): 1, 8.
15. I. D. Novikov and Ya. B. Zeldovich, "Physical Processes Near Cosmological Singularities," *Annual Review of Astronomy and Astrophysics* 11 (1973): 401–402.
16. John Gribbin, "Oscillating Universe Bounces Back," *Nature* 259 (1976): 16.
17. P. C. W. Davies, *The Physics of Time Asymmetry* (London: Surrey University Press, 1974), p. 104.
18. David Hume to John Stewart, February 1754, in *The Letters of David Hume*, ed. J. Y. T. Greig (Oxford, England: Clarendon Press, 1932), 1:187.
19. Paul Davies, *God and the New Physics* (New York: Simon & Schuster, 1983), p. 214.
20. Ibid., p. 215.
21. Ibid., p. 31.
22. Ibid., pp. 215, 216.

Study Questions

1. What is the kalam cosmological argument? How does it differ from the version of the cosmological argument in the previous reading?
2. How does Craig argue against the possibility of an actual infinite?
3. What does the Big Bang theory have to do with showing that the universe had a beginning?
4. How does Craig argue that the first cause was a personal being?

J. L. Mackie

Critique of the Cosmological Argument

J. L. Mackie (1917–1981) considers and critiques various versions of the cosmological argument. Versions that appeal to the principle of sufficient reason he rejects on the ground that there is no reason to think that this principle is true or that its denial commits one to the unintelligibility of things. He rejects versions of the argument (e.g., Thomas Aquinas's) that appeal to the impossibility of an infinite regress of causes on the grounds that they presuppose that contingent things must depend on something else for their existence. He argues to the contrary that there might simply be permanent matter whose existence is independent of anything else. He rejects the kalam argument on the ground that the alleged paradoxes found in infinite sets can be resolved by the careful application of two criteria for determining the size of groups in the series; "smaller than" and "equal to" don't apply to infinites. Further, even if the universe were finite in time, there is no reason for holding that it could not have originated by itself. Finally, for Mackie, the same problem of why something exists applies to God as well. Indeed, if God has always existed, the same problems of being an actual infinite would also apply to God.

CONTINGENCY AND SUFFICIENT REASON

Leibniz gives what is essentially the same proof in slightly different forms in different works; we can sum up his line of thought as follows.[1] He assumes the *principle of sufficient reason*, that nothing occurs without a sufficient reason why it is so and not otherwise. There must, then, be a sufficient reason for the world as a whole, a reason why something exists rather than nothing. Each thing in the world is contingent, being causally determined by other things: it would not occur if other things were otherwise. The world as a whole, being a collection of such things, is therefore itself contingent. The series of things and events, with their causes, with causes of those causes, and so on, may stretch back infinitely in time; but, if so, then however far back we go, or if we consider the series as a whole, what we have is still contingent and therefore requires a sufficient reason outside this series. That is, there must be a sufficient reason *for* the world which is *other than* the world. This will have to be a necessary being, which contains its own sufficient reason for existence. Briefly, things must have a sufficient reason for their existence, and this must be found ultimately in a necessary being. There must be something free from the disease of contingency, a disease which affects everything in the world and the world as a whole, even if it is infinite in past time.

This argument, however, is open to criticisms of two sorts, summed up in the questions "How do we know that everything must have a sufficient reason?" and "How can there be a necessary being, one that contains its own sufficient reason?" These challenges are related: if the second question cannot be answered satisfactorily, it will follow that things as a whole cannot have a sufficient reason, not merely that we do not know that they must have one....

Perhaps we can still make something like Kant's point, even if we are relying only on a criticism of the second sort. Since it is always a further question whether a concept is instantiated or not, no matter how much it contains, the existence even of a being whose essence included existence would not be self-explanatory: there might have failed to be any such thing. This "might" expresses at least a conceptual possibility; if it is alleged that this being nonetheless exists by a metaphysical necessity, we are still waiting for an explanation of this kind of necessity. The existence of this being is not logically necessary; it does not exist in all logically possible worlds; in what way, then, does it necessarily exist in this world and satisfy the demand for a sufficient reason?

It might be replied that we understand what it is for something to exist contingently, in that it would not have existed if something else had been otherwise: to exist necessarily is to exist but not contingently in this sense. But then the premise that the natural world as a whole is contingent is not available: though we have some ground for thinking that each part, or each finite temporal stretch, of the world is contingent in this sense upon something else, we have initially no ground for thinking that the world as a whole would not have existed if something else had been otherwise; inference from the contingency of every part to the contingency *in this sense* of the whole is invalid. Alternatively, we might say that something exists contingently if and only if it might not have existed, and by contrast that something exists necessarily if and only if it exists, but it is not the case that it might not have existed. In this sense we could infer the contingency of the whole from the

contingency of every part. But once it is conceded, for reasons just given, that it is not logically impossible that the alleged necessary being might not have existed, we have no understanding of how it could be true of this being that it is not the case that it might not have existed. We have as yet no ground for believing that it is even possible that something should exist necessarily in the sense required.

This criticism is reinforced by the other objection, "How do we know that everything must have a sufficient reason?" I see no plausibility in the claim that the principle of sufficient reason is known a priori to be true. Leibniz thought that reliance on this principle is implicit in our reasoning both about physics and about human behaviour....

The principle of sufficient reason expresses a demand that things should be intelligible *through and through*. The simple reply to the argument which relies on it is that there is nothing that justifies this demand, and nothing that supports the belief that it is satisfiable even in principle. As we have seen in considering the other main objection to Leibniz's argument, it is difficult to see how there even could be anything that would satisfy it. If we reject this demand, we are not thereby committed to saying that things are utterly unintelligible. The sort of intelligibility that is achieved by successful causal inquiry and scientific explanation is not undermined by its inability to make things intelligible through and through. Any particular explanation starts with premises which state "brute facts," and although the brutally factual starting-points of one explanation may themselves be further explained by another, the latter in turn will have to start with something that it does not explain, *and so on however far we go*. But there is no need to see this as unsatisfactory....

The principle of sufficient reason, then, is more far-reaching than the principle that every occurrence has a preceding sufficient cause: the latter, but not the former, would be satisfied by a series of things or events running back infinitely in time, each determined by earlier ones, but with no further explanation of the series as a whole. Such a series would give us only what Leibniz called "physical" or "hypothetical" necessity, whereas the demand for a sufficient reason for the whole body of contingent things and events and laws calls for something with "absolute" or "metaphysical" necessity. But even the weaker, deterministic, principle is not a priori truth, and indeed it may not be a truth at all; much less can this be claimed for the principle of sufficient reason. Perhaps it just expresses an arbitrary demand; it may be intellectually satisfying to believe that there is, objectively, an explanation for everything together, even if we can only guess at what the explanation might be. But we have no right to assume that the universe will comply with our intellectual preferences. Alternatively, the supposed principle may be an unwarranted extension of the determinist one, which, in so far as it is supported, is supported only empirically, by our success in actually finding causes, and can at most be accepted provisionally, not as an a priori truth. The form of the cosmological argument which relies on the principle of sufficient reason therefore fails completely as a demonstrative proof.

THE REGRESS OF CAUSES

There is a popular line of thought, which we may call the first cause argument, and which runs as follows: things must be caused, and their causes will be other things that must have causes, and so on; but this series of causes cannot go back indefinitely; it must terminate in a first cause, and this first cause will be God. This argument envisages a regress of causes in time, but says (as Leibniz, for one, did not) that this regress must stop somewhere. Though it has some initial plausibility, it also has obvious difficulties. Why must the regress terminate at all? Why, if it terminates, must it lead to a single termination, to one first cause, rather than to a number—perhaps an indefinitely large number—of distinct uncaused causes? And even if there is just one first cause, why should we identify this with God? I shall come back to this argument and to possible replies to these objections; but first I want to look at a more elaborate philosophical argument that has some, though not much, resemblance to it.

Of Aquinas's "five ways," the first three are recognizably variants of the cosmological proof, and all three involve some kind of terminated regress of

cause.[2] But all of them are quite different from our first cause argument. The first way argues to a first mover, using the illustration of something's being moved by a stick only when the stick is moved by a hand; here the various movings are simultaneous, we do not have a regress of causes in time. Similarly the "efficient causes" in the second way are contemporary agents. Both these arguments, as Kenny has shown, depend too much on antiquated physical theory to be of much interest now. The third way is much more significant....

This argument is quite different from our first cause argument and also from Leibniz's argument from contingency. Although it uses the contrast between things which are able-not-to-be (and therefore contingent) and those which are necessary, it is not satisfied with the conclusion that there is something necessary; it allows that there may be many necessary things, and reaches God only at the end of the second stage, as what has its necessity "through itself" (per se). Clearly "necessary" does not mean the same for Aquinas as for Leibniz. What it does mean will become clearer as we examine the reasoning.

In the first stage, the premise "what is able-not-to-be, at some time is not" seems dubious: why should not something which is *able* not to be nevertheless just happen to exist always? But perhaps Aquinas means by "things that are able-not-to-be" (*possibilia non esse*) something like "impermanent things," so that this premise is analytic. Even so, the statement that if everything were such, at some time there would have been nothing, does not follow: some impermanent things might have lasted through all past time, and be going to display their impermanence by perishing only at some time in the future. But we may be able to understand Aquinas's thought by seeing what is said more explicitly by Maimonides, by whom Aquinas appears to have been influenced here.[3] His corresponding proof seems to assume that past time has been finite—and reasonably so, for if past time has been finite there would seem to be an easier argument for a divine creator, such as we shall consider below. The suggestion is that it would not have been possible for impermanent things to have lasted throughout an infinite time, and hence they would have perished already.

However, another objection is that there might be a series of things, each of which was impermanent and perished after a finite period, but whose periods of existence overlapped so that there never was a time when there was nothing. It would be clear logical fallacy (of which some commentators have accused Aquinas) to infer "at some time everything is not" from "each thing at some time is not." But we might defend Aquinas in either of two ways. First, if each thing were impermanent, it would be the most improbable good luck if the overlapping sequence kept up through infinite time. Secondly, even if this improbable luck holds, we might regard the series of overlapping things as itself a thing which had already lasted through infinite time, and so could not be impermanent. Indeed, if there were such a series which never failed, this might well indicate that there was some *permanent* stock of material of which the perishable things were composed and into which they disintegrated, thereby contributing to the composition of other things.

A third objection concerns the premise that "what does not exist cannot begin to be except through something that is." This is, of course, a form of the principle that nothing can come from nothing; the idea then is that if our series of impermanent things had broken off, it could never have started again after a gap. But is this an a priori truth? As Hume pointed out, we can certainly conceive an uncaused beginning-to-be of an object; if what we can thus conceive is nevertheless in some way impossible, this still requires to be shown.[4] Still, this principle has some plausibility, in that it is constantly confirmed in our experience (and also used, reasonably, in interpreting our experience).

Altogether, then, the first stage of Aquinas's argument falls short of watertight demonstration, but it gives some lower degree of support to the conclusion that there is at least one thing that is necessary in the sense, which has now become clear, that it is permanent, that *for some reason* it is not able-not-to-be.

The second stage takes this conclusion as its starting-point. One permanent thing, it allows, may be caused to be permanent, sustained always in existence, by another. But, it holds, there cannot be an infinite regress of such things. Why not? Aquinas refers us to his earlier proof about efficient causes, in the second way. This runs:

> It is not possible to go to infinity in a series of efficient causes. For in all ordered efficient causes the first item is the cause of the intermediate one and the intermediate is the cause of the last (whether there is only one intermediate or more than one); now if the cause is removed, so is the effect. Therefore if there has not been a first item among efficient causes there will not be a last or an intermediate. But if one goes to infinity in a series of efficient causes, there will not be a first efficient cause, and so there will not be a last effect or intermediate efficient causes.

Unfortunately this argument is unsound. Although in a *finite* ordered series of causes the intermediate (or the earliest intermediate) is caused by the first item, this would not be so if there were an infinite series. In an infinite series, every item is caused by an earlier item. The way in which the first item is "removed" if we go from a finite to an infinite series does not entail the removal of the later items. In fact, Aquinas (both here and in the first way) has simply begged the question against an infinite regress of causes. But is this a sheer mistake, or is there some coherent thought behind it? Some examples (some of which would not themselves have been available to Aquinas, though analogues of them would have been) may suggest that there is. If we were told that there was a watch without a mainspring, we would hardly be reassured by the further information that it had, however, an infinite train of gear-wheels. Nor would we expect a railway train consisting of an infinite number of carriages, the last pulled along by the second last, the second last by the third last, and so on, to get along without an engine. Again, we see a chain, consisting of a series of links, hanging from a hook; we should be surprised to learn that there was a similar but infinite chain, with no hook, but links supported by links above them for ever. The point is that in these examples, and in the series of efficient causes or of necessary things, it is assumed that there is a relation of *dependence*—or, equivalently, one in the reverse direction of *support*—and, if the series were infinite, there would in the end be nothing for the effects to depend on, nothing to support them.

And the same would be true if the regress were not infinite but circular.

There is here an implicit appeal to the following general principle: Where items are ordered by a relation of dependence, the regress must end somewhere; it cannot be either infinite or circular. Perhaps this principle was intended by al Farabi in the dictum that is translated "But a series of contingent beings which would produce one another cannot proceed to infinity or move in a circle" (p. 83). As our examples show, this principle is at least highly plausible; the problem will be to decide when we have such a relation of dependence.

In the second stage of Aquinas's argument, therefore, the key notion is that any necessary—that is, permanent—thing either depends for its permanence on something else or is *per se necessarium* in a sense which can apply only to God. The actual text of the third way does not reveal Aquinas's thinking about this. But comparison of it with other passages in his writings and with Maimonides' proof suggests that the implicit assumption is that anything whose essence does not involve existence must, even if it is permanent, depend for its existence on something else.[5] His assumption would give the dependence which would call for an end to the regress and also ensure that nothing could end it but a being whose essence involved existence which would explain the assertion that what is *per se necessarium* is what men all call God.

But the final objection to the argument is that we have no reason for accepting this implicit assumption. Why, for example, might there not be a permanent stock of matter whose essence did not involve existence but which did not derive its existence from anything else?...

But what about the popular first cause argument? Can we not now answer our earlier queries? Why must the regress of causes in time terminate? Because things, states of affairs, and occurrences *depend* on their antecedent causes. Why must the regress lead to one first cause rather than to many uncaused causes, and why must that one cause be God? Because anything other than God would need something else causally to depend upon. Moreover, the assumption needed for this argument is more plausible than that needed for Leibniz's proof, or for Aquinas's. The notion that everything must have a sufficient reason is a metaphysician's demand, as is the notion that anything permanent must depend for its permanence on something else unless its essence involves existence. But the notion that an effect *depends* on a temporally earlier cause is part of our ordinary understanding of causation: we all have some grasp of this asymmetry between cause and effect, however hard it may be to give an exact analysis of it.[6]

Nevertheless, this argument is not demonstratively cogent. Though we understand that where something has a temporally antecedent cause, it depends somehow upon it, it does not follow that everything (other than God) needs something else to depend on in this way. Also, what we can call al Farabi's principle, that where items are ordered by a relation of dependence, the regress must terminate somewhere, and cannot be either infinite or circular, though plausible, may not be really sound. But the greatest weakness of this otherwise attractive argument is that some reason is required for making God the one exception to the supposed need for something else to depend on: why should God, rather than anything else, be taken as the only satisfactory termination of the regress? If we do not simply accept this as a sheer mystery (which would be to abandon rational theology and take refuge in faith), we shall have to defend it in something like the ways that the metaphysicians have suggested. But then this popular argument takes on board the burdens that have sunk its more elaborate philosophical counterparts.

FINITE PAST TIME AND CREATION

There is, as Craig explains, a distinctive kind of cosmological argument which, unlike those of Aquinas, Leibniz, and many others, assumes or argues that the past history of the world is finite.[7] This, which Craig calls, by its Arabic name, the kalam type of argument, was favoured by Islamic thinkers who were suspicious of the subtleties of the philosophers and relied more on revelation than on reason. Nevertheless, they did propound this as a rational proof of

God's existence, and some of them used mathematical paradoxes that are descended from Zeno's, or that anticipate Cantor's, to show that there cannot be an actual infinite—in particular, an infinite past time. For example, if time past were infinite, an infinite stretch would have actually to have been traversed in order to reach the present, and this is thought to be impossible. Then there is an ingenious argument suggested by al Ghazali: the planet Jupiter revolves in its orbit once every twelve years, Saturn once every thirty years; so Jupiter must have completed more than twice as many revolutions as Saturn; yet if past time were infinite they would each have completed the same (infinite) number; which is a contradiction. The first of these (which Kant also uses in the thesis of his First Antinomy) just expresses a prejudice against an actual infinity. It assumes that, even if past time were infinite, there would still have been a starting-point of time, but one infinitely remote, so that an actual infinity would have had to be traversed to reach the present from there. But to take the hypothesis of infinity seriously would be to suppose that there was no starting-point, not even an infinitely remote one, and that from any specific point in past time there is only a finite stretch that needs to be traversed to reach the present. Al Ghazali's argument uses an instance of one of Cantor's paradoxes, that in an infinite class a part can indeed be equal to the whole: for example, there are just as many even numbers (2, 4, 6, etc.) as there are whole numbers (1, 2, 3, etc.), since these classes can be matched one-one with each other. But is this not a contradiction? Is not the class of even numbers both equal to that of the integers (because of this one-one correlation) and smaller than it (because it is a proper part of it, the part that leaves out the odd numbers)? But what this brings out is that we ordinarily have and use a criterion for one group's being smaller than another—that it is, or can be correlated one-one with, a proper part of the other—and a criterion for two groups' being equal in number—that they can be correlated one-one with each other—which together ensure that *smaller than* and *equal to* exclude one another for all pairs of finite groups, but not for pairs of infinite groups. Once we understand the relation between the two criteria, we see that there is no real contradiction.

In short, it seems impossible to disprove, a priori, the possibility of an infinite past time. Nevertheless, many people shared, and many still do share, these doubts about an actual infinite in the real world, even if they are willing to leave mathematicians free to play their Cantorian games—which, of course, not all mathematicians, or all philosophers of mathematics, want to play. Also the view that, whatever we say about *time*, the *universe* has a finite past history, has in recent years received strong empirical support from the cosmology that is a branch of astronomy. So let us consider what the prospects would be for a proof of the existence of a god if we were supplied, from whatever source, with the premise that the world has only a finite past history, and therefore a beginning in time, whether or not this is also the beginning of time. Here the crucial assumption is stated by al Ghazali: "[We] know by rational necessity that nothing which originates in time originates by itself, and that, therefore, it needs a creator" (p. 102). But *do* we know this by rational necessity? Surely the assumption required here is just the same as that which is used differently in the first cause argument, that anything other than a god needs a cause or a creator to depend on. But there is a priori no good reason why a sheer origination of things, not determined by anything, should be unacceptable, whereas the existence of a god with the power to create something out of nothing is acceptable.

When we look hard at the latter notion we find problems within it. Does God's existence have a sheer origination in time? But then this would be as great a puzzle as the sheer origination of a material world. Or has God existed for ever through an infinite time? But this would raise again the problem of the actual infinite. To avoid both of these, we should have to postulate that God's own existence is not in time at all; but this would be a complete mystery.

Alternatively, someone might not share al Ghazali's worries about the actual infinite, and might rely on an empirical argument—such as the modern cosmological evidence for the "big bang"—to show that the material world had a beginning in time. For him, therefore, God's existence through an infinite time would be unproblematic. But he is still using the crucial assumptions that God's existence and creative power would be self-explanatory whereas the unexplained origination of a material world would be unintelligible and therefore unacceptable. But the first of these leads us back to the criticism stated [earlier]. The notion, embedded in the ontological argument, of a being whose existence is self-explanatory because it is not the case that it might not have existed, is *not* defensible; so we cannot borrow that notion to complete any form of the cosmological argument. The second assumption is equally questionable. We have no good ground for an a priori certainty that there could not have been a sheer unexplained beginning of things. But in so far as we find this improbable, it should cast doubt on the interpretation of the big bang as an absolute beginning of the material universe; rather, we should infer that it must have had *some* physical antecedents, even if the big bang has to be taken as a discontinuity so radical that we cannot explain it, because we can find no laws which we can extrapolate backwards through this discontinuity.

In short, the notion of creation seems more acceptable than any other way out of the cosmological maze only because we do not look hard either at it or at the human experiences of making things on which it is modelled. It is vaguely explanatory, apparently satisfying; but these appearances fade away when we try to formulate the suggestion precisely.

NOTES

1. The clearest account is in "On the Ultimate Origination of Things," printed, e.g., in G. W. Leibniz, *Philosophical Writings* (London: Dent, 1934), pp. 32–41.
2. A. Kenny, *The Five Ways* (London: Routledge & Kegan Paul, 1969).
3. William L. Craig, *The Cosmological Argument from Plato to Leibniz* (London: Macmillan, 1980), chap. 4.
4. *Treatise*, Book I, Part 3, Section 3; contrast Kenny, op. cit., p. 67.
5. Craig, op. cit., pp. 142–143, 146–148.
6. Cf. chapter 7 of J. L. Mackie, *The Cement of the Universe* (Oxford, England: Clarendon Press, 1974).
7. Craig, op. cit., Chapter 3.

STUDY QUESTIONS

1. What questions does Mackie raise against the possibility that a necessary being exists?
2. Using the reading by Reichenbach, how might Mackie respond to Reichenbach's contention that the Principle of Sufficient Reason is true?
3. Reconstruct Aquinas's cosmological argument from Mackie's text. What two major objections does Mackie raise against Aquinas's argument?
4. What two major objections does Mackie raise against the kalam argument? From Craig's reading, how might Craig respond to these two objections?

William Paley

The Analogical Teleological Argument

William Paley (1743–1805) notes that one would have a different reaction to finding a watch than to finding a stone. On finding a watch, one would note its intricate means–ends structure, which suggests that it had an intelligent maker. Paley then notes that human and animal eyes also have means–ends ordering, which indicates that nature too had an intelligent creator. That we have not seen watches or eyes made, that sometimes they do not work, that we do not know the functions of all their parts or even that we can invoke laws governing them does not mitigate the force of the argument. Paley also notes that as we would reject mere natural explanations for the watch, so too should we reject mere natural explanations for organs like eyes. Granted, there are defects in nature, but these are due to causes of which we are ignorant, not to God's lack of knowledge.

Chapter I. State of The Argument

In crossing a heath, suppose I pitched my foot against a *stone*, and were asked how the stone came to be there, I might possibly answer, that, for anything I knew to the contrary, it had lain there for ever; nor would it, perhaps, be very easy to show the absurdity of this answer. But suppose I had found a *watch* upon the ground, and it should be inquired how the watch happened to be in that place, I should hardly think of the answer which I had before given, that, for anything I knew, the watch might have always been there. Yet why should not this answer serve for the watch as well as for the stone? Why is it not as admissible in the second case as in the first? For this

reason, and for no other, viz., that, when we come to inspect the watch, we perceive (what we could not discover in the stone) that its several parts are framed and put together for a purpose, e.g., that they are so formed and adjusted as to produce motion, and that motion so regulated as to point out the hour of the day; that, if the different parts had been differently shaped from what they are, of a different size from what they are, or placed after any other manner, or in any other order than that in which they are placed, either no motion at all would have been carried on in the machine, or none which would have answered the use that is now served by it. To reckon up a few of the plainest of these parts, and of their offices, all tending to one result: We see a cylindrical

William Paley, *Natural Theology* (New York: Harper and Brothers, 1845), pp. 37–38, 40–42, 49–51, 82–83.

box containing a coiled elastic spring, which, by its endeavor to relax itself, turns round the box. We next observe a flexible chain communicating the action of the spring from the box to the fusee. We then find a series of wheels, the teeth of which catch in, and apply to, each other, conducting the motion from the fusee to the balance, and from the balance to the pointer, and, at the same time, by the size and shape of those wheels, so regulating that motion as to terminate in causing an index, by an equable and measured progression, to pass over a given space in a given time. We take notice that the wheels are made of brass in order to keep them from rust; the springs of steel, no other metal being so elastic; that over the face of the watch there is placed a glass, a material employed in no other part of the work; but in the room of which, if there had been any other than a transparent substance, the hour could not be seen without opening the case. This mechanism being observed, the inference, we think, is inevitable, that the watch had a maker: that there must have existed at some time, and some place or other, an artificer or artificers who formed it for the purpose which we find it actually to answer: who comprehended its construction and designed its use.

I. Nor would it, I apprehend, weaken the conclusion that we had never seen a watch made; that we had never known an artist capable of making one: that we are altogether incapable of executing such a piece of workmanship ourselves, or of understanding in what manner it was performed; all this being no more than what is true of some exquisite remains of ancient art, of some lost arts, and to the generality of mankind, of the more curious productions of modern manufacture....

II. Neither, secondly, would it invalidate our conclusion, that the watch sometimes went wrong, or that it seldom went exactly right. The purpose of the machinery, the design, and the designer, might be evident, and, in the case supposed, would be evident, in whatever way we account for the irregularity of the movement, or whether we could account for it or not. It is not necessary that a machine be perfect in order to show with what design it was made: still less necessary where the only question is whether it were made with any design at all.

III. Nor, thirdly, would it bring any uncertainty into the argument, if there were a few parts of the watch, concerning which we could not discover or had not yet discovered, in what manner they conduced to the general effect; or even some parts, concerning which we could not ascertain whether they conduced to that effect in any manner whatever....

IV. Nor, fourthly, would any man in his senses think the existence of the watch, with its various machinery, accounted for by being told that it was one out of possible combinations of material forms; that whatever he had found in the place where he found the watch, must have contained some internal configuration or other; and that this configuration might be the structure now exhibited, viz., of the works of a watch, as well as a different structure.

V. Nor fifthly, would it yield his inquiry more satisfaction to be answered that there existed in things a principle of order, which had disposed the parts of the watch into their present form and situation. He never knew a watch made by the principle of order; nor can he even form to himself an idea of what is meant by a principle of order, distinct from the intelligence of the watchmaker.

VI. Sixthly, he would be surprised to hear that the mechanism of the watch was not proof of contrivance, only a motive to induce the mind to think so:

VII. And not less surprised to be informed that the watch in his hand was nothing more than the result of the laws of *metallic* nature. It is a perversion of language to assign any law as the efficient operative cause of anything. A law presupposes an agent: for it is only the mode according to which an agent proceeds: it implies a power; for it is the order according to which that power acts. Without this agent, without this power, which are both distinct from itself, the *law* does nothing, is nothing....

VIII. Neither, lastly, would our observer be driven out of his conclusion, or from his confidence in its truth, by being told that he knew nothing at all about the matter. He knows enough for his argument: he knows the utility of the end: he knows the subservience and adaptation of the means to the end. These points being known, his ignorance of other points, his doubts concerning other points, affect not the certainty of his reasoning....

CHAPTER III. APPLICATION OF THE ARGUMENT

Every indication of contrivance, every manifestation of design, which existed in the watch, exists in the works of nature; with the difference, on the side of nature, of being greater and more, and that in a degree which exceeds all computation. I mean that the contrivances of nature surpass the contrivances of art in the complexity, subtlety, and curiosity of the mechanism; and still more if possible, do they go beyond them in number and variety; yet, in a multitude of cases, are not less evidently mechanical, not less evidently contrivances, not less evidently accommodated to their end, or suited to their office, than are the most perfect productions of human ingenuity.

[Compare] an eye, for example, with a telescope. As far as the examination of the instrument goes, there is precisely the same proof that the eye was made for vision, as there is that the telescope was made for assisting it. They are made upon the same principles; both being adjusted to the laws by which the transmission and refraction of the rays of light are regulated.... For instance these laws require, in order to produce the same effect, that the rays of light, in passing from water into the eye, should be refracted by a more convex surface than when it passes out of air into the eye. Accordingly, we find that the eye of a fish, in that part of it called the crystalline lens, is much rounder than the eye of terrestrial animals.

What plainer manifestation of design can there be in their difference? What could a mathematical instrument maker have done more to show his knowledge of his principle, his application of that knowledge, his suiting of his means to his end. [It testifies to] counsel, choice, consideration, purpose....

CHAPTER V. APPLICATION OF THE ARGUMENT CONTINUED

Every observation which was made in our first chapter concerning the watch, may be repeated with strict propriety concerning the eye.... As,

I. When we are inquiring simply after the *existence* of an intelligent Creator, imperfection, inaccuracy, liability to disorder, occasional irregularities, may subsist in a considerable degree, without inducing any doubt into the question: just as a watch may frequently go wrong.... When the argument respects his attributes, they are of weight; but are then to be taken in conjunction ... with the unexceptionable evidences which we possess of skill, power, and benevolence displayed in other instances; which evidences may, in strength, number, and variety, be such, and may so overpower apparent blemishes, as to induce us, upon the most reasonable ground, to believe that these last ought to be referred to some cause, though we be ignorant of it, other than defect of knowledge or of benevolence in the author.

STUDY QUESTIONS

1. What analogy does Paley use to construct his teleological argument for the existence of a Creator?
2. Consider two of the objections Paley raises against the view that a watch requires a designer, and apply them to the eye. Then show how Paley answers these objections.

David Hume

Critique of the Analogical Teleological Argument

This section begins with a statement of the teleological argument by Cleanthes, a defender of the rationalist view that God's existence can be argued by empirical evidence. Then Philo, a skeptic generally held to represent Hume's own views, proceeds to attack the argument. (We have omitted the fideist Demea from the *Dialogues* for considerations of space.) First, Philo argues that an analogical argument is only as strong as the analogues are similar, but the universe bears little resemblance to human artifacts like houses and ships. Cleanthes replies that this objection misses the point: the analogy is not between these things but is found in the fact that both have means–ends ordering. Second, Philo asks, why should reason be taken as the fundamental ordering principle, when there are other ordering principles, like vegetation or magnetism, that might be equally effective? Just because reason is effective in organizing in one area does not mean that it is necessary for order in other areas (like biology) or that it even governs the universe. Third, Philo argues that Cleanthes cannot make this move from items where he has experienced the cause and effect to a universe that he has not experienced and of whose principles he is largely ignorant. Further, Philo argues that if we say that ideas can fall into order by themselves, without a cause, why can we not say that matter also can organize itself? By appeal to divine Mind, we have achieved no advance in explaining material order. Finally, Philo contends that if we argue from this analogy, we have no reason to think that God is perfect (given the imperfections in nature) or even a single being, since order can arise from the combined work of many. In sum, we should look to principles other than reason to explain the order in the world.

PART II

CLEANTHES:...I shall briefly explain how I conceive this matter. Look round the world: contemplate the whole and every part of it: you will find it to be nothing but one great machine, subdivided into an infinite number of lesser machines, which again admit of subdivisions to a degree beyond what human senses and faculties can trace and explain. All these various machines, and even their most minute parts, are adjusted to each

---

From David Hume, *Dialogues Concerning Natural Religion*. Indianapolis, Ind.: Hackett, 1980.

other with an accuracy which ravishes into admiration all men who have ever contemplated them. The curious adapting of means to ends, throughout all nature, resembles exactly, though it much exceeds, the productions of human contrivance; of human designs, thought, wisdom, and intelligence. Since, therefore, the effects resemble each other, we are led to infer, by all the rules of analogy, that the causes also resemble; and that the Author of Nature is somewhat similar to the mind of man, though possessed of much larger faculties, proportioned to the grandeur of the work which he has executed. By this argument a posteriori, and by this argument alone, do we prove at once the existence of a Deity, and his similarity to human mind and intelligence....

PHILO: What I chiefly scruple in this subject is not so much that all religious arguments are by Cleanthes reduced to experience, as that they appear not to be even the most certain and irrefragable of that inferior kind. That a stone will fall, that fire will burn, that the earth has solidity, we have observed a thousand and a thousand times; and when any new instance of this nature is presented, we draw without hesitation the accustomed inference. The exact similarity of the cases gives us a perfect assurance of a similar event; and a stronger evidence is never desired nor sought after. But wherever you depart, in the least, from the similarity of the cases, you diminish proportionably the evidence; and may at last bring it to a very weak analogy, which is confessedly liable to error and uncertainty. After having experienced the circulation of the blood in human creatures, we make no doubt that it takes place in Titius and Maevius. But from its circulation in frogs and fishes, it is only a presumption, though a strong one, from analogy, that it takes place in men and other animals. The analogical reasoning is much weaker, when we infer the circulation of the sap in vegetables from our experience that the blood circulates in animals; and those, who hastily followed that imperfect analogy, are found, by more accurate experiments, to have been mistaken.

If we see a house, Cleanthes, we conclude, with the greatest certainty, that it had an architect or builder; because this is precisely that species of effect which we have experienced to proceed from that species of cause. But surely you will not affirm, that the universe bears such a resemblance to a house that we can with the same certainty infer a similar cause, or that the analogy is here entire and perfect. The dissimilitude is so striking, that the utmost you can here pretend to is a guess, a conjecture, a presumption concerning a similar cause; and how that pretension will be received in the world, I leave you to consider.

CLEANTHES: ... But is the whole adjustment of means to ends in a house and in the universe so slight a resemblance? The economy of final causes? The order, proportion, and arrangement of every part? Steps of a stair are plainly contrived, that human legs may use them in mounting; and this inference is certain and infallible. Human legs are also contrived for walking and mounting; and this inference, I allow, is not altogether so certain, because of the dissimilarity which you remark; but does it, therefore, deserve the name only of presumption or conjecture?...

PHILO: [reformulating Cleanthes's argument] Now, according to this method of reasoning, it follows (and is, indeed, tacitly allowed by Cleanthes himself), that order, arrangement, or the adjustment of final causes, is not of itself any proof of design; but only so far as it has been experienced to proceed from that principle. For ought we can know a priori, matter may contain the source or spring of order originally within itself as well as mind does; and there is no more difficulty in conceiving, that the several elements, from an internal unknown cause, may fall into the most exquisite arrangement, than to conceive that their ideas, in the great universal mind, from a like internal unknown cause, fall into that arrangement. The equal possibility of both these suppositions is allowed. But, by experience, we find, (according to Cleanthes) that there is a difference between them. Throw several pieces of steel together, without shape or form; they will never arrange themselves so as to compose a watch. Stone, and mortar, and wood, without an architect, never erect a house. But the ideas in a human mind, we see, by an unknown, inexplicable economy, arrange themselves so as to form the plan of a watch or house. Experience, therefore, proves, that there is an original principle of order in mind, not in matter. From similar effects we infer similar causes. The adjustment of means to ends is alike in the universe, as in a machine of human contrivance. The causes, therefore, must be resembling....

That all inferences, Cleanthes, concerning fact, are founded on experience; and that all experimental reasonings are founded on the supposition that similar causes prove similar effects, and similar effects similar causes; I shall not at present much dispute with you. But observe, I entreat you, with what extreme caution all just reasoners proceed in the transferring of experiments to similar cases. Unless the cases be exactly similar, they repose no perfect confidence in applying their past observation to any particular phenomenon. Every alteration of circumstances occasions a doubt concerning the event; and it requires new experiments to prove certainly, that the new circumstances are of no moment or importance. A change in bulk, situation, arrangement, age, disposition of the air, or surrounding bodies; any of these particulars may be attended with the most unexpected consequences: and unless the objects be quite familiar to us, it is the highest temerity to expect with assurance, after any of these changes, an event similar to that which before fell under our observation....

But can you think, Cleanthes, that your usual phlegm and philosophy have been preserved in so wide a step as you have taken, when you compared to the universe houses, ships, furniture, machines, and, from their similarity in some circumstances, inferred a similarity in their causes? Thought, design, intelligence, such as we discover in men and other animals, is no more than one of the springs and principles of the universe, as well as heat or cold, attraction or repulsion, and a hundred others, which fall under daily observation. It

is an active cause, by which some particular parts of nature, we find, produce alterations on other parts. But can a conclusion, with any propriety, be transferred from parts to the whole? Does not the great disproportion bar all comparison and inference? From observing the growth of a hair, can we learn any thing concerning the generation of a man? Would the manner of a leaf's blowing, even though perfectly known, afford us any instruction concerning the vegetation of a tree?

But, allowing that we were to take the operations of one part of nature upon another, for the foundation of our judgment concerning the origin of the whole, (which never can be admitted,) yet why select so minute, so weak, so bounded a principle, as the reason and design of animals is found to be upon this planet? What peculiar privilege has this little agitation of the brain which we call thought, that we must thus make it the model of the whole universe? Our partiality in our own favour does indeed present it on all occasions; but sound philosophy ought carefully to guard against so natural an illusion.

So far from admitting, continued Philo, that the operations of a part can afford us any just conclusion concerning the origin of the whole, I will not allow any one part to form a rule for another part, if the latter be very remote from the former. Is there any reasonable ground to conclude, that the inhabitants of other planets possess thought, intelligence, reason, or any thing similar to these faculties in men? When nature has so extremely diversified her manner of operation in this small globe, can we imagine that she incessantly copies herself throughout so immense a universe? And if thought, as we may well suppose, be confined merely to this narrow corner, and has even there so limited a sphere of action, with what propriety can we assign it for the original cause of all things? The narrow views of a peasant, who makes his domestic economy the rule for the government of kingdoms, is in comparison a pardonable sophism.

But were we ever so much assured, that a thought and reason, resembling the human, were to be found throughout the whole universe, and were its activity elsewhere vastly greater and more commanding than it appears in this globe; yet I cannot see, why the operations of a world constituted, arranged, adjusted, can with any propriety be extended to a world which is in its embryo state, and is advancing towards that constitution and arrangement. By observation, we know somewhat of the economy, action, and nourishment of a finished animal; but we must transfer with great caution that observation to the growth of a foetus in the womb, and still more in the formation of an animalcule in the loins of its male parent. Nature, we find, even from our limited experience, possesses an infinite number of springs and principles, which incessantly discover themselves on every change of her position and situation. And what new and unknown principles would actuate her in so new and unknown a situation as that of the formation of a universe, we cannot, without the utmost temerity, pretend to determine.

A very small part of this great system, during a very short time, is very imperfectly discovered to us; and do we then pronounce decisively concerning the origin of the whole?

Admirable conclusion! Stone, wood, brick, iron, brass, have not, at this time, in this minute globe of earth, an order or arrangement without human art and contrivance; therefore the universe could not originally attain its order and arrangement, without something similar to human art. But is a part of nature a rule for another part very wide of the former? Is it a rule for the whole? Is a very small part a rule for the universe? Is nature in one situation, a certain rule for nature in another situation vastly different from the former?...

In this cautious proceeding of the astronomers, you may read your own condemnation, Cleanthes; or rather may see, that the subject in which you are engaged exceeds all human reason and enquiry. Can you pretend to shew any such similarity between the fabric of a house, and the generation of a universe? Have you ever seen nature in any such situation as resembles the first arrangement of the elements? Have worlds ever been formed under your eye; and have you had leisure to observe the whole progress of the phenomenon, from the first appearance of order to its final consummation? If you have, then cite your experience, and deliver your theory....

PART IV

PHILO:...If Reason (I mean abstract reason, derived from enquiries a priori) be not alike mute with regard to all questions concerning cause and effect, this sentence at least it will venture to pronounce, That a mental world, or universe of ideas, requires a cause as much, as does a material world, or universe of objects; and, if similar in its arrangement, must require a similar cause. For what is there in this subject, which should occasion a different conclusion or inference? In an abstract view, they are entirely alike; and no difficulty attends the one supposition, which is not common to both of them.

Again, when we will needs force Experience to pronounce some sentence, even on these subjects which lie beyond her sphere, neither can she perceive any material difference in this particular, between these two kinds of worlds; but finds them to be governed by similar principles, and to depend upon an equal variety of causes in their operations. We have specimens in miniature of both of them. Our own mind resembles the one; a vegetable or animal body the other. Let experience, therefore, judge from these samples. Nothing seems more delicate, with regard to its causes, than thought; and as these causes never operate in two persons after the same manner, so we never find two persons who think exactly alike. Nor indeed does the same person think exactly alike at any two different periods of time. A difference of age, of the disposition of his body, of weather, of food, of company, of books, of passions; any of these particulars, or others more minute, are sufficient to alter the curious machinery of thought, and communicate to it very different movements and operations. As far as we can judge, vegetables and animal bodies are not more delicate in their motions, nor depend upon a greater variety or more curious adjustment of springs and principles.

How, therefore, shall we satisfy ourselves concerning the cause of that Being whom you suppose the Author of Nature, or, according to your system of Anthropomorphism, the ideal world, into which you trace the material? Have we not the same reason to trace that ideal world into another ideal world, or new intelligent principle? But if we stop, and go no further; why go so far? why not stop at the material world? How can we satisfy ourselves without going on in infinitum? And, after all, what satisfaction is there in that infinite progression? Let us remember the story of the Indian philosopher and his elephant. It was never more applicable than to the present subject. If the material world rests upon a similar ideal world, this ideal world must rest upon some other; and so on, without end. It were better, therefore, never to look beyond the present material world. By supposing it to contain the principle of its order within itself, we really assert it to be God; and the sooner we arrive at that Divine Being, so much the better. When you go one step beyond the mundane system, you only excite an inquisitive humour which it is impossible ever to satisfy.

To say, that the different ideas which compose the reason of the Supreme Being, fall into order of themselves, and by their own nature, is really to talk without any precise meaning. If it has a meaning, I would fain know, why it is not as good sense to say, that the parts of the material world fall into order of themselves and by their own nature. Can the one opinion be intelligible, while the other is not so?

We have, indeed, experience of ideas which fall into order of themselves, and without any known cause. But, I am sure, we have a much larger experience of matter which does the same; as, in all instances of generation and vegetation, where the accurate analysis of the cause exceeds all human comprehension. We have also experience of particular systems of thought and of matter which have no order; of the

first in madness, of the second in corruption. Why, then, should we think, that order is more essential to one than the other? And if it requires a cause in both, what do we gain by your system, in tracing the universe of objects into a similar universe of ideas? The first step which we make leads us on for ever. It were, therefore, wise in us to limit all our enquiries to the present world, without looking further. No satisfaction can ever be attained by these speculations, which so far exceed the narrow bounds of human understanding....

An ideal system, arranged of itself, without a precedent design, is not a whit more explicable than a material one, which attains its order in a like manner; nor is there any more difficulty in the latter supposition than in the former.

PART V

PHILO:...Now, Cleanthes, mark the consequences. First, by this method of reasoning, you renounce all claim to infinity in any of the attributes of the Deity. For, as the cause ought only to be proportioned to the effect, and the effect, so far as it falls under our cognizance, is not infinite; what pretensions have we, upon your suppositions, to ascribe that attribute to the Divine Being? You will still insist, that, by removing him so much from all similarity to human creatures, we give in to the most arbitrary hypothesis, and at the same time weaken all proofs of his existence.

Secondly, you have no reason, on your theory, for ascribing perfection to the Deity, even in his finite capacity, or for supposing him free from every error, mistake, or incoherence, in his undertakings. There are many inexplicable difficulties in the works of Nature, which, if we allow a perfect author to be proved a priori, are easily solved, and become only seeming difficulties, from the narrow capacity of man, who cannot trace infinite relations. But according to your method of reasoning, these difficulties become all real; and perhaps will be insisted on, as new instances of likeness to human art and contrivance. At least, you must acknowledge, that it is impossible for us to tell, from our limited views, whether this system contains any great faults, or deserves any considerable praise, if compared to other possible, and even real systems. Could a peasant, if the *Aeneid* were read to him, pronounce that poem to be absolutely faultless, or even assign to it its proper rank among the productions of human wit, he, who had never seen any other production?

But were this world ever so perfect a production, it must still remain uncertain, whether all the excellences of the work can justly be ascribed to the workman. If we survey a ship, what an exalted idea must we form of the ingenuity of the carpenter who framed so complicated, useful, and beautiful a machine? And what surprise must we feel, when we find him a stupid mechanic, who imitated others, and copied an art, which, through a long succession of ages, after multiplied trials, mistakes, corrections, deliberations, and controversies, had been gradually improving? Many worlds might have been botched and bungled, throughout an eternity, ere this system was struck out; much labour lost, many fruitless trials made; and a slow, but continued improvement carried on during infinite ages in the art of world-making. In such subjects, who can determine, where the truth; nay, who can conjecture where the probability lies, amidst a great number of hypotheses which may be proposed, and a still greater which may be imagined?

And what shadow of an argument can you produce, from your hypothesis, to prove the unity of the Deity? A great number of men join in building a house or ship, in rearing a city, in framing a commonwealth; why may not several deities combine in contriving and framing a world? This is only so much greater similarity to human affairs. By sharing the work among several, we may so much further limit the attributes of each, and get rid of that extensive power and knowledge, which must be supposed in one deity, and which, according to you, can only serve to weaken the proof of his existence. And if such foolish, such vicious creatures as man, can yet often unite in framing and executing one plan, how much more those deities or demons, whom we may suppose several degrees more perfect!...

PART VII

PHILO:...But here, in examining the ancient system of the soul of the world, there strikes me, all on a sudden, a new idea, which, if just, must go near to subvert all your reasoning, and destroy even your first inferences, on which you repose such confidence. If the universe bears a greater likeness to animal bodies and to vegetables, than to the works of human art, it is more probable that its cause resembles the cause of the former than that of the latter, and its origin ought rather to be ascribed to generation or vegetation, than to reason or design. Your conclusion, even according to your own principles, is therefore lame and defective....

Our friend Cleanthes, as you have heard, asserts, that since no question of fact can be proved otherwise than by experience, the existence of a Deity admits not of proof from any other medium. The world, says he, resembles the works of human contrivance; therefore its cause must also resemble that of the other. Here we may remark, that the operation of one very small part of nature, to wit man, upon another very small part, to wit that inanimate matter lying within his reach, is the rule by which Cleanthes judges of the origin of the whole; and he measures objects, so widely disproportioned, by the same individual standard. But to waive all objections drawn from this topic, I affirm, that there are other parts of the universe (besides the machines of human invention) which bear still a greater resemblance to the fabric of the world, and which, therefore, afford a better conjecture concerning the universal origin of this system. These parts are animals and vegetables. The world plainly resembles more an animal or a vegetable, than it does a watch or a knitting-loom. Its cause, therefore, it is more probable, resembles the cause of the former. The cause of the former is generation or vegetation. The cause, therefore, of the world, we may infer to be something similar or analogous to generation or vegetation....

CLEANTHES: I must confess, Philo, that of all men living, the task which you have undertaken, of raising doubts and objections, suits you best, and seems, in a manner, natural and unavoidable to you. So great is your fertility of invention, that I am not ashamed to acknowledge myself unable, on a sudden, to solve regularly such out-of-the-way difficulties as you incessantly start upon me: though I clearly see, in general, their fallacy and error. And I question not, but you are yourself, at present, in the same case, and have not the solution so ready as the objection: while you must be sensible, that common sense and reason are entirely against you; and that such whimsies as you have delivered, may puzzle, but never can convince us.

STUDY QUESTIONS

1. How does Cleanthes' teleological argument compare with that given by William Paley in the previous reading?
2. Present three objections that Philo raises against the teleological argument.
3. How does Paley attempt to answer Hume's objections, and how successful do you think Paley is?

L. Stafford Betty with Bruce Cordell

The Anthropic Teleological Argument

L. Stafford Betty (b. 1942) and Bruce Cordell (b. 1949) develop a cumulative argument that cites various features of the universe to establish the probability that God exists. They think that a universe described by a grand universal theory (GUT) or by a theory of superstrings is unlikely to have evolved this way merely by chance. Also, the Anthropic Principle indicates that a large number of basic physical constants of particular values were needed for conscious life to arise; yet, each individual constant, let alone all of them together, are a priori extraordinarily improbable. Thus, the fact that we exist and are able to observe the universe inductively suggests a universal, creative intelligence. For Betty and Cordell, the existence of an intelligent creator explains the origin of life better than any neo-Darwinian account. They propose the law that the significantly greater cannot come from the significantly less, with the result that it is reasonable to hold that the supermind behind the universe is superior to us in every respect.

The Teleological Argument (*telos* in the Greek means "purpose," "end," or "design") presented here is akin to, yet somewhat different from the "wider teleological argument" of F. R. Tennant. Tennant did not think that his arguments were conclusive; taken together they only *suggested* "an intelligent Designer." The present argument, however, is largely based on mathematics and physics, and these yield probabilities. Quite a few neo-teleologists in the scientific community hold that the orthodox model of randomly evolving complexity and order in the universe is *overwhelmingly improbable*, for, they argue, the mathematics of the case makes it so. An intelligent designer, they say, is, by a very wide margin, the best available explanation of the universe....

This paper will present, under four headings, the most important evidences which, we believe, point to an intelligent designer as the best explanation of our orderly universe. These headings are the following: (a) intuitive factors, (b) cosmology, (c) the fossil record, and (d) biochemical complexity. [(a) and (c) are omitted.]

Cosmology

...We will consider three arguments for the existence of a cosmic orderer. They are based on the Big Bang and the anthropic principle.

From *International Philosophical Quarterly 27*, no. 4 (December 1987). Footnotes are omitted. Reprinted by permission.

The Big Bang. The first of these, the argument based on the Big Bang, is in many ways the most impressive. But it does not lend itself to mathematical analysis, and hence to a probability calculus (with odds computed for or against the argument), as readily as the other two arguments. Thus, we will treat it first and regard it as the weakest, i.e., the most "intuitive" of the arguments.

Most scientists and philosophers stop well short of reasoning backward from the cosmos as it exists today to the necessary existence of an ultimate mind and will behind the primeval explosion. But at least one, Hannes Alfvén, concluded that the Big Bang "necessarily presupposes a divine creation," while another, the British physicist Edmund Whitaker, maintained that there "is no ground for supposing that matter and energy existed before [the Big Bang] and was suddenly galvanized into action...It is simpler to postulate creation *ex nihilo*—Divine will constituting Nature from nothingness." Whatever one's particular view of the ultimate cause of the Big Bang, it is certainly the case that a universe with a beginning in time—anywhere from thirteen to twenty billion years ago, according to latest estimates—is more likely to arouse speculation about a Creator than a steady-state, apparently beginningless universe of infinite duration.

This is reasonable because the Big Bang refers, according to latest refinements of the theory, to a time when matter-energy arose out of a condition which is mysterious to us, and will probably always be. Even if the Big Bang is the result of a "zero-point fluctuation," as some physicists have recently speculated, it would be necessary to ask what caused this fluctuation. At best this theory only moves back the unexplainable one step; the order, immensity, complexity, and beauty of our present universe remains anchored in an irresistible surd.

At this point we must ask ourselves what is easier to imagine and thus to believe: that the cosmos' entire history should have arisen from this self-creating and self-explaining surd; or that a pre-existing mind and power of vast magnitude should have created the ingredients of the universe and triggered it at the Big Bang? This second alternative seems to us somewhat more likely. It is certainly no more preposterous....

Many scientists hold that it is impossible to extrapolate as far back into the past. The distinguished MIT physicist Victor Weisskopf is one of these. "It is very difficult," he says, "to know what happened at periods earlier than about 10^{-6} sec...but scientists like to speculate and to construct hypotheses." And they do. One speculation that has enjoyed wide currency is called the grand unification theory (GUT), so called because it postulates a time when all forces of nature, apart from gravity, were reduced to a single force.

GUT yields a universe which not only boggles the imagination, but which is utterly spectacular in its elegantly simple unfolding. Could such a universe have unfurled by chance alone? Or was there a mind of indescribable magnitude behind the whole thing? Mike Corwin, a physicist who has studied and written about the universe's beginning according to the GUT scenario, is "filled with a sense of wonder and mystery" at "the natural miracle of our existence." Corwin is, of course, speaking poetically, but that is exactly the point. A study of the universe's beginning leaves some people speechless or stammering; or inclined to write poetry; or, in a few cases, to believe.

Potentially more revolutionary than GUT—or supersymmetry, or the electroweak theory, or quantum chromodynamics (QCD), which are alternative attempts to reduce the universe to a sublime primeval simplicity—is superstrings. "Superstrings," writes Gary Taubes in *Discover*, "is a theory of the universe, a ten-dimensional one, in which the fundamental building blocks of matter and energy aren't infinitesimal points but infinitesimal strings." So comprehensive is superstrings—it neatly and elegantly accommodates all four of the fundamental forces of the universe—that physicists are calling it the Theory of Everything (T.O.E.). Not even taken seriously by the huge majority of physicists until 1984, today it is considered to be the theory with the best chance of reducing the universe, including gravity, to a single fundamental force. "It's beautiful, wonderful, majestic—and strange, if you like," says mathematician Edward Witten of Princeton. It still remains to reduce superstrings' ivory-tower ten-dimensional universe to the common-sense four-dimensional one in which we live, but many physicists and mathematicians are confident that this will be done. If so, then "all matter and energy, all forces, all people, planets, stars, cats and dogs, quasars, atoms, automobiles and everything else, from the instant of the Big Bang to the end of time," will be shown to be the result of the twitchings, vibrations, and interactions of these infinitesimal strings.

Again the question arises: How likely is it that our spectacularly complex, orderly universe should have arisen from the *chance* twitchings and interactions of these strings? Is it not more likely that there is an ordering, creating intelligence attached (if you'll forgive us) to the strings? . . .

The Anthropic Principle. One scientist who did take Dirac's principle seriously was Robert H. Dicke of Princeton. Influenced by Dirac's reasoning, Dicke in 1961 introduced the scientific world to the "anthropic principle." Like Dirac's large-number hypothesis, the anthropic principle derives its force from certain "coincidences" in the values of the basic physical constants. Dicke was specifically concerned to show that the Hubble constant, which governs the rate of expansion of the universe, could not have been much different from what it in fact is, or otherwise life could not have evolved. Cambridge University physicist Brandon Carter, whose name is more often associated with the anthropic principle, applied Dicke's reasoning to all of the initial conditions of the universe (temperature, chemical environment, etc.). According to Carter, if the initial conditions at the Big Bang had been any different from what they were, life as we know it could not have evolved. Paraphrasing Descartes, Carter writes, *"Cogito ergo mundus talis est"* (I think, therefore, the world is as it is).

According to Dewey Schwartzenburg, the anthropic principle (*anthropos*, Greek for "man") boils down to this: " . . . if the universe were in fact different in any significant way from the way it is, we wouldn't be here to wonder why it is the way it is." B. J. Carr and M. J. Rees, whose 1979 article in *Nature* is perhaps the most impressive scientific statement of the principle yet to appear, explain that the "possibility of life as we know it evolving in the Universe depends on the values of a few basic physical constants—and is in some respects remarkably sensitive to their numerical values."

What are those constants? Physicists speak of "coupling constants," but these in turn depend on such basic constants as the charge of the proton, the mass of the proton, the speed of light, the gravitational constant G in Newton's law of universal gravitation, and Planck's constant, h which allows us to determine a quantum of energy emitted by an electron radiating at a particular frequency. In mathematical notation, h is equal to 6.626×10^{-34} J-sec, and "Big G" the gravitational constant, is equal to 6.67×10^{-11} Newton-m^2/kg^2.

What is remarkable—and it is this that forms the basis of the anthropic principle—is that if, for instance, Planck's constant had a different value, say 6.626×10^{-33} instead of 10^{-34}, the whole universe would be different from the way it is. More importantly, intelligent life could not have evolved in a substantially altered universe. For example, if gravity were significantly stronger than it is, stars would exhaust their hydrogen fuels much faster, and humanoid life (as we know it) could not appear in a universe where stars "died young." Or if the "strong force," which binds the nuclei of atoms together, were stronger, helium nuclei would dominate the universe, and no hydrogen would be left over; without hydrogen there would be no water, and without water there could not be life as we know it. This list of examples could go on indefinitely. The point is that, as far as we can tell, intelligent humanoid life could have evolved in only one narrowly select set of universes: the set including the universe we find ourselves in, a universe whose physical processes are governed by the precise basic constants that it possesses. Corwin states the case well:

> Life as we conceive it demands severe constraints on the initial conditions of the universe. Life and consciousness are not only the direct result of the initial conditions, but could only have resulted from a narrow range of initial conditions (i.e., the constants had to be precisely as they are). It is not that changes in the initial conditions would have changed the character of life, but rather that any significant change in the initial conditions would have ruled out the possibility of life evolving later . . . the universe would have evolved as a life-less, unconscious entity.

It is no wonder that today a few scientists who are aware of the anthropic principle are asking the question, "Does all this mean that cosmology has come to the point of having to postulate a 'Creator'?" The answer would seem, at first glance, to be Yes. For how else can we explain all these "coincidences"? Let us use an analogy: Imagine nine jars, each containing ten slips of paper with one number from 0 to 9, one number to a slip, with each number represented, placed side by side. Suppose now that a mechanical device drew at random one slip from each jar, and that the numbers drawn in sequence happened to correspond *exactly* to your nine-numbered Social Security Number. What are the chances of a random drawing giving such a result? They are exactly one in a billion. Now suppose, unlike a legitimate, genuinely random lottery drawing, there was no special reason dictating that the drawing had to be random, even though the mechanical device *suggested* randomness. If your number were drawn, would it not be far more reasonable to assume that the drawing was *not* random, that it was instead being superintended by some intelligence behind the scenes who was in some way invisibly manipulating the mechanical device? Would it not, in other words, be reasonable to conclude that the drawing was fixed—fixed in your favor?

Don N. Page of the Institute for Advanced Study in Princeton, N.J., recently calculated the odds against the formation of our universe, and the figure was a good deal more than one in a billion. His exact computation was in fact one in $10,000,000,000^{124}$, a number so large that to call it "astronomical" would be to engage in a wild understatement. But are the odds *against a Cosmic Designer* so high? If we must make a forced choice between an unintelligent random process and an invisible Intelligence behind the scenes, as it appears we must, and if, furthermore, the chance against a random process accounting for the precise values of the basic constants of physics is well in excess of a billion to one, then a designer may be considered highly probable. In other words, the anthropic principle looks as if it might succeed, after careful analysis, in making highly probable the existence of a universal designer-creator.

There are three reasons, however, to think that it might not. Though they may seem like quibbles to some, they have been thought by others to tip the balance back in the opposite direction, or if not in the opposite direction, then in a new direction leading to a destination that altogether baffles the human mind.

First, as Carr and Rees point out, the anthropic principle

> is based on what may be an unduly anthropocentric concept of an observer. The arguments invoked here assume that life requires elements heavier than hydrogen and helium, water, galaxies, and special types of stars and planets. It is conceivable [however] that some form of intelligence could exist without all of these features.

In other words, intelligent life might have evolved out of a very different kind of universe, and not just the one we know, with its particular governing constants. Of course, this "life" would have almost nothing in common (at least physically) with the biological life forms to which our universe has given rise. But what, except our own narrow experience, is guiding us when we limit life to conditions such as our universe provides?

Second, it is possible that an infinite number of universes coexist alongside our own or have existed sequentially in the beginningless past prior to our own. University of Texas physicist John Archibald Wheeler, who helped develop the many-worlds theory of coexisting universes first proposed in 1957 by Princeton physicist Hugh Everett, championed the "Everett Hypothesis" as a way of explaining the anthropic coincidences. He reasoned that, given enough universes, it is not unlikely that one would come along which had the right ingredients for life; and our universe is it. As for the others, "nothing 'interesting' would ever happen—there would be universes without stars, and others without atoms, and still others without even matter." Wheeler's view has found few supporters, largely for the reason that such universes have never been observed and, moreover, are in principle unobservable. Even Wheeler himself is now looking elsewhere for the clue to our universe's existence, namely, to the "magic central idea" which will at last make intelligible quantum theory, and with it our seemingly improbable universe. In any case, there is nothing intrinsically absurd about this many-worlds hypothesis.

The third refutation is very much the brainchild of Wheeler. Though it might at first sound fantastic because incompatible with our commonsense realism, it is in fact consistent with quantum mechanics, which describes the activity of tiny particles (electrons, for example) on an atomic or molecular scale. Wheeler predicted that an experimenter would be able to observe either the particle's diffraction pattern (single slit) or its interference pattern (double slit), whichever one he chose, *even though the particle had already moved* and, as it were, "committed itself" to one, and *only* one, of these patterns. Wheeler writes: "After the quantum of energy has *already* gone through the doubly slit screen, a last-instant free choice on our part—we have found—gives at will a double slit interference record or a one-slit-beam count." On the basis of this extraordinary prediction, scientists in France, West Germany, and at the University of Maryland recently set up "delayed choice" experiments to test the prediction. All of the findings seemed to support Wheeler: "…whether you make the choice before or after the event occurs, the effect of the choice [is] the same." As Corwin puts it, "observership becomes the mechanism of genesis.…What we choose to measure, argues Wheeler, is really an inseparable part of a phenomenon that in earlier thinking one would have said has 'already happened.'"

How is this way of thinking—"observership becomes the mechanism of genesis"—a threat to the thesis that our universe was created by a supermind ("God")? In this way: if we are capable of creating the experimental outcome that we desire, the next logical step is to suggest that scientists in some way create (imagine?) the basic constants of physics that our argument is based on. In that case there would be nothing special about the constants, and the only mind proven by them would be our own. One could not say of them that they were "true"; nor could one say that the "universe" they described really existed. A cosmic creator would become an unnecessary hypothesis.

What defense can we give against these three arguments? We admit that the theory of life's emergence from conditions greatly dissimilar to what we know on Earth, however unlikely this scenario may be, and the theory of an infinite number of universes, however farfetched it may seem, are at least not intrinsically absurd; but with this last hypothesis just sketched, although it is seemingly more plausible, there are grave philosophical difficulties. Indeed such a position can be regarded as self-refuting. Wheeler states that the experimenter would have ended up with a "different story for the doings of the electron if he had done different measurements in a different sequence." In other words, there is not "a world sitting 'out there'" for us to discover, measure, and describe. But if this is so, we would argue, then human observation is intrinsically suspect, and truth ceases to have any meaning. In such a solipsistic universe, or what Wheeler calls a "participatory universe," where we in some sense create what we set out to find, science is turned into a creative art; elegance and beauty, rather than correspondence to reality, might conceivably become the ultimate meaningful measures of "good science."

Philosophy aside, Wheeler's controversial views are rejected by physicists who call themselves realists, such as Fritz Rohrlich. Although the apparatus "plays a much more important role in measurements of the quantum world than in measurements of the classical world," as Rohrlich says, that does not mean "that reality is created by the observer.… The world of electrons, protons, and all the rest does exist out there even if we do not observe it." Three physicists working in England—David Bohm, C. Dewdney, and B. H. Hiley—would agree. They recently published a paper in which they claim to give "a simple and intelligible account of a typical delayed-choice experiment." If their account holds up, they will have succeeded to a degree in demystifying the quantum, and Wheeler's hypothesis that a quantum phenomenon does not exist until we observe it, will be discardable, and with it the threat to our present thesis.

To summarize, the anthropic principle presents us with a potentially powerful argument for the existence of a universal creating intelligence. Although three refutations can be brought forth, each has its problems. Nevertheless, there is nothing intrinsically implausible about the first two, and it is too early to dispose of the third. We must look elsewhere—to biology—for a more compelling argument.…

BIOCHEMICAL COMPLEXITY

So far we have concentrated on the fossil record and restricted our investigation to the last six hundred million years of Earth's 4.6 billion year history; we have said nothing about the evolution of life itself during the first billion or so years of Earth's history. What do we find when we try to account for the earliest, simplest life forms on Earth? How did the first protein, the first enzyme, the first DNA or RNA molecule come to be? Does the Neo-Darwinian Synthesis, with its dependence on exclusively random processes, give a plausible account of the appearance of these early biomolecules? Does it adequately account for the jump from nonlife to life? Or are we forced to look elsewhere for a more plausible explanation? These are the questions that this last section will address.

Charles-Eugene Guye, a Swiss physicist who died in 1942, was the first to apply the probability calculus to the question of life's origin. He calculated the mathematical odds against the random formation of a single protein molecule (protein is an essential ingredient in every organism) at $1:2.02 \times 10^{321}$....

Thirty-four years later another book appeared.... This was Fred Hoyle's and N. C. Wickramasinghe's *Evolution from Space*. Reasoning and calculating in much the same way as Guye, they tried to show that mathematical probability is stacked against Neo-Darwinism. Far more likely is it, they believe, that some kind of Super-Intelligence is behind the evolution of life on our planet.

Hoyle, one of the great astronomers of our century, and Wickramasinghe, currently (1987) Head of the Department of Applied Mathematics and Astronomy at University College in Cardiff, Wales, base their argument on the molecular structure of enzymes, which are complex macromolecules essential for the evolution of life. The two scientists hold that the "usual theory of mutation and natural selection cannot produce complex biomolecules from a random association of atoms," and, therefore, that the essential building blocks of even the most rudimentary forms of life could not have formed in the way in which Neo-Darwinists say they did.

Hoyle and Wickramasinghe are especially interested in refuting the "organic soup myth." This is the theory that the primeval stew of water (H_2O), ammonia (NH_3), methane (CH_4), and other simple compounds which made up our planet in its infancy, *randomly* generated, when subjected to lightning

flashes or other energy sources, the enzymes so critical to life. After pointing out that there are "some ten to twenty distinct amino acids which determine the basic backbone of the enzyme" and that these "simply must be in the correct position in the polypeptide structure," Hoyle and Wickramasinghe calculate the chance of one enzyme forming anywhere on earth through the random ordering of amino acids at one in 10^{20}. The brunt of their argument follows:

> By itself, this small probability could be faced, because one must contemplate not just a single shot at obtaining the enzyme, but a very large number of trials such as are supposed to have occurred in an organic soup early in the history of the Earth. The trouble is that there are about two thousand enzymes, and the chance of obtaining them all in a random trial is only one part in $(10^{20})^{2000} = 10^{40,000}$ an outrageously small probability that could not be faced even if the whole universe consisted of organic soup.

This immense figure is only the beginning. They continue:

> Nothing has been said of the origin of DNA itself, nothing of DNA transcription to RNA, nothing of the origin of the program whereby cells organize themselves, nothing of mitosis or meiosis. These issues are too complex to set numbers to.

The two scientists go on to say that the chance of these biochemical systems being formed "through random shufflings of simple organic molecules is exceedingly minute, to a point where it is insensibly different from zero."

Hoyle and Wickramasinghe are now poised for the strike. If Neo-Darwinism cannot account for the biochemical complexity necessary for the origin of life, what can? They answer:

> Any theory with a probability of being correct that is larger than one part in $10^{40,000}$ must be judged superior to random shuffling. The theory that life was assembled by an intelligence has, we believe, a probability vastly higher than one part in $10^{40,000}$ of being the correct explanation.... Indeed, such a theory is so obvious that one wonders why it is not widely accepted as being self-evident....

A trio of scientists headed by chemist Charles Thaxton, director of Curriculum Research for the

Foundation for Thought and Ethics in Dallas, provide another angle of vision on the problem of life's origin; and their conclusions are just as vexatious for traditional Neo-Darwinists as were the above. Their 1984 book *The Mystery of Life's Origin* is especially valuable for its summary of experiments—thousands of them—undertaken all over the world to show how life might have arisen on earth. All these experiments try to simulate earth's primitive geological condition ("the prebiotic soup") and atmosphere. In some experiments ultraviolet light is directed through the system, in others heat, in others special chemical reactants, and so forth. Many energy sources have been tried, and just as many varieties and conditions of "soup." Has anything like proteins, enzymes, RNA, or DNA ever turned up? Thaxton offers this summary: "The uniform failure in literally thousands of experimental attempts to synthesize protein or DNA under even questionable prebiotic conditions is a monument to [its] difficulty...." By "questionable" Thaxton and his colleagues mean "illegitimate." In their survey of the kinds of experiments being carried out, they show that most investigators, in an effort to achieve the hoped for results, more or less fudge; in other words, they create conditions that were not likely to have existed on the primitive earth. Thaxton and his colleagues find that the less fudging there is, the less satisfactory are the results.

The conclusion of their study is that chemical evolution along the lines of the Neo-Darwinian synthesis "is highly implausible." It is noteworthy that the esteemed biologist Sidney W. Fox, one of the leading proponents and a veteran of early-earth simulation experiments, agrees. Fox views amino acids as "self-ordering," not at all the lucky result of random processes. He is convinced that "matter organizes itself" and that "all evolutionary processes are highly nonrandom." Many biologists, chemists, and philosophers of science agree with Fox. While declining to say what it is which might account for the self-ordering—or more precisely, what it is which might account for the fortuitous morphology of amino acids that results in "molecular selection"—they nevertheless acknowledge that self-ordering, as opposed to random interaction, is a fact of pre-life.

Thaxton and his colleagues, however, do not decline to say what they think is behind the "self-ordering." Risking certain censure by fellow scientists, they conclude, in agreement with Hoyle and Wickramasinghe, that an ordering intelligence is the most plausible way of accounting for the evolution of proteins, RNA, and DNA on early earth. They do not regard this conclusion as "religious," but as solidly scientific:

> We have observational evidence in the present that intelligent investigators can (and do) build ways to bring about some complex chemical synthesis, even gene building. May not the principle of uniformity then be used in a broader frame of consideration to suggest that DNA had an intelligent cause at the beginning?

All in all, the biochemical argument, with an assist from the probability calculus, is a most imposing argument for the existence of a universal creative intelligence. In conjunction with the arguments centering on the physical constants (see the second argument, considered earlier) and on the inadequacy of Neo-Darwinism's doctrine of gradualism (our third argument), this last acquires even stronger force; just as three sticks held together in a bunch are harder to break as a module than each by itself. We can liken the argument to the reasoning process of an archaeologist. He sees no designer, no maker, no orderer physically laid out alongside the shard that he uncovers. If he finds only one shard, dirty and worn, he might wonder if it is after all merely a strangely shaped rock, an anomaly. But if he finds two others alongside the first, he confidently infers a designer, though the designer is never seen. Why should we not do this with respect to the earth (and, by extension, the universe)?

We are struck by the way that the old notion of a "God of the gaps"—a God needed to explain a diminishing number of mysteries, until at some time in the future He Himself fades away when the last mystery is unfolded—has been stood on its head. The gaps are proving to be more and more resistant to conventional scientific theory. It is as if they are fighting back, resisting closure, frustrating every attempt to bridge them, and widening in the process. If anything, science nowadays is creating new gaps, not closing old ones. We find ourselves wondering if the term "God of the gaps" may someday be used not by atheists to make fun of theists but by theists to remind atheists of the facts. In the meantime, we have on our hands a formidable teleological argument for the existence of a creative supermind.

With that, we come to the last question that we must treat.

WHAT GOD MIGHT BE

If our argument is sound, if we are justified in concluding that a supermind exists, can we say anything about what He, She, or It might be? Might It be something so impersonal that, besides its consciousness and computational skills, there is nothing else at all to which we can relate? Or might She be a Cosmic Mother who loves her creatures, especially her more intelligent species, analogously to the way we love our children, and who is as perfect in goodness as She is immense and unfathomable in her intelligence? Or is He a Cosmic Scientist experimenting with life forms in his laboratory, which we call the universe—a God neither loving nor callous by nature, but exceedingly curious? Does this God pre-exist the universe and create it out of nothing, or coexist everlastingly alongside it? Does this God suffuse our beings, and can we experience Her within, as the mystics of all the great religions have proclaimed? Is this God essentially spiritual, and does He have a body, perhaps the universe itself, as the Hindu theologian Ramanuja supposed? Or is God an all-comprehending Absolute that specifies Itself in conscious persons, only to draw them back into unity with It in some ineffable perfection, as the modern philosopher J. N. Findlay thinks? Does our argument help us answer such questions as these?

Strictly speaking, it doesn't. All it can do is point to the existence of a supermind behind nature's orderly, evolving processes. But there is a certain logic that we have been using throughout which, if applied to the question now before us, allows us to say more, if at great risk. We have seen in our investigation of biomolecular processes that there is good reason to believe that the significantly greater does not *randomly* come forth out of the significantly less. Simple amino acids,

to be sure, are randomly generated, not surprisingly, by inorganic compounds; but the *significantly* greater (because vastly more complex) enzymes have never revealed how they might be randomly generated by the amino acids. Indeed it seems there is no way they *could* have been generated without the help of intelligent orchestration.

In order to learn more about the *nature* of the proposed supermind, let's indulge in a little speculation and see where it takes us. We have just seen that there is good reason to think that the significantly greater cannot evolve unaided from the significantly less. Now let's postulate that it is a *universal law* that the significantly greater cannot be generated by the significantly less, and then apply it to the supermind, which is exponentially, perhaps even infinitely greater than we are. Would it not be a violation of this law if so much moral goodness as appears in this world were to exceed the goodness of the supermind? Consider for a moment the world we live in. We occasionally meet Mahatmas, more frequently little old ladies who unfailingly greet us with cheerful smiles in spite of severe arthritis. Not only is there much nobility and goodness in our own species; there is also a reverence for truth and a love of beauty. Beauty, truth, and goodness: those three fundamental values of the Greeks. Do large numbers of human beings significantly surpass the supermind in these "constants of the spirit?" This would have to be so if the supermind were merely a mind. We, its creations, would significantly surpass it in the area of values. It would have succeeded in creating a good that it knows nothing of, and the law that the significantly greater cannot come from the significantly less would have been violated.

This universal law—if it in fact is a law, as I tentatively propose—has enormously important implications for our discussion of the supermind's nature. If such a law holds, then it would follow that the supermind must be superior to us, not only with respect to intelligence (which seems obvious), but in every other important way as well. That mind must be characterized by knowledge, power, beauty, goodness, and love to a degree not known to us mortals. If so, it must in some sense be personal (perhaps "superpersonal" is a better way of putting it), for such traits as goodness and love would seem to adhere only in that which is at least analogous to persons. Whether or not the supermind has these perfections to an *infinite* degree—whatever that might involve—cannot be predicted by our argument. Nonetheless, it is clear that we are not too far away from a God whom we can at least admire. And if admiration should grow to love—a not unnatural progression—then the God of the great theistic religions is not far away. Religion and science will have joined hands.

Study Questions

1. What is the big bang argument for God's existence developed by Betty and Cordell?
2. What is the anthropic argument for God's existence? Develop one objection to the anthropic argument and comment on that objection's plausibility.
3. How does the difficulty of finding an explanation for the origin of life form an argument for God's existence?
4. Why do Betty and Cordell think that God is best understood theistically?

Robert Merrihew Adams

Moral Arguments for God's Existence

Robert Adams (b. 1937) advances three moral arguments for God's existence (the third is omitted here). First, he contends that the divine command theory, which claims that rightness or wrongness consists in agreement or disagreement with God's will or commands, provides the most adequate ethical theory because it treats moral rightness and wrongness as objective, nonnatural facts and is relatively intelligible. This moral theory entails the existence of God. Second, we have pragmatic reasons for believing in the moral order of the universe, for not to believe in it is demoralizing, and demoralization is morally undesirable. Since theism provides the most adequate theory of moral order, it follows that we have a pragmatic reason for believing in the existence of God. Finally, the moral argument has the advantage of providing a reason for thinking that if there is a God, he is morally very good, for to deny this would run counter to the respect that we pay to the moral law and hence would be morally intolerable.

Moral arguments were the type of theistic argument most characteristic of the nineteenth and early twentieth centuries. More recently they have become one of philosophy's abandoned farms. The fields are still fertile, but they have not been cultivated systematically since the latest methods came in.... This paper is intended to contribute to the remedy of this neglect. It will deal with quite a number of arguments, because I think we can understand them better if we place them in relation to each other....

I

Let us begin with one of the most obvious, though perhaps never the most fashionable, arguments on the farm: an Argument from the Nature of Right and Wrong. We believe quite firmly that certain things are morally right and others are morally wrong—for example, that it is wrong to torture another person to death just for fun. Questions may be raised about the nature of that which is believed in these beliefs: what does the rightness or wrongness of an act consist in? I believe that the most adequate answer is provided by a theory that entails the existence of God—specifically, by the theory that moral rightness and wrongness consist in agreement and disagreement, respectively, with the will or commands of a loving God. One of the most generally accepted reasons for believing in the existence of anything is that its existence is implied by the theory that seems to account most adequately for some subject matter. I take it, therefore, that my metaethical views provide me with a reason of some weight for believing in the existence of God.

Perhaps some will think it disreputably "tender-minded" to accept such a reason where the subject matter is moral. It may be suggested that the epistemological status of moral beliefs is so far inferior to that of physical beliefs, for example, that any moral belief found to entail the existence of an otherwise unknown object ought simply to be abandoned. But in spite of the general uneasiness about morality that pervades our culture, most of us do hold many moral beliefs with almost the highest degree of confidence. So long as we think it reasonable to argue at all from grounds that are not absolutely certain, there is no clear reason why such confident beliefs, in ethics as in other fields, should not be accepted as premises in arguing for the existence of anything that is required for the most satisfactory theory of their subject matter.

The divine command theory of the nature of right and wrong combines two advantages not jointly possessed by any of its non-theological competitors. These advantages are sufficiently obvious that their nature can be indicated quite briefly to persons familiar with the metaethical debate, though they are also so controversial that it would take a book-length review of the contending theories to defend my claims. The first advantage of divine command metaethics is that it presents facts of moral rightness and wrongness as objective, non-natural facts—objective in the sense that whether they obtain or not does not depend on whether any human being thinks they do; and non-natural in the sense that they cannot be stated entirely in the language of physics, chemistry, biology, and human or animal psychology. For it is an objective but not a natural fact that God commands, permits,

or forbids something. Intuitively this is an advantage. If we are tempted to say that there are only natural facts of right and wrong, or that there are no objective facts of right and wrong at all, it is chiefly because we have found so much obscurity in theories about objective, non-natural ethical facts. We seem not to be acquainted with the simple, nonnatural ethical properties of the Intuitionists, and we do not understand what a Platonic Form of the Good or the Just would be. The second advantage of divine command metaethics is that it is relatively intelligible. There are certainly difficulties in the notion of a divine command, but at least it provides us more clearly with matter for thought than the Intuitionist and Platonic conceptions do....

What we cannot avoid discussing, and at greater length than the advantages, are the alleged disadvantages of divine command metaethics. The advantages may be easily recognized, but the disadvantages are generally thought to be decisive. I have argued elsewhere, in some detail, that they are not decisive. Here let us concentrate on three objections that are particularly important for the present argument.

(1) In accordance with the conception of metaethics as analysis of the meanings of terms, a divine command theory is often construed as claiming that "right" *means* commanded (or permitted) by God, and that "wrong" *means* forbidden by God. This gives rise to the objection that people who do not believe that there exists a God to command or forbid still use the terms "right" and "wrong," and are said (even by theists) to believe that certain actions are right and others wrong. Surely those atheists do not mean by "right" and "wrong" what the divine command theory seems to say they must mean. Moreover, it may be objected that any argument for the existence of God from the premise that certain actions are right and others wrong will be viciously circular if that premise *means* that certain actions are commanded or permitted by God and others forbidden by God.

One might reply that it is not obviously impossible for someone to disbelieve something that is analytically implied by something else that he asserts. Nor is it impossible for the conclusion of a perfectly good, non-circular argument to be analytically implied by its premises. But issues about the nature of conceptual analysis, and of circularity in argument, can be avoided here. For in the present argument, a divine command theory need not be construed as saying that the existence of God is analytically implied by ascriptions of rightness and wrongness. It can be construed as proposing an answer to a question left open by the meaning of "right" and "wrong," rather than as a theory of the meaning of those terms. The ordinary meanings of many terms that signify properties, such as "hot" and "electrically charged," do not contain enough information to answer all questions about the nature (or even in some cases the identity) of the properties signified. Analysis of the meaning of "wrong" might show, for example, that "Nuclear deterrence is wrong" ascribes to nuclear deterrence a property about which the speaker may be certain of very little except that it belongs, independently of his views, to many actions that he opposes, such as torturing people just for fun. The analysis of meaning need not completely determine the identity of this property, but it may still be argued that a divine command theory identifies it most adequately.

(2) The gravest objection to the more extreme forms of divine command theory is that they imply that if God commanded us, for example, to make it our chief end in life to inflict suffering on other human beings, for no other reason than that He commanded it, it would be *wrong* not to obey. Finding this conclusion unacceptable, I prefer a less extreme, or modified, divine command theory, which identifies the ethical property of wrongness with the property of being contrary to the commands of a *loving* God. Since a God who commanded us to practice cruelty for its own sake would not be a loving God, this modified divine command theory does not imply that it would be wrong to disobey such a command.

But the objector may continue his attack: "Suppose that God did not exist, or that He existed but did not love us. Even the modified divine command theory implies that in that case it would not be wrong to be cruel to other people. But surely it would be wrong."

The objector may have failed to distinguish sharply two claims he may want to make: that some acts *would* be wrong even if God *did* not exist, and that some acts *are* wrong even if God *does* not exist. I grant the latter. Even if divine command metaethics

is the best theory of the nature of right and wrong, there are other theories which are more plausible than denying that cruelty is wrong. If God does not exist, my theory is false; but presumably the best alternative to it is true, and cruelty is still wrong.

But suppose there is in fact a God—indeed a loving God—and that the ethical property of wrongness is the property of being forbidden by a loving God. It follows that no actions would be wrong in a world in which no loving God existed, if 'wrong' designates rigidly (that is, in every possible world) the property that it actually designates. For no actions would have that property in such a world. Even in a world without God, however, the best remaining alternative to divine command metaethics might be correct in the following way. In such a world there could be people very like us who would say truly, "Kindness is right," and "Cruelty is wrong." They would be speaking about kindness and cruelty, but not about rightness and wrongness. That is, they would not be speaking about the properties that *are* rightness and wrongness, though they might be speaking about properties (perhaps natural properties) that they would be *calling* "rightness" and "wrongness." But they would be using the words "right" and "wrong" with the same *meaning* as we actually do. For the meaning of the words, I assume, leaves open some questions about the identity of the properties they designate.

Some divine command theorists could not consistently reply as I have suggested to the present objection. Their theory is about the meaning of "right" and "wrong," or they think all alternatives to it (except the complete denial of moral distinctions) are too absurd to play the role I have suggested for alternative theories. But there is another reply that is open to them. They can say that although wrongness is not a property that would be possessed by cruelty in a world without God, the possibility or idea of cruelty-in-a-world-without-God *does* possess, in the actual world (with God), a property that is close kin to wrongness: the property of being frowned on, or viewed with disfavor, by God. The experience of responding emotionally to fiction should convince us that it is possible to view with the strongest favor or disfavor events regarded as taking place in a world that would not, or might not, include one's own existence—and if possible for us, why not for God? If we are inclined to say that cruelty in a world without God would be wrong, that is surely because of an attitude of disfavor that we have in the actual world toward such a possibility. And if our attitude corresponds to an objective, non-natural moral fact, why cannot that fact be one that obtains in the actual world, rather than in the supposed world without God?

(3) It may be objected that the advantages of the divine command theory can be obtained without an entailment of God's existence. For the rightness of an action might be said to consist in the fact that the action *would* agree with the commands of a loving God if one existed, *or* does so agree if a loving God exists. This modification transforms the divine command theory into a non-naturalistic form of the ideal observer theory of the nature of right and wrong. It has the advantage of identifying rightness and wrongness with properties that actions could have even if God does not exist. And of course it takes away the basis of my metaethical argument for theism.

The flaw in this theory is that it is difficult to see what is supposed to be the force of the counterfactual conditional that is centrally involved in it. If there is no loving God, what makes it the case if there were one, He would command this rather than that? Without an answer to this question, the crucial counterfactual lacks a clear sense. I can see only two possible answers: either that what any possible loving God would command is logically determined by the concept of a loving God, or that it is determined by a causal law. Neither answer seems likely to work without depriving the theory of some part of the advantages of divine command metaethics.

No doubt some conclusions about what He would not command follow *logically* or analytically from the concept of a loving God. He would not command us to practice cruelty for its own sake, for example. But in some cases, at least, in which we believe the act is wrong, it seems only contingent that a loving God does or would frown on increasing the happiness of other people by the painless and undetected killing of a person who wants to live but will almost certainly not live happily. Very diverse preferences about what things are to be treated as personal rights seems compatible with love and certainly with deity.

Of course, you could explicitly build all your moral principles into the definition of the kind of hypothetical divine commands that you take to make facts of right and wrong. But then the fact that your principles *would* be endorsed by the commands of such a God adds nothing to the principles themselves; whereas endorsement by an *actual* divine command would add something, which is one of the advantages of divine command metaethics.

Nor is it plausible to suppose that there are *causal* laws that determine what would be commanded by a loving God, if there is no God. All causal laws, at bottom, are about actual things. There are no causal laws, though there could be legends, about the metabolism of chimeras or the susceptibility of centaurs to polio. There are physical laws about frictionless motions which never occur, but they are extrapolated from facts about actual motions. And we can hardly obtain a causal law about the commands of a possible loving God by extrapolating from causal laws governing the behavior of monkeys, chimpanzees, and human beings, as if every possible God would simply be a very superior primate. Any such extrapolation, moreover, would destroy the character of the theory of hypothetical divine commands as a theory of *non-natural* facts.

Our discussion of the Argument from the Nature of Right and Wrong may be concluded with some reflections on the nature of the God in whose existence it gives us some reason to believe. (1) The appeal of the argument lies in the provision of an explanation of moral facts of whose truth we are already confident. It must therefore be taken as an argument for the existence of a God whose commands—and presumably, whose purposes and character as well—are in accord with our most confident judgments of right and wrong. I have suggested that He must be a loving God. (2) He must be an intelligent being, so that it makes sense to speak of His having a will and issuing commands. Maximum adequacy of a divine command theory surely requires that God be supposed to have enormous knowledge and understanding of ethically relevant facts, if not absolute omniscience. He should be a God "unto whom all hearts are open, all desires known, and from whom no secrets are hid." (3) The argument does not seem to imply very much about God's power, however—certainly not that He is omnipotent. (4) Nor is it obvious that the argument supports belief in the unity or uniqueness of God. Maybe the metaethical place of divine commands could be taken by the unanimous deliverances of a senate of deities—although that conception raises troublesome questions about the nature of the morality or quasi-morality that must govern the relations of the gods with each other.

II

The most influential moral arguments for theistic belief have been a family of arguments that may be called Kantian. They have a common center in the idea of a moral order of the universe and are arguments for belief in a God sufficiently powerful to establish and maintain such an order. The Kantian family has members on both sides of one of the most fundamental distinctions in this area—the distinction between *theoretical* and *practical* arguments. By "a theoretical moral argument for theistic belief" I mean an argument having an ethical premise and purporting to prove the *truth*, or enhance the *probability*, of theism. By "a practical argument for theistic belief" I mean an argument purporting only to give ethical or other practical reasons for *believing* that God exists. The practical argument may have no direct bearing at all on the truth or probability of the belief whose practical advantage it extols....

Elsewhere Kant argues quite differently. He even denies that a command to promote the highest good is contained in, or analytically derivable from, the moral law. He claims rather that we will be "hindered" from doing what the moral law commands us to do unless we can regard our actions as contributing to the realization of "a final end of all things" which we can also make a "final end for all our actions and abstentions." He argues that only the highest good can serve morally as such a final end and that we therefore have a compelling moral need to believe in the possibility of its realization. This yields only a practical argument for theistic belief. Stripped of some of its more distinctively Kantian dress, it can be stated in terms

of "demoralization," by which I mean a weakening or deterioration of moral motivation.

(E) It would be demoralizing not to believe there is a moral order of the universe; for then we would have to regard it as very likely that the history of the universe will not be good on the whole, no matter what we do.

(F) Demoralization is morally undesirable.

(G) Therefore, there is moral advantage in believing that there is a moral order of the universe.

(H) Theism provides the most adequate theory of a moral order of the universe.

(J) Therefore, there is a moral advantage in accepting theism.

What is a moral order of the universe? I shall not formulate any necessary condition. But let us say that the following is *logically sufficient* for the universe's having a moral order: (1) a good world-history requires something besides human virtue (it might, as Kant thought, require the happiness of the virtuous); but (2) the universe is such that morally good actions will probably contribute to a good world-history. (I use "world" as a convenient synonym for "universe.")

Theism has several secular competitors as a theory of a moral order of the universe in this sense. The idea of scientific and cultural progress has provided liberal thinkers, and Marxism has provided socialists, with hopes of a good world-history without God. It would be rash to attempt to adjudicate this competition here. I shall therefore not comment further on the truth of (H) but concentrate on the argument from (E) and (F) to (G). It is, after all, of great interest in itself, religiously and in other ways, if morality gives us a reason to believe in a moral order of the universe.

Is (E) true? Would it indeed be demoralizing not to believe there is a moral order of the universe? The issue is in large part empirical. It is for sociologists and psychologists to investigate scientifically what are the effects of various beliefs on human motivation. And the motivational effects of religious belief form one of the central themes of the classics of speculative sociology. But I have the impression that there has not yet been very much "hard" empirical research casting light directly on the question whether (E) is true.

It may be particularly difficult to develop empirical research techniques subtle enough philosophically to produce results relevant to our present argument. One would have to specify which phenomena count as a weakening or deterioration of moral motivation. One would also have to distinguish the effects of belief in a moral world-order from the effects of other religious beliefs, for (E) could be true even if, as some have held, the effects of actual religious beliefs have been predominantly bad from a moral point of view. The bad consequences might be due to doctrines which are separable from faith in a moral order of the universe.

Lacking scientifically established answers to the empirical aspects of our question, we may say, provisionally, what seems plausible to us. And (E) does seem quite plausible to me. Seeing our lives as contributing to a valued larger whole is one of the things that gives them a point in our own eyes. The morally good person cares about the goodness of what happens in the world and not just about the goodness of his own actions. If a right action can be seen as contributing to some great good, that increases the importance it has for him. Conversely, if he thinks that things will turn out badly no matter what he does, and especially if he thinks that (as often appears to be the case) the long-range effects of right action are about as likely to be bad as good, that will diminish the emotional attraction that duty exerts on him. Having to regard it as very likely that the history of the universe will not be good on the whole, no matter what one does, seems apt to induce a cynical sense of futility about the moral life, undermining one's moral resolve and one's interest in moral considerations. My judgment on this issue is subject to two qualifications, however.

(1) We cannot plausibly ascribe more than a demoralizing *tendency* to disbelief in a moral order of the universe. There are certainly people who do not believe in such an order, but show no signs of demoralization.

(2) It may be doubted how much most people are affected by beliefs or expectations about the history of the universe as a whole. Perhaps most of us could

sustain with comparative equanimity the bleakest of pessimism about the twenty-third century if only we held brighter hopes for the nearer future of our own culture, country, or family, or even (God forgive us!) our own philosophy department. The belief that we can accomplish something significant and good for our own immediate collectivities may be quite enough to keep us going morally. On the other hand, belief in a larger-scale moral order of the universe might be an important bulwark against demoralization if all or most of one's more immediate hopes were being dashed. I doubt that there has ever been a time when moralists could afford to ignore questions about the motivational resources available in such desperate situations. Certainly it would be unimaginative to suppose that we live in such a time.

Some will object that those with the finest moral motivation can find all the inspiration they need in a tragic beauty of the moral life itself, even if they despair about the course of history. The most persuasive argument for this view is a presentation that succeeds in evoking moral emotion in connection with the thought of tragedy; Bertrand Russell's early essay "A Free Man's Worship" is an eloquent example. But I remain somewhat skeptical. Regarded aesthetically, from the outside, tragedy may be sublimely beautiful; lived from the inside, over a long period of time, I fear it is only too likely to end in discouragement and bitterness, though no doubt there have been shining exceptions.

But the main objection to the present argument is an objection to all practical arguments. It is claimed that none of them give justifying reasons for believing anything at all. If there are any practical advantages that are worthy to sway us in accepting or rejecting a belief, the advantage of not being demoralized is surely one of them. But can it be right, and intellectually honest, to believe something, or try to believe it, for the sake of any practical advantage, however noble?

I believe it can. This favorable verdict on practical arguments for theoretical conclusions is particularly plausible in "cases where faith creates its own verification," as William James puts it—or where your wish is at least more likely to come true if you believe it will. Suppose you are running for Congress and an unexpected misfortune has made it doubtful whether you still have a good chance of winning. Probably it will at least be clear that you are more likely to win if you continue to believe that your chances are good. Believing will keep up your spirits and your alertness, boost the morale of your campaign workers, and make other people more likely to take you seriously. In this case it seems to me eminently reasonable for you to cling, for the sake of practical advantage, to the belief that you have a good chance of winning.

Another type of belief for which practical arguments can seem particularly compelling is trust in a person. Suppose a close friend of mine is accused of a serious crime. I know him well and can hardly believe he would do such a thing. He insists he is innocent. But the evidence against him, though not conclusive, is very strong. So far as I can judge the total evidence (including my knowledge of his character) in a cool, detached way, I would have to say it is quite evenly balanced. I want to believe in his innocence, and there is reason to think that I ought, morally, to believe in it if I can. For he may well be innocent. If he is, he will have a deep psychological need for someone to believe him. If no one believes him, he will suffer unjustly a loneliness perhaps greater than the loneliness of guilt. And who will believe him if his close friends do not? Who will believe him if I do not? Of course I could try to *pretend* to believe him. If I do that I will certainly be less honest with him, and I doubt that I will be more honest with myself, than if I really cling to the belief that he is innocent. Moreover, the pretense is unlikely to satisfy his need to be believed. If he knows me well and sees me often, my insincerity will probably betray itself to him in some spontaneous reaction.

The legitimacy of practical arguments must obviously be subject to some restrictions. Two important restrictions were suggested by William James. (1) Practical arguments should be employed only on questions that "cannot…be decided on intellectual grounds." There should be a plurality of alternatives that one finds intellectually plausible. (The option should be "living," as James would put it.) Faith ought not to be "believing what you know ain't so." It also ought not to short-circuit rational inquiry; we ought not to try to settle by practical argument an issue that we could settle by further investigation of evidence in the time available for settling it. (2) The question to be

decided by practical argument should be urgent and of practical importance ("forced" and "momentous," James would say). If it can wait or is pragmatically inconsequential, we can afford to suspend judgment about it; and it is healthier to do so.

To these I would add a third important restriction: it would be irrational to accept a belief on the ground that it gives you a *reason* for doing something that you want to do. To the extent that your belief is based on a desire to do *x,* it cannot add to your reasons for doing *x.*…

IV

Perhaps moral arguments establish at most subsidiary advantages of belief in God's existence. They are more crucial to the case for His goodness. Causal arguments, in particular, from the existence and qualities of the world, may have some force to persuade us that there is a God; but they plainly have much less support to offer the proposition,

(K) If there is a God, He is morally very good.

(Here I define "a God" as a creator and governor of the whole universe, supreme in understanding and knowledge as well as in power, so that (K) is not a tautology.)

There is a powerful moral argument for (K). Belief in the existence of an evil or amoral God would be morally intolerable. In view of His power, such belief would be apt to carry with it all the disadvantages, theoretical and practical, of disbelief in a moral order of the universe. But I am even more concerned about the consequences it would have in view of His knowledge and understanding. We are to think of a being who understands human life much better than we do—understands it well enough to create and control it. Among other things, He must surely understand our moral ideas and feelings. He understands everyone's point of view, and has a more objective, or at least a more complete and balanced view of human relationships than any of us can have. He has whatever self-control, stability, and integration of purpose are implied in His having produced a world as constant in its causal order as our own. And now we are to suppose that that being does not care to support with His will the moral principles that we believe are true. We are to suppose that He either opposes some of them, or does not care enough about some of them to act on them. I submit that if we really believed there is a God like that, who understands so much and yet disregards some or all of our moral principles, it would be extremely difficult for us to continue to regard those principles with the respect that we believe is due them. Since we believe that we ought to pay them that respect, this is a great moral disadvantage of the belief that there is an evil or amoral God.

I think the same disadvantage attends even the belief that there is a morally slack God, since moral slackness involves some disregard of moral principles. There might seem to be less danger in the belief that there is a morally weak God—perhaps one who can't resist the impulse to toy with us immorally, but who feels guilty about it. At least He would be seen as caring enough about moral principles to feel guilty. But He would not be seen as caring enough about them to control a childish impulse. And I think that our respect for the moral law will be undermined by any belief which implies that our moral sensibilities were created, and are thoroughly understood, by a being who does not find an absolutely controlling importance in the ends and principles of true morality.

I shall not offer here a definitive answer to the question, whether this moral argument for belief in God's goodness is theoretical or practical. There may be metaethical views—perhaps some ideal observer theory—which imply that nothing could be a true moral principle if there is a God who does not fully accept it. Such views, together with the thesis that there are true moral principles, would imply the truth of (K) and not merely the desirability of believing (K). That would produce a theoretical argument.

On the other hand, it might be claimed that moral principles would still be true, and the respect that is due them undiminished, if there were an evil or amoral God, but that it would be psychologically difficult or impossible for us to respect them as we ought if we believed them to be disregarded or lightly regarded by an all-knowing Creator. This claim implies that there is a morally important advantage in believing that if there is a God He is morally very good. I think that this practical argument for believing (K) is sound, if the theoretical argument is not.

In closing, I shall permit myself an argument *ad hominem*. The hypothesis that there is an amoral God is not open to the best known objection to theism, the argument from evil. Whatever may be said against the design argument for theism, it is at least far from obvious that the world was not designed. Yet hardly any philosopher really takes seriously the hypothesis that it was designed by an amoral or evil being. Are there any good grounds for rejecting that hypothesis? Only moral grounds. One ought to reflect on that before asserting that moral arguments are out of place in these matters.

STUDY QUESTIONS

1. What is the divine command theory of ethics? How does Adams see this theory providing a reason to think that God exists?
2. Give one objection to the divine command theory and note how Adams responds to it.
3. What is Adams's second argument, from practical considerations, for God's existence?
4. Why does Adams think that the moral argument helps us to understand the nature of God?

SUGGESTED READING

Barrow, John D., and Frank J. Tipler. *The Anthropic Cosmological Principle.* Oxford, England: Clarendon Press, 1986.

Copan, Paul, and William Lane Craig. *Creation Out of Nothing.* Grand Rapids, Mich.: Baker, 2004.

Craig, William L. *The Cosmological Argument from Plato to Leibniz.* New York: Barnes & Noble, 1980.

——— . *The Kalam Cosmological Argument*. London: Macmillan, 1979.

——— and Quentin Smith. *Theism, Atheism, and Big Bang Cosmology*. New York: Oxford University Press, 1993.

Davis, Stephen T. *God, Reason, and Theistic Proofs*. Grand Rapids, Mich.: William B. Eerdmans, 1997.

Dombrowski, Daniel A. *Rethinking the Ontological Argument: A Neoclassical Theistic Response*. Cambridge, England: Cambridge University Press, 2006.

Edwards, Rem B. *What Caused the Big Bang?* Atlanta Ga.: Rodopi, 2001.

Flew, Antony, and Roy Abraham Varghese. *There Is a God: How the World's Most Notorious Atheist Changed His Mind*. New York: HarperCollins, 2007.

Gale, Richard. *On the Nature and Existence of God*. Cambridge, England: Cambridge University Press, 1991.

Hick, John, and Arthur C. McGill, eds. *The Many-Faced Argument*. New York: Macmillan, 1967.

Hume, David. *Dialogues Concerning Natural Religion*. Indianapolis, Ind.: Hackett, 1980.

Kenny, Anthony. *The Five Ways*. New York: Schocken Books, 1969.

Layman, Stephen. *Letters to Doubting Thomas: A Case for the Existence of God*. Oxford, England: Oxford University Press, 2007.

Leslie, John, ed. *Modern Cosmology and Philosophy*. Amherst, N.Y.: Prometheus, 1998.

Mackie, J. L. *The Miracle of Theism*. Oxford, England: Clarendon Press, 1982.

Manson, Neil. *God and Design: The Teleological Argument and Modern Science*. London: Routledge, 2003.

Martin, Michael. *Atheism: A Philosophical Justification*. Philadelphia: Temple University Press, 1990.

——— . *The Case Against Christianity*. Philadelphia: Temple University Press, 1991.

Messer, Richard. *Does God's Existence Need Proof?* New York: Oxford University Press, 1993.

Miller, Barry. *From Existence to God: A Contemporary Philosophical Argument*. London: Routledge, 1992.

Moreland, James P., and Kai Neilson. *Does God Exist?: The Great Debate*. Nashville, Tenn.: Thomas Nelson, 1990.

O'Connor, Timothy. *Theism and Ultimate Explanation: The Necessary Shape of Contingency*. London: Wiley-Blackwell, 2008.

Oppy, Graham. *Arguing About Gods*. Cambridge, England: Cambridge University Press, 2006.

——— . *Ontological Arguments and Belief in God*. Cambridge, England: Cambridge University Press, 1996.

Owen, H. P. *The Moral Argument for Christian Theism*. London: Allen & Unwin, 1965.

Plantinga, Alvin. *God, Freedom, and Evil*. New York: Harper and Row, 1974, Part II.

——— . *The Nature of Necessity*. New York: Oxford University Press, 1989.

Prevost, Robert. *Probability and Theistic Explanation*. Oxford, England: Clarendon Press, 1990.

Pruss, Alexander. *The Principle of Sufficient Reason: A Reassessment*. Cambridge, England: Cambridge University Press, 2006.

Reichenbach, Bruce R. *The Cosmological Argument: A Reassessment*. Springfield, Ill.: Charles C Thomas, 1972.

Robson, John M., ed. *Origin and Evolution of the Universe: Evidence for Design?* Kingston, Ontario: McGill-Queen's University Press, 1987.

Rowe, William L. *The Cosmological Argument*. Princeton, N.J.: Princeton University Press, 1975.

Silk, Joseph. *The Big Bang*. San Francisco, Calif.: W. H. Freeman, 2001.

Swinburne, Richard. *The Existence of God*. 2nd ed. Oxford, England: Clarendon Press, 2004.

——— . *Is There a God?* Oxford, England: Oxford University Press, 1996.

Wainwright, William. *Religion and Morality*. Aldershot, England: Ashgate, 2005.

PART SIX

Knowing God Without Arguments

The selections in the previous section illustrate what has undoubtedly been the most common approach among philosophers in considering the question of the existence of God. Theists marshal the available arguments, do their best to formulate them in the best way possible, and defend them against objections. Atheists, on the other hand, look for flaws and loopholes in the theistic arguments; they also develop arguments against belief in God. (By far the most common argument of this sort is the problem of evil, which is discussed in Part Seven). The debate between the two sides rages on, with no final resolution in sight.

One of the most interesting developments in recent philosophy of religion is the rise of a way of addressing belief in God that circumvents the debate described above. The philosophers who support this approach see no need for arguments proving the existence of God; they may even believe that such arguments are harmful. These philosophers, however, are not fideists (see Part Three, on faith and reason); they are very much concerned that their faith be rationally justified, and they are at pains to defend their belief against the problem of evil and other arguments against theism. Their approach is often referred to as "Reformed epistemology," because of a certain affinity with the Reformed, or Calvinistic, branch of Christianity. However, one need not be a Calvinist, or even a Christian, to be a Reformed epistemologist.

BASIC AND DERIVED BELIEFS

But how is it possible to rationally defend belief in God, while ignoring the arguments for God's existence? In order to understand this, there are a few concepts of epistemology (the theory of knowledge) that we need to have in mind. First of all, there is the distinction between *basic beliefs* and *derived beliefs*. A derived belief is a belief that one accepts because it is supported by (and thus derived from) other beliefs that one holds. A detective's belief about who is guilty of a crime is a derived belief, based on the evidence the detective is aware of. Now, a little thought will suggest that not all of our beliefs can be derived beliefs; this would mean that whatever we believe is supported by some other belief, which is in turn supported by still another belief, and so on forever. And that does not seem possible. There must be some beliefs of ours, then, that are *basic*, beliefs that do not need to be supported by other beliefs we hold. If during lunch I ask you, "What are you eating?" and you reply that it is a ham sandwich, it doesn't occur to me to ask, "On what do you base that belief?" If I did ask that, you might reply, "What do you mean? It just *is* a ham sandwich, and I am eating it right now." This is a basic belief, one that doesn't need to be based on anything else you believe. And our basic beliefs are the foundation of all of the other, derived beliefs, so that our entire belief structure ultimately rests on those basic beliefs.

Next, we need the concept of a *properly basic belief*. A properly basic belief is a basic belief such that, given the circumstances in which you hold the belief, it is rationally appropriate—right and proper, we might say—that you hold that belief in a basic way. Your belief about the ham sandwich, at the time when you are eating it, is undoubtedly a properly basic belief. On the other hand, suppose you see a stranger's face on television and immediately say to yourself, "I don't trust that fellow at all." This again expresses a basic belief, but it may well be *improperly* basic; most likely, you cannot reasonably or reliably conclude under those circumstances that the person in question is not trustworthy.

Strong Foundationalism

Now, an important question in the theory of knowledge is, What are the requirements for a belief to be properly basic? What sorts of beliefs is it legitimate to hold in a basic way, so that they do not need to be supported by other beliefs? One approach to this question that has historically been popular can be labeled as *strong foundationalism*. The key idea of strong foundationalism is that the properly basic beliefs are limited to those concerning which it is impossible, or nearly impossible, that we should go wrong. These may include beliefs about one's own immediate experience ("My tooth is hurting me"), simple perceptual beliefs ("This is a ham sandwich"), and "self-evident" truths of logic and mathematics ("$2+3=5$"). If we can show how all of our other legitimate beliefs can be based on these "maximally certain" kinds of beliefs, we should be able to erect a belief structure that is very nearly flawless. René Descartes is famous for having set up his own theory of knowledge along these lines, but many other philosophers have made similar attempts. A strong foundationalist will think that belief in God, if it is to be rational, needs to be supported by good arguments, perhaps including some of the arguments discussed in the previous chapter. (It should be clear that a strong foundationalist will also be a *strong rationalist*, of the sort discussed in Part Three of this book.)

Unfortunately, this inspiring project cannot be carried out; it simply is not possible to base all of our knowledge on these few sorts of maximally certain beliefs. One reason for this is that we can't know much of anything without relying heavily on memory. But memory, as all of us realize from time to time, is far from being infallible; to the extent that we rely on it, we have to give up the goal of maximal certainty for our belief system. Yet another problem arises from strong foundationalism itself. Strong foundationalism asserts that *the only propositions that are properly basic are those that concern one's own immediate experience, or are self-evident, or are simple perceptual beliefs.* Now, just try to work out how *that* assertion is supposed to be based on those few kinds of maximally certain beliefs! If you can't do it—and it certainly seems that you can't—then strong foundationalism is *self-refuting*. And unfortunately, that does indeed seem to be the case.

"God Exists" as Properly Basic

But if strong foundationalism is wrong, what *are* the criteria for a belief to be properly basic? It's clear that any reasonable answer to this question will have to be more permissive than the one given by strong foundationalism. And this means that the goal of maximal certainty for our entire belief system will have to be given up. On the other hand, we can't just assume that anything goes—that just anything a person believes can be properly basic. Some sorts of beliefs clearly stand in need of evidential support; the detective who "just knows" who committed a crime but does not have any evidence to support his claim will not stand much of a chance of convincing a jury.

The task of working out a full set of criteria for properly basic beliefs is a challenging one that requires a lot of hard work from epistemologists. At this point, however, the Reformed episte-mologists have a radical suggestion to make: why can't the belief that *there is a God* be properly basic? Why can't this be one of the beliefs a person is rationally entitled to hold, even if she has no arguments in support of it and does not base it on any other beliefs that she holds? If this is so, then for such a person the arguments of natural theology are unnecessary and irrelevant—yet she is perfectly rational and justified in her belief that God exists.

Stated thus baldly, the Reformed epistemologist's proposal will strike many people as arbitrary and implausible. *Why* should we suppose that belief in God qualifies as a properly basic belief? Can just *any* belief qualify for that status? If not, then how does belief in God qualify? This is a natural question, but the Reformed epistemologist has an answer for it. When we introduced the idea of a properly basic belief, we said that such a belief is "a basic belief such that, *given the circumstances in which you hold the belief*, it is rationally appropriate...that you hold that belief in a basic way." So when we ask whether the belief in God can be properly basic, we need to consider the circumstances in which that belief is held. Alvin Plantinga has described some of these circumstances as follows:

> There is in us a disposition to believe propositions of the sort *this flower was created by God* or *this vast and intricate universe was created by God* when we contemplate the flower or behold the starry heavens....Upon reading the Bible, one may be impressed with a deep sense that God is speaking to him. Upon having done what I know is cheap, or wrong, or wicked, I may feel guilty in God's sight and form the belief *God disapproves of what I have done*. Upon confession and repentance I may feel forgiven, forming the belief *God forgives me for what I have done*. (From his essay "Reason and Belief in God")

Keeping Plantinga's examples in mind, we see that the basic belief in God's existence does not just come out of the blue. The belief has, in a broad sense, *experiential grounds*; the sorts of experiences he described provide the occasion for beliefs concerning God to be formed. But we must be careful to understand this in the right way. It is not a matter of first observing certain characteristics of the flower and then inferring from those characteristics that the flower must have had an "intelligent designer." That is the way things go when one is employing the teleological argument (discussed in the Part Five), and in that case the belief in God would be a derived belief. In Plantinga's account, however, one simply contemplates the flower and *finds oneself believing* that God created it; there is no inference from one belief to another. Nor does one have a certain sort of experience and infer from that experience that there must be a God who is causing the experience. One has the experience and *finds oneself believing* that God is speaking to one, or is displeased with one, and so on. The resulting beliefs are basic beliefs, not derived beliefs, and they are properly basic in virtue of the circumstances in which the beliefs are formed.

DEFEATERS FOR BASIC BELIEFS

There is one further matter that deserves comment. I said early on that the Reformed epistemologists were very much concerned to defend their belief in God against objections such as the problem of evil. But you might be inclined to ask, "Isn't that unnecessary? If the belief in God is properly basic, as they claim, isn't it 'home free,' so to speak? Why do they have to pay attention to objections?" This, however, would be a misunderstanding. That a belief is properly basic means that one is rational and justified in holding the belief, *other things being equal*. But the fact that a belief is properly basic does not guarantee that the belief is true, because the ways in which these beliefs are formed are not infallible. (Even simple perceptual beliefs can be mistaken: the "ham" in your ham sandwich may really be ham-flavored turkey.) So if there are plausible reasons to think a basic belief is mistaken (that is, if there are "defeaters" for the belief), they need to be considered and, if possible, refuted. And that is how it is for belief in God, according to Reformed epistemology. But that does not mean that one needs to give arguments in favor of the belief itself; in fact, nothing of the sort is called for.

It should be obvious by now that the contentions of the Reformed epistemologists are highly debatable; and, in fact, they have been extensively debated. The selections in this section give you a sampling of some of the questions that have been discussed.

In the first selection, Alvin Plantinga, one of the pioneers of Reformed epistemology, sets out some of the basic concepts of that viewpoint. He also shows the connection between this type of religious epistemology and some traditional themes of Reformed theology; he shows how these ideas account for the sometimes hostile attitude of Reformed theologians to the traditional enterprise of natural theology.

In the next selection, Robert Pargetter considers the Reformed epistemologists' claim that belief in God is properly basic. In particular, he examines several potential defeaters for this claim and considers whether they make belief in God unreasonable. Perhaps the most interesting part of his article, however, is the parallel he draws between the experience of God and the experience of "the Force" in the *Star Wars* film series: the way in which Luke Skywalker and others came to believe in the Force bears an interesting resemblance to the way in which, according to Reformed epistemology, a person may come to believe in God.

In the final selection, William Hasker comments on a debate between Alvin Plantinga and Philip Quinn. The disagreement between Plantinga and Quinn does not concern the existence of God as such: both men are Christian theists. Nor is it over the question of whether religious experience can provide someone with a justification for believing in God that does not depend on inference and argument: they agree that it can. What they disagree about is the strength of the justification enjoyed by the average well-educated contemporary theist, and how this stands up against the defeaters of theistic belief. Quinn holds that, in virtue of the defeaters, most such persons will need the arguments of natural theology to supplement the justification received from experience. Plantinga, however, disagrees; he thinks that most will have no need for natural theology.

Alvin Plantinga

The Reformed Objection to Natural Theology

In this essay, Alvin Plantinga (b. 1932) sets out the essentials of an approach to religious knowledge that has come to be known as Reformed epistemology. Plantinga notes that the tradition of natural theology, which seeks to prove God's existence on the basis of premises that are obvious to any thinking person, has often met with resistance in the Reformed (or Calvinistic) branch of Christianity. Not only have the Reformed Christians felt that the arguments of natural theology are insufficient as a basis for religious belief, but they have considered the whole idea of basing belief on arguments to be misguided. This is not to say, however, that their belief in God is irrational. On the contrary, Reformed Christians have typically held that belief in God is a *properly basic* belief, one that is not held on the basis of any other belief and does not need to be justified in terms of other beliefs—or arguments. In the following piece, Plantinga briefly develops the epistemological position that seeks to make sense of these claims.

Suppose we think of natural theology as the attempt to prove or demonstrate the existence of God. This enterprise has a long and impressive history—a history stretching back to the dawn of Christendom and boasting among its adherents many of the truly great thinkers of the Western world. Chief among these is Thomas Aquinas, whose work, I think, is the natural starting point for Christian philosophical reflection, Protestant as well as Catholic. Here we Protestants must be, in Ralph McInerny's immortal phrase, Peeping Thomists. Recently—since the time of Kant, perhaps—the tradition of natural theology has not been as overwhelming as it once was: yet it continues to have able defenders both within and without officially Catholic philosophy.[1]

Many Christians, however, have been less than totally impressed. In particular Reformed or Calvinist theologians have for the most part taken a dim view of this enterprise. A few Reformed thinkers—B. B. Warfield[2] for example,—endorse the theistic proofs; but for the most part the Reformed attitude has ranged from indifference, through suspicion and hostility, to outright accusations of blasphemy. And this stance is initially puzzling. It looks a little like the

From *Christian Scholar's Review* 11, no. 3 (1982): 187–198. Reprinted by permission of *Christian Scholars Review*.

attitude some Christians adopt towards faith healing: it can't be done, but even if it could, it shouldn't be. What exactly, or even approximately, do these sons and daughters of the Reformation have against proving the existence of God? What *could* they have against it? What could be less objectionable to any but the most obdurate atheist?

PROOF AND BELIEF IN GOD

Let's begin with the nineteenth-century Dutch theologian Herman Bavinck:

> Scripture urges us to behold heaven and earth, birds and flowers and lilies, in order that we may see and recognize God in them. "Lift up your eyes on high, and see who hath created these" Is. 40:26. Scripture does not reason in the abstract. It does not make God the conclusion of a syllogism, leaving it to us whether we think the argument holds or not. But it speaks with authority. Both theologically and religiously it proceeds from God as the starting point.[3]
>
> We receive the impression that belief in the existence of God is based entirely upon these proofs. But indeed that would be "a wretched faith, which, before it invokes God, must first prove his existence." The contrary, however, is the truth.... Of the existence of self, of the world round about us, of logical and moral laws, etc., we are so deeply convinced because of the indelible impressions which all these things make upon our consciousness that we need no arguments or demonstration. Spontaneously, altogether involuntarily: without any constraint or coercion, we accept that existence. Now the same is true in regard to the existence of God. The so-called proofs are by no means the final grounds of our most certain conviction that God exists: This certainly is established only by faith; i.e., by the spontaneous testimony which forces itself upon us from every side.[4]

According to Bavinck, then, a Christian's belief in the existence of God is not based upon proofs or arguments. By "argument" here, I think he means arguments in the style of natural theology—the sort given by Aquinas and Scotus and later by Descartes, Leibniz, Clarke, and others. And what he means to say, I think, is that Christians don't *need* such arguments. Don't need them for what?

Here I think Bavinck means to hold two things. First, arguments or proofs are not, in general, the source of the believer's confidence in God. Typically, the believer does not believe in God on the basis of arguments; nor does he believe such truths as, for example, that God has created the world on the basis of arguments. Secondly, argument is not needed for *rational justification*; the believer is entirely within his epistemic right in believing that God has created the world, even if he has no argument at all for that conclusion. The believer doesn't need natural theology in order to achieve rationality or epistemic propriety in believing; his belief in God can be perfectly rational even if he knows of no cogent argument, deductive or inductive, for the existence of God—indeed, even if there *isn't* any such argument.

Bavinck has three further points. First he means to add, I think, that we *cannot* come to knowledge of God on the basis of argument; the arguments of natural theology just don't work. (And he follows this passage with a more or less traditional attempt to refute the theistic proofs, including an endorsement of some of Kant's fashionable confusions about the ontological argument.) Secondly, Scripture "proceeds from God as the starting point," and so should the believer. There is nothing by way of proofs or arguments for God's existence in the Bible; that is simply presupposed. The same should be true of the Christian believer then; he should *start* from belief in God, rather than from the premises of some argument whose conclusion is that God exists. What is it that makes those premises a better starting point anyway? And third, Bavinck points out that belief in God relevantly resembles belief in the existence of the self and of the external world—and, we might add, belief in other minds and the past. In none of these areas do we typically *have* proof or arguments, or *need* proofs or arguments.

According to John Calvin, who is as good a Calvinist as any, God has implanted in us all an innate tendency, or nisus, or disposition to believe in him:

> "There is within the human mind, and indeed by natural instinct, an awareness of divinity." This we take to be beyond controversy. To prevent anyone from taking refuge in the pretense of ignorance, God himself has implanted in all men a certain understanding of his

divine majesty. Ever renewing its memory, he repeatedly sheds fresh drops. Since, therefore, men one and all perceive that there is a God and that he is their Maker, they are condemned by their own testimony because they have failed to honor him and to consecrate their lives to his will. If ignorance of God is to be looked for anywhere, surely one is most likely to find an example of it among the more backward folk and those more remote from civilization. Yet there is, as the eminent pagan says, no nation so barbarous, no people so savage, that they have not a deep-seated conviction that there is a God. So deeply does the common conception occupy the minds of all, so tenaciously does it inhere in the hearts of all! Therefore, since from the beginning of the world there has been no region, no city, in short, no household, that could do without religion, there lies in this a tacit confession of a sense of deity inscribed in the hearts of all.[5]

Indeed, the perversity of the impious, who though they struggle furiously are unable to extricate themselves from the fear of God, is abundant testimony that this conviction, namely, that there is some God, is naturally inborn in all, and is fixed deep within, as it were in the very marrow.... From this we conclude that it is not a doctrine that must first be learned in school, but one of which each of us is master from his mother's womb and which nature itself permits no one to forget.[6]

Calvin's claim, then, is that God has created us in such a way that we have a strong propensity or inclination towards belief in him. This tendency has been in part overlaid or suppressed by sin. Were it not for the existence of sin in the world, human beings would believe in God to the same degree and with the same natural spontaneity that we believe in the existence of other persons, an external world, or the past. This is the natural human condition; it is because of our presently unnatural sinful condition that many of us find belief in God difficult or absurd. The fact is, Calvin thinks, one who doesn't believe in God is in an epistemically substandard position—rather like a man who doesn't believe that his wife exists, or thinks she is like a cleverly constructed robot and has no thoughts, feelings, or consciousness.

Although this disposition to believe in God is partially suppressed, it is nonetheless universally present. And it is triggered or actuated by widely realized conditions:

Lest anyone, then, be excluded from access to happiness, he not only sowed in men's minds that seed of religion of which we have spoken, but revealed himself and daily discloses himself in the whole workmanship of the universe. As a consequence, men cannot open their eyes without being compelled to see him.[7]

Like Kant, Calvin is especially impressed in this connection, by the marvelous compages of the starry heavens above:

Even the common folk and the most untutored, who have been taught only by the aid of the eyes, cannot be unaware of the excellence of divine art, for it reveals itself in this innumerable and yet distinct and well-ordered variety of the heavenly host.[8]

And Calvin's claim is that one who accedes to this tendency and in these circumstances accepts the belief that God has created the world—perhaps upon beholding the starry heavens, or the splendid majesty of the mountains, or the intricate, articulate beauty of a tiny flower—is entirely within his epistemic rights in so doing. It isn't that such a person is justified or rational in so believing by virtue of having an implicit argument—some version of the teleological argument, say. No; he doesn't need any argument for justification or rationality. His belief need not be based on any other propositions at all; under these conditions he is perfectly rational in accepting belief in God in the utter absence of any argument, deductive or inductive. Indeed, a person in these conditions, says Calvin, *knows* that God exists, has knowledge of God's existence, apart from any argument at all.

Elsewhere Calvin speaks of "arguments from reason" or rational arguments:

The prophets and apostles do not boast either of their keenness or of any thing that obtains credit for them as they speak; nor do they dwell upon rational proofs. Rather, they bring forward God's holy name, that by it the whole world may be brought into obedience to him. Now we ought to see how apparent it is not only by plausible opinion but by dear truth that they do not call upon God's name heedlessly or falsely. If we desire to provide in the best way for our consciences—that they may not be perpetually beset by the instability of doubt or vacillation, and that they may not also boggle at the smallest quibbles—we ought to seek our conviction, in a higher place than human reasons, judgments, or conjectures, that is, in the secret testimony of the Spirit.[9]

Here the subject for discussion is not belief in the existence of God, but belief that God is the author of the Scriptures; I think it is clear, however, that Calvin would say the same thing about belief in God's existence. The Christian doesn't need natural theology, either as the source of his confidence or to justify his belief. Furthermore, the Christian *ought* not to believe on the basis of argument; if he does, his faith is likely to be unstable and wavering. From Calvin's point of view, believing in the existence of God on the basis of rational argument is like believing in the existence of your spouse on the basis of the analogical argument for other minds—whimsical at best and not at all likely to delight the person concerned.

FOUNDATIONALISM

We could look further into the precise forms taken by the Reformed objection to natural theology; time is short, however; what I shall do instead is tell you what I think underlies these objections, inchoate and unfocused as they are. The reformers mean to say, fundamentally, that belief in God can properly be taken as basic. That is, a person is entirely within his epistemic rights, entirely rational, in believing in God, even if he has no argument for this belief and does not believe it on the basis of any other beliefs he holds. And in taking belief in God as properly basic, the reformers were implicitly rejecting a whole picture or way of looking at knowledge and rational belief; call it *classical foundationalism*. This picture has been enormously popular ever since the days of Plato and Aristotle; it remains the dominant way of thinking about knowledge, justification, belief, faith, and allied topics. Although it has been thus dominant, Reformed theologians and thinkers have, I believe, meant to reject it. What they say here tends to be inchoate and not well-articulated; nevertheless the fact is they meant to reject classical foundationalism. But how shall we characterize the view rejected? The first thing to see is that foundationalism is a *normative* view. It aims to lay down conditions that must be met by anyone whose system of beliefs is *rational;*

and here "rational" is to be understood normatively. According to the foundationalist, there is a right way and a wrong way with respect to belief. People have responsibilities, duties and obligations with respect to their believings just as with respect to their (other) actions. Perhaps this sort of obligation is really a special case of a more general moral obligation; or perhaps, on the other hand, it is *sui generis*. In any event there are such obligations: to conform to them is to be rational and to go against them is to be irrational. To be rational, then, is to exercise one's epistemic powers *properly*—to exercise them in such a way as to go contrary to none of the norms for such exercise.

Foundationalism, therefore, is in part a normative thesis. I think we can understand this thesis more fully if we introduce the idea of a *noetic structure*. A person's noetic structure is the set of propositions he believes together with certain epistemic relations that hold among him and these propositions. Thus some of his beliefs may be *based on* other things he believes; it may be that there are a pair of propositions A and B such that he believes A on the basis of B. Although this relation isn't easy to characterize in a revealing and nontrivial fashion, it is nonetheless familiar. I believe that the word "umbrageous" is spelled u-m-b-r-a-g-e-o-u-s: this belief is based on another belief of mine, the belief that that's how the dictionary says it's spelled. I believe that $72 \times 71 = 5112$. This belief is based upon several other beliefs I hold—such beliefs as that $1 \times 72 = 72$; $7 \times 2 = 14$; $7 \times 7 = 49$; $49 + 1 = 50$; and others. Some of my beliefs, however, I accept but don't accept on the basis of any other beliefs. I believe that $2 + 1 = 3$, for example, and don't believe it on the basis of other propositions. I also believe that I am seated at my desk, and that there is a mild pain in my right knee. These too are basic for me; I don't believe them on the basis of any other propositions.

An account of a person's noetic structure, then, would include a specification of which of his beliefs are basic and which are non-basic. Of course it is abstractly possible that *none* of his beliefs is basic; perhaps he holds just three beliefs, A, B, and C, and believes each of them on the basis of the other two. We might think this improper or irrational, but that is not to say it couldn't be done. And it is also possible that *all* of his beliefs are basic; perhaps he believes a lot of propositions, but doesn't believe any of them on the basis of any others. In the typical case, however, a noetic structure will include both basic and non-basic beliefs.

Secondly, an account of a noetic structure will include what we might call an index of degree of belief. I hold some of my beliefs much more firmly than others. I believe both that $2+1=3$ and that London, England, is north of Saskatoon, Saskatchewan; but I believe the former more resolutely than the latter. Here we might make use of the personalist[10] interpretation of probability theory; think of an index of degree of belief as a function $Ps(A)$ from the set of propositions a person S believes or disbelieves into the real numbers between 0 and 1. $Ps(A)=n$, then, records something like the degree to which S believes A, or the strength of his belief that A. $Ps(A)=1$ proclaims S's utter and abandoned commitment to A; $Ps(A)=0$ records a similar commitment to not-A; $Ps(A)=.5$ means that S, like Buridan's ass, is suspended in equilibrium between A and not-A. We could then go on to consider whether the personalist is right in holding that a rational noetic structure conforms to the Calculus of Probability.[11]

Thirdly, a somewhat vaguer notion; an account of S's noetic structure would include something like an index of *depth of ingression*. Some of my beliefs are, we might say, on the periphery of my noetic structure. I accept them, and may even accept them quite firmly; but if I were to give them up, not much else in my noetic structure would have to change. I believe there are some large boulders on the top of the Grand Teton. If I come to give up this belief, however (say by climbing it and not finding any), that change wouldn't have extensive reverberations throughout the rest of my noetic structure; it could be accommodated with minimal alteration elsewhere. So its depth of ingression into my noetic structure isn't great. On the other hand, if I were to come to believe that there simply is no such thing as the Grand Teton, or no mountains at all, or no such thing as the state of Wyoming, that would have much greater reverberations. And if, *per impossible*, I were to come to think there hadn't been much of a past (that the world was created just five minutes ago, complete with all its apparent memories and traces of the past), or that there weren't any other persons, that would have even greater reverberations; these beliefs of mine have great depth of ingression into my noetic structure.

Now classical foundationalism is best construed, I think, as a thesis about *rational* noetic structures. A noetic structure is rational if it could be the noetic structure of a person who was completely rational. To be completely rational, as I am here using the term, is not to believe only what is true, or to believe all the logical consequences of what one believes, or to believe all necessary truths with equal firmness, or to be uninfluenced by emotion; it is, instead, to do the right thing with respect to one's believings. As we have seen, the foundationalist holds that there are responsibilities and duties that pertain to believings as well as to actions, or other actions; these responsibilities accrue to us just by virtue of our having the sorts of noetic capabilities we do have. There are norms or standards for beliefs. To criticize a person as irrational, then, is to criticize her for failing to fulfill these duties or responsibilities, or for failing to conform to the relevant norms or standards. From this point of view, a rational person is one whose believings meet the appropriate standards. To draw the ethical analogy, the irrational is the impermissible; the rational is the permissible.

A rational noetic structure, then, is one that could be the noetic structure of a perfectly rational person. And classical foundationalism is, in part, a thesis about such noetic structures. The foundationalist notes, first of all, that some of our beliefs are based upon others. He immediately adds that a belief can't properly be accepted on the basis of just *any* other belief; in a rational noetic structure, A will be accepted on the basis of B only if B *supports* A, or is a member of a set of beliefs that together support A. It isn't clear just what this supports relation is; different foundationalists propose different candidates. One candidate, for example, is *entailment*; A supports B only if B is entailed by A, or perhaps is self-evidently entailed by A, or perhaps follows from A by an argument where each step is a self-evident entailment. Another and more permissive candidate is probability; perhaps A supports B if B is likely or probable with respect to A. And of course there are other candidates.

More important for present purposes, however, is the following claim: in a rational noetic structure, there will be some beliefs that are not based upon others: call these its *foundations*. If every belief in a rational noetic structure were based upon other beliefs, the structure in question would contain infinitely many beliefs. However things may stand for more powerful intellects—angelic intellects, perhaps—human beings aren't capable of believing infinitely many propositions. Among other things, one presumably doesn't believe a proposition one has never heard of, and no one has had time, these busy days, to have heard of infinitely many propositions. So every rational noetic structure has a foundation.

Suppose we say that *weak* foundationalism is the view that (1) every rational noetic structure has a foundation, and (2) in a rational noetic structure, non-basic belief is proportional in strength to support from the foundations. When I say Reformed thinkers have meant to reject foundationalism, I do not mean to say that they intended to reject weak foundationalism. On the contrary; the thought of many of them tends to support or endorse weak foundationalism. What then do they mean to reject? Here we meet a further and fundamental feature of classic varieties of foundationalism: they all lay down certain conditions of proper or rational basicality. From the foundationalist point of view, not just any kind of belief can be found in the foundations of a rational noetic structure; a belief, to be properly basic (i.e., basic in a rational noetic structure) must meet certain conditions. It is plausible to see Thomas Aquinas, for example, as holding that a proposition is properly basic for a person only if it is self-evident to him (such that his understanding or grasping it is sufficient for his seeing it to be true) or "evident to the senses," as he puts it. By this latter term I think he means to refer to propositions whose truth or falsehood we can determine by looking or listening or employing some other sense—such propositions as

(1) There is a tree before me
(2) I am wearing shoes

and

(3) That tree's leaves are yellow.

Many foundationalists have insisted that propositions basic in a rational noetic structure must be

certain in some important sense. Thus it is plausible to see Descartes as holding that the foundations of a rational noetic structure don't include such propositions as (1)–(3) but more cautious claims—claims about one's own mental life, for example:

(4) It seems to me that I see a tree
(5) I seem to see something green

or, as Professor Chisholm puts it,

(6) I am appeared greenly to.

Propositions of this latter sort seem to enjoy a kind of immunity from error not enjoyed by those of the former. I could be mistaken in thinking I see a pink rat; perhaps I am hallucinating or the victim of an illusion. But it is at the least very much harder to see that I could be mistaken in believing that I *seem* to see a pink rat, in believing that I am appeared pinkly (or pink ratly) to. Suppose we say that a proposition with respect to which I enjoy this sort of immunity from error is *incorrigible* for me; then perhaps Descartes means to hold that a proposition is properly basic for S only if it is either self-evident or incorrigible for S.

Aquinas and Descartes, we might say, are *strong* foundationalists; they accept weak foundationalism and add some conditions for proper basicality. Ancient and medieval foundationalists tended to hold that a proposition is properly basic for a person only if it is either self-evident or evident to the senses; modern foundationalists—Descartes, Locke, Leibniz, and the like—tended to hold that a proposition is properly basic for S only if either self-evident or incorrigible for S. Of course this is a historical generalization and is thus subject to contradiction by scholars, such being the penalty for historical generalization; but perhaps it is worth the risk. And now suppose we say that *classical foundationalism* is the disjunction of ancient and medieval with modern foundationalism.

THE REFORMED REJECTION OF CLASSICAL FOUNDATIONALISM

These Reformed thinkers, I believe, are best understood as rejecting classical foundationalism.[12] They were inclined to accept weak foundationalism, I think; but they were completely at odds with the idea that the foundations of a rational noetic structure can at most include propositions that are self-evident or evident to the senses or incorrigible. In particular, they were prepared to insist that a rational noetic structure can include belief in God as basic. As Bavinck put it "Scripture...does not make God the conclusion of a syllogism, leaving it to us whether we think the argument holds or not. But it speaks with authority." Both theologically and religiously it proceeds from God as the starting point. And of course Bavinck means to say that we must emulate Scripture here.

In the passages I quoted earlier on, Calvin claims the believer doesn't need argument—doesn't need it, among other things, for epistemic respectability. We may understand him as holding, I think, that a rational noetic structure may perfectly well contain belief in God among its foundations. Indeed, he means to go further, and in two separate directions. In the first place, he thinks a Christian *ought* not believe in God on the basis of other propositions; a proper and well formed Christian noetic structure will *in fact* have belief in God among its foundations. And in the second place Calvin claims that one who takes belief in God as basic can nonetheless know that God exists. Calvin holds that one can *rationally accept* belief in God as basic; he also claims that one can *know* that God exists even if he has no argument, even if he does not believe on the basis of other propositions. A weak foundationalist is likely to hold that some properly basic beliefs are such that anyone who accepts them, *knows* them. More exactly, he is likely to hold that among the beliefs properly basic for a person S, some are such that if S accepts them S knows them. A weak foundationalist could go on to say that *other* properly basic beliefs can't be known, if taken as basic, but only rationally believed; and he might think of the existence of God as a case in point. Calvin will have none of this; as he sees it, one needs no arguments to know that God exists.

Among the central contentions of these Reformed thinkers, therefore, are the claims that belief in God is properly basic, and the view that one who takes belief in God as basic can also *know* that God exists.

THE GREAT PUMPKIN OBJECTION

Now I enthusiastically concur in these contentions of Reformed epistemology, and by way of conclusion I want to defend them against a popular objection. It is tempting to raise the following sort of question. If belief in God is properly basic, why can't just any belief be properly basic? Couldn't we say the same for any bizarre aberration we can think of? What about voodoo or astrology? What about the belief that the Great Pumpkin returns every Halloween? Could I properly take *that* as basic? And if I can't, why can I properly take belief in God as basic? Suppose I believe that if I flap my arms with sufficient vigor, I can take off and fly about the room; could I defend myself against the charge of irrationality by claiming this belief is basic? If we say that belief in God is properly basic, won't we be committed to holding that just anything, or nearly anything, can properly be taken as basic, thus throwing wide the gates to irrationalism and superstition?

Certainly not. What might lead one to think the Reformed epistemologist is in this kind of trouble? The fact that he rejects the criteria for proper basicality purveyed by the classical foundationalist? But why should *that* be thought to commit him to such tolerance of irrationality? Consider an analogy. In the palmy days of positivism, the positivists went about confidently wielding their verifiability criterion and declaring meaningless much that was obviously meaningful. Now suppose someone rejected a formulation of that criterion—the one to be found in the second edition of A. J. Ayer's *Language, Truth and Logic*, for example. Would that mean she was committed to holding that

(7) Twas brillig; and the slithy toves did gyre and gymble in the wabe,

contrary to appearances, makes good sense? Of course not. But then the same goes for the Reformed epistemologist; the fact that he rejects the criteria of classical foundationalism does not mean that he is committed to supposing just anything is properly basic.

But what then is the problem? Is it that the Reformed epistemologist not only rejects those criteria for proper basicality, but seems in no hurry to produce what he takes to be a better substitute? If he has no such criterion, how can he fairly reject belief in the Great Pumpkin as properly basic?

This objection betrays an important misconception. How *do* we rightly arrive at or develop criteria for meaningfulness, or justified belief, or proper basicality? Where do they come from? Must one have such a criterion before one can sensibly make any judgments—positive or negative—about proper basicality? Surely not. Suppose I don't know of a satisfactory substitute for the criteria proposed by classical foundationalism; I am nevertheless entirely within my rights in holding that certain propositions are not properly basic in certain conditions. Some propositions seem self-evident when in fact they are not; that is the lesson of some of the Russell Paradoxes.[13] Nevertheless it would be irrational to take as basic the denial of a proposition that seems self-evident to you. Similarly, suppose it seems to you that you see a tree; you would then be irrational in taking as basic the proposition that you don't see a tree, or that there aren't any trees. In the same way, even if I don't know of some illuminating criterion of meaning, I can quite properly declare (7) meaningless, even if I don't have a successful substitute for the positivist's verifiability criterion.

And this raises an important question—one Roderick Chisholm has taught us to ask.[14] What is the status of criteria for meaningfulness, or proper basicality, or justified belief? These are typically universal statements. The modern foundationalist's criterion for proper basicality, for example, is doubly universal:

(8) For any proposition *A* and person *S*, *A* is properly basic for *S* if and only if *A* is incorrigible for *S* or self-evident to *S*.

But how does one know a thing like that? Where does it come from? (8) certainly isn't self-evident or just obviously true. But if it isn't, how does one arrive at it? What sorts of arguments would be appropriate? Of course a philosopher might find (8) so appealing that he simply takes it to be true, neither offering argument for it, nor accepting it on the basis of other things he believes. If he does so, however, his noetic structure will be self-referentially incoherent.

(8) itself is neither self-evident nor incorrigible; hence in accepting (8) as basic, the classical foundationalist violates the condition of proper basicality he himself lays down in accepting it. On the other hand, perhaps the philosopher has some argument for it from premises that are self-evident; it is exceeding hard to see, however, what such arguments might be like. And until he has produced such arguments, what shall the rest of us do—we who do not find (8) at all obvious or compelling? How could he use (8) to show us that belief in God, for example, is not properly basic? Why should we believe (8), or pay it any attention?

The fact is, I think, that neither (8) nor any other revealing necessary and sufficient condition for proper basicality follows from obviously self-evident premises by obviously acceptable arguments. And hence the proper way to arrive at such a criterion is, broadly speaking, *inductive*. We must assemble examples of beliefs and conditions such that the former are obviously properly basic in the latter, and examples of beliefs and conditions such that the former are obviously not properly basic in the latter. We must then frame hypotheses as to the necessary and sufficient conditions of proper basicality and test these hypotheses by reference to those examples. Under the right conditions, for example, it is clearly rational to believe that you see a human person before you: a being who has thoughts and feelings, who knows and believes things, who makes decisions and acts. It is clear, furthermore, that you are under no obligation to reason to this belief from others you hold; under those conditions that belief is properly basic for you. But then (8) must be mistaken; the belief in question, under those circumstances, is properly basic, though neither self-evident nor incorrigible for you. Similarly, you may seem to remember that you had breakfast this morning, and perhaps you know of no reason to suppose your memory is playing you tricks. If so, you are entirely justified in taking that belief as basic. Of course it isn't properly basic on the criteria offered by classical foundationalists; but that fact counts not against you but against those criteria.

Accordingly, criteria for proper basicality must be reached from below rather than above; they should not be presented as *obiter dicta*, but argued to and tested by a relevant set of examples. But there is no reason to assume, in advance, that everyone will agree on the examples. The Christian will of course suppose that belief in God is entirely proper and rational; if he doesn't accept this belief on the basis of other propositions, he will conclude that it is basic for him and quite properly so. Followers of Bertrand Russell and Madalyn Murray O'Hair may disagree; but how is that relevant? Must my criteria, or those of the Christian community, conform to their examples? Surely not. The Christian community is responsible to its set of examples, not to theirs.

Accordingly, the Reformed epistemologist can properly hold that belief in the Great Pumpkin is not properly basic, even though he holds that belief in God is properly basic and even if he has no full fledged criterion of proper basicality. Of course he is committed to supposing that there is a relevant *difference* between belief in God and belief in the Great Pumpkin, if he holds that the former but not the latter is properly basic. But this should be no great embarrassment; there are plenty of candidates. Thus the Reformed epistemologist may concur with Calvin in holding that God has implanted in us a natural tendency to see his hand in the world around us; the same cannot be said for the Great Pumpkin, there being no Great Pumpkin and no natural tendency to accept beliefs about the Great Pumpkin.

By way of conclusion then, the Reformed objection to natural theology, unformed and inchoate as it is, may best be seen as a rejection of classical foundationalism. As the Reformed thinker sees things, being self-evident, or incorrigible, or evident to the senses is not a necessary condition of proper basicality. He goes on to add that belief in God is properly basic. He is not thereby committed, even in the absence of a general criterion of proper basicality, to suppose that just any or nearly any belief—belief in the Great Pumpkin, for example—is properly basic. Like everyone should, he begins with examples; and he may take belief in the Great Pumpkin as a paradigm of irrational basic belief.

Notes

1. See, for example, James Ross, *Philosophical Theology* (Indianapolis, Ind.: Bobbs-Merrill, 1969), and Richard Swinburne, *The Existence of God* (Oxford, England: Clarendon Press, 1979).
2. "God," in *Studies in Theology* (New York: Oxford University Press, 1932), pp. 110–11.
3. *The Doctrine of God*, trans. William Hendriksen (Grand Rapids, Mich.: William B. Eerdmans, 1951). This is a translation of vol. 2 of Bavinck's *Gereformeerde Dogmatiek* (Kampen, the Netherlands: Kok, 1918), p. 76.
4. Ibid., p. 78.
5. *Institutes of the Christian Religion*, ed. J. T. McNeill and trans. Ford Lewis Battles (Philadelphia: Westminster Press, 1960), Book I, Chap. iii, sec. 1.
6. *Institutes*, I, iii, 3.
7. *Institutes*, V, v, 1.
8. *Institutes*, V, v, 2.
9. *Institutes*, I, vii, 4.
10. See, for example, Richard Jeffrey's *The Logic of Decision* (New York: McGraw-Hill, 1965).
11. See my paper "The Probabilistic Argument from Evil," *Philosophical Studies* 30 (1979): 21.
12. Here I think they were entirely correct; both ancient and modern foundationalism are self-referentially incoherent. See my paper "Is Belief in God Rational?" [*Rationality and Religious Belief*, ed. C. Delany (South Bend, Ind.: University of Notre Dame Press, 1979)] p. 26.
13. "Is Belief in God Rational?" p. 22.
14. *The Problem of the Criterion* (Milwaukee, Wis.: Marquette University Press, 1973).

STUDY QUESTIONS

1. Discuss briefly the reasons why thinkers in the Reformed tradition have tended to dismiss natural theology.
2. What is a basic belief? What is a derived belief? What is a properly basic belief?
3. What is classical foundationalism? Explain briefly Plantinga's objections to classical foundationalism as a theory of knowledge.
4. Plantinga's main contention is that religious beliefs, specifically belief in God, can be properly basic. Why does he think so? Do you find this contention to be plausible?
5. Explain briefly the "Great Pumpkin objection" to the claim that religious beliefs can be properly basic. Do you find the objection to be a serious problem for Reformed epistemology? Why, or why not?

Robert Pargetter

Experience, Proper Basicality,
and Belief in God

Robert Pargetter (b. 1944) agrees with Plantinga that many theists believe in God in a "basic" way, grounding this belief in experience rather than supporting it by other beliefs they hold. But is such a belief *properly* basic, so that it is *reasonable* to hold one's belief in this way? That depends on whether there are effective "defeaters" for theistic belief—other propositions the believer accepts, or ought to accept, that provide compelling reasons for rejecting the experientially based belief in God. Pargetter examines several potential defeaters in order to see whether they do in fact make a basic belief in God unreasonable. He illuminates his discussion by pointing out the analogies between a properly basic belief in God and belief in "the Force" by characters in the popular *Star Wars* film series.

Luke Skywalker did not know about the Force until he met Obi-Wan Kenobi. Obi-Wan, a Jedi Knight, knew of the Force by direct experience. His belief was grounded in his feeling of the Force. Perhaps this had not always been the case—he had been trained by Yoda, the Jedi Master—and this is the sort of result such training can have. But Luke believed in the Force on the testimony of Obi-Wan, a testimony he was rational to accept given the kind of system of beliefs this gave him. He was able to explain and make sense of so much he saw about him: the lives and powers of Obi-Wan and Yoda, the struggle between the Emperor and the Rebels, the history of his own family. It gave him direction and survival potential, and he found a new meaning and purpose to life.

In time with training as a Jedi Knight by Obi-Wan and Yoda, Luke too could feel the power of the Force. He sensed disturbances in it, and gained knowledge and power directly from it. His belief then too was grounded in experience, and rationally so. There was no relevant defeater for such a belief for Luke, and his belief system, including such a basic belief, had all the required holistic features of rationality in a fairly rational community. Han Solo was a skeptic about the Force, but with time he also came to believe in it. He never experienced the Force, and his belief was always warranted by beliefs based on the testimony of others. But his resulting belief system was made more rational by accepting the beliefs based on the testimony of Luke, Obi-Wan, and Princess Leia.[1]

From *International Journal for Philosophy of Religion* 27 (1990). Reprinted with kind permission from Kluwer Academic Publishers.

Alvin Plantinga argues that many theists believe in God for reasons which seem to be of exactly the same kind of reasons as those which Luke Skywalker and Obi-Wan Kenobi have for believing in the Force in our story. Their belief in God is caused by and grounded in experience, and is not inferred from nor does it gain warrant from other beliefs. Given there are no defeaters of this belief for them, their belief is *properly basic*, and thus is rational.[2]

Let us grant Plantinga's empirical claim, for clearly this is an accurate reconstruction of why many theists take their theism to be rational. Plantinga identifies such theism as being of a Calvinist tradition, but perhaps he underestimates how widely his reconstrual applies. This probably depends on some of the detailed points concerning the nature of the experience. Plantinga's list of experiences include being directly aware of God speaking to one, feeling a Divine disapproval, and the feelings of God's forgiveness, all such experiences being in the appropriate circumstances. He also mentions the possibility of humans having a disposition to believe in a supreme designer in circumstances where they are confronted with natural beauty or order. He notes that a belief in God may be inferential from such basic beliefs, but (rightly) notes that, for simplicity, it is harmless enough to treat belief in God itself as being properly basic.[3]

Some theists would claim that they do in fact experience the direct presence of God, and that the experience may range over a great diversity of circumstances, perhaps even over all circumstances, though the nature of the experience is plausibly not exactly the same in all circumstances. These experiences are not usually episodes of extreme religious or mystical experience, such as those reported by St. Teresa and St. John of the Cross, though it is not out of the question that some such episodes could be made compatible with this sort of justified theistic belief. But the kinds of experiences that John Hick has pointed to as giving an experiential basis for rational belief in God would certainly be taken as experiences which could ground properly basic theistic belief.[4]

There are three matters that we will address in considering the proper basicality of belief in God. First, the question as to whether there are defeaters

for the theist for such a basic belief, and which the theist should rationally hold. Second, the significance and implication of the empirical fact that many persons do *not* have these experiences in very similar circumstances, and how this bears on the question of rational theistic belief both for those who do, and for those who do not, have the experiences. Third, the question as to whether consideration of holistic features of systems of beliefs relevant for rationality will lead to the proper basicality of belief in God.

DEFEATERS

Suppose A forms the belief, or is disposed to form the belief, that God exists, as a result of some experience in some particular circumstance. What could act as a defeater for such a belief for A?

Obviously it could be a belief about the circumstances. If it was in the circumstance of having tried a new drug, or having had doubtful scallops the night before, or some similar such circumstance, it seems that there is an obvious defeater which should prevent A from rationally accepting a belief grounded in an unusual experience. It is for this reason that the experiences of St. John of the Cross and other mystics are problematic. Their mode of preparation seems to be exactly right for producing hallucinations, and in such circumstances we should be cautious about their beliefs grounded in experience. We certainly have rational defeaters which may well prevent us accepting their beliefs on their testimony and it seems that they also ought to have, if rational, such defeaters.

But let us suppose that A's circumstances seem normal, and that there is a range of circumstances in which A's experiences are such that they lead, via the internal mechanism S_A, to the formation of a basic belief that there is a God, a belief that is grounded in those experiences. What then are the possible defeaters? Plantinga considers and (rightly) rejects the suggestion that there is a general sophisticated intellectual belief in the community that God does not exist which A should share with others, and which would act as a defeater for A for the basic belief that God exists.[5]

There are two worries about taking this belief as a defeater. First, why does A accept the defeater belief, that is, what would make it rational for A? Because others accept it. But this should only be a rational belief if it is justified on holistic grounds as part of the most rational system of beliefs for A, or because A has reasons which justify atheism. But what are these reasons, and are they *still* reasons given the experiences A now has had? This will again require further provision of rational reasons for atheism, or it leads us again to those holistic features relevant to assessing A's belief system and modifications to it. Second, suppose there is a potential defeater. There is the question of what belief defeats what belief. Does the defeater prevail, or does the new basic belief grounded in experience prevail? As there is a prima facie case that each is rational, the answer to this question will be determined by consideration of those holistic features of systems of beliefs.

Plantinga also considers an obvious defeater (perhaps related to the one just discussed). The belief A has, or ought to have, about the existence of evil. But this is not straightforwardly a defeater.[6] What is required is that A has the belief that there is evil which is unnecessary if God exists. Now it seems *that* belief is either question begging or plain unjustified. But allowing it for the moment, it is again a question of which belief defeats which, and this again is a matter that will require holistic consideration of the alternative belief systems.

A passing note on the belief that there is evil. What is surprising to many atheists is that this is not taken by many theists to even give a prima facie case against the existence of God. For some theists, this could be because they regard such a case as question begging.[7] But for those who widely (or even continuously) experience the presence of God, the experience of evil does not alleviate that experience of God The nature of the experience could vary, but it does not need to take on a "Godless" nature. (Even Obi-Wan Kenobi experienced disturbances in the Force when the power of the Dark Side was manifested, but the experience of the Force was not lost.)

It may be thought that we are sidestepping the obvious defeater. A had the experience, but many do not have such an experience in the same or very similar circumstances. Hence this lack of agreement or corroboration itself supplies A with a defeater.

And certainly it might be thought to supply anyone who does not experience the presence of God with a defeater to accepting the belief on the grounds of A's testimony. This brings us to our second matter for consideration.

VARIATION IN EXPERIENCE

A experiences the presence of God, B does not, and the circumstances are as similar as we can make them. What are we to make of this?

We noted earlier that this does not necessarily provide the basis for a rational defeater for A, or for a belief that would prevent B and others from adopting A's belief which for A is grounded in experience, on the basis of A's testimony. We need to examine the details.

B is not having the same experiences as A in the circumstances, but A is not alone. There is at least a reasonably large group of theists who claim to have experiences of this kind, in a large range of circumstances. Hence the view that there is a malfunction in S_A seems implausible. It also seems implausible seeing A (and the others) generally agree about experiences with most other people most of the time. It does not rule out the possibility [that] A and the others all have something wrong with their perception and belief-forming mechanisms. Or perhaps they have special perception abilities. But given there are no discernible differences in these mechanisms, it seems very unlikely. It is also implausible that there really are different external stimuli acting on A and B, unless God is only stimulating the perception mechanisms in A. Perhaps such stimuli are *internal*, which would explain why B and many others do not have the experiences.

But is it true that we have no reason to doubt the reliability of A's relevant perceptual mechanism S_A? For unlike the case of the perceptual experiences considered earlier, aren't we ignorant about the mechanism by which A has her theistic experiences? We may have no reason to doubt that A and B differ in their modular delivery mechanisms, the sensory organs, which are responsible for normal perceptual experiences, but why do we think that the same mechanisms are responsible for A's "God experiences," and if they are not, then isn't it the case that we know nothing about the mechanism in A which is responsible?

The reason for not doubting the reliability of the S_A involved in the formation of A's basic theistic belief rests on two considerations. First, the similarity between A and B is not limited to mere similarity of the sensory organs, but includes general physical and neurological similarity. If there is a special mechanism in A, it would need to be nonphysical. Second, there is no reason to suppose the experiential input should not be by the normal sensory mechanisms. The fact that the beliefs formed are not simple perceptual beliefs does not require a special sensory input. The belief "There is a hand in front of me" is a belief about a hand, not about hand-like sensations. Similarly the belief "God is present" is a belief about God, not a belief about God-like sensations. Difference in beliefs does not require a corresponding difference in the kind of sensory input. Consider how mathematical beliefs might form after sensory input, yet no special mathematics sensory mechanism is required.

If A and B have similar, reliable, sensory mechanisms, how are we to account for the difference in the beliefs formed? It may be that A has an acquired skill or improved awareness required to have the perceptual experience. Musicians have such skills. Also, one can improve auditory and visual perception with training. Luke Skywalker was trained to feel the Force. Many theists claim to have developed the ability to directly experience God. Or it just may be left as unexplained why A and B differ in their experiences.

These brief discussions seem to demonstrate that variation in experience, that is, some people having the experiences while others do not, does not *in itself* constitute grounds for A adopting a defeater for a belief in God grounded in her direct experience. Maybe, on careful examination, particular details will warrant A accepting a defeater, but this should not be presumed without the provision of such details, and there is no reason in advance for A adopting a defeater on the basis of variation in experience. Thus if A is to be denied proper basicality for her belief in God grounded in experience, it must be because that belief leads to a system of beliefs which does not score well on a holistic evaluation of rationality as a system of beliefs.

What should be the attitude of B and others to A's testimony about her experiences? There is at least a prima facie plausibility to the claim that B should adopt A's belief. We have pointed out that A has generally been reliable in beliefs based on experience, and we know that some do have experiences which others do not which are the basis for rational beliefs. So providing B has no independent reasons for accepting defeaters for this belief of A, or independent reasons for not accepting A's belief on the basis of A's testimony, and providing there are no discernible features of A's internal mechanisms to suggest selective unreliability, there is a strong prima facie case that B ought to accept A's belief on the basis of A's testimony. There is, in fact, a problem in rejecting A's testimony. A's testimonies in the past have been reliable, and the testimony itself constitutes an experience for B which would in most circumstances effect a corresponding belief in B. Why not accept A's testimony—what is B's defeater for this?[8]

It is plausible that perhaps in time B too could gain this ability to directly perceive God—as Luke and Princess Leia learnt to feel The Force. Or maybe B will always be like Han Solo. But this is unimportant. What will determine whether B should accept A's testimony will be exactly the same as what will determine A's claim to proper basicality. It will depend on the holistic features that determine the rationality of B's, and A's, overall systems of beliefs.

HOLISTIC EVALUATION

A's claim, for proper basicality for her belief in God, grounded as it is in her experience, will ultimately depend on the holistic evaluation of the system of beliefs that A has with this belief compared with that which she would have if she rejected this belief. Similarly with B and others concerning whether they should accept A's testimony, and accept A's belief as their own on that basis.

Note that A and B will never be the same again. Before the experience A has the belief that she can reliably base beliefs on her perceptual experience. If she now rejects the belief in the presence of God, she also has modified her belief in her own perceptual reliability. And if she accepts the belief as properly basic, her belief system is also radically different.

Similarly with B. B has the belief that A's testimony is reliable, and that she can accept beliefs on the basis of A's testimony. If now she rejects such testimony, then B's system of beliefs is still quite different, and it also would be very different if B accepts theistic belief on the basis of A's testimony.

What holistic evaluation comes to is to consider the survival potential, meaningfulness, usefulness, cohesiveness, explanatory potential, contribution to general well-being, and so forth, of the two competing systems of beliefs for each of A and B. And of course there is the contention, common among theists, that the theistic belief system is clearly advantageous in these regards. Many atheists deny this, but of course questions about futility are held to be particularly troublesome for the atheist.[9]

We shall not here consider this holistic evaluation in detail, for, as we noted earlier, it is not completely clear exactly which features are relevant, and there is no general agreement about how such an evaluation should be carried out. But it seems plausible that the required comparisons can be made, and the matter is, at least in principle, decideable.

Notice that this is independent of what B experiences. B may claim to have no experiences of God's presence, or even claim to experience God's

nonexistence (whatever that kind of experience could be like). What is needed is the holistic evaluation of B's system of beliefs if B were to accept a belief grounded in A's testimony, and a comparison of this with the system formed if B were to reject A's testimony.

It is not new to argue for the rationality of belief in God on the grounds of the overall, holistic, rationality of various systems of beliefs which include theistic belief.[10] But that is not what is here being suggested. The suggestion is that theism for many may be a basic belief grounded in experience, and the proper basicality of such belief for any such person is established by the holistic rationality of the resulting overall belief system. Similarly theism for many others may be grounded in the experience of others' testimonies, others who have experienced God's existence, and the rationality of such resulting belief systems will again depend on holistic evaluation.

In summary, then, the claim of proper basicality for belief in God, grounded in experience, will depend ultimately on reliable persons having such experiences in circumstances which do not undermine their reliability, and for the resulting systems of beliefs to fare well on holistic evaluation for rationality. The rationality of those who do not share these experiences in accepting such beliefs on the basis of testimony, will similarly depend on the holistic evaluation for rationality of their resulting systems of beliefs.

Notes

1. The popular *Star Wars* films and paperback books by George Lucas form the basis for this story.
2. See Alvin Plantinga, "Is Belief in God Properly Basic?," *Noûs* 15 (1981): 41–53; and "Reason and Belief in God," in Alvin Plantinga and Nicholas Wolterstorff, eds., *Faith and Rationality: Reason and Belief in God* (Notre Dame, Ind.: University of Notre Dame Press, 1983), pp. 16–93. See also William P. Alston, "Religious Experience and Religious Belief," *Noûs* 16 (1982): 3–12.
3. See "Is Belief in God Properly Basic?"
4. See the section of William P. Alston and Richard B. Brandt, *The Problems of Philosophy* (Boston: Allyn and Bacon, 1967) citing William James, "Are Men Ever Directly Aware of God?" and F. C. Happold, *Mysticism* (Harmondsworth, Middlesex [England]: Pelican, 1963). Also see Chapter 7 of John Hick's *Arguments for the Existence of God* (New York: Macmillan, 1970).
5. The question of various defeaters is discussed in Phillip L. Quinn, "In Search of the Foundations of Theism," *Faith and Philosophy* 2 (1985): 469–86, and also in Alvin Plantinga, "The *Foundations of Theism*: A Reply," *Faith and Philosophy* 3 (1986): 298–313.

6. See Plantinga, "A Reply"; and Quinn, "In Search of Foundations."

7. See Robert Pargetter, "Evil as Evidence Against the Existence of God," *Mind* 85 (1976): 242–45; and "Evil as Evidence," *Sophia* 21 (1982): 11–15.

8. The inductive basis for such practices is discussed in Plantinga, "Is Belief in God Properly Basic?" which follows the thinking of Roderick Chisholm, *Theory of Knowledge*, 2nd ed. (Englewood Cliffs, N.J. Prentice-Hall, 1977), and *The Problem of the Criterion* (Milwaukee, Wis.: Marquette University Press, 1973).

9. See, for example, the section "Flight from Meaninglessness" in A. K. Bierman and James A. Gould, *Philosophy for a New Generation* (New York: Macmillan, 1970); see also W. D. Joske, "Philosophy and the Meaning of Life," *Australasian Journal of Philosophy* 52 (1974): 93–104.

10. See Bierman and Gould, *Philosophy for a New Generation*; and W. D. Joske, "Philosophy and the Meaning of Life."

Study Questions

1. Pargetter compares Reformed epistemology's view of religious knowledge with the ways in which persons in the *Star Wars* films come to know about "the Force." Explain briefly the parallel between the two situations. Does the comparison strike you as appropriate? Why, or why not?

2. Pargetter maintains that whether or not religious beliefs are properly basic depends on a "holistic evaluation" of a person's system of beliefs. Explain what is meant by a holistic evaluation. Why does Pargetter think such an evaluation is necessary?

William Hasker

The Case of the Intellectually Sophisticated Theist

Philip Quinn (1940–2004) grants that belief in God can have a justification or warrant that is based directly on experience, in the way described by Plantinga. But is this justification sufficient by itself to make belief in God rational for well-informed contemporary adults? Plantinga thinks the answer to this is yes, but Quinn disagrees. He contends that for most well-informed theists in our culture, there are "defeaters" for theistic belief (notably, the problem of evil and "projective" psychological explanations of religious belief) that outweigh the warrant provided by religious experience. For such persons, an additional positive case, in the form of some kind of natural theology, is needed if their belief in God is to be rational. In this selection, William Hasker (b. 1935) summarizes and assesses this disagreement between Quinn and Plantinga.

We now come to the area of disagreement between Quinn and Plantinga which, I believe, both of them regard as most important. It concerns, on the one hand, the epistemic status of theistic belief for well-informed contemporary theists, and, on the other hand, the importance or unimportance of natural theology. The discussion revolves around "the intellectually sophisticated adult theist in our culture," a person Quinn supposes to "know a good deal about standard objections to belief in God ... [including] various versions of the problem of evil as well as the tradition of explaining theistic belief projectively that stems from Feuerbach and comes down to us through Freud and Durkheim."[1] (Later on I shall suggest a modification of this description.)

Granted that theistic beliefs *can* be basic under the appropriate circumstances, are they *in fact* basic for typical, well-informed theists in our culture? Plantinga thinks they are, but Quinn thinks they are not. Quinn is not denying that such theists have experiences which confer non-inferential justification on their beliefs. But he thinks that, in the typical case, this non-inferential justification will be outweighed by the kinds of objections to theism that are so prevalent in contemporary intellectual culture. So if these theists are to be rational in their beliefs, the non-inferential justification of the beliefs through experience needs to be supplemented by a broad case for the rationality of theistic belief— that is, by natural theology. On this point, Plantinga says, "I find myself in solid disagreement."[2]

From "The Foundations of Theism: Scoring the Quinn-Plantinga Debate," *Faith and Philosophy* 15, no. 1 (January 1998): 60–67. Reprinted by permission.

Pretty clearly, Quinn and Plantinga disagree about the strength of the justification most theists possess in virtue of their religious experience. Quinn thinks that for the typical theist, who has not been spoken to from a burning bush but who (for example) senses God speaking to him as he reads the Bible, these beliefs "have only a modest amount of [non-inferential] warrant" (*Rejoinder*, p. 40). I think Plantinga believes the warrant is stronger than this, though he says little about this directly. Both men devote most of their discussion to the potential defeaters of theistic belief, and we shall follow their example.

Concerning the problem of evil, Quinn writes, "What I know, partly from experience and partly from testimony, about the amount and variety of nonmoral evil in the universe confirms highly for me the proposition expressed by…

(28) God does not exist" (*Rejoinder,* p. 40).

Quinn adds that this claim of his is consistent with (28) being highly disconfirmed by his total evidence. But clearly, additional evidence is needed, to overcome the strong objection to theism based on natural evil.

Plantinga concedes that the problem of evil initially seems to present a strong reason for rejecting theism, but he thinks this initial impression is misleading. He notes that atheologians have pretty well given up the claim that evil is logically inconsistent with theism, and have retreated to the claim that theism is improbable with respect to the evidence of evil. In response to this, Plantinga observes that "no atheologian has given a successful or cogent way of working out or developing a probabilistic atheological argument from evil, and I believe there are good reasons for thinking it can't be done" (*Reply*, p. 309). (He refers the reader interested in these reasons to his own article on the subject.[3]) Quinn replies that the failure to construct a successful probabilistic argument from evil shows that evil does not disconfirm theism only if we assume that confirmation must be understood probabilistically, an assumption Quinn rejects. He writes, "I take intuitively clear cases of scientific confirmation and disconfirmation as data against which philosophical accounts of confirmation are to be tested.… And I am inclined to think

that the claim [that] (28) is highly confirmed by the non-moral evil in the universe is another such datum for confirmation theory" (*Rejoinder*, p. 41).

I suspect that quite a few theists will fail to be satisfied by Plantinga's approach to this problem. There is the initial difficulty that understanding Plantinga's objections to probabilistic arguments from evil requires a level of logical sophistication which is not possessed by all philosophers, let alone non-philosophers. But even for those who understand his arguments (or accept the assurance of experts that the arguments are successful), there remains the larger challenge exemplified by Quinn's response to Plantinga. To Quinn it seems simply evident that the world's evil disconfirms theism, and the failure of a particular philosophical strategy for showing this (e.g., by arguments based on probability theory) leaves that troubling conviction unaffected. If one sees the problem of evil primarily as a group of arguments devised by atheistic philosophers to make life difficult for theists, then showing that, for technical reasons, these arguments are unsuccessful may be a sufficient response. (Showing this is in any case an important thing to do, and Plantinga has done it brilliantly.) But if one is deeply troubled and perplexed by the actual phenomena of evil, a purely negative and defensive strategy may be insufficient. What one needs, in that case, is some positive account of evil, something that offers some actual understanding of why evil exists and how it fits into God's plan for the world. In other words, a theodicy.[4]

The disagreement between Quinn and Plantinga about projective explanations of religious belief is sharp. Plantinga writes, "Freud's jejune speculations as to the psychological origin of religion and Marx's careless claims about its social role can't sensibly be taken as providing argument or reason for (28), i.e., for the nonexistence of God; so taken they present text-book cases…of the genetic fallacy" (*Reply*, p. 308). Quinn admits there are flaws in Freud's writings on this topic, but insists that "to construe Freud's contribution to our understanding of religion as nothing but jejune speculation strikes me as uncharitable in the extreme." He goes on to discuss various projection theories, and concludes "I believe that projection theories have so far achieved a real, but limited, success in explaining religious beliefs of some sorts, and I think this success does give the intellectually sophisticated adult theist in our culture substantial reason for thinking that (28) is true" (*Rejoinder*, pp. 41, 42).

Plantinga thinks the projection theories (considered as an argument for God's non-existence) commit the genetic fallacy, because they assume that an account of the origin of religious belief is determinative for its subsequent status, in this case its truth or falsity. This assessment may be correct.[5] But what Plantinga overlooks is that psychological projection theories, if they are successful, constitute a powerful undercutting defeater for the claim that theistic beliefs are non-inferentially justified by religious experience. The view that such experiences do provide significant non-inferential justification for theistic beliefs is plausible only on the supposition that, in the experience, the believer is genuinely in contact with God. I don't mean by this that one must *first* establish that there is contact with God, and only then conclude that the experiences afford justification; that would be falling back into the trap of evidentialism. But evidence that the experience can be completely and correctly explained *without reference* to the presence and activity of God strongly undermines the claim of those experiences to afford justification for beliefs about God's character and activities.[6] And this kind of explanation is just what the projection theories claim to provide. Furthermore, it's not necessary, in order to have this effect, for the projection theories to show that all religious experience is a result of projection. The non-inferential justification of religious beliefs by experience is largely, if not entirely, a "first-person" affair, and if one comes to suspect that one's *own* religious experiences are the result of psychological projection, wish-fulfillment, and the like, then that tends to both to discredit the experiences themselves and to undermine any warrant they might otherwise provide for one's religious beliefs.[7]

That is not to say that the projection theories are in fact successful in discrediting religious experience and religious beliefs. This is a large topic, and no doubt there is much to be said against such theories, especially when they are taken as a *general* explanation for religious belief and practice. But there is work here

that needs to be done, and once a person has begun to recognize the elements of plausibility, and indeed of partial truth, in these theories, an offhand dismissal like Plantinga's is not apt to be convincing.[8]

At this point I wish to suggest a modest addition to Quinn's description of the intellectually sophisticated adult theist in our culture. I believe the addition will be both realistic, in that many contemporary theists in fact conform to the augmented description, and helpful for the present topic. I will ask us to assume that our typical theist has a modicum of knowledge about the plurality of religions in the modern world. In particular, she knows that there are several different "world religions" with mutually incompatible doctrines, each of them boasting elaborate, intellectually developed systems of belief and espoused by intelligent, thoughtful advocates who can testify to experiences confirmatory of their respective beliefs.[9]

Now, how does this affect the rationality of our theist's belief in God? It does not necessarily lend support to atheism; indeed one might seek to argue from the prevalence of religious experience that there is "something out there" to which the religious are responding. It seems clear, however, that religious pluralism does to some extent weaken the support, whether inferential or non-inferential, of religious experience for any particular system of beliefs about the nature of God or ultimate reality. This does not, I think, mean that the theist ought to *give up* her beliefs; they are, after all, *her* beliefs, grounded in part in her own experience, and she should give them up only if, after thorough reflection, they seem insufficiently likely to be true, or to be close to the truth in important respects. But the fact that others—Buddhists and Hindu advaitists, for example—experience the divine as having significantly different characteristics has to constitute a problem for her. And it is exceedingly difficult to see how she is going to find a satisfying resolution of the problem apart from a large-scale apologetic enterprise which will argue for the superiority of theism as a worldview and, indeed, for the particular variety of theism she espouses.[10]

What shall we conclude from all this? I think we have seen that each of the three problem areas we have considered may well present genuine difficulty for well-informed contemporary theists, and the resolution of these difficulties is likely to demand answers going well beyond the kinds of responses Plantinga has indicated. Are the difficulties so severe as to overwhelm the non-inferential justification the theist has for her belief in God, and render that belief no longer properly basic for her? That is a difficult question to answer, and in fact no general answer is possible; the answer in each case will depend both on the strength of the theist's non-inferential justification for her belief, and on the strength *for her* of the various objections to it. But even if her non-inferential justification for theism is sufficient to outweigh the combined force of the objections, the latter is great enough that sooner or later it is going to take its toll, creating genuine discomfort and perplexity. It seems, then, that it will be to her advantage, even if it is not absolutely essential for justified belief, to have available to her further answers which defeat the objections and contribute to an over-all case for the rationality of theistic belief.

Now in principle, these further answers could be limited to "defeater-defeaters"; they could consist of considerations which lessen or eliminate the force of the objections to theism, but do not attempt to provide any positive support for belief in the existence of God or for a particular system of religious belief. But while the further support *could* be so limited, is there any intelligible reason why it *ought* to be? Should the theist not, on the contrary, avail herself of plausible theistic arguments, if there are any, and permit them to add their force to her "cumulative case" for the reality of God and the truthfulness of her faith? If not, why not? To be sure, if the various objections could be defeated conclusively and without remainder, it may be the theist would find it superfluous to attempt to add anything by way of positive argumentative support; in her reclaimed innocence, she could again assume the stance of the "rational basic believer." In practice, though, that is not how things are likely to go. All of the objections we have mentioned, even when answered as completely as possible, are likely to leave behind a lingering aura of tension not fully

resolved. And unless we, like Kierkegaard, revel in intellectual uncertainty as the lifeblood of faith, it is only sensible to marshal all our resources in order to exhibit to the greatest degree possible the rational excellence of the faith we profess.[11]

So who wins the debate? Obviously the issues in this part of the paper are many and complex, and it would be rash in the extreme to assert that either Quinn or Plantinga (or the author of this paper!) is right about all of them. But on the main points at issue, the seriousness of the challenges to theism and the importance of natural theology, I cannot help but conclude that Quinn is more nearly right than Plantinga....

In the end of course, it is artificial and perhaps even wrong-headed to think of "scoring" a debate like this one. Insofar as issues are clarified and light is thrown on them, both Quinn and Plantinga are winners—as are all the rest of us who have benefited from their exchange. And if the general conclusions drawn in this final section are correct, there is another sense in which the debate has many winners and no losers. We have envisioned a situation in which there is a large number of philosophical and apologetic tasks waiting to be performed. Much work remains to be done in clarifying the nature, scope and force of the non-inferential justification of religious belief by experience. There is also the task of traditional natural theology, in developing and advancing arguments and analyses supportive of belief in God and the religious worldview.[12] Insofar as our faith is crucially rooted in historical narratives, there is philosophical work (as well as historical work) to be done in clarifying the nature, credibility, and evidential force of those narratives. And of course, there is a great deal that needs to be said in response to the many potential defeaters of religious belief. There is occupation here for virtually every philosophical taste and talent—and what more could a philosopher ask for?[13] But all this work needs to be done—we intellectually sophisticated contemporary adult theists need all the help we can get.

NOTES

1. "The Foundations of Theism Again: A Rejoinder to Plantinga," in Linda Zagzebski, ed., *Rational Faith: Catholic Responses to Reformed Epistemology* (Notre Dame, Ind.: University of Notre Dame Press, 1993), p. 35 (hereafter cited as *Rejoinder*).

2. "The Foundations of Theism: A Reply," *Faith and Philosophy* 3:3 (1986), p. 308 (hereafter cited as *Reply*).

3. See "The Probabilistic Argument from Evil," *Philosophical Studies*, 1980, pp. 1–53.

4. I believe Plantinga *is* troubled and perplexed by the phenomena of evil, but his sense of the greatness of God and the insufficiency of human reason makes him despair of our ability to provide much in the way of constructive understanding of it. If so, this is a classically Reformed response—and as such, it will be appealing to some contemporary theists, but certainly not to all.

5. It may be, however, that Marx, Freud, and other projection theorists were not actually committing this fallacy. Rather they may have concluded on evidentialist grounds that God does not exist.

6. It will not be sufficient for the theist to claim in the connection that, since God's sustaining activity is required for the existence of all objects, persons, and events, *no* experience can be explained "without reference to the presence and activity of God." In order to claim that the experiences confer justification, the theist must hold that God is involved in those experiences in a direct and specific way.

7. My own mother, an extremely devout person, once mentioned to me that, when she first learned of the psychological explanations of religion, she was unable to pray for several months. I suspect that, for many contemporary theists, the thought that one's own religious affections may be the projections of psychological needs is a sort of lingering undercurrent of the religious life.

8. Alvin Plantinga's book, *Warranted Christian Belief* (New York: Oxford University Press, 2000), contains an extensive discussion of projection theories.

9. In correspondence, Quinn states: "I agree completely that the intellectually sophisticated theist will need to deal with the problem of religious diversity or pluralism. My thoughts on this topic are contained in my 'Towards Thinner Theologies: Hick and Alston on Religious Diversity' (*International Journal for the Philosophy of Religion* 38 [1995], pp. 145–64)."

10. This point has been made by a number of authors. Consider, e.g., William Hasker, "On Justifying the Christian Practice," *The New Scholasticism* 60 (1986), pp. 129–44; David Basinger, "Hick's Religious Pluralism and 'Reformed Epistemology': A Middle Ground," *Faith and Philosophy* 5:5 (1988), pp. 421–32; and William Wainwright, "Religious Language, Religious Experience, and Religious Pluralism," in Thomas D. Senor, ed., *The Rationality of Belief and the Plurality of Faith: Essays in Honor of William P. Alston* (Ithaca, N.Y.: Cornell University Press, 1995), pp. 170–88. Alston now agrees that it is advisable to use all available means, including metaphysical and historical arguments, to resolve the ambiguity created by the plurality of mystical practices; see his *Perceiving God* (Ithaca, N.Y.: Cornell University Press, 1991), chapter 7. Plantinga, so far as I am aware, has not yet addressed the issue.

11. It would be premature to claim that there is a consensus on this point, but I believe it is possible to discern a movement in the direction of such a consensus. In addition to the sources cited in the previous note, several of the essays in *Rational Faith* call for such a broad-based apologetic strategy, one which includes the non-inferential justification of belief by experience as well as metaphysical and historical argument and responses to the various potential defeaters of religious belief. Even Plantinga has softened in his attitude towards natural theology; he has delivered (but not so far published) a paper entitled "Two Dozen (or So) Arguments for the Existence of God."

12. It will, of course, be important to refrain from the excessive claims to demonstrative certainty characteristic of much traditional natural theology—claims which provide all too easy a target for critics of theism.

13. Even the atheists gain by this; they will have more and better grist for their mills than ever before!

STUDY QUESTIONS

1. According to Quinn, "projective explanations of religious belief" create an obstacle for thoughtful theists, an obstacle that must be overcome if their beliefs are to be justified. What exactly is a projective explanation of belief, and why does it constitute a problem?

2. Hasker states, and Quinn agrees, that religious diversity also constitutes a problem that must be overcome in order for one's religious beliefs to be justified. Do you agree that it does constitute such a problem? Why or why not?

3. From your own observations of thoughtful religious believers, do you agree with Quinn that they need support from rational theology if their beliefs are to be rationally justified? Or do you agree with Plantinga that such support is not needed? Give reasons for your answer.

Suggested Reading

Alston, William P. "Christian Experience and Christian Belief," in *Faith and Rationality: Reason and Belief in God*, ed. Alvin Plantinga and Nicholas Wolterstorff, pp. 103–34. Notre Dame, Ind.: University of Notre Dame Press, 1983.

———. *Perceiving God: The Epistemology of Religious Experience*. Ithaca, N.Y.: Cornell University Press, 1991.

Gellman, Jerome I. *Experience of God and the Rationality of Theistic Belief*. Ithaca, N.Y.: Cornell University Press, 1997.

Hasker, William. "Proper Function, Reliabilism, and Religious Knowledge: A Critique of Plantinga's Epistemology," in C. Stephen Evans and Merold Westphal, eds., *Christian Perspectives on Religious Knowledge*, pp. 66–86. Grand Rapids, Mich.: Eerdmans, 1993.

———. "The Epistemic Value of Religious Experience: Perceptual and Explanatory Models," in Thomas Senor, ed., *The Rationality of Belief and the Plurality of Faith*, pp. 150–69. Ithaca, N.Y.: Cornell University Press, 1995.

Hester, Marcus, ed. *Faith, Reason, and Skepticism*. Philadelphia: Temple University Press, 1991.

Hoitenga, Dewey. *From Plato to Plantinga: An Introduction to Reformed Epistemology*. Albany: State University of New York Press, 1991.

Kvanvig, Jonathan, ed. *Warrant in Contemporary Epistemology; Essays in Honor of Plantinga's Theory of Knowledge*. Totowa, N.J.: Rowman and Littlefield, 1996.

McLeod, Mark S. *Rationality and Theistic Belief: An Essay on Reformed Epistemology*. Ithaca, N.Y.: Cornell University Press, 1993.

Plantinga, Alvin. "Reason and Belief in God," in *Faith and Rationality: Reason and Belief in God*, ed. Alvin Plantinga and Nicholas Wolterstorff, pp. 16–93. Notre Dame, Ind.: University of Notre Dame Press, 1983.

———. "The Foundations of Theism: A Reply," *Faith and Philosophy* 3:3 (1986), pp. 298–313.

———. "Coherentism and the Evidentialist Objection to Belief in God," in *Rationality, Religious Belief, and Moral Commitment*, ed. Robert Audi and William J. Wainwright, pp. 109–38. Ithaca, N.Y.: Cornell University Press, 1986.

———. *Warranted Christian Belief*. New York: Oxford University Press, 2000.

Plantinga, Alvin, R. Douglas Geivett, Greg Jesson, Richard Fumerton, Keith E. Yandell, and Paul K. Moser. Symposium on Warranted Christian Belief. *Philosophia Christi* 3:2 (2001), pp. 327–400.

Quinn, Philip. "On Finding the Foundations of Theism," *Faith and Philosophy* 2 (1985), pp. 469–86.

———. "The Foundations of Theism Again: A Rejoinder to Plantinga," in Linda Zagzebski, ed., *Catholic Responses to Reformed Epistemology*. pp. 14–47. Notre Dame, Ind.: University of Notre Dame Press, 1993.

Swinburne, Richard. "Plantinga on Warrant," *Religious Studies* 37:2 (2001), pp. 203–14.

Wolterstorff, Nicholas, "Can Belief in God Be Rational If It Has No Foundations?" in *Faith and Rationality: Reason and Belief in God*, ed. Alvin Plantinga and Nicholas Wolterstorff, pp. 135–86. Notre Dame, Ind.: University of Notre Dame Press, 1983.

Wykstra, Stephen. "Toward a Sensible Evidentialism: On the Notion of 'Needing Evidence,' "in *Philosophy of Religion: Selected Readings*, 2nd ed., ed. William L. Rowe and William J. Wainwright, pp. 426–37. New York: Harcourt Brace Jovanovich, 1989.

Zagzebski, Linda, ed. *Catholic Responses to Reformed Epistemology.* Notre Dame, Ind.: University of Notre Dame Press, 1993.

PART SEVEN

The Problem of Evil

Evil in our world perplexes us and demands understanding. It is not surprising that every major worldview, whether religious or secular, offers some explanation for the presence of evil. Historically, the "problem of evil" has been a serious difficulty for theistic believers who want to square their lofty claims about God's perfect power, knowledge, and goodness with claims about evil in the world, whether to clarify their own commitments or to give reasonable answers to critics. Of course, the problem of evil has long been a stronghold for nonbelievers who object to theistic faith.

Important Definitions and Distinctions

Philosophers typically distinguish between two broad types of evil. *Moral evils* are the wrongful actions of persons (such as murder, cruelty, fraud, etc.), but they also include bad intentions and vicious character traits. *Natural evils* are caused by the physical or impersonal objects and forces of our environment when they threaten or destroy human interests, health, or safety. Such evils include tuberculosis, mental disorders, famine, and many more too numerous to list. Problems may be raised either with respect to evil in general (its proportion to good or its justification) or with respect to a specific type of evil (moral or natural) or even a specific instance of evil (e.g., torture of an infant).

The problem of evil is best interpreted as an argument—actually, as a cluster of different arguments. An argument becomes a problem when its premises are perceived to be plausible or true but the conclusion opposes one's current beliefs. Obviously, the problem of evil is a problem for the theist because it supports an atheistic conclusion. The arguments coming under the rubric "problem of evil" reflect two different strategies. *Logical arguments* contend that theism is irrational because it includes an inconsistent set of beliefs—the belief that God is omnipotent, omniscient, and wholly good and the belief that evil exists in God's created world. Since these two beliefs seem inconsistent with one another, theism itself may be incoherent, in which case it is not rational to accept it. *Evidential arguments* seek to show that theism is implausible, improbable, or rationally unacceptable in light of evil. Such arguments treat theism as a kind of global metaphysical and theological hypothesis that implies certain things about the disposition of evil in the world—for instance, that evil would be less severe or less unfairly distributed than it is. So, the facts of evil become evidence against the truth of theism.

There are also different strategies of theistic response. A *defense* aims at refuting an argument from evil by showing that the argument does not establish that theism is incoherent or improbable. A *theodicy* offers an explanation for why theism can actually be true or plausible in light of evil by offering one or more reasons why God would allow evil. Theodicies often correct misunderstandings of key divine attributes (e.g., omniscience and omnipotence) and develop key themes (e.g., that the potential for evil is inherent in free will, that evil builds character, that evil provides meaningful contrast to good, etc.). Traditionally, theodicies were deployed to answer the problem of evil, whether stated as a logical or evidential argument. In recent decades, however, defense has become the strategy of choice for responding to logical arguments, and theodicy has largely become the strategy for responding to evidential arguments. The "skeptical theist defense" (or "cognitive limitation defense") has also emerged as an alternative response to evidential arguments that are based the apparent pointlessness of some evils. This defense contends that finite human epistemic capabilities cannot know whether many of the evils are connected to greater goods, leaving open the possibility that there are such connections and that only God's infinite knowledge can understand them. Critics and some other theists observe that this maneuver assumes a particular version of theism and the meanings it assigns to the divine attributes.

A CLASSIC STATEMENT OF THE PROBLEM AND A CLASSIC RESPONSE

David Hume's *Dialogues Concerning Natural Religion* present a forceful statement of the problem of evil in which both logical and evidential arguments can be detected. Hume creatively frames a dialogue (or trialogue) among three fictional speakers—Demea, Cleanthes, and Philo—who take different approaches to the subject. Demea, a theist, argues that the existence of God can be known a priori—that is, deduced by reason using self-evident principles—much as mathematics and logic deduce their conclusions. For Demea, it is not only rational to believe that there is a God, it is positively irrational to deny it. For Demea's rationalist approach, then, the existence of the infinite God is a sufficient reason for the universe, and therefore there must be some reason for evil, even if it is beyond the capacity of human beings to understand it. With the existence of God assured, evils must somehow be rectified in a future period of existence. Demea's general attitude has been called "dogmatic" and "mystical." The position of Gottfried Leibniz—that reason can show that this is the best of all possible worlds—is perhaps a prototype for Hume's Demea.

Cleanthes, on the other hand, represents an a posteriori approach to the discussion: that features of the world are a kind of empirical evidence for a Deity whose power, knowledge, and goodness resemble those attributes in humans. This means that evils in the world have to be construed as part of the evidence supporting the traditional belief in the existence and nature of God—partly by Cleanthes' claim that the world contains a greater amount of happiness and enjoyment than evil. This inductive argument resembles, say, the familiar reasoning process of citing evidence in support of a hypothesis—whether in ordinary life or science. For example, we might infer the existence of mice from bite marks on cheese, or a magnetic field from the pattern of iron filings on a smooth surface. Cleanthes reflects the type of position the eighteenth-century thinker Joseph Butler held regarding the empirical evidence provided by ordinary life and nature for the truth of traditional religion and morality. Similarly, William Paley's teleological argument concludes that God exists because of the order of the world.

Philo is a religious skeptic, like Hume himself, and verbalizes the most convincing arguments. He argues, for instance, that a consideration of evil shows us that we cannot follow Cleanthes in saying that divine attributes such as power and goodness resemble our understanding of these traits in human life. For we know that in human affairs, a person who is both able and willing to prevent or eliminate evil would in fact to so. Yet God does not. Even Cleanthes' point that pleasure and benefits are more plentiful than pain and hardships is met by Philo's skeptical counterpoint that we are not in a position to perform such an assessment.

Gottfried Leibniz attempted to reconcile evil with the existence of God. Representing the long-standing tradition of theodicy, Leibniz argues that even including evil, the actual world is the best of all possible worlds. He reasons that God, being perfect, would choose the best world to bring about. In surveying all possible worlds, God's unlimited knowledge would allow him to know the best world, his unlimited goodness would make him want it, and his unlimited power would enable him to bring it about. Some people interpret Leibniz to say that this world contains the least possible amount of evil that is compatible with there being a world at all. However, it is entirely conceivable that there are other possible worlds that are not as good as ours but that also contain less evil. So, it is more accurate to interpret Leibniz as saying that this world contains the least amount of evil commensurate with its being the best possible. Obviously, some great goods are made possible only by the presence of evil (e.g., compassion is made possible by engaging suffering; fortitude by hardship). Worlds with less evil as well as worlds with more evil, Leibniz argues, simply do not contain the exact entities and events, connected in the exact ways, that make them candidates for being the best. The moral principle Leibniz employs to justify the permission of evil is that it must be necessary for a greater good. Furthermore, he argues that for God to foreknow that free creatures would sin in the best of all possible worlds is not for God to predetermine that they sin and thus undermine their freedom. Instead, in choosing the best possible world, God consents to all that happens in that world, including freely chosen sin. Although the world contains sin and evil, Leibniz points out that it also contains the incarnation of the Son of God and his atoning work for humanity, which are very great goods that offer to humanity the prospect of life in God. So, the best possible world admittedly contains a great deal of evil but also contains an unsurpassably great good that outweighs all finite evils.

Best-of-all-possible-worlds theodicy bristles with issues for discussion, including the following. First, some contend that the concept of a best possible world is logically incoherent, just as the concept of the highest possible integer is logically incoherent. There simply is no end to the system of integers. So, why would we think that there is some best possible world? Second, the Leibnizian approach seems to imply that our world is not capable of improvement, an implication that runs counter to our ordinary moral judgments and attempts to enlist moral energies. The third, and perhaps most serious, problem regards the question of why a good God chose to create a world at all, given that it had to have this much suffering. In *The Brothers Karamazov*, Ivan Karamozov recites a list of situations involving the torture and murder of small children to his brother Alyosha, a Russian Orthodox priest. Alyosha admits that he would not create the present world if its being the best possible world depended upon the unimaginable suffering of even one small child.

The Logical Argument and the Free Will Defense

Twentieth-century philosopher J. L. Mackie argues that theism is logically inconsistent since it involves two propositions that cannot both be true:

1. An omnipotent, omniscient, perfectly good God exists

and

2. Evil exists.

If the two statements are indeed inconsistent, then theism does not simply lack rational support, it is positively irrational.

Of course, the contradiction between 1 and 2 is not immediately obvious, putting the burden on the critic to make it explicit. Mackie and other critics have proposed additional statements—or "quasi-logical rules"—to show how the contradiction arises. Their suggestions include the following: that an omniscient being knows how to eliminate evil; that an omnipotent being has the power to eliminate evil; that a perfectly good being will want to or have an obligation to eliminate evil; that evil is not logically necessary; and so forth. These statements specify more fully the meaning of key terms. The critic reasons that if God has the knowledge, power, and desire to eliminate evil, and if evil is not necessary, then no evil should exist.

Theistic philosopher Alvin Plantinga developed a rebuttal of the charge of inconsistency known as the Free Will Defense. Since the critic alleges that it is *logically impossible* that both God and evil exist, the theistic defender must show that it is *logically possible*. A defense here, in other words, is produced when the defender is able to show not that both claims *are in fact* true, but that it is *possible* for both claims to be true. As Plantinga indicates, the general strategy for proving consistency between any two statements involves finding a *third* statement that is possibly true, that is consistent with the first statement, and that, in conjunction with the first statement, implies the second statement. The third statement, of course, need not actually be true or known to be true; it need not even be plausible. What the Free Will defender must do, therefore, is to find a statement that meets these conditions.

Plantinga's argument uses ideas from contemporary logic about *possible worlds*. A possible world is a total possible state of affairs, a total possible way things could have been. The needed third statement is then drawn from a description of a possible world, a brief scenario of human freedom in relation to divine omnipotence. God brings about a world containing "significantly" free creatures who can choose right or wrong, because he knows that such a world is more valuable than a world containing no free creatures. Significant free will means that God cannot determine the right creaturely choices. For if God causes right choices, then creatures are not free. Therefore, to create a world in which moral good is possible, God must create a world in which moral evil is also possible. Yet the fact that free creatures sometimes go wrong does not count against God's power or goodness, because he could have prevented moral evil only by eliminating the possibility of moral good.

For any world God might create, populated by whatever significantly free creatures, it is not within God's power to ensure that those significantly free creatures never go wrong. In other words,

3. God is omnipotent, and it was not within his power to create a world containing moral good but no moral evil.

This new statement, together with one asserting the existence of God, implies that evil is possible in worlds with free creatures. The point is that it is *possible* (or possibly true) that

4. God would create a world of free creatures who choose to do evil.

Thus, the critic's charge—that it is not possible for God and evil to exist—is refuted. The Free Will Defense depends, of course, on an *incompatibilist* view of free will—that is, that free will is not compatible with any form of determinism, either natural or divine. Yet Mackie, Antony Flew, and other critics have pressed the inconsistency argument by endorsing a compatibilist view of free will—the view that God could actualize a world containing creatures who only choose the good without violating free will.

SOUL-MAKING THEODICY

Continuing with the theme of freedom of will, John Hick offers a theodicy—that is, a justification of the ways of God in light of evil in the world. Most people are familiar with variations of St. Augustine of Hippo's theodicy, which are popular to the present day: the evil we witness and experience is a result of the human fall from the original, pristine state of the world. However, Hick's theodicy follows the thinking of Irenaeus, also a bishop of the ancient Church, who held that evil is better understood as a phase in the development of an imperfect world into a more perfect one. After all, it is not clear that moral perfection can be created instantaneously, since moral maturity must be developed over time in response to a variety of conditions. So, Irenaean theodicy does not rest on a theory of the causal genesis of evil but on a theory of how God is working for the gradual progress and development of the human race. In this vein, Hick views the world as a necessary stage in the evolution of a relatively immature creation into a more mature state. God is seeking to bring forth mature moral and spiritual beings who are capable of freely exercising faith in him and love toward their fellows. If this is God's overall aim, then it makes sense that his universe exhibits certain structural features so that it can be an environment conducive to bringing about these results. For example, there is "epistemic distance" between the creature and God, such that the world does not make clear whether God exists and thus leaves open the possibility of real faith. And the world is structured so that we humans are mutually vulnerable to one another—and are thus able to give comfort and support, or create pain and suffering, in our relationships. Furthermore, since it seems apparent that not all persons reach moral maturity and connection to God in temporal life, Hick believes that the divine program of soul making will culminate in the afterlife, which must involve "universal salvation."

The Evidential Argument

By the 1980s, challenges to theism based on the presence of evil had transitioned from a focus on logical arguments about the inconsistency of an omnipotent God and evil in the world to an emphasis on evidential arguments in which the facts of evil were construed as evidence against the claim that God exists. Specifically, such arguments assume that if God were indeed omnipotent, omniscient, and wholly good, evils must be necessary to greater goods. Thus, evils in the world that do not seem to be connected greater goods would support the conclusion that it is more rational to reject theism. The burden for theists, then, is to explain why God allows the evils in question (i.e., give a theodicy) or to somehow uncover a flaw in the evidential argument itself (i.e., provide a defense).

William Rowe, Edward Madden, Wesley Salmon, and others have advanced various versions of the evidential argument. Rowe's formulation is now a standard in philosophical discussions:

1. There exist instances of intense suffering, which an omnipotent, omniscient being could have prevented without thereby losing some greater good or permitting some evil equally bad or worse. (Factual premise)
2. An omnipotent, wholly good being would prevent the occurrence of any intense suffering it could, unless it could not do so without thereby losing some greater good or permitting some evil equally bad or worse. (Theological premise)
3. There does not exist an omnipotent, omniscient, wholly good being. (Conclusion)

Since the logic of the argument is sound, the debate must deal with the credibility of its premises. In support of premise 1, Rowe often cites the cases of a fawn that suffered and died in a forest fire (natural evil) and a five-year-old girl who was horribly abused and beaten to death by her mother's drunken boyfriend (moral evil). Neither of these events appear to be connected to any greater good or the prevention of an equally bad or worse evil. Furthermore, Rowe believes that premise 2 is essential to theistic belief because, surely, the only morally sufficient justification for God's permission of an evil is that it be necessary to the existence of a greater good or to the prevention of some equally bad or worse evil.

Typically, both theists and nontheists think that debate over the evidential argument centers on its factual premise, which is essentially the claim that pointless or unjustified evil exists. Rowe and other critics of theism maintain that the factual premise is more reasonable than not to believe. Theists who try to rebut the factual premise divide into two camps: those who say that we can know it to be false and those who say that we cannot know it to be true. Theists who contend that premise 1 is false advance a theodicy or some element of a theodicy explaining what sorts of greater goods are connected to what sorts of evils. (e.g., suffering builds character, provides meaningful contrast to the good, etc.). Other theists call into question the epistemic grounds for accepting the premise 1. Stephen Wykstra and William Alston think that a defense is called for, rather than a positive theodicy. Wykstra, for example, challenges Rowe's claim that it "does not appear" that there are goods that justify the evils in question. Wykstra contends that accepting an "appearance-claim" in a given situation is warranted only when it is reasonable to believe that, given our cognitive faculties and our use of them, the truth of the claim would be discernible by us. Explaining that God's knowledge is infinitely higher than human knowledge. Wykstra concludes that it is not reasonable to think that if God has some justifying good for a given evil, we would know it or it would be apparent to us—i.e., that we would have "reasonable epistemic access." Since God's ways are beyond the power of finite minds to comprehend, we are not justified in thinking that evils have no point simply because they do not "appear" to us to have a point. Interestingly, Rowe has replied that Wykstra's argument relies on a particular interpretation of the inscrutability of divine reasons for the permission of evil. Clearly, other theistic traditions do not dichotomize divine and human knowledge so drastically and instead affirm that humans have divinely created capacities to comprehend something of the personal, moral, and spiritual meanings of the universe, including those related to evil and suffering.

RESPONDING TO HORRENDOUS EVILS

In the past couple of decades, Marilyn Adams has addressed that special class of evils that are difficult if not impossible to connect to any justifying or offsetting goods. Whether the problem is framed as a logical argument or an evidential argument, Adams observes that the discussion usually revolves around the credibility of "global and generic" theodicies that seek to show that a good God allows evil because it contributes to a world that is good on the whole or that contains certain kinds of goods that could not otherwise be achieved. However, Adams observes that such approaches do not address the need to show how God's goodness addresses those cases in which individual human beings experience evil so destructive that it threatens to destroy the value and meaning of their lives (e.g., Rowe's murdered child example). For these cases, no finite goods seem adequate to balance, let alone mitigate, what she labels "horrendous evils."

Adams' task is to show how God deals with—and, indeed, defeats—horrendous evils. She distinguishes between God's goodness conceived as involved in the global production of goods and his goodness conceived as love toward each individual created person. She argues that theists must relinquish the shared methodological assumption that they are obligated to answer the problem of evil by reference to goods that nontheists also accept. She argues that these goods will be secular, finite, and temporal, whereas theism contains a rich arsenal of infinite and eternal goods as well. She argues that the metaphysical nature of God is such that God is the source of value and thus good in that sense; but she also argues that God is not subject to the normal network of creaturely rights and obligations which so many formulations of the problem of evil assume. Her argument ultimately concludes that God can defeat horrors only by bringing those the individuals involved into relationship with himself, since he is infinite in value and the ultimate source of meaning.

David Hume

Evil Makes a Strong Case Against God's Existence

David Hume (1711–1776) was a major thinker in the Scottish Enlightenment and is considered one of the greatest philosophers of all time. Hume's *Dialogues Concerning Natural Religion* is applauded as the most sophisticated and elegant philosophical dialogue written in English. The three principal (fictional) speakers in the *Dialogues* are Demea, Cleanthes, and Philo. Demea, something of a dogmatist, defends the existence of God on a priori grounds and, in that regard, reflects a Leibnizian approach. Cleanthes believes that experience provides evidence for the existence of a deity who is immensely powerful and benevolent, perhaps reflecting the approach of William Paley. Philo, probably Hume's protagonist, is a skeptic who attempts to rebut arguments for God from reason and experience. The following discussion from the *Dialogues* contains two renditions of the problem of evil. The first argument is quite direct: the claim that "God exists" and "evil exists" are logically incompatible; and since we can be sure that evil does exist, we know that God does not exist. We see this type of logical argument advanced by J. L. Mackie and other contemporary philosophers. The second argument is less direct: even if "God exists" and "evil exists" are logically compatible claims, the truth of the latter provides strong, although not conclusive, grounds or evidence for rejecting the former. Among contemporary critics, William Rowe advances this type of argument.

PHILO AND DEMEA DISCUSS SUFFERING

It is my opinion,…replied Demea, that each man feels, in a manner, the truth of religion within his own breast, and, from a consciousness of his imbecility and misery rather than from any reasoning, is led to seek protection from that Being on whom he and all nature is dependent. So anxious or so tedious are even the best scenes of life that futurity is still the object of all our hopes and fears. We incessantly look forward and endeavour, by prayers, adoration, and sacrifice, to appease those unknown powers whom we find, by experience, so able to afflict and oppress us. Wretched creatures that we are! What resource for us amidst the innumerable ills of life did not religion

From *Dialogues Concerning Natural Religion*, Part X.

suggest some methods of atonement, and appease those terrors with which we are incessantly agitated and tormented?

I am indeed persuaded, said Philo, that the best and indeed the only method of bringing everyone to a due sense of religion is by just representations of the misery and wickedness of men. And for that purpose a talent of eloquence and strong imagery is more requisite than that of reasoning and argument. For is it necessary to prove what everyone feels within himself? It is only necessary to make us feel it, if possible, more intimately and sensibly.

The people, indeed, replied Demea, are sufficiently convinced of this great and melancholy truth. The miseries of life, the unhappiness of man, the general corruptions of our nature, the unsatisfactory enjoyment of pleasures, riches, honours—these phrases have become almost proverbial in all languages. And who can doubt of what all men declare from their own immediate feeling and experience?

In this point, said Philo, the learned are perfectly agreed with the vulgar; and in all letters, *sacred* and *profane*, the topic of human misery has been insisted on with the most pathetic eloquence that sorrow and melancholy could inspire. The poets, who speak from sentiment, without a system, and whose testimony has therefore the more authority, abound in images of this nature. From Homer down to Dr. Young, the whole inspired tribe have ever been sensible that no other representation of things would suit the feeling and observation of each individual.

As to authorities, replied Demea, you need not seek them. Look round this library of Cleanthes. I shall venture to affirm that, except authors of particular sciences, such as chemistry or botany, who have no occasion to treat of human life, there is scarce one of those innumerable writers from whom the sense of human misery has not, in some passage or other, extorted a complaint and confession of it. At least, the chance is entirely on that side; and no one author has ever, so far as I can recollect, been so extravagant as to deny it.

There you must excuse me, said Philo: Leibniz has denied it, and is perhaps the first who ventured upon so bold and paradoxical an opinion; at least, the first who made it essential to his philosophical system.

And by being the first, replied Demea, might he not have been sensible of his error? For is this a subject in which philosophers can propose to make discoveries especially in so late an age? And can any man hope by a simple denial (for the subject scarcely admits of reasoning) to bear down the united testimony of mankind, founded on sense and consciousness?

And why should man, added he, pretend to be an exemption from the lot of all other animals? The whole earth, believe me, Philo, is cursed and polluted. A perpetual war is kindled amongst all living creatures. Necessity, hunger, want stimulate the strong and courageous; fear, anxiety, terror agitate the weak and infirm. The first entrance into life gives anguish to the new-born infant and to its wretched parent; weakness, importance, distress attend each stage of that life, and it is, at last, finished in agony and horror.

Observe, too, says Philo, the curious artifices of nature in order to embitter the life of every living being. The stronger prey upon the weaker and keep them in perpetual terror and anxiety. The weaker, too, in their turn, often prey upon the stronger, and vex and molest them without relaxation. Consider that innumerable race of insects, which either are bred on the body of each animal or, flying about, infix their stings in him. These insects have others still less than themselves which torment them. And thus on each hand, before and behind, above and below, every animal is surrounded with enemies which incessantly seek his misery and destruction.

WHETHER HUMANKIND IS AN EXCEPTION

Man alone, said Demea, seems to be, in part, an exception to this rule. For by combination in society he can easily master lions, tigers, and bears, whose greater strength and agility naturally enable them to prey upon him.

On the contrary, it is here chiefly, cried Philo, that the uniform and equal maxims of nature are most apparent. Man, it is true, can, by combination, surmount all his *real* enemies and become master of the whole animal creation; but does he not immediately raise up to himself *imaginary* enemies, the demons of his fancy, who haunt him with superstitious terrors and blast every enjoyment of life? His pleasure, as he imagines, becomes in their eyes a crime; his food and repose give them umbrage and offence; his very sleep and dreams furnish new materials to anxious fear; and even death, his refuge from every other ill, presents only the dread of endless and innumerable woes. Nor does the wolf molest more the timid flock than superstition does the anxious breast of wretched mortals.

Besides, consider, Demea: This very society by which we surmount those wild beasts, our natural enemies, what new enemies does it not raise to us? What woe and misery does it not occasion? Man is the greatest enemy of man. Oppression, injustice, contempt, contumely, violence, sedition, war, calumny, treachery, fraud—by these they mutually torment each other, and they would soon dissolve that society which they had formed were it not for the dread of still greater ills which must attend their separation.

But though these external insults, said Demea, from animals, from men, from all the elements, which assault us form a frightful catalogue of woes, they are nothing in comparison of those which arise within ourselves, from the distempered condition of our mind and body. How many lie under the lingering torment of diseases? Hear the pathetic enumeration of the great poet.

> Intestine stone and ulcer, colic-pangs,
> Demoniac frenzy, moping melancholy,
> And moon-struck madness, pining atrophy,
> Marasmus, and wide-wasting pestilence.
> Dire was the tossing, deep the groans: *Despair*
> Tended the sick, busiest from couch to couch.
> And over them triumphant *Death* his dart
> Shook: but delay'd to strike, though oft invok'd
> With vows, as their chief good and final hope.

The disorders of the mind, continued Demea, though more secret, are not perhaps less dismal and vexatious. Remorse, shame, anguish, rage, disappointment, anxiety, fear, dejection, despair—who has ever passed through life without cruel inroads from these tormentors? How many have scarcely ever felt any better sensations? Labour and poverty, so abhorred by everyone, are the certain lot of the far greater number; and those few privileged persons who enjoy ease and opulence never reach contentment or true felicity. All the goods of life united would not make a very happy man, but all the ills united would make a wretch indeed; and any one of them almost (and who can be free from every one?), nay, often the absence of one good (and who can possess all?) is sufficient to render life ineligible.

Were a stranger to drop on a sudden into this world, I would show him, as a specimen of its ills, an hospital full of diseases, a prison crowded with malefactors and debtors, a field of battle strewed with carcases, a fleet foundering in the ocean, a nation languishing under tyranny, famine, or pestilence. To turn the gay side of life to him and give him a notion of its pleasures—whither should I conduct him? To a ball, to an opera, to court? He might justly think that I was only showing him a diversity of distress and sorrow.

There is no evading such striking instances, said Philo, but by apologies which still further aggravate the charge. Why have all men, I ask, in all ages, complained incessantly of the miseries of life?...They have no reason, says one: these complaints proceed only from their discontented, repining, anxious disposition....And can there possibly, I reply, be a more certain foundation of misery than such a wretched temper?

But if they were really as unhappy as they pretend, says my antagonist, why do they remain in life?...

Not satisfied with life, afraid of death—this is the secret chain, say I, that holds us. We are terrified, not bribed to the continuance of our existence.

It is only a false delicacy, he may insist, which a few refined spirits indulge, and which has spread these complaints among the whole race of mankind....And what is this delicacy, I ask, which you blame? Is it anything but a greater sensibility to all the pleasures and pains of life? And if the man of a delicate, refined temper, by being so much more alive than the rest of the world, is only so much more unhappy, what judgment must we form in general of human life?

Let men remain at rest, says our adversary, and they will be easy. They are willing artificers of their own misery....No! reply I: an anxious languor follows their repose; disappointment, vexation, trouble, their activity and ambition.

Is Happiness More Common Than Suffering?

I can observe something like what you mention in some others, replied Cleanthes, but I confess I feel little or nothing of it in myself, and hope that it is not so common as you represent it.

If you feel not human misery yourself, cried Demea, I congratulate you on so happy a singularity. Others, seemingly the most prosperous, have not been ashamed to vent their complaints in the most melancholy strains. Let us attend to the great, the fortunate emperor, Charles V, when, tired with human grandeur, he resigned all his extensive dominions into the hands of his son. In the last harangue which he made on that memorable occasion, he publicly avowed *that the greatest prosperities which he had ever enjoyed had been mixed with so many adversities that he might truly say he had never enjoyed any satisfaction or contentment.* But did the retired life in which he sought for shelter afford him any greater happiness? If we may credit his son's account, his repentance commenced the very day of his resignation.

Cicero's fortune, from small beginnings, rose to the greatest lustre and renown; yet what pathetic complaints of the ills of life do his familiar letters, as well as philosophical discourses, contain? And suitably to his own experience, he introduces Cato, the great, the fortunate Cato protesting in his old age that had he a new life in his offer he would reject the present.

Ask yourself, ask any of your acquaintance, whether they would live over again the last ten or twenty years of life. No! but the next twenty, they say, will be better:

And from the dreges of life, hope to receive
What the first sprightly running could not give.

Thus, at last, they find (such is the greatness of human misery, it reconciles even contradictions) that they complain at once of the shortness of life and of its vanity and sorrow.

What About God?

And is it possible, Cleanthes, said Philo, that after all these reflections, and infinitely more which might be suggested, you can still persevere in your anthropomorphism, and assert the moral attributes of the Deity, his justice, benevolence, mercy, and rectitude, to be of the same nature with these virtues in human creatures? His power, we allow, is infinite; whatever he wills is executed; but neither man nor any other animal is happy; therefore, he does not will their happiness. His wisdom is infinite; he is never mistaken in choosing the means to any end; but the course of nature tends not to human or animal felicity; therefore, it is not established for that purpose. Through the whole compass of human knowledge there are no inferences more certain and infallible than these. In what respect, then, do his benevolence and mercy resemble the benevolence and mercy of men?

Epicurus' old questions are yet unanswered.

Is he willing to prevent evil, but not able? then is he impotent. Is he able, but not willing? then is he malevolent. Is he both able and willing? whence then is evil?

You ascribe, Cleanthes, (and I believe justly) a purpose and intention to nature. But what, I beseech you, is the object of that curious artifice and machinery which she has displayed in all animals—the preservation alone of individuals, and propagation of the species? It seems enough for her purpose, if such a rank be barely upheld in the universe, without any care or concern for the happiness of the members that compose it. No resource for this purpose: no machinery in order merely to give pleasure or ease; no fund of pure joy and contentment; no indulgence without some want or necessity accompanying it. At least, the few phenomena of this nature are overbalanced by opposite phenomena of still greater importance.

Our sense of music, harmony, and indeed beauty of all kinds, gives satisfaction, without being absolutely necessary to the preservation and propagation of the species. But what racking pains, on the other hand, arise from gouts, gravels, megrims, toothaches, rheumatisms, where the injury to the animal machinery is either small or incurable? Mirth, laughter, play, frolic seem gratuitous satisfactions which have no further tendency; spleen, melancholy, discontent, superstition are pains of the same nature. How then does the Divine benevolence display itself, in the sense of you anthropomorphites? None but we mystics, as you were pleased to call us, can account for this strange mixture of phenomena, by deriving it from attributes infinitely perfect but incomprehensible.

And have you, at last, said Cleanthes smiling, betrayed your intentions, Philo? Your long agreement with Demea did indeed a little surprise me, but I find you were all the while erecting a concealed battery against me. And I must confess that you have now fallen upon a subject worthy of your noble spirit of opposition and controversy. If you can make out the present point, and prove mankind to be unhappy or corrupted, there is an end at once of all religion. For to what purpose establish the natural attributes of the Deity, while the moral are still doubtful and uncertain?

You take umbrage very easily, replied Demea, at opinions the most innocent and the most generally received, even amongst the religious and devout themselves; and nothing can be more surprising than to find a topic like this—concerning the wickedness and misery of man—charged with no less than atheism and profaneness. Have not all pious divines and preachers who have indulged their rhetoric on so fertile a subject, have they not easily, I say, given a solution of any difficulties which may attend it? This world is but a point in comparison of the universe; this life but a moment in comparison of eternity. The present evil phenomena, therefore, are rectified in other regions, and in some future period of existence. And the eyes of men, being then opened to larger views of things, see the whole connection of general laws, and trace, with adoration, the benevolence and rectitude of the Deity through all the mazes and intricacies of his providence.

No! replied Cleanthes, no! These arbitrary suppositions can never be admitted, contrary to matter of fact, visible and uncontroverted. Whence can any cause be known but from its known effects? Whence can any hypothesis be proved but from the apparent phenomena? To establish one hypothesis upon another is building entirely in the air; and the utmost we ever attain by these conjectures and fictions is to ascertain the base possibility of our opinion, but never can we, upon such terms, establish its reality.

The only method of supporting Divine benevolence—and it is what I willingly embrace—is to deny absolutely the misery and wickedness of man. Your representations are exaggerated; your melancholy views mostly fictitious; your inferences contrary to fact and experience. Health is more common than sickness; pleasure than pain; happiness than misery. And for one vexation which we meet with, we attain, upon computation, a hundred enjoyments.

Admitting your position, replied Philo, which yet is extremely doubtful, you must at the same time allow that, if pain be less frequent than pleasure, it is infinitely more violent and durable. One hour of it is often able to outweigh a day, a week, a month of our common insipid enjoyments; and how many days, weeks, and months are passed by several in the most acute torments? Pleasure, scarcely in one instance, is ever able to reach ecstasy and rapture; and in no one instance can it continue for any time at its highest pitch and altitude. The spirits evaporate, the nerves relax, the fabric is disordered, and the enjoyment quickly degenerates into fatigue and uneasiness. But pain often, good God, how often! rises to torture and agony; and the longer it continues, it becomes still more genuine agony and torture. Patience is exhausted, courage languishes, melancholy seizes us, and nothing terminates our misery but the removal of its cause or another event which is the sole cure of all evil, but which, from our natural folly, we regard with still greater horror and consternation.

But not to insist upon these topics, continued Philo, though most obvious, certain, and important, I must use the freedom to admonish you, Cleanthes, that you have put the controversy upon a most dangerous issue, and are unawares introducing a total scepticism into the most essential articles of natural and revealed theology. What! no method of fixing a just foundation for religion unless we allow the happiness of human life, and maintain a continued existence even in this world, with all our present pains, infirmities, vexations, and follies, to be eligible and desirable! But this is contrary to everyone's feeling and experience; it is contrary to an authority so established as nothing can subvert. No decisive proofs can ever be produced against this authority; nor is it possible for you to compute, estimate, and compare all the pains and all the pleasures in the lives of all men and of all animals; and thus, by your resting the whole system of religion on a point which, from its very nature, must for ever be uncertain, you tacitly confess that that system is equally uncertain.

But allowing you what never will be believed, at least, what you never possibly can prove, that animal or, at least, human happiness in this life exceeds its misery, you have yet done nothing; for this is not, by any means, what we expect from infinite power, infinite wisdom, and infinite goodness. Why is there any misery at all in the world? Not by chance, surely. From some cause then. Is it from the intention of the Deity? But he is perfectly benevolent. Is it contrary to his intention? But he is almighty. Nothing can shake the solidity of this reasoning, so short, so clear, so decisive, except we assert that these subjects exceed all human capacity, and that our common measures of truth and falsehood are not applicable to them—a topic which I have all along insisted on, but which you have, from the beginning, rejected with scorn and indignation.

But I will be contented to retire still from this intrenchment, for I deny that you can ever force me in it. I will allow that pain or misery in man is *compatible* with infinite power and goodness in the Deity, even in your sense of these attributes: what are you advanced by all these concessions? A mere possible compatibility is not sufficient. You must *prove* these pure, unmixt, and uncontrollable attributes from the present mixed and confused phenomena, and from these alone. A hopeful undertaking! Were the phenomena ever so pure and unmixed, yet, being finite, they would be insufficient for that purpose. How much more, where they are also so jarring and discordant!

Here, Cleanthes, I find myself at ease in my argument. Here I triumph. Formerly, when we argued concerning the natural attributes of intelligence and design, I needed all my sceptical and metaphysical subtilty to elude your grasp. In many views of the universe and of its parts, particularly the latter, the beauty and fitness of final causes strike us with such irresistible force that all objections appear (what I believe they really are) mere cavils and sophisms; nor can we then imagine how it was ever possible for us to repose any weight on them. But there is no view of human life or of the condition of mankind from which, without the greatest violence, we can infer the moral attributes or learn that infinite benevolence, conjoined with infinite power and infinite wisdom, which we must discover by the eyes of faith alone. It is your turn now to tug the labouring oar, and to support your philosophical subtilties against the dictates of plain reason and experience.

STUDY QUESTIONS

1. Summarize and evaluate the respective positions of the three speakers on the nature and extent of suffering in the world.
2. What can you discern, if anything, about each speaker's position on the issue of whether humankind is, on balance, happy?
3. Reconstruct and evaluate Philo's case that anthropomorphism in religious descriptions of the attributes of the Deity (e.g., benevolence, goodness, mercy, intention, knowledge, etc.) has implications for how a being who possesses them would act with respect to evil.
4. Cleanthes is pictured as resting the credibility of both natural theology (theological truths known by reason) and revealed theology (theological truths known from sacred scripture and tradition) on what debatable claim? How do Demea and Philo reply to this claim?

Gottfried Leibniz

Best of All Possible Worlds Theodicy

Gottfried Wilhelm von Leibniz (1646–1716), a German philosopher who held rationalist and idealist positions, articulated a comprehensive theodicy. He argues that God, who possesses perfect power, knowledge, and goodness, would choose to bring about the best possible world. Many interpret this point to mean that this world contains the least possible amount of evil, but it is better interpreted as meaning that this world contains the least amount of evil commensurate with its being the best world possible. As Leibniz points out, God knows which evils are necessarily connected to greater goods such that those goods could not otherwise be achieved—and it is the whole collection of goods and evils in the actual world make that it the best one possible. Leibniz also argues that the presence of sin and evil allowed for the incarnation of the Son of God and his redemptive work for humanity, which is an unsurpassably great good. Because of this fact, Leibniz reasons, the human fall into sin was a *felix culpa* (a "fortunate flaw" or "happy fault"). Also, on Leibniz's view, God's foreknowledge of human acts does not prevent those acts from being free.

God Would Choose the Best World

I. *Objection.* Whoever does not choose the best is lacking in power, or in knowledge, or in goodness.

God did not choose the best in creating this world.

Therefore, God has been lacking in power, or in knowledge, or in goodness.

Answer. I deny the minor, that is, the second premise of this syllogism; and our opponent proves it by this.

Prosyllogism. Whoever makes things in which there is evil, which could have been made without any evil, or the making of which could have been omitted, does not choose the best.

God has made a world in which there is evil; a world, I say, which could have been made without any evil, or the making of which could have been omitted altogether.

Therefore, God has not chosen the best.

Answer. I grant the minor of this prosyllogism; for it must be confessed that there is evil in this world which God has made, and that it was possible to make

From Gottfried Leibniz, *The Theodicy: Abridgement of the Argument Reduced to Syllogistic Form* (1710).

a world without evil, or even not to create a world at all, for its creation has depended on the free will of God; but I deny the major, that is, the first of the two premises of the prosyllogism, and I might content myself with simply demanding its proof; but in order to make the matter clearer, I have wished to justify this denial by showing that the best plan is not always that which seeks to avoid evil, since it may happen that *the evil is accompanied by a greater good*. For example, a general of an army will prefer a great victory with a slight wound to a condition without wound and without victory. We have proved this more fully in the large work by making it clear, by instances taken from mathematics and elsewhere, that an imperfection in the part may be required for a greater perfection in the whole. In this I have followed the opinion of St. Augustine, who has said a hundred times, that God has permitted evil in order to bring about good, that is, a greater good; and that of Thomas Aquinas (in libr. II. sent. dist. 32, qu. I, art. 1), that the permitting of evil tends to the good of the universe. I have shown that the ancients called Adam's fall *felix culpa*, a happy sin, because it had been retrieved with immense advantage by the incarnation of the Son of God, who has given to the universe something nobler than anything that ever would have been among creatures except for it. For the sake of a clearer understanding, I have added, following many good authors, that it was in accordance with order and the general good that God allowed to certain creatures the opportunity of exercising their liberty, even when he foresaw that they would turn to evil, but which he could so well rectify; because it was not fitting that, in order to hinder sin, God should always act in an extraordinary manner. To overthrow this objection, therefore, it is sufficient to show that a world with evil might be better than a world without evil; but I have gone even farther, in the work, and have even proved that this universe must be in reality better than every other possible universe....

FOREKNOWLEDGE IS COMPATIBLE WITH HUMAN FREEDOM

III. *Objection*. If it is always impossible not to sin, it is always unjust to punish.

Now, it is always impossible not to sin; or, in other words, every sin is necessary.

Therefore, it is always unjust to punish.

The minor of this is proved thus:

1. *Prosyllogism*. All that is predetermined is necessary.

Every event is predetermined.

Therefore, every event (and consequently sin also) is necessary.

Again this second minor is proved thus:

2. *Prosyllogism*. That which is future, that which is foreseen, that which is involved in the causes, is predetermined.

Every event is such.

Therefore, every event is predetermined.

Answer. I admit in a certain sense the conclusion of the second prosyllogism, which is the minor of the first; but I shall deny the major of the first prosyllogism, namely, that every thing predetermined is necessary; understanding by the *necessity* of sinning, for example, or by the impossibility of not sinning, or of not performing any action, the necessity with which we are here concerned, that is, that which is essential and absolute, and which destroys the morality of an action and the justice of punishments. For if anyone understood another necessity or impossibility, namely, a necessity which should be only moral, or which was only hypothetical (as will be explained shortly); it is clear that I should deny the major of the objection itself. I might content myself with this answer and demand the proof of the proposition denied; but I have again desired to explain my procedure in this work, in order to better elucidate the matter and to throw more light on the whole subject, by explaining the necessity which ought to be rejected and the determination which must take place. That *necessity* which is contrary to morality and which ought to be rejected, and which would render punishment unjust, is an insurmountable necessity which would make all opposition useless, even if we should wish with all our heart to avoid the necessary action, and should make all possible efforts to that end. Now, it is manifest that this is not applicable to voluntary actions, because we would not perform them if we did not choose to. Also their prevision and predetermination are not absolute, but presuppose the will: if it is certain that we shall perform them, it is not less certain that we shall choose to perform them. These voluntary actions and their consequences will not take place no matter what we do or whether we wish them or not; but, *through* that which we shall do and through that which we shall wish to do, which leads to them. And this is involved in prevision and in predetermination, and even constitutes their ground. And the necessity of such an event is called conditional or hypothetical, or the necessity of consequence, because it supposes the will, and the other *requisites*; whereas the necessity which destroys morality and renders punishment unjust and reward useless, exists in things which will be whatever we may do or whatever we may wish to do, and, in a word, is in that which is essential; and this is what is called an absolute necessity. Thus it is to no purpose, as regards what is absolutely necessary, to make prohibitions or commands, to propose penalties or prizes, to praise or to blame; it will be none the less. On the other hand, in voluntary actions and in that which depends upon them, precepts armed with power to punish and to recompense are very often of use and are included in the order of causes which make an action exist. And it is for this reason that not only cares and labors but also prayers are useful; God having had these prayers in view before he regulated things and having had that consideration for them which was proper. This is why the precept which says *ora et labora* (pray and work), holds altogether good; and not only those who (under the vain pretext of the necessity of events) pretend that the care which business demands may be neglected, but also those who reason against prayer, fall into what the ancients even then called the *lazy sophism*. Thus the predetermination of events by causes is just what contributes to morality instead of destroying it, and causes incline the will, without compelling it. This is why the *determination* in question is not a necessitation—it is certain (to him who knows all) that the effect will follow this inclination; but this effect does not follow by a necessary consequence, that is, one the contrary of which implies contradiction. It is also by an internal inclination such as this that the will is determined, without there being any necessity. Suppose that one has the greatest passion in the world (a great thirst, for example), you will admit to me that the soul can find some reason for resisting it, if it were only that of

showing its power. Thus, although one may never be in a perfect indifference of equilibrium and there may be always a preponderance of inclination for the side taken, it, nevertheless, never renders the resolution taken absolutely necessary.

God Wills Perfection but Permits Sin

IV. *Objection*. Whoever can prevent the sin of another and does not do so, but rather contributes to it although he is well informed of it, is accessory to it.

God can prevent the sin of intelligent creatures; but he does not do so, and rather contributes to it by his concurrence and by the opportunities which he brings about, although he has a perfect knowledge of it.

Hence, etc.

Answer. I deny the major of this syllogism. For it is possible that one could prevent sin, but ought not, because he could not do it without himself committing a sin, or (when God is in question) without performing an unreasonable action. Examples have been given and the application to God himself has been made. It is possible also that we contribute to evil and that sometimes we even open the road to it, in doing things which we are obliged to do; and, when we do our duty or (in speaking of God) when, after thorough consideration, we do that which reason demands, we are not responsible for the results, even when we foresee them. We do not desire these evils; but we are willing to permit them for the sake of a greater good which we cannot reasonably help preferring to other considerations. And this is a *consequent* will, which results from *antecedent* wills by which we will the good. I know that some persons, in speaking of the antecedent and consequent will of God, have understood by the *antecedent* that which wills that all men should be saved; and by the consequent, that which wills, in consequence of persistent sin, that some should be damned. But these are merely illustrations of a more general idea, and it may be said for the same reason that God, by his antecedent will, wills that men should not sin; and by his consequent or final and decreeing will (that which is always followed by its effect), he wills to permit them to sin, this permission being the result of superior reasons. And we have the right to say in general that the antecedent will of God tends to the production of good and the prevention of evil, each taken in itself and as if alone (*particulariter et secundum quid*, Thom. I, qu. 19, art. 6), according to the measure of the degree of each good and each evil; but that the divine consequent or final or total will tends toward the production of as many goods as may be put together, the combination of which becomes in this way determined, and includes also the permission of some evils and the exclusion of some goods, as the best possible plan for the universe demands. Arminius, in his *Antiperkinsus*, has very well explained that the will of God may be called consequent, not only in relation to the action of the creature considered beforehand in the divine understanding, but also in relation to other anterior divine acts of will. But this consideration of the passage cited from Thomas Aquinas, and that from Scotus (I. dist. 46, qu. XI), is enough to show that they make this distinction as I have done here. Nevertheless, if anyone objects to this use of terms let him substitute *deliberating* will, in place of antecedent, and final or decreeing will, in place of consequent. For I do not wish to dispute over words.

GOD DOES NOT CAUSE SIN

V. *Objection*. Whoever produces all that is real in a thing, is its cause.

God produces all that is real in sin.

Hence, God is the cause of sin.

Answer. I might content myself with denying the major or the minor, since the term real admits of interpretations which would render these propositions false. But in order to explain more clearly, I will make a distinction. *Real* signifies either that which is positive only, or, it includes also privative beings: in the first case, I deny the major and admit the minor; in the second case, I do the contrary. I might have limited myself to this, but I have chosen to proceed still farther and give the reason for this distinction. I have been very glad therefore to draw attention to the fact that every reality purely positive or absolute is a perfection; and that imperfection comes from limitation, that is, from the privative: for to limit is

to refuse progress, or the greatest possible progress. Now God is the cause of all perfections and consequently of all realities considered as purely positive. But limitations or privations result from the original imperfection of creatures, which limits their receptivity. And it is with them as with a loaded vessel, which the river causes to move more or less slowly according to the weight which it carries: thus its speed depends upon the river, but the retardation which limits this speed comes from the load. Thus in the *Theodicy*, we have shown how the creature, in causing sin, is a defective cause; how errors and evil inclinations are born of privation; and how privation is accidentally efficient; and I have justified the opinion of St. Augustine (lib. I, ad Simpl. qu. 2) who explains, for example, how God makes the soul obdurate, not by giving it something evil, but because the effect of his good impression is limited by the soul's resistance and by the circumstances which contribute to this resistance, so that he does not give it all the good which would overcome its evil. *Nec* (inquit) *ab illo erogatur aliquid quo homo fit deterior, sed tantum quo fit melior non erogatur*. But if God had wished to do more, he would have had to make either other natures for creatures or other miracles to change their natures, things which the best plan could not admit. It is as if the current of the river must be more rapid than its fall admitted or that the boats should be loaded more lightly, if it were necessary to make them move more quickly. And the original limitation or imperfection of creatures requires that even the best plan of the universe could not receive more good, and could not be exempt from certain evils, which, however, are to result in a greater good. There are certain disorders in the parts which marvelously enhance the beauty of the whole; just as certain dissonances, when properly used, render harmony more beautiful. But this depends on what has already been said in answer to the first objection.

GOD IS NOT CULPABLE FOR NOT PREVENTING SIN

VII. *Objection*. Whoever gives only to some, and not to all, the means which produces in them effectively a good will and salutary final faith, has not sufficient goodness.

God does this.

Hence, etc.

Answer. I deny the major of this. It is true that God could overcome the greatest resistance of the human heart; and does it, too, sometimes, either by internal grace, or by external circumstances which have a great effect on souls; but he does not always do this. Whence comes this distinction? it may be asked, and why does his goodness seem limited? It is because, as I have already said in answering the first objection, it would not have been in order always to act in an extraordinary manner, and to reverse the connection of things. The reasons of this connection, by means of which one is placed in more favorable circumstances than another, are hidden in the depths of the wisdom of God; they depend upon the universal harmony. The best plan of the universe, which God could not fail to choose, made it so. We judge from the event itself; since God has made it, it was not possible to do better. Far from being true that this conduct is contrary to goodness, it is supreme goodness which led him to it. This objection with its solution might have been drawn from what was said in regard to the first objection; but it seemed useful to touch upon it separately.

God Freely Chooses The Best World

VIII. *Objection.* Whoever cannot fail to choose the best, is not free.

God cannot fail to choose the best.

Hence, God is not free.

Answer. I deny the major of this argument; it is rather true liberty, and the most perfect, to be able to use one's free will for the best, and to always exercise this power, without ever being turned aside either by external force or by internal passions, the first of which causes slavery of the body, the second, slavery of the soul. There is nothing less servile, and nothing more in accordance with the highest degree of freedom, than to be always led toward the good, and always by one's own inclination, without any constraint and

without any displeasure. And to object therefore that God had need of external things, is only a sophism. He created them freely; but having proposed to himself an end, which is to exercise his goodness, wisdom has determined him to choose the means best fitted to attain this end. To call this a need, is to take that term in an unusual sense which frees it from all imperfection, just as when we speak of the wrath of God.

Seneca has somewhere said that God commanded but once but that he obeys always, because he obeys laws which he willed to prescribe to himself: *semel jussit, semper paret.* But he might better have said that God always commands and that he is always obeyed; for in willing, he always follows the inclination of his own nature, and all other things always follow his will. And as this will is always the same, it cannot be said that he obeys only that will which he formerly had. Nevertheless, although his will is always infallible and always tends toward the best, the evil, or the lesser good, which he rejects, does not cease to be possible in itself; otherwise the necessity of the good would be geometrical (so to speak), or metaphysical, and altogether absolute; the contingency of things would be destroyed, and there would be no choice. But this sort of necessity, which does not destroy the possibility of the contrary, has this name only by analogy; it becomes effective, not by the pure essence of things, but by that which is outside of them, above them, namely, by the will of God. This necessity is called moral, because, to the sage, *necessity* and *what ought to be* are equivalent things; and when it always has its effect, as it really has in the perfect sage, that is, in God, it may be said that it is a happy necessity. The nearer creatures approach to it, the nearer they approach to perfect happiness. Also this kind of necessity is not that which we try to avoid and which destroys morality, rewards, and praise. For that which it brings, does not happen whatever we may do or will, but because we will it so. And a will to which it is natural to choose well, merits praise so much the more; also it carries its reward with it, which is sovereign happiness. And as this constitution of the divine nature gives entire satisfaction to him who possesses it, it is also the best and the most desirable for the creatures who are all dependent on God. If the will of God did not have for a rule the principle of the best, it would either tend toward evil, which would be the worst; or it would be in some way indifferent to good and to evil, and would be guided by chance: but a will which would allow itself always to act by chance, would not be worth more for the government of the universe than the fortuitous concourse of atoms, without there being any divinity therein. And even if God should abandon himself to chance only in some cases and in a certain way (as he would do, if he did not always work entirely for the best and if he were capable of preferring a lesser work to a greater, that is, an evil to a good, since that which prevents a greater good is an evil), he would be imperfect, as well as the object of his choice; he would not merit entire confidence; he would act without reason in such a case, and the government of the universe would be like certain games, equally divided between reason and chance. All this proves that this objection which is made against the choice of the best, perverts the notions of the free and of the necessary, and represents to us the best even as evil: which is either malicious or ridiculous.

STUDY QUESTIONS

1. Reconstruct Leibniz's argument that God would choose to create the best of all possible worlds. Which aspects of this argument seem strong to you? Which ones seem weak?
2. How effective is the argument that all evil in the world is justified by being connected to a greater good—that is, to the world's being the best possible? Is this sufficient to justify the divine permission of evil?
3. Leibniz claims that foreknowledge is compatible with human freedom and that a good God could consent to creaturely sin that he foreknows. Explain and evaluate both parts of this position.

J. L. Mackie

Evil and Omnipotence

J. L. Mackie (1917–1981) offers a contemporary statement of what professional philosophers call the "logical problem of evil." Essentially, he argues that theism is logically incoherent and therefore irrational. He claims that the theistic belief that God is omnipotent, omniscient, and wholly good and the belief that there is evil in the world are logically inconsistent. Since the alleged inconsistency in theism is implicit rather than explicit, Mackie offers various supplementary statements to highlight the inconsistency, mostly in the form of definitions of key terms, such as *omnipotence*. Omnipotence, he says, is the power to bring about any logically possible state of affairs, including the prevention or elimination of evil. Mackie then goes on to show why various theistic attempts to eliminate the inconsistency are weak and unsuccessful, concluding that any adequate theistic answer would have to modify at least one key theistic concept. For example, theists unwittingly modify the concept of omnipotence by saying that God limits himself to allow for creaturely freedom to commit evil because this is a corollary to the freedom to do good. For Mackie, this kind of move implicitly surrenders the core theistic position by denying a strong definition of omnipotence. The Paradox of Omnipotence, which he explains, is the problem of whether an omnipotent Deity can create finite creatures that it cannot subsequently control. He argues that it is not possible both that God is genuinely omnipotent and that he was unable to create a universe containing moral good but no moral evil.

The traditional arguments for the existence of God have been fairly thoroughly criticised by philosophers. But the theologian can, if he wishes, accept this criticism. He can admit that no rational proof of God's existence is possible. And he can still retain all that is essential to his position, by holding that God's existence is known in some other, non-rational way.

I think, however, that a more telling criticism can be made by way of traditional problem of evil. Here it can be shown, not that religious beliefs lack rational support, but that they are positively irrational, that the several parts of the essential theological doctrine are inconsistent with one another, so that the theologian can maintain his position as a whole only by a

Mind 64 (1955): 200–212. Reprinted by permission of Oxford University Press.

much more extreme rejection of reason than in the former case. He must now be prepared to believe, not merely what cannot be proved, but what can be *disproved* from other beliefs that he also holds.

The problem of evil, in the sense in which I shall be using the phrase, is a problem only for someone who believes that there is a God who is both omnipotent and wholly good. And it is a logical problem, the problem of clarifying and reconciling a number of beliefs: it is not a scientific problem that might be solved by further observations, or a practical problem that might be solved by a decision or an action. These points are obvious; I mention them only because they are sometimes ignored by theologians, who sometimes parry a statement of the problem with such remarks as "Well, can you solve the problem yourself?" or "This is a mystery which may be revealed to us later" or "Evil is something to be faced and overcome, not to be merely discussed."

In its simplest form the problem is this: God is omnipotent; God is wholly good; and yet evil exists. There seems to be some contradiction between these three propositions, so that if any two of them were true the third would be false. But at the same time all three are essential parts of most theological positions: the theologian, it seems, at once *must* adhere and *cannot consistently* adhere to all three. (The problem does not arise only for theists, but I shall discuss it in the form in which it presents itself for ordinary theism.)

However, the contradiction does not arise immediately; to show it we need some additional premises, or perhaps some quasi-logical rules connecting the terms "good," "evil," and "omnipotent." These additional principles are that good is opposed to evil, in such a way that a good thing always eliminates evil as far as it can, and that there are no limits to what an omnipotent thing can do. From these it follows that a good omnipotent thing eliminates evil completely, and then the propositions that a good omnipotent thing exists, and that evil exists, are incompatible.

Adequate Solutions

Now once the problem is fully stated it is clear that it can be solved, in the sense that the problem will not arise if one gives up at least one of the propositions that constitute it. If you are prepared to say that God is not wholly good, or not quite omnipotent, or that evil does not exist, or that good is not opposed to the kind of evil that exists, or that there are limits to what an omnipotent thing can do, then the problem of evil will not arise for you.

There are, then, quite a number of adequate solutions of the problem of evil, and some of these have been adopted, or almost adopted, by various thinkers. For example, a few have been prepared to deny God's omnipotence, and rather more have been prepared to keep the term "omnipotence" but severely to restrict its meaning, recording quite a number of things that an omnipotent being cannot do. Some have said that evil is an illusion, perhaps because they held that the whole world of temporal, changing things is an illusion, and that what we call evil belongs only to this world, or perhaps because they held that although temporal things *are* much as we see them, those that we call evil are not really evil. Some have said that what we call evil is merely the privation of good, that evil in a positive sense, evil that would really be opposed to good, does not exist. Many have agreed with Pope that disorder is harmony not understood, and that partial evil is universal good. Whether any of these views is *true* is, of course, another question. But each of them gives an adequate solution of the problem of evil in the sense that if you accept it this problem does not arise for you, though you may, of course, have *other* problems to face.

But often enough these adequate solutions are only *almost* adopted. The thinkers who restrict God's power, but keep the term "omnipotence," may reasonably be suspected of thinking, in other contexts, that his power is really unlimited. Those who say that evil is an illusion may also be thinking, inconsistently, that this illusion is itself an evil. Those who say that "evil" is merely privation of good may also be thinking, inconsistently, that privation of good is an evil. (The fallacy here is akin to some forms of the "naturalistic fallacy" in ethics, where some think, for example, that "good" is just what contributes to evolutionary progress, and that evolutionary progress is itself good.) If Pope meant what he said in the first line of his couplet, that "disorder" is only harmony not understood, the "partial evil" of the second line must, for consistency, mean "that which, taken in isolation, falsely appears to be evil," but it would more naturally mean "that which, in isolation, really is evil." The second line, in fact, hesitates between two views, that "partial evil" isn't really evil, since only the universal quality is real, and that "partial evil" is really an evil, but only a little one.

In addition, therefore, to adequate solutions, we must recognise unsatisfactory inconsistent solutions, in which there is only a half-hearted or temporary rejection of one of the propositions which together constitute the problem. In these, one of the constituent propositions is explicitly rejected, but it is covertly re-asserted or assumed elsewhere in the system.

Fallacious Solutions

Besides these half-hearted solutions, which explicitly reject but implicitly assert one of the constituent propositions, there are definitely fallacious solutions which explicitly maintain all the constituent propositions, but implicitly reject at least one of them in the course of the argument that explains away the problem of evil.

There are, in fact, many so-called solutions which purport to remove the contradiction without abandoning any of its constituent propositions. These must be fallacious, as we can see from the very statement of the problem, but it is not so easy to see in each case precisely where the fallacy lies. I suggest that in all cases the fallacy has the general form suggested above: in order to solve the problem one (or perhaps more) of its constituent propositions is given up, but in such a way that it appears to have been retained, and can therefore be asserted without qualification in other contexts. Sometimes there is a further complication: the supposed solution moves to and fro between, say, two of the constituent propositions, at one point asserting the first of these but covertly abandoning the second, at another point asserting the second but covertly abandoning the first. These fallacious solutions often turn upon some equivocation with the words "good" and "evil," or upon some vagueness about the way in which good and evil

are opposed to one another, or about how much is meant by "omnipotence." I propose to examine some of these so-called solutions, and to exhibit their fallacies in detail. Incidentally, I shall also be considering whether an adequate solution could be reached by a minor modification of one or more of the constituent propositions, which would, however, still satisfy all the essential requirements of ordinary theism.

1. "Good Cannot Exist Without Evil" or "Evil Is Necessary as a Counterpart to Good"

It is sometimes suggested that evil is necessary as a counterpart to good, that if there were no evil there could be no good either, and that this solves the problem of evil. It is true that it points to an answer to the question "Why should there be evil?" But it does so only by qualifying some of the propositions that constitute the problem.

First, it sets a limit to what God can do, saying that God *cannot* create good without simultaneously creating evil, and this means either that God is not omnipotent or that there are *some* limits to what an omnipotent thing can do. It may be replied that these limits are always presupposed, that omnipotence has never meant the power to do what is logically impossible, and on the present view the existence of good without evil would be a logical impossibility. This interpretation of omnipotence may, indeed, be accepted as a modification of our original account which does not reject anything that is essential to theism, and I shall in general assume it in the subsequent discussion. It is, perhaps, the most common theistic view, but I think that some theists at least have maintained that God can do what is logically impossible. Many theists, at any rate, have held that logic itself is created or laid down by God, that logic is the way in which God arbitrarily chooses to think. (This is, of course, parallel to the ethical view that morally right actions are those which God arbitrarily chooses to command, and the two views encounter similar difficulties.) And *this* account of logic is clearly inconsistent with the view that God is bound by logical necessities—unless it is possible for an omnipotent being to bind himself, an issue which we shall consider later, when we come to the Paradox of Omnipotence. This solution of the problem of evil cannot, therefore, be consistently adopted along with the view that logic is itself created by God.

But, secondly, this solution denies that evil is opposed to good in our original sense. If good and evil are counterparts, a good thing will not "eliminate evil as far as it can." Indeed, this view suggests that good and evil are not strictly qualities of things at all. Perhaps the suggestion is that good and evil are related in much the same way as great and small. Certainly, when the term "great" is used relatively as a condensation of "greater than so-and-so," and "small" is used correspondingly, greatness and smallness are counterparts and cannot exist without each other. But in this sense greatness is not a quality, not an intrinsic feature of anything; and it would be absurd to think of a movement in favour of greatness and against smallness in this sense. Such a movement would be self-defeating, since relative greatness can be promoted only by a simultaneous promotion of relative smallness. I feel sure that no theists would be content to regard God's goodness as analogous to this—as if what he supports were not the *good* but the *better*, and as if he had the paradoxical aim that all things should be better than other things.

This point is obscured by the fact that "great" and "small" seem to have an absolute as well as a relative sense. I cannot discuss here whether there is absolute magnitude or not, but if there is, there could be an absolute sense for "great," it could mean of at least a certain size, and it would make sense to speak of all things getting bigger, of a universe that was expanding all over, and therefore it would make sense to speak of promoting greatness. But in *this* sense great and small are not logically necessary counterparts: either quality could exist without the other. There would be no logical impossibility in everything's being small or in everything's being great.

Neither in the absolute nor in the relative sense, then, of "great" and "small" do these terms provide an analogy of the sort that would be needed to support this solution of the problem of evil. In neither case are greatness and smallness *both* necessary counterparts *and* mutually opposed forces or possible objects for support and attack.

It may be replied that good and evil are necessary counterparts in the same way as any quality and its logical opposite: redness can occur, it is suggested, only if non-redness also occurs. But unless evil is merely the privation of good, they are not logical opposites, and some further argument would be needed to show that they are counterparts in the same way as genuine logical opposites. Let us assume that this could be given. There is still doubt of the correctness of the metaphysical principle that a quality must have a real opposite: I suggest that it is not really impossible that everything should be, say, red, that the truth is merely that if everything were red we should not notice redness, and so we should have no word "red"; we observe and give names to qualities only if they have real opposites. If so, the principle that a term must have an opposite would belong only to our language or to our thought, and would not be an ontological principle, and, correspondingly, the rule that good cannot exist without evil would not state a logical necessity of a sort that God would just have to put up with. God might have made everything good, though *we* should not have noticed it if he had.

But, finally, even if we concede that this is an ontological principle, it will provide a solution for the problem of evil only if one is prepared to say, "Evil exists, but only just enough evil to serve as the counterpart of good." I doubt whether any theist will accept this. After all, the *ontological* requirement that non-redness should occur would be satisfied even if all the universe, except for a minute speck, were red, and, if there were a corresponding requirement for evil as a counterpart to good, a minute dose of evil would presumably do. But theists are not usually willing to say, in all contexts, that all the evil that occurs is a minute and necessary dose.

2. "Evil Is Necessary as a Means to Good"

It is sometimes suggested that evil is necessary for good not as a counterpart but as a means. In its simple form this has little plausibility as a solution of the problem of evil, since it obviously implies a severe restriction of God's power. It would be a *causal* law that you cannot have a certain end without a certain means, so that if God has to introduce evil as a means to good, he must be subject to at least some causal laws. This certainly conflicts with what a theist normally means by omnipotence. This view of God as limited by causal laws also conflicts with the view that causal laws are themselves made by God, which is more widely held than the corresponding view about the laws of logic. This conflict, would, indeed, be resolved if it were possible for an omnipotent being to bind himself, and this possibility has still to be considered. Unless a favourable answer can be given to this question, the suggestion that evil is necessary as a means to good solves the problem of evil only by denying one of its constituent propositions, either that God is omnipotent or that "omnipotent" means what it says.

3. "The Universe Is Better with Some Evil in It Than It Could Be If There Were No Evil"

Much more important is a solution which at first seems to be a mere variant of the previous one, that evil may contribute to the goodness of a whole in which it is found, so that the universe as a whole is better as it is, with some evil in it, than it would be if there were no evil. This solution may be developed in either of two ways. It may be supported by an aesthetic analogy, by the fact that contrasts heighten beauty, that in a musical work, for example, there may occur discords which somehow add to the beauty of the work as a whole. Alternatively, it may be worked out in connexion with the notion of progress, that the best possible organisation of the universe will not be static, but progressive, that the gradual overcoming of evil by good is really a finer thing than would be the eternal unchallenged supremacy of good.

In either case, this solution usually starts from the assumption that the evil whose existence gives rise to the problem of evil is primarily what is called physical evil, that is to say, pain. In Hume's rather half-hearted presentation of the problem of evil, the evils that he stresses are pain and disease, and those who reply to him argue that the existence of pain and disease makes possible the existence of sympathy, benevolence, heroism, and the gradually successful struggle of doctors and reformers to overcome these evils. In fact, theists often seize the opportunity to accuse those who stress the problem of evil of taking a low, materialistic view of good and evil, equating these with pleasure and pain, and of ignoring the more spiritual goods which can arise in the struggle against evils.

But let us see exactly what is being done here. Let us call pain and misery "first order evil" or "evil (1)." What contrasts with this, namely, pleasure and happiness, will be called "first order good" or "good (1)." Distinct from this is "second order good" or "good (2)" which somehow emerges in a complex situation in which evil (1) is a necessary component—logically, not merely causally, necessary. (Exactly *how* it emerges does not matter: in the crudest version of this solution good (2) is simply the heightening of happiness by the contrast with misery, in other versions it includes sympathy with suffering, heroism in facing danger, and the gradual decrease of first order evil and increase of first order good.) It is also being assumed that second order good is more important than first order good or evil, in particular that it more than outweighs the first order evil it involves.

Now that is a particularly subtle attempt to solve the problem of evil. It defends God's goodness and omnipotence on the ground that (on a sufficiently long view) this is the best of all logically possible worlds, because it includes the important second order goods, and yet it admits that real evils, namely first order evils, exist. But does it still hold that good and evil are opposed? Not, clearly, in the sense that we set out originally: good does not tend to eliminate evil in general. Instead, we have a modified, a more complex pattern. First order good (e.g. happiness) *contrasts with* first order evil (e.g. misery): these two are opposed in a fairly mechanical way; some second order goods (e.g. benevolence) try to maximize first order good and minimize first order evil; but God's goodness is not this, it is rather the will to maximize second order good. We might, therefore, call God's goodness an example of a third order goodness, or good (3). While this account is different from our original one, it might well be held to be an improvement on it, to give a more accurate description of the way in which good is opposed to evil, and to be consistent with the essential theist position.

There might, however, be several objections to this solution.

First, some might argue that such qualities as benevolence—and a fortiori the third order goodness which promotes benevolence—have a merely derivative value, that they are not higher sorts of good, but merely means to good (1), that is, to happiness, so that it would be absurd for God to keep misery in existence in order to make possible the virtues of benevolence, heroism, etc. The theist who adopts the present solution must, of course, deny this, but he can do so with some plausibility, so I should not press this objection.

Secondly, it follows from this solution that God is not in our sense benevolent or sympathetic: he is not concerned to minimise evil (1), but only to promote good (2); and this might be a disturbing conclusion for some theists.

But, thirdly, the fatal objection is this. Our analysis shows clearly the possibility of the existence of a *second* order evil, an evil (2) contrasting with good (2) as evil (1) contrasts with good (1). This would include malevolence, cruelty, callousness, cowardice, and states in which good (1) is decreasing and evil (1) increasing. And just as good (2) is held to be the important kind of good, the kind that God is concerned to promote, so evil (2) will, by analogy, be the important kind of evil, the kind which God, if he were wholly good and omnipotent, would eliminate. And yet evil (2) plainly exists, and indeed most theists (in other contexts) stress its existence more than that of evil (1). We should, therefore, state the problem of evil in terms of second order evil, and against this form of the problem the present solution is useless.

An attempt might be made to use this solution again, at a higher level, to explain the occurrence of evil (2): indeed the next main solution that we shall examine does just this, with the help of some new notions. Without any fresh notions, such a solution would have little plausibility: for example, we could hardly say that the really important good was a good (3), such as the increase of benevolence in proportion to cruelty, which logically required for its occurrence the occurrence of some second order evil. But even if evil (2) could be explained in this way, it is fairly clear that there would be third order evils contrasting with this third order good: and we should be well on the way to an infinite regress, where the solution of a problem of evil, stated in terms of evil (n), indicated the existence of an evil ($n+1$), and a further problem to be solved.

4. "Evil Is Due to Human Free Will"

Perhaps the most important proposed solution of the problem of evil is that evil is not to be ascribed to God at all, but to the independent actions of human beings, supposed to have been endowed by God with freedom of the will. This solution may be combined with the preceding one: first order evil (e.g. pain) may be justified as a logically necessary component in second order good (e.g. sympathy) while second order evil (e.g. cruelty) is not *justified*, but is so ascribed to human beings that God cannot be held responsible for it. This combination evades my third criticism of the preceding solution.

The freewill solution also involves the preceding solution at a higher level. To explain why a wholly good God gave men free will although it would lead to some important evils, it must be argued that it is better on the whole that men should act freely, and sometimes err, than that they should be innocent automata, acting rightly in a wholly determined way. Freedom, that is to say, is now treated as a third order good, and as being more valuable than second order goods (such as sympathy and heroism) would be if they were deterministically produced, and it is being assumed that second order evils, such as cruelty, are logically necessary accompaniments of freedom, just as pain is a logically necessary pre-condition of sympathy.

I think that this solution is unsatisfactory primarily because of the incoherence of the notion of freedom of the will: but I cannot discuss this topic adequately here, although some of my criticisms will touch upon it.

First I should query the assumption that second order evils are logically necessary accompaniments of freedom. I should ask this: if God has made men such that in their free choices they sometimes prefer what is good and sometimes what is evil, why could He not have made men such that they always freely choose the good? If there is no logical impossibility in a man's freely choosing the good on one, or on several, occasions, there cannot be a logical impossibility in his freely choosing the good on every occasion. God was not, then, faced with a choice between making innocent automata and making beings who, in acting freely, would sometimes go wrong: there was open to him the obviously better possibility of making beings who would act freely but always go right. Clearly, his failure to avail himself of this possibility is inconsistent with his being both omnipotent and wholly good.

If it is replied that this objection is absurd, that the making of some wrong choices is logically necessary for freedom, it would seem that "freedom" must here mean complete randomness or indeterminacy, including randomness with regard to the alternatives good and evil, in other words that men's choices and consequent actions can be "free" only if they are not determined by their characters. Only on this assumption can God escape the responsibility for men's actions; for if he made them as they are, but did not determine their wrong choices, this can only be because the wrong choices are not determined by men as they are. But then if freedom is randomness, how can it be a characteristic of *will*? And, still more, how can it be the most important good? What value or merit would there be in free choices if these were random actions which were not determined by the nature of the agent?

I conclude that to make this solution plausible two different senses of "freedom" must be confused, one sense which will justify the view that freedom is a third order good, more valuable than other goods would be without it, and another sense, sheer randomness, to prevent us from ascribing to God a decision to make men such that they sometimes go wrong when he might have made them such that they would always freely go right.

This criticism is sufficient to dispose of this solution. But besides this there is a fundamental difficulty in the notion of an omnipotent God creating men with free will, for if men's wills are really free this must mean that even God cannot control them, that is, that God is no longer omnipotent. It may be objected that God's gift of freedom to men does not mean that he *cannot* control their wills, but that he always *refrains* from controlling their wills. But why,

we may ask, should God refrain from controlling evil wills? Why should he not leave men free to will rightly, but intervene when he sees them beginning to will wrongly? If God could do this, but does not, and if he is wholly good, the only explanation could be that even a wrong free act of will is not really evil, that its freedom is a value which outweighs its wrongness, so that there would be a loss of value if God took away the wrongness and the freedom together. But this is utterly opposed to what theists say about sin in other contexts. The present solution of the problem of evil, then, can be maintained only in the form that God has made men so free that he *cannot* control their wills.

This leads us to what I call the Paradox of Omnipotence: can an omnipotent being make things which he cannot subsequently control? Or, what is practically equivalent to this, can an omnipotent being make rules which then bind himself? (These are practically equivalent because any such rules could be regarded as setting certain things beyond his control, and vice versa.) The second of these formulations is relevant to the suggestions that we have already met, that an omnipotent God creates the rules of logic or causal laws, and is then bound by them.

It is clear that this is a paradox: the questions cannot be answered satisfactorily either in the affirmative or in the negative. If we answer "Yes," it follows that if God actually makes things which he cannot control, or makes rules which bind himself, he is not omnipotent once he has made them: there are *then* things which he cannot do. But if we answer "No," we are immediately asserting that there are things which he cannot do, that is to say that he is already not omnipotent.

It cannot be replied that the question which sets this paradox is not a proper question. It would make perfectly good sense to say that a human mechanic has made a machine which he cannot control: if there is any difficulty about the question it lies in the notion of omnipotence itself.

This, incidentally, shows that although we have approached this paradox from the free will theory, it is equally a problem for a theological determinist. No one thinks that machines have free will, yet they may well be beyond the control of their makers. The determinist might reply that anyone who makes anything determines its ways of acting, and so determines its subsequent behaviour: even the human mechanic does this by his *choice* of materials and structure for his machine, though he does not know all about either of these: the mechanic thus determines, though he may not foresee, his machine's actions. And since God is omniscient, and since his creation of things is total, he both determines and foresees the ways in which his creatures will act. We may grant this, but it is beside the point. The question is not whether God *originally* determined the future actions of his creatures, but whether he can *subsequently* control their actions, or whether he was able in his original creation to put things beyond his subsequent control. Even on determinist principles the answers "Yes" and "No" are equally irreconcilable with God's omnipotence.

Before suggesting a solution of this paradox, I would point out that there is a parallel Paradox of Sovereignty. Can a legal sovereign make a law restricting its own future legislative power? For example, could the British parliament make a law forbidding any future parliament to socialise banking, and also forbidding the future repeal of this law itself? Or could the British parliament, which was legally sovereign in Australia in, say, 1899, pass a valid law, or series of laws, which made it no longer sovereign in 1933? Again, neither the affirmative nor the negative answer is really satisfactory. If we were to answer "Yes," we should be admitting the validity of a law which, if it were actually made, would mean that parliament was no longer sovereign. If we were to answer "No," we should be admitting that there is a law, not logically absurd, which parliament cannot validly make, that is, that parliament is not now a legal sovereign. This paradox can be solved in the following way. We should distinguish between first order laws, that is laws governing the actions of individuals and bodies other than the legislature, and second order laws, that is laws about laws, laws governing the actions of the legislature itself. Correspondingly, we should distinguish two orders of sovereignty, first order sovereignty (sovereignty (1)) which is unlimited authority to make first order laws, and second-order sovereignty (sovereignty (2)) which is unlimited authority to make second order laws. If we say that parliament is sovereign we might mean that any parliament at any time has sovereignty (1), or we might mean that parliament has both sovereignty (1) and sovereignty (2) at present, but we cannot without contradiction mean both that the present parliament has sovereignty (2) and that every parliament at every time has sovereignty (1), for if the present parliament has sovereignty (2) it may use it to take away the sovereignty (1) of later parliaments. What the paradox shows is that we cannot ascribe to any continuing institution legal sovereignty in an inclusive sense.

The analogy between omnipotence and sovereignty shows that the paradox of omnipotence can be solved in a similar way. We must distinguish between first order omnipotence (omnipotence (1)), that is unlimited power to act, and second order omnipotence (omnipotence (2)), that is unlimited power to determine what powers to act things shall have. Then we could consistently say that God all the time has omnipotence (1), but if so no beings at any time have powers to act independently of God. Or we could say that God at one time had omnipotence (2), and used it to assign independent powers to act to certain things, so that God thereafter did not have omnipotence (1). But what the paradox shows is that we cannot consistently ascribe to any continuing being omnipotence is an inclusive sense.

An alternative solution of this paradox would be simply to deny that God is a continuing being, that any times can be assigned to his actions at all. But on this assumption (which also has difficulties of its own) no meaning can be given to the assertion that God made men with wills so free that he could not control them. The paradox of omnipotence can be avoided by putting God outside time, but the freewill solution of the problem of evil cannot be saved in this way, and equally it remains impossible to hold that an omnipotent God *binds himself* by causal or logical laws.

CONCLUSION

Of the proposed solutions of the problem of evil which we have examined, none has stood up to criticism. There may be other solutions which require examination, but this study strongly suggests that there is no valid solution of the problem which does not modify at least one of the constituent propositions in a way which would seriously affect the essential core of the theistic position.

Quite apart from the problem of evil, the paradox of omnipotence has shown that God's omnipotence must in any case be restricted in one way or another, that unqualified omnipotence cannot be ascribed to any being that continues through time. And if God and his actions are not in time, can omnipotence, or power of any sort, be meaningfuly ascribed to him?

STUDY QUESTIONS

1. How does Mackie frame the problem of evil as a problem of logical inconsistency within the set of theistic beliefs? What theistic beliefs exactly? What rational force does he think this problem has against the believer in theism? According to Mackie, what must be the essential strategy of the theist who seeks to solve the problem he poses?

2. Mackie thinks that the problem of evil is completely formed only when key divine attributes are defined in particular ways. Review Mackie's definitions here and evaluate their accuracy.

3. Mackie reviews and criticizes various fallacious solutions to the problem of evil. State the main theme of each solution, state Mackie's criticism, and then evaluate the effectiveness of the criticism.

4. What does Mackie call the paradox of omnipotence? Evaluate the negative import of this paradox for theism, regardless of the problem of evil.

Alvin Plantinga

The Free Will Defense

Alvin Plantinga (b. 1932) seeks to refute J. L. Mackie's basic contention that it is not possible both that God is omnipotent and that he was unable to create a universe containing moral good but no moral evil. Plantinga's famous argument has become known as the Free Will Defense. Using the language of "possible worlds" (related to modal logic), he develops a scenario of human freedom in relation to divine omnipotence. In his scenario, God actualizes a world that contains creatures with free will so that they have the power to do good; but they sometimes choose to do evil. That is the danger and risk of free choice. Given that God decided to initiate a world containing free creatures, it was not possible to for God to ensure that the free creatures would always do good and never go wrong. Obviously, Mackie's *compatibilist* view of free will leads him to conclude that omnipotence can bring about any logically possible world, including worlds in which free creatures never commit evil. And certainly there are such possible worlds. However, working from an *incompatibilist* view of free will, Plantinga shows that the essence of created freedom is that things can happen in the world that are decided by free creatures and are not under God's control. So, it is not within the scope of omnipotence to determine the outcome of free creaturely choice. Plantinga, then, claims to have shown—contrary to Mackie—that it is logically possible for God to exist and for evil to exist, thus defending against the charge of inconsistency.

In a widely discussed piece entitled "Evil and Omnipotence" John Mackie repeats this claim:

> I think, however, that a more telling criticism can be made by way of the traditional problem of evil. Here it can be shown, not that religious beliefs lack rational support, but that they are positively irrational, that the several parts of the essential theological doctrine are *inconsistent* with one another.[1]

Is Mackie right? Does the theist contradict himself? But we must ask a prior question: just what is being claimed here? That theistic belief contains an inconsistency or contradiction, of course. But what, exactly, is an inconsistency or contradiction? There are several kinds. An *explicit* contradiction is a proposition of a certain sort— a conjunctive *proposition*, one conjunct of which is the denial or negation of the other conjunct. For example:

Paul is a good tennis player, and it's false that Paul is a good tennis player.

(People seldom assert explicit contradictions.) Is Mackie charging the theist with accepting such a contradiction? Presumably not; what he says is:

> In its simplest form the problem is this: God is omnipotent; God is wholly good; yet evil exists. There seems to be some contradiction between these three propositions, so that if any two of them were true the third would be false. But at the same time all three are essential parts of most theological positions; the theologian, it seems, at once *must* adhere and *cannot consistently* adhere to all three.[2]

According to Mackie, then, the theist accepts a group or set of three propositions; this set is inconsistent. Its members, of course are,

(1) God is omnipotent
(2) God is wholly good

and

(3) Evil exists.

Call this set A; the claim is that A is an inconsistent set. But what is it for a *set* to be inconsistent or contradictory? Following our definition of an explicit contradiction, we might say that a set of propositions is explicitly contradictory if one of the members is the denial or negation of another member. But then, of course, it is evident that the set we are discussing is not explicitly contradictory; the denials of (1), (2), and (3), respectively, are

(1′) God is not omnipotent (or it's false that God is omnipotent)
(2′) God is not wholly good

and

(3′) There is no evil

none of which is in set A.

Of course many sets are pretty clearly contradictory, in an important way, but not *explicitly* contradictory. For example, set B:

(4) If all men are mortal, then Socrates is mortal
(5) All men are mortal
(6) Socrates is not mortal.

This set is not explicitly contradictory; yet surely *some* significant sense of that term applies to it. What is important here is that by using only the rules of ordinary logic—the laws of propositional logic and quantification theory found in any introductory text on the subject—we can deduce an explicit contradiction from the set. Or to put it differently, we can use the laws of logic to deduce a proposition from the set, which proposition, when added to the set, yields a new set that is explicitly contradictory. For by using the law *modus ponens* (if *p*, then *q*; *p*; therefore *q*) we can deduce

(7) Socrates is mortal

from (4) and (5). The result of adding (7) to B is the set {(4), (5), (6), (7)}. This set, of course, is explicitly contradictory in that (6) is the denial of (7). We might say that any set which shares this characteristic with set B is *formally* contradictory. So a formally contradictory set is one from whose members an explicit contradiction can be deduced by the laws of logic. Is Mackie claiming that set A is formally contradictory?

If he is, he's wrong. No laws of logic permit us to deduce the denial of one of the propositions in A from the other members. Set A isn't formally contradictory either.

But there is still another way in which a set of propositions can be contradictory or inconsistent. Consider set C, whose members are

(8) George is older than Paul
(9) Paul is older than Nick

and

(10) George is not older than Nick.

This set is neither explicitly nor formally contradictory; we can't, just by using the laws of logic, deduce the denial of any of these propositions from the others. And yet there is a good sense in which it is inconsistent or contradictory. For clearly it is *not possible* that its three members all be true. It is *necessarily true* that

(11) If George is older than Paul, and Paul is older than Nick, then George is older than Nick.

And if we add (11) to set C, we get a set that is formally contradictory; (8), (9), and (11) yield, by the laws of ordinary logic, the denial of (10).

I say that (11) is *necessarily true*; but what does *that* mean? Of course we might say that a proposition is necessarily true if it is impossible that it be false, or if its negation is not possibly true. This would be to explain necessity in terms of possibility. Chances are, however, that anyone who does not know what necessity is will be equally at a loss about possibility; the explanation is not likely to be very successful. Perhaps all we can do by way of explanation is to give some examples and hope for the best. In the first place many propositions can be established by the laws of logic alone—for example,

(12) If all men are mortal and Socrates is a man, then Socrates is mortal.

Such propositions are truths of logic; and all of them are necessary in the sense of question. But truths of arithmetic and mathematics generally are also necessarily true. Still further, there is a host of propositions that are neither truths of logic nor truths of mathematics but are nonetheless necessarily true; (11) would be an example, as well as

(13) Nobody is taller than himself
(14) Red is a color
(15) No numbers are persons
(16) No prime number is a prime minister

and

(17) Bachelors are unmarried.

So here we have an important kind of necessity—let's call it "broadly logical necessity." Of course there is a correlative kind of *possibility*: a proposition *p* is possibly true (in the broadly logical sense) just in case its negation or denial is not necessarily true (in that same broadly logical sense). This sense of necessity and possibility must be distinguished from another that we may call *causal* or *natural* necessity and possibility. Consider

(18) Henry Kissinger has swum the Atlantic.

Although this proposition has an implausible ring, it is not necessarily false in the broadly logical sense (and its denial is not necessarily true in that sense). But there is a good sense in which it is impossible: it is *causally* or *naturally* impossible. Human beings, unlike dolphins, just don't have the physical equipment demanded for this feat. Unlike Superman, furthermore, the rest of us are incapable of leaping tall buildings at a single bound or (without auxiliary power of some kind) traveling faster than a speeding bullet. These things are *impossible* for us—but not *logically* impossible, even in the broad sense.

So there are several senses of necessity and possibility here. There are a number of propositions, furthermore, of which it's difficult to say whether they are or aren't possible in the broadly logical sense; some of these are subjects of philosophical controversy. Is it possible, for example, for a person never to be conscious during his entire existence? Is it possible for a (human) person to exist *disembodied*? If that's possible, is it possible that there be a person who *at no time at all* during his entire existence has a body? Is it possible to see without eyes? These are propositions about whose possibility in that broadly logical sense there is disagreement and dispute.

Now return to set C. What is characteristic of it is the fact that the conjunction of its members—the proposition expressed by the result of putting "and's" between (8), (9), and (10)—is necessarily false. Or we might put it like this: what characterizes set C is the fact that we can get a formally contradictory set by adding a necessarily true proposition—namely (11). Suppose we say that a set is *implicitly contradictory* if it resembles C in this respect. That is, a set *S* of propositions is implicitly contradictory if there is a necessary proposition *p* such that the result of adding *p* to *S* is a formally contradictory set. Another way to put it: *S* is implicitly contradictory if there is some necessarily true proposition *p* such that by using just the laws of ordinary logic, we can deduce an explicit contradiction from *p* together with the members of *S*. And when Mackie says that set A is contradictory, we may properly take him, I think, as holding that it is implicitly contradictory in the explained sense. As he puts it:

However, the contradiction does not arise immediately; to show it we need some additional premises, or perhaps some quasi-logical rules connecting the terms "good" and "evil" and "omnipotent." These additional principles are that good is opposed to evil, in such a way that a good thing always eliminates evil as far as it can, and that there are no limits to what an omnipotent thing can do. From these it follows that a good omnipotent thing eliminates evil completely, and then the propositions that a good omnipotent thing exists, and that evil exists, are incompatible.[3]

Here Mackie refers to "additional premises"; he also calls them "additional principles" and "quasi-logical rules"; he says we need them to show the contradiction. What he means, I think, is that to get a formally contradictory set we must add some more propositions to set A; and if we aim to show that set A is implicitly contradictory, these propositions must be necessary truths—"quasi-logical rules" as Mackie calls them. The two additional principles he suggests are

(19) A good thing always eliminates evil as far as it can

and

(20) There are no limits to what an omnipotent being can do.

And, of course, if Mackie means to show that set A is implicitly contradictory, then he must hold that (19) and (20) are not merely *true* but *necessarily true.*

But, are they? What about (20) first? What does it mean to say that a being is omnipotent? That he is *all-powerful,* or *almighty,* presumably. But are there no limits at all to the power of such a being? Could he create square circles, for example, or married bachelors? Most theologians and theistic philosophers who hold that God is omnipotent, do not hold that He can create round squares or bring it about that He both exists and does not exist. These theologians and philosophers may hold that there are no *nonlogical* limits to what an omnipotent being can do, but they concede that not even an omnipotent being can bring about logically impossible states of affairs or cause necessarily false propositions to be true. Some theists, on the other hand—Martin Luther and Descartes, perhaps—have apparently thought that God's power is unlimited even by the laws of logic.

For these theists the question whether set A is contradictory will not be of much interest. As theists they believe (1) and (2), and they also presumably, believe (3). But they remain undisturbed by the claim that (1), (2), and (3) are jointly inconsistent—because, as they say, God can do what is logically impossible. Hence He can bring it about that the members of set A are all true, even if that set is contradictory (concentrating very intensely upon this suggestion is likely to make you dizzy). So the theist who thinks that the power of God isn't limited *at all*, not even by the laws of logic, will be unimpressed by Mackie's argument and won't find any difficulty in the contradiction set A is alleged to contain. This view is not very popular, however, and for good reason; it is quite incoherent. What the theist typically means when he says that God is omnipotent is not that there are *no* limits to God's power, but at most that there are no nonlogical limits to what He can do; and given this qualification, it is perhaps initially plausible to suppose that (20) is necessarily true.

But what about (19), the proposition that every good thing eliminates every evil state of affairs that it can eliminate? Is that necessarily true? Is it true at all? Suppose, first of all, that your friend Paul unwisely goes for a drive on a wintry day and runs out of gas on a deserted road. The temperature dips to –10°, and a miserably cold wind comes up. You are sitting comfortably at home (twenty-five miles from Paul) roasting chestnuts in a roaring blaze. Your car is in the garage; in the trunk there is the full five-gallon can of gasoline you always keep for emergencies. Paul's discomfort and danger are certainly an evil, and one which you could eliminate. You don't do so. But presumably you don't thereby forfeit your claim to being a "good thing"—you simply didn't know of Paul's plight. And so (19) does not appear to be necessary. It says that every good thing has a certain property—the property of eliminating every evil that it can. And if the case I described is possible—a good person's failing through ignorance to eliminate a certain evil he can eliminate—then (19) is by no means necessarily true.

But perhaps Mackie could sensibly claim that if you *didn't know* about Paul's plight, then in fact you were *not*, at the time in question, able to eliminate the evil in question; and perhaps he'd be right. In any event he could revise (19) to take into account the kind of case I mentioned:

> (19a) Every good thing always eliminates every evil that *it knows about* and can eliminate.

{(1), (2), (3), (20), (19a)}, you'll notice is not a formally contradictory set—to get a formal contradiction we must add a proposition specifying that God *knows about* every evil state of affairs. But most theists do believe that God is omniscient or all-knowing; so if this new set—the set that results when we add to set A the proposition that God is omniscient—is implicitly contradictory then Mackie should be satisfied and the theist confounded. (And, henceforth, set A will be the old set A together with the proposition that God is omniscient.)

But is (19a) necessary? Hardly. Suppose you know that Paul is marooned as in the previous example, and you also know another friend is similarly marooned fifty miles in the opposite direction. Suppose, furthermore, that while you can rescue one or the other, you simply can't rescue both. Then each of the two evils is such that it is within your power to eliminate it; and you know about them both. But you can't eliminate *both*; and you don't forfeit your claim to being a good person by eliminating only one—it wasn't within your power to do more. So the fact that you don't doesn't mean that you are not a good person. Therefore (19a) is false; it is not a necessary truth or even a truth that every good thing eliminates every evil it knows about and can eliminate.

We can see the same thing another way. You've been rock climbing. Still something of a novice, you've acquired a few cuts and bruises by inelegantly using your knees rather than your feet. One of these bruises is fairly painful. You mention it to a physician friend, who predicts the pain will leave of its own accord in a day or two. Meanwhile, he says, there's nothing he can do, short of amputating your leg above the knee, to remove the pain. Now the pain in your knee is an evil state of affairs. All else being equal, it would be better if you had no such pain. And it is within the power of your friend to eliminate this evil state of affairs. Does his failure to do so mean that he is not a good person? Of course not; for he could eliminate this evil

state of affairs only by bringing about another, much worse evil. And so it is once again evident that (19a) is false. It is entirely possible that a good person can fail to eliminate an evil state of affairs that he knows about and can eliminate. This would take place, if, as in the present example, he couldn't eliminate the evil without bringing about a *greater* evil.

A slightly different kind of case shows the same thing. A really impressive good state of affairs G will *outweigh* a trivial E—that is, the conjunctive state of affairs G *and* E is itself a good state of affairs. And surely a good person would not be obligated to eliminate a given evil if he could do so only by eliminating a good that outweighed it. Therefore (19a) is not necessarily true; it can't be used to show that set A is implicitly contradictory.

These difficulties might suggest another revision of (19); we might try

> (19b) A good being eliminates every evil E that it knows about and that it can eliminate without either bringing about a greater evil or eliminating a good state of affairs that outweighs E.

Is this necessarily true? It takes care of the second of the two difficulties afflicting (19a) but leaves the first untouched. We can see this as follows. First, suppose we say that a being *properly eliminates* an evil state of affairs if it eliminates that evil without either eliminating an outweighing good or bringing about a greater evil. It is then obviously possible that a person find himself in a situation where he could properly eliminate an evil E and could also properly eliminate another evil E', but couldn't properly eliminate them both. You're rock climbing again, this time on the dreaded north face of the Grand Teton. You and your party come upon Curt and Bob, two mountaineers stranded 125 feet apart on the face. They untied to reach their cigarettes and then carelessly dropped the rope while lighting up. A violent, dangerous thunderstorm is approaching. You have time to rescue one of the stranded climbers and retreat before the storm hits; if you rescue both, however, you and your party and the two climbers will be caught on the face during the thunderstorm, which will very likely destroy your entire party. In this case you can eliminate one evil (Curt's being stranded on the face) without causing more evil or eliminating a greater good; and you are also able to properly eliminate the other evil (Bob's being thus stranded). But you can't properly eliminate them *both*. And so the fact that you don't rescue Curt, say, even though you could have, doesn't show that you aren't a good person. Here, then, each of the evils is such that you can properly eliminate it; but you can't properly eliminate them both, and hence can't be blamed for failing to eliminate one of them.

So neither (19a) nor (19b) is necessarily true. You may be tempted to reply that the sort of counterexamples offered—examples where someone is able to eliminate an evil *A* and also able to eliminate a different evil *B*, but unable to eliminate them both—are irrelevant to the case of a being who, like God, is both omnipotent and omniscient. That is, you may think that if an omnipotent and omniscient being is able to eliminate *each* of two evils, it follows that he can eliminate them *both*. Perhaps this is so; but it is not strictly to the point. The fact is the counterexamples show that (19a) and (19b) are not necessarily true and hence can't be used to show that set A is implicitly inconsistent. What the reply does suggest is that perhaps the atheologian will have more success if he works the properties of omniscience and omnipotence into (19). Perhaps he could say something like

(19c) An omnipotent and omniscient good being eliminates every evil that it can properly eliminate.

And suppose, for purposes of argument, we concede the necessary truth of (19c). Will it serve Mackie's purposes? Not obviously. For we don't get a set that is formally contradictory by adding (20) and (19c) to set A. This set (call it A′) contains the following six members:

(1) God is omnipotent
(2) God is wholly good
(2′) God is omniscient
(3) Evil exists
(19c) An omnipotent and omniscient good being eliminates every evil that it can properly eliminate

and

(20) There are no nonlogical limits to what an omnipotent being can do.

Now if A′ were formally contradictory, then from any five of its members we could deduce the denial of the sixth by the laws of ordinary logic. That is, any five would *formally entail* the denial of the sixth. So if A′ were formally inconsistent, the denial of (3) would be formally entailed by the remaining five. That is, (1), (2), (2′), (19c), and (20) would formally entail

(3′) There is no evil.

But they don't; what they formally entail is not that there is no evil *at all* but only that

(3″) There is no evil that God can properly eliminate.

So (19c) doesn't really help either—not because it is not necessarily true but because its addition [with (20)] to set A does not yield a formally contradictory set.

Obviously, what the atheologian must add to get a formally contradictory set is

(21) If God is omniscient and omnipotent, then he can properly eliminate every evil state of affairs.

Suppose we agree that the set consisting in A plus (19c), (20), and (21) is formally contradictory. So if (19c), (20), and (21) are all necessarily true, then set A is implicitly contradictory. We've already conceded that (19c) and (20) are indeed necessary. So we must take a look at (21). Is this proposition necessarily true?

No. To see this let us ask the following question. Under what conditions would an omnipotent being be unable to eliminate a certain evil *E* without eliminating an outweighing good? Well, suppose that *E* is *included* in some good state of affairs that outweighs it. That is, suppose there is some good state of affairs *G* so related to *E* that it is impossible that *G* obtain or be actual and *E* fail to obtain. (Another way to put this: a state of affairs *S* includes *S′* if the conjunctive state of affairs *S but not S′* is impossible, or if it is necessary that *S′* obtains if *S* does.) Now suppose that some good state of affairs *G* includes an evil state of affairs *E* that it outweighs. Then not even an omnipotent being could eliminate *E* without eliminating *G*. But *are* there any cases where a good state of affairs includes, in this sense, an evil that it outweighs?[4] Indeed there are such states of affairs. To take an artificial example, let's suppose that *E* is Paul's suffering from a minor abrasion and *G* is your being deliriously happy. The conjunctive state of affairs, *G and E*—the state of affairs that obtains if and only if both *G* and *E* obtain—is then a good state of affairs: it is better, all else being equal, that you be intensely happy and Paul suffer a mildly annoying abrasion than that this state of affairs not obtain. So *G and E* is a good state of affairs. And clearly *G and E* includes *E*: obviously it is necessarily true that if you are deliriously happy and Paul suffering from an abrasion, then Paul is suffering from an abrasion.

But perhaps you think this example trivial, tricky, slippery, and irrelevant. If so, take heart; other examples abound. Certain kinds of values, certain familiar kinds of good states of affairs, can't exist apart from evil of some sort. For example, there are people who display a sort of creative moral heroism in the face of suffering and adversity—a heroism that inspires others and creates a good situation out of a bad one. In a situation like this the evil, of course, remains evil; but the total state of affairs—someone's bearing pain magnificently, for example—may be good. If it is, then the good present must outweigh the evil; otherwise the total situation would not be *good*. But, of course, it is not possible that such a good state of affairs obtain unless some evil also obtain. It is a necessary truth that if someone bears pain magnificently, then someone is in pain.

The conclusion to be drawn, therefore, is that (21) is not necessarily true. And our discussion thus far shows at the very least that it is no easy matter to find necessarily true propositions that yield a formally contradictory set when added to set *A*.[5] One wonders, therefore, why the many atheologians who confidently assert that this set is contradictory make no attempt whatever to *show* that it is. For the most part they are content just to *assert* that there is a contradiction here. Even Mackie, who sees that some "additional premise" or "quasi-logical rules" are needed, makes scarcely a beginning towards finding some additional premises that are necessarily true and that together with the members of set A formally entail an explicit contradiction.

CAN WE SHOW THAT THERE IS NO INCONSISTENCY HERE?

To summarize our conclusions so far: although many atheologians claim that the theist is involved in contradiction when he asserts the members of set A, this set, obviously, is neither *explicitly* nor *formally* contradictory; the claim, presumably, must be that it is *implicitly* contradictory. To make good this claim the atheologian must find some necessarily true proposition *p* (it could be a conjunction of several propositions) such that the addition of *p* to set A yields a set that is formally contradictory. No atheologian has produced even a plausible candidate for this role, and it certainly is not easy to see what such a proposition might be. Now we might think we should simply declare set A implicitly consistent on the principle that a proposition (or set) is to be presumed consistent or possible until proven otherwise. This course, however, leads to trouble. The same principle would impel us to declare the atheologian's claim—that set A is *in*consistent—possible or consistent. But the claim that a given set of propositions is implicitly contradictory is itself either necessarily true or necessarily false; so if such a claim is *possible*, it is not necessarily false and is, therefore, true (in fact, necessarily true). If we followed the suggested principle, therefore, we should be obliged to declare set A implicitly consistent (since it hasn't been shown to be otherwise), but we should have to say the same thing about the atheologian's claim, since we haven't shown *that* claim to be inconsistent or impossible. The atheologian's claim, furthermore, is necessarily true if it is possible. Accordingly, if we accept the above principle, we shall have to declare set A both implicitly consistent and implicitly inconsistent. So all we can say at this point is that set A has not been shown to be implicitly inconsistent.

Can we go any further? One way to go on would be to try to *show* that set A is implicitly consistent or possible in the broadly logical sense. But what is involved in showing such a thing? Although there are various ways to approach this matter, they all resemble one another in an important respect. They all amount to this: to show that a set *S* is consistent you think of a *possible state of affairs* (it needn't *actually obtain*) which is such that if it were actual, then all of the members of *S* would be true. This procedure is sometimes called *giving a model of S*. For example, you might construct an axiom set and then show that it is consistent by giving a model of it; this is how it was shown that the denial of Euclid's parallel postulate is formally consistent with the rest of his postulates.

There are various special cases of this procedure to fit special circumstances. Suppose, for example, you have a pair of propositions *p* and *q* and wish to show them consistent. And suppose we say that a proposition p_1 *entails* a proposition p_2 if it is impossible that p_1 be true and p_2 false—if the conjunctive proposition p_1 *and not p_2* is necessarily false. Then one way to show that *p* is consistent with *q* is to find some proposition *r* whose conjunction with *p* is both possible, in the broadly logical sense, and entails *q*. A rude and unlettered behaviorist, for example, might hold that thinking is really nothing but movements of the larynx; he might go on to hold that

P Jones did not move his larynx after April 30

is inconsistent (in the broadly logical sense) with

Q Jones did some thinking during May.

By way of rebuttal, we might point out that *P* appears to be consistent with

R While convalescing from an April 30 laryngotomy, Jones whiled away the idle hours by writing (in May) a splendid paper on Kant's *Critique of Pure Reason*.

So the conjunction of *P* and *R* appears to be consistent; but obviously it also entails *Q* (you can't write even a passable paper on Kant's *Critique of Pure Reason* without doing some thinking); so *P* and *Q* are consistent.

We can see that this is a special case of the procedure I mentioned above as follows. This proposition

R is consistent with *P*; so the proposition *P and R* is possible, describes a possible state of affairs. But *P and R* entails *Q*; hence if *P and R* were true, *Q* would also be true, and hence both *P* and *Q* would be true. So this is really a case of producing a possible state of affairs such that, if it were actual, all the members of the set in question (in this case the pair set of *P* and *Q*) would be true.

How does this apply to the case before us? As follows, let us conjoin propositions (1), (2), and (2′) and henceforth call the result (1):

(1) God is omniscient, omnipotent, and wholly good.

The problem, then, is to show that (1) and (3) (evil exists) are consistent. This could be done, as we've seen, by finding a proposition *r* that is consistent with (1) and such that (1) and (*r*) together entail (3). One proposition that might do the trick is

(22) God creates a world containing evil and has a good reason for doing so.

If (22) is consistent with (1), then it follows that (1) and (3) (and hence set A) are consistent. Accordingly, one thing some theists have tried is to show that (22) and (1) are consistent.

One can attempt this in at least two ways. On the one hand, we could try to apply the same method again. Conceive of a possible state of affairs such that, if it obtained, an omnipotent, omniscient, and wholly good God would have a good reason for permitting evil. On the other, someone might try to specify *what God's reason* is for permitting evil and try to show, if it is not obvious, that it is a good reason. St. Augustine, for example, one of the greatest and most influential philosopher-theologians of the Christian Church, writes as follows:

> …some people see with perfect truth that a creature is better if, while possessing free will, it remains always fixed upon God and never sins; then, reflecting on men's sins, they are grieved, not because they continue to sin, but because they were created. They say: He should have made us such that we never willed to sin, but always to enjoy the unchangeable truth.
>
> They should not lament or be angry. God has not compelled men to sin just because He created them and

gave them the power to choose between sinning and not sinning. There are angels who have never sinned and never will sin.

> Such is the generosity of God's goodness that He has not refrained from creating even that creature which He foreknew would not only sin, but remain in the will to sin. As a runaway horse is better than a stone which does not run away because it lacks self-movement and sense perception, so the creature is more excellent which sins by free will than that which does not sin only because it has no free will.[6]

In broadest terms Augustine claims that God could create a better, more perfect universe by permitting evil than He could by refusing to do so:

> Neither the sins nor the misery are necessary to the perfection of the universe, but souls as such are necessary, which have the power to sin if they so will, and become miserable if they sin. If misery persisted after their sins had been abolished, or if there were misery before there were sins, then it might be right to say that the order and government of the universe were at fault. Again, if there were sins but no consequent misery, that order is equally dishonored by lack of equity.[7]

Augustine tries to tell us *what God's reason* is for permitting evil. At bottom, he says, it's that God can create a more perfect universe by permitting evil. A really top-notch universe requires the existence of free, rational, and moral agents; and some of the free creatures He created went wrong. But the universe with the free creatures it contains and the evil they commit is better than it would have been had it contained neither the free creatures nor this evil. Such an attempt to specify God's reason for permitting evil is what I earlier called a *theodicy*; in the words of John Milton it is an attempt to "justify the ways of God to man," to show that God is just in permitting evil. Augustine's kind of theodicy might be called a Free Will Theodicy, since the idea of rational creatures with free will plays such a prominent role in it.

A theodicist, then, attempts to tell us why God permits evil. Quite distinct from a Free Will Theodicy is what I shall call a Free Will Defense. Here the aim is not to say what God's reason *is*, but at most what God's reason *might possibly be*. We could put the difference like this. The Free Will theodicist and Free Will defender are both trying to show that (1) is consistent with (22), and of course if so, then set A is consistent. The Free Will theodicist tries to do this by finding some proposition *r* which in conjunction with (1) entails (22); he claims, furthermore, that this proposition is *true*, not just consistent with (1). He tries to tell us what God's reason for permitting evil *really is*. The Free Will defender, on the other hand, though he also tries to find a proposition *r* that is consistent with (1) and in conjunction with it entails (22), does *not* claim to know or even believe that *r* is true. And here, of course, he is perfectly within his rights. His aim is to show that (1) is consistent with (22); all he need do then is find an *r* that is consistent with (1) and such that (1) and (*r*) entail (22); whether *r* is *true* is quite beside the point.

So there is a significant difference between a Free Will Theodicy and a Free Will Defense. The latter is sufficient (if successful) to show that set A is consistent; in a way a Free Will Theodicy goes beyond what is required. On the other hand, a theodicy would be much more satisfying, if possible to achieve. No doubt the theist would rather know what God's reason *is* for permitting evil than simply that it's possible that He has a good one. But in the present context (that of investigating the consistency of set A), the latter is all that's needed. Neither a defense or a theodicy, of course, gives any hint to what God's reason for some *specific* evil—the death or suffering of someone close to you, for example—might be. And there is still another function—a sort of pastoral function[8]—in the neighborhood that neither serves. Confronted with evil in his own life or suddenly coming to realize more clearly than before the *extent* and *magnitude* of evil, a believer in God may undergo a crisis in faith. He may be tempted to follow the advice of Job's "friends"; he may be tempted to "curse God and die." Neither a Free Will Defense nor a Free Will Theodicy is designed to be of much help or comfort to one suffering from such a storm in the soul (although in a specific case, of course, one or the other could prove useful). Neither is to be thought of first of all as a means of pastoral counseling. Probably neither will enable someone to find peace with himself and with God in the face of the evil the world contains. But then, of course, neither is intended for that purpose.

THE FREE WILL DEFENSE

In what follows I shall focus attention upon the Free Will Defense. I shall examine it more closely, state it more exactly, and consider objections to it; and I shall argue that in the end it is successful. Earlier we saw that among good states of affairs there are some that not even God can bring about without bringing about evil: those goods, namely, that *entail* or *include* evil states of affairs. The Free Will Defense can be looked upon as an effort to show that there may be a very different kind of good that God can't bring about without permitting evil. These are good states of affairs that don't include evil; they do not entail the existence of any evil whatever; nonetheless God Himself can't bring them about without permitting evil.

So how does the Free Will defense work? And what does the Free Will defender mean when he says that people are or may be free? What is relevant to the Free Will Defense is the idea of *being free with respect to an action*. If a person is free with respect to a given action, then he is free to perform that action and free to refrain from performing it; no antecedent conditions and/or causal laws determine that he will perform the action, or that he won't. It is within his power, at the time in question, to take or perform the action and within his power to refrain from it. Freedom so conceived is not to be confused with unpredictability. You might be able to predict what you will do in a given situation even if you are free, in that situation, to do something else. If I know you well, I may be able to predict what action you will take in response to a certain set of conditions; it does not follow that you are not free with respect to that action. Secondly, I shall say that an action is *morally significant*, for a given person, if it would be wrong for him to perform the action but right to refrain or vice versa. Keeping a promise, for example, would ordinarily be morally significant for a person, as would refusing induction into the army. On the other hand, having Cheerios for breakfast (instead of Wheaties) would not normally be morally significant. Further, suppose we say that a person is *significantly free*, on a given occasion, if he is then free with respect to a morally significant action. And finally we must distinguish between *moral evil* and *natural evil*. The former is evil that results from free human activity; natural evil is any other kind of evil.[9]

Given these definitions and distinctions, we can make a preliminary statement of the Free Will Defense as follows. A world containing creatures who are significantly free (and freely perform more good than evil actions) is more valuable, all else being equal, than a world containing no free creatures at all. Now God can create free creatures, but He can't *cause* or *determine* them to do only what is right. For if He does so, then they aren't significantly free after all; they do not do what is right *freely*. To create creatures capable of *moral good*, therefore, He must create creatures capable of moral evil; and He can't give these creatures the freedom to perform evil and at the same time prevent them from doing so. As it turned out, sadly enough, some of the free creatures God created went wrong in the exercise of their freedom; this is the source of moral evil. The fact that free creatures sometimes go wrong, however, counts neither against God's omnipotence nor against His goodness; for He could have forestalled the occurrence of moral evil only by removing the possibility of moral good.

I said earlier that the Free Will defender tries to find a proposition that is consistent with

(1) God is omniscient, omnipotent, and wholly good

and together with (1) entails that there is evil. According to the Free Will Defense, we must find this proposition somewhere in the above story. The heart of the Free Will Defense is the claim that it is *possible* that God could not have created a universe containing moral good (or as much moral good as this world contains) without creating one that also contained moral evil. And if so, then it is possible that God has a good reason for creating a world containing evil.

Now this defense has met with several kinds of objections. For example, some philosophers say that *causal determinism* and *freedom*, contrary to what we might have thought, are not really incompatible.[10] But if so, then God could have created free creatures who were free, and free to do what is wrong, but nevertheless were causally determined to do only what is right. Thus He could have created creatures who were free to do what was wrong, while nevertheless preventing them from ever performing any wrong actions—simply by seeing to it that they were causally determined to do only what is right. Of course this contradicts the Free Will Defense, according to which there is inconsistency in supposing that God determines free creatures to do only what is right. But is it really possible that all of a person's actions are causally determined while some of them are free? How could that be so? According to one version of the doctrine in question, to say that George acts freely on a given occasion is to say only this: *if George had chosen to do otherwise, he would have done otherwise.* Now George's action A is causally determined if some event E—some event beyond his control—has already occurred, where the state of affairs consisting in E's occurrence conjoined with George's *refraining* from performing A, is a causally impossible state of affairs. Then one can consistently hold both that all of a man's actions are causally determined and that some of them are free in the above sense. For suppose that all of a man's actions are causally determined and that he *couldn't*, on any occasion, have made any choice or performed any action different from the ones he did make and perform. It could still be true that if he *had* chosen to do otherwise, he would have done otherwise. Granted, he couldn't have chosen to do otherwise; but this is consistent with saying that if he had, things would have gone differently.

This objection to the Free Will Defense seems utterly implausible. One might as well claim that being in jail doesn't really limit one's freedom on the grounds that if one were *not* in jail, he'd be free to come and go as he pleased. So I shall say no more about this objection here.[11]

A second objection is more formidable. In essence it goes like this. Surely it is possible to do only what is right, even if one is free to do wrong. It is *possible*, in that broadly logical sense, that there would be a world containing free creatures who always do what is right. There is certainly no *contradiction* or *inconsistency* in this idea. But God is omnipotent; his power has no nonlogical limitations. So if it's possible

that there be a world containing creatures who are free to do what is wrong but never in fact do so, then it follows that an omnipotent God could create such a world. If so, however, the Free Will Defense must be mistaken in its insistence upon the possibility that God is omnipotent but unable to create a world containing moral good without permitting moral evil. J. L. Mackie . . . states this objection:

> If God has made men such that in their free choices they sometimes prefer what is good and sometimes what is evil, why could he not have made men such that they always freely choose the good? If there is no logical impossibility in a man's freely choosing the good on one, or on several occasions, there cannot be a logical impossibility in his freely choosing the good on every occasion. God was not, then, faced with a choice between making innocent automata and making beings who, in acting freely, would sometimes go wrong; there was open to him the obviously better possibility of making beings who would act freely but always go right. Clearly, his failure to avail himself of this possibility is inconsistent with his being both omnipotent and wholly good.[12]

Now what, exactly, is Mackie's point here? This. According to the Free Will Defense, it is possible both that God is omnipotent and that He was unable to create a world containing moral good without creating one containing moral evil. But, replies Mackie, this limitation on His power to create is inconsistent with God's omnipotence. For surely it's *possible* that there be a world containing perfectly virtuous persons—persons who are significantly free but always do what is right. Surely there are *possible worlds* that contain moral good but no moral evil. But God, if He is omnipotent, can create any possible world he chooses. So it is *not* possible, contrary to the Free Will Defense, both that God is omnipotent and that he could create a world containing moral good only by creating one containing moral evil. If He is omnipotent, the only limitations of His power are *logical* limitations; in which case there are no possible worlds He could not have created.

This is a subtle and important point. According to the great German philosopher G. W. Leibniz, *this* world, the actual world, must be the best of all possible worlds. His reasoning goes as follows. Before God created anything at all, He was confronted with an enormous range of choices; He could create or bring into actuality any of the myriads of different possible worlds. Being perfectly good, He must have chosen to create the best world He could; being omnipotent, He was able to create any possible world He pleased. He must, therefore, have chosen the best of all possible worlds; and hence *this* world, the one He did create, must be the best possible. Now Mackie, of course, agrees with Leibniz that God, if omnipotent, could have created any world He pleased and would have created the best world he could. But while Leibniz draws the conclusion that this world, despite appearances, must be the best possible, Mackie concludes instead that there is no omnipotent, wholly good God. For, he says, it is obvious enough that this present world is not the best of all possible worlds.

The Free Will defender disagrees with both Leibniz and Mackie. In the first place, he might say, what is the reason for supposing that *there* is such a thing as the best of all possible worlds? No matter how marvelous a world is containing no matter how many persons enjoying unalloyed bliss—isn't it possible that there be an even better world containing even more persons enjoying even more unalloyed bliss? But what is really characteristic and central to the Free Will Defense is the claim that God, though omnipotent, could not have actualized just any possible world He pleased.

WAS IT WITHIN GOD'S POWER TO CREATE ANY POSSIBLE WORLD HE PLEASED?

This is indeed the crucial question for the Free Will Defense. If we wish to discuss it with insight and authority, we shall have to look into the idea of *possible worlds*. And a sensible first question is this: what sort of thing is a possible world? The basic idea is that a possible world is a *way things could have been*; it is a *state of affairs* of some kind. Earlier we spoke of states of affairs, in particular of good and evil states of affairs. Suppose we look at this idea in more detail. What sort of thing is a state of affairs? The following would be examples:

Nixon's having won the 1972 election
7 + 5's being equal to 12
All men's being mortal

and

Gary, Indiana's, having a really nasty pollution problem.

These are *actual* states of affairs: states of affairs that do in fact *obtain*. And corresponding to each such actual state of affairs there is a true proposition—in the above cases, the corresponding propositions would be *Nixon won the 1972 presidential election, 7 + 5 is equal to 12, all men are mortal,* and *Gary, Indiana, has a really nasty pollution problem.* A proposition *p corresponds* to a state of affairs *s,* in this sense, if it is impossible that *p* be true and *s* fail to obtain and impossible that *s* obtain and *p* fail to be true.

But just as there are false propositions, so there are states of affairs that do not obtain or are *not* actual. *Kissinger's having swum the Atlantic* and *Hubert Horatio Humphrey's having run a mile in four minutes* would be examples. Some states of affairs that do not obtain are *impossible:* e.g., *Hubert's having drawn a square circle, 7 + 5's being equal to 75,* and *Agnew's having a brother who was an only child.* The propositions corresponding to these states of affairs, of course, are necessarily false. So there are states of affairs that *obtain* or *are actual* and also states of affairs that don't obtain. Among the latter some are *impossible* and others are possible. And a possible world is a possible state of affairs. Of course not every possible state of affairs is a possible world; *Hubert's having run a mile in four minutes* is a possible state of affairs but not a possible world. No doubt it is an *element* of many possible worlds, but it isn't itself inclusive enough to be one. To be a possible world, a state of affairs must be very large—so large as to be *complete* or *maximal.*

To get at this idea of completeness we need a couple of definitions. As we have already seen a state of affairs *A includes* a state of affairs *B* if it is not possible that *A* obtain and *B* not obtain or if the conjunctive state of affairs *A but not B*—the state of affairs that obtains if and only if *A* obtains and *B* does not—is not possible. For example, *Jim Whittaker's being the first American to climb Mt. Everest* includes *Jim*

Whittaker's being an American. It also includes *Mt. Everest's being climbed, something's being climbed, no American's having climbed Everest before Whittaker did*, and the like. *Inclusion* among states of affairs is like *entailment* among propositions; and where a state of affairs *A* includes a state of affairs *B*, the proposition corresponding to *A* entails the one corresponding to *B*. Accordingly, *Jim Whittaker is the first American to climb Everest* entails *Mt. Everest has been climbed, something has been climbed*, and *no American climbed Everest before Whittaker did*. Now suppose we say further that a state of affairs *A precludes* a state of affairs *B* if it is not possible that *both* obtain, or if the conjunctive state of affairs *A and B* is impossible. Thus *Whittaker's being the first American to climb Mt. Everest* precludes *Luther Jerstad's being the first American to climb Everest*, as well as *Whittaker's never having climbed any mountains*. If *A* precludes *B*, then *A*'s corresponding proposition entails the denial of the one corresponding to *B*. Still further, let's say that the *complement* of a state of affairs is the state of affairs that obtains just in case *A* does not obtain. [Or we might say that the complement (call it $\bar{A}$) of *A* is the state of affairs corresponding to the *denial* or *negation* of the proposition corresponding to *A*.] Given these definitions, we can say what it is for a state of affairs to be *complete*: *A* is a complete state of affairs if and only if for every state of affairs *B*, either *A includes B* or *A precludes B*. (We could express the same thing by saying that if *A* is a complete state of affairs, then for every state of affairs *B*, either *A* includes *B* or *A* includes $\bar{B}$, the complement of *B*.) And now we are able to say what a possible world is: a possible world is any possible state of affairs that is complete. If *A* is a possible world, then it says something about everything; every state of affairs *S* is either included in or precluded by it.

Corresponding to each possible world *W*, furthermore, there is a set of propositions that I'll call *the book on W*. A proposition is in the book on *W* just in case the state of affairs to which it corresponds is included in *W*. Or we might express it like this. Suppose we say that a proposition *P is true in a world W* if and only if *P would have been true if W had been actual*—if and only if, that is, it is not possible that *W* be actual and *P* be false. Then the book on *W* is the set

of propositions true in *W*. Like possible worlds, books are *complete*; if *B* is a book, then for any proposition *P*, either *P* or the denial of *P* will be a member of *B*. A book is a *maximal consistent set* of propositions; it is so large that the addition of another proposition to it always yields an explicitly inconsistent set.

Of course, for each possible world there is exactly one book corresponding to it (that is, for a given world *W* there is just one book *B* such that each member of *B* is true in *W*); and for each book there is just one world to which it corresponds. So every world has its book.

It should be obvious that exactly one possible world is actual. At *least* one must be, since the set of true propositions is a maximal consistent set and hence a book. But then it corresponds to a possible world, and the possible world corresponding to this set of propositions (since it's the set of *true* propositions) will be actual. On the other hand there is at *most* one actual world. For suppose there were two: *W* and *W'*. These worlds cannot include all the very same states of affairs; if they did, they would be the very same world. So there must be at least one state of affairs *S* such that *W* includes *S* and *W'* does not. But a possible world is maximal; *W'* therefore, includes the complement $\bar{S}$ of *S*. So if both *W* and *W'* were actual, as we have supposed, then both *S* and $\bar{S}$ would be actual—which is impossible. So there can't be more than one possible world that is actual.

Leibniz pointed out that a proposition *p* is necessary if it is true in every possible world. We may add that *p* is possible if it is true in one world and impossible if true in none. Furthermore, *p entails q* if there is no possible world in which *p* is true and *q* is false, and *p is consistent with q* if there is at least one world in which both *p* and *q* are true.

A further feature of possible worlds is that people (and other things) *exist* in them. Each of us exists in the actual world, obviously; but a person also exists in many worlds distinct from the actual world. It would be a mistake, of course, to think of all these worlds as somehow "going on" at the same time, with the same person reduplicated through these worlds and actually existing in a lot of different ways. This is not what is meant by saying that the same person exists in different possible worlds. What is meant, instead, is this: a person Paul exists in each of those possible worlds *W* which is such that, if *W had been actual*, Paul would have existed—actually existed. Suppose Paul had been an inch taller than he is, or a better tennis player. Then the world that does in fact obtain would not have been actual; some other world—*W'*, let's say—would have obtained instead. If *W'* had been actual, Paul would have existed; so Paul exists in *W'*. (Of course there are still other possible worlds in which Paul does not exist—worlds, for example, in which there are no people at all). Accordingly, when we say that Paul exists in a world *W*, what we mean is that Paul *would have* existed had *W* been actual. Or we could put it like this: Paul exists in each world *W* that includes the state of affairs consisting in Paul's existence. We can put this still more simply by saying that Paul exists in those worlds whose books contain the proposition *Paul exists*.

But isn't there a problem here? *Many* people are named "Paul": Paul the apostle, Paul J. Zwier, John Paul Jones, and many other famous Pauls. So who goes with "Paul exists"? Which Paul? The answer has to do with the fact that books contain *propositions*—not sentences. They contain the sort of thing sentences are used to express and assert. And the same sentence—"Aristotle is wise," for example—can be used to express many different propositions. When Plato used it, he asserted a proposition predicating wisdom of his famous pupil; when Jackie Onassis uses it, she asserts a proposition predicating wisdom of her wealthy husband. These are distinct propositions (we might even think they differ in truth value); but they are expressed by the same sentence. Normally (but not always) we don't have much trouble determining which of the several propositions expressed by a given sentence is relevant in the context at hand. So in this case a given person, Paul, exists in a world *W* if and only if *W*'s book contains the proposition that says that *he*—that particular person—exists. The fact that the sentence we use to express this proposition can also be used to express *other* propositions is not relevant.

After this excursion into the nature of books and worlds we can return to our question. Could God have created just any world He chose? Before

addressing the question, however, we must note that God does not, strictly speaking, *create* any possible worlds or states of affairs at all. What He creates are the heavens and the earth and all that they contain. But He has not created states of affairs. There are, for example, the state of affairs consisting in God's existence and the states of affairs consisting in His nonexistence. That is, there is such a thing as the state of affairs consisting in the existence of God, and there is also such a thing as the state of affairs consisting in the nonexistence of God, just as there are the two propositions *God exists* and *God does not exist*. The theist believes that the first state of affairs is actual and the first proposition true, the atheist believes that the second state of affairs is actual and the second proposition true. But, of course, both propositions *exist*, even though just one is true. Similarly, there are two states of affairs here, just one of which is actual. So both states of affairs *exist*, but only one *obtains*. And God has not created either one of them since there never was a time at which either did not exist. Nor has He created the state of affairs consisting in the earth's existence; there was a time when the *earth* did not exist, but none when the state of affairs consisting in the earth's existence didn't exist. Indeed, God did not bring into existence any states of affairs at all. What He did was to perform actions of a certain sort—the. heavens and the earth, for example—which resulted in the *actuality* of certain states of affairs. God *actualizes* states of affairs. He actualizes the possible world that does in fact obtain; He does not create it. And while He has created Socrates, He did not create the state of affairs consisting in Socrates' existence.[13]

Bearing this in mind, let's finally return to our question. Is the atheologian right in holding that if God is omnipotent, then he could have actualized or created any possible world He pleased? Not obviously. First, we must ask ourselves whether God is a *necessary* or a *contingent* being. A *necessary* being is one that exists in every possible world—one that would have existed no matter which possible world had been actual; a contingent being exists only in some possible worlds. Now if God is not a necessary being (and many, perhaps most, theists think that He is not), then clearly enough there will be many possible worlds He could not have actualized—all those, for example, in which He does not exist. Clearly, God could not have created a world in which He doesn't even exist.

So, if God is a contingent being then there are many possible worlds beyond His power to create. But this is really irrelevant to our present concerns. For perhaps the atheologian can maintain his case if he revises his claim to avoid this difficulty; perhaps he will say something like this: if God is omnipotent, then He could have actualized any of those possible worlds *in which He exists*. So if He exists and is omnipotent, He could have actualized (contrary to the Free Will Defense) any of those possible worlds in which He exists and in which there exist free creatures who do no wrong. He could have actualized worlds containing moral good but no moral evil. Is this correct?

Let's begin with a trivial example. You and Paul have just returned from an Australian hunting expedition: your quarry was the elusive double-wattled cassowary. Paul captured an aardvark, mistaking it for a cassowary. The creature's disarming ways have won it a place in Paul's heart; he is deeply attached to it. Upon your return to the States you offer Paul $500 for his aardvark, only to be rudely turned down. Later you ask yourself, "What would he have done if I'd offered him $700?" Now what is it, exactly, that you are asking? What you're really asking in a way is whether, under a *specific set of conditions*, Paul would have sold it. These conditions include your having offered him $700 rather than $500 for the aardvark, everything else being as much as possible like the conditions that did in fact obtain. Let S' be this set of conditions or state of affairs. S' includes the state of affairs consisting in your offering Paul $700 (instead of the $500 you did offer him); of course it does not include his *accepting* your offer, and it does not include his *rejecting* it; for the rest, the conditions it includes are just like the ones that did obtain in the actual world. So, for example, S' includes Paul's being free to accept the offer and free to refrain; and if in fact the going rate for an aardvark was $650, then S' includes the state of affairs consisting in the going rate's being $650. So we might put your question by asking which of the following conditionals is true:

(23) If the state of affairs S' had obtained, Paul would have accepted the offer

(24) If the state of affairs S' had obtained, Paul would not have accepted the offer.

It seems clear that at least one of these conditionals is true, but naturally they can't both be; so exactly one is.

Now since S' includes neither Paul's accepting the offer nor his rejecting it, the antecedent of (23) and (24) does not entail the consequent of either. That is,

(25) S' obtains

does not entail either

(26) Paul accepts the offer

or

(27) Paul does not accept the offer.

So there are possible worlds in which both (25) and (26) are true, and other possible worlds in which both (25) and (27) are true.

We are now in a position to grasp an important fact. Either (23) or (24) is in fact true; and either way there are possible worlds God could not have actualized. Suppose, first of all, that (23) is true. Then it was beyond the power of God to create a world in which (1) Paul is free to sell his aardvark and free to refrain, and in which the other states of affairs included in S' obtain, and (2) Paul does not sell. That is, it was beyond His power to create a world in which (25) and (27) are both true. There is at least one possible world like this, but God, despite His omnipotence, could not have brought about its actuality. For let W be such a world. To actualize W, God must bring it about that Paul is free with respect to this action, and that the other states of affairs included in S' obtain. But (23), as we are supposing, is true; so if God had actualized S' and left Paul *free* with respect to this action, he would have sold: in which case W would not have been actual. If, on the other hand, God had *brought it about* that Paul didn't sell or had *caused him* to refrain from selling, then Paul would not have been free with respect to this action; then S' would not have been actual (since S' includes Paul's being free with respect to it), and *W* would not have been actual since *W* includes *S'*.

Of course if it is (24) rather than (23) that is true, then another class of worlds was beyond God's power to actualize—those, namely, in which *S'* obtains and Paul *sells* his aardvark. These are the worlds in which both (25) and (26) are true. But either (23) or (24) is true. Therefore, there are possible worlds God could not have actualized. If we consider whether or not God could have created a world in which, let's say, both (25) and (26) are true, we see that the answer depends upon a peculiar kind of fact; it depends upon what Paul would have freely chosen to do in a certain situation. So there are any number of possible worlds such that it is partly up to Paul whether God can create them.[14]

That was a past tense example. Perhaps it would be useful to consider a future tense case, since this might seem to correspond more closely to God's situation in choosing a possible world to actualize. At some time *t* in the near future Maurice will be free with respect to some insignificant action—having freeze-dried oatmeal for breakfast, let's say. That is, at time *t* Maurice will be free to have oatmeal but also free to take something else—shredded wheat, perhaps. Next, suppose we consider *S'*, a state of affairs that is included in the actual world and includes Maurice's being free with respect to taking oatmeal at time *t*. That is, *S'* includes Maurice's being free at time *t* to take oatmeal and free to reject it. *S'* does not include Maurice's taking oatmeal, however; nor does it include his rejecting it. For the rest *S'* is as much as possible like the actual world. In particular there are many conditions that do in fact hold at time *t* and are *relevant* to his choice—such conditions, for example, as the fact that he hasn't had oatmeal lately, that his wife will be annoyed if he rejects it, and the like; and *S'* includes each of these conditions. Now God no doubt knows what Maurice will do at time *t*, if S obtains; He knows which action Maurice would freely perform if S were to be actual. That is, God knows that one of the following conditionals is true:

(28) If *S'* were to obtain, Maurice will freely take the oatmeal

or

(29) If *S'* were to obtain, Maurice will freely reject it.

We may not know which of these is true, and Maurice himself may not know; but presumably God does.

So either God knows that (28) is true, or else He knows that (29) is. Let's suppose it is (28). Then there is a possible world that God, though omnipotent, cannot create. For consider a possible world *W'* that shares *S'* with the actual world (which for ease of reference I'll name "Kronos") and in which Maurice does *not* take oatmeal. (We know there is such a world, since *S'* does not include Maurice's taking the oatmeal.) *S'* obtains in *W'* just as it does in Kronos. Indeed, everything in *W'* is just as it is in Kronos up to time *t*. But whereas in Kronos Maurice takes oatmeal at time *t*, in *W'* he does not. Now *W'* is a perfectly possible world; but it is not within God's power to create it or bring about its actuality. For to do so He must actualize *S'*. But (28) is in fact true. So if God actualizes *S'* (as He must to create *W'*) and leaves Maurice free with respect to the action in question, then he will take the oatmeal; and then, of course, *W'* will not be actual. If, on the other hand, God causes Maurice to *refrain* from taking the oatmeal, then he is not *free* to take it. That means, once again, that *W'* is not actual; for in *W'* Maurice is free to take the oatmeal (even if he doesn't do so). So if (28) is true, then this world *W'* is one that God can't actualize, it is not within His power to actualize it even though He is omnipotent and it is a possible world.

Of course, if it is (29) that is true, we get a similar result; then too there are possible worlds that God can't actualize. These would be worlds which share *S'* with Kronos and in which Maurice *does* take oatmeal. But either (28) or (29) *is* true; so either way there is a possible world that God can't create. If we consider a world in which *S'* obtains and in which Maurice freely chooses oatmeal at time *t*, we see that whether or not it is within God's power to actualize it depends upon what Maurice would do if he were free in a certain situation. Accordingly, there are any number of possible worlds such that it is partly up to Maurice whether or not God can actualize them. It is, of course, up to God whether or not to create Maurice and also up to God whether or not to make him free with respect to the action of taking oatmeal at time *t*. (God could, if He chose, cause him to succumb to the dreaded *equine obsession*, a condition shared by some people and most horses, whose victims find it *psychologically impossible* to refuse oats or oat products.) But if He creates Maurice and creates him free with respect to this action, then whether or not he actually performs the action is up to Maurice—not God.[15]

Now we can return to the Free Will Defense and the problem of evil. The Free Will defender, you recall, insists on the possibility that it is not within God's power to create a world containing moral good without creating one containing moral evil. His atheological opponent—Mackie, for example—agrees with Leibniz in insisting that *if* (as the theist holds) God is omnipotent, then it *follows* that He could have created any possible world He pleased. We now see that this contention—call it "Leibniz's Lapse"—is a mistake. The atheologian is right in holding that there are many possible worlds containing moral good but no moral evil; his mistake lies in endorsing Leibniz's Lapse. So one of his premises—that God, if omnipotent, could have actualized just any world He pleased—is false.

Could God Have Created a World Containing Moral Good but No Moral Evil?

Now suppose we recapitulate the logic of the situation. The Free Will Defender claims that the following is possible:

(30) God is omnipotent, and it was not within His power to create a world containing moral good but no moral evil.

By way of retort the atheologian insists that there are possible worlds containing moral good but no moral evil. He adds that an omnipotent being could have actualized any possible world he chose. So if God is omnipotent, it follows that He could have actualized a world containing moral good but no moral evil, hence (30), contrary to the Free Will defender's claim, is not possible. What we have seen so far is that his second premise—Leibniz's Lapse—is false.

Of course, this does not settle the issue in the Free Will defender's favor. Leibniz's Lapse (appropriately enough for a lapse) is false; but this doesn't show that (30) is possible. To show this latter we must demonstrate the possibility that among the worlds God could not have actualized are all the worlds containing moral good but no moral evil. How can we approach this question?

Instead of choosing oatmeal for breakfast or selling an aardvark, suppose we think about a morally significant action such as taking a bribe. Curley Smith, the mayor of Boston, is opposed to the proposed freeway route; it would require destruction of the Old North Church along with some other antiquated and structurally unsound buildings. L. B. Smedes, the director of highways, asks him whether he'd drop his opposition for $1 million. "Of course," he replies. "Would you do it for $2?" asks Smedes. "What do you take me for?" comes the indignant reply. "That's already established," smirks Smedes; "all that remains is to nail down your price." Smedes then offers him a bribe of $35,000; unwilling to break with the fine old traditions of Bay State politics, Curley accepts. Smedes then spends a sleepless night wondering whether he could have bought Curley for $20,000.

Now suppose we assume that Curley was free with respect to the action of taking the bribe—free to take it and free to refuse. And suppose, furthermore, that he would have taken it. That is, let us suppose that

(31) If Smedes had offered Curley a bribe of $20,000, he would have accepted it.

If (31) is true, then there is a state of affairs S' that (1) includes Curley's being offered a bribe of $20,000; (2) does not include either his accepting the bribe or his rejecting it; and (3) is otherwise as much as possible like the actual world. Just to make sure S' includes every relevant circumstance, let us suppose that it is a *maximal world segment*. That is, add to S' any state of affairs compatible with but not included in it, and the result will be an entire possible world. We could think of it roughly like this: S' is included in at least one world W in which Curley takes the bribe and in at least one world W' in which he rejects it. If S' is a maximal world segment, then S' is what remains of W when *Curley's taking the bribe* is deleted; it is also what remains of W' when *Curley's rejecting the bribe* is detected. More exactly, if S' is a maximal world segment, then every possible state of affairs that includes S', but isn't included by S', is a possible world. So if (31) is true, then there is a maximal world segment S' that (1) includes Curley's being offered a bribe of $20,000; (2) does not include either his accepting the bribe or his rejecting it; (3) is otherwise as much as possible like the actual world—in particular, it includes Curley's being free with respect to the bribe; and (4) is such that if it were actual then Curley would have taken the bribe. That is,

> (32) If S' were actual, Curley would have accepted the bribe is true.

Now, of course, there is at least one possible world W' in which S' is actual and Curley does not take the bribe. But God could not have created W'; to do so, He would have been obliged to actualize S', leaving Curley free with respect to the action of taking the bribe. But under these conditions Curley, as (32) assures us, would have accepted the bribe, so that the world thus created would not have been S'.

Curley, as we see, is not above a bit of Watergating. But there may be worse to come. Of course, there are possible worlds in which he is significantly free (i.e., free with respect to a morally significant action) and never does what is wrong. But the sad truth about Curley may be this. Consider W', any of these worlds: in W' Curley is significantly free, so in W' there are some actions that are morally significant for him and with respect to which he is free. But at least one of these actions—call it A—has the following peculiar property. There is a maximal world segment S' that obtains in W' and is such that (1) S' includes Curley's being free *re* A but neither his performing A nor his refraining from A; (2) S' is otherwise as much as possible like W'; and (3) if S' had been actual, Curley would have gone wrong with respect to A.[16] (Notice that this third condition holds in fact, in the actual world; it does not hold in that world W'.)

This means, of course, that God could not have actualized W'. For to do so He'd have been obliged to bring it about that S' is actual; but then Curley would go wrong with respect to A. Since in W' he always does what is right, the world thus actualized would not be W'. On the other hand, if God *causes* Curley to go right with respect to A or *brings it about that* he

does so, then Curley isn't free with respect to A; and so once more it isn't W' that is actual. Accordingly God cannot create W'. But W' was just any of the worlds in which Curley is significantly free but always does only what is right. It therefore follows that it was not within God's power to create a world in which Curley produces moral good but no moral evil. Every world God can actualize is such that if Curley is significantly free in it, he takes at least one wrong action.

Obviously Curley is in serious trouble. I shall call the malady from which he suffers *transworld depravity*. (I leave as homework the problem of comparing transworld depravity with what Calvinists call "total depravity.") By way of explicit definition:

> (33) A person P *suffers from transworld depravity* if and only if the following holds: for every world W such that P is significantly free in W and, P does only what is right in W, there is an action A and a maximal world segment S' such that
>
> (1) S' includes A's being morally significant for P
> (2) S' includes P's being free with respect to A
> (3) S' is included in W and includes neither P's performing A nor P's refraining from performing A

and

> (4) If S' were actual, P would go wrong with respect to A.

(In thinking about this definition, remember that (4) is to be true in fact, in the actual world—not in that world W.)

What is important about the idea of transworld depravity is that if a person suffers from it, then it wasn't within God's power to actualize any world in which that person is significantly free but does no wrong—that is, a world in which he produces moral good but no moral evil.

We have been here considering a crucial contention of the Free Will defender: the contention, namely, that

> (30) God is omnipotent, and it was not within His power to create a world containing moral good but no moral evil.

How is transworld depravity relevant to this? As follows. Obviously it is possible that there be persons who suffer from transworld depravity. More generally, it is possible that *everybody* suffers from it. And if this possibility were actual, then God, though omnipotent, could not have created any of the possible worlds containing just the persons who do in fact exist, and containing moral good but no moral evil. For to do so He'd have to create persons who were significantly free (otherwise there would be no moral good) but suffered from transworld depravity. Such persons go wrong with respect to at least one action in any world God could have actualized and in which they are free with respect to morally significant actions; so the price for creating a world in which they produce moral good is creating one in which they also produce moral evil.

Notes

1. John Mackie, "Evil and Omnipotence," in *The Philosophy of Religion*, ed. Basil Mitchell (London: Oxford University Press, 1971), p. 92.
2. Ibid., pp. 92–93.
3. Ibid., p. 93.
4. More simply the question is really just whether any good state of affairs includes an evil; a little reflection reveals that no good state of affairs can include an evil that it does *not* outweigh.
5. In Plantinga, *God and Other Minds* (Ithaca, N.Y.: Cornell University Press, 1967), chap. 5, I explore further the project of finding such propositions.
6. *The Problem of Free Choice*, vol. 22 of *Ancient Christian Writers* (Westminster, Md.: Newman Press, 1955), bk. 2, pp. 4–15.
7. Ibid., bk. 3, p. 9.
8. I am indebted to Henry Schuurman (in conversation) for helpful discussion of the difference between this pastoral function and those served by a theodicy or a defense.
9. This distinction is not very precise (how, exactly, are we to construe "results from"?), but perhaps it will serve our present purposes.
10. See, for example, A. Flew, "Divine Omnipotence and Human Freedom," in *New Essays in Philosophical Theology*, eds. A. Flew and A. MacIntyre (London: SCM, 1955), pp. 150–153.
11. For further discussion of it see Plantinga, *God and Other Minds*, pp. 132–135.
12. Mackie, in *The Philosophy of Religion*, pp. 100–101.
13. Strict accuracy demands, therefore, that we speak of God as *actualizing* rather than creating possible worlds. I shall continue to use both locutions, thus sacrificing accuracy to familiarity. For more about possible worlds see my book *The Nature of Necessity* (Oxford, England: Clarendon Press, 1974), chaps. 4–8.
14. For a fuller statement of this argument see Plantinga, *The Nature of Necessity*, chap. 9, secs. 4–6.
15. For a more complete and more exact statement of this argument see Plantinga, *The Nature of Necessity*, chap. 9, secs. 4–6.
16. A person goes wrong with respect to an action if he either wrongfully performs it or wrongfully fails to perform it.

Study Questions

1. Engaging Mackie's logical problem of evil, Plantinga examines different kinds of contradiction and different kinds of necessity and possibility. Cite as many logical concepts as you can in Plantinga's case and then show that they clarify the nature of the debate.
2. Explore how Plantinga critiques Mackie's definitions of omnipotence and perfect moral goodness.
3. In a general way, how can one refute the charge that a set of statements is logically inconsistent—that is, how can one show consistency? How does Plantinga's case reflect this strategy?
4. Plantinga's defense of theism against the logical problem of evil involves the concept of significant free will. Discuss and evaluate in depth how this concept plays into the Free Will Defense.

John Hick

Soul-Making Theodicy

John Hick (b. 1922) offers an explanation for evil in the world that contrasts to the well-known Augustinian type of theodicy. Whereas Augustinian theodicy sees present evil as representing a fall from a pristine, original state of the world, Hick follows St. Irenaeus in arguing that an adequate answer lies not in seeking the causal genesis of evil but in interpreting evil as a stage in human progress and development. In other words, rather than view the present state of the world as fallen from a kind of previous perfection, Hick views the world as a necessary stage in the evolution of a relatively immature creation into a more mature state. God seeks to bring forth mature moral and spiritual beings who are capable of freely exercising faith in him and love toward their fellows. Hick discusses the main features of an environment that would be conducive to bringing about these results. Two such features are ambiguity about the existence of God and human vulnerability to one another—both of which provide opportunities for moral and spiritual growth. In the larger context of Hick's writings, we find that the divine program of soul making will culminate in the afterlife, which Hick believes must involve universal salvation.

Can a world in which sadistic cruelty often has its way, in which selfish lovelessness is so rife, in which there are debilitating diseases, crippling accidents, bodily and mental decay, insanity, and all manner of natural disasters be regarded as the expression of infinite creative goodness? Certainly all this could never by itself lead anyone to believe in the existence of a limitlessly powerful God. And yet even in a world which contains these things innumerable men and women have believed and do believe in the reality of an infinite creative goodness, which they call God. The theodicy project starts at this point, with an already operating belief in God, embodied in human living, and attempts to show that this belief is not rendered irrational by the fact of evil. It attempts to explain how it is that the universe, assumed to be created and ultimately ruled by a limitlessly good and limitlessly powerful Being, is as it is, including all the pain and suffering and all the wickedness and folly that we find around us and within us. The theodicy project is thus an exercise in metaphysical construction, in the sense that it consists in the formation and criticism of large-scale hypotheses concerning the nature and process of the universe.

Since a theodicy both starts from and tests belief in the reality of God, it naturally takes different forms in relation to different concepts of God. In this essay I shall be discussing the project of a specifically Christian theodicy; I shall not be attempting the further and even more difficult work of comparative theodicy, leading in turn to the question of a global theodicy.

The two main demands upon a theodicy hypothesis are (1) that it be internally coherent, and (2) that it be consistent with the data both of the religious tradition on which it is based, and of the world, in respect both of the latter's general character as revealed by scientific enquiry and of the specific facts of moral and natural evil. These two criteria demand, respectively, possibility and plausibility.

Traditionally, Christian theology has centered upon the concept of God as both limitlessly powerful and limitlessly good and loving; and it is this concept of deity that gives rise to the problem of evil as a threat to theistic faith. The threat was definitively expressed in Stendhal's bombshell, "The only excuse for God is that he does not exist!" The theodicy project is the attempt to offer a different view of the universe which is both possible and plausible and which does not ignite Stendhal's bombshell.

Christian thought has always included a certain range of variety, and in the area of theodicy it offers two broad types of approach. The Augustinian approach, representing until fairly recently the majority report of the Christian mind, hinges upon the idea of the fall, which has in turn brought about the disharmony of nature. This type of theodicy is developed today as "the free will defense." The Irenaean approach, representing in the past a minority report, hinges upon the creation of humankind through the evolutionary process as an immature creature living in a challenging and therefore person-making world. I shall indicate very briefly why I do not find the first type of theodicy satisfactory, and then spend the remainder of this essay in exploring the second type.

In recent years the philosophical discussion of the problem of evil has been dominated by the free will defense. A major effort has been made by Alvin Plantinga and a number of other Christian philosophers to show that it is logically possible that a limitlessly powerful and limitlessly good God is responsible for the existence of this world. For all evil may ultimately be due to misuses of creaturely freedom. But it may nevertheless be better for God to have created free than unfree beings; and it is logically possible that any and all free beings whom God might create would, as a matter of contingent fact, misuse their freedom by falling into sin. In that case it would be logically impossible for God to have created a world containing free beings and yet not containing sin and the suffering which sin brings with it. Thus it is logically possible, despite the fact of evil, that the existing universe is the work of a limitlessly good creator.

These writers are in effect arguing that the traditional Augustinian type of theodicy, based upon the fall from grace of free finite creatures—first angels and then human beings—and a consequent going wrong of the physical world, is not logically impossible. I am in fact doubtful whether their argument is sound, and will return to the question later. But even if it should be sound, I suggest that their argument wins only a Pyrrhic victory, since the logical possibility that it would establish is one which, for very many people today, is fatally lacking in plausibility. For most educated inhabitants of the modern world regard the biblical story of Adam and Eve, and their temptation by the devil, as myth rather than as history; and they believe that so far from having been created finitely perfect and then failing, humanity evolved out of lower forms of life, emerging in a morally, spiritually, and culturally primitive state. Further, they reject as incredible the idea that earthquake and flood, disease, decay, and death are consequences either of a human fall, or of a prior fall of angelic beings who are now exerting an evil influence upon the earth. They see all this as part of a pre-scientific world view, along with the stories of the world having been created in six days and of the sun standing still for twenty-four hours at Joshua's command. One cannot, strictly speaking, disprove any of these ancient biblical myths and sagas, or refute their confident elaboration in the medieval Christian picture of the universe. But those of us for whom the resulting theodicy, even if logically possible, is radically implausible, must look elsewhere for light on the problem of evil.

I believe that we find the light that we need in the main alternative strand of Christian thinking, which goes back to important constructive suggestions by the early Hellenistic Fathers of the Church, particularly St. Irenaeus (A.D. 120–202). Irenaeus himself did not develop a theodicy, but he did—together with other Greek-speaking Christian writers of that period, such as Clement of Alexandria—build a framework of thought within which a theodicy became possible which does not depend upon the idea of the fall, and which is consonant with modern knowledge concerning the origins of the human race. This theodicy cannot, as such, be attributed to Irenaeus. We should rather speak of a type of theodicy, presented in varying ways by different subsequent thinkers (the greatest of whom has been Friedrich Schleiermacher), of which Irenaeus can properly be regarded as the patron saint.

The central theme out of which this Irenaean type of theodicy has arisen is the two-stage conception of the creation of humankind, first in the "image" and then in the "likeness" of God. Re-expressing this in modern terms, the first stage was the gradual production of homo sapiens, through the long evolutionary process, as intelligent ethical and religious animals. The human being is an animal, one of the varied forms of earthly life and continuous as such with the whole realm of animal existence. But the human being is uniquely intelligent, having evolved a large and immensely complex brain. Further, the human being is ethical—that is, a gregarious as well as an intelligent animal, able to realize and respond to the complex demands of social life. And the human being is a religious animal, with an innate tendency to experience the world in terms of the presence and activity of supernatural beings and powers. This then is early homo sapiens, the intelligent social animal capable of awareness of the divine. But early homo sapiens is not the Adam and Eve of Augustinian theology, living in perfect harmony with self, with nature, and with God. On the contrary, the life of this being must have been a constant struggle against a hostile environment, and capable of savage violence against one's fellow human beings, particularly outside one's

own immediate group; and this being's concepts of the divine were primitive and often bloodthirsty. Thus existence "in the image of God" was a potentiality for knowledge of and relationship with one's Maker rather than such knowledge and relationship as a fully realized state. In other words, people were created as spiritually and morally immature creatures, at the beginning of a long process of further growth and development, which constitutes the second stage of God's creative work. In this second stage, of which we are a part, the intelligent, ethical, and religious animal is being brought through one's own free responses into what Irenaeus called the divine "likeness." The human animal is being created into a child of God. Irenaeus' own terminology (*eikon, homoiosis; imago, similitudo*) has no particular merit, based as it is on a misunderstanding of the Hebrew parallelism in Genesis 1:26; but his conception of a two-stage creation of the human, with perfection lying in the future rather than in the past, is of fundamental importance. The notion of the fall was not basic to this picture, although it was to become basic to the great drama of salvation depicted by St. Augustine and accepted within Western Christendom, including the churches stemming from the Reformation, until well into the nineteenth century. Irenaeus himself however could not, in the historical knowledge of his time, question the fact of the fall; though he treated it as a relatively minor lapse, a youthful error, rather than as the infinite crime and cosmic disaster which has ruined the whole creation. But today we can acknowledge that there is no evidence at all of a period in the distant past when humankind was in the ideal state of a fully realized "child of God." We can accept that, so far as actual events in time are concerned, there never was a fall from an original righteousness and grace. If we want to continue to use the term fall, because of its hallowed place in the Christian tradition, we must use it to refer to the immense gap between what we actually are and what in the divine intention is eventually to be. But we must not blur our awareness that the ideal state is not something already enjoyed and lost, but is a future and as yet unrealized goal. The reality is not a perfect creation which has gone tragically wrong, but a still continuing creative process whose completion lies in the eschaton.

Let us now try to formulate a contemporary version of the Irenaean type of theodicy, based on this suggestion of the initial creation of humankind, not as a finitely perfect, but as an immature creature at the beginning of a long process of further growth and development. We may begin by asking why one should have been created as an imperfect and developing creature rather than as the perfect being whom God is presumably intending to create? The answer, I think, consists in two considerations which converge in their practical implications, one concerned with the human's relationship to God and the other with the relationship to other human beings. As to the first, we could have the picture of God creating finite beings, whether angels or persons, directly in God's own presence, so that in being conscious of that which is other than one's self the creature is automatically conscious of God, the limitless divine reality and power, goodness and love, knowledge and wisdom, towering above one's self. In such a situation the disproportion between Creator and creatures would be so great that the latter would have no freedom in relation to God; they would indeed not exist as independent autonomous persons. For what freedom could finite beings have in an immediate consciousness of the presence of the one who has created them, who knows them through and through, who is limitlessly powerful as well as limitlessly loving and good, and who claims their total obedience? In order to be a person, exercising some measure of genuine freedom, the creature must be brought into existence, not in the immediate divine presence, but at a "distance" from God. This "distance" cannot of course be spatial; for God is omnipresent. It must be an epistemic distance, a distance in the cognitive dimension. And the Irenaean hypothesis is that this "distance" consists, in the case of humans, in their existence within and as part of a world which functions as an autonomous system and from within which God is not overwhelmingly evident. It is a world, in Bonhoeffer's phrase, *etsi deus non daretur*, as if there were no God. Or rather, it is religiously ambiguous, capable both of being seen as a purely natural phenomenon and of being seen as God's creation and experienced as mediating God's presence. In such a world one can exist as a person over against the Creator. One has

space to exist as a finite being, a space created by the epistemic distance from God and protected by one's basic cognitive freedom, one's freedom to open or close oneself to the dawning awareness of God which is experienced naturally by a religious animal. This Irenaean picture corresponds, I suggest, to our actual human situation. Emerging within the evolutionary process as part of the continuum of animal life, in a universe which functions in accordance with its own laws and whose workings can be investigated and described without reference to a creator, the human being has a genuine, even awesome, freedom in relation to one's Maker. The human being is free to acknowledge and worship God; and is free—particularly since the emergence of human individuality and the beginnings of critical consciousness during the first millennium B.C.—to doubt the reality of God.

Within such a situation there is the possibility of the human being coming freely to know and love one's Maker. Indeed, if the end state which God is seeking to bring about is one in which finite persons have come in their own freedom to know and love God, this requires creating them initially in a state which is not that of their already knowing and loving God. For it is logically impossible to create beings already in a state of having come into that state by their own free choices.

The other consideration, which converges with this in pointing to something like the human situation as we experience it, concerns our human moral nature. We can approach it by asking why humans should not have been created at this epistemic distance from God, and yet at the same time as morally perfect beings? That persons could have been created morally perfect and yet free, so that they would always in fact choose rightly, has been argued by such critics of the free-will defense in theodicy as Antony Flew and J. L. Mackie, and argued against by Alvin Plantinga and other upholders of that form of theodicy. On the specific issue defined in the debate between them, it appears to me that the criticism of the free-will defense stands. It appears to me that a perfectly good being, although formally free to sin, would in fact never do so. If we imagine such a being in a morally frictionless environment, involving no stresses or temptation, then we must assume that one would exemplify the ethical equivalent of Newton's first law of motion, which states that a moving body will continue in uniform motion until interfered with by some outside force. By analogy, a perfectly good being would continue in the same moral course forever, there being nothing in the environment to throw one off it. But even if we suppose the morally perfect being to exist in an imperfect world, in which one is subject to temptations, it still follows that, in virtue of moral perfection, one will always overcome those temptations—as in the case, according to orthodox Christian belief, of Jesus Christ. It is, to be sure, logically possible, as Plantinga and others argue, that a free being, simply as such, may at any time contingently decide to sin. However, a responsible free being does not act randomly, but on the basis of moral nature. And a free being whose nature is wholly and unqualifiedly good will accordingly never in fact sin.

But if God could, without logical contradiction, have created humans as wholly good free beings, why did God not do so? Why was humanity not initially created in possession of all the virtues, instead of having to acquire them through the long hard struggle of life as we know it? The answer, I suggest, appeals to the principle that virtues which have been formed within the agent as a hard-won deposit of her own right decisions in situations of challenge and temptation, are intrinsically more valuable than virtues created within her ready made and without any effort on her own part. This principle expresses a basic value judgment, which cannot be established by argument but which one can only present, in the hope that it will be as morally plausible, and indeed compelling, to others as to oneself. It is, to repeat, the judgment that a moral goodness which exists as the agent's initial given nature, without ever having been chosen by her in the face of temptations to the contrary, is intrinsically less valuable than a moral goodness which has been built up through the agent's own responsible choices through time in the face of alternative possibilities.

If, then, God's purpose was to create finite persons embodying the most valuable kind of moral goodness, God would have to create them, not as already perfect beings but rather as imperfect creatures who can then attain to the more valuable kind of goodness

through their own free choices as in the course of their personal and social history new responses prompt new insights, opening up new moral possibilities, and providing a milieu in which the most valuable kind of moral nature can be developed.

We have thus far, then, the hypothesis that one is created at an epistemic distance from God in order to come freely to know and love the Maker; and that one is at the same time created as a morally immature and imperfect being in order to attain through freedom the most valuable quality of goodness. The end sought, according to this hypothesis, is the full realization of the human potentialities in a unitary spiritual and moral perfection in the divine kingdom. And the question we have to ask is whether humans as we know them, and the world as we know it, are compatible with this hypothesis.

Clearly we cannot expect to be able to deduce our actual world in its concrete character, and our actual human nature as part of it, from the general concept of spiritually and morally immature creatures developing ethically in an appropriate environment. No doubt there is an immense range of possible worlds, any one of which, if actualized, would exemplify this concept. All that we can hope to do is to show that our actual world is one of these. And when we look at our human situation as part of the evolving life of this planet we can, I think, see that it fits this specification. As animal organisms, integral to the whole ecology of life, we are programmed for survival. In pursuit of survival, primitives not only killed other animals for food but fought other human beings when their vital interests conflicted. The life of prehistoric persons must indeed have been a constant struggle to stay alive, prolonging an existence which was, in Hobbes's phrase, "poor, nasty, brutish and short." And in his basic animal self-regardingness humankind was, and is, morally imperfect. In saying this I am assuming that the essence of moral evil is selfishness, the sacrificing of others to one's own interests. It consists, in Kantian terminology, in treating others, not as ends in themselves, but as means to one's own ends. This is what the survival instinct demands. And yet we are also capable of love, of self-giving in a common cause, of a conscience which responds to others in their needs and dangers. And with the development of civilization we see the growth of moral insight, the glimpsing and gradual assimilation of higher ideals, and tension between our animality and our ethical values. But that the human being has a lower as well as a higher nature, that one is an animal as well as a potential child of God, and that one's moral goodness is won from a struggle with one's own innate selfishness, is inevitable given one's continuity with the other forms of animal life. Further, the human animal is not responsible for having come into existence as an animal. The ultimate responsibility for humankind's existence, as a morally imperfect creature, can only rest with the Creator. The human does not, in one's own degree of freedom and responsibility, choose one's origin, but rather one's destiny.

This then, in brief outline, is the answer of the Irenaean type of theodicy to the question of the origin of moral evil: the general fact of humankind's basic self-regarding animality is an aspect of creation as part of the realm of organic life; and this basic self-regardingness has been expressed over the centuries both in sins of individual selfishness and in the much more massive sins of corporate selfishness, institutionalized in slavery and exploitation and all the many and complex forms of social injustice.

But nevertheless our sinful nature in a sinful world is the matrix within which God is gradually creating children of God out of human animals. For it is as men and women freely respond to the claim of God upon their lives, transmuting their animality into the structure of divine worship, that the creation of humanity is taking place. And in its concrete character this response consists in every form of moral goodness, from unselfish love in individual personal relationships to the dedicated and selfless striving to end exploitation and to create justice within and between societies.

But one cannot discuss moral evil without at the same time discussing the non-moral evil of pain and suffering. (I propose to mean by "pain" physical pain, including the pains of hunger and thirst; and by "suffering" the mental and emotional pain of loneliness, anxiety, remorse, lack of love, fear, grief, envy, etc.) For what constitutes moral evil as evil is the fact that it causes pain and suffering. It is impossible to conceive of an instance of moral evil, or sin, which is not productive of pain or suffering to anyone at any time. But in addition to moral evil there is another source of pain and suffering in the structure of the physical world, which produces storms, earthquakes, and floods and which afflicts the human body with diseases—cholera, epilepsy, cancer, malaria, arthritis, rickets, meningitis, etc.—as well as with broken bones and other outcomes of physical accident. It is true that a great deal both of pain and of suffering is humanly caused, not only by the "inhumanity of man to man" but also by the stresses of our individual and corporate lifestyles, causing many disorders—not only lung cancer and cirrhosis of the liver but many cases of heart disease, stomach and other ulcers, strokes, etc.—as well as accidents. But there remain nevertheless, in the natural world itself, permanent causes of human pain and suffering. And we have to ask why an unlimitedly good and unlimitedly powerful God should have created so dangerous a world, both as regards its purely natural hazards of earthquake and flood, etc., and as regards the liability of the human body to so many ills, both psychosomatic and purely somatic.

The answer offered by the Irenaean type of theodicy follows from and is indeed integrally bound up with its account of the origin of moral evil. We have the hypothesis of humankind being brought into being within the evolutionary process as a spiritually and morally immature creature, and then growing and developing through the exercise of freedom in this religiously ambiguous world. We can now ask what sort of a world would constitute an appropriate environment for this second stage of creation? The development of human personality—moral, spiritual, and intellectual—is a product of challenge and response. It does not occur in a static situation demanding no exertion and no choices. So far as intellectual development is concerned, this is a well-established principle which underlies the whole modern educational process, from preschool nurseries designed to provide a rich and stimulating environment, to all forms of higher education designed to challenge the intellect. At a basic level the essential part played in learning by the learner's own active response to environment was strikingly demonstrated by the Held and Heim experiment with kittens. Of two litter-mate kittens in the same artificial environment one was free to exercise its own freedom and intelligence in exploring the environment, while the other was suspended in a kind of "gondola" which moved whenever and wherever the free kitten moved. Thus the second kitten had a similar succession of visual experiences as the first, but did not exert itself or make any choices in obtaining them. And whereas the first kitten learned in the normal way to conduct itself safely within its environment, the second did not. With no interaction with a challenging environment there was no development in its behavioral patterns. And I think we can safely say that the intellectual development of humanity has been due to interaction with an objective environment functioning in accordance with its own laws, an environment which we have had actively to explore and to cooperate with in order to escape its perils and exploit its benefits. In a world devoid both of dangers to be avoided and rewards to be won we may assume that there would have been virtually no development of the human intellect and imagination, and hence of either the sciences or the arts, and hence of human civilization or culture.

The fact of an objective world within which one has to learn to live, on penalty of pain or death, is also basic to the development of one's moral nature. For it is because the world is one in which men and women can suffer harm—by violence, disease, accident, starvation, etc.—that our actions affecting one another have moral significance. A morally wrong act is, basically, one which harms some part of the human community; while a morally right action is, on the contrary, one which prevents or neutralizes harm or which preserves or increases human wellbeing. Now we can imagine a paradise in which no one can ever come to any harm. It could be a world which, instead of having its own fixed structure, would be plastic to human wishes. Or it could be a world with a fixed structure, and hence the possibility of damage and pain, but whose structure is suspended or adjusted by special divine action whenever necessary to avoid human pain. Thus, for example, in such a miraculously pain-free world one who falls accidentally off a high building would presumably float unharmed to the ground; bullets would become insubstantial when fired at a human body; poisons would cease to poison; water to drown, and so

on. We can at least begin to imagine such a world. And a good deal of the older discussion of the problem of evil—for example in Part xi of Hume's *Dialogues Concerning Natural Religion*—assumed that it must be the intention of a limitlessly good and powerful Creator to make for human creatures a pain-free environment; so that the very existence of pain is evidence against the existence of God. But such an assumption overlooks the fact that a world in which there can be no pain or suffering would also be one in which there can be no moral choices and hence no possibility of moral growth and development. For in a situation in which no one can ever suffer injury or be liable to pain or suffering there would be no distinction between right and wrong action. No action would be morally wrong, because no action could have harmful consequences; and likewise no action would be morally right in contrast to wrong. Whatever the values of such a world, it clearly could not serve a purpose of the development of its inhabitants from self-regarding animality to self-giving love.

Thus the hypothesis of a divine purpose in which finite persons are created at an epistemic distance from God, in order that they may gradually become children of God through their own moral and spiritual choices, requires that their environment, instead of being a pain-free and stress-free paradise, be broadly the kind of world of which we find ourselves to be a part. It requires that it be such as to provoke the theological problem of evil. For it requires that it be an environment which offers challenges to be met, problems to be solved, dangers to be faced, and which accordingly involves real possibilities of hardship, disaster, failure, defeat, and misery as well as of delight and happiness, success, triumph and achievement. For it is by grappling with the real problems of a real environment, in which a person is one form of life among many, and which is not designed to minister exclusively to one's well-being, that one can develop in intelligence and in such qualities as courage and determination. And it is in the relationships of human beings with one another, in the context of this struggle to survive and flourish, that they can develop the higher values of mutual love and care, of self-sacrifice for others, and of commitment to a common good.

Study Questions

1. What is theodicy? How does theodicy differ from defense in the problem of evil? Using the theme of free will in Plantinga and Hick, respectively, show how it functions differently in theodicy than it does in defense.
2. What is Hick's distinction between moral and natural evil?
3. How is Hick's Irenaean-type theodicy different from theodicy in the Augustinian tradition?
4. In your own words, explain the concept of a person-making environment. Be sure to include all the elements for such an environment that Hick brings to the discussion.

William Rowe

The Evidential Argument from Evil

William Rowe (b. 1931) is a well-known exponent of the evidential argument from evil. Although it is *logically possible* that God has a morally sufficient reason for permitting the evils in our world, Rowe develops the case that it is not likely to be a morally sufficient reason for some, perhaps many, evils of which we are aware. For a deity who is perfect in power and goodness, a morally sufficient reason for a given evil would be that its occurrence is necessary in order to obtain a greater good or to prevent an evil that is comparably bad or worse. Rowe cites specific cases of evils for which we can think of no morally sufficient reason—that is, evils that an all-powerful, all-good God could have prevented without losing a greater good or allowing an equivalent or worse evil. In the following piece, he uses the example of a natural evil: a fawn trapped in a forest fire and suffering for days before finally dying a horrible death. In other pieces, he has also used an example of moral evil: a small child beaten, raped, and killed by the mother's drunken boyfriend. His basic point is that it seems quite unlikely that all such horrible evils are necessary for bringing about a greater good or for preventing an even more monstrous evil. In Rowe's argument, the facts of evil are marshaled as *evidence* against the claim that God exists: if an all-powerful, all-good God exists, then pointless evils (i.e., evils for which there is no morally sufficient reason) would not exist. Rowe concludes that it is more probable than not that God does not exist.

This paper is concerned with three interrelated questions. The first is: Is there an argument for atheism based on the existence of evil that may rationally justify someone in being an atheist? To this first question I give an affirmative answer and try to support that answer by setting forth a strong argument for atheism based on the existence of evil.[1] The second question is: How can the theist best defend his position against the argument for atheism based on the existence of evil? In response to this question I try to describe what may be an adequate rational defense for theism against any argument for atheism based on the existence of evil. The final question is: What position should the informed atheist take

From William Rowe, "Evil and Theodicy," *Philosophical Topics* 16, no. 2 (1988).

concerning the rationality of theistic belief? Three different answers an atheist may give to this question serve to distinguish three varieties of atheism: unfriendly atheism, indifferent atheism, and friendly atheism. In the final part of the paper I discuss and defend the position of friendly atheism.

Before we consider the argument from evil, we need to distinguish a narrow and a broad sense of the terms "theist," "atheist," and "agnostic." By a "theist" in the narrow sense I mean someone who believes in the existence of an omnipotent, omniscient, eternal, supremely good being who created the world. By a "theist" in the broad sense I mean someone who believes in the existence of some sort of divine being or divine reality. To be a theist in the narrow sense is also to be a theist in the broad sense, but one may be a theist in the broad sense—as was Paul Tillich—without believing that there is a supremely good, omnipotent, omniscient, eternal being who created the world. Similar distinctions must be made between a narrow and a broad sense of the terms "atheist" and "agnostic." To be an atheist in the broad sense is to deny the existence of any sort of divine being or divine reality. Tillich was not an atheist in the broad sense. But he was an atheist in the narrow sense, for he denied that there exists a divine being that is all-knowing, all-powerful and perfectly good. In this paper I will be using the terms "theism," "theist," "atheism," "atheist," "agnosticism," and "agnostic" in the narrow sense, not in the broad sense.

I

In developing the argument for atheism based on the existence of evil, it will be useful to focus on some particular evil that our world contains in considerable abundance. Intense human and animal suffering, for example, occurs daily and in great plentitude in our world. Such intense suffering is a clear case of evil. Of course, if the intense suffering leads to some greater good, a good we could not have obtained without undergoing the suffering in question, we might conclude that the suffering is justified, but it remains an evil nevertheless. For we must not confuse the intense suffering in and of itself with the good things to which it sometimes leads or of which it may be a necessary part. Intense human or animal suffering is in itself bad, an evil, even though it may sometimes be justified by virtue of being a part of, or leading to, some good which is unobtainable without it. What is evil in itself may sometimes be good as a means because it leads to something that is good in itself. In such a case, while remaining an evil in itself, the intense human or animal suffering is, nevertheless, an evil which someone might be morally justified in permitting.

Taking human and animal suffering as a clear instance of evil which occurs with great frequency in our world, the argument for atheism based on evil can be stated as follows:

(1) There exist instances of intense suffering which an omnipotent, omniscient being could have prevented without thereby losing some greater good or permitting some evil equally bad or worse.[2]

(2) An omniscient, wholly good being would prevent the occurrence of any intense suffering it could, unless it could not do so without thereby losing some greater good or permitting some evil equally bad or worse.

(3) There does not exist an omnipotent, omniscient, wholly good being.

What are we to say about this argument for atheism, an argument based on the profusion of one sort of evil in our world? The argument is valid; therefore, if we have rational grounds for accepting its premises, to that extent we have rational grounds for accepting atheism. Do we, however, have rational grounds for accepting the premises of this argument?

Let's begin with the second premise. Let s_1 be an instance of intense human or animal suffering which an omniscient, wholly good being could prevent. We will also suppose that things are such that s_1 will occur unless prevented by the omniscient, wholly good (OG) being. We might be interested in determining what would be a *sufficient* condition of OG failing to prevent s_1. But, for our purpose here, we need only try to state a *necessary* condition for OG failing to prevent s_1. That condition, so it seems to me, is this:

Either (i) there is some greater good, G, such that G is obtainable by OG only if OG permits s_1,[3]

or (ii) there is some greater good, G, such that G is obtainable by OG only if OG permits either s_1 or some evil equally bad or worse,

or (iii) s_1 is such that it is preventable by OG only if OG permits some evil equally bad or worse.

It is important to recognize that (iii) is not included in (i). For losing a good greater than s_1 is not the same as permitting an evil greater than s_1. And this because the *absence* of a good state of affairs need not itself be an evil state of affairs. It is also important to recognize that s_1 might be such that it is preventable by OG *without* losing G (so condition (i) is not satisfied) but also such that if OG did prevent it, G would be lost *unless* OG permitted some evil equal to or worse than s_1. If this were so, it does not seem correct to require that OG prevent s_1. Thus, condition (ii) takes into account an important possibility not encompassed in condition (i).

Is it true that if an omniscient, wholly good being permits the occurrence of some intense suffering it could have prevented, then either (i) or (ii) or (iii) obtains? It seems to me that it is true. But if it is true then so is premise (2) of the argument for atheism. For that premise merely states in more compact form what we have suggested must be true if an omniscient, wholly good being fails to prevent some intense suffering it could prevent. Premise (2) says that an omniscient, wholly good being would prevent the occurrence of any intense suffering it could, unless it could not do so without thereby losing some greater good or permitting some evil equally bad or worse. This premise (or something not too distant from it) is, I think, held in common by many atheists and nontheists. Of course, there may be disagreement about whether something is good, and whether, if it is good, one would be morally justified in permitting some intense suffering to occur in order to obtain it. Someone might hold, for example, that no good is great enough to justify permitting an innocent child to suffer terribly.[4] Again, someone might hold that the mere

fact that a given good outweighs some suffering and would be lost if the suffering were prevented, is not a morally sufficient reason for permitting the suffering. But to hold either of these views is not to deny (2). For (2) claims only that *if* an omniscient, wholly good being permits intense suffering *then* either there is some greater good that would have been lost, or some equally bad or worse evil that would have occurred, had the intense suffering been prevented. (2) does not purport to describe what might be a *sufficient* condition for an omniscient, wholly good being to permit intense suffering, only what is a *necessary* condition. So stated, (2) seems to express a belief that accords with our basic moral principles, principles shared by both theists and nontheists. If we are to fault the argument for atheism, therefore, it seems we must find some fault with its first premise.

Suppose in some distant forest lightning strikes a dead tree, resulting in a forest fire. In the fire a fawn is trapped, horribly burned, and lies in terrible agony for several days before death relieves its suffering. So far as we can see, the fawn's intense suffering is pointless. For there does not appear to be any greater good such that the prevention of the fawn's suffering would require either the loss of that good or the occurrence of an evil equally bad or worse. Nor does there seem to be any equally bad or worse evil so connected to the fawn's suffering that it would have had to occur had the fawn's suffering been prevented. Could an omnipotent, omniscient being have prevented the fawn's apparently pointless suffering? The answer is obvious, as even the theist will insist. An omnipotent, omniscient being could have easily prevented the fawn from being horribly burned, or, given the burning, could have spared the fawn the intense suffering by quickly ending its life, rather than allowing the fawn to lie in terrible agony for several days. Since the fawn's intense suffering was preventable and, so far as we can see, pointless, doesn't it appear that premise (1) of the argument is true, that there do exist instances of intense suffering which an omnipotent, omniscient being could have prevented without thereby losing some greater good or permitting some evil equally bad or worse?

It must be acknowledged that the case of the fawn's apparently pointless suffering does not *prove* that (1) is true. For even though we cannot see how the fawn's suffering is required to obtain some greater good (or to prevent some equally bad or worse evil), it hardly follows that it is not so required. After all, we are often surprised by how things we thought to be unconnected turn out to be intimately connected. Perhaps, for all we know, there is some familiar good outweighing the fawn's suffering to which that suffering is connected in a way we do not see. Furthermore, there may well be unfamiliar goods, goods we haven't dreamed of, to which the fawn's suffering is inextricably connected. Indeed, it would seem to require something like omniscience on our part before we could lay claim to *knowing* that there is no greater good connected to the fawn's suffering in such a manner that an omnipotent, omniscient being could not have achieved that good without permitting that suffering or some evil equally bad or worse. So the case of the fawn's suffering surely does not enable us to *establish* the truth of (1).

The truth is that we are not in a position to prove that (1) is true. We cannot know with certainty that instances of suffering of the sort described in (1) do occur in our world. But it is one thing to *know* or *prove* that (1) is true and quite another thing to have *rational grounds* for believing (1) to be true. We are often in the position where in the light of our experience and knowledge it is rational to believe that a certain statement is true, even though we are not in a position to prove or to know with certainty that the statement is true. In the light of our past experience and knowledge it is, for example, very reasonable to believe that neither Goldwater nor McGovern will ever be elected President, but we are scarcely in the position of knowing with certainty that neither will ever be elected President. So, too, with (1), although we cannot know with certainty that it is true, it perhaps can be rationally supported, shown to be a rational belief.

Consider again the case of the fawn's suffering. Is it reasonable to believe that there is some greater good so intimately connected to that suffering that even an omnipotent, omniscient being could not have obtained that good without permitting that suffering or some evil at least as bad? It certainly does not appear reasonable to believe this. Nor does it

seem reasonable to believe that there is some evil at least as bad as the fawn's suffering such that an omnipotent being simply could not have prevented it without permitting the fawn's suffering. But even if it should somehow be reasonable to believe either of these things of the fawn's suffering, we must then ask whether it is reasonable to believe either of these things of *all* the instances of seemingly pointless human and animal suffering that occur daily in our world. And surely the answer to this more general question must be no. It seems quite unlikely that *all* the instances of intense suffering occurring daily in our world are intimately related to the occurrence of greater goods or the prevention of evils at least as bad; and even more unlikely, should they somehow all be so related, that an omnipotent, omniscient being could not have achieved at least some of those goods (or prevented some of those evils) without permitting the instances of intense suffering that are supposedly related to them. In the light of our experience and knowledge of the variety and scale of human and animal suffering in our world, the idea that none of this suffering could have been prevented by an omnipotent being without thereby losing a greater good or permitting an evil at least as bad seems an extraordinary absurd idea, quite beyond our belief. It seems then that although we cannot *prove* that (1) is true, it is, nevertheless, altogether *reasonable* to believe that (1) is true, that (1) is a *rational* belief.[5]

Returning now to our argument for atheism, we've seen that the second premise expresses a basic belief common to many theists and nontheists. We've also seen that our experience and knowledge of the variety and profusion of suffering in our world provides *rational support* for the first premise. Seeing that the conclusion, "There does not exist an omnipotent, omniscient, wholly good being" follows from these two premises, it does seem that we have *rational support* for atheism, that it is reasonable for us to believe that the theistic God does not exist.

II

Can theism be rationally defended against the argument for atheism we have just examined? If it can, how might the theist best respond to that argument? Since the argument from (1) and (2) to (3) is valid, and since the theist, no less than the nontheist, is more than likely committed to (2), it's clear that the theist can reject this atheistic argument only by rejecting its first premise, the premise that states that there are instances of intense suffering which an omnipotent, omniscient being could have prevented without thereby losing some greater good or permitting some evil equally bad or worse. How, then, can the theist best respond to this premise and the considerations advanced in its support?

There are basically three responses a theist can make. First, he might argue not that (1) is false or probably false, but only that the reasoning given in support of it is in some way *defective*. He may do this either by arguing that the reasons given in support of (1) are *in themselves* insufficient to justify accepting (1), or by arguing that there are other things we know which, when taken in conjunction with these reasons, do not justify us in accepting (1). I suppose some theists would be content with this rather modest response to the basic argument for atheism. But given the validity of the basic argument and the theist's likely acceptance of (2), he is thereby committed to the view that (1) is false, not just that we have no good reasons for accepting (1) as true. The second two responses are aimed at showing that it is reasonable to believe that (1) is false. Since the theist is committed to this view, I shall focus the discussion on these two attempts, attempts which we can distinguish as "the direct attack" and "the indirect attack."

By a direct attack, I mean an attempt to reject (1) by pointing out goods, for example, to which suffering may well be connected, goods which an omnipotent, omniscient being could not achieve without permitting suffering. It is doubtful, however, that the direct attack can succeed. The theist may point out that some suffering leads to moral and spiritual development impossible without suffering. But it's reasonably clear that suffering often occurs in a degree far beyond what is required for character development. The theist may say that some suffering results from free choices of human beings and might

be preventable only by preventing some measure of human freedom. But, again, it's clear that much intense suffering occurs not as a result of human free choices. The general difficulty with this direct attack on premise (1) is twofold. First, it cannot succeed, for the theist does not know what greater goods might be served, or evils prevented, by each instance of intense human or animal suffering. Second, the theist's own religious tradition usually maintains that in this life it is not given to us to know God's purpose in allowing particular instances of suffering. Hence, the direct attack against premise (1) cannot succeed and violates basic beliefs associated with theism.

The best procedure for the theist to follow in rejecting premise (1) is the indirect procedure. This procedure I shall call "the G. E. Moore shift," so-called in honor of the twentieth century philosopher, G. E. Moore, who used it to great effect in dealing with the arguments of the skeptics. Skeptical philosophers such as David Hume have advanced ingenious arguments to prove that no one can know of the existence of any material object. The premises of their arguments employ plausible principles, principles which many philosophers have tried to reject directly, but only with questionable success. Moore's procedure was altogether different. Instead of arguing directly against the premises of the skeptic's arguments, he simply noted that the premises implied, for example, that he (Moore) did not know of the existence of a pencil. Moore then proceeded indirectly against the skeptic's premises by arguing:

> I do know that this pencil exists.
>
> If the skeptic's principles are correct I cannot know of the existence of this pencil.
> _____
>
> ∴ The skeptic's principles (at least one) must be incorrect.

Moore then noted that his argument is just as valid as the skeptic's, that both of their arguments contain the premise "If the skeptic's principles are correct Moore cannot know of the existence of this pencil," and concluded that the only way to choose between the two arguments (Moore's and the skeptic's) is by deciding which of the first premises it is more rational to believe—Moore's premise "I do know that this pencil exists" or the skeptic's premise asserting that his skeptical principles are correct. Moore concluded that his own first premise was the more rational of the two.[6]

Before we see how the theist may apply the G. E. Moore shift to the basic argument of atheism, we should note the general strategy of the shift. We're given an argument: p, q, therefore, r. Instead of arguing directly against p, another argument is constructed—not-r, q, therefore, not-p—which begins with the denial of the conclusion of the first argument, keeps its second premise, and ends with the denial of the first premise as its conclusion. Compare, for example, these two:

I. p II. not-r

$$\frac{q}{r} \qquad \frac{q}{\text{not-}p}$$

It is a truth of logic that if I is valid II must be valid as well. Since the arguments are the same so far as the second premise is concerned, any choice between them must concern their respective first premises. To argue against the first premise (p) by constructing the counter argument II is to employ the G. E. Moore shift.

Applying the G. E. Moore shift against the first premise of the basic argument for atheism, the theist can argue as follows:

not-3. There exists an omnipotent, omniscient, wholly good being.

2. An omniscient, wholly good being would prevent the occurrence of any intense suffering it could, unless it could not do so without thereby losing some greater good or permitting some evil equally bad or worse.

therefore,

not-1. It is not the case that there exist instances of intense suffering which an omnipotent, omniscient being could have prevented without thereby losing some greater good or permitting some evil equally bad or worse.

We now have two arguments: the basic argument for atheism from (1) and (2) to (3), and the theist's best response, the argument from (not-3) and (2) to (not-1). What the theist then says about (1) is that he has rational grounds for believing in the existence of the theistic God (not-3), accepts (2) as true, and sees that (not-1) follows from (not-3) and (2). He concludes, therefore, that he has rational grounds for rejecting (1). Having rational grounds for rejecting (1), the theist concludes that the basic argument for atheism is mistaken.

III

We've had a look at a forceful argument for atheism and what seems to be the theist's best response to that argument. If one is persuaded by the argument for atheism, as I find myself to be, how might one best view the position of the atheist? Of course, he will view the theist as having a false belief, just as the theist will view the atheist as having a false belief. But what position should the atheist take concerning the *rationality* of the theist's belief? There are three major positions an atheist might take, positions which we may think of as some varieties of atheism. First, the atheist may believe that no one is rationally justified in believing that the theistic God exists. Let us call this position "unfriendly atheism." Second, the atheist may hold no belief concerning whether any theist is or isn't rationally justified in believing that the theistic God exists. Let us call this view "indifferent atheism." Finally, the atheist may believe that some theists are rationally justified in believing that the theistic God exists. This view we shall call "friendly atheism." In this final part of the paper I propose to discuss and defend the position of friendly atheism.

If no one can be rationally justified in believing a false proposition then friendly atheism is a paradoxical, if not incoherent position. But surely the truth of a belief is not a necessary condition of someone's being rationally justified in having that belief. So in holding that someone is rationally justified in believing that the theistic God exists, the friendly atheist is not committed to thinking that the theist has a true belief. What he is committed to is that the theist has rational grounds for his belief, a belief the atheist rejects and is convinced he is rationally justified in rejecting. But is this possible? Can someone, like our friendly atheist, hold a belief, be convinced that he is rationally justified in holding that belief, and yet believe that someone else is equally justified in believing the opposite? Surely this is possible. Suppose your friends see you off on a flight to Hawaii. Hours after take-off they learn that your plane has gone down at sea. After a twenty-four hour search, no survivors have been found. Under these circumstances they are rationally justified in believing that you have perished. But it is hardly rational for you to believe this, as you bob up and down in your life vest, wondering why the search planes have failed to spot you. Indeed, to amuse yourself while awaiting your fate, you might very well reflect on the fact that your friends are rationally justified in believing that you are now dead, a proposition you disbelieve and are rationally justified in disbelieving. So, too, perhaps an atheist may be rationally justified in his atheistic belief and yet hold that some theists are rationally justified in believing just the opposite of what he believes.

What sort of grounds might a theist have for believing that God exists? Well, he might endeavor to justify his belief by appealing to one or more of the traditional arguments: Ontological, Cosmological, Teleological, Moral, etc. Second, he might appeal to certain aspects of religious experience, perhaps even his own religious experience. Third, he might try to justify theism as a plausible theory in terms of which we can account for a variety of phenomena. Although an atheist must hold that the theistic God does not exist, can he not also believe, and be justified in so believing, that some of these "justifications of theism" do actually rationally justify some theists in their belief that there exists a supremely good, omnipotent, omniscient being? It seems to me that he can.

If we think of the long history of theistic belief and the special situations in which people are sometimes placed, it is perhaps as absurd to think that no one was ever rationally justified in believing that the theistic God exists as it is to think that no one was ever justified in believing that human beings would never walk on the moon. But in suggesting that friendly atheism is preferable to unfriendly atheism, I don't mean to rest the case on what some human beings might reasonably have believed in the eleventh or thirteenth century. The more interesting question is whether some people in modern society, people who are aware of the usual grounds for belief and disbelief and are acquainted to some degree with modern science, are yet rationally justified in accepting theism. Friendly atheism is a significant position only if it answers this question in the affirmative.

It is not difficult for an atheist to be friendly when he has reason to believe that the theist could not reasonably be expected to be acquainted with the grounds for disbelief that he (the atheist) possesses. For then the atheist may take the view that some theists are rationally justified in holding to theism, but would not be so were they to be acquainted with the grounds for disbelief—those grounds being sufficient to tip the scale in favor of atheism when balanced against the reasons the theist has in support of his belief.

Friendly atheism becomes paradoxical, however, when the atheist contemplates believing that the theist has all the grounds for atheism that he, the atheist, has, and yet is rationally justified in maintaining his theistic belief. But even so excessively friendly a view as this perhaps can be held by the atheist if he also has some reason to think that the grounds for theism are not as telling as the theist is justified in taking them to be.[7]

In this paper I've presented what I take to be a strong argument for atheism, pointed out what I think is the theist's best response to that argument, distinguished three positions an atheist might take concerning the rationality of theistic belief, and made some remarks in defense of the position called "friendly atheism." I'm aware that the central points of the paper are not likely to be warmly received by many philosophers. Philosophers who are atheists tend to be tough minded—holding that there are no good reasons for supposing that theism is true. And theists tend either to reject the view that the existence of evil provides rational grounds for atheism or to hold that religious belief has nothing to do with reason and evidence at all. But such is the way of philosophy.

NOTES

1. Some philosophers have contended that the existence of evil is *logically inconsistent* with the existence of the theistic God. No one, I think, has succeeded in establishing such an extravagant claim. Indeed, granted incompatibilism, there is a fairly compelling argument for the view that the existence of evil is logically consistent with the existence of the theistic God. [For a lucid statement of this argument see Alvin Plantinga, *God, Freedom, and Evil* (New York: Harper and Row, 1974), pp. 29–59.] There remains, however, what we may call the *evidential* form—as opposed to the *logical* form—of the problem of evil: the view that the variety and profusion of evil in our world, although perhaps not logically inconsistent with the existence of the theistic God, provides, nevertheless, *rational support* for atheism. In this paper I shall be concerned solely with the evidential form of the problem, the form of the problem which, I think, presents a rather severe difficulty for theism.

2. If there is some good, G, greater than any evil, (1) will be false for the trivial reason that no matter what evil, E, we pick the conjunctive good state of affairs consisting of G and E that will outweigh E and be such that an omnipotent being could not obtain it without permitting E. [See Alvin Plantinga, *God and Other Minds* (Ithaca, N.Y.: Cornell University Press, 1967), 167.] To avoid this objection we may insert "unreplaceable" into our premises (1) and (2) between "some" and "greater." If E isn't required for G, and G is better than G plus E, then the good conjunctive state of affairs composed of G and E would be *replaceable* by the greater good of G alone. For the sake of simplicity, however, I will ignore this complication both in the formulation and discussion of premises (1) and (2).

3. Three clarifying points need to be made in connection with (1). First, by "good" I don't mean to exclude the fulfilment of certain moral principles. Perhaps preventing s_1 would preclude certain actions prescribed by the principles of justice. I shall allow that the satisfaction of certain principles of justice may be a good that outweighs the evil of s_1. Second, even though (1) may suggest it, I don't mean to limit the good in question to something that would follow in *time* the occurrence of s_1. And, finally, we should perhaps not fault OG if the good G, that would be loss were s_1 prevented, is not actually greater than s_1, but merely such that allowing s_1, and G, as opposed to preventing s_1 and thereby losing G, would not alter the balance between good and evil. For reasons of simplicity, I have left this point out in stating (i), with the result that (i) is perhaps a bit stronger than it should be.

4. See Ivan's speech in bk. v, ch. iv, of *The Brothers Karamazov*.

5. One might object that the conclusion of this paragraph is stronger than the reasons given warrant. For it is one thing to argue that it is unreasonable to think that (1) is false and another thing to conclude that we are therefore justified in accepting (1) as true. There are propositions such that believing them is much more reasonable than disbelieving them, and yet are such that *withholding judgment* about them is more reasonable than believing them. To take an example of Chisholm's: It is more reasonable to believe that the Pope will be in Rome (on some arbitrarily picked future date) than to believe that he won't: but it is perhaps more reasonable to suspend judgment on the question of the Pope's whereabouts on that particular date, than to believe that he will be in Rome. Thus it might be objected, that while we've shown that believing (1) is more reasonable than disbelieving (1), we haven't shown that believing (1) is more reasonable than withholding belief. My answer to this objection is that there are things we know which render (1) probable to the degree that it is more reasonable to believe (1) than to suspend judgment on (1). What are these things we know? First, I think, is the fact that there is an enormous variety and profusion of intense human and animal suffering in our world. Second, is the fact that much of this suffering seems quite unrelated to any greater goods (or the absence of equal or greater evils) that might justify it. And, finally, there is the fact that such suffering as is related to greater goods (or the absence of equal or greater evils) does not, in many cases, seem so intimately related as to require its permission by an omnipotent being bent on securing those goods (the absence of those evils). These facts, I am claiming, make it more reasonable to accept (1) than to withhold judgment on (1).

6. See, for example, the two chapters on Hume in G. E. Moore, *Some Main Problems of Philosophy* (London: George, Allen, and Unwin, 1953).

7. Suppose that I add a long sum of numbers three times and get result x. I inform you of this so that you have pretty much the same evidence I have for the claim that the sum of the numbers is x. You then use your calculator twice over and arrive at result y. You, then, are justified in believing that the sum of the numbers is not x. However, knowing that your calculator has been damaged and is therefore unreliable, and that you have no reason to think that it is damaged, I may reasonably believe not only that the sum of the numbers is x, but also that you are justified in believing that the

sum is not *x*. Here is a case, then, where you have all of my evidence for *p*, and yet I can reasonably believe that you are justified in believing not-*p*—for I have reason to believe that your grounds for not-*p* are not as telling as you are justified in taking them to be.

STUDY QUESTIONS

1. Rowe spends a great deal of time marshaling rational grounds to accept the premises of his argument from evil. State the two premises and rehearse Rowe's very careful reasoning behind each of them. Do you accept the premises? If not, which do you doubt or reject—and what is your reasoning?
2. Rowe anticipates both an indirect and a direct attack on his premise (2). What would each of these attacks involve? Rowe cites the Hick-type theodicy as one auspicious direct attack, but why does he think it fails? What do you think?
3. The theist may claim that apart from considerations of evil, we have other rational grounds for knowing the existence of God. Therefore, the theist would conclude that there are no instances of intense suffering that God could have prevented without losing a greater good or permitting some equally bad or worse evil. Explain how this argument seems poised against Rowe's.

Marilyn McCord Adams

Horrendous Evils and the Goodness of God

Marilyn McCord Adams (b. 1943) argues that the existence of disproportionate suffering makes it theoretically unfruitful to pursue the question of why evils happen. Instead she addresses the question of how God deals with—and, indeed, defeats—evils. She calls the class of evils that are of utmost concern "horrors"—i.e., evils that threaten to engulf a person and destroy all meaning in his or her life. She is critical of standard approaches to theodicy, which justify God's actions from a global perspective by arguing that the goods of the world offset or outweigh the evils and that the world is good on the whole. Obviously, much philosophical discussion and debate surrounds theodicies based on this understanding of God's goodness. Adams, on the other hand, believes that, for cases of horrors, theodicy must show how God's goodness is related to each individual sufferer. Although standard theodicies generally connect created and temporal goods to various evils being explained, and although they tend to use only those goods that are also recognized by their critics, Adams argues that horrors are so deep and destructive that no finite goods can overcome them. The worst evils ("horrors") demand to be overcome by the greatest good, which is the infinite good of God himself. Only intimate connection to God—the "beatific vision" in classical terms—can engulf the most horrible evils, make the sufferer's life a great good to him or her, and eliminate any doubt that that life is worth living.

1. INTRODUCTION

Over the past thirty years, analytic philosophers of religion have defined "the problem of evil" in terms of the prima-facie difficulty in consistently maintaining

(1) God exists, and is omnipotent, omniscient, and perfectly good

and

(2) Evil exists.

In a crisp and classic article, "Evil and Omnipotence"[1] J. L. Mackie emphasized that the problem is not that (1) and (2) are logically inconsistent by themselves, but that they together with quasi-logical rules formulating attribute-analyses, such as

Marilyn McCord Adams, "Horrendous Evils and the Goodness of God," first published in *Proceedings of the Aristotelian Society*, Supplementary Vol. 63 (1989), pp. 297–310, slightly revised by the author, with the addition of notes that respond to the comments of Professor Stewart Sutherland, commentator at the 1989 Joint Session of the Mind Association and Aristotelian Society at which the paper was presented. © The Aristotelian Society 1989. Reprinted by courtesy of the editor.

(P1) A perfectly good being would always eliminate evil so far as it could,

and

(P2) There are *no limits* to what an omnipotent
being can do—

constitute an inconsistent premise set. He added,
of course, that the inconsistency might be removed
by substituting alternative and perhaps more subtle
analyses, but cautioned that such replacements of
(P1) and (P2) would save "ordinary theism" from
his charge of positive irrationality, only if true to its
essential requirements.[2]

In an earlier paper, "Problems of Evil: More
Advice to Christian Philosophers,"[3] I underscored
Mackie's point and took it a step further. In debates
about whether the argument from evil can establish the irrationality of religious belief, care must be
taken, both by the atheologians who deploy it and
by the believers who defend against it, to ensure that
the operative attribute-analyses accurately reflect
that religion's understanding of divine power and
goodness. It does the atheologian no good to argue
for the falsity of Christianity on the ground that the
existence of an omnipotent, omniscient, pleasure-
maximizer is incompossible with a world such as
ours, because Christians never believed God was a
pleasure-maximizer anyway. But equally, the truth of
Christianity would be inadequately defended by the
observation that an omnipotent, omniscient egoist
could have created a world with suffering creatures,
because Christians insist that God loves other (created) persons than Himself. The extension of "evil" in
(2) is likewise important. Since Mackie and his successors are out to show that "the several parts of the
essential theological doctrine are inconsistent with
one another,"[4] they can accomplish their aim only
if they circumscribe the extension of "evil" as their
religious opponents do. By the same token, it is not
enough for Christian philosophers to explain how
the power, knowledge, and goodness of God could
coexist with some evils or other; a full account must
exhibit the compossibility of divine perfection with
evils in the amounts and of the kinds found in the
actual world (and evaluated as such by Christian
standards).

The moral of my earlier story might be summarized thus: where the internal coherence of a system
of religious beliefs is at stake, successful arguments
for its inconsistency must draw on premises (explicitly or implicitly) internal to that system or obviously
acceptable to its adherents; likewise for successful
rebuttals or explanations of consistency. The thrust
of my argument is to push both sides of the debate
towards more detailed attention to and subtle understanding of the religious system in question.

As a Christian philosopher, I want to focus in
this paper on the problem for the truth of Christianity raised by what I shall call "horrendous" evils.
Although our world is riddled with them, the biblical record punctuated by them, and one of them—
namely, the passion of Christ; according to Christian
belief, the judicial murder of God by the people of
God—is memorialized by the Church on its most
solemn holiday (Good Friday) and in its central sacrament (the Eucharist), the problem of horrendous
evils is largely skirted by standard treatments for the
good reason that they are intractable by them. After
showing why, I will draw on other Christian materials to sketch ways of meeting this, the deepest of
religious problems.

2. DEFINING THE CATEGORY

For present purposes, I define "horrendous evils" as
"evils the participation in (the doing or suffering of)
which gives one reason prima facie to doubt whether
one's life could (given their inclusion in it) be a great
good to one on the whole."[5] Such reasonable doubt
arises because it is so difficult humanly to conceive
how such evils could be overcome. Borrowing Chisholm's contrast between *balancing off* (which occurs
when the opposing values of *mutually exclusive* parts
of a whole partially *or* totally cancel each other out)
and *defeat* (which cannot *occur* by the mere addition to the whole of a new part of opposing value,
but involves some "organic unity" among the values
of parts and wholes, as when the positive aesthetic
value of a whole painting defeats the ugliness of a

small colour patch),[6] horrendous evils seem prima facie, not only to balance off but to engulf the positive value of a participant's life. Nevertheless, that very horrendous proportion, by which they threaten to rob a person's life of positive meaning, cries out not only to be engulfed, but to be made meaningful through positive and decisive defeat.

I understand this criterion to be objective, but relative to individuals. The example of habitual complainers, who know how to make the worst of a good situation, shows individuals not to be incorrigible experts on what ills would defeat the positive value of their lives. Nevertheless, nature and experience endow people with different strengths; one bears easily what crushes another. And a major consideration in determining whether an individual's life is/has been a great good to him/her on the whole, is invariably and appropriately how it has seemed to him/her.[7]

I offer the following list of paradigmatic horrors: the rape of a woman and axing off of her arms, psychophysical torture whose ultimate goal is the disintegration of personality, betrayal of one's deepest loyalties, cannibalizing one's own offspring, child abuse of the sort described by Ivan Karamazov, child pornography, parental incest, slow death by starvation, participation in the Nazi death camps, the explosion of nuclear bombs over populated areas, having to choose which of one's children shall live and which be executed by terrorists, being the accidental and/or unwitting agent of the disfigurement or death of those one loves best. I regard these as *paradigmatic,* because I believe most people would find in the doing or suffering of them prima-facie reason to doubt the positive meaning of their lives.[8] Christian belief counts the crucifixion of Christ another: on the one hand, death by crucifixion seemed to defeat Jesus' messianic vocation; for according to Jewish law, death by hanging from a tree made its victim ritually accursed, definitively excluded from the compass of God's people, *a fortiori* disqualified from being the Messiah. On the other hand, it represented the defeat of its perpetrators' leadership vocations, as those who were to prepare the people of God for the Messiah's coming killed and ritually accursed the true Messiah, according to later theological understanding, God Himself.

3. The Impotence of Standard Solutions

For better and worse, the by now standard strategies for "solving" the problem of evil are powerless in the face of horrendous evils.

3.1. Seeking the Reason-Why

In his model article "Hume on Evil,"[9] Pike takes up Mackie's challenge, arguing that (P1) fails to reflect ordinary moral intuitions (more to the point, I would add, Christian beliefs), and traces the abiding sense of trouble to the hunch that an omnipotent, omniscient being could have no reason compatible with perfect goodness for permitting (bringing about) evils, because all legitimate excuses arise from ignorance or weakness. Solutions to the problem of evil have thus been sought in the form of counter-examples to this latter claim—i.e., logically possible reasons—why that would excuse even an omnipotent, omniscient God! The putative logically possible reasons offered have tended to be *generic* and *global*: generic in so far as some *general* reason is sought to cover all sorts *of* evils; global in so far as they seize upon some feature of the world as a whole. For example, philosophers have alleged that the desire to make a world with one of the following properties—"the best *of* all possible worlds,"[10] "a world a more perfect than which is impossible," "a world exhibiting a perfect balance of retributive justice,"[11] "a world with as favorable a balance of (created) moral good over moral evil as God can weakly actualize"[12] would constitute a reason compatible with perfect goodness for God's creating a world with evils in the amounts and of the kinds found in the actual world. Moreover, such general reasons are presented as so powerful as to do away with any need to catalogue types of evils one by one, and examine God's reason for permitting each in particular. Plantinga explicitly hopes that the problem of horrendous evils can thus be solved without being squarely confronted.[13]

3.2. The Insufficiency of Global Defeat

A pair of distinctions is in order here: (i) between two dimensions of divine goodness in relation to creation—namely, "producer of global goods" and "goodness to" or "love of individual created persons"; and (ii) between the overbalance/defeat of evil by good on the global scale, and the overbalance/defeat of evil by good within the context of an individual person's life.[14] Correspondingly, we may separate two problems of evil parallel to the two sorts of goodness mentioned in (i).

In effect, generic and global approaches are directed to the first problem: they defend divine goodness along the first (global) dimension by suggesting logically possible strategies for the global defeat of evils. But establishing God's excellence as a producer of global goods does not automatically solve the second problem, especially in a world containing horrendous evils. For *God* cannot be said to be good or loving to any created persons the positive meaning of whose lives He allows to be engulfed in and/or defeated by evils—that is, individuals within whose lives horrendous evils remain undefeated. Yet, the only way unsupplemented global and generic approaches could have to explain the latter, would be by applying their general reasons-why to particular cases of horrendous suffering.

Unfortunately, such an exercise fails to give satisfaction. Suppose for the sake of argument that horrendous evil could be included in maximally perfect world orders; its being partially constitutive of such an order would assign it that generic and global positive meaning. But would knowledge of such a fact defeat for a mother the prima-facie reason provided by her cannibalism of her own infant to wish that she had never been born? Again, the aim of perfect retributive balance confers meaning on evils imposed. But would knowledge that the torturer was being tortured give the victim who broke down and turned traitor under pressure any more reason to think his/her life worth while? Would it not merely multiply reasons for the torturer to doubt that his/her life could turn out to be a good to him/her on the whole? Could the truck-driver who accidentally runs over his beloved child find consolation in the idea that this middle-known[15] but unintended side-effect was part of the price *God* accepted for a world with the best balance of moral good over moral evil he could get?

Not only does the application to horrors of such generic and global reasons for divine permission of evils fail to solve the second problem of evil; it makes it worse by adding *generic prima-facie* reasons to doubt whether human life would be a great good to individual human beings in possible worlds where such divine motives were operative. For, taken in isolation and made to bear the weight of the whole explanation, such reasons-why draw a picture of divine indifference or even hostility to the human plight. Would the fact that *God* permitted horrors because they were constitutive means to His end of global perfection, or that He tolerated them because He could obtain that global end anyway, make the participant's life more tolerable, more worth living for him/her? Given radical human vulnerability to horrendous evils, the ease with which humans participate in them, whether as victim or perpetrator, would not the thought that God visits horrors on anyone who caused them, simply because he/she deserves it, provide one more reason to expect human life to be a nightmare?

Those willing to split the two problems of evil apart might adopt a divide-and-conquer strategy, by simply denying divine goodness along the second dimension. For example, many Christians do not believe that God will ensure an overwhelmingly good life to each and every person He creates. Some say the decisive defeat of evil with good is promised only within the lives of the obedient, who enter by the narrow gate. Some speculate that the elect may be few. Many recognize that the sufferings of this present life are as nothing compared to the hell of eternal torment, designed to defeat goodness with horrors within the lives of the damned.

Such a road can be consistently travelled only at the heavy toll of admitting that human life in worlds such as ours is a bad bet. Imagine (adapting Rawls's device) persons in a pre-original position, considering possible worlds containing managers of differing power, wisdom, and character, and subjects of varying fates. The question they are to answer about each world is whether they would willingly enter it as a human being, from behind a veil of ignorance as to which position they would occupy. Reason would,

I submit, dictate a negative verdict for worlds whose omniscient and omnipotent manager permits ante-mortem horrors that remain undefeated within the context of the human participant's life; *a fortiori*, for worlds in which some or most humans suffer eternal torment.

3.3. Inaccessible Reasons

So far, I have argued that generic and global solutions are at best incomplete: however well their account of divine motivating reasons deals with the first problem of evil, the attempt to extend it to the second fails by making it worse. This verdict might seem prima facie tolerable to standard generic and global approaches and indicative of only a minor modification in their strategy: let the above-mentioned generic and global reasons cover divine permission of nonhorrendous evils, and find other *reasons* compatible with perfect goodness *why* even an omnipotent, omniscient God would permit horrors.

In my judgment, such an approach is hopeless. As Plantinga[16] points out, where horrendous evils are concerned, not only do we not know God's *actual* reason for permitting them; we cannot even *conceive* of any plausible candidate sort of reason consistent with worthwhile lives for human participants in them.

4. The How of God's Victory

Up to now, my discussion has given the reader cause to wonder whose side I am on anyway. For I have insisted, with rebels like Ivan Karamazov and John Stuart Mill, on spotlighting the problem horrendous evils pose. Yet, I have signalled my preference for a version of Christianity that insists on both dimensions of divine goodness, and maintains not only *(a)* that God will be good enough to created persons to make human life a good bet, but also *(b)* that each created person will have a life that is a great good to him/her on the whole. My critique of standard approaches to the problem of evil thus seems to reinforce atheologian Mackie's verdict of "positive irrationality" for such a religious position.

4.1. Whys Versus Hows

The inaccessibility of reasons-why seems especially decisive. For surely an all-wise and all-powerful God. who loved each created person enough *(a)* to defeat any experienced horrors within the context of the participant's life, and *(b)* to give each created person a life that is a great good to him/her on the whole, would not permit such persons to suffer horrors for no reason.[17] Does not our inability even to conceive of plausible candidate reasons suffice to make belief in such a God positively irrational in a world containing horrors? In my judgment, it does not.

To be sure, motivating reasons come in several varieties relative to our conceptual grasp: There are (i) reasons of the sort we can readily understand when we are informed of them (e.g., the mother who permits her child to undergo painful heart surgery because it is the only humanly possible way to save its life). Moreover, there are (ii) reasons we would be cognitively, emotionally, and spiritually equipped to grasp if only we had a larger memory or wider attention span (analogy: I may be able to memorize small town street plans; memorizing the road networks of the entire country is a task requiring more of the same, in the way that proving Gödel's theorem is not). Some generic and global approaches insinuate that divine permission of evils has motivating reasons of this sort. Finally, there are (iii) reasons that we are cognitively, emotionally, and/or spiritually too immature to fathom (the way a two-year-old child is incapable of understanding its mother's reasons for permitting the surgery). I agree with Plantinga that our ignorance of divine reasons for permitting horrendous evils is not of types (i) or (ii), but of type (iii).

Nevertheless, if there are varieties of ignorance, there are also varieties of reassurance.[18] The two-year-old heart patient is convinced of its mother's love, not by her cognitively inaccessible reasons, but by her intimate care and presence through its painful experience. The story of Job suggests something similar is true with human participation in horrendous suffering: God does not give Job His reasons-why, and implies that Job isn't smart enough to grasp them; rather Job is lectured on the extent of divine power, and sees God's goodness face to face! Likewise, I suggest, to exhibit the logical compossibility of both dimensions of divine goodness with horrendous suffering, it is not necessary to find logically possible reasons *why* God might permit them. It is enough to show *how* God can be good enough to, created persons despite their participation in horrors-by defeating them within the context of the individual's life and by giving that individual a life that is a great good to him/her on the whole.

4.2. What Sort of Valuables?

In my opinion, the reasonableness of Christianity can be maintained in the face of horrendous evils only by drawing on resources of religious value theory, for one way for God to be *good to* created persons is by relating them appropriately to relevant and great goods. But philosophical and religious theories differ importantly on what valuables they admit into their ontology. Some maintain that "what you see is what you get," but nevertheless admit a wide range of valuables, from sensory pleasures, the beauty of nature and cultural artifacts, the joys of creativity, to loving personal intimacy. Others posit a transcendent good (e.g., the Form of the Good in Platonism, or God, the Supremely Valuable Object, in Christianity). In the spirit of Ivan Karamazov, I am convinced that the depth of horrific evil cannot be accurately estimated without recognizing it to be incommensurate with any package of merely non-transcendent goods and so unable to be balanced off, much less defeated, thereby.

Where the *internal* coherence of Christianity is the issue, however, it is fair to appeal to its own store of valuables. From a Christian point of view, God is a being a greater than which cannot be conceived, a good incommensurate with both created goods and temporal evils. Likewise, the good of beatific, face-to-face intimacy with God is simply incommensurate with any merely non-transcendent goods or ills a person might experience. Thus, the good of beatific face-to-face intimacy with God would *engulf* (in a sense analogous to Chisholmian balancing off) even the horrendous evils humans experience in this present life here below, and overcome any prima-facie reasons the individual had to doubt whether his/her life would or could be worth living.

4.3. Personal Meaning, Horrors Defeated

Engulfing personal horrors within the context of the participant's life would vouchsafe to that individual a life that was a great good to him/her on the whole. I am still inclined to think it would guarantee that immeasurable divine goodness to any person thus benefited. But there is good theological reason for Christians to believe that God would go further, beyond engulfment to defeat. For it is the nature of persons to look for meaning, both in their lives and in the world. Divine respect for and commitment to created personhood would drive God to make all those sufferings which threaten to destroy the positive meaning of a person's life meaningful through positive defeat.[19]

How could God do it? So far as I can see, only by integrating participation in horrendous evils into a person's relationship with God. Possible dimensions of integration are charted by Christian soteriology. I pause here to sketch three:[20] (i) First, because God in Christ participated in horrendous evil through His passion and death, human experience of horrors can be a means of *identifying* with Christ, either through *sympathetic* identification (in which each person suffers his/her own pains, but their similarity enables each to know what it is like for the other) or through *mystical* identification (in which the created person is supposed literally to experience a share of Christ's pain[21]). (ii) Julian of Norwich's description of heavenly welcome suggests the possible defeat of horrendous evil through divine gratitude. According to Julian, before the elect have a chance to thank God for all He has done for them, God will say, "Thank you for all your suffering, the suffering of your youth." She says that the creature's experience of divine gratitude will bring such full and unending joy as could not be merited by the whole sea of human pain and suffering throughout the ages.[22] (iii) A third idea identifies temporal suffering itself with a vision into the inner life of God, and can be developed several ways. Perhaps, contrary to medieval theology, God is not impassible, but rather has matched capacities for joy and for suffering. Perhaps, as the Heidelberg catechism suggests, God responds to human sin and the sufferings of Christ with an agony beyond human conception.[23] Alternatively, the inner life of God may be, strictly speaking and in and of itself, beyond both joy and sorrow. But, just as (according to Rudolf Otto) humans experience divine presence now as *tremendum* (with deep dread and anxiety), now as *fascinans* (with ineffable attraction), so perhaps our deepest suffering as much as our highest joys may themselves be direct visions into the inner life of God, imperfect but somehow less obscure in proportion to their intensity. And if a face-to-face vision of God is a good for humans incommensurate with any nontranscendent goods or ills, so any vision of God (including horrendous suffering) would have a good aspect in so far as it is a vision of God (even if it has an evil aspect in so far as it is horrendous suffering). For the most part, horrors are not recognized as experiences of God (any more than the city slicker recognizes his visual image of a brown patch as a vision of Beulah the cow in the distance). But, Christian mysticism might claim, at least from the post-mortem perspective of the beatific vision, such sufferings will be seen for what they were, and retrospectively no one will wish away any intimate encounters with God from his/her life-history in this world. The created person's experience of the beatific vision together with his/her knowledge that intimate divine presence stretched back over his/her ante-mortem life and reached down into the depths of his/her worst suffering, would provide retrospective comfort independent of comprehension of the reasons-why akin to the two-year-old's assurance of its mother's love. Taking this third approach, Christians would not need to commit themselves about what in any event we do not know: namely, whether we will (like the two-year-old) ever grow up enough to understand the reasons why God permits our participation in horrendous evils. For by contrast with the best of earthly mothers, such divine intimacy is an incommensurate good and would cancel out for the creature any need to know why.

5. Conclusion

The worst evils demand to be defeated by the best goods. Horrendous evils can be overcome only by the goodness of God. Relative to human nature, participation in horrendous evils and loving intimacy with God are alike disproportionate: for the former threatens to engulf the good in an individual human life with evil, while the latter guarantees the reverse engulfment of evil by good. Relative to one another, there is also disproportion, because the good that God *is*, and intimate relationship with Him, is incommensurate with created goods and evils alike. Because intimacy with God so outscales relations (good or bad) with any creatures, integration into the human person's relationship with God confers significant meaning and positive value even on horrendous suffering. This result coheres with basic Christian intuition: that the powers of darkness are stronger than humans, but they are no match for God!

Standard generic and global solutions have for the most part tried to operate within the territory common to believer and unbeliever, within the confines of religion-neutral value theory. Many discussions reflect the hope that substitute attribute-analyses, candidate reasons-why, and/or defeaters could issue out of values shared by believers and unbelievers alike. And some virtually make this a requirement on an adequate solution. Mackie knew better how to distinguish the many charges that may be levelled against religion. Just as philosophers mayor may not find the existence of God plausible, so they may be variously attracted or repelled by Christian values of grace and redemptive sacrifice. But agreement on truth-value is not necessary to consensus on internal consistency. My contention has been that it is not only legitimate, but, given horrendous evils, necessary for Christians to dip into their richer store of valuables to exhibit the consistency of (1) and (2).[24] I would go one step further: assuming the pragmatic and/or moral (I would prefer to say, broadly speaking, religious) importance of believing that (one's own) human life is worth living, the ability of Christianity to exhibit how this could be so despite human vulnerability to horrendous evil, constitutes a pragmatic/moral/religious consideration in its favour, relative to value schemes that do not.

To me, the most troublesome weakness in what I have said lies in the area of conceptual under-development. The contention that God suffered in Christ or that one person can experience another's pain requires detailed analysis and articulation in metaphysics and philosophy of mind. I have shouldered some of this burden elsewhere,[25] but its full discharge is well beyond the scope of this paper.

NOTES

1. J. L. Mackie, "Evil and Omnipotence," *Mind*, 64 (1955); repr. in Nelson Pike (ed.), *God and Evil* (Englewood Cliffs, N.J.: Prentice-Hall, 1964), pp. 46–60.
2. Ibid. 47.
3. Marilyn McCord Adams, "Problems of Evil: More Advice to Christian Philosophers," *Faith and Philosophy* (Apr. 1988): 121–43.
4. Mackie, "Evil and Omnipotence," pp. 46–47. Emphasis mine.
5. Stewart Sutherland (in his comment "Horrendous Evils and the Goodness of God-II," *Proceedings of the Aristotelian Society*, suppl. vol. 63 [1989]: 311–23, esp. 311) takes my criterion to be somehow "first-person." This was not my intention. My definition may be made more explicit as follows: an evil *e* is horrendous if and only if participation in *e* by person *p* gives everyone prima-facie reason to doubt whether *p*'s life can, given *p*'s participation in *e*, be a great good to *p* on the whole.
6. Roderick Chisholm, "The Defeat of Good and Evil".
7. Cf. Malcolm's astonishment at Wittgenstein's dying exclamation that he had had a wonderful life, *Ludwig Wittgenstein: A Memoir* (London: Oxford University Press, 1962), p. 100.
8. Once again, more explicitly, most people would agree that a person *p*'s doing or suffering of them constitutes prima-facie reason to doubt whether *p*'s life can be, given such participation, a great good to *p* on the whole.
9. "Hume on Evil," *Philosophical Review*, 72 (1963): 180–97; reprinted in Pike (ed.), *God and Evil*, p. 88.
10. Following Leibniz, Pike draws on this feature as part of what I have called his Epistemic Defence ("Problems of Evil: More Advice to Christian Philosophers," pp. 124–25).
11. Augustine, *On Free Choice of Will*, iii. 93–102, implies that there is a maximum value for created worlds, and a plurality of worlds that meet it. All of these contain rational free creatures; evils are foreseen but unintended side-effects of their creation. No matter what they choose, however, God can order their choices into a maximally perfect universe by establishing an order of retributive justice.
12. Plantinga takes this line in numerous discussions, in the course of answering Mackie's objection to the Free Will Defence, that God should have made sinless free creatures. Plantinga insists that, given incompatibilist freedom in creatures, God cannot strongly actualize any world He wants. It is logically possible that a world with evils in the amounts and of the kinds found in this world is the best that He could do, Plantinga argues, given His aim of gelling some moral goodness in the world.
13. Alvin Plantinga, "Self-Profile," in James E. Tomberlin and Peter van Inwagen, eds., *Profiles: Alvin Plantinga* (Dordrecht, the Netherlands: Reidel, 1985), p. 38.
14. I owe the second of these distinctions to a remark by Keith De Rose in our fall 1987 seminar at UCLA on the problem of evil.
15. Middle knowledge, or knowledge of what is "in between" the actual and the possible, is the sort of knowledge of what a free creature *would do* in every situation in which that creature could possibly find himself. Following Luis de Molina and Francisco Suarez, Alvin Plantinga ascribes such knowledge to God, prior in the order of explanation to God's decision about which free creatures to actualize (in *The Nature of Necessity* (Oxford, England: Clarendon Press, 1974), pp. 164–93, Robert Merrihew Adams challenges this idea in his article "Middle Knowledge and the Problem of Evil," *American Philosophical Quarterly*, 14 (1977); repr. in *The Virtue of Faith* (New York: Oxford University Press, 1987), pp. 77–93.
16. Alvin Plantinga, "Self-Profile," pp. 34–35.
17. This point was made by William Fitzpatrick in our fall 1987 seminar at UCLA on the problem of evil.
18. Contrary to what Sutherland suggests ("Horrendous Evils," pp. 314–15), so far as the compossibility problem is concerned, I intend no illicit shift from reason to emotion. My point is that intimacy with a loving other is a good, participation in which can defeat evils, and so provide everyone with reason to think a person's life can be a great good to him/her on the whole, despite his/her participation in evils.
19. Note, once again, contrary to what Sutherland suggests ("Horrendous Evils," pp. 321–23) "horrendous evil *e* is defeated" entails *none* of the following propositions: "*e* was not horrendous," "*e* was not unjust," "*e* was not so bad after all." Nor does my suggestion that even horrendous evils can be defeated by a great enough (because incommensurate

and uncreated) good in any way impugn the reliability of our moral intuitions about injustice, cold-bloodedness, or horror. The judgment that participation in *e* constitutes prima-facie reason to believe that *p*'s life is ruined, stands and remains a daunting measure of *e*'s horror.

20. In my paper "Redemptive Suffering: A Christian Solution to the Problem of Evil," in Robert Audi and William J. Wainwright (eds.), *Rationality, Religious Belief, and Moral Commitment: New Essays in Philosophy of Religion* (Ithaca, N.Y.: Cornell University Press, 1986), pp. 248–67, I sketch how horrendous suffering can be meaningful by being made a vehicle of divine redemption for victim, perpetrator, and onlooker, and thus an occasion of the victim's collaboration with God. In "Separation and Reversal in Luke–Acts," in Thomas Morris (ed.), *Philosophy and the Christian Faith* (Notre Dame, Ind.: University of Notre Dame Press, 1988), pp. 92–117, I attempted to chart the redemptive plot-line whereby horrendous sufferings are made meaningful by being woven into the divine redemptive plot. My considered opinion is that such collaboration would be too strenuous for the human condition were it not to be supplemented by a more explicit and beatific divine intimacy.

21. For example, Julian of Norwich tells us that she prayed for and received the latter (*Revelations of Divine Love*, ch. 17). Mother Theresa of Calcutta seems to construe Matthew 25:31–46 to mean that the poorest and the least *are* Christ, and that their sufferings *are* Christ's (Malcolm Muggeridge, *Something Beautiful for God* [New York: Harper & Row, 1960], pp. 72–75).

22. *Revelations of Divine Love*, ch. 14. I am grateful to Houston Smith for recognizing this scenario of Julian's as a case of Chisholmian defeat.

23. Cf. Plantinga, "Self-Profile," p. 36.

24. I develop this point at some length in "Problems of Evil: More Advice to Christian Philosophers," pp. 127–35.

25. For example, in "The Metaphysics of the Incarnation in Some Fourteenth-Century Franciscans," in William A. Frank and Girard J. Etzkorn (eds.), *Essays Honoring Allan B. Woller* (St. Bonaventure, N.Y.: The Franciscan Institute, 1985), pp. 21–57.

26. In the development of these ideas, I am indebted to the members of our fall 1987 seminar at UCLA on the problem of evil—especially to Robert Merrihew Adams (its co-leader) and to Keith De Rose, William Fitzpatrick, and Houston Smith. I am also grateful to the Very Revd. Jon Hart Olson for many conversations in mystical theology.

STUDY QUESTIONS

1. Adams speaks of the standard discussion of the problem of evil as one about whether the existence of God and evil are compatible in general. Likewise, standard solutions try to show that they are compatible in general. What is Adams' criticism of this level of discussion?

2. How does Adams frame up the version of the problem of evil that she wants to address? What difference does it make that she is committed to Christian faith and not just to basic theism?

3. Precisely what are horrendous evils? Adams thinks that some answers to the problem of horrendous evils are appropriate, while others are inappropriate. Explain and evaluate.

4. Adams raises the interesting consideration of distinctively Christian attribute-analyses and value theory. Elaborate and show how these elements figure into her overall case. Why does she claim that without such elements, there is no hope of overcoming horrendous evils?

SUGGESTED READING

Adams, Marilyn. *Christ and Horrors: The Coherence of Christology*. Cambridge, England: Cambridge University Press, 2006.

———. *Horrendous Evils and the Goodness of God*. Ithaca, N.Y.: Cornell University Press, 1999.

Adams, Robert, and Marilyn Adams, eds. *The Problem of Evil*. New York: Oxford University Press, 1990.

Basinger, David. *The Case for Free Will Theism*. Downers Grove, Ill.: InterVarsity Press, 1996.

Drange, Theodore. *Nonbelief and Evil: Two Arguments for the Nonexistence of God.* Buffalo, N.Y.: Prometheus Books, 1998.

Griffin, David Ray. *God, Power, and Evil: A Process Theodicy.* Philadelphia: Westminster Press, 1976.

———. *Evil Revisited: Responses and Reconsiderations.* Albany, N.Y.: SUNY Press, 1991.

Hasker, William. *The Triumph of God over Evil: Theodicy for a World of Suffering.* Downers Grove, Ill.: InterVarsity Press, 2008.

Hick, John. *Evil and the God of Love.* Rev. ed. San Francisco, Calif: Harper and Row, 1978.

Howard-Snyder, Daniel, ed. *The Evidential Argument from Evil.* Bloomington: Indiana University Press, 1996.

Lewis, C. S. *The Problem of Pain.* New York: Touchstone Books, 1996.

Mackie, J. L. *The Miracle of Theism.* Oxford, England: Clarendon Press, 1982, ch. 9.

Madden, Edward, and Peter Hare. *Evil and the Concept of God.* Springfield, Ill.: Charles C. Thomas, 1968.

O'Connor, David. *God and Inscrutable Evil: In Defense of Theism and Atheism.* Lanham, Md.: Rowman and Littlefield, 1998.

Peterson, Michael. *Evil and the Christian God.* Grand Rapids, Mich.: Baker Book House, 1982.

———. *God and Evil: An Introduction to the Issues.* Boulder, Colo.: Westview Press, 1998.

Plantinga, Alvin. *The Nature of Necessity.* Oxford, England: Clarendon Press, 1973.

———. *God, Freedom, and Evil.* 1974 Reprint. Grand Rapids, Mich.: William B. Eerdmans, 1977.

Reichenbach, Bruce. *Evil and a Good God.* New York: Fordham University Press, 1982.

Swinburne, Richard. *Providence and the Problem of Evil.* Oxford, England: Clarendon Press, 1998.

Van Inwagen, Peter, ed. *Christian Faith and the Problem of Evil.* Grand Rapids, Mich.: William B. Eerdmans, 2004.

PART EIGHT

Divine Action

INTRODUCTION

Belief in a personal God and belief in divine action in the world are closely tied together. In order to act in the world, God must be able to know what goes on in the world, must be capable of preferring one possible state of the world to another, and must have some capacity to bring about the preferred states—which is to say, God must be a personal agent. And yet, if God does know about the world, does prefer some ways the world could be to others, and does have some ability to affect the world, it is difficult to understand why God would never act to bring about those preferred states. Furthermore, much of theistic religion revolves around beliefs concerning actions God has performed or is expected to perform in the future. For Christianity, the central events are those involved in the life, death, and resurrection of Jesus Christ. The crucial events for Judaism are those surrounding the Exodus: God's leading Israel out of Egypt and into the promised land through Moses' leadership. For Islam, the Hegira of Mohammed from Mecca to Medina and the giving of the Qur'an to Mohammed by the angel Gabriel are supremely important.

These particular events need to be investigated historically and also through the theological interpretations given in the different faiths. What can be done by philosophy in these matters is of a more general nature, but still important. Philosophers will not seek to determine what God has actually done, but rather what sorts of actions it is possible to attribute to God, in the light of various other considerations. The crucial variables for a theory of divine action are the power of God, the knowledge possessed by God, and the nature of human freedom. There are important questions to be asked about each of these variables, the answers to which distinguish the primary ways of understanding divine action.

Process Theism and God's Persuasive Power

The view known as *process theism* is distinguished from other theories of divine action by its characterization of God's power as persuasive rather than coercive. According to this view, each entity in the world is at every moment subject to God's "persuasion"—which means that God is continually showing to each created entity, and in particular to each person, what would be best for that entity or person to do, from among the options that are available to it. But having done that, there is nothing more that God can do: he completely lacks any "coercive power" to compel creatures to do what he wills for them. This results in a conception in which God's power and God's control over events are much more limited than has traditionally been assumed by the major theistic religions—and more limited than in any of the other views discussed in this section. In certain respects, this limitation can be seen as an advantage: if God has less control over events in the world than has often been supposed, God is also less responsible for the world's evils than has been generally thought. (The problem of evil, discussed in the previous section, plays an important role in weighing the advantages and disadvantages of the different theories of divine action.) Many believers, however, have felt that such a restricted conception of divine power detracts from much that is important in their faith.

Divine Determinism and Compatibilist Free Will

All of the other main theories of divine action reject the limitation on God's power postulated by process theism. In general, they are in agreement on a view similar to that of Thomas Aquinas (in Part Four): God can do anything that is logically possible and consistent with God's perfect nature. If God had power like this, it might seem to follow the world would be exactly the way God wants it to be: since nothing can resist God's will, how could God fail to get exactly what he wants? A possible answer to this question is that God has endowed human beings with *free will*. But if humans have the power to make their own decisions about some matters, then in spite of God's power some things may not go as God wants them to go.

Whether this is so or not, however, depends on how we understand free will. According to one major tradition in religious thought, free will is best understood in a *compatibilist* way: this means, roughly, that we are free if we are able to do whatever it is we most want to do. Freedom in this sense is entirely "compatible" with our actions' being controlled by our desires, whatever these happen to be. So our free actions can be, and according to some theologians are in fact, the inevitable result of a chain of causes going all the way back to God: in the end, what we desire and what we do are the predetermined result that flows from God's decrees concerning the sort of world he desired to create.

A view of this sort can be termed *divine determinism*, in that God's will is the ultimate determining cause of whatever happens. Among Protestants the view is often called Calvinism, after the Swiss reformer John Calvin; among Roman Catholics it is often referred to as Thomism, after Thomas Aquinas. The determinist view is also characteristic of orthodox or Sunni Islam. Adherents find the view admirable because it fully recognizes God's sole, ultimate control—his "sovereignty"—over everything that takes place, in a way no other view of divine action can match. On the other hand, divine determinism encounters severe difficulties with the problem of evil: if everything that happens is the result of God's decrees, this applies to all the evil and suffering in the world as well as to the good. Divine determinism further entails that *everything in the world and in human life is exactly as God wants it to be.* And this creates a problem, in that the Scriptures of all the theistic religions state clearly that there are some things that happen that are definitely *not* as God desires. Some careful maneuvering is required if divine determinism is to avoid this apparent contradiction.

MOLINISM AND THE COUNTERFACTUALS OF FREEDOM

The views that remain to be considered all affirm that human beings possess *libertarian* free will. This means that it is often the case that persons find themselves in circumstances where it is genuinely possible for them to do any of two or more different things. And since the choice in these situations is up to the persons involved, God may not, and in fact often does not, get the result he most desires. To be sure, it is by God's own choice that this comes about. God need not have created people with free will, and even after they have been created he has the superior power that would enable him to negate and overrule their decisions. What he cannot do, however, is to create them with free will, allow them to exercise that freedom, and still guarantee that they will make the choices he desires for them to make; to do that would be contradictory.

There is, however, a view that affirms libertarian free will and still retains for God a very large degree of control over what takes place. The name of this view is Molinism, after the sixteenth-century Jesuit theologian Luis de Molina, who developed it. According to this theory, God knows certain propositions, termed *counterfactuals of creaturely freedom*, which inform him of exactly what each actual or possible creature would freely choose to do in any situation in which it might find itself. God's knowledge of these truths is termed "middle knowledge," and it enables God to plan the course of events in full and exact detail, with complete confidence that his plan will be carried out: he needs only to place created persons in circumstances in which they will do what God intends for them to do. Yet if the creatures do evil, it is they and not God who are responsible for the evil, since it was fully in their power to make morally good choices instead. Almost certainly, Molinism affords God the greatest degree of control that is possible, consistent with libertarian free will. According to this view, God may not get everything he wants from the world and human history, but he can be sure to get exactly the world history he plans for. However, there are serious questions concerning whether the "middle knowledge" postulated by Molinism is even possible: the counterfactuals of freedom may not exist for God to know them. The debate over Molinism has played an important role in recent discussions concerning divine action.

SIMPLE FOREKNOWLEDGE AND DIVINE TIMELESS KNOWLEDGE

Suppose that we reject divine determinism, and we do not believe God has the "counterfactual knowledge" postulated by Molinism. A remaining option, which has been embraced by many, is that God has "simple foreknowledge": he knows everything about the actual future, even if he lacks Molinism's knowledge of hypothetical futures. A related view, which is similar in its consequences for divine action, is that God is timeless and possesses timeless knowledge of everything that takes place in time. (For this view, see the selection from Boethius in Part Four.)

There is a widely discussed argument that claims to show that comprehensive divine knowledge of the future is incompatible with libertarian free will. (For one version, see the article by Nelson Pike in Part Four.) The view that God's knowledge is timeless has been held to circumvent this argument, but this also is controversial. But even if we assume that this argument can be met, there is a further difficulty that affects both the simple foreknowledge view and the view that God possesses timeless knowledge of what transpires in time. For either of these views, it can be argued that the knowledge God has of the future is *completely useless* from the standpoint of guiding his decisions about his actions in the world. That is to say, if God has complete knowledge of the actual future, this knowledge does not provide any better guidance for his actions than if he has "only" full knowledge of the past and present. To see this, suppose that in the first decade of the twenty-first century, God looks into the future and sees something happening in 2050 that is contrary to his wishes. Can God do something now, early in the century, that will prevent that undesired future event from occurring? A little reflection shows that this is incoherent. By hypothesis, what God sees happening in 2050 is the *actual future* as of that date, and to suppose that God might do something that would cause it *not* to be the actual future is self-contradictory. This argument has come to the fore only recently, and it is still very much under discussion, but so far the attempts to circumvent it do not appear promising.

OPEN THEISM AND DIVINE RISK TAKING

Suppose, then, that we conclude that humans are free in the libertarian sense, and that this freedom is inconsistent both with divine middle knowledge and with comprehensive divine knowledge of the actual future. If we accept these conclusions, we have come to a view that is known as *open theism*—so called because God is "open" to an as-yet-undetermined future, which will become definite and determinate only as a result of the free choices that are yet to be made by human beings (and other free creatures, if there are any). This view, perhaps even more than the others surveyed above, is extremely controversial. (Actually all are controversial, but since open theism has only recently become a prominent option, the controversy over it is especially intense at present.) Let us see exactly what the view amounts to.

Since open theism and process theism both deny that God has complete, comprehensive knowledge of the future, they have often been compared. However, this is the *only* major point of agreement between the views, which in other respects are quite different. Open theism affirms that God is omnipotent, just as do Calvinism, Molinism, and the simple foreknowledge theory. (The question is not how much power God has, but how God has chosen to exercise his power.) And open theists also subscribe to divine omniscience: they may hold that, concerning the specific events of the as-yet-undetermined future, there are no truths to be known, and thus no truths of which God is ignorant. God does, to be sure, know infinitely more about the future than any human being does, but this knowledge, insofar as it concerns free creaturely actions, is a knowledge of possibilities and probabilities rather than knowledge of what will definitely occur. Because of this, God's plans for the future involve an element of risk: if humans do not respond in the way needed to fulfill certain of God's objectives, God will need either to find another way to his goals or to abandon that specific objective. (If the argument given above is correct, this riskiness applies also to the simple foreknowledge and divine timeless knowledge views, but proponents of those views have often failed to recognize the fact.) Open theists insist, however, that in view of God's power and wisdom his ultimate purposes are not endangered.

They further claim that open theism fits very well with the dynamic, interactive character of God's relationships with human beings, as portrayed in the Scriptures. But whether the limitations concerning God's knowledge of the future postulated by open theism are acceptable remains very much in debate.

In our first selection, the Calvinist theist Paul Helm argues for divine determinism by insisting that it is unacceptable to view divine providence as involving risk. Helm admits that there are biblical passages that might seem to support such a view, but he believes that they are outweighed by others that imply God's absolute control over everything that happens; the former passages, then, must be viewed as anthropomorphic rather than exact.

In the next selection, David Basinger discusses the importance of middle knowledge for Christian theology. He sets out the main ideas of this theory, and argues that if libertarian freedom is assumed, middle knowledge plays an important role. Given libertarian freedom, certain assumptions concerning divine providence and biblical prophecy that have been commonly made by theologians become untenable unless God is assumed to possess middle knowledge.

In the third selection, Robert Adams sets out what is perhaps the commonest objection to middle knowledge: there seems to be no way in which the "counterfactuals of freedom," which are crucial for the middle knowledge, can be true. This "grounding objection" to middle knowledge has generated considerable discussion; it is fair to say that no resolution of the issue has been generally accepted.

Next, J. R. Lucas sets out the basic ideas of the theory of divine action that has come to be known as open theism. Insofar as the future depends on the free actions of human beings and other creatures, there is no definite and knowable truth concerning it. God's providence should not be thought of as a blueprint with every detail already in place, but as a plan of action that develops along with the process of human history. This view, Lucas asserts, gives the most adequate and satisfying account of God's love, which is not only creative but also, like all love, vulnerable.

In our final selection, John B. Cobb and David Ray Griffin sketch the view of divine action that is implied by process theism. They emphasize the superiority of this view—in which God is affected by, and responsive to, his creatures—to a deterministic view in which God is impassive and unaffected by human beings. God's love is both creative and responsive; he "lures" the creatures in the way that is best for them to go, but the outcome depends on their free and uncoerced response.

Paul Helm

Providence: Risky or Risk-Free?

Paul Helm (b. 1940) contends for the "risk-free" view of divine providence that is characteristic of Calvinism or theological determinism. He acknowledges that the Bible provides support for both "risky" and risk-free views, but he holds that the former type of passages must
be understood as "accommodation," in which God adapts himself to "human incapacity and
weakness." On Helm's view, only a risk-free view gives us a proper estimation of the greatness
and majesty of God.

Does God's providence, according to Scripture, extend to all that he has created, including the choices of men and women? Or is his providence limited, perhaps limited by God himself, so that he does not infallibly know how the universe is going to unfold? Let us call the first of these views (it is in fact a family of views) the "risk-free" or "no-risk" view of providence, and the second family, the "risky" view.[1] Our question then is: which view of providence does Scripture favour?

It is clear that there are different kinds of risk. For example, if we start something, not knowing how it will turn out, and if how it turns out matters to us then we take a risk. A risk of another, perhaps lesser, kind is where we have no formulated or expressed prefer-ence as to how we want things to turn out, but only expectations; and we set in motion events which may lead only to the partial fulfilment of our expectations,

or to their non-fulfilment. In what follows we shall use "risk" in the stronger of these senses, where both preferences and expectations are at stake. We take no risk if we knowingly set in motion events which will turn out exactly as we want them to do.

In the case of divine providence the events in ques-tion are all those which, in the history of the entire universe, are to become actual. We shall assume that if at least one of these events could be caused to turn out in a way other than the way that God believes that it will, then God is taking a risk. The risk may not be very great, and its inherent riskiness may be softened by remembering that even if God does not infallibly determine what will happen in this particular case, his control of what will happen will be considerable. Nevertheless, a risk is a risk.

It will be noted that we have formulated riskiness and risk-freeness in terms of God's *knowledge*.[2] It is

Paul Helm, *The Providence of God* (Downers Grove, Ill.: Inter Varsity Press, 1994), pp. 39–55.

also possible to formulate it in terms of God's decreeing or ordaining, and it might be thought that such a formulation would be more in accord with divine providence. If God takes a risk, however, where this is understood in terms of knowledge, then it would follow logically that he also takes a risk in terms of what he ordains. For what he ordains must be similarly risky.

Numerous contemporary theologians and philosophers take the view that God's providence must be a risky affair. Here are some representative statements:

> It is evident that the view of God's governance of the world here proposed differs from others that are commonly held. But wherein precisely does the difference lie? I believe it can be formulated in a simple, yet crucial question: *Does God take risks?* Or, to put the matter more precisely, we may ask: *Does God make decisions that depend for their outcomes on the responses of free creatures in which the decisions themselves are not informed by knowledge of the outcomes?* If he does, then creating and governing a world is for God a risky business. That this is so is evidently an implication of the views here adopted, and it is equally evident that it would be rejected by some Christian thinkers—those, for example, who hold to a theory of predestination according to which everything that occurs is determined solely by God's sovereign decree.[3]

> The value that regards knowledge as a good can be more fully realised by forgoing the possibility of being a complete know-all, and creating a world in which the future actions of others can often only be surmised, and sometimes not even that. If God created man in His own image, He must have created him capable of new initiatives and new insights which cannot be precisely or infallibly foreknown, but which give to the future a perpetual freshness as the inexhaustible variety of possible thoughts and actions, on the part of His children as well as Himself, crystallizes into actuality.[4]

> …God must take real risks if He makes free creatures (thousands, millions, or trillions of risks, if each creature makes thousands of morally significant free choices). No matter how shrewdly God acted in running so many risks, His winning on *every* risk would not be antecedently probable.[5]

> That God is omniscient only in the attenuated sense would of course—given that he is perfectly free and omnipotent—have resulted from his own choice. In choosing to preserve his own freedom (and to give others freedom), he limits his own knowledge of what

is to come. He continually limits himself in this way by not curtailing his or men's future freedom.

> As regards men, their choices are much influenced by circumstances and this makes it possible for a being who knows all the circumstances to predict human behaviour correctly most of the time, but always with the possibility that men may falsify those predictions.[6]

The following are some representative statements of the no-risk view of providence:

> Even though it may seem to us that all things happen equally to the good and to the evil since we are ignorant of the reasons for God's providence in allotting these things, there is no doubt that in all these good and evil things happening to the good or to the evil there is operative a well worked out plan by which God's providence directs all things.[7]

> But God protects and governs by His providence all things which He created, "teaching from end to end mightily and ordering all things sweetly" (Wisdom 8:1). For "all things are naked and open to his eyes" (Heb. 4:13), even those which by the free action of creatures are in the future.[8]

> God, the great Creator of all things, doth uphold, direct, dispose, and govern all creatures, actions and things, from the greatest even to the least, by his most wise and holy providence, according to his infallible foreknowledge, and the free and immutable counsel of his own will, to the praise of the glory of his wisdom, power, justice, goodness, and mercy.[9]

It will be noted from this selection of views on providence that the chief (if not the only) reason why a "risk" view of providence is taken is a concern to preserve human freedom, and (in the case of Swinburne at least) to preserve divine freedom as well. All the writers hold the view that only if providence is risky will there be room for the exercise of human freedom.

"Freedom" is a term that has many meanings, and so it is important to understand what is the sense of human freedom that these writers believe it is essential to safeguard. One way of explaining this sense is as follows. If we are free, then we have the power to do some particular action, or to refrain from doing it, even though the entire history of the universe up to the moment of that choice is the same whichever choice is made. The entire history of the universe, up to the point of our choice, is consistent either with our performing of that action or with our refraining from it. So which action is performed is up to us, to the exercise of our free choice. An alternative way of expressing this, though not a strictly equivalent way, is to say that we are free in doing an action only if, every circumstance other than our decision remaining the same, we could have decided otherwise.

This is a sense of freedom which is incompatible with determinism. Only if freedom in this sense is maintained (writers such as Lucas and Swinburne believe) can justice be done to human dignity and creativity, and to human responsibility.... At this stage we shall consider what the consequences are for the idea of divine providence of taking a non-deterministic view of human freedom (or, more accurately, what consequences the writers just quoted are prepared to accept). These consequences have chiefly to do with God's character—his knowledge, his will and his goodness, including the character of God's saving grace. This latter point, though, is not something that looms large in current discussion. We shall briefly comment on each of these in turn.

The Character of God

1. God's Knowledge

As traditionally understood, God is omniscient. This is not only a consequence of the perfection of God in the abstract (for how could a perfect God be ignorant of anything?), but also of attending to the relevant data of Scripture. In Scripture God is said to be one who knows the end from the beginning; all things are naked and open before his eyes; he has numbered the hairs of our heads; he knows our downsitting and uprising, he understands our ways afar off; he knows what we need before we ask; he ordains all things after the counsel of his own will, and so on.

But if in fact God has created a universe in which there is risk, then he cannot be omniscient. Most writers who take the "risk" view accept this. They are prepared, as a consequence, to sacrifice or to attenuate the classical and scriptural doctrine of divine omniscience in the interests of a risky providence. There are several different arguments by which such

attentuation is defended, but in order to simplify and focus our discussion I shall concentrate upon one of these: that provided by Richard Swinburne in *The Coherence of Theism*.

Swinburne develops his account out of a concern not only for the preservation of human freedom, but for divine freedom. Because of his concern to safeguard freedom, Swinburne proposes the following restricted definition of omniscence:

> A person P is omniscient at a time t if and only if he knows of every true proposition about t or an earlier time that it is true *and* also he knows of every true proposition about a time later than t, such that what it reports is physically necessitated by some cause at t or earlier, that it is true.[10]

This definition may require a little explanation. Note in the first place that what is proposed is a general definition of omniscience, one that could apply not only to God but to any person. Also, whoever it applies to is in time, for the definition refers to omniscience *at a time*. If God is timelessly eternal, as some have argued, then this definition could not apply to him. Perhaps, though, it could be suitably modified.

The basic thought behind the definition, however, is that an omniscient being knows everything about the past and about the present, and he also knows whatever is "physically necessitated" by any cause in the present or past. Such an omniscient being would know, for example, that I am typing these sentences on my word processor now, and he would also know what the movements of the planets will be tomorrow, and what the state of any remote forest, physically inaccessible to human interference, will be tomorrow. What he will not know today is anything whatever about tomorrow which depends upon non-physically necessitated choices, particularly human decisions. Thus, if I have not yet made up my mind whether or not, by a free action, to chop down my cherry tree tomorrow, then God cannot yet know what the state of that tree will be tomorrow. He would of course otherwise know what its state tomorrow will be, since its state tomorrow (freely decided-upon interference apart) is physically necessitated by its state today.

Swinburne stresses the importance for limiting omniscience of what is not *physically* necessitated, but this restriction may not cover all the cases that he has in mind. For some have argued, not that human choices are physically necessitated, but that they are psychologically necessitated or even rationally necessitated. That is, they have claimed that human choices are the outcome not of prior physical states, but of prior psychological states such as desires, wishes and preferences of various kinds. Still, Swinburne's account can be modified to cover such cases, simply by dropping the word "physical" from it.

In saying that God (for example) does not *know* what a person (including himself) will freely choose tomorrow, Swinburne is not denying that God may have *beliefs* about the future.

> In choosing to preserve his own freedom (and to give others freedom), he (that is, God) limits his own knowledge of what is to come. He continually limits himself in this way by not curtailing his or men's future freedom. As regards men, their choices are much influenced by circumstances and this makes it possible for a being who knows all the circumstances to predict human behaviour correctly most of the time, but always with the possibility that men may falsify those predictions.[11]

Knowing what he does about the present and the past, God may (as we noted earlier) have very accurate beliefs. Nonetheless these beliefs do not amount to knowledge. God has beliefs (we may presume), many of which turn out to be false as, due to the free decisions of men and women, what he supposes will happen does not in fact happen. Not only, therefore, is God's omniscience restricted in the way indicated, but his infallibility must also be surrendered. We shall return to this point later.

Such an account of omniscience differs markedly from that given by the great theologians of Christianity. For example:

> Now, if the infinity of numbers cannot be beyond the limits of the knowledge of God which comprehends it, who are we little men that we should presume to put limits to His knowledge? ... The fact is that God, whose knowledge is simple in its multiplicity and one in its diversity, comprehends all incomprehensible things with an incomprehensible comprehension.[12]

> Whatever can be produced or thought or said by a creature, and also whatever God himself can produce, all is known by God, even if it is not actually existing.[13]
>
> Concerning repentance, we ought so to hold that it is no more chargeable against God than is ignorance.[14]

While Swinburne acknowledges that his account of omniscience is less strict than that usually attributed to God by Christian theologians, he nevertheless claims scriptural support for it. He cites, for example, the fact that in the Old Testament God has certain plans which he on occasion changes. He changed his plan regarding Sodom when Abraham interceded, and spared Israel when Moses interceded; he spared Nineveh when Jonah preached, and so on. In general, Swinburne says, God would not need to make conditional promises if he knew what men would do.

> By contrast, the New Testament talks a great deal of God's "foreknowledge," but, at any rate sometimes, it does not seem to regard this as absolute. Man can upset God's plans.[15]

So there are, in effect, two types of scriptural data. One type indicates that God's knowledge is unqualified. The other type of data represents God as learning, as forgetting, as changing his mind, as being surprised, and the like. What, then, ought we to conclude? What part do such data play in an account of divine providence which is not only coherent in itself but in accordance with all the data of Scripture? We shall consider an answer to this question shortly.

2. God's Will

There are several senses in which God is said to have a will. God may will in the sense of *command*, and he may will in the sense of *decree*. My cherry tree exists by God's decree, but God has not commanded the tree to exist. (We might say that he has commanded that the tree exist, but not that he has commanded it *to* exist.) After all, it is possible to issue commands only to what already exists, and until God has commanded that the tree exist there is no tree for him to issue commands to.

It is not easy to suppose that God might issue commands to trees. But according to Scripture, from time to time he has commanded men and women.

Sometimes these commands have to do with particular people, times and places; sometimes they are more general, even universal, in their scope. God's command to Abraham to sacrifice Issac was specific. His command forbidding stealing was issued to Israel, and perhaps applies more widely still.

Not every command of God is obeyed. Scripture teaches, however, that even on those occasions when the command of God is disobeyed, the disobedience is in accordance with his will, in the sense of his decree. Scripture is littered with examples of such cases. It was against the command of God (presumably) that Joseph's brothers should sell him, but in this way God decreed a saviour for Israel. Through Saul's disobedience David became king. Again, through the murderous intentions of the Jews and the weakness of Pilate, Jesus was crucified.

Perhaps these events could have been brought about without violations of God's command. We shall not speculate on this. It is sufficient to note that *in fact* they did not come about in such ways, but what God decreed involved violations of commands that he himself had given. To put the point paradoxically, the breaking of his will became part of the fulfilling of his will. We shall consider the character of God's will in more detail in chapter 5.

If, however, one supposes a "risk" view of providence, this picture appears to change in a radical way. According to some Christian theologians who support such a view, there are at least some significant occasions which contain elements undecreed by God, or on which, though God has decreed a certain definite outcome, that decree is thwarted or modified by the exercise of human libertarian free will. While, on this view God *unconditionally* decrees much (for example, those aspects of his creation never affected by libertarian choices), he also *conditionally* decrees much, thereby taking risks. Similarly, just as his commands (for instance, not to steal) may be broken, so may what he has decreed, if what he has decreed falls foul of free choice. Those who make such a choice may not know that they are thwarting God's decree (for that decree may not have been disclosed to anyone), but this does not alter the fact of the matter.

In fact, however, the matter runs deeper than this. On the "risk" view of divine providence, not only may a free decision thwart the decree of God, but God's decreeing any human action is inconsistent with that action's being indeterministically free. For, as we have seen, the essence of indeterministic freedom is a power to choose either A or not–A in a situation where the character of the universe, up to the moment of the choice, is fixed. So what God may or may not have decreed about the choice, prior to its exercise, is *irrelevant* to the exercise of such a choice.

Various ways have been proposed to mitigate the effects of this collision between God's decree and human libertarian freedom, to minimize or eliminate the risk. It has been proposed, for example, that we should think of the relation of God to his free creatures as like that of a chess Grand Master, who is able effortlessly to outwit the freely made chess moves of any number of novices.[16] . . .

3. God's Goodness

The question whether or not providence is risky also affects the character of God's goodness.

God's goodness may be considered from various aspects, and in almost all these aspects it is a bone of contention. Chief controversial interest is at present focused on the extensiveness of God's goodness. Granted that many men and women lead tolerable and personally fulfilling lives, why does God not bring it about that everyone does? Why are God's blessings uneven? Why is there discrimination? Why do the wicked prosper? If God is good, and all-powerful, why has he not arranged matters so as to minimize suffering and to maximize individual pleasure? These questions form the heart of the problem of evil. . . .

There is, however, another way in which the goodness of God may be considered which is less frequently debated at present. We might call this the *intensiveness* question. Given that God wishes to do good, how effective can these wishes be? Can he wish to do good to a person and be thwarted by that person? In other words, in carrying out his plans to do good, does God take risks?

Historically, this question has been at the centre of a controversy about divine saving grace. Is that grace merely *enabling*, or is it *effective*? How that question is answered will vitally affect the providence of God as it concerns the existence and character of the Christian church. Is the church formed as a result of men and women taking advantage of certain favourable conditions and circumstances provided by God in his goodness? Or does God's goodness actually cause the church to be formed by bringing about the conversion of men and women to Christ?

In Scripture God's grace in conversion is powerful (1 Thes. 1:5); it is an effective call (Rom. 1:6; 9:11; 1 Cor. 1:9; Eph. 4:4); it is compared to a creation (2 Cor. 4:6), and to a resurrection (Eph. 2:5), and to a new birth (1 Pet. 1:23). The Holy Spirit gives repentance (2 Tim. 2:25) and faith (Eph. 2:8). Both the plain and the figurative language used about conversion seems to point unmistakably to the idea that God's grace is effective in securing the ends at which it aimed.

It is hard to see how one can hold both (a) that God's goodness is effective in the way that these verses describe (*i.e.*, that it is causally sufficient for making a person a Christian) and (b) that people have indeterministic freedom to choose whether or not to be converted. It would certainly be possible to hold that there are many indeterministic choices but that Christian conversion does not include any, though this is not a view that is readily found in the history of Christian thought. If, at the point of conversion, we have indeterministic power, then we have indeterministic power to reject the efforts of God's goodness to bring about our conversion. It would then follow that in offering his goodness in these circumstances God was taking a risk.

Yet what is one to make of the scriptural references to men and women resisting the grace of God (Acts 7:51) and rejecting the message of salvation (Acts 13:46)? Is Scripture simply contradictory at this point, or "paradoxical"? Can the data be combined together consistently by taking certain expressions to have priority over others? It is here that we need to return to the point raised earlier in the discussion of Swinburne's position.

ACCOMMODATION

We are faced with apparently incompatible data— data which on the one hand stress God's omniscience and the power of his grace, and on the other portray him as changing his mind, and men and women resisting his grace. How then is one to proceed in constructing from Scripture an account of divine omniscience or goodness, and with it an account of divine providence? Which of these apparently inconsistent or incompatible sets of data is to take priority? Which data control the remainder?

One alternative would be to say that the language about God's ignorance, about his changes of mind and resistance to his grace, is more basic to our understanding of God than the more general statements (quoted earlier) about the extent of God's knowledge or the efficacy of his grace. Statements which imply God's ignorance and powerlessness thus take precedence over statements which do not. As a consequence, we should be committed to maintaining that God is at times ignorant, that he changes his mind, that he is open to persuasion, that his purposes of goodness are thwarted, and so on. Not only this; but by parity of reasoning from the language of Scripture about God, we should also be committed to the view that God has a rich, ever-changing emotional life, and perhaps that he has a body, and a physical location in heaven.

As a consequence of accepting this principle of biblical interpretation, the scriptural language which ascribes omniscience or gracious power to God would be understood as hyperbolic; to ascribe omniscience to God is exactly like ascribing it to a human expert, to someone who knows everything about his subject. To say that God is gracious is rather like saying that a generous friend, whose gifts may be spurned, is gracious.

The alternative hermeneutical position would be to say that general scriptural statements of the omniscience, will and effective goodness of God take precedence. The other language of Scripture, the language of ignorance, of indecision and of change, is then to be interpreted in the light of these statements.

There is therefore a straight choice. Put in such a stark way it seems obvious (to me at least) what that choice ought to be. The statements about the extent and intensity of God's knowledge, power and goodness must control the anthropomorphic and weaker statements, and not vice versa. The alternative approach would appear to be quite unacceptable, for it would result in a theological reductionism in which God is distilled to human proportions.

But why, if the biblical language which portrays God as ignorant or vacillating or ultimately resistible, cannot be literally true, is it employed in Scripture? No better general answer has been given to this question, to my mind, that the one found throughout the writings of John Calvin; namely, that God uses such language to accommodate himself to human incapacity and weakness.

Accommodation, the need for God to address men and women in terms that they can understand and respond to, would seem to be a good general explanation for the occurrence of such language in Scripture, for two interconnected reasons. To begin with, it preserves the proper sense of direction. The presence of anthropomorphic language in Scripture is not a human attempt to express the inexpressible, but is one of the ways in which God graciously condescends to his creatures. As Calvin put it, referring to passages where God is said to "repent":

> What, therefore, does the word "repentance" mean? Surely its meaning is like that of all other modes of speaking that describe God for us in human terms. For because our weakness does not attain to his exalted state, the description of him that is given to us must be accommodated to our capacity so that we may understand it. Now the mode of accommodation is for him to represent himself to us not as he is in himself, but as he seems to us.[17]

In Calvin's eyes the movement of direction is from God to mankind, and not vice versa. Furthermore, because such language is an act of accommodation it is also an act of grace. Divine revelation is evangelical in motive and in manner, as well as in content.

But does this not reduce much of the language of Scripture to a mere teaching tool, a concession to those of weak capacity (as thinkers as different as Philo and John Locke have maintained)? While this may be our initial reaction, behind what may seem a psychological or epistemological economy on God's part, there lies a logical point of some importance.

Calvin's claim is not that human beings will not understand God at all unless he condescends to speak to us in human-like, activistic ways. For there

is much in the writings of Calvin to show that he took the opposite view. The very fact that he regards certain expressions as divine *accommodations* implies that it is possible to think of God in ways which are exact and unaccommodated.

What then lies behind Calvin's view? He recognizes that it is because God wishes people to respond to him that he *must* represent himself to them as one to whom response is possible, and as one who is responsive, who acts in space and time in reaction to human actions in space and time. Only on such an understanding is it possible to provide for that divine—human interaction which is at the heart of biblical religion.

At the centre of Calvin's doctrine of divine accommodation, therefore, is a logical point: namely that it is a logically necessary condition of dialogue between people that those people should act and react in time. Omniscience and omnipotence have priority because they are essential properties of God, whereas his creating a universe in which there are creatures with whom he converses is a contingent matter. Nevertheless, if dialogue between God and mankind is to be real and not make-believe, then God cannot inform those with whom he converses of what they will decide to do, for then they would not *decide* to do it, and dialogue would be impossible.

God is portrayed in Scripture as separate from his creation, as self-sufficient, and as bringing into being a creation which is distinct from himself. On the other hand, God is also shown in anthropomorphic ways, and his action and character are also likened to non-human animals and to inanimate things. The reason for such portrayals is both pragmatic and logical: the need to represent God to human beings in ways which do not (as Calvin would have put it) pander to the natural, sinful torpor and sluggishness of the human mind; and also the need for God to reveal himself in such a way as to make dialogue possible between himself and his human creatures.

Both the anthropomorphic and the exact language of Scripture are, of course, equally important, but in constructing a coherent account of God one set of data must take priority over the other. If readers believe that to give priority to the metaphysical over the apparently figurative is a mistaken decision, then it will be possible for them to make the necessary adjustments through the discussion that follows. These adjustments, however, are not small, and, if they are carried through consistently, a substantially different account of divine providence will ensue.

COSTS AND BENEFITS

We are now in a position to summarize briefly our discussion so far. The costs of a "risk" view of providence, however minimal the degree of risk is judged to be, are that God cannot be regarded as infallibly omniscient of his creation, nor is he able to bring to pass everything that he might wish to do. There will, in the life of God, necessarily be some frustration as those ends that he wishes to secure cannot be achieved, or must be achieved by a different route. God will have many true beliefs about the future; he will be highly informed and expert, but his knowledge will be like your knowledge and mine—it will be fallible. Alternatively, infallibility will be purchased at the expense of ignorance.

Similarly, it will follow that the exercise of God's redeeming grace can never, on the "risk" view of divine providence, be efficacious. His grace is always resistible by the person on whom it operates. If it were not resistible, the action which results from such grace could not be a free action in the sense of the concept of "freedom" being defended. For nothing that has been ensured to happen by the power of divine grace can be indeterministically free.

This would be a somewhat ironic result given the teaching of Christ that whoever the Son makes free is free indeed (Jn. 8:36). The New Testament appears to find no incoherence in the idea of being made to be free, and has little concern with the prospect that any person whose action is caused cannot be free in performing that action.

Further, as we noted briefly earlier, it appears that the "risk" view of providence carries with it the consequence that God is in time, and so is not timelessly eternal. For a God whose knowledge and purposes are both modifiable by human, free decisions must be in time, for any such modifications must take place in time. This consequence is one that is certainly recognized and even welcomed by, for example, Swinburne and Lucas.

The benefits of the "risk" view can be put down to the presence of one factor—an indeterministic view of free will, a view of freedom which gives an individual power, in identical circumstances, either to act or not to act, as he or she chooses.

NOTES

1. The idea of risk as a central motif in Christian theology is to be found, for example, in *The Divine Risk*, ed. Richard Holloway (London: Darton, Longman and Todd, 1990).
2. In *God, Time, and Knowledge* (Ithaca, N.Y.: Cornell University Press, 1989), William Hasker offers reasons for objecting to this. According to him God's knowledge of future events is derived from the actual occurrence of those events (p. 197). If this point were to be granted then God's knowledge would simply "record" (by anticipating) the events known, including, presumably, his own frustrated attempts to change human wills. Would this mean that God has knowledge of some of his own actions only after he has carried them out, that he could not anticipate the effects his actions would have? If so, this would appear to be incompatible with his omniscience. As Hasker says, such foreknowledge would be useless. The reader must judge whether this view does justice to such scriptural statements of divine foreknowledge as Rom. 8:29; 11:2; 1 Pet. 1:2.
3. Ibid., p. 197.
4. J. R. Lucas, *The Future* (Oxford, England: Blackwell, 1989), p. 233.
5. Robert Merrihew Adams, "Middle Knowledge and the Problem of Evil," in *The Problem of Evil*, ed. Robert Merrihew Adams and Marilyn McCord Adams (Oxford, England: Oxford University Press, 1990), p. 125.
6. Richard Swinburne, *The Coherence of Theism* (Oxford, England: Clarendon Press, 1977), p. 176.
7. Thomas Aquinas, *Providence and Predestination*, trans. R. W. Mulligan (Chicago: Regnery, 1953), p. 44.

8. Vatican I, Session III. Quoted from Denzinger, *Sources of Catholic Dogma* (St. Louis, Mo., and London: B. Herder Book Company, 1957), p. 443.
9. Westminster Confession of Faith (1647), V. 1.
10. R. Swinburne, op. cit., p. 175.
11. Ibid., p. 176.
12. *City of God*, trans. Gerald G. Walsh and Grace Monahan (*Fathers of the Church*, vol. 14) (Washington, D.C.: Catholic University of America Press, 1952), XII. 19.
13. Thomas Aquinas, *Summa Theologiae*, Ia. 14. 9.
14. John Calvin, *Institutes of the Christian Religion*, I, 17, 12.
15. R. Swinburne, op. cit., p. 177.
16. William James, *The Will to Believe and Other Essays in Popular Philosophy* (New York: Longmans, 1897), pp. 180–81. See also P. T. Geach, *Providence and Evil* (Cambridge, England: Cambridge University Press, 1977), p. 58.
17. *Institutes* I, 17, 13. Compare Aquinas: "To speak of God as repenting is to use the language of metaphor. Men are said to repent when they do not carry out what they threatened to do" (*Summa Theologiae* Ia. 19.7).

STUDY QUESTIONS

1. Explain briefly the difference between a "risky" and a "risk-free" account of divine providence. What are Helm's reasons for preferring a "risk-free" account?
2. Explain briefly the difference between "libertarian" and "compatibilist" views of free will. What are Helm's reasons for preferring the compatibilist view?
3. What does it mean to say that a passage of Scripture is an instance of "accommodation"? Why does Helm believe that certain passages must be viewed as accommodation? Does this view of Helm's strike you as plausible and satisfying?

David Basinger

Middle Knowledge and Classical Christian Thought

David Basinger (b. 1947) sets out the central ideas of the theory of divine *middle knowledge*, or Molinism. If God has knowledge of the counterfactuals of freedom—that is, if God knows what his free creatures *would do* under hypothetical circumstances that may never actually arise—this is a great advantage for God's providential governance of the world. Basinger argues that if libertarian free will is accepted, important aspects of the traditional doctrine of divine providence stand or fall with middle knowledge; thus, challenges to the coherence of middle knowledge need to be taken seriously.

To say that God is omniscient, most philosophers and theologians agree, is to say that he knows all true propositions and none that are false.[1] But there is a great deal of disagreement about what is knowable. Some believe that God's knowledge is limited to everything that is (or has been) actual and that which will follow deterministically from it. He knows, for example, exactly what Caesar was thinking when he crossed the Rubicon and how many horses he had in his army that day. And he knows exactly how Gorbachev feels about the use of nuclear weapons. And since he knows how the "laws of nature" (which he has purportedly created) function, he knows, for example, how certain weather systems will develop and what their effects will be on certain natural environments. But with respect to any future state of affairs which includes free human decision-making as a causal component, God is said not to know what will occur. God, as the ultimate psychoanalyst or behaviourist, can with great accuracy predict what we will freely decide to do in the future in many cases. He might well, for example, be able to predict quite accurately who will win the 1988 Presidential election. But a God who possesses only "present knowledge" cannot know who will win. Given that the election in question is dependent on free choices which have yet to be made, there is presently nothing for God to know.[2]

Proponents of what we shall call "simple foreknowledge" disagree. Statements describing what

David Basinger, "Middle Knowledge and Classical Christian Thought," *Religious Studies* 22 (1986): 407–22.

will actually happen, they argue, including those statements describing events related to what humans will freely choose to do, are true *now*. It is now true or false that "Gary Hart *will* be elected in 1996 in the actual world." The relevant decisions have, of course, not yet been made. But Hart will either choose to run or choose not to run, he will either be nominated or not be nominated, and he will either be elected or not be elected. Thus, since God knows all true propositions, he knows now if Hart will be elected President in the actual world in 1996.[3]

It is important to add parenthetically that timeless knowledge also normally fits into this category. The proponent of timeless knowledge usually maintains that God's knowledge of all actual occurrences (those which are from *our perspective* past, present or future) is not "in time." All occurrences are being viewed by him in the "eternal now." This differs from simple foreknowledge in that God is not said to *foreknow* anything. But it is similar in that both models maintain that God knows all that which *from our perspective* was, is or will be actual.[4]

But what about counterfactual claims? What, for example, should we say about the following statement: "If Ted Kennedy had won the Presidential election in 1980, he would have run again in 1984." The antecedent is false, so that statement cannot be true by virtue of the fact that it describes what has occurred or will actually occur. But is it not either true or false that *if* Kennedy had won in 1980, he would have run again? And, thus, ought we not maintain that God knows the truth or falsity of such hypothetical propositions?

There are many philosophers and theologians who believe that God has such "middle knowledge." They believe, that is, not only that God knows what *will* in fact happen in the actual world or what *could* in fact happen in all worlds, but also what *would* in fact happen in every possible situation, including what every possible free creature would do in every possible situation in which that creature could find itself. They believe that God does know, for example, whether Ted Kennedy would have chosen freely to run again in 1984 if he had been elected President in 1980. We as humans, as Alvin Plantinga states it, "may not know what the answer is" in such a case. But "one thing we would take for granted," he argues,

"is there is a right answer here . . . we would reject out of hand . . . the suggestion that there simply is none."[5]

A proponent of timeless knowledge, it should be added, could in principle also affirm a version of middle knowledge although I am not aware of any who do. It could be claimed that in addition to "timelessly" seeing the actual world in its entirety, God timelessly "sees" not only all other possible worlds in their entirety, but can identify which of these worlds would have been actual, given that other creative decisions had been made.

Does the model of divine omniscience one affirms make much difference? Specifically, do such models have important implications for God's ability to influence earthly affairs? The answer depends in part on the perceived relationship between divine sovereignty and human freedom. Some orthodox Christians are theological determinists. They, like their non-theistic counterparts, argue that an action is voluntary (free) as long as the action is willed or chosen by the agent herself—i.e., as long as the agent is not forced to perform the action against her will. Thus, they see nothing inconsistent in claiming that, although God irresistibly influences the desires (will) of his created moral agents in such a manner that he can insure that they will perform the exact states of affairs he desires, such moral agents are still acting freely. For such actions are still seen as willed by the agents in question.[6]

In such a universe, God does in fact have a form of middle knowledge. That is, in addition to knowing what has happened and will happen in the actual world, he knows exactly what would have happened in any other world he could have actualized. But his decisions are not based on what he foreknows. He does not, in other words, utilize his middle knowledge when deciding how to act. For the compatibilistic God just the opposite is true. His knowledge is based on his decisions. Since he can create any self-consistent state of affairs of which he can conceive, he knows what will or would happen in any context because he knows how he has decided or would have decided to respond to that which he encounters. Accordingly, for the Christian compatibilist, the nature of God's knowledge is irrelevant to his ability to control earthly affairs.

Theistic indeterminists strongly disagree with a deterministic conception of human freedom. They insist that a person (*P*) can only be free with respect to an action (*A*) if God does not bring it about (casually determine) that *P* do *A*. Most, therefore, openly acknowledge that in a world containing significantly free individuals, God cannot retain total control over all earthly affairs regardless of the type of knowledge he possesses.[7]

But in a world containing indeterministic freedom, the nature of God's knowledge *is* extremely relevant to the amount of influence God can wield. The purpose of this paper is to document this fact and draw out some of its implications for classical Christian thought. I shall conclude that classical Christian theism (in its indeterministic forms) is much more dependent on middle knowledge than most realize and, thus, that recent attempts to criticize this form of knowledge must be taken seriously by those in the classical camp.

I

Let us first assume that God has only present knowledge. It might appear that this would greatly limit his ability to control earthly affairs. For if God cannot make people freely do what he wants and he does not know what they will freely do, then it appears that to the extent to which he makes them free, he is committed to accepting the unknowable results of their actions. To the extent, for example, to which God has decided to give individuals the freedom to treat their spouses and children as they wish, it seems that he has committed himself to living with an unknown amount of family happiness and/or spouse and child abuse. It seems, in other words, that to the extent to which a God with present knowledge gives humans freedom, he becomes a "cosmic gambler."

But this assessment is open to challenge. We can logically and chronologically separate a person's decision to perform a certain action from the performance of that action, itself, and the performance from the consequences it will produce. For example, we can logically and chronologically distinguish a person's decision to fire a gun from the actual firing

and the actual firing from that which the firing will bring about—e.g., someone's death, a dent in a tin can, etc. Accordingly, it appears that even a God with just present knowledge would know what a person had chosen to do *before* the decision resulted in the desired action and thus before the consequences of the action occurred. But if this is so, then it appears that he could "veto" any human action or modify its natural consequences even [after] the relevant decision, itself, has been *freely* made. It appears, for example, that he could protect a bank employee whom he sees a robber has freely decided to shoot by distracting the robber before the gun is actually fired or by making the gun jam or by changing the angle of the bullet. And if this is so, it might be argued, then it appears that even a God with present knowledge can be said to retain control over all earthly affairs in the sense that no state of affairs occurs which God does not desire to occur.[8]

This line of reasoning, however, is subject to serious criticism. For most theistic indeterminists, to say that a person is significantly free does not mean only that such a person has it within her power to choose to perform actions not in keeping with God's will. It also means that this person has it within her power to bring it about that events not necessarily desired by God will actually occur. But if this is so, then God cannot stop the actualization of a *freely* chosen decision or modify its consequences. He must tolerate the results or be considered guilty of "determining" human behaviour.[9]

However, let us grant for the sake of argument that a God with present knowledge does have the power to "veto" the actualization of any free choice. It does then follow that no human action (as distinguished from a human choice) will ever occur which God does not desire to occur. But a God with only present knowledge still does not know with certainty what free choices will be made in the future or how his "present" choices will effect the future. And this has significant implications for classical Christian thought.

Consider, for example, God's initial creative act. According to classical theism, there was once a time (chronologically or logically) when only God existed. Everything else was created by God *ex nihilo*. But what kind of creative options did God have "before" creation if he had only present knowledge? He could have conceived of many possibilities. And if he had not wanted to create a world containing free individuals, he could have known exactly what he would always bring about. But assuming that he desired to create a universe containing significantly free individuals, he did not know "before" creation exactly what would happen. He knew he would veto anything he did not want. But he did not know with certainty which type of free will universe—i.e., which type of free creatures in which environmental context—would develop into a universe most closely approximating his ideal. He did not know how many times he would have to "veto" human action in the type of world he did choose to initiate. And he did not know how such vetoes might ultimately affect his work. He did not even have the assurance that he would not need ultimately to remove freedom totally to "save" his creation from destruction. In short, for a God with present knowledge, the creative act was a significant gamble.

This characterization of the act of creation, however, hardly seems compatible with classical Christian thought. Even those classical Christians who affirm indeterministic freedom normally agree with Augustine that:

> God is called almighty for no other reason than that he can do what ever he willeth and because the efficacy of his omnipotent will is not impeded by the will of any creature.[10]

Accordingly, the vast majority of classical theists, both past and present, have affirmed with William Craig that:

> History is not an unpredictably unfolding sequence of events plunging haphazardly without purpose or direction; rather God…directs the course of world history toward His previsioned ends.… God's salvific plan was not an afterthought necessitated by an unforeseen circumstance, but was an eternal plan brought to realization in history.[11]

In other words, for classical theism, God is definitely not a cosmic gambler. He may have voluntarily given humans some freedom to determine their own destiny. But even this is seen as a pre-ordained aspect of the creative plan God "saw" and sanctioned in its entirety before creation.

The affirmation of present knowledge also has significant implications for personal divine guidance—i.e., the process whereby God gives useful information to individuals about present or future events in their lives. A God with present knowledge can give excellent personal and predictive advice based on what he now knows. He can promise to "manipulate" or stop certain affairs if they happen to eventuate. But to the extent to which human choice will play a part in any future sequence of events, God does not know exactly how things will turn out. Thus, he cannot be certain that his advice will, if followed, actually lead to the best possible outcome (or even a good outcome). For example, let us assume that both Tom and Fred have proposed to Sue and that she has turned to God for guidance. A God with present knowledge knows whether Tom or Fred would at present be a better partner for Sue. But he does not know all that Tom and Fred will encounter in the future or what they will freely choose to do in response. Accordingly, unless God is willing directly to manipulate the lives of those involved, he may not presently know which person would ultimately be a better partner. And Sue, accordingly, can never be sure that her choice was the best, even if she follows God's leading. She must be content with knowing that God will always be there to help her respond to that which eventuates, no matter which choice she makes.

Analogous limitations also apply to God's ability to make infallible public prophetic utterances which presuppose knowledge of future free choices. A God with present knowledge could not, for example, have infallibly known before creation or even during the time the Bible was written to what extent people would freely choose to accept or reject Christ's teachings or anything concerning the "end times" which involves human choice. He could only have predicted how humanity would freely behave. And such predictions would have weakened as they "stretched" further into the future.

All this, however, will hardly do for classical Christian theists. Most have uniformly held that God's personal guidance and "public" prophetic utterances are based on his total and infallible knowledge of what will (at least from our human perspective) happen in the future. Most, in fact, would agree with Stephen Charnock that:

> If God knows not future things but only by conjecture, then there is no God, because a certain knowledge, so as infallibly to predict things to come, is an inseparable perfection of the Deity.[12]

Such "problems" readily disappear if God possesses middle knowledge. A God with middle knowledge knew *before* creation what would in fact eventuate, given every option open to him. This does not necessarily mean that he had the ability to actualize the most desirable state of affairs of which he could conceive. For he may have desired to create a world containing individuals with indeterministic freedom and even God, as we have seen, cannot totally control all of the activities in such a world. But the fact that he knew *before* creation what would eventuate given any creative option does, of course, mean that no gambling was involved in the creative process. He did not have to worry about any surprises; he knew no second guessing would be necessary. For he had the ability to consider all the actualizable worlds and choose the one which best mirrored his creative options.

Nor need a God with middle knowledge rely on prediction when giving personal guidance. For example, in the case of Sue's marriage proposals, a God with middle knowledge is not limited to knowing what might or will in fact happen. He knows before he gives guidance to Sue exactly what would happen if she marries Tom, exactly what would happen if she marries Fred, and exactly what would happen if she marries neither. He knows, for instance, if Tom would still love her thirty years after their marriage or if Sue would meet someone better if she refused both proposals. Accordingly, Sue can be assured she is getting infallible, long-term advice. To the extent to which she believes she has correctly discerned God's guidance on this issue, and acted in accordance with it, she need never wonder whether she has made a mistake—i.e., whether things would have been better if she had acted differently. No matter what problems develop, she can steadfastly believe that she is pursuing the best "life-plan" available to her.

And, of course, since a God with middle knowledge knows all that will happen in the actual world, he can make infallible public prophetic claims about future states of affairs. In fact, he can even make accurate conditional prophecies involving human choice. That is, he can say exactly what will happen *if* certain decisions are made and exactly what will happen if they are not. For he sees both possibilities with equal clarity.

But the concept of middle knowledge is coming under increasing criticism. Everyone agrees that if hypothetical conditions of freedom *were* true, God would have knowledge of them. But some philosophers deny or at least doubt, in the words of Robert Adams, that such conditionals "ever were or ever will be true."[13] Some, such as Adams and Bruce Reichenbach, hold this view because they do not see any comprehensible grounds on which such propositions can be true.[14] Others, for example, William Hasker, go even further, claiming that the concept of a true counterfactual of freedom is self-contradictory.[15]

Let us assume for the sake of argument that these criticisms hold—i.e., let us assume that God does not have middle knowledge. This fact would be extremely damaging to classical Christian thought if God were limited to either present knowledge or middle knowledge for, as we have seen, present knowledge is incompatible with a number of classical beliefs. But there is also the concept of simple foreknowledge to consider. Thus, the crucial questions for the classical theist become: To what extent does simple foreknowledge allow God to influence earthly affairs? And does this amount of influence resolve the problems inherent in assuming God only possesses present knowledge?

Proponents of simple foreknowledge who believe God makes meaningful (indeterministically) free decisions are faced with a seeming dilemma. If they maintain, as they must, that God has always known exactly what he will decide *before* his decisions are made, then it appears that such decisions are not truly free. For an agent can only be said to be making a meaningful, free decision if what will be decided has not already been determined. But if, on the other hand, they claim that God does make meaningful, free decisions, then it seems they must acknowledge that God does not know what will be decided *before* his decisions are made and thus that God has not *always* known all that will occur.

The only viable way I see of attempting to resolve this tension is to separate, as many proponents of simple foreknowledge do, the *chronological* and *epistemological* (*logical*) relationships which exist between God's decisions and his knowledge of them.[16] Since God has always had knowledge of all that will be actual, it is argued, it is true that his knowledge of what he will decide to do in any given situation *chronologically* precedes the actual decisions themselves. But his knowledge of what he will decide to do in any given situation has its basis in (is grounded on) the decision itself—i.e., he knows at time t' what he will do at time t^2 *because of* the decision made at t^2. Thus, epistemologically (logically) his decisions precede his knowledge of them.[17]

Or, to make the point less formally, to allow for meaningful, free divine decision-making, proponents of simple foreknowledge must make a distinction between God's role as observer of all earthly affairs and God's role as participant in earthly affairs. They must claim that although God in his role as observer has always known what he as a participant in earthly affairs will decide to do, such knowledge is based on (and thus epistemologically preceded by) what he, as participant, actually decides....

This means that a God with simple foreknowledge is no less a reacting, cosmic gambler than is a God with present knowledge. He has, in his role as observer, always known how his gamble will turn out. But he, no more than a God with present knowledge, has access to such information when making his decisions. Only a God with middle knowledge has this luxury.[18]

The same is true for a God who has "timeless" knowledge of that which is actual. Such a God, remember, *foreknows* nothing. All is seen as existing in the "eternal now." But proponents of this model also want to affirm that God makes meaningful free decisions. Thus, the question we have just been discussing arises again: What information is known by God when he freely makes his decisions? And the same response must again be given. What cannot be seen by a timeless God in his role as decision-maker are the consequences of his decisions because until (in a logical sense) the decision is made, there is nothing actual for God as decision-maker timelessly to see. He, like a God with simple foreknowledge, must base his decisions on prediction in such cases.

This fact, of course, has significant implications for our understanding of God's act of creation. In his role as observer of earthly affairs, a God with simple foreknowledge knew before creation which creative option he would choose and what the exact outcome would be. But since, as we have seen, his "foreknowledge" of his decisions and what they would produce were based on (epistemologically preceded by) these choices themselves, he, in his role as participant in earthly affairs, had no knowledge of what would actually occur until the relevant creative choices were made. Accordingly, he, no more than a God with present knowledge, can be said to be "directing the course of world history toward his previsioned ends." Both can react to what occurs in an attempt to bring about desired goals. But neither, in his role as creator, was able "before" creation to envision what would happen and use this information as a basis for determining the exact nature of the creative act. Both, in their role as creator, approached (and continue to approach) creation as cosmic gamblers....

Will a line of reasoning be developed which will show clearly to the satisfaction of most philosophers and theologians that the concept of middle knowledge must be rejected? I am not sure. But if the general thesis of this paper is correct, this question cannot be dismissed lightly or ignored by those interested in classical Christian thought. For what is at stake is the very coherence of classical Christian theism itself.

Notes

1. There are, of course, other ways of defining omniscience. Some say, for example, that God's omniscience does not necessarily consist in his knowing all true propositions but rather in his knowing everything that it is logically possible from him to know. Such conceptions of omniscience, however, yield the same basic categories of divine knowledge with which I will be concerned, so I have chosen not to explicitly identify and discuss them in the text.

2. See, for example, Clark Pinnock, *Predestination and Free Will*, ed. by David and Randall Basinger (Downer's Grove, Ill.: InterVarsity Press, 1986), pp. 141–162. Donald Bloesch, *Essentials of Evangelical Theology* (New York: Harper and Row, 1978), pp. 29–30.

3. See, for example, Bruce Reichenbach, *Evil and a Good God* (New York: Fordham Press, 1982), pp. 14–16, 68–74.

4. See, for example, Norman Geisler, *Predestination and Free Will*, pp. 11–84.

5. Alvin Plantinga, *The Nature of Necessity* (Oxford, England: Clarendon Press, 1974), p. 180.

6. John S. Feinberg, *Predestination and Free Will*, pp. 99–124.

7. See Plantinga, pp. 169–84.

8. See, for example, Susan Anderson, "Plantinga and the Free Will Defense," *Pacific Philosophical Quarterly*, LXII (1981), 274–81.

9. This is argued more fully in David Basinger, "Anderson on Plantinga: A Response," *Philosophy Research Archives*, VII (1982), 315–20.

10. Augustine, *Enchiridion* XIV. 96.

11. William Craig, "Divine Foreknowledge and Future Contingency," sermons (forthcoming in reader on Process thought).

12. Craig, p. 5.

13. Robert Adams, "Middle Knowledge and the Problem of Evil," *American Philosophical Quarterly, XIV* (1977), 110.

14. Reichenbach, pp. 68–74.

15. William Hasker, "A Refutation of Middle Knowledge," forthcoming in *Noûs*.

16. An interesting alternative response has recently been proposed by Bruce Reichenbach, "Omniscience and Deliberation," *International Journal for Philosophy of Religion*, XVI (1984), 225–36. Omniscience, Reichenbach argues, is only incompatible with divine decision-making if we conceive of such decision-making in terms of deliberation, i.e., if we see God as weighing viable options before a decision is made. But intentional decision-making, he continues, can be non-deliberative—i.e., can simply be a decision to implement certain goals or objectives. Thus this type of intentional divine activity is not ruled out by the fact that God knows what he will decide to do before the decision is made. Reichenbach's argument, however, is only helpful if it is the case that God never has or will make a deliberative decision. But there appears to be no good theological basis for believing that this is the case. In fact, there appears to be a strong theological argument against this contention in that while most theists have wanted to claim that God's decisions are freely made, it is not clear that non-deliberative decisions are truly free.

17. See, for example, Jock Cottrell, "Conditional Election," *Grace Unlimited*, ed., Clark Pinnock (Minneapolis, Min.: Bethany Fellowship, 1975), pp. 68–70.

18. Some proponents of SFK may wish to hold that God's decisions are made "outside of time" or "before all worlds" rather than at the time at which he acts. But even granting this possibility, the basic point still holds: knowledge of the actual results of a decision *cannot* be presupposed in making the decision.

Study Questions

1. Explain briefly Basinger's reasons for saying that a God with middle knowledge is much better able to exercise providential control in the world than a God with only "present knowledge."

2. Basinger argues that if God has only "simple foreknowledge" of the actual future, this does not give God significantly more control than if he has only present knowledge. Explain Basinger's reasons for this claim.

Robert Merrihew Adams

An Objection to Middle Knowledge

Robert Merrihew Adams (b. 1937) approaches the topic of middle knowledge through a historical overview of the rise of this theory. He then poses what many regard as the most formidable difficulty facing the proponents of middle knowledge: it is very difficult to see how the propositions God is alleged to know—the counterfactuals of creaturely freedom—can be true. And of course, if they are not true, God cannot know them to be true!

If President Kennedy had not been shot, would he have bombed North Vietnam? God only knows. Or does He? Does even He know what Kennedy would have done?

There is a little known but interesting literature on the general issue exemplified by this question. In the 1580s a fierce controversy erupted between the Jesuits and the Dominicans about the relation between God's grace and human free will. The Jesuits held, among other things, that many human actions are free in the sense that their agents are not logically or causally determined to do them. ("Free" will always be used in this sense in the present essay.) How then does God maintain control over human history? Not by causally determining human actions, as the Dominicans seemed to believe,[1] but by causing circumstances in which He knew that we would *freely* act in accordance with His plans. This answer was developed with great ingenuity by Luis de Molina, and defended by other Jesuit theologians, notably by Francisco Suarez. Their theory includes the thesis that God knows with certainty what every possible free creature would freely do in every situation in which that creature could possibly find himself. Such knowledge was called "middle knowledge" by the Jesuits, because they thought it had a middle status between other kinds of knowledge—between God's knowledge of the merely possible and His knowledge of the actual; or between His knowledge of necessary truths, which all follow from the divine nature, and His knowledge of His own will and everything that is causally determined by His will.[2]

This paper [asks] ... whether middle knowledge is possible, even for God. I shall argue that it is not, on the ground that conditional propositions of the sort that are supposed to be known by middle knowledge cannot be true. I will examine (in section II) the attempts of Molina and Suarez to explain how God

Robert Merrihew Adams, "Middle Knowledge and the Problem of Evil," *American Philosophical Quarterly* 14 (1977): 109–17.

can have middle knowledge.…But first of all (in section I) I will try to explain why there seems to me to be a problem about the possibility of middle knowledge.

I

In the twenty-third chapter of the first book of Samuel it is written that after David had rescued the Jewish city of Keilah from the Philistines, and settled his men there, Saul made plans to besiege Keilah in order to capture David. When David heard of Saul's plans, he consulted God by means of an ephod, which apparently was an instrument of divination that yielded a yes-or-no answer to questions. David asked, "Will Saul come down, as thy servant has heard?" The Lord answered affirmatively. Then David asked, "Will the men of Keilah surrender me and my men into the hand of Saul?" And the Lord replied, "They will surrender you." Thereupon David evacuated his men from Keilah, and hid out in the hills, with the result that Saul did not have the opportunity to besiege him in Keilah, and the men of Keilah did not have occasion to betray him to Saul (I Samuel 23:1–14, RSV).

This passage was a favorite proof text for the Jesuit theologians. They took it to prove that God knew the following two propositions to be true:

(1) If David stayed in Keilah, Saul would besiege the city.
(2) If David stayed in Keilah and Saul besieged the city, the men of Keilah would surrender David to Saul.

This is a case of middle knowledge; for it is assumed that all the actions mentioned in (1) and (2) would have been *free,* in the relevant sense, if they had occurred.

If we suppose that God is omniscient we cannot consistently doubt that He had this middle knowledge unless we doubt that (1) and (2) were true. Therefore, as Suarez says, "the whole controversy comes back to this, that we should see whether those conditionals have a knowable determinate truth."[3]

But I do doubt that propositions (1) and (2) ever were, or ever will be, true. This is not because I am inclined to assert the truth of their opposites,

(3) If David stayed in Keilah, Saul would *not* besiege the city.
(4) If David stayed in Keilah and Saul besieged the city, the men of Keilah would *not* surrender David to Saul.

Suarez would say that (1) and (3), and (2) and (4), respectively, are pairs of contradictories, and therefore that one member of each pair must be true. He thus affirms what has been called the law of Conditional Excluded Middle. But this is a mistake. One does not obtain the contradictory of a conditional proposition by negating the consequent; one must negate the whole conditional, as was pointed out by Suarez's Dominican opponent, Diego Alvarez.[4] It is true that in everyday speech we might deny (1) by asserting (3), as we may deny a proposition by asserting any belief we hold that is obviously enough inconsistent with it. But we might also deny both of them by asserting, "If David stayed in Keilah, Saul might or might not besiege the city." I believe the case of what Saul would or might have done if David stayed in Keilah provides a plausible counterexample to the proposed law of Conditional Excluded Middle; and philosophers have found even more convincing counterexamples.[5]

I do not understand what it would be for any of propositions (1)–(4) to be true, given that the actions in question would have been free, and that David did not stay in Keilah. I will explain my incomprehension.

First we must note that middle knowledge is not simple *fore*knowledge. The answers that David got from the ephod—"He will come down," and "They will surrender you"—are not understood by the theologians as categorical predictions. If they were categorical predictions, they would be false. Most philosophers (including Suarez but not Molina) have supposed that categorical predictions, even about contingent events, can be true by corresponding to the actual occurrence of the event that they predict. But propositions (1) and (2) are not true in this way. For there never was nor will be an actual besieging of Keilah by Saul, nor an actual betrayal of David to Saul by the men of Keilah, to which those propositions might correspond.[6]

Some other grounds that might be suggested for the truth of (1) and (2) are ruled out by the assumption that the actions of Saul and the men of Keilah are and would be free in the relevant sense. The suggestion that Saul's besieging Keilah follows by *logical* necessity from David's staying there is implausible in any case.[7] It would be more plausible to suggest that Saul's besieging Keilah follows by *causal* necessity from David's staying there, together with a number of other features of the situation which in fact obtained. But both of these suggestions are inconsistent with the assumption that Saul's action would have been free.

Since necessitation is incompatible with the relevant sort of free will, we might seek non-necessitating grounds for the truth of (1) and (2) in the actual intentions, desires, and character of Saul and the Keilahites. It does appear from the Biblical narrative that Saul actually intended to besiege David in Keilah if he could. Perhaps proposition (1) is true by virtue of its correspondence with Saul's intention. One might also suppose that (2) was true by virtue of correspondence with the desires and character of the leading men of Keilah, if not their fully formed intentions. Maybe they were cowardly, untrustworthy, and ungrateful. And I take it that neither the Jesuits nor Plantinga would say that Saul's intentions, or the desires and character of the Keilahites, necessitated their actions or interfered in any way with their freedom of will.

But the basis thus offered for the truth of (1) and (2) is inadequate precisely because it is not necessitating. A free agent may act out of character, or change his intentions, or fail to act on them. Therefore the propositions which may be true by virtue of correspondence with the intentions, desires and character of Saul and the men of Keilah are not (1) and (2) but

    (5) If David stayed in Keilah, Saul would *probably* besiege the city.

    (6) If David stayed in Keilah and Saul besieged the city, the men of Keilah would *probably* surrender David to Saul.

(5) and (6) are enough for David to act on, if he is prudent; but they will not satisfy the partisans of middle knowledge. It is part of their theory that God knows infallibly what definitely would happen, and not just what would probably happen or what free creatures would be likely to do.[8]

II

I trust that it is clear by this point that there is reason to doubt the possibility of middle knowledge. Those who believe it possible have some explaining to do.

In Molina's explanation the superiority of God's cognitive powers bears the heaviest burden. He holds "that the certainty of that middle knowledge comes from the depth and unlimited perfection of the divine intellect, by which [God] knows certainly what is in itself uncertain."[9] This came to be known as the theory of "supercomprehension." According to it God's intellect so immensely surpasses, in its perfection, all created free will, that it "supercomprehends" them— that is, it understands more about them than would be necessary merely to comprehend them.[10] But as Suarez pointed out in rejecting the theory of supercomprehension, to comprehend something is already to understand about it everything that is there to be understood, and it is absurd to suppose that anyone, even God, could understand more than that.[11] Molina seems to want to say that what free creatures would do under various possible conditions is not there, objectively, to be known, but that God's mind is so perfect that He knows it anyway. But that is impossible. The problem to be solved is how the relevant subjunctive conditionals can be true, and nothing that may be said about the excellence of God's cognitive powers contributes anything to the solution of that problem.

Suarez offers what seems to me the least clearly unsatisfactory type of explanation for the alleged possibility of middle knowledge. He appeals, in effect, to a primitive understanding, which needs no analysis, of what it is for the relevant subjunctive conditionals to be true. Consider a possible free creature, c, who may not ever exist, and a possible free action, a, which c may freely do or refrain from doing in a possible situation s. We are to consider c, not as actually existing, but as having "possible being" in the cause (God) that is able to produce c. So considered, according to Suarez, c has a property (a *habitudo*, as Suarez puts it) which is either the property of being a possible agent who would in s freely do a, or the property of being a possible agent who would in s freely refrain from doing a. c has one of these properties, although there is nothing either internal or external to *c*, except the property itself, which would make or determine *c* to have one of these properties rather than the other. God has middle knowledge of what *c* would do in *s*, because God knows which of the two properties *c* has.[12]

Many philosophers would object to Suarez's ontology of merely possible entities, but perhaps one could develop a similar account of the relevant conditionals without such an ontology. God's *idea* of *c*, for example, is presumably an *existing* subject of properties. And one might ascribe to it, as a primitive property, the property of being an idea which, if it were satisfied by anything in *s*, would be satisfied by an agent that freely did *a* in *s*. This would have the disadvantage, however, of implying that whether *c* would do *a*

in *s* depends, not on a property of *c*, but on a property of God's idea of *c*. That consequence might seem to compromise *c*'s freedom of will.

My principal objection to Suarez's defense of the possibility of middle knowledge is not based on ontological considerations, however. I do not think I have any conception, primitive or otherwise, of the sort of *habitudo* or property that Suarez ascribes to possible agents with respect to their acts under possible conditions. Nor do I think that I have any other primitive understanding of what it would be for the relevant subjunctive conditionals to be true. My reason for saying that Suarez's defense is of the least clearly unsatisfactory type is that it is very difficult to refute someone who claims to have a primitive understanding which I seem not to have.

Notes

1. An acutely argued Dominican contribution to the debate is Diego (Didacus) Alvarez, OP, *De auxiliis divinae gratiae et humani arbitrii viribus, et libertate, ac legitima eius cum efficacia eorundem auxiliorum concordia* (Rome, 1590); see especially the seventh disputation.
2. I believe Molina originated the term "middle knowledge" (*scientia media*). I have given a very simplified account of his reasons for thinking it appropriate. See his *Liberi arbitrii cum gratiae donis, divina praescientia, providentia, praedestinatione et reprobatione concordia* [hereafter abbreviated, *Concordia*], ed. John Rabeneck (Ona and Madrid, 1953), qu. 14, art. 13, disp. 52, nn. 9–10, and disp. 53, memb. 1, n. 6, and memb. 4, n. 4 (pp. 339 f., 360, 394).
3. Suarez, *De gratia*, prol. 3, c. 7, n. 1, in his *Opera omnia* (Paris, 1856–78), vol. vii, p. 85. (All my page references to *De gratia* will be to this edition and volume.)
4. Alvarez, *De auxiliis divinae gratiae et humani arbitrii viribus*, Bk. 2, disp. 7, n. 30 (p. 74). See Suarez, *De gratia*, prol. 2, c. 7, n. 24 (p. 95).
5. David Lewis, *Counterfactuals* (Oxford, 1973), 79 f.; John H. Pollock, "Four Kinds of Conditionals," *American Philosophical Quarterly*, 12 (1975), 53. The law of Conditional Excluded Middle was defended by Robert C. Stalnaker, in "A Theory of Conditionals," *American Philosophical Quarterly Monograph Series*, no. 2, *Studies in Logical Theory*, ed. Nicholas Rescher (Oxford, 1968), 106 f.
6. Suarez saw this point pretty clearly; see his "De scientia Dei futurorum contingentium" [hereafter abbreviated, DSDFC], Bk. 2, c. 5, n. 6 (*Opera omnia*, vol. xi, p. 357).
7. Suarez makes a similar point: DSDFC, Bk. 2, c. 5, n. 11 (p. 358).
8. See Suarez, DSDFC, Bk. 2, c. 1, nn. 1–2, and c. 5, n. 9 (pp. 343 f., 357 f.).
9. Molina, *Concordia*, qu. 14, art. 13, disp. 53, memb. 3, n. 10 (pp. 389 f.).
10. Ibid., disp. 52, nn. 11, 17 (pp. 341, 345).
11. Suarez, DSDFC, Bk. 2, c. 7, n. 6 (pp. 366 f.).
12. I believe this is what Suarez's views come to, as they are found in *De gratia*, prol. 2, c. 7, nn. 21, 24, 25 (pp. 94–96).

STUDY QUESTIONS

1. Explain why Adams thinks that there is a problem about the counterfactuals of freedom that, according to the theory of middle knowledge, God is alleged to know. Does this seem to you to be a serious problem?

2. Adams suggests that future-tense conditionals should be understood probabilistically—for instance, as "If David stayed in Keilah, Saul would *probably* besiege the city." Does this seem to be a good way to understand these statements? Why or why not?

J. R. Lucas

The Vulnerability of God

If humans do possess libertarian free will, ruling out theological determinism, and if the theory of middle knowledge is mistaken, what sort of conception of divine providence results? This question is answered by J. R. Lucas (b. 1929), who sets forth a version of the view known as "open theism," because of its insistence that the future is open, not closed. We should not, says Lucas, think of God's providence as a blueprint for everything that is to take place. Rather, God is like a "Persian rug-maker, who lets his children work at one end while he does the other." When the children make mistakes, he "adapts the design at his end to take into account each error at the children's end." Lucas also discusses the implications of this view for our understanding of the world's evil.

Our understanding of time has deep implications for our view of reality and God, the ultimate reality. If time is a perpetual becoming, a weaving rather than an unrolling, we cannot take a static view of the universe, but must see it as dynamic, in which something is always happening, vague possibilities crystallizing out into sharp actuality. Reality is through and through temporal. Equally, God is temporal, though not merely that. Although we can properly say that God is more than merely temporal, that He transcends time, and to that extent is beyond and outside time, we cannot say that He is timeless, or that for Him there is no difference between future and past....

If we are to characterize God at all, we must say that He is personal, and if personal then temporal, and if temporal then in some sense in time, not outside it. That God cannot alter the past should be seen not as a lamentable lack of power on the part of the Almighty, but as a corollary of His being an agent. To be an agent is to be crystallizing potentiality into actuality, thereby making it unalterable thereafter. No unalterability, no agency. To bewail unalterability is like bewailing God's inability to make a world so big that He cannot move it, and to project an inconsistency in our concepts into an inability in what they are being applied to.

Traditionally time, like space, has been thought of as a thing, and therefore something created by God, and not existing before He created it. Before God created time, we are sometimes encouraged to think, time did not exist, and then God certainly

J. R. Lucas, *The Future: An Essay on God, Temporality, and Truth* (Oxford, England: Blackwell, 1989), pp. 209, 213, 220–33.

was a timeless being. But the very formulation of the statement that purports to tell us what God was like before time existed is incoherent. Time is not a thing that God might or might not create, but a category, a necessary concomitant of the existence of a personal being, though not of a mathematical entity. This is not to say that time is an independent category, existing independently of God. It exists because of God: not because of some act of will on His part, but because of His nature: if the ultimate reality is personal, then it follows that time must exist. God did not make time, but time stems from God....

An omniscient being can know all there is to know of temporal reality. He has immediate, undimmed knowledge of the present and past. He can view things from any temporal standpoint He pleases, experiencing both what is occurring and what has occurred, and envisaging the sort of thing that would occur or might have occurred, were certain conditions fulfilled.

We can thus give a coherent account of God's temporal relations with His creation. It is a matter of distinguishing what is conceptually necessary, if there is to be a coherent concept at all, from what is only a contingent limitation, due to human weakness and imperfection. God is not limited in the way we are. We forget: God does not. We are impatient: God is not. We fail to think ahead: God does not. Although temporal predicates can be applied to God in a full sense, and though God changes in some respects with the passage of time, He does not grow old and wear out, and instead of being subject to time, as we are, can properly be said to transcend it.

FOREKNOWLEDGE AND FOREBELIEF

Boethius was led to the conclusion that God was timeless as an escape from the problem of foreknowledge and free will. In fact, however, foreknowledge, rightly understood, is compatible with freedom, partly because it is first-personal, partly because it invokes a number of different modalities, not all of them Procrustean, and is therefore inherently defeasible.

I know what I am going to do tomorrow. You may too. God also can. Each of us is privy to his own counsels, and often by his explicit avowals makes others privy too. If God is about my path, and about my bed, and if there is not a word in my tongue He does not altogether know,[1] then He will have a fair idea of my future course of action, far from complete, of course, since I have not made up my mind about many things, and do not know myself what I am going to do, but enough none the less to predict some things with a fair degree of certainty. Even if God did not know the secrets of men's hearts, but only what they explicitly told Him or implied in their importunate petitions, He would still be better informed than most of us, who nonetheless manage to predict quite a number of future events with success. But this sort of foreknowledge does not foreclose freedom. It is either entirely, or else vicariously, first-personal foreknowledge, resting on an internal rather than an external modality, which, rather than restricting one's freedom of action, gives it definition and structure. I can decide what I am going to do but that does not mean that thereafter I am absolutely not free not to do it, but only with respect to my upholding my previous decision. Only an internal necessity binds me. I cannot do other than do it, except at the cost of abandoning my own previous decision, which I am rationally reluctant to do.

But of course I always can. My decisions, however binding, are not irreversible. Internal modalities are always subject to a *homine volente* ["the person being willing"] escape clause. And then my own and other men's well-founded predictions will be falsified, and what had seemed to be foreknowledge will prove to have been merely mistaken, though well-grounded, belief. Foreknowledge can become, *ex post facto*, not knowledge at all, and for this reason lacks the Procrustean power to bind the future.

God, having vicarious first-personal knowledge of our future actions, and knowing also the ways and waywardness of man, can foreknow much, but in a non-threatening, because in a not external and not infallible, way, and always subject, so far as particular actions of particular individuals are concerned, to a *homine volente* clause. But still we may press specific questions. Did God foreknow the Second World War? The misery of the Germans during the slump, the wickedness of Hitler, the blindness and irresolution of Britain and France, were grounds enough for pre-dicting war, if not over the Sudetenland then over Danzig, if not over Danzig then over the Saar, or Denmark, or Alsace-Lorraine. But always there was the possibility of things going differently. If Britain had not caved in at Munich, and if the General Staff had then succeeded in removing Hitler, then the inevitable would not have happened, and foreknowl-edge, even God's foreknowledge, would have proved not knowledge after all.

...Some unease remains. Whatever account we give of knowledge, belief is not defeasible. It is a hard, unalterable fact that you believed I would go to Professor Strawson's lecture tomorrow, and if, when tomorrow comes, I do not go, then there is no ques-tion of your not having really believed it: you did believe it, and were wrong. So too with God. If God had a belief yesterday that I should do something, and I do not do it, then God was wrong in His belief. If God had believed that Peter would deny Him, and Peter, when questioned, rose courageously to the occasion, and confessed that he was one of Jesus' dis-ciples, then God would have been wrong. Nor is this a merely hypothetical possibility. In the Old Testa-ment He is often represented as changing His mind, and not carrying out the threatened consequences of the Jews' bad behaviour He had announced that He would bring about. Elijah foretold evil for Ahab in the name of the Lord. "I will bring evil upon thee, and will take away thy posterity, and will cut off every male of the house of Ahab, bond or free, in Israel."... But when he heard those words, he rent his clothes, and put sackcloth upon his flesh, and fasted and lay in the sackcloth, and went about dejectedly. And the word of the Lord came to Elijah saying "Seest thou how Ahab has humbleth himself before me? Because he humbleth himself before me, I will not bring the evil in his days, but in his son's days will I bring evil upon his house."[2]

The natural reading is that God changed his mind. He did not speak mendaciously to Elijah the first time, but at that time intended to sweep away the house of Ahab in his own lifetime so that he could appreciate his punishment, but later, in the light of his penitence, suspended part of the sentence for the remainder of his life. And he might have done more,

had he repented more. Suppose Ahab had not merely fasted and put on sackcloth himself, but, besides giv-ing back the vineyard to Naboth's heirs, had universa-lised the prescription, "Let neither man nor beast, herd nor flock, taste anything; let them not feed, nor drink water, but let man and beast be covered with sack-cloth, and let them cry mightily to God";...thinking to himself "who can tell if God will turn and repent, and turn away from his fierce anger, so that we per-ish not?"[3] Certainly, when Hezekiah had been told by Isaiah that he was going to die, God heard his prayer and changed His mind, giving Hezekiah another fif-teen years of life.[4]

Such changes of heart were a problem for thought-ful theists. The author of the book of Jonah points out that an unrelenting God, who secures His absolute veracity at the cost of never showing mercy, would be less perfect than one whose ears are open to our prayers.[5] In the New Testament the good news is that if we repent, we can escape the consequences of our ill-doing that would otherwise ensue. "Except ye repent, ye shall all likewise perish."[6] The clear picture is of a God who can change His mind, and is pre-pared to make prophecies, issued in His name and on His explicit commands, come false....

PERFECTION

God is perfect, but perfection, like infinity, is easily misunderstood. As we saw earlier with infallibility, it is easy, by insisting on one apparent excellence, to narrow, rather than widen, the range of divine competence. So, more generally, as Findlay, Kenny, and Blumenfeld have pointed out,[7] it is easy to set one superlative against another, and conclude that no entity at all could possibly be superlative in all respects. If God is absolutely omnipotent, and can always change His mind, He cannot be absolutely omniscient, and know infallibly that He never will. In any case, He cannot make a world so big He cannot move it, nor know absolutely everything, false propo-sitions as well as true.

We need to construe the the *omni* of omnipotence and omniscience, not in terms of some inconsist-ent, absolute all, but negatively, as contrasting with various forms of non-omnipotence and non-omniscience. I am not omnipotent because there are lots of things I cannot do, and it is a defect of mine that I cannot. I cannot write Greek elegiacs, I cannot jump over the moon, I cannot swim across the Behring Strait. But other people can, and it is only because I am not as good as they that I cannot. Equally, I am not omniscient: I do not know French, I do not know Twister theory, I do not know American history. Other people do, and I should be less ignorant if I did too. In other cases, however, it is no defect of mine that I cannot do, or do not know, something. I cannot make a flag that is red and green all over, not on account of any inadequacy of mine, but because it is logically impossible task. It is no skin off my nose that I cannot alter the past—it is not something I ought to remedy, or could try to overcome with effort. . . . Where the question "Why can't you?" or "Why don't you know?" has to be met with a confession of inability or ignorance on my part, it is reasonable to look for God's not being subject to any such limitation. But where it is not due to an incapacity of the person but is in the nature of the case that something cannot be done or known, then it is no derogation from God that He cannot do it or know it either.[8] God cannot sin: God cannot know first-hand what it is to have sinned: God cannot infallibly know what He is going to do until He has made up His mind—else omniscience would have foreclosed His freedom, and curtailed His omnipotence—and God cannot, so long as He has created us free and autonomous agents, infallibly know what we are going to do until we have done it. But this is no imperfection, but a corollary of His creative love.

The theological superlative is a potent source of error. There is a sense in which God is the mostest. There is a sense in which God is the bestest. God is the ultimate reality. But there are many sorts of greatness, many sorts of goodness, incommensurate and not always compatible, and in ascribing maximality to God, we need to have in mind in what way He is the greatest or the best. Questions of ontology and value are involved, and as we come to understand more fully what it really is to exist and what values are truly worth espousing, we advance also in our understanding of the perfection of God.

PROVIDENCE

An omnipotent God could have chosen to create a world in which not everything could be known, even by Him. Einstein said he could not believe in a dice-playing God, but unless quantum mechanics is logically inconsistent, an almighty God could have chosen to make a world that exemplified the laws of quantum mechanics. And if He did, then He would be unable to have detailed knowledge of its future development.

Many thinkers have felt that it would run counter to the doctrine of providence if the details of the future course of events were not foreknown and foreordained. But such a doctrine, though widely held, is un-Christian. Apart from leaving no room for human freedom, it poses the problem of evil in irresoluble form, and subverts the moral teaching of Jesus.

There are many tribulations in human life that are not attributable to the wickedness of men. Earthquakes, famines, disease and death are evils. Good may come out of them in the fortitude with which they are met, or the sympathy they evoke, but they are evils none the less. If God "freely and knowingly plans, orders, and provides for all the effects that constitute His artefact, the created universe with its entire history, and executes His chosen plan by playing an active causal role sufficient to ensure its exact realisation,"[9] then He is directly and immediately responsible for these evils. And then the project of justifying the ways of God to man becomes impossible to carry through.

Many thinkers have set their face against any such project. There is no searching of God's understanding, and He giveth no account of any of His matters. We cannot question the inscrutable decrees of God's providence, and should simply trust Him that, despite any appearances to the contrary, all will be well. Such a response, though expressing an important insight, does not capture the main thrust of the Christian revelation. Admittedly, it is important to emphasize the great gap between our very limited understanding and the profundity of the Divine Reason itself. There is a tendency for modern man . . . to tell God what he is, and is not, prepared to accept, and to call God to account for Himself to his complete satisfaction. He needs to be answered out of the whirlwind. But he is not typical of the whole human race, and to insist upon the nothingness of man in comparison with the greatness of God belies the concern for His children expressed by God in the Old Covenant, and His sending His Son to save them in the New. Although there is a great gap between selfish, unredeemed humanity and the perfection of God, there is not intended to be a complete barrier between man and God—God became man in order that man might become like God—and the breaking down of the barrier opens the way to, and indeed is partly constituted by, the asking of questions. The faithful Christian, caring about the immense suffering many men have to undergo, must wonder why a good, all-powerful God should allow such terrible things to happen.

It could be that God is improving us or using us. Theages was saved by ill health from dissipation. A touch of arthritis may make us more sympathetic to the weakness of others. Only if I am ill can doctors have the opportunity to make me better and nurses the occasion to care for me. Only at my funeral will old friends renew old acquaintanceships. But such a justification, however applicable in general, cannot cover every particular case. Not every disaster can be accounted for as a providential means to a greater good. I am not invariably improved by disease or death. Although sometimes good may come out of ill, the loss remains and is real. Nor is it consonant with God's fatherly care for His children simply to use them as means towards some external end.

It could be that God is punishing us. That is what the Jews thought. But Jesus taught otherwise. Neither the cripple nor his parents had done wrong; neither the casualties of the collapse of the tower of Siloam, nor the victims of Herod's vendetta against Judaism, were sinners more than the rest of us.[10] It is, furthermore, contrary to the thrust of the New Covenant to see everything that happens as God's immediate response to our previous actions. The rigid moralism of the Pharisees could accommodate the Old Understanding that if we walk in God's ways it will be well for us, but such a legalism destroys the spontaneity of the heart and all personal relations. Unless God sends the rain on the unjust as well as the just, the disinterested love of justice cannot be made manifest

or distinguished from meteorological prudence. We need to live in a world in which we do not always get what we deserve, so that we can exercise the good will uncontaminated by ulterior motives. I cannot be friends on a strict *quid pro quo* basis. If whenever I do a good turn, it earns me a good turn in return, my good will is merged in the self-interested motive of doing well by number one. I can do business on that basis, but not manifest friendship. In order to be friends there needs to be some separation between the nicely calculated less and more of merit and reward on the one hand and the free expression of feelings and attitudes on the other. To enter into personal relations I need room to be myself, not constrained by prudential reckonings with providence. It follows that the Christian view of providence must be, on purely theological grounds, different from the traditional one.

Not everything that happens can be attributed directly to the detailed decision of God. Although He knows how many hairs I have on my head, He has not decided how many there shall be.[11] He distances Himself from the detailed control of the course of events in order, among other things, to give us the freedom of manoeuvre we need both to be moral agents and to go beyond morality into the realm of personal relations. Although He could, and perhaps on occasion does, intervene directly to avert a particular evil or guide things towards an appropriate end, He could not do it often or as a matter of course without destroying the conditions of freedom in which alone man could come to, and exercise, mature autonomy.

Questions of theodicy and providence remain. If we deny the doctrine of detailed providence, then we can attribute suffering to accident rather than to God, but still ask why God created such an accident-prone world, and what reason we have to think that He cares for us at all. The general considerations outlined earlier are a partial answer to the first question: accident-proneness is a concomitant of freedom: only through trial and error can we develop as self-reliant and autonomous individuals: only in an accident-prone world can we manifest sympathy and fortitude. There still remains a justified complaint on the part of latter-day Jobs, but the terms of the complaint are altered, and the possibility of a further answer is open.

God's ordering of the world does not have to be detailed in order to manifest His goodness towards us. God provides for us also in securing generally beneficent conditions for our existence, and in there being certain tendencies in natural phenomena and human affairs that work to our advantage, often redressing some of the ill consequences of our bad decisions. God's providence is shown not in the fact that everything happens as it does, but in some good things happening when they might well have not happened. The providential ordering of the world is shown both in its general arrangements being conducive to our welfare, and in that setbacks, though real, can characteristically be overcome. In an earlier work I suggested that instead of thinking of God's providence as a sort of blueprint with the inevitably Procrustean overtones of that metaphor, we should liken it to the Persian rug-maker, who lets his children work at one end while he does the other. The children make mistakes, but so great is his skill that he adapts the design at his end to take into account each error at the children's end, and works it into a new, constantly updated pattern.[12] The analogy is helpful so far as the relatively rare direct interventions of God are concerned, and the, perhaps more frequent, occasions when men are guided by God to do His will. But we need also to note a certain self-correcting tendency in the course of events, whereby if one thing fails another is likely to happen that will bring about the same effect. Were it not for this, the universe might get out of hand and become beyond saving. But the element of chaos introduced by chance and men's arbitrary bad decisions is not the only factor at work in a universe inhabited by men who are also partly rational and sometimes well-intentioned. There is a natural propensity for those governed by self-will to lose contact with reality, and ultimately to compass their own destruction, as Hitler, Amin and Galtieri did, and for those who are sensitive to the will of God to be able to work together in achieving their reasonable and realistic ends. The good we do is often taken up and amplified by other men: our evil plans are often self-frustrating, and our selfish failures interred with our bones. We may thwart God's purposes for a season, but in the long run the pervasive pressures of rationality and love will circumvent our petty resistances and secure a wider measure of cooperation than our self-isolating selfishness can defeat.

VULNERABILITY AND VALUE

The perfection of God raises questions of value. Christian values go beyond those of ordinary morality. Love, rather than duty, is the keynote, and love is many-faceted. Instead of the monolithic scale of values assumed by Plato and most moralists, there are many different forms of fulfilment, and many different goals we should set ourselves to achieve with the passing of time. We are moral agents, but not mere units of morality, whose sole job is to carry out the behests of the moral law, as in the dreary moral determinism preached by the Stoics and by Kant. Though bounded by moral considerations, fulfilment for the Christian is personal fulfilment, different for different individuals.

If individuals are valuable in their own right, as children are in the eyes of their father, the traditional doctrine of impassibility loses its appeal. It was thought to be incompatible with the ultimacy of God that He should be moved by anything outside Himself. But if God has created independent centres of value, He is not being constrained by some external force, if He then values them for what they are and what they become, independently of any further choice of His. Having created men in His own image, He has endowed their choices and predilections with a value in their own right. A father does not merely leave his children free to make up their own minds for themselves on occasion: he so much respects their choices that the fact that they want something is valuable in his eyes too. Likewise God is guided in the things He wants to happen by the things we want to happen. But this is not the constraint of external necessity, but the free first-personal choice of creative love.

Love is not only creative, but vulnerable. If I care for somebody I can be hurt. God, on the Christian view, is highly passible and was hurt. Instead of the impassive Buddha untroubled by the tribulations of mortal existence, the Christians see God on a cross: instead of the Aristotelian ideal of a self-sufficient

God who devotes His time to enjoying the contemplation of His own excellence, the Christians worship a God who shared the human condition and came among us.

The greatness of God is understood very differently on this view from the traditional account of His absolute perfection. God is a father, first and foremost, and His kingdom, power and glory are that of a father rather than an absolute monarch. Power, as ordinarily understood, is not the great good we think it is, but must, as Gregory of Nyssa pointed out, be understood in an altered perspective.

That the omnipotence of God's divine nature should have had strength to descend to the lowliness of humanity furnishes a more manifest proof of power than even the supernatural character of the miracles.... It is not the vastness of the heavens and the bright shining of the constellations, the order of the universe and the unbroken administration over all existence, that so manifestly

displays the transcendent power of Deity as the condescension to the weakness of our nature in the way in which the sublimity is seen in lowliness, and yet the loftiness descends not.[13]

And much as it can be an exercise of omnipotence for God to limit Himself and make Himself vulnerable to the will of others, so the value that regards knowledge as a good can be more fully realised by forgoing the possibility of being a complete know-all, and creating a world in which the future actions of others can often only be surmised, and sometimes not even that. If God created man in His own image, He must have created him capable of new initiatives and new insights which cannot be precisely or infallibly foreknown, but which give to the future a perpetual freshness as the inexhaustible variety of possible thoughts and actions, on the part of His children as well as Himself, crystallizes into actuality.

Notes

1. Psalm 139:2, 3.
2. 1 Kings 21:17–24, 27–9.
3. cf. Jonah 3:7–9.
4. 2 Kings 20:1–6.
5. Psalm 34:15.
6. Luke 13:3 and 5.
7. J. N. Findlay, "Can God's Existence Be Disproved?," *Mind*, *57*(1948): 108–18; Anthony Kenny, *The God of the Philosophers*, Oxford, 1979; David Blumenfeld, "On the Compossibility of the Divine Attributes," *Philosophical Studies*, 34(1978): 91–103.
8. Compare Thomas P. Flint and Alfred J. Freddoso, "Maximal Power," in Alfred J. Freddoso, ed., *Existence and Nature of God*, reprinted in Thomas V. Morris, ed. *The Concept of God* (New York: Oxford University Press, 1987), p. 151: "Therefore... there will be some state of affairs... which even an omnipotent agent is incapable of actualizing. And since this inability results solely from the logically necessary truth that one being cannot causally determine how another will freely act, it should not be viewed... as a kind of inability which disqualifies an agent from ranking as omnipotent."
9. Luis de Molina, *On Divine Foreknowledge: Part IV of the Concordia*, translated, with an introduction and notes by Alfred J. Freddoso (Ithaca, N.Y.: Cornell University Press, 1988), p. 3.
10. John 9:2; Luke 13:1–5.
11. Luke 12:7. The parallel passage in Matthew 10:30 is, however, more predestinarian in tone. That the point at issue is one of God's concern rather than control is one of many I owe to D. J. Bartholemew, *God of Chance* (London: SCM, 1984.)
12. I have tried to work out the analogy more fully in J. R. Lucas, *Freedom and Grace* (London: SPCK, 1976), chs. 4 and 5, esp. p. 39. See also Jacques Maritain, *God and the Permission of Evil*, cited by Flint and Freddoso, "Maximal Power," in Freddoso, ed., *Existence and Nature of God*, reprinted in Morris, ed., *The Concept of God*, p. 163, n. 30.

13. *Oratio Catechetica*, in J-P. Migne, *Patrologia Graeca-Latina*, 24; quoted A. M. Ramsey, "Christian Belief—an Under-lying Essence," *Religious Studies*, 11 (1975): 198.

Study Questions

1. Why does Lucas think that God must be temporal, rather than timeless? Do you find his reasoning convincing?

2. In contrast to much traditional thinking about God, Lucas contends that God in his love has made himself vulnerable and is hurt when his creatures go against his loving intentions for them. Do you think religious believers ought to accept this idea of God? Why or why not?

3. Lucas contrasts the idea of God's plan as a blueprint for all of history, with the idea that it is adaptable and is modified in the light of human responses. (The weaver modifies the pattern at his end, taking account of the mistakes made by his children at the other end.) Which conception of divine providence is better, and why?

John B. Cobb and David Ray Griffin

God Is Creative-Responsive Love

The theory of process theism differs from those espoused the previous selections, and with almost all of the theistic tradition in philosophy and theology, in holding a much more restricted view of God's power and God's activity in the world. God exercises "persuasive power," but never "coercive power"; once God has communicated to creatures his intentions for them, he has no further control over what they actually do. In setting out this view, John B. Cobb (b. 1925) and David Ray Griffin (b. 1939) emphasize God's responsiveness to and empathy for his creatures, an aspect of divine love that is lacking in deterministic views of providence. God's love is also creative, but the outcome of God's creative activity always depends on the free, uncoerced responsiveness of the creatures.

GOD AS RESPONSIVE LOVE

Whitehead noted that whereas in a primitive religion "you study the will of God in order that He may preserve you," in a universal religion "you study his goodness in order to be like him."[1] The Taoist tries to live in harmony with the Tao; the Hindu Vedantist seeks to realize the identity of Atman with Brahman; the Moslem bows to the will of Allah; the Marxist aligns with the dialectical process of history. Accordingly, the statement in Matt. 5:48, "You, therefore, must be perfect, as your heavenly Father is perfect," is a particular expression of the universal religious aspiration of humanity to participate in or be in harmony with perfection. By definition the divine

reality is perfect. The question concerns the nature of this perfection.

Christian faith has held that the basic character of this divine reality is best described by the term "love." However, the meaning of the statement "God is love" is by no means self-evident. Whitehead helps us to recover much of the meaning of that phrase as it is found in the New Testament.

We are told by psychologists, and we know from our own experience, that love in the fullest sense involves a sympathetic response to the loved one. Sympathy means feeling the feelings of the other, hurting with the pains of the other, grieving with the grief, rejoicing with the joys. The "others" with whom we sympathize most immediately are the members

John B. Cobb, Jr., and David Ray Griffin, *Process Theology, an Introductory Exposition* (Philadelphia: Westminster Press, 1981).

of our own bodies. When the cells in our hands, for example, are in pain, we share in the pain; we do not view their condition impassively from without. When our bodies are healthy and well exercised, we feel good with them. But we also feel sympathy for other human beings. We would doubt that a husband truly loved his wife if his mood did not to some extent reflect hers.

Nevertheless, traditional theism said that God is completely impassive, that there was no element of sympathy in the divine love for the creatures. The fact that there was an awareness that this Greek notion of divine impassibility was in serious tension with the Biblical notion of divine love for the world is most clearly reflected in this prayer of the eleventh-century theologian Anselm:

> Although it is better for thee to be…compassionate, passionless, than not to be these things; how art thou…compassionate, and, at the same time, passionless? For, if thou art passionless, thou does not feel sympathy; and if thou does not feel sympathy, thy heart is not wretched from sympathy for the wretched; but this it is to be compassionate.[2]

Anselm resolved the tension by saying: "Thou art compassionate in terms of our experience, and not compassionate in terms of thy being."[3] In other words, God only *seems* to us to be compassionate; he is not *really* compassionate! In Anselm's words: "When thou beholdest us in our wretchedness, we experience the effect of compassion, but thou dost not experience the feeling."[4] Thomas Aquinas in the thirteenth century faced the same problem. The objection to the idea that there is love in God was stated as follows: "For in God there are no passions. Now love is a passion. Therefore love is not in God."[5] Thomas responds by making a distinction between two elements within love, one which involves passion and one which does not. He then says, after quoting Aristotle favorably, that God "loves without passion."[6]

This denial of an element of sympathetic responsiveness to the divine love meant that it was entirely creative. That is, God loves us only in the sense that he does good things for us. In Anselm's words:

> Thou art both compassionate, because thou dost save the wretched, and spare those who sin against thee; and not compassionate, because thou art affected by no sympathy for wretchedness.[7]

In Thomas's words: "To sorrow, therefore, over the misery of others belongs not to God, but it does most properly belong to Him to dispel that misery."[8]

Accordingly, for Anselm and Thomas the analogy is with the father who has no feeling for his children, and hence does not feel their needs, but "loves" them in that he gives good things to them. Thomas explicitly states that "love" is to be understood in this purely outgoing sense, as active goodwill: "To love anything is nothing else than to will good to that thing." He points out that God does not love as we love. For our love is partly responsive, since it is moved by its object, whereas the divine love is purely creative, since it creates its object.[9]

This notion of love as purely creative has implications that are in tension with the Biblical idea of God's equal love for all persons. All persons are obviously not equal in regard to the "good things of life" (however these be defined) that they enjoy (especially in the context of traditional theism, where the majority are consigned to eternal torment). And yet, if God's love is purely creative, totally creating the goodness of the beings loved, this implies that God loves some persons more than others. As Thomas said: "No one thing would be better than another if God did not will greater good for one than for another."[10] This is one of the central ways in which the acceptance of the notion of divine impassibility undercuts the Biblical witness to the love of God.

Since we mold ourselves partly in terms of our image of perfect human existence, and this in turn is based upon our notion of deity, the notion of God as an Impassive Absolute whose love was purely creative could not help but have practical consequences for human existence. Love is often defined by theologians as "active goodwill." The notion of sympathetic compassion is missing. Indeed, one of the major theological treatises on the meaning of agape, or Christian love, portrays it as totally outgoing, having no element of responsiveness to the qualities of the loved one.[11] This notion of love has promoted a "love" that is devoid of genuine sensitivity to the deepest needs of the "loved ones." Is this not why the word "charity," which is derived from *caritas* (the Latin word for agape), today has such heavily negative connotations? Also, the word "do-gooder" is a word of reproach, not because we do not want people to do good things, but because people labeled "do-gooders" go around trying to impose their own notions of the good that needs doing, without any sensitive responsiveness to the real desires and needs of those they think they are helping. This perverted view of love as purely active goodwill is due in large part to the long-standing notion that this is the kind of love which characterizes the divine reality.

This traditional notion of love as solely creative was based upon the value judgment that independence or absoluteness is unqualifiedly good, and that dependence or relativity in any sense derogates from perfection. But while perfection entails independence or absoluteness in some respects, it also entails dependence or relativity in other respects. It entails ethical independence, in the sense that one should not be deflected by one's passions from the basic commitment to seek the greatest good in all situations. But this ethical commitment, in order to be actualized in concrete situations, requires responsiveness to the actual needs and desires of others. Hence, to promote the greatest good, one must be informed by, and thus relativized by, the feelings of others. Furthermore, we do not admire someone whose enjoyment is not in part dependent upon the condition of those around them. Parents who remained in absolute bliss while their children were in agony would not be perfect—unless there are such things as perfect monsters!

In other words, while there is a type of independence or absoluteness that is admirable, there is also a type of dependence or relativity that is admirable. And, if there is an example of absoluteness that is *unqualifiedly* admirable, this means that there is a divine absoluteness; and the same holds true of relativity. Process thought affirms that both of these are true. While traditional theism spoke only of the divine absoluteness, process theism speaks also of "the divine relativity" (this is the title of one of Hartshorne's books).

Process theism is sometimes called "dipolar theism," in contrast to traditional theism with its doctrine of divine simplicity. For Charles Hartshorne, the two "poles" or aspects of God are the abstract essence of God, on the one hand, and God's concrete actuality on the other. The abstract essence is eternal, absolute, independent, unchangeable. It includes those abstract attributes of deity which characterize the divine existence at every moment. For example, to say that God is omniscient means that in every moment of the divine life God knows everything which is knowable at that time. The concrete actuality is temporal, relative, dependent, and constantly changing. In each moment of God's life there are new, unforeseen happenings in the world which only then have become knowable. Hence, God's concrete knowledge is dependent upon the decisions made by the worldly actualities. God's knowledge is always relativized by, in the sense of internally related to, the world.

Whitehead's way of conceiving the divine dipolarity was not identical with Hartshorne's. Whitehead distinguished between the Primordial Nature of God and the Consequent Nature. The former will be discussed in the following section. The latter is largely identical with what Hartshorne has called God's concrete actuality. Since the Consequent Nature is God as fully actual,[12] the term "consequent" makes the same point as Hartshorne's term "relative," that God as fully actual is responsive to and receptive of the worldly actualizations.

This divine relativity is not limited to a "bare knowledge" of the new things happening in the world. Rather, the responsiveness includes a sympathetic feeling with the worldly beings, all of whom have feelings. Hence, it is not merely the content of God's knowledge which is dependent, but God's own emotional state. God enjoys our enjoyments, and suffers with our sufferings. This is the kind of responsiveness which is truly divine and belongs to the very nature of perfection. Hence it belongs to the ideal for human existence. Upon this basis, Christian agape can come to have the element of sympathy, of compassion for the present situation of others, which it should have had all along.

GOD AS CREATIVE LOVE

If sympathetic responsiveness is an essential aspect of Christian love, creative activity is no less essential.

Whether it be considered a theme or a presupposition, the notion that God is active in the world, working to overcome evil and to create new things, is central to the Biblical tradition. To be in harmony with the God of Israel and of Jesus is to be involved in the struggle to overcome the various impediments to the fullness of life. In Luke 4:18, Jesus quotes from Isaiah, who indicates that the Spirit of the God he worships impels one to "set at liberty those who are oppressed."

The impetus in Western civilization for individual acts and social programs aimed at alleviating human misery and injustice has come in large part from the belief that God not only loves all persons equally, and hence desires justice, but also is directly acting in the world to create just conditions. The reason is that the basic religious drive of humanity is not only to be in harmony with deity, it is also to be in contact with this divine reality. It is because God is personally present and active in the world that contact with the sacred reality does not necessitate fleeing from history. Our activity aimed at creating good puts us in harmony and contact with God. Indeed, this activity can be understood in part as God's acting through us.

Accordingly, the loss of belief in the creative side of God's love would tend to undermine the various liberation movements that have been originally inspired by belief in divine providence, since it is largely this belief which has lent importance to these movements. Cultures in which the sacred is not understood as involved in creating better conditions for life in the world have had difficulty in generating the sustained commitments necessary to bring about significant change.

It is precisely this notion of divine creative activity in the world which has been most problematic in recent centuries, both within theological circles and in the culture at large. In traditional popular Christian thought, God was understood as intervening here and there in the course of the world. The notion of "acts of God" referred to events which did not have natural causes, but were directly caused by God. In traditional theological thought, all events were understood to be totally caused by God, so all events were "acts of God." However, most events were understood to be caused by God through the mediation of worldly or natural causes. God was the "primary cause" of these events, while the natural antecedents were called "secondary causes." However, a few events were thought to be caused directly by God, without the use of secondary causes. These events were "miracles." Accordingly, while all events were in one sense acts of God, these miracles were acts of God in a special sense. Thus, both in popular and theological circles, there was meaning to be given to the idea that God was creatively active in the world.

However, there are two major problems with this notion. First, it raises serious doubt that the creative activity of God can be understood as *love*, since it creates an enormous problem of evil by implying that *every* event in the world is *totally* caused by God, with or without the use of natural causes. Second, since the Renaissance and Enlightenment, the belief has grown that there are no events which happen without natural causes. Accordingly, the notion of "acts of God" has lost all unambiguous referents. Every event termed an act of God was said also, from another perspective, to be totally explainable in terms of natural causation. This rendered the notion of "act of God" of doubtful meaning. If an event can be totally explained in terms of natural forces, i.e., if these provide a "sufficient cause" for it, what justification is there for introducing the idea of "another perspective?" This seems like special pleading in order to retain a vacuous idea....

In Western culture generally, the problem of evil, and the widespread belief that the nexus of natural cause and effect excludes divine "intervention," have combined to render the notion of divine creative love problematic. When the leading secular thinkers then see that the leading theologians have provided no intelligible means for speaking of God's activity in the world, they are confirmed in their suspicion that this belief belongs to the myths of the past. Process theology provides a way of recovering the conviction that God acts creatively in the world and of understanding this creative activity as the expression of divine *love* for the world. The notion that there is a creative power of love behind and within the worldly process is no longer one which can only be confessed in spite of all appearances to the contrary. Instead it illuminates our experience.

DIVINE CREATIVE LOVE AS PERSUASIVE

Traditional theism portrayed God as the Controlling Power. The doctrine of divine omnipotence finally meant that God controlled every detail of the world process. Some traditional theologians, such as Thomas Aquinas, muted this implication of their thought as much as possible (in order to protect the doctrine of human freedom). Others, such as Luther and Calvin, proclaimed the doctrine from the housetops (in order to guard against both pride and anxiety). But, in either case, the doctrine followed logically from other doctrines that were affirmed. The notion that God knows the world, and that this knowledge is unchanging, suggests that God must in fact determine every detail of the world, lest something happen which was not immutably known. The doctrine that God is completely independent of the world implies that the divine knowledge of it cannot be dependent upon it, and this can only be if the world does nothing which was not totally determined by God. The doctrine of divine simplicity involves the assertion that all the divine attributes are identical; hence God's knowing the world is identical with God's causing it. The Biblical record is quite ambivalent on the question of whether God is in complete control of the world. There is much in the Bible which implies that divine providence is not all-determining. But the interpretation of the Biblical God in terms of valuations about perfection derived from Greek philosophy ruled out this side of the Biblical witness, thereby making creaturely freedom vis-à-vis God merely apparent.

Process thought, with its different understanding of perfection, sees the divine creative activity as based upon responsiveness to the world. Since the very meaning of actuality involves internal relatedness, God as an actuality is essentially related to the world. Since actuality as such is partially self-creative, future events are not yet determinate, so that even perfect knowledge cannot know the future, and God does not wholly control the world. Any divine creative influence must be persuasive, not coercive.

Whitehead's fundamentally new conception of divine creativity in the world centers around the notion that God provides each worldly actuality with an "initial aim." This is an impulse, initially felt conformally by the occasion, to actualize the best possibility open to it, given its concrete situation. But this initial aim does not automatically becomes the subject's own aim. Rather, this "subjective aim" is a product of its own decision. The subject may choose to actualize the initial aim; but it may also choose from among the other real possibilities open to it, given its context. In other words, God seeks to persuade each occasion toward that possibility for its own existence which would be best for it; but God cannot control the finite occasion's self-actualization. Accordingly, the divine creative activity involves risk. The obvious point is that, since God is not in complete control of the events of the world, the occurrence of genuine evil is not incompatible with God's beneficence toward all his creatures.

A less obvious but equally important consequence is that, since persuasion and not control is the divine way of doing things, this is the way we should seek to accomplish our ends. Much of the tragedy in the course of human affairs can be attributed to the feeling that to control others, and the course of events, is to share in divinity. Although traditional theism said that God was essentially love, the divine love was subordinated to the divine power. Although the result of Jesus' message, life, and death should have been to redefine divine power in terms of the divine love, this did not happen. Power, in the sense of controlling domination, remained the *essential* definition of deity. Accordingly, the control of things, events, and other persons, which is to some extent a "natural" human tendency, took on that added sense of satisfaction which comes from participating in an attribute understood (more or less consciously) to be divine.

Process theology's understanding of divine love is in harmony with the insight, which we can gain both from psychologists and from our own experience, that if we truly love others we do not seek to control them. We do not seek to pressure them with promises and threats involving extrinsic rewards and punishments. Instead we try to persuade them to actualize those possibilities which they themselves will find intrinsically rewarding. We do this by providing ourselves as an environment that helps open up new, intrinsically attractive possibilities.

Insofar as the notion that divine love is persuasive is accepted, the exercise of persuasive influence becomes intrinsically rewarding. It takes on that aura of extra importance that has too often been associated with the feeling of controlling others. This change has implications in all our relations, from one-to-one I–thou encounters to international relations. It does not mean that coercive control could be eliminated, but it does mean that such control is exercised as a last resort and with a sense of regret rather than with the thrill that comes from the sense of imitating deity.

NOTES

1. Alfred North Whitehead, *Religion in the Making* (New York: Macmillan, 1926), p. 40.
2. Anselm, *Proslogium*, VI and VII, in *Proslogium; Monologium; An Appendix, In Behalf of the Fool, by Gaunilon; and Cur Deus Homo*, trans. S. N. Deane (Chicago: The Open Court Publishing Company, 1903, 1945), pp. 11, 13.
3. Ibid., p. 13.
4. Ibid.
5. *Summa Theologica* I, Q. 20, art. 1, obj. 1.
6. Ibid., ans. 1.
7. *Proslogium*, VII, loc. cit. pp. 13–14.
8. *Summa Theologica* I, Q, 21, art. 3, ans.
9. *Summa Theologica* I, Q. 20, art. 2, ans.
10. *Summa Theologica* I, Q. 20, art. 3, ans.
11. Anders Nygren, *Agape and Eros* (Philadelphia: Westminster Press, 1953), pp. 77–78.
12. Alfred North Whitehead, *Process and Reality* (New York: Macmillan, 1929), pp. 524, 530.

STUDY QUESTIONS

1. Cobb and Griffin, like Lucas, insist that God's love is responsive to his creatures, and that God feels with them when things go badly for them. Explain their reasons for thinking that this view is superior to the traditional doctrine of God as "impassible," incapable of suffering.
2. According to Cobb and Griffin, the idea of divine love as creative has become "problematic" in the modern world. Explain briefly why this is so.
3. Explain briefly process theology's idea that divine creative love is "persuasive, but never coercive."

SUGGESTED READING

Basinger, David. *The Case for Freewill Theism: A Philosophical Assessment,* Downers Grove, Ill.: InterVarsity Press, 1996.

Berkouwer, G. C. *The Providence of God,* trans. L. B. Smedes. Grand Rapids, Mich.: William B. Eerdmans, 1952.

Cobb, John B., and David Ray Griffin. *Process Theology: An Introductory Exposition.* Philadelphia: Westminster Press, 1976.

Flint, Thomas. *Divine Providence: The Molinist Account.* Ithaca, N.Y.: Cornell University Press, 1998.

Griffin, David Ray. *God, Freedom, and Evil: A Process Theodicy.* Philadelphia: Westminster Press, 1976.

Hasker, William. *Providence, Evil, and the Openness of God.* London: Routledge, 2004.

Helm, Paul. *The Providence of God.* Downers Grove, Ill.: InterVarsity Press, 1994.

Lucas, J. R. *The Future: An Essay on God, Temporality, and Truth.* Oxford, England: Blackwell, 1989.

Pinnock, Clark, Richard Rice, John Sanders, William Hasker, and David Basinger. *The Openness of God.* Downers Grove, Ill.: InterVarsity Press, 1994.

Sanders, John. *The God Who Risks: A Theology of Providence.* Downers Grove, Ill.: InterVarsity Press, 1998.

Swinburne, Richard. *Providence and the Problem of Evil.* Oxford, England: Clarendon Press, 1998.

Tiessen, Terrance. *Providence and Prayer: How Does God Work in the World?* Downers Grove, Ill.: InterVarsity Press, 2000.

Tracy, Thomas F., ed. *The God Who Acts: Philosophical and Theological Explorations.* University Park, Pa.: Pennsylvania State University Press, 1994.

PART NINE

Religious Language

Philosophers have always had an intense interest in language, and particularly in problems of reference and meaning. Contemporary philosophers of language have focused attention on many important domains of human language—including language about mental phenomena, about ethics and character, and about theological entities. Of course, the theological entity at the heart of the controversy is God. One of the key issues for philosophers of religious language is, How can we can speak meaningfully of God? Another question is, To what does the word "God" refer, if anything? And does it need to refer to something in order to be meaningful? Obviously, all we have at our disposal is human language, however imperfect it is, and yet religious language speaks of something drastically different from the ordinary realities about which we normally use language. This is the fundamental problem of religious language. As with all philosophical issues, a wide variety of viewpoints are available on the nature of religious language.

THE THEORY OF ANALOGY

The classical theory of analogy, formulated by the great medieval thinker Thomas Aquinas, holds that the meaning of terms used theologically is neither identical with nor totally disconnected from their meaning when applied to creaturely realities. Instead, these terms have analogical meaning, with some similarities and some dissimilarities. Clearly, there is a realist backdrop to the theory: the conviction that there is a real world and a real being, God, that is the target of our terms. The theory of "analogy" or "analogical predication" has been standard fare in discussions of religious language throughout the centuries.

A predicate term in a sentence attaches some property, relation, or activity to the subject term. An example is the statement "God is wise." How shall we understand the meaning of this sentence? Aquinas held that when a word—e.g., "wise"—is applied both to a created being and to God, it is not being used *univocally* (i.e., with exactly the same meaning) in the two instances. Yet neither is the word being used *equivocally* (i.e., with two completely different meanings), as when "hot" is used to apply to peppercorns and race cars. There is continuity between divine wisdom and human wisdom, a similarity between this quality in God and in persons. This allows the word to be used *analogically*. Thomists believe that analogy theory provides a helpful middle way between *anthropomorphism* and *agnosticism*, respectively. The theory assumes, then, that ordinary terms already have meaning when used appropriately in religious contexts and that there is an appropriate transfer of meaning from ordinary to religious contexts.

Transfers of meaning obviously occur in common situations, making analogy part of the structure of ordinary discourse—e.g., "John is faithful" and "Lassie is faithful." Of course, a theory of religious language must describe the transfer of meaning from contexts where terms are used to speak of the familiar creaturely realities to contexts where those terms speak of God and spiritual realities. That is why Aquinas and other Scholastic philosophers developed rules reflecting constraints on analogical predication. For example, the rule of proper proportionality states that God and creatures have qualities and engage in activities in proportion to their respective modes of being—infinite and finite, respectively. So, saying "God is wise" and "Socrates is wise" requires a shift in meaning between the two sentential contexts. And the shift is proportional to the two modes of being to which the predicate term "wise" is related. There is similarity or continuity, but there is also difference. Some critics, of course, wonder whether the notion of "similarity" can be given any clear definition.

The Verification/Falsification Challenge

In the twentieth century, wholesale challenges to the meaningfulness of religious language were waged. Logical positivists insisted that religious (or theological) language meet the same sorts of standards imposed on scientific language. Religious language is meaningful, it was argued, only if religious statements are nonanalytic and are either verifiable or falsifiable on empirical grounds. A. J. Ayer wrote, "A sentence is factually significant to any given person, if, and only if, he knows how to verify the proposition which it purports to express—that is, if he knows what observations would lead him, under certain conditions, to accept the proposition as being true, or reject it as being false." Truth and falsity, of course, apply only to propositions that have cognitive meaning. If religious propositions lack meaning because they are neither verifiable nor falsifiable, then they cannot be discussed in the intellectual arena in terms of truth and falsity. Ayer and other positivists maintain that theological language fails to meet the empirical standard of verifiability and thus has no cognitive meaning. Therefore, for them, theistic claims—as well as antitheistic claims—are not false but meaningless.

Continuing in this vein, Anthony Flew proposed a "falsification challenge" to religious language. He tells a story about two explorers in the jungle who come across a clearing where many flowers and also many weeds are growing. One explorer claims that a gardener tends this plot, but the other explorer disagrees. Through a series of experiments (use of a barbed-wire fence, bloodhounds, etc.), they fail to detect the gardener. Yet the Believer persists, saying that the gardener is invisible, intangible, insensible to electric shocks, etc. Frustrated, the Skeptic demands that the Believer declare exactly what would have to happen in order for him to withdraw his claim that there is a gardener—i.e., specify the claim's "falsification conditions."

Flew's essential point is that religious believers allow nothing to count against their claims and continually modify and qualify them in order to prevent them from being falsified. When believers state that "God loves us as a father loves his children," we would expect divine help in times of serious trouble or disease. Yet God seems distant, absent. So believers make some qualification—"God's love is not like human love" or "God's love is an inscrutable love"—making misfortune and suffering compatible with the original theological pronouncement. In response to this maneuvering, Flew puts forth this central question: "'What would have to occur or to have occurred to constitute for you a disproof of the love of, or of the existence of, God?'" If there is no state of affairs that would count against the original theological statement, then it is not really a genuine assertion at all. It says nothing, neither affirming nor denying that any state of affairs is actually the case.

The falsificationist critique of religious language prompted spirited discussion about whether religious claims have factual (i.e., empirical) significance. No doubt, for many critics, the only kind of cognitive significance is factual significance. Philosophers who agreed that the falsification principle defines the issue divided into two camps: those who thought that theological language is nonfalsifiable and those who thought that it could be shown falsifiable. R. M. Hare argued that religious utterances are not falsifiable for most believers and thus are not direct statements of fact. In an effort to distinguish religious assertions from factual assertions, Hare calls the former "bliks," a term he coined to designate something like an unshakable mindset. He says that the religious believer just has a "blik" that God exists and that a certain religious way of life is correct. Although Hare's terminology tends to trivialize religious assertions, an important point here is that religious faith is rooted in deeply held interpretive beliefs or assumptions about the world that cannot be readily overturned by direct empirical observation.

Basil Mitchell maintains that religious assertions are not straightforwardly falsifiable by empirical experience. Trust and commitment, he argues, play a role in filtering circumstances that might appear to falsify a belief. Mitchell tells a story about a member of a resistance movement meeting a stranger who impresses him very much. The partisan remains convinced of the stranger's trustworthiness throughout all changing circumstances, even when the stranger is seen capturing and imprisoning his comrades. Mitchell leaves open the possibility that religious assertions might at some point be abandoned by believers; but he tries to expose the oversimplification involved in the falsification challenge. Continuing the discussion, John Hick provides specific verification and falsification conditions for establishing the factual significance of religious claims: believers and nonbelievers will one day experience the afterlife, in which the empirical conditions tied to the meaning of religious statements either will or will not be met. Technically, Hick may have satisfied the logic of a verification/falsification challenge, but one wonders what benefit it is to us in temporal life to suppose that actual verification or falsification is located in the afterlife, which is something we cannot now experience!

As discussions of religious language based on positivistic criteria ran their course, many thinkers saw promise in the thinking of the later Wittgenstein for addressing and, indeed, transcending previous concerns. Following Ludwig Wittgenstein's declaration that the meaning of any stretch of language is related to its use in a certain human context rather than to its reference to an object, D. Z. Phillips and Paul van Buren, for example, urge that we need to study the function or use of key linguistic expressions within the religious "language-game." Interest in meaning-as-use actually led Wittgensteinian philosophers to consider questions of truth inappropriate.

Must Talk of God Be Nonliteral?

Although the verification/falsification challenge denied cognitive meaning to religious discourse, and functional analysis sought to find uses for it that were basically noncognitive, some thinkers wanted to restore some kind of cognitive meaning to religious language. Most were persuaded that whatever cognitive meaning may be there cannot be *literal*—that, instead, "religious narrative" or "metaphor" or "parable" must be the essential mode of religious discourse. Paul Tillich holds that talk of God is *symbolic*. Clearly, statements such as "Yahweh spoke to the prophets" and "The Lord is my shepherd" are not commonly considered to be capable of literal interpretation. God does not "speak" by expelling air across physical vocal chords; nor is he a "shepherd" in the typical sense. Tillich's position is that religious language is irreducibly symbolic. For, when God is the subject of predication, all properties, relationships, and activities are ascribed to something that is "wholly other" i.e., radically unlike anything else we know in the creaturely realm. Mistaken attempts to talk literally of God must be banned, for they treat God as a particular, discrete being rather than as the "ground of being." Therefore, it is impossible to specify literally or "cash out" what is being asserted of God.

In the strictest sense, then, God cannot be described in terms of the predicates in our language—because one can never claim with respect to some property or attribute that God really possesses it and the claim is true if, and only if, God actually possesses the property or attribute. Nevertheless, Tillich believes that the power of religious symbols is to reflect our "ultimate concern" and open us up to deeper levels of reality. The Holy, or the Ultimate, transcends every concrete symbol of the Holy. The history of religion contains a rich diversity of material that at some point in time has become a symbol of the Holy. According to Tillich, the key to understanding this otherwise confusing history is to see religions as employing symbols (e.g., a lotus blossom, a star, a cross) that rest on the Ultimate considered as the "ground of being," and provide an avenue through which the Ultimate can be experienced.

According to feminist theologians, however, we can no longer rely on a symbolic analysis of religious language because we no longer have a sacramental understanding of the world it assumes. The disunity, materialism, and skepticism of our age prevents us from viewing ordinary things as continuous with sacred things such that the former can properly symbolize the latter. Unfortunately, traditional religious expressions persist and become absolutized apart from their original context. The feminist critique of traditional Western religious language centers on the expression "God the father." This patriarchal image has been identified as the exclusive way of understanding the divine and has dominated to the exclusion of other images of the divine. The patriarchal model, then, becomes a grid or filter that interprets the nature of God, our relations to the divine, and our interactions with one another. Feminist theologians warn that the twin dangers of the patriarchal model to religion are idolatry and irrelevance. Mary Daly recommends that idolatry of the paternal image is countered by the insight of the *apophatic tradition*, which holds that, because of the gap between the Infinite and the finite, God can only be named by what God is *not*. Irrelevance to large numbers of women as well as to ethnic minorities and residents of the third world is countered by eliminating the hierarchical, male, white, Western elements of our image of God.

The selection here by Rosemary Ruether argues that historic monotheism—originating among the ancient Hebrews and expressed in Judaism, Christianity, and Islam—is a radical departure from earlier religious consciousness in the Ancient Near East. "Male monotheism," writes Ruether, "becomes the vehicle of a psychocultural revolution of the male ruling class in its relationship to surrounding reality." This hierarchy became sacralized as though it were a cosmic principle essential to monotheism: that maleness is the best symbol of deity. By contrast, Ruether points out, the much older, polytheistic religions that were supplanted by monotheism actually envisioned a realm of paired gods and goddesses within a matrix of one physical-spiritual reality, thus validating both masculine and feminine images for the divine. To correct the male monopoly on God-language, then, she recommends using "inclusive language" for God that draws on the images and experiences of both genders. Although there are precedents for using inclusive language for God within the Christian tradition, religions of the Ancient Near East also provide examples in which positive qualities are attributed to a feminine deity, the Goddess figure. Ruether uses the term "God/ess" which must be invested with both female and male metaphors.

Can Talk of God Be Literal?

William P. Alston rejects claims that all talk of God must be nonliteral. He draws an initial distinction between the form of our language and the reality it addresses. The *subject–predicate structure* of language assumes a distinction between an *object* and its *properties*, whereas the classical doctrine of divine simplicity maintains there are no such distinctions in God. So, when a predicate term (e.g., "love") connects a property to some subject term (e.g., "Mother Teresa"), the subject–predicate structure of the sentence assumes a distinction between Mother Teresa and her love. However, we have to use the same subject–predicate language, with its distinctions, to speak of God and God's love, although there is no parallel distinction in God. Alston states therefore that our conceptual grid, reflected in our language, cannot fully capture the divine reality.

For Alston, the limitations of our subject–predicate language do not necessarily preclude the literal application of all predicate terms to God. That is, there can be a genuine reality that is the intended target of our terms. Although we typically apply concepts such as love or knowledge or power or action in a literal fashion to human beings, and human beings possess creaturely characteristics (e.g., finitude, temporality, embodiment), Alston contends that the concepts of love, knowledge, power, and action do not necessarily involve creaturely conditions. Thus, he believes that there is a core of meaning for these concepts that can be literally attributed to God. Alston argues this point by focusing on *personalistic predicates*, which apply to personal agents who carry out intentions and plans in light of knowledge or belief, express attitudes guided by principles, and communicate with and relate to other such agents. Personalistic predicates—such as "commands," "loves," and "guides"—are obviously used in sentences with God as the subject: "God loves humanity," "Yahweh is righteous," "Allah is merciful," etc. The key issue is whether any personalistic predicate term, used literally, can be *true* of God, or *truly applied* to God, or just *literally true* of God. For nonliteralists, God's radical "otherness" preempts personalistic predicates from literally applying to God. For others, God's positive attributes—such as incorporeality, infinity, and timelessness—are obstacles to literal predication.

A comprehensive defense of speaking literally of God would address each aspect of the divine that is alleged to prohibit applying literal predication to God. As an initial foray into the topic, Alston shows that incorporeality is not incompatible with *personalistic predicates* and, therefore, that it does not rule out the possibility of their true application to an incorporeal being. He argues that *mental predicates* (having to do with cognitions, feelings, and other internal psychological states) and *action predicates* (having to do with what an agent does) can be applied to God. Regarding action predicates, part of his contention is that our concept of overt action does not require bodily movements, although perhaps all *human* actions with which we are familiar involve bodily movements. But it does not follow that *no* action concepts whatsoever are applicable to an incorporeal being, which can be conceived to bring about events without physical movements. So, there is no conceptual impossibility in applying mental predicates and action predicates to an incorporeal being. Thus, the prospects for speaking literally about God are not as dim as often thought. If Alston is right, then he has gone a considerable way toward showing that theistic thinkers are not asserting and discussing propositions about God that are obviously extraneous or absurd. By the same token, he has shown that critiques and denials of theistic beliefs, which are also framed largely as literal predications, are also not beside the point.

Thomas Aquinas

The Doctrine of Analogy

The theory of analogy plays an important role in the philosophy of Thomas Aquinas (1224–1274). Misunderstood by some critics as an analogical strategy for arguing that God exists, this scholastic doctrine really pertains to how it is possible to say anything meaningful about God using human language. For Aquinas, it is a general theory about the way in which we actually extend meaningful discourse from familiar circumstances to circumstances in which normal experience no longer applies. Technically, the theory of analogy is a theory about how ordinary predicates (e.g., "good" and "wise") apply to God. By means of this view, Aquinas is able to steer a middle course between saying that such predicates have *univocal* meaning when applied to God (i.e., exactly the same meaning as when they are applied to creatures) and that they have *equivocal* meaning (i.e., completely different meaning as when they are applied to creatures). The Angelic Doctor's middle course was to give an explication of how ordinary terms have *analogical* meaning, replete with a number of technical rules. A confident realist, Aquinas was trying to account for the fact that discourse about God has already been taking place in human affairs in spite of various considerations that might seem to rule out the possibility. The implicit claim throughout is that finite language is neither exhaustive nor complete in referring to God, but that its capacity for analogical predication makes it adequate for this purpose.

It is impossible that anything should be predicated of both creatures and God univocally. Any effect that falls short of the power of its cause resembles its cause inadequately because it differs from it. Thus, what is found diversely and in various ways in the effect exists simply and in a single way in the cause; so, the sun by a single power produces many different kinds of lower things. In just that way,...all the perfections which are found among creatures in diverse and various ways preexist in God as united in one.

When we predicate of creatures some term which indicates a perfection, that term signifies the perfection as something distinct by its definition from every other perfection; for instance, when we predicate the term "wise" of some man, we signify some

From *Summa Theologica*, 1.13.5 and *Disputed Questions: On Truth*, 2.11, trans. by James Ross. Used by permission of James Ross.

perfection which is distinct from the essence of the man, and also from his powers and from his existence. But when we predicate such a term of God, we do not intend to signify something which is distinct from His essence, power and existence. Also, when we predicate the term "wise" of some man, it circumscribes and isolates what is signified; but this is not so when the term "wise" is predicated of God because the reality signified by the term remains unisolated and exceeds the signification (the linguistic intention) of the term. Therefore, it is obvious that the term "wise" does not have exactly the same meaning when predicated of God and of some creature. And the same reasoning holds for all the other terms which indicate perfection. So no term is predicated of God and creatures univocally.

But the terms are not used purely equivocally either, as some have claimed. For, if that were so, nothing would be knowable or demonstrable concerning God from our knowledge of creatures; our reasoning would always commit the fallacy of equivocation. Such a view would be as discordant with the philosophers who demonstrate a number of things about God, as it would be with the Apostle Paul who said: "The invisible things of God are made known by the things that are made."

We have to say, then, that terms are used of creatures and God analogously, that is, according to an ordering between them. We can distinguish two ways in which analogy based upon the order among things can be found among terms: First, one word may be used of two things because each of them has some order or relation to a third thing. Thus we use the term "healthy" of both medicine and urine because both things have a relation to another thing, namely, the health of the animal, of which the latter is the sign and the former the cause. Secondly, one word may be used of two things because of the relation the one thing has to the other; thus "healthy" is used of both the medicine and the animal because the medicine is the cause of the health in the man. In this way some terms are used of creatures and God, neither univocally nor purely equivocally, but analogously.

We are unable to speak of God except in the language we use of creatures.... And so, whatever is said of both creatures and God is said on the basis of the order or relation which holds between the creature and God, namely, that God is the source and cause in which all the perfections of things preexist eminently.

This kind of community is a middle-ground between pure equivocation and simply univocity. For among those terms which are used analogously, there is not a common or single concept, as there is among univocal terms; but neither are the concepts wholly diverse, as is the case among equivocal terms. Rather, the term which is predicated in different ways signifies different relations to some one thing; thus "healthy" when predicated of urine means "is a sign of the health of the animal," whereas when predicated of the medicine it means "is a cause of the health of the animal."

Nothing can be predicated of a creature and of God univocally. For when a term is used univocally of more than one thing, what the term signifies is common to each of the things of which it is univocally predicated. So far as the signification of the term is concerned, the things of which it is univocally predicated are undifferentiated, even though they may precede one another in being; for instance, all numbers are equally numbers although one is prior to another. But no matter how much a creature may resemble God, a point cannot be reached at which something belongs to it and to God for the same reason. For things which are in different subjects and have the same formal definition are common to the subjects in substance and quiddity but are distinct in *esse*. Whatever is in God, however, is His own *esse*; for just as His essence is the same as His *esse*, so His knowledge is the same as His knowing. Since the *esse* which is proper to one thing cannot be communicated to another, it cannot happen that a creature should ever attain to having something for the same reason that God has it because it is impossible that the creature should come into possession of the same *esse* as is God's. The same is true for us; if "man" and "to *be* as a man" did not differ in Peter and Paul it would not be possible for the term "man" to be predicated univocally of Peter and of Paul whose *esse* is distinct.

Still, it cannot be maintained that whatever is predicated of God and a creature is predicated purely equivocally because if there were not some real resemblance between the creature and God, His essence would not be a likeness of creatures, and thus He could not understand creatures by understanding His essence. Similarly, we would not be able to come to know God from created things either; nor would it be that from among the terms which apply to creatures, one rather than another, ought to be predicated of God; for with equivocal terms it makes no difference which is applied since the term does not imply any real agreement among the things to which it applies.

So we have to say that the term "knowledge" is predicated of God's knowledge and of ours neither wholly univocally nor purely equivocally. Instead it is predicated analogously, which is the same as proportionally.

Resemblance on account of a proportion (relation) can be of two kinds, and so two kinds of analogous community can be distinguished. There is a community between things of which one is related to another in virtue of their having a fixed distance or other determinate relationship to each other, as the number 2 to the number 1, in that the former is the double of the latter. Sometimes there is a community (or resemblance) between two things, not accounted for because the one is a function of the other but rather, because of a likeness of two relations; for instance, 6 resembles 4 in that as 6 is the double of 3, so is 4 the double of 2. The first kind of resemblance is one of proportion; the second is one of parity of proportion or proportionality.

We find something said analogically of two things in virtue of the first type of resemblance when one of them has a direct and determinate relationship to the other, as, for instance, "being" is predicated of accident and of substance because of the relationship which accident has to substance; and "healthy" is predicated of urine and of an animal because urine has some relation to the health of the animal. Sometimes something is predicated analogically in virtue of the second type of resemblance, as when the term insight is predicated of bodily sight and of understanding, because sight is to the eye what understanding is to the mind.

There must be some determinate (definite) relationship between things to which something is common by analogy of the first sort; consequently, it cannot be that anything is predicated of God and creatures by this type of analogy because no creature has such a determinate relationship to God. But the other type of analogy requires no determinate type of relationship between the things in which something is common by analogy; and so nothing excludes some term's being predicated analogously of God and creatures in this manner.

This can happen in two ways: sometimes the term implies that some-thing, which cannot be common to God and a creature even in a proportionality, belongs to what it primarily designated. This is so of everything which is predicated metaphorically of God as when He is said to be a lion, the sun, and so forth, because the definitions include matter which cannot be attributed to God. In other cases, a term which is used of God and creatures has no implications in its primary uses which preclude a resemblance of the kind described between God and creatures. To this class belong all those predicates which do not imply a defect (limitation) and which do not depend upon matter for their *esse*; for instance, "being," "good," and so forth.

STUDY QUESTIONS

1. What does it mean to apply predicates to something? What is the relation between predicates (linguistic elements) and attributes (ontological elements)?
2. According to Aquinas, in applying predicates to creatures and to God, what are the problems at each extreme? What, according to Aquinas, is the middle way? Evaluate.

Antony Flew and Basil Mitchell
The Falsification Debate

The following piece is part of the famous "university discussion" among several British analytic philosophers over the application of positivist criteria of meaning to religious language. Antony Flew (b. 1923) argues that religious statements must be empirically falsifiable in order to be cognitively meaningful. Here Flew reflects the widespread opinion during the last century that empirical falsifiability is necessary for any statement to be factually significant. Science—with its rigorous demand that claims of fact be empirically testable—was considered to set the standard of human knowledge that all other claims must emulate. Flew thinks that religious believers refuse to specify falsification conditions for their claims—e.g., the claim that a loving God exists. Although religious believers offer many qualifications to their claims about God, it appears that in the final analysis they will not articulate what would have to happen to get them to withdraw their claims. Thus, Flew concludes, those claims must be rejected not as false but as meaningless, totally devoid of conceptual content. In reply, Basil Mitchell (b. 1917) explains that religious claims are not straightforwardly falsifiable because they involve trust in and commitment to God, which cannot be subjected to an empirical formula. Similarly, one's claims about another person's character involve trust and commitment, which factor into an interpretation of various circumstances. Mitchell argues that we must appreciate this more subtle evaluative process when we see religious believers retain their faith in the face of circumstances that would otherwise seem to provide conclusive falsification of their beliefs. Other participants in this discussion were R. M. Hare and I. M. Crombie.

FLEW

Let us begin with a parable. It is a parable developed from a tale told by John Wisdom in his haunting and revelatory article "Gods."[1] Once upon a time two explorers came upon a clearing in the jungle. In the clearing were growing many flowers and many weeds. One explorer says, "Some gardener must tend this plot." The other disagrees, "There is no gardener." So they pitch their tents and set a watch. No gardener is ever seen. "But perhaps he is an invisible gardener." So they set up a barbed-wire fence. They electrify it. They patrol with bloodhounds. (For they remember how H. G. Wells's *The Invisible Man* could be both smelt and touched though he could not be seen.) But no shrieks ever suggest that some intruder has received a shock. No movements of the wire ever betray an invisible climber. The blood hounds never give cry. Yet still the Believer is not convinced. "But there is a gardener, invisible, intangible, insensible to electric shocks, a gardener who has no scent and makes no sound, a gardener who comes secretly to look after the garden which he loves." At last the Sceptic despairs, "But what remains of your original assertion? Just how does what you call an invisible, intangible, eternally elusive gardener differ from an imaginary gardener or even from no gardener at all?"

In this parable we can see how what starts as an assertion, that something exists or that there is some analogy between certain complexes of phenomena, may be reduced step by step to an altogether different status, to an expression perhaps of a "picture preference."[2] The Sceptic says there is no gardener. The Believer says there is a gardener (but invisible, etc.). One man talks about sexual behaviour. Another man prefers to talk of Aphrodite (but knows that there is not really a superhuman person additional to, and somehow responsible for, all sexual phenomena).[3] The process of qualification may be checked at any point before the original assertion is completely withdrawn and something of that first assertion will remain (Tautology). Mr. Wells's invisible man could not, admittedly, be seen, but in all other respects he was a man like the rest of us. But though the process of qualification may be, and of course usually is, checked in time, it is not always judiciously so halted. Someone may dissipate his assertion completely without noticing that he has done so. A fine brash hypothesis may thus be killed by inches, the death by a thousand qualifications.

And in this, it seems to me, lies the peculiar danger, the endemic evil, of theological utterance. Take such utterances as "God has a plan," "God created the world," "God loves us as a father loves his children." They look at first sight very much like assertions, vast cosmological assertions. Of course, this is no sure sign that they either are, or are intended to be, assertions. But let us confine ourselves to the cases where those who utter such sentences intend them to express assertions. (Merely remarking parenthetically that those who intend or interpret such utterances as crypto-commands, expressions of wishes, disguised ejaculations, concealed ethics, or as anything else but assertions, are unlikely to succeed in making them either properly orthodox or practically effective.)

Now to assert that such and such is the case is necessarily equivalent to denying that such and such is not the case.[4] Suppose then that we are in doubt as to what someone who gives vent to an utterance is asserting, or suppose that, more radically, we are sceptical as to whether he is really asserting anything at all, one way of trying to understand (or perhaps it will be to expose) his utterance is to attempt to find what he would regard as counting against, or as being incompatible with, its truth. For if the utterance is indeed an assertion, it will necessarily be equivalent to a denial of the negation of that assertion. And anything which would count against the assertion, or which would induce the speaker to withdraw it and to admit that it had been mistaken, must be part of (or the whole of) the meaning of the negation of that assertion. And to know the meaning of the negation of an assertion, is as near as makes no matter, to know the meaning of that assertion.[5] And if there is nothing which a putative assertion denies then there is nothing which it asserts either: and so it is not really an assertion. When the Sceptic in the parable asked the Believer, "Just how does what you call an invisible, intangible, eternally elusive gardener differ from an imaginary gardener or even from no gardener at all?" he was suggesting that the Believer's earlier statement had been so eroded by qualification that it was no longer an assertion at all.

Now it often seems to people who are not religious as if there was no conceivable event or series of events the occurrence of which would be admitted by sophisticated religious people to be a sufficient reason for conceding "There wasn't a God after all" or "God does not really love us then." Someone tells us that God loves us as a father loves his children. We are reassured. But then we see a child dying of inoperable cancer of the throat. His earthly father is driven frantic in his efforts to help, but his Heavenly Father reveals no obvious sign of concern. Some qualification is made—God's love is "not a merely human love" or it is "an inscrutable love," perhaps—and we realize that such sufferings are quite compatible with the truth of the assertion that "God loves us as a father (but, of course,).... " We are reassured again. But then perhaps we ask: what is this assurance of God's (appropriately qualified) love worth, what is this apparent guarantee really a guarantee against? Just what would have to happen not merely (morally and wrongly) to tempt but also (logically and rightly) to entitle us to say "God does not love us" or even "God does not exist"? I therefore put to the succeeding symposiasts the simple central questions, "What would have to occur or to have occurred to constitute for you a disproof of the love of, or the existence of, God?"

MITCHELL

Flew's article is searching and perceptive, but there is, I think, something odd about his conduct of the theologian's case. The theologian surely would not deny that the fact of pain counts against the assertion that God loves men. This very incompatibility generates the most intractable of theological problems—the problem of evil. So the theologian *does* recognize the fact of pain as counting against Christian doctrine. But it is true that he will not allow it—or anything—to count decisively against it; for he is committed by his faith to trust in God. His attitude is not that of the detached observer, but of the believer.

Perhaps this can be brought out by yet another parable. In time of war in an occupied country, a member of the resistance meets one night a stranger who deeply impresses him. They spend that night together in conversation. The Stranger tells the partisan that he himself is on the side of the resistance—indeed that he is in command of it, and urges the partisan to have faith in him no matter what happens. The partisan is utterly convinced at that meeting of the Stranger's sincerity and constancy and undertakes to trust him.

They never meet in conditions of intimacy again. But sometimes the Stranger is seen helping members of the resistance, and the partisan is grateful and says to his friends, "He is on our side."

Sometimes he is seen in the uniform of the police handing over patriots to the occupying power. On these occasions his friends murmur against him: but the partisan still says, "He is on our side." He still believes that, in spite of appearances, the Stranger did not deceive him. Sometimes he asks the Stranger for help and receives it. He is then thankful. Sometimes he asks and does not receive it. Then he says, "The Stranger knows best." Sometimes his friends, in exasperation, say, "Well, what *would* he have to do for you to admit that you were wrong and that he is not on our side?" But the partisan refuses to answer. He will not consent to put the Stranger to the test. And sometimes his friends complain, "Well, if *that's* what you mean by his being on our side, the sooner he goes over to the other side the better."

The partisan of the parable does not allow anything to count decisively against the proposition "The Stranger is on our side." This is because he has committed himself to trust the Stranger. But he of course recognizes that the Stranger's ambiguous behaviour *does* count against what he believes about him. It is precisely this situation which constitutes the trial of his faith.

When the partisan asks for help and doesn't get it, what can he do? He can *(a)* conclude that the stranger is not on our side; or *(b)* maintain that he is on our side, but that he has reasons for withholding help.

The first he will refuse to do. How long can he uphold the second position without its becoming just silly?

I don't think one can say in advance. It will depend on the nature of the impression created by the Stranger in the first place. It will depend, too, on the manner in which he takes the Stranger's behaviour. If he blandly dismisses it as of no consequence, as having no bearing upon his belief, it will be assumed that he is thoughtless or insane. And it quite obviously won't do for him to say easily, "Oh, when used of the Stranger the phrase 'is on our side' *means* ambiguous behaviour of this sort." In that case he would be like the religious man who says blandly of a terrible disaster "It is God's will." No, he will only be regarded as sane and reasonable in his belief, if he experiences in himself the full force of the conflict.

It is here that my parable differs from Hare's. The partisan admits that many things may and do count against his belief: whereas Hare's lunatic who has *blik* about dons doesn't admit that anything counts against his *blik*. Nothing *can* count against *bliks*. Also the partisan has a reason for having in the first instance committed himself, viz., the character of the Stranger; whereas the lunatic has no reason for his *blik* about dons—because, of course, you can't have reasons for *bliks*.

This means that I agree with Flew that theological utterances must be assertions. The partisan is making an assertion when he says, "The Stranger is on our side."

Do I want to say that the partisan's belief about the Stranger is, in any sense, an explanation? I think I do. It explains and makes sense of the Stranger's behaviour: it helps to explain also the resistance movement in the context of which he appears. In each case it differs from the interpretation which the others put upon the same facts.

"God loves men" resembles "the Stranger is on our side" (and many other significant statements, e.g., historical ones) in not being conclusively falsifiable. They can both be treated in at least three different ways: (1) as provisional hypotheses to be discarded if experience tells against them, (2) as significant articles of faith, (3) as vacuous formulae (expressing, perhaps, a desire for reassurance) to which experience makes no difference and which make no difference to life.

The Christian, once he has committed himself, is precluded by his faith from taking up the first attitude: "Thou shalt not tempt the Lord thy God." He is in constant danger, as Flew has observed, of slipping into the third. But he need not; and, if he does, it is a failure in faith as well as in logic.

Notes

1. *P.A.S.,* 1944–45, reprinted as Ch. X of *Logic and Language,* vol. I (Blackwell, 1951), and in his *Philosophy and Psychoanalysis* (Blackwell, 1953).
2. Cf. J. Wisdom, "Other Minds," *Mind,* 1940; reprinted in his *Other Minds* (Blackwell, 1952).
3. Cf. Lucretius, *De Rerum Natura,* II, 655–60:

Hic siquis mare Neptunum Cereremque vocare
Constituet fruges et Bacchi nomine abuti
Mavolat quam laticis proprium proferre vocamen
Consedamus ut hic terrarum dictitet orbem
Esse deum matrem dum vera re tamen ipse
Religione animum turpi contingere parcat.

4. For those who prefer symbolism: $p \equiv \sim\sim p$.
5. For by simply negating $\sim p$ we get $p{:}\sim\sim p{\equiv}p$.

Study Questions

1. Flew lays down a challenge to religious believers to provide meaning to their claims. What theory of meaning does Flew use as the standard by which to judge? What are the strengths and weaknesses of this theory? What if scientific claims were made the focus of evaluation?
2. Essentially, Flew's point is that religious claims and beliefs are meaningless, not that they have been falsified or that they are false. How does he make this point by way of story? Exactly how does this kind of challenge differ from other direct challenges to the truth of religious claims?
3. Mitchell disagrees with Flew that nothing counts against religious beliefs but argues that religious faith does not let anything count decisively against its beliefs. How does his story make this point?

Paul Tillich

Religious Language as Symbolic

Paul Tillich (1886–1965) develops the view that religious language cannot be understood literally but must be understood symbolically. For him, God is the "ground of being" and not simply one being among many others. Since literal language is designed to talk of the finite beings that populate our world, it must fail in any attempt to represent this ultimate reality, or what he often speaks of as the "dimension of the Holy." A study of the function of symbols in general in human life shows that they "open up" levels of reality for which nonsymbolic speaking is inadequate—whether in visual art, poetry, music, etc. This opening of new levels pertains both to new and deeper vistas on the object and to the subject's finding new depths and insights within his or her own soul. With religious symbols, then, whether linguistic or nonlinguistic, new levels are opened up on divine reality and on our own relation to it. For Tillich, religious symbols "participate" in the reality and power of the Holy, mediating the Holy to us. All religions and cultures take the infinity of material in their experience and create the symbols that are powerful for them—what Tillich calls the "sacramental function." Since the Holy is not an individual being but is "Being Itself," there can be an amazing variety of compelling symbols across the world's religions, according to their different historical journeys and experiences. Tillich's article here provides a thorough analysis of the aspects of religious symbols and their function in human life.

Symbols and Signs

Words do not communicate to us any more what they originally did and what they were invented to communicate. This has something to do with the fact that our present culture has no clearing house such as medieval scholasticism was, Protestant scholasticism in the seventeenth century at least tried to be, and philosophers like Kant tried to renew....

Let us proceed with the intention of clearing concepts as much as we are able, and let us take five steps, the first of which is the discussion of "symbols and signs." Symbols are similar to signs in one decisive respect: both symbols and signs point beyond

From "The Nature of Religious Language," *The Christian Scholar* 38, no. 3 (September 1955).

themselves to something else. The typical sign, for instance the red light at the corner of the street, does not point to itself but it points to the necessity of cars stopping. And every symbol points beyond itself to a reality for which it stands. In this, symbols and signs have an essential identity—they point beyond themselves. And this is the reason that the confusion of language mentioned above has also conquered the discussion about symbols for centuries and has produced confusion between signs and symbols. The first step in any clearing up of the meaning of symbols is to distinguish it from the meaning of signs.

The difference, which is a fundamental difference between them is that signs do not participate in any way in the reality and power of that to which they point. Symbols, although they are not the same as that which they symbolize, participate in its meaning and power. The difference between symbol and sign is the participation in the symbolized reality which characterizes the symbols, and the nonparticipation in the "pointed-to" reality which characterizes a sign. For example, letters of the alphabet as they are written, an "A" or an "R" do not participate in the sound to which they point; on the other hand, the flag participates in the power of the king or the nation for which it stands and which it symbolizes....

Language is a very good example of the difference between signs and symbols. Words in a language are signs for a meaning which they express. The word "desk" is a sign which points to something quite different—namely, the thing on which a paper is lying and at which we might be looking. This has nothing to do with the word "desk," with these four letters. But there are words in every language which are more than this, and in the moment in which they get connotations which go beyond something to which they point as signs, then they can become symbols; and this is a very important distinction for any speaker. He can speak almost completely in signs, reducing the meaning of his words almost to mathematical signs, and this is the absolute ideal of the logical positivist. The other pole of this is liturgical or poetic language where words have a power through centuries, or more than centuries. They have connotations in situations in which they appear so that they cannot be replaced. They have become not only signs pointing to a meaning which is defined, but also symbols standing for a reality in the power of which participate.

THE FUNCTION OF SYMBOLS

Now we come to a second consideration dealing with the functions of symbols. This first function is implied in what has already been said—namely, the representative function. The symbol represents something which is not itself, for which it stands and in the power and meaning of which it participates. This is a basic function of every symbol, and therefore, if that word had not been used in so many other ways, one could perhaps even translate "symbolic" as "representative," but for some reason that is not possible. If the symbols stand for something which they are not, then the question is, "Why do we not have that for which they stand directly? Why do we need symbols at all?" And now we come to something which is perhaps the main function of the symbol—namely, the opening up of levels of reality which otherwise are hidden and cannot be grasped in any other way.

Every symbol opens up a level of reality for which nonsymbolic speaking is inadequate. Let us interpret this, or explain this, in terms of artistic symbols. The more we try to enter into the meaning of symbols, the more we become aware that it is a function of art to open up levels of reality; in poetry, in visual art, and in music, levels of reality are opened up which can be opened up in no other way. Now if this is the function of art, then certainly artistic creations have symbolic character. You can take that which a landscape of Rubens, for instance, mediates to you. You cannot have this experience in any other way than through this painting made by Rubens. This landscape has some heroic character; it has character of balance, of colors, of weights, of values, and so on. All this is very external. What this mediates to you cannot be expressed in any other way than through the painting itself. The same is true also in the relationship of poetry and philosophy. The temptation may often be to confuse the issue by bringing too many philosophical concepts into a poem. Now this is really the problem; one cannot do this. If one uses philosophical language or scientific language, it does not mediate the same thing which is mediated in the use of really poetic language without a mixture of any other language.

This example may show what is meant by the phrase "opening up of levels of reality." But in order to do this, something else must be opened up—namely, levels of the soul, levels of our interior reality. And they must correspond to the levels in exterior reality which are opened up by a symbol. So every symbol is two-edged. It opens up reality and it opens up the soul. There are, of course, people who are not opened up by music or who are not opened up by poetry, or more of them (especially in Protestant America) who are not opened up at all by visual arts. The "opening up" is a two-sided function—namely, reality in deeper levels and the human soul in special levels. . . .

"Out of what womb are symbols born?" Out of the womb which is usually called today the "group unconscious" or "collective unconscious," or whatever you want to call it—out of a group which acknowledges, in this thing, this word, this flag, or whatever it may be, its own being. It is not invented intentionally; even if somebody would try to invent a symbol, as sometimes happens, then it becomes a symbol only if the unconscious of a group says "yes" to it. It means that something is opened up by it in the sense which I have just described. Now this implies further that in the moment in which this inner situation of the human group to a symbol has ceased to exist, then the symbol dies. The symbol does not "say" anything any more. In this way, all of the polytheistic gods have died; the situation in which they were born, has changed or does not exist any more, and so the symbols died. But these are events which cannot be described in terms of intention and invention.

The Nature of Religious Symbols

Now we come to a third consideration—namely, the nature of religious symbols. Religious symbols do exactly the same thing as all symbols do—namely, they open up a level of reality, which otherwise is not opened at all, which is hidden. We can call this the depth dimension of reality itself, the dimension of reality which is the ground of every other dimension and every other depth, and which therefore, is not one level beside the others but is the fundamental level, the level below all other levels, the level of being itself, or the ultimate power of being. Religious symbols open up the experience of the dimension of this depth in the human soul. If a religious symbol has ceased to have this function, then it dies. And if new symbols are born, they are born out of a changed relationship to the ultimate ground of being, i.e., to the Holy.

The dimension of ultimate reality is the dimension of the Holy. And so we can also say, religious symbols are symbols of the Holy. As such they participate in the holiness of the Holy according to our basic definition of a symbol. But participation is not identity; they are not themselves *the* Holy. The wholly transcendent transcends every symbol of the Holy. Religious symbols are taken from the infinity of material which the experienced reality gives us. Everything in time and space has become at some time in the history of religion a symbol for the Holy. And this is naturally so, because everything that is in the world we encounter rests on the ultimate ground of being. This is the key to the otherwise extremely confusing history of religion. Those of you who have looked into this seeming chaos of the history of religion in all periods of history from the earliest primitives to the latest developments, will be extremely confused about the chaotic character of this development. The key which makes order out of this chaos is comparatively simple. It is that everything in reality can impress itself as a symbol for a special relationship of the human mind to its own ultimate ground and meaning. So in order to open up the seemingly closed door to this chaos of religious symbols, one simply has to ask, "What is the relationship to the ultimate which is symbolized in these symbols?" And then they cease to be meaningless; and they become, on the contrary, the most revealing creations of the human mind, the most genuine ones, the most powerful ones, those who control the human consciousness, and perhaps even more the unconsciousness, and have therefore this tremendous tenacity which is characteristic of all religious symbols in the history of religion.

Religion, as everything in life, stands under the law of ambiguity, "ambiguity" meaning that it is creative and destructive at the same time. Religion has its holiness and its unholiness, and the reason for this is obvious from what has been said about religious symbolism. Religious symbols point symbolically to that which transcends all of them. But since, as symbols, they participate in that to which they point, they always have the tendency (in the human mind, of course) to replace that to which they are supposed to point, and to become ultimate in themselves. And in the moment in which they do this, they become idols. All idolatry is nothing else than the absolutizing of symbols of the Holy, and making them identical with the Holy itself. In this way, for instance, holy persons can become a god. Ritual acts can take on unconditional validity, although they are only expressions of a special situation. In all sacramental activities of religion, in all holy objects, holy books, holy doctrines, holy rites, you find this danger which we call "demonization." They become demonic at the moment in which they become elevated to the unconditional and ultimate character of the Holy itself.

Now we turn to a fourth consideration—namely, the levels of religious symbols. There are two fundamental levels in all religious symbols: the transcendent level, the level which goes *beyond* the empirical reality we encounter, and the immanent level, the level which we find *within* the encounter with reality. Let us look at the first level, the transcendent level. The basic symbol on the transcendent level would be God himself. But we cannot simply say that God is a symbol. We must always say two things about him: we must say that there is a non-symbolic element in our image of God—namely, that he is ultimate reality, being itself, ground of being, power of being; and the other, that he is the highest being in which everything that we have does exist in the most perfect way. If we say this we have in our mind the image of a highest being, a being with the characteristics of highest perfection. That means, we have a symbol for that which is not symbolic in the idea of God—namely, "Being Itself."

It is important to distinguish these two elements in the idea of God. Thus all of these discussions going on about God being a person or not a person, God being

similar to other things or not similar, these discussions which have a great impact on the destruction of the religious experience through false interpretations of it, could be overcome if we would say, "Certainly the awareness of something unconditional is in itself what it is, is not symbolic." We can call it *"Being Itself,"* *esse qua esse, esse ipsum*, as the scholastics did. But in our relationship to this ultimate we symbolize and must symbolize. We could not be in communication with God if he were only "ultimate being." But in our relationship to him we encounter him with the highest of what we ourselves are, *person*. And so in the symbolic form of speaking about him, we have both that which transcends infinitely our experience of ourselves as persons, and that which is so adequate to our being persons that we can say, "Thou" to God, and can pray to him....

The second is the qualities, the attributes of God, whatever you say about him: that he is love, that he is mercy, that he is power, that he is omniscient, that he is omnipresent, that he is almighty. These attributes of God are taken from experienced qualities we have ourselves. They cannot be applied to God in the literal sense. If this is done, it leads to an infinite amount of absurdities....

A third element on the transcendent level is the acts of God, for example, when we say, "He has created the world," "He has sent his Son," "He will fulfill the world." In all these temporal, causal, and other expressions we speak symbolically of God. As an example, look at the one small sentence: *"God has sent his son."* Here we have in the word "has" temporality. But God is beyond our temporality, though not beyond every temporality. Here is space; "sending somebody" means moving him from one place to another place. This certainly is speaking symbolically, although spatiality is in God as an element in his creative ground. We say that he "has sent"—that means that he has caused something. In this way God is subject to the category of causality. And when we speak of him and his Son, we have two different substances and apply the category of substance to him. Now all this, if taken literally, is absurd. If it is taken symbolically, it is profound expression, the ultimate Christian expression, of the relationship between God and man in the Christian experience....

Now consider the immanent level, the level of the appearances of the divine in time and space. Here we have first of all the incarnations of the divine, different beings in time and space, divine beings transmuted into animals or men or any kinds of other beings as they appear in time and space. This is often forgotten by those within Christianity who like to use in every second theological proposition the word "incarnation." They forget that this is not an especially Christian characteristic, because incarnation is something which happens in paganism all the time. The divine beings always incarnate in different forms....

Out of this identity of the immanent and the transcendent, the gods of the great mythologies have developed in Greece and in the Semitic nations and in India. There we find incarnations as the immanent element of the divine....

[T]he second element in the immanent religious symbolism [is] the sacramental. The sacramental is nothing else than some reality becoming the bearer of the Holy in a special way and under special circumstances. In this sense, the Lord's Supper, or better the materials in the Lord's Supper, are symbolic. Now you will ask perhaps, "only symbolic?" That sounds as if there were something more than symbolic, namely, "literal." But the literal is not more but less than symbolic. If we speak of those dimensions of reality which we cannot approach in any other way than by symbols, then symbols are not used in terms of "only" but in terms of that which is necessary, of that which we *must* apply. Sometimes, because of nothing more than the confusion of signs with symbols, the phrase "only a symbol" means "only a sign." And then the question is justified. "Only a sign?" "No." The sacrament is not only a sign....

Then there is the third element on the immanent level. Many things—like special parts of the church building, like the candles, like the water at the entrance of the Roman Church, like the cross in all churches, especially Protestant churches—were originally only signs, but in use became symbols; call them sign-symbols, signs which have become symbols.

The Truth of Religious Symbols

And now a last consideration—namely, the truth of religious symbols. Here we must distinguish a negative, a positive, and an absolute statement. First the negative statement. Symbols are independent of any empirical criticism. You cannot kill a symbol by criticism in terms of natural sciences or in terms of historical research. As was said, symbols can only die if the situation in which they have been created has passed. They are not on a level on which empirical criticism can dismiss them. Here are two examples, both connected with Mary, the mother of Jesus, as Holy Virgin. First of all you have here a symbol which has died in Protestantism by the changed situation of the relation to God. The special, direct, immediate relationship to God, makes any mediating power impossible. Another reason which has made this symbol disappear is the negation of the ascetic element which is implied in the glorification of virginity. And as long as the Protestant religious situation lasts it cannot be reestablished....

Another example is the story of the virginal birth of Jesus. This is from the point of view of historical research a most obviously legendary story, unknown to Paul and to John. It is a late creation, trying to make understandable the full possession of the divine Spirit of Jesus of Nazareth. [This symbol will die because] it is theologically quasiheretical. It takes away one of the fundamental doctrines of Chalcedon, viz., the classical Christian doctrine that the full humanity of Jesus must be maintained beside his whole divinity. A human being who has no human father has no full humanity. This story then has to be criticized on inner-symbolic grounds, but not on historical grounds. This is the negative statement about the truth of religious symbols. Their truth is their adequacy to the religious situation in which they are created, and their inadequacy to another situation is their untruth. In the last sentence both the positive and the negative statement about symbols are contained.

Religion is ambiguous and every religious symbol may become idolatrous, may be demonized, may elevate itself to ultimate validity although nothing is ultimate but the ultimate itself; no religious doctrine and no religious ritual may be. If Christianity claims to have a truth superior to any other truth in its symbolism, then it is the symbol of the cross in which this is expressed, the cross of the Christ. He who himself embodies the fullness of the divine's presence sacrifices himself in order not to become an idol, another god beside God, a god into whom the disciples wanted to make him. And therefore the decisive story is the story in which he accepts the title "Christ" when Peter offers it to him. He accepts it under the one condition that he has to go to Jerusalem to suffer and to die, which means to deny the idolatrous tendency even with respect to himself. This is at the same time the criterion of all other symbols, and it is the criterion to which every Christian church should subject itself.

STUDY QUESTIONS

1. Discuss Tillich's distinction between signs and symbols. Include the many important functions of symbols.
2. For Tillich, religious symbols, which include religious language, open up a dimension of reality that literal language cannot describe. He posits God as the transcendent and ultimate reality, ground of being, wholly other. Exactly how, then, does religious language apply to God? How does Tillich think of the transcendent on the immanent level of appearances of the divine in space and time?
3. To take religious language literally, for Tillich, is to engage in idolatry. How so? To think that Jesus *is* God is idolatry on this account. What do you think?

Rosemary Radford Ruether

Sexism and God-Talk

Rosemary Radford Ruether (b. 1936) provided what was probably the first systematic critique of Christian theology from a feminist point of view. In the following selection, she argues that there is a superior–subordinate mind-set reflected in the patriarchal model of God. The traditional monotheistic language of "God as father" operates on the basis of a fundamental metaphor, deeply rooted in Western culture, which takes God as authoritative and male. Ruether believes that this perspective—tied to male-dominant language—has historically reinforced the oppression of women in a male-dominated, hierarchical social structure. But it has also reinforced aristocratic superiority of masters over slaves, king over subjects, etc. As a remedy to this improper hierarchical orientation, she develops a way of recovering female qualities in the divine that uses inclusive language for God, which draws from the experiences of both genders. For example, God is not simply to be understood as powerful but also as nurturing. Ruether's analysis includes treatment of the ancient nature religions in which male images and analogies for the deities were not superior to female ones. Reminding us of the biblical prohibition against idolatry, she warns that even masculine language that suggests that God is male and not female is a form of verbal idolatry with very severe consequences in society. Reminding us further that Christianity teaches that God is Spirit and not a bodily being, she recommends that we speak of and name the Divine—or "God/ess"—with female as well as male metaphors.

MALE GENDER AND MONOTHEISM

Male monotheism has been so taken for granted in Judeo-Christian culture that the peculiarity of imaging God solely through one gender has not been recognized. But such an image indicates a sharp departure from all previous human consciousness.

It is possible that the social origins of male monotheism lie in nomadic herding societies. These cultures lacked the female gardening role[1] and tended to image God as the Sky-Father.[2] Nomadic religions were characterized by exclusivism and an aggressive, hostile relationship to the agricultural people of the land and their religions.

Male monotheism reinforces the social hierarchy of patriarchal rule through its religious system in a way that was not the case with the paired images of God and Goddess. God is modeled after the patriarchal ruling class and is seen as addressing this class of males directly, adopting them as his "sons." They are his representatives, the responsible partners of the covenant with him. Women as wives now become symbolically repressed as the dependent servant class. Wives, along with children and servants, represent those ruled over and owned by the patriarchal class. They relate to man as he relates to God. A symbolic hierarchy is set up: God-male-female. Women no longer stand in direct relation to God; they are connected to God secondarily, through the male. This hierarchical order is evident in the structure of patriarchal law in the Old Testament, in which only the male heads of families are addressed directly. Women, children, and servants are referred to indirectly through their duties and property relations to the patriarch.[3] In the New Testament this hierarchical "order" appears as a cosmic principle:

> But I want to understand that the head of every man is Christ, the head of a woman is her husband, and the head of Christ is God…For a man ought not to cover his head, since he is the image and glory of God, but the woman is the glory of man. (1 Cor. 11:3, 7)

Male monotheism becomes the vehicle of a psychocultural revolution of the male ruling class in its relationship to surrounding reality. Whereas ancient myth had seen the Gods and Goddesses as within the matrix of one physical-spiritual reality, male monotheism begins to split reality into a dualism of transcendent Spirit (mind, ego) and inferior and dependent physical nature. Bodiless ego or spirit is seen as primary, existing before the cosmos. The physical world is "made" as an artifact by transcendent, disembodied mind or generated through some process of devolution from spirit to matter.

Both the Hebrew Genesis story and the Platonic creation story of *Timaeus* retain reminiscences of the idea of primal matter as something already existing that is ordered or shaped by the Creator God. But this now becomes the lower pole in the hierarchy of being. Thus the hierarchy of God-male-female does not merely make woman secondary in relation to

God, it also gives her a negative identity in relation to the divine. Whereas the male is seen essentially as the image of the male transcendent ego or God, woman is seen as the image of the lower, material nature. Although both are seen as "mixed natures," the male identity points "above" and the female "below." Gender becomes a primary symbol for the dualism of transcendence and immanence, spirit and matter.

THE GODDESS IN JEWISH AND CHRISTIAN MONOTHEISM

In Hebrew religious development, male monotheism does not, by any means, succeed in simply supplanting the older world of Gods and Goddesses or the cult of salvation through renewal of nature-society. Rather it imposes itself on this older world, assimilating, transforming, and reversing its symbol systems. Thus, for example, the ancient myth of the Sacred Marriage lives on in Yahwism, but in a reversed form that uses this story to exert the possessive and judgmental relation of the patriarchal God over the people of agricultural society. The patriarchal God, not the Goddess, is the dominant partner in the Sacred Marriage. The female has been reduced to the human partner as servant to God. In the prophet Hosea, the marriage symbol is taken over judgmentally as a diatribe against the "harlotry" of Israelites, who prefer Baal, the vegetation and rain God of the Canaanites, to Yahweh, the nomadic patriarch. Yahweh is depicted as the angry and threatening husband who will punish his unfaithful bride with summary divorce.

But he is also described as winning her back and making her faithful to him by drawing her out into the desert wildness.…

BEYOND MALE GENDER GOD-LANGUAGE IN THE BIBLICAL TRADITION

The Prophetic God

Although the predominantly male images and roles of God make Yahwism an agent in the sacralization of patriarchy, there are critical elements in Biblical theology that contradict this view of God. By patriarchy we mean not only the subordination of females to males, but the whole structure of Father-ruled society: aristocracy over serfs, masters over slaves, king over subjects, racial overlords over colonized people. Religions that reinforce hierarchical stratification use the Divine as the apex of this system of privilege and control. The religions of the ancient Near East link the Gods and Goddesses with the kings and queens, the priests and priestesses, the warrior and temple aristocracy of a stratified society. The Gods and Goddesses mirror this ruling class and form its heavenly counter-part. The divinities also show mercy and favor to the distressed, but in the manner of noblesse oblige....

The Davidic monarchy represents a capitulation of Judaic leadership to the city-state model of power, but the prophets of Israel continue the tradition of protest against the hierarchical, urban, landowning society that deprives and oppresses the rural peasantry. This established at the heart of Biblical religion a motif of protest against the status quo of ruling-class privilege and the deprivation of the poor. God is seen as a critic of this society, a champion of the social victims. Salvation is envisioned as deliverance from systems of social oppression and as restoration of an egalitarian peasant society of equals, "where each have their own vine and fig tree and none need be afraid" (Mic. 4:4).

Although Yahwism dissents against class hierarchy, it issues no similar protest against gender discrimination. There are several reasons (not to be seen as "excuses") for this. First, there is always a sociology of knowledge in social ideology, even in liberation ideology. Those male prophets who were aware of oppression by rich urbanites or dominating empires were not similarly conscious of their own oppression of dependents—women and slaves—in the patriarchal family. Only the emergence of women conscious of their oppression could have applied the categories of protest to women. This did not happen in Yahwism. Second, although Hebrew religion was to shape systems of patriarchal law that emphasize gender dualism and hierarchy, in its protest against Canaanite urban society it would have known powerful females,

queens, priestesses, and wealthy landowners who functioned as oppressors. It would have been difficult to recognize women as an oppressed gender group when the primary social stratification integrated some women into roles of power. Indeed, perhaps it was not until the early modern period that the perception of women as marginalized by gender became stronger than the perception of women as divided by class. Only then could a feminist movement arise that protested the subjugation of women as a group.

The New Testament contains a renewal and radicalization of prophetic consciousness, now applied to marginalized groups in a universal, nontribal context. Consequently, it is possible to recognize as liberated by God social groups overlooked in Old Testament prophecy. Class, ethnicity, and gender are now specifically singled out as the divisions overcome by redemption in Christ. In the New Testament stories, gender is recognized as an additional oppression within oppressed classes and ethnic groups.[4]...

The Liberating Sovereign

A second antipatriarchal use of God-language occurs in the Old and New Testaments when divine sovereignty and fatherhood are used to break the ties of bondage under human kings and fathers. Abraham is called into an adoptive or covenanted relation with God only by breaking his ties with his family, leaving behind the graves of his ancestors.[5] The God of Exodus establishes a relationship with the people that breaks their ties with the ruling overlords. As the people flee from the land of bondage, Pharaoh and his horsemen are drowned. God's kingship liberates Israel from human kings. The antimonarchical tradition inveighs against Israel's capitulation to the customs of the surrounding people by adopting kingship.

These Old Testament traditions are developed in Jesus' teaching. It has been often pointed out that Jesus uses a unique word for God. By adopting the word *Abba* for God, he affirms a primary relationship to God based on love and trust; *Abba* was the intimate word used by children in the family for their fathers. It is not fully conveyed by English terms such as *Daddy*, for it was also a term an adult could use of an older man to signify a combination of respect and affection.[6] But is it enough to conclude from this use of *Abba* that Jesus transforms the patriarchal concept of divine fatherhood into what might be called a maternal or nurturing concept of God as loving, trustworthy parent?

The early Jesus movement characteristically uses this concept of God as *Abba* to liberate the community from human dominance-dependence relationships based on kinship ties or master-servant relationships. In the Gospel tradition, joining the new community of Jesus creates a rupture with traditional family ties and loyalties. In order to follow Jesus one must "hate" (that is, put aside one's loyalty to) father and mother, sisters and brothers (Luke 14:26; Matt. 10:37–38). The patriarchal family is replaced by a new community of brothers and sisters (Matt. 12:46–50; Mark 3:31–35; Luke 8:19–21). This new community is a community of equals, not of master and servants, father and children. Matthew 23:1–10 states that the relationship to God as *Abba* abolishes all father-child, master-servant relations between people within the Jesus community: "You are to call no man father, master or Lord." The relationship between Christians is to be one of mutual service and not of mastery and servitude....

The Proscription of Idolatry

A third Biblical tradition that is important to a feminist theology is the proscription of idolatry. Israel is to make no picture or graven image of God; no pictorial or verbal representation of God can be taken literally. By contrast, Christian sculpture and painting represents God as a powerful old man with a white beard, even crowned and robed in the insignia of human kings or the triple tiara of the Pope. The message created by such images is that God is both similar to and represented by the patriarchal leadership, the monarchs and the Pope. Such imaging of God should be judged for what it is—as idolatry, as the setting up of certain human figures as the privileged images and representations of God. To the extent that such political and ecclesiastical patriarchy incarnates unjust and oppressive relationships, such images of God become sanctions of evil.

The proscription of idolatry must also be extended to verbal pictures. When the word *Father* is taken literally to mean that God is male and not female, represented by males and not females, then this word becomes idolatrous. The Israelite tradition is circumspect about the verbal image, printing it without vowel signs. The revelation to Moses in the burning bush gives as the name of God only the enigmatic "I am what I shall be." God is person without being imaged by existing social roles. God's being is open-ended, pointing both to what is and to what can be.

Classical Christian theology teaches that all names for God are analogies. The tradition of negative or *apophatic* theology emphasizes the unlikeness between God and human words for God. That tradition corrects the tendency to take verbal images literally; God is like but also unlike any verbal analogy. Does this not mean that male words for God are not in any way superior to or more appropriate than female analogies? God is both male and female and neither male nor female. One needs inclusive language for God that draws on the images and experiences of both genders. This inclusiveness should not become more abstract. Abstractions often conceal androcentric assumptions and prevent the shattering of the male monopoly on God-language, as in "God is not male. He is Spirit." Inclusiveness can happen only by naming God/ess in female as well as male metaphors.

Notes

1. M. Kay Martin and Barbara Voorheis, *The Female of the Species* (New York: Columbia University Press, 1975).
2. E. O. James, *The Worship of the Sky God: A Comparative Study of Semitic and Indo-European Religion* (London: Athlone Press, 1963).
3. Phyllis Bird, "Women in the Old Testament," in *Religion and Sexism: Images of Women in the Jewish and Christian Traditions,* ed. R. Ruether (New York: Simon and Schuster, 1974), pp. 48–57.

4. See, for example, Matt. 15:21–28; Mark 5:25–33; Luke 7:11–17, 7:36–50, 10:38–42, 13:10–17.
5. Robert Hamerton-Kelly, *God the Father: Theology and Patriarchy in the Teachings of Jesus* (Philadelphia: Fortress, 1979), pp. 21–28.
6. Ibid., pp. 70–81.

Study Questions

1. Describe how Ruether thinks that ancient patriarchal societies gave rise to male monotheism, that is, a masculine concept of God. According to Ruether, what problems has male monotheism caused?

2. As a corrective to male monotheism, Ruether proposes reviving goddess imagery. Describe the goddess religious orientation and explain how she thinks it will help solve problems that are caused by male monotheism. Although she identifies a biblical tradition of male dominance, how does Ruether argue that there are biblical grounds for overthrowing it?

3. Ruether recognizes that God, as spirit, is neither male nor female, which are physical realities. She speaks of the tradition of apophatic theology, which emphasizes the unlikeness between God and creatures, and argues for inclusive language for God that is inherently metaphorical. Review her points related to these issues and evaluate.

William P. Alston

Speaking Literally of God

⤚⟶

William P. Alston (1921–2009) brings his widely recognized expertise in the philosophy of language to bear upon issues related to religious language. In the following essay, he explores the question of whether we can speak literally of God. Recognizing the popular professional opinion that our talk of God must be somehow nonliteral (e.g., symbolic, metaphorical, figurative), he develops an argument for how religious language can be used literally. Alston carefully frames the question as follows: can we form subject-predicate sentences that can possibly be asserted truly of God conceived as an incorporeal being? In pursuing this question, he restricts his study to *personalistic predicates*—what he calls "P-predicates"—that distinctively apply to personal agents. The range of personalistic predicates, of course, includes *mental predicates* (pertaining to cognitions, feelings, and other psychological states) and *action predicates* (pertaining to what an agent does). Alston looks at the concept of God's incorporeality to see whether it provides a sovereign objection to applying personalistic predicates to God and concludes that it does not. There simply is nothing inherent in the concept of God's incorporeality to prevent such predicates from applying to God. Alston appreciates the fact that much more work remains to be done to build a comprehensive argument that we can speak literally of God—work that would include an analysis of timelessness, immutability, and other classical divine attributes to see if they might constitute a bar to speaking literally of God. Nonetheless, Alston believes that his present argument shows that in principle we can indeed speak literally of God.

LITERAL PREDICATION
AND THEOLOGY

In this essay we shall be concerned with only one stretch of talk about God, but a particularly central stretch—subject-predicate statements in which the subject term is used to refer to God. I mean this to be limited to *statements* in a strict sense, utterances that are put forward with a "truth claim." This is a crucial stretch of the territory, because any other talk that involves reference to God presupposes the truth of one or more statements about God. For example, if I ask God to give me courage, I am presupposing that God is the sort of being to whom requests can be sensibly addressed. Thus our more specific topic concerns whether terms can be literally predicated of God.

According to contemporary Protestant theologians of a liberal cast, it is almost an article of faith that this is impossible. Let us be somewhat more explicit than people like that generally are, as to just what is being denied. When someone says that we cannot speak literally of God, that person does not mean to deny us the capacity to form a subject-predicate sentence that contains a subject term used to refer to God, making a literal use of the predicate term and uttering the sentence with the claim that the predicate is true of the subject. I could easily refute that denial here and now—"God has commanded us to love one another." I have just done it. But presumably it is not that sort of ability that is in question. It is rather a question as to whether any such truth claim can succeed. What is being denied is that any predicate term, used literally, can be *truly applied* to God, or as we might say, that any predicate is *literally true* of God.

But even this is stronger than a charitable interpretation would require. Presumably, no one who thinks it possible to refer to God would deny that some negative predicates are literally true of God—for instance, incorporeal, immutable, or not-identical-with-Richard-Nixon. Nor would all extrinsic predicates be ruled out; it would be difficult to deny that "thought of now by me" could be literally true of God. Now it is notoriously difficult to draw an exact line between positive and negative predicates; and the class of predicates I am calling "extrinsic" is hardly easier to demarcate. It is either very difficult or impossible to give a precise characterization of the class of predicates to which the deniers of literal talk should be addressing themselves. Here I shall confine myself to the following brief statement. The reason various predicates are obvious examples of "negative" or "extrinsic" predicates is that they do not "tell us anything" about the subject—about the nature or operations of the subject. Let us call predicates that do "tell us something" about such matters "intrinsic" predicates. We may then take it that an opponent of literal theological talk is denying that any *intrinsic*

predicate can be literally true of God. It will be noted that "intrinsic" predicates include various *relational* predicates, such as "made the heavens and the earth" and "spoke to Moses."

Various reasons have been given for the impossibility of literal predication in theology. Among the most prominent have been the following.

1. Since God is an absolutely undifferentiated unity, and since all positive predications impute complexity to their subject, no such predications can be true of God. This line of thought is most characteristic of the mystical tradition, but something like it can be found in other theologies as well.
2. God is so "transcendent," so "wholly other," that no concepts we can form would apply to him.
3. The attempt to apply predicates literally to God inevitably leads to paradoxes.

It is the second reason that bulks largest in twentieth-century Protestant theology. It has taken several forms, one of the more fashionable being the position of Paul Tillich that (a) God is not *a* being but Being-Itself, since anything that is *a* being would not be an appropriate object of "ultimate concern"; and (b) only what is *a* being can be literally characterized.

In my opinion, all these arguments are radically insufficient to support the sweeping denial that *any* intrinsic predicate can be literally true of God. But this is not the place to go into that. Nor will I take up the cudgel for the other side on this issue and argue that it must be possible for *some* intrinsic predicates or other to be literally true of God. Instead I will focus on a particularly important class of predicates—those I shall call "personalistic" (or, following Strawson, "P-predicates")—and consider the more specific question, whether any P-predicates can be literally true of God. Or rather, as I shall make explicit shortly, I will consider one small part of this very large question. By "personalistic" predicates, I mean those that, as a group, apply to a being only if that being is a "personal agent"—an agent that carries out intentions, plans, or purposes in its actions, that acts in the light of knowledge or belief; a being whose actions express attitudes and are guided by standards and principles; a being capable of communicating with other such agents and entering into other forms of personal relations with them. The conception of God as a personal agent is deeply embedded in Christianity and in other theistic religions. Communication between God and man, verbal and otherwise, is at the heart of the Judaeo-Christian tradition. Equally fundamental is the thought of God as a being who lays down commands, injunctions, rules, and regulations, and who monitors compliance or noncompliance; who created the world and directs it to the attainment of certain ends; who enters into covenants; who rewards and punishes; who loves and forgives; who acts in history and in the lives of men to carry out His purposes. The last few sentences indicate some of the kinds of P-predicates that have traditionally been applied to God.

WHAT DOES IT MEAN TO SPEAK LITERALLY?

Before coming to grips with this problem, we must provide some clarification of the central term "literal." To begin on a negative note, despite the frequent occurrence of phrases such as "literal *meaning*" and "literal *sense*," I believe that such phrases constitute a confused or at least a loose way of thinking about the subject. To get straight about the matter, we need to keep a firm hold on the distinction between *language* and *speech*. A (natural) language is an abstract system, a system of sound types or, in principle, types of other sorts of perceptible items. The systematicity involved is both "internal" and "external." The phonology, morphology, and syntax of a language reveal its internal system—the ways its elements can be combined to form larger units. The external system is revealed by the semantics of the language—the way units of language have the function of "representing" things in the world and features of the world.[1] A language serves as a means of communication; in fact, it is plausible to look on the entire complex structure as "being there" in order to make a language an effective device for communication. Speech, on the other hand, is the *use* of language in communication (using "speech" in an extended sense, to cover written as well as oral communication). It is what we *do* in the

course of exploiting a linguistic system for purposes of communication.

Now the fact that a given word or phrase has the meaning(s) or sense(s) that it has is a fact about the language; it is part of the semantic constitution of the language.[2] Thus it is a semantic fact about English that "player" has among its meanings:

1. an idler;
2. one who plays some (specified) game;
3. a gambler;
4. an actor.[3]

It is partly the fact that a word *has* a certain meaning in a language that gives the word its usability for communication; this fact constitutes one of the linguistic resources we draw upon in saying what we have to say.

The term "literal," on the other hand, stands for a certain way of *using* words, phrases, and so on; it stands for a mode of *speech* rather than for a type of meaning or any other feature of *language*. As such, it stands in contrast with a family of *figurative* uses of terms—"figures of speech," as they are appropriately termed in the tradition—the most familiar of which is metaphor. Let us make explicit the difference between literal and metaphorical uses, restricting ourselves to uses of predicates in subject-predicate statements.

We may think of each meaning of a predicate term as "correlating" the term with some, possibly very complex, property.[4] Different theories of meaning provide differing accounts of the nature of this correlation. Thus the "ideational" theory of meaning, found for example in Locke's *Essay*, holds that a meaning of a predicate term correlates it with a certain property—P—*iff* the term functions as a sign of the *idea* of P in communication. Other theories provide other accounts. It will be convenient to speak of the predicate term as "signifying" or "standing for" the correlated property.

Now when I make a *literal* use of a predicate term (in one of its meanings) in a subject-predicate statement, I utter the sentence with the claim that the property signified by the predicate term is possessed by the subject (i.e., the referent of the subject term), or holds between the subject, if the predicate is a relational one. Thus, if I make a literal use of "player" in saying "He's one of the players," I am claiming, let us say, that the person referred to has the property specified in the fourth definition listed above. And if my statement is true, if the person referred to really does have that property, we may say that "player" is *literally true* of him in that sense—does *literally apply* to him in that sense.

But suppose I say, as Shakespeare has Macbeth say, "Life's...a poor player that struts and frets his hour upon the stage and then is heard no more." It is clear that life is not really an actor; nor, if we surveyed the other established meanings of "player," would we find any properties signified that are exemplified by life. Hence in uttering Macbeth's sentence, I will, if I am sensible, be using the term "player" metaphorically rather than literally. Since figurative uses appear in this paper only as a foil for literal uses, I will not be able to embark on the complex task of characterizing the figures of speech. Suffice it to say that when I use a term metaphorically, I exploit some meaning the term has in the language, but not in the straightforward way that is involved in literal usage. Rather than claiming that the property signified by the predicate does apply to the subject(s), I do something more complex, more indirect. I first, so to speak, "present" the hearer with the sort of thing to which the term literally applies (call it an exemplar) and then suggest that the exemplar can be taken as a "model" of the subject(s); I suggest that by considering the exemplar, one will thereby be put in mind of certain features of the subject(s). In the example just given, the exemplar is an (insignificant) actor who plays his part in a stage production and then disappears from the view of the audience; the suggestion is that a human life is like that in some significant respect(s).[5]

The term "literal" has picked up a number of adventitious associations in recent times. I think particularly of "precise," "univocal," "specific," "empirical," and "ordinary." However common the conflation, it is simply a confusion to suppose that "literal," in the historically distinctive sense just set out, implies any of the features just mentioned. Meanings that words have in a language can be more or less vague, open-textured, unspecific, and otherwise indeterminate. Hence I can be using words literally and still be speaking vaguely, ambiguously, or unspecifically.

Again, I can be using my words just as literally when asking questions, cursing fate, or expressing rage, as when I am soberly asserting that the cat is on the mat. The conflation of "literal" with "empirical," however, is more than a vulgar error; it reflects a conviction as to the conditions under which a word can acquire a meaning in the language. If this requires contact with "experience" in one or another of the ways spelled out in empiricist theories of meaning, then only terms with empirical meanings can be used literally, for only such terms *have* established senses. But that does not follow merely from the meaning of "literal"; it also requires an empiricist theory of meaning, and it is by no means clear that any such theory is acceptable.

It might be thought that after the term "literal" has been stripped of all these interesting connotations, the question as to whether we can speak literally of God has lost its importance. Not so. To demonstrate its importance, we merely need appeal to some highly plausible principles which connect meanings and concepts. It seems clear that I can attach a certain meaning to a predicate term only if I have a concept of the property signified by the term when used with that meaning; otherwise, how can I "get at" the property so as to signify it by that term? And on the other hand, if I do have a concept of that property, it could not be impossible for me to use a term to signify that property. And if a sufficient number of members of my linguistic community share that concept, it could not be, in principle, impossible for a term to signify that property in the language. Thus it is possible for a term in a certain language to signify a certain property *iff* speakers of that language have or can have a concept of that property. Hence our language can contain terms that stand for intrinsic properties of God *iff* we can form concepts of intrinsic properties of God. And since we can make true literal predications of God *iff* our language contains terms that stand for properties exemplified by God, we may say, finally, that we can speak literally of God (in the relevant sense of true literal predication) *iff* we can form concepts of intrinsic divine properties.[6] And whether this last is true is *obviously* an important issue—one that has been at the very center of metatheology from the beginning.

The question whether certain terms can be literally applied to God is often identified with the question whether those terms are literally true of God in senses they bear outside theology. Thus with respect to P-predicates, it is often supposed that God can be spoken of as literally having knowledge and intentions, as creating, commanding, and forgiving, only if those terms are literally true of God in the same senses as those in which they are literally true of human beings. The reason usually given for this supposition is that we first come to attach meaning to these terms by learning what it is for human beings to command, forgive, and so on, and that there is no other way we can proceed. We cannot begin by learning what it is for God to know, command, or forgive. I do not want to contest this claim about the necessary order of language learning, though there is much to be said on both sides. I will confine myself to pointing out that even if this claim is granted, it does not follow that terms can be literally applied to God only in senses in which they also are true of human beings and other creatures. For the fact that we must begin with creatures is quite compatible with the supposition that at some later stage terms take on special technical senses in theology. After all, that is what happens in science. There, too, it can be plausibly argued that we can learn theoretical terms in science only if we have already learned commonsense meanings of these and other terms—senses in which the terms are true of ordinary middle-sized objects. But even if that is true, it does not prevent such terms as "force" and "energy" from taking on new technical senses in the development of sophisticated theories. Why should not the same be true of theology?

Many will claim that the same cannot be true of theology, because the conditions that permit technical senses to emerge in science do not obtain in theology. For example, it may be claimed that theological systems do not have the kind of explanatory efficacy possessed by scientific theories. These are important questions, but I can sidestep them for now, because I will restrict myself here to whether (some) P-predicates can be true of God in (some of) the senses in which they are true of human beings. The only qualification I make on that is that I shall

consider a simple transformation of certain human action predicates—"simple," in that the change does not involve any radical conceptual innovation. The revised action predicates are fundamentally of the same sort as human action predicates, though different in some details.

Whether certain predicates are literally true of God depends on both parties to the transaction; it depends both on what God is like and on the content of the predicates. To carry out a proper discussion of the present issue, I would need to (a) present and defend an account of the nature of God, and (b) present and defend an analysis of such P-predicates as will be considered. That would put us in a position to make some well-grounded judgments as to whether such predicates could be literally true of God. Needless to say, I will not have time for all that; I would not have had time, even if I had cut the preliminary cackle and buckled down to the job straight away. Hence I must scale down my aspirations. Instead of trying to "tell it like it is" with God, I shall simply pick one commonly recognized attribute of God—incorporeality—which has been widely thought to rule out personal agency, and I shall consider whether it does so. My main reasons for focusing on incorporeality, rather than on simplicity, infinity, timelessness, or immutability, are that it, much more than the others, is widely accepted today as a divine attribute and that it has bulked large in some recent arguments against the literal applicability of P-predicates. On the side of the predicates, I shall consider those types of analyses that are, in my judgment, the strongest contenders and ask what each of them implies as to literal applicability to an incorporeal being.[7]

This investigation is only a fragment of the total job. It is radically incomplete from both sides, and especially from the side of the divine nature. Even if we satisfy ourselves that personalistic terms can be literally true of an incorporeal being, that will by no means suffice to show that they are literally true of God. God is not just any old incorporeal being. There may well be other divine attributes that inhibit us from thinking literally of God as a personal agent—simplicity, infinity, immutability, and timelessness. But sufficient unto the day is the problem thereof.

MENTAL PREDICATES AND GOD

P-predicates may be conveniently divided into mental or psychological predicates (M-predicates) and action predicates (A-predicates). M-predicates have to do with cognitions, feelings, emotions, attitudes, wants, thoughts, fantasies, and other internal psychological states, events, and processes. A-predicates have to do with what, in a broad sense, an agent *does*. For reasons that will emerge in the course of the discussion, it will be best to begin with theories of M-predicates. I shall oscillate freely between speaking of the *meanings* of predicates and the *concepts* those predicates express by virtue of having those meanings.

The main divide in theories of M-predicates concerns whether they are properly defined in terms of their behavioral manifestations.[8] On the negative side of that issue is the view that was dominant from the seventeenth through the nineteenth century—what we may call the Private Paradigm (PP) view. According to this position, the meaning of an M-predicate—for example, "feels depressed"—is given, for each person, by certain paradigms of feelings of depression within his own experience. By "feels depressed" I mean a state such as X, Y, Z,..., where these are clear cases of feeling depressed that I can remember having experienced. We might say that on this model an M-predicate acquires meaning through "inner ostension"; I attach meaning to the term by "associating" it with samples of the state it signifies. On the PP view, an M-predicate is not properly defined in terms of its invariable, normal, or typical behavioral manifestations. Even if feelings of depression are typically manifested by droopy appearance, slowness of response, and lack of vigor, it is no part of the *meaning* of the term that these are the typical manifestations. Our *concept* of feeling depressed is such that it makes sense to think of a world in which feelings of depression typically manifest themselves in alert posture and vigorous reactions. Since the term simply designates certain feeling qualities, it is just a matter of fact that feelings of depression manifest themselves in the way they do.[9]

There are solid reasons for the PP view, especially for feeling and sensation terms. (1) If I have never felt depressed, then in an important sense, I do not understand the term, for I do not know *what it is like* to feel depressed; I simply do not have the concept of that sort of feeling. (2) My knowledge of my own feelings is quite independent of my knowledge of my behavior or demeanor; I do not have to watch myself in a mirror to know how I feel. Hence it seems that what I know when I know how I feel cannot consist in any behavioral manifestations or tendencies thereto. (3) It does seem an *intelligible* supposition that the kind of feeling we call a feeling of depression should be manifested in ways that are radically different from those that do in fact obtain. And the PP account allows for this.

However, the PP account has been under attack throughout this century. There are four main motives for dissatisfaction. (1) If feeling depressed is not, by definition, typically manifested in certain ways, then how can I tell what other people are feeling, on the basis of their behavior and demeanor? For I can discover a correlation between a certain kind of feeling and certain kinds of behavior only in my own case; and how can I generalize from one case? Thus the PP view has been felt to rule out knowledge of the mental states of others. (2) How can you and I have any reason to suppose that we attach the same meaning to any M-predicate, if each of us learns the meaning from nonshareable paradigms? How can I tell whether my paradigms of feeling depressed are like your paradigms? Thus the PP view has been thought to sap our conviction that we share a public language for talking about the mind. (3) On the widely influential Verifiability Theory of Meaning, the meaning of a term is given by specifying the ways in which we can tell that it applies. Since we can tell whether M-predicates apply to others by observing their demeanor and behavior, the latter must enter into the meaning of the term. (4) Wittgenstein mounted a very influential attack on the possibility of attaching meaning to terms by private ostension.[10]

These arguments against PP support the idea that mental states are identified in terms of their typical manifestations in overt behavior and demeanor. We may use the term Logical Connectionism (LC) as a general term for views of this sort, on the ground that these views hold that there is a logical (conceptual) connection between a mental state and its manifestations.

The general concept of LC allows plenty of room for variation. The simplest form that is not wildly implausible is Logical Behaviorism (LB). LB may be formulated as the view that an M-predicate signifies a set of behavioral dispositions—dispositions to behave a certain way, given certain conditions.[11] Thus a logical behaviorist would explain "S feels depressed" in some such way as this: If someone makes a suggestion to S, S will respond slowly and without enthusiasm; if S is presented with something S usually likes, S will not smile as S normally does in such situations, and so on.[12] LB is not nearly as prominent now as a decade or so ago, and in my opinion, there are excellent reasons for this decline. The fatal difficulty is this. The response tendencies associated with a particular case of a mental state will depend upon the total psychological field of the moment—that is, the other mental states present at the time. For example, whether a person who feels depressed will react in a characteristically depressed way depends upon whether he is sufficiently motivated to conceal his condition. If he is, the typical manifestation may well not be forthcoming. Thus any particular behavioral reaction emerges from the total contemporary psychological field and is not wholly determined by any one component thereof. This consideration should inhibit us from attempting to identify any particular M-concept with the concept of any particular set of behavioral dispositions.

Under the impact of these considerations, more subtle forms of LC have developed, for which we may use the generic term, "Functionalism." The general idea of Functionalism is that each M-concept is a concept of a certain functional role in the operation of the psyche. A major emphasis in this position has been the functional character of M-concepts. In attributing a certain belief, attitude, or feeling to S, we are committing ourselves to the position that a certain function is being carried out in S's psyche, or at least that S is prepared to carry it out if the need arises. We are not committing ourselves on the physical (or spiritual) structure or composition of whatever is performing this function; our concept is neutral as to that. M-concepts, on this position, are

functional in essentially the same way as the concept of a mousetrap. A mousetrap, by definition, is a device for catching mice; the definition is neutral as to the composition and structure of devices that perform this function. That is why it is possible to build a better mousetrap.[13]

To exploit this initial insight, the functionalist will have to find a way of specifying functional roles in the psyche. It is now generally assumed by functionalists that the basic function of the psyche as a whole is the production of overt behavior. That is why Functionalism counts as a form of LC. To understand the concept of belief is, at least in part, to understand the role of beliefs in the production of behavior. But "at least in part" is crucial; it is what enables Functionalism to escape the above objections to LB. Functionalism is thoroughly systemic. The vicissitudes of LB have taught it to avoid the supposition that each distinguishable mental state is related separately to overt behavior. It has thoroughly internalized the point that a given belief, attitude, or feeling gives rise to a certain distinctive mode of behavior only in conjunction with the rest of the contemporary psychological field. Therefore in specifying the function of an enthusiasm for Mozart, for example, in the production of behavior, we must specify the way that enthusiasm combines with each of various other combinations of factors to affect behavioral output. It also recognizes that intrapsychic functions enter into M-concepts. Our concept of the belief that it is raining now includes (a) the way this belief will combine with others to inferentially generate other beliefs, and (b) the way it will combine with an aversion to rainy weather, to produce dismay, as well as (c) the way it will combine with an aversion to getting wet, to produce the behavior of getting out one's umbrella. Clearly, a full functionalist specification of an M-concept would be an enormously complicated affair.[14]

With an eye to putting some flesh on this skeleton, consider this attempt by R. B. Brandt and Jaegwon Kim to formulate a functionalist analysis of the ordinary concept of *want*, conceived in a broad sense as any state in which the object of the "want" has what Lewin called positive valence for the subject.[15]

"X wants p" has the meaning it does for us because we believe roughly the following statements.

1. If, given that x had not been expecting p but now suddenly judged that p would be the case, x would feel joy, then x wants p.

2. If, given that x had been expecting p but then suddenly judged that p would not be the case, x would feel disappointment, then x wants p.

3. If daydreaming about p is pleasant to x, then x wants p.

4. If x wants p, then, under favorable conditions, if x judges that doing A will probably lead to p and that not doing A will probably lead to not p, x will feel some impulse to do A.

5. If x wants p, then, under favorable conditions, if x thinks some means M is a way of bringing p about, x will be more likely to notice an M than he would otherwise have been.

6. If x wants p, then, under favorable conditions, if p occurs, without the simultaneous occurrence of events x does not want, x will be pleased.[16]

In terms of our general characterization of Functionalism, we can think of each of these lawlike generalizations as specifying a *function* performed by wants. Thus a "want" is the sort of state that (a) together with unexpected fulfillment, gives rise to feelings of joy; (b) renders daydreaming about its object pleasant, and so on. (c) is the crucial connection with behavior, though in this formulation it is quite indirect, coming through a connection with an "impulse" to perform a certain action.[17] This is in contrast to PP, which would view a want for p as a certain kind of introspectable state, event, or process with a distinctive "feel"—for instance, a sense of the attractiveness of p, or a felt urge to realize p.[18]

Now let us turn to the way these views bear upon the applicability of M-predicates to an incorporeal being. I believe it would be generally supposed that our two views have opposite consequences: that on a PP view, M-predicates could be applied to an incorporeal being, but not on an LC view. However, I will contest this received position to the extent of arguing that neither position presents any conceptual bar to the literal application of M-predicates.

First, a brief word about the bearing of the PP view before turning to the debate over LC, which is my main concern in this section. Presumably, an incorporeal subject could have states of consciousness with distinctive phenomenological qualities, just as well as we could. Hence terms that signify such states of consciousness would not be inapplicable in principle to such a being. But though I believe this is correct, I do not feel that it is of much significance for theology, and this for two reasons.

First, the PP account is most plausible with respect to feelings, sensations, and other M-states which clearly have a distinctive "feel." It is much less plausible with respect to "colorless" mental states such as beliefs, attitudes, thoughts, and intentions. We cannot hold an intention or a belief "before the mind" as we can a feeling of dismay, and thereby form a conception of "what it is like." But it is M-predicates of the colorless sort that are of most interest to theology. In thinking of God as a personal agent, we think of God as possessing (and using) knowledge, purpose, intention, and the like. Feelings and sensations either are not applicable to God at all, or they are of secondary importance. Theology quite properly avoids trying to figure out what it *feels* like to be God.

Second, suppose that one defends the applicability of M-predicates on a PP basis because he considers them inapplicable on an LC construal. This latter conviction would presumably be based on an argument similar to the one to be given shortly, to the effect that M-predicates, as analyzed in LC, are inapplicable to God because, as an incorporeal being, God is incapable of overt behavior. In that case, even if our theorist succeeds in showing that PP predicates can apply, he has won, at most a Pyrrhic victory. To secure application of M-predicates at the price of abandoning the idea that God acts in the world is to doom the enterprise to irrelevance. Whatever may be the case with the gods of Aristotle and the Epicureans, the God of the Judaeo-Christian tradition is preeminently a God who *acts*, in history and in the lives of individuals, not to mention His creation and preservation of the world. Hence even if, on the PP view, M-predicates are applicable to an incorporeal being incapable of overt action, that does nothing to show that M-predicates are applicable to the Judaeo-Christian God.

Turning now to LC, let us look at a typical statement by one who is arguing from an LC position.

> What would it be like for an x to be just loving without doing anything or being capable of doing anything?...Surely "to do something," "to behave in a certain way," is to make—though this is not all that it is—certain bodily movement....For it to make sense to speak of x's acting or failing to act, x must have a body. Thus if "love" is to continue to mean anything at all near to what it normally means, it is meaningless to say that God loves mankind. Similar considerations apply to the other psychological predicates tied to the concept of God.[19]

It will help us in evaluating this argument to set it out more carefully.

1. On LC, an M-concept is, at least in part, a concept of dispositions to overt behavior (perhaps through the mediation of other mental states).[20]
2. Overt behavior requires bodily movements of the agent.
3. An incorporeal being, lacking a body, cannot move its body.
∴4. An incorporeal being cannot engage in overt behavior.
5. A being that is, in principle, incapable of overt behavior cannot have dispositions to overt behavior.
∴6. M-concepts are, in principle, inapplicable to an incorporeal being.

This argument is certainly on sound ground in claiming that, on LC, an M-predicate is applicable to S only if A-predicates are so applicable. Its Achilles' heel, I will claim, is 2, the thesis that overt behavior requires bodily movements of the agent. My attack on that thesis will occupy the next section. Let us take the upshot of this section to be that, on the most plausible account of the M-predicates that are of most interest to theology, God can literally know, purpose, and will, only if God can literally perform overt actions. This result nicely mirrors the fundamental place of divine agency in Judaeo-Christian theology.

Before embarking on the discussion of A-predicates, I want to make two points.

First, there are forms of LC that do rule out the application of M-predicates to an incorporeal being. I am thinking of those views that put certain kinds of restrictions on the input, or output, of the psyche. Some forms of LB, for example, require that the behavioral output be specified in terms of bodily movements of the agent, and the input in terms of stimulations of the agent's sense receptors. Functionalist theories may also be so restricted. Clearly, M-predicates analyzed in this way are applicable only to beings capable of such inputs and outputs. But our concern in this paper is to determine whether any version of LC would allow the application of M-predicates to an incorporeal being.

Second, we should not suppose that the question of the applicability of A-predicates to an incorporeal being is prejudged by the fact that all cases of overt action with which we are most familiar involve bodily movements of the agent. A feature that is common to the familiar *denotata* of a term may not be reflected in the meaning of that term, even if this class of *denotata* is the one from which we learn the meaning of the term, and even if it contains the only *denotata* with which we are acquainted. It is doing small honor to human powers of conception to suppose that one must form one's concept of P in such a way as to be limited to the class of Ps from which the concept was learned. Surely we can think more abstractly and generically than that. Even though our concept of *animal* was formed solely from experience of land creatures, that concept might still be such that it contains only features that are equally applicable to fish. And even if that were not the case—even if the capacity to walk on legs is part of our concept of an animal—it may be that it can be easily extended to fish, merely by dropping out the feature just mentioned. The moral of the story is obvious. We cannot assume in advance that our concept of making, commanding, or forgiving includes the concept of bodily movements of the maker, commander, or forgiver. And even if it does, this may be a relatively peripheral component which can be sheared off, leaving intact a distinctive conceptual core.

ACTION PREDICATES AND GOD

Let us consider, then, whether it is conceptually possible for an incorporeal being to perform overt actions. Our entrée to that discussion will be a consideration of the vulnerable premise in the argument, the thesis that overt behavior requires bodily movements.

To understand the grounds for this thesis, we must introduce the notion of a *basic action*. Roughly speaking, a basic action is one that is performed *not* by or in (simultaneously) performing some other action. Thus if I sign my name, *that* is done by moving my hand in a certain way, so the action is not basic; but if moving my hand is *not* done *by* doing something else, it will count as a basic action. Just where to locate basic human actions is philosophically controversial. If contracting muscles in my hand is something I do (in the intended sense of "do"), then it seems that I move my hand *by* contracting my muscles, and moving my hand will not count as a basic action. Again, if sending neural impulses to the muscles is something I *do*, then it seems that I contract the muscles *by* sending neural impulses to them, and so the contraction of muscles will not count as a basic action. Since I do not have time to go into this issue, I shall simply follow a widespread practice and assume that all overt human basic actions consist in the movements of certain parts of the body which ordinarily would be thought to be under "voluntary control," such as the hand.

It follows from our explanation of the term "basic action" that every nonbasic action is done *by* performing a basic action. If we are further correct in ruling that every human basic action consists in moving some part of one's body, then it follows that every human nonbasic action is built on, or presupposes, some bodily movement of the agent. The relationship differs in different cases: Sometimes the nonbasic action involves an effect of some bodily movement(s), as in the action of knocking over a vase; sometimes it involves the bodily movement's falling under a rule or convention of some kind, as in signaling a turn. But whatever the details, it follows from what has been laid down thus far that a human being cannot do anything overt without moving some part of the body. Either the action is basic,

in which case it merely *consists* in moving some part of one's body; or it is not, in which case it is done by moving some part of one's body.

But granted that this is the way it is with human action, what does this have to do with A-*concepts*? As noted earlier, our concept of a ϕ never includes all the characteristics that are in fact common to ϕs we have experienced. So why should we suppose that our concepts of various human actions—making or commanding, for example—contain any reference to bodily movement?

Again it will be most useful to divide this question in accordance with the basic–nonbasic distinction. Our concepts of particular types of human basic actions certainly do involve specifications of bodily movements. This is because that is what such actions *are*. Their whole content is a certain kind of movement of a certain part of the body. That is what distinguishes one type of human basic action from another. Hence we cannot say what kind of basic action we are talking about without mentioning some bodily movement—stretching, kicking, raising the arm, or whatever. Clearly, A-predicates such as these are not literally applicable to an incorporeal being. But this will be no loss to theology. I take it that none of us is tempted to think that it could be literally true that God stretches out His arm or activates His vocal organs.

The more relevant question concerns the status of such human nonbasic A-predicates as "makes," "speaks," "commands," "forgives," "comforts," and "guides." In saying of S that he commanded me to love my neighbor, am I thereby committing myself to the proposition that S moved some part of his body? Is bodily movement of the agent part of what is *meant* by commanding?

One point at least is clear. Nonbasic human A-concepts do not, in general, carry any reference to particular types of bodily movements. There is indeed wide variation in this regard. At the specific end of the continuum, we have a predicate such as "kicks open the door," which clearly requires a certain kind of motion of a leg. But "make a soufflé" and "command" are more typical, in that the concept is clearly not tied to any particular *kind* of underlying bodily movement. I can issue a command orally or in writing. Indeed, in view of the fact that no limit can be placed on what can be used as a system of communication, any bodily movements whatever could, with the appropriate background, subserve the issuing of a command. In like manner, although there are normal or typical ways of moving the body for making a soufflé, we cannot suppose that these exhaust the possibilities. In this age of electronic marvels, one could presumably make a soufflé by pushing some buttons on a machine with one's toes.

Thus, if any reference to bodily movement is included in such A-concepts as making and commanding, it will have to be quite unspecific. The most we could have would be along these lines:

> Making a soufflé—causing a soufflé to come into being by some movements of one's body.
> Commanding—producing a command by some movements of one's body.[21]

But can we have even this much? Is it any part of the meaning of these terms, in the sense in which they are applied to human beings, that the external effects in question are produced by movements of the agent's body? No doubt it is completely obvious to all of us that human beings cannot bring about such consequences except by moving their bodies. But to repeat the point once more, it does not follow that this fact is built into human A-concepts. Perhaps our *concept* of making a soufflé is simply that of *bringing a soufflé into existence*, the concept being neutral as to how this is done.

What we have here is one of the numerous difficulties in distinguishing between what we mean by a term and what we firmly believe to be true of the things to which the term applies—in other words, distinguishing between analytic and synthetic truths. These persistent difficulties have been among the factors leading to widespread skepticism about the viability of such distinctions. But for our purpose we need not decide the issue. Let us yield to our opponent. If we can make our case even on the position most favorable to our opponent, we can ignore the outcome of this skirmish.

Let us suppose, then, that all human A-concepts do contain a bodily movement requirement. It clearly follows that no *human* A-concepts are applicable to an incorporeal being. But that by no means shows that no A-concepts are applicable. Why should we suppose that the A-concepts we apply to human beings exhaust the field? We must at least explore the possibility that we can form A-concepts that are (a) distinctively and recognizably action concepts and (b) do not require any bodily movements of the agent.

In order to do this we must bring out the distinctive features of A-concepts that make them concepts of *actions*. Thus far in discussing human A-concepts, we have gone only as far as the thesis that every human A-concept involves some reference to bodily movement. But that by no means suffices to make them concepts of *actions*. The concept of a heart beat or of a facial tic involves reference to bodily movements, but it is not a concept of an action. What else is required?

I will continue to use human A-concepts as my point of departure for the exploration of the general field, since that is where we get our general concept of action. And I will continue to concentrate on concepts of *basic* actions; since they are relatively simple, the crucial features of A-concepts stand out more clearly there.[22] To focus the discussion further, I shall restrict attention to *intentional* actions—those the agent "meant" to perform.[23]

Now, as intimated above, although every human basic action consists in moving some part of the body, not just any bodily movement constitutes a basic *action*. It is possible for my arm to move without my having *moved* it, as in automatic twitches and jerks. In order for it to be the case that I performed the basic action of raising my arm, some further condition must hold, over and above the fact that my arm rose. Thus we can pose the crucial question about the constitution of human basic actions in the classic Wittgensteinian form: "What is left over if I subtract the fact that my arm goes up from the fact that I raise my arm?"[24] Or, putting it the other way round, what must be added to the fact that my arm goes up, to make it the case that I raise my arm?

The recent literature contains many attempts to answer this question, and I shall not have time for a survey. Leaving aside views that, in my opinion, do not survive critical scrutiny (such as the "ascriptive" view, according to which it is an action because we hold the agent responsible for it[25] and the view that "It all depends on context,"[26] we have two serious contenders.

1. *Psychological causation (explanation) view.* What distinguishes the action from the "mere" movement is the psychological background of the movement, what gives rise to it, or issues in it.[27]

2. *Agent causation view.* A bodily movement is an action *iff* it is caused in a certain special way— not by some other event or state, but by the agent itself.[28]

The psychological causation view exists in many forms, depending on just what psychological factors are specified and just what relation to the bodily movement is required. As for the former, popular candidates have been the will, volitions, intentions, and wants-and-beliefs. On the second score, it is generally required that the movement occur "because of" the psychological factor in question, but there has been considerable controversy over whether to regard the relation as "causal." So as to have a simple form of the view to work with, let us focus on the position that what makes a case of my arm's rising into a case of my raising my arm, is that my arm rose because it was in accordance with my dominant *intentions* at the moment that it should rise.

So the model of a basic action that we get from the human case is:

1. bodily movement
2. caused by _____

To construct an analogous model for incorporeal action that will be an unmistakable model for *action*, we must (a) find a suitable replacement for bodily movements and (b) show that incorporeality is no bar to the satisfaction of a causal condition that will make the whole package into an *action*. It will prove best to begin with the second task, since that poses the more complex and difficult, as well as more controversial, issues. It shall proceed as I did with M-concepts—by considering, with respect to each of our contenders,

whether that condition could be satisfied by an incorporeal being.

As for the agent causation view, the concept of agent causation may well be obscure, and it certainly runs violently counter to some deeply rooted contemporary prejudices, but at least it is clear that it does not carry a restriction to *corporeal* substances. The theory avoids, on principle, any specification of the internal machinery by which an agent exercises its causal efficacy—"on principle," since the whole thrust of the position is that when I bring about a bodily movement in performing a basic action, I am not bringing about that movement by initiating certain other events which, in turn, bring about the movement by "event causation." Rather, I directly bring about the bodily movement simply by exploiting my basic capacity to do so. Hence the agent causality interpretation is not restricted to substances possessing one kind of internal structure or equipment rather than another.

On the psychological explanation view, things are a bit more complicated. Let us recall that the "causal condition" on this view is that the bodily movement results from an intention, or the like. So our question divides into two parts. (1) Can an incorporeal being have intentions, or whatever kind of psychological cause is required by the particular version of the theory under discussion? (2) Can an intention cause whatever substitutes for bodily movement in incorporeal basic action? As for (2), it is difficult to discuss this without deciding what does play the role of bodily movement in incorporeal basic actions. Hence we will postpone this question until we specify that substitute.

That leaves us with the question as to whether an incorporeal being can have intentions and the like. And now we find ourselves in a curious position. For that is exactly the question we were asking in the previous section on M-concepts. The conclusion we reached there, on an LC position, was that these concepts are applicable to a subject only if A-concepts are applicable. And now we see that, on the psychological explanation view, A-concepts are applicable to S only if M-concepts are applicable. Where does that leave us? We obviously are in some kind of circle. But is it the vicious circle of chasing our own tail, or a

virtuous circle of the sort in which the heavenly bodies were once deemed to move?

Here it is crucial to remember the task we set out
to accomplish. If we were trying to *prove* that M- and
A-concepts *are* applicable to an incorporeal being, we
would have reached an impasse. For since each application depends on the other as a necessary condition,
we would not have established either, unless we had
some independent argument for the applicability of
one or the other. But in fact, we set ourselves a more
modest goal—to determine whether the incorporeality of a being is sufficient ground for *denying* the
applicability of such concepts. We are considering
whether incorporeality renders their applicability
impossible. And from that standpoint, the circle is
virtuous. The reciprocity we have uncovered provides
no reason for *denying* the applicability of either sort
of concept. Psychological concepts are applicable only
if action concepts are applicable, and vice versa. As
far as that consideration goes, it is quite possible that
both kinds are applicable. This circle leaves standing
the *possibility* that an incorporeal being is such that
actions and intentions fit smoothly into the economy
of its operations.

Let us now return to the first condition of human
basic action concepts, to the problem of finding
something that could play the same role for incorporeal basic actions that bodily movements play for corporeal basic actions. I believe that the entrée to this
question is an appreciation of the difference between
the general concept of a basic action and specific concepts of particular human basic actions. Although
concepts of the latter sort contain concepts of particular types of bodily movements, this is not because
it is required by the general concept of a basic action.
That general concept, as we set it out initially, is simply the concept of an action that is not performed *by*
or *in* (simultaneously) performing some other action.
This general concept is quite neutral as to what kinds
of actions have that status for one or another type of
agent. It is just a fact about human beings (*not* a general constraint on action or basic action) that only
movements of certain parts of their bodies are under
their direct voluntary control and that anything else
they bring off, they must accomplish *by* moving their
bodies in certain ways. If I am to knock over a vase

or make a soufflé or communicate with someone, I
must do so by moving my hands, legs, vocal organs,
or whatever. But that is only because of my limitations. We can conceive of agents, corporeal or otherwise, such that things other than their bodies (if any)
are under their direct voluntary control. Some agents
might be such that they could knock over a vase or
bring a soufflé into being without doing something
else in order to do so.[29]

What these considerations suggest is that it is conceptually possible for any change whatsoever to be
the core of a basic action. Movements of an agent's
body are only what we happen to be restricted to in
the human case. Just what changes are within the
basic action repertoire of a given incorporeal agent
would depend upon the nature of that agent. But the
main point is that since such changes are not necessarily restricted to bodily movements of the agent, a
subject's bodilessness is no conceptual bar to the performance of basic actions by that subject.

I believe that the case in which we are particularly
interested, divine action, can be thought of along the
lines of the preceding discussion. Of course, one can
think of God as creating light by saying to himself,
"Let there be light," or as parting the sea of reeds by
saying to himself, "Let the sea of reeds be parted."
In that case the basic actions would be mental actions.
But what the above discussion indicates is that we are
not conceptually required to postulate this mental
machinery. We could think just as well of the coming
into being of light or of the parting of the sea of reeds
as directly under God's voluntary control.

This further suggests that all God's actions might
be basic actions. If any change whatsoever could conceivably be the core of a basic action, and if God is
omnipotent, then clearly, God *could* exercise direct
voluntary control over every change in the world
which he influences by his activity. However, I do not
claim to have done more than exhibit this as a possibility. It is equally possible that God chooses to influence some situations *indirectly*. He might choose to
lead or inspire Cyrus to free the Israelites, thus using
Cyrus as an instrument to bring about that result. In
that case, freeing the Israelites would be a nonbasic
action. I am quite willing to leave the decision on this
one up to God.[30]

Now let us just glance at the question I postponed—whether it is possible for intentions, and the like, to give rise directly to changes outside the agent's body (if any). I do not have much to say about this—it obviously is something outside our ordinary experience. But I can see nothing in our present understanding of the psyche and of causality that would show it to be impossible in principle. So, pending further insights into those matters, I am inclined to take a quasi-Humean line and say that what can cause what is "up for grabs." And of course, if it is an omnipotent deity that is in question, I suppose He could ordain that intentions can directly cause a parting of waters, provided this is a logical possibility.

Let me sum up these last two sections. Action concepts applicable to an incorporeal being can be constructed that would differ from human action concepts (on the most plausible accounts of the latter) only by the substitution of other changes for bodily movements of the agent in basic action concepts. Hence there is no conceptual bar to the performance of *overt* actions by incorporeal agents and hence no conceptual bar, even on an LC position, to the application of M-predicates to incorporeal beings.

As indicated earlier, this paper constitutes but a fragment of a thoroughgoing discussion of the title question. Other fragments would go into the question as to whether timelessness, immutability, and other traditional attributes constitute a bar to the literal predication of one or another kind of predicate. And of course we would have to discuss whether God is timeless, immutable, and so on. Moreover, we would have to scrutinize the classical arguments for the denial that *any* intrinsic predicates can be literally predicated of God. But perhaps even this fragment has sufficed to show that the prospects for speaking literally about God are not as dim as is often supposed by contemporary thinkers.[31]

Notes

1. This is a crude characterization of semantics, but it will have to do for now. There is no general agreement on what an adequate semantics would look like.
2. We shall not distinguish between *meaning* and *sense*.
3. *Webster's New Collegiate Dictionary* (Springfield, Mass.: Merriam, 1959). I am far from claiming that this is the most adequate way to meanings. Indeed, it is far from clear what that way would be. But it is clear that "player" has the meanings thus specified, however lamely and haltingly, and that its having these meanings is (a small) part of what makes the English language what it is at this stage of its history.
4. I want this supposition to be compatible with the fact that most or all predicate terms have meanings that are vague, exhibit "open texture," or suffer from indeterminacy in other ways. This implies that an adequate formulation would be more complicated than the one given here.
5. Metaphor is a topic of unlimited subtlety and complexity, and the above formulation barely scratches the surface. For a bit more detail, see my "Irreducible Metaphors in Theology," reprinted in my *Divine Nature and Human Language* (Ithaca, N.Y.: Cornell University Press, 1989), pp. 17–38.
6. This argument is developed more fully in "Irreducible Metaphors in Theology."
7. The question as to whether P-predicates could be applied to an incorporeal being presupposes that we can form a coherent notion of an incorporeal substance or other concrete subject of attributes. This has often been denied on the grounds that it is, in principle, impossible to identify, reidentify, or individuate such a being. See Antony Flew, *God and Philosophy* (London: Hutchinson, 1966), chap. 2; Terence Penelhum, *Survival and Disembodied Existence* (New York: Humanities Press, 1970), chap. 6; Sydney Shoemaker, *Self-Knowledge and Self-Identity* (Ithaca, N.Y.: Cornell University Press, 1963), chaps. 4 and 5. If arguments like this were successful, as I believe they are not, our problem would not arise.
8. Note that the issue here concerns the content (character, correct analysis) of psychological predicates or *concepts*, not the *nature of* the human psyche or the *nature of* human thought, intention, etc. Obviously the divine psyche, if there be such, is radically different in nature from the human psyche. The only question is as to whether there are any psychological concepts that apply to both. Hence our specific interest is in what we are saying about a human being

when we say of that person that she is thinking, has a certain attitude, or whatever. Thus the classification to follow is not a classification of theories of the nature of human mind—dualism, materialism, epiphenomenalism, etc.

9. The PP view was espoused or presupposed by the great seventeenth- and eighteenth-century philosophers: Descartes, Spinoza, Locke, Leibniz, Berkeley, Hume, and Reid. It surfaces as an explicit dogma in Book II of Locke's *Essay Concerning Human Understanding*, throughout Hume's *Treatise of Human Nature*, and in Essay I of Reid's *Essays on the Intellectual Powers of Man*.

10. Ludwig Wittgenstein, *Philosophical Investigations*, trans. G. E. M. Anscombe (Oxford, England: Basil Blackwell, 1953), nos. 258–70. In briefly indicating the main arguments for and against the PP view, I am merely trying to convey some sense of why various positions have seemed plausible. No endorsement of any particular argument is intended.

11. For an important statement of LB, see Rudolf Carnap, "Psychologie in physikalischer Sprache," *Erkenntnis*, vol. 3 (1932). English translation, "Psychology in Physical Language," by George Schick in *Logical Positivism*, ed. A. J. Ayer (New York: The Free Press, 1959). Gilbert Ryle's *The Concept of Mind* (London: Hutchinson, 1949) is an influential work that is often regarded as a form of LB.

12. In this quick survey I am ignoring many complexities. For example, the most plausible LB account of feeling depressed would involve some categorical overt manifestations, such as "looking droopy," as well as response tendencies like those cited in the text. I am also forced to omit any consideration of the relation of LB to behaviorism in psychology.

13. I am indebted to Jerry Fodor, *Psychological Explanation* (New York: Random House, 1968), pp. 15–16, for this felicitous analogy.

14. The functionalist is not committed to holding that all functional relations in which a given mental state stands will enter into our ordinary concept of that state. Picking out those that do is admittedly a tricky job; but that difficulty is by no means restricted to Functionalism.

15. I follow Brandt and Kim in taking Functionalism, as well as the other views canvassed, to be an account of the ordinary meanings of M-predicates. Some theorists present it as a proposal for developing psychological concepts for scientific purposes, or as an account of the *nature* of mental states.

16. R. B. Brandt and Jaegwon Kim, "Wants as Explanations of Actions," *Journal of Philosophy*, 60 (1963), 427.

17. Different forms of Functionalism display special features not mentioned in this brief survey. Cybernetic analogies are prominent in many versions, with psychological functions thought of on the model of the machine table of a computer. Some, like the Brandt and Kim account, find a useful model in the way in which theoretical terms in science get their meaning from the ways in which they figure in the theory.

18. It may be doubted that "want" is a serious candidate for theological predication. It would not be if the term were being used in a narrow sense that implies felt craving or lack of need. But I, along with many philosophers, mean to be using it in the broad sense just indicated. To indicate how the term might be applied to God in this sense, Aquinas uses the term "appetition" more or less in the way Brandt and Kim explain "want." *Will* for Aquinas is "intellectual appetition," and he applies "will" to God.

19. Kai Nielsen, *Contemporary Critiques of Religion* (London: Macmillan, 1971), p. 117. See also Paul Edwards, "Difficulties in the Idea of God," in *The Idea of God*, ed. E. H. Madden, R. Handy, and M. Farber (Springfield, Ill.: Charles C. Thomas, 1968), pp. 45 ff.

20. Let us define "overt" behavior as action that essentially involves some occurrence outside the present consciousness of the agent. This will exclude, e.g., "mental" actions such as focusing one's attention on something or resolving to get out of bed. The kinds of actions that are crucial to the Judaeo-Christian concept of God—creating the world, issuing commands, and guiding and comforting individual—count as overt on this definition.

21. These formulations raise questions that are not directly relevant to our concerns in this paper, e.g., how to think of a "command" in such a way that it might be "produced" by an agent. I should note, however, that the causation involved is not restricted to direct causation; intermediaries are allowed.

22. There is another reason for this procedure. Since nonbasic actions presuppose basic actions, and not vice versa, there could conceivably be only basic actions, but it is not possible that there should be only nonbasic actions. We shall see that it is a live possibility that all God's actions are basic.

23. Again, the basic (but not as obvious) point is that intentional actions are conceptually more basic. It seems that the analysis of action concepts is best set out by beginning with intentional actions and then defining unintentional actions as a certain derivation from that, rather than beginning by analyzing a neutral concept and then explaining intentional

and unintentional as different modifications of that. On the former approach it turns out that all basic actions are intentional. See Alvin I. Goldman, *A Theory of Human Action* (Englewood Cliffs, N.J.: Prentice-Hall, 1970), chap. 3.

24. Wittgenstein, *Philosophical Investigations*, no. 621.
25. H. L. A. Hart, "The Ascription of Responsibility and Rights," *Proceedings of the Aristotelian Society*, 69 (1949), 171–94.
26. A. I. Melden, *Free Action* (New York: Humanities Press, 1961).
27. Goldman, *Theory*, chaps. 1–3; Charles Taylor, *The Explanation of Behavior* (New York: Humanities Press, 1964), chaps. 2 and 3; W. P. Alston, "Conceptual Prolegomena to a Prolegomena to a Psychological Theory of Intentional Action," in *Philosophy of Psychology*, ed. S. C. Brown (London: Macmillan, 1974), pt. 2.
28. Roderick M. Chisholm, "The Descriptive Element in the Concept of 'Action'," *Journal of Philosophy*, 61 (1964), 613–24; Richard Taylor, *Action and Purpose* (Englewood Cliffs, N.J.: Prentice-Hall, 1966), chaps. 1–9.
29. Be careful to envisage this situation just as I have described it. The agent knocks over the vase not by doing anything else—even anything mental. Telekinesis is often thought of as an agent saying to himself something like "Let the vase be knocked over," and *this* causes the vase to fall over. But that does not make knocking over the vase a basic action. It is still a matter of knocking over the vase by doing something else, albeit something mental. In order for knocking over a vase to be a basic action, it would have to be just as immediate as is my raising my arm in the normal case, where I do this not by saying to myself "Let the arm rise," whereupon it rises; but where I just raise the arm intentionally.
30. It might be contended that if the physical universe, or any part thereof, is under God's direct voluntary control, this implies that the world is the body of God, which in turn implies that God is not an incorporeal being; that would mean that our case for *incorporeal* basic action fails. That is, the contention would be that in order to ascribe basic actions to S we have to pay the price of construing the changes in question as movements of S's body. This claim could be supported by the thesis that a sufficient condition for something to be part of my body is that it be under my direct voluntary control. So if the physical universe is under God's direct voluntary control, it is His body. Against this, I would argue that we have many different ways of picking out the body of a human being. In addition to the one just mentioned, my body is distinctive in that it is the perspective from which I perceive the world; it provides the immediate causal conditions of my consciousness; and it constitutes the phenomenological locus of my "bodily sensations." With multiple criteria there is room for maneuver. Holding the other criteria constant, we can envisage a state of affairs in which *something other than my body*, e.g., my wristwatch, is under my direct voluntary control. Thus I deny that my position requires God to have a body.
31. This paper grew out of material presented in my NEH Summer Seminars on Theological Language, given in 1978 and 1979, and more directly out of a lecture delivered at the 1978 Wheaton College Philosophy Conference. I am grateful to the participants in my summer seminars and at the Wheaton Conference for many valuable reactions.

Study Questions

1. Many thinkers, including many in this part of the book, argue that we cannot speak literally of God. Alston interprets them as holding that we cannot form subject-predicate sentences that are literally true of God. How does Alston respond to apparent obstacles to literal talk of God?
2. In showing that it is not impossible to speak literally of God, Alston selects two kinds of predicates for close analysis. Which types of predicates? Why are they so germane to the issue at hand? How do you evaluate the effectiveness of Alston's case?

Suggested Reading

Alston, William P. "Religious Language." In *The Oxford Handbook of Philosophy of Religion*, ed. William Wainwright, pp. 221–24. Oxford, England: Oxford University Press, 2005.

Ayer, A. J. *Language, Truth, and Logic*. New York: Dover, 1952.

———. "The Principle of Verifiability." *Mind* 45, no. 178 (1936): 199–203.

Burrell, David. *Knowing the Unknowable God: Ibn-Sina, Maimonides, Aquinas*. Notre Dame, Ind.: University of Notre Dame Press, 1986.

Diamond, Malcolm, and Thomas V. Lizenbury, Jr., eds. *The Logic of God*. Indianapolis, Ind.: Bobbs-Merrill, 1975.

Durrant, Michael. *The Logical Status of "God."* London: Macmillan, 1973.

Ferré, Frederick. *Language, Logic, and God*. New York: Harper and Row, 1969.

Fodor, Jerry. *Christian Hermeneutics: Paul Ricoeur and the Refiguring of Theology*. Oxford, England: Oxford University Press, 1995.

Gilkey, Langdon. *Naming the Whirlwind*. Indianapolis, Ind.: Bobbs-Merrill, 1969.

Gilson, Etienne. *Linguistics and Philosophy*. Notre Dame, Ind.: University of Notre Dame Press, 1988.

High, Dallas, ed. *New Essays in Religious Language*. New York: Oxford University Press, 1969.

Kellenberger, James. *Religious Discovery, Faith, and Knowledge*. Englewood Cliffs, N.J.: Prentice-Hall, 1972.

Kiel, Alvin F., Jr. *Speaking the Christian God*. Grand Rapids, Mich.: William B. Eerdmans, 1992.

Mascall, E. L. *Existence and Analogy*. New York: Longmans, Green, & Co., Ltd., 1949.

———. *Words and Images*. New York: Ronald Press, 1957.

McFague, Sallie. *Metaphorical Theology*. Philadelphia: Fortress Press, 1982.

Mitchell, Basil. *Faith and Logic*. London: Allen & Unwin, 1957.

Ramsey, Ian. *Religious Language*. London: SCM Press, 1957.

———, ed. *Words About God: The Philosophy of Religion*. New York: Harper and Row, 1971.

Ross, James F. *Portraying Analogy*. Cambridge, England: Cambridge University Press, 1981.

Ruether, Rosemary Radford. *Sexism and God-Talk: Toward a Feminist Theology*. Boston: Beacon Press, 1983.

Soskice, Janet Martin. *Metaphor and Religious Language*. Oxford, England: Oxford University Press, 1984.

Stiver, Dan. *The Philosophy of Religious Language: Sign, Symbol, and Story*. Oxford, England: Blackwell, 1996.

Wisdom, John. "Gods." Chapter 10 in *Language and Logic*, vol. 1. Oxford, England: Blackwell, 1951.

PART TEN

Miracles

Many religions claim that God has miraculously intervened in earthly affairs. Within Christianity, one of the most significant of these claims is that Jesus was miraculously resurrected from the dead on the third day after his crucifixion. When assessing this claim, at least three related, but distinct questions can be raised. Is it rational to believe that this event actually occurred as reported? Is it rational to believe that, if it did occur, this is an event that could never be explained naturally? And whether or not it is held that laws of nature were "violated," is it rational to believe that divine intervention is the most plausible explanation for this event (assuming that it occurred as reported)?

In the first reading in this section, Stephen Davis considers whether one can rationally believe that the answer to all three of these questions is yes—that God actually did raise Jesus from the dead in a manner that cannot be explained by an appeal to natural laws alone. The answer, he tells us, depends in part on one's worldview. For someone who is a *naturalist*—who believes that nature alone exists and thus that every event is explainable solely in terms of natural processes—it is rational to deny that the resurrection occurred. On the other hand, for one who is a *supernaturalist*—who believes that God exists and can intervene in early affairs—there is enough evidence to make it perfectly rational to believe that Jesus Christ did in fact rise from the dead.

To help us determine whether Davis and others who claim that it can be rational to believe in miracles are correct, we need to define miracle more precisely and then look individually at the three basic epistemological questions that come into play.

MIRACLE DEFINED

The term "miracle" is sometimes used in general discussions to refer to any unexpected event—from the unanticipated passing of a difficult exam to the rediscovery of a lost item of great value to the rapid and total recovery from a bout with cancer. However, when "miracle" is used in its distinctively religious sense, what most have in mind is not only the occurrence of an unusual or expected event but the occurrence of an unusual, remarkable event that would not have occurred in the exact manner in which it did if God had not intentionally brought it about—that is, if God had not at some point and in some manner directly imposed his divine will on the natural order.

MIRACLES AS EVENTS THAT CANNOT
BE EXPLAINED NATURALLY

There remains, however, significant debate about the relationship between miraculous events and the natural order. At least since the time of David Hume (1711–1776), miracles have often been defined by proponents and critics alike as *violations of natural laws*. One oft-repeated critical response to this characterization is that to conceive of a violation of natural laws in this manner is incoherent. Natural laws, it is argued, are simply statements that describe the actual course of events. Thus, we could never find ourselves justified in claiming both that our current set of natural laws is adequate and that some acknowledged occurrence is a violation of these laws in the sense that it is a true counterinstance to them, an event for which no natural explanation could ever be forthcoming. To acknowledge that an event is a true counterinstance to established laws only demonstrates that the laws in question are inadequate, since we must always be willing, in principle, to expand our natural laws to accommodate any occurrence, no matter how unusual. So a violation of our natural laws—if viewed as a true counterinstance to true (i.e., adequate) laws—is conceptually impossible.

Some, though, view this criticism as question begging. Since it cannot be demonstrated in an objective manner (without begging the question) that supernatural activity is impossible—that is, since it cannot be demonstrated that forces from outside the natural system cannot influence observed activity in our world—the concept of a divinely induced true counterinstance to natural laws, it is argued, remains coherent. And if this is so, then for those who grant that a true counterinstance to a natural law can rightly be labeled a violation regardless of the type of causal factors involved, a violation of natural laws can be considered a coherent concept.

However, even if we dismiss the concept of a violation and think of the miraculous only in terms of a true counterinstance to natural laws, this leaves open the question of whether the label of "miracle" should be reserved for only those occurrences that are permanently inexplicable in the sense that no event of this type could ever be given a fully natural explanation—that is, that nature could never produce such an event on its own. And this continues to be the subject of considerable debate.

Those theists and nontheists who believe it unwise to conceive of a miracle as a permanently inexplicable event type offer a straightforward, seemingly compelling argument. To define a miracle as permanently inexplicable in this sense allows a person to claim that any given event is actually a miracle only if we are, or could be, in a position to state with certainty or high probability that a given type of event could never be given a fully natural explanation. However, the scientific enterprise is continually discovering new, often startling and unexpected, information about the causal relationships that operate in our universe. And the annals of science record numerous instances in which counterinstances to supposedly well-established natural laws were later demonstrated—sometimes only after significant conceptual shifts—to in fact be consistent with such laws or revisions thereof. Accordingly, it is argued, would it not be the height of scientific provincialism for a theist (or anyone else) ever to decide, solely on the basis of the data presently available, that it was now justifiable to label a given occurrence as permanently inexplicable by nature? Given our necessarily limited understanding of the true nature of reality, wouldn't the more reasonable response to even the most unusual of anomalies be for theists to assume that the scientist should continue to run tests indefinitely or simply label the occurrence a "freak event" and await the occurrence of similar phenomena before seriously investigating further?

A number of philosophers aren't convinced. Let us assume, for instance, that a person who lost a leg to cancer experienced the leg's immediate regeneration under the most stringent, fraud-detecting conditions—for instance, in the presence of doctors or TV cameras. Such an event, it is argued, would conflict with so many accepted scientific facts that any attempt to revise our present scientific laws to accommodate events of this type would so weaken the predictive power of such laws that they would no longer be of practical value. Accordingly, it is argued, if such an event were actually to occur, the scientist, of necessity, would be forced to identify it as a permanently unexplainable phenomenon.

Others, however, see this as a false dilemma. When encountering real or imaginable occurrences that are seeming counterinstances to well-established laws, our choice is not solely between declaring the type of event in question permanently inexplicable naturally or declaring that there is a fully natural explanation (even if it is yet to be found). The more reasonable alternative is to acknowledge that the type of event in question *might* be inexplicable naturally while continuing to search for a natural explanation. To do so would not functionally damage the natural laws in question, since only repeatable or frequent counterinstances falsify natural laws. So the practical value of the relevant laws for predicting the behavior of the natural order would remain.

There have always been, however, a significant number of theists who do not believe that an observable event need be of a type that cannot be explained naturally to be considered miraculous. Take, for instance, the classic story by R. F. Holland (*American Philosophical Quarterly*, 1965). A child riding his toy motorcar strays onto an unguarded railway crossing near his house, whereupon a wheel of his car gets stuck beside of one of the rails. At that exact moment, an express train is approaching with the signals in its favor. Also, a curve in the track will make it impossible for the driver to see the boy soon enough to stop his train in time to avoid hitting him. Moreover, the child is so engrossed in freeing his wheel that he hears neither the train whistle nor his mother, who has just come out of the house and is trying to get his attention. The child appears to be doomed. But just before the train rounds the curve, its brakes are applied and it comes to rest a few feet from the child. The mother thanks God for the miracle, although she learns in due course that there was not necessarily anything supernatural about the manner in which the brakes came to be applied. The driver had fainted for a reason that had nothing to do with the presence of the child on the line, and the brakes were applied automatically as his hand ceased to exert pressure on the control lever.

The event sequence described in this situation includes no component for which a natural explanation is not available. Boys sometimes play on train tracks, drivers sometimes faint, and the brakes of trains have been constructed to become operative when a driver's hand releases the control lever. But another explanation presents itself in this case: that God directly intervened to cause the driver to faint at that precise moment. And as the theists in question see it, if God did directly intervene in this instance, the event can be considered a miracle, even though a totally natural explanation would also be available.

In short, there are a number of theists who do not want to limit the range of the term "miracle" to only those direct acts of God for which no natural explanation can presently be offered. They want to expand the definition to cover events in relation to which God can be viewed as having directly manipulated the natural order, regardless of anyone's ability to construct plausible alternate natural causal scenarios.

Miracles as Historical Events

Many theists do not claim only that certain types of events could justifiably be considered miracles if they were to occur. They claim that certain events meriting the label of miraculous have actually occurred in the past. If these events have natural explanations available, as is the case in Holland's story about the boy and the train, the accuracy of such claims can be assessed in the same way we assess any historical report. We can, for example, try to determine whether the original source was trustworthy and whether what was originally reported has been faithfully transmitted.

Yet what of those allegedly miraculous events that are incompatible with current natural laws? What, for instance, of the Christian belief that Jesus came back to life after he had been dead for three days, or that Jesus turned water into wine? Or what of the claim made today by some that God restores malformed body parts such as arms and legs to their original shape? Are we ever in a position to claim justifiably that seemingly unexplainable events of this sort have actually occurred as reported?

David Hume, in the second reading in this section, argues that the answer is no. The wise person, he tells us, proportions his or her belief to the evidence. And when we consider the evidence rationally, it is not difficult to see the problem at hand. We have well-known natural laws that are based on uniform past and present experience. On the other hand, alleged miraculous violations of these laws are supported only by the personal testimony of a few, and such testimonial evidence will by its very nature always be weaker than the evidence for the laws they contradict, since human memory is often unreliable, humans are gullible, humans by nature want to find mystery and wonder where there is none, and those reporting alleged miracles want passionately to believe that miracles occur. Accordingly, Hume concludes, we can establish "as a maxim that no human testimony can have such force as to prove a miracle."

In the third reading, J. L. Mackie offers an updated version of Hume's argument. After acknowledging that Hume's understanding of natural law needs revision and that certain forms of evidence can be more powerful than Hume's discussion would suggest, Mackie presents what he sees as the strongest evidential argument against accepting that allegedly miraculous events, understood as violations (true counterinstances), have occurred as reported. The real problem here, we are told, is that the person wanting to accept such a claim has the double burden of holding both that the event took place and that it "violated" a law of nature. If this person has very strong evidence that a seeming counterinstance to natural law has occurred, then she or he has a very strong reason to believe that the law as currently understood is inadequate. On the other hand, if this person has very strong evidence that a law of nature is adequate, then she or he has a very strong reason to believe that the seeming counterinstance didn't occur as reported. Accordingly, to hold both that one has strong evidence for the adequacy of the law and a counter instance to this law is by its very nature extremely difficult—so difficult that it is more reasonable to assume that the alleged miracle did not occur exactly as reported.

In the final reading in this section, Richard Swinburne challenges these types of arguments. We have, Swinburne notes, four types of evidence about what happened in the past: our own memories, the testimony of others, physical traces, and our contemporary understanding of what's possible. Our experience, codified in natural laws, does give us a reason not to believe that alleged counterinstances to natural laws have actually occurred as reported. However, while personal memories can be faulty, past experience gives us reason to believe they should rightly be given strong credence. The testimony of others can also be faulty, but we have sound methods for determining the reliability of such testimony. And we have increasingly sophisticated ways of determining the reliability of physical traces—e.g., increasingly accurate methods for the dating of ancient documents. In short, we have available to us reliable, objective methods for assessing whether a seeming counterinstance to a nature law has actually occurred. And there is no reason to believe that these forms of evidence could not, in principle, sometimes outweigh the evidence of physical impossibility and thus furnish us with a sound basis for maintaining that the accuracy of reports of counterinstances to adequate natural laws cannot be ruled out in an *a priori* manner.

Miracles as Acts of God

Yet another aspect of the epistemological debate over miracles is the question of whether the undisputed occurrence of certain events could ever require all honest, thoughtful individuals to acknowledge that God has supernaturally intervened in earthly affairs. Some philosophers believe the answer to be yes. They maintain that, in the face of certain conceivable events, divine intervention would have to be acknowledged by all. For example, let us imagine that there is a man who claims to have healing powers from God and that we are able to capture on film that after his prayers to God on behalf of someone who had lost fingers to leprosy, the fingers immediately regrew. Let us suppose also that trickery can be objectively ruled out. In a case such as this, would it not require a greater act of faith to interpret such events naturally than to assume that natural explanations could never be forthcoming because supernatural causal intervention was involved?

Other philosophers believe not. They have argued in response that, given all we experience—for instance, the tremendous amount of horrific evil in our world—no single event or series of events could ever compel all thoughtful individuals to acknowledge the existence of a perfectly good supernatural intervening causal agent.

For many theists, though, the crucial question is not whether there are imaginable conditions under which all rational individuals would have to acknowledge divine intervention. The important issue, as they see it, is whether they as theists can (could) justifiably claim that God is, at least in part, directly responsible for certain occurrences. That is, the important question is whether there are conditions under which the theist can reasonably claim that certain events are direct acts of God.

One of the most common responses by theists is that they have acquired—from written revelation or oral tradition or personal experience—accurate information about God's general "patterns of action" in our world. And when they observe (or at least if they were to observe) some specific event fitting such a pattern, they can (or at least could) justifiably label it a direct act of God.

Since few philosophers today maintain that God's existence can be conclusively disproved or that the concept of divine communication with humans is self-contradictory, it should not be surprising that few today wish to argue that theists cannot rationally maintain belief in the accuracy of certain divine action patterns and thus cannot justifiably label events that fit such patterns miraculous direct acts of God.

The Relationship Between Miracle and Evil

Finally, in addition to epistemological challenges, those theists who believe that God can and does at time miraculously intervene in earthly affairs find themselves facing the following theological question: if God can miraculously intervene, why would a good God not intervene more frequently in order to prevent particularly horrendous evils? Theists normally maintain in response either that God's respect for human freedom prohibits God from more frequent intervention or that we are not in a position to understand the ways of God. But even these theists acknowledge that two general points remain: To the extent that a theist responds to specific instances of evil by claiming that God is barred from removing them because of the nature of our moral universe, this theist has less reason to expect beneficial (miraculous) intervention in any specific situation. And to the extent that a theist resolves the tension in question by claiming that "God's ways are above our ways," the less able she or he is to predict when and where any such intervention might occur.

We see, then, that miracle is a very complex concept, with every aspect the basis for significant debate. However, the issues raised—especially those concerning our ability to identify miracles—are of vital importance for both religion and science. Moreover, new perspectives on these questions continue to appear. Accordingly, it seems quite likely that the miraculous will justifiably continue to be one of the most popular topics for discussion in philosophy of religion.

Stephen T. Davis

Is It Possible to Know That Jesus Was Raised from the Dead?

Many religions claim that God has miraculously intervened in early affairs. Within Christianity, one of the most significant of these claims is that Jesus was miraculously resurrected from the dead on the third day after his crucifixion. In this selection, Stephen T. Davis (b. 1940) discusses whether one can rationally believe that this resurrection actually occurred. The answer, he tells us, depends in part on one's worldview. For someone who is a naturalist—who believes that nature alone exists and thus that every event is explainable solely in terms of natural processes— it is rational to deny that the resurrection occurred. On the other had, for someone who is a supernaturalist—who believes that God exists and can intervene in early affairs—there is enough evidence to make it perfectly rational to believe that Jesus Christ did in fact rise from the dead.

Philosophical discussions of religious knowledge are often general in nature, i.e. they take place quite apart from consideration of actual items religious people claim to know or rationally believe. In this paper, I propose to approach the broad epistemological topic of religious knowledge by taking a specific tenet of a specific religion and asking whether it can be known or rationally believed. The moral I hope to draw is that the vastly different conclusions religious believers and nonbelievers reach about religious knowledge is due to differences in the worldviews they accept.

The resurrection of Jesus from the dead is by universal consent a crucial doctrine of the Christian faith. Thus it is natural for Christian philosophers who believe the doctrine to ask what they can or ought to do as philosophers to defend it. Naturally, their first impulse is to engage in some kind of rational apologetic. Although apologetics is an enterprise that is often maligned, I believe this is an understandable and quite acceptable impulse. I will argue in this paper against a certain way of doing apologetics, but I believe that all Christians engage in the enterprise.

Let me distinguish between two sorts of apologetic arguments in favor of the resurrection of Jesus. Let us call a "soft apologetic argument" one that attempts to demonstrate the rationality of belief in the resurrection of Jesus. And let us call a "hard apologetic argument" one that attempts to demonstrate the irrationality of unbelief in the resurrection of Jesus. One of my aims in this paper is to show the limits of what philosophy can achieve on this issue. I am opposing what I consider to be overblown claims that are made on both sides of the issue, i.e., by those who hold that rational argument can either verify or falsify the resurrection. I do not believe that it can do either, as

From *Faith and Philosophy: Journal of the Society of Christian Philosophers.* Volume 1, no. 2, 1984. Used by permission of the Editor.

I will try to show. As a believer in the resurrection, I naturally hold (and will argue) that Christians are within their intellectual rights in believing that Jesus was raised from the dead.[1] But I do not believe it can be shown that religious skeptics are not within their intellectual rights in rejecting the doctrine.

There is a paradox that faces any philosopher who writes about the possibility of the resurrection of Jesus. On the one hand, some believers in the resurrection hold that the evidence in its favor is overwhelming. (I once knew a seminary professor who was known to say, "Any rational person who honestly looks at the evidence for the resurrection of Jesus must be convinced by it and become a Christian.") On the other hand, many nonbelievers in the resurrection hold that the claim that Jesus was raised from the dead is perfectly absurd. (As an undergraduate, I studied under a man who liked to debunk the biblical miracles; one day in class he dismissed the resurrection with the statement "I hope everybody here knows that dead people stay dead.")

What is the reason for this puzzling phenomenon? Why is it that people on both sides are so convinced that they are obviously correct and the others obviously wrong? Of course, we do notice that both sides can offer explanations of the strange behavior of the other—believers can claim that nonbelievers are blinded by sin; nonbelievers can claim that believers are blinded by credulity and wishful thinking. But is there anything Christian philosophers can helpfully say at this point? Perhaps not, but I will try.

One difficulty that needs to be cleared up concerns the term "miracle." For quite understandable reasons, the word is usually defined in terms of transgressions or violations of natural laws. Critics have been quick to point out a complication, however. Since laws of nature are human inventions, i.e., descriptions of observed regularities, if we really became aware of a violation of (what we understood to be) a law of nature, they say, we should not proclaim a miracle but rather simply amend our understanding of the law of nature in question—even reject it altogether, if necessary. The issue here is complex, and I do not wish to explore it in detail. But fortunately it need not be explored, even in a paper on the resurrection of Jesus, an event often considered the paradigmatic miracle.

For Christians won't mind one bit if it turns out, through some sound process of reasoning, that no miracles occur, i.e., that no true natural laws are ever violated but rather that some weak ones are just occasionally discovered to be inadequate. As long as it is still true, for example, that Jesus was born of a virgin, was raised from the dead, healed people, turned water into wine, etc., it will be a matter of profound indifference to them whether natural laws are ever violated.

However, since the issue *is* unclear, I will continue in this paper to speak of the resurrection as a miracle. For it must be admitted that with the resurrection we are talking not just about a highly unusual event but an event that, given our best knowledge of the workings of the world, seems causally impossible. Almost any event that occurs can be described in such a way as to have been or at least rationally seemed to have been highly improbable before it occurred. In 1875, or even in 1975, what would have been the odds that in 1981 a Claremont philosopher who coaches soccer and whose father was a Nebraska cattle rancher would write a paper entitled "Is It Possible to Know That Jesus Was Raised from the Dead?" and that thirty years later you would read it? The odds would have been low indeed, but the point is that there is nothing in this description (as there *is* in a description of the resurrection) that seems causally impossible given our best knowledge. The resurrection is not just a unique and improbable event but an intellectual scandal. Accordingly, an event should probably only be considered a miracle if no purported explanation of it that crucially omits God is a good explanation. It just might be possible to offer a good explanation of my writing and your reading this paper that fails to mention God. And so our doing so, however improbable it may be, is not a miracle. But the resurrection of Jesus, if it occurred, in all probability could not be explained without God, and so (if it occurred) is probably a miracle.

It is sometimes said that every miracle is ambiguous in that it can be interpreted either as an act of God or as a surprising and perhaps inexplicable natural event. But surely this can be said not just about miracles but about almost any event, as John Hick has often argued.[2] Name virtually any event, and the religious believer and the religious skeptic can disagree on how to interpret it. The one may well see it as an act of God whereas the other will not. They do not differ, so to speak, on the facts (both experience the event and acknowledge that it has occurred) but on how to interpret or account for the facts.

However, there is a difference between miracles and natural events in this regard. With natural events (e.g., someone's recovering from a serious illness), the believer and the skeptic do not differ on the question of whether the event occurred; both will agree that it did. Their difference concerns the cause and meaning of the event. With miracles, however (or at least with certain of them, e.g., the resurrection of Jesus), the believer and the skeptic will typically differ on the fundamental question of what precisely occurred. They differ here on the facts.

Accordingly, influenced by our earlier distinction between hard and soft apologetics, let us make a distinction between hard and soft miracles. A *soft miracle*, let us say, is a miracle that religious skeptics can consistently agree has occurred; it is just that they will disagree with religious believers on its cause and meaning. If Jones, apparently doomed with cancer, is after prayer and fasting found to be well and free of cancer, this may well constitute a soft miracle. Skeptics can consistently agree that Jones was gravely ill but now is well—they will simply deny that Jones's recovery was due to God. A *hard miracle*, on the other hand, is one that is very difficult for religious skeptics to explain naturalistically,[3] and so skeptics will not want to allow that it has occurred. The resurrection of Jesus appears to be a hard miracle—skeptics apparently cannot agree that it has occurred (not as the event is recorded in the gospels, at any rate) without abandoning religious skepticism. The strategy of consistent skeptics must accordingly be to argue that the event has not in fact occurred.

Hard miracles are obviously going to be appealing to rational apologists for religious faith. It is tempting to think of them as good devices for evangelism, i.e., for converting people from religious skepticism to religious faith. But have any hard miracles occurred? Religious believers hold that the answer is yes, and religious skeptics will say no. As a Christian, I hold that certain hard miracles have occurred, and I believe that the resurrection of Jesus is one of them.

But have any events occurred that can be *shown* to be hard miracles? Here I am doubtful. It certainly seems *possible* to me for an event to occur that would be irrational for anyone to deny is a hard miracle, but to my knowledge no such events have occurred—not even the resurrection. Soft miracles, then, are religiously ambiguous, because they can be interpreted as natural events; hard miracles are religiously ambiguous, because the ones that have purportedly occurred can apparently be rationally denied. How the resurrection can rationally be denied I will consider presently.

In order to make the problem we face more concrete, let us look at the way believers and nonbelievers in the resurrection of Jesus can most persuasively present their respective cases.

Believers in the resurrection first stress the unity of the New Testament witness to the resurrection. Despite differences in some details—believers will argue—the biblical writers, who give us our earliest testimony to the events after the crucifixion, unanimously agree that Jesus rose from the dead.

Second, believers in the resurrection will point out that there are certain facts surrounding the resurrection that have virtually been demonstrated by historical scholarship and that no competent biblical, theological, or historical scholar denies them. They are, preeminently, that Jesus died on a cross, that certain people later came to believe that God had raised him from the dead, and that the firm belief in the resurrection that these people had was the heart of the message they proclaimed and the reason they so radically changed. Disheartened, confused, and fearful immediately after the crucifixion, they quickly became determined, bold, and courageous. The most plausible explanation of these facts—so believers in the resurrection will argue—is that Jesus did indeed rise from the dead and show himself to the disciples. It does not seem sensible to claim that the Christian Church, a spiritual movement whose vitality changed the world, was started by charlatans or dupes. If the disciples knew that Jesus was not really risen, they were charlatans. If they believed he was risen when in fact he was not, they were dupes.

Third, something of an embarrassment in the position of nonbelievers in the resurrection can be pointed out: their inability to offer an acceptable alternative explanation of the known facts surrounding the resurrection of Jesus. The old nineteenth-century rationalistic explanations (swoon theory, stolen body, wrong tomb, etc.) all seem to collapse of their own weight once spelled out, and no strong new theory has emerged as the consensus of scholars who deny that the resurrection occurred. One recent full-blooded attempt to offer such an explanation is Hugh Schonfield's *The Passover Plot*,[4] a bold and entertaining book. But with its highly fanciful hypotheses and selective use of evidence, it has drawn much criticism and precious little support from scholars.

The plain fact is that most contemporary Christian theologians who do not believe that Jesus was dead for three days and then actually lived again offer no explanation. Many suggest only vague poetic metaphors like "spiritual resurrection," the "Easter vision of the disciples," or "dramatic imagery seen through the eyes of faith." Some hint that parapsychological phenomena were at work. "But does all this vague talk mean anything?" the believer in the resurrection will bluntly ask. Isn't it just theological jargon amounting to this: "I can't bring myself to believe that a real resurrection happened, but *something* (I don't know what) must have happened to account for the disciples' faith"? And surely all this is odd, the believer continues: if the resurrection did not occur, it is at least *prima facie* puzzling that no consensus alternative explanation of the known facts has emerged. All in all, the believer will say, the most rational position is to believe that Jesus really did, as claimed, rise from the dead.

But nonbelievers in the resurrection can make an impressive case too. They will first argue that the biblical testimony is unreliable. It was written years after the event by unsophisticated, myth-prone people who were more interested in formulating statements of faith and in furthering Christian ends than in writing accurate history. Furthermore, the evidence they present is contradictory: How many women visited the tomb? Had the sun risen or was it still dark? Was there one angel (or young man) or two? Were they inside the tomb or outside? Did the women keep silent or run to tell the disciples? Were the disciples told to stay in Jerusalem or to go to Galilee? Was the resurrected Jesus in physical or spiritual form? Did

the ascension occur immediately after the resurrection, or forty days later?

But the nonbeliever's strongest argument will run as follows: "Granted I have no plausible alternative explanation of the known facts; and granted that on the basis of the known facts and available possible explanations of them, the chances are (let's be as generous as possible) 99 out of 100 that the resurrection really happened; still we must ask the following fatal question: *What are the chances that a man dead for three days would live again?*" In short, the nonbeliever will claim that even if the believer's arguments are strong, and even if nonbelievers can't say for sure what *did* happen, by far the most sensible position is to deny that the resurrection occurred, for the probability that we should assign to the statement "People dead for three days stay dead" is very, very high. Thus, the position of the nonbeliever amounts to this: "I don't know exactly what happened after the crucifixion—it was, after all, nearly two thousand years ago, and by now it's very hard to tell—but whatever happened, it certainly wasn't a resurrection."

But a truly vital factor in the debate would be omitted if we stopped here. For we must consider the very different metaphysical worldviews typically held by those who do and do not believe in the resurrection. The nonbeliever's position is probably convincing to the nonbeliever not primarily because of evidence or arguments in its favor but because it is entailed by the worldview he or she accepts. Let's call that worldview *naturalism*. It is the view, we will say, that holds that the following four statements are true: (1) Nature alone exists. The word "nature" is difficult to define precisely, but let us say that it is the sum total of what could in principle be observed by human beings or be studied by methods analogous to those used in the natural sciences. Accordingly, naturalism excludes God, or at least the theistic God. (2) Nature is eternal. Nature is an uncreated thing; there is no moment in time when it does not exist; it is not contingent. (3) Nature is uniform. There are no nonnatural events (e.g. miracles); rather, nature is regular, continuous. (4) Every event is explicable. In principle at least, any event can be explained in terms of nature or natural processes, i.e., by explanatory methods similar to those used in the natural sciences.

Similarly, the believer's position is probably convincing to the believer not primarily because of evidence or arguments in its favor but because it dovetails with the worldview he or she accepts. Let's call that world view *supernaturalism*. It is the view, we will say, that holds (1) that something besides nature exists, viz. God; (2) that nature depends for its existence on God; (3) that the regularity of nature can be and occasionally is interrupted by miraculous acts of God; and (4) that such events are humanly quite unpredictable and inexplicable.[5]

All people interpret their experience within a certain philosophical framework. For many people, their philosophical assumptions exclude God's existence and the possibility of miracles. Such people presumably reject the resurrection, but not because the evidence for it is weak. Surely, if the resurrection were not essentially miraculous (if it were like, say, the crucifixion), few rational persons would doubt it. They reject the resurrection because it does not fit with their naturalistic world view. The essentially miraculous nature of the resurrection impels them to discount the evidence for it despite their inability to explain what *did* happen or how the disciples came to believe in the resurrection.

Well then—you will want to ask at this point— did the resurrection of Jesus occur? Which is more likely—that the resurrection occurred, or not? To put it in Hume's terms, which is the lesser miracle? My own view will come as no surprise. As a supernaturalist and as a Christian, I find the evidence in favor of the resurrection strong. Perhaps it can even be said to be compelling for those Christians who admit the possibility of miracles.[6] But the problem is that for those who don't, the available evidence is not likely to be compelling.

For as we have seen, the odd thing is that a person's decision about whether to believe in the resurrection is usually made on some basis other than the evidence pro and con. (Is this why miracles seem to bring so few people to faith, why Jesus was reluctant to perform spectacular public miracles?) Those who believe in Christ believe in the resurrection; those who accept naturalism do not.

There is a curious circularity here. I believe that philosophers have shown over against Hume that miracles *can* occur; the real question is whether any *have* occurred. But when we turn to historical evidence for a purported miracle, e.g., the resurrection, it turns out that a decision whether or not it occurred normally turns on whether or not one believes that miracles *can* occur. Perhaps this circularity explains the puzzle with which we began, viz. why Christians find the evidence for the resurrection so utterly compelling, while nonbelievers think it sheer foolishness to believe in the resurrection. From the perspective of naturalism, the resurrection does seem like a prescientific myth. From the perspective of supernaturalism, or at least Christian supernaturalism, the resurrection seems the best explanation of the evidence.

The upshot of what I have been arguing is that both belief and disbelief in the resurrection of Jesus can be rational. It is a mistake to argue either (1) that it is *never* rational to believe in the resurrection of Jesus, or (2) that belief in the resurrection of Jesus is the *only* rational position. Both arguments have been presented; let me comment briefly on each.

(1) Some Christian theologians in recent years have argued against belief in a real resurrection of Jesus from what clearly amounts to a perspective very near naturalism. Rather than rejecting talk of the resurrection entirely, as a religious skeptic might do, they typically offer what might be called reductive theories of the resurrection. "What 'Jesus rose from the dead' really means," they say, "is____," where the blank is filled in with a way of understanding the resurrection that does not actually involve a dead man's coming back to life. Thus, Rudolf Bultmann:

> Indeed, *faith in the resurrection is really the same as faith in the saving efficacy of the cross*, faith in the cross as the cross of Christ.[7]

And Willi Marxsen:

> Talk of the resurrection of Jesus is an interpretation designed to express the fact that my faith has a source and that source is Jesus.... Jesus is risen in that his offer meets us today and in that, if we accept it, he gives us this new life.[8]

Bultmann does not try to hide the fact that his understanding of the resurrection of Jesus rests on a basically naturalist position (I say *basically* naturalist because he does believe in God). Modern people can no longer believe in mythological stories, he says. The idea of dead people rising is utterly inconceivable and incredible to us. In a famous passage, Bultmann says,

> It is impossible to use the electric light and the wireless and to avail ourselves of modern medical and surgical discoveries, and at the same time to believe in the New Testament world of spirits and miracles. We may think we can manage it in our own lives, but to expect others to do so is to make the Christian faith unintelligible and unacceptable to the modern world.[9]

Although much could be said in response to this point of view, let me limit myself to two comments. First, the rather condescending air theologians such as Bultmann and Marxsen typically take toward pre-modern people, e.g., people in New Testament times, seems to me altogether unwarranted. "Such people could believe in myths, spirits, and miracles," it is said, "but we moderns cannot." The implication is that the poor devils just didn't have the benefit of our modern scientific knowledge and reasoning power—and that is why they believed such silly things. But surely this is grossly exaggerated. If miracles and resurrections were supposed to be so commonplace in ignorant times like the first century, why was the resurrection of Jesus taken to be so significant? I would have thought that the idea of a man dead for three days living again was no less intellectually scandalous to first-century people than it is to us. (Notice the reaction of the apostle Thomas in John 20 and of the Stoic and Epicurean philosophers in Acts 17 to talk of the resurrection.) On the whole, I would have thought that first-century people were no more superstitious, credulous, or just plain stupid than we are.

Second, naturalism is not the only rational position a person can take. Bultmann's statement about the wireless is admirably picturesque and pointed, but I see no reason to believe it. Precisely why (or in what sense) is it impossible for a person who uses the wireless and the electric light to believe that miracles occur? I am unable to find any plausible construal of Bultmann's remarks, especially when there are today so many apparently quite rational people who both use the wireless and believe in miracles.

Interpreting Bultmann's remark, Van Harvey says,

He meant that the act of turning a switch, speaking over a microphone, visiting a doctor or a psychiatrist is a practical commitment to a host of beliefs foreign to those of the New Testament. It is to say that the world of modern theory—be it electrical, atomic, biological, even psychological—is a part of the furniture of our minds and that we assume this in our reading of the newspapers, in our debates over foreign policy, in our law courts, and, it needs to be added, in our writing of history. In other words, our daily intercourse reveals that we, in fact, do not believe in a three-story universe or in the possession of the mind by either angelic or demonic beings.[10]

I do not wish to comment here on demon-possession or on the famed three-story universe Bultmann and others think the New Testament writers believed in. The real question is, Do our modern beliefs and practices somehow commit us to naturalism or near naturalism? Again, I am unable to see why. It is quite correct that we are committed to giving naturalistic explanations (i.e., explanations that do not involve appeals to miracles) of the vast majority of the events we see occurring. But so were first-century people. I fail to see any good reason, either from Bultmann or Harvey, why a contemporary person cannot consistently be a supernaturalist.

(2) Other Christian thinkers, especially theologically conservative ones, try to show that belief in the resurrection of Jesus is the *only* rational position.[11] But one lesson Christian philosophers and apologists can draw from this paper is that if God's existence and the possibility of miracles are not first allowed, i.e., if naturalism is not first abandoned, it is difficult for evidence for, or arguments for, the resurrection to produce a conversion. The seminary professor who thought that any rational person who fairly examines the evidence must convert was wrong. A naturalist can say—and unless we can refute naturalism, such a position seems to me rational—"Yes, the evidence for the resurrection of Jesus is strong; I can't produce a good alternative explanation of what happened, but a resurrection just couldn't have happened."

Apologists for the resurrection are quick to criticize this position, and if we are careful only to look at it from a certain rather acute angle it does look weak. "True"—the apologist says—"secular historians will not accept the resurrection because they insist, on a priori grounds, that it could not have happened. But why so insist? Why not be open-minded rather than dogmatic about what we might find in history or in our experience? Let history speak for itself; don't interpret it only from the perspective of preconceived assumptions."

Although I am ultimately in sympathy with this criticism of naturalism, I believe it is often presented in far too facile a manner. It ignores the rationality of our bias against extraordinary events. I ask, How would you respond if somebody in all apparent sincerity told you that Bauer Hall levitated for an hour last night? Or, How would you respond if someone in all sincerity told you that John Lennon came back to life three days after his death?

What follows from this, I believe, is that the aim of Christian philosophers who want to defend the resurrection ought not to be hard apologetics. Unless naturalism can first be refuted, it is pointless to try to produce rational arguments that by their logical power will coerce conversions, so to speak. Disbelief in the resurrection does seem to be a rational position. The aim of Christian philosophers ought to be soft apologetics. They ought to try to defend belief in the resurrection against the objections of critics;

demonstrate the rationality of supernaturalism; and show that given supernaturalist assumptions, belief in the resurrection makes good sense.

What, then, about the question that forms this paper's title? Is it possible to know that Jesus was raised from the dead? Naturally, the answer will depend on what is meant by the word "know." If we accept a Cartesian notion of knowledge, whereby I know p if and only if I believe p and p is immune to all conceivable doubt, the answer is no. The same negative answer holds even if we accept the much weakened but far more plausible notion that I know p if and only if I believe p and p is immune to all *rational* doubt. As I have argued, the resurrection can rationally be doubted.

We did note, however, that the crucial difference in how one is likely to evaluate the claim that Jesus was raised is made by the worldview one accepts. The deepest question we can ask in this area accordingly emerges: which world view is more plausible, naturalism or supernaturalism? Unfortunately, answering that question is far beyond the scope of this paper and, perhaps, of my ability.

But if we ask the question with which we began in this way, Can it be rationally believed that Jesus was raised from the dead? the answer is yes.

Notes

1. And indeed that he was *bodily* raised from the dead, which in my opinion is the most acceptable interpretation of the doctrine for Christians.
2. See John Hick, *Faith and Knowledge* (Ithaca, N.Y.: Cornell University Press, 1957), pp. 182–191.
3. But perhaps not impossible. A skeptic who is present at the resurrection of a person dead for three days may well try to offer a naturalistic explanation ("psychosomatic cure of death"?), but the point is that based on our present knowledge, such an explanation would undoubtedly be highly improbable.
4. New York: Bantam Books, 1966.
5. Furthermore, while perhaps not a worldview per se, there is another difference between most believers and non-believers that is crucial to their different attitudes toward the resurrection. The believer accepts the view that the Bible is in some sense revelatory and reliable, and the nonbeliever does not. See, for example, Antony Flew, *God and Philosophy* (London: Hutchinson, 1966), p. 158: "We must never forget that it is only if we take for granted that these events were part of a unique divine revelation that we have any reason to be sure that the available evidence must be sufficient."
6. And who accept the reliability of the Bible. On this point, it should be added that there are, of course, many supernaturalists who allow for miracles but not the miracle of the resurrection of Jesus Christ. Typically, adherents of other religions than Christianity would take such a position. It is not part of my purpose to argue that belief in the resurrection of Jesus is compelling for all supernaturalists, but rather that belief in the resurrection of Jesus is rational

from the perspective of supernaturalism. It may indeed be compelling for those supernaturalists (Christian ones, of course) who hold that the Bible is revelatory and reliable, but that is not my main claim.

7. Rudolf Bultmann, *Kerygma and Myth*, ed. H. W. Bartsch (New York: Harper and Row, 1961), p. 41.

8. Willi Marxsen, *The Resurrection of Jesus of Nazareth* (Philadelphia: Fortress Press, 1970), pp. 143, 184.

9. *Ibid.*, p. 5; cf, p. 39.

10. Van Harvey, *The Historian and the Believer* (Philadelphia: Westminster Press, 1966), pp. 114–115.

11. This seems, for example, to be the aim of some books of conservative apologetics, e.g., Josh McDowell's *The Resurrection Factor* (San Bernardino, Calif.: Here's Life Publishers, Inc., 1981) and Gary Habermas's *The Resurrection of Jesus* (Grand Rapids, Mich.: Baker Book House, 1980).

Study Questions

1. Explain the difference between a soft miracle and a hard miracle. Into which category, if either, do you think the resurrection of Jesus fits best?

2. Why does Davis say that whether it is rational to believe that Jesus was raised from the dead is dependent on one's worldview? Does your worldview allow for the possibility that this event actually occurred?

David Hume

The Evidence for Miracles Is Weak

David Hume (1711–1776) crafted a number of arguments against miracles understood as violations of natural laws. In this selection, Hume considers how we should respond to reports of alleged miracles. The wise person, we are told, will always believe in proportion to the evidence. However, although our belief in the relevant laws of nature is based on uniform, public, past experience—which provides an overwhelming amount of objective evidence for questioning whether any alleged miraculous violation to these laws has occurred—the evidence supporting alleged violations of these laws consists solely of the personal testimonies of a small number of biased individuals, testimonies that cannot be substantiated by independent testing. Accordingly, Hume concludes, it is always most reasonable to assume that alleged miracles did not occur as reported.

…A miracle is a violation of the laws of nature; and as a firm and unalterable experience has established these laws, the proof against a miracle, from the very nature of the fact, is as entire as any argument from experience can possibly be imagined. Why is it more than probable, that all men must die; that lead cannot, of itself, remain suspended in the air; that fire consumes wood, and is extinguished by water; unless it be, that these events are found agreeable to the laws of nature, and there is required a violation of these laws, or in other words, a miracle to prevent them? Nothing is esteemed a miracle, if it ever happen in the common course of nature. It is no miracle that a man, seemingly in good health, should die of a sudden, because such a kind of death, though more unusual than any other, has yet been frequently observed to happen. But it is a miracle, that a dead man should come to life; because that has never been observed in any age or country. There must, therefore, be a uniform experience against every miraculous event, otherwise the event would not merit that appellation. And as a uniform experience amounts to a proof, there is here a direct and full *proof*, from the nature of the fact, against the existence of any miracle; nor can such a proof be destroyed, or the miracle rendered credible, but by an opposite proof, which is superior.

The plain consequence is (and it is a general maxim worthy of our attention), "That no testimony is sufficient to establish a miracle, unless the testimony be of such a kind, that its falsehood would be

From "Of Miracles," in *An Enquiry Concerning Human Understanding.*

more miraculous, than the fact, which it endeavors to establish; and even in that case there is a mutual destruction of arguments, and the superior only gives as an assurance suitable to that degree of force, which remains, after deducting the inferior." When anyone tells me, that he saw a dead man restored to life, I immediately consider with myself, whether it be more probable, that this person should either deceive or be deceived, or that the fact, which he relates, should really have happened. I weigh the one miracle against the other; and according to the superiority, which I discover, I pronounce my decision, and always reject the greater miracle. If the falsehood of his testimony would be more miraculous, than the event which he relates; then, and not till then, can he pretend to command my belief or opinion.

Why We Should Doubt Reports of Miraculous Events

In the foregoing reasoning we have supposed, that the testimony, upon which a miracle is founded, may possibly amount to an entire proof, and that the falsehood of that testimony would be a real prodigy: But it is easy to show, that we have been a great deal too liberal in our concession, and that there never was a miraculous event established on so full an evidence.

The Witnesses Are Not Reliable

For *first*, there is not to be found, in all history, any miracle attested by a sufficient number of men, of such unquestioned good sense, education, and learning, as to secure us against all delusion in themselves; of such undoubted integrity, as to place them beyond all suspicion of any design to deceive others; of such credit and reputation in the eyes of mankind, as to have a great deal to lose in case of their being detected in any falsehood; and at the same time, attesting facts performed in such a public manner and in so celebrated a part of the world, as to render the detection unavoidable: All which circumstances are requisite to give us a full assurance in the testimony of men.

Humans Are Gullible

Secondly. We may observe in human nature a principle which, if strictly examined, will be found to diminish extremely the assurance, which we might, from human testimony, have, in any kind of prodigy. The maxim, by which we commonly conduct ourselves in our reasonings, is, that the objects, of which we have no experience, resemble those, of which we have; that what we have found to be most usual is always most probable; and that where there is an opposition of arguments, we ought to give the preference to such as are founded on the greatest number of past observations. But though, in proceeding by this rule, we readily reject any fact which is unusual and incredible in an ordinary degree; yet in advancing farther, the mind observes not always the same rule; but when anything is affirmed utterly absurd and miraculous, it rather the more readily admits of such a fact, upon account of that very circumstance, which ought to destroy all its authority, the passion of *surprise* and *wonder*, arising from miracles, being an agreeable emotion, gives a sensible tendency towards the belief of those events, from which it is derived. And this goes so far, that even those who cannot enjoy this pleasure immediately, nor can believe those miraculous events, of which they are informed, yet love to partake of the satisfaction at second-hand or by rebound, and place a pride and delight in exciting the admiration of others.

With what greediness are the miraculous accounts of travelers received, their descriptions of sea and land monsters, their relations of wonderful adventures, strange men, and uncouth manners? But if the spirit of religion join itself to the love of wonder, there is an end of common sense; and human testimony, in these circumstances, loses all pretensions to authority. A religionist may be an enthusiast, and imagine he sees what has no reality: he may know his narrative to be false, and yet persevere in it, with the best intentions in the world, for the sake of promoting so holy a cause: or even where this delusion has not place, vanity, excited by so strong a temptation, operates on him more powerfully than on the rest of mankind in any other circumstances; and self-interest with equal force. His auditors may not have, and commonly have not, sufficient judgment to canvass his evidence: what judgment they have, they renounce by principle, in these sublime and mysterious subjects: or if they were ever so willing to employ it, passion and a heated imagination disturb the regularity of its operations. Their credulity increases his impudence: and his impudence overpowers their credulity.

Eloquence, when at its highest pitch, leaves little room for reason or reflection; but addressing itself entirely to the fancy or the affections, captivates the willing hearers, and subdues their understanding....Do not the same passions, and others still stronger, incline the generality of mankind to believe and report, with the greatest vehemence and assurance, all religious miracles?

Educated People Are Seldom Convinced

Thirdly. It forms a strong presumption against all supernatural and miraculous relations, that they are observed chiefly to abound among ignorant and barbarous nations; or if a civilized people has ever given admission to any of them, that people will be found to have received them from ignorant and barbarous ancestors, who transmitted them with that inviolable sanction and authority, which always attend received opinions. When we peruse the first histories of all nations, we are apt to imagine ourselves transported into some new world; where the whole frame of nature is disjointed, and every element performs its operations in a different manner, from what it does at present. Battles, revolutions, pestilence, famine and death, are never the effect of those natural causes, which we experience. Prodigies, omens, oracles, judgments, quite obscure the few natural events, that are intermingled with them. But as the former grow thinner every page, in proportion as we advance nearer the enlightened ages, we soon learn, that there is nothing mysterious or supernatural in the case, but that all proceeds from the usual propensity of mankind towards the marvelous, and that, though this inclination may at intervals receive a check from sense and learning, it can never be thoroughly extirpated from human nature.

It is strange, a judicious reader is apt to say, upon the perusal of these wonderful historians, *that such prodigious events never happen in our days*. But it is nothing strange, I hope, that men should lie in all ages. You must surely have seen instances enough of that frailty. You have yourself heard many such marvelous relations started, which, being treated with scorn by all the wise and judicious, have at last been abandoned even by the vulgar. Be assured, that those renowned lies, which have spread and flourished to such a monstrous height, arose from like beginnings; but being sown in a more proper soil, shot up at last into prodigies almost equal to those which they relate....

The advantages are so great, of starting an imposture among an ignorant people, that, even though the delusion should be too gross to impose on the generality of them (*which, though seldom, is sometimes the case*) it has a much better chance for succeeding in remote countries, than if the first scene had been laid in a city renowned for arts and knowledge. The most ignorant and barbarous of these barbarians carry the report abroad. None of their countrymen have a large correspondence, or sufficient credit and authority to contradict and beat down the delusion. Men's inclination to the marvelous has full opportunity to display itself. And thus a story, which is universally exploded in the place where it was first started, shall pass for certain at a thousand miles distance....

The Counterevidence Is Always Stronger

I may add as a *fourth* reason, which diminishes the authority of prodigies, that there is no testimony for any, even those which have not been expressly detected, that is not opposed by an infinite number of witnesses; so that not only the miracle destroys the credit of testimony, but the testimony destroys itself. To make this the better understood, let us consider, that, in matters of religion, whatever is different is contrary; and that it is impossible the religions of ancient Rome, of Turkey, of Siam, and of China should, all of them, be established on any solid foundation. Every miracle, therefore, pretended to have been wrought in any of these religions (and all of them abound in miracles), as its direct scope is to establish the particular system to which it is attributed; so has it the same force, though more indirectly, to overthrow every other system. In destroying a rival system, it likewise destroys the credit of those miracles, on which that system was established; so that all the prodigies of different religions are to be regarded as contrary facts; and the evidences of these prodigies, whether weak or strong, as opposite to each other. According to this method of reasoning, when we believe any miracle of Mahomet or his successors, we have for our warrant the testimony of a few barbarous Arabians: And on the other hand, we are to regard the authority of Titus Livius, Plutarch, Tacitus, and, in short, of all the authors and witnesses, Grecian, Chinese, and Roman Catholic, who have related any miracle in their particular religion; I say, we are to regard their testimony in the same light as if they had mentioned that Mahometan miracle, and had in express terms contradicted it, with the same certainty as they have for the miracle they relate. This argument may appear over subtile and refined; but is not in reality different from the reasoning of a judge, who supposes, that the credit of two witnesses, maintaining a crime against any one, is destroyed by the testimony of two others, who affirm him to have been two hundred leagues distant, at the same instant when the crime is said to have been committed....

There is also a memorable story related by Cardinal de Retz, which may well deserve our consideration. When that intriguing politician fled into Spain, to avoid the persecution of his enemies, he passed through Saragossa, the capital of Arragon, where he was shown, in the cathedral, a man, who had served seven years as a doorkeeper, and was well known to everybody in town, that had ever paid his devotions at that church. He had been seen, for so long a time, wanting a leg; but recovered that limb by the rubbing of holy oil upon the stump; and the cardinal assures us that he saw him with two legs. This miracle was vouched by all the canons of the church; and the whole company in town were appealed to for a confirmation of the fact: whom the cardinal found, by their zealous devotion, to be thorough believers of the miracle. Here the relater was also contemporary to the supposed prodigy, of an incredulous and libertine character, as well as of great genius; the miracle of so *singular* a nature as could scarcely admit of a counterfeit, and the witnesses very numerous, and all

of them, in a manner, spectators of the fact, to which they gave their testimony. And what adds mightily to the force of the evidence, and may double our surprise on this occasion, is, that the cardinal himself, who relates the story, seems not to give any credit to it, and consequently cannot be suspected of any concurrence in the holy fraud. He considered justly, that it was not requisite, in order to reject a fact of this nature, to be able accurately to disprove the testimony, and to trace its falsehood, through all the circumstances of knavery and credulity which produced it. He knew, that, as this was commonly altogether impossible at any small distance of time and place; so was it extremely difficult, even where one was immediately present, by reason of the bigotry, ignorance, cunning, and roguery of a great part of mankind. He therefore concluded, like a just reasoner, that such an evidence carried falsehood upon the very face of it, and that a miracle, supported by any human testimony, was more properly a subject of derision than of argument.

There surely never was a greater number of miracles ascribed to one person, than those, which were lately said to have been wrought in France upon the tomb of Abbé Paris, the famous Jansenist, with whose sanctity the people were so long deluded. The curing of the sick, giving hearing to the deaf, and sight to the blind, were every where talked of as the usual effects of that holy sepulchre. But what is more extraordinary; many of the miracles were immediately proved upon the spot, before judges of unquestioned integrity, attested by witnesses of credit and distinction, in a learned age, and on the most eminent theatre that is now in the world. Nor is this all: a relation of them was published and dispersed everywhere; nor were the *Jesuits*, though a learned body, supported by the civil magistrate, and determined enemies to those opinions, in whose favor the miracles were said to have been wrought, ever able distinctly to refute or detect them. Where shall we find such a number of circumstances, agreeing to the corroboration of one fact? And what have we to oppose to such a cloud of witnesses, but the absolute impossibility or miraculous nature of the events, which they relate? And this surely, in the eyes of all reasonable people, will alone be regarded as a sufficient refutation....

The wise lend a very academic faith to every report which favors the passion of the reporter; whether it magnifies his country, his family, or himself, or in any other way strikes in with his natural inclinations and propensities. But what greater temptation than to appear a missionary, a prophet, an ambassador from heaven? Who would not encounter many dangers and difficulties, in order to attain so sublime a character? Or if, by the help of vanity and a heated imagination, a man has first made a convert of himself, and entered seriously into the delusion; who ever scruples to make use of pious frauds, in support of so holy and meritorious a cause?

The smallest spark may here kindle into the greatest flame; because the materials are always prepared for it. The *avidum genus auricularum*,[1] the gazing populace, receive greedily, without examination, whatever soothes superstition, and promotes wonder.

How many stories of this nature have, in all ages, been detected and exploded in their infancy? How many more have been celebrated for a time, and have afterwards sunk into neglect and oblivion? Where such reports, therefore, fly about, the solution of the phenomenon is obvious; and we judge in conformity to regular experience and observation, when we account for it by the known and natural principles of credulity and delusion. And shall we, rather than have a recourse to so natural a solution, allow of a miraculous violation of the most established laws of nature?…

In the infancy of new religions, the wise and learned commonly esteem the matter too inconsiderable to deserve their attention or regard. And when afterwards they would willingly detect the cheat, in order to undeceive the deluded multitude, the season is now past, and the records and witnesses, which might clear up the matter, have perished beyond recovery.

No means of detection remain, but those which must be drawn from the very testimony itself of the reporters: and these, though always sufficient with the judicious and knowing, are commonly too fine to fall under the comprehension of the vulgar.

Upon the whole, then, it appears, that no testimony for any kind of miracle has ever amounted to a probability, much less to a proof; and that,

even supposing it amounted to a proof, it would be opposed by another proof; derived from the very nature of the fact, which it would endeavor to establish. It is experience only, which gives authority to human testimony; and it is the same experience, which assures us of the laws of nature. When, therefore, these two kinds of experience are contrary, we have nothing to do but subtract the one from the other, and embrace an opinion, either on one side or the other, with that assurance which arises from the remainder. But according to the principle here explained, this subtraction, with regard to all popular religions, amounts to an entire annihilation; and therefore we may establish it as a maxim, that no human testimony can have such force as to prove a miracle, and make it a just foundation for any such system of religion.

WHY MIRACULOUS REPORTS USED TO SUPPORT RELIGIOUS BELIEF ARE EVEN MORE DUBIOUS

I beg the limitations here made may be remarked, when I say, that a miracle can never be proved, so as to be the foundation of a system of religion. For I own, that otherwise, there may possibly be miracles, or violations of the usual course of nature, of such a kind as to admit of proof from human testimony, though, perhaps, it will be impossible to find any such in all the records of history. Thus, suppose, all authors, in all languages, agree, that, from the first of January 1600, there was a total darkness over the whole earth for eight days: suppose that the tradition of this extraordinary event is still strong and lively among the people: that all travelers, who return from foreign countries, bring us accounts of the same tradition, without the least variation or contradiction: it is evident, that our present philosophers, instead of doubting the fact, ought to receive it as certain, and ought to search for the causes whence it might be derived. The decay, corruption, and dissolution of nature, is an event rendered probable by so many analogies, that any phenomenon, which seems to have a tendency towards that catastrophe, comes within the reach of human testimony, if that testimony be very extensive and uniform.

But suppose, that all the historians who treat of England, should agree, that, on the first of January 1600, Queen Elizabeth died; that both before and after her death she was seen by her physicians and the whole court, as is usual with persons of her rank; that her successor was acknowledged and proclaimed by the Parliament; and that, after been interred a month, she again appeared, resumed the throne, and governed England for three years: I must confess that I should be surprised at the concurrence of so many odd circumstances, but should not have the least inclination to believe so miraculous an event. I should not doubt of her pretended death, and of those other public circumstances that followed it: I should only assert it to have been pretended, and that it neither was, nor possibly could be real. You would in vain object to me the difficulty, and almost impossibility of deceiving the world in an affair of such consequence; the wisdom and solid judgment of that renowned queen; with the little or no advantage which she could reap from so poor an artifice: All this might astonish me; but I would still reply, that the knavery and folly of men are such common phenomena, that I should rather believe the most extraordinary events to arise from their concurrence, than admit of so signal a violation of the laws of nature.

But should this miracle be ascribed to any new system of religion; men, in all ages, have been so much imposed on by ridiculous stories of that kind, that this very circumstance would be a full proof of a cheat, and sufficient, with all men of sense, not only to make them reject the fact, but even reject it without farther examination. Though the Being to whom the miracle is ascribed, be, in this case, Almighty, it does not, upon that account, become a whit more probable; since it is impossible for us to know the attributes or actions of such a Being, otherwise than from the experience which we have of his productions, in the usual course of nature. This still reduces us to past observation, and obliges us to compare the instances of the violation of truth in the testimony of men, with those of the violation of the laws of nature by miracles, in order to judge which of them is most likely and probable. As the violations of truth are more

common in the testimony concerning religious miracles, than in that concerning any other matter of fact; this must diminish very much the authority of the former testimony, and make us form a general resolution, never to lend any attention to it, with whatever specious pretence it may be covered.

Lord Bacon seems to have embraced the same principles of reasoning. "We ought," says he, "to make a collection or particular history of all monsters and prodigious births or productions, and in a word of every thing new, rare, and extraordinary in nature. But this must be done with the most severe scrutiny, lest we depart from truth. Above all, every relation must be considered as suspicious, which depends in any degree upon religion, as the prodigies of Livy: And no less so, every thing that is to be found in the writers of natural magic or alchemy, or such authors, who seem, all of them, to have an unconquerable appetite for falsehood and fable."[2]

I am the better pleased with the method of reasoning here delivered, as I think it may serve to confound those dangerous friends or disguised enemies to the *Christian Religion*, who have undertaken to defend it by the principles of human reason. Our most holy religion is founded on *Faith*, not on reason; and it is a sure method of exposing it to put it to such a trial as it is, by no means, fitted to endure. To make this more evident, let us examine those miracles, related in scripture; and not to lose ourselves in too wide a field, let us confine ourselves to such as we find in the *Pentateuch*, which we shall examine, according to the principles of these pretended Christians, not as the word or testimony of God himself, but as the production of a mere human writer and historian. Here then we are first to consider a book, *presented* to us by a barbarous and ignorant people, written in an age when they were still more barbarous, and in all probability long after the facts which it relates, corroborated by no concurring testimony, and resembling those fabulous accounts, which every nation gives of its origin. Upon reading this book, we find it full of prodigies and miracles. It gives an account of a state of the world and of human nature entirely different from the present: Of our fall from that state: Of the age of man, extended to near a thousand years: Of the destruction of the world by a deluge: Of the arbitrary choice of one people, as the favorites of heaven; and that people the countrymen of the author: Of their deliverance from bondage by prodigies the most astonishing imaginable: I desire any one to lay his hand upon his heart, and after a serious consideration declare, whether he thinks that the falsehood of such a book, supported by such a testimony, would be more extraordinary and miraculous than all the miracles it relates; which is, however, necessary to make it be received, according to the measures of probability above established.

Notes

1. Lucret.
2. Nov. Org. Lib. ii. aph. 29.

Study Questions

1. Hume maintains that it is always most reasonable to assume that an alleged miracle did not occur as reported. What do you see as his strongest argument for this claim? What do you see as his weakest argument for this claim? Elaborate.
2. The reported reappearance of a missing leg is the type of claim that Hume thinks we ought to reject. Are there conceivable conditions under which you would consider it reasonable to believe that such a claim was true?
3. Hume seems to believe that educated people are less likely to believe that violations of natural laws have occurred. Do you agree? Why, or why not?

J. L. Mackie

Miracles and Testimony

In this selection, J. L. Mackie (1917–1981) presents an updated version of Hume's argument against accepting reports of miracles. Mackie acknowledges that Hume's argument needs revision because certain forms of evidence for the occurrence of alleged counterinstances to natural laws are stronger than Hume is willing to grant. However, those who want to accept the report that a violation of a natural law has actually occurred, he argues, have a double burden: to establish that the event has occurred and that it has violated a natural law. Mackie emphasizes that the attempt to establish both points simultaneously is quite problematic, since the stronger the evidence for believing that an event has actually violated a natural law, the weaker the evidence for believing that this event actually occurred as reported.

... Hume's case against miracles is an epistemological argument: it does not try to show that miracles never do happen or never could happen, but only that we never have good reasons for believing that they have happened. It must be clearly distinguished from the suggestion that the very concept of a miracle is incoherent. That suggestion might be spelled out as follows. A miracle is, by definition, a violation of a law of nature, and a law of nature is, by definition, a regularity—or the statement of a regularity—about what happens, about the way the world works; consequently, if some event actually occurs, no regularity which its occurrence infringes (or, no regularity-statement which it falsifies) can really be a law of nature; so this event, however unusual or surprising, cannot after all be a miracle. The two definitions together entail that whatever happens is not a miracle, that is, that miracles never happen. This, be it noted, is not Hume's argument. If it were correct, it would make Hume's argument unnecessary. Before we discuss Hume's case, then, we should consider whether there is a coherent concept of a miracle which would not thus rule out the occurrence of miracles a priori.

MIRACLES COULD OCCUR

If miracles are to serve their traditional function of giving spectacular support to religious claims—whether general theistic claims, or the authority of some specific religion or some particular sect or individual teacher—the concept must not be so weakened that anything at all unusual or remarkable counts as a miracle. We must keep in the definition the notion of a violation of natural law. But then, if it is to be even possible that a miracle should occur, we must modify the definition given above of a law of nature. What we want to do is to contrast the order of nature with a possible divine or supernatural intervention. The laws of nature, we must say, describe the ways in which the world—including, of course, human beings—works when left to itself, when not interfered with. A miracle occurs when the world is not left to itself, when something distinct from the natural order as a whole intrudes into it.

Natural Laws Could Be Violated

This notion of ways in which the world works is coherent and by no means obscure. We know how to discover causal laws, relying on a principle of the uniformity of the course of nature—essentially the assumption that there are some laws to be found—in conjunction with suitable observations and experiments, typically varieties of controlled experiment whose underlying logic is that of Mill's "method of difference." Within the laws so established, we can further mark off basic laws of working from derived laws which hold only in a particular context or contingently upon the way in which something is put together. It will be a derived law that a particular clock, or clocks of a particular sort, run at such a speed, and this will hold only in certain conditions of temperature, and so on; but this law will be derived from more basic ones which describe the regular behavior of certain kinds of material, in view of the way in which the clock is put together, and these more basic laws of materials may in turn be derived from yet more basic laws about sub-atomic particles, in view of the ways in which those materials are made up of such particles. In so far as we advance towards a knowledge of such a system of basic and derived laws, we are acquiring an understanding of ways in which the world works. As well as what we should ordinarily call causal laws, which typically concern interactions, there are similar laws

with regard to the ways in which certain kinds of things simply persist through time, and certain sorts of continuous process just go on. These too, and in particular the more basic laws of these sorts, help to constitute the ways in which the world works. Thus there are several kinds of basic "laws of working."[1] For our present purpose, however, it is not essential that we should even be approaching an understanding of how the world works; it is enough that we have the concept of such basic laws of working, that we know in principle what it would be to discover them. Once we have this concept, we have moved beyond the definition of laws of nature merely as (statements of) what always happens. We can see how, using this concept and using the assumption that there are some such basic laws of working to be found, we can hope to determine what the actual laws of working are by reference to a restricted range of experiments and observations. This opens up the possibility that we might determine that something is a basic law of working of natural objects, and yet also, independently, find that it was occasionally violated. An occasional violation does not in itself necessarily overthrow the independently established conclusion that this *is* a law of working.

Supernatural Intervention Is Not Impossible

Equally, there is no obscurity in the notion of intervention. Even in the natural world we have a clear understanding of how there can be for a time a closed system, in which everything that happens results from factors within that system in accordance with its laws of working, but how then something may intrude from outside it, bringing about changes that the system would not have produced of its own accord, so that things go on after this intrusion differently from how they would have gone on if the system had remained closed. All we need do, then, is to regard the whole natural world as being, for most of the time, such a closed system; we can then think of a supernatural intervention as something that intrudes into that system from outside the natural world as a whole.

If the laws by which the natural world works are deterministic, then the notion of a violation of them is quite clear-cut: such a violation would be an event which, given that the world was a closed system working in accordance with these laws, and given some actual earlier complete state of the world, simply could not have happened at all. Its occurrence would then be clear proof that either the supposed laws were not the real laws of working, or the earlier state was not as it was supposed to have been, or else the system was not closed after all. But if the basic laws of working are statistical or probabilistic, the notion of a violation of them is less precise. If something happens which, given those statistical laws and some earlier complete state of the world, is extremely improbable—in the sense of physical probability: that is, something such that there is a strong propensity or tendency for it *not* to happen—we still cannot say firmly that the laws have been violated: laws of this sort explicitly allow that what is extremely improbable may occasionally come about. Indeed it is highly probable (both physically and epistemically) that some events, each of which is very improbable, will occur at rare intervals.[2] If tosses of a coin were governed by a statistical law that gave a 50 percent propensity to heads at each toss, a continuous run of ten heads would be a highly improbable occurrence; but it would be highly probable that there would be some such runs in a sequence of a million tosses. Nevertheless, we can still use the contrast between the way of working of the natural world as a whole, considered as a normally closed system, and an intervention or intrusion into it. This contrast does not disappear or become unintelligible merely because we lack decisive tests for its application. We can still define a miracle as an event which would not have happened in the course of nature, and which came about only through a supernatural intrusion. The difficulty is merely that we cannot now say with certainty, simply by reference to the relevant laws and some antecedent situation, that a certain event would not have happened in the course of nature, and therefore must be such an intrusion. But we may still be able to say that it is very probable—and this is now an epistemic probability—that it would not have happened naturally, and so is likely to be such an intrusion. For if the laws made it physically improbable that it would come about, this tends

to make it epistemically improbable that it did come about through those laws, if there is any other way in which it could have come about and which is not equally improbable or more improbable. In practice the difficulty mentioned is not much of an extra difficulty. For even where we believe there to be deterministic laws and an earlier situation which together would have made an occurrence actually impossible in the course of nature, it is from our point of view at best epistemically very probable, not certain, that those are the laws and that that was the relevant antecedent situation.

Consequently, whether the laws of nature are deterministic or statistical, we can give a coherent definition of a miracle as a supernatural intrusion into the normally closed system that works in accordance with those laws, and in either case we can identify conceivable occurrences, and alleged occurrences, which if they were to occur, or have occurred, could be believed with high probability, though not known with certainty, to satisfy that definition.

However, the full concept of a miracle requires that the intrusion should be purposive, that it should fulfil the intention of a god or other supernatural being. This connection cannot be sustained by any ordinary causal theory; it presupposes a power to fulfil intentions directly, without physical means, which... is highly dubious; so this requirement for a miracle will be particularly hard to confirm. On the other hand it is worth noting that successful prophecy could be regarded as a form of miracle for which there could in principle be good evidence. If someone is reliably recorded as having prophesied at t_1 an event at t_2 which could not be predicted at t_1 on any natural grounds, and the event occurs at t_2, then at any later time t_3 we can assess the evidence for the claims both that the prophecy was made at t_1 and that its accuracy cannot be explained either causally (for example, on the ground that it brought about its own fulfilment) or as accidental, and hence that it was probably miraculous.

There is, then, a coherent concept of miracles. Their possibility is not ruled out a priori, by definition. So we must consider whether Hume's argument shows that we never have good reason for believing that any have occurred.

We Have Good Reasons to Believe Miracles Never Do Occur

Hume's Argument Clarified

Hume's general principle for the evaluation of testimony, that we have to weigh the unlikelihood of the event reported against the unlikelihood that the witness is mistaken or dishonest, is substantially correct. It is a corollary of the still more general principle of accepting whatever hypothesis gives the best overall explanation of all the available and relevant evidence. But some riders are necessary. First, the likelihood or unlikelihood, the epistemic probability or improbability, is always relative to some body of information, and may change if additional information comes in. Consequently, any specific decision in accordance with Hume's principle must be provisional. Secondly, it is one thing to decide which of the rival hypotheses in the field at any time should be provisionally accepted in the light of the evidence then available; but it is quite another to estimate the weight of this evidence, to say how well supported this favored hypothesis is, and whether it is likely that its claims will be undermined either by additional information or by the suggesting of further alternative hypotheses. What is clearly the best-supported view of some matter at the moment may still be very insecure, and quite likely to be overthrown by some further considerations. For example, if a public opinion poll is the only evidence we have about the result of a coming election, this evidence may point, perhaps decisively, to one result rather than another; yet if the poll has reached only a small sample of the electorate, or if it was taken some time before the voting day, it will not be very reliable. There is a dimension of reliability over and above that of epistemic probability relative to the available evidence. Thirdly, Hume's description of what gives support to a prediction, or in general to a judgment about an unobserved case that would fall under some generalization, is very unsatisfactory. He seems to say that if *all* so-far observed As have been Bs, then this amounts to a "proof" that some unobserved A will be (or is, or was) a B, whereas if some observed As have been Bs, but some have not, there is only a "probability" that an unobserved A will

be a B.[3] ... [However] a good deal of other information and background knowledge is needed, in either case, before the generalization, whether universal or statistical, is at all well supported, and hence before the stage is properly set for either proof or probabilification about an as yet unobserved A. It is harder than Hume allows here to arrive at well-supported generalizations of either sort about how the world works.

These various qualifications together entail that what has been widely and reasonably thought to be a law of nature may not be one, perhaps in ways that are highly relevant to some supposed miracles. Our present understanding of psychosomatic illness, for example, shows that it is not contrary to the laws of nature that someone who for years has seemed, to himself as well as to others, to be paralyzed should rapidly regain the use of his limbs. On the other hand, we can still be pretty confident that it is contrary to the laws of nature that a human being whose heart has stopped beating for forty-eight hours in ordinary circumstances—that is, without any special life-support systems—should come back to life, or that what is literally water should without addition or replacement turn into what is literally good-quality wine.

However, any problems there may be about establishing laws of nature are neutral between the parties to the present debate, Hume's followers and those who believe in miracles; for both these parties need the notion of a well-established law of nature. The miracle advocate needs it in order to be able to say that the alleged occurrence is a miracle, a violation of natural law by supernatural intervention, no less than Hume needs it for his argument against believing that this event has actually taken place.

It is therefore not enough for the defender of a miracle to cast doubt (as he well might) on the certainty of our knowledge of the law of nature that seems to have been violated. For he must himself say that this is a law of nature: otherwise the reported event will not be miraculous. That is, he must in effort *concede* to Hume that the antecedent improbability of this event is as high as it could be, hence that, apart from the testimony, we have the strongest possible grounds for believing that the alleged event did not occur. This event must, by the miracle advocate's own admission, be contrary to a genuine, not merely a supposed, law of nature, and therefore maximally improbable. It is this maximal improbability that the weight of the testimony would have to overcome.

One further improvement is needed in Hume's theory of testimony. It is well known that the agreement of two (or more) *independent witnesses* constitutes very powerful evidence. Two independent witnesses are more than twice as good as each of them on his own. The reason for this is plain. If just one witness says that *p*, one explanation of this would be that it was the case that *p* and that he has observed this, remembered it, and is now making an honest report; but there are many alternative explanations, for example that he observed something else which he mistook for its being that *p*, or is misremembering what he observed, or is telling a lie. But if two witnesses who can be shown to be quite independent of one another both say that *p*, while again one explanation is that each of them has observed this and remembered it and is reporting honestly, the alternative explanations are not now so easy. They face the question "How has there come about this *agreement* in their reports, if it was not the case that *p*? How have the witnesses managed to misobserve to the same effect, or to misremember in the same way, or to hit upon the same lie?" It is difficult for even a single liar to keep on telling a *consistent* false story; it is much harder for two or more liars to do so. Of course if there is any collusion between the witnesses, or if either has been influenced, directly or indirectly, by the other, or if both stories have a common source, this question is easily answered. That is why the independence of the witnesses is so important. This principle of the improbability of coincident error has two vital bearings upon the problem of miracles. On the one hand, it means that a certain sort of testimony can be more powerful evidence than Hume's discussion would suggest. On the other, it means that where we seem to have a plurality of reports, it is essential to check carefully whether they really are independent of one another; the difficulty of meeting this requirement would be an important supplement to the points made in Part II of Hume's essay. Not only in remote and barbarous times, but also in recent ones, we are usually justified in suspecting that what look like distinct reports of a remarkable occurrence arise from different strands of a single tradition between which there has already been communication.

The Key Problem Summarized

We can now put together the various parts of our argument. Where there is some plausible testimony about the occurrence of what would appear to be a miracle, those who accept this as a miracle have the double burden of showing both that the event took place and that it violated the laws of nature. But it will be very hard to sustain this double burden. For whatever tends to show that it would have been a violation of natural law tends for that very reason to make it most unlikely that it actually happened. Correspondingly, those who deny the occurrence of a miracle have two alternative lines of defense. One is to say that the event may have occurred, but in accordance with the laws of nature. Perhaps there were unknown circumstances that made it possible; or perhaps what were thought to be the relevant laws of nature are not strictly laws; there may be as yet unknown kinds of natural causation through which this event might have come about. The other is to say that this event would indeed have violated natural law, but that for this very reason there is a very strong presumption against its having happened, which it is most unlikely that any testimony will be able to outweigh. Usually one of these defenses will be stronger than the other. For many supposedly miraculous cures, the former will be quite a likely sort of explanation, but for such feats as the bringing back to life of those who are really dead the latter will be more likely. But the *fork*, the disjunction of these two sorts of explanation, is as a whole a very powerful reply to any claim that a miracle has been performed.

MIRACLES CAN'T OFFER SUPPORT FOR BELIEF IN GOD

However, we should distinguish two different contexts in which an alleged miracle might be discussed. One possible context would be where the parties in debate already both accept some general theistic doctrines, and the point at issue is whether a miracle has occurred which would enhance the authority of a specific sect or teacher. In this context supernatural intervention, though prima facie unlikely on any particular occasion, is, generally speaking, on the cards: it is not altogether outside the range of reasonable expectation for these parties. Since they agree that there is an omnipotent deity, or at any rate one or more powerful supernatural beings, they cannot find it absurd to suppose that such a being will occasionally interfere with the course of nature, and this *may* be one of these occasions. For example, if one were already a theist and a Christian, it would not be unreasonable to weigh seriously the evidence of alleged miracles as some indication whether the Jansenists or the Jesuits enjoyed more of the favor of the Almighty. But it is a very different matter if the context is that of fundamental debate about the truth of theism itself. Here one party to the debate is initially at least agnostic, and does not yet concede that there is a supernatural power at all. From this point of view the intrinsic improbability of a genuine miracle, as defined above, is very great, and one or other of the alternative explanations in our fork will always be much more likely—that is, either that the alleged event is not miraculous, or that it did not occur, that the testimony is faulty in some way.

This entails that it is pretty well impossible that reported miracles should provide a worthwhile argument for theism addressed to those who are initially inclined to atheism or even to agnosticism. Such reports can form no significant part of what, following Aquinas, we might call a *Summa contra Gentiles*, or what, following Descartes, we could describe as being addressed to infidels. Not only are such reports unable to carry any rational conviction on their own, but also they are unable even to contribute independently to the kind of accumulation or battery of arguments referred to in the Introduction. To this extent Hume is right, despite the inaccuracies we have found in his statement of the case.

There is, however, a possibility which Hume's argument seems to ignore—though, as we shall see, he did not completely ignore it. The argument has been directed against the acceptance of miracles on testimony; but what, it may be objected, if one is not reduced to reliance on testimony, but has observed a miracle for oneself? Surprisingly, perhaps, this possibility does not make very much difference. The first of the above-mentioned lines of defense is still available: maybe the unexpected event that one has oneself observed did indeed occur, but in accordance with the laws of nature. Either the relevant circumstances or the operative laws were not what one had supposed them to be. But at least a part of the other line of defense is also available. Though one is not now relying literally on another witness or other witnesses, we speak not inappropriately of the evidence of our senses, and what one takes to be an observation of one's own is open to questions of the same sort as is the report of some other person. I may have misobserved what took place, as anyone knows who has ever been fooled by a conjurer or "magician," and, though this is somewhat less likely, I may be misremembering or deceiving myself after an interval of time. And of course, the corroboration of one or more independent witnesses would bring in again the testimony of others which it was the point of this objection to do without. Nevertheless, anyone who is fortunate enough to have carefully observed and carefully recorded, for himself, an apparently miraculous occurrence is no doubt rationally justified in taking it very seriously; but even here it will be in order to entertain the possibility of an alternative natural explanation.

As I said, Hume does not completely ignore this possibility. The Christian religion, he says, cannot at this day be believed by any reasonable person without a miracle. "Mere reason is insufficient to convince us of its veracity: And whoever is moved by *Faith* to assent to it, is conscious of a continued miracle in his own person, which subverts all the principles of his understanding."[4] But of course this is only a joke. What the believer is conscious of in his own person, though it may be a mode of thinking that goes against "custom and experience," and so is contrary to the ordinary rational principles of the understanding, is not, as an occurrence, a violation of natural law. Rather it is all too easy to explain immediately by the automatic communication of beliefs between persons and the familiar psychological processes of wish fulfillment, and ultimately by what Hume himself was later to call "the natural history of religion."

Notes

1. The notion of basic laws of working is fully discussed in chaps. 8 and 9 of my *The Cement of the Universe: A Study of Causation* (Oxford, England: Oxford University, Press, 1974 and 1980).
2. The distinction between physical and epistemic probability has been drawn in my Introduction; the exact form of statistical laws is discussed in chap. 9 of *The Cement of the Universe*.
3. David Hume, "Of Miracles," reprinted in *Miracles* (New York: Macmillan, 1989), pp. 24–26.
4. Hume, "Of Miracles," p. 40.

Study Questions

1. Why does Mackie believe that any evidence supporting the belief that an event is really a violation of a natural law is at the same time evidence against the belief that the event actually occurred as reported or observed? Did you find his argument convincing?
2. Some claim that the stronger the evidence for violations of natural laws, the more probable it is that God exists. Others claim that the stronger the evidence that God exists, the more probable it is that violations of natural laws occur. Would Mackie accept either statement as true? Do you believe either to be true?

Richard Swinburne

Miracles and Historical Evidence

Hume argues that the minimal, subjective evidence supporting the report of an allegedly miraculous event can never outweigh the widespread, objective evidence supporting the contention that it did not occur as reported. In the selection presented here, Richard Swinburne (b. 1934) challenges this argument, claiming that the objective evidence for such an event is not insignificant. Such evidence can be furnished by our own apparent memories, which our past experience gives us good reason to believe should be given strong credence; the testimony of others, which can be tested for reliability by common methods; and by the relevant physical traces, which can be tested for reliability by such means as carbon dating, x-rays, and videos. The combination of these forms of evidence could in some cases, Swinburne concludes, outweigh the familiar and seemingly incontrovertible counterevidence against the accuracy of reports of alleged miracles.

CONSIDERATIONS WHEN ASSESSING MIRACULOUS CLAIMS

[I have claimed] that we could have good reason to suppose that event *E*, if it occurred, was a violation of a law of nature *L*. But could one have good evidence that such an event *E* occurred? At this point we must face the force of Hume's own argument. This, it will be remembered, runs as follows. The evidence, which *ex hypothesi* is good evidence, that *L* is a law of nature is evidence that *E* did not occur. We have certain other evidence that *E* did occur. In such circumstances, writes Hume, the wise man "weighs the opposite experiments. He considers which side is supported by the greater number of experiments."

Since he supposes that the evidence that *E* occurred would be that of testimony, Hume concludes "that no testimony is sufficient to establish a miracle, unless the testimony be of such a kind, that its falsehood would be more miraculous, than the fact which it endeavors to establish."

We have four kinds of evidence about what happened at some past instant–our own apparent memories of our past experiences, the testimony of others about their past experiences, physical traces and our contemporary understanding of what things are physically impossible or improbable. (The fourth is only a corrective to the other three, not an independent source of detailed information.) A piece of evidence gives grounds for believing that some past event occurred, except in so far as it conflicts with other pieces of evidence. In so far as pieces of evidence conflict, they have to be weighed against each other....

The fundamental idea involved in...weighing evidence seems to be to obtain as coherent a picture as possible of the past as consistent as possible with the evidence. We can express this idea in the form of one basic principle for assessing evidence and several subsidiary principles limiting its operation. The most basic principle is to accept as many pieces of evidence as possible. If one witness says one thing, and five witnesses say a different thing, then, in the absence of further evidence (e.g., about their unreliability) take the testimony of the latter. If one method of dating an artifact gives one result, and five methods give a different result, then, in the absence of further information accept the latter result.

What Types of Evidence Are Most Trustworthy?

The first subsidiary principle is—apart from any empirical evidence about their relative reliability—that evidence of different kinds ought to be given different weights. How this is to be done can only be illustrated by examples. Thus one's own apparent memory ought as such to count for more than the testimony of another witness (unless and until evidence of its relative unreliability is forthcoming). If I appear to remember having seen Jones yesterday in Hull, but Brown says that he had Jones under observation all day yesterday and that he went nowhere near to Hull, then—*ceteris paribus*—I ought to stand by my apparent memory. This is because when someone else gives testimony it always makes sense to suppose that he is lying; whereas, when I report to myself what I appear to remember, I cannot be lying. For the liar is someone who says what he believes to be false. But if I report what I appear to remember (and I can *know* for certain what I appear to remember), I cannot be lying. Secondly, if I feel highly confident that I remember some event, my apparent memory ought to count for more than if I am only moderately confident. My apparent memory has a built-in weight, apart from empirical evidence which may be

forthcoming about its reliability in different circumstances (e.g., that it is not reliable when I am drunk). In these and other ways for non-empirical reasons different pieces of evidence ought to be given different weights in assessing the balance of evidence.

Is the Evidence from a Reliable Source?

The second subsidiary principle is that different pieces of evidence ought to be given different weights in accordance with any empirical evidence which may be available about their different reliability, obtained by a procedure which I may term narrowing the evidence class. In general we necessarily assume or have reason to believe that apparent memory, testimony and states of particular types are reliable evidence about past states and events. But clash of evidence casts doubt on this. So we test the reliability of a piece of evidence by classifying it as a member of a narrow class, and investigating the reliability of other members of that class which...would have to be classes whose members were described by projectible predicates. If the testimony of Jones conflicts with the testimony of Smith, then we must investigate not the worth of testimony in general, but the worth of Jones' testimony and of Smith's testimony. We do this by seeing if on all other occasions when we can ascertain what happened Jones or Smith correctly described what happened. In so far as each did, his testimony is reliable....

Similar tests to these tests of the reliability of testimony can be made of the reliability of traces, e.g., of methods of dating ancient documents.

Can the Evidence Be Explained Away?

The third subsidiary principle is not to reject coincident evidence (unless the evidence of its falsity is extremely strong) unless an explanation can be given of the coincidence; and the better substantiated is that explanation, the more justified the rejection of the coincident evidence. If five witnesses all say the same thing and we wish to reject their evidence, we are in general not justified in doing so unless we can explain why they all said the same thing. Such explanations could be that they were subject to common illusions, or all plotted together to give false testimony. The better substanti-ated is such an explanation the better justified is our rejection of the evidence. Substantiation of the theory of a common plot would be provided by evidence that the witnesses were all seen together before the event, that they stood to gain from giving false testimony, etc. But ultimately the evidence rests on evidence about particular past events and would itself need to be sub-stantiated in ways earlier described.

These subsidiary principles, and perhaps others which I have not described, then qualify the basic prin-ciple of accepting the majority of the evidence. They are the standards of investigation adopted, I would claim, by and large by all historical investigators....

Assessing Conflicts Between Historical and Scientific Evidence for Miraculous Claims

Flew's Support for Scientific Evidence

Bearing in mind these considerations about conflict-ing evidence and these principles for assessing dif-ferent ways of weighing evidence, what are we to say when there is a conflict between evidence of the first three kinds that an event E occurred and evidence of the fourth kind that an event of the type of E is physi-cally impossible? Hume's official answer...was that exceedingly strong evidence of other kinds, in partic-ular testimony, would be needed for evidence about physical impossibility to be outweighed. A more extreme answer is given by Antony Flew in a passage in his *Hume's Philosophy of Belief.*

> The justification for giving the "scientific" this ultimate precedence here over the "historical" lies in the nature of the propositions concerned and in the evidence which can be displayed to sustain them...the candidate his-torical proposition will be particular, often singular, and in the past tense....But just by reason of this very past-ness and particularity it is no longer possible for anyone to examine the subject directly for himself...the law of nature will, unlike the candidate historical proposition, be a general nomological. It can thus in theory, though obviously not always in practice, be tested at any time by any person.

Flew seems here to be taking the view that evidence of the fourth kind ("scientific" evidence) could never be outweighed by evidence of the first three kinds ("historical" evidence), an answer suggested also by Hume's detailed discussions of three purported mir-acles. Flew's justification for this view is that while a historical proposition concerns a past event of which we have only the present remains (viz. evidence of the first three kinds), the scientific proposition, being a general statement (viz. about all entities of some kind at all times and places), can go on and on being tested by any person who wishes to test it. Flew's suggestion seems to be that the historical proposition cannot go on and on being tested by any person at any time.

If this is Flew's contrast, it is mistaken. Particular experiments on particular occasions only give a cer-tain and far from conclusive support to claims that a purported scientific law is true. Any person can test for the truth of a purported scientific law, but a posi-tive result to one test will give only limited support to the claim. Exactly the same holds for purported historical truths. Anyone can examine the evidence, but a particular piece of evidence gives only limited support to the claim that the historical proposition is true. But in the historical as in the scientific case, there is no limit to the testing which we can do.... This indirect evidence could mount up in just the way in which the evidence of the physical impossibility of an event could mount up. Hence by his examining the reliability of the direct evidence, the truth of the "historical" proposition like the "scientific" can also "be tested at any time by any person."

Swinburne's Support for Historical Evidence

But if Flew's justification of his principle is mistaken, what can we say positively for or against the principle itself? Now I would urge that it is an unreasonable principle since claims that some formula L is a law of nature, and claims that apparent memory, testimony or traces of certain types are to be relied on are claims established ultimately in a similar kind of way...and will be strong or weak for the same reasons, and so neither ought to take automatic preference over the other. To make the supposition that they are to be treated differently is to introduce a complicating *ad hoc* procedure for assessing evidence. As we have seen, formulae about how events succeed each other are shown to be laws of nature by the fact that they provide the most simple and coherent account of a large number of observed data. Likewise testimony given by certain kinds of people or traces of certain kinds are established as reliable by well-established correlations between present and past phenomena. (The reliability of apparent memory could also be assessed in the same way, but we will ignore this for the moment, as important only for the few who claim to have observed miracles.) The reliability of C_{14} dating is established by showing that the postulated correlation between the proportion of C_{14} in artifacts and their age since manufacture clearly established by other methods holds of the large number of cases studied without exception and is the simplest correlation that does. That testimony given by Jones on oath is to be relied on is to be established by showing that whatever Jones said on oath is often by other methods shown to be true and never shown to be false, and there is no other simple account of the matter coherent with the data than that Jones tells the truth on oath (e.g., the account that in each of these cases he told the truth because he knew that a lie could be detected).

So then a claim that a formula L is a law of nature and a claim that testimony or trace of a certain type is reliable are established in basically the same way—by showing that certain formulae connect observed data in a simple coherent way. This being so, whether we take the evidence of an established law of nature that E did not occur or the evidence of trace or testimony that it did would seem to be a matter of the firmness with which the law, if reliable, forbids and the firmness with which the trace or testimony, if reliable, establishes the occurrence of E, and of the reliability of each. If the law is universal, it will firmly rule out an exception; if it is statistical, it will merely show an exception to be highly improbable.... Likewise traces or testimony may, in virtue of the correlation used, either show to be certain or show to be highly probable the event in question.

If the correlation between (e.g.) testimony of a certain kind of witness and the past event testified to is statistical (e.g., "witnesses of such and such a type are reliable in 99 percent of cases") then it shows that the event in question (what the witness reported) having happened is highly probable. If the correlation is universal ("witnesses of such and such a type are invariably reliable") then it makes certain the occurrence of the event in question (viz. given the truth of the correlation, it is then certain that the event happened). So whether the evidence on balance supports or opposes the occurrence of E is firstly a matter of whether the law or correlation in question is universal or statistical in form. It is secondly a matter of how well established the law or correlation is: a statistical law may have very strong evidence in its favor. The basic laws of quantum theory are statistical in form but the evidence in their favor is enormously strong. On the other hand, some universal laws are, though established, not very strongly established. Such are, for example, many of the generalizations of biology or anthropology. If L is a law, universal or statistical, to which the occurrence of E would be an exception, and T is a trace or piece of testimony of the occurrence of E, shown to be such by an established correlation C, whether the evidence on balance supports or opposes the occurrence of E is a matter of whether L and C are universal or statistical, and how well established respectively are L and C.

If C is universal and better established than L, then, surely, whether L is universal or statistical, the evidence on balance supports the occurrence of E; whereas if L is universal and is better established than C, then, whether C is universal or merely statistical, the evidence is against the occurrence of E. If C and L are both statistical, and C is no less well established than L, and C renders the occurrence of E more probable than L renders it improbable, then the evidence on balance supports the occurrence of E. If C and L are both statistical, and L is no less well established than C, and L renders the occurrence of E more improbable than C renders it probable, then the evidence on balance is against the occurrence of E. What we are to say in other cases depends on whether we can measure antitatively how well established are C and L and compare these figures with the probability and the improbability which they respectively ascribe to E. How well established or confirmed are L or C is a matter of how well they (or the scientific theory of which they are part) integrate a large number of data into a simple and coherent pattern....

It is not always easy to compare the strength of support for various proposed laws or correlations, let alone measure such strength quantitatively. But, as we have seen, laws and correlations are supported in a similar kind of way by instances. Hence it seems reasonable to suppose that in principle the degree of support for any correlation C or disjunction of correlations could exceed the degree of support for any law and hence render it more probable than not that the cited event E occurred. Flew's principle can only be saved if we suppose that support for the C's and support for L are to be treated differently just because of the different role which the C's and L play in supporting or opposing the occurrence of E. But this seems to be to make a complicating, *ad hoc* supposition. Flew's principle advocates treating evidence for generalizations in a different way from the way in which we ordinarily treat it, and is therefore for this reason to be rejected.

It must however be admitted that in general any one correlation C will be less well established than L, and since L will usually be a universal law, its evidence will in general be preferred to that of C. However, the more pieces of evidence there are that E occurred (e.g., the testimony of many independent witnesses), the more such evidence by its cumulative effect will tend to outweigh the counter-evidence of L. This accounts for our previous third subsidiary principle.

Although we do not yet have any exact laws about the reliability of testimony of different kinds, we have considerable empirical information which is not yet precisely formulated. We know that witnesses with axes to grind are less to be relied on than witnesses with no stake in that to which they testify; that primitive people whose upbringing conditions them to expect unusual events are more likely to report the occurrence of unusual events which do not occur than are modern atheists (perhaps too that modern atheists are more likely to deny the occurrence of unusual events which in fact occur in their environment than are primitive people); and so on.

I venture to suggest that generalizations of this kind about the reliability of testimony, although statistical in character, are extremely well established, perhaps better established than many laws of nature. However it must be added that while we can construct wide and narrow generalizations about the reliability of contemporary witnesses which are well confirmed, generalizations about the reliability of past witnesses will be more shaky, for we have less information about them and it is in practice often difficult to obtain more.

Now, although we are in no position yet (if ever we will be) to work out numerically the degree or balance of support for a violation E of a law of nature L having taken place, since a priori objections have been overruled, we can surely cite examples where the combined testimony of many witnesses to such an event is in the light of the above considerations to be accepted.

One interesting such example is given by Hume himself:

> Thus, suppose, all authors in all languages agree, that, from the first of January 1600, there was a total darkness over the whole earth for eight days: suppose that the tradition of this extraordinary event is still strong and lively among the people: that all travellers, who return from foreign countries, bring us accounts of the same tradition, without the least variation or contradiction: it is evidence, that our present philosophers, instead of doubting the fact, ought to receive it as certain, and ought to search for the causes whence it might be derived.

...The example is similar to many which might be artificially constructed in which the amount, diversity, and detail of testimony to the occurrence of E surely suffices to overwhelm any information provided by science that E is physically impossible.

So I conclude that although standards for weighing evidence are not always clear, apparent memory, testimony and traces could sometimes outweigh the evidence of physical impossibility. It is just a question of how much evidence of the former kind we have and how reliable we can show it to have been. Hume's general point must be admitted, that we should accept the historical evidence, viz. a man's apparent memory, the testimony of others and traces, only if the falsity of the latter would be "more miraculous," i.e., more improbable "than the event *which* he relates." However, my whole discussion in this chapter has ignored "background evidence." In so far as there is substantial other evidence in favor of the existence of God, less would be required in the way of historical evidence in favor of the occurrence of a miracle than this chapter has supposed hitherto. If we have already good grounds for believing that there is a gorilla loose in snowy mountains, we require less by way of evidence of footprints to show that he has visited a particular place. Conversely, if there is substantial evidence against the existence of God, more is required in the way of historical evidence in favor of the occurrence of a miracle than this chapter has supposed—for we have then substantial evidence for supposing that nothing apart from laws of nature determines what happens.

Study Questions

1. Swinburne argues that the evidence from memories, personal testimony, and physical traces could be strong enough to justify believing that a counterinstance to well-established natural law has occurred. What do you see as the strongest aspect of his argument? What do you see as the weakest aspect?
2. Direct observation is considered strong evidence for the occurrence of an event. Are there conceivable events that seem to you so unlikely that you would not accept that they had actually occurred, even if you were seemingly observing them yourself?

Suggested Reading

Adams, Robert Merrihew. "Miracles, Laws and Natural Causation (II)." *Proceedings of the Aristotelian Society* (Supplementary Volume) 66 (June 1992): 207–24.

Basinger, David, and Randall Basinger. *Philosophy and Miracle: The Contemporary Debate*. Lewiston, N.Y.: Edwin Mellen Press, 1986.

Earman, John. *Hume's Abject Failure: The Argument Against Miracles*. New York: Oxford University Press, 2000.

Flew, Antony. "The Impossibility of Miracles." *Hume's Philosophy of Religion*, ed. Flew et al. Winston-Salem, N.C.: Wake Forest University Press, 1986.

Fogelin, Robert J. *A Defense of Hume on Miracles* (Princeton Monographs in Philosophy). Princeton, N.J.: Princeton University Press, 2003.

Hughes, Christopher. "Miracles, Laws and Natural Causation (I)." *Proceedings of the Aristotelian Society* (Supplementary Volume) 66 (June 1992): 179–205.

Houston, J. *Reported Miracles: A Critique of Hume*. Cambridge, England: Cambridge University Press, 1994.

Hume, David. *Enquiries Concerning the Human Understanding and Concerning the Principles of Morals*, 2nd ed., L. A. Selby-Bigge, ed. Oxford, England: Clarendon Press, 1972.

Johnson, David. *Hume, Holism and Miracles*. Ithaca, N.Y.: Cornell University Press, 1999.

Larmer, Robert, ed. *Questions of Miracle*. Montreal: McGill-Queen's University Press, 1996.

Lewis, C. S. *Miracles*. Rev. ed. London: Collins, Fontana Books, 1960.

Mavrodes, George. "Hume and the Probability of Miracles." *International Journal for the Philosophy of Religion* 43 (1998): 167–82.

Otte, Richard. "Mackie's Treatment of Miracles." *International Journal for the Philosophy of Religion* 39 (1996): 151–58.

Swinburne, Richard. *The Concept of Miracle*. London: Macmillan, 1970.

———, ed. *Miracles*. New York: Macmillan, 1989.

Williams, T. C. *The Idea of the Miraculous: The Challenge of Science and Religion*. New York: St. Martin's Press, 1991.

PART ELEVEN

Life After Death

Someone once said that belief in life after death is so important to us that if God does not exist, we would have to invent God to satisfy this longing. Philosophers of religion, too, are interested in whether there is any reason to think that people can live subsequent to their death. The topic involves two major questions.

IS LIFE AFTER DEATH POSSIBLE?

Immortality and the Soul

First, given the fact of universal human mortality and bodily corruption, is life after death possible? The classic response is that life after death would be possible if humans possess or are, in essence, souls that can be immortal. The soul is considered the locus of one's personal identity and is characterized by mental functions like memory and conscious awareness. The existence of a soul would allow individual persons to survive bodily corruption, remember their past life, and possibly even perceive their own unique world and communicate with others in it by using paranormal abilities such as mental telepathy. In our first selection, H. H. Price suggests a scenario in which a disembodied soul would engage its world through mental images. It would take this image-world to be real, possessing a full range of visual, auditory, olfactory, and tactile images. This world might seem to be solipsistic, but Price thinks that it could also allow for interpersonal interaction through the telepathic meeting of images conveyed by other disembodied souls. In this sense, the world of ideas would be public, a joint product of many minds. With an immortal soul, we would live on, disembodied, but supplied with a rich plethora of images coming from ourselves and others.

Other philosophers, like Richard Swinburne in our second selection, agree that the soul could exist apart from the physical world but are dubious that the soul could function disembodied. Almost overwhelming evidence seems to confirm that brain activity of some sort is necessary for humans to have cognitive powers. However, Swinburne notes, this evidence presents no insurmountable difficulties for belief in life after death. For one thing, the connection between physical systems and brains cannot be absolutely established since we have no postmortem experience of souls. At best we get a correlation between brain and mental activity in this life. For another, after death God could create for a person/soul another body that would allow the soul to function. Since the soul has continued in the meantime, our personal identity throughout the loss of the original body is protected.

Serious difficulties afflict the view that humans have souls. The traditional problem concerns how the spiritual soul interacts with the physical body, since they have nothing in common. But having common properties is necessary for interaction. To this may be added questions about how one reconciles a belief in the soul with the evolution of human beings. If there is a continued lineage, and if animals do not have souls, it is probably unreasonable to think that one generation was not human, whereas the next generation was a souled human (although some like William Hasker see the possibility of the soul's emerging from our corporeal nature). Further, the fact that genetics plays such an important role in determining mental abilities suggests that the connection between the body and mind is not mere correlation: the mind is the functioning of the brain. Researchers are tantalizingly close to stimulating particular ideas by stimulating individual neurons. Finally, how can appeal to a soul satisfy the demand for personal identity? If the soul is conceived of as my awareness of myself–which is constantly changing because it is the subject of my conscious experiences—it lacks the continuity necessary to establish personal identity. For this, we must turn to physical continuity, which is missing if we speak about immortality as the continuance of disembodied souls after death.

Life After Death Without a Soul

Although traditionally those who denied the existence of a human soul also denied immortality, some, such as John Hick in our fourth selection, argue that God could create an entirely new being with the same or similar-enough properties as the deceased so that this being would be identical with the deceased. What matters is not the persistence of particular physical parts (the hardware), but the pattern of code (the software) that makes us what we are, and this can be re-created in a different space-time. In this scenario, human existence would be "gap inclusive"; at some (unspecified) time after our death, God would re-create us to take up living where we left off when we died, perhaps even in the context of a space that is unrelated to our present space.

This position faces the problem that the re-created person may be merely a replica of, and not identical with, the deceased. For example, if God made multiple replicas of the deceased, one could not distinguish the real person (the deceased) from persons merely like the deceased. And if no identification of the deceased were possible, one could not say that the same person continued to live rather than that a new person (a replica) was created. Hick's reply to this objection is that since two persons who are identical to the deceased cannot both be the deceased, and since God cannot do the logically impossible, it would be impossible for him to create two persons who are identical to the deceased. But from the fact that God cannot create two persons identical to the deceased, it does not follow that he cannot create one person identical to the deceased.

This view also faces the question of whether spatial–temporal continuity is a criterion of personal identity. If persons are gap inclusive, they lack causal, material continuity. Peter van Inwagen seeks to ground this causal, material continuity in a continuing basic element that, surviving decomposition, provides a core around which God can re-form the person. That there is any such thing, however, is empirically problematic. Others have suggested a kind of fission or split at death, when the real physical person splits off, leaving the corpse behind. Perhaps the most likely position for a materialist to take is to deny the necessity of causal, material continuity for identity. For example, Lynn Baker asserts that what gives us our identity is the first-person perspective that we have over time, a perspective that, though it may require a physical embodiment, does not require a continuous embodiment.

Is It Rational to Believe That People Live Subsequent to Their Death?

A Priori Arguments

The second major question concerns whether evidence exists that people live subsequent to their death. Traditionally, philosophers have presented *a priori* arguments for life after death. Plato argued that since the soul was simple, it was indestructible and therefore immortal. Aquinas contended that we are made for an ultimate end, namely, happiness or beatitude. Since God would not make us in vain, we must be able to obtain this end. But since this end is unobtainable in this life, the soul must continue to live after this life, in conjunction with the self-same body that died. But since we no longer think of biological beings as having a teleology, this argument has largely fallen out of favor.

Immanuel Kant contended that immortality was a postulate of the moral law. Since we are obligated to achieve the highest good, and since if we are obligated to achieve something the achievement must be possible, we must be able to achieve the highest good, which is the perfect alignment of our will with the moral law. But since we cannot achieve this perfect alignment of our wills in this life, we need subsequent lives for this to occur. Hence, we must postulate life after death for this to be achieved. In one sense, however, this argument is counterintuitive, for life after death has usually been associated with providing an opportunity to improve one's virtue. On Kant's view, should persons have perfected their virtue, we would have no reason to continue to postulate life after death for those persons.

A Posteriori Arguments

Some believers in life after death focus on *a posteriori* evidence for life after death. Some appeal to near-death and alleged paranormal experiences; if one can have experiences after one has died and then can recall them when one is resuscitated, or if one can communicate with people who have died, then there are experiential reasons for thinking that life after death actually occurs. However, there is significant doubt surrounding mediumistic communication with deceased persons, not only because of the lack of significant information received from such communication but also because of the possible and proven cases of fraud. Mediumist reports do not convey the impression that the immortal person has continued with a meaningful, experientially rich, developing life. Although there is little doubt that people have near-death experiences, there is much doubt about what these experiences show. For one thing, as Linda Badham points out in our third selection, one can give explanations of these events without having to appeal to a life that continues after death. They might be due to the presence of drugs or stress, both of which can produce vivid visions. Indeed, although near-death experiences invoke physical events such as seeing a tunnel of light or other persons, there is no physical mechanism to account for these events, since the body lies visible to others and the soul allegedly has departed the body.

Some theologians and philosophers within the Christian faith point to the tradition that affirms that since Jesus was raised from the dead, we have theological reason to believe that the same will happen to us. Critics point to alleged inconsistencies in the resurrection accounts of Jesus and contend that even if God raised Jesus from the dead, that event has little implication for us.

Life After Death in Non-Western Traditions

Hindu and Buddhist philosophers reject the general tenor of the previous discussion, believing that it unduly focuses on the individual person as a continuing self. As developed in our fifth selection from the dialogue of King Milinda with the sage Nāgasena, Buddhists deny the existence a continuing self. Belief in the existence of a self misidentifies groups of momentary events as some enduring reality. What is reborn is not a self but a series of events, including sensations, perceptions, dispositions, and consciousness, conditioned by karma (prior actions). The connection of the future with the past is through the causation by the past of future events. The series of rebirths comes to an end with the attainment of Nirvana. In Nirvana we cannot say that there is a self or that there is not a self, that there both is and is not a self, or that there neither is nor is not a self. Nirvana is a state that lies beyond causation and predication, making discourse about any possible life in that state impossible.

Vedantic Hindus hold that the empirical self, which goes through a cycle of rebirths, should not be confused with the absolute self (*Atman* or *Purusha*), which neither changes nor is reborn. From our human perspective, as empirical selves or souls we go through a series of rebirths. Because of the misery of this life, we seek liberation from this cycle of rebirths by achieving union with the Nondual. From the perspective of the Absolute Self, which is the foundational reality that undergirds the conscious powers of the individual, change or rebirth is only an appearance, not a reality, arising as the Self manifests itself in finite existence. We have always been identical with the Absolute Reality. This view is developed in our sixth selection from Sri Aurobindo.

In both Buddhism and Vedantic Hinduism, the ultimate goal is not individual immortality but termination of the unsatisfactory existence of empirical selfhood, either in Nirvana or in the liberation that realizes our already-state of union with the Nondual. Hence, the question of life after death is treated differently in light of a different view of reality.

The lack of direct experience of life after death should not curtail the investigation of whether beliefs about it are justified on any of the previous schemes. The believer, contending that reason can only proceed so far, may want to appeal to something more, such as revelation or meditative or yogic experience, whereas the skeptic, with a differing perspective, will push for empirical evidence. Perhaps that is why, in many religious traditions, life after death is more a hope than a belief justified by rigorous argument.

H. H. Price

The Soul Survives and Functions After Death

H. H. Price (1899–1984) attempts to give meaning to the idea of a next world inhabited by disembodied persons, which he refers to as the Survival Hypothesis. In this world, disembodied beings would entertain mental images (visual, auditory, olfactory, and tactile) that would be real to those who have them and give the impression of perceiving physical objects. The imaging, centered on a fundamental body image, would replace sense-perception, and encounters with other disembodied persons would occur by telepathy. Price suggests that the location of this world has nothing to do with a change of place but with a change of consciousness. Although one might wonder whether such a world is real, the matter of what is real and unreal is contextual, not a matter of physicality. Finally, this world could be public—the joint product of many telepathically interacting minds, expressing desires and entertaining memories.

I am here only concerned with the conception of Survival; with the *meaning* of the Survival Hypothesis, and not with its truth or falsity. When we consider the Survival Hypothesis, whether we believe it or disbelieve it, what is it that we have in mind? Can we form any idea, even a rough and provisional one, of what a disembodied human life might be like? Supposing we cannot, it will follow that what is called the Survival Hypothesis is a mere set of words and not a hypothesis at all. The evidence adduced in favour of it might still be evidence for something, and perhaps for something important, but we should no longer have the right to claim that it is evidence for Survival. There cannot be evidence for something which is completely unintelligible to us.

Now let us consider the situation in which we find ourselves after seventy years of psychical research. A very great deal of work has been done on the problem of Survival.... Yet there are the widest differences of opinion about the result. A number of intelligent persons would maintain that we now have a very large mass of evidence in favour of Survival; that some of it is of very good quality indeed, and cannot be explained away unless we suppose that the supernormal cognitive powers of some embodied human minds are vastly more extensive and more accurate than we can easily believe them to be; in short, that on the evidence available the Survival Hypothesis is more probable than not. Some people—and not all of them are silly or credulous—would even maintain that the Survival Hypothesis is proved, or as near to being so as any empirical hypothesis can be. On the other hand, there are also many intelligent persons who entirely reject these conclusions. Some of them, no doubt, have not taken the trouble to examine the evidence. But others of them have; they may even have given years of study to it. They would agree that the evidence is evidence of *something*, and very likely of something important. But, they would say, it cannot be evidence of Survival; there *must* be some alternative explanation of it, however difficult it may be to find out. Why do they take this line? I think it is because they find the very conception of Survival unintelligible. The very idea of a "discarnate human personality" seems to them a muddled or absurd one; indeed not an idea at all, but just a phrase—an emotionally exciting one, no doubt—to which no clear meaning can be given....

Now why should it be thought that the very idea of life after death is unintelligible? Surely it is easy enough to conceive (whether or not it is true) that experiences might occur after Jones's death which are linked with experiences which he had before his death, in such a way that his personal identity is preserved? But, it will be said, the idea of after-death *experiences* is just the difficulty. What kind of experiences could they conceivably be? In a disembodied state, the supply of sensory stimuli is perforce cut off, because the supposed experiment has no sense organs and no nervous system. There can therefore be no sense-perception. One has no means of being aware of material objects any longer; and if one has not, it is hard to see how one could have any emotions or wishes either. For all the emotions and wishes we have in this present life are concerned directly or indirectly with material objects, including of course our own organisms and other organisms, especially other human ones. In short, one could only be said to have experiences at all, if one is aware of some sort of a *world*. In this way, the idea of Survival is bound up with the idea of "another world" or a "next world." Anyone who maintains that the idea of Survival is after all intelligible must also be claiming that we can form some conception, however rough and provisional, of what "the next world" or "the other world" might be like....

The Next World, I think, might be conceived as a kind of dream-world. When we are asleep, sensory stimuli are cut off, or at any rate are prevented from having their normal effects upon our brain-centres. But we still manage to have experiences. It is true that sense-perception no longer occurs, but something sufficiently like it does. In sleep, our image-producing powers, which are more or less inhibited in waking life by a continuous bombardment of sensory stimuli, are released from this inhibition. And then we are provided with a multitude of objects of awareness, about which we employ our thoughts and towards which we have desires and emotions. Those objects which we are aware of behave in a way which seems very queer to us when we wake up. The laws of their behaviour are not the laws of physics. But however queer their behaviour is, it does not at all disconcert us at the time, and our personal identity is not broken.

In other words, my suggestion is that the Next World, if there is one, might be a world of mental images. Nor need such a world be so "thin and unsubstantial" as you might think. Paradoxical as it may sound, there is nothing imaginary about a mental image. It is an actual entity, as real as anything can be. The seeming paradox arises from the ambiguity of the verb "to imagine." It does sometimes mean "to have mental images." But more usually it means "to entertain propositions without believing them," and very often they are false propositions, and moreover we *dis*believe them in the act of entertaining them. This is what happens, for example, when we read Shakespeare's play *The Tempest*, and that is why we say that Prospero and Ariel are "imaginary characters." Mental images are not in this sense imaginary at all. We do actually experience them, and they are no more imaginary than sensations. To avoid the paradox, though at the cost of some pedantry, it would be well to distinguish between *imagining* and *imaging*, and to have two different adjectives "imaginary" and "imagy." In this terminology, it is imaging, and not imagining, that I wish to talk about; and the Next World, as I am trying to conceive of it, is an *imagy* world, but not on that account an imaginary one.

Indeed, to those who experience it an image-world would be just as "real" as this present world is; and perhaps so like it, that they would have considerable difficulty in realising that they were dead. We are, of course, sometimes told in mediumistic communications that quite a lot of people do find it difficult to realise that they are dead; and this is just what we should expect if the Next World is an image-world.... So far as I can see, there might be a set of visual images related to each other perspectively, with front views and side views and back views all fitting neatly together in the way that ordinary visual appearances do now. Such a group of images might contain tactual images too. Similarly it might contain auditory images and smell images. Such a family of inter-related images would make a pretty good object. It would be quite a satisfactory substitute for the material objects which we perceive in this present life. And a whole world composed of such families of mental images would make a perfectly good world.

It is possible, however, and indeed likely, that some of those images would be what Francis Galton called *generic* images. An image representing a dog or a tree need not necessarily be an exact replica of some individual dog or tree one has perceived. It might rather be a representation of a *typical* dog or tree. Our memories are more specific on some subjects than on others. How specific they are, depends probably on the degree of interest we had in the individual objects or events at the time when we perceived them.... Left to our own resources, as we should be in the Other World, with nothing but our memories to depend on, we should probably be able to form only generic images of such objects. In this respect, an image-world would not be an exact replica of this one, not even of those parts of this one which we have actually perceived. To some extent it would be, so to speak, a generalised picture, rather than a detailed reproduction.

Let us now put our question in another way, and ask what kind of experience a disembodied human mind might be supposed to have. We can then answer that it might be an experience in which *imaging* replaces sense-perception; "replaces" it, in the sense that imaging would perform much the same function as sense-perception performs now, by providing us with objects about which we could have thoughts, emotions, and wishes. There is no reason why we

should not be "as much alive," or at any rate *feel* as much alive, in an image-world as we do now in this present material world, which we perceive by means of our sense-organs and nervous systems. And so the use of the word "survival" ("life after death") would be perfectly justifiable.

It will be objected, perhaps, that one cannot be said to be alive unless one has a body. But what is meant here by "alive"? It is surely conceivable (whether or not it is true) that *experiences* should occur which are not causally connected with a physical organism. If they did, should we or should we not say that "life" was occurring? I do not think it matters much whether we answer Yes or No. It is purely a question of definition. If you define "life" in terms of certain very complicated physico-chemical processes, as some people would, then of course life after death is by definition impossible, because there is no longer anything to be alive. In that case, the problem of survival (*life* after bodily death) is misnamed. Instead, it ought to be called the problem of after-death *experiences*. And this is in fact the problem with which all investigators of the subject have been concerned. After all, what people want to know, when they ask whether we survive death, is simply whether experiences occur after death, or what likelihood, if any, there is that they do; and whether such experiences, if they do occur, are linked with each other and with *ante mortem* ones in such a way that personal identity is preserved. It is not physico-chemical processes which interest us, when we ask such questions. But there is another sense of the words "life" and "alive" which may be called the psychological sense; and in this sense "being alive" just *means* "having experiences of certain sorts." In this psychological sense of the word "life" it is perfectly intelligible to ask whether there is life after death, even though life in the physiological sense does *ex hypothesi* come to an end when someone dies. Or, if you like, the question is whether one could *feel* alive after bodily death, even though (by hypothesis) one would not *be* alive at that time. It will be just enough to satisfy most of us if the *feeling* of being alive continues after death. It will not make a halfpennyworth of difference that one will not then *be* alive in the physiological or biochemical sense of the word.

It may be said, however, that "feeling alive" (life in the psychological sense) cannot just be equated with having experiences in general. Feeling alive, surely, consists in having experiences of a special sort, namely *organic sensations*—bodily feelings of various sorts. In our present experience, these bodily feelings are not as a rule separately attended to unless they are unusually intense or unusually painful. They are a kind of undifferentiated mass in the background of consciousness. All the same, it would be said, they constitute our feeling of being alive; and if they were absent (as surely they must be when the body is dead) the feeling of being alive could not be there.

I am not at all sure that this argument is as strong as it looks. I think we should still feel alive—or alive enough—provided we experienced emotions and wishes, even if no organic sensations accompanied these experiences, as they do now. But in case I am wrong here, I would suggest that *images* of organic sensations could perfectly well provide what is needed. We can quite well image to ourselves what it feels like to be in a warm bath, even when we are not actually in one; and a person who has been crippled can image what it felt like to climb a mountain. Moreover, I would ask whether we do not feel alive when we are dreaming. It seems to me that we obviously do—or at any rate quite alive enough to go on.

This is not all. In an image-world, a dream-like world such as I am trying to describe, there is no reason at all why there should not be *visual* images resembling the body which one had in this present world. In this present life (for all who are not blind) visual percepts of one's own body form as it were the constant centre of one's perceptual world. It is perfectly possible that visual images of one's own body might perform the same function in the next. They might form the continuing centre or nucleus of one's image world, remaining more or less constant while other images altered. If this were so, we should have an additional reason for expecting that recently dead people would find it difficult to realise that they were dead, that is, disembodied. To all appearances they *would* have bodies just as they had before, and pretty much the same ones. But, of course, they might discover in time that these image-bodies were subject to rather peculiar causal laws. For example, it might be found that in an image world our wishes tend ipso facto to fulfil themselves in a way they do not now. A wish to go to Oxford might be immediately followed by the occurrence of a vivid and detailed set of Oxford-like images; even though, at the moment before, one's images had resembled Piccadilly Circus or the palace of the Dalai Lama in Tibet. In that case, one would realise that "going somewhere"—transferring one's body from one place to another—was a rather different process from what it had been in the physical world. Reflecting on such experiences, one might come to the conclusion that one's body was not after all the same as the physical body one had before death. One might conclude perhaps that it must be a "spiritual" or "psychical" body, closely resembling the old body in appearance, but possessed of rather different causal properties. It has been said, of course, that phrases like "spiritual body" or "psychical body" are utterly unintelligible, and that no conceivable empirical meaning could be given to such expressions. But I would suggest that they might be a way (rather a misleading way perhaps) of referring to a set of body-like images. . . .

I think, then, that there is no difficulty in conceiving that the experience of feeling alive could occur in the absence of a physical organism; or, if you prefer to put it so, a disembodied personality could *be* alive in the psychological sense, even though by definition it would not be alive in the physiological or biochemical sense.

Moreover, I do not see why disembodiment need involve the destruction of personal identity. It is, of course, sometimes supposed that personal identity depends on the continuance of a background of organic sensation—the "mass of bodily feeling" mentioned before. (This may be called the Somato-centric Analysis of personal identity.) We must notice, however, that this background of organic sensation is not literally the same from one period of time to another. The very most that can happen is that the organic sensations which form the background of my experience now should be *exactly similar* to those which were the background of my experience a minute ago. And as a matter of fact the present ones need not *all* be exactly similar to the previous ones. I might have a twinge of toothache now which I did not have then.

I may even have an overall feeling of lassitude now which I did not have a minute ago, so that the whole mass of bodily feeling, and not merely one part of it, is rather different; and this would not interrupt my personal identity at all. The most that is required is only that the majority (not all) of my organic sensations should be closely (not exactly) similar to those I previously had. And even this is only needed if the two occasions are close together in my private time series; the organic sensations I have now might well be very unlike those I used to have when I was one year old: I say "in my private time series." For when I wake up after eight hours of dreamless sleep my personal identity is not broken, though in the physical or public time series there has been a long interval between the last organic sensations I experienced before falling asleep, and the first ones I experience when I wake up. But if similarity, and not literal sameness, is all that is required of this "continuing organic background," it seems to me that the continuity of it could be perfectly well preserved if there were organic *images* after death very like the organic *sensations* which occurred before death.

As a matter of fact, this whole "somato-centric" analysis of personal identity appears to me highly disputable. I should have thought that Locke was much nearer the truth when he said that personal identity depends on memory. But I have tried to show that even if the "somato-centric" theory of personal identity is right, there is no reason why personal identity need be broken by bodily death, provided there are images after death which sufficiently resemble the organic sensations one had before; and this is very like what happens when one falls asleep and begins dreaming.

There is, however, another argument against the conceivability of a disembodied person, to which some present-day Linguistic Philosophers would attach great weight. It is neatly expressed by Mr. A.G.N. Flew when he says, "People are what you meet."...

As a matter of fact, however, we can quite easily conceive that "meeting" of a kind might still be possible between discarnate experiments. And therefore, even if we do make it part of the definition of "a person," that he is capable of being met by others, it will still make sense to speak of "discarnate persons," provided we allow that telepathy is possible between them. It is true that a special sort of telepathy would be needed; the sort which in this life produces *telepathic apparitions*. It would not be sufficient that A's thoughts or emotions should be telepathically affected by B's. If such telepathy were sufficiently prolonged and continuous, and especially if it were reciprocal, it would indeed have some of the characteristics of social intercourse; but I do not think we should call it "meeting," at any rate in Mr. Flew's sense of the word. It would be necessary, in addition, that A should be aware of something which could be called's "B's body," or should have an experience not too unlike the experience of *seeing* another person in this life. This additional condition would be satisfied if A experienced a telepathic apparition of B. It would be necessary, further, that the telepathic apparition by means of which B "announces himself" (if one may put it so) should be recognisably similar on different occasions. And if it were a case of meeting some person *again* whom one had previously known in this world, the telepathic apparition would have to be recognisably similar to the physical body which that person had when he was still alive.

There is no reason why an image-world should not contain a number of images which are telepathic apparitions; and if it did, one could quite intelligently speak of "meeting other persons" in such a world. All the experiences I have when I meet another person in this present life could still occur, with only this difference, that percepts would be replaced by images. It would also be possible for another person to "meet" me in the same manner, if I, as telepathic agent, could cause him to experience a suitable telepathic apparition, sufficiently resembling the body I used to have when he formerly "met" me in this life.

I now turn to another problem which may have troubled some of you. If there be a next world, *where* is it?...Surely the next world, if it exists, must be somewhere; and, yet, it seems, there is nowhere for it to be.

The answer to this difficulty is easy if we conceive of the Next World in the way I have suggested, as a dream-like world of mental images. Mental images, including dream images, are in a space of their own.

They do have spatial properties. Visual images, for instance, have extension and shape, and they have spatial relations to one another. But they have no spatial relation to objects in the physical world. If I dream of a tiger, my tiger-image has extension and shape. The dark stripes have spatial relations to the yellow parts, and to each other; the nose has a spatial relation to the tail. Again, the tiger image as a whole may have spatial relations to another image in my dream, for example to an image resembling a palm tree. But suppose we have to ask how far it is from the foot of my bed, whether it is three inches long, or longer, or shorter; is it not obvious that these questions are absurd ones? We cannot answer them, not because we lack the necessary information or find it impracticable to make the necessary measurements, but because the questions themselves have no meaning. In the space of the physical world these images are nowhere at all. But in relation to other images of mine, each of them is somewhere. Each of them is extended, and its parts are in spatial relations to one another. There is no a priori reason why all extended entities must be in physical space.

If we now apply these considerations to the Next World, as I am conceiving of it, we see that the question "where is it?" simply does not arise. An image-world would have a space of its own. We could not find it anywhere in the space of the physical world, but this would not in the least prevent it from being a spatial world all the same. If you like, it would be its own "where."...

It follows that when we speak of "passing" from this world to the next, this passage is not to be thought of as any sort of movement in space. It should rather be thought of as a change of consciousness, analogous to the change which occurs when we "pass" from waking experience to dreaming. It would be a change from the perceptual type of consciousness to another type of consciousness in which perception ceases and imaging replaces it, but unlike the change from waking consciousness to dreaming in being irreversible....

I now turn to another difficulty. It may be felt that an image-world is some how a deception and a sham, not a *real* world at all. I have said that it would be a kind of dream-world. Now when one has a dream in this life, surely the things one is aware of in the dream are not *real* things. No doubt the dreamer really does have various mental images. These images do actually occur. But this is not all that happens. As a result of having these images, the dreamer believes, or takes for granted, that various material objects exist and various physical events occur; and these beliefs are mistaken. For example, he believes that there is a wall in front of him and that by a mere effort of will he succeeds in flying over the top of it. But the wall did not really exist, and he did not really fly over the top of it. He was in a state of delusion. Because of the images which he did really have, there *seemed* to him to be various objects and events which did not really exist at all. Similarly, you may argue, it may *seem* to discarnate minds (if indeed there are such) that there is a world in which they live, and a world not unlike this one. If they have mental images of the appropriate sort, it may even *seem* to them that they have bodies not unlike the ones they had in this life. But surely they will be mistaken....

I would suggest, however, that this argument about the "delusiveness" or "unreality" of an image-world is based on a confusion.

One may doubt whether there is any clear meaning in using the words "real" and "unreal" *tout court*, in this perfectly general and unspecified way. One may properly say, "this is real silver, and that is not," "this is a real pearl and that is not," or again "this is a real pool of water, and that is only a mirage." The point here is that something X is mistakenly believed to be something else Y, because it does resemble Y in some respects. It makes perfectly good sense, then, to say that X is not really Y. This piece of plated brass is not real silver, true enough. It only looks like silver. But for all that, it cannot be called "unreal" in the unqualified sense, in the sense of not existing at all. Even the mirage is something, though it is not the pool of water you took it to be. It is a perfectly good set of visual appearances, though it is not related to other appearances in the way you thought it was; for example, it does not have the relations to tactual appearances, or to visual appearances from other places, which you expected it to have. You may properly say that the mirage is not a real pool of water, or even that it is not a real physical object, and that anyone who thinks it is must be in a state of delusion. But there is no clear meaning in saying that it is just "unreal" *tout court*, without any further specification or explanation. In short, when the word "unreal" is applied to something, one means that it is different from something else, with which it might be mistakenly identified; what that something else may not be explicitly stated, but it can be gathered from the context.

What, then, could people mean by saying that a next world such as I have described would be "unreal"? If they are saying anything intelligible, they must mean that it is different from something else, something else which it does resemble in some respects, and might therefore be confused with. And what is that something else? It is this present physical world in which we now live. An image-world, then, is only "unreal" in the sense that it is not really physical, though it might be mistakenly thought to be physical by some of those who experience it. But this only amounts to saying that the world I am describing would be an *other* world, other than this present physical world, which is just what it ought to be; other than this present physical world, and yet sufficiently like it to be possibly confused with it, because images do resemble percepts. And what would this otherness consist in? First, in the fact that it is in a *space* which is other than physical space; secondly, and still more important, in the fact that the *causal laws* of an image-world would be different from the laws of physics. And this is also our ground for saying that the events we experience in dreams are "unreal," that is, not really physical, though mistakenly believed by the dreamer to be so. They do in some ways closely resemble physical events, and that is why the mistake is possible. But the causal laws of their occurrence are quite different, as we recognise when we wake up; and just occasionally we recognise it even while we are still asleep....

Let us now try to explore the conception of a world of mental images a little more fully. Would it not be a "subjective" world? And surely there would be many *different* next worlds, not just one; and each of them would be private. Indeed, would there not be as many

next worlds as there are discarnate minds, and each of them wholly private to the mind which experiences it? In short, it may seem that each of us, when dead, would have his own dream world, and there would be no common or public Next World at all.

"Subjective," perhaps, is rather a slippery word. Certainly, an image world would have to be subjective in the sense of being mind-dependent, dependent for its existence upon mental processes of one sort or another; images, after all, are mental entities. But I do not think that such a world need be completely private, if telepathy occurs in the next life.... It is reasonable to suppose that in a disembodied state telepathy would occur more frequently than it does now. It seems likely that in this present life our telepathic powers are constantly being inhibited by our need to adjust ourselves to our physical environment. It even seems likely that many telepathic "impressions" which we receive at the unconscious level are shut out from consciousness by a kind of biologically-motivated censorship. Once the pressure of biological needs is removed, we might expect that telepathy would occur continually, and manifest itself in consciousness by modifying and adding to the images which one experiences. (Even in this life, after all, some dreams are telepathic.)

If this is right, an image-world such as I am describing would not be the product of one single mind only, nor would it be purely private. It would be the joint-product of a group of telepathically-interacting minds and public to all of them. Nevertheless, one would not expect it to have unrestricted publicity. It is likely that there would still be *many* next worlds, a different one for each group of like-minded personalities. I admit I am not quite sure what might be meant by "like-minded" and "unlike-minded" in this connection. Perhaps we could say that two personalities are like-minded if their memories or their characters are sufficiently similar. It might be that Nero and Marcus Aurelius do not have a world in common, but Socrates and Marcus Aurelius do.

So far, we have a picture of many "semi-public" next worlds, if one may put it so; each of them composed of mental images, and yet not wholly private for all that, but public to a limited group of telepathically-interacting minds. Or, if you like, after death everyone does have his own dream, but there is still some overlap between one person's dream and another's, because of telepathy.

I have said that such a world would be mind-dependent, even though dependent on a group of minds rather than a single mind. In what way would it be mind-dependent? Presumably in the same way as dreams are now. It would be dependent on the *memories* and the *desires* of the persons who experienced it. Their memories and their desires would determine what sort of images they had. If I may put it so, the "stuff" or "material" of such a world would come in the end from one's memories, and the "form" of it from one's desires. To use another analogy, memory would provide the pigments, and desire would paint the picture. One might expect, I think, that desires which had been unsatisfied in one's earthly life would play a specially important part in the process. That may seem an agreeable prospect. But there is another which is less agreeable. Desires which had been *repressed* in one's earthly life, because it was too painful or too disgraceful to admit that one had them, might also play a part, and perhaps an important part, in determining what images one would have in the next. And the same might be true of repressed memories. It may be suggested that what Freud (in one stage of his thought) called "the censor"—the force or barrier or mechanism which keeps some of our desires and memories out of consciousness, or only lets them in when they disguise themselves in symbolic and distorted forms—operates only in this present life and not in the next. However we conceive of "the censor," it does seem to be a device for enabling us to adapt ourselves to our environment. And when we no longer have an environment, one would expect that the barrier would come down.

We can now see that an after-death world of mental images can also be quite reasonably described in the terminology of the Hindu thinkers as "a world of desire" (*Kama Loka*). Indeed, this is just what we should expect if we assume that dreams, in this present life, are the best available clue to what the next life might be like. Such a world could also be described as "a world of memories"; because imaging, in the end, is a function of memory, one of the ways in which our memory-dispositions manifest themselves. But this description would be less apt, even though correct as far as it goes. To use the same rather inadequate language as before, the "materials" out of which an image-world is composed would have to come from the memories of the mind or group of minds whose world it is. But it would be their desires (including those repressed in earthly life) which determined the ways in which these memories were used, the precise kind of dream which was built up out of them or on the basis of them.

It will, of course, be objected that memories cannot exist in the absence of a physical brain, nor yet desires, nor images either. But this proposition, however plausible, is after all just an empirical hypothesis, not a necessary truth. Certainly there is empirical evidence in favour of it. But there is also empirical evidence against it. Broadly speaking one might say, perhaps, that the "normal" evidence tends to support this Materialistic or Epiphenomenalist theory of memories, images and desires, whereas the "supernormal" evidence on the whole tends to weaken the Materialist or Epiphenomenalist theory of human personality (of which this hypothesis about the brain-dependent character of memories, images and desires is a part). Moreover, any evidence which directly supports the Survival Hypothesis (and there is quite a lot of evidence which does, provided we are prepared to admit that the Survival Hypothesis is intelligible at all) is *pro tanto* evidence against the Materialistic conception of human personality.

In this lecture, I am not of course trying to argue in favour of the Survival Hypothesis. I am only concerned with the more modest task of trying to make it intelligible. All I want to maintain, then, is that there is nothing self-contradictory or logically absurd in the hypothesis that memories, desires and images can exist in the absence of a physical brain. The hypothesis may, of course, be false. My point is only that it is not absurd; or, if you like, that it is at any rate intelligible, whether true or not.

Study Questions

1. How does Price show that disembodied souls can have experiences after death?
2. How does Price use somatic images to solve the problem of bodily (somatic) identity after death?
3. How does Price account for "meeting other persons" in a disembodied state?
4. In what sense would this image-world be or not be a public world?
5. Would Price's description of the afterlife make life after death attractive to you? Why or why not?

Richard Swinburne

The Soul Needs a Brain to Continue to Function

According to Richard Swinburne (b. 1934), humans consist of a physical body plus a soul that forms beliefs and has desires. The function—but not the existence—of the soul depends on a functioning physical brain that connects the soul to its surroundings. Since it is unlikely that brains can be reassembled, the soul may continue to exist after death but is unlikely to be able to function. Arguments from psychical research, near-death experiences, and philosophers like Plato also fail to show that souls can function without brains. However, since there is no natural law requiring the connection of souls with brains, the way is open for a metaphysical theory like theism to claim that it is possible that God could create the requisite conditions under which the soul could live and function after death. For example, God might create a different body for souls to inhabit after death so that they could still have a connection to a functioning brain.

A man's having a mental life must be understood as a non-bodily part of the man, his soul, having a mental life....

THE EXISTENCE OF THE SOUL

What I have argued so far is that without a functioning brain, the soul will not function (i.e., have conscious episodes)—not that it will not exist. But what does it mean to suppose that the soul exists at some time without functioning? The distinction between existence and functioning is clear enough in the case of a material substance, which has some sort of life (e.g., a plant) or some sort of working (e.g., a machine).

The substance continues to exist so long as the matter of which it is made continues to exist in roughly the same shape (with the possibility perhaps of gradual replacement of parts). But it functions only so long as normal life-processes or machine-use continue. The clock exists, when it no longer tells the time, so long as the parts remain joined in roughly the normal way; and a dead tree is still a tree, although it no longer takes in water through its roots and sunlight through its leaves.

The distinction is not, however, at all clear in the case of the soul, an immaterial substance. The soul functions while it is the subject of conscious episodes—while it has sensations or thoughts or purposes. But is it still there when the man is asleep, having no conscious episodes? This calls for a decision of what (if anything) we are to mean by saying of some soul that it exists but is not functioning.

We suppose that persons continue to exist while asleep, having no conscious life. In saying that some such person still exists, we mean, I suggest, that the sleeping body will again by normal processes give rise to a conscious life, or can be caused to give rise to a conscious life (e.g., by shaking it), a conscious life which will be the life of the person existing before sleep. Now, we could describe this latter fact by saying that, although persons only exist while they are conscious, the bodies which they previously owned continue to exist during the periods of unconsciousness and become thereafter the bodies of persons again (indeed the same persons who previously owned those bodies). However, that would be a very unnatural way to talk, largely because it has the consequence that certain substances (persons) are continually popping in and out of existence. Although there seems to me nothing contradictory in allowing to a substance many beginnings of existence, it seems a less cumbersome way to describe the cited fact to say that persons exist while not conscious, and mean by this that normal bodily processes or available artificial techniques can make those persons conscious. This will have the consequence that persons normally have only one beginning of existence during their life on Earth.

Our grounds for saying that persons exist while not conscious are similar to the grounds for saying that persons have desires and beliefs when they are not aware of them, i.e., that they can easily be made aware of them and that those desires and beliefs will influence their actions when they are put in appropriate circumstances.

Conscious persons consist of body and soul. We could say that souls exist only while conscious; while a person is asleep, his soul ceases to exist but it is made to exist again when he is woken up. But this would be a cumbersome way of talking. It is better to understand by a soul existing when not functioning that normal bodily processes on their own will, or available artificial techniques can, make that soul function. In saying this I am laying down rules for the use of a technical term, "soul." With this usage, a soul

exists while its owner exists; and a soul will normally have only one beginning of existence during a man's life on Earth....

Four thousand million years of evolution produced man, a body and soul in continuing interaction. A human soul is more dependent for its development on its own states than is an animal soul, for it has complex beliefs and desires kept in place and changing in accord with other beliefs and desires. Other animals having only much simpler beliefs and desires are much more dependent for their continuing beliefs and desires directly on their bodily states. Can this complex evolved human soul survive on its own apart from the body which sustains it? I have argued so far that the functioning of the human soul (i.e., its having conscious episodes) is guaranteed by the functioning of the brain currently connected with it (connected, in that the soul's acquisition of beliefs about its surroundings and action upon those surroundings is mediated by that brain). I have considered what it is for a man or his soul to exist unconscious, and I have argued that that was a matter which required to be settled by definition. The definition which I suggested was that a soul exists if normal bodily processes or available artificial techniques can bring the man to be conscious, i.e., his soul to function again.

When the body dies and the brain ceases to function, the evidence suggests that the soul will cease to function also. For that evidence suggests that the soul functions only when the brain has rhythms of certain kinds, and at death the brain ceases to function altogether. If the soul does not function before there is a functioning brain, or during deep sleep, when the brain is not functioning at a certain level, surely it will not function after there ceases to be a functioning brain. However, there are arguments and evidence of less usual kinds which purport to show that things are different after death from what they are before birth.

Before we face the question of whether the soul can function without the functioning of the brain currently connected with it, we must consider the question of whether, after death, the brain which ceases to function at death can be made to function again and whether thereby the soul can be revived.

CAN THE BRAIN BE REACTIVATED?

A crucial problem is that we do not know how much of the brain that was yours has to be reassembled and within what time interval in order that we may have *your* brain and so your soul function again. We saw this earlier in the split brain cases. If both half-brains are transplanted into empty skulls and the transplants take, both subsequent persons will satisfy to some extent the criterion of apparent memory (as well as the brain criterion) for being the original person. One subsequent person might satisfy the criterion better than the other, and that would be evidence that he was the original person; but the evidence could be misleading. The situation is equally unclear with possible developments at death.

Suppose you die of a brain haemorrhage which today's doctors cannot cure, but your relatives take your corpse and put it straight into a very deep freeze in California. Fifty years later your descendants take it out of the freeze; medical technology has improved and the doctors are able quickly to mend your brain, and your body is then warmed up. The body becomes what is clearly the body of a living person, and one with your apparent memory and character. Is it you? Although we might be mistaken, the satisfaction of the criterion of apparent memory (together with the—at any rate partial—satisfaction of the criterion of brain continuity) would suggest that we ought to say "Yes." So long as the same brain is revived, the same functioning soul would be connected with it—whatever the time interval. But what if the brain is cut up into a million pieces and then frozen? Does the same hold? Why should there be any difference? Suppose that the brain is reduced to its component atoms; and then these are reassembled either by chance or because they have been labelled radioactively. Again, if the subsequent person makes your memory claims, surely we ought to say that it is you. But how many of the original atoms do we need in the original locations? That we do not know. So long as the subsequent person had many similar atoms in similar locations in his brain, he would claim to have been you. So, the criterion of apparent memory will be satisfied. Total non-satisfaction of the brain criterion would defeat the claims of apparent memory (in

the absence of any general failure of coincidence in results between these criteria). But it remains unclear and indeed insoluble exactly how much of the original brain is needed to provide satisfaction of the brain criterion.

This problem of how much of the original body is physically necessary when other matter is added to it so as to make a fully functioning body, in order that the original soul may be present and function, is a problem which concerned the thinkers of the early Christian centuries and of the Middle Ages. They considered the imaginary case of the cannibal who eats nothing but human flesh. Given that both the cannibal and his victims are to be brought to life in the General Resurrection, to whom will the flesh of the cannibal belong? Aquinas[1] begins his answer by saying that "if something was materially present in many men, it will rise in him to whose perfection it belonged," i.e., that part of the body which is necessary for a man being the person he is will belong to him in the General Resurrection. But what part is that, and what guarantee is there that the matter of that part cannot come to form the essential part of a different man who cannot therefore be reconstituted at the same time as the original man (given the operation of normal processes)? Aquinas goes on to produce an argument that the "radical seed" (i.e., the sperm, which according to Aristotle formed the original matter of the embryo) forms the minimum essential bodily core around which a man could be rebuilt. But we know now, as Aquinas did not, that the sperm does not remain as a unit within the organism, and there seems to me no reason why all the atoms which originally formed it should not be lost from the body, and indeed come to form parts of original cells of many subsequent men. The atoms of the original cell are not therefore the most plausible candidate for being the part of the body physically necessary for human personal identity. Aquinas's problem remains without modern solution.

Nevertheless, although neurophysiology cannot tell us which part of his brain is physically necessary for the embodiment of a given man, it does tell us, as I argued earlier, that some of the brain is thus necessary. For the functioning of a given human soul, there has to be a man whose brain contains certain of the matter of his original brain (but which matter we do not know), similarly arranged. A certain amount of the original brain matter has to be reassembled in a similar arrangement and reactivated by being joined to other brain matter and a body if the soul is to function again. And how likely is it that physical processes will bring about such a reassembly? As the time since death increases, and brain cells and then brain molecules are broken up, burnt by fire, or eaten by worms— it becomes very, very unlikely indeed that chance will reassemble them; or even that human agents can do so for they will not be able to reidentify the atoms involved....I conclude that it is very, very unlikely (and with increasing time virtually impossible) that after death souls will again have reassembled the brain basis which we know makes them function.

Is there any good reason to suppose that the soul continues to function without the brain functioning? Arguments to show that the soul continues to function without the brain functioning may be divided into three groups, involving different amounts of theoretical structure, to reach their conclusions. First, we may consider arguments which purport to show that certain men have survived death, in the sense that their souls have functioned without their brains functioning, directly—i.e., without needing first to establish anything about the nature of the soul or any more systematic metaphysical structure. Arguments of this kind may be called parapsychological arguments.

Arguments from Parapsychology

First, there is the alleged evidence of reincarnation, that souls function in new bodies with new brains on Earth. There are Indian children who claim to remember having lived a certain past life, and whose memory claims coincide with the events of some real past life about which—allegedly—they could not have learnt by what they were told or had read.[2] Now, it is of course open to serious question whether perhaps those Indian children had read or were told or learnt in some other perfectly normal way the details of those past lives. But even if for a few Indian children there was this coincidence between their memory claims

and the events of a certain past person's life, without there being any normal cause of the accuracy of their memory claims that would not be enough evidence to show their identity with those persons. For, given the general coincidence of sameness of memory with continuity of brain, we must take continuity of brain as a criterion of identity; and the nonsatisfaction of that in the case of the few Indian children (who do not have the same brain matter as the cited past persons), must remain substantial evidence against the supposition that they are those persons.

Next, there is the alleged evidence of spiritualism, that souls function without bodies or with new bodies and brains in another world. Mediums purport to have telepathic communication with dead persons. The evidence that they do is allegedly provided by the knowledge of the details of the dead person's life on Earth (not obtainable by the medium by normal means) which the medium's reports of the telepathic communications reveal. In the reincarnation case there is no doubt that there exists in the present a living conscious person; the debatable question concerns his identity with the past person. In the spiritualism case the crucial issue concerns whether there is a conscious person with whom the medium is in communication.

A serious issue in medium cases, like the similar issue in the supposed reincarnation cases, concerns the source of the mysterious knowledge. Perhaps the medium gets her knowledge from some spy who has done research on the dead person's life. But even if investigation showed clearly that the mediums had gained their knowledge of the past lives of dead persons by no normal route, the evidence would still, I suggest, not support the hypothesis of telepathic communication with the dead. For also compatible with the evidence would be the hypothesis that the mediums have clairvoyance—they see directly into the past and acquire their knowledge thus. (Adopting the latter hypothesis would involve supposing either that the mediums were deceiving us about the kind of experiences they were having (apparent two-way traffic with a living person), or that they were deceiving themselves, or that their experiences were illusory.) On the choice between the two hypotheses there seem to me to be two important reasons for preferring the clairvoyance hypothesis. First, there are no cross-checks between mediums about the alleged present experiences of the dead in the afterlife. Mediums never give independently verifiable reports on this. Secondly, their reports about the present alleged experiences of the dead are themselves very banal. Yet one would expect because of the total lack of dependence of the dead on their past bodies, that they would live in a very different world, and that this would emerge in their reports on that world.[3]

Finally, there is the interesting and recently published alleged evidence that souls function while their bodies are out of action. There has been careful analysis of the experiences of those who clinically were as good as dead and then recovered. Such experiences are often called "near-death experiences."[4] Fifteen percent of subjects resuscitated after being in such a condition report strange experiences of one of two kinds. Many of them report the following "transcendental experiences":

> an initial period of distress followed by profound calm and joy; out-of-the-body experiences with the sense of watching resuscitation events from a distance; the sensation of moving rapidly down a tunnel or along a road, accompanied by a loud buzzing or ringing noise or hearing beautiful music; recognising friends and relatives who have died previously; a rapid review of pleasant incidents from throughout the life as a panoramic playback (in perhaps twelve per cent of cases); a sense of approaching a border or frontier and being sent back; and being annoyed or disappointed at having to return from such a pleasant experience—"I tried not to come back," in one patient's words. Some describe frank transcendent experiences and many state that they will never fear death again. Similar stories have been reported from the victims of accidents, falls, drowning, anaphylaxis, and cardiac or respiratory arrest.[5]

Resuscitated patients other than those who had transcendental experiences have undergone "a wide variety of vivid dreams, hallucinations, nightmares and delusions," but some of those who had transcendental experiences also experienced these and sharply distinguished between the two kinds of experience. The "dreams" were regarded as dreams, and were quickly forgotten; the "supposed glimpses of a future life" were regarded as real and permanently remembered. These glimpses were reported as having occurred at moments when "breathing had ceased, the heart had stopped beating, and the patients showed no visible signs of life." The principle of credulity might suggest that we ought to take such apparent memories seriously, especially in view of the considerable coincidences between them, as evidence that what subjects thought they experienced, they really did. But although the subjects referred these experiences to moments at which the heart had stopped beating, etc., I do not know of any evidence that at these moments their brains had ceased to function. And if the brain was still functioning then, what the evidence would show is not that the soul may function when the brain does not, but only that its perceptual experiences (i.e., sensations and acquisitions of belief about far away places) are not dependent on normal sensory input.

The same conclusion will follow with respect to the considerable but not overwhelming evidence of those resuscitated patients who had experiences of the other strange kind, "out-of-body-experiences," i.e., being able to view their own bodies and events in the operating theatre from a distance, obtaining thereby information which they would not have been able to obtain by normal means (e.g., having visual experiences of events which they would not have got from use of their eyes, such as views of parts of the theatre hidden from their eyes).[6] This again suggests that the subject's acquisition of information is dependent on some factor quite other than normal sensory input to the brain. But again I know of no evidence that these experiences occurred while the brain was not functioning; and so the available evidence does not support the suggestion that the soul can function without the brain functioning.

My conclusion on parapsychology is that it provides no good evidence that the soul continues to function without the brain to which it is currently connected, functioning.

ARGUMENTS FOR NATURAL SURVIVAL

The second class of arguments purporting to show that the soul survives death purport to show from a consideration of what the soul is like when it functions normally that its nature is such that the failure of the brain to function would make no difference to the operation of the soul. Such arguments verge from very general arguments of what the soul must be like to be conscious at all to arguments which appeal to particular empirical data.

Dualist philosophers of the past have usually affirmed the natural immortality of the soul—that the soul has such a nature, or the laws of nature are such, that (barring suspension of natural laws) it will continue to function forever. There have been a variety of general arguments for the natural immortality of the soul. Each argument has, in my view, its own fallacies; and the fallacies being fairly evident today, there is no need for any extensive discussion of such arguments. (Expositions of the arguments do, incidentally, usually suffer from confusing the existence of the soul with its functioning; wrongly supposing that when it exists, necessarily it will function.)

To illustrate the fallacies of such arguments, I take just one famous argument, put forward by Plato.[7] Plato argues that the soul being an immaterial thing is unextended, and so does not have parts; but the destruction of a thing consists in separating from each other its parts; whence it follows that souls cannot be destroyed and must continue to exist forever.

Now certainly the normal way by which most material objects cease to exist is that they are broken up into parts. The normal end of a table is to be broken up; likewise for chairs, houses, and pens. But this need not be the way in which a material object ceases to exist. Things cease to exist when they lose their essential properties. The essential properties of a table include being solid. If a table was suddenly liquified, then, even if its constituent molecules remained arranged in the shape of a table by being contained in a table-shaped mould, the table would have ceased to exist. So if even material objects can cease to exist without being broken up into parts, souls surely can cease to exist by some other route than by being broken up into parts....

Is the Soul Naturally Embodied?

If it cannot be shown that the soul has a nature so as to survive death without its connected brain functioning, can it be shown that the soul has a nature such that its functioning is dependent on that of the brain with which it is connected? Can we show that there is a natural law which (i) connects consciousness of a soul with the functioning of some material system, and (ii) connects the consciousness of each soul with the functioning of a particular material system; so that of natural necessity a soul can only function if the brain or other complex system with which it is at some time connected continues to function?

The answer given [previously] is that this cannot be shown. It has not been shown and probably never can be shown that there is any naturally necessary connection of these kinds between soul and body. All we are ever likely to get is correlations—between this kind of brain-event and that kind of mental event. And in the absence of a theory which explains why a material system of this kind is needed to produce a soul, how this sort of physical change will produce this kind of mental state, how just so much of the brain and no more is needed for the continuity of a certain soul (as opposed to the mere functioning of a soul with similar apparent memories), we have no grounds for saying that souls *cannot* survive the death of their brains. We do not know and are not likely to find out what if any natural necessity governs the functioning of souls.

The situation is simply that the fairly direct kinds of evidence considered so far give no grounds for supposing that anyone has survived death, but we know of no reason to suppose that it is not possible for anyone to survive death. The situation is thus similar to that in many areas of enquiry when no one has yet found a so-and-so but no one has shown that so-and-sos do not exist. Maybe there are living persons on other planets, naturally occurring elements with atomic numbers of over 1,000, or magnetic monopoles; but as yet no one has found them. Someone may argue that failure to find something when you have looked for it is evidence that it does not exist. But that is so only if you would recognize the object when you found it, and if there is a limited region within which the object can exist and you have explored quite a lot of the region. Failure to find oil in the English Channel after you have drilled in most parts of it, or to find the Abominable Snowman if you have explored most of the Himalayas, is indeed evidence that the thing does not exist. But that is hardly the case with souls whose brains have ceased to function. Maybe they are reincarnate in new bodies and brains on Earth but, as they have lost their memories, the evidence of their identity has gone. Or maybe they are where we cannot at present look. They may still function without being embodied... and so there be no place which they occupy. Or if they are re-embodied in another body with another brain, they may be anywhere in this universe or some other. Failure to find souls who have survived death shows no more than that if they do exist, they are not in the very few places where we have looked for them or that if they are, the marks of their identity (e.g., apparent memories of past lives) have been removed. In the absence of any further evidence as to whether souls do survive death we can only remain agnostic and wait until further evidence does turn up.

EVIDENCE OF SURVIVAL VIA METAPHYSICAL THEORY

There is however a third kind of evidence about whether men survive death which we have not yet considered. This is evidence of a wide ranging character which is most simply explained by a very general metaphysical theory of the world, which has as its consequence that human souls survive death as a result of their nature or as a result of the predictable action of some agent who has the power to bring them to life.

One such theory is the Hindu-Buddhist metaphysic of karma, a deep law of retribution in nature whereby an agent who lives a life thereafter lives another in which he gets the deserts (reward or punishment) for the previous life. (The establishment of such a system would have the consequence that, despite the lack of evidence for this on which I commented [previously], souls exist before birth; in order to be reborn they must then normally lose much of the character which, I have argued, comes to characterize the soul by the time of death.)

Another such theory is of course Christian theism. The theist has first to argue for the existence of God, a person (in a wide sense) of infinite power, wisdom,

goodness, and freedom. He may argue that the existence of God provides the simplest explanation of the existence of the universe, the virtual total regularity of its behaviour in its conformity to natural laws, and various more particular phenomena within the universe. It would then follow that God, being omnipotent, would have the power to give to souls life after death (and if there is no natural law which ties the functioning of a soul to the operation of a brain, God would not need to suspend natural laws in order to do this). The Christian theist will need further to show that God intends to bring souls to function after death. He could show this either by showing that it was an obligation on an omnipotent being to do such a thing, and so that, being good, God would do it; or by showing that God had announced his intention of doing this (e.g., by doing something which God alone could do such as suspending a law of nature, in connection with the work of a prophet as a sign that the prophet who had said that God so intended was to be trusted).

It will be evident that any argument via metaphysical theory to the survival of death by human souls will have a lengthy and complicated structure. But of course those who produce such arguments are equally concerned about most of the other things which need to be proved on the way. Few people are interested in the existence of God solely for its value in proving life after death. And if I am right in my claim that we cannot show that the soul has a nature such that it survives "under its own steam," and that we cannot show that it has a nature such that it cannot survive without its sustaining brain, the only kind of argument that can be given is an argument which goes beyond nature, i.e., that shows there is something beyond the natural order embodied in laws of nature, and that the operation of that something is to some extent predictable.

If God did give to souls life after death in a new body or without a body, he would not in any way be violating natural laws—for, if I am right, there are no natural laws which dictate what will happen to the soul after death. The soul doesn't have a nature which has consequences for what will happen to it subsequent to the dissolution of its links to the body.

In the last chapter I argued that the human soul at death had a structure, a system of beliefs and desires which might be expected to be there to some degree in the soul if that soul were to be revived. If a man does survive death, he will take his most central desires and beliefs with him, which is the kind of survival for which, I suspect, most men hope. In hoping to survive death, a man hopes not only that subsequent to his death, he will have experiences and perform actions. He hopes also to take with him a certain attitude to the world. That attitude certainly does not always include all aspects of a man's present character. Much, no doubt, many a man would be happy to dispense with. But it does include some of his character, and that part just because it is the part which he desires should continue, is the most central part.

Note that if there does occur a general resurrection of souls with new bodies in some other world, yet with apparent memories of their past lives (or a general reincarnation on Earth with such memories), they would have grounds for reidentifying each other correctly. For then the general failure of the results of the criterion of bodily continuity to coincide with those of apparent memory would by arguments [I have offered elsewhere] justifiably lead us to abandon the former criterion and rely entirely on the latter. Not merely is a general resurrection logically possible but it would be known by the subjects to have occurred.

CONCLUSION

The view of the evolved human soul which I have been advocating may be elucidated by the following analogy. The soul is like a light bulb and the brain is like an electric light socket. If you plug the bulb into the socket and turn the current on, the light will shine. If the socket is damaged or the current turned off, the light will not shine. So, too, the soul will function (have a mental life) if it is plugged into a functioning brain. Destroy the brain or cut off the nutriment supplied by the blood, and the soul will cease to function, remaining inert. But it can be revived and made to function again by repairing or reassembling the brain—just as the light can be made to shine again by repairing the socket or turning on the current. But now, my analogy breaks down slightly (as all analogies do—else they would not be analogies). Humans can repair light sockets. But there is a practical limit to the ability of humans to repair brains; the bits get lost. Humans can move light bulbs and put them into entirely different sockets. But no human knows how to move a soul from one body and plug it into another; nor does any known natural force do this. Yet the task is one involving no contradiction and an omnipotent God could achieve it; or maybe there are other processes which will do so. And just as light bulbs do not have to be plugged into sockets in order to shine (loose wires can be attached to them), maybe there are other ways of getting souls to function than by plugging them into brains. But investigation into the nature of the soul does not reveal those ways. And humans cannot discover what else is needed to get souls to function again, unless they can discover the ultimate force behind nature itself.

NOTES

1. *Summa Contra Gentiles*, 4. 81. 12 and 13. (Book IV, translated under the title *On the Truth of the Catholic Faith*, Book IV, by C. J. O'Neill, Image Books, New York, 1957.)
2. For references to the literature, see John Hick, *Death and Eternal Life* (London: Collins, 1976), pp. 373–78.
3. On the alleged evidence of spiritualism, see John Hick, op. cit., ch. 7.
4. There is a brief and well-balanced survey of this evidence in Paul and Linda Badham, *Immortality or Extinction?* (London: Macmillan, 1982), ch. 5. My summary of the evidence is based on this chapter, but I also make use of a very careful and balanced account of a new programme of investigations by Michael B. Sabom, *Recollections of Death* (New York: Harper and Row, 1982).
5. Lancet, 24 June 1978, quoted in Badham, op. cit.
6. On this, see Sabom, op. cit., chs. 3, 6, 7, and 8.
7. *Phaedo* 78b–80c.

Study Questions

1. How does Swinburne distinguish between the existence of the soul and its function? Why is this distinction important to Swinburne's argument?
2. Why does Swinburne conclude that it is unlikely that after death souls would be able to use their brain to function? What follows from Swinburne's view about the soul?
3. Why is Swinburne unpersuaded by parapsychology to believe that souls function after death?
4. How could God make it possible that the soul could function after death? Why does Swinburne think that this account does not violate any natural laws?

Linda Badham

Problems with Accounts of Life After Death

Linda Badham (b. 1950) raises objections to various conceptions of life after death. She argues that people who believe that we will be resurrected with the same body we have now encounter three problems: that we share atoms with other persons over a lifetime, that a resurrected body would again have to face its mortality, and that all the resurrected people would have be located somewhere. Badham objects to a scenario in which the person is re-created after death on the grounds that one cannot distinguish the re-created person, which would be the same person, from its replica, which would not be the same person. She says that the case for immortality of the soul fails to understand the person's intrinsic connection with his or her body. She also believes that the evolution of the species presents the problem of deciding which beings do or do not have souls. Moreover, for souls to have identity, they must have continuity, but it is physical, not mental, continuity that creates identity, and souls lack physical continuity. Finally, Badham observes that near-death experiences do not require a theistic interpretation; indeed, they invoke all the problems of connecting with the physical that face an anthropological dualist. She concludes that there is no good reason to believe that life after death or immortality is possible.

It is a popularly held view that science and religion are antithetical. And this view is supported by the sociological fact that leading scholars and scientists are significantly less likely to be Christian than other groups in society. Yet even so, there are a number of very eminent scientists, and particularly physicists, who claim that there is no real conflict between their scientific and religious beliefs. And many Christian apologists have drawn comfort from such claims in an age where the tide of secularism threatens to engulf the ancient citadel of Christian belief. However, I have my doubts as to whether or not Christianity is secure from attack by science in general on some of its most crucial tenets. And, in particular, what I want to argue in this chapter is that the implications of modern science are far more damaging to doctrines of life after death than many Christian writers have supposed.

From *Death and Immortality in the Religions of the World*, ed. Paul Badham and Linda Badham. Reprinted by permission of Paragon Press. Footnotes are omitted.

RESURRECTION OF THE BODY (THIS FLESH)

Although many might think that belief in the resurrection of this flesh at the end of time is now unthinkable, it has to be recognized that this is the form that orthodox Christian belief took from at least the second century onwards. Thus the Apostles' Creed affirms belief in the resurrection of the flesh; the Nicene Creed looks for the "upstanding of the dead bodies"; and the Christian Fathers were utterly explicit that the resurrection was definitely a physical reconstitution. Moreover, such belief is still Catholic orthodoxy: a recent *Catholic Catechism for Adults* declares that each one of us will rise one day "the same person he was, in the same flesh made living by the same spirit."...Hence it seems reasonable to suppose that this form of resurrection belief is still held among Christians. Yet a minimal knowledge of modern science seems sufficient to undermine it completely.

First, there is the problem that "this flesh" is only temporarily mine. I am not like a machine or artifact, which keeps its atoms and molecules intact throughout its existence, save for those lost by damage or replaced during repair. Rather, I am a biological system in dynamic equilibrium (more or less) with my environment, in that I exchange matter with that environment continually. As J. D. Bernal writes, "It is probable that none of us have more than a few atoms with which we started life, and that even as adults we probably change most of the material of our bodies in a matter of a few months." Thus it might prove an extremely difficult business to resurrect "this" flesh at the end of time, for the atoms that will constitute me at the moment of death will return to the environment and will doubtless become part of innumerable other individuals. Augustine discussed the case of cannibals having to restore the flesh they had "borrowed" as an exception. But in the light of our current knowledge, shared atoms would seem the rule rather than the exception.

Moreover, there is the further problem that even if the exact atoms that constituted me at death could all be reassembled without leaving some other people bereft of vital parts, then the reconstituted body would promptly expire again. For whatever caused the systems' failure in my body, which led to my death originally, would presumably still obtain if the body exactly as it was prior to death were remade. But perhaps we can overcome this problem with a fairly simple proviso: the resurrection body should be identical to the body that died, malfunctions apart. After all, it might be said, we have no difficulty in accepting our television set returned in good working order from the repair shop after a breakdown as one and the same television set that we took to be repaired, even though some or even several of its components have been replaced. But people are not television sets. What counts as malfunction? Increasing age usually brings some diminution in physical and mental powers. Are all these to be mended too? How much change can a body take and still be the same person? Nor is it possible to suggest that the resurrection environment might be such as to reverse the effects of aging and disease. For this move implies such a great change in the properties of the matter that is "this flesh" as to make it dubious whether "this" flesh really had been resurrected. The more one actually fills out the vague notion of the resurrection of the same flesh that perished, the more problems arise.

And even if the problem of reconstituting each one of us to the same (healthy) flesh he was (or might have been) could be overcome, there would remain the question of where we could all be resurrected. There is a space problem. If the countless millions of human beings who have ever lived and may live in the future were all to be resurrected on this earth, then the overcrowding would be acute. Now there are at least two theological maneuvers that we could make to circumvent this embarrassment. If we want to retain resurrection on this earth, then we might say that only the chosen will be resurrected and thereby limit the numbers. But that solution raises insuperable problems about the morality of a God who would behave in such a way. Alternatively, it might be argued that the resurrection will be to a new life in heaven and not to eternal life on earth. But in that case it has to be noted that resurrected bodies would need a biological environment markedly similar to the one we now live in. This leads to the implication that heaven would have to be a planet, or series of planets, all suitable for human life. The further one pushes this picture, the more bizarre and religiously unsatisfying it becomes.

In sum, then, a little knowledge of the biochemistry of living organisms together with a brief consideration of the physicochemical conditions that such organisms require if they are to live, ought to have rendered the traditional notion of literal bodily resurrection unthinkable.

RESURRECTION OF THE BODY TRANSFORMED

It might be argued, as John Polkinghorne claims, that all this is irrelevant: "We know that there is nothing significant about the material which at any one time constitutes our body.... It is the pattern they [the atoms] form which persists and evolves. We are liberated, therefore, from the quaint medieval picture of the reassembly of the body from its scattered components. In very general terms it is not difficult to imagine the pattern recreated (the body resurrected) in some other world."

At this point we should note that the doctrine being proposed here has shifted in a very significant way. The old doctrine of resurrection of the flesh guaranteed personal survival because the resurrected body was physically identical with the one laid in the grave. Physical continuity supplied the link between the person who died and the one who was resurrected. But Polkinghorne's version of the resurrection envisages recreation of a *pattern* in some other world. This is open to a host of philosophical problems about the sense in which the recreation of a replica can count as the survival of the person who died.

What would we say, for example, if the replica were created *before* my death? Would I then die happily knowing that someone was around to carry on, as it were, in my place? Would I think to myself that the replica really was me? Consider the possibility of cloning. Let us imagine that science reaches a stage where a whole adult human individual can be regenerated from a few cells of a person in such a way that the original—Jones I—and the copy—Jones II—are

genetically identical, and that the clone knows everything that Jones I knows. We may imagine that the purpose of doing this is to give a healthy body to house the thoughts of the physically ailing, but brilliant, Jones I. Now does Jones I die secure in the knowledge that he will live again? I would suggest that he might feel relieved to know that his life's work would carry on, and that his project would be entrusted to one incomparably suited to continue with it. He might also feel exceptionally close to Jones II and be deeply concerned for his welfare. But the other would not *be* him. In the end, Jones I would be dead and the other, Jones II, would carry on in his place. As far as Jones I was concerned, he himself would not live again, even though most other people would treat Jones II as if he were Jones I rejuvenated.

If these intuitions are correct, then they suggest that whatever it is that we count as essential for being one and the same person, it is not a "pattern." And I would suggest that all theories of resurrection that speak of our rising with new and transformed bodies fall foul of what I term the replica problem. For without some principle of continuity between the person who died and the one who was resurrected, then what was resurrected would only be something very similar to the one who died, a replica, and not a continuation of the dead person.

THE SOUL

Such considerations have led theologians at least from Aquinas onwards to argue that any tenable resurrection belief hinges on a concept of the soul. For even if we hold to a belief in the resurrection of some "new and glorious body," then we need the soul to avoid the replica problem. There has to be a principle of continuity between this world and the next if what is raised to new life really is one and the same person as the one who died. Moreover, this principle of continuity must encapsulate enough of the real "me" for both "old" and "new" versions to count as the same person. Might this requirement be fulfilled if we were to espouse a dualist concept of the person and say, with Descartes, that my essential personhood is to be identified with my mind, that is, with the subject of conscious experiencing. However, I want argue that not even this move is sufficient to rescue the Christian claim.

First, there are the practical problems of which contemporary dualists are very much aware. Our personal experience and emotions are intimately linked to our body chemistry. Indeed, the limits to what we are able to think at all are set by our genetic endowment; so that one man's physicochemical equipment enables him to be a brilliant mathematician, while another's lack condemns him to lifelong imbecility. If our diet is imbalanced and inadequate, or if certain of our organs are malfunctioning, then our bodies may be starved of essential nutrients or poisoned by the excessive production of some hormone. In such cases, the whole personality may be adversely affected. The "subject of my conscious experiences" would seem to be very much at the mercy of my physico-chemical constitution.

A second difficulty lies in deciding which organisms count as having souls and which do not. And if God is to give eternal life to the former class and not to the latter, then even He has to be able to draw a line somewhere, and that nonarbitrarily. The problem occurs both in considering the evolution of the species Homo sapiens and the individual development of human beings. Even if we ignore the problem of nonhuman animals and restrict the possibility of possessing a soul to humans, there are still insuperable difficulties.

Consider first the evolutionary pathway that led from the early mammals to man. Somewhere along that line we would be fairly secure in denying that such and such a creature had any awareness of self. And it is also true to say that most normal adult humans possess such an awareness. But between these extremes lies a gray area. To have a nonarbitrary dividing line, it has to be possible for us to decide (at least in principle) where a sharp division can be drawn between the last generation of anthropoid apes and the first generation of true Homo sapiens. Are we to suppose that in one generation there were anthropoid apes who gave birth to the next generation of true *Homo sapiens*, and that the changes between one generation and the next were so great that the children counted in God's eyes

as the bearers of immortality while their parents were "mere animals"? Yet unless dualists are prepared to fly in the face of evolutionary biology, how can they avoid this unpalatable conclusion? . . .

There are, in addition, some further objections of a more purely philosophical nature, which I think need mentioning at this point. The subject of my conscious experiencing is singularly unconvincing as a principle of continuity that guarantees persistence of the "same" person through change. Moreover, defining the "real" me in this way actually misses a lot of what most of us would want to say is a part of the "real" me. I shall begin by discussing the question of a principle of continuity.

One great problem with my awareness of self is its lack of persistence, its transitoriness. My stream of consciousness is far from being a constant or even ever-present (though varying) flow. When I am unconscious, in a dreamless sleep, or even in a vacant mood, it just is not there. Yet *I* do not cease to exist whenever my conscious mind is, as it were, switched off temporarily. Secondly, we have to face the problem that this awareness of self is ever-changing. What I was as a child is very different from what I, as I am in myself, am today; and if I live to be an old lady, doubtless the subject of my conscious experiences will look back with a mixture of wry amusement and nostalgia at that other her of forty years ago. Now it might be thought that this problem of continual change is no greater a problem for the notion of same "self" than it is for the notion of same "body" since the body is also in a continual state of flux. But I would suggest that what supplies continuity through change is matter. It may be that all my constituent atoms will have changed in the next few months, but they will not have all changed simultaneously. Moreover, the physically-based blueprints from the chemistry that keeps my body going are passed on from one generation of cells to another in a direct physical line of succession. Thus, I would argue that what keeps the subject of my conscious experiencing belonging to one and the same person is this physical continuity.

The essential requirement of physical continuity can be illustrated if we return to the clone example. Let us modify the thought experiment a little, and make Jones II a copy of a perfectly healthy Jones I. And let us also stipulate that the two Joneses emerge from the cloning laboratory not knowing who is the original and who the copy. In other words, Jones I and II are, seemingly, wholly similar. Neither they nor we can tell which is which, unless we trace the histories of the two bodies to ascertain which grew from a fertilized ovum and which developed as the result of cloning. Now if we apply the implications of this to the question of what might live again after death, we see that being "the subject of my conscious experiences" is not sufficient to guarantee that I am one and the same person as the one who died. For what the clone example shows is that both Jones I and Jones II may believe (or doubt) equally that he really is the same person as Jones I while he relies solely on his personal experience of himself as Jones. Only when he traces the path of physical continuity can he know whether he truly is Jones I or not. (Of course, we might want to say that where there had been one person, Jones, there were now two distinct individuals, both of whom were physically continuous with the original. But in that case the possibility of defining "same person" in terms of "same stream of consciousness" does not even arise.)

Thus I contend, a dualist definition of what I really am fails because it cannot provide adequate criteria for recognizing the "same" person through change. I can think of no other case where we would even be tempted to accept something as transitory and ever-changing as "consciousness of self" to be the essential criterion for defining what it is that an entity has to retain if it is to count as remaining the same individual through change.

I move on now to the problems that arise from the restrictedness of defining me as the subject of my conscious experiences. A great deal of what I am does not involve my conscious thoughts at all, even when I am fully awake. Take the familiar example of driving a car. When I was learning to drive, I certainly employed a great amount of conscious effort. But nowadays my conscious thoughts are fairly free to attend to other matters when I am driving, even though, of course, intense conscious attention instantly returns if danger threatens. I certainly do not want to say "my body" drove here. I drove here, even though most of the time the subject of my conscious experiences was not much involved.

Moreover, we cannot ignore the possibility that the conscious subject might actually fail to recognize a significant part of all that I really am. To exemplify the point: imagine someone who believes himself to be a great wit, when most of his colleagues find him a crashing bore. If he were to arrive in the resurrection world without his familiar characteristics—clumsiness of speech, repetitiveness, triviality, self-centeredness—would he really be the person who had died? Yet could he bring these characteristics with him if the subject of his conscious experiences, the "real" him, was wholly unaware of having been like this?

In sum, what I have been arguing against dualism is that this concept of the soul cannot bear the weight put on it. Yet it has to bear this weight if it is to be the sine qua non of my surviving bodily death. Considerations from the natural sciences and philosophy, and even religious implications, combine to render it far from convincing. But, it might be countered, no amount of argument on the basis of current scientific theory, philosophy, or religious sentiments can count against hard empirical fact. So what about the reports that exist of near-death experiences, which seem to show that some people really do have experiences apart from their bodies?

NEAR-DEATH EXPERIENCES

Let me begin by stating quite clearly that I shall not be concerned to discuss the merits or otherwise of individual cases. I am going to suppose, for the purposes of discussion, that there is strong, bona fide evidence that some people come back from the brink of death fully convinced that they had left their bodies and had had apparently veridical experiences as if from a vantage point different from that of the body. The question then is, how do we interpret these "travelers, tales."

I have three main points to make here. The first is that a present absence of satisfactory normal explanations for these cases does not imply that there are no such explanations ever to be found. We should not be hurried into a supernaturalist account merely because we can find no other, as if the God-of-the-gaps lesson had yet to be learned....

My second point is that even if we take near-death experiences as supplying empirical proof of the existence, nay persistence, of the human soul or mind, that would not smooth out all the difficulties. All the problems that I have discussed earlier would still be there, awaiting some kind of resolution. And there would arise yet further problems. Take, for example, the question of how the soul actually "sees" physical objects while it supposedly hovers below the ceiling. William Rushton puts the point thus: "What is this out-of-the-body eye that can encode the visual scene exactly as does the real eye, with its hundred million photoreceptors and its million signaling optic nerves? Can you imagine anything but [that] a replica of a real eye could manage to do this? But if this floating replica is to see, it must catch light, and hence cannot be transparent, and so must be visible to people in the vicinity. In fact floating eyes are not observed, nor would this be expected, for they exist only in fantasy." And if it be countered that the soul perceives without using the normal physicochemical mechanisms, then we might ask why on earth did such a complicated organ as the eye ever evolve (or remain unatrophied) if human beings possess souls that can "see" without normal eyes. Moreover, one might expect that blind people, deprived of normal visual stimuli, would use this psychic ability, if it really existed. These, and kindred problems concerned with modes of perception, would need answers if we were to take seriously supernatural interpretations of OBEs.

Finally, I suggest that to accept the existence of some nonmaterial soul in man would be to embrace a notion fundamentally at variance with other well-founded convictions about the nature of reality. For we would then have to allow for events happening in the world that rest on no underlying physicochemical mechanisms. Now I am very well aware that scientists are continually changing their theories to accommodate new data, and that from time to time some wholesale replacement of outmoded ideas has been necessary. So, it might be asked, can we not envisage some new scientific outlook that embraces both the normal data and the paranormal? Just so. A new scientific outlook, which could encompass both normal and paranormal data, would clearly be more satisfactory than one which could in no way account for the paranormal. But it must be remembered that the whole scientific enterprise presupposes the existence of underlying mechanisms whose discovery enables us to understand the "how" of an event. So it is hard to see how any unified scientific theory could embrace both the notion that most events in the world depend on underlying physico-chemical mechanisms, and also that there are some events that do not utilize any such mechanisms at all. And if paranormal data are taken as support for the belief in the existence of nonmaterial entities (like souls) then these data fly in the face of normal science. Thus I concur with C. D. Broad that "it is certainly right to demand a much higher standard of evidence for events which are alleged to be paranormal than those which would be normal.... For in dealing with evidence we have always to take into account the antecedent probability or improbability of the alleged event, i.e., its probability or improbability relative to all the rest of our knowledge and well-founded belief other than the special evidence adduced in its favour."

In sum then, it seems that at present paranormal data cannot be accommodated within naturalist science. But to move from that to claiming that we have empirical evidence for the existence of immaterial souls seems unwarranted, not least because to explicate the paranormal in terms of the activities of immaterial souls may appear to solve one explanatory difficulty, but only at the expense of raising a host of other problems.

CONCLUSION

When Christianity was originally formulated, man's entire world view was very different from our current beliefs. It was plausible to think in terms of a three-decker universe in which the center of God's interest was this Earth and its human population. The idea that God would raise man from the dead to an eternal life of bliss fitted neatly into this schema. However, the erosion of this picture, beginning from at least the time of Copernicus and Galileo, has cut the traditional Christian hope adrift from the framework of ideas in which it was originally formulated. What I have tried to show in this chapter is that various attempts, which have been made to try to accommodate some form of resurrection/immortality belief within our current world view, are inadequate and fail. I conclude, then, that a due consideration of man's place in nature leads us to the view that he belongs there and nowhere else.

STUDY QUESTIONS

1. What three major problems does Badham see facing the view that life after death involves the resurrection of the actual flesh or body?
2. How does Badham's example of cloning show that re-creation of the person out of new material cannot account for personal life after death?
3. Why does Badham believe that appeal to a soul cannot account for personal identity over time? Why is this point important to the question of life after death?
4. Do you think that Badham successfully shows the impossibility of life after death? Why or why not?

John Hick

Resurrection of the Person

John Hick (b. 1922) explores an understanding of life after death that invokes a view of the person as a psycho-physical unity (having no soul). Hick develops three scenarios where a person disappears or dies and subsequently a "replica" exists elsewhere. He suggests that the most reasonable explanation in each case is that the same person again exists in a different place at a subsequent time. He goes on to respond to three objections to his view. One objection is that personal identity is a matter of decision. Hick responds that even if it is a matter of decision, some decisions are more reasonable than others, and deciding on identity is reasonable. A second objection concerns how to understand time according to his theory. Hick proposes a single time sequence, with events occurring simultaneously in different places and with each space's measurement of time determined only by occurrences in that space. The last objection is that multiple replicas could be possible, which would destroy identity. To this, Hick replies that although logically there cannot be more than one being, it does not follow that there cannot be exactly one. Finally, he speculates about possible ways that the "replica" might differ from the deceased without destroying the identity.

THE IDEA OF RESURRECTION

"I believe," says the Apostles' Creed, "in the resurrection of the body and the life everlasting." The resurrection of the body, or of the flesh, has been given a variety of meanings in different ages and different theological circles; but we are not at present concerned with the history of the concept. We are concerned with the meaning that can be given to it today in terms of our contemporary scientific and philosophical understanding.

The prevailing view of man among both contemporary scientists and Western philosophers is that he is an indissoluble psycho-physical unity. The only self of which we know is the empirical self, the walking, talking, acting, sleeping individual who lives, it may be, for some sixty to eighty years and then dies. Mental events and mental characteristics are analysed into the modes of behaviour and behavioural dispositions of this empirical self. The human being is described as an organism capable of acting in the high-level ways which we characterize as intelligent, resentful, humorous, calculating and the like. The concept of mind or soul is thus not that of a "ghost in the machine" but of the more flexible and sophisticated ways in which human beings behave and have it in them to behave. On this view there is no room for the notion of soul in distinction from body; and if there is no soul in distinction from body there can be no question of the soul surviving the death of the body. Against this background of thought the specifically Christian and Jewish belief in the resurrection of the body, in contrast to the Hellenic idea of the survival of a disembodied soul, might be expected to have attracted more attention than it has. For it is consonant with the conception of man as an indissoluble psycho-physical unity and yet it also offers the possibility of an empirical meaning for the idea of life after death.

St. Paul is the chief biblical expositor of the idea of the resurrection of the body. His basic conception, as I understand it, is this. When someone has died he is, apart from any special divine action, extinct. A human being is by nature mortal and subject to annihilation at death. But in fact God, by an act of sovereign power, either sometimes or always resurrects or reconstitutes or recreates him—not however as the identical physical organism that he was before death, but as a *soma pneumatikon* ("spiritual body") embodying the dispositional characteristics and memory traces of the deceased physical organism, and inhabiting an environment with which the *soma pneumatikon* is continuous as our present bodies are continuous with our present world. We are not concerned here with the difficult exegetical question of how precisely Paul thought of the resurrection body but with the conceptual question as to how, if at all, we can intelligibly think of it today.

THE "REPLICA" THEORY

I wish to suggest that we can think of it as the divine creation in another space of an exact psycho-physical "replica" of the deceased person.

The first point requiring clarification is the idea of spaces in the plural.[1] In this context the possibility of two spaces is the possibility of two sets of extended objects such that each member of each set is spatially related to each other member of the same set but not spatially related to any member of the other set. Thus everything in the space in which I am is at a certain distance and in a certain direction from me, and vice versa; but if there is a second space, nothing in it is at any distance or in any direction from where I now am. In other words, from my point of view the other space is nowhere and therefore does not exist. But if there *is* a second space, unobservable by me, the objects in it are entirely real to an observer within that space, and our own world is to him nowhere—not at any distance nor in any direction—so that from his point of view it does not exist. Now it is logically possible for there to be any number of worlds, each in its own space, these worlds being all observed by the universal consciousness of God but only one of them being observed by an embodied being who is part of one of these worlds. And the idea of bodily resurrection requires (or probably requires) that there be at least two such worlds, and that when an individual dies in our present world in space number one he is either immediately or after a lapse of time re-created in a world in space number two.

In order to develop this idea more fully I shall present a series of three cases, which I claim to be logically possible of fulfilment.

We begin with the idea of someone suddenly ceasing to exist at a certain place in this world and the next instant coming into existence at another place which is not contiguous with the first. He has not moved from A to B by making a path through the intervening space but has disappeared at A and reappeared at B. For example, at some learned gathering in London one of the company suddenly and inexplicably disappears and the next moment an exact "replica" of him suddenly and inexplicably appears at some comparable meeting in New York. The person who appears in New York is exactly similar, as to both bodily and mental characteristics, to the person who disappears in London. There is continuity of memory, complete similarity of bodily features, including fingerprints, hair and eye coloration and stomach contents, and also of beliefs, habits, and mental propensities. In fact there is everything that would lead us to identify the one who appeared with the one who disappeared, except continuous occupancy of space.

It is I think clear that this is a logically possible sequence of events. It is of course factually impossible: that is to say, so long as matter functions in accordance with the "laws" which it has exhibited hitherto, such things will not happen. But nevertheless we can imagine changes in the behaviour of matter which would allow it to happen, and we can ask what effect this would have upon our concept of personal identity. Would we say that the one who appears in New York is the same person as the one who disappeared in London? This would presumably be a matter for decision, and perhaps indeed for a legal decision affecting such matters as marriage, property, debts, and other social rights and obligations. I believe that the only reasonable and generally acceptable decision would be to acknowledge identity. The man himself would be conscious of being the same person, and I suggest that his fellow human beings would feel obliged to recognize him as being the one whom he claims to be. We may suppose, for example, that a deputation of the colleagues of the man who disappeared fly to New York to interview the "replica" of him which is reported there, and find that he is in all respects but one exactly as though he had travelled from London to New York by conventional means. The only difference is that he describes how, as he was listening to Dr. Z reading a paper, on blinking his eyes he suddenly found himself sitting in a different room listening to a different paper by an American scholar. He asks his colleagues how the meeting had gone after he had ceased to be there, and what they had made of his disappearance, and so on. He clearly thinks of himself as the one who was present with them at their meeting in London. He is presently reunited with his wife, who is quite certain that he is her husband; and with his children, who are quite certain that he is their father. And so on. I suggest that faced with all these circumstances those who know him would soon, if not immediately, find themselves thinking of him and treating him as the individual who had so inexplicably disappeared from the meeting in London; and that society would accord legal

recognition of his identity. We should be extending our normal use of "same person" in a way which the postulated facts would both demand and justify if we said that the person who appears in New York is the same person as the one who disappeared in London. The factors inclining us to identify them would, I suggest, far outweigh the factors disinclining us to do so. The personal, social, and conceptual cost of refusing to make this extension would so greatly exceed the cost of making it that we should have no reasonable alternative but to extend our concept of *the* "same person" to cover this strange new case.

This imaginary case, bizarre though it is, establishes an important conceptual bridgehead for the further claim that a post-mortem "replica" of Mr. X in another space would likewise count as the same person as the this-world Mr. X before his death. However, let me strengthen this bridgehead at two points before venturing upon it.

The cyberneticist Norbert Wiener has graphically emphasized the nondependence of human bodily identity through time upon the identity of the physical matter momentarily composing the body. He points out that the living human body is not a static entity but a pattern of change: "The individuality of the body is that of a flame rather than that of a stone, of a form rather than that of a bit of substance."[2] The pattern of the body can be regarded as a message that is in principle capable of being coded, transmitted, and then translated back into its original form, as sight and sound patterns may be transmitted by radio and translated back into sound and picture. Hence "there is no absolute distinction between the types of transmission which we can use for sending a telegram from country to country and the types of transmission which at least are theoretically possible for transmitting a living organism such as a human being."[3] Strictly, one should not speak, as Wiener does here, of a living organism or body being transmitted; for it would not be the body itself but its coded form that is transmitted. At other times, however, Wiener is more precise. It is, he says, possible to contemplate transmitting "the whole pattern of the human body, of the human brain with its memories and cross connections, so that a hypothetical receiving instrument could re-embody these messages in appropriate matter, capable of continuing the processes already in the body and the mind, and of maintaining the integrity needed for this continuation by a process of homeostasis."[4] Accordingly Wiener concludes that the telegraphing of the pattern of a man from one place to another is theoretically possible even though it remains at the present time technically impossible.[5] And it does indeed seem natural in discussing this theoretical possibility to speak of the bodily individual who is constituted at the end of the process as being the same person as the one who was "encoded" at the beginning. He is not composed of numerically the same parcel of matter; and yet it is more appropriate to describe him as the same person than as a different person because the matter of which he is composed embodies exactly the same "information." Similarly, the rendering of Beethoven's ninth symphony which reaches my ears from the radio loudspeaker does not consist of numerically the same vibrations that reached the microphone in the concert hall; those vibrations have not travelled on through another three hundred miles to me. And yet it is more appropriate to say that I am hearing this rendering of the ninth symphony than that I am hearing something else....

Wiener's contribution to the present argument is his insistence that psycho-physical individuality does not depend upon the numerical identity of the ultimate physical constituents of the body but upon the pattern of "code" which is exemplified. So long as the same "code" operates, different parcels of matter can be used, and those parcels can be in different places.[6]

The second strengthening of the bridgehead concerns the term "replica" which, it will be observed, I have used in quotes. The quotes are intended to mark a difference between the normal concept of a replica and the more specialized concept in use here. The paradigm sense of "replica" is that in which there is an original object, such as a statue, of which a more or less exact copy is then made. It is logically possible (though not of course necessary) for the original and the replica to exist simultaneously; and also for there to be any number of replicas of the same original. In contrast to this, in the case of the disappearance in London and reappearance in New York it is not logically possible for the original and the "replica" to exist

simultaneously or for there to be more than one "replica" of the same original. If a putative "replica" did exist simultaneously with its original it would not be a "replica" but a replica; and if there were more than one they would not be "replicas" but replicas. For "replica" is the name that I am proposing for the second entity in the following case. A living person ceases to exist at a certain location, and a being exactly similar to him in all respects subsequently comes into existence at another location. And I have argued so far that it would be a correct decision, causing far less linguistic and conceptual disruption than the contrary one, to regard the "replica" as the same person as the original.

Let us now move on to a second imaginary case, a step nearer to the idea of resurrection. Let us suppose that the event in London is not a sudden and inexplicable disappearance, and indeed not a disappearance at all, but a sudden death. Only, at the moment when the individual dies a "replica" of him as he was at the moment before his death, and complete with memory up to that instant, comes into existence in New York. Even with the corpse on our hands it would still, I suggest, be an extension of "same person" required and warranted by the postulated facts to say that the one who died has been miraculously re-created in New York. The case would, to be sure, be even odder than the previous one because of the existence of the dead body in London contemporaneously with the living person in New York. And yet, striking though the oddness undoubtedly is, it does not amount to a logical impossibility.... Once again the factors inclining us to say that the one who died and the one who appeared are the same person would far outweigh the factors inclining us to say that they are different people. Once again we should have to extend our usage of "same person" to cover the new case.

However, rather than pause longer over this second picture let us proceed to the idea of "replication" in another space, which I suggest can give content to the notion of resurrection. For at this point the problem of personal identity shifts its focus from second- and third-person criteria to first-person criteria. It is no longer a question of how we in this world could know that the "replica" Mr. X is the same person as the now deceased Mr. X, but of how the "replica"

Mr. X himself could know this. And since this raises new problems it will be well to move directly to this case and the issues which it involves.

The picture that we have to consider is one in which Mr. X dies and his "replica," complete with memory, etc., appears, not in America, but as a resurrection "replica" in a different world altogether, a resurrection world inhabited by resurrected "replicas"—this world occupying its own space distinct from the space with which we are familiar. It is, I think, manifestly an intelligible hypothesis that after my death I shall continue to exist as a consciousness and shall remember both having died and some at least of my states of consciousness both before and after death. Suppose then that I exist, not as a disembodied consciousness but as a psycho-physical being, a psycho-physical being exactly like the being that I was before death, though existing now in a different space. I have the experience of waking up from unconsciousness, as I have on other occasions woken up from sleep; and I am no more inclined in the one case than in the others to doubt my own identity as an individual persisting through time. I realize, either immediately or presently, that I have died, both because I can remember being on my death-bed and because my environment is now different and is populated by people some of whom I know to have died. Evidences of this kind could mount up to the point at which they are quite as strong as the evidence which, in the previous two pictures, convinces the individual in question that he has been miraculously translated to New York. Resurrected persons would be individually no more in doubt about their own identity than we are now, and would presumably be able to identify one another in the same kinds of ways and with a like degree of assurance as we do now.

IDENTITY FROM WORLD TO WORLD

I suggest that if we knew it to be a "law of nature" that re-creation or "replication" occurs in another space, we should be obliged to modify our concept of "same person" to permit us to say that the "replica" Mr. X in space two is the same person as the former Mr. X in space one. For such an extension of use involves

far less arbitrariness and paradox than would be generated by saying either that they are not the same person or that it is uncertain whether they are the same person. They have everything in common that they could possibly have, given that they exist successively in different spaces. They are physically alike in every particular; psychologically alike in every particular; and the Mr. X stream of consciousness, memory, emotion and volition continues in "replica" Mr. X where it left off at the death of earthly Mr. X. In these circumstances it would, I submit, be wantonly paradoxical to rule that they are not the same person and that the space-two "replica" ought not to think of himself as the person whose past he remembers and whom he is conscious of being.

Terence Penelhum has discussed this concept of resurrection and suggests that although the identification of resurrection-world Mr. X with the former earthly Mr. X is permissible it is not mandatory. He argues that in my cases number two and number three (and probably number one also) it would be a matter for decision as to whether or not to make the identification. The general principle on which he is working is that there can only be an automatic and unquestionable identification when there is bodily continuity. As soon as this is lost, identity becomes a matter for decision, with arguments arising both for and against. He concludes that although "the identification of the former and the latter persons in each of the three pictures is not absurd," yet "in situations like these it is a matter of decision whether to say that physical tests of identity reveal personal identity or very close similarity. We can, reasonably, decide for identity, but we do not have to. And this seems to leave the description of the future life in a state of chronic ambiguity."[7] In response to this I would agree, and have indeed already acknowledged, that these are cases for decision. Indeed, I would say that *all* cases other than ordinary straightforward everyday identity require a decision. Even physical identity, as such, is no guarantee against the need for decisions, as is shown by such imaginary cases as that of the prince whose consciousness, memory, and personality is transferred into the body of a cobbler, and vice versa.[8] Thus all cases outside the ordinary require linguistic legislation. My contention is not that the identification of resurrection-world Mr. X with the former this-world Mr. X is entirely unproblematic, but that the decision to identify is much more reasonable, and is liable to create far fewer problems, than would be the decision to regard them as different people.

TIMES AND SPACES

But if the notion of spaces in the plural, and of resurrection as psycho-physical re-creation after death in another space, is accepted as meaningful, how can we understand the time relationship between the two spaces? Is not time so closely linked with space that the this-world series of events would have to be temporally as well as spatially unrelated to the resurrection-world series of events? And in that case how could someone be said to appear in the resurrection world *after* he had died in this world? ...

Why should there not be a single time sequence in which events can occur simultaneously in different spaces, even though within each space the measurement of time must be in relation to physical movements peculiar to that space? Presumably the divine mind, conscious of all spaces and of the elapse of singular time, would be aware of the temporal relationship between events in different spaces. But the inhabitants of a given space could only be aware of the continuity of time through spaces as an inference from their own memories of life in another space. It could then be the case that "replica" Mr. X in space two comes into existence subsequently to the death of Mr. X in space one, although the only direct evidence of this available to him is his own memory. Reversing Olding's conclusion: he remembers dying, and therefore his dying must have been a past event.

MULTIPLE REPLICATION?[9]

A further difficulty has been raised, based upon the logical spectre of the existence of two or more identical resurrection Mr. X's.[10] If it makes sense to suppose that God might create a second-space reproduction of Mr. X, then it makes sense to suppose that he might create two or more such second-space reproductions, namely X^2, X^3, etc. However, since X^2 and X^3 would then each be the same person as X^1, they would both be the same person; which is absurd. Thus the existence of X^3 would prohibit us from identifying X^2 as being the same person as X^1. Further, it has been argued by J. J. Clarke that the bare logical possibility of X^3 has the same effect. Speaking of several Hicks, H_1, H_2 and H_3, he says, "It is not even necessary to suppose that God has *actually* created H_3, for the mere *possibility* of his doing so is as much a threat to H_2's identity as is H_3's actual existence. If the actual *existence* of H_3 alongside H_2 obliges us to refrain from identifying H_2 as Hick, then the mere *possibility* of H_3 ought similarly to restrain us from conferring identity. This is pinpointed by the fact that if H_3 became reconstituted some while after H_2, one would have to say that for a while H_2 *could* conceivably have been H_1, but then on H_3's arrival in the resurrection world this identification ceased to be possible. This is incoherent."[11] That is to say, so long as it is true that it could turn out, through the arrival of H_3 that H_2 was not after all identical with H_1, that identification is not permissible. Accordingly, since there cannot be two or more re-created X's, there cannot be one re-created X. Applying his argument, appropriately, to myself, Mr. Clarke concludes: "Since multiples of re-embodied Hick cannot enter the resurrection world, then neither can one."[12]

It might perhaps be thought that this difficulty has been avoided by so defining "replica" that there cannot at any given time be more than one "replica" of the same individual. As was said above, if there were two or more they would not be "replicas" but replicas. But whilst this is, I believe, the correct conception of the entity whose existence would constitute the resurrected existence of a deceased individual, it does not obviate the "if not two, then not one" argument. For if there were two (or more) identical post-mortem persons, none of them could be "replica" Mr. X, and thus their existence would render "replication" impossible.

We are asked, then, to contemplate the idea of God re-creating Mr. X, not as a "one off" act but as the re-creation of a plurality of "Mr. X's," each starting life in the world to come as a re-creation of the earthly Mr.

X, complete with his memories, etc. I think it must be granted that if this were to happen our present system of concepts would be unable to deal with it. We should simply not know how to identify the multiple "Mr. X's." Our concept of "the same person" has not been developed to cope with such a situation. It can tolerate a great deal of change in an individual—the changes, for example, that occur as between the baby, the young man, the middle-aged man and the very old man. And I have argued that it could if necessary tolerate gaps in occupancy of space (an instantaneous quantum jump from one point in space to another, or divine decreation at one place and re-creation at another), or even in occupancy of time (a person ceasing to exist at t^1 and existing again after a, preferably short, time lapse at t^2). But one thing that it will not tolerate is multiplicity. A person is by definition unique. There cannot be two people who are exactly the same in every respect, including their consciousness and memories. That is to say, if there were a situation satisfying this description, our present concept of "person" would utterly break down under the strain.

The question, then, is whether we can properly move from the premise that there cannot be two beings in the world to come each of whom is the same person as Mr. X in this world, to the conclusion that there cannot be one being in the world to come who is the same person as Mr. X in this world. And it seems clear to me that we cannot validly reach any such conclusion. Suppose that last week I was in New York and now I am in London. It would be absurd for someone to argue that since there cannot now be *two* JH's in London who are the same person as JH in New York last week, therefore there cannot be *one* JH in London now who is the same person as JH in New York last week! I freely grant that if there were two resurrection "Mr. X's" neither of them could be identified as the same person as the earthly Mr. X, and that therefore, so far from there being two, there would not even be one. But I deny that the unrealized logical possibility of their being two resurrection "Mr. X's" makes it logically impossible for there to be one. It is a conceptual truth that if there were one resurrected "Mr. X" there could not be another; but this truth does not prohibit there being one and only one.

The fact that if there were two or more "Mr. X's," none of them would be Mr. X, does not prevent there being the only kind of resurrected "Mr. X" that could exist, namely, a single one.

In other words, it is impossible for the universe in which we are to have incompatible characteristics. If we are in a universe in which an individual can die and be re-created elsewhere, then we are not in a universe in which an individual can die and be multiply re-created elsewhere. But this fact does not show, or even tend to show, that we cannot be in the first kind of universe....

It is in fact possible to conceive of a great number of situations and worlds in which our present understanding of personal identity would fail to apply and in which we should simply not know what to say. But these do not properly tell against the claim that our ordinary concept of the "same person" can be applied, extended but not disrupted, to the resurrection situation which I have described. It is not an acceptable form of argument that because all manner of other conceivable situations would be unintelligible, or would undermine some of our basic concepts, therefore the possibility that I have outlined is to be rejected as either unintelligible or impossible. It has to be considered on its own merits. And I hope that this discussion has in fact established the conceivability of resurrection as the divine re-creation of the individual after his earthly death as a total psycho-physical "replica" in another space. This can, however, in relation to our present knowledge, be no more than a logical possibility; and if in due course we each discover that this possibility is realized we shall undoubtedly also discover that our present bare outline of it is filled out in ways which we do not foresee. That the basic notion of psycho-physical re-creation can only be the beginning of a full picture becomes evident when we remember that an exact "replica" of a dying man at his last moment of life would be a dying man at his last moment of life! In other words, the first thing that the resurrection body would do is to expire. For we have thus far supposed that the body being replicated is one whose heart is failing, or whose breathing is being fatally obstructed, or which is in the terminal stage of cancer—or whatever other condition is the immediate cause of death. If, then, life is to continue in the postmortem world we must suppose a change in the condition of the resurrection body. But what might be the nature of such a change? Could we, for example, suppose that the resurrection body, instead of being identical in form with the earthly body at the moment of death, is a "replica" of it at some earlier point of life, when it was in full health and vigour?[13] No doubt we can conceive of this; but the cost would be high. For if we envisage the resurrection body as "replicating" the individual in the physical prime of his life at, let us say, around the age of thirty or perhaps twenty-five, he will presumably lose in the resurrection all the memories and all the development of character that had accrued to him on earth since that age. It would seem, then, that we must think of the resurrection body as being created in the condition of the earthly body, not necessarily precisely at the last moment of physical life (which can be defined in several different ways), but perhaps at the last moment of conscious personal life. And then, instead of its immediately or soon dying, we must suppose that in its new environment it is subjected to processes of healing and repair which bring it into a state of health and activity. In the case of old people—and most people die in relatively old age—we might even conceive of a process of growing physically younger to an optimum age.

The reason for postulating full initial bodily similarity between the resurrected person and the pre-resurrection person is to preserve a personal identity which we are supposing to be wholly bound up with the body. If the person is an indissoluble psycho-physical unity, it would seem that he must begin his resurrection life as identically the person who has just died, even though he may then proceed to undergo changes which are not possible in our present world.

This, at least, represents the simplest model for a resurrection world. But this model is only the most accessible of a range of possibilities. It is conceivable that in the resurrection world we shall have bodies which are the outward reflection of our inner nature but which reflect it in ways quite different from that in which our present bodies reflect our personality. In supposing this we have already begun a process of speculation which we cannot profitably pursue. The consideration of logically coherent extrapolations can take us as far as the bare idea of divine reconstitution in another world which is not spatially related to our present world; but beyond this only creative imagination can paint pictures of the possible conditions of such a world and of human life within it.

Notes

1. The conceivability of plural spaces is argued by Anthony Quinton in an important article to which I should like to draw the reader's attention: "Spaces and Times," in *Philosophy*, April 1962.
2. Norbert Wiener, *The Human Use of Human Beings* (London: Sphere Books, 1968), p. 91.
3. Ibid.
4. Ibid., p. 86.
5. Ibid., p. 92.
6. For a discussion of Norbert Wiener's ideas in this connection, see David L. Mouton, "Physicalism and Immortality," in *Religious Studies*, March 1972.
7. Terence Penelhum, *Survival and Disembodied Existence* (London: Routledge, 1970), pp. 100–101.
8. Locke's *Essay Concerning Human Understanding*, book II, ch. 27, para. 15.
9. Much of this section repeats, with the editor's permission, material in "Mr. Clarke's Resurrection Also," in *Sophia*, October 1972.
10. This spectre was first raised in a different context by Bernard Williams in "Personal Identity and Individuation," in *Proc. Aristot. Soc.*, 1956–7, reprinted in *Problems of the Self,* particularly pp. 8–11. Williams's article provoked a valuable discussion in *Analysis*, with articles by C. B. Martin (March 1958), G. C. Nerlich (June 1958 and October 1960), R. C. Coburn (April 1960), Bernard Williams (December 1960), and J. M. Shorter (March 1962). See also: Robert Young, "The Resurrection of the Body," in *Sophia*, July 1970.

11. J. J. Clarke, "John Hick's Resurrection," in *Sophia*, October 1971, p. 20.

12. Ibid., p. 22.

13. In some medieval Christian books about death it was stated that the blessed "would be in the full vigour of their age, for at the Resurrection of the Dead they would have the same age as that of Christ at his death, thirty-two years and three months, regardless of the age at which they died" (T. S. R. Boase, *Death in the Middle Ages* [New York: McGraw Hill, 1972], pp. 19–21). Cf. Aquinas, *Summa Theologica, III* a (Suppl.) Q81, art. 1.

STUDY QUESTIONS

1. What is the point of Hick's three scenarios of the re-creation or replication of the professor?

2. What does the idea of the transmission of a person as data from one point to another (one might think of beaming someone up in *Star Trek*) contribute to the idea that persons can be re-created after their death?

3. What is Hick's distinction between "replica" and replica, and why is this distinction important for his case?

4. What reply does Hick give to the objection that since there could be two replicas of the deceased person (which would make it impossible to identify either as the deceased), there cannot be one "replica" of the deceased?

Anonymous

Buddhist View of Rebirth

Buddhists hold that there is no permanent, persisting self or soul. Rather, we bundle mental (name) and physical (form) events together to form the fiction or concept of a self or person. In this dialogue between King Milinda and the venerable Nāgasena, the latter identifies these constructed bundles as name-and-form (person) and considers whether the name-and-form continues after death. He gives two responses. First, the name-and-form that is taken to be us will exist after death if we still have cravings and ignorance and have not achieved liberation. Second, when we do live on, each name-and-form gives rise to a subsequent name-and-form. Life after death occurs not because of any persisting soul, but because of the causal relationships that hold between bundles of events (attachment groups or *khandas*). For humans beings, this causal connection is especially evident in their karma, which is the fruit of the actions done out of desire. The Buddhist view of rebirth differs significantly from traditional Indian views that emphasize the immortality of some persisting self or soul.

6. The king said: "What is it, Nāgasena, that is reborn?"

"Name-and-form is reborn."

"Is it this same name-and-form that is reborn?"

"No, but by this name-and-form deeds are done, good or evil, and by these deeds (karma) another name-and-form is reborn."

"If that be so, Sir, would not the new being be released from its evil karma?"

Nāgasena replied: "Yes, if it were not reborn. But just because it is reborn, O king, it is therefore not released from its evil karma."

"Give me an illustration."

"Suppose, O king, some man were to steal a mango from another man, and the owner of the mango were to seize him and bring him before the king, and charge him with the crime. And the thief were to say: 'Your Majesty! I have not taken away this man's mangoes. Those that he put in the ground are different from the ones I took. I do not deserve to be punished.' How then? Would he be guilty?"

"Certainly, Sir. He would deserve to be punished."

"But on what ground?"

The Questions of King Milinda, trans. T. W. Rhys Davids, II, 2, 6–9 (Oxford, England: Clarendon Press, 1890).

"Because in spite of whatever he may say, he would be guilty in respect of the last mango which resulted from the first one that the owner set in the ground."

"Just so, great king, deeds good or evil are done by this name-and-form and another is reborn. But that other is not thereby released from its karma."

"Give me a further illustration."

"...It is like the fire which a man, in the cold season, might kindle, and when he had warmed himself, leave still burning, and go away. Then if that fire were to set another man's field on fire, and the owner of the field were to seize him and bring him before the king and charge him with the injury, and he were to say: 'Your Majesty! It was not I who set this man's field on fire. The fire I left burning was a different one from that which burnt his field. I am not guilty.' Now would the man, O king, be guilty?"

"Certainly, Sir."

"But why?"

"Because, in spite of whatever he might say, he would be guilty in respect of the subsequent fire that resulted from the previous one."

"Just so, great king, deeds good or evil are done by this name-and-form and another is reborn. But the other is not thereby released from its karma."...

"Give me a further illustration."

"Suppose, O king, a man were to choose a young girl in marriage, and give a price for her and go away. And she in due course should grow up to full age, and then another man were to pay a price for her and marry her. And when the first one had come back he should say: 'Why, you fellow, have you carried off my wife?' And the other were to reply: 'It is not your wife I have carried off! The little girl, the mere child, whom you chose in marriage and paid a price for is one; the girl grown up to full age whom I chose in marriage and paid a price for, is another.' Now, if they, thus disputing, were to go to law about it before you, O king, in whose favor would you decide the case?"

"In favor of the first."

"But why?"

"Because, in spite of whatever the second might say, the grown-up girl would have been derived from the other girl."

"Just so, great king, it is one name-and-form which has its end in death, and another name-and-form which is reborn. But the second is the result of the first, and is therefore not set free from its evil deeds."...

7. The king said: "Will you, Nāgasena, be reborn?"

"No, great king, what is the use of asking that question again? Have I not already told you that if, when I die, I die with craving in my heart, I shall be reborn; but if not, not be reborn."...

8. The king said: "You were talking just now of name-and-form. What does 'name' mean in that expression, and what does 'form' mean?"

"Whatever is gross is 'form'; whatever is subtle, mental is 'name.'"

"Why it is, Nāgasena, that name is not reborn separately, or form separately?"

"These conditions, great king, are connected one with the other; and spring into being together."

"Give me an illustration."

"As a hen, great king, would not get a yoke or an egg-shell separately, but both would arise in one, they two being intimately dependent one on the other; just so, if there were no name there would be no form. What is meant by name in that expression being intimately dependent on what is meant by form; they spring up together. And this is, through time immemorial, their nature."...

9. ... "Where there are beings who, when dead, will be reborn, there time is. Where there are beings who, when dead, will not be reborn, there time is not; and where there are beings who are altogether set free (who, having attained nirvana in their present life, have come to the end of that life), there time is not—because of their having been quite set free."

Study Questions

1. What is the Buddhist view of the human person?
2. What possibilities face persons after they die?
3. If there is no persisting self, how can one hold the subsequent person responsible for the moral actions done by the first person at a prior time?

Sri Aurobindo

Rebirth

Sri Aurobindo (1872–1950) contends that traditional objections to the theory of rebirth, such as the absence of memories of past lives, the suggestion that paranormal phenomena have other explanations, and the scientific understanding of heredity, do not disprove the theory of rebirth, for science really has nothing to say to the question of the nonphysical soul. At the same time, he rejects the common notion that we are an unchanging, persistent soul or personality that simply undergoes a series of reincarnations. Rather, he distinguishes between the empirical self or personality, which is an aspect of nature (*Prakriti*) that reincarnates, going from death to death, and the true Self (*Purusha*), which is the force or reality behind the empirical self. The empirical self, usually unconsciously, draws on the experiences it gains through numerous rebirths, but it is never more than a distorted image of the real Self, which is unchanging and imperishable. The Self neither is born nor dies, but is one with Reality, watching and enjoying the cycle of rebirths but not itself participating in them.

The theory of rebirth is almost as ancient as thought itself and its origin is unknown. We may, according to our prepossessions, accept it as the fruit of ancient psychological experience always renewable and variable and therefore true, or dismiss it as a philosophical dogma and ingenious speculation; but in either case the doctrine...is likely also to endure as long as human beings continue to think.

In former times the doctrine used to pass in Europe under the grotesque name of transmigration....Reincarnation is the now popular term, but the idea in the word leans to the gross or external view of the fact and begs many questions. I prefer "rebirth,"...which commits us to nothing but the fundamental idea which is the essence and life of the doctrine.

Rebirth is for the modern mind no more than a speculation and a theory; it has never been proved by the methods of modern science or to the satisfaction of the new critical mind formed by a scientific culture. Neither has it been disproved; for modern science knows nothing about a before-life or an after-life for the human soul, knows nothing indeed about a soul at all, nor can know; its province stops with the flesh and brain and nerve, the embryo and

Reprinted with the kind permission of Sri Aurobindo Ashram Trust.

its formation and development. Neither has modern criticism any apparatus by which the truth or untruth of rebirth can be established....

The arguments, which are usually put forward by supporters and opponents, are often sufficiently futile and at their best certainly insufficient either to prove or to disprove anything. One argument, for instance, often put forward triumphantly in disproof is this that we have no memory of our past lives and therefore there were no past lives! One smiles to see such reasoning seriously used.... The argument proceeds on psychological grounds and yet it ignores the very nature of our ordinary or physical memory which is all that the normal man can employ. How much do we remember of our actual lives which we are undoubtedly living at the present moment? Our memory is normally good for what is near, becomes vaguer or less comprehensive as its objects recede into the distance, farther off seizes only some salient points and, finally, for the beginning of our lives falls into a mere blankness. Do we remember even the mere fact, the simple state of being an infant on the mother's breast? And yet that state of infancy was, on any but a Buddhist theory, part of the same life and belonged to the same individual—the very one who cannot remember it just as he cannot remember his past life. Yet we demand that this physical memory, this memory of the brute brains of man which cannot remember our infancy and has lost so much of our later years, shall yet recall that which was before infancy, before birth, before itself was formed. And if it cannot, we are to cry, "disproved your reincarnation theory!"... Obviously, if our past lives are to be remembered whether as fact and state or in their events and images, it can only be by a psychical memory awaking which will overcome the limits of the physical and resuscitate impressions other than those stamped on the physical being by physical cerebration.

I doubt whether, even if we could have evidence of the physical memory of past lives or of such a psychical awakening, the theory would be considered any better proved than before. We now hear of many such instances confidently alleged, though without that apparatus of verified evidence responsibly examined which gives weight to the results of psychical research. The sceptic can always challenge them as mere fiction

and imagination unless and until they are placed on firm basis of evidence.... And even supposing the evidence were too strong and unexceptionable to be got rid of by these familiar devices, they might yet not be accepted as proof of rebirth; the mind can discover a hundred theoretical explanations for a single group of facts. Modern speculation and research have brought in this doubt to overhang all psychical theory and generalization.

We know, for instance, that in the phenomena, say, of automatic writing or of communication from the dead, it is disputed whether the phenomena proceed from outside, from disembodied minds, or from within, from the subliminal consciousness, or whether the communication is actual and immediate from the released personality or is the uprising to the surface of a telepathic impression which came from the mind of the then living man but has remained submerged in our subliminal mentality. The same kind of doubts might be opposed to the evidences of reincarnate memory. It might be maintained that they prove the power of a certain mysterious faculty in us, a consciousness that can have some inexplicable knowledge of past events, but that these events belong to other personalities than ours and that our attribution of them to our personality in past lives is an imagination, a hallucination.... Much would be proved by an accumulation of such evidences but not, to the sceptic at least, rebirth....

In absence of external proof which to our matter-governed sensational intellects is alone conclusive, we have the argument of the reincarnationists that their theory accounts for all the facts better than any other yet advanced. The claim is just, but it does not create any kind of certitude. The theory of rebirth coupled with that of Karma gives us a simple, symmetrical, beautiful explanation of things.... [But] the simplicity, symmetry, beauty, satisfactoriness of the reincarnation theory is no warrant of its certitude.

When we go into details, the uncertainty increases. Rebirth accounts, for example, for the phenomenon of genius, inborn faculty, and so many other psychological mysteries. But then Science comes in with its all-sufficient explanation by heredity....

The true foundation of the theory of rebirth is the evolution of the soul, or rather its efflorescence out of the veil of Matter and its gradual self-finding. Buddhism contained this truth involved in its theory of Karma and emergence out of Karma but failed to bring it to light; Hinduism knew it of old, but afterwards missed the right balance of its expression.... But what is the aim of that evolution? Not conventional or interested virtue and the faultless counting out of the small coin of good in the hope of an apportioned material reward, but the continual growth of a divine knowledge, strength, love and purity. These things alone are real virtue and this virtue is its own reward....

The soul needs no proof of its rebirth any more than it needs proof of its immortality. For there comes a time when it is consciously immortal, aware of itself in its eternal and immutable essence. Once that realisation is accomplished, all intellectual questionings for and against the immortality of the soul fall away like a vain clamour of ignorance around the self-evidence and everpresent truth.... There comes a time when the soul becomes aware of itself in its eternal and mutable moment; it is then aware of the ages behind that constituted the present organisation of the movement, sees how this was prepared in an uninterrupted past, remembers the bygone soul-states, environments, particular forms of activity which built up its present constituents, and knows to what it is moving by developments in an uninterrupted future. This is the true dynamic belief in rebirth, and there too the play of the questioning intellect ceases; the soul's vision and the soul's memory are all. Certainly, there remains the question of the mechanism of the development and of the laws of rebirth where the intellect and its inquiries and generalisations can still have some play. And here the more one thinks and experiences, the more the ordinary, simple, cut-and-dried account of reincarnation seems to be of doubtful validity. There is surely here a greater complexity, a law evolved with a more difficult movement and a more intricate harmony out of the possibility of the Infinite....

In the ordinary, the vulgar conception there is no birth of a soul at all, but only the birth of a new body into the world occupied by an old personality unchanged from that which once left some now-discarded physical frame. It is John Robinson who has gone out of the form of flesh he once occupied; it is John Robinson who tomorrow or some centuries hence will reincarnate in another form of flesh and resume the course of his terrestrial experiences with another name and in another environment.... The one objection that really stands in the way of its acceptance is the obvious nonsurvival of memory. Memory is the man, says the modern psychologist, and what is the use of the survival of my personality, if I do not remember my past, if I am not aware of being the same person still and always? What is the utility? What is the enjoyment?

The old Indian thinkers—I am not speaking of the popular belief which was crude enough and thought not at all about the matter—[and] the old Buddhistic and Vedantist thinkers surveyed the whole field from a very different standpoint. They were not attached to the survival of the personality; they did not give to that survival the high name of immortality; they saw that personality being what it is, a constantly changing composite, the survival of an identical personality was a non-sense, a contradiction in terms. They perceived indeed that there is a continuity, and they sought to discover what determines this continuity and whether the sense of identity which enters into it is an illusion or the representation of a fact, of a real truth, and, if the latter, then what that truth may be. The Buddhist denied any real identity. There is, he said, no self, no person; there is simply a continuous stream of energy in action like the continuous flowing of a river or the continuous burning of a flame. It is this continuity which creates in the mind the false sense of identity. I am not now the same person that I was a year ago, not even the same person that I was a moment ago, any more than the water flowing past yonder ghaut is the same water that flowed past it a few seconds ago; it is the persistence of the flow in the same channel that preserves the false appearance of identity. Obviously, then, there is no soul that reincarnates, but only Karma that persists in flowing continuously down the same apparently uninterrupted channel. It is Karma that incarnates; Karma creates the form of a constantly changing mentality and physical bodies that are, we may presume, the result of that changing composite of ideas and sensations which I call myself. The identical "I" is not, never was, never will be. Practically, so long as error of personality persists, this does not make much difference, and I can say in the language of ignorance that I am reborn in a new body; practically, I have to proceed on the basis of that error. But there is this important point gained that it is all an error and an error which can cease; the composite can be broken up for good without any fresh formation, the flame can be extinguished, the channel which called itself a river destroyed. And then there is non-being, there is cessation, there is the release of the error from itself.

The Vedantist comes to a different conclusion; he admits an identical, a self, a persistent immutable reality—but other than my personality, other than this composite which I call myself. In the Katha Upanishad the question is raised in a very instructive fashion. Nachiketas, sent by his father to the world of Death, thus questions Yama, the lord of that world: Of the man who has gone forward, who has passed away from us, some say that he is and other "this he is not"; which then is right? What is the truth of the great passage? Such is the form of the question and at first sight it seems simply to raise the problem of immortality in the European sense of the word, the survival of the identical personality. But this is not what Nachiketas asks. He has already taken as the second of three boons offered to him by Yama, the knowledge of the sacred Flame by which man crosses over hunger and thirst, leaves sorrow and fear far behind him, and dwells in heaven securely rejoicing. Immortality in that sense he takes for granted as, already standing in that farther world, he must surely do. The knowledge he asks for involves the deeper, finer problem.... Something survives that appears to be the same person, that descends into hell, that ascends into heaven, that returns upon the earth with a new body, but is it really the same person that thus survives? Can we really say of the man "He still is," or must we not rather say "This he no longer is"? Yama too in his answer speaks not at all of the survival of death, and he only gives a verse or two to a bare description of that constant rebirth which all serious thinkers admitted as a universally acknowledged truth. What he speaks of is the Self, the real Man, the Lord of all these changing appearances; without the knowledge of that Self the survival of the personality is not immortal life but a constant passing

from death to death; he only who goes beyond personality to the real Person [who] becomes the Immortal. Till then a man seems indeed to be born again and again by the force of his knowledge and works, name succeeds to name, form gives place to form, but there is no immortality.

Such then is the real question put and answered so divergently by the Buddhist and the Vedantin. There is a constant re-forming of personality in new bodies, but this personality is a mutable creation of force at its work streaming forward in Time and never for a moment the same, and the ego-sense that makes us cling to the life of the body and believe readily that it is the same idea and form, that it is John Robinson who is reborn as Sidi Hossain, is a creation of the mentality. Achilles was not reborn as Alexander, but the stream of force in its works which created the momentarily changing mind and body of Achilles [that] flowed on and created the momentarily changing mind and body of Alexander. Still, said the Ancient Vedanta, there is yet something beyond this force in action, Master of it, one who makes it create for him new names and forms, and that is the Self, the Purusha, the Man, the Real Person. The ego-sense is only its distorted image reflected in the flowing stream of embodied mentality.

Is it then the Self that incarnates and reincarnates? But the Self is imperishable, immutable, unborn, undying. The Self is not born and does not exist in the body; rather, the body is born and exists in the Self. For the Self is one every where,—*in* all bodies, we say, but really it is not confined and parceled out in different bodies except as the all-constituting ether seems to be formed into different objects and is in a sense in them. Rather all these bodies are in the Self; but that also is a figment of space-conception, and rather than these bodies are only symbols and figures of itself created by it in its own consciousness. Even what we call the individual soul is greater than its body and not less, more subtle than it, and therefore not confined by its grossness. At death it does not leave its form, but casts it off, so that a great departing soul can say of this death in vigorous phrase, "I have spat out the body."

What then is it that we feel to inhabit the physical frame? What is it that the Soul draws out from the body when it casts off this partial physical robe which enveloped not it, but part of its members?...The answer does not help us much. It is the subtle or psychical frame which is tied to the physical by the heart-strings, by the cords of life-force, of nervous energy which has been woven into every physical fibre. This the Lord of the body draws out and the violent snapping or the rapid or tardy loosening of the life-cords, the exit of the connecting force constitutes the pain of death and its difficulty.

Let us then change the form of the question and ask rather what it is that reflects and accepts the mutable personality, since the Self is immutable? We have, in fact, an immutable Self, a Real Person, Lord of this ever-changing personality which, again, assumes ever-changing bodies, but the real Self knows itself always as above the mutation, watches and enjoys it, but is not involved in it. Through what does it enjoy the changes and feel them to be its own, even while knowing itself to be unaffected by them? The mind and ego-sense are only inferior instruments; there must be some more essential form of itself which the Real Man puts forth, puts in front of itself, as it were, and at the back of the changings to support and mirror them without being actually changed by them. This more essential form is the mental being or mental person which the Upanishads speak of as the mental leader of the life and body. It is that which maintains the ego-sense as a function in the mind and enables us to have the firm conception of continuous identity in Time as opposed to the timeless identity of the Self.

The changing personality is not this mental person; it is a composite of various stuff of Nature, a formation of Prakriti and is not at all the Purusha.

And it is a very complex composite with many layers; there is a layer of physical, a layer of nervous, a layer of mental, even final stratum of supramental personality; and within these layers themselves there are strata within each stratum....The mental being in resuming bodily life forms a new personality for its new terrestrial existence; it takes material from the common matter-stuff, life-stuff, mind-stuff of the physical world, and during earthly life it is constantly absorbing fresh material, throwing out what is used up, changing its bodily, nervous, and mental tissues. But all this is surface work; behind is the foundation of past experience held back from the physical memory so that the superficial consciousness may not be troubled or interfered with by the conscious burden of the past, but may concentrate on the work immediately in hand. Still that foundation of past experience is the bedrock of personality; and it is more than that. It is our real fund on which we can always draw even apart from our present superficial commerce with our surroundings. That commence adds to our gain, modifies the foundation for subsequent existence.

Moreover, all this is, again, on the surface. It is only a small part of ourselves which lives and acts in the energies of our earthly existence....Behind is the Person, the unchanging entity, the Matter who manipulates this complex material, the Artificer of this wondrous artifice....The body is a convenience, the personality is a constant formation for whose development action and experience are the instruments; but the Self by whose will and for whose delight all this is, is other than the body, other than the action and experience, other than the personality which they develop. To ignore it is to ignore the whole secret of our being.

Study Questions

1. Why does Aurobindo believe that the appeal to memory neither establishes nor refutes life after death?
2. Why does Aurobindo conclude that the psychological person or personality does not experience immortal life but only the passing from death to death?
3. What is Aurobindo's view of the Self? How does the Self relate to the individual personality and to the question of our immortality?

SUGGESTED READING

Badham, Paul. *Christian Beliefs About Immortality*. London: Macmillan, 1976.

———, and Linda Badham. *Immortality or Extinction?* London: Macmillan, 1982.

Baker, Lynne Rudder. *Persons and Bodies: A Constitution View*. Cambridge, England: Cambridge University Press, 2000.

Blackmore, Susan. *Dying to Live: Near-Death Experiences*. Buffalo, N.Y.: Prometheus, 1993.

Cooper, John. *Body, Soul, and Life Everlasting*. Grand Rapids, Mich.: William B. Eerdmans, 1989.

Corcoran, Kevin. *Soul, Body, and Survival*. Ithaca, N.Y.: Cornell University Press, 2001.

Davis, Stephen T., ed. *Death and Afterlife*. London: Macmillan, 1989.

Edwards, Paul, ed. *Immortality*. New York: Macmillan, 1992.

———. *Reincarnation: A Critical Examination*. Buffalo, N.Y.: Prometheus, 1996.

Hasker, William. *The Emergent Self*. Ithaca, N.Y.: Cornell University Press, 1999.

Hick, John. *Death and Eternal Life*. New York: Harper and Row, 1976.

Lewis, H. D. *Persons and Life After Death*. London: Macmillan, 1978.

———. *The Self and Immortality*. New York: Seabury, 1973.

Mittal, Kewal, ed. *Perspectives on Karma and Rebirth*. Delhi, India: Department of Buddhist Studies, 1990.

Moody, Raymond A., Jr. *The Light Beyond*. New York: Bantam Books, 1989.

Murphy, Nancey. *Bodies and Souls, or Spirited Bodies?* Cambridge, England: Cambridge University Press, 2006.

Paterson, R. W. K. *Philosophy and the Belief in Life After Death*. London: Macmillan, 1995.

Penelhum, Terence. *Survival and Disembodied Existence*. London: Routledge & Kegan Paul, 1970.

Preston, Ted M. and Scott Dixon. "Who Wants to Live Forever? Immortality, Authenticity, and Living Forever in the Present," *International Journal for Philosophy of Religion* 61, no. 2 (April 2007): 99–117.

Reichenbach, Bruce R. *Is Man the Phoenix? A Study of Immortality*. Grand Rapids, Mich.: William B. Eerdmans, 1978.

———. *The Law of Karma: A Philosophical Study*. London: Macmillan, 1990.

Shoemaker, Sidney, and Richard Swinburne. *Personal Identity*. Oxford, England: Blackwell, 1984.

Swinburne, Richard. *The Evolution of the Soul*. Oxford, England: Oxford University Press, 1986.

Tipler, Frank. *The Physics of Immortality*. New York: Doubleday, 1994.

PART TWELVE

Religion and Science

Historically, there have been many positive aspects to the relationship of religion and science, but the controversies between them have attracted much more attention in popular culture and academic circles. From the Catholic Church's condemnation of the writings of Galileo to court battles waged by Protestant fundamentalists against evolutionary theory in public school textbooks, each issue generates its own measure of heat and light! The selections to follow provide a sampling of important perspectives. Stephen Jay Gould and Richard Dawkins try to define the relationship of religion and science in very different ways; William Dembski and Phillip Kitcher debate the credibility of intelligent design theory; and John Polkinghorne and John Lennox seek to identify a way of thinking about an intelligence behind the universe that transcends the current intelligent design controversy.

A Taxonomy of Views

There are different ways of understanding the relationship of religion and science as human activities. And since theology is the organized system of beliefs of a given religion, it inevitably enters the discussion. It is helpful to clarify the respective objects, aims, and methods of theology and science: What are the objects of study that constitute the subject matter addressed by theology and science? Is there any overlap? And what is the aim of the theological enterprise compared to the aim of the scientific enterprise? That is, do both disciplines aim at explaining or providing rational support for believing something? What about their respective methods, the way they go about their intellectual tasks, the way they arrive at knowledge—how different or how similar are these methods? In light of such questions, Ian Barbour identifies four models for understanding the relationship of religion and science: *independence, conflict, dialogue,* and *integration.*

The *independence* model asserts that the objects, aims, and methods of religion and science are utterly different—resulting in total compartmentalization. Neo-orthodox theology, existentialist philosophy, positivism, and Wittgenstein-inspired ordinary language philosophy take this position. Neo-Wittgensteinians, for example, claim that science and religion are two different "language-games," each with its own vocabulary and rules of usage and particular function in human affairs. Scientist Stephen Gould expresses this opinion and quotes various documents of the Catholic Church endorsing the independence of science and religion as two legitimate authorities. For the Church, all truth is a unity and cannot conflict; so the apparent conflicts of science and religion are explained as two different types of truth, and as addressing different questions. For example, the Church endorses evolution and sees it as consistent with Catholic theology, but stresses the doctrine of creation as a statement of the dependency of everything on God and the special status of humanity in the image of God. Gould concludes that the independence model has the double effect of preventing religion from dictating to science and of prohibiting science from claiming higher moral or intellectual insight than religion. He believes that the groundwork is laid for mutual humility, productive dialogue, and the search for a larger vision of reality.

In contrast, the *conflict* model envisages the objects or the aims or the methods, or perhaps all of them, as being much the same between religion and science. So, religion and science are genuinely competitive, thereby opening the door for a clash. Religious fundamentalists seeking to refute scientific claims on theological grounds fall into this category. Conversely, philosophical naturalists give priority to science, maintaining that it discredits religion. Daniel Dennett and Richard Dawkins, for example, argue that evolutionary biology shows religion to be a purely natural phenomenon and discredits belief in a deity. Dawkins points out that religious claims that miracles have occurred are about a public realm of facts that can be subjected to the scrutiny of science. He rejects the Catholic Church's attempt to reconcile the evolution of *Homo sapiens* from lower forms of life with the theological affirmation that human beings are "created in the image of God"—because to argue that God endows an evolved material body with a divinely created "immaterial soul" is fundamentally anti-evolutionary.

The third model—that of *dialogue* or interaction between religion and science—is more positive, acknowledging differences between the two disciplines and yet recognizing avenues for discussion. Some approaches to dialogue engage the presuppositions on which science rests (e.g., the reality and intelligibility of physical nature, its lawlike structure, etc.) because theistic theology, for example, has much to say about theistic beliefs in a rational Creator of a rational world that is rationally knowable. Other approaches seek interaction about the limits of explanation that science reaches in its most general and comprehensive theories. At such points, Ernan McMullin says that there is "consonance but not direct implication" between the statements of science and those of religion. This is apparent when modern cosmology tells us about the Big Bang 13.7 billion years ago, since this invites dialogue on a question science cannot answer: why should anything exist all? (See discussions of the cosmological argument in Part Five of this anthology.) And some thinkers even identify methodological parallels between science and theology. Nancey Murphy, for instance, compares theology to scientific inquiry because they both follow a "research program," which is a coherent network of theories that guides research among a community of inquirers.

The fourth model seeks the actual *integration* of science and religion. Traditional natural theology promotes integration by beginning with the findings and theories of science (about the cosmos, its structure, etc.) and supplementing them or putting them in larger contexts with theological explanations that are not available to science per se. The cosmological and anthropic teleological arguments (discussed in Part Five of this book) are good examples of attempts to augment science with theological understandings of how a supreme power and intelligence are at work in the universe. Proponents of a "theology of nature" embrace current science to reformulate and refine theological doctrines (e.g., creation, providence, and human freedom)—so that science inevitably affects our understanding of God–world interaction. Contemporary theologies of nature generally include themes of stewardship of the environment and even of the sacramental character of matter as an avenue of divine grace. Still other attempts at integration try to synthesize all that we know—from the sciences, the humanities, theology, and philosophy—into a coherent metaphysical picture of reality or worldview. The Thomistic synthesis is a classical example, whereas both process metaphysics and openness theology are more recent examples of the search for a comprehensive vision of God, humanity, and the universe.

Evolution and Intelligent Design

Darwinian evolutionary theory, as commonly understood, maintains that relatively complex organisms develop from simpler ones, over extremely long periods of time, due to random genetic variations, from which the process of "natural selection" determines which variations provide greater reproductive success, such that these organisms pass on their genetic information to subsequent generations. Some people interpret the role of chance in Darwin's "descent with modification" to exclude a divine creator and represent a purely naturalistic view of reality. Critics charge that naturalism is reductionistic, assuming a mechanistic system of "causes and effects" as the basis of scientific explanation—such that purpose and intentionality are excluded. The "methodological naturalism" of science is equated with *philosophical* naturalism.

A much debated reaction to Darwinism is known as intelligent design theory, or IDT. According to William Dembski, "the key to overturning naturalism is design, and not just the design of the universe taken as a whole but design within the universe." IDT attempts to replace the unquestioned scientific assumption of blind causation with openness to evidence of design. According to Dembski, three characteristics of an object or event—*contingency, complexity*, and *specification*—lead us to a warranted "design inference." "Contingency" means that the object did not result from an automatic process; "complexity" means that it is not so simple that it can be explained by chance. "Specification" refers to the type of pattern that reveals intelligence. In the third reading, Dembski makes the case that finding these features in biological organisms supports an inductive conclusion of design with very high probability. Citing biochemist Michael Behe's work on "irreducible complexity" as a compelling example of design in biology, Dembski explains that some organisms possess complex structures—such as the tail of the bacterial flagellum—that could not have been produced by slow, gradual, incremental development of the various interactive parts, as the Darwinian paradigm envisions. The argument is that the removal of any one of the parts of the mechanism destroys the whole system's function. Such cases necessitate that the parts all be present at once—presenting us with a phenomenon natural selection cannot account for and facing us with the need to leave room for the activity of an intelligent designer.

ID theorists see themselves as inferring design strictly from observational features of the world, not as importing theological bias or metaphysical preconceptions into science. IDT, they claim, simply unpacks and gives logical and statistical rigor to our common, everyday activity of inferring that certain things are intelligently designed rather than produced by natural causes. Of course, since the examples they identify for inferring intelligent design allegedly cannot be explained by natural causes operating purely by chance, and certainly cannot be explained by human causes, IDT opens the door for the discussion of a nonnatural or supernatural cause that intentionally produces particular effects in the natural world. Methodological naturalism (with its alleged reductionism) is then said to be overturned. Especially in the area of biology, where Darwinism has reigned supreme for well over a century, ID theorists believe that they have established the need for a new paradigm that empirically recognizes design. One key issue here is whether this nonnatural intelligence acts in nature by "special creation" of certain biological stuctures or "guides" the course of evolution so that they emerge. (Direct creation relates to the issue of miracles discussed in Part Ten, guidance relates to the issue of divine action in the world in Part Eight.)

Philip Kitcher claims that IDT fundamentally misunderstands chance and design to be mutually exclusive. Equating the role of chance in biological evolution with purposelessness, proponents of IDT attempt to connect design to biological science. Kitcher works at two broad levels: he analyzes IDT's negative arguments (the concrete case argument and the computational argument, both aimed at pointing out unsolved problems with evolution) and IDT's positive arguments (for intelligent causation beyond what natural selection can recognize).

The concrete case argument—most famously advanced by Behe—focuses on "irreducibly complex" biological structures that are supposedly impossible for natural selection to explain (e.g., the flagellum-bearing bacterium or the eye). In response, Kitcher points out that all sciences face unsolved problems that motivate further research but calls it a logical fallacy to conclude that the currently unsolved problems are unsolvable. He further argues that, since science has acquired the ability to map the genome, intensive research into genetic factors has shown that already-present proteins are often modified for new uses.

The computational argument—advanced by William Dembski, David Berlinski, Michael Behe, and others—has several variations. The thrust of the argument is that certain features of life on earth are so complex that it is highly improbable that they could arise through natural selection, even given the extreme amount of time available for the evolutionary process. In regard to the blood-clotting mechanism, Behe calculates that the odds of getting the relevant alignment of 10,000 genes, each with three subordinate pieces, falling into four domains, are 30,000 to the fourth power. Kitcher corrects Behe's faulty math in this instance (for he surely means 1/30,000 to the fourth power), but he also shows that Behe's understanding of how to calculate probability skews his argument. Behe assumes both that the probability that independent events will occur is a product of the individual probabilities and that possible outcomes are equiprobable. But Kitcher argues that these notions bias Behe's argument. For instance, we obviously do not know the initial state of the organisms in the population in which blood clotting emerged—and so we are not justified either in assigning complete independence to the different molecular factors or in imputing equiprobability to the outcome they produce.

After creating an opening via its negative arguments against natural selection, IDT advances its positive argument: that certain events in the formation of life can only be understood in terms of the operation of "Intelligence." Kitcher contends that, among other problems with this argument, the appeal to an abstract Intelligence lacks any set of principles regarding its powers, limitations, intentions, and pattern of operation, and therefore cannot make predictions—which are crucial to scientific testability. Moreover, the claim that there is an Intelligence operative in some aspects of nature faces serious problems of explaining why this alleged Intelligence acts in nonbeneficial ways in the natural world—allowing disease bacteria to flourish, not removing useless vestigial structures, and committing many wasteful genetic "blunders." As Hume astutely observed, the apparent arbitrariness and indifference of this Intelligence give rise to questions of whether it good, wise, or aims for our best interests. (See Part Seven of this anthology, on the problem of evil.)

A Look at the Broader Issues

John Polkinghorne seeks to rehabilitate the concepts of creation and intelligent design, which he considers to have been greatly damaged by the cultural and intellectual oddity of North American "creation-ism" (creation science) as well as by more recent IDT proposals. He admits that science studies natural processes (employs "methodological naturalism") but explains that it is theology that offers a larger understanding of important features of the world that science investigates. Of course, debates are endless in Western culture over whether theism or naturalism provides the more adequate ultimate explanation for the natural world—and science is extremely relevant because its character and findings constrain, but do not determine, the outcome of this debate. For Polkinghorne, the broad structural aspects of nature revealed by the sciences find deep resonance with features of the creation as understood in classical theology. (For example, unpredictability in quantum physics suggests genuine openness to unfolding future possibilities allowed by divine self-limitation, and relationality in an Einsteinian universe suggests the interconnectedness of creation.) Clearly, Polkinghorne is expressing a version of theistic evolution in which the universe is indeed seen as the "creation" of a "divine intelligence"; but he strongly opposes IDT because it anchors its argument on miscellaneous and ostensibly arbitrary tinkerings by the divine in specific cases. Transcending IDT, he argues that a divine intelligence created the universe and its laws, guides events largely by those laws, and can perform miracles within the relatively stable natural order—a position seeks the thorough integration of science and religion.

Fortunately, the debate over intelligent design is not irreducibly complex. In the final selection in this section, John Lennox clarifies the basis and structure of the different sorts of design arguments. Observing that eminent scientists fall on both sides of the question of whether there is a God, he concludes that the fundamental conflict is not a scientific issue but is clearly a clash between the worldviews of naturalism (or materialism) and theism. This raises the issue of whether and in what particular way science can be construed to support either of these worldviews. According to Lennox, Level I design arguments are metaphysical and theological in nature, maintaining that the laws of the universe are designed and that the phenomena they generate are evidence of their fruitfulness. Level II arguments maintain that some phenomena studied by science can only be explained by direct input from a designing intelligence rather than as a consequence of designed laws. Both levels break into two subordinate types—Type I arguments, from the history, philosophy, and methodology of science and Type II arguments, on detailed results from the sciences themselves (cosmology, physics, biology). The types can be further divided into A-arguments, which flow from an acceptance of mainstream science, and B-arguments, which challenge mainstream science.

Level I arguments have been employed for centuries in one form or another, largely under the rubric of teleological arguments, which, in effect, maintain that God explains the rational order and intelligibility of the universe in which science works. Since science cannot explain itself, it is argued that theism offers a comprehensive worldview context in which science makes sense. Naturalists, by contrast, are committed to explaining the rational intelligibility of the universe by purely natural or material causes. (A more detailed discussion of design can be found in Part Five, on arguments for God's existence.) In physics and cosmology, Level II, Type IIA arguments look to the big bang origin of the universe as an event requiring direct input from a designing intelligence: clearly, the beginning of the universe and its laws constitute a novel event that cannot be explained by prior conditions and laws. Type IIA arguments are also used in biology and typically interpret the process of evolution (mechanistic cause) as compatible with—and perhaps requiring—an intelligent agent's activity to account for is purposeful order. Dawkins, Dennett, and other naturalists see mechanistic causation and agency causation as mutually exclusive. So, theistic evolutionists and atheistic evolutionists are not arguing so much about what science per se says about evolution but about which total worldview provides the best explanation of all we know.

The controversy over ID is best seen as a Level II, Type IIB argument in biology, because it challenges the accepted Darwinian approach. As we have seen, IDT seeks to point out a variety of instances in biology that warrant inference to the direct involvement of an intelligent designer—again, calling into question the power of Darwinian evolution to explain all relevant phenomena. Critics counter that such arguments take a "God-of-the-gaps" approach—i.e., there is no plausible material process for X, therefore X must involve the input of intelligence. This approach was employed during the Enlightenment, when religious apologists invoked God whenever science failed to account for all of the phenomena. As science advanced, God was expelled from nature. Kitcher argues that evolutionary science will eventually close the gaps cited by IDT, as it discovers the appropriate material processes. He argues further that science already knows how to fill the explanatory gaps identified by IDT—i.e., by providing purely natural explanations of certain allegedly irreducibly complex biological structures. Lennox calls these "bad gaps," because they make IDT vulnerable to the progressive development of scientific understanding and thus create the perception of IDT as antiscience.

Lennox recognizes that discussions of IDT can alert us to an important concept that is not the exclusive property of IDT: the concept of *information*—in the present instance, *biological information* as contained in the genome. Without staking the case on whether certain complex biological structures must be novelty creations, he reminds us of the deeper problem that there is simply no naturalist account of how complex information can be created in the first place. Although natural processes can transmit complex specified information, they cannot generate it. This gap, accentuated by discussions of IDT, is what Lennox deems a "good gap," which is revealed by arguments of Type IIB—a good gap in that naturalism cannot successfully fill it. If arguments that it is impossible in principle for a naturalist account to fill the information gap are successful, there is strong reason to consider theism over naturalism. Then the sciences, which are tremendously successful on their own terms in studying the natural world, will have actually revealed and allowed us to formulate the information gap in very precise terms. Or, better, reflecting philosophically on science, and, in particular, asking penetrating philosophical questions about science, reveals the gaps (e.g., regarding ultimate origins). So, then, it is not accurate to say that a straightforward case for God can be made within science, but it is now obvious that science provides deeper understanding of exactly what it is about the world that requires fuller context and explanation from theology.

Stephen Jay Gould

Two Separate Domains

Stephen Jay Gould (1941–2002), a Harvard scientist who distinguished himself in geology, zoology, and paleontology, maintains that religion and science occupy separate spheres of human inquiry. As an exponent of a compartmentalization or independence model, he argues that there is no real conflict between religion and science, because each has its own legitimate domain of authority and the two domains do not overlap. Gould does, however, recognize that these two intellectual territories share a joint border that creates many complex interactions between them. He welcomes the progress reflected in the statement of Pope John Paul II that the Church accepts evolution as a fact which that stimulate serious theological reflection.

Incongruous places often inspire anomalous stories. In early 1984, I spent several nights at the Vatican housed in a hotel built for itinerant priests. While pondering over such puzzling issues as the intended function of the bidet in each bathroom, and hungering for something more than plum jam on my breakfast rolls (why did the basket only contain hundreds of identical plum packets and not a one of, say, strawberry?), I encountered yet another among the innumerable issues of contrasting cultures that can make life so expansive and interesting. Our crowd (present in Rome to attend a meeting on nuclear winter, sponsored by the Pontifical Academy of Sciences) shared the hotel with a group of French and Italian Jesuit priests who were also professional scientists. One day at lunch, the priests called me over to their table to pose a problem that had been troubling them. What, they wanted to know, was going on in America with all this talk about "scientific creationism"? One of the priests asked me: "Is evolution really in some kind of trouble; and, if so, what could such trouble be? I have always been taught that no doctrinal conflict exists between evolution and Catholic faith, and the evidence for evolution seems both utterly satisfying and entirely overwhelming. Have I missed something?"

A lively pastiche of French, Italian, and English conversation then ensued for half an hour or so, but the priests all seemed reassured by my general answer—"Evolution has encountered no intellectual trouble; no new arguments have been offered. Creationism is a home-grown phenomenon of American sociocultural history—a splinter movement

Reprinted by permission of Stephen Jay Gould.

(unfortunately rather more of a beam these days) of Protestant fundamentalists who believe that every word of the Bible must be literally true, whatever such a claim might mean." We all left satisfied, but I certainly felt bemused by the anomaly of my role as a Jewish agnostic, trying to reassure a group of priests that evolution remained both true and entirely consistent with religious belief.

Another story in the same mold: I am often asked whether I ever encounter creationism as a live issue among my Harvard undergraduate students. I reply that only once, in thirty years of teaching, did I experience such an incident. A very sincere and serious freshman student came to my office with a question that had clearly been troubling him deeply. He said to me, "I am a devout Christian and have never had any reason to doubt evolution, an idea that seems both exciting and well documented. But my roommate, a proselytizing evangelical, has been insisting with enormous vigor that I cannot be both a real Christian and an evolutionist. So tell me, can a person believe both in God and in evolution?" Again, I gulped hard, did my intellectual duty, and reassured him that evolution was both true and entirely compatible with Christian belief—a position that I hold sincerely, but still an odd situation for a Jewish agnostic.

These two stories illustrate a cardinal point, frequently unrecognized but absolutely central to any understanding of the status and impact of the politically potent, fundamentalist doctrine known by its self-proclaimed oxymoron as "scientific creationism"—the claim that the Bible is literally true, that all organisms were created during six days of twenty-four hours, that the earth is only a few thousand years old, and that evolution must therefore be false. Creationism does not pit science against religion (as my opening stories indicate), for no such conflict exists. Creationism does not raise any unsettled intellectual issues about the nature of biology or the history of life. Creationism is a local and parochial movement, powerful only in the United States among Western nations, and prevalent only among the few sectors of American Protestantism that choose to read the Bible as an inerrant document, literally true in every jot and tittle.

I do not doubt that one could find an occasional nun who would prefer to teach creationism in her parochial school biology class, or an occasional rabbi who does the same in his yeshiva, but creationism based on biblical literalism makes little sense either to Catholics or Jews, for neither religion maintains any extensive tradition for reading the Bible as literal truth, other than illuminating literature based partly on metaphor and allegory (essential components of all good writing), and demanding interpretation for proper understanding. Most Protestant groups, of course, take the same position—the fundamentalist fringe notwithstanding.

The argument that I have just outlined by personal stories and general statements represents the standard attitude of all major Western religions (and of Western science) today. (I cannot, through ignorance, speak of Eastern religions, though I suspect that the same position would prevail in most cases.) The *lack of conflict* between science and religion arises from a *lack of overlap* between their respective domains of professional expertise—science in the empirical constitution of the universe, and religion in the search for proper ethical values and the spiritual meaning of our lives. The attainment of wisdom in a full life requires extensive attention to both domains—for a great book tells us both that the truth can make us free, and that we will live in optimal harmony with our fellows when we learn to do justly, love mercy, and walk humbly.

In the context of this "standard" position, I was enormously puzzled by a statement issued by Pope John Paul II on October 22, 1996, to the Pontifical Academy of Sciences, the same body that had sponsored my earlier trip to the Vatican. In this document, titled "Truth Cannot Contradict Truth," the Pope defended both the evidence for evolution and the consistency of the theory with Catholic religious doctrine. Newspapers throughout the world responded with front-page headlines, as in the *New York Times* for October 25: "Pope Bolsters Church's Support for Scientific View of Evolution."

Now I know about "slow news days," and I do allow that nothing else was strongly competing for headlines at that particular moment. Still, I couldn't help feeling immensely puzzled by all the attention paid to the Pope's statement (while being wryly pleased, of course, for we need all the good press we can get, especially from respected outside sources). The Catholic Church does not oppose evolution, and has no reason to do so. Why had the Pope issued such a statement at all? And why had the press responded with an orgy of worldwide front-page coverage?

I could only conclude at first, and wrongly as I soon learned, that journalists throughout the world must deeply misunderstand the relationship between science and religion, and must therefore be elevating a minor papal comment to unwarranted notice. Perhaps most people really do think that a war exists between science and religion, and that evolution cannot be squared with a belief in God. In such a context, a papal admission of evolution's legitimate status might be regarded as major news indeed—a sort of modern equivalent for a story that never happened, but would have made the biggest journalistic splash of 1640: Pope Urban VIII releases his most famous prisoner from house arrest and humbly apologizes: "Sorry, Signor Galileo... the sun, er, is central."

But I then discovered that such prominent coverage of papal satisfaction with evolution had not been an error of non-Catholic anglophone journalists. The Vatican itself had issued the statement as a major news release. And Italian newspapers had featured, if anything, even bigger headlines and longer stories. The conservative *Il Giornale*, for example, shouted from its masthead: "Pope Says We May Descend from Monkeys."

Clearly, I was out to lunch; something novel or surprising must lurk within the papal statement, but what could be causing all the fuss?—especially given the accuracy of my primary impression (as I later verified) that the Catholic Church values scientific study, views science as no threat to religion in general or Catholic doctrine in particular, and has long accepted both the legitimacy of evolution as a field of study and the potential harmony of evolutionary conclusions with Catholic faith.

As a former constituent of Tip O'Neill, I certainly know that "all politics is local"—and that the Vatican undoubtedly has its own internal reasons, quite opaque to me, for announcing papal support of evolution in a major statement. Still, I reasoned that I must be missing some important key, and I felt quite frustrated. I then remembered the primary rule of

intellectual life: When puzzled, it never hurts to read the primary documents—a rather simple and self-evident principle that has, nonetheless, completely disappeared from large sectors of the American experience.

I knew that Pope Pius XII (not one of my favorite figures in twentieth-century history, to say the least) had made the primary statement in a 1950 encyclical entitled *Humani Generis*. I knew the main thrust of his message: Catholics could believe whatever science determined about the evolution of the human body, so long as they accepted that, at some time of his choosing, God had infused the soul into such a creature. I also knew that I had no problem with this argument—for, whatever my private beliefs about souls, science cannot touch such a subject and therefore cannot be threatened by any theological position on such a legitimately and intrinsically religious issue. Pope Pius XII, in other words, had properly acknowledged and respected the separate domains of science and theology. Thus, I found myself in total agreement with *Humani Generis*—but I had never read the document in full (not much of an impediment to stating an opinion these days).

I quickly got the relevant writings from, of all places, the Internet. (The Pope is prominently on line, but a luddite like me is not. So I got a cyberwise associate to dredge up the documents. I do love the fracture of stereotypes implied by finding religion so hep and a scientist so square.) Having now read in full both Pope Pius's *Humani Generis* of 1950 and Pope John Paul's proclamation of October 1996, I finally understand why the recent statement seems so new, revealing, and worthy of all those headlines. And the message could not be more welcome for evolutionists, and friends of both science and religion.

The text of *Humani Generis* focuses on the *Magisterium* (or Teaching Authority) of the Church—a word derived not from any concept of majesty or unquestionable awe, but from the different notion of teaching, for *magister* means "teacher" in Latin. We may, I think, adopt this word and concept to express the central point of this essay and the principled resolution of supposed "conflict" or "warfare" between science and religion. No such conflict should exist because each subject has a legitimate magisterium, or domain of reaching authority—and these magisteria do not overlap (the principle that I would like to designate as NOMA, or "nonoverlapping magisteria"). The net of science covers the empirical realm: what is the universe made of (fact) and why does it work this way (theory). The net of religion extends over questions of moral meaning and value. These two magisteria do not overlap, nor do they encompass all inquiry (consider, for starters, the magisterium of art and the meaning of beauty). To cite the usual clichés, we get the age of rocks, and religion retains the rock of ages; we study how the heavens go, and they determine how to go to heaven.

This resolution might remain entirely neat and clean if the non-overlapping magisteria of science and religion stood far apart, separated by an extensive no-man's-land. But, in fact, the two magisteria bump right up against each other, interdigitating in wondrously complex ways along their joint border. Many of our deepest questions call upon aspects of both magisteria for different parts of a full answer—and the sorting of legitimate domains can become quite complex and difficult. To cite just two broad questions involving both evolutionary facts and moral arguments: Since evolution made us the only earthly creatures with advanced consciousness, what responsibilities are so entailed for our relations with other species? What do our genealogical ties with other organisms imply about the meaning of human life?

Pius XII's *Humani Generis* (1950), a highly traditionalist document written by a deeply conservative man, faces all the "isms" and cynicisms that rode the wake of World War II and informed the struggle to rebuild human decency from the ashes of the Holocaust. The encyclical bears the subtitle "concerning some false opinions which threaten to undermine the foundations of Catholic doctrine," and begins with a statement of embattlement:

> Disagreement and error among men on moral and religious matters have always been a cause of profound sorrow to all good men, but above all to the true and loyal sons of the Church, especially today, when we see the principles of Christian culture being attacked on all sides.

Pius lashes out, in turn, at various external enemies of the Church: pantheism, existentialism, dialectical materialism, historicism, and, of course and preeminently, communism. He then notes with sadness that some well-meaning folks within the Church have fallen into a dangerous relativism—"a theological pacifism and egalitarianism, in which all points of view become equally valid"—in order to include those who yearn for the embrace of Christian religion, but do not wish to accept the particularly Catholic magisterium.

Speaking as a conservative's conservative, Pius laments:

> Novelties of this kind have already borne their deadly fruit in almost all branches of theology....Some question whether angels are personal beings, and whether matter and spirit differ essentially....Some even say that the doctrine of Transubstantiation, based on an antiquated philosophic notion of substance, should be so modified that the Real Presence of Christ in the Holy Eucharist be reduced to a kind of symbolism.

Pius first mentions evolution to decry a misuse by overextension among zealous supporters of the anathematized "isms":

> Some imprudently and indiscreetly hold that evolution...explains the origin of all things....Communists gladly subscribe to this opinion so that, when the souls of men have been deprived of every idea of a personal God, they may the more efficaciously defend and propagate their dialectical materialism.

Pius presents his major statement on evolution near the end of the encyclical, in paragraphs 35 through 37. He accepts the standard model of nonoverlapping magisteria (NOMA) and begins by acknowledging that evolution lies in a difficult area where the domains press hard against each other. "It remains for Us now to speak about those questions which, although they pertain to the positive sciences, are nevertheless more or less connected with the truths of the Christian faith."[1]

Pius then writes the well-known words that permit Catholics to entertain the evolution of the human body (a factual issue under the magisterium of science), so long as they accept the divine creation and infusion of the soul (a theological notion under the magisterium of religion).

The Teaching Authority of the Church does not forbid that, in conformity with the present state of human sciences and sacred theology, research and discussions, on the part of men experienced in both fields, take place with regard to the doctrine of evolution, in as far as it inquires into the origin of the human body as coming from pre-existent and living matter—for the Catholic faith obliges us to hold that souls are immediately created by God.

I had, up to here, found nothing surprising in *Humani Generis*, and nothing to relieve my puzzlement about the novelty of Pope John Paul's recent statement. But I read further and realized that Pius had said more about evolution, something I had never seen quoted, and something that made John Paul's statement most interesting indeed. In short, Pius forcefully proclaimed that while evolution may be legitimate in principle, the theory, in fact, had not been proven and might well be entirely wrong. One gets the strong impression, moreover, that Pius was rooting pretty hard for a verdict of falsity.

Continuing directly from the last quotation, Pius advises us about the proper study of evolution:

> However, this must be done in such a way that the reasons for both opinions, that is, those favorable and those unfavorable to evolution, be weighed and judged with the necessary seriousness, moderation and measure.... Some however, rashly transgress this liberty of discussion, when they act as if the origin of the human body from preexisting and living matter were already completely certain and proved by the facts which have been discovered up to now and by reasoning on those facts, and as if there were nothing in the sources of divine revelation which demands the greatest moderation and caution in this question.

To summarize, Pius generally accepts the NOMA principle of nonoverlapping magisteria in permitting Catholics to entertain the hypothesis of evolution for the human body so long as they accept the divine infusion of the soul. But he then offers some (holy) fatherly advice to scientists about the status of evolution as a scientific concept: the idea is not yet proven, and you all need to be especially cautious because evolution raises many troubling issues right on the border of my magisterium. One may read this second theme in two rather different ways: either as

a gratuitous incursion into a different magisterium, or as a helpful perspective from an intelligent and concerned outsider. As a man of goodwill, and in the interest of conciliation, I am content to embrace the latter reading.

In any case, this rarely quoted second claim (that evolution remains both unproven and a bit dangerous)—and not the familiar first argument for the NOMA principle (that Catholics may accept the evolution of the body so long as they embrace the creation of the soul)—defines the novelty and the interest of John Paul's recent statement.

John Paul begins by summarizing Pius's older encyclical of 1950, and particularly by reaffirming the NOMA principle—nothing new here, and no cause for extended publicity:

> In his encyclical "Humani Generis" (1950) my predecessor Pius XII had already stated that there was no opposition between evolution and the doctrine of the faith about man and his vocation.

To emphasize the power of NOMA, John Paul poses a potential problem and a sound resolution: How can we possibly reconcile science's claim for physical continuity in human evolution with Catholicism's insistence that the soul must enter at a moment of divine infusion?

> With man, then, we find ourselves in the presence of an ontological difference, an ontological leap, one could say. However, does not the posing of such ontological discontinuity run counter to that physical continuity which seems to be the main thread of research into evolution in the field of physics and chemistry? Consideration of the method used in the various branches of knowledge makes it possible to reconcile two points of view which would seem irreconcilable. The sciences of observation describe and measure the multiple manifestations of life with increasing precision and correlate them with the time line. The moment of transition to the spiritual cannot be the object of this kind of observation.

The novelty and news value of John Paul's statement lies, rather, in his profound revision of Pius's second and rarely quoted claim that evolution, while conceivable in principle and reconcilable with religion, can cite little persuasive evidence in support, and may well be false. John Paul states—and I can only say amen, and thanks for noticing—that the half century between Pius surveying the ruins of World War II and his own pontificate heralding the dawn of a new millennium has witnessed such a growth of data, and such a refinement of theory, that evolution can no longer be doubted by people of goodwill and keen intellect:

> Pius XII added...that this opinion [evolution] should not be adopted as though it were a certain, proven doctrine...Today, almost half a century after the publication of the encyclical, new knowledge has led to the recognition of the theory of evolution as more than a hypothesis.[2] It is indeed remarkable that this theory has been progressively accepted by researchers, following a series of discoveries in various fields of knowledge. The convergence, neither sought nor fabricated, of the results of work that was conducted independently is in itself a significant argument in favor of the theory.

In conclusion, Pius had grudgingly admitted evolution as a legitimate hypothesis that he regarded as only tentatively supported and potentially (as he clearly hoped) untrue. John Paul, nearly fifty years later, reaffirms the legitimacy of evolution under the NOMA principle—no news here—but then adds that additional data and theory have placed the factuality of evolution beyond reasonable doubt. Sincere Christians must now accept evolution not merely as a plausible possibility, but also as an effectively proven fact. In other words, official Catholic opinion on evolution has moved from "say it ain't so, but we can deal with it if we have to" (Pius's grudging view of 1950) to John Paul's entirely welcoming "it has been proven true; we always celebrate nature's factuality, and we look forward to interesting discussions of theological implications." I happily endorse this turn of events as gospel—literally good news. I may represent the magisterium of science, but I welcome the support of a primary leader from the other major magisterium of our complex lives. And I recall the wisdom of King Solomon: "As cold waters to a thirsty soul, so is good news from a far country" (Proverbs 25:25).

Just as religion must bear the cross of its hardliners, I have some scientific colleagues, including a few in prominent enough positions to wield influence by their writings, who view this rapprochement of the separate magisteria with dismay. To colleagues like me—agnostic scientists who welcome and celebrate the rapprochement, especially the Pope's latest statement—they say, "C'mon, be honest; you know that religion is addlepated, superstitious, old-fashioned BS. You're only making those welcoming noises because religion is so powerful, and we need to be diplomatic in order to buy public support for science." I do not think that many scientists hold this view, but such a position fills me with dismay—and I therefore end this essay with a personal statement about religion, as a testimony to what I regard as a virtual consensus among thoughtful scientists (who support the NOMA principle as firmly as the Pope does).

I am not, personally, a believer or a religious man in any sense of institutional commitment or practice. But I have great respect for religion, and the subject has always fascinated me, beyond almost all others (with a few exceptions, like evolution and paleontology). Much of this fascination lies in the stunning historical paradox that organized religion has fostered, throughout Western history, both the most unspeakable horrors and the most heartrending examples of human goodness in the face of personal danger. (The evil, I believe, lies in an occasional confluence of religion with secular power. The Catholic Church has sponsored its share of horrors, from Inquisitions to liquidations—but only because this institution held great secular power during so much of Western history. When my folks held such sway, more briefly and in Old Testament times, we committed similar atrocities with the same rationales.)

I believe, with all my heart, in a respectful, even loving, concordat between our magisteria—the NOMA concept. NOMA represents a principled position on moral and intellectual grounds, not a merely diplomatic solution. NOMA also cuts both ways. If religion can no longer dictate the nature of factual conclusions residing properly within the magisterium of science, then scientists cannot claim higher insight into moral truth from any superior knowledge of the world's empirical constitution. This mutual humility leads to important practical consequences in a world of such diverse passions.

Religion is too important for too many people to permit any dismissal or denigration of the comfort still sought by many folks from theology. I may, for example, privately suspect that papal insistence on divine infusion of the soul represents a sop to our fears, a device for maintaining a belief in human superiority within an evolutionary world offering no privileged position to any creature. But I also know that the subject of souls lies outside the magisterium of science. My world cannot prove or disprove such a notion, and the concept of souls cannot threaten or impact my domain. Moreover, while I cannot personally accept the Catholic view of souls, I surely honor the metaphorical value of such a concept both for grounding moral discussion, and for expressing what we most value about human potentiality: our decency, our care, and all the ethical and intellectual struggles that the evolution of consciousness imposed upon us.

As a moral position (and therefore not as a deduction from my knowledge of nature's factuality), I prefer the "cold bath" theory that nature can be truly "cruel" and "indifferent" in the utterly inappropriate terms of our ethical discourse—because nature does not exist for us, didn't know we were coming (we are, after all, interlopers of the latest geological moment), and doesn't give a damn about us (speaking metaphorically). I regard such a position as liberating, not depressing, because we then gain the capacity to conduct moral discourse—and nothing could be more important—in our own terms, free from the delusion that we might read moral truth passively from nature's factuality.

But I recognize that such a position frightens many people, and that a more spiritual view of nature retains broad appeal (acknowledging the factuality of evolution, but still seeking some intrinsic meaning in human terms, and from the magisterium of religion).

I do appreciate, for example, the struggles of a man who wrote to the *New York Times* on November 3, 1996, to declare both his pain and his endorsement of John Paul's statement:

> Pope John Paul II's acceptance of evolution touches the doubt in my heart. The problem of pain and suffering in a world created by a God who is all love and light is hard enough to bear, even if one is a creationist. But at least a creationist can say that the original creation, coming from the hand of God, was good, harmonious, innocent and gentle. What can one say about evolution, even a spiritual theory of evolution? Pain and suffering, mindless cruelty and terror are its means of creation. Evolution's engine is the grinding of predatory teeth upon the screaming, living flesh and bones of prey.... If evolution be true, my faith has rougher seas to sail.

I don't agree with this man, but we could have a terrific argument. I would push the "cold bath" theory; he would (presumably) advocate the theme of inherent spiritual meaning in nature, however opaque the signal. But we would both be enlightened and filled with better understanding of these deep and ultimately unanswerable issues. Here, I believe, lies the greatest strength and necessity of NOMA, the nonoverlapping magisteria of science and religion. NOMA permits—indeed enjoins—the prospect of respectful discourse, of constant input from both magisteria toward the common goal of wisdom. If human beings can lay claim to anything special, we evolved as the only creatures that must ponder and talk. Pope John Paul II would surely point out to me that his magisterium has always recognized this uniqueness, for John's gospel begins by stating *in principio erat verbum*—in the beginning was the word.

Notes

1. Interestingly, the main thrust of these paragraphs does not address evolution in general, but lies in refuting a doctrine that Pius calls "polygenism," or the notion of human ancestry from multiple parents—for he regards such an idea as incompatible with the doctrine of original sin "which proceeds from a sin actually committed by an individual Adam and which, through generation, is passed on to all and is in everyone as his own." In this one instance, Pius may be transgressing the NOMA principle—but I cannot judge, for I do not understand the details of Catholic theology and therefore do not know how symbolically such a statement may be read. If Pius is arguing that we cannot entertain a theory about derivation of all modern humans from an ancestral population rather than through an ancestral individual (a potential fact) because such an idea would question the doctrine of original sin (a theological construct),

then I would declare him out of line for letting the magisterium of religion dictate a conclusion within the magisterium of science.

2. This passage, here correctly translated, provides a fascinating example of the subtleties and inherent ambiguities in rendering one language into another. Translation may be the most difficult of all arts, and meanings have been reversed (and wars fought) for perfectly understandable reasons. The Pope originally issued his statement in French, where this phrase read "…*de nouvelles connaissances conduisent à reconnaître dans la théorie de l'évolution plus qu'une hypothèse*." *L'Osservatore Romano*, the official Vatican newspaper, translated this passage as: "new knowledge has led to the recognition of more than one hypothesis in the theory of evolution." This version (obviously, given the official Vatican source) then appeared in all English commentaries, including the original version of this essay.

I included this original translation, but I was profoundly puzzled. Why should the Pope be speaking of *several* hypotheses within the framework of evolutionary theory? But I had no means to resolve my confusion, so I assumed that the Pope had probably fallen under the false impression (a fairly common misconception) that, although evolution had been documented beyond reasonable doubt, natural selection had fallen under suspicion as a primary mechanism, while other alternatives had risen to prominence.

Other theologians and scientists were equally puzzled, leading to inquiries and a resolution of the problem as an error in translation (as many of us would have realized right away if we had seen the original French, or even known that the document had been issued in French). The problem lies with ambiguity in double meaning for the indefinite article in French—where *un* (feminine *une*) can mean either "a" or "one." Clearly, the Pope had meant that the theory of evolution had now become strong enough to rank as "more than *a* hypothesis" (*plus qu'une hypothèse*), but the Vatican originally read *une* as "one" and gave the almost opposite rendition: "more than *one* hypothesis." *Caveat emptor.*

I thank about a dozen correspondents for pointing out this error, and the Vatican's acknowledgment, to me. I am especially grateful to Boyce Rensberger, one of America's most astute journalists on evolutionary subjects, and David M. Byers, executive director of the National Conference of Catholic Bishops' Committee on Science and Human Values. Byers affirms the NOMA principle by writing to me: "Thank you for your recent article…. It admirably captures the relationship between science and religion that the Catholic Bishops' Committee works to promote and to realize. The text of the October 1996 papal statement from which you were working contains a mistranslation of a key phrase; the correct translation supports your thesis with even greater force."

Study Questions

1. Gould uses the troubled relationship between evolutionary science and "scientific creationism" as a springboard for addressing the general relationship between science and religion. How does he describe evolution and creationism, respectively, as intellectual pursuits?

2. How does Gould explain Catholic support for the claim that science and religion, properly understood, do not conflict because they occupy separate intellectual domains, or "magesteria"?

3. Do you think that total independence of the two domains is the most reasonable view? Why or why not? And, then, how does one work toward a comprehensive, integrated perspective in light of everything we know?

Richard Dawkins

Science Discredits Religion

Richard Dawkins (b. 1941) of Oxford University is arguably the world's leading evolutionary biologist who is now considered a public intellectual. He argues that religion and science can and do conflict—and that science wins the conflict. Dawkins opposes Gould's view, which he takes as too conciliatory. First, he argues, the independence view fails to establish religion as the sole authority on meaning and value, since moral understanding changes over time with social progress. Second, it can be inconsistent, since the Catholic Church has used the independence view to assert that human beings are unique on a spiritual level while admitting that the facts of evolution show continuity with all other species on the physical level. Religion intrudes into the domain of science, according to Dawkins, since it claims divine intervention into the evolutionary process—making religion deeply antievolutionary. The putative independence of religion and science is a ruse, then, since religion makes a number of factual claims (e.g., about divine action in the world and the resurrection of Jesus) that science discredits.

A cowardly flabbiness of the intellect afflicts otherwise rational people confronted with long-established religions (though, significantly, not in the face of younger traditions such as Scientology or the Moonies). S. J. Gould, commenting...on the Pope's attitude to evolution, is representative of a dominant strain of conciliatory thought, among believers and nonbelievers alike:

> Science and religion are not in conflict, for their teachings occupy distinctly different domains...I believe,

with all my heart, in a respectful, even *loving* concordat [my emphasis]....

Well, what are these two distinctly different domains, these "Nonoverlapping Magisteria" which should snuggle up together in a respectful and loving concordat? Gould again:

> The net of science covers the empirical universe: what is it made of (fact) and why does it work this way (theory). The net of religion extends over questions of moral meaning and value.

From the *Quarterly Review of Biology* 72 (1997): 397–399. Reprinted by permission of the University of Chicago Press and Richard Dawkins.

Would that it were that tidy. In a moment I'll look at what the Pope actually says about evolution, and then at other claims of his church, to see if they really are so neatly distinct from the domain of science. First though, a brief aside on the claim that religion has some special expertise to offer us on moral questions. This is often blithely accepted even by the nonreligious, presumably in the course of a civilized "bending over backwards" to concede the best point your opponent has to offer—however weak that best point may be.

The question, "What is right and what is wrong?" is a genuinely difficult question which science certainly cannot answer. Given a moral premise or a priori moral belief, the important and rigorous discipline of secular moral philosophy can pursue scientific or logical modes of reasoning to point up hidden implications of such beliefs, and hidden inconsistencies between them. But the absolute moral premises themselves must come from elsewhere, presumably from unargued conviction. Or, it might be hoped, from religion—meaning some combination of authority, revelation, tradition and scripture.

Unfortunately, the hope that religion might provide a bedrock, from which our otherwise sand-based morals can be derived, is a forlorn one. In practice no civilized person uses scripture as ultimate authority for moral reasoning. Instead, we pick and choose the nice bits of scripture (like the Sermon on the Mount) and blithely ignore the nasty bits (like the obligation to stone adulteresses, execute apostates, and punish the grandchildren of offenders). The God of the Old Testament himself, with his pitilessly vengeful jealousy, his racism, sexism, and terrifying bloodlust, will not be adopted as a literal role model by anybody you or I would wish to know. Yes, *of course* it is unfair to judge the customs of an earlier era by the enlightened standards of our own. But that is precisely my *point*! Evidently, we have some alternative source of ultimate moral conviction which overrides scripture when it suits us.

That alternative source seems to be some kind of liberal consensus of decency and natural justice which changes over historical time, frequently under the influence of secular reformists. Admittedly, that doesn't sound like bedrock. But in practice we, including the religious among us, give it higher priority than scripture. In practice we more or less ignore scripture, quoting it when it supports our liberal consensus, quietly forgetting it when it doesn't. And, wherever that liberal consensus comes from, it is available to all of us, whether we are religious or not.

Similarly, great religious teachers like Jesus or Gautama Buddha may inspire us, by their good example, to adopt their personal moral convictions. But again we pick and choose among religious leaders, avoiding the bad examples of Jim Jones or Charles Manson, and we may choose good secular role models such as Jawaharlal Nehru or Nelson Mandela. Traditions too, however anciently followed, may be good or bad, and we use our secular judgment of decency and natural justice to decide which ones to follow, which to give up.

But that discussion of moral values was a digression. I now turn to my main topic of evolution, and whether the Pope lives up to the ideal of keeping off the scientific grass. His Message on Evolution to the Pontifical Academy of Sciences begins with some casuistical doubletalk designed to reconcile what John Paul is about to say with the previous, more equivocal pronouncements of Pius XII whose acceptance of evolution was comparatively grudging and reluctant. Then the Pope comes to the harder task of reconciling scientific evidence with "revelation."

Revelation teaches us that [man] was created in the image and likeness of God...if the human body takes its origin from pre-existent living matter, the spiritual soul is immediately created by God...Consequently, theories of evolution which, in accordance with the philosophies inspiring them, consider the mind as emerging from the forces of living matter, or as a mere epiphenomenon of this matter, are incompatible with the truth about man...With man, then, we find ourselves in the presence of an ontological difference, an ontological leap, one could say.

To do the Pope credit, at this point he recognizes the essential contradiction between the two positions he is attempting to reconcile:

However, does not the posing of such ontological discontinuity run counter to that physical continuity which seems to be the main thread of research into evolution in the field of physics and chemistry?

Never fear. As so often in the past, obscurantism comes to the rescue:

Consideration of the method used in the various branches of knowledge makes it possible to reconcile two points of view which would seen irreconcilable. The sciences of observation describe and measure the multiple manifestations of life with increasing precision and correlate them with the time line. The moment of transition to the spiritual cannot be the object of this kind of observation, which nevertheless can discover at the experimental level a series of very valuable signs indicating what is specific to the human being.

In plain language, there came a moment in the evolution of hominids when God intervened and injected a human soul into a previously animal lineage (When? A million years ago? Two million years ago? Between *Homo erectus* and *Homo sapiens*? Between "archaic" *Homo sapiens* and *H. sapiens sapiens*?). The sudden injection is necessary, of course, otherwise there would be no distinction upon which to base Catholic morality, which is speciesist to the core. You can kill adult animals for meat, but abortion and euthanasia are murder because *human* life is involved.

Catholicism's "net" is not limited to moral considerations, if only because Catholic morals have scientific implications. Catholic morality demands the presence of a great gulf between *Homo sapiens* and the rest of the animal kingdom. Such a gulf is fundamentally anti-evolutionary. The sudden injection of an immortal soul in the time-line is an anti-evolutionary intrusion into the domain of science.

More generally it is completely unrealistic to claim, as Gould and many others do, that religion keeps itself away from science's turf, restricting itself to morals and values. A universe with a supernatural presence would be a fundamentally and qualitatively different kind of universe from one without. The difference is, inescapably, a scientific difference. Religions make existence claims, and this means scientific claims.

The same is true of many of the major doctrines of the Roman Catholic Church. The Virgin Birth, the bodily Assumption of the Blessed Virgin Mary, the Resurrection of Jesus, the survival of our own souls after death: these are all claims of a clearly scientific nature. Either Jesus had a corporeal father or he didn't.

This is not a question of "values" or "morals," it is a question of sober fact. We may not have the evidence to answer it, but it is a scientific question, nevertheless. You may be sure that, if any evidence supporting the claim were discovered, the Vatican would not be reticent in promoting it.

Either Mary's body decayed when she died, or it was physically removed from this planet to Heaven. The official Roman Catholic doctrine of Assumption, promulgated as recently as 1950, implies that Heaven has a physical location and exists in the domain of physical reality—how else could the physical body of a woman go there? I am not, here, saying that the doctrine of the Assumption of the Virgin is necessarily false (although of course I think it is). I am simply rebutting the claim that it is outside the domain of science. On the contrary, the Assumption of the Virgin is transparently a scientific theory. So is the theory that our souls survive bodily death and so are all stories of angelic visitations, Marian manifestations, and miracles of all types.

There is something dishonestly self-serving in the tactic of claiming that all religious beliefs are outside the domain of science. On the one hand miracle stories and the promise of life after death are used to impress simple people, win converts, and swell congregations. It is precisely their scientific power that gives these stories their popular appeal. But at the same time it is considered below the belt to subject the same stories to the ordinary rigors of scientific criticism: these are religious matters and therefore outside the domain of science. But you cannot have it both ways. At least, religious theorists and apologists should not be allowed to get away with having it both ways. Unfortunately all too many of us, including nonreligious people, are unaccountably ready to let them get away with it.

I suppose it is gratifying to have the Pope as an ally in the struggle against fundamentalist creationism. It is certainly amusing to see the rug pulled out from under the feet of Catholic creationists such as Michael Behe. Even so, given a choice between honest-to-goodness fundamentalism on the one hand, and the obscurantist, disingenuous doublethink of the Roman Catholic Church on the other, I know which I prefer.

STUDY QUESTIONS

1. Unlike Gould, Dawkins is not content to allow religion to occupy its own sphere of theological and spiritual truth while science occupies the sphere of empirical and factual truth. For Dawkins, religion and science really do conflict in terms of their methods for obtaining knowledge, and therefore it is not surprising that they conflict in their resultant truth-claims. Explain Dawkins's view of the difference in methods.

2. Evaluate Dawkins's criticism of how the Church reconciles the theological teaching on the high status and value of humanity as "created in the image of God" with the findings of evolutionary science.

3. Since science studies the realm of public facts, and since religion often makes claims of fact, the potential for conflict is present. Explore whether conflict is necessary or whether there can be some kind of agreement about some or all of the public facts.

William Dembski

Reinstating Design Within Science

William Dembski (b. 1960) is a philosopher and mathematician who is a leader in the intelligent design movement. As discussion of intelligent design has expanded in the broader culture, he has assumed the role of public intellectual, lecturing, debating, and giving interviews. Dembski argues that there are objects studied by science that cannot be explained simply as the result of natural causes—i.e., by employing methodological naturalism. He offers the complexity-specification criterion for discriminating events and objects that are caused by an intelligent agent and those that are not. If an event or object is sufficiently complex that its occurrence is highly improbable, he believes that a "design inference" is warranted. Dembski believes that the reinstatement of design within science will help it escape the limitations of methodological naturalism and expand its explanatory power.

[T]he] worry of falsely attributing something to design (here identified with creation) only to have it overturned later prevents design from entering science proper.

This worry, though perhaps justified in the past, is no longer tenable. There does in fact exist a rigorous criterion for distinguishing intelligently caused objects from unintelligently caused ones. Many special sciences already use this criterion, though in a pretheoretic form (e.g., forensic science, artificial intelligence, cryptography, archaeology, and the search for extraterrestrial intelligence [SETI]). The great breakthrough of the intelligent design movement has been to isolate and make precise this criterion. Michael

Behe's criterion of irreducible complexity for establishing the design of biochemical systems is a special case of this general criterion for detecting design.

Yet before examining this criterion, I want briefly to clarify the word *design*. I'm using *design* in three distinct senses. First, I use it to denote the scientific theory that distinguishes intelligent agency from natural causes, a theory that increasingly is being referred to as *design theory* or *intelligent design* (ID). Second, I use *design* to denote what it is about intelligently produced objects that enables us to tell that they are intelligently produced and not simply the result of natural causes. When intelligent agents act, they leave behind a characteristic trademark or signature. The scholastics used

From *Intelligent Design: The Bridge Between Science and Theology.* Downers Grove, Ill.: InterVarsity Press, 1999.

to refer to the "vestiges in creation." The Latin *vestigium* means footprint. It was thought that God, though not directly present to our senses, had nonetheless left his "footprints" throughout creation. Hugh Ross has referred to the "fingerprint of God." It is *design* in this sense—as a trademark, signature, vestige, or fingerprint—that this criterion for discriminating intelligently from unintelligently caused objects is meant to identify. Last, I use "*design*" to denote intelligent agency itself. Thus, to say that something is designed is to say that an intelligent agent caused it. But note, to say that an intelligent agent caused something is not to prescribe how an intelligent agent caused it. In particular, design in this last sense is separate from miracle.

The Complexity-Specification Criterion

What does this criterion for detecting design look like? Although a detailed explanation and justification of this criterion is fairly technical, the basic idea is straightforward and easily illustrated. Consider how the radio astronomers in the movie *Contact* detected an extraterrestrial intelligence. This movie, based on a novel by Carl Sagan, was an enjoyable piece of propaganda for the SETI research program—the search for extraterrestrial intelligence. To make the movie interesting, the SETI researchers in *Contact* actually did find an extraterrestrial intelligence. (The *nonfictional* SETI program has yet to be so lucky.)

How then did the researchers in *Contact* convince themselves that they had found an extraterrestrial intelligence? To increase their chances of finding an extraterrestrial intelligence, SETI researchers monitor millions of radio signals from outer space. Many natural objects in space produce radio waves (e.g., pulsars). Looking for signs of design among all these naturally produced radio signals is like looking for a needle in a haystack. To sift through the haystack, SETI researchers run the signals they monitor through computers programmed with pattern-matchers. So long as a signal doesn't match one of the present patterns, it will pass through the pattern-matching sieve (and that even if it has an intelligent source). On the other hand, if it does match one of these patterns, then depending on the pattern matched, the SETI researchers may have cause for celebration.

The SETI researchers in *Contact* did find a signal worthy of celebration:

```
1101110111110111111101111111111101111111111111101111111
1111111111101111111111111111111101111111111111111111111
0111111111111111111111111111111101111111111111111111111
1111111101111111111111111111111111111111111111101111111
1111111111111111111111111111111111101111111111111111111
1111111111111111111111110111111111111111111111111111111
1111111111111111101111111111111111111111111111111111111
1111111111111111101111111111111111111111111111111111111
1111111111111111111111111011111111111111111111111111111
1111111111111111111111111111111111111111101111111111111
1111111111111111111111111111111111111111111111111111111
1111011111111111111111111111111111111111111111111111111
1111111111111111111111110111111111111111111111111111111
1111111111111111111111111111111111111111111111111110111
1111111111111111111111111111111111111111111111111111111
1111111111111111111111111011111111111111111111111111111
1111111111111111111111111111111111111111111111111111111
1111111101111111111111111111111111111111111111111111111
1111111111111111111111111111111111111111111111111111101
1111111111111111111111111111111111111111111111111111111
1111111111111111111111111111111111111111111111111111
```

They received this signal as a sequence of 1,126 beats and pauses, where 1s correspond to beats and 0s to pauses. This sequence represents the prime numbers from 2 to 101, where a given prime number is represented by the corresponding number of beats (i.e., 1s) and the individual prime numbers are separated by pauses (i.e., 0s). The SETI researchers in *Contact* took this signal as decisive confirmation of an extraterrestrial intelligence.

What characteristic about this signal implicates design? Whenever we infer design, we must establish three things: *contingency*, *complexity*, and *specification*. Contingency ensures that the object in question is not the result of an automatic and therefore unintelligent process that had no choice in its production. Complexity ensures that the object is not so simple that it can readily be explained by chance. Finally, specification ensures that the object exhibits the type of pattern characteristic of intelligence. Let us examine these three requirements more closely.

In practice, to establish the contingency of an object, event, or structure, one must establish that it is compatible with the regularities involved in its production but that these regularities also permit any number of alternatives to it. Typically these regularities are conceived as natural laws or algorithms. By being compatible with but not required by the regularities involved in its production, an object, event, or structure becomes irreducible to any underlying physical necessity. Michael Polanyi and Timothy Lenoir have both described this method of establishing contingency. The method applies quite generally: the position of Scrabble pieces on a game board is irreducible to the natural laws governing the motion of scrabble pieces; the configuration of ink on a sheet of paper is irreducible to the physics and chemistry of paper and ink; the sequencing of DNA bases is irreducible to the bonding affinities between the bases; and so on. In the case at hand, the sequence of 0s and 1s to form a sequence of prime numbers is irreducible to the laws of physics that govern the transmission of radio signals. We therefore regard the sequence as contingent.

To see next why complexity is crucial for inferring design, consider the following sequence of bits:

110111011111

These are the first twelve bits in the previous sequence representing the prime numbers 2, 3, and 5 respectively. Now it is a sure bet that no SETI researcher, if confronted with this twelve-bit sequence, is going to contact the science editor at the *New York Times*, hold a press conference and announce that an extraterrestrial intelligence has been discovered. No headline is going to read, "Aliens Master First Three Prime Numbers!"

The problem is that this sequence is much too short (and thus too simple) to establish that an extraterrestrial intelligence with knowledge of prime numbers produced it. A randomly beating radio source might by chance just happen to output this sequence. A sequence of 1,126 bits representing the prime numbers from 2 to 101, however, is a different story. Here the sequence is sufficiently long (and therefore sufficiently complex) that only an extraterrestrial intelligence could have produced it.

Complexity as I am describing it here is a form of probability. Later in this chapter I will require a more general conception of complexity to unpack the logic of design inferences. But for now, complexity as a form of probability is all we need. To see the connection between complexity and probability, consider a combination lock. The more possible combinations of the lock, the more complex the mechanism and, correspondingly, the more improbable that the mechanism can be opened by chance. Complexity and probability therefore vary inversely: the greater the complexity, the smaller the probability. Thus to determine whether something is sufficiently complex to warrant a design inference is to determine whether it has sufficiently small probability.

Even so, complexity (or improbability) isn't enough to eliminate chance and establish design. If I flip a coin thousand times, I'll participate in a highly complex (i.e., highly improbable) event. Indeed, the sequence I end up flipping will be one in a trillion trillion trillion...(where the ellipsis needs twenty-two more *trillions*). This sequence of coin tosses won't, however, trigger a design inference. Though complex, this sequence won't exhibit a suitable pattern. Contrast this with the previous sequence representing the prime numbers from 2 to 101. Not only is this sequence complex, but it also embodies a suitable pattern. The SETI researcher who in the movie *Contact* discovered this sequence put it this way: "This isn't noise; this has structure."

What is a *suitable* pattern for inferring design? Not just any pattern will do. Some patterns can legitimately be employed to infer design whereas others cannot. The intuition underlying the distinction between patterns that alternately succeed or fail to implicate design is, however, easily motivated. Consider the case of an archer. Suppose an archer stands fifty meters from a large wall, with bow and arrow in hand. The wall, let us say, is sufficiently large that the archer cannot help but hit it. Now suppose each time the archer shoots an arrow at the wall, the archer paints a target around the arrow so that the arrow sits squarely in the bull's-eye. What can be concluded from this scenario? Absolutely nothing about the archer's ability as an archer. Yes, a pattern is being matched, but it is a pattern fixed only after the arrow has been shot. The pattern is thus purely ad hoc.

But suppose instead the archer paints a fixed target on the wall and then shoots at it. Suppose the archer shoots a hundred arrows and each time hits a perfect bull's-eye. What can be concluded from this second scenario? We are obligated to infer that here is a world-class archer, one whose shots cannot legitimately be referred to luck but rather must be referred to the archer's skill and mastery. Skill and mastery are of course instances of design.

The archer example introduces three elements that are essential for inferring design:

1. a reference class of possible events (the arrow hitting the wall at some unspecified place)
2. a pattern that restricts the reference class of possible events (a target on the wall)
3. the precise event that has occurred (the arrow hitting the wall at some precise location)

In a design inference, the reference class, the pattern, and the event are linked, with the pattern's mediating between event and reference class and helping to decide whether the event is due to chance or design.

Note that in determining whether an event is sufficiently improbable or complex to implicate design, the relevant improbability is not that of the precise event that occurred but that of the target/pattern. Indeed, the bigger the target, the easier it is to hit it by chance and thus apart from design.

The type of pattern where an archer fixes a target first and then shoots at it is common to statistics, where it is known as setting a *rejection region* prior to an experiment. In statistics, if the outcome of an experiment falls within a rejection region, the chance hypothesis supposedly responsible for the outcome is rejected. The reason for setting a rejection region prior to an experiment is to forestall what statisticians call "data snooping" or "cherry picking." Just about any data set will contain strange and improbable patterns if we look hard enough. By forcing experimenters to set their rejection regions prior to an experiment, the statistician protects the experiment from spurious patterns that could just as well result from chance.

Now a little reflection makes clear that a pattern need not be given prior to an event to eliminate chance and implicate design. Consider the following cipher text:

nfuijolt ju jt mjlf b xfbtfm

Initially this looks like a random sequence of letters and spaces—initially you lack any pattern for rejecting chance and inferring design.

But suppose next that someone comes along and tells you to treat this sequence as a Caesar cipher, in which each letter has shifted one notch down the alphabet. The deciphered sequence then reads,

methinks it is like a weasel

Even though the pattern (in this case, the decrypted text) is given after the fact, it still is the right sort of pattern for eliminating chance and inferring design. In contrast to statistics, which always identifies its patterns before an experiment is performed, cryptanalysis must discover its patterns after the fact. In both instances, however, the patterns are suitable for inferring design.

Patterns thus divide into two types, those that in the presence of complexity warrant a design inference and those that despite the presence of complexity do not warrant a design inference. The first type of pattern I call a *specification*, the second a *fabrication*. Specifications are the non–ad hoc patterns that can legitimately be used to eliminate chance and warrant a design inference. In contrast, fabrications are the ad hoc patterns that cannot legitimately be used to warrant a design inference. This distinction between specifications and fabrications can be made with full statistical rigor.

To sum up, the complexity-specification criterion detects design by establishing three things: contingency, complexity, and specification. When called to explain an event, object, or structure, we have a decision to make—are we going to attribute it to *necessity, chance,* or *design*? According to the complexity-specification criterion, to answer this question is to answer three simpler questions: Is it contingent? Is it complex? Is it specified? Consequently the complexity-specification criterion can be represented as a flowchart with three decision nodes. I call this flowchart the explanatory filter:

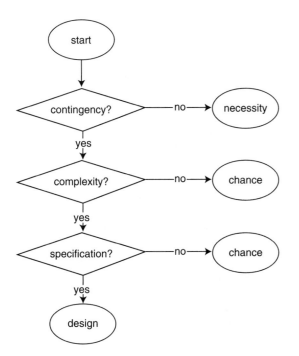

SPECIFICATION

Because specification is so central to inferring design, I need to elaborate it. For a pattern to count as a specification, the important thing is not when it was identified but whether in a certain well-defined sense it is *independent* of the event it describes. Drawing a target around an arrow already embedded in a wall is not independent of the arrow's trajectory. Consequently such a target/pattern cannot be used to attribute the arrow's trajectory to design. Patterns that are specifications cannot simply be read off the events whose design is in question. Rather, to count as specifications, patterns must be suitably independent of events. I refer to this relation of independence as *detachability* and say that a pattern is *detachable* just in case it satisfies that relation.

Detachability can be understood as asking the following question: given an event whose design is in question and a pattern describing it, would we be able to construct that pattern if we had no knowledge which event occurred? Here is the idea. An event has occurred. A pattern describing the event is given. The event is one from a range of possible events. If all we knew was the range of possible events without any specifics about which event actually occurred, could we still construct the pattern describing the event? If so, the pattern is detachable from the event.

To see what's at stake, we will use the example that finally clarified for me what transforms a pattern simpliciter into a pattern qua specification. Consider, therefore, the event E, an event that to all appearances was obtained by flipping a fair coin a hundred times:

THTTTHHTHHTTTTTHTHTTHHHTT
HTHHHTHHHTTTTTTTHTTHTTTHH
THTTTHTHTHTHHTTHHHHHTTTHTTHH
THTHTHHHHTTHHTHHHHTHHHHTT

Is E the product of chance or not? A standard trick of statistics professors with an introductory statistics class is to divide the class in two, having students in one half of the class each flip a coin a hundred times, writing down the sequence of heads and tails on a slip of paper, and having students in the other half each generate purely with their minds a "random looking" string of coin tosses that mimics the tossing of a coin a hundred times, also writing down the sequence of heads and tails on a slip of paper. When the students hand in their lists of sequences, the professor must sort them into two piles, those generated by flipping a fair coin and those concocted in the students' heads. To the amazement of the students, the statistics professor is typically able to sort the papers with 100 percent accuracy.

There's no mystery here. The statistics professor simply looks for a repetition of six or seven heads or tails in a row to distinguish the truly random from the pseudorandom sequences. In a hundred coin flips, one is quite likely to see six or seven such repetitions. On the other hand, people concocting pseudorandom sequences with their minds tend to alternate between heads and tails too frequently. Whereas with a truly random sequence of coin tosses there is a 50 percent chance that one toss will differ from the next, as a matter of human psychology people expect that one toss will differ from the next around 70 percent of the time.

How then will our statistics professor fare when confronted with E? Will E be attributed to chance or to the musings of someone trying to mimic chance? According to the professor's crude randomness checker, E would be assigned to the pile of sequences presumed to be truly random, for E contains a repetition of seven tails in a row. Everything that at first blush would lead us to regard E as truly random checks out. There are exactly fifty alternations between heads and tails (as opposed to the seventy that would be expected from humans trying to mimic chance). What's more, the relative frequencies of heads and tails check out: there were forty-nine heads and fifty-one tails. Thus it's not as though the coin supposedly responsible for generating E was heavily biased in favor of one side versus the other.

Suppose, however, that our statistics professor suspects that she is not up against a neophyte statistics student but instead a fellow statistician who is trying to put one over on her. To help organize her problem, study it more carefully, and enter it into a computer, she will find it convenient to let strings of 0s and 1s represent the outcomes of coin flips, with 1

corresponding to heads and 0 to tails. In that case, the following pattern D will correspond to the event E.

01000110110000010110011100
10111011100000010010001 1
01000101011001111100010011
01010111100110111101 11100

Now the mere fact that the event E conforms to the pattern D is no reason to think that E did not occur by chance. As things stand, the pattern D has simply been read off the event E.

But D need not have been read off of E. Indeed, D could have been constructed without recourse to E. To see this, let us rewrite D as follows:

0
1
00
01
10
11
000
001
010
011
100
101
110
111
0000
0001
0010
0011
0100
0101
0110
0111
1000
1001
1010
1011
1100
1101
1110
1111
00

By viewing D this way, anyone with the least exposure to binary arithmetic immediately recognizes that D was constructed simply by writing binary numbers in ascending order, starting with the one-digit binary numbers (i.e., 0 and 1), proceeding then to the two-digit binary numbers (i.e., 00, 01, 10, and 11) and continuing on until a hundred digits were recorded. It's therefore intuitively clear that D does not describe a truly random event (i.e., an event gotten by tossing a fair coin) but rather a pseudorandom event, concocted by doing a little binary arithmetic.

Although it's now intuitively clear why chance cannot properly explain E, we need to consider more closely why this mode of explanation fails here. We started with a putative chance event E, supposedly gotten by flipping a fair coin a hundred times. Since heads and tails each have probability 1/2, and since this probability gets multiplied for each flip of the coin, it follows that the probability of E is 2^{-100}, or approximately 10^{-30}. In addition, we constructed a pattern D to which E conforms. Initially D proved insufficient to eliminate chance as the explanation of E since in its construction, D was simply read off of E. Rather, to eliminate chance, we had also to recognize that D could have been constructed quite easily by performing some simple arithmetic operations with binary numbers. Thus to eliminate chance, we needed to employ additional *side information*, which in this case consisted of our knowledge of binary arithmetic. This side information detached the pattern D from the event E and thereby rendered D a specification.

For side information to detach a pattern from an event, it must satisfy two conditions, a *conditional independence condition* and a *tractability condition*. According to the conditional independence condition, the side information must be conditionally independent of the event E. Conditional independence is a well-defined notion from probability theory. It means that the probability of E doesn't change once the side information is taken into account. Conditional independence is the standard probabilistic way of unpacking epistemic independence. Two things are epistemically independent if knowledge about one thing (in this case the side information) does not affect knowledge about the other (in this case the occurrence of E). This is certainly the case here since our knowledge of binary arithmetic does not affect the probabilities we assign to coin tosses.

The second condition, the tractability condition, requires that the side information enable us to construct the pattern D to which E conforms. This is evidently the case here as well since our knowledge of binary arithmetic enables us to arrange binary numbers in ascending order and thereby construct the pattern D. But what exactly is this *ability to construct a pattern on the basis of side information*? Perhaps the most slippery words in philosophy are *can*, *able*, and *enable*. Fortunately, just as there is a precise theory for characterizing the epistemic independence between an event and side information—namely, probability theory—so, too, there is a precise theory for characterizing the ability to construct a pattern on the basis of side information—namely, *complexity theory*.

Complexity theory, conceived now quite generally and not merely as a form of probability, assesses the difficulty of tasks, given the resources available for accomplishing those tasks. As a generalization of computational complexity theory, complexity theory ranks tasks according to difficulty and then determines which tasks are sufficiently manageable to be doable or tractable. For instance, given current technology we find sending a person to the moon tractable, but sending a person to the nearest galaxy intractable. In the tractability condition the task to be accomplished is the construction of a pattern, and the resources for accomplishing that task are side information. Thus for the tractability condition to be satisfied, side information must provide the resources necessary for constructing the pattern in question. All of this admits a precise complexity-theoretic formulation and makes definite what I called *the ability to construct a pattern on the basis of side information*.

Taken jointly, the tractability and conditional independence conditions mean that side information enables us to construct the pattern to which an event conforms, yet without recourse to the actual event. This is the crucial insight. Because the side information is conditionally and therefore epistemically independent of the event, any pattern constructed from this side information is obtained without recourse to the event. In this way any pattern that is constructed from such side information avoids the charge of being ad hoc. These then are the detachable patterns. These are the specifications.

FALSE NEGATIVES AND FALSE POSITIVES

As with any criterion, we need to make sure that the judgments of the complexity-specification criterion agree with reality. Consider medical tests. Any medical test is a criterion. A perfectly reliable medical test would detect a disease whenever it is present and fail to detect the disease whenever it is absent. Unfortunately, no medical test is perfectly reliable, and so the best we can do is keep the proportion of false positives and false negatives as low as possible.

All criteria, and not just medical tests, face the problem of false positives and false negatives. A criterion attempts to classify individuals with respect to a target group (in the case of medical tests, those who have a certain disease). When the criterion places in the target group an individual who should not be there, it commits a false positive. Alternatively, when the criterion fails to place in the target group an individual who should be there, it commits a false negative.

Take medical tests again. A medical test checks whether an individual has a certain disease. The target group comprises all those individuals who actually have the disease. When the medical test classifies an individual who doesn't have the disease with those who do, it commits a false positive. When the medical test classifies an individual who does have the disease with those who do not, it commits a false negative.

Let us now apply these observations to the complexity-specification criterion. This criterion purports to detect design. Is it a reliable criterion? The target group for this criterion comprises all things intelligently caused. How accurate is this criterion at correctly assigning things to this target group and correctly omitting things from it? The things we are trying to explain have causal stories. In some of those causal stories intelligent causation is indispensable, whereas in others it is dispensable. An inkblot can be explained without appealing to intelligent causation; ink arranged to form meaningful text cannot. When the complexity-specification criterion assigns

something to the target group, can we be confident that it actually is intelligently caused? If not, we have a problem with false positives. On the other hand, when this criterion fails to assign something to the target group, can we be confident that no intelligent cause underlies it? If not, we have a problem with false negatives.

Consider first the problem of false negatives. When the complexity-specification criterion fails to detect design in a thing, can we be sure no intelligent cause underlies it? The answer is no. For determining that something is not designed, this criterion is not reliable. False negatives are a problem for it. This problem of false negatives, however, is endemic to detecting intelligent causes.

One difficulty is that intelligent causes can mimic necessity and chance, thereby rendering their actions indistinguishable from such unintelligent causes. A bottle of ink may fall off a cupboard and spill onto a sheet of paper. Alternatively a human agent may deliberately take a bottle of ink and pour it over a sheet of paper. The resulting inkblot may look identical in both instances, but the one case results by chance, the other by design.

Another difficulty is that detecting intelligent causes requires background knowledge on our part. It takes an intelligent cause to know an intelligent cause. But if we don't know enough, we'll miss it. Consider a spy listening in on a communication channel whose messages are encrypted. Unless the spy knows how to break the cryptosystem used by the parties on whom he is eavesdropping, any messages passing the communication channel will be unintelligible and might in fact be meaningless.

The problem of false negatives therefore arises either when an intelligent agent has acted (whether consciously or unconsciously) to conceal one's actions or when an intelligent agent in trying to detect design has insufficient background knowledge to determine whether design actually is present. Detectives face this problem all the time. A detective confronted with a murder needs first to determine whether a murder has indeed been committed. If the murderer was clever and made it appear that the victim died by accident, then the detective will mistake the murder for an accident. So, too, if the detective is stupid and misses certain obvious clues, the detective will mistake the murder for an accident. In mistaking a murder for an accident, the detective commits a false negative. Contrast this, however, with a detective facing a murderer intent on revenge and who wants to leave no doubt that the victim was intended to die. In that case, the problem of false negatives is unlikely to arise (though we can imagine an incredibly stupid detective, like Chief Inspector Clouseau, mistaking a rather obvious murder for an accident).

Intelligent causes can do things that unintelligent causes cannot and can make their actions evident. When for whatever reason an intelligent cause fails to make its actions evident, we may miss it. But when an intelligent cause succeeds in making its actions evident, we take notice. This is why false negatives do not invalidate the complexity-specification criterion. This criterion is fully capable of detecting intelligent causes intent on making their presence evident. Masters of stealth intent on concealing their actions may successfully evade the criterion. But masters of self-promotion intent on making sure their intellectual property gets properly attributed find in the complexity-specification criterion a ready friend.

This brings us to the problem of false positives. Even though specified complexity is not a reliable criterion for *eliminating* design, it is, I shall argue, a reliable criterion for *detecting* design. The complexity-specification criterion is a net. Things that are designed will occasionally slip past the net. We would prefer that the net catch more than it does, omitting nothing due to design. But given the ability of design to mimic unintelligent causes and the possibility of our own ignorance's passing over things that are designed, this problem cannot be fixed. Nevertheless we want to be very sure that whatever the net does catch includes only what we intend it to catch—things that are designed. Only things that are designed had better end up in the net. If this is the case, we can have confidence that whatever the complexity-specification criterion attributes to design is indeed designed. On the other hand, if things end up in the net that are not designed, the criterion will be worthless.

I want then to argue that specified complexity is a reliable criterion for detecting design. Alternatively

I want to argue that the complexity-specification criterion successfully avoids false positives. Thus whenever this criterion attributes design, it does so correctly. Let us now see why this is the case. I offer two arguments. The first is a straightforward inductive argument: in every instance where the complexity-specification criterion attributes design and where the underlying causal story is known, it turns out design actually is present; therefore design actually is present whenever the complexity-specification criterion attributes design. The conclusion of this argument is a straightforward inductive generalization. It has the same logical status as concluding that all ravens are black given that all ravens observed to date have been found to be black.

The naturalist is likely to object at this point, claiming that the only things we can know to be designed are artifacts manufactured by intelligent beings that are in turn the product of blind evolutionary processes (e.g., humans). Hence, to use the complexity-specification criterion to extrapolate design beyond such artifacts is illegitimate. This argument doesn't work. It is circular reasoning to invoke naturalism to underwrite an evolutionary account of intelligence and then in turn to employ this account of intelligence to insulate naturalism from critique. Naturalism is a metaphysical position, not a scientific theory based on evidence. Any account of intelligence it entails is therefore suspect and needs to be subjected to independent checks. The complexity-specification criterion provides one such check.

If we dismiss, as we ought, the naturalist's evolutionary account of intelligence, a more serious objection remains. I am arguing inductively that the complexity-specification criterion is a reliable criterion for detecting design. The conclusion of this argument is that whenever the criterion attributes design, design actually is present. The premise of this argument is that whenever the criterion attributes design and the underlying causal story can be verified, design actually is present. Now even though the conclusion follows as an inductive generalization from the premise, the premise itself seems false. There are a lot of coincidences out there that seem best explained without invoking design. Consider, for instance, the Shoemaker-Levy comet. The

Shoemaker-Levy comet crashed into Jupiter exactly twenty-five years to the day after the Apollo 11 moon landing. What are we to make of this coincidence? Do we really want to explain it in terms of design? What if we submitted this coincidence to the complexity-specification criterion and out popped design? Our intuitions strongly suggest that the comet's trajectory and NASA's space program were operating independently, and that at best this coincidence should be referred to chance—certainly not design.

This objection is readily met. The fact is that the complexity-specification criterion does not yield design all that easily, especially if the complexities are kept high (or correspondingly, the probabilities are kept small). It is simply not the case that unusual and striking coincidences automatically trigger design. Martin Gardner is no doubt correct when he notes, "The number of events in which you participate for a month, or even a week, is so huge that the probability of noticing a startling correlation is quite high, especially if you keep a sharp outlook." The implication he means to draw, however, is incorrect, namely, that therefore startling correlations/coincidences may uniformly be relegated to chance. Yes, the fact that the Shoemaker-Levy comet crashed into Jupiter exactly twenty-five years to the day after the Apollo 11 moon landing is a coincidence best referred to chance. But the fact that Mary Baker Eddy's writings on Christian Science bear a remarkable resemblance to Phineas Parkhurst Quimby's writings on mental healing is a coincidence that cannot be explained by chance and is properly explained by positing Quimby as a source for Eddy.

The complexity-specification criterion is robust and easily resists counterexamples of the Shoemaker-Levy variety. Assuming, for instance, that the Apollo 11 moon landing serves as a specification for the crash of Shoemaker-Levy into Jupiter (a generous concession at that), that the comet could have crashed at any time within a period of a year, and that the comet crashed to the very second precisely twenty-five years after the moon landing, a straightforward probability calculation indicates that the probability of this coincidence is no smaller than 10^{-8}. This simply isn't all that small a probability (i.e., high complexity), especially when considered in relation to all the events astronomers are observing in the solar system. Certainly this probability is nowhere near the universal probability bound of 10^{-150} that I propose in *The Design Inference*. I have yet to see a convincing application of the complexity-specification criterion in which coincidences better explained by chance get attributed to design. I challenge anyone to exhibit a specified event of probability less than my universal probability bound for which intelligent causation can be convincingly ruled out.

WHY THE CRITERION WORKS

My second argument for showing that specified complexity reliably detects design considers the nature of intelligent agency and, specifically, what it is about intelligent agents that makes them detectable. Even though induction confirms that specified complexity is a reliable criterion for detecting design, induction does not explain why this criterion works. To see why the complexity-specification criterion is exactly the right instrument for detecting design, we need to understand what it is about intelligent agents that makes them detectable in the first place. The principal characteristic of intelligent agency is choice. Even the etymology of the word *intelligent* makes this clear. *Intelligent* derives from two Latin words, the preposition *inter*, meaning between, and the verb *lego*, meaning to choose or select. Thus according to its etymology, intelligence consists in *choosing between*. For an intelligent agent to act is therefore to choose from a range of competing possibilities.

This is true not just of humans but also of animals as well as of extraterrestrial intelligences. A rat navigating a maze must choose whether to go right or left at various points in the maze. When SETI researchers attempt to discover intelligence in the extraterrestrial radio transmissions they are monitoring, they assume an extraterrestrial intelligence could have chosen any number of possible radio transmissions and then attempt to match the transmissions they observe with certain patterns as opposed to others. Whenever a human being utters meaningful speech, a choice is made from a range of possible sound-combinations that might have been uttered. Intelligent agency always entails discrimination, choosing certain things, ruling out others.

Given this characterization of intelligent agency, the crucial question is how to recognize it. Intelligent agents act by making a choice. How then do we recognize that an intelligent agent has made a choice? A bottle of ink spills accidentally onto a sheet of paper; someone takes a fountain pen and writes a message on a sheet of paper. In both instances ink is applied to paper. In both instances one among an almost infinite set of possibilities is realized. In both instances a contingency is actualized and others are ruled out. Yet in one instance we ascribe agency; in the other, chance.

What is the relevant difference? Not only do we need to observe that a contingency was actualized, but we ourselves need also to be able to specify that contingency. The contingency must conform to an independently given pattern, and we must be able independently to construct that pattern. A random ink blot is unspecified; a message written with ink on paper is specified. To be sure, the exact message recorded may not be specified. But orthographic, syntactic, and semantic constraints will nonetheless specify it.

Actualizing one among several competing possibilities, ruling out the rest, and specifying the one that was actualized encapsulates how we recognize intelligent agency, or equivalently, how we detect design. Experimental psychologists who study animal learning and behavior have known this all along. To learn a task an animal must acquire the ability to actualize behaviors suitable for the task as well as the ability to rule out behaviors unsuitable for the task. Moreover, for a psychologist to recognize that an animal has learned a task, it is necessary not only to observe the animal making the appropriate discrimination but also to specify the discrimination.

Thus, to recognize whether a rat has successfully learned how to traverse a maze, a psychologist must first specify which sequence of right and left turns conducts the rat out of the maze. No doubt a rat randomly wandering a maze also discriminates a sequence of right and left turns. But by randomly wandering the maze, the rat gives no indication that it can discriminate the appropriate sequence of right and left turns for exiting the maze. Consequently the psychologist studying the rat will have no reason to think the rat has learned how to traverse the maze.

Only if the rat executes the sequence of right and left turns specified by the psychologist will the psychologist recognize that the rat has learned how to traverse the maze. Now it is precisely these learned behaviors that we regard as intelligent in animals. Hence it is no surprise that the same scheme for recognizing animal learning recurs for recognizing intelligent agency generally: actualizing one among several competing possibilities, ruling out the others, and specifying the one actualized.

Note that complexity is implicit here as well. To see this, consider again a rat traversing a maze, but now take a very simple maze in which two right turns conduct the rat out of the maze. How will a psychologist studying the rat determine whether it has learned to exit the maze? Just putting the rat in the maze will not be enough. Because the maze is so simple, the rat could by chance just happen to take two right turns and thereby exit the maze. The psychologist will therefore be uncertain whether the rat actually learned to exit this maze, or whether the rat just got lucky.

But contrast this with a complicated maze in which a rat must take just the right sequence of left and right turns to exit the maze. Suppose that the rat must take one hundred appropriate right and left turns and that any mistake will prevent the rat from exiting the maze. A psychologist who observes the rat taking no erroneous turns and in short order exiting the maze will be convinced that the rat has indeed learned how to exit the maze and that this was not dumb luck.

This general scheme for recognizing intelligent agency is but a thinly disguised form of the complexity-specification criterion. In general, to recognize intelligent agency, we must observe an actualization of one among several competing possibilities, note which possibilities were ruled out, and then be able to specify the possibility that was actualized. What's more, the competing possibilities that were ruled out must be live possibilities and sufficiently numerous so that specifying the possibility that was actualized cannot be attributed to chance. In terms of complexity, this is just another way of saying that the range of possibilities is complex. In terms of probability this is just another way of saying that the possibility that was actualized has small probability.

All the elements in this general scheme for recognizing intelligent agency (i.e., actualizing, ruling out, and specifying) find their counterpart in the complexity-specification criterion. It follows that this criterion formalizes what we have been doing right along when we recognize intelligent agency. The complexity-specification criterion pinpoints how we detect design.

IRREDUCIBLE COMPLEXITY

Design is present in biology. Perhaps the most compelling evidence for design in biology comes from biochemistry. In a February 1998 issue of *Cell*, Bruce Alberts, president of the National Academy of Sciences, remarked,

> The entire cell can be viewed as a factory that contains an elaborate network of interlocking assembly lines, each of which is composed of large protein machines.... Why do we call the large protein assemblies that underlie cell function *machines*? Precisely because, like the machines invented by humans to deal efficiently with the macroscopic world, these protein assemblies contain highly coordinated moving parts.

Even so, Alberts sides with the majority of biologists in regarding the cell's marvelous complexity as only apparently designed. The Lehigh University biochemist Michael Behe disagrees. In *Darwin's Black Box*, Behe presents a powerful argument for actual design in the cell. Central to his argument is his notion of *irreducible complexity*. A system is irreducibly complex if it consists of several interrelated parts so that removing even one part completely destroys the system's function. As an example of irreducible complexity Behe offers the mousetrap. A mousetrap consists of a platform, a hammer, a spring, a catch, and a holding bar. Remove any one of these five components, and it is impossible to construct a functional mousetrap.

Irreducible complexity needs to be contrasted with *cumulative complexity*. A system is cumulatively complex if the components of the system can be arranged sequentially so that the successive removal of components never leads to the complete loss of function. An example of a cumulatively complex system is a city. It is possible successively to remove people and services from a city until one is down to a tiny village—all without losing the sense of community, which in this case constitutes function.

From this characterization of cumulative complexity, it is clear that the Darwinian mechanism of selection and mutation can readily account for cumulative complexity. Indeed the gradual accrual of complexity via selection mirrors the retention of function as components are successively removed from a cumulatively complex system.

But what about irreducible complexity? Can the Darwinian mechanism account for irreducible complexity? Certainly, if selection acts with reference to a goal, it can produce irreducible complexity. Take Behe's mousetrap. Given the goal of constructing a mousetrap, one can specify a goal-directed selection process that in turn selects a platform, a hammer, a spring, a catch, and a holding bar, and at the end puts all these components together to form a functional mousetrap. Given a prespecified goal, selection has no difficulty producing irreducibly complex systems.

But the selection operating in biology is Darwinian natural selection. And this form of selection operates without goals, has neither plan nor purpose, and is wholly undirected. The great appeal of Darwin's selection mechanism was, after all, that it would eliminate teleology from biology. Yet by making selection an undirected process, Darwin drastically abridged the type of complexity biological systems could manifest. Henceforth biological systems could manifest only cumulative complexity, not irreducible complexity.

Why is this? As Behe explains in *Darwin's Black Box*,

> An irreducibly complex system cannot be produced...by slight, successive modifications of a precursor system, because any precursor to an irreducibly complex system that is missing a part is by definition nonfunctional....Since natural selection can only choose systems that are already working, then if a biological system cannot be produced gradually it would have to arise as an integrated unit, in one fell swoop, for natural selection to have anything to act on.

For an irreducibly complex system, function is attained only when all components of the system are in place simultaneously. It follows that natural selection, if it is going to produce an irreducibly complex system, has to produce it all at once or not at all. This would not be a problem if the systems in question were simple. But they're not. The irreducibly complex biochemical systems Behe considers are protein machines consisting of numerous distinct proteins, each indispensable for function and together beyond what natural selection can muster in a single generation.

One such irreducibly complex biochemical system that Behe considers is the bacterial flagellum. The flagellum is a whiplike rotary motor that enables a bacterium to navigate through its environment. The flagellum includes an acid-powered rotary engine, a stator, O-rings, bushings, and a drive shaft. The intricate machinery of this molecular motor requires approximately fifty proteins. Yet the absence of any one of these proteins results in the complete loss of motor function.

The irreducible complexity of such biochemical systems counts powerfully against the Darwinian mechanism and indeed against any naturalistic evolutionary mechanism proposed to date. Moreover, because irreducible complexity occurs at the biochemical level, there is no more fundamental level of biological analysis to which the irreducible complexity of biochemical systems can be referred and at which a Darwinian analysis in terms of selection and mutation can still hope for success. Undergirding biochemistry are ordinary chemistry and physics, neither of which can account for biological information. Also, whether a biochemical system is irreducibly complex is a fully empirical question: individually knocking out each protein constituting a biochemical system will determine whether function is lost. If it is, we are dealing with an irreducibly complex system. Protein knock-out experiments of this sort are routine in biology.

The connection between Behe's notion of irreducible complexity and my complexity-specification criterion is now straightforward. The irreducibly complex systems Behe considers require numerous components specifically adapted to each other and each necessary for function. On any formal complexity-theoretic analysis, they are complex in the sense required by the complexity-specification criterion. Moreover, in virtue of their function, these systems embody patterns independent of the actual living systems. Hence these systems are also specified in the sense required by the complexity-specification criterion.

Biological specification always denotes function. An organism is a functional system comprising many functional subsystems. The functionality of organisms can be cashed out in any number of ways. Arno Wouters cashes it out globally in terms of the *viability* of whole organisms. Michael Behe cashes it out in terms of the *minimal function* of biochemical systems. Even the staunch Darwinist Richard Dawkins will admit that life is specified functionally, cashing out functionality in terms of the *reproduction* of genes. Thus, in *The Blind Watchmaker*, Dawkins will write, "Complicated things have some quality, specifiable in advance, that is highly unlikely to have been acquired by random chance alone. In the case of living things the quality that is specified in advance is…the ability to propagate genes in reproduction."

So What?

There exists a reliable criterion for detecting design. This criterion detects design strictly from observational features of the world. Moreover it belongs to probability and complexity theory, not to metaphysics and theology. And although it cannot achieve logical demonstration, it does achieve statistical justification so compelling as to demand assent. This criterion is relevant to biology. When applied to the complex, information-rich structures of biology, it detects design. In particular, the complexity-specification criterion shows that Michael Behe's irreducibly complex biochemical systems are designed.

What are we to make of these developments? Many scientists remain unconvinced. So what, if we have a reliable criterion for detecting design, and so what, if that criterion tells us that biological systems are designed? How is looking at a biological system and inferring it's designed any better than shrugging our shoulders and saying God did it? The fear is that design cannot help but stifle scientific inquiry.

Design is not a science-stopper. Indeed design can foster inquiry where traditional evolutionary approaches obstruct it. Consider the term "junk DNA." Implicit in this term is the view that because the genome of an organism has been cobbled together through a long, undirected evolutionary process, the genome is a patchwork of which only limited portions are essential to the organism. Thus, on an evolutionary view, we expect a lot of useless DNA. If, on the other hand, organisms are designed, we expect DNA as much as possible to exhibit function. And indeed the most recent findings suggest that designating DNA as "junk" merely cloaks our current lack of knowledge about function. For instance, in a 1997 issue of the *Journal of Theoretical Biology*, John Bodnar and his colleagues describe how "non-coding DNA in eukaryotic genomes encodes a language which programs organismal growth and development." Design encourages scientists to look for function where evolution discourages it.

Or consider vestigial organs that later are found to have a function after all. Evolutionary biology texts often cite the human coccyx as a "vestigial structure" that hearkens back to vertebrate ancestors with tails. Yet if one looks at a recent edition of *Gray's Anatomy*, one finds that the coccyx is a crucial point of contact with muscles that attach to the pelvic floor. Now anatomy is nothing other than an exercise in design, studying the large-scale design plans/blueprints for bodies. Thus here again we find design encouraging scientists to look for function where evolution discourages it. Examples where the phrase "vestigial structure" merely cloaks our current lack of knowledge about function can be multiplied. The human appendix, formerly thought to be vestigial, is now known to be a functioning component of the immune system.

Reinstating design within science can only enrich science. All the tried-and-true tools of science remain intact. But design also adds new tools to the scientist's explanatory tool chest. Moreover design raises a whole new set of research questions. Once we know that something is designed, we will want to know how it was produced, to what extent the design

is optimal, and what is its purpose. Note that we can detect design without knowing what something was designed for. There is a room at the Smithsonian filled with obviously designed objects for which no one has a clue about their purpose.

Design also implies constraints. An object that is designed functions within certain design constraints. Transgress those constraints, and the object functions poorly or breaks. Moreover we can discover those constraints empirically by seeing what does and doesn't work. This simple insight has tremendous implications not just for science but also for ethics. If humans are in fact designed, then we can expect psychosocial constraints to be hardwired into us. Transgress those constraints, and we personally as well as our society will suffer. There's plenty of empirical evidence to suggest that many of the attitudes and behaviors our society promotes undermine human flourishing. Design promises to reinvigorate that ethical stream running from Aristotle through Aquinas known as natural law.

By reinstating design within science, we do much more than simply critique scientific reductionism. Scientific reductionism holds that everything is reducible to scientific categories. Scientific reductionism is self-refuting and easily seen to be self-refuting. The existence of the world, the laws by which the world operates, the intelligibility of the world, and the unreasonable effectiveness of mathematics for comprehending the world are just a few of the questions that science raises but is incapable of answering.

Simply critiquing scientific reductionism, however, is not enough. Critiquing scientific reductionism does nothing to change science—and it is science that must change. By eschewing design, science has for too long operated with an inadequate set of conceptual categories. This has led to a constricted vision of reality, skewing how science understands not just the world but also ourselves. Evolutionary psychology, which justifies everything from infanticide to adultery, is just one symptom of this inadequate conception of science. Barring design from science distorts science, making it a mouthpiece for materialism instead of a search for truth.

Martin Heidegger remarked in *Being and Time*, "A science's level of development is determined by the extent to which it is *capable* of a crisis in its basic concepts." The basic concepts with which science has operated these last several hundred years are no longer adequate, certainly not in an information age, certainly not in an age where design is empirically detectable. Science faces a crisis of basic concepts. The way out of this crisis is to expand science to include design. To reinstate design within science is to liberate science, freeing it from restrictions that were always arbitrary and now have become intolerable.

STUDY QUESTIONS

1. Explain how Dembski treats chance and design as mutually exclusive alternatives in explaining natural biological phenomena. Is there any other way to treat these two concepts?
2. Rehearse in detail what Dembski means by "specified complexity."
3. By finding biological structures that exhibit specified complexity that cannot be explained by Darwinian natural selection, Dembski believes that he is setting up the inference to an intelligent designer for those structures. Do you believe that science must be open to such reasoning? Why or why not?
4. How do discussions of specified complexity—or irreducible complexity—in biology relate to the discussion of miracles as violations of the laws of nature?

Philip Kitcher

At the Mercy of Chance?

Philip Kitcher (b. 1947) is a philosopher who writes on bioethics, creationism, sociobiology, and the genetic revolution. Having commented and published frequently on the general clash between science and religion in the modern world, Kitcher approaches intelligent design in part by showing how it raises antiselectionist issues in biology long settled since Darwin. He argues that IDT claims about cases that supposedly cannot be explained by natural selection in terms of gradual, incremental development fail to grasp existing scientific information (e.g, regarding the blood-clotting mechanism) and jump to the conclusion that science will never provide an explanation based on natural selection. He also exposes flaws in the calculations that are wielded by ID proponents to argue that it is extremely improbable that natural processes produced certain biological structures but highly probable that they are the result of intelligent agency. Confronting the more positive IDT argument for an intelligence behind specified complexity, Kitcher requests a coherent account of its power and direction in the world.

[I]ntelligent design is a two-part doctrine. Despite the fact that its negative part, its antiselectionism, occupies almost all the movement's writings, there's also a positive claim, the thesis that whatever cause produced particular changes in the history of life deserves the label "intelligent." Hence, two issues need to be addressed. First, how troublesome are the complaints, the versions of the concrete case and computational arguments? Second, even if we were to wonder whether natural selection can yield the outcomes to which the complainers point, what reasons are there for supposing that the actual cause, whatever it is, is intelligent?

THE CONCRETE CASE ARGUMENT

Darwin's own consideration of the *concrete case argument* focused on some complex organs and structures that he rightly believed to be hard to understand in terms of natural selection. Two examples are prominent in the *Origin*, the eye and the electric organs found in some fish....

Darwin himself offered a tentative proposal about the evolution of the eye. He supposed that sensitivity to light might come in degrees, and that it might be possible to find, among existing organisms, some with a crude ability to respond to light, others with a

From *Living with Darwin: Evolution, Design, and the Future of Faith*. Oxford, England: Oxford University Press, 2007.

more refined capacity, and so on in something like a series. Perhaps, he speculated, research on these creatures might expose reasons why the different levels of sensitivity provided an advantage over rival organisms who had less, thus providing a way of answering (or sidestepping) the creationist quip, "What use is half an eye?"

It has taken more than a century of research on a wide variety of organisms to demonstrate that Darwin's hunch was basically right. Appearances to the contrary, organs and structures sensitive to light can be assembled piecemeal, with the intermediates enjoying some advantage over the competition. Biologists have studied organisms that respond to the light that impinges on their surfaces, organisms with indentations of the superficial layer that are able to acquire information about the direction of the light, organisms with deeper indentations whose light detection is more fine grained, organisms that have a structure resembling a pinhole camera, organisms that interpose a translucent medium between the surface and the aperture through which the light comes—and so on. By studying this sequence of organisms, they have been able to explore the transitions through which relatively crude abilities to detect light were successively refined. One feature of the story deserves emphasis. Darwin didn't start with a comparison between the fully formed eye—in a human being or an octopus, say—and then think of the component parts as being introduced, one at a time. He resisted the challenge to explain first the advantage of an eighth of an eye, then the advantage of a quarter of an eye, and so on, and focused instead on a function, light sensitivity, that might have been refined from an initial state of absence. To put it more bluntly, he didn't allow his envisaged challengers to define the sequence of "intermediates" for him.

Savvy champions of the concrete case argument know this story. They appreciate Darwin's ingenuity in responding to the challenge, and, although they think the response ultimately fails, their reasons for this judgment depend on a more general problem for evolution under natural selection. That more general problem derives from the fine structure of the components of complex organs (like eyes), the molecular mechanisms that have to be in place for eyes to work.

For all Darwin's cleverness, he failed to appreciate the full depth, and the full generality, of the difficulty confronting him.

The principal exponent of the complex case argument is Michael Behe, a professor of biochemistry, who argues at length in *Darwin's Black Box* that the real troubles of natural selection become visible when you appreciate the molecular components of complex biological systems. Almost everywhere you look in nature, there are complicated structures and processes, with many molecular constituents, and all the constituents need to be present and to fit together precisely for things to work as they should. Biochemical pathways require numerous enzymes to interact with one another, in appropriate relative concentrations, so that some important process can occur. If you imagine a mutation in one of the genes that directs the formation of some essential protein, or if you suppose that the genetic material becomes shuffled in a way that allows for differences in the rates at which proteins are formed, it looks as though disaster will ensue. Crucial pieces will be missing, or won't be present in the right proportions, so that everything will break down. How then could organisms with the pertinent structures or processes have evolved from organisms that lacked them?

Behe offers numerous instances of molecular machines that, he claims, could not have been built up in stages by natural selection. Among his most influential examples is a discussion of devices that some bacteria use for motion, flagella. He contrasts the bacterial flagellum with a different motor, used by other cells, the cilium: "In 1973 it was discovered that some bacteria swim by rotating their flagella. So the bacterial flagellum acts as a rotary propeller—in contrast to the cilium, which acts more like an oar." Both flagella and cilia are intricate structures, and Behe describes the many molecular parts and systems that have to be present if they are to do their jobs. He concludes that the complexity of the organization dooms any attempt to explain its emergence as the result of natural selection: "As biochemists have begun to examine apparently simple structures like cilia and flagella, they have discovered staggering complexity, with dozens or even hundreds of precisely tailored parts. It is very likely that many of the parts we have not considered here are required for any cilium to function in a cell. As the number of required parts increases, the difficulty of gradually putting the system together skyrockets, and the likelihood of indirect scenarios plummets. Darwin looks more and more forlorn." Indeed, the most famous portraits of Darwin hardly make him look exactly cheerful, but it's worth asking why examples like these should render him more forlorn.

Perhaps it seems obvious. Natural selection depends upon mutations that are not produced in response to the organism's needs. The bacteria are at the mercy of chance, which will fling in this variant protein or that, with negligible probability that the latest novelty will fit with what went before or will contribute to the design project of building a flagellum. In essentials, however, this is precisely parallel to an old creationist strategy, just the one that Darwin sidestepped in the case of the eye. Behe has specified how the intermediates are to be formed, and it isn't surprising that his preferred scenario has the air of impossibility.

What exactly is known about the bacterial flagellum? During the past few decades, careful molecular studies have identified the genes that direct the assembly of the motor, and have explored the ways in which it is put together in the development of an individual bacterium. Some mutations in these genes allow for bacteria to move, albeit less efficiently. What is currently missing, however, is that systematic study of the differences among bacteria with flagella and bacteria without that would parallel the knowledge attained in the case of vision. A sufficiently intensive study of the genomes of bacteria that lack flagella would enable biologists to explore the potential role of some of the crucial genes, and of the proteins they give rise to, when others are absent, and thus enable them to make more progress with Behe's apparently formidable challenge.

Most sciences face unsolved problems—indeed the exciting unsolved problems are the motivators for talented people to enter a field. . . . Unsolved questions are not typically written off as unsolvable—nobody proposes that there's some special force, unknown to current chemistry (an "intelligent force" perhaps?) that guides the proteins to their proper forms, or some hand that assembles the cilium in the development of an individual bacterium. Why, then, should we believe that the problem of the bacterial flagellum is unsolvable? Just because, in the absence of systematic molecular studies of bacteria with and without flagella, we can't currently give a satisfactory scenario for the evolution of the bacterial flagellum under natural selection, why should we conclude that further research couldn't disclose how that evolution occurred?

We are beguiled by the simple story line Behe rehearses. He invites us to consider the situation by supposing that the flagellum requires the introduction of some number—twenty, say—of proteins that the ancestral bacterium doesn't originally have. So Darwinians have to produce a sequence of twenty-one organisms, the first having none of the proteins, and each subsequent organism having one more than its predecessor. Darwin is forlorn because however he tries to imagine the possible pathway along which genetic changes successively appeared, he appreciates the plight of numbers 2–20, each of which is clogged with proteins that can't serve any function, proteins that interfere with important cellular processes. These organisms will be targets of selection, and will wither in the struggle for existence. Only number 1, and number 21, in which all the protein constituents come together to form the flagellum, have what it takes. Because of the dreadful plight of the intermediates, natural selection couldn't have brought the bacterium from there to here.

The story is fantasy, and Darwinians should disavow any commitment to it. First, there is no good reason for supposing that the ancestral bacterium lacked all, or even any, of the proteins needed to build the flagellum. It's a common theme of evolutionary biology that constituents of a cell, a tissue, or an organism are put to new uses because of a modification of the genome. Perhaps the immediate precursor of the bacterium with the flagellum is an organism in which all the protein constituents are already present, but are employed in different ways. Then, at the very last step, there's a change in the genome that removes whatever chemical barrier previously prevented the building of the flagellum. In this organism (the precursor), the function of one of the proteins is to increase the efficiency of a particular energy-transfer process. The precursor of the precursor lacked that protein, so that the genetic change that led to the precursor improved a process that was previously adequate. So it goes, back down a sequence of ancestors, all quite capable of functioning in their environments but all at a selective disadvantage to the bacteria that succeeded them....

The serious way forward is to amend our ignorance, by sequencing the genomes of different bacteria, with and without flagella. Using our current knowledge of the genetic basis of the flagellum, researchers would be able to specify more clearly what the intermediate forms—those with some, but not all, of the crucial genes—might have been like, and what functions the relevant proteins might have served. Until we know these things, efforts to describe intermediates will be so much whistling in the dark. Behe's examples rely on guesses that simply anticipate what this hard work would reveal....

THE COMPUTATIONAL ARGUMENT

The computational argument occurs in a variety of forms in current intelligent design literature, sometimes with relatively simple calculations of infinitesimal probabilities, on other occasions with much more technical specification of conditions under which we should make the "design inference" and conclude that some aspect of life has been intelligently designed. Whether or not intelligent design-ers attempt to be fully explicit about the requirements for invoking design, all their versions require the preliminary step of arguing that it is highly improbable that various aspects of life on earth could have emerged through natural selection. To use an analogy much beloved by earlier creationists, Darwinian claims about selection and the organization of life are equivalent to the idea that a hurricane in a junkyard could assemble a functioning airplane.

Besides providing the concrete case argument, Behe offers several versions of its computational cousin. Here's his attack on a scenario for the evolution of a blood-clotting mechanism, tentatively proposed by the eminent biochemist Russell Doolittle:

Let's do our own quick calculation. Consider that animals with blood-clotting cascades have roughly 10,000 genes, each of which is divided into an average of three pieces. This gives a total of about 30,000 gene pieces. TPA [tissue plasminogen activator] has four different types of domains. By "variously shuffling," the odds of getting those four domains together is 30,000 to the fourth power [presumably Behe means that the chance is one-thirty-thousandth to the fourth power], which is approximately one-tenth to the eighteenth power. Now, if the Irish Sweepstakes had odds of winning of one-tenth to the eighteenth power, and if a million people played the lottery each year, it would take about a thousand billion years before *anyone* (not just a particular person) won the lottery....Doolittle apparently needs to shuffle and deal himself a number of perfect bridge hands to win the game.

At first sight, this looks very powerful, since, given the time available for the evolution of life on earth (four billion or so years), it seems extremely improbable that the clotting mechanism could have evolved through natural selection.

Yet we should think carefully about the ways in which the pertinent probabilities are calculated. Behe is relying on two general ideas about probability. One is the thought that, when events are independent of one another, the probability that both will occur is the product of the individual probabilities—if you toss a fair die twice, then the chance of getting two sixes is 1 in 36; for, on each toss, the probability is 1 in 6, and, since the tosses are independent of one another, you multiply. The other idea is that, when you have a range of alternatives and don't have any reasons for thinking that one is more likely to occur than another, each of the possibilities has an equal chance. This idea, the notorious "principle of indifference," is known to be problematic, but, judiciously employed, it serves us well in some everyday contexts—as, for example, when we conclude that each side of the die has the same probability of falling uppermost.

Even in ordinary life, however, there are occasions on which applications of these principles would lead us to obviously unacceptable conclusions, so that we would rethink our computations. Consider a humdrum phenomenon suggested by Behe's analogy with bridge. You take a standard deck of cards and deal 13 to yourself. What is the probability that you get exactly those cards in exactly that order? The answer is 1 in 4×10^{21}. Suppose you repeat the process 10 times. You'll now have received 10 standard bridge hands, 10 sets of 13 cards; each one delivered in a particular order. Scrupulously, you record just the order in which all these cards were received, and calculate the chance that this event occurs. The probability, you claim, is 1 in $4^{10} \times 10^{210}$, which is approximately 1 in 10^{216}—notice that this denominator is enormously larger than Behe's 10^{18}. It must be really improbable that you (or anyone else) would ever receive just those cards in just that order in the entire history of the universe. But you did, and you have witnesses to testify that your records are correct. Excitedly, you contact Michael Behe to announce this quite miraculous event, surely evidence of some kind of Intelligence at work in the universe.

Your report would not be well received. Like everyone else, Behe knows how to understand this commonplace occurrence. Given the way in which the cards were initially arranged, the first deal was bound to go as it did. Given the shuffling that produced the ordering prior to the second deal, that deal, too, was sure to give rise to just those cards in that order; and so on. So there was a perspective, unknown to you, from which the probability of that sequence of cards wasn't some infinitesimally small number, but one (as high as chances go). If you describe events that actually occur from a perspective that lacks crucial items of knowledge, you can make them look improbable. We know enough about card dealing and coin tossing to understand this, and to see the calculation I attributed to you as perverse—for, although you don't know what the initial setup was, you should have recognized that there was some initial setup that would determine the sequence. Hence you should have known that application of the two general principles of probability in this context would provide a misleading view of the chance that this particular sequence would result.

In the case of the evolution of blood clotting, our ignorance is deeper. Not only do we not know what the initial molecular conditions—the prior state of the organisms in the population in which blood clotting emerged—were, we also don't know whether that initial state favored certain sorts of molecular changes rather than others. We have reason to think that Behe's assumption that there's a precise chance of 1 in 30,000 that each gene piece will participate in the "shuffling" process is incorrect. For, given what we know about mechanisms within the genome, the idea of exactly equal chances is suspect. But we don't know whether, given the initial molecular state, the chance of the cascade Doolittle hypothesizes remains infinitesimally small or whether it is actually one. Any estimate of the probability here is an irresponsible guess.

My imagined experiment with the deck of cards suggests a different way to think about the problem. Imagine that all the hands you were dealt were mundane—fairly evenly distributed among the four suits, with a scattering of high cards in each. If you calculated the probability of receiving ten mundane hands in succession, it would naturally be a lot higher than the chance of being dealt those very particular mundane hands, with the cards arriving in precisely that sequence (although it wouldn't be as high as you might expect). Blood clotting might also work in the same way, depending on how many candidates there are among the 30,000 "gene pieces" to which Behe alludes, that would yield a protein product able to play the necessary role. Suppose that there are a thousand acceptable candidates for each of the four positions in the molecule we need (TPA). The chance of success on any particular draw is now about 1 in 2.5 million. If there were 10,000 tries a year, it would take, on average, two or three centuries to find an appropriate combination, a flicker of an instant in evolutionary time.

My assumptions are no better—and no worse—than Behe's, for neither of us knows how tolerant the blood-clotting system is of the molecular combinations that the animals in question (whatever they were) might have supplied. We simply don't know what the right way to look at this problem is. But, given our ignorance, we shouldn't make wild guesses and then declare that the probabilities are so low that evolution under natural selection is impossible. A better research strategy would be to try to assemble information that will replace the guesses with serious estimates.

Moreover, even when the chance of a particular event turns out to be extremely small, it is important to resist the idea that that event could not have occurred. Imagine that you own a ticket in a lottery with an extremely large number of tickets—a million, say—and that the lottery is decided by a fundamentally random process, one that has no underlying causal basis by which the outcome will be determined. (You might suppose that each ticket is associated with a specific atomic nucleus of some radioactive element, and that the prize will go to the person whose nucleus decays first.) On any perspective we might justifiably adopt, there is a probability of one in a million that you will win, and similarly for all the other ticket holders (nobody has more than one ticket). Clearly, somebody will be lucky, and, after the fact, we'll have to admit that something very improbable has occurred. That shows that an extremely improbable outcome, one much less probable than alternatives, is still possible.

[Yet] champions of intelligent design declare that the probabilities that simple living things could arise "by chance"—or, more exactly, by the mechanisms adduced by Darwinians—are so low that some quite different explanation is required.

THE POSITIVE DOCTRINE

So far I have focused on the negative doctrine of intelligent design, the identification of unsolved evolutionary problems. We now have to consider the positive thesis, the claim that the phenomena to which Darwin's detractors point are produced by a process that deserves the label "intelligent." Two issues need to be considered. First, on what grounds should we apply the label? Second, what help can intelligent design provide in understanding the phenomena in question?

It's important to play by the rules. We mustn't personify Intelligence. Instead, according to the official doctrine, the acquiescence in a single tree of life, there are some evolutionary transitions—the original formation of life from nonlife, the emergence of the bacterial flagellum and the blood-clotting cascade—that can only be understood in terms of the action of a mechanism other than selection, that is, in terms of the operation of Intelligence.

As I've noted, there are some scientists who focus on kindred phenomena and try to find alternative physical mechanisms that would substitute for or complement natural selection. They don't dignify their proposed mechanisms with the label "intelligent." So we must inquire what grounds might support this title.

Making any judgment about whether a mechanism is intelligent or not appears rather difficult until we have been told considerably more about the way in which that mechanism operates. Officially, of course, we aren't supposed to personify this mechanism, and it's hard to understand just what the attribution of Intelligence even means if we resist the personification. If something counts as intelligent, wouldn't it have psychological states and engage in psychological processes—and wouldn't anything like that be very like a person? Intelligent design-ers do not address such questions. All we learn from the full gamut of their literature is that they conceive of Intelligence as whatever it is that produces the outcomes they identify as too complex to be attained through the operation of selection. The line of reasoning seems to be this: these phenomena, unattainable by selection, look designed or planned, and, as a result, the mechanism that produced them must be intelligent.

There is a fallacy here. Even without the slightest characterization of the mechanism, we're meant to infer one of its characteristics from the appearances of its products. One of Darwin's great achievements was to argue that you can have the appearance of design without a designer. Of course, even if they allow a limited role to natural selection, intelligent design-ers will contend that the kinds of complex organization to which they point couldn't have been produced by Darwin's surrogate for a designer—natural selection. Yet if we forget about natural selection, and ignore the controversies about what it can and cannot do, there are plenty of other instances in which striking order, pattern, and even beauty emerge from processes in which there is no planning, no design, but only the operation of blind and simple rules....

[C]onsider some contemporary studies of the ways in which the arrangements of petals in flowers, the banding patterns on seashells, the "designs" on the wings of butterflies and moths, and the coat patterns of mammals are generated in the development of those organisms—studies that give rise to strikingly beautiful computer graphics. In all these cases, researchers have been able to show how relatively simple—unintelligent, unplanned—processes can be iterated to yield structures that look so intricate that one would naively take them to have been planned by an intelligent designer.…

[Such] examples can be found in the phenomena of chemical reactions that organize striking patterns, in the honeycombs of the beehive, and in the structures of snowflakes—reveal that we have to be careful in inferring the character of a causal process from the order we think we discern in its outcome. It's simply a fallacy to suppose that because a particular structure or mechanism appears complex, then the causal agent that brought it about must be appropriately characterized as having "foreseen" or "planned" or "designed" the outcome. Even if intelligent designers were right in supposing that the phenomena they indicate couldn't have evolved by natural selection, only a more explicit identification of the causal mechanism that was at work could justify the conclusion that that mechanism is intelligent.

So, turning to the second question posed above, what help can intelligent design provide when we try to understand the difficulties it takes to beset Darwinism? How does it deal with the bacterial flagellum, for example?

If we take Behe at his word when he declares that he finds "the idea of common descent" to be "fairly convincing," and that he has "no particular reason to doubt it," then we should suppose that bacteria with flagella emerged from ancestors who lacked flagella. In line with the simple additive story he uses to make a history of natural selection appear implausible, he must suppose that the ancestors were missing a number of crucial proteins that the lucky descendants acquired, proteins that, once present, fit themselves together in the flagellum. If the intelligent design perspective is to help settle the unsolved problems of evolution, it would be good to have an alternative account that tells us how Intelligence facilitated the transition.

Unfortunately, the rest is silence. Neither in Behe's writings, nor in those of any other intelligent design-er, is there the slightest indication of how Intelligence performs the magic that poor, limited, natural selection cannot. On the face of it, there are just two basic possibilities. The first option is that Intelligence arranges the environment so that the intermediates—the apparently hapless organisms, cluttered with useless proteins—are protected against elimination under natural selection. (If we were unofficially inclined, we might say that the good Lord tempers the wind to the shorn bacterium.) The second option is that Intelligence provides for coordinated mutations to arise. If twenty genetic changes are needed, it brings about all of them at once. Or we can mix elements of both options and suppose that Intelligence introduces mutations in clumps—first ten, say, and then another ten, or first seven, then another seven, then six—and arranges protective environments for the intermediates. Of course, any story along these lines raises serious doubts. Just how does the coordination of the genetic changes or the modification of the environment work?

In presenting the possibilities in this way, I may seem to be forcing words into the mouths of the intelligent design-ers. Their core position, after all, is that at crucial moments in the history of life, descendants of some ancestors who lacked some trait (or organ or structure) came to possess the pertinent trait (organ, structure) by some causal process that is, unlike natural selection, intelligent. Why, then, do they have to talk about genes, mutations, and the need for protection against natural selection? The answer is that the traits in question are heritable—they are not introduced in each generation by some continued activity on the part of Intelligence, but emerge through the interactions of genes and environments. As in the case of the bacterial flagellum, there are underlying genes, and hence there have to be genetic changes in the passages from the ancestors to the descendants. If these changes occur over several generations, then, on the intelligent design-ers' own principles, there has to be protection against the tendency of natural selection to weed out the hapless intermediates. If they happen in one step, then, again by the favored principles, there must be coordinated mutations. Hence, even if the position would prefer to talk more vaguely of "novelties," it is committed to one of the options I have presented.

What intelligent design urgently needs if it's going to make any progress in understanding these transitions, in tackling the problems it claims to raise, is a set of coherent principles that identify the ways in which Intelligence is directed and what its powers and limitations are. If we lapse from the official story for a moment, we have to have some idea about what Intelligence "wants to achieve" and what kinds of things "it can do to work toward what it wants." What basis do we have to think that Intelligence aims to remedy the plight of the flagellumless bacteria, who can't evolve into bacteria-with-a-flagellum under natural selection? What basis is there to believe that Intelligence—or anything else, for that matter—can coordinate genetic changes or modify environments?

In fact, we need two distinct kinds of principles. First, there have to be principles that specify when Intelligence swings into action. Perhaps they will tell us that Intelligence operates when there are potentially advantageous complex traits that can't evolve by natural selection. Second, there must be principles that explain what Intelligence does when it acts. Perhaps these will identify the sorts of genetic changes Intelligence can arrange, or the ways in which it can inhibit the normal operation of selection.

It is already clear that these principles will be hard to state precisely. For, if Intelligence has been waiting in the wings throughout the history of life, seizing opportunities as they arise, we know that there are all sorts of things it hasn't done. Apparently Intelligence isn't directed toward eliminating the junk from genomes or removing vestigial structures like the whale's pelvis or generating radically new arrangements for mammalian forelimbs. It's possible, of course, that although directed toward these ends, Intelligence is simply unable to bring them about. So any satisfactory principles must differentiate between the bacterial flagellum, blood-clotting cascade, and similar places where Intelligence shows its prowess, and the accumulated junk, vestigial structures, and genetic blunders, where it remains in abeyance.

Drawing this distinction is even more difficult than I have made it appear. For there are really simple genetic problems with respect to which Intelligence seems to be impotent.

As I noted earlier, sickle-cell anemia has persisted because the gene that gives rise to the disease when present in double dose, the S allele, confers an advantage when it appears in combination with the standard A allele, by providing resistance to malaria. This is the simple part of a classic evolutionary story, one routinely taught to those schoolchildren fortunate enough to learn something about evolution.

However, there is a twist, one not so widely known. In some African populations, there appears another form of the gene, the C allele, usually only present at a low frequency. The comparative rarity of the C allele is initially puzzling, for people who have two copies have the best of both worlds—they enjoy the resistance to malaria, and they aren't silent carriers of a deadly disease. Given its apparent advantages, why doesn't the C allele drive the others out? Why do inferior genes persist?

The sad answer is that natural selection tends to drive the C allele out of the populations in which it makes its cameo appearances. When it is relatively rare, its carriers tend to produce offspring with people who have the standard alleles—the A allele and the S allele—and, unfortunately, the combinations of C with A and C with S are inferior to both the more frequent genotypes (AA and AS). If only the C allele could reach a threshold frequency, then the chances of its bearers mating with one another and having children with the CC genotype would be sufficiently great to outweigh the defects of the CA and CS combinations—and, at that point, natural selection would eliminate the A and S alleles, producing a population with a genotype that would offer greater protection against disease.

If Intelligence can handle the transition to the bacterial flagellum, then, according to the story on which Behe relies to discredit natural selection, it must be able to coordinate genetic changes or to provide environmental protection for otherwise vulnerable intermediates. Indeed, since there are, on Behe's hypothesis, a number of proteins that must be introduced to make the flagellum, it must be able to perform one or the other of these tricks on a rather grand scale. By contrast, the genetic problem with the C

allele is trivial. It could be solved if Intelligence could protect a few organisms—those with the *CA* and *CS* genotypes—from the rigors of selection until the *C* allele had reached the requisite threshold frequency. It could also be solved if Intelligence could arrange for some coordinated mutations, not a long series as with the bacteria, but just some extra *C* mutants. In fact, if Intelligence could simply produce one *C* allele in a human male and, simultaneously, a *C* allele in a human female, and then ensure that *C*-bearers mated with one another for a few generations, everything would work out beautifully. Apparently, however, Intelligence isn't up to these jobs. But if it can't perform these easy tasks, why should we think it can manage the transition to the bacterial flagellum?

Perhaps, however, the problem isn't with the power of Intelligence, but with its direction. Intelligent design-ers might suppose that their favored mechanism responds to the "needs" of the flagellum-less bacteria, but not to those of human populations in which the *S* allele—and the debilitating disease it brings—is maintained by natural selection. If we were to talk illicitly, we might wonder why Intelligence is more "worried about" the disadvantages that beset unflagellated bacteria than about the human beings who are, according to religious tradition, the foci of divine concern. Even if we play by the rules, however, it's appropriate to ask for the set of principles that govern the direction and power of Intelligence. Can intelligent design-ers explain how the problematic evolutionary transitions—those beyond the scope of natural selection—are accomplished, how Intelligence fails to overcome relatively small genetic barriers, and fails to clean up the repetitive DNA, purge the vestigial structures, and so on?

Why do intelligent design-ers ignore the basic problem of explaining the power and direction of the mechanism they invoke, a problem that strikes at the heart of their theory? Apparently, their preferred perspective faces a multitude of currently unsolved puzzles about the scope and direction of Intelligence. Yet, unlike their counterparts in other scientific ventures, they are reluctant to suggest their strategies for seeking solutions. Their reticence provokes the charge that what they are doing is not science, but perhaps breaking their silence would be theologically unwise. Saying too much might disrupt the harmony between the sanitized version of intelligent design elaborated in the classroom during the week and the richer account delivered from the pulpit on Sunday. Moreover, saying anything that would genuinely respond to the puzzles might be saying too much.

STUDY QUESTIONS

1. How does Kitcher explain the role of chance as essential to natural selection and thus to evolution?
2. Kitcher states that the intelligent design viewpoint relies heavily on two types of argument against selectionism: the concrete case argument and the computational argument. Be very specific in articulating these two arguments and then evaluating their effectiveness.
3. Granting that we can talk about an Intelligent Designer that has directly created certain biological structures, what criticisms of this Intelligence does Kitcher offer? What specific issues treated in previous sections of this book relate to do these criticisms?

John Polkinghorne

The Universe as Creation

John Polkinghorne (b. 1930) is a mathematical physicist who played an important role in the discovery of the quark. In the middle of his career, he became an Anglican priest. He has published many books on issues in science and religion, including *The Way the World Is: The Christian Perspective of a Scientist* and *One World: The Interaction of Science and Theology*. He is a co-director of the Psychology and Religion Research Group at Cambridge University. His career reflects his deep conviction that the universe (literally "one-truth") must be known through the fullest cooperation of all the disciplines—particularly the sciences, theology, and philosophy. He is disturbed by both well-worn creationism and the more recent intelligent design theory, which both try to gain traction for the idea of a transcendent being or God by alleging inadequacies within science. In the present selection, he tries to move beyond such approaches and explores important themes on which both science and theology, upon deeper reflection, are congruent.

Scientists are motivated by the desire to understand what is happening in the world. Their quest has been remarkably successful, extending its scope far beyond those everyday processes whose comprehension might plausibly be explained by evolutionary necessity's having shaped our brains to be apt for this purpose. Science helps us understand the realm of subatomic physics and the nature of cosmic space-time, regimes remote from direct impact upon us and with a character whose understanding calls for modes of thought quite different from those required to cope with mundane necessity. Yet science's success has been purchased by the modesty of its explanatory ambition. It does not attempt to ask and answer every question that one might legitimately raise. Instead, it confines itself to investigating natural processes, attending to the question of how things happen. Other questions, such as those relating to meaning and purpose, are deliberately bracketed out. This scientific stance is taken simply as a methodological strategy with no implication that those other questions, of what one might call a "why" kind, are not fully meaningful and necessary to ask if complete understanding is to be attained.

Yet, even in relation to its own self-limited field of enquiry, science cannot function as a wholly free-standing discipline, capable of answering fully its "how" kind of questions. Considering causal issues illustrates this point. The consideration of causality is certainly constrained by what science has to

From "The Universe as Creation" in *Intelligent Design: William A. Dembski and Michael Ruse in Dialogue*, edited by Robert B. Stewart. Minneapolis: Fortress Press, 2007.

say, but the outcome of that discussion is not fully determined by science alone. Understanding the nature of causality calls also for acts of metaphysical decision. Quantum theory makes the point clearly enough. The quantum world is necessarily characterized by the presence of intrinsic unpredictabilities, and epistemic access to it is restricted by Heisenberg's uncertainty principle. So much physics can say. But do these facts arise from an unavoidable ignorance of certain fine details relating to a physical reality whose underlying nature is actually fully deterministic, or are they signs of the intrinsically indeterministic character of the quantum world? It turns out that either answer is compatible with the empirical evidence that physics can offer. While most physicists follow Niels Bohr in giving the second answer, there is an ingenious theory due to David Bohm that demonstrates that the first answer is also a possibility. The choice between these two options cannot be made on purely scientific grounds, but appeal has to be made to metascientific criteria, such as judgments of economy, elegance, and naturalness (the absence of contrivance).

Those who have a thirst for understanding will not find it quenched by science alone. While many scientists exhibit a kind of professional distrust of the notion of metaphysics, the truth is that no one can do without a wider view than the strictly scientific. The scientist reductionist who proclaims that scientific knowledge is all we have, or need to have, is making a statement that has not been derived from science itself, properly understood. Human beings think metaphysics as naturally and as unavoidably as we speak prose.

Nothing comes of nothing, and any metaphysical scheme must rest on an underived and unexplained basis, which then serves as the foundation for subsequent explanatory development. In the Western tradition, there have been two fundamentally distinct kinds of metaphysical starting points. One takes as its basic brute fact the existence of the material world, treating the laws of nature as the given basis for all further explanation. David Hume was a notable proponent of this kind of materialistic metaphysics. The other approach takes the brute fact of a self-subsistent divine agent as its basic foundation, seeing the world as being ordered according to that agent's will and its

history as expressive of that agent's purpose. Theism is the metaphysical stance that seeks to understand the universe in terms of its being a divine creation.

Arguments for and against these two great explanatory traditions have raged for many centuries. Recently a new kind of defense of the theistic position has been proposed—or perhaps one might better say an old kind of defense has reappeared dressed in novel intellectual clothing. Under the rubric of ID [intelligent design], this new movement claims to be able to discern scientific aspects of our knowledge of the living world whose existence cannot be understood without appeal to the direct action of a designing intelligence at work within the course of history. While the proponents of this view are very discreet about saying anything definite concerning the nature of this active intelligence—it is a tactic of their discourse to eschew the use of words such as *God* or *Creator*—it seems pretty clear that the underlying agenda of the ID movement is to offer a particular kind of tacit defense of theistic metaphysics. Before attempting to evaluate this approach, it is necessary to make a preliminary survey of the scientific and theological contexts within which it has to be considered.

Science

We have seen that physics does not determine metaphysics, but it certainly constrains it, rather as the foundations of a house do not determine the edifice that will be erected on them, but they do constrain its possible form. Five aspects of science's view of reality are particularly relevant to the present discussion.

1. *Fragmentary Accounts.* Physics proceeds by the detailed investigation of particular domains: subatomic physics, condensed matter physics, continuum mechanics, and so on. Within each domain, considerable understanding can be gained of the processes involved, but the relationships between the different domains are often far from being properly understood. To be perfectly frank, physics' contribution to an account of the causal nexus of the world is distinctly patchy.

A striking example of the fragmentary nature of physical understanding is provided by the perplexities that are still unresolved concerning how quantum physics and classical physics should be thought to relate to each other. This problem remains challenging even after eighty years of highly successful calculational achievement. We know how to do the sums, but we do not fully understand what is happening. The most notorious difficulty relates to the measurement problem. Quantum physics is based on the superposition principle, permitting the combination of states that Newtonian thinking, or common sense, would say were strictly immiscible. An electron can be in a state that is a mixture of being here and being there. Not only does this possibility reflect the unpicturable strangeness of the quantum world, but it also relates to the probabilistic nature of quantum physics. If the position of an electron in such a superposed state is actually measured, sometimes the result will be here and sometimes it will be there. The formalism enables one to calculate with impressive accuracy the relative probabilities of obtaining these two answers, but there is no widely agreed upon and satisfactory theoretical explanation of why a particular result is found on a particular occasion. This scientific aporia is the measurement problem. In other words, it is embarrassing for a physicist to have to confess that he or she does not understand how the cloudy quantum world and the clear classical world are joined to each other by the bridge of measurement. As a result, there is a yawning gap in physics' account of causal structure.

A second example of patchiness is the failure to combine quantum theory and chaos theory in a coherent manner. Chaotic systems possess such exquisite sensitivity to the smallest detail of their circumstances that prediction of future behavior would soon require a degree of accurate knowledge that Heisenberg uncertainty forbids. This implies that there should be an intertwining of quantum theory and chaos theory but, in fact, the two formalisms as they now stand are incompatible with each other. Quantum theory has a scale, given by Planck's constant, but the fractal character of chaotic dynamics means that it is scale-free, having the same characteristics whatever size is sampled. The two just do not fit together.

Physics is unable to offer a seamless account of what is going on in the world. It is clear that it has failed to establish the causal closure of the universe on its own physicalist terms.

2. *Unpredictability*. Twentieth-century science discovered the existence of intrinsic unpredictabilities in physical process. They first came to light at the subatomic level of quantum physics, and then later more were discovered at the macroscopic level of chaos theory. It is important to give full weight to the word *intrinsic*. We are not referring to situations where better measurement techniques, or more powerful means of calculation, could remove the unpredictabilities. Unpredictability is an epistemological property, referring to what we can or cannot know about future behavior. There is no logically necessary link between epistemology and ontology (what is actually the case). As we have seen already in the case of Heisenberg uncertainty, a metaphysical decision is required concerning what kind of ontological interpretation to espouse (determinism or indeterminism?). It is a perfectly coherent and acceptable strategy to interpret physical unpredictabilities as signals of the presence of a causal openness, permitting the operation of causal influences over and above those resulting from the exchange of energy between constituents that has been the traditional story told by science. An obvious candidate for such an additional causal principle would be the willed acts of intentional human agents. Another possibility would be divine providential action, continuously operating within the open grain of nature. An honest science is not in the position to forbid either of these possibilities.

3. *Relationality*. Newtonian thinking thought of physical process in terms of the collisions of particles moving in the container of absolute space and in the course of the unfolding of absolute time. The twentieth century replaced this picture with something altogether more intrinsically relational; Einstein's theory of general relativity combined space, time, and matter in a single integrated account. Matter curves space-time, and the curvature of space-time influences the paths of matter. In the quantum world, once two particles have interacted, they remain mutually entangled, effectively becoming a single system so that, however far they separate, acting on one will produce an immediate effect on the other. (This is the

celebrated "EPR effect.") Even the subatomic world, it appears, cannot be treated atomistically.

4. *Evolving and Emergent Complexity.* The universe 13.7 billion years ago was just a small, almost uniform, expanding ball of energy. Today it is a vast cosmos, populated by rich and diverse structures. That ball of energy has become the home of saints and scientists. The processes that have brought about this astonishingly fruitful transformation have been evolutionary in character, whether one is considering early cosmic history, in the course of which the universe became lumpy and grainy with stars and galaxies, or the 3.5-billion-year story of the development of life on earth. Evolutionary process is the result of the fertile interplay of two contrasting tendencies that one may label "Chance" and "Necessity." Necessity stands for the lawful regularity of the world. Chance stands for contingent particularity, the happenstance that this occurs rather than that. The range of possible events is so vast that even in 13.7 billion years only a small fraction of what might have happened has actually happened. Many illustrations could be given of the symbiotic interplay of these two tendencies.

Science has learned to recognize that true novelty can only emerge in regimes that may be said to be at the edge of chaos, a realm where order and contingency interlace to constitute the domain of chance and necessity. Pure necessity would correspond to a world too rigid in its nature to permit anything really new to emerge. Pure chance would correspond to a world too haphazard in its nature to allow anything really new to persist. Without a degree of genetic mutation, there would be no new forms of life. Without a degree of stable genetic transfer between the generations, there would be no metastable species established on which the sifting process of natural selection could operate.

The powerful fertility of the universe is made apparent by the punctuated emergence of wholly new forms of complexity, whose natures were unforeseeable in terms of what had preceded them: life from inanimate matter; consciousness from life; human self-consciousness (the very means by which the universe became aware of itself, thereby making science an eventual possibility). However, it is not clear that conventional evolutionary thinking is the complete

scientific account of how this has come about. It is just becoming possible to study the behavior of moderately complex systems, treated in their entirety rather than being decomposed into constituent parts. Presently, most of this work is at the natural-history stage of simply looking at specific instances, often computer-generated models. However, it is already clear that complex systems frequently manifest astonishing powers of spontaneous self-organization, resulting in the generation of novel patterns of structure and behavior. It is entirely conceivable that the emergence of novelty is partly influenced by holistic pattern-forming laws of nature, of a kind not previously considered by science and as yet far from being fully understood.

5. *Fine-tuned Potentiality.* Much discussion of evolutionary significance has concentrated on the chance half of the duality, but necessity should not be taken as being in any lesser degree significant. A surprising development in scientific understanding has been the recognition that lawful regularity had to take a very specific, quantitatively precise form, if it were to be possible for carbon-based life to evolve anywhere at all in the course of cosmic history. A universe capable of being the home of life is a very special kind of universe indeed. While life only seems to have developed after about ten billion years of cosmic history, our universe was pregnant with this possibility from the big bang onward, in the sense that its given physical fabric had just the right character to permit this to happen. The collection of scientific insights that led to this remarkable and unanticipated conclusion has been given the name of the Anthropic Principle. One example must suffice to indicate the kind of thinking that underlies it.

Because the very early universe is very simple, it only produces very simple consequences. The only chemical elements it can generate are the two simplest, hydrogen and helium. For life, one needs much more diversity of chemical resources. In particular, one needs carbon, whose capacity to generate long chain molecules lies at the basis of all living beings. There is only one place in the whole universe where carbon can be made: in the interior nuclear furnaces of the stars. We are people of stardust, made out of the ashes of dead stars. The person who first understood this process was Fred Hoyle. In a moment of great insight, he saw that stellar carbon production was just possible, in a beautiful and delicate way, because there was an enhancement effect (a resonance, as we say) at just the right energy to permit what would otherwise have been a forbidden process. Hoyle also realized that if the nuclear forces had been only slightly different, there would have been no suitable resonance and so no carbon-based life. Despite a lifelong commitment to atheism, he is reported to have said that the universe is a "put-up job." In other words, Hoyle could not believe that the existence of carbon was just a happy accident. Because he did not care for the word *God*, he said there must be some intelligence that had fixed the laws of nature to make it so. We could say that Hoyle felt he had perceived intelligent design present in the fabric of the world. This would, of course, be quite different from the ID movement's claim to discern a different kind of intelligent design, present in the actual detailed structures of some living beings. The former relates to the rules of the cosmic game; the latter refers to specific moves in that game.

Theology

The foregoing discussion has concentrated on scientific insights concerning which there would be widespread agreement in the competent community. But full understanding of the implications of these remarkable discoveries requires locating them in the deeper context of intelligibility afforded by an overarching metaphysical point of view. We have already noted that there will be no logical inevitability or necessary uniqueness about such a move and, consequently, there will not be universal agreement about which metascientific scheme to adopt. The thesis of this essay is that seeing the universe as a divine creation provides the most intellectually satisfying context of understanding. Exploring that claim requires identifying some of the resources of insight that theism can offer. Three concepts are of particular relevance.

1. *Creation.* To see the world as creation is to believe that the mind of God lies behind its marvelous order

and the will of God behind its fruitful history. The astonishing power of the human mind to understand the deep structures of the world—the very fact that has made science possible, but which science itself is unable to explain—can be rendered intelligible by the ancient belief that humans are made in the image of God (Gen. 1:26–27). The rational beauty disclosed in fundamental physics, which affords scientists the reward of wonder as a recompense for all the labor of their research, is not then seen as some happy accident, but it is recognized as a true reflection of the mind of the Creator, encountered through the marvelously ordered fabric of creation. The anthropic fine-tuning of that fabric, which has been necessary to enable the astonishing fertility of cosmic and terrestrial history, is understood from a theistic point of view to be the endowment given by the Creator to enable creation to fulfill the divinely willed purpose of its creative history.

These insights all refer to aspects of the laws of nature that a materialistic metaphysics would have to treat as mere brute fact, but whose significant character seems to call for an explanation if the thirst for understanding is truly to be quenched. To see the universe as creation is to discern intelligent design built into its physical fabric. In this perspective God is not pictured as the great Artificer, contriving ingenious and particular structures, but as the grand Ordainer of inherent potentiality and order without which the world would be a chaos rather than a cosmos. This understanding meets Hume's criticism of the physico-theologians of the eighteenth century, people like John Ray and William Paley, whose appeal to the functional aptness of living beings was an argument at the level of organisms similar to the arguments now being made by the ID movement at the level of molecular mechanisms. Hume said that the picture of God offered by the physico-theologians was too anthropomorphic, treating the act of creation as if it were comparable to a carpenter making a ship. But bringing into existence a world endowed with inherent potentiality is quite different from manipulating existing material in order to produce new forms. In Hebrew terminology, the former is *bara* (a distinctive word used only of divine creativity) rather than *'asah* (the ordinary word for any form of making).

2. *Kenosis.* Christian theology understands love to be the nature of God. In consequence, it can neither picture the Creator as an indifferent deistic Spectator, who having set it all going just lets it all happen, nor as the cosmic Puppet Master pulling every string in the theatre of creation. The gift of love must always include some due degree of independence granted to the object of love. Recognizing this has led many contemporary theologians to understand the act of creation to be an act of creatorly kenosis, involving a divine self-limitation in order to permit the created other truly to be itself and, indeed, to make itself.

The thought of creaturely self-making (as old as Charles Kingsley's initial response to the publication of the *Origin of Species*) is the theological way to interpret evolution, seen as the shuffling explorations of chance by which the divinely given potentiality of the universe is brought to specifically realized actuality. It can be claimed that a world of that kind of evolving fruitfulness is a greater good than a ready-made creation would have been. Yet that goodness has a necessary cost. There is an inevitable shadow side to the evolutionary process, as contingent exploration results not only in new kinds of fruitfulness, but it also leads to ragged edges and blind alleys. In an evolving world, the death of one generation is the necessary cost of the new life of the next. We know that biological evolution has been driven by genetic mutation, but if germ cells are to be able to mutate and produce new forms of life, then somatic cells will also, by the same process, be able to mutate and sometimes they will then become malignant. Some help is offered here to theology as it struggles with the deep perplexities of theodicy. The anguishing fact of cancer is not something gratuitous, as if a Creator who was a bit more competent or a bit less callous could easily have eliminated it. It is the necessary cost of creation in which creatures are allowed to make themselves.

3. *Providence.* We have seen that an honest evaluation of science's actual knowledge of the causal nexus of the world is compatible with understanding its process to be more subtle and more supple than the picture of creation as a gigantic piece of cosmic clockwork. There are no adequate scientific grounds

requiring us to exclude a metaphysics of agency, including the possibility of divine providential interaction in the course of unfolding history. The idea of a universe of becoming, open to its future, permits an understanding of divine providence as operating within the open grain of created nature, rather than as acting against that nature, whose character, after all, is itself an expression of the Creator's will. It was suggested earlier that the locus of the necessary causal flexibility might lie in those cloudy domains of intrinsic unpredictability that have been discovered by science. If that is the case, it follows that the process of the world cannot be taken apart and exhaustively itemized, as if one could assert that nature did this, human will did that, and divine providence did the third thing. There is intrinsic entanglement. Acts of providence may be discernible by faith, but they will never be demonstrable by experiment.

What, then, about miracles? Christianity has to face the issue, since at the heart of its belief is the resurrection of Christ, and no one could pretend that a man rising from death to a transformed life of unending glory came about through clever exploitation of quantum or chaotic unpredictabilities. Here there must have been a direct act of God of a completely unprecedented kind. Since science is concerned with what usually happens, it cannot logically forbid the possibility of unique occurrences. Yet theology itself forbids thinking of God as a kind of whimsical celestial conjurer, doing an occasional trick just to astonish people. If unprecedented events like miracles actually happen, it can only be because unprecedented circumstances have made that a possibility, which is consonant with the consistency of divine will. If Jesus was the incarnate Son of God, as Christians believe, then his resurrection can indeed be seen as a consistent form of divine action, and also understood as the signal and seal within history of what God intends to do for all humanity beyond history (1 Cor. 15:22). This approach to the question of miracles sees them as events that open windows onto deep levels of the divine nature, affording more profound insight than is revealed by everyday experience. It corresponds to ways in which John's gospel calls them signs.

INTELLIGENT DESIGN

The concept of providence just proposed is one that pictures God as ceaselessly interacting with creation by means of continuous action taking place within the divinely ordained open grain of nature. Special divine acts in special circumstances of revelational disclosure are not excluded, but the expectation is that these acts will be comparatively rare and that they will occur for highly significant reasons. If the purpose of miracles is truly to be signs of deep significance, they will not be rashly and prodigally scattered throughout history. In fact, consideration of the biblical miracle stories shows that they concentrate around times of particular importance in salvation history: the exodus, the dawn of prophecy in Israel, the life of Jesus Christ, and the foundation of the Church.

Although the carefully chosen language of the ID movement recoils from using the word *miracle*, its picture of the developing history of life carries the clear implication that it is seeded with numerous miraculous interventions, discontinuous acts in which new entities are specially created. How else could one suppose complex designed systems to have sprung into being, other than through a direct act of intervention by an intelligent designing agent? And to be perfectly frank, what credible designing agent could there be other than God? One has to ask what evidence could be offered to support this extremely strong claim.

William Dembski set out to discuss what would be the kind of evidence that could be held to point in a logically persuasive manner to the presence of intelligent design. His key concept is what he calls the *complexity-specification criterion*. Three elements are identified as necessary for the satisfaction of the criterion: contingency, complexity, and specification. *Contingency* means that the entity is not something that was bound to be formed through processes of inexorable necessity. When using a personal computer, if you click on "print," the resulting text will inevitably correspond to the words that were already on the screen. Whatever intelligence went into the original composition, no further intelligence was involved making an automatic copy. *Complexity* means that the entity is not so simple that its formation by mere chance is perfectly likely. If you type four letters at random, occasionally they will correspond to an English word, and this is sufficiently likely that, when it does happen, no great significance attaches to the event. However, if you type a hundred letters at random and find that they can be split up into a sequence of English words, one may rightly think that this occurrence calls for some further explanation. *Specification* is the most elusive of the conditions to define. It requires the presence of a pattern whose character is such as naturally to suggest a role for intelligence in its formation. If those hundred letters are found to correspond to the words of a Shakespearean sonnet, then surely something is going on of a highly significant kind. A problem with the specification condition lies in the identification of the presence of significance. If the hundred letters formed the translation of the sonnet into Urdu, that would also be a significant fact, but one that would be likely to be overlooked by a monoglot English speaker.

It seems reasonable to agree that an act of intelligent design would be expected in some way to fulfill the complexity-specification criterion. What is much more controversial is the assertion that fulfilling that criterion is a sufficient condition for establishing intelligent design. After all, the Darwinian thesis of natural selection specifically suggests a way in which the winnowing effects of environmental sifting and preservation, continuously operating on small random differences and accumulating over long periods of time, can bring about consequences for the adaptation of living entities to their environments that are contingent and complex, and which can be considered to fulfill specification, not in a preset sense, but in the sense that the results are functionally effective to a high degree. It was precisely the ability of evolutionary thinking to explain the appearance of design without needing to invoke the direct intervention of a designer that subverted the arguments of the physico-theologians. On both sides of the argument, however, more is needed than highly generalized argument. What will be persuasive is the careful investigation of particular cases.

Here, the ID theorists turn to a concept that has been discussed extensively by Michael Behe. It is the idea of irreducible complexity, which Behe defines as meaning "a single system composed of several well-matched, interacting parts that contribute to the basic function, wherein the removal of one of the parts causes the system to effectively cease functioning." It is clear that the evolution of such a system, at least if treated as being isolated, could not be explained by the Darwinian notion of gradual incremental development, at each stage of which some further degree of survival efficiency is supposed to be gained. Behe believes that he can identify several such irreducibly complex systems. One of his favorite examples is provided by the cilia that enable organelles to swim. This argument is the molecular counterpart of the difficulties raised soon after the publication of *On the Origin of Species*, concerning how complex organs such as the eye could have evolved. Darwin himself was troubled about this, though later thinking has been able to propose plausible evolutionary pathways, and the fact that eyes have developed several times independently in the course of evolutionary history is suggestive that there is not a real problem. Are matters at the molecular level really that different?

I do not think that Behe has established the irrefutable existence of irreducible complexity. It is not sufficient to consider a single system as if it were simply an isolated system. Evolutionary process is entangled in complex ways, and it is characterized by the improvising cooption of subsystems, developed for one purpose and then appropriated for an entirely different purpose. It would be very difficult to prove that there was no pathway by which what was claimed to be an irreducibly complex structure could have evolved, just as it would be difficult to establish for certain the actual route of its evolutionary development. At the present stage, an open verdict is the utmost that might be claimed. Yet, since the ID claim is of such potential significance, the burden of proof must surely rest with those who assert it. I do not think that burden has been discharged.

If irreducible complexity could be established, it would be a *scientific* achievement of substantial magnitude. In fact, one might think it to be a discovery of Nobel caliber. The frequent criticism made of the ID movement—that it is not at all scientific because its proponents perform no experiments—is unfair.

Historical-observational sciences do not have ready access to direct experimental verification. Their argument must depend upon proposing the best explanation of a complex set of processes, whose details are only fragmentarily known. Darwin's account in the *Origin* has just that character. The ID people are asking an important scientific question. The trouble is that they do not as yet know the answer.

A significant criticism of ID is that its covert theological program is based on a mistaken strategy. The God who is the ordainer of nature can be understood to act as much through the processes of nature as in any other way. There is no distinction that has to be enforced between natural explanation and the work of the Creator. God's will is as much expressed in the evolutionary process that results in the continuous exploration of potentiality as in any supposed events of direct divine intervention. God is present both in the chance and in the necessity of creation.

THEISTIC EVOLUTION

The latter way is exactly how theistic evolution interprets the doctrine of creation. The anthropically fine-tuned necessity of the universe is seen as a manifestation of the will of its Creator, while divine providence is believed to be at work within the contingencies of cosmic history, according to the picture already given of continuous providential action operating within the open grain of nature. To use a musical metaphor employed by Arthur Peacocke, the fugue of creation is not the performance of a fixed score already written in eternity, but it is a grand unfolding improvisation in which Creator and creatures both participate. This collaborative process is made possible by the Creator's kenotic love for creation, according to which creatures are allowed to be themselves and to make themselves. The grand fugue of creation will come to its final resolution, for it is an entirely coherent belief that God will achieve determinate purposes along contingent paths. Meanwhile, the present counterpoint accords with the intentions that the divine Musician has for the shape of its development, even if there is significant creaturely influence on the harmonic details. It was not decreed from all eternity that *Homo sapiens* should appear in our contingent five-fingered specificity, but the emergence of self-conscious beings able to know and worship their Creator was ordained by the divine will.

The balance struck between creatorly guidance and creaturely independence is a delicate matter, not open to clear specification. This is a familiar theological problem, for it is simply the issue of grace and free will, now written cosmically large. We have seen already that acknowledging the independence granted to creatures offers theology some help in its wrestling with the perplexities of disease and disaster. God does not directly will either a murder or an earthquake, but both are allowed to happen in a creation that is something more subtle and flexible than a divine puppet theater. The concept of theistic evolution also helps us understand the apparent imperfections of design observed in evolved beings. Vestigial organs such as the human appendix, serving no currently useful purpose, are simply leftovers from earlier functional necessities, rather than otiose features of an imperfect design. Anyone who has suffered from back pain will be aware that the human skeleton is not perfectly intelligently designed for bipedal motion.

An irritating feature of some contemporary religious discourse is the way in which important words have been hijacked in an attempt to make them the private property of a minority. Like other theists, I am a creationist in the true sense of believing that the divine will is the source of the universe's being and the divine purpose is expressed in its history, but I am certainly not a "creationist" in the curious North American sense of believing in a flat-footed literal interpretation of the first two chapters of Genesis. I believe also in intelligent design, built into the physical fabric of the world and finding its emergent expression through processes that are guided, but not solely determined, by God, but I do not believe that the Creator has chosen to act by episodic acts of direct intervention, as if the great act of creation needed continual reconstructive tinkering in its details.

STUDY QUESTIONS

1. How does Polkinghorne distinguish the classical doctrine of creation from "creation science"? And how does he affirm that the universe is intelligently designed but avoid endorsing the recent intellectual and cultural movement based on intelligent design theory?
2. What are Polkinghorne's criticisms of "scientific reductionism"?
3. Rather than dichotomize chance and necessity, or contingency and law, Polkinghorne describes the universe as exhibiting their "fertile interplay." Explain what he means here and how he thinks this provides important contact between science and theology.
4. Explore Polkinghorne's assertion that there is "deep resonance" between the theories and findings of science, on the one hand, and classical theological themes, on the other. In light of this reading, how would you classify Polkinghorne in terms of the four models of the religion–science relationship discussed in the introduction to this section? Explain.

John Lennox

Reflections on the Intelligent Design Debate

John Lennox (b. 1943) is a mathematician and philosopher at Oxford University. He has lectured widely in academic and popular venues, and has debated scientific naturalists, such as Richard Dawkins. His piece here attempts to sort out the structure and strategy of the various design arguments that have been constructed—arguments about an intelligence outside of, yet operating on, nature. He reviews the various arguments that have been used historically and offers observations about why these arguments are sometimes resisted in the name of science. Students of the debate will find the taxonomy of argument types that he creates to be very helpful. Whatever the strengths and weaknesses of the controversial intelligent design arguments may be, Lennox observes, what is fundamentally at stake is the concept of *information*: whether they provide a vision of reality that can adequately account for its origin and existence.

The intelligent design debate is part of a wider discussion about the relationship of science to religion that is often felt to be one of deep hostility and antagonism as, for instance, encapsulated by Richard Dawkins's recent popular book *The God Delusion*. The inadequacy of this conflict thesis is reflected in the equally recent book *The Language of God* by Francis Collins, director of the Human Genome Project, and has been admirably documented by John Brooke. Indeed, the fact that there are eminent scientists who believe in God and eminent scientists who do not shows that the real conflict is not between science and religion at all but between the diametrically opposed worldviews of materialism and theism, and there are scientists on both sides. The central issue at stake, therefore, is which worldview is supported by

science? It is in that context that I wish to reflect on the matter of intelligent design.

At a 2006 discussion in Oxford, I asked a group of scientists and theologians whether it was legitimate to look for scientific evidence of the involvement of intelligence in the origin of the universe and in its laws of operation. The response was overwhelmingly positive. However, protest was elicited when it was suggested that this question lay behind the notion of intelligent design. The ensuing discussion revealed that now ID is freighted with very different connotations, namely, that of a stealth creationism that concentrates solely on attacking evolutionary biology and is antiscience in spirit.

This semantic shift spawns unfortunate consequences. It obscures the long and distinguished

From "Intelligent Design: Some Critical Reflections on the Current Debate" in *Intelligent Design: William A. Dembski and Michael Ruse in Dialogue*, edited by Robert B. Stewart. Minneapolis: Fortress Press, 2007.

philosophical and theological pedigree of the idea of intelligent causation. It fails to do justice to the divergence of scholarly interpretations of the Genesis account, even among those who ascribe final authority to the biblical record, and shifts the focus away from the fact of creation to the timing of creation. Finally, concentration on evolutionary biology alone can lead to failure to take account of wider evidence for intelligent causation from other sciences such as physics and cosmology and, importantly, from the philosophy of science.

It may be helpful to distinguish between a broader theory of intelligent design that deals with that wider evidence and a narrower theory that concentres on biology. For example, William Dembski says, "Intelligent design is the field of study that investigates signs of intelligence. It identifies those features of objects that reliably signal the action of an intelligent cause" (the broader perspective) whereas Dembski and Michael Ruse define intelligent design as "the hypothesis that in order to explain life it is necessary to suppose the action of an unevolved intelligence" (the narrower perspective).

The term *intelligent design* is intended to separate the recognition of design from the identification of the designer with a view to regarding the first issue as falling within the remit of science. However, this attempt can be misunderstood in that highlighting the first issue has led to accusations of avoiding the second in order to conceal a theistic or even a creationist agenda. Now it is, of course, difficult to think of design at the big-picture level of the universe and life without thinking of God as the putative designer, and many if not most of those people espousing intelligent design are theists. Perhaps it would be best if worldview commitments, since we all have them, were made explicit so that we could then concentrate on the arguments themselves and avoid the all-too-common genetic fallacy: "you believe X only because you are a Y."

The other danger of too forced a separation between the recognition of design and the identification of the designer is the inadvertent communication of the erroneous impression that the former question is strictly scientific whereas the latter, not being strictly scientific, is nonrational and the sciences (of whatever kind) can contribute nothing to it.

Nevertheless, it is surely clear that the two questions are logically separate. If the first Earth visitors to Mars were to see a sequence of thousands of piles of titanium cubes where each pile contained a prime number of cubes and the piles were arranged in ascending order—2, 3, 5, 7, 11, 13, 17, 19, and so forth—they might well conclude that intelligent life had been there before them, but they would not be able to say anything about the identity of the intelligence involved. SETI raises the same issue and is discussed in detail in Dembski's *The Design Inference*.

IS ID SCIENCE?

This question can be somewhat misleading. Consider the parallel questions: Is theism science? Is atheism science? Most people would probably give a negative answer to both. But if we interpret the question as, Is there any scientific evidence for theism or atheism, then the answer might well be positive. For instance, E. O. Wilson holds that "scientific humanism" is "the only worldview compatible with science's growing knowledge of the real world and the laws of nature." Incidentally, atheists of his persuasion can scarcely object to Christians using science to support the New Testament claim that there is evidence of God in the created universe. We deal below with the related question as to whether ID is science in the sense of making testable predictions.

WHY IS ID PERCEIVED TO BE ANTISCIENCE?

For context we need to consider design arguments in general. They come in two levels. Level I consists of arguments that the scientific laws by which the universe operates are designed (in the sense that they are the result of intelligent input) and the phenomena of the universe are the evidence of their fruitfulness. Level II consists of arguments that the phenomena themselves involve direct input from a designing intelligence rather than emerging as a consequence of the (designed) laws.

The arguments at each level fall into two types: Type I are arguments from the history, philosophy, and methodology of science; and Type II are arguments from the detailed results of the sciences—cosmology, physics, biology.

Crucial for our understanding of the ID debate is the observation that Type II arguments split into two very different kinds. Type IIA are arguments that flow from an acceptance of mainstream science; and Type IIB are arguments that involve challenging mainstream science. Obviously IIB arguments are much more controversial than IIA arguments and inevitably attract more (media) attention.

Now, Type IIB arguments are not unimportant—indeed, science in general is kept healthy and advances as a result of being challenged, sometimes even resulting in a paradigm shift that leads to great advance (Galileo's questioning of Aristotle and Wegener's work on plate tectonics, to give but two examples). It is understandable, however, that arguments of Type IIB are not likely to be taken seriously unless they are supported (and preceded) by other arguments of Types I and IIA.

Type I Arguments: The History, Philosophy, and Methodology of Science

At the heart of all science lies the conviction that the universe is rationally intelligible. For Albert Einstein this was something to be wondered at:

> You find it strange that I consider the comprehensibility of the world…as a miracle or as an eternal mystery. Well, a priori, one should expect a chaotic world, which cannot be grasped by the mind in any way…the kind of order created by Newton's theory of gravitation, for example, is wholly different. Even if man proposes the axioms of the theory, the success of such a project presupposes a high degree of ordering of the objective world, and this could not be expected a priori. That is the "miracle" which is being constantly reinforced as our knowledge expands.

Sir Roger Penrose, whose understanding of the depth and subtlety of the relationship between physics and mathematics is unquestioned, writes:

It is hard for me to believe…that such SUPERB theories could have arisen merely by some random natural selection of ideas leaving only the good ones as survivors. The good ones are simply much too good to be the survivors of ideas that have arisen in a random way. There must be, instead, some deep underlying reason for the accord between mathematics and physics.

Now science itself cannot account for this resonance. "Science does not explain the mathematical intelligibility of the physical world, for it is part of science's founding faith that this is so." What does account for it? Our answer will depend not so much on whether we are scientists or not, but on our worldview. From a theistic perspective, the rational intelligibility of the universe makes perfect sense in light of the rationality of God the Creator. Indeed, it would seem that this was the driving force behind the rise of science. Melvin Calvin, Nobel Prize winner in biochemistry, writes:

> As I try to discern the origin of that conviction [that the universe is orderly], I seem to find it in a basic notion discovered 2,000 or 3,000 years ago, and enunciated first in the Western world by the ancient Hebrews: namely that the universe is governed by a single God, and is not the product of the whims of many gods, each governing his own province according to his own laws. This monotheistic view seems to be the historical foundation for modern science.

More recently, Peter Harrison has made a strong case that a dominant feature in the rise of modern science was the Protestant attitude to the interpretation of biblical texts, which spelled an end to the symbolic approach of the Middle Ages. We are not, of course, suggesting that there never has been religious antagonism to science. T.F. Torrance points out that the development of science was often "seriously hindered by the Christian church even when within it the beginnings of modern ideas were taking their rise." He nevertheless supports Melvin Calvin: "In spite of the unfortunate tension that has so often cropped up between the advance of scientific theories and traditional habits of thought in the Church, theology can still claim to have mothered throughout long centuries the basic beliefs and impulses which have given rise especially to modern empirical science, if only through its unflagging faith in the reliability of God the Creator and in the ultimate intelligibility of his creation."

It is sometimes claimed that notions of intelligent design fail to be scientific because they make no testable predictions. But this is surely as far from the truth as it could be if one of the major impulses behind the rise of science is the confirmation of a prediction, based on biblical texts, of the rational intelligibility of the universe. Putting it a different way, Richard Swinburne writes: "Note that I am not postulating a 'God of the gaps,' a god merely to explain the things that science has not yet explained. I am postulating a God to explain why science explains; I do not deny that science explains, but I postulate God to explain why science explains. The very success of science in showing us how deeply ordered the natural world is provides strong grounds for believing that there is an even deeper cause for that order."

The Reductionist Alternative

The alternative, indeed, the only possible option under atheistic assumptions, is ultimately to ascribe the rational intelligibility of the universe to purely material causes. An example of this extreme kind of (ontological or conceptual) reductionism is given by Francis Crick: "You, your joys and your sorrows, your memories and ambitions, your sense of personal identity and free will, are in fact no more than the behaviour of a vast assembly of nerve cells and their associated molecules."[21] The telltale words that reveal such reductionism are "no more than" or "nothing but." Remove them and usually something unobjectionable remains—our memories certainly involve the behavior of nerve cells. Add the words "nothing but" and we have changed a scientific statement into a statement of materialistic belief—and nothing more.

If Crick's thesis is true, we could never know it, as John Polkinghorne shows when he describes such a reductionist program as containing the seeds of its own destruction:

> Ultimately it is suicidal. Not only does it relegate our experiences of beauty, moral obligation, and religious encounter to the epiphenomenal scrap-heap. It also destroys rationality. Thought is replaced by

electro-chemical neural events. Two such events cannot confront each other in rational discourse. They are neither right nor wrong. They simply happen.... The very assertions of the reductionist himself are nothing but blips in the neural network of his brain. The world of rational discourse dissolves into the absurd chatter of firing synapses. Quite frankly, that cannot be right and none of us believes it to be so.

Indeed. None of us believes that a Rembrandt painting is nothing but a distribution of molecules of paint on canvas. Any adequate explanation of the painting both involves the materials and mechanisms involved—the canvas, the paint, and the tools by which it is applied—and the intelligent agent Rembrandt. The fundamental point at issue in intelligent design (in the broad sense) is the same: Is a mechanistic description of the universe adequate as explanation in the fullest sense?

Type IIA Arguments in Physics and Cosmology

A complete explanation of a Rembrandt painting involves both mechanism and agency seen as complementary levels of explanation. They neither compete nor are they the same kind of explanation. Rembrandt will not be found in a minute analysis of the chemistry of the paint: it is rather the organization and execution of the whole painting that points to him. Similarly, when Kepler made his brilliant obser'vational deduction that the planets move in ellipses 'round the sun as focus and Newton later explained these motions in terms of his law of gravity, they did not conclude that their discoveries of law or mechanism obviated God. Kepler said: "The chief aim of all investigations of the external world should be to discover the rational order which has been imposed on it by God, and which he revealed to us in the language of mathematics." Sir John Houghton has captured the idea well: "Our science is God's science. He holds the responsibility for the whole scientific story.... The remarkable order, consistency, reliability and fascinating complexity found in the scientific description of the universe are reflections of the order, consistency, reliability and complexity of God's activity."

Thus, the two explanations, the first in terms of law and mechanism, the second in terms of agency (God), run in parallel and, far from the second inhibiting work on the first, it was, certainly for many of the pioneers of science, their central motivation. Similar things may be said for the fine-tuning arguments from cosmology that have been discussed by many authors. Arno Penzias, who won the Nobel Prize for discovering the microwave background radiation that indicated a finite age to the universe, sums up his position: "Astronomy leads us to a unique event, a universe which was created out of nothing, one with the very delicate balance needed to provide exactly the right conditions required to permit life, and one which has an underlying (one might say 'supernatural') plan." It needs to be emphasized that these design arguments flow out of mainstream science, in this case the Standard Model in cosmology. They do not arise out of ignorance of science but out of knowledge of science.

At the heart of the majority of the fine-tuning arguments lies the conviction that space-time had a beginning some thirteen to fifteen billion years ago, which is of interest in connection with the question mentioned earlier of whether intelligent design theories make testable predictions. For centuries the Genesis account has been available with its magisterial opening words: "In the beginning God created the heavens and the earth." It must be fairly obvious, surely, that if these words had been taken seriously by scientists, the attempt to find scientific evidence for such a beginning, and thus challenge the Aristotelian paradigm of an eternal universe, would have started long before it did. In the event, when evidence began to pile up that the cosmos had a beginning, ironically it was fiercely resisted by prominent scientists (like Sir John Maddox, then editor of *Nature*) because they thought it would give too much leverage to those who believed in creation! It is particularly apposite that it was Penzias who wrote, "The best data we have [concerning the big bang] are exactly what I would have predicted, had I nothing to go on but the five books of Moses, the Psalms and the Bible as a whole." Note the word *predicted*.

TYPE IIA ARGUMENTS IN BIOLOGY

Type IIA arguments are not restricted to physics and cosmology. They are used to question the notion that evolutionary biology demands atheism (a Type IIA anti–intelligent design argument). For instance, chapter 4 of Dawkins's recent book, *The God Delusion*, titled "Why There Is Almost Certainly No God," is devoted to showing, "Far from pointing to a designer, the illusion of design in the living world is explained with far greater economy and with devastating elegance by Darwinian natural selection." For Dawkins, God and evolution are alternative, mutually exclusive explanations. However, he commits the category mistake of failing to distinguish agency from mechanism. Dennett does the same, but in such a way that the reader thinks he has dealt with the matter of agency, when he has not even addressed it: "Love it or hate it, phenomena like this [DNA] exhibit the heart of the power of the Darwinian idea. An impersonal, unreflective, robotic, mindless little scrap of molecular machinery is the ultimate basis of all agency, and hence meaning, and hence consciousness in the universe." Leaving aside the question of whether Dennett's grandiose claim for DNA is true, DNA as a molecular machine may well be impersonal, unreflective, robotic, and mindless. Most machines are. But that says absolutely nothing about whether they have been designed or not—in fact, most machines have been.

To quote Sir John Houghton once more, "The fact that we understand some of the mechanisms of the working of the universe or of living systems does not preclude the existence of a designer, any more than the possession of insight into the processes by which a watch has been put together, however automatic these processes may appear, implies there can be no watchmaker."

On this view, the evolutionary viewpoint, far from invalidating inference to intelligent origin, simply backs it up one level—from primary to secondary causation. On seeing a car for the first time, a person might suppose that it is made directly by humans, only later to discover it is made in a robotic factory by robots which, in turn, were made by machines made by humans. It was not the inference to intelligent origin that was wrong but the concept of the nature of the implementation of that intelligence. Direct human activity was not seen in the factory because it is the existence of the factory itself that is the product of that activity.

In this vein Charles Kingsley wrote to Darwin suggesting that his theory of natural selection provided "just as noble a conception of Deity, to believe that He created primal forms capable of self-development…as to believe that He required a fresh act of intervention to supply the lacunas which He Himself had made." Though Kingsley was not a scientist, Darwin was so impressed by his words that he cited them in the second edition of *On the Origin of Species*, possibly with an eye to influencing his more skeptical clerical readers.

The fine-tuning arguments from physics and cosmology are, of course, independent of evolutionary theory, yet it is important to note that the theory demands the existence of a fine-tuned universe producing exactly the right kind of materials and operating according to complex laws that are consistent with supporting life. Such anthropic fruitfulness could then be regarded as evidence of creative intelligent activity. Keith Ward speaks of evolution as "having been chosen by a rational agent for the sake of some good that it, and perhaps it alone, makes possible." John Polkinghorne speaks of creation as "realising the inbuilt potentiality with which the Creator has endowed it." Theistic evolution has thus commended itself to many scientists, from Asa Gray and Richard Owen in Darwin's day to the present.

Even the late Stephen Jay Gould thought that regarding Darwinism as necessarily atheistic was going beyond the evidence: "Either half of my colleagues are enormously stupid, or else the science of Darwinism is fully compatible with conventional religious beliefs—and equally compatible with atheism." However, Dawkins and Dennett think not. Dennett regards Darwin's idea as a kind of corrosive acid, which "threatens to destroy all pre-Darwinian views of the world; in that, instead of the universe's matter being a product of mind, the minds in the universe are a product of matter. They are nothing more than the results of an undirected, mindless, purposeless process." He claims that "natural selection somehow designs without either itself being designed or having any purpose in view" characterizing it as "mindless, motiveless, mechanicity." In the language of Aristotle, Dennett's claim is that it is the very nature of the efficient cause (evolution) that rules out the existence of a final cause (divine intention).

TYPE IIB ARGUMENTS IN BIOLOGY

It is, in part, this kind of assertion that leads to the Type IIB question whether the evolutionary mechanism will bear all the weight that is put on it, for instance, by Richard Dawkins: "Natural selection, the blind, unconscious, automatic process which Darwin discovered, and which we now know is the explanation for the existence and apparently purposeful form of all life, has no purpose in mind."

Does natural selection really account for the existence of life as distinct from its variations? Surely it cannot be quite so straightforward for the simple reason that, until life exists, there is no mutating replicator on which natural selection can operate. Theodosius Dobzhansky, one of the pioneers of evolutionary biology, who said that "nothing makes sense in biology except in light of evolution," also said that "prebiological evolution is a contradiction in terms."

This question of what accounts for life's existence is at the heart of the (narrower) ID debate, a debate that received an unexpected stimulus when eminent philosopher Antony Flew gave as the reason for his conversion to theism after over fifty years of atheism that the investigation of DNA by biologists "has shown, by the almost unbelievable complexity of the arrangements which are needed to produce life, that intelligence must have been involved.…It has become inordinately difficult even to begin to think about constructing a naturalistic theory of the evolution of that first reproducing organism."

It will be objected that this is an antiscientific God-of-the-gaps solution of the sort "there is no plausible material process for X, therefore X must involve the input of intelligence." We must take this objection seriously, though we first of all record a warning by an expert on the origin of life, Nobel laureate Robert Laughlin, of the danger of an evolution of the gaps:

Evolution by natural selection which Darwin conceived as a great theory has lately come to function as an anti-theory called upon to cover up embarrassing experimental shortcomings and legitimize findings that are at worst not even wrong. Your protein defies the laws of mass action—evolution did it! Your complicated mess of chemical reactions turns into a chicken—evolution did it! The human brain works on logical principles no computer can emulate—evolution is the cause!

The origin of life has not been observed, so scientists use the historical methods appropriate to the investigation of unrepeatable past events and make inferences to the best explanation. It is therefore clear how an evolution-of-the-gaps could be just as metaphysically motivated for an incautious atheist as a God-of-the-gaps could be for an incautious theist. For materialists there simply must eventually be a solution in terms of material processes alone, so they might as well call it evolution, filling in the details as they are found—for they must be found.

Now many scientists who are theists and all who are atheists insist that science restricts its explanation to material processes. They therefore reject Level II arguments. The theists among them often use Level I arguments for the existence of God. To warn of the dangers of Level II God-of-the-gaps arguments, they might cite Newton's letter in which he said that his law of gravitation could explain the motion of planets around the sun but not their motion around their own axes, which needed a "divine arm." Progress in physics, they might well add, has removed the need for this kind of divine intervention and has led us to a seamless scientific understanding of the evolution of the cosmos in terms of material processes involving cause and effect, chance and necessity. There are no singularities—except (for many) at the beginning. We can see all of this cosmic development as the fruit of mathematical and physical laws that express the Creator's mind. So why can the same not hold for the origin of life?

As a scientist, the author takes such reasoning and the concomitant charge of intellectual laziness that is often leveled at God-of-the-gaps-type arguments very seriously indeed but, nevertheless, thinks there is more to be said both from a scientific and from a theological perspective. Let us take the theological

perspective first. If there is a God who does anything in the world indirectly, then, as Alvin Plantinga argues, logic would tell us that God must do something directly. What is that direct something? Most theists would agree that it was causing the universe to exist, creating it originally, and maintaining it throughout its history. The initial act of creation would then appear as a singularity to any scientific analysis based on purely material processes.

Cosmology speaks of precisely such a singularity and is not embarrassed to do so. Its understanding of physics leads back to the big bang singularity where, according to Stephen Hawking, "the laws of physics break down." Once we admit that God has acted directly at least once in the past to create the universe, what is there in principle to prevent God's acting directly more than once, whether in the past or in the future? For nature's laws are not independent of God. From a Level I perspective, they are mathematical formulations of the regularities with which God has endowed the physical universe and so, as C. S. Lewis has argued, it would be absurd to think that they constrained God so that the Divine could never do anything special: "Could we not sensibly conclude, for example, that God created life, or human life, or something else specially?"

Apparently not, says Paul Davies: "There's no need to invoke anything supernatural in the origins of the universe or of life. I have never liked the idea of divine tinkering: for me it is much more inspiring to believe that a set of mathematical laws can be so clever as to bring all these things into being." So Davies assumes that if God created life specially, it would demean God into a kind of cosmic magician who constantly interferes with the universe. However, this reaction is surely unwarranted. After all, if the claim that God created and upholds the universe is not demeaning, why should the claim that God created life, especially if human life bears the Divine image, be demeaning?

1. It is not as if claims were being made (from a biblical perspective, now) that God was constantly tinkering with the universe. For instance, in the Genesis creation narrative it is interesting that the number of special commandments—"And God said..." is relatively small and the series

of such commandments (however long it took) came to an end. Indeed, the surprise is how few such special actions of God are claimed in the Bible as a whole.

2. To say that the universe and life have been brought into existence by mathematical laws is astonishing. Apart from begging the question of where the laws came from, such laws are abstract mathematical formulations that by their very nature (laws are not material), far from bringing anything into existence, cannot even cause anything. Newton's laws of motion will tell you a billiard ball's trajectory once it has been hit and the fact that it will remain at rest if it is never hit—but the laws will never move the ball. Or, more simply, $2 + 2 = 4$, but this fact has never put any money in anyone's pocket.

3. Davies says that he does not "like the idea of divine tinkering" to which one might respond, first, that it is perhaps unwise to decide the nature of reality by our likes or dislikes but rather on the basis of evidence and, second, that the pejorative word *tinkering* scarcely does justice to a God who has the power to create the universe and life.

David Hume has persuaded many scientists that special activity by God (miracle) involves a breaking of the laws of nature and is therefore ruled out *a priori* as scientifically impossible. However, C. S. Lewis and others have shown that Hume's objection involves the misunderstanding of the nature of law mentioned in my second point above. The laws are a description of what normally happens in the universe, but God the Creator can do something special directly without breaking the laws. For example, at the heart of Christianity is the claim that Jesus was raised from the dead by a direct injection of the power of God. It is noteworthy that a mathematical physicist of the eminence of Sir John Polkinghorne does not think that his position as a scientist is compromised by his belief in the resurrection of Jesus, even though, from the perspective of explanation in terms of unguided material processes, the resurrection is a singularity.

Thus, scientists who are Christians would appear to be committed to at least two singularities, (1) creation itself, the beginning of space-time, and (2) the resurrection of Jesus within space-time. There is therefore, surely, no in-principle reason not to consider the origin of life as a potential third singularity, provided, of course, that the evidence warrants it.

This is the key question. However, since many scientists will feel that we have long since left the realm of science for fairyland, it is important first to discuss what kind of scientific evidence we might expect if the origin of life has a supernatural dimension and is not explicable solely in terms of purely material processes.

First, we should expect that explanations in terms of material processes fail at certain points. This logical observation, however, is the focus of a major objection, hinted at earlier: is it not an intellectually lazy, antiscientific attitude simply to give up the attempt at material explanation after the first few tries and say God did it?

Our response is that it might well be. However, pure mathematics has something to teach us here. If mathematicians have tried to prove a conjecture in pure mathematics for a long time, like the anciently posed task of trisecting an angle with straightedge and compasses, and they fail, there will come a time when they will try to mount an attack in the opposite direction and try to *prove* that the conjecture is false. This was done after many centuries in the case of angle trisection by Pierre Wantzel in 1836. Consequently, no one tries to do it any more.

Now, origin-of-life research burst on the world in 1953 with the announcement of the results of the Miller-Urey experiment—the production of some of the amino acid building blocks of protein in a simulated primeval soup bombarded by electricity. However, over the subsequent fifty-four years, it has been realized that the real problem was not obtaining the building blocks of life (although that problem is still with us) but getting those building blocks in the right order as revealed by the genetic code whose discovery ranks as perhaps the greatest ever scientific achievement.

Subsequent research has produced several emergent and self-organizing scenarios that, although of great interest, seem rather to highlight and intensify this problem rather than solve it, as is, somewhat ironically, very well expressed by Paul Davies:

> Life is actually *not* an example of *self*-organisation. Life is in fact *specified*, i.e. genetically directed, organisation. Living things are instructed by the genetic software encoded in their DNA (or RNA). Convection cells form spontaneously by self-organisation. There is no gene for a convection cell. The source of order is not encoded in software; it can instead be traced to the boundary conditions in the fluid....In other words, a convection cell's order is imposed *externally*, from the system's environment. By contrast, the order of a living cell derives from *internal* control....The theory of self-organisation as yet gives no clue how the transition is to be made between spontaneous, or self-induced organisation—which in even the most elaborate non-biological examples still involves relatively simple structures—and the highly complex, information-based, genetic organisation of living things.

This brings us to the meat of the problem—to explain the genesis of the specified computer-language-like structure of DNA that Dennett calls a "mindless scrap of molecular machinery." Now it may justifiably be said that fifty-four years is not a very long time in science. So why not simply keep on trying to establish the truth of the conjecture that the origin of biological information is a purely material process and not give in to a God-of-the-gaps thinking? Well, that might be the thing to do provided that, to use mathematical terminology, the conjecture is not provably false.

But is this not to fall afoul of the "impossibility of proving a negative" dictum? Not in principle, as is seen from my mathematical example. More importantly, physics gives us more relevant examples. Take, for instance, the law of conservation of energy that prohibits the existence of certain material things, such as perpetual-motion machines. It is therefore pointless to argue that, although people have failed to construct perpetual-motion machines in the past, it would be against the spirit of science to give up on the construction of such a machine. Physics itself says they are impossible constructions. Any machine will use more energy than it produces.

Of immediate relevance to our discussion are the following parallel observations. The first is due to a pioneer of information theory, Leonard Brillouin: "A machine does not create any new information, but it performs a very valuable transformation of known information." The second comes from the brilliant mathematician Kurt Gödel, who proved certain far-reaching impossibility theorems in mathematics, like the incompleteness of arithmetic:

> The complexity of living bodies has to be present in the material [from which they are derived] or in the laws [governing their formation]. In particular, the materials forming the organs, if they are governed by mechanical laws, have to be of the same order of complexity as the living body....More generally, Gödel believes [Gödel sometimes expressed himself in the third person] that mechanism in biology is a prejudice of our time which will be disproved. In this case, one disproval, in Gödel's opinion, will consist in a mathematical theorem to the effect that the formation within geological times of a human body by the laws of physics (or any other laws of a similar nature), starting from a random distribution of the elementary particles and the field, is as unlikely as the separation by chance of the atmosphere into its components.

Nobel Laureate Sir Peter Medawar thought there might be some kind of law of conservation of information and, more recently, William Dembski argues for a nondeterministic law of conservation of information along the lines suggested by Brillouin to the effect that, although natural processes (involving only chance and necessity) can effectively transmit complex specified information, they cannot generate it so that information is not reducible to physics and chemistry.

Now there is clearly a great deal at stake here—in particular a radical challenge to materialistic philosophy and, if we add in the fact that the concept of information, especially information with a semantic dimension, is notoriously difficult to define, it is not surprising that the question of the validity of such a law of conservation of information is still a topic of hot debate. Making due allowance for this fact, however, just as we can test the plausibility of the law of conservation of energy by finding the energy flaw in a putative perpetual-motion machine, we can test the plausibility of a theory of information conservation. If information is conserved in some meaningful sense, then we would expect that any scenario that claimed to get information for free (by chance and necessity) was flawed and that information had to be smuggled in somewhere. That seems to be exactly what is found in all scenarios hitherto offered, for instance, by Dawkins and others.

To put it another way, there seem to be two kinds of gaps: bad gaps and good gaps. The bad gaps are those that are targeted in God-of-the-gaps accusations, those that science will eventually fill. The good gaps are those that are revealed by science, such as the information gap discussed just now. We emphasize that it is science that reveals the good gaps, and not theology. However, theology can help illuminate where they are likely to be (witness creation). We would therefore argue that, just as the beginning of space-time is a good gap in the explanatory power of physics, the origin of life is a good gap in the explanatory power of molecular biology. Biology is not reducible to physics and chemistry.

John Polkinghorne also suggests a similar differentiation:

We must never rest content with a discussion in such soft-focus that it never begins to engage our intuitions about God's action with our knowledge of physical process.... If the physical world is really open, and top-down intentional causality operates within it, there must be intrinsic "gaps" ("an envelope of possibility") in the bottom-up account of nature to make room for intentional causality.... We are unashamedly "people of the gaps" in this intrinsic sense and there is nothing unfitting in a "God of the gaps" in this sense either.

These arguments amplify work by scientist and philosopher Michael Polanyi, who asks us to think of the various levels of process involved in constructing an office building with bricks. First, there is the process of extracting the raw materials out of which the bricks have to be made. Then there are the successively higher levels of making the bricks—they do not make themselves; bricklaying—the bricks do not self-assemble; designing the building—it does not design itself; and planning the town in which the building is to be built—it does not organize itself. Each level has its own rules. The laws of physics and chemistry govern the raw material of the bricks; technology prescribes the art of brickmaking; architecture

teaches the builders; and the architects are controlled by the town planners. Each level is controlled by the level above. But the reverse is not true. The laws of a higher level cannot be derived from the laws of a lower level; although what can be done at a higher level will, of course, depend on the lower levels. For example, if the bricks are not strong, there will be a limit on the height of the building that can safely be built with them.

The same is true of a printed page. As Nobel laureate Roger Sperry has said: "The meaning of the message is not to be found in the physics and chemistry of the paper and ink." We are suggesting here that information and intelligence are fundamental to the existence of the universe and life and, far from being the end-products of an unguided natural process starting with mass energy, they were involved from the very beginning. Interestingly, Paul Davies writes,

The increasing application of the information concept to nature has prompted a curious conjecture. Normally we think of the world as composed of simple, clod-like, material particles, and information as a derived phenomenon attached to special, organised states of matter. But maybe it is the other way around: perhaps the universe is really a frolic of primal information, and material objects a complex secondary manifestation.

However, the proposal that information be regarded as a fundamental quantity has been around for centuries. "In the beginning was the Word...all things were made by him" wrote John, the author of the fourth gospel. The Greek for "Word" is *Logos*, a term used by Stoic philosophers for the rational principle behind the universe and subsequently invested with additional meaning by Christians to describe the Second Person of the Trinity. The term *Word* itself conveys to us notions of command, code, communication, meaning, and thus information, as well as the creative power needed to realise what was specified by that information. The Word, therefore, is more fundamental than mass energy. Mass energy belongs to the category of the created. The Word does not.

It is surely very striking indeed that at the heart of the biblical analysis of the creative acts, so readily dismissed by many, we find the very concept which science has shown to be of paramount importance—the concept of information. Perhaps if these profound biblical ideas had been taken more seriously by scientists they would have concluded more rapidly that information is important. Just as with the fact of the beginning, a scientific prediction could have been theologically informed in this way.

I have spent a relatively long time on these arguments of Type IIB, not because they are more important—although I believe that the last point is of immense significance—but because they are the most controversial and the most misunderstood. I would conclude, however, by recalling once more that the main arguments to intelligent causation are of Types I and IIA. The evidence of God is to be seen mainly in the things that we do understand and not in the things we don't. If those of us who favor such arguments keep this perspective, we can then evaluate and use some arguments of Type IIB without giving the impression that all our eggs are in the God-of-the-Bad-Gaps basket.

STUDY QUESTIONS

1. As clearly as you can, describe Lennox's classificatory scheme for sorting out the different types of design arguments.
2. Lennox divides design arguments into one class that reflects on the history, philosophy, and methodology of science and another class that deals with specific findings within science in order to conclude that there is an Intelligence behind the universe. Which scientific disciplines are involved? Discuss and assess.
3. In the eighteenth century, the God-of-the-gaps had to retreat from nature as science advanced more explanations for natural phenomena. Explore how contemporary ID theory could be seen as a reiteration of a God-of-the-gaps fallacy of offering agency explanations for matters eventually covered by mechanistic explanations.
4. Explore the claim that the concept of information is one of the most important points of contact between science and theology.

SUGGESTED READING

Austin, William H. *The Relevance of Natural Science to Theology*. London: Macmillan, 1976.

Ayala, Francisco. *Darwin's Gift to Science and Religion*. Washington, D.C.: Joseph Henry Press, 2007.

Babour, Ian G., ed. *Science and Religion: New Perspectives on the Dialogue*. New York: Harper and Row, 1968.

———, ed. *Religion in an Age of Science*. San Francisco, Calif.: Harper and Row, 1990.

Behe, Michael. *Darwin's Black Box*. New York: Touchstone, 1996.

Brooke, John Hedley. *Science and Religion*. Cambridge: Cambridge University Press, 1991.

Clayton, Philip, ed. *The Oxford Handbook of Religion and Science*. New York: Oxford University Press, 2006.

Collins, Francis. *The Language of God: A Scientist Presents Evidence for Belief*. New York: Free Press, 2006.

Davies, Paul. *God and the New Physics*. New York: Simon and Schuster, 1983.

Dawkins, Richard. *The God Delusion*. Boston: Houghton Mifflin, 2006.

———. *Unweaving the Rainbow: Science, Delusion, and the Appetite for Wonder*. Boston: Houghton Mifflin, 1998.

Dembski, William. *The Design Inference: Eliminating Chance Through Small Probabilities*. Cambridge, England: Cambridge University Press, 1998.

Dennett, Daniel. *Breaking the Spell: Religion as a Natural Phenomenon*. New York: Viking Press, 2006.

Dillenberger, John. *Protestant Thought and Natural Science*. New York: Doubleday, 1960.

Flew, Antony. *There Is a God: How the World's Most Notorious Atheist Changed His Mind*. New York: Harper-Collins, 2007.

Gingerich, Owen. *God's Universe*. Cambridge, Mass.: Harvard University Press, 2006.

Gould, Stephen Jay. *Rocks of Ages: Science and Religion in the Fullness of Life*. New York: Ballantine Books, 1999.

Hawking, Steven. *A Brief History of Time*. New York: Bantam, 1988.

Hempel, Carl. *Philosophy of Natural Science*. Englewood Cliffs, N.J.: Prentice-Hall, 1966.

Mascall, E. L. *Christian Theology and Natural Science*. London: Oxford University Press, 1979.

Murphy, Nancey. *Theology in the Age of Scientific Reasoning*. Ithaca, N.Y.: Cornell University Press, 1990.

O'Connor, Daniel, and Francis Oakley, eds. *Creation: The Impact of an Idea*. New York: Scribners, 1969.

Peacocke, Arthur. *Theology for a Scientific Age: Being and Becoming—Natural, Divine, and Human*. Minneapolis, Minn.: Fortress Press, 1993.

Polkinghome, John. *The Way the World Is*. Grand Rapids, Mich.: William B. Eerdmans, 1983.

——. *Reason and Reality: The Relationship Between Science and Theology*. Philadelphia: Trinity Press International, 1991.

——. *Belief in God in an Age of Science*. New Haven, Conn.: Yale University Press, 1998.

——. *Science and Theology: An Introduction*. London: SPCK; Minneapolis, Minn.: Fortress Press, 1998.

Popper, Karl. *Conjectures and Refutations*. New York: Harper and Row, 1963.

Rolston, Holmes. *Science and Religion: A Critical Survey*. New York: Random House, 1987.

Ruse, Michael. *Can a Darwinian Be a Christian: The Relationship Between Science and Religion*. Cambridge, England: Cambridge University Press, 2001.

——. *Darwinism and Its Discontents*. Cambridge, England: Cambridge University Press, 2008.

Stegner, Victor. *God: The Failed Hypothesis*. Amherst, N.Y.: Prometheus Press, 2007.

Wilson, David B., ed., with Warren D. Dolphin. *Did the Devil Make Darwin Do It? Modern Perspectives on the Creation–Evolution Controversy*. Ames, Iowa: Iowa State University Press, 1983.

PART THIRTEEN

Religious Diversity

Diversity, which stands as a hallmark of contemporary culture, is no less significant in religion than elsewhere. Religions engage in practices and rituals, many similar but some different, such as using candles, burning incense, washing feet, handling prayer beads, raising prayer flags, making pilgrimages, dancing, donating to the poor, burning faux money for ancestors, and meditating. Of particular interest to philosophers of religion are the beliefs and doctrines that the diverse religions hold. Even a cursory analysis shows that the religions of the world make both compatible and incompatible claims. For example, Christians maintain that there is a personal trinitarian God; Muslims and Jews are strict monotheists; Vedantic Hindus believe that Ultimate Reality lacks any distinctions, whereas other Hindus are polytheistic; and Theravada Buddhists do not believe in a god at all. Some people believe that salvation/liberation is achieved through divine forgiveness of sins, others by keeping some sort of law, others by removing bad karma through benevolent acts, and still others by yogic practice and meditation. But if religions make incompatible statements about the nature of reality and about what is necessary to achieve salvation or liberation, how are we to understand those statements? In particular, can one discuss religion in terms of truth, and what are the implications of doing so?

Religious Exclusivism

The problem of religious diversity is often discussed in terms of three categories: *exclusivism*, *inclusivism*, and *pluralism*. Exclusivists argue that all religions express some important truths (especially moral truths about how to live); otherwise they would not have persisted. However, basic and central claims about the nature of God or Reality and salvation/liberation are not only different in the various religions but at points are so incompatible that all their claims cannot possibly be true. Consequently, one set of claims about religious reality (and hence the religion that incorporates that set) is more true than others; it more correctly describes the nature of Reality and the way of salvation or liberation. Further, exclusivists hold that to achieve salvation/

573

liberation, it is essential that individuals know these salvific truths so that they can apply them to their own lives.

For example, Karl Barth does not deny that religions other than Christianity contain truths and high moral values, or that their adherents can be moral or sincere. But he believes that, because of the uniqueness of Jesus, Christianity is the locus of true religion. He does not want to call Christianity a "religion," however, because he sees religions as human attempts to reach and understand God, rather than the proper course of God's revealing himself to us.

In our second selection, Paul Griffiths argues that whatever the religion—whether Christianity, Buddhism, or another—from the perspective of that religion, its religious beliefs are unique. He points to five factors that strengthen this claim: the rules that govern community life, the beliefs that delineate the life of the community, the doctrines that define community boundaries and separate orthodox from heterodox beliefs, the beliefs that shape the community by being taught to its members, and the beliefs that express salvifically significant truths. To water down these beliefs and doctrines does a disservice to the integrity of the religion. To be treated authentically, religions must have their diverse beliefs acknowledged and understood.

Critics of exclusivism wonder how God could justly hold people accountable if they have never had access to the saving or liberating knowledge afforded to the advantaged group. It would seem that God would not so exclusively bind his revelation of the way to salvation/liberation to a particular time or place but would make it available to everyone, especially through each person's own religious tradition. In effect, exclusivism constitutes a form of arrogance.

Exclusivists correctly note, however, that the fact that many people hold a belief does not imply that what they believe is true. Hence, the recognition that various people have differing religious beliefs should not compel any individuals to abandon their own doctrines, for those doctrines function centrally in their respective religious communities. Indeed, as Alvin Plantinga notes, the arrogance that critics see in exclusivism can also be found in the same critics who hold that exclusivists are mistaken and their views unjustified.

Religious Inclusivism

Inclusivists, like Karl Rahner, whose views are expressed in the third selection, agree with exclusivists that the absolute provision for salvation is revealed in one religion. From a Christian perspective, God has acted in the life and death of Jesus in a particular way that makes salvation available for all. For Muslims, God revealed himself uniquely and finally in revelations to Mohammed. At the same time, since God may reveal himself or act graciously in diverse ways in a variety of places and times, people can encounter God and receive God's grace in diverse religions. Christianity had a prehistory in the ancient Jewish culture. The New Testament says that in these pre-Christian times people were saved by their faith, despite their ignorance of what was to come. In effect, adherents of other religions can be saved/liberated because God has placed his moral law in their religious traditions. Similarly, Islam has a prehistory; a line of prophets delineated God's message, but this was incomplete until the revelations to Mohammed.

Buddhists like the Dalai Lama hold that adherents of other religions can achieve the self-transformation necessary for happiness and moral living through their particular religious practices. But the achievement of mindfulness and emptiness ultimately necessary for entrance into nirvana is found only in the Buddha's teachings. This view is developed in the first selection by the Dalai Lama. In short, although what is ultimately necessary for salvation or liberation—forgiveness of sins through the death of Christ, acceptance by God through obedience to the five pillars, cultivation of emptiness through the Eightfold Noble Path—is specified by the true religion, persons can achieve salvation/liberation without knowing anything about the religion or practices that embody the objective provision for salvation. Thus, using Rahner's terminology, someone from another religious faith might be an "anonymous Christian" or an "anonymous Muslim" or an "anonymous Buddhist" in that he or she is moving along the correct path without knowing he or she is doing so.

Critics of inclusivism ask why, if salvation/liberation can occur apart from knowledge of or incorporation into a particular religious tradition, one has to use concepts and ideas from that tradition to interpret their experience. Thus, questions are raised about the term "anonymous Christians." Isn't calling someone an anonymous X from a particular perspective a bald piece of ethnocentrism? Furthermore, if individuals can achieve salvation/liberation in another tradition, what incentive is there for evangelization or conversion? It would seem not only to be unnecessary but to create unnecessary tension and conflict between the various religions. Rahner replies that having the correct belief is significant and beneficial in this life and that this justifies evangelization. There are intrinsic, lasting benefits to be found in practicing the true religion.

RELIGIOUS PLURALISM

Pluralists like John Hick, whose views are presented in the fourth selection, disagree with both exclusivists and inclusivists: no single religion is true. Rather, many paths lead to the goal of salvation/liberation. Each religion specifies its own unique way that, for its adherents, can bring them release from the human predicament, self-transformation, and contact with the Real. Religions have different accounts of the Real because they have differing perspectives, conceptual backgrounds, and traditions. Hick recalls the old Indian story of the blind men and the elephant. Each man felt a different part of the elephant's body and reported that what was before him was a great pillar, a great snake, a sharp plough, etc. Each was correct in a way, from his own perspective. So likewise, we are blind concerning the Real and hence cannot give an unbiased description or account of it; we can only project from our own experience what it might be like or seem to be for us.

In effect, individual conceptions of the Real are human projections, affecting the way the Real is perceived or understood by various individuals and traditions. Any attempt to give a definitive account must be demythologized. Of course, religious claims must have checks and balances; not just anything counts as a religion. But these checks are provided for when, over the centuries, the religious tradition has produced profound scriptures, impressive intellectual systems, new visions of human existence, and saintly lives.

Critics of pluralism wonder how such incompatible religious conceptions of God or the Real can all be true. Some pluralists, who are religious nonrealists, respond that since religions do not make truth claims, diverse claims present no problem; religion's sole concern is to make life meaningful, not to make truth claims. Other pluralists hold that religious concepts express not the Real itself, but our attempt to understand the Real. These concepts express how the Real appears to us and hence should not be taken as literally descriptive of it. Moreover, they cannot be contradictory, for how I perceive something may differ from how another experiences the same thing, but our claims do not conflict with one another because the language used only talks about our experience. But, the objection goes, if we have no clear concept of the Real, what distinguishes religious belief from agnosticism? Indeed, what would it mean to claim that the Real exists? It would seem that all discussion of the Real would have to be abandoned on the same grounds the pluralists used to reject traditional religious conceptions of God and the transcendent.

Is It Possible to Assess Religions?

If religions make truth claims, a final issue concerns how one might assess religious systems. The criteria employed must be carefully chosen so that they do not bias the evaluation in favor of any one religion. Some philosophers, like Keith Yandell and Harold Netland, suggest some cross-cultural criteria that may be employed in such an assessment. For example, the propositions essential to a religion must be consistent with one another and be compatible with what exists and with other well-established data; the religion must deliver on the solutions to the problems that it promises to solve; and the religion should account for and explain a great deal of human experience. Other philosophers, like Gavin D'Costa, question such a possibility. For one thing, the appeal to rational consistency seems to beg the question in favor of "rational" over "nonrational" religions (such as Zen Buddhism).

Whatever position we take on the matter of religious diversity, we need to attempt to understand and appreciate the religious claims made by others before raising questions about the truth of religious beliefs. It is also important to distinguish between the question of whether particular religious claims are true and the question of whether we should espouse religious tolerance. Engaging in the evaluation of claims should never interfere with the acceptance of others as valuable human persons or with the desire to enter into genuine dialogue with them. At the same time, dialogue can be seriously undertaken when one attends to the views of others and seeks to understand their unique contributions to the discussion.

Dalai Lama

Buddhism and Other Religions

Responding to questions about the relation between Buddhism and other religious, the Dalai Lama (b. 1940) affirms that real differences exist between the various world religions, so that they cannot be syncretized. People in different religions not only have different techniques and practices but believe in different liberations or salvations. What matters are not these differences, but rather the fact that all religions aim at transforming persons so that they can achieve permanent human happiness. Since the practice of religion is highly personal, the religion that is suitable for one person may not be suitable for another. The important thing is that persons practice a religion that is effective for their spiritual development. At the same time, the Dalai Lama believes that Buddhism has techniques and ideas that may enrich other religions, and that Buddhist liberation can only come through the practice of Buddhism.

QUESTIONER: Do you see any possibility of an integration of Christianity and Buddhism in the West? An overall religion for Western society?

HIS HOLINESS: It depends upon what you mean by integration. If you mean by this the possibility of the integration of Buddhism and Christianity within a society, where they co-exist side by side, then I would answer affirmatively. If, however, your view of integration envisions all of society following some sort of composite religion which is neither pure Buddhism nor pure Christianity, then I would have to consider this form of integration implausible.

It is, of course, quite possible for a country to be predominantly Christian, and yet that some of the people of that country choose to follow Buddhism. I think it is quite possible that a person who is basically a Christian, who accepts the idea of a God, who believes in God, could at the same time incorporate certain Buddhist ideas and techniques into his or her practice. The teaching of love, compassion, and kindness are present in Christianity and also in Buddhism. Particularly in the Bodhisattva vehicle there are many techniques which focus on developing compassion, kindness, etc. These are things which can be practiced at the same time by Christians and by Buddhists. While remaining committed to Christianity, it is quite conceivable that a person may choose to undergo training in meditation, concentration, and one-

From Dalai Lama, *Answers*, edited by José Ignacio Cabezón (Ithaca, N.Y.: Snow Lion Pub., 1988).

pointedness of mind, that, while remaining a Christian, one may choose to practice Buddhist ideas. This is another possibility and very viable kind of integration.

QUESTIONER: Is there any conflict between the Buddhist teachings and the idea of a creator God who exists independently from us?

HIS HOLINESS: If we view the world's religions from the widest possible viewpoint, and examine their ultimate goal, we find that all of the major world religions, whether Christianity or Islam, Hinduism or Buddhism, are directed to the achievement of permanent human happiness. They are all directed toward that goal. All religions emphasize the fact that the true follower must be honest and gentle, in other words, that a truly religious person must always strive to be a better human being. To this end, the different world's religions teach different doctrines which will help transform the person. In this regard, all religions are the same, there is no conflict. This is something we must emphasize. We must consider the question of religious diversity from this viewpoint. And when we do, we can find no conflict.

Now from the philosophical point of view, the theory that God is the creator, is almighty and permanent, is in contradiction to the Buddhist teachings. From this point of view there is disagreement. For Buddhists, the universe has no first cause and hence no creator, nor can there be such a thing as a permanent, primordially pure being. So, of course, doctrinally, there is conflict. The views are opposite to one another. But if we consider the purpose of these different philosophies, then we see that they are the same. This is my belief.

Different kinds of food have different tastes: one may be very hot, one may be very sour, and one very sweet. They are opposite tastes, they conflict. But whether a dish is concocted to taste sweet, sour, or hot, it is nonetheless made in this way so as to taste good. Some people prefer very spicy hot foods with a lot of chili peppers. Many Indians and Tibetans have a liking for such dishes. Others are very fond of bland-tasting foods. It is a wonderful thing to have variety. It is an expression of individuality; it is a personal thing.

Likewise, the variety of the different world religious philosophies is a very useful and beautiful thing. For certain people, the idea of God as creator and of everything depending on his will is beneficial and soothing, and so for that person such a doctrine is worthwhile For someone else, the idea that there is no creator, that ultimately, one is oneself the creator—in that everything depends upon oneself—is more appropriate. For certain people, it may be a more effective method of spiritual growth, it may be more beneficial. For such persons, this idea is better and for the other type of person, the other idea is more suitable. You see, there is no conflict, no problem. This is my belief.

Now conflicting doctrines are something which is not unknown even within Buddhism itself. The Mādhymikas and Cittamātrins, two Buddhist philosophical subschools, accept the theory of emptiness. The Vaibhāṣikas and Sautrāntikas, two others, accept another theory, the theory of selflessness, which, strictly speaking, is not the same as the doctrine of emptiness as posited by the two higher schools. So there exists this difference, some schools accepting the emptiness of phenomena and others not....

So you see, conflict in the philosophical field is nothing to be surprised at. It exists even within Buddhism itself....

QUESTIONER: It is generally said that teachers of other religions, no matter how great, cannot attain liberation without turning to the Buddhist path. Now suppose that there is a great teacher, say he is a Śaivite, and suppose he upholds very strict discipline and is totally dedicated to other people all of the time, always giving of himself. Is this person, simply because he follows Śiva, incapable of attaining liberation, and if so, what can be done to help him?

HIS HOLINESS: During the Buddha's own time, there were many non-Buddhist teachers whom the

Buddha could not help, for whom he could do nothing. So he just let them be.

The Buddha Śākyamuni was an extraordinary being, he was the manifestation (nirmānakāya), the physical appearance, of an already enlightened being. But while some people recognized him as a Buddha, others regarded him as a black magician with strange and evil powers. So, you see, even the Buddha Śākyamuni himself was not accepted as an enlightened being by all of his contemporaries. Different human beings have different mental predispositions, and there are cases when even the Buddha himself could not do much to overcome these—there was a limit.

Now today, the followers of Śiva have their own religious practices, and they reap some benefit from engaging in their own forms of worship. Through this, their life will gradually change. Now my own position on this question is that Śiva-ji's followers should practice according to their own beliefs and traditions, Christians must genuinely and sincerely follow what they believe, and so forth. That is sufficient.

QUESTIONER: But they will not attain liberation!

HIS HOLINESS: We Buddhists ourselves will not be liberated at once. In our own case, it will take time. Gradually we will be able to reach *mokṣa* or *nirvāṇa*, but the majority of Buddhists will not achieve this within their own lifetimes. So there's no hurry. If Buddhists themselves have to wait, perhaps many lifetimes, for their goal, why should we expect that it be different for non-Buddhists? So, you see, nothing much can be done.

Suppose, for example, you try to convert someone from another religion to the Buddhist religion, and you argue with them trying to convince them of the inferiority of their position. And suppose you do not succeed, suppose they do not become Buddhist. On the one hand, you have failed in your task, and on the other hand, you may have weakened the trust they have in their own religion, so that they may come to doubt their own faith. What have you accomplished by all this? It is of no use. When we come into contact with the followers of different religions, we should not argue. Instead, we should advise them to follow their own beliefs as sincerely and as truthfully as possible. For if they do so, they will no doubt reap certain benefit. Of this there is no doubt. Even in the immediate future they will be able to achieve more happiness and more satisfaction....

This is the way I usually act in such matters, it is my belief. When I meet the followers of different religions, I always praise them, for it is enough, it is sufficient, that they are following the moral teachings that are emphasized in every religion. It is enough, as I mentioned earlier, that they are trying to become better human beings. This in itself is very good and worthy of praise.

QUESTIONER: But is it only the Buddha who can be the ultimate source of refuge?

HIS HOLINESS: Here, you see, it is necessary to examine what is meant by liberation or salvation. Liberation in which "a mind that understands the sphere of reality annihilates all defilements in the sphere of reality" is a state that only Buddhists can accomplish. This kind of *mokṣa* or *nirvāṇa* is only explained in the Buddhist scriptures and is achieved only through Buddhist practice. According to certain religions, however, salvation is a place, a beautiful paradise, like a peaceful valley. To attain such a state as this, to achieve such a state of *mokṣa*, does not require the practice of emptiness, the understanding of reality. In Buddhism itself, we believe that through the accumulation of merit one can obtain rebirth in heavenly paradises like Tusita.

QUESTIONER: So, if one is a follower of Vedānta, and one reaches the state of satcitānanda, would this not be considered ultimate liberation?

HIS HOLINESS: Again, it depends upon how you interpret the words, "ultimate liberation." The *mokṣa* which is described in the Buddhist religion is achieved only through the practice of emptiness. And this kind of *nirvāṇa* or liberation, as I have defined it above, cannot be achieved even by Svātantrika Mādhyamikas, by Cittamātras, Sautrāntikas or Vaibhāṣikas. The followers of these schools, *though Buddhists*, do not understand the actual doctrine of emptiness. Because they cannot realize emptiness, or reality, they cannot accomplish the kind of liberation I defined previously.

QUESTIONER: To what do you attribute, in this particular age, the reasons for this fascination [with Eastern religions], and would you encourage people who are dissatisfied with their own Western way of life, having been brought up in the Mosaic religions (Christianity, Judaism, and Islam), dissatisfied with their lack of spiritual refreshment, to search further in their own religions or to look into Buddhism as an alternative?

HIS HOLINESS: That's a tricky question. Of course, from the Buddhist viewpoint, we are all human beings and we all have every right to investigate either one's own religion or another religion. That is our right. It think that on the whole a comparative study of different religious traditions is useful.

I generally believe that every major religion has the potential for giving any human being good advice; there is no question that this is so. But we must always keep in mind that different individuals have different mental predispositions. This means that for some individuals one religious system or philosophy will be more suitable than another. The only way one can come to a proper conclusion as to what is most suitable for *oneself* is through comparative study. Hence, we look and study, and we find a teaching that is most suitable to our own taste. This, you see, is my feeling.

I cannot advise everyone to practice Buddhism. That I cannot do. Certainly, for some people the Buddhist religion or ideology is most suitable, most effective. But that does not mean it is suitable for all.

STUDY QUESTIONS

1. According to the Dalai Lama, what is the purpose of religion?
2. How does the Dalai Lama address contradictions among religious beliefs?
3. What does the Dalai Lama claim about the role or necessity of Buddhist practices for liberation?
4. Given the discussion of the nature of religion in Part One of this anthology, what view of religion does the Dalai Lama presuppose in his discussion, and why do you say this?

Paul J. Griffiths

The Uniqueness of Religious Doctrines

Paul Griffiths (b. 1947) holds that each religion is unique not only in its historical particularity, but in its religious doctrines, rooted in and definitive of that respective community, that make universal and exclusivist claims. He employs examples from Buddhism and Christianity to illustrate five central features of religious doctrine: religious doctrines express rules that govern a religious community's life; they delineate the boundaries a religion uses to distinguish acceptable and orthodox beliefs from inadequate, false, or heretical beliefs; they exist in constructive engagement with the spiritual experiences of the particular religious community; they function to recruit members to the community through both catechism and evangelism; and they delineate salvifically significant truths that are espoused by the community. This rich understanding of religious doctrine conflicts with a pluralistic, functional view of religious diversity that reduces religious doctrine to its transformative effect on believers. Griffiths believes that not only does an analysis of religious doctrine show the uniqueness or particularity of the respective religious traditions, but a proper understanding of the distinctive doctrines of any religious tradition is a prerequisite for interreligious dialogue.

PROLEGOMENA

The doctrines, self-understandings, and attitudes of many non-Christian religious communities will require drastic revision if pluralism should turn out to be true. Christians are not the only ones to have developed doctrines that are, prima facie at least, particularist and exclusivist; they are not the only ones to have engaged in extensive missionary activity, activity often predicated upon an assumption of the possession of some significant salvific truth not possessed by those being evangelized; and they are therefore not the only ones to have judged that both their community and its doctrines are unique....Such judgments and attitudes are apparent, for example, in the standard Islamic position on the revelatory status of the Qur'an vis-à-vis other, sacred books; in the usual Buddhist judgments as to the salvific inefficacy

From *Christian Uniqueness Reconsidered: The Myth of a Pluralistic Theology of Religions*, ed. by Gavin D'Costa (Maryknoll: Orbis Books, 1990). Reprinted by permission of Orbis Books.

of Hindu doctrine and practice—and, by extension, of all non-Buddhist doctrine and practice; and in the traditional Jewish morning prayer, which includes a heartfelt expression of thanks to God for not having been made a non-Jew....

I shall offer what I take to be a more proper and fullblooded analysis of what religious doctrine is, both formally and functionally, and in so doing shall suggest that a proper understanding of its nature makes adherence to the kind of a priori pluralism espoused by Hick and others effectively impossible. This analysis will be buttressed with examples from both Christianity and Buddhism. Finally, in the brief concluding section I shall state and argue for my conviction that the pluralists' misunderstandings and partial understandings of what religious doctrine is mean that they also drastically misunderstand and misappropriate the Christian tradition. I shall argue, that is, that there is a sense in which Christian doctrine is unique,... and that an acknowledgment of this is required by a proper appropriation of the tradition, a proper understanding of its syntax and semantics. Such an acknowledgment is the ground and prerequisite for a properly Christian engagement in interreligious dialogue, just as its Buddhist analogue is the ground and prerequisite for a properly Buddhist engagement in such dialogue.... What, then, might a fuller and more defensible analysis of religious doctrine look like?

Some Buddhist and Christian Perspectives on the Nature of Doctrine

I shall here offer a brief characterization of what I take to be the five most important dimensions of religious doctrine, dimensions that must be addressed by any responsible analysis of the category. These five aspects overlap to some extent and cannot be rigidly separated one from another; many specific doctrines can and should be understood to fit into more than one of the five. So, like any categorical schema, the one offered here must be understood principally as a heuristic device... In sketching these five dimensions

of doctrine I shall mention both Buddhist and Christian examples thereof; these examples will be further drawn upon for the normative comments made in the brief concluding section.

Religious Doctrines as Community Rules

First, religious doctrines function as rules governing the life of the communities that profess them. Among other things they delineate the kinds of conduct that are appropriate for and required of members; provide rubrics for the ritual acts of the community; supply conceptual categories to be used by members in thinking about and analyzing their religious lives; and, most generally, structure and order the intellectual, affective, and practical life of the community. This dimension of religious doctrines is perhaps the most basic of all; from it the others flow, as I shall try to show.

An example: There is a whole complex of doctrines in Buddhism about the making of merit. Certain acts are deemed by the community to be especially productive of religious merit and thus to have beneficial effects upon those who engage in them, most obviously, for lay Buddhists, the donation of money, food, and other material goods to the Sangha, the monastic community. The complex of rules governing the relations between the monastic and lay communities in most forms of Buddhism is indicated by the fundamentally important doctrine that *the Sangha is a great field of merit*. On its face this looks like a straightforwardly descriptive claim about a property of the monastic community, that it is a "great field of merit." And so, on one level, it is, but its most important function, for Buddhists, is clearly the set of rule-governed activities toward which it points. Taking it seriously issues in a rich and complex set of religious behaviors.

To take a more abstract conceptual example: Yogacara Buddhists typically claim that *all existents are mental events*, a doctrine-expressing sentence which has many and complex metaphysical implications. It was clearly intended by its formulators in part as what William Christian would call a doctrine "about the setting of human life," that is, as a claim with cognitive content about the way things really are.

But also, and equally important, it is a rule governing the intellectual life of the community that professes it, a rule which tells the members of that community which kinds of conceptual category are appropriate for discussing what exists and how it exists. The doctrine-expressing sentence quoted above, then, functions for its community both syntactically (as a rule supplying a category to be employed in metaphysical discourse), and semantically (as a substantive claim with cognitive content).

Examples of Christian doctrine-expressing sentences that function regulatively in this way are easy to come by. Consider, for example, the eighteenth of the thirty-nine articles of religion that inform the life of Christians within the Anglican communion:

> They also are to be had accursed that presume to say, That every man shall be saved by the Law or Sect which he professeth, so that he be diligent to frame his life according to that Law and the light of Nature. For Holy Scripture doth set out to us only the Name of Jesus Christ, whereby men must be saved. (*Book of Common Prayer*, 871)

The two doctrine-expressing sentences given in this article regulate what it is possible for the community to say about salvation; they reject, in very clear terms, the application of the category "salvation" to those outside the community, and in so doing tell the community that the category can be applied only to those inside. This is the syntactic function of the doctrine; it provides the community with rules for the employment of a conceptual category. The article also, of course, makes a clear substantive claim, and thus functions semantically as well as syntactically, but my interest at this point is in the regulative function rather than cognitive content of doctrines.

Religious Doctrines as Definitions of Community Boundaries

The second dimension of religious doctrines, again one that focuses upon one of their functions for religious communities, is that many of them exclude what is unacceptable to the community, reject heresy and so define, conceptually and practically, the bounds of the community. There is no doubt that, for most religious communities most of the time, doctrine-expressing sentences have taken form precisely as a result of the desire of those communities to exclude what they came to feel to be untrue, inadequate, or misleading.

To consider a Buddhist example: There is little doubt that one of the formative influences upon the development of scholastic doctrinal thought among Yogacara Buddhists in India from the fourth century A.D. onward was the desire of Yogacara intellectuals to reject, or at least to modify, what they had come to regard as the excessive negativity, of Nagarjuna's (second century A.D.) dialectical deconstruction of all theoretical thought. The (doctrinal) assertion that all doctrinal assertions are misleading—which is one way of understanding what Nagarjuna and his followers were trying to show—was felt by Yogacara intellectuals to be excessively depressing and so not conducive to the attainment of Nirvana. It therefore needed to be rejected and replaced by a complex and detailed analysis of the workings of consciousness, an analysis centered upon the key Yogacara doctrinal idea of the "three patterns" (*trisvabhava*) of consciousness and their salvific significance. A significant function of the doctrine of the three patterns for Yogacara Buddhists, then, is precisely to reject an excessively apophatic understanding of the basic Buddhist doctrine of emptiness (*sunyata*).

Christian examples are equally easy to come by. Most Christological doctrine came into being, at least in part, as a result of the need to exclude what the community came to feel were partial, mistaken, or simply inappropriate delineations of the person and work of Jesus Christ. And the same is true of the development of Trinitarian doctrine. The Chalcedonian formulae, whatever one may think of their substantive merits, were historically the product of controversy. And as a final example, it is very clear that many of the thirty-nine articles of the Anglican church were explicitly designed primarily to exclude positions that the community regarded as false or misleading. Consider the twenty-second article, on purgatory and associated matters, which is an extreme example since it propounds nothing positive, claiming only that a certain doctrine belonging to another community must not be assented to by members of this one:

The Romish Doctrine concerning Purgatory, Pardons, Worshipping and Adoration, as well as Images as of Relics, and also Invocation of Saints, is a fond thing, vainly invented, and grounded upon no warranty of Scripture, but rather repugnant to the Word of God. (*Book of Common Prayer*, 872)

Religious Doctrines and the Spiritual Experience of Communities

Third, religious doctrines are both shaped by and formative of the spiritual experience of the communities that profess them. In Christian theology this fact is summarized by the tag *lex orandi, lex credendi*. To say that what one believes is governed or controlled by how one prays is no doubt too strong; there are many other influences that are operative. But the tag nevertheless expresses an important truth; and it is clear, if a specific example is needed, that the formation of doctrines about the Blessed Virgin (up to and including the doctrine of the Immaculate Conception) was causally influenced by the prayer habits of Christians, and that the doctrines, once formed, had a significant effect upon those prayer habits and upon the phenomenology of the experience had by Christians during prayer.

The same points can be made, *mutatis mutandis*, for Buddhism. A strict doctrine of momentariness came to be defined by Buddhist intellectuals in India, a doctrine which says in its strongest forms that everything which exists is momentary. It is very clear that this doctrine both expressed and shaped the experience of meditating Buddhists. Buddhist intellectuals have always held that the apparent continuities and solidities of ordinary human experience—the experience of the substantive continuity of one's own identity, the experience of the unbroken continuing identity of medium-sized physical objects, and so forth—are to a significant degree misleading, salvifically detrimental, and the result of bad cognitive and perceptual habits. Meditational practice was in part designed to break down, to deconstruct, just these experienced solidities, and to replace them with a stream (*samtana*) of specific intentional mental events each of which lasts no more than an instant. Buddhist metaphysicians (*abhidharmikas*) developed

a complex set of classifications for these momentary mental events, classifications which were intended to be (and were) learned by meditators and employed by them as tools to shape their meditational experience. There is thus a complex symbiosis between the doctrines of Yogacara Buddhist scholastics and their spirituality. The doctrine of radical momentariness is just one example of this.

Religious Doctrines—Catechesis and Evangelism

Fourth, religious doctrines function as instruments for the making of members of religious communities. There are two modes in which this is done, the traditional Christian terms for which are *catechesis* and *evangelism*. The term *doctrine* in English, as also *doctrina* in Latin, means both "the act of teaching" and "the content of what is taught," and hence overlaps significantly with the terms *catechesis* and *catechism*. *Doctrina* was used in the Vulgate to translate the Greek words *didaskalia* and *didache*; entirely typical is the use of *didaskalia* and cognate terms in 1 Timothy 4. The author of this letter asks Timothy to beware of the "doctrines of demons" (*didaskaliais daimonion*, 4:1), and to pay attention instead to the "good doctrines" (*kales didaskalias*, 4:6). "indoctrinating" (*didaske*, 4:11) others with them and centering his own spiritual practice around public reading of scripture, exhortation, and "doctrine" (*didaskalia*, 4:13), and finally to keep close watch on himself and his "doctrine" (*didaskalia*, 4:16). The term—whether it is translated into English by "doctrine" and derivatives, following the Latin *doctrina*, or whether "teaching" and derivatives are preferred—clearly embraces both act and object.

Catechesis in the fullest and richest sense possible—the formation of faithful Christians by a deep and detailed exposure to the narratives, teachings, practices, and so forth of a Christian community—obviously includes, then, an important doctrinal element, as is already suggested by the etymology and use of the word. Christians need to know and (ideally) to understand the doctrine-expressing sentences contained in their creeds and dramatized in their liturgies, and historically this has been ensured by various forms of rote learning, usually in question-and-answer form. Enculturation into a religious community, Christian or other, cannot occur without catechesis in this sense, and so also cannot occur without doctrine.

There are many Buddhist analogues to the catechetical function of doctrine in Christianity. Most striking, perhaps, is the development of the catechetical method evident in the Indian scholastic texts that began to be composed shortly before the beginning of the common era, texts classified as *abhidharma* by the tradition. The term *abhidharma* is derived from the more basic term *dharma*, which, like *doctrine*, covers both the act and the content of Buddhist teaching (and much more besides). The earliest uses of the term *abhidharma* link it with doctrinal debates and expositions, and often with specific numbered lists of doctrinal terms. Buddhism has delighted in such numerical lists from the very earliest times (four truths, eight-membered path, twelve-membered chain of dependent origination), largely for mnemonic purposes, and the development of the canonical *abhidharma* texts was very closely linked to the elaboration of these lists, an elaboration which occurred in a number of different ways.

There are references in the discourses, early texts that generally predate the systematic catechetics of the *abhidharma*, to monks versed in these doctrinal lists. Such statements are usually connected with others to the effect that one should question and interrogate such monks, and that they will then dispel doubt about disputed doctrinal issues and will open up the meaning of the doctrine by their answers. Even at this early stage, then, the use of a question-and-answer method for communicating doctrinal norms is evident in the Buddhist tradition. Historically it seems fairly clear that at a very early period in the history of Buddhist thought (certainly within a century of the Buddha's death, and in some cases probably before that), these numerical ordered lists of items of doctrine were developed and formalized as mnemonic aids and then began to be used as catechetical tools. In these standardized forms we have the kernels of the canonical *abhidharma* texts. The expansion of these kernels into the texts as they now stand took longer, and in the texts as we now have them there is

clear evidence of intellectual interests far more extensive than the development of mnemotechnical aids. But the main point for the purpose of this study is that Buddhists have always been aware of the importance of catechetics as a way of using doctrine for the formation of members, and that this awareness is also clearly evident in most Mahayana schools.

Rather less need be said about the other aspect of the use of doctrine by religious communities for the making of members, that which is usually called evangelism by Christians. Both Buddhism and Christianity have it as an essential part of their own self-definition that the conversion of non-Buddhists and non-Christians is desirable; and such conversion, when it occurs, often does so as a result of the conviction of such outsiders that certain heretofore unknown or rejected items of doctrine are in fact both true and desirable. When evangelism has had its effect, catechesis can begin. And doctrine is integral to both processes.

Religious Doctrines and Salvation

Fifth, and finally, almost all religious communities take most of their doctrines—at least those that make prima facie claims about the nature of human persons and the world in which they live, as well as those that make recommendations about what kinds of action are desirable—to have cognitive content and to be expressive of salvifically significant truths. Consider the eighteenth of the thirty-nine articles of religion, cited above, or the Buddhist assertion of strict momentariness. Both of these are not only rules governing the life of the community and instruments to exclude what the community finds unacceptable, but also complex and interesting claims as to what is the case, claims whose truth the communities that profess them take to be of considerable salvific significance.

Let us assume for the moment that the analysis of religious doctrine sketched here is preferable to that implicit (and at times explicit) in the work of John Hick.... What then is suggested about the validity and desirability of following them into the kind of pluralism they recommend? First, it should be evident that the central doctrines of any religious community cannot be abandoned easily by that community, and certainly not for the kind of superficial, pragmatic reasons suggested by Hick and others. The central doctrines of any community will almost always have a key catechetical role to play for the members of that community; they will almost always have deep historical roots in the tradition, having been formed by repeated attempts on the part of the community to exclude what it finds doctrinally unacceptable; and they will almost always be intimately, symbiotically, linked with the spirituality and the ritual practice of the community that professes them. And finally, of course, religious communities (or at least their representative intellectuals) will almost always take their doctrines, even the most apparently exclusivist ones, to be, simply, true.

For Buddhists, to let go of the idea that the *buddhadharma* is the supreme expression of truth, that the Buddha is superior to men and gods, and that all other religious communities (when they are not simply abominations) are partial reflections of and preparations for the real truth (which is Buddhism), means much more than simply tinkering with the system. It means an abandonment of almost everything that has been of key importance for Buddhist spirituality, intellectual life, ritual and ethical practice, and the rest. It is akin to asking a native speaker of English to please try and do without nouns, since we have reason to think that using them leads to an inappropriately reified view of the world. Vital and pressing reasons are needed for such changes, since they will almost always mean, for those who make them, death—or such a radical transformation that the new is not recognizable as the old. And pluralists, and here Hick is entirely typical, give us no such pressing reasons, nothing more, in fact, than a weak pragmatic argument based upon an impoverished understanding of what doctrine is and how it functions.

The Uniqueness of Christian Doctrine

There is a trivial sense in which Christian doctrine is unique and an equally trivial sense in which it is not. Its trivial uniqueness lies simply in its historical particularity, a particularity shared by no other doctrinal system; but every doctrinal system is, by definition, unique in just this formal sense. Hence also the trivial sense in which Christian doctrine is not unique: It shared the formal characteristic of being unique in its historical particularity with every doctrinal system. Any interesting uniqueness that Christian doctrine may have, then, must lie not at the formal level but at the substantive level. And any attempt to delineate and to flesh out in what this substantive uniqueness consists must in turn rest upon some particular attempt to construct a referent for the term *Christian doctrine*. But since all such attempts are partial and tendentious, because they are all themselves undertaken in unique historical circumstances by individuals or communities with a particular interest and a particular *Tendenz*, no single attempt to do this will meet with universal approval.

I have not attempted, then, to construct such a referent in the preceding sections of this study. Neither shall I attempt it here in anything other than a suggestive way. To do it fully would be a lifetime's work, and one that would remain always unfinished. I shall simply make some suggestions, unavoidably in a confessional way—for to be confessional is simply to be open about one's historical and religious locatedness, one's specificity, an openness that is essential for serious theological work and indeed for any serious intellectual work that is not in thrall to the myth of the disembodied and unlocated scholarly intellect— and shall try to link them to what I have said earlier about the nature and functions of religious doctrine.

I am writing these words a few days after the feast of Christ the King, a feast at which Christ's kingship and his crucifixion are celebrated together by the church. Part of the liturgical celebration of that feast is (in the Anglican communion) the reading of the Christological hymn in Colossians 1:11–20, a hymn which concludes with these words:

> For in him the complete being of God, by God's own choice, came to dwell. Through him God chose to reconcile the whole universe to himself, making peace through the shedding of his blood upon the cross— to reconcile all things, whether on earth or in heaven, through him alone.

A strong and interesting doctrinal claim is being made here, a claim as to the singularity and salvific centrality of a particular historical event. It is a claim that functions in almost all the ways distinguished in the analysis of religious doctrine given above: It is a rule governing what may properly be said by the communities for which this text is authoritative; it excludes, if taken seriously, other less daring and universalistic conceptual alternatives for understanding the work of Jesus Christ that the community has found and still finds largely unacceptable; and it is used catechetically, as well as dramatized and reinforced liturgically, in ways which make it enter the very heart of Christian spirituality. It, and its like, have deep roots and a strong grip upon the spirit, intellect, and imagination of Christian communities and it is here, in the linked doctrines of the universal significance of the incarnation and the atonement, that I would begin my construction of the referent of the term *Christian doctrine*. It is also from here that I would begin my engagement, serious and deep-going as I hope it is and intend it to be, with Buddhists and their equally (though very different) universalistic and exclusivistic doctrinal claims. These matters must be on the agenda and openly so, of interreligious dialogue if it is to be anything other than a futile exercise in the exchange of ethical platitudes for all concerned. As Rowan Williams has put it:

> The problem was, is, and always will be the Christian attitude to the historical order, the human past. By affirming that all "meaning," every assertion about the significance of life and reality, must be judged by reference to a brief succession of contingent events in Palestine, Christianity—almost without realizing it—closed off the path to "timeless truth." (*Christian Spirituality*, p. 1)

Here lies the uniqueness of Christian doctrine, and here lies also the "problem" that pluralists are trying to dissolve. The universalistic and apparently exclusivistic claims made here and throughout the tradition may of course turn out to be false, to have been misconceived and to be in need of abandonment; but such a judgment needs to be made in full awareness of what it entails and of how such claims function for Christians and are rooted in and definitive of their communities. Pluralists show no such awareness. My attempt to sketch the lineaments of such an awareness in this study has been intended to suggest that a certain kind of uniqueness, a uniqueness that includes both universalism and exclusivism, is integral to both the syntax and the semantics of the Christian life. I also want to suggest that this syntax and semantics are worth preserving in default of pressing and detailed reasons to abandon them, and that pluralists have offered no such reasons. Their preservation will mean that the Christian life will continue to be structured around and given meaning by a certain kind of universalism and exclusivism, and this must also therefore be a constitutive factor in the Christian engagement with religiously committed non-Christians. That the preservation of this universalism and exclusivism need not lead to the military or economic oppression by Christians of non-Christians is obvious; and that a frank acknowledgment of the universalistic and exclusivistic dimension of Christian syntax and semantics by Christians committed to interreligious dialogue will lead to the crossing of new frontiers in interreligious dialogue, frontiers inaccessible from within the pluralist paradigm, is the hope that informs this essay.

Study Questions

1. What five functions does Griffiths see for religious doctrines?
2. What does Griffiths see as the implications of his account of religious doctrines for John Hick's pluralist view of religions?
3. Why does Griffiths believe that we need to take seriously the universalistic and exclusivist claims made by religions?

Karl Rahner

Religious Inclusivism

Karl Rahner (1904–1984) maintains that Christianity is the true, absolute religion for everyone, portraying God's grace as coming in his self-revelation in Jesus Christ. However, before Christianity historically introduced the obligation to believe in Christ, there were other lawful religions that admittedly embodied an imperfect knowledge of God and yet contained supernatural elements of grace. This grace was effective for the salvation of many righteous but non-Christian persons who practiced those religions. He considers religions today to be similarly situated to those that preceded the coming of Jesus in that their adherents likewise have no meaningful historical encounter with Christian saving truths. Christianity becomes necessary for salvation when it becomes historically real for them. In the meantime, he is confident that these religions too can be lawful because God, desiring that all be saved, gives people his grace through these religions. The social religion, endowed with supernatural elements, can be absolutely legitimate for the individual because God's intent of salvation reached the person through it. Faithful adherents of these religions must be regarded as "anonymous Christians" until the gospel brings them to an explicit knowledge of God's self-revelation in Jesus.

"Open Catholicism" involves two things. It signifies the fact that the Catholic Church is opposed by historical forces which she herself cannot disregard as if they were purely "worldly" forces and a matter of indifference to her but which, on the contrary, although they do not stand in a positive relationship of peace and mutual recognition to the Church, do have a significance for her. "Open Catholicism" means also the task of becoming related to these forces in order to understand their existence (since this cannot be simply acknowledged), in order to bear with and overcome the annoyance of their opposition and in order to form the Church in such a way that she will be able to overcome as much of this pluralism as should not exist, by understanding herself as the higher unity of this opposition.

"Open Catholicism" means therefore a certain attitude towards the present-day pluralism of powers with different outlooks on the world. We do not, of course, refer to pluralism merely as a fact which one simply acknowledges without explaining it. Pluralism is meant here as a fact which ought to be thought about and one which, without denying that—in part at least—it should not exist at all, should be incorporated once more from a more elevated viewpoint into the totality and unity of the Christian understanding of human existence. For Christianity, one of the gravest elements of this pluralism in which we live and with which we must come to terms, and indeed the element most difficult to incorporate, is the pluralism of religions....

This pluralism is a greater threat and a reason for greater unrest for Christianity than for any other religion. For no other religion—not even Islam—maintains so absolutely that it is *the* religion, the one and only valid revelation of the one living God, as does the Christian religion.

The fact of the pluralism of religions, which endures and still from time to time becomes virulent anew even after a history of two thousand years, must therefore be the greatest scandal and the greatest vexation for Christianity. And the threat of this vexation is also greater for the individual Christian today than ever before. For in the past, the other religion was in practice the religion of a completely different cultural environment. It belonged to a history with which the individual only communicated very much on the periphery of his own history; it was the religion of those who were even in every other respect alien to oneself. It is not surprising, therefore, that people did not wonder at the fact that these "others" and "strangers" had also a different religion. No wonder that in general people could not seriously consider these other religions as a challenge posed to themselves or even as a possibility for themselves. Today things have changed. The West is no longer shut up in itself; it can no longer regard itself simply as the centre of the history of this world and as the centre of culture, with a religion which even from this point of view (i.e., from a point of view which has really nothing to do with a decision of faith but which simply carries the weight of something quite self-evident) could appear

as the obvious and indeed sole way of honouring God to be thought of for a European. Today everybody is the next-door neighbour and spiritual neighbour of everyone else in the world. And so everybody today is determined by the intercommunication of all those situations of life which affect the whole world. Every religion which exists in the world is—just like all cultural possibilities and actualities of other people—a question posed, and a possibility offered, to every person.... Hence, the question about the understanding of and the continuing existence of religious pluralism as a factor of our immediate Christian existence is an urgent one and part of the question as to how we are to deal with today's pluralism.

This problem could be tackled from different angles. In the present context we simply wish to try to describe a few of those basic traits of a Catholic dogmatic interpretation of the non-Christian religions which may help us to come closer to a solution of the question about the Christian position in regard to the religious pluralism in the world of today....

First Thesis

We must begin with the thesis...that Christianity understands itself as the absolute religion, intended for all men, which cannot recognize any other religion beside itself as of equal right. This proposition is self-evident and basic for Christianity's understanding of itself. There is no need here to prove it or to develop its meaning. After all, Christianity does not take valid and lawful religion to mean primarily that relationship of man to God which man himself institutes on his own authority. Valid and lawful religion does not mean man's own interpretation of human existence....

Valid and lawful religion for Christianity is rather God's action on men, God's free self-revelation by communicating himself to man. It is God's relationship to men, freely instituted by God himself and revealed by God in this institution. *This* relationship of God to man is basically the same for all men, because it rests on the Incarnation, death and resurrection of the one Word of God become flesh. Christianity is God's own interpretation in his Word of this relationship of God to man founded in Christ by God himself. And so Christianity can recognize itself as the true and lawful religion for all men only where and when it enters with existential power and demanding force into the realm of another religion and—judging it by itself—puts it in question. Since the time of Christ's coming—ever since he came in the flesh as the Word of God in absoluteness and reconciled, i.e., united, the world with God by his death and resurrection, not merely theoretically but really—Christ and his continuing historical presence in the world (which we call "Church") is *the* religion which binds man to God.

Already we must, however, make one point clear as regards this first thesis....It is true that the Christian religion itself has its own pre-history which traces this religion back to the beginning of the history of humanity—even though it does this by many basic steps. It is also true that this fact of having a pre-history is of much greater importance, according to the evidence of the New Testament, for the theoretical and practical proof of the claim to absolute truth made by the Christian religion than our current fundamental theology is aware of. Nevertheless, the Christian religion as such has a beginning in history; it did not always exist but began at some point in time. It has not always and everywhere been *the* way of salvation for men—at least not in its historically tangible ecclesio-sociological constitution and in the reflex fruition of God's saving activity in, and in view of, Christ. As a historical quantity Christianity has, therefore, a temporal and spatial starting point in Jesus of Nazareth and in the saving event of the unique Cross and the empty tomb in Jerusalem. It follows from this, however, that this absolute religion—even when it begins to be this for practically all men—must come in a historical way to men, facing them as the only legitimate and demanding religion for them. It is therefore a question of whether this moment, when the existentially real demand is made by the absolute religion in its historically tangible form, takes place really at the same chronological moment for all people, or whether the occurrence of this moment has itself a history and thus is not chronologically simultaneous for all people, cultures and spaces of history....Normally the beginning of

the objective obligation of the Christian message for all men—in other words, the abolition of the validity of the Mosaic religion *and* of all other religions which (as we will see later) may also have a period of validity and of being-willed-by-God—is thought to occur in the apostolic age. Normally, therefore, one regards the time between this beginning and the actual acceptance of the personally guilty refusal of Christianity in a non-Jewish world and history as the span between the already given promulgation of the law and the moment when the one to whom the law refers takes cognizance of it.

It is not just an idle academic question to ask whether such a conception is correct or whether, as we maintain, there could be a different opinion in this matter, i.e., whether one could hold that the beginning of Christianity for actual periods of history, for cultures and religions, could be postponed to those moments in time when Christianity became a real historical factor in an individual history and culture—a real historical moment in a particular culture....

From this there follows a delicately differentiated understanding of our first thesis: we maintain positively only that, as regards destination, Christianity is the absolute and hence the only religion for all men. We leave it, however, an open question (at least in principle) at what exact point in time the absolute obligation of the Christian religion has in fact come into effect for every man and culture, even in the sense of the *objective* obligation of such a demand. Nevertheless—and this leaves the thesis formulated still sufficiently exciting—wherever in practice Christianity reaches man in the real urgency and rigour of his actual existence, Christianity—once understood—presents itself as the only still valid religion for this man, a necessary means for his salvation and not merely an obligation with the necessity of a precept. It should be noted that this is a question of the necessity of a *social* form for salvation. Even though this is Christianity and not some other religion, it may surely still be said without hesitation that this thesis contains implicitly another thesis which states that in concrete human existence as such, the nature of religion itself must include a social constitution—which means that religion can exist only in a social form. This means, therefore, that man, who is commanded to have a religion, is also commanded to seek and accept a social form of religion. It will soon become clear what this reflection implies for the estimation of non-Christian religions.

Finally, we may mention one further point in this connection. What is vital in the *notion* of *paganism* and hence also of the non-Christian pagan religions (taking "pagan" here as a theological concept without any disparaging intent) is not the actual refusal to accept the Christian religion but the absence of any sufficient historical encounter with Christianity which would have enough historical power to render the Christian religion really present in this pagan society and in the history of the people concerned. If this is so, then paganism ceases to exist in this sense by reason of what is happening today. For the Western world is opening out into a universal world history in which every people and every cultural sector becomes an inner factor of every other people and every other cultural sector. Or rather, paganism is slowly entering a new phase: there is *one* history of the world, and in this *one* history both the Christians and the non-Christians (i.e., the old and new pagans together) live in one and the same situation and face each other in dialogue, and thus the question of the theological meaning of the other religions arises once more and with even greater urgency.

Second Thesis

Until the moment when the Gospel really enters into the historical situation of an individual, a non-Christian religion (even outside the Mosaic religion) does not merely contain elements of a natural knowledge of God, elements, moreover, mixed up with human depravity which is the result of original sin and later aberrations. It contains also supernatural elements arising out of the grace which is given to men as a gratuitous gift on account of Christ. For this reason a non-Christian religion can be recognized as a *lawful* religion (although only in different degrees) without thereby denying the error and depravity contained in it. This thesis requires a more extensive explanation.

We must first of all note the point up to which this evaluation of the non-Christian religions is valid. This is the point in time when the Christian religion becomes a historically real factor for those who are of this religion. . . .

The thesis itself is divided into two parts. It means first of all that it is a priori quite possible to suppose that there are supernatural, grace-filled elements in non-Christian religions. Let us first of all deal with this statement. It does not mean, of course, that all the elements of a polytheistic conception of the divine, and all the other religious, ethical and metaphysical abberations contained in the non-Christian religions, are to be or may be treated as harmless either in theory or in practice. There have been constant protests against such elements throughout the history of Christianity and throughout the history of the Christian interpretation of the non-Christian religions, starting with the Epistle to the Romans and following on the Old Testament polemics against the religion of the "heathens." Every one of these protests is still valid in what was really meant and expressed by them. Every such protest remains a part of the message which Christianity and the Church has to give to the peoples who profess such religions. Furthermore, we are not concerned here with an a posteriori history of religions. Consequently, we also cannot describe empirically what should not exist and what is opposed to God's will in these non-Christian religions, nor can we represent these things in their many forms and degrees. We are here concerned with dogmatic theology and so can merely repeat the universal and unqualified verdict as to the unlawfulness of the non-Christian religions right from the moment when they came into real and historically powerful contact with Christianity (and at first only thus!). It is clear, however, that this condemnation does not mean to deny the very basic differences within the non-Christian religions especially since the pious, God-pleasing pagan was already a theme of the Old Testament, and especially since this God-pleasing pagan cannot simply be thought of as living absolutely outside the concrete socially constituted religion and constructing his own religion on his native foundations—just as St. Paul in his speech on the Areopagus did not simply exclude a positive and basic view of the pagan religion.

The decisive reason for the first part of our thesis is basically a theological consideration. This consideration (prescinding from certain more precise qualifications) rests ultimately on the fact that, if we wish to be Christians, we must profess belief in the universal and serious salvific purpose of God towards all men which is true even within the post-paradisean phase of salvation dominated by original sin. We know, to be sure, that this proposition of faith does not say anything certain about the *individual* salvation of man understood as something which has in fact been reached. But God desires the salvation of everyone. And this salvation willed by God is the salvation won by Christ, the salvation of supernatural grace which divinizes man, the salvation of the beatific vision. It is a salvation really intended for all those millions upon millions of people who lived perhaps a million years before Christ—and also for those who have lived after Christ—in nations, cultures and epochs of a very wide range which were still completely shut shut off from the viewpoint of those living in the light of the New Testament. If, on the one hand, we conceive salvation as something specifically *Christian*, if there is no salvation apart from Christ, if according to Catholic teaching the supernatural divinization of mankind can never be replaced merely by goodwill on the part of man but is necessary as something itself given in this earthly life; and if, on the other hand, God has really, truly and seriously intended this salvation for all men—then these two aspects cannot be reconciled in any other way than by stating that every human being is really and truly exposed to the influence of divine, supernatural grace which offers an interior union with God and by means of which God communicates himself whether the individual takes up an attitude of acceptance or of refusal towards this grace. It is senseless to suppose cruelly—and without any hope of acceptance by the man of today, in view of the enormous extent of the extra-Christian history of salvation and damnation—that nearly all men living outside the official and public Christianity are so evil and stubborn that the offer of supernatural grace ought not even to be made in fact in most cases, since these individuals have already rendered themselves unworthy of such an offer by previous, subjectively grave offences against the natural moral law.

If one gives more exact theological thought to this matter, then one cannot regard nature and grace as two phases in the life of the individual which follow each other in time. It is furthermore impossible to think that this offer of supernatural, divinizing grace made to all men on account of the universal salvific purpose of God, should in general (prescinding from the relatively few exceptions) remain ineffective in most cases on account of the personal guilt of the individual. For, as far as the Gospel is concerned, we have no really conclusive reason for thinking so pessimistically of men. On the other hand, and contrary to every merely human experience, we do have every reason for thinking optimistically of God and his salvific will which is more powerful than the extremely limited stupidity and evil-mindedness of men. However little we can say with certitude about the final lot of an individual inside or outside the officially constituted Christian religion, we have every reason to think optimistically—i.e., truly hopefully and confidently in a Christian sense—of God who has certainly the last word and who has revealed to us that he has spoken his powerful word of reconciliation and forgiveness into the world....

Once we take all this into consideration, we will not hold it to be impossible that grace is at work, and is even being accepted, in the spiritual, personal life of the individual, no matter how primitive, unenlightened, apathetic, and earth-bound such a life may at first sight appear to be. We can say quite simply that, wherever, and in so far as, the individual makes a moral decision in his life... this moral decision can also be thought to measure up to the character of a supernaturally elevated, believing and thus saving act, and hence to be more in actual fact than merely "natural morality." Hence, if one believes seriously in the universal salvific purpose of God towards all men in Christ, it need not and cannot really be doubted that gratuitous influences of properly Christian supernatural grace are conceivable in the life of all men (provided they are first of all regarded as individuals) and that these influences can be presumed to be accepted in spite of the sinful state of men and in spite of their apparent estrangement from God.

Our second thesis goes even further than this, however, and states in its second part that, from what has been said, the actual religions of "pre-Christian" humanity too must not be regarded as simply illegitimate from the very start, but must be seen as quite capable of having a positive significance. This statement must naturally be taken in a very different sense which we cannot examine here for the various particular religions. This means that the different religions will be able to lay claim to being lawful religions only in very different senses and to very different degrees. But precisely this variability is not at all excluded by the notion of a "lawful religion," as we will have to show in a moment. A lawful religion means here an institutional religion whose "use" by man at a certain period can be regarded on the whole as a positive means of gaining the right relationship to God and thus for the attaining of salvation, a means which is therefore positively included in God's plan of salvation.

That such a notion and the reality to which it refers can exist even where such a religion shows many theoretical and practical errors in its concrete form becomes clear in a theological analysis of the structure of the Old Covenant. We must first of all remember in this connection that only in the New Testament—in the Church of Christ understood as something which is eschatologically final and *hence* (and only for this reason) "indefectible" and infallible—is there realized the notion of a Church which, because it is instituted by God in some way or other, already contains the permanent norm of differentiation between what is right (i.e., willed by God) and what is wrong in the religious sphere, and contains it both as a permanent institution and as an intrinsic element of this religion. There was nothing like this in the Old Testament, although it must undoubtedly be recognized as a lawful religion....

Hence it cannot be a part of the notion of a lawful religion in the above sense that it should be free from corruption, error, and objective moral wrong in the concrete form of its appearance, or that it should contain a clear objective and permanent final court of appeal for the conscience of the individual to enable the individual to differentiate clearly and with certainty between the elements willed and instituted by God and those which are merely human and corrupt.

We must therefore rid ourselves of the prejudice that we can face a non-Christian religion with the dilemma that it must either come from God in everything it contains and thus correspond to God's will and positive providence, or be simply a purely human construction. If man is under God's grace even in these religions—and to deny this is certainly absolutely wrong—then the possession of this supernatural grace cannot but show itself, and cannot but become a formative factor of life in the concrete, even where (though not only where) this life turns the relationship to the absolute into an explicit theme, viz. in religion....

Furthermore, it must be borne in mind that the individual ought to and must have the possibility in his life of partaking in a genuine saving relationship to God, and at all times and in all situations of the history of the human race. Otherwise there could be no question of a serious and also actually effective salvific design of God for all men, in all ages and places. In view of the social nature of man and the previously even more radical social solidarity of men, however, it is quite unthinkable that man, being what he is, could actually achieve this relationship to God—which he must have and which if he is to be saved, is and must be made possible for him by God—in an absolutely private interior reality and this outside of the actual religious bodies which offer themselves to him in the environment in which he lives. If man had to be and could always and everywhere be a *homo religiosus* in order to be able to save himself as such, then he was this *homo religiosus* in the concrete religion in which "people" lived and had to live at that time. He could not escape this religion, however much he may have and did take up a critical and selective attitude towards this religion on individual matters, and however much he may have and did put different stresses in practice on certain things which were at variance with the official theory of this religion. If, however, man can always have a positive, saving relationship to God, and if he always had to have it, then he has always had it within *that* religion which in practice was at his disposal by being a factor in his sphere of existence. As already stated above, the inherence of the individual exercise of religion in a social religious order is one of the essential traits of true religion as it exists in practice. Hence, if one were to expect from someone who lives outside the Christian religion that he should have exercised his genuine, saving relationship to God absolutely outside the religion which society offered him, then such a conception would turn religion into something intangibly interior, into something which is always and everywhere performed only indirectly, a merely transcendental religion without anything which could become tangible in categories. Such a conception would annul the above-mentioned principle regarding the necessarily social nature of all religion in the concrete, so that even the Christian Church would then no longer have the necessary presupposition of general human and natural law as proof of her necessity. And since it does not at all belong to the notion of a lawful religion intended by God for man as something positively salvific that it should be pure and positively willed by God in all its elements, such a religion can be called an absolutely legitimate religion for the person concerned. That which God has intended as salvation for him, reached him, in accordance with God's will and by his permission (no longer adequately separable in practice), in the *concrete* religion of his actual realm of existence and historical condition, but this fact did not deprive him of the right and the limited possibility to criticize and to heed impulses of religious reform which by God's providence kept on recurring within such a religion....

The morality of a people and of an age, taken in its totality, is therefore the legitimate and concrete form of the divine law (even though, of course, it can and may have to be corrected), so that it was not until the New Testament that the institution guaranteeing the purity of this form became (with the necessary reservations) an element of this form itself. Hence, if there existed a divine moral law and religion in the life of man *before* this moment, then its absolute purity (i.e., its constitution by divinely willed elements alone) must not be made the condition of the lawfulness of its existence. In fact, if every man who comes into the world is pursued by God's grace—and if one of the effects of this grace, even in its supernatural and salvifically elevating form, is to cause changes in

consciousness (as is maintained by the better theory in Catholic theology) even though it cannot be simply as such a direct object of certain reflection—then it cannot be true that the actually existing religions do not bear any trace of the fact that all men are in some way affected by grace. These traces may be difficult to distinguish even to the enlightened eye of the Christian. But they must be there....

The second part of this second thesis, however, states two things positively. It states that even religions other than the Christian and the Old Testament religions contain quite certainly elements of a supernatural influence by grace which must make itself felt even in these objectifications. And it also states that by the fact that in practice man as he really is can live his proffered relationship to God only in society, man must have had the right and indeed the duty to live this his relationship to God within the religious and social realities offered to him in his particular historical situation.

THIRD THESIS

If the second thesis is correct, then Christianity does not simply confront the member of an extra-Christian religion as a mere non-Christian but as someone who can and must already be regarded in this or that respect as an anonymous Christian. It would be wrong to regard the pagan as someone who has not yet been touched in any way by God's grace and truth. If, however, he has experienced the grace of God—if, in certain circumstances, he has already accepted this grace as the ultimate, unfathomable entelechy of his existence by accepting the immeasurableness of his dying existence as opening out into infinity—then he has already been given revelation in a true sense even before he has been affected by missionary preaching from without. For this grace, understood as the priori horizon of all his spiritual acts, accompanies his consciousness subjectively, even though it is not known objectively. And the revelation, which comes to him from without is not in such a case the proclamation of something as yet absolutely unknown....But if it is true that a person who becomes the object of the Church's missionary efforts is or may be already someone on the way towards his salvation, and some-one who in certain circumstances finds it, without being reached by the proclamation of the Church's message—and if it is at the same time true that this salvation which reaches him in this way is Christ's salvation, since there is no other salvation—then it must be possible to be not only an anonymous the-ist but also an anonymous Christian. And then it is quite true that in the last analysis, the proclamation of the Gospel does not simply turn someone abso-lutely abandoned by God and Christ into a Christian, but turns an anonymous Christian into someone who now also knows about his Christian belief in the depths of his grace-endowed being by objective reflection and in the profession of faith which is given a social form in the Church.

It is not thereby denied, but on the contrary implied, that this explicit self-realization of his pre-viously anonymous Christianity is itself part of the development of this Christianity itself—a higher stage of development of this Christianity demanded by his being—and that it is therefore intended by God in the same way as everything else about salva-tion. Hence, it will not be possible in any way to draw the conclusion from this conception that, since man is already an anonymous Christian even without it, this explicit preaching of Christianity is superfluous. Such a conclusion would be just as false (and for the same reasons) as to conclude that the sacraments of baptism and penance could be dispensed with because a person can be justified by his subjective acts of faith and contrition even before the reception of these sacraments.

The reflex self-realization of a previously anony-mous Christianity is demanded (1) by the incarna-tional and social structure of grace and of Christi-anity, and (2) because the individual who grasps Christi-anity in a clearer, purer and more reflective way has, other things being equal, a still greater chance of sal-vation than someone who is merely an anonymous Christian. If, however, the message of the Church is directed to someone who is a "non-Christian" only in the sense of living by an anonymous Christianity not as yet fully conscious of itself, then her missionary work must take this fact into account and must draw the necessary conclusions when deciding on its mis-sionary strategy and tactics....

FOURTH THESIS

It is possibly too much to hope, on the one hand, that the religious pluralism which exists in the concrete situation of Christians will disappear in the foreseeable future. On the other hand, it is nevertheless absolutely permissible for the Chris-tian himself to interpret this non-Christianity as Christianity of an anonymous kind which he does always still go out to meet as a missionary, seeing it as a world which is to be brought to the explicit consciousness of what already belongs to it as a divine offer or already pertains to it also over and above this as a divine gift of grace accepted unre-flectedly and implicitly....

Non-Christians may think it presumption for the Christian to judge everything which is sound or restored (by being sanctified) to be the fruit in every man of the grace of his Christ, and to interpret it as anonymous Christianity; they may think it presump-tion for the Christian to regard the non-Christian as a Christian who has not yet come to himself reflec-tively. But the Christian cannot renounce this "pre-sumption" which is really the source of the greatest humility both for himself and for the Church. For it is a profound admission of the fact that God is greater than man and the Church. The Church will go out to meet the non-Christian of tomorrow with the attitude expressed by St. Paul when he said: What therefore you do not know and yet worship [and yet *worship*!] that I proclaim to you (Acts 17:23). On such a basis one can be tolerant, humble and yet firm towards all non-Christian religions.

STUDY QUESTIONS

1. What is Rahner's first thesis regarding Christianity, and how does he qualify this thesis in terms of the historical development of religion?
2. In his second thesis, what does Rahner mean by a lawful religion? In what sense would a religion be lawful?
3. What are implications of Rahner's claim that humans can live out their relationship to God only in society?
4. What does Rahner mean by "anonymous Christian"? Could believers from a religion other than Christianity apply the term "anonymous X" to a person who has not yet encountered their religious tradition? Why, or why not?

John Hick

Religious Pluralism

John Hick (b. 1922) believes that the various world faiths embody different views of Ultimate Reality and thus provide different ways to attain what is called in different religions salvation, liberation, enlightenment, or fulfillment. This transformation is essentially the same in all religions, just portrayed differently. To those who object by insisting that Christianity is unique because it was founded by God incarnate in Jesus, Hick replies that God can act through many individuals who are open to God. Jesus was not uniquely divine but merely one of many such persons. To those who point out that the different religions provide incompatible descriptions of Reality, he responds that each tradition believes that Reality exceeds our creaturely understanding. Each person experiences Reality as it appears to him or her in a unique cultural situation. In other words, each religious tradition conditions its adherents' understanding of Reality and provides authentic and appropriate ways for them to respond to it.

Wilfred Cantwell Smith in his work on the concepts of religion and of religions has been responsible, more than any other one individual, for the change which has taken place within a single generation in the way in which many of us perceive the religious life of mankind.

Seen through pre–Cantwell Smith eyes there are a number of vast, long-lived historical entities or organisms known as Christianity, Hinduism, Islam, Buddhism, and so on. Each has an inner skeletal framework of beliefs, giving shape to a distinctive form of religious life, wrapped in a thick institutional skin which divides it from other religions and from the secular world within which they exist. Thus Buddhism, Islam, Christianity, and the rest, are seen as contraposed socio-religious entities which are the bearers of distinctive creeds; and every religious individual is a member of one or other of these mutually exclusive groups.

This way of seeing the religious life of humanity, as organised in a number of communities based upon rival sets of religious beliefs, leads to the posing of questions about religion in a certain way. For the beliefs which a religion professes are beliefs about God, or the Ultimate, and as such they define a way of human salvation or liberation and are accordingly a matter of spiritual life and death. Looking at the religions of the world, then, in the plural we are presented with competing claims to possess the saving truth. For each community believes that its own gospel is true and that other gospels are false in so far as they differ from it. Each believes that the way of salvation to which it witnesses is the authentic way, the only sure path to eternal blessedness. And so the proper question in face of this plurality of claims is, which is the true religion?

In practice, those who are concerned to raise this question are normally fully convinced that theirs is the true religion; so that for them the task is to show the spiritual superiority of their own creed and the consequent moral superiority of the community which embodies it. A great deal of the mutual criticism of religions, and of the derogatory assessment of one by another, has been in fulfilment of this task.

This view of mankind's religious life as divided into great contraposed entities, each claiming to be the true religion, is not however the only possible way of seeing the religious situation. Cantwell Smith has offered an alternative vision.

He shows first that the presently dominant conceptuality has a history that can be traced back to the European Renaissance. It was then that the different streams of religious life began to be reified in Western thought as solid structures called Christianity, Judaism, and so forth. And having reified their own faith in this way Westerners have then exported the notion of "a religion" to the rest of the world, causing others to think of themselves as belonging to the Hindu, or the Confucian, or the Buddhist religion, and so on, over against others. But an alternative perception can divide the scene differently. It sees something of vital religious significance taking different forms all over the world within the contexts of the different historical traditions. This "something of vital religious significance" Cantwell Smith calls faith. I would agree with some of his critics that this is not the ideal word for it; for "faith" is a term that is more at home in the Semitic than in the Indian family of traditions and which has, as his own historical researches have shown, become badly overintellectualised. But I take it that he uses the term to refer to the spiritual state, or existential condition, constituted by a person's present response to the ultimate divine Reality. This ranges from the negative response of a self-enclosed consciousness which is blind to the divine presence, whether beyond us or in the depths of our own being,

to a positive openness to the Divine which gradually transforms us and which is called salvation or liberation or enlightenment. This transformation is essentially the same within the different religious contexts within which it occurs: I would define it formally as the transformation of human existence from self-centredness to Reality-centredness. This is the event or process of vital significance which one can see to be occurring in individuals all over the world, taking different forms within the contexts of the different perceptions of the Ultimate made available by the various religious traditions.

These cumulative traditions themselves are the other thing that one sees with the aid of the new conceptuality suggested by Cantwell Smith. They are distinguishable strands of human history in each of which a multitude of religious and cultural elements interact to form a distinctive pattern, constituting, say, the Hindu, Buddhist, Confucian, Jewish, Christian, or Muslim tradition. These traditions are not static entities but living movements; and they are not tightly homogeneous but have each become in the course of time internally highly various. Thus there are large differences between, for example, Buddhism in the time of Gautama and Buddhism after the development of the Mahāyāna and its expansion northwards into China; or between the Christian movement in Roman Palestine and that in medieval Europe. And there are large differences today between, say, Zen and Amida Buddhism in Japan, or between Southern Baptist and Northern Episcopalian Christianity in the United States. Indeed, since we cannot always avoid using the substantives, we might do well to speak of Buddhisms, Christianities, and so on, in the plural. A usage consonant with Cantwell Smith's analysis has however already become widespread, and many of us now often prefer to speak not of Christianity but of the Christian tradition, the Hindu tradition, and so on, when referring to these historically identifiable strands of history.

These cumulative traditions are composed of a rich complex of inner and outer elements cohering in a distinctive living pattern which includes structures of belief, life-styles, scriptures and their interpretations, liturgies, cultic celebrations, myths, music, poetry, architecture, literature, remembered history and its heroes. Thus the traditions constitute religious cultures, each with its own unique history and ethos. And each such tradition creates human beings in its own image. For we are not human in general, participating in an eternal Platonic essence of humanity. We are human in one or other of the various concrete ways of being human which constitute the cultures of the earth. There is a Chinese way of being human, an African way, an Arab way, a European way, or ways, and so on. These are not fixed moulds but living organisms which develop and interact over the centuries, so that the patterns of human life change, usually very slowly but sometimes with startling rapidity. But we are all formed in a hundred ways of which we are not normally aware by the culture into which we were born, by which we are fed, and with which we interact.

Let us then enter, with Cantwell Smith, into the experiment of thinking, on the one hand, of "faith," or human response to the divine, which in its positive and negative forms is salvation and non-salvation and, on the other hand, of the cumulative religious traditions within which this occurs; and let us ask what the relation is between these two realities—on the one hand salvation/liberation and on the other the cumulative traditions....

[We omit Hick's discussion of "exclusivism."]

However, we may now turn to a second Christian answer to our question, which can be labelled "inclusivism." This can be expressed in terms either of a juridical or of a transformation-of-human-existence conception of salvation. In the former terms it is the view that God's forgiveness and acceptance of humanity have been made possible by Christ's death, but that the benefits of this sacrifice are not confined to those who respond to it with an explicit act of faith. The juridical transaction of Christ's atonement covered all human sin, so that all human beings are now open to God's mercy, even though they may never have heard of Jesus Christ and why he died on the cross of Calvary....

Rahner's is a brave attempt to attain an inclusivist position which is in principle universal but which does not thereby renounce the old exclusivist dogma. But the question is whether in this new context the old dogma has not been so emptied of content as

no longer to be worth affirming. When salvation is acknowledged to be taking place without any connection with the Christian Church or Gospel, in people who are living on the basis of quite other faiths, is it not a somewhat empty gesture to insist upon affixing a Christian label to them? Further, having thus labelled them, why persist in the aim of gathering all humankind into the Christian Church? Once it is accepted that salvation does not depend upon this, the conversion of the people of the other great world faiths to Christianity hardly seems the best way of spending one's energies.

The third possible answer to the question of the relation between salvation/liberation and the cumulative religious traditions can best be called pluralism. As a Christian position this can be seen as an acceptance of the further conclusion to which inclusivism points. If we accept that salvation/liberation is taking place within all the great religious traditions, why not frankly acknowledge that there is a plurality of saving human responses to the ultimate divine Reality? Pluralism, then, is the view that the transformation of human existence from self-centredness to Reality-centredness is taking place in different ways within the contexts of all the great religious traditions. There is not merely one way but a plurality of ways of salvation or liberation. In Christian theological terms, there is a plurality of divine revelations, making possible a plurality of forms of saving human response.

What however makes it difficult for Christians to move from inclusivism to pluralism, holding the majority of Christian theologians today in the inclusivist position despite its evident logical instability, is of course the traditional doctrine of the Incarnation, together with its protective envelope, the doctrine of the Trinity. For in its orthodox form, as classically expressed at the Councils of Nicaea and Chalcedon, the incarnational doctrine claims that Jesus was God incarnate, the Second Person of the Triune God living a human life. It is integral to this faith that there has been (and will be) no other divine incarnation. This makes Christianity unique in that it, alone among the religions of the world, was founded by God in person. Such a uniqueness would seem to demand Christian exclusivism—for must God not want all human beings to enter the way of salvation which he has provided for them? However, since such exclusivism seems so unrealistic in the light of our knowledge of the wider religious life of mankind, many theologians have moved to some form of inclusivism, but now feel unable to go further and follow the argument to its conclusion in the frank acceptance of pluralism. The break with traditional missionary attitudes and long-established ecclesiastical and liturgical language would, for many, be so great as to be prohibitive.

There is however the possibility of an acceptable Christian route to religious pluralism in work which has already been done, and which is being done, in the field of Christology with motivations quite other than to facilitate pluralism, and on grounds which are internal to the intellectual development of Christianity. For there is a decisive watershed between what might be called all-or-nothing Christologies and degree Christologies. The all-or-nothing principle is classically expressed in the Chalcedonian Definition, according to which Christ is "to be acknowledged in Two Natures," "Consubstantial with the Father according to his Deity, Consubstantial with us according to his Humanity." Substance is an all-or-nothing notion, in that A either is or is not composed of the same substance, either has or does not have the same essential nature, as B. Using this all-or-nothing conceptuality Chalcedon attributed to Christ two complete natures, one divine and the other human, being in his divine nature of one substance with God the Father. Degree Christologies, on the other hand, apply the term "incarnation" to the activity of God's Spirit or of God's grace in human lives, so that the divine will is done on earth.... In so far as a human being is open and responsive to God, so that God is able to act in and through that individual, we can speak of the embodiment in human life of God's redemptive activity. And in Jesus this "paradox of grace"—the paradox expressed by St. Paul when he wrote "it was not I, but the grace of God which is in me" (1 Corinthians 15:10)—or the inspiration of God's Spirit, occurred to a startling extent. The paradox, or the inspiration, are not however confined to the life of Jesus; they are found, in varying degrees, in all free human response to God....

These modern degree Christologies were not in fact for the most part developed in order to facilitate a Christian acceptance of religious pluralism. They were developed as alternatives to the old substance Christology, in which so many difficulties, both historical and philosophical, had become apparent. They claim to be compatible with the teachings of Jesus and of the very early Church, and to avoid the intractable problem, generated by a substance Christology, of the relation between Jesus's two natures. But, as an unintended consequence, degree Christologies open up the possibility of seeing God's activity in Jesus as being of the same kind as God's activity in other great human mediators of the divine. The traditional Christian claim to the unique superiority of Christ and of the Christian tradition is not of course precluded by a degree Christology; for it may be argued that Christ was the *supreme* instance of the paradox of grace or of the inspiration of the Spirit, so that Christianity is still assumed to be the *best* context of salvation/liberation. But, whereas, starting from the substance Christology, the unique superiority of Christ and the Christian Church are guaranteed a priori, starting from a degree Christology they have to be established by historical evidence. Whether this can in fact be done is, clearly, an open question. It would indeed be an uphill task today to establish that we know enough about the inner and outer life of the historical Jesus, and of the other founders of great religious traditions, to be able to make any such claim; and perhaps an even more uphill task to establish from the morally ambiguous histories of each of the great traditions, complex mixtures of good and evil as each has been, that one's own tradition stands out as manifestly superior to all others.

I think, then, that a path exists along which Christians can, if they feel so drawn, move to an acceptance of religious pluralism. Stated philosophically such a pluralism is the view that the great world faiths embody different perceptions and conceptions of, and correspondingly different responses to, the Real or the Ultimate from within the major variant cultural ways of being human; and that within each of them the transformation of human existence from self-centredness to Reality-centredness is manifestly taking place—and taking place, so far as human observation can tell, to much the same extent. Thus the great religious traditions are to be regarded as alternative soteriological "spaces" within which, or "ways" along which, men and women can find salvation/liberation/enlightenment/fulfilment.

But how can such a view be arrived at? Are we not proposing a picture reminiscent of the ancient allegory of the blind men and the elephant, in which each runs his hands over a different part of the animal, and identifies it differently, a leg as a tree, the trunk as a snake, the tail as a rope, and so on? Clearly, in the story the situation is being described from the point of view of someone who can observe both elephant and blind men. But where is the vantage-point from which one can observe both the divine Reality and the different limited human standpoints from which that Reality is being variously perceived? The advocate of the pluralist understanding cannot pretend to any such cosmic vision. How then does he profess to know that the situation is indeed as he depicts it? The answer is that he does not profess to *know* this, if by knowledge we mean infallible cognition. Nor indeed can anyone else properly claim to have knowledge, in this sense, of either the exclusivist or the inclusivist picture. All of them are, strictly speaking, hypotheses. The pluralist hypothesis is arrived at inductively. One starts from the fact that many human beings experience life in relation to a limitlessly greater transcendent Reality—whether the direction of transcendence be beyond our present existence or within its hidden depths. In theory such religious experience is capable of a purely naturalistic analysis which does not involve reference to any reality other than the human and the natural. But to participate by faith in one of the actual streams of religious experience—in my case, the Christian stream—is to participate in it as an experience of transcendent Reality. I think that there is in fact a good argument for the rationality of trusting one's own religious experience, together with that of the larger tradition within which it occurs, so as both to believe and to live on the basis of it; but I cannot develop that argument here. Treating one's own form of religious experience, then, as veridical—as an experience (however dim, like "seeing through a glass, darkly") of transcendent divine Reality—one then has to take account of the fact that there are other great streams of religious experience which take different forms, are shaped by different conceptualities,

and embodied in different institutions, art forms, and lifestyles. In other words, besides one's own religion, sustained by its distinctive form of religious experience, there are also other religions, through each of which flows the life blood of a different form of religious experience. What account is one to give of this plurality? . . .

But if we look for the transcendence of egoism and a recentring in God or in the transcendent Real, then I venture the proposition that, so far as human observation and historical memory can tell, this occurs to about the same extent within each of the great world traditions.

If this is so, it prompts us to go beyond inclusivism to a pluralism which recognises a variety of human religious contexts within which salvation/liberation takes place.

But such a pluralistic hypothesis raises many questions. What is this divine Reality to which all the great traditions are said to be oriented? Can we really equate the personal Yahweh with the non-personal Brahman, Shiva with the Tao, the Holy Trinity with the Buddhist Trikāya, and all with one another? Indeed, do not the Eastern and Western faiths deal incommensurably with different problems?

As these questions indicate, we need a pluralistic theory which enables us to recognise and be fascinated by the manifold differences between the religious traditions, with their different conceptualisations, their different modes of religious experience, and their different forms of individual and social response to the divine. I should like in these final pages to suggest the ground plan of such a theory—a theory which is, I venture to think, fully compatible with the central themes of Cantwell Smith's thought.

Each of the great religious traditions affirms that in addition to the social and natural world of our ordinary human experience there is a limitlessly greater and higher Reality beyond or within us, in relation to which or to whom is our highest good. The ultimately real and the ultimately valuable are one, and to give oneself freely and totally to this One is our final salvation/liberation/enlightenment/fulfilment. Further, each tradition is conscious that the divine Reality exceeds the reach of our earthly speech and thought. It cannot be encompassed in human concepts. It is infinite, eternal, limitlessly rich beyond the scope of our finite conceiving or experiencing. Let us then both avoid the particular names used within the particular traditions and yet use a term which is consonant with the faith of each of them—Ultimate Reality, or the Real.

Let us next adopt a distinction that is to be found in different forms and with different emphases within each of the great traditions, the distinction between the Real *an sich* (in him/her/itself) and the Real as humanly experienced and thought. In Christian terms this is the distinction between God in God's infinite and eternal self-existent being, "prior" to and independent of creation, and God as related to and known by us as creator, redeemer and sanctifier. In Hindu thought it is the distinction between *nirguṇa* Brahman, the Ultimate in itself, beyond all human categories, and *saguṇa* Brahman, the Ultimate as known to finite consciousness as a personal deity, Iśvara. In Taoist thought, "The Tao that can be expressed is not the eternal Tao" (*Tao-Te Ching*, 1). There are also analogous distinctions in Jewish and Muslim mystical thought in which the Real *an sich* is called *en Soph* and *al Haqq*. In Mahāyāna Buddhism there is the distinction between the *dharmakāya*, the eternal cosmic Buddha-nature, which is also the infinite Void (*śūnyatā*), and on the other hand the realm of heavenly Buddha figures (*sambhogkāya*) and their incarnations in the earthly Buddhas (*nirmāṇakāya*). This varied family of distinctions suggests the perhaps daring thought that the Real *an sich* is one but is nevertheless capable of being humanly experienced in a variety of ways. This thought lies at the heart of the pluralistic hypothesis which I am suggesting.

The next point of which we need to take account is the creative part that thought, and the range of concepts in terms of which it functions, plays in the formation of conscious experience. It was above all Immanuel Kant who brought this realisation into the stream of modern reflection, and it has since been confirmed and amplified by innumerable studies, not only in general epistemology but also in cognitive psychology, in the sociology of knowledge, and in the philosophy of science. The central fact, of which the epistemology of religion also has to take account, is that our environment is not reflected in our consciousness in a simple and straightforward way, just as it is, independently of our perceiving it. At the physical level, out of the immense richness of structure and detail around us, only that minute selection that is relevant to our biological survival and flourishing affects our senses; and these inputs are interpreted in the mind/brain to produce our conscious experience of the familiar world in which we live. Its character as an environment within which we can learn to behave appropriately can be called its *meaning* for us. This all-important dimension of meaning, which begins at the physical level as the habitability of the material world, continues at the personal, or social, level of awareness as the moral significance of the situations of our life, and at the religious level as a consciousness of the ultimate meaning of each situation and of our situation as a whole in relation to the divine Reality. This latter consciousness is not however a general consciousness of the divine, but always takes specific forms; and, as in the case of the awareness of the physical and of the ethical meaning of our environment, such consciousness has an essential dispositional aspect. To experience in this way rather than in that involves being in a state of readiness to behave in a particular range of ways, namely, that which is appropriate to our environment having the particular character that we perceive (or of course misperceive) it to have. Thus to be aware of the divine as "the God and Father of our Lord Jesus Christ," in so far as this is the operative awareness which determines our dispositional state, is to live in the kind of way described by Jesus in his religious and moral teaching—in trust towards God and in love towards our neighbours.

How are these various specific forms of religious awareness formed? Our hypothesis is that they are formed by the presence of the divine Reality, this presence coming to consciousness in terms of the different sets of religious concepts and structures of religious meaning that operate within the different religious traditions of the world. If we look at the range of actual human religious experience and ask ourselves what basic concepts and what concrete images have operated in its genesis, I would suggest that we arrive at something like the following answer. There are, first, the two basic religious concepts which between them dominate the entire range of the forms of religious experience. One is the concept of Deity, or God, i.e., the Real as personal; and the other is the concept of the Absolute, i.e., the Real as non-personal. (The term "Absolute" is by no means ideal for the purpose, but is perhaps the nearest that we have.) We do not however, in actual religious experience, encounter either Deity in general or the Absolute in general, but always in specific forms. In Kantian language, each general concept is schematised, or made concrete. In Kant's own analysis of sense-experience the schematisation of the basic categories is in terms of time; but religious experience occurs at a much higher level of meaning, presupposing and going beyond physical meaning and involving much more complex and variable modes of dispositional response. Schematisation or concretisation here is in terms of "filled" human time, or history, as diversified into the different cultures and civilisations of the earth. For there are different concrete ways of being human and of participating in human history, and within these different ways the presence of the divine Reality is experienced in characteristically different ways.

To take the concept of God first, this becomes concrete as the range of specific deities to which the history of religion bears witness. Thus the Real as personal is known in the Christian tradition as God the Father; in Judaism as Adonai; in Islam as Allah, the Qur'ānic Revealer; in the Indian traditions as Shiva, or Vishnu, or Paramātmā, and under the many other lesser images of deity which in different regions of India concretise different aspects of the divine nature. This range of personal deities who are the foci of worship within the theistic traditions constitutes the range of the divine personae in relation to mankind. Each persona, in his or her historical concreteness, lives within the corporate experience of a particular faith-community. Thus the Yahweh persona exists and has developed in interaction with the Jewish people. He is a part of their history, and they are a part of his; and he cannot be extracted from this historical context. Shiva, on the other hand, is a quite different divine persona existing in the experience of hundreds of millions of people in the Shaivite stream of Indian religious life. These two personae, Yahweh and Shiva, live within different worlds of faith, partly creating and partly created by the features of different human

cultures, being responded to in different patterns of life, and being integral to different strands of historical experience. Within each of these worlds of faith great numbers of people find the ultimate meaning of their existence, and are carried through the crises of life and death; and within this process many are, in varying degrees, challenged and empowered to move forward on the way of salvation/liberation from self-centredness to Reality-centredness. From the pluralist point of view Yahweh and Shiva are not rival gods, or rival claimants to be the one and only God, but rather two different concrete historical personae in terms of which the ultimate divine Reality is present and responded to by different large historical communities within different strands of the human story.

This conception of divine personae, constituting (in Kantian language) different divine phenomena in terms of which the one divine noumenon is humanly experienced, enables us to acknowledge the degree of truth within the various projection theories of religion from Feuerbach through Freud to the present day. An element of human projection colours our mental images of God, accounting for their anthropomorphic features—for example, as male or female. But human projection does not—on this view—bring God into existence; rather it affects the ways in which the independently existing divine Reality is experienced.

Does this epistemological pattern of the schematisation of a basic religious concept into a range of particular correlates of religious experience apply also to the non-theistic traditions? I suggest that it does. Here the general concept, the Absolute, is schematised in actual religious experience to form the range of divine impersonae—Brahman, the Dharma, the Tao, nirvāṇa, śūyatā, and so on—which are experienced within the Eastern traditions. The structure of these impersonae is however importantly different from that of the personae. A divine persona is concrete, implicitly finite, sometimes visualisable and even capable of being pictured. A divine impersona, on the other hand, is not a "thing" in contrast to a person. It is the infinite being—consciousness—bliss (saccidānanda) of Brahman; or the beginningless and endless process of cosmic change (pratītya samutpāda) of Buddhist teaching; or again the ineffable "further shore" of *nirvāṇa*, or the eternal Buddha-nature (*dharmakāya*); or the ultimate Emptiness (*śūnyatā*) which is also the fullness or suchness of the world; or the eternal principle the Tao. It is thus not so much an entity as a field of spiritual force, or the ultimate reality of everything, that which gives final meaning and joy. These non-personal conceptions of the Ultimate inform modes of consciousness varying from the advaitic experience of becoming one with the Infinite, to the Zen experience of finding a total reality in the present concrete moment of existence in the ordinary world. And according to the pluralistic hypothesis these different modes of experience constitute different experiences of the Real as non- or trans-personal. As in the case of the divine *personae*, they are formed by different religious conceptualities which have developed in interaction with different spiritual disciplines and methods of mediation. The evidence that a range of *impersonae* of the one Ultimate Reality are involved in the non-theistic forms of religious experience, rather than the direct unmediated awareness of Reality itself, consists precisely in the differences between the experiences reported within the different traditions. How is it that a "direct experience" of the Real can take such different forms? One could of course at this point revert to the exclusivism or the inclusivism whose limitations we have already noted. But the pluralist answer will be that even the most advanced form of mystical experience, as an experience undergone by an embodied consciousness whose mind/brain has been conditioned by a particular religious tradition, must be affected by the conceptual framework and spiritual training provided by that tradition, and accordingly takes these different forms. In other words the Real is experienced not *an sich*, but in terms of the various non-personal images or concepts that have been generated at the interface between the Real and different patterns of human consciousness.

These many different perceptions of the Real, both theistic and nontheistic, can only establish themselves as authentic by their soteriological efficacy. The great world traditions have in fact all proved to be realms within which or routes along which people are enabled to advance in the transition from self-centredness to Reality-centredness. And, since they reveal the Real in such different lights, we must conclude that they are independently valid. Accordingly, by attending to other traditions than one's own one may become aware of other aspects or dimensions of the Real, and of other possibilities of response to the Real, which had not been made effectively available by one's own tradition. Thus a mutual mission of the sharing of experiences and insights can proceed through the growing network of interfaith dialogue and the interactions of the faith communities. Such mutual mission does not aim at conversion—although occasionally individual conversions, in all directions, will continue to occur—but at mutual enrichment and at cooperation in face of the urgent problems of human survival in a just and sustainable world society.

STUDY QUESTIONS

1. How does Hick understand the relationships among the various religious traditions?
2. What objections does Hick raise against Rahner's inclusivism?
3. How does the story of the blind men and the elephant illustrate Hick's pluralism?
4. How does Hick's use of Kant's philosophy help him to account for the diverse views religions have of the Real or Absolute?

SUGGESTED READING

Barnes, Michael. *Religions in Conversation*. London: SPCK, 1989.

Basinger, David. *Religious Diversity: A Philosophical Assessment*. Aldershot, England: Ashgate, 2001.

Coward, Harold, ed. *Modern Indian Responses to Religious Pluralism*. Albany: State University Press of New York Press, 1987.

D'Costa, Gavin, ed. *Christian Uniqueness Reconsidered: The Myth of a Pluralistic Theology of Religions*. Maryknoll, N.Y.: Orbis, 1990.

———. *Theology and Religious Pluralism: The Challenge of Other Religions*. London: Blackwell, 1986.

Dean, Thomas, ed. *Religious Pluralism and Truth: Essays on Cross-Cultural Philosophy of Religion*. Albany: State University of New York Press, 1995.

DiNoia, J. A. *The Diversity of Religions: A Christian Perspective*. Washington, D.C.: Catholic University of America Press, 1992.

Eck, Diana L. *Encountering God: A Spiritual Journey from Bozeman to Banaras*. Boston: Beacon, 1993.

Griffiths, Paul J. *An Apology for Apologetics: A Study in the Logic of Interreligious Dialogue*. Maryknoll, N.Y.: Orbis, 1991.

———. *Problems of Religious Diversity*. London: Blackwell, 2001.

Heim, S. Mark. *Salvations: Truth and Difference in Religion*. Maryknoll, N.Y.: Orbis, 1995.

Hick, John. *An Interpretation of Religion: Human Responses to the Transcendent*. New Haven, Conn.: Yale University Press, 1991.

———, ed. *Problems of Religious Pluralism*. New York: St. Martin's Press, 1988.

———, and Brian Hebblethwaite, eds. *Christianity and Other Religions*. Glasgow: Collins, 1980.

———, and Paul Knitter. *The Myth of Christian Uniqueness: Toward a Pluralistic Theology of Religions*. Maryknoll, N.Y.: Orbis, 1990.

Kiblinger, Kristin Beise. *Buddhist Inclusivism*. Aldershot, England: Ashgate, 2005.

Knitter, Paul. *No Other Name? A Critical Survey of Christian Attitudes Toward World Religions*. Maryknoll, N.Y.: Orbis, 1985.

Kung, Hans, et al. *Christianity and the World Religions: Paths to Dialogue with Islam, Hinduism, and Buddhism*. Garden City, N.Y.: Doubleday & Company, 1986.

McKim, Robert. *Religious Ambiguity and Religious Diversity*. New York: Oxford University Press, 2001.

Nash, Ronald. *Is Jesus the Only Saviour?* Grand Rapids, Mich.: Zondervan, 1994.

Netland, Harold. *Dissonant Voices: Religious Pluralism and the Question of Truth*. Grand Rapids, Mich: William B. Eerdmans, 1991.

Ogden, Shubert. *Is There Only One True Religion or Are There Many?* Dallas, Tex.: Southern Methodist Press, 1992.

Pinnock, Clark H. *A Wideness in God's Mercy*. Grand Rapids, Mich.: Zondervan, 1992.

Quinn, Philip L., and Kevin Meeker, eds. *The Philosophical Challenge of Religious Diversity*. New York: Oxford University Press, 2000.

Sanders, John. *No Other Name! A Biblical, Historical, and Theological Investigation into the Destiny of the Unevangelized*. Grand Rapids, Mich.: William B. Eerdmans, 1992.

Smith, Wilfred Cantwell. *Towards a World Theology*. Philadelphia: Westminster, 1981.

Yandell, Keith E. *Christianity and Philosophy*. Grand Rapids, Mich.: William B. Eerdmans, 1984.

PART FOURTEEN

Religion and Morality

The Source of Religious Ethical Truth

All of us affirm ethical principles related to almost every aspect of our lives. That is, we believe we have some understanding of how we, our family and friends, and even those with whom we will never have any direct contact *ought* to behave. But what is the origin of the ethical principles we believe to be true? At one level an answer is readily available. We initially acquired the vast majority of these principles in the same fashion we initially acquired many other beliefs: from respected authorities such as our parents, teachers, and religious leaders.

What, however, is the *ultimate* origin of the ethical principles we hold to be true? A great many religious persons maintain that the basic moral principles they affirm have their origin in God, as opposed to human thought or some source totally independent of both. Yet this claim has generated a significant number of philosophical debates, some as old as the famed discussion between Socrates and Euthyphro.

One important debate emerges over an apparent dilemma for believers. If believers say that whatever God wills is morally right, then do they mean that anything—even rape or torture—could be morally permissible or even obligatory as long as it is commanded by God? This horn of the dilemma seems to make God's morality something alien to our highest ideals. On the other hand, if believers say that God cannot contravene fundamental moral laws, then must they acknowledge that such laws are somehow independent of God and beyond God's control? This horn seems to admit something that is binding upon God.

Some believers think that they successfully avoid the dilemma by arguing that God's commands must be consistent with absolute moral norms but that these norms themselves have their origin in God's nature. Other theists, however, do not grant this "moral continuity" thesis. God, it is argued, has created a consistent, thoughtful ethical standard for humans—a standard that, if followed, will bring about what God desires and the greatest fulfillment for all. But God is not bound by such a standard. God can do whatever God wants for whatever reasons God has, and such actions are ethically justifiable simply because God has performed them.

The Authoritative Basis of Religious Ethical Truth

Whatever one's position on this issue, a significant question remains: what gives the ethical principles that originate in God their authority? To put it another way, why ought the theist obey what God communicates? Or, as Alasdair MacIntyre poses this question in the first reading, What conditions must be satisfied for it to be rational for someone to treat God's [ethical] beliefs as authoritative? It is true, Macintyre maintains, that believers are to consider God's commands authoritative and are thus obligated to follow them. However, this is only problematic if it is possible that God could command something that is unjust. And this cannot be the case. Specifically, "it is incompatible with the nature of . . . God that he should ever command anyone to do what it would be right for that person to do with a divided mind, feeling, or will, in which obedience to the divine command was combined with a justified judgment that in some respects it was bad to do what God commanded." It might appear, Macintyre acknowledges, that this means we in some sense judge God by a standard external to God. However, since our understanding of what is just has its source in God, we can justifiably maintain that we must assess God's commands before following them and yet consider God's commands authoritative.

The Acquisition of Religiously Based Ethical Truth

Let us assume, then, for the sake of argument, that theists can justifiably maintain not only that ethical truth originates in God but also that such truth is authoritative for this reason. This still leaves us with the question of how theists acquire this ethical insight.

Three distinct, although not mutually exclusive, methods of acquisition are mentioned most frequently. First, theists often claim that God has communicated ethical truths through some form of written revelation—for example, the Bible or the Qur'an. Opinions differ widely on the extent of God's involvement in the production of this revelation. Some believe that God is directly responsible for every word; others believe that God is responsible for the basic concepts; and still others believe that God is responsible only for helping to collate the most accurate human ethical insights. But many, if not most, theists hold that written revelation is a very important source of information about the ethical principles by which God wants us to live.

A second method of acquisition, often labeled the "natural law" tradition, is explicated by Thomas Aquinas in the second reading in this section. God, Aquinas maintains, is the ultimate source of all ethical knowledge. That is, God establishes the ultimate distinction between good and evil. However, as the result of being created in God's image, we as humans possess the rational capacities to comprehend those aspects of this ethical standard that have been revealed in nature. That is, from our observation of the natural order, we can deduce how human beings are to act and to be treated.

This does not mean, Thomas argues elsewhere, that such ethical reflection is a more trustworthy avenue for discerning ethical truth than written revelation. In fact, he argues that written revelation must be given precedence in the event of a conflict. However, although written revelation is *sufficient* for giving us God's basic ethical perspective, it is not always *necessary*. Human reflection on the nature of things can uncover much about God's basic ethical standards and their application to our daily lives.

Third, as has already been implicitly noted, some theists also claim that divine ethical truth is at least in part innate. Each of us, they maintain, has been created in the "image of God," including God's "ethical image." And this means that our basic ethical intuitions—for example, the belief that we should not kill innocent children—automatically mirror God's basic ethical perspectives. Some have argued that such innate intuitions may require some external illumination before we become consciously aware of them. We may, for instance, need to understand what a child is, and what killing means, before we become consciously aware of the fact that killing children is wrong. Moreover, not all available ethical insight comes to us in this fashion. Written revelation and reason are also necessary. But some of the basic ethical principles we believe to be true, these theists argue, were not "learned." We, as divine creations, were simply "born" with them.

There is, however, a seemingly serious problem that proponents of all three of these modes of acquiring divine ethical truth must face. Why is there so much ethical diversity among theists? That is, why do seemingly sincere, knowledgeable theists differ significantly on so many issues related to human thought and action? If theists have access to basic ethical truth, as they claim, why is there not greater ethical consensus?

In response, many theists emphasize the important distinction between affirming *different* basic ethical principles and ranking the *same* basic ethical principles differently. Take, for example, the case of Christians who were hiding Jews in their homes during World War II. All of the Christians involved thought it was their God-sanctioned duty both to protect innocent lives *and* not to lie. They differed on the question of which principle was properly to be given precedence in this case.

Other theists hold that the human ability to identify divine ethical principles accurately has been severely damaged by "the fall"—that is, by a break in the relationship between humans beings and God that was precipitated by a human act of rebellion. Thus, they claim that although many of us at times are able to discern with relative accuracy the ethical principles affirmed by God, some of us will inevitably be unable to do so, or at least be unable to do so consistently.

Finally, those theists who maintain that some ethical truth is "inborn" often emphasize the significance of cultural conditioning. It is one thing, they argue, to say that each human has some basic understanding of the divine ethical law, but quite another thing to say that such an understanding will always be consciously felt as predominant. Individuals are greatly influenced by their culture. If, for instance, they are raised in a culture where stealing or cheating or lying is condoned, they will have a strong disposition to believe it is right to engage in such activities.

Of course, even if all this is granted, pervasive ethical diversity among and within religious perspectives still leaves us with the following question: which religious ethical standard most closely resembles God's standard? And this surely is an important question, in that much strife throughout history has been the result of individuals or groups acting on what they perceived to be the correct set of divinely sanctioned ethical principles. In fact, it is so important that the reality of pervasive diversity might be a good reason for theists to periodically reassess their ethical beliefs (and the behavior such beliefs are likely to generate). That is, such diversity may well stand as a real challenge to ethical dogmatism, especially in action.

However, just as the reality of diversity in political opinion does not necessarily require us to become political relativists or skeptics, the reality of ethical diversity does not necessarily require us to become ethical relativists or skeptics. Ethical diversity ought to be recognized and considered by theists as they put their ethical beliefs into action. But acknowledged diversity doesn't invalidate justified belief. Thus, it does not follow from the fact that theists acknowledge the reality of ethical diversity that they cannot justifiably claim that an ethical truth exists, that such truth is divine in origin, or even that they have access to it.

ETHICS WITHOUT RELIGION

What does all this mean for those individuals who are not religious? Nontheistic and explicitly atheistic ethical systems abound. If theists are correct in holding that ethical truth originates in God and that they have access to such truth, what are the implications for those who do not believe in God (or who deny that ethical truth is in any sense dependent on God)?

In our third reading, Jean-Paul Sartre speaks directly to this question. It is true, Sartre maintains, that if there is no God, then there are no absolute values externally imposed on all of us. Rather, if there is no God, morality is relative in the sense that we must all create our own values. And it is true that to be in this state is sobering, since it means that we alone must decide how to act, that we must acknowledge that our actions have important consequences not only for ourselves but for others, and that we live in a world in which we cannot always know exactly what the consequences of our actions will be. This doesn't mean, though, Sartre adds, that the life we choose for ourselves cannot have personal meaning. Nor does it mean that arbitrary and capricious behavior would be justified because that would not be compatible with a proper understanding of the fact that our actions always have significant consequences for others.

Sartre's claim that we can have personal meaning in our lives, even if there exists no God and thus no ultimate meaning for the world in which we live, has been the subject of continuing debate. But the consensus seems to be that although a nonreligious worldview may require some reworking of the traditional concept of personal meaning, and although some nontheists may in fact not experience personal meaning, it does not follow necessarily that nontheists cannot justifiably affirm an enduring sense of personal meaning. That is, it does not necessarily follow that although a world without God may well not have any cosmic meaning, the values created in a godless world cannot give us adequate personal meaning. A separate argument is needed for this claim, an argument that does not already assume the truth of what is to be proved.

There are also questions concerning the "moral status" of nonbelievers. For instance, some have argued that if ethical truth originates in God, this mean that those who do not believe in God do not have access to such truth, or at least cannot appropriate it as fully as believers can. Other believers maintain, though, that some of God's truths—including moral truths—are available to all human beings God has created. And many nonbelievers maintain that there are perfectly good reasons why we should have the institution of morality as we now have it without positing a God—that morality has an objective rationale completely independent of religion.

CURRENT ISSUES

One approach to ethics to which philosophers have recently been giving considerable attention is called *virtue ethics*, and this has carried over into the religious realm. Religious virtue ethicists question the common assumption that to be ethical from a religious perspective is to act in accordance with revealed rules (duties) that have their grounding in God. Why, they ask, do we continue to conceive of ethical activity primarily in terms of doing what God wants, or even wanting to do what God wants, rather than in terms of being the type of person God wants us to be? We would be better served, we are told, by understanding that the essence of ethical living is to *be* religious—for example, to be Christian or to be Islamic—because then we would quite naturally find ourselves living as we should.

Or, to state this point differently, for the religious virtue ethicist, the essence of ethical activity is not seen as conscious adherence to a set of duties. Specifically, the key to ethical living is not thought to be something that can be abstracted from the religious tradition and rationally applied to culture. We must become part of a tradition—a faith community—in which the character of this community—its intentions, desires, and values—becomes our own. We will then quite naturally find ourselves living as we should. Once we *become* religious, we will act in a properly religious—i.e., ethical—manner. The development of our religious character occurs prior to the realization of our religious duty.

Another approach to ethics currently receiving considerable attention is often labeled "feminist ethics." Although religious feminists differ on the extent to which any ethical system needs general moral rules from which we can deduce appropriate behavior in specific contexts, there is general agreement that traditional ethical systems rely too heavily on abstract generalized principles applied to hypothetical situations, often at the expense of the immediate needs of actual individuals. Specifically, they maintain that these traditional systems speak primarily to the experience of men in power. What is needed, it is argued, is an ethic that not only frees women from patriarchal oppression, but also encourages women's self-affirmation as equal participants in the religious and ethical arenas.

All these complex issues, and *many* others, continue to make the field of religious ethics a fertile area for philosophical discussion.

Alasdair MacIntyre

Which God Ought We to Obey?

Proponents of many religious perspectives have claimed that what is right or good is what God commands. In this reading, Alasdair MacIntyre (b. 1929) acknowledges that we would be under no obligation to consider God's commands authoritative, and thus binding on us, if those commands were unjust. However, it cannot possibly be the case that authentic divine commands are unjust, he argues, since justice is an essential component of God's nature. This means, he acknowledges, that we in some sense judge God by a standard external to God. However, since our understanding of what is just has its source in God, we can justifiably maintain that we must assess God's commands before following them and yet consider God's commands authoritative. And since God's commands can rightly be considered authoritative, they should be obeyed.

THE NATURE OF GOD'S COMMANDS

Some Believe God's Commands Could Be Unjust

Consider first a psychologically primitive version of the relationship between beliefs about right and wrong, justice and injustice, and beliefs about divine commands, one to be found in many social orders in which the father plays a dominant authoritarian role in the life of the young child. This is the version of that relationship identified by Freud, in which what is heard in later life as the commanding voice of god is in fact a numinously and unconsciously disguised echo of the commanding voice of the father. What renders deference to such ostensibly divine commands objectionable is in part the arbitrariness of their content. For whatever the father had in the past happened to have commanded, no matter how contrary to the requirements of justice or of the other virtues, will now be reproduced as the content of the seemingly divine commands. Even if in a particular case what someone's father had in fact commanded was nothing other than what justice and the other virtues require, it would nonetheless be true of that father's offspring that, if his or her father had commanded what was contrary to justice or to any other virtue the same unjust or otherwise vicious content would now be attributed to the divine commands. So believers in a god thus conceived, the god who functions as deified superego, the god whom William Blake named Nobodaddy (see Poems XX and LII from the

From *Faith and Philosophy* 3, no. 4 (October 1986): 359–371. Reprinted by permission.

Notebook, c. 91–2, and "When Klopstock England Defied" pp. 155, 168 and 467 in *The Poems of William Blake* ed. by W. H. Stevenson London: 1971) will if they become aware of the logical relationships informing their beliefs have to acknowledge that if their god had commanded them to perform unjust actions, for example, actions of those kinds that we and they now call "theft" or "adultery," then those commands would have the same authority, would impose upon them the same kind of requirement as do the commands which their god actually utters.... They are committed to acknowledging that Nobodaddy's commands could involve the infliction of unmerited harm upon human beings of a kind incompatible with what some of us now call justice, the justice of desert.

This distinguishes Nobodaddy significantly from any god whose essential identifying attributes include not only that he is just, never inflicting unmerited harm in a way incompatible with the justice of desert, and that his only departures from the justice of desert in cases where desert is relevant to actions are actions of mercy, but also that, just because these are essential attributes, he could not be otherwise. The difference between such a god and Nobodaddy emerges most clearly in the difference in the canon of interpretation which believers must use in interpreting divine actions directed towards them. If a believer in an omnipotent Nobodaddy is apparently confronted by a divine action which seems to him or her from the standpoint which he or she has hitherto adopted the infliction of an unjust gratuitous and unmerited harm upon him or her by Nobodaddy, he or she has no good reason to rule out the possibility that matters just are as they seem to be: Nobodaddy has inflicted or has commanded the infliction by someone else of just such a harm.

It is quite otherwise with the God of the Jewish and Christian scriptures. When in the fable constructed by the author of the Book of Job Job confronts the harms which have befallen him, the one canon of interpretation of God's will which is presupposed both by Job's so-called comforters and also by the utterances of God Himself is that what has happened to Job cannot be, necessarily is not, unmerited harm of a kind incompatible with the justice of desert. Job's so-called comforters argue from the premises that Job has undergone

harm and that God could not ever inflict unmerited harm. They conclude that Job has done something to merit such harm. When God speaks, His message is that Job is owed nothing by Him, for no question of desert arises; Job like the rest of creation owes everything to Him. What we learn—among other things—from the portrait of God in the Book of Job is that the divine infliction of harm of a kind incompatible with justice is not a possible state of affairs.

The essential characteristics then which distinguish the God of the Jewish and Christian scriptures from any of the Nobodaddies whose worship is part of the psychopathology of religious life are that He is just and that He cannot possibly not be. And this is a kind of impossibility which is not derived from defining or partially defining "just" as meaning "commanded by God." The concept of justice and the standard of justice which are required in order to characterize God so as to distinguish him adequately from the class of divine pretenders whom we have been considering are and have to be a concept and a standard elaborated independently of our knowledge of God....

Some Believe Obeying God's Commands Could Be Wrong

Another god from whom it is important to distinguish God is Jupiter. In the *Aeneid* Virgil represents Jupiter as sending Mercury to convey his command to Aeneas to leave Dido and to sail on to Italy (IV,237). Aeneas does obey the divine command, but he is divided not only in his feelings, but also in his will (IV, 361; VI, 460). And Virgil makes it clear that this division of feeling and will does Aeneas credit. The divine command gives Aeneas a good, indeed an overridingly good reason for doing what Jupiter commands, but Aeneas also has good reasons for doing what is contrary to the divine command. It can on Virgil's view be right for someone to obey Jupiter and yet also to have justified regrets for so doing.

The Commands of the Judeo-Christian God Are Just, and Obeying Them, Never Wrong

Jupiter is not the only god of whom this is true. But a god of whom it is signally false is once again the God of the Jewish and Christian scriptures.... It is incompatible with the nature of this God that he should ever command anyone to do what it would be right for that person to do with a divided mind, feelings or will, in which obedience to the divine command was combined with a justified judgment that in some respects it was bad to do what God commanded. Anyone who takes this to be logically possible when the God spoken of is the God of Abraham, Isaac and Jacob has failed to distinguish adequately between God and Jupiter.

Yet that just this may be logically possible is argued by Robert Merrihew Adams in "A Modified Divine Command-Theory of Ethical Wrongness" (*Divine Commands and Morality*, ed. by Paul Helm, Oxford: 1981, pp. 83–108). I say "may be" rather than "is," because Adams says of the theory which he is expounding that he believes it to be defensible, but is not sure that it is correct (p. 83). That theory involves a rejection of what Adams calls the unmodified divine command theory—in essence, Occam's theory—according to which it is logically impossible that it should be true of any action both that it is commanded by God and that it would not be wrong not to do it; it allows by contrast that "there is a logically possible situation which [the modified divine command theorist] would describe by saying 'God commands cruelty for its own sake'" (p. 92). So on this view there is the logical possibility of a situation in which the divine command's prescription is incompatible with what the believer, on other grounds, judges to be wrong. But such a situation would be one in which the believer would be justifiably divided in feelings and will. And thus it would be one in which God would not have been adequately distinguished from Jupiter....

Let me now formulate a more general claim. It is that moral theories of the type advanced by Occam and Adams are unlikely to be able to distinguish adequately between the claims to human allegiance made in the name of a variety of different gods who allegedly issue commands to us, because they approach these claims with too meagre a set of resources, conceptual and otherwise, with which to evaluate such claims. And this meagreness is itself surely due to the attempt to make divine commands in some way

foundational for morality. Adams's discussion is instructive on this point.

On Adams's account "It is contrary to God's commands to do X" only implies "It is wrong to do X" when conjoined with statements about God's nature, more particularly about God's love for human beings (p. 86). It is because believers encounter God as loving that they call Him good. But what, on Adams's view, are we doing when we call God good? We are "normally expressing a favorable emotional attitude" towards God and we are also often saying that God has done things which we regard as beneficial to us (p. 100). If we ask what it is to regard something as beneficial, nothing is said to carry this account of goodness any further. Adams presumably does not mean to assert that from the premises "God commands us to do so" and "God is loving and confers benefits" we can somehow derive the conclusion: "We ought to do what God commands." For that conclusion, derived from those premises, would at best express a piece of prudential advice and not at all any strict obligation to obedience, such as we are under in respect of God's commands. What would have to be added to these premises for there to be such an obligation?

WHY ONLY JUST DIVINE COMMANDS ARE WORTHY OF OBEDIENCE

The crucial concept that is characteristically missing from divine command theories, modified or unmodified, is that of just authority. It is when, and only when, effective power is wielded so that the ends of justice are served by the exercise of power, that authority is justly ascribed to whomsoever it is who wields that power. And the ends of justice are only served when power is exercised in accordance with, and by means of, a duly promulgated law. So it is only insofar as the commands of just authority are themselves just, that is, are in accord with the justice expressed in justly promulgated law, that the utterance of commands imposes any obligation. Power without justice may give us reasons to obey commands because we fear to do otherwise; beneficence without justice may give us reasons to obey commands either from gratitude or because we have been provided with expectations of future beneficence. So that if we know of some god, such as Nobodaddy or Jupiter, that he is powerful, or if we know of God that he is beneficent, we may indeed have good reason to obey the relevant set of commands, but not at all the kind of reason that we need to treat obedience as obligatory. Hence any account of divine commands as foundational to morality, as antecedent to and partially or wholly definitive of justice, such as we are offered in one version by Occam, in another by Adams, has to fail. It is noteworthy that when Adams lists those human virtues to which he takes it that there are analogues in God's attributes, he omits all mention of justice (pp. 100–101). And Occam is precluded by the whole tenor of his theory from appealing to any conception of a justice not itself derived definitionally from the divine commands. It would follow that since divine commands cannot be identified as those of a just authority, except tautologically, they cannot be treated as obligatory, as binding. And if and insofar as we follow Occam and Adams in also explaining such notions as those of "right" and "wrong" by appeal only to divine commands or to divine commands and attributes other than justice, it will be the case that "It is wrong to commit theft" or "It is right to honor one's parents" will not be binding rules....

If then Occamists and post-Occamist theologians or philosophers cannot derive the obligatoriness, the bindingness of divine commands either from God's justice, which their own view of the matter precludes them from doing, or from some conception provided by legal positivism...whence can they derive it? The answer that some theologians of this kind at least seem to presuppose is that the obligatoriness of divine commands cannot be derived or justified in any way. For if it were derived or justified, either in one of the two ways that I have discussed, or in some other way, then we would have to say that it is right to obey the divine commands because they are the just commands of a just authority or because they are the effectively enforcible commands of a legal sovereign power or because....But on the view taken by such theologians it cannot be right to obey the divine commands for any reason....We are simply to be obedient. Karl Barth has written that "Christian philosophy, which starts by hearing God's word,...cannot indeed

view the good other than as obedience. An action is obedience, however, when its goodness obviously lies not in doing it or in doing it in a particular way but in doing what is commanded because it is commanded..." (*Ethics*, ed. Dietrich Braun, trans. Geoffrey W. Bromiley, New York: 1981, pp. 42–43).

If there is nothing to the good other than obedience qua obedience, then we can indeed have no conception of goodness in terms of which to justify obedience to the commands of any one god rather than of any other. For the question of why we should obey divine commands has been decisively separated from the question of what attributes a god must have whose commands are to be worthy of obedience. Nobodaddy, Jupiter, Satan, and God all compete for our allegiance on equal terms—apart, that is, from inequalities in their power. There are of course Christian theologians who have not blanched at accepting a conclusion very like this. We, on their view, do not and cannot choose to obey the divine commands, and so the question of our justifying our choice of one good rather than another does not arise; we are either chosen by the most powerful of the gods to be his subject or we are rejected and those rejected are handed over to the sovereignty of some lesser power, such as Satan. Such theologians however also want to assert that the damned still owe God their allegiance and that they are unjustly disobedient to God. But there appears to be no way in which they can intelligibly and coherently make both sets of assertions....

HOW WE ACQUIRED OUR UNDERSTANDING OF A JUST GOD

When we first acquire some concept, it is characteristically, perhaps always, in terms of its application in some restricted context....Concepts, that is to say, their acquisition, their understanding, and their transformations have a history both in the life of an individual and in that of a culture. And at some later stage in the history of a concept, we may be able to recognize both that some earlier stage in our understanding of that same concept was indispensable to the conceptual education which has issued in our present formulation of that concept, but that nonetheless that present formulation also embodies a correction either of some degree of misunderstanding or of some inadequacy at that earlier stage. So it is, for example, with the concept of justice. And so it is also with the related concepts of goodness and of the divine. For the history of these three concepts over long periods is one single complex history. From that history I select three types of episode—understood for the moment as ideal types—for particular attention.

Stage 1

The first is that in which the members of some community have already come to share a conception of justice which they justify by relating it to their conception of the human good. That good, on their view, consists in the achievement of a form of life in which the goods and excellences of a variety of types of human activity have been integrated into an overall good, the realization of which is the end of political activity. To act justly is in key part to give to each person what that person deserves in respect of their contribution to that overall good, both in the distribution of public offices and in that of honor and of other rewards. Justice in exchange is governed by a scale of worth consistent with that same conception of overall good. And the rules which define just actions and transactions are constitutive of that form of life in and through which the good and the best is achieved. So the conception of justice is inseparable from that of the good and the best. And so too is the corresponding conception of the divine....

Of the divine thus conceived little can be affirmed, but rather more denied. And among what must be denied is the possibility of the divine exhibiting imperfection by engaging in injustice. But if the perfection of the divine thus conceived excludes injustice, this is partly because the divine thus conceived is incapable of actively engaging in any transaction with human beings whatsoever.

Stage 2

It is one of the marks which distinguish a second quite different type of stage in the history of these conceptual relationships...that the divine is now conceived of as initiating transactions with human beings, by in the first instance creating them and later by entering into covenants with some of them. When and if it happens that those who have been educated into the conceptual scheme of the first stage encounter the theological claims made for God so understood in this second way (when, for example, those who have been educated by Plato and Aristotle encounter Yahweh), the question of how to judge the justice or otherwise of Yahweh becomes inescapable. For at both types of stage the evaluation of the claims of rival claimants to the place of divine supremacy has involved the use of standards which make reference to justice. The rational grounds for the rejection of Zeus/Jupiter as unjust in favor of the Unmoved Mover and for the rejection of the Unmoved Mover insofar as it is necessarily incapable of either justice or injustice impose constraints upon the acceptance of Yahweh. And what has to be learned is both in what way the standards of justice involved in those rejections are applicable to Yahweh and in what way they are not.

Stage 3

Yahweh, as partner in covenant, puts Himself into a relationship in which the standards of the justice of exchange not only can be employed without inappropriateness, but ought to be so employed. And Yahweh presents Himself as one who certainly will not fail in his pledges just because he cannot so fail, and who thus has to be judged as just or unjust, as deserving or undeserving from those with whom He has covenanted, in respect of his truthfulness. And in calling Yahweh just or truthful in these respects we are evaluating Him by the same standards as each of us would another human being. But if we suppose that we can with equal appropriateness judge God by these same standards when we confront Him not as partner in covenant, but either as creator or as law-giver and judge, we shall have to learn that we err.

It is from the Book of Job that we have to learn, as I said earlier, that our creator owes us nothing and that we owe Him everything (Job is a Kedemite and not in a covenant relation with God). And about God as creator we can only learn from what is revealed in the scriptures. But it is not only from the scriptures, but also from our own rational reflection upon our own natures, that we are able to learn to recognize that the standards of justice which we have used in judging God as well as each other have themselves the force and authority of law, and that the law-giver who makes them law by promulgating them is God. We learn this by following through two lines of argument. One of these begins by subjecting the standards of justice, which were originally acknowledged as constituting the life of particular political communities, to enquiry in order to discern how they must be reformulated if they are to be the standards necessary to constitute any form of human association in and through which the good and the best is to be pursued. A second begins by criticizing the conception of the good and the best which was originally acknowledged, and moving from a conception of that type of human life which is the good and the best as consisting in the life of the political virtues, supplemented in its later stages by the contemplation of the Unmoved Mover, to a conception of it as consisting in rational friendship and therefore ultimately in friendship with God. We move, that is to say, from Aristotle to Aquinas. And in so doing of course we not only reject certain aspects of our earlier conceptions, including conceptions of justice, as inadequate, we reject certain aspects of them as false. But we also learn that part of what we took to be true is indeed true and that the justice in terms of which we judged God's claims, in order to distinguish them from those of Jupiter and Nobodaddy, is a justice which is commanded by God Himself. This I take it is why, even although Job had misunderstood the relationship between himself as creature and God as creator he had not been mistaken in calling God to account in terms of justice, something that God himself affirms in saying that Job, unlike Eliphaz, had spoken as he ought (42:7–8).

The concept of justice which we use in speaking of God is therefore an analogically and historically ordered concept, which in some of its uses is no different from those in which it is applied by human beings to each other and in others very different indeed, although not so different as not to preserve the core unity of the concept. J. S. Mill asserted against H. L. Mansel that "I take my stand on the acknowledged principle of logic and morality, that when we mean different things we have no right to call them by the same name, and to apply to them the same predicates, moral and intellectual. Language has no meaning for the words Just, Merciful, Benevolent, save that in which we apply them to our fellow-creatures.... If in affirming them of God, we do not mean to affirm these very qualities, differing only as greater in degree, we are neither philosophically nor morally entitled to affirm them at all" (p. 102, *An Examination of Sir William Hamilton's Philosophy*, edited by J. M. Robson, Toronto: 1979). Mill's doctrine in this passage is defensible only if generalized into a denial that any concept can be justifiably used in an analogically and historically ordered way. If enforced, it would deprive us of the linguistic means necessary for rational progress in a number of areas and not just in theology.... And I take it that it is in consequence of these consequences of Mill's doctrine having been well understood that almost no philosopher—perhaps no philosopher at all—now holds it. But it seems still to exert an influence upon a certain type of theology.

The contention that, were we to define and to understand our key evaluative terms independently of any knowledge of God or of His commands and then proceed to apply them to God, we should be treating God as if He were a merely finite being, is surely true only if something very like Mill's doctrine is presupposed.... And the identification of Mill's mistake has now put us in a position to see what is mistaken in this theological doctrine.

From the fact that we can at one stage in our progress towards God evaluate the divine claims, using a standard of justice acquired and elaborated independently of the knowledge of God, it does not follow that in so doing we are judging the Word of God by something external to it. This may indeed seem to be the case if we restrict our attention to that preliminary stage. But if we progress beyond it, something we are able to do rationally only because and insofar as we first assented to the divine claims because we judged them to be just (and also, of course, true), then we discover, as our analogically and historically ordered concept of justice develops, that the standard by which we judged God is itself a work of God, and that the judgments which we made earlier were made in obedience to the divine commands, even although we did not and could not have recognized this at that earlier stage. God, it turns out, cannot be truly judged of by something external to his Word, but that is because natural justice recognized by natural reason is itself divinely uttered and authorized. . . .

STUDY QUESTIONS

1. MacIntyre claims that it would be wrong for a theist to follow God's commands if such commands were incompatible with our basic concept of justice. Why does he say this? Do you agree?
2. Compare and contrast the three "gods" that MacIntyre discusses: Nobodaddy, Jupiter, and the Judeo-Christian God.
3. MacIntyre seems to presuppose that there is a basic, objective standard of justice to which we as humans have access. Do you agree? Why, or why not?

Thomas Aquinas

Ethics and Natural Law

Even if we assume that theists can justifiably maintain that ethical truth originates in God, this still leaves the question of how such truth is communicated from God to humans. In this reading, Thomas Aquinas (1224–1274) argues that as the result of being created in God's image, we as humans possess the rational capacities to comprehend those aspects of God's ethical standard that have been revealed in nature. Moreover, he maintains that from these observations, we can often deduce how human beings are to act and be treated. This is not, he maintains, to place natural reason above divine revelation. However, although written revelation is *sufficient* for giving us God's basic moral perspective, it is not always *necessary*. Human reflection on the nature of things can discover much about God's basic ethical standards and their application to our daily lives.

The precepts of the law of nature are related to practical reason in the same way that the first principles of demonstration are to speculative reason. Both are principles that are self-known [*per se nota*]. Now, we speak of something as self-known in two ways: first, in itself; second, in relation to us.

Any proposition is called self-known in itself when its predicate belongs to the intelligible meaning of its subject. However, it is possible for such a proposition not to be evident to a person ignorant of the definition of the subject. Thus, this proposition, *man is rational*, is self-evident in its own nature, since to say man is to say rational; yet, for a person who is ignorant of what man is, this proposition is not self-known.

Consequently, as Boethius says (*De Hebdomadibus*, PL 64, 1311), there are some axioms or propositions that are in general self-known to all. Of this type are those propositions whose terms are known to all; for example, *every whole is greater than its part*, and *things equal to one and the same thing are equal to each other*. But there are some propositions that are self-known only to the wise, those who understand the meaning of the terms of these propositions. Thus, to one who understands that an angel is not a body, it is self-known that an angel is not present circumscriptively in place. This is not obvious to uninstructed people, who fail to grasp this point.

A definite order is found among items that fall under the apprehension of men. For, that which first

Reprinted with the permission of Simon & Schuster from *The Pocket Aquinas* by Vernon J. Bourke. Copyright © 1960 by Washington Square Press. Copyright renewed © 1988 by Simon & Schuster.

falls under apprehension is *being* [*ens*]: the understanding of it is included in all things whatsoever that one apprehends. So, the first indemonstrable principle is: *It is not proper at once to affirm and to deny.* This is based on the intelligible meaning of being and nonbeing. On this principle all others are founded, as is said in the *Metaphysics* (III, 3, 1005b29).

Now, just as "being" is the first item that falls within apprehension without any qualification, so "good" is the first that falls within the apprehension of practical reason, which is directed toward work: *for every agent acts for the sake of an end*, which has the intelligible meaning of good. Thus, the first principle in the practical reason is what is based on the meaning of "good"; and it is: *The good is what all desire.* This is, then, the first principle of law: *Good is to be done and sought after, evil is to be avoided.* On this all the other precepts of the law of nature are based, in the sense that all things to be done or avoided belong to the precepts of the law of nature, if practical reason apprehends them as human goods.

Now, since the good has the rational character of an end, and evil has the contrary meaning, as a consequence reason naturally apprehends all things to which man has a natural inclination as goods and, therefore, as things to be sought after in working, and their contraries are apprehended as evils and as things to be avoided.

Our Natural Moral Inclinations

So, the order of the precepts of the law of nature is in accord with the order of natural inclinations. First, there is present in man the inclination toward the good on the level of the nature which he shares with all substances, inasmuch as each substance desires the preservation of its own existence according to its own nature. Now, those things whereby the life of man is preserved, and whereby its contrary is impeded, pertain to the natural law according to this inclination.

Second, there is present in man an inclination toward some more special things, on the level of the nature which he shares with other animals. And on this level, those things are said to belong to natural law "which nature teaches to all animals" (*Corpus Juris Civilis, Digesta*, I, tit. 1, leg. 1), as, for instance, the union of male and female, the upbringing of offspring, and similar things.

Third, there is present in man an inclination toward the good that is in accord with the nature of reason, and this is proper to him. Thus, man has a natural inclination toward knowing the truth about God, and toward living in society. On this level, those things within the scope of this inclination pertain to the natural law; for instance, that man should avoid ignorance, that he should not offend those with whom he must associate, and others of this kind that are concerned with this level.

[The difficulties mentioned at the beginning of the article boil down to this: Why are there many precepts of natural law, when man's nature is one and so is his reason?]

1. All these precepts of the law of nature, insofar as they are referred to one first precept, do have the rational character [*ratio*] of one natural law.
2. All inclinations of this kind, of whatsoever parts of human nature, for instance, of the concupiscible or irascible powers, belong to the natural law inasmuch as they are regulated by reason, and they are reduced to one first precept, as has been said. According to this, there are many precepts in themselves of the law of nature but they share in one common root.
3. Although reason is one in itself, it is directive of all things that pertain to men. For this reason, all things that can be regulated by reason are contained under the law of reason....

Moral rules are concerned with those matters that essentially pertain to good behavior. Now, since human morals are spoken of in relation to reason (for it is the proper principle of human acts), those customs that are in conformity with reason are called good, and those that are in discord with reason are deemed bad. Just as every judgment of speculative reason proceeds from the natural knowledge of first principles, so, too, does every judgment of practical reason issue from certain naturally known principles, as we have explained before.

How These Inclinations Guide Us

Now, it is possible to proceed in different ways from these principles in making judgments on different problems. There are some cases in human actions that are so explicit that they can be approved or condemned at once, with very little thought, by reference to those general and primary principles. Then, there are other problems for the judgment of which a good deal of thinking on the different circumstances is required. Careful consideration of such problems is not the prerogative of just any person but of the wise. In the same way, it is not the function of all men to consider the conclusions of the sciences but only of the philosophers. Again, there are still other matters for the judgment of which man stands in need of help by divine instruction, as is so in the case of items of belief.

And so, it becomes evident that since moral precepts belong among the matters that pertain to good behavior, and since these are items that are in conformity with reason, and since every judgment of human reason is derived in some fashion from natural reason,

it must be true that all moral rules belong to the law of nature, but not all in the same way.

For, there are some things that the natural reason of every man judges immediately and essentially as things to be done or not done; for example, *Honor thy father and mother*, and *Thou shalt not kill; Thou shalt not steal*. Precepts of this kind belong in an unqualified way to the law of nature.

Then, there are other things that are judged by a more subtle rational consideration, on the part of the wise men, to be matters of obligation. Now, these belong to the law of nature in this way: they of course require instruction, by which less favored people are taught by those who are wise; for example, *Rise up before the hoary head, and honor the person of the aged man* (Lev. 19:32), and other injunctions of this kind.

Finally, there are other matters for the judgment of which human reason needs divine instruction, whereby we are taught concerning matters of divinity; for example, *Thou shalt not make to thyself a graven thing, nor the likeness of any thing.... Thou shalt not take the name of thy God in vain* (Exod. 20:4, 7).

Study Questions

1. Aquinas believes that all of us "just know" that some actions—for example, killing innocent people—are wrong. Do you agree? If so, list some actions or behaviors that you think fit into this category.
2. Aquinas does not make reference to the influence of culture and experience on moral beliefs. To what extent do you think moral beliefs are influenced by these factors?

Jean-Paul Sartre

Ethics Without Religion

Theists sometimes contend that a world without God necessarily has at least two undesirable characteristics: life can have no meaning, and all moral values are relative. In this reading, Jean-Paul Sartre (1905–1980) acknowledges that a world without God is different. In a godless world there are no absolute values superimposed on us from without; we must of necessity create our own values. And this, he maintains, should be sobering. We experience the forlornness resulting from the fact that we alone must decide how to act, the anguish that follows from recognizing that our actions have important consequences for others, and the despair that comes from realizing that that we can never know beforehand with any certainty the outcome of our actions. However, Sartre denies that we can find no personal meaning in world without God. He also challenges the contention that creating our own values would enable us to justify arbitrary and capricious behavior by pointing out that such behavior would not be compatible with a proper understanding of the fact that our actions always have significant consequences for others.

VALUES IN A GODLESS WORLD

Atheistic existentialism, which I represent,...states that if God does not exist, there is at least one being in whom existence precedes essence, a being who exists before he can be defined by any concept, and that this being is man, or,...human reality. What is meant here by saying that existence precedes essence? It means that, first of all, man exists, turns up, appears on the scene, and, only afterwards, defines himself. If man, as the existentialist conceives him, is indefinable, it is because at first he is nothing. Only afterward will he be something, and he himself will have made what he will be. Thus, there is no human nature, since there is no God to conceive it. Not only is man what he conceives himself to be, but he is also only what he wills himself to be after this thrust toward existence.

Man is nothing else but what he makes of himself. Such is the first principle of existentialism. It is also what is called subjectivity—the name we are labeled with when charges are brought against us. But what do we mean by this, if not that man has a

From *Existentialism and Human Emotions* (Secaucus, N.J.: Citadel Press, 1985).

greater dignity than a stone or table? For we mean that man first exists, that is, that man first of all is the being who hurls himself toward a future and who is conscious of imagining himself as being in the future. Man is at the start a plan which is aware of itself, rather than a patch of moss, a piece of garbage, or a cauliflower; nothing exists prior to this plan; there is nothing in heaven; man will be what he will have planned to be. Not what he will want to be. Because by the word "will" we generally mean a conscious decision, which is subsequent to what we have already made of ourselves. I may want to belong to a political party, write a book, get married; but all that is only a manifestation of an earlier, more spontaneous choice that is called "will." But if existence really does precede essence, man is responsible for what he is. Thus, existentialism's first move is to make every man aware of what he is and to make the full responsibility of his existence rest on him. And when we say that a man is responsible for himself, we do not only mean that he is responsible for his own individuality, but that he is responsible for all men.

The word subjectivism has two meanings, and our opponents play on the two. Subjectivism means, on the one hand, that an individual chooses and makes himself; and, on the other, that it is impossible for man to transcend human subjectivity. The second of these is the essential meaning of existentialism. When we say that man chooses his own self, we mean that every one of us does likewise; but we also mean by that that in making this choice he also chooses all men. In fact, in creating the man that we want to be, there is not a single one of our acts which does not at the same time create an image of man as we think he ought to be. To choose to be this or that is to affirm at the same time the value of what we choose, because we can never choose evil. We always choose the good, and nothing can be good for us without being good for all.

If, on the other hand, existence precedes essence, and if we grant that we exist and fashion our image at one and the same time, the image is valid for everybody and for our whole age. Thus, our responsibility is much greater than we might have supposed, because it involves all mankind. If I am a workingman and

choose to join a Christian trade-union rather than be a communist, and if by being a member I want to show that the best thing for man is resignation, that the kingdom of man is not of this world, I am not only involving my own case—1 want to be resigned for everyone. As a result, my action has involved all humanity. To take a more individual matter, if I want to marry, to have children; even if this marriage depends solely on my own circumstances or passion or wish, I am involving all humanity in monogamy and not merely myself. Therefore, I am responsible for myself and for everyone else. I am creating a certain image of man of my own choosing. In choosing myself, I choose man.

PRACTICAL IMPLICATIONS

This helps us understand what the actual content is of such rather grandiloquent words as anguish, forlornness, despair. As you will see, it's all quite simple.

Anguish

First, what is meant by anguish? The existentialists say at once that man is anguish. What that means is this: the man who involves himself and who realizes that he is not only the person he chooses to be, but also a law-maker who is, at the same time, choosing all mankind as well as himself, cannot help escape the feeling of his total and deep responsibility. Of course, there are many people who are not anxious; but we claim that they are hiding their anxiety, that they are fleeing from it. Certainly, many people believe that when they do something, they themselves are the only ones involved, and when someone says to them, "What if everyone acted that way?" they shrug their shoulders and answer, "Everyone doesn't act that way." But really, one should always ask himself, "What would happen if everybody looked at things that way?" There is no escaping this disturbing thought except by a kind of double-dealing. A man who lies and makes excuses for himself by saying "not everybody does that," is someone with an uneasy conscience, because the act of lying implies that a universal value is conferred upon the lie.

Anguish is evident even when it conceals itself. This is the anguish that Kierkegaard called the anguish of Abraham. You know the story: an angel has ordered Abraham to sacrifice his son; if it really were an angel who has come and said, "You are Abraham, you shall sacrifice your son," everything would be all right. But everyone might first wonder, "Is it really an angel, and am I really Abraham? What proof do I have?"

There was a madwoman who had hallucinations; someone used to speak to her on the telephone and give her orders. Her doctor asked her, "Who is it who talks to you?" She answered, "He says it's God." What proof did she really have that it was God? If an angel comes to me, what proof is there that it's an angel? And if I hear voices, what proof is there that they come from heaven and not from hell, or from the subconscious, or a pathological condition? What proves that they are addressed to me? What proof is there that I have been appointed to impose my choice and my conception of man on humanity? I'll never find any proof or sign to convince me of that. If a voice addresses me, it is always for me to decide that this is the angel's voice; if I consider that such an act is a good one, it is I who will choose to say that it is good rather than bad.

Now, I'm not being singled out as an Abraham, and yet at every moment I'm obliged to perform exemplary acts. For every man, everything happens as if all mankind had its eyes fixed on him and were guiding itself by what he does. And every man ought to say to himself, "Am I really the kind of man who has the right to act in such a way that humanity might guide itself by my actions?" And if he does not say that to himself, he is masking his anguish.

There is no question here of the kind of anguish which would lead to quietism, to inaction. It is a matter of a simple sort of anguish that anybody who has had responsibilities is familiar with. For example, when a military officer takes the responsibility for an attack and sends a certain number of men to death, he chooses to do so, and in the main he alone makes the choice. Doubtless, orders come from above, but they are too broad; he interprets them, and on this interpretation depend the lives often of fourteen or twenty men. In making a decision he can not help having a certain anguish. All leaders know this anguish. That doesn't keep them from acting; on the contrary, it is the very condition of their action. For it implies that they envisage a number of possibilities, and when they choose one, they realize that it has value only because it is chosen. We shall see that this kind of anguish, which is the kind that existentialism describes, is explained, in addition, by a direct responsibility to the other men whom it involves. It is not a curtain separating us from action, but is part of action itself.

Forlornness

When we speak of forlornness, we mean only that God does not exist and that we have to face all the consequences of this. The existentialist is strongly opposed to a certain kind of secular ethics which would like to abolish God with the least possible expense. About 1880, some French teachers tried to set up a secular ethics which went something like this: God is a useless and costly hypothesis; we are discarding it; but, meanwhile, in order for there to be an ethics, a society, a civilization, it is essential that certain values be taken seriously and that they be considered as having an a priori existence. It must be obligatory, a priori, to be honest, not to lie, not to beat your wife, to have children, etc., etc. So we're going to try a little device which will make it possible to show that values exist all the same, inscribed in a heaven of ideas, though otherwise God does not exist. In other words—and this, I believe, is the tendency of everything called reformism in France—nothing will be changed if God does not exist. We shall find ourselves with the same norms of honesty, progress, and humanism, and we shall have made of God an outdated hypothesis which will peacefully die off by itself.

The existentialist, on the contrary, thinks it very distressing that God does not exist, because all possibility of finding values in a heaven of ideas disappears along with Him; there can no longer be an a priori Good, since there is no infinite and perfect consciousness to think it. Nowhere is it written that the Good exists, that we must be honest, that we must not lie; because the fact is we are on a plane where there are only men. Dostoyevsky said, "If God didn't exist, everything would be possible." That is the very starting point of existentialism. Indeed, everything is permissible if God does not exist, and as a result man is forlorn, because neither within him nor without does he find anything to cling to. He can't start making excuses for himself.

If existence really does precede essence, there is no explaining things away by reference to a fixed and given human nature. In other words, there is no determinism, man is free, man is freedom. On the other hand, if God does not exist, we find no values or commands to turn to which legitimize our conduct. So, in the bright realm of values, we have no excuse behind us, nor justification before us. We are alone, with no excuses.

That is the idea I shall try to convey when I say that man is condemned to be free. Condemned, because he did not create himself, yet, in other respects is free; because, once thrown into the world, he is responsible for everything he does. The existentialist does not believe in the power of passion. He will never agree that a sweeping passion is a ravaging torrent which fatally leads a man to certain acts and is therefore an excuse. He thinks that man is responsible for his passion.

The existentialist does not think that man is going to help himself by finding in the world some omen by which to orient himself. Because he thinks that man will interpret the omen to suit himself. Therefore, he thinks that man, with no support and no aid, is condemned every moment to invent man....

To give you an example which will enable you to understand forlornness better, I shall cite the case of one of my students who came to see me under the following circumstances: his father was on bad terms with his mother, and, moreover, was inclined to be a collaborationist; his older brother had been killed in the German offensive of 1940, and the young man, with somewhat immature but generous feelings, wanted to avenge him. His mother lived alone with him, very much upset by the half-treason of her husband and the death of her older son; the boy was her only consolation.

The boy was faced with the choice of leaving for England and joining the Free French Forces—that is, leaving his mother behind—or remaining with his mother and helping her to carry on. He was fully aware that the woman lived only for him and that his going-off—and perhaps his death—would plunge her into despair. He was also aware that every act that he did for his mother's sake was a sure thing, in the sense that it was helping her to carry on, whereas every effort he made toward going off and fighting was an uncertain move which might run aground and prove completely useless; for example, on his way to England he might, while passing through Spain, be detained indefinitely in a Spanish camp; he might reach England or Algiers and be stuck in an office at a desk job. As a result, he was faced with two very different kinds of action: one, concrete, immediate, but concerning only one individual; the other concerned an incomparably vaster group, a national collectivity, but for that very reason was dubious, and might be interrupted en route. And, at the same time, he was wavering between two kinds of ethics. On the one hand, an ethics of sympathy, of personal devotion; on the other, a broader ethics, but one whose efficacy was more dubious. He had to choose between the two.

Who could help him choose? Christian doctrine? No. Christian doctrine says, "Be charitable, love your neighbor, take the more rugged path, etc., etc." But which is the more rugged path? Whom should he love as a brother? The fighting man or his mother? Which does the greater good, the vague act of fighting in a group, or the concrete one of helping a particular human being to go on living? Who can decide a priori? Nobody. No book of ethics can tell him. The Kantian ethics says, "Never treat any person as a means, but as an end." Very well, if I stay with my mother, I'll treat her as an end and not as a means; but by virtue of this very fact, I'm running the risk of treating the people around me who are fighting as means; and, conversely, if I go to join those who are fighting, I'll be treating them as an end, and, by doing that, I run the risk of treating my mother as a means.

If values are vague, and if they are always too broad for the concrete and specific case that we are considering, the only thing left for us is trust our instincts. That's what this young man tried to do; and when I saw him, he said, "In the end, feeling is what counts. I ought to choose whichever pushes me in one direction. If I feel that I love my mother enough to sacrifice everything else for her—my desire for vengeance, for action, for adventure—then I'll stay with her. If, on the contrary, I feel that my love for my mother isn't enough, I'll leave."

But how is the value of a feeling determined? What gives his feeling for his mother value? Precisely the fact that he remained with her. I may say that I like so-and-so well enough to sacrifice a certain amount of money for him, but I may say so only if I've done it. I may say "I love my mother well enough to remain with her" if I have remained with her. The only way to determine the value of this affection is, precisely, to perform an act which confirms and defines it. But, since I require this affection to justify my act, I find myself caught in a vicious circle....

In other words, the feeling is formed by the acts one performs; so, I cannot refer to it in order to act upon it. Which means that I can neither seek within myself the true condition which will impel me to act, nor apply to a system of ethics for concepts which will permit me to act. You will say, "At least, he did go to a teacher for advice." But if you seek advice from a priest, for example, you have chosen this priest; you already knew, more or less, just about what advice he was going to give you. In other words, choosing your adviser is involving yourself. The proof of this is that if you are a Christian, you will say, "Consult a priest." But some priests are collaborating, some are just marking time, some are resisting. Which to choose? If the young man chooses a priest who is resisting or collaborating, he has already decided on the kind of advice he's going to get. Therefore, in coming to see me he knew the answer I was going to give him, and I had only one answer to give: "You're free, choose, that is, invent." No general ethics can show you what is to be done; there are no omens in the world. The Catholics will reply, "But there are." Granted—but, in any case, I myself choose the meaning they have.

When I was a prisoner, I knew a rather remarkable young man who was a Jesuit. He had entered the Jesuit order in the following way: he had had a number of very bad breaks; in childhood, his father died, leaving him in poverty, and he was a scholarship student at a religious institution where he was constantly made to feel that he was being kept out of charity; then, he failed to get any of the honors and distinctions that children like; later on, at about eighteen, he

bungled a love affair; finally, at twenty-two, he failed in military training, a childish enough matter, but it was the last straw.

This young fellow might well have felt that he had botched everything. It was a sign of something, but of what? He might have taken refuge in bitterness or despair. But he very wisely looked upon all this as a sign that he was not made for secular triumphs, and that only the triumphs of religion, holiness, and faith were open to him. He saw the hand of God in all this, and so he entered the order. Who can help seeing that he alone decided what the sign meant?

Some other interpretation might have been drawn from this series of setbacks; for example, that he might have done better to turn carpenter or revolutionist. Therefore, he is fully responsible for the interpretation. Forlornness implies that we ourselves choose our being. Forlornness and anguish go together.

Despair

As for despair, the term has a very simple meaning. It means that we shall confine ourselves to reckoning only with what depends upon our will, or on the ensemble of probabilities which make our action possible. When we want something, we always have to reckon with probabilities. I may be counting on the arrival of a friend. The friend is coming by rail or street-car; this supposes that the train will arrive on schedule, or that the street-car will not jump the track. I am left in the realm of possibility; but possibilities are to be reckoned with only to the point where my action comports with the ensemble of these possibilities, and no further. The moment the possibilities I am considering are not rigorously involved by my action, I ought to disengage myself from them, because no God, no scheme, can adapt the world and its possibilities to my will. When Descartes said, "Conquer yourself rather than the world," he meant essentially the same thing....

OBJECTIONS

We are told, "So you're able to do anything, no matter what!" This is expressed in various ways. First we are accused of anarchy; then they say, "You're unable to pass judgment on others, because there's no reason to prefer one configuration to another"; finally they tell us, "Everything is arbitrary in this choosing of yours. You take something from one pocket and pretend you're putting it into the other."

These three objections aren't very serious. Take the first objection. "You're able to do anything, no matter what" is not to the point. In one sense choice is possible, but what is not possible is not to choose. I can always choose, but I ought to know that if I do not choose, I am still choosing. Though this may seem purely formal, it is highly important for keeping fantasy and caprice within bounds. If it is true that in facing a situation, for example, one in which, as a person capable of having sexual relations, of having children, I am obliged to choose an attitude, and if I in any way assume responsibility for a choice which, in involving myself, also involves all mankind, this has nothing to do with caprice, even if no *a priori* value determines my choice.

If anybody thinks that he recognizes here Gide's theory of the arbitrary act, he fails to see the enormous difference between this doctrine and Gide's. Gide does not know what a situation is. He acts out of pure caprice. For us, on the contrary, man is in an organized situation in which he himself is involved. Through his choice, he involves all mankind, and he cannot avoid making a choice: either he will remain chaste, or he will marry and have children; anyhow, whatever he may do, it is impossible for him not to take full responsibility for the way he handles this problem. Doubtless, he chooses without referring to pre-established values, but it is unfair to accuse him of caprice. Instead, let us say that moral choice is to be compared to the making of a work of art. And before going any further, let it be said at once that we are not dealing here with an aesthetic ethics, because our opponents are so dishonest that they even accuse us of that. The example I've chosen is a comparison only.

Having said that, may I ask whether anyone has ever accused an artist who has painted a picture of not having drawn his inspiration from rules set up a priori? Has anyone ever asked, "What painting ought he to make?" It is clearly understood that there is no definite painting to be made, that the artist is engaged in the making of his painting, and that the painting to be made is precisely the painting he will have made. It is clearly understood that there are no a priori aesthetic values, but that there are values which appear subsequently in the coherence of the painting, in the correspondence between what the artist intended and the result. Nobody can tell what the painting of tomorrow will be like. Painting can be judged only after it has once been made. What connection does that have with ethics? We are in the same creative situation. We never say that a work of art is arbitrary. When we speak of a canvas of Picasso, we never say that it is arbitrary; we understand quite well that he was making himself what he is at the very time he was painting, that the ensemble of his work is embodied in his life.

The same holds on the ethical plane. What art and ethics have in common is that we have creation and invention in both cases. We cannot decide a priori what there is to be done. I think that I pointed that out quite sufficiently when I mentioned the case of the student who came to see me, and who might have applied to all the ethical systems, Kantian or otherwise, without getting any sort of guidance. He was obliged to devise his law himself. Never let it be said by us that this man—who, taking affection, individual action, and kind-heartedness toward a specific person as his ethical first principle, chooses to remain with his mother, or who, preferring to make a sacrifice, chooses to go to England—has made an arbitrary choice. Man makes himself. He isn't ready made at the start. In choosing his ethics, he makes himself and the force of circumstances is such that he cannot abstain from choosing one. We define man only in relationship to involvement. It is therefore absurd to charge us with arbitrariness of choice.

In the second place, it is said that we are unable to pass judgment on others. In a way this is true, and in another way, false. It is true in this sense, that, whenever a man sanely and sincerely involves himself and chooses his configuration, it is impossible for him to prefer another configuration, regardless of what his own may be in other respects. It is true in this sense, that we do not believe in progress. Progress is betterment. Man is always the same. The situation confronting him varies. Choice always remains a choice in a situation. The problem has not changed since the time one could choose between those for and those against slavery, for example, at the time of the Civil War, and the present time, when one can side with the Maquis Resistance Party, or with the Communists.

But, nevertheless, one can still pass judgment, for, as I have said, one makes a choice in relationship to others. First, one can judge (and this is perhaps not a judgment of value, but a logical judgment) that certain choices are based on error and others on truth. If we have defined man's situation as a free choice, with no excuses and no recourse, every man who takes refuge behind the excuse of his passions, every man who sets up determinism, is a dishonest man.

The objection may be raised, "But why mayn't he choose himself dishonestly?" I reply that I am not obliged to pass moral judgment on him, but that I do define his dishonesty as an error. One cannot help considering the truth of the matter. Dishonesty is obviously a falsehood because it belies the complete freedom of involvement. On the same grounds, I maintain that there is also dishonesty if I choose to state that certain values exist prior to me; it is self-contradictory for me to want them and at the same state that they are imposed on me. Suppose someone says to me, "What if I want to be dishonest?" I'll answer, "There's no reason for you not to be, but I'm saying that that's what you are, and that the strictly coherent attitude is that of honesty."

Besides, I can bring moral judgment to bear. When I declare that freedom in every concrete circumstance can have no other aim than to want itself, if man has once become aware that in his forlornness he imposes values, he can no longer want but one thing, and that is freedom, as the basis of all values. That doesn't mean that he wants it in the abstract. It means simply that the ultimate meaning of the acts of honest men is the quest for freedom as such. A man who belongs to a communist or revolutionary union wants concrete goals; these goals imply an abstract desire for freedom; but this freedom is wanted in something concrete. We want freedom for freedom's sake and in every particular circumstance. And in wanting freedom we discover that it depends entirely on the freedom of others, and that the freedom of others depends on ours. Of course, freedom as the

definition of man does not depend on others, but as soon as there is involvement, I am obliged to want others to have freedom at the same time that I want my own freedom. I can take freedom as my goal only if I take that of others as a goal as well. Consequently, when, in all honesty, I've recognized that man is a being in whom existence precedes essence, that he is a free being who, in various circumstances, can want only his freedom, I have at the same time recognized that I can want only the freedom of others.

Therefore, in the name of this will for freedom, which freedom itself implies, I may pass judgment on those who seek to hide from themselves the complete arbitrariness and the complete freedom of their existence. Those who hide their complete freedom from themselves out of a spirit of seriousness or by means of deterministic excuses, I shall call cowards; those who try to show that their existence was necessary, when it is the very contingency of man's appearance on earth, I shall call stinkers. But cowards or stinkers can be judged only from a strictly unbiased point of view.

Therefore though the content of ethics is variable, a certain form of it is universal. Kant says that freedom desires both itself and the freedom of others. Granted. But he believes that the formal and the universal are enough to constitute an ethics. We, on the other hand, think that principles which are too abstract run aground in trying to decide action. Once again, take the case of the student. In the name of what, in the name of what great moral maxim do you think he could have decided, in perfect peace of mind, to abandon his mother or to stay with her? There is no way of judging. The content is always concrete and thereby unforeseeable; there is always the element of invention. The one thing that counts is knowing whether the inventing that has been done, has been done in the name of freedom.

For example, let us look at the following two cases. You will see to what extent they correspond, yet differ. Take *The Mill on the Floss*. We find a certain young girl, Maggie Tulliver, who is an embodiment of the value of passion and who is aware of it. She is in love with a young man, Stephen, who is engaged to an insignificant young girl. This Maggie Tulliver, instead of heedlessly preferring her own happiness, chooses, in the name of human solidarity, to sacrifice herself and give up the man she loves. On the other hand, Sanseverina, in *The Charterhouse of Parma*, believing that passion is man's true value, would say that a great love deserves sacrifices; that it is to be preferred to the banality of the conjugal love that would tie Stephen to the young ninny he had to marry. She would choose to sacrifice the girl and fulfill her happiness; and, as Stendhal shows, she is even ready to sacrifice herself for the sake of passion, if this life demands it. Here we are in the presence of two strictly opposed moralities. I claim that they are much the same thing; in both cases what has been set up as the goal is freedom.

You can imagine two highly similar attitudes: one girl prefers to renounce her love out of resignation; another prefers to disregard the prior attachment of the man she loves out of sexual desire. On the surface these two actions resemble those we've just described. However, they are completely different. Sanseverina's attitude is much nearer that of Maggie Tulliver, one of heedless rapacity.

Thus, you see that the second charge is true and, at the same time, false. One may choose anything if it is on the grounds of free involvement.

The third objection is the following: "You take something from one pocket and put it into the other. That is, fundamentally, values aren't serious, since you choose them." My answer to this is that I'm quite vexed that that's the way it is; but if I've discarded God the Father, there has to be someone to invent values. You've got to take things as they are. Moreover, to say that we invent values means nothing else but this: life has no meaning a priori. Before you come alive, life is nothing; it's up to you to give it a meaning, and value is nothing else but the meaning that you choose. In that way, you see, there is a possibility of creating a human community.

I've been reproached for asking whether existentialism is humanistic. It's been said, "But you said in *Nausea* that the humanists were all wrong. You made fun of a certain kind of humanist. Why come back to it now?" Actually, the word humanism has two very different meanings. By humanism one can mean a theory which takes man as an end and as a higher value. Humanism in this sense can be found in Cocteau's tale *Around the World in Eighty Hours* when a character, because he is flying over some mountains in an airplane, declares, "Man is simply amazing." That means that I, who did not build the airplanes, shall personally benefit from these particular inventions, and that I, as man, shall personally consider myself responsible for, and honored by, acts of a few particular men. This would imply that we ascribe a value to man on the basis of the highest deeds of certain men. This humanism is absurd, because only the dog or the horse would be able to make such an overall judgment about man, which they are careful not to do, at least to my knowledge.

But it cannot be granted that a man may make a judgment about man. Existentialism spares him from any such judgment. The existentialist will never consider man as an end because he is always in the making. Nor should we believe that there is a mankind to which we might set up a cult in the manner of Auguste Comte. The cult of mankind ends in the self-enclosed humanism of Comte, and, let it be said, of fascism. This kind of humanism we can do without.

But there is another meaning of humanism. Fundamentally it is this: man is constantly outside of himself; in projecting himself, in losing himself outside of himself; he makes for man's existing; and, on the other hand, it is by pursuing transcendent goals that he is able to exist; man, being this state of passing beyond, and seizing upon things only as they bear upon this passing-beyond, is at the heart, at the center of this passing-beyond. There is no universe other than a human universe, the universe of human subjectivity. This connection between transcendency, as a constituent element of man—not in the sense that God is transcendent, but in the sense of passing beyond—and subjectivity, in the sense that man is not closed in on himself but is always present in a human universe, is what we call existentialist humanism. Humanism, because we remind man that there is no law-maker other than himself, and that in his forlornness he will decide by himself; because we point out that man will fulfill himself as man, not in turning toward himself, but in seeking outside of himself a goal which is just this liberation, just this particular fulfillment.

STUDY QUESTIONS

1. What does Sartre mean when he says that life in a godless world is likely to produce forlornness, anguish, and despair? Do you agree?
2. Sartre maintains that everything is permissible if God exists but denies that this means that we can do just anything we want. Why does he claim this? Do you believe he is being consistent at this point?

SUGGESTED READING

Broom, Donald M. *The Evolution of Morality and Religion.* Cambridge, England: Cambridge University Press, 2003.

Castelli, Elizabeth A. *Women, Gender, Religion: A Reader.* New York: Palgrave Macmillan, 2001.

Donagan, Allan. *The Theory of Morality.* Chicago: University of Chicago Press, 1977.

Drywall, Stephen L., ed. *Virtue Ethics.* Oxford, England: Blackwell, 2002.

Hare, John. *God and Morality: A Philosophical History.* Oxford, England: Blackwell, 2006.

Hursthouse, Rosalind. *On Virtue Ethics.* Oxford, England: Oxford University Press, 2002.

MacIntyre, Alasdair. *After Virtue.* Notre Dame, Ind.: University of Notre Dame Press, 1981.

McClendon, James W., Jr. *Ethics: Systematic Theology,* vol. 1. Nashville, Tenn.: Abingdon, 1986.

Mitchell, Basil. *Morality: Religious and Secular.* Oxford, England: Oxford University Press, 1980.

Murphy, Mark. *An Essay on Divine Authority.* Ithaca, N.Y.: Cornell University Press, 2002.

Nielsen, Kai. *Ethics Without God.* London: Pemberton, 1973.

Parsons, Susan Frank. *The Ethics of Gender* (New Dimension to Religious Ethics). Oxford, England: Blackwell, 2002.

Phillips, D. Z., ed. *Religion and Morality* (Claremont Studies in the Philosophy of Religion). New York: Palgrave Macmillan, 1996.

Quinn, Philip. *Divine Commands and Moral Requirements.* Oxford, England: Oxford University Press, 1978.

Wainwright, William, J. *Religion and Morality* (Ashgate Philosophy of Religion Series). Burlington, Vt.: Ashgate, 2005.

Schweiker, William, ed. *The Blackwell Companion to Religious Ethics.* Oxford, England: Blackwell, 2004.

Zagzebski, Linda. *Divine Motivation Theory.* Cambridge, England: Cambridge University Press, 2004.

GLOSSARY

A posteriori proposition A proposition that is known after or by means of experience or observation.

A priori proposition A proposition that is known prior to experience or observation.

Accommodation The view that in some portions of Scripture, God has "accommodated" himself to human understanding by saying things that are not strictly true but that are helpful in enabling us to grasp the intended message. (See *double meaning*.)

Actual infinite A timeless totality that can neither increase nor decrease in the number of its members.

Analogical language Language that draws meaning from being like another thing in a certain respect. "God is our father" gets meaning insofar as God is like an earthly father.

Analytic proposition A proposition that is true in virtue of the meaning of the words in which it is expressed; for example, "All bachelors are unmarried."

Anthropomorphism Using essentially human categories for understanding God.

Anti-realism In any field of inquiry or in metaphysics generally, the view that objects of inquiry do not exist or are not real independently of the human mind. Also, in epistemology, the view that the human mind contributes either the existence or structure of objects.

Apophatic theology A way of doing theology based on the conviction that the divine transcends human categories of thought and therefore human language. It is often said that we can speak of God in terms of what he is not, or *via negativa*.

Atheistic existentialism The view that there are no absolute ethical values to guide our lives. We must create for ourselves the ethical values by which we will live.

Basic belief A belief that is accepted without being based on other beliefs that one holds, for example, "I am now seeing a tree." (Contrasts with *derived belief*.)

Brahman In Hinduism, the ultimate Being that includes everything else within itself. (See *pantheism*.)

Coercive power The power to "make things happen," to unilaterally determine that things shall occur in a certain way. (Contrasts with *persuasive power*.)

Coincidence miracle An event that has a natural explanation available but for which the event sequencing—the fact that an event occurred in the time and place that it did—makes it probable that God was directly involved.

Compatibilism The view that free will is compatible with *determinism*; one is free if one is able to act upon one's strongest desire, even if that desire was itself determined by previously existing causes.

Cosmological argument An argument for God's existence from the need to provide the best explanation for the existence of contingent beings or the universe.

Counterfactuals of freedom Propositions that state, concerning each actual or possible free creature, what that creature would freely (in the *libertarian* sense) choose to do in any possible situation in which that creature might find itself.

Critical dialog See *critical rationalism.*

Critical rationalism The view that it is possible and appropriate to reflect critically upon religious beliefs, considering their rational coherence and evidential support or lack thereof, even though it is often not possible to show such beliefs to be true or false in a way that is convincing to all rational inquirers.

Defeater (for beliefs) A defeater for a belief is another belief that, if accepted, makes it unreasonable to accept the first belief. For example, the credibility of a witness in a trial may be defeated if it is shown that the witness was bribed to testify as he or she did.

Defense (against the problem of evil) An argument that some argument from evil fails to show that theism is inconsistent, irrational, improbable, and so forth. No attempt is made to show that theism is true, plausible, probable, and the like.

Derived belief A belief that is accepted because it is supported by other beliefs that one holds. (Contrasts with *basic belief.*)

Design Intelligent structure and order in the universe and its objects; the subject of a family of arguments that attributes structure and order to an intelligent agency distinct from the universe.

Determinism The view that everything that occurs, particularly every action of every person, must necessarily occur as it does because of previous circumstances.

Direct act of God An event that occurs because God has directly modified or circumvented the relevant natural laws.

Divine command theory The theory that whatever God commands us to do is morally right and ought to be obeyed.

Double meaning (of Scripture) The view that some parts of Scripture have both a literal meaning, which is understood by uneducated persons, and an allegorical meaning, which is understood only by the learned. (See *accommodation.*)

Duty (epistemic) An epistemic duty is an obligation that persons are thought to have with respect to what they believe and disbelieve, in particular, an obligation to believe that which is supported by sufficient evidence.

Epistemic Referring to the capacity or process for gaining knowledge.

Epistemology The branch of philosophy that is concerned with the nature, sources, and justification of belief and knowledge.

Ethics The branch of philosophy that is concerned with right and wrong, good and bad, character and virtue.

Everlasting Something that is everlasting exists at every moment of time; it has neither a beginning nor an ending. (Contrasts with *timeless.*)

Evidentialism The view that religious beliefs are *derived beliefs*, to be accepted if and only if they are sufficiently supported by the evidence.

Falsificationism Advanced by logical positivists, it requires that all cognitively meaningful statements be able to be empirically falsified in principle.

Fideism The view that it is inappropriate to subject religious beliefs to critical evaluation that goes beyond the religious belief system.

Foundationalism (strong) Foundationalism divides all beliefs into *basic beliefs* and *derived beliefs* and holds that derived beliefs should be accepted to the extent that they are supported by basic beliefs. Strong foundationalism adds that basic beliefs should be limited to those concerning which we are (nearly) infallible, such as self-evident beliefs and those things that are "evident to the senses."

Genuine option A choice between alternatives that are "living" (both sides of the choice represent real possibilities for the person making the choice), "forced" (one has to choose one way or the other; it is impossible to remain neutral), and "momentous" (the choice has important consequences for one's life).

God of the gaps Pejorative term for a concept of God that is used to explain phenomena not explained by the operation of scientific laws. As science advances to fill the gaps, God is pushed out of nature.

Gratuitous evil Evil that is not necessary to a greater good or to the prevention of an evil equally bad or worse.

Grounding objection The objection to the theory of *middle knowledge* that the *counterfactuals of freedom* cannot be true because there is no "ground" or basis in reality for their being true.

Horrendous evil Evil that has come to be defined as so overwhelming to an individual person that the meaning of his or her life is threatened or destroyed.

Impassibility (of God) The view that God cannot be affected by human beings or other creatures; in particular, God cannot suffer or undergo negative emotions of any kind.

Indeterminism The view that *determinism* is false, that there are some events that are not determined to occur as they do by anything in the past. (See *libertarianism*.)

Indirect act of God An event that occurs as a result of the outworking of the natural laws created and sustained by God.

Ineffable experience Experience that cannot be expressed or described by language.

Intelligent design Narrowly, the label for an intellectual movement (with some political and religious associations) focusing on special cases in biology that allegedly cannot be explained by Darwinian evolution. Broadly, any theistic view of the universe as a created and in some sense ordered by God.

Irreducible complexity A term often applied to biological systems meaning that the whole system of intricately interworking parts could not come to exist by gradual evolutionary addition of the constituent parts and could not continue to function without any part.

Kenosis Greek for "self-emptying." Used in Christian theology to describe God's condescension to humanity in Jesus Christ; also used more broadly to speak of God's willing self-limitation in order to allow creation to exist and have its own powers and abilities.

Libertarianism The view that free will requires *indeterminism* because in a free decision it must be genuinely possible for the agent to choose in either of two or more ways, with all previous circumstances remaining the same.

Logically necessary being A being whose nonexistence is logically impossible.

Maximal greatness A property a being has in virtue of being maximally excellent in every possible world; it includes having such properties as being omnipotent, omniscient, and omnibenevolent.

Memes The cultural analogues of genes, these are strings of informational code that pass easily from one mind to another, and thus are the building blocks of culture.

Metaphysics The branch of philosophy that is concerned with the nature and structure of reality. The related term *ontology* refers to a theory of what sorts of things exist.

Middle knowledge The theory that God knows the *counterfactuals of freedom* with respect to all actual and possible free creatures, and thus God can make his plan for creation in complete assurance that the creatures will act in accordance with it.

Moral absolutes Moral principles that apply to all people at all times and places, regardless of what a culture or specific individuals think is right.

Moral argument An argument for God's existence from the existence of an objective moral law.

Moral continuity thesis The moral principles given to us by God have their origin in God's moral nature. God, therefore, would never act in ways that are contrary to how God would have us act.

Mystical experience Experience that somehow allows the person to perceive or feel related to a divine realm, receive a divine message, and so forth.

Natural law ethics Many of the basic moral principles by which God would have us live can be discovered by reflecting upon what we have been given in the rational capacity to learn about the nature of God's world.

Natural theology The project of proving or giving reasons for the existence of God, and other truths concerning God, on the basis of knowledge that is naturally available to all human beings.

Necessary being A being that, if it exists, cannot not exist.

Necessary existence A being has necessary existence if it "cannot not exist"; its nonexistence is impossible. Often said to be true of God.

Negative theology The project of speaking about God by saying what God is not; for example, God does not have a body.

Neutralism The view that one ought to approach religion and other important philosophical topics from a "neutral" standpoint, which assumes only what is known and accepted by all reasonable people.

Noetic Having to do with the acquisition or employment of knowledge.

Nonanalytic proposition See *synthetic proposition*.

Omnipotence God's property of being "perfect in power"; the precise definition is controversial.

Omniscience God's property of being "perfect in knowledge"; the precise definition is controversial.

Ontological argument An argument for God's existence that begins with the idea of supreme perfection or unsurpassable greatness.

Open theism The view that God is both omnipotent and omniscient, but does not have complete knowledge of what will occur in the future because the future does not yet exist to be known.

Pantheism The view that God is not a personal being, but an all-encompassing reality that includes all beings within itself. (See *Brahman*.)

Persuasive power Power that is exercised by "persuading" other beings to act according to one's desires, but without the ability to compel them to do so. (Contrasts with *coercive power*.)

Potential infinite A finite number that can always be increased in time by adding to its members.

Principle of credulity If something seems to be the case, and if there is reason to think that one's faculties are functioning reliably and past experience of this sort has not proved false, then it is probably true that it really is the case.

Principle of sufficient reason For everything contingent that exists or happens, there must be a reason or explanation for why it exists or happens.

Problem of evil The philosophical argument to the effect that belief in God is either false, improbable, implausible in light of evil. Frequently divided into logical and evidential types of argument.

Process theism A version of *theism*, derived from the thought of A. N. Whitehead, which holds that God has only *persuasive power* but not *coercive power*.

Projective explanation (of religious belief) The explanation of religious belief as produced by "projection" of our psychological needs; for example, God fills the need created by the fact that, after we are grown, our parents can no longer guarantee our safety and comfort.

Properly basic belief A properly basic belief is a *basic belief* that is properly so; that is, it is rationally justified and appropriate for a person to accept it in a basic way.

Rationalism (strong) The view that in order to be reasonably accepted, religious beliefs must be shown to be true (or, at least, to be probably true) on the basis of evidence that is accepted by all reasonable people, regardless of their previous state of belief or disbelief. (See *evidentialism*, *neutralism*, and *strong foundationalism*.)

Realism In any field of inquiry or in metaphysics generally, the view that objects of inquiry exist independently of the human mind. Also, in epistemology, the view that the human mind is basically reliable to know the objects presented to it. Often qualified as "critical realism" which is sophisticated and not naïve about the complex conditions of knowledge.

Rebirth The individual is reborn subsequent to his or her death.

Reformed epistemology A theory of religious knowledge that holds that religious beliefs can be (and in appropriate circumstances are, in fact) *properly basic beliefs* that do not need to be supported by other beliefs one accepts.

Religious virtue ethics The essence of ethical living is not to act in accordance with revealed rules (duty) but, rather, to be ethical, that is, to develop proper moral character.

Research programme An approach to a set of problems in science that is widely shared by a community of scientists.

Self-transcendence Moving from a primary occupation with oneself or the false self to realizing the true self in relation to the Other.

Simple foreknowledge The view that God has complete and precise knowledge of the actual future, but not hypothetical knowledge concerning choices that persons would make under circumstances that never actually occur (see *counterfactuals of freedom*).

Soul A nonphysical feature of humans that is responsible for personal identity and certain mental functions like memory and rationality.

Specified complexity An event or phenomenon that is contingent (not necessary), complex (not easily repeatable by chance), and specified in that it exhibits an independently given pattern. Interpreted by some as an indicator of intelligence or product of intelligence.

Statistical law of nature A summary statement about the natural regularity we observe that maintains that counterinstances are highly improbable.

Supernatural A person, object, or event is supernatural if it is not a part of the ordinary system of nature and natural laws as studied by the sciences.

Symbol, symbolic language Nonliteral language that is particularly able to represent deep and important meaning.

Synthetic proposition A proposition that is true or false in virtue of whether it corresponds to some state of affairs.

Teleological argument An argument for God's existence that attempts to explain the significant means-ends order found in the world.

Telepathy The ability of one mind to communicate with another mind without the use of the senses or signals.

Theism The belief in a personal God who is the creator of the world and is perfect in knowledge, power, and goodness.

Theistic evolution The view that God created and ordered the universe to operate by laws, with some variation of opinions possible about the degree and nature of God's guidance in its ongoing operation. Typically opposed to the position of creationism on the young age of the earth and the special creation of all species positions.

Theodicy Literally, "justification of God" in light of evil.

Theological determinism The belief that everything whatsoever that occurs is predetermined to occur by divine decrees.

Theology The intellectual discipline that is concerned with the knowledge of God, its coherent articulation, systematization, implications, and so forth.

Theory of appearing A view of perception in which what is perceived is understood in terms of how it appears to someone.

Timeless A being is timeless if it exists, but does not exist in time; it has neither duration nor temporal location. (Often said to be true of God; contrasts with *everlasting*.)

Transcendence The characteristic of the divine of being that it is other than everything else in the created world.

Universal law of nature A summary statement about the natural regularity that we observe that admits of no exceptions.

Virtue ethics An ethical theory focusing on the development of moral qualities that constitute character as distinct from other theories focusing on actions, rules, or motives.